Critical Values of t

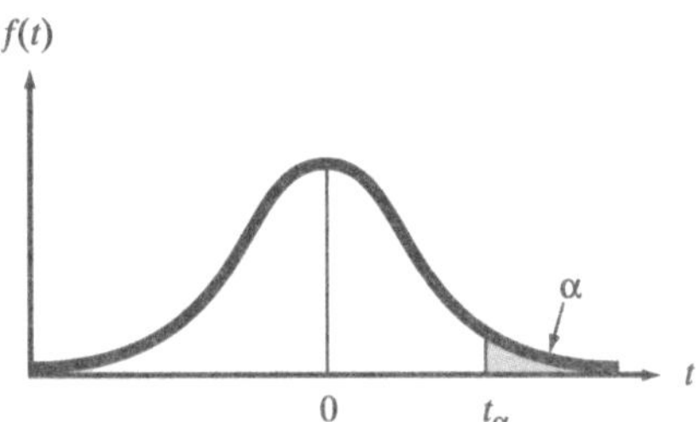

ν	$t_{.100}$	$t_{.050}$	$t_{.025}$	$t_{.010}$	$t_{.005}$	$t_{.001}$	$t_{.0005}$
1	3.078	6.314	12.706	31.821	63.657	318.31	636.62
2	1.886	2.920	4.303	6.965	9.925	22.326	31.598
3	1.638	2.353	3.182	4.541	5.841	10.213	12.924
4	1.533	2.132	2.776	3.747	4.604	7.173	8.610
5	1.476	2.015	2.571	3.365	4.032	5.893	6.869
6	1.440	1.943	2.447	3.143	3.707	5.208	5.959
7	1.415	1.895	2.365	2.998	3.499	4.785	5.408
8	1.397	1.860	2.306	2.896	3.355	4.501	5.041
9	1.383	1.833	2.262	2.821	3.250	4.297	4.781
10	1.372	1.812	2.228	2.764	3.169	4.144	4.587
11	1.363	1.796	2.201	2.718	3.106	4.025	4.437
12	1.356	1.782	2.179	2.681	3.055	3.930	4.318
13	1.350	1.771	2.160	2.650	3.012	3.852	4.221
14	1.345	1.761	2.145	2.624	2.977	3.787	4.140
15	1.341	1.753	2.131	2.602	2.947	3.733	4.073
16	1.337	1.746	2.120	2.583	2.921	3.686	4.015
17	1.333	1.740	2.110	2.567	2.898	3.646	3.965
18	1.330	1.734	2.101	2.552	2.878	3.610	3.922
19	1.328	1.729	2.093	2.539	2.861	3.579	3.883
20	1.325	1.725	2.086	2.528	2.845	3.552	3.850
21	1.323	1.721	2.080	2.518	2.831	3.527	3.819
22	1.321	1.717	2.074	2.508	2.819	3.505	3.792
23	1.319	1.714	2.069	2.500	2.807	3.485	3.767
24	1.318	1.711	2.064	2.492	2.797	3.467	3.745
25	1.316	1.708	2.060	2.485	2.787	3.450	3.725
26	1.315	1.706	2.056	2.479	2.779	3.435	3.707
27	1.314	1.703	2.052	2.473	2.771	3.421	3.690
28	1.313	1.701	2.048	2.467	2.763	3.408	3.674
29	1.311	1.699	2.045	2.462	2.756	3.396	3.659
30	1.310	1.697	2.042	2.457	2.750	3.385	3.646
40	1.303	1.684	2.021	2.423	2.704	3.307	3.551
60	1.296	1.671	2.000	2.390	2.660	3.232	3.460
120	1.289	1.658	1.980	2.358	2.617	3.160	3.373
∞	1.282	1.645	1.960	2.326	2.576	3.090	3.291

Source: This table is reproduced with the kind permission of the Trustees of Biometrika from E. S. Pearson and H. O. Hartley (eds.), *The Biometrika Tables for Statisticians*, Vol. 1, 3d ed., Biometrika, 1966.

A FIRST COURSE IN BUSINESS Statistics

A FIRST COURSE IN BUSINESS Statistics

Eighth Edition

JAMES T. McCLAVE
Info Tech, Inc.
University of Florida

P. GEORGE BENSON
Terry College of Business
University of Georgia

TERRY SINCICH
University of South Florida

PRENTICE HALL
Upper Saddle River, NJ 07458

Library of Congress Cataloging-in-Publication Data

McClave, James T.
A first course in business statistics / James T. McClave, P. George Benson, Terry Sincich.—8th ed.
p. cm.
Includes bibliographical references and index.
ISBN 0-13-018679-1
1. Commercial statistics. 2. Statistics—Data processing. 3. Commercial statistics—Case studies. I. Title: 1st course in business statistics. II. Benson, P. George, 1946– . III. Sincich, Terry. IV. Title.

HF1017.M358 2001
519.5—dc21 00-061971

Acquisition Editor: Kathleen Boothby Sestak
Editor-in-Chief: Sally Yagan
Assistant Vice President of Production and Manufacturing: David W. Riccardi
Executive Managing Editor: Kathleen Schiaparelli
Senior Managing Editor: Linda Mihatov Behrens
Project Management: Elm Street Publishing Services, Inc.
Manufacturing Buyer: Alan Fischer
Manufacturing Manager: Trudy Pisciotti
Marketing Manager: Angela Battle
Marketing Assistant: Vince Jansen
Director of Marketing: John Tweeddale
Associate Editor, Mathematics/Statistics Media: Audra J. Walsh
Editorial Assistant/Supplements Editor: Joanne Wendelken
Art Director: Maureen Eide
Assistant to the Art Director: John Christiana
Interior Designer: Donna Aiello
Cover Designer: Laura Gardner
Art Editor: Grace Hazeldine
Art Manager: Gus Vibal
Director of Creative Services: Paul Belfanti
Cover Photo: Michael Aveto/SIS, Inc.
Art Studio: Elm Street Publishing Services, Inc.

Printed in the United States of America
10 9 8 7 6 5 4 3 2 1

0-13-018679-1

Prentice-Hall International (UK) Limited, *London*
Prentice-Hall of Australia Pty. Limited, *Sydney*
Prentice-Hall Canada, Inc., *Toronto*
Prentice-Hall Hispanoamericano, S.A., *Mexico*
Prentice-Hall of India Private Limited, *New Delhi*
Prentice-Hall of Japan, Inc., *Tokyo*
Pearson Education Asia Pte. Ltd.
Editora Prentice-Hall do Brasil, *Rio De Janeiro*

Contents

CHAPTER 3 PROBABILITY 117

CHAPTER 4 RANDOM VARIABLES AND PROBABILITY DISTRIBUTIONS 167

CHAPTER 5

INFERENCES BASED ON A SINGLE SAMPLE: ESTIMATION WITH CONFIDENCE INTERVALS 259

CHAPTER 6

INFERENCES BASED ON A SINGLE SAMPLE: TESTS OF HYPOTHESIS 299

CHAPTER 7

COMPARING POPULATION MEANS 345

APPENDICES

Preface

This eighth edition of *A First Course in Business Statistics* is an introductory business text emphasizing inference, with extensive coverage of data collection and analysis as needed to evaluate the reported results of statistical studies and to make good decisions. As in earlier editions, the text stresses the development of statistical thinking, the assessment of credibility and value of the inferences made from data, both by those who consume and those who produce them. It assumes a mathematical background of basic algebra.

A more comprehensive version of the book, *Statistics for Business and Economics (8/e),* is available for two-term courses or those that include more extensive coverage of special topics.

NEW IN THE EIGHTH EDITION

Major Content Changes

Chapter 2 includes two new optional sections: methods for detecting outliers (Section 2.8) and graphing bivariate relationships (Section 2.9).

Chapter 4 now covers descriptive methods for assessing whether a data set is approximately normally distributed (Section 4.8) and normal approximation to the binomial distribution (Section 4.9).

Exploring Data with Statistical Computer Software and the Graphing Calculator—Throughout the text, computer printouts from five popular Windows-based statistical software packages (SAS, SPSS, MINITAB, STATISTIX and EXCEL) are displayed and used to make decisions about the data. New to this edition, we have included instruction boxes and output for the TI-83 graphing calculator.

Statistics in Action—One feature per chapter examines current real-life, high-profile issues. Data from the study is presented for analysis. Questions prompt the students to form their own conclusions and to think through the statistical issues involved.

Real-World Business Cases—Six extensive business problem-solving cases, with real data and assignments. Each case serves as a good capstone and review of the material that has preceded it.

Real-Data Exercises—Almost all the exercises in the text employ the use of current real data taken from a wide variety of publications (e.g., newspapers, magazines, and journals).

Quick Review—Each chapter ends with a list of key terms and formulas, with reference to the page number where they first appear.

Language Lab—Following the Quick Review is a pronunciation guide for Greek letters and other special terms. Usage notes are also provided.

TRADITIONAL STRENGTHS

We have maintained the features of *A First Course in Business Statistics* that we believe make it unique among business statistics texts. These features, which assist the student in achieving an overview of statistics and an understanding of its relevance in the business world and in everyday life, are as follows:

The Use of Examples as a Teaching Device

Almost all new ideas are introduced and illustrated by real data-based applications and examples. We believe that students better understand definitions, generalizations, and abstractions *after* seeing an application.

Many Exercises—Labeled by Type

The text includes more than 1,000 exercises illustrated by applications in almost all areas of research. Because many students have trouble learning the mechanics of statistical techniques when problems are couched in terms of realistic applications, all exercise sections are divided into two parts:

Learning the Mechanics. Designed as straightforward applications of new concepts, these exercises allow students to test their ability to comprehend a concept or a definition.

Applying the Concepts. Based on applications taken from a wide variety of journals, newspapers, and other sources, these exercises develop the student's skills to comprehend real-world problems and describe situations to which the techniques may be applied.

A Choice in Level of Coverage of Probability (Chapter 3)

One of the most troublesome aspects of an introductory statistics course is the study of probability. Probability poses a challenge for instructors because they must decide on the level of presentation, and students find it a difficult subject to comprehend. We believe that one cause for these problems is the mixture of probability and counting rules that occurs in most introductory texts. We have included the counting rules and worked examples in a separate appendix (Appendix A) at the end of the text. Thus, the instructor can control the level of coverage of probability.

Nonparametric Topics Integrated

In a one-term course it is often difficult to find time to cover nonparametric techniques when they are relegated to a separate chapter at the end of the book. Consequently, we have integrated the most commonly used techniques in optional sections as appropriate.

Coverage of Multiple Regression Analysis (Chapter 10)

This topic represents one of the most useful statistical tools for the solution of applied problems. Although an entire text could be devoted to regression modeling, we believe we have presented coverage that is understandable, usable, and much more comprehensive than the presentations in other introductory statistics texts.

Footnotes

Although the text is designed for students with a non-calculus background, footnotes explain the role of calculus in various derivations. Footnotes are also used to inform the student about some of the theory underlying certain results. The footnotes allow additional flexibility in the mathematical and theoretical level at which the material is presented.

SUPPLEMENTS FOR THE INSTRUCTOR

The supplements for the eighth edition have been completely revised to reflect the revisions of the text. To ensure adherence to the approaches presented in the main text, each element in the package has been accuracy checked for clarity and freedom from computational, typographical, and statistical errors.

Annotated Instructor's Edition (AIE) (ISBN 0-13-027985-4)

Marginal notes placed next to discussions of essential teaching concepts include:

- Teaching Tips—suggest alternative presentations or point out common student errors
- Exercises—reference specific section and chapter exercises that reinforce the concept
- —disk icon identifies data sets and file names of material found on the data CD-ROM in the back of the book.
- Short Answers—section and chapter exercise answers are provided next to the selected exercises

Instructor's Notes by Mark Dummeldinger (ISBN 0-13-027410-0)

This printed resource contains suggestions for using the questions at the end of the Statistics in Action boxes as the basis for class discussion on statistical ethics and other current issues, solutions to the Real-World Cases, a complete short answer book with letter of permission to duplicate for student use, and many of the exercises and solutions that were removed from previous editions of this text.

Instructor's Solutions Manual by Nancy S. Boudreau (ISBN 0-13-027421-6)

Solutions to all of the even-numbered exercises are given in this manual. Careful attention has been paid to ensure that all methods of solution and notation are consistent with those used in the core text. Solutions to the odd-numbered exercises are found in the *Student's Solutions Manual.*

Test Bank by Mark Dummeldinger (ISBN 0-13-027419-4)

Entirely rewritten, the *Test Bank* now includes more than 1,000 problems that correlate to problems presented in the text.

Test Gen-EQ (ISBN 0-13-027367-8)

- Menu-driven random test system
- Networkable for administering tests and capturing grades online
- Edit and add your own questions—or use the new "Function Plotter" to create a nearly unlimited number of tests and drill worksheets

PowerPoint Presentation Disk by Mark Dummeldinger (ISBN 0-13-027365-1)

This versatile Windows-based tool may be used by professors in a number of different ways:

- Slide show in an electronic classroom
- Printed and used as transparency masters
- Printed copies may be distributed to students as a convenient note-taking device

Included on the software disk are learning objectives, thinking challenges, concept presentation slides, and examples with worked-out solutions. The PowerPoint Presentation Disk may be downloaded from the FTP site found at the McClave Web site.

Data CD-ROM—available free with every text purchased from Prentice Hall (ISBN 0-13-027293-0)

The data sets for all exercises and cases are available in ASCII format on a CD-ROM in the back of the book. When a given data set is referenced, a disk symbol and the file name will appear in the text near the exercise.

McClave Internet Site (http://www.prenhall.com/mcclave)

This site will be updated throughout the year as new information, tools, and applications become available. The site contains information about the book and its supplements as well as FTP sites for downloading the PowerPoint Presentation Disk and the Data Files. Teaching tips and student help are provided as well as links to useful sources of data and information such as the Chance Database, the STEPS project (interactive tutorials developed by the University of Glasgow), and a site designed to help faculty establish and manage course home pages.

SUPPLEMENTS AVAILABLE FOR STUDENTS

Student's Solutions Manual by Nancy S. Boudreau (ISBN 0-13-027422-4)

Fully worked-out solutions to all of the odd-numbered exercises are provided in this manual. Careful attention has been paid to ensure that all methods of solution and notation are consistent with those used in the core text.

Companion Microsoft Excel Manual by Mark Dummeldinger (ISBN 0-13-029347-4)

Each companion manual works hand-in-glove with the text. Step-by-step keystroke level instructions, with screen captures, provide detailed help for using the technology to work pertinent examples and all of the technology projects in the text. A cross-reference chart indicates which text examples are included and the exact page reference in both the text and technology manual. Output with brief instruction is provided for selected odd-numbered exercises to reinforce the examples. A Student Lab section is included at the end of each chapter.

The Excel Manual includes ***PH*stat**, a statistics add-in for Microsoft Excel (CD-ROM) featuring a custom menu of choices that lead to dialog boxes to help perform statistical analyses more quickly and easily than off-the-shelf Excel permits.

Student Version of SPSS

Student versions of SPSS, the award-winning and market-leading commercial and data analysis package, and MINITAB are available for student purchase. Details on all current products are available from Prentice Hall or via the SPSS Web site at http://www.spss.com.

Learning Business Statistics with Microsoft® Excel by John L. Neufeld (ISBN 0-13-234097-6)

The use of Excel as a data analysis and computational package for statistics is explained in clear, easy-to-follow steps in this self-contained paperback text.

A MINITAB Guide to Statistics by Ruth Meyer and David Krueger (ISBN 0-13-784232-5)

This manual assumes no prior knowledge of MINITAB. Organized to correspond to the table of contents of most statistics texts, this manual provides step-by-step instruction to using MINITAB for statistical analysis.

ConStatS by Tufts University (ISBN 0-13-502600-8)

ConStatS is a set of Microsoft Windows-based programs designed to help college students understand concepts taught in a first-semester course on probability and statistics. ConStatS helps improve students' conceptual understanding of statistics by engaging them in an active, experimental style of learning. A companion ConStatS workbook (ISBN 0-13-522848-4) that guides students through the labs and ensures they gain the maximum benefit is also available.

ACKNOWLEDGMENTS

This book reflects the efforts of a great many people over a number of years. First we would like to thank the following professors whose reviews and feedback on organization and coverage contributed to the eighth and previous editions of the book.

Reviewers Involved with the Eighth Edition

Mary C. Christman, University of Maryland; James Czachor, Fordham–Lincoln Center, AT&T; William Duckworth II, Iowa State University; Ann Hussein, Ph.D., Philadelphia University; Lawrence D. Ries, University of Missouri–Columbia.

Reviewers of Previous Editions

Atul Agarwal, GMI Engineering and Management Institute; Mohamed Albohali, Indiana University of Pennsylvania; Gordon J. Alexander, University of Minnesota; Richard W. Andrews, University of Michigan; Larry M. Austin, Texas Tech University; Golam Azam, North Carolina Agricultural & Technical University; Donald W. Bartlett, University of Minnesota; Clarence Bayne, Concordia University; Carl Bedell, Philadelphia College of Textiles and Science; David M. Bergman, University of Minnesota; William H. Beyer, University of Akron; Atul Bhatia, University of Minnesota; Jim Branscome, University of Texas at Arlington; Francis J. Brewerton, Middle Tennessee State University; Daniel G. Brick, University of St. Thomas; Robert W. Brobst, University of Texas at Arlington; Michael Broida, Miami University of Ohio; Glenn J. Browne, University of Maryland, Baltimore; Edward Carlstein, University of North Carolina at Chapel Hill; John M. Charnes, University of Miami; Chih-Hsu Cheng, Ohio State University; Larry Claypool, Oklahoma State University; Edward R. Clayton, Virginia Polytechnic Institute and State University; Ronald L. Coccari, Cleveland State University; Ken Constantine, University of New Hampshire; Lewis Coopersmith, Rider University; Robert Curley, University of Central Oklahoma; Joyce Curley-Daly, California Polytechnic State University; Jim Daly, California Polytechnic State University; Jim Davis, Golden Gate University; Dileep Dhavale, University of Northern Iowa; Bernard Dickman, Hofstra University; Mark Eakin, University of Texas at Arlington; Rick L. Edgeman, Colorado State University; Carol Eger, Stanford University; Robert Elrod, Georgia State University; Douglas A. Elvers, University of North Carolina at Chapel Hill; Iris Fetta, Clemson University; Susan Flach, General Mills, Inc.; Alan E. Gelfand, University of Connecticut; Joseph Glaz, University of Connecticut; Edit Gombay, University of Alberta; Jose Luis Guerrero-Cusumano, Georgetown University; Paul W. Guy, California State University, Chico; Judd Hammack, California State University–Los Angeles; Michael E. Hanna, University of Texas at Arlington; Don Holbert, East Carolina University; James Holstein, University of Missouri, Columbia; Warren M. Holt, Southeastern Massachusetts University; Steve Hora, University of Hawaii, Hilo; Petros Ioannatos, GMI Engineering & Management Institute; Marius Janson, University of Missouri, St. Louis; Ross H. Johnson, Madison College; P. Kasliwal, California State University–Los Angeles; Timothy J. Killeen, University of Connecticut; Tim Krehbiel, Miami University of Ohio; David D. Krueger, St. Cloud State University; Richard W. Kulp, Wright-Patterson AFB, Air Force Institute of Technology; Mabel T. Kung, California State University–Fullerton; Martin Labbe, State University of New York College at New Paltz; James Lackritz, California State University at San Diego; Lei Lei, Rutgers University; Leigh Lawton, University of St. Thomas; Peter Lenk, University of Michigan; Benjamin Lev, University of Michigan–Dearborn; Philip Levine, William Patterson College; Eddie M. Lewis, University of Southern Mississippi; Fred Leysieffer, Florida State University; Xuan Li, Rutgers University; Pi-Erh Lin, Florida State University; Robert Ling, Clemson University; Benny Lo; Karen Lundquist, University of Minnesota; G. E. Martin,

Clarkson University; Brenda Masters, Oklahoma State University; William Q. Meeker, Iowa State University; Ruth K. Meyer, St. Cloud State University; Edward Minieka, University of Illinois at Chicago; Rebecca Moore, Oklahoma State University; June Morita, University of Washington; Behnam Nakhai, Millersville University; Paul I. Nelson, Kansas State University; Paula M. Oas, General Office Products; Dilek Onkal, Bilkent University, Turkey; Vijay Pisharody, University of Minnesota; Rose Prave, University of Scranton; P. V. Rao, University of Florida; Don Robinson, Illinois State University; Beth Rose, University of Southern California; Jan Saraph, St. Cloud State University; Lawrence A. Sherr, University of Kansas; Craig W. Slinkman, University of Texas at Arlingon; Robert K. Smidt, California Polytechnic State University; Toni M. Somers, Wayne State University; Donald N. Steinnes, University of Minnesota at Duluth; Virgil F. Stone, Texas A & M University; Katheryn Szabet, La Salle University; Alireza Tahai, Mississippi State University; Kim Tamura, University of Washington; Zina Taran, Rutgers University; Chipei Tseng, Northern Illinois University; Pankaj Vaish, Arthur Andersen & Company; Robert W. Van Cleave, University of Minnesota; Charles F. Warnock, Colorado State University; Michael P. Wegmann, Keller Graduate School of Management; William J. Weida, United States Air Force Academy; T. J. Wharton, Oakland University; Kathleen M. Whitcomb, University of South Carolina; Edna White, Florida Atlantic University; Steve Wickstrom, University of Minnesota; James Willis, Louisiana State University; Douglas A. Wolfe, Ohio State University; Gary Yoshimoto, St. Cloud State University; Doug Zahn, Florida State University; Fike Zahroom, Moorhead State University; Christopher J. Zappe, Bucknell University.

Special thanks are due to our ancillary authors, Nancy Shafer Boudreau and Mark Dummeldinger, and to typist Kelly Barber, who have worked with us for many years. Laurel Technical Services has done an excellent job of accuracy checking the eighth edition and has helped us to ensure a highly accurate, clean text. Wendy Metzger and Stephen M. Kelly should be acknowledged for their help with the TI-83 boxes. The Prentice Hall staff of Kathy Boothby Sestak, Joanne Wendelken, Gina Huck, Angela Battle, Linda Behrens, and Alan Fischer, and Elm Street Publishing Services' Martha Beyerlein helped greatly with all phases of the text development, production, and marketing effort. We acknowledge University of Georgia Terry College of Business MBA students Brian F. Adams, Derek Sean Rolle, and Misty Rumbley for helping us to research and acquire new exercise/case material. Our thanks to Jane Benson for managing the exercise development process. Finally, we owe special thanks to Faith Sincich, whose efforts in preparing the manuscript for production and proofreading all stages of the book deserve special recognition.

For additional information about texts and other materials available from Prentice Hall, visit us on-line at http://www.prenhall.com.

James T. McClave
P. George Benson
Terry Sincich

How to Use This Book

TO THE STUDENT

The following four pages will demonstrate how to use this text effectively to make studying easier and to understand the connection between statistics and your world.

Chapter Openers Provide a Roadmap

Where We've Been quickly reviews how information learned previously applies to the chapter at hand.

Where We're Going highlights how the chapter topics fit into your growing understanding of statistical inference.

Chapter 9

SIMPLE LINEAR REGRESSION

CONTENTS

STATISTICS IN ACTION

Can "Dowsers" Really Detect Water?

Where We've Been

We've learned how to estimate and test hypotheses about population parameters based on a random sample of observations from the population. We've also seen how to extend these methods to allow for a comparison of parameters from two populations.

Where We're Going

Suppose we want to predict the assessed value of a house in a particular community. We could select a single random sample of n houses from the community, use the methods of Chapter 5 to estimate the mean assessed value μ, and then use this quantity to predict the house's assessed value. A better method uses information that is available to any property appraiser, e.g., square feet of floor space and age of the house. If we measure square footage and age at the same time as assessed value, we can establish the relationship between these variables—one that lets us use these variables for prediction. This chapter covers the simplest situation—relating two variables. The more complex problem of relating more than two variables is the topic of Chapter 10.

471

SECTION 4.12 The Central Limit Theorem 251

STATISTICS IN Action

IQ, Economic Mobility, and the Bell Curve

In their controversial book *The Bell Curve* (Free Press, 1994), Professors Richard J. Herrnstein (a Harvard psychologist who died while the book was in production) and Charles Murray (a political scientist at MIT) explore, as the subtitle states, "intelligence and class structure in American life." *The Bell Curve* heavily employs statistical analyses in an attempt to support the authors' positions. Since the book's publication, many expert statisticians have raised doubts about the authors' statistical methods and the inferences drawn from them. (See, for example, "Wringing *The Bell Curve:* A cautionary tale about the relationships among race, genes, and IQ," *Chance,* Summer 1995.) In Chapter 10's Statistics in Action, we explore a few of these problems.

One of the many controversies sparked by the book is the authors' tenet that level of intelligence (or lack thereof) is a cause of a wide range of intractable social problems, including constrained economic mobility. "America has taken great pride in the mobility of generations," state Herrnstein and Murray, "but this mobility has its limits .... The son of a father whose earnings are in the bottom five percent of the [income] distribution has something like one chance in twenty (or less) of rising to the top fifth of the income distribution and almost a fifty-fifty chance of staying in the bottom fifth. He has less than one chance in four of rising above even the median income .... Most people at present are stuck near where their parents were on the income distribution in part because [intelligence], which has become a ...dictor of income, passes on sufficiently from one ... the next to constrain eco... mobility."

able having a normal distribution with mean $\mu = 100$ and standard deviation $\sigma = 15$. This distribution, or *bell curve,* is shown in Figure 4.49.

In their book, Herrnstein and Murray refer to five cognitive classes of people defined by percentiles of the normal distribution. Class I ("very bright") consists of those with IQs above the 95th percentile; Class II ("bright") are those with IQs between the 75th and 95th percentiles; Class III ("normal") includes IQs between the 25th and 75th percentiles; Class IV ("dull") are those with IQs between the 5th and 25th percentiles; and Class V ("very dull") are IQs below the 5th percentile. These classes are also illustrated in Figure 4.49.

Focus

a. Assuming that the distribution of IQ is accurately represented by the bell curve in Figure 4.49, determine the proportion of people with IQs in each of the five cognitive classes defined by Herrnstein and Murray.

b. Although the cognitive classes above are defined in terms of percentiles, the authors stress that IQ scores should be compared with z-scores, not percentiles. In other words, it is more informative to give the difference in z-scores for two IQ scores than it is to give the difference in percentiles. To demonstrate this point, calculate the difference in z-scores for IQs at the 50th and 55th percentiles. Do the same for IQs at the 94th and 99th percentiles. What do you obs...

"Statistics in Action" Boxes Explore High-Interest Issues

- Highlight controversial, contemporary issues that involve statistics.
- Work through the **"Focus"** questions to help you evaluate the findings.
- Integration of Real-World Data helps students see relevance to their daily lives.

Shaded Boxes Highlight Important Information

- Definitions, Strategies, Key Formulas, Rules, and other important information is highlighted in easy-to-read boxes.
- Prepare for quizzes and tests by reviewing the highlighted information.

Probability Rules for Sample Points

1. All sample point probabilities *must* lie between 0 and 1 inclusive.
2. The probabilities of all the sample points within a sample space *must* sum to 1.

Assigning probabilities to sample points is easy for some experiments. For example, if the experiment is to toss a fair coin and observe the face, we would probably all agree to assign a probability of $\frac{1}{2}$ to the two sample points, Observe a head and Observe a tail. However, many experiments have sample points whose probabilities are more difficult to assign.

EXAMPLE 3.2 A retail computer store sells two basic types of personal computers (PCs): standard desktop units and laptop units. Thus the owner must decide how many of each type of PC to stock. An important factor affecting the solution is the proportion of customers who purchase each type of PC. Show how this problem might be formulated in the framework of an experiment with sample points and a sample space. Indicate how probabilities might be assigned to the sample points.

Solution If we use the term *customer* to refer to a person who purchases one of the two types of PCs, the experiment can be defined as the entrance of a customer and the observation of which type of PC is purchased. There are two sample points in the sample space corresponding to this experiment:

D: {The customer purchases a standard desktop unit}

L: {The customer purchases a laptop unit}

The difference between this and the coin-toss experiment becomes apparent when we attempt to assign probabilities to the two sample points. What probability should we assign to the sample point *D*? If you answer .5, you are assuming that the events *D* and *L* should occur with equal likelihood, just like the sample points Heads and Tails in the coin-toss experiment. But assignment of sample point probabilities for the PC purchase experiment is not so easy. Supp... of the store's reco... might...

Interesting Examples with Solutions

- Examples, with complete step-by-step solutions and explanations, illustrate every concept and are numbered for easy reference.
- Solutions are carefully explained to prepare for the section exercise set.
- The end of the solution is clearly marked by a ✳ symbol.

Then we use*

$$s^2 = \frac{\sum_{i=1}^{n} x_i^2 - \frac{\left(\sum_{i=1}^{n} x_i\right)^2}{n}}{n-1} = \frac{47 - \frac{(15)^2}{5}}{5-1} = \frac{2}{4} = .5$$

$$s = \sqrt{.5} = .71$$ ✳

EXAMPLE 2.10 Use the computer to find the sample variance s^2 and the sample standard deviation s for the 50 companies' percentages of revenues spent on R&D.

Solution The SAS printout describing the R&D percentage data is displayed in Figure 2.19. The variance and standard deviation, highlighted on the printout, are: $s^2 = 3.922792$ and $s = 1.980604$. ✳

FIGURE 2.19
SAS printout of numerical descriptive measures for 50 R&D percentages

```
                         UNIVARIATE PROCEDURE
Variable=RDPCT
                               Moments

              N               50   Sum Wgts           50
              Mean         8.492   Sum             424.6
              Std Dev   1.980604   Variance     3.922792
              Skewness  0.854601   Kurtosis     0.419288
              USS        3797.92   CSS          192.2168
              CV        23.32317   Std Mean       0.2801
              T:Mean=0  30.31778   Prob>|T|       0.0001
              Sgn Rank     637.5   Prob>|S|       0.0001
              Num ^= 0        50

                           Quantiles(Def=5)

               100% Max     13.5        99%        13.5
                75% Q3       9.6        95%        13.2
                50% Med     8.05        90%        11.2
                25% Q1       7.1        10%         6.5
                 0% Min      5.2         5%         5.9
                                         1%         5.2

              Range          8.3
              Q3-Q1          2.5
              Mode           6.5
```

You now know that the standard deviation measures the variability of a set of data and how to calculate it. B... can we interpret and ... dard deviation... topi...

Computer Output Integrated Throughout

- Statistical software packages such as SPSS, MINITAB, SAS, and EXCEL crunch data quickly so you can spend time analyzing the results. Learning how to interpret statistical output will prove helpful in future classes or on the job.
- When computer output appears in examples, the solution explains how to read and interpret the output.

EXERCISES 2.30–2.42

Learning the Mechanics

2.30 Calculate the mode, mean, and median of the following data:

18 10 15 13 17 15 12 15 18 16 11

2.31 Calculate the mean and median of the following grade point averages:

3.2 2.5 2.1 3.7 2.8 2.0

2.32 Calculate the mean for samples where
a. $n = 10, \sum x = 85$ b. $n = 16, \sum x = 400$
c. $n = 45, \sum x = 35$ d. $n = 18, \sum x = 242$

2.33 Calculate the mean, median, and mode for each of the following samples:
a. 7, −2, 3, 3, 0, 4 b. 2, 3, 5, 3, 2, 3, 4, 3, 5, 1, 2, 3, 4
c. 51, 50, 47, 50, 48, 41, 59, 68, 45, 37

2.34 Describe how the mean compares to the median for a distribution as follows:
a. Skewed to the left b. Skewed to the right
c. Symmetric

Applying the Concepts

2.35 The total number of passengers handled in 1998 by eight cruise ships based in Port Canaveral (Florida) are listed in the table below. Find and interpret the mean and median of the data set.

2.36 *Fortune* (Oct. 25, 1999) magazine's second annual ranking of the 50 most powerful women in America is provided in the table on page 60. In addition to salary, position, and profile, *Fortune* based these rankings on the woman's influence within her company and her company's effect on culture in society. Consider the age (in years) distribution of these 50 women. Numerical descriptive statistics for the data are shown in the MINITAB printout below.
a. Find the mean, median, and modal age of the distribution. Interpret these values.
b. What do the mean and the median indicate about the skewness of the age distribution?
c. What percentage of these women are in their forties? Their fifties? Their sixties?

CRUISE.DAT

Cruise Line (Ship)	Number of Passengers
Canaveral (Dolphin)	152,240
Carnival (Fantasy)	480,924
Disney (Magic)	73,504
Premier (Oceanic)	270,361
Royal Caribbean (Nordic Empress)	106,161
Sun Cruz Casinos	453,806
Sterling Cruises (New Yorker)	15,782
Topaz Int'l. Shipping (Topaz)	28,280

Source: Florida Trend, Vol. 41, No. 9, Jan. 1999.

MINITAB Output for Exercise 2.36

```
Descriptive Statistics

Variable        N      Mean    Median   Tr Mean    StDev   SE Mean
Age            50    48.160    47.000    47.795    6.015     0.851

Variable      Min       Max        Q1        Q3
Age        36.000    68.000    45.000    51.250
```

Lots of Exercises for Practice

Every section in the book is followed by an Exercise Set divided into two parts:

- **Learning the Mechanics** has straightforward applications of new concepts. Test your mastery of definitions, concepts, and basic computation. Make sure you can answer all of these questions before moving on.
- **Applying the Concepts** tests your understanding of concepts and requires you to apply statistical techniques in solving real-world problems.

Real Data

- Most of the exercises contain data or information taken from newspaper articles, magazines, and journals. Statistics are all around you.

Computer Output

- Computer output screens appear in the exercise sets to give you practice in interpretation.

End of Chapter Review

- Each chapter ends with information designed to help you check your understanding of the material, study for tests, and expand your knowledge of statistics.
- **Quick Review** provides a list of key terms and formulas with page number references.
- **Language Lab** helps you learn the language of statistics through pronunciation guides, descriptions of symbols, names, etc.
- **Supplementary Exercises** review all of the important topics covered in the chapter and provide additional practice learning statistical computations.

Data sets for use with the problems are available on a CD-ROM in the back of the book. The disk icon indicates when to use the CD.

QUICK REVIEW

Key Terms

Note: Starred (*) items are from the optional sections in this chapter.

Analysis of Vairance (ANOVA) 400
Blocking 365
F-distribution* 377
F-test* 381
mean square for error* 402
mean square for treatments* 402
Paired difference experiment 365
Pooled sample estimate of variance 351
Randomized block experiment 365
Rank Sum* 385
Robust Method* 410
Sum of squares for error* 402
Standard error 347
Treatments* 400
Wilcoxon rank sum test* 384
Wilcoxon signed rank text* 393

LANGUAGE LAB

Symbol	Pronunciation	Description
$(\mu_1 - \mu_2)$	mu-1 minus mu-2	Difference between population means
$(\bar{x}_1 - \bar{x}_2)$	*x*-bar-1 minus *x*-bar-2	Difference between sample means
$\sigma_{(\bar{x}_1-\bar{x}_2)}$	sigma of *x*-bar-1 minus *x*-bar-2	Standard deviation of the sampling distribution of $(\bar{x}_1 - \bar{x}_2)$

Note: Starred (*) symbols are from the optional sections in this chapter.

SUPPLEMENTARY EXERCISES 7.89–7.110

Starred (*) exercises refer to the optional sections in this chapter.

Learning the Mechanics

7.89 Independent random samples were selected from two normally distributed populations with means μ_1 and μ_2, respectively. The sample sizes, means, and variances are shown in the following table.

Sample 1	Sample 2
$n_1 = 135$	$n_2 = 148$
$\bar{x}_1 = 12.2$	$\bar{x}_2 = 8.3$
$s_1^2 = 2.1$	$s_2^2 = 3.0$

c. What sample sizes would be required if you wish to estimate $(\mu_1 - \mu_2)$ to within .2 with 90% confidence? Assume that $n_1 = n_2$.

Real-World Case The Kentucky Milk Case–Part 1
(A Case Covering Chapters 1 and 2)

Many products and services are purchased by governments, cities, states, and businesses on the basis of sealed bids, and contracts are awarded to the lowest bidders. This process works extremely well in competitive markets, but it has the potential to increase the cost of purchasing if the markets are noncompetitive or if collusive practices are present. An investigation that began with a statistical analysis of bids in the Florida school milk market in 1986 led to the recovery of more than $33,000,000 from dairies who had conspired to rig the bids there in the 1980s. The investigation spread quickly to other states, and to date settlements and fines from dairies exceed $100,000,000 for school milk bidrigging in twenty other states. This case concerns a school milk bidrigging investigation in Kentucky.

Each year the Commonwealth of Kentucky invites bids ... containers of ...

DATA. ASCII file name: MILK.DAT
Number of observations: 392

Variable	Column(s)	Type	Description
YEAR	1–4	QN	Year in which milk contract awarded
MARKET	6–15	QL	Northern Kentucky Market (TRI-COUNTY or SURROUND)
WINNER	17–30	QL	Name of winning dairy
WWBID	32–38	QN	Winning bid price of whole white milk (dollars per half-pint)
WWQTY	40–46	QN	Quantity of whole white milk purchased (number of half-pints)

Real-World Cases

- Six real-business cases put you in the position of the business decision maker or consultant. Use the data provided and the information you have learned in preceding chapters to reach a decision and support your arguments about the questions being asked.

Finding One-Variable Descriptive Statistics

USING THE TI-83 GRAPHING CALCULATOR

Step 1 *Enter the data*
Press **STAT** **1** for **STAT Edit**
Enter the data into one of the lists.

Step 2 *Calculate descriptive statistics*
Press **STAT**
Press the right arrow key to highlight **CALC**
Press **ENTER** for **1-Var Stats**

Enter the name of the list containing your data.
Press **2nd** **1** for **L1** (or **2nd 2** for **L2** etc.)
Press **ENTER**

... the statistics on your screen. Some of the ... are off the bottom ...

Using the TI-83 Graphing Calculator

- Provides you with step-by-step instruction on using the TI-83 in a variety of applications.

Chapter 1

STATISTICS, DATA, AND STATISTICAL THINKING

CONTENTS

STATISTICS IN ACTION

Where We're Going

Statistics? Is it a field of study, a group of numbers that summarizes the state of our national economy, the performance of a stock, or the business conditions in a particular locale? Or, as one popular book (Tanur *et al.*, 1989) suggests, is it "a guide to the unknown"? We'll see in Chapter 1 that each of these descriptions is applicable in understanding what statistics is. We'll see that there are two areas of statistics: *descriptive statistics,* which focuses on developing graphical and numerical summaries that describe some business phenomenon, and *inferential statistics,* which uses these numerical summaries to assist in making business decisions. The primary theme of this text is inferential statistics. Thus, we'll concentrate on showing how you can use statistics to interpret data and use them to make decisions. Many jobs in industry, government, medicine, and other fields require you to make data-driven decisions, so understanding these methods offers you important practical benefits.

1.1 THE SCIENCE OF STATISTICS

What does statistics mean to you? Does it bring to mind batting averages, Gallup polls, unemployment figures, or numerical distortions of facts (lying with statistics!)? Or is it simply a college requirement you have to complete? We hope to persuade you that statistics is a meaningful, useful science whose broad scope of applications to business, government, and the physical and social sciences is almost limitless. We also want to show that statistics can lie only when they are misapplied. Finally, we wish to demonstrate the key role statistics play in critical thinking—whether in the classroom, on the job, or in everyday life. Our objective is to leave you with the impression that the time you spend studying this subject will repay you in many ways.

The *Random House College Dictionary* defines *statistics* as "the science that deals with the collection, classification, analysis, and interpretation of information or data." Thus, a statistician isn't just someone who calculates batting averages at baseball games or tabulates the results of a Gallup poll. Professional statisticians are trained in *statistical science.* That is, they are trained in collecting numerical information in the form of **data,** evaluating it, and drawing conclusions from it. Furthermore, statisticians determine what information is relevant in a given problem and whether the conclusions drawn from a study are to be trusted.

DEFINITION 1.1

Statistics is the science of data. It involves collecting, classifying, summarizing, organizing, analyzing, and interpreting numerical information.

In the next section, you'll see several real-life examples of statistical applications in business and government that involve making decisions and drawing conclusions.

1.2 TYPES OF STATISTICAL APPLICATIONS IN BUSINESS

Statistics means "numerical descriptions" to most people. Monthly unemployment figures, the failure rate of a new business, and the proportion of female executives in a particular industry all represent statistical descriptions of large sets of data collected on some phenomenon. Often the data are selected from some larger set of data whose characteristics we wish to estimate. We call this selection process *sampling.* For example, you might collect the ages of a sample of customers at a video store to estimate the average age of *all* customers of the store. Then you could use your estimate to target the store's advertisements to the appropriate age group. Notice that statistics involves two different processes: (1) describing sets of data and (2) drawing conclusions (making estimates, decisions, predictions, etc.) about the sets of data based on sampling. So, the applications of statistics can be divided into two broad areas: *descriptive statistics* and *inferential statistics.*

DEFINITION 1.2

Descriptive statistics utilizes numerical and graphical methods to look for patterns in a data set, to summarize the information revealed in a data set, and to present the information in a convenient form.

DEFINITION 1.3

Inferential statistics utilizes sample data to make estimates, decisions, predictions, or other generalizations about a larger set of data.

Although we'll discuss both descriptive and inferential statistics in the following chapters, the primary theme of the text is **inference.**

Let's begin by examining some business studies that illustrate applications of statistics.

Study 1 "U.S. Market Share for Credit Cards" (*The Nilson Report,* Oct. 8, 1998)

The Nilson Report collected data on all credit or debit card purchases in the United States during the first six months of 1998. The amount of each purchase was recorded and classified according to type of card used. The results are shown in the Associated Press graphic, Figure 1.1. From the graph, you can clearly see that half of the purchases were made with a VISA card and one-fourth with a MasterCard. Since Figure 1.1 describes the type of card used in all credit card purchases for the first half of 1998, the graphic is an example of descriptive statistics.

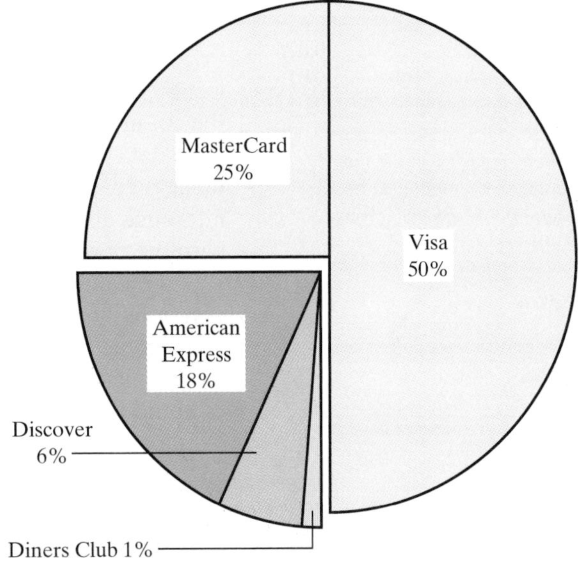

FIGURE 1.1
U.S. Credit Card Market Shares
Source: The Nilson Report, Oct. 8, 1998.

Study 2 "The Executive Compensation Scoreboard" (*Business Week,* Apr. 19, 1999)

How much are the top corporate executives in the United States being paid and are they worth it? To answer these questions, *Business Week* magazine compiles its "Executive Compensation Scoreboard" each year based on a survey of executives at the highest-ranking companies listed in the *Business Week 1000.* The average* total pay of chief executive officers (CEOs) at 365 companies sampled in the 1998 scoreboard was $10.6 million—an increase of 36% over the previous year.

*Although we will not formally define the term *average* until Chapter 2, *typical* or *middle* can be substituted here without confusion.

To determine which executives are worth their pay, *Business Week* also records the ratio of total shareholder return (measured by the dollar value of a $100 investment in the company made 3 years earlier) to the total pay of the CEO (in thousand dollars) over the same 3-year period. For example, a $100 investment in Walt Disney Corporation in 1995 was worth $156 at the end of 1998. When this shareholder return ($156) is divided by CEO Michael Eisner's total 1996–1998 pay of $594.9 million, the result is a return-to-pay ratio of only .0003, one of the lowest among all other chief executives in the survey.

An analysis of the sample data set reveals that CEOs in the industrial high-technology industry have one of the highest average return-to-pay ratios (.046) while the CEOs in the transportation industry have one of the lowest average ratios (.015). (See Table 1.1.) Armed with this sample information *Business Week* might *infer* that, from the shareholders' perspective, typical chief executives in transportation are overpaid relative to industrial high-tech CEOs. Thus, this study is an example of *inferential statistics.*

TABLE 1.1 Average Return-to-Pay Ratios of CEOs, by Industry

Industry	Average Ratio
Industrial high-tech	0.046
Services	0.046
Telecommunications	0.045
Utilities	0.039
Financial	0.031
Consumer products	0.029
Resources	0.016
Industrial low-tech	0.015
Transportation	0.015

Source: Analysis of data in "Executive Compensation Scoreboard," *Business Week,* April 19, 1999.

Study 3 "The Consumer Price Index" *(U.S. Department of Labor)*

A data set of interest to virtually all Americans is the set of prices charged for goods and services in the U.S. economy. The general upward movement in this set of prices is referred to as *inflation*; the general downward movement is referred to as *deflation*. In order to *estimate* the change in prices over time, the Bureau of Labor Statistics (BLS) of the U.S. Department of Labor developed the Consumer Price Index (CPI). Each month, the BLS collects price data about a specific collection of goods and services (called a *market basket*) from 85 urban areas around the country. Statistical procedures are used to compute the CPI from this sample price data and other information about consumers' spending habits. By comparing the level of the CPI at different points in time, it is possible to *estimate* (make an inference about) the rate of inflation over particular time intervals and to compare the purchasing power of a dollar at different points in time.

One major use of the CPI as an index of inflation is as an indicator of the success or failure of government economic policies. A second use of the CPI is to escalate income payments. Millions of workers have *escalator clauses* in their collective bargaining contracts; these clauses call for increases in wage rates based on increases in the CPI. In addition, the incomes of Social Security beneficiaries and retired military and federal civil service employees are tied to the CPI. It has been estimated that a 1% increase in the CPI can trigger an increase of over $1 billion in income payments. Thus, it can be said that the very livelihoods of millions of Americans depend on the behavior of a statistical estimator, the CPI.

Like Study 2, this study is an example of *inferential statistics.* Market basket price data from a sample of urban areas (used to compute the CPI) are used to make inferences about the rate of inflation and wage rate increases.

These studies provide three real-life examples of the uses of statistics in business, economics, and government. Notice that each involves an analysis of data, either for the purpose of describing the data set (Study 1) or for making inferences about a data set (Studies 2 and 3).

1.3 FUNDAMENTAL ELEMENTS OF STATISTICS

Statistical methods are particularly useful for studying, analyzing, and learning about *populations.*

DEFINITION 1.4

A **population** is a set of units (usually people, objects, transactions, or events) that we are interested in studying.

For example, populations may include (1) *all* employed workers in the United States, (2) *all* registered voters in California, (3) *everyone* who has purchased a particular brand of cellular telephone, (4) *all* the cars produced last year by a particular assembly line, (5) the *entire* stock of spare parts at United Airlines' maintenance facility, (6) *all* sales made at the drive-through window of a McDonald's restaurant during a given year, and (7) the set of *all* accidents occurring on a particular stretch of interstate highway during a holiday period. Notice that the first three population examples (1–3) are sets (groups) of people, the next two (4–5) are sets of objects, the next (6) is a set of transactions, and the last (7) is a set of events. Also notice that each set includes all the units in the population of interest.

In studying a population, we focus on one or more characteristics or properties of the units in the population. We call such characteristics *variables*. For example, we may be interested in the variables age, gender, income, and/or the number of years of education of the people currently unemployed in the United States.

DEFINITION 1.5

A **variable** is a characteristic or property of an individual population unit.

The name "variable" is derived from the fact that any particular characteristic may vary among the units in a population.

In studying a particular variable it is helpful to be able to obtain a numerical representation for it. Often, however, numerical representations are not readily available, so the process of measurement plays an important supporting role in statistical studies. **Measurement** is the process we use to assign numbers to variables of individual population units. We might, for instance, measure the preference for a food product by asking a consumer to rate the product's taste on a scale from 1 to 10. Or we might measure workforce age by simply asking each worker how old she is. In other cases, measurement involves the use of instruments such as stopwatches, scales, and calipers.

If the population we wish to study is small, it is possible to measure a variable for every unit in the population. For example, if you are measuring the starting salary for all University of Michigan MBA graduates last year, it is at least feasible to obtain every salary. When we measure a variable for every unit of a population, the result is called a **census** of the population. Typically, however, the populations of interest in most applications are much larger, involving perhaps many thousands or even an infinite number of units. Examples of large populations include those following Definition 1.4, as well as all invoices produced in the last year by a *Fortune* 500 company, all potential buyers of a new fax machine, and all stockholders of a firm listed on the New York Stock Exchange. For such populations, conducting a census would be prohibitively time-consuming and/or costly.

A reasonable alternative would be to select and study a *subset* (or portion) of the units in the population.

DEFINITION 1.6

A **sample** is a subset of the units of a population.

For example, suppose a company is being audited for invoice errors. Instead of examining all 15,472 invoices produced by the company during a given year, an auditor may select and examine a sample of just 100 invoices (see Figure 1.2). If he is interested in the variable "invoice error status," he would record (measure) the status (error or no error) of each sampled invoice.

FIGURE 1.2
A sample of all company invoices

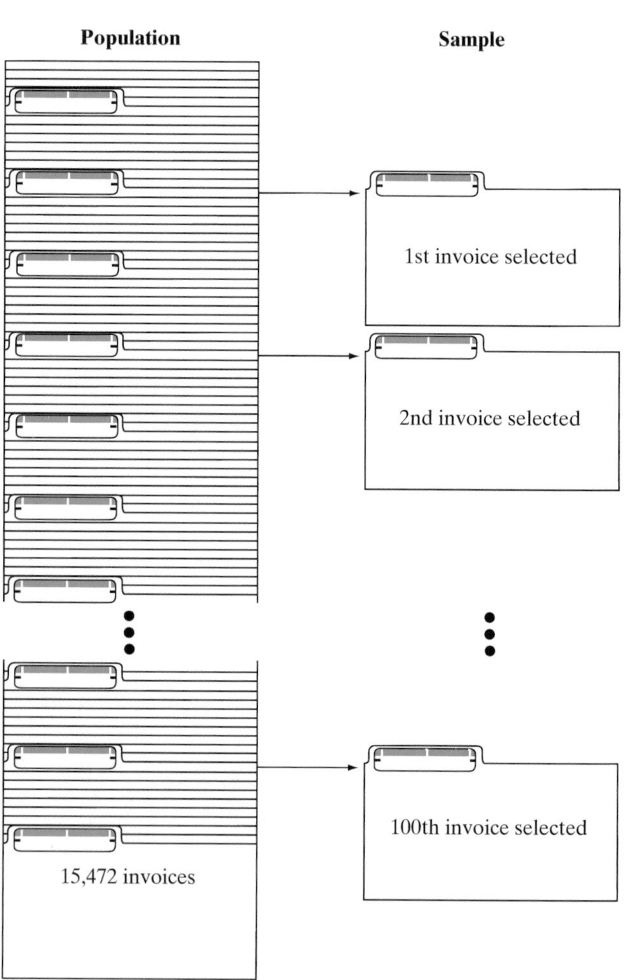

After the variable(s) of interest for every unit in the sample (or population) is measured, the data are analyzed, either by descriptive or inferential statistical methods. The auditor, for example, may be interested only in *describing* the error rate in the sample of 100 invoices. More likely, however, he will want to use the information in the sample to make *inferences* about the population of all 15,472 invoices.

DEFINITION 1.7

A **statistical inference** is an estimate or prediction or some other generalization about a population based on information contained in a sample.

*That is, we use the information contained in the sample to learn about the larger population.** Thus, from the sample of 100 invoices, the auditor may estimate the total number of invoices containing errors in the population of 15,472 invoices. The auditor's inference about the quality of the firm's invoices can be used in deciding whether to modify the firm's billing operations.

EXAMPLE 1.1

A large paint retailer has had numerous complaints from customers about underfilled paint cans. As a result, the retailer has begun inspecting incoming shipments of paint from suppliers. Shipments with underfill problems will be returned to the supplier. A recent shipment contained 2,440 gallon-size cans. The retailer sampled 50 cans and weighed each on a scale capable of measuring weight to four decimal places. Properly filled cans weigh 10 pounds.

a. Describe the population.

b. Describe the variable of interest.

c. Describe the sample.

d. Describe the inference.

Solution

a. The population is the set of units of interest to the retailer, which is the shipment of 2,440 cans of paint.

b. The weight of the paint cans is the variable the retailer wishes to evaluate.

c. The sample is a subset of the population. In this case, it is the 50 cans of paint selected by the retailer.

d. The inference of interest involves the *generalization* of the information contained in the weights of the sample of paint cans to the population of paint cans. In particular, the retailer wants to learn about the extent of the underfill problem (if any) in the population. This might be accomplished by finding the average weight of the cans in the sample and using it to estimate the average weight of the cans in the population.

EXAMPLE 1.2

"Cola wars" is the popular term for the intense competition between Coca-Cola and Pepsi displayed in their marketing campaigns. Their campaigns have featured movie and television stars, rock videos, athletic endorsements, and claims of consumer preference based on taste tests. Suppose, as part of a Pepsi marketing campaign, 1,000 cola consumers are given a blind taste test (i.e., a taste test in which the two brand names are disguised). Each consumer is asked to state a preference for brand A or brand B.

a. Describe the population.

b. Describe the variable of interest.

*The terms *population* and *sample* are often used to refer to the sets of measurements themselves, as well as to the units on which the measurements are made. When a single variable of interest is being measured, this usage causes little confusion. But when the terminology is ambiguous, we'll refer to the measurements as *population data sets* and *sample data sets,* respectively.

c. Describe the sample.

d. Describe the inference.

Solution

a. The population of interest is the collection or set of all cola consumers.

b. The characteristic that Pepsi wants to measure is the consumer's cola preference as revealed under the conditions of a blind taste test, so cola preference is the variable of interest.

c. The sample is the 1,000 cola consumers selected from the population of all cola consumers.

d. The inference of interest is the *generalization* of the cola preferences of the 1,000 sampled consumers to the population of all cola consumers. In particular, the preferences of the consumers in the sample can be used to *estimate* the percentage of all cola consumers who prefer each brand. ✶

The preceding definitions and examples identify four of the five elements of an inferential statistical problem: a population, one or more variables of interest, a sample, and an inference. But making the inference is only part of the story. We also need to know its **reliability**—that is, how good the inference is. The only way we can be certain that an inference about a population is correct is to include the entire population in our sample. However, because of *resource constraints* (i.e., insufficient time and/or money), we usually can't work with whole populations, so we base our inferences on just a portion of the population (a sample). Consequently, whenever possible, it is important to determine and report the reliability of each inference made. Reliability, then, is the fifth element of inferential statistical problems.

The measure of reliability that accompanies an inference separates the science of statistics from the art of fortune-telling. A palm reader, like a statistician, may examine a sample (your hand) and make inferences about the population (your life). However, unlike statistical inferences, the palm reader's inferences include no measure of reliability.

Suppose, as in Example 1.1, we are interested in estimating the average weight of a population of paint cans from the average weight of a sample of cans. Using statistical methods, we can determine a *bound on the estimation error.* This bound is simply a number that our estimation error (the difference between the average weight of the sample and the average weight of the population of cans) is not likely to exceed. We'll see in later chapters that this bound is a measure of the uncertainty of our inference. The reliability of statistical inferences is discussed throughout this text. For now, we simply want you to realize that an inference is incomplete without a measure of its reliability.

DEFINITION 1.8

A **measure of reliability** is a statement (usually quantified) about the degree of uncertainty associated with a statistical inference.

Let's conclude this section with a summary of the elements of both descriptive and inferential statistical problems and an example to illustrate a measure of reliability.

Four Elements of Descriptive Statistical Problems

1. The population or sample of interest
2. One or more variables (characteristics of the population or sample units) that are to be investigated
3. Tables, graphs, or numerical summary tools
4. Conclusions about the data based on the patterns revealed

Five Elements of Inferential Statistical Problems

1. The population of interest
2. One or more variables (characteristics of the population units) that are to be investigated
3. The sample of population units
4. The inference about the population based on information contained in the sample
5. A measure of reliability for the inference

EXAMPLE 1.3 Refer to Example 1.2, in which the cola preferences of 1,000 consumers were indicated in a taste test. Describe how the reliability of an inference concerning the preferences of all cola consumers in the Pepsi bottler's marketing region could be measured.

Solution When the preferences of 1,000 consumers are used to estimate the preferences of all consumers in the region, the estimate will not exactly mirror the preferences of the population. For example, if the taste test shows that 56% of the 1,000 consumers chose Pepsi, it does not follow (nor is it likely) that exactly 56% of all cola drinkers in the region prefer Pepsi. Nevertheless, we can use sound statistical reasoning (which is presented later in the text) to ensure that our sampling procedure will generate estimates that are almost certainly within a specified limit of the true percentage of all consumers who prefer Pepsi. For example, such reasoning might assure us that the estimate of the preference for Pepsi from the sample is almost certainly within 5% of the actual population preference. The implication is that the actual preference for Pepsi is between 51% [i.e., $(56 - 5)\%$] and 61% [i.e., $(56 + 5)\%$]—that is, $(56 \pm 5)\%$. This interval represents a measure of reliability for the inference. ✶

1.4 PROCESSES (OPTIONAL)

Sections 1.2 and 1.3 focused on the use of statistical methods to analyze and learn about populations, which are sets of *existing* units. Statistical methods are equally useful for analyzing and making inferences about *processes.*

DEFINITION 1.9

A **process** is a series of actions or operations that transforms inputs to outputs. A process produces or generates output over time.

The most obvious processes that are of interest to businesses are production or manufacturing processes. A manufacturing process uses a series of operations performed by people and machines to convert inputs, such as raw materials and parts, to finished products (the outputs). Examples include the process used to produce the paper on which these words are printed, automobile assembly lines, and oil refineries.

Figure 1.3 presents a general description of a process and its inputs and outputs. In the context of manufacturing, the process in the figure (i.e., the transformation process) could be a depiction of the overall production process or it could be a depiction of one of the many processes (sometimes called subprocesses) that exist within an overall production process. Thus, the output shown could be finished goods that will be shipped to an external customer or merely the output of one of the steps or subprocesses of the overall process. In the latter case, the output becomes input for the next subprocess. For example, Figure 1.3 could represent the overall automobile assembly process, with its output being fully assembled cars ready for shipment to dealers. Or, it could depict the windshield assembly subprocess, with its output of partially assembled cars with windshields ready for "shipment" to the next subprocess in the assembly line.

FIGURE 1.3 Graphical depiction of a manufacturing process

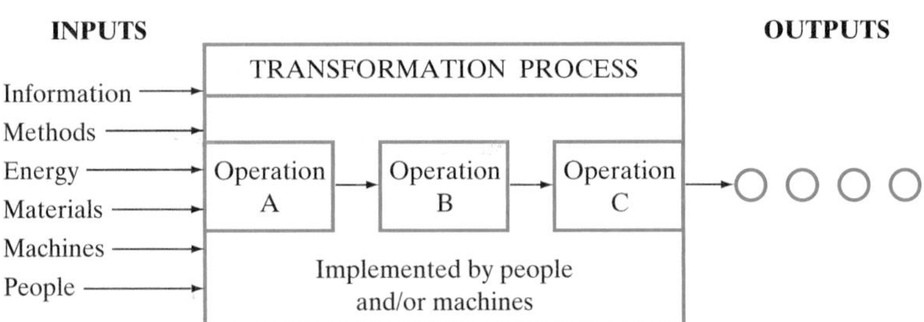

Besides physical products and services, businesses and other organizations generate streams of numerical data over time that are used to evaluate the performance of the organization. Examples include weekly sales figures, quarterly earnings, and yearly profits. The U.S. economy (a complex organization) can be thought of as generating streams of data that include the Gross Domestic Product (GDP), stock prices, and the Consumer Price Index (see Section 1.2). Statisticians and other analysts conceptualize these data streams as being generated by processes. Typically, however, the series of operations or actions that cause particular data to be realized are either unknown or so complex (or both) that the processes are treated as *black boxes.*

DEFINITION 1.10

A process whose operations or actions are unknown or unspecified is called a **black box.**

Frequently, when a process is treated as a black box, its inputs are not specified either. The entire focus is on the output of the process. A black box process is illustrated in Figure 1.4.

FIGURE 1.4
A black box process with numerical output

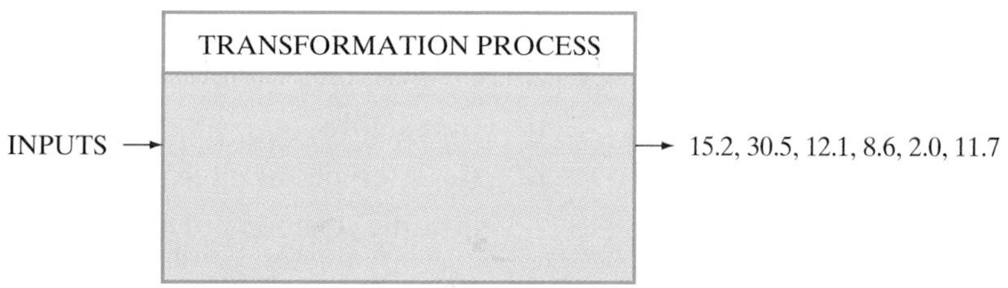

In studying a process, we generally focus on one or more characteristics, or properties, of the output. For example, we may be interested in the weight or the length of the units produced or even the time it takes to produce each unit. As with characteristics of population units, we call these characteristics *variables*. In studying processes whose output is already in numerical form (i.e., a stream of numbers), the characteristic, or property, represented by the numbers (e.g., sales, GDP, or stock prices) is typically the variable of interest. If the output is not numeric, we use *measurement processes* to assign numerical values to variables.* For example, if in the automobile assembly process the weight of the fully assembled automobile is the variable of interest, a measurement process involving a large scale will be used to assign a numerical value to each automobile.

As with populations, we use sample data to analyze and make inferences (estimates, predictions, or other generalizations) about processes. But the concept of a sample is defined differently when dealing with processes. Recall that a population is a set of existing units and that a sample is a subset of those units. In the case of processes, however, the concept of a set of existing units is not relevant or appropriate. Processes generate or create their output *over time*—one unit after another. For example, a particular automobile assembly line produces a completed vehicle every four minutes. We define a sample from a process in the box.

DEFINITION 1.11

Any set of output (objects or numbers) produced by a process is called a **sample.**

Thus, the next 10 cars turned out by the assembly line constitute a sample from the process, as do the next 100 cars or every fifth car produced today.

EXAMPLE 1.4

A particular fast-food restaurant chain has 6,289 outlets with drive-through windows. To attract more customers to its drive-through services, the company is considering offering a 50% discount to customers who wait more than a specified number of minutes to receive their order. To help determine what the time limit should be, the company decided to estimate the average waiting time at a particular drive-through window in Dallas, Texas. For seven consecutive days, the worker taking customers' orders recorded the time that every order was placed. The worker who handed the order to the customer recorded the time of delivery. In both cases, workers used synchronized digital clocks that reported the time to the nearest second. At the end of the 7-day period, 2,109 orders had been timed.

*A process whose output is already in numerical form necessarily includes a measurement process as one of its subprocesses.

a. Describe the process of interest at the Dallas restaurant.
b. Describe the variable of interest.
c. Describe the sample.
d. Describe the inference of interest.
e. Describe how the reliability of the inference could be measured.

Solution

a. The process of interest is the drive-through window at a particular fast-food restaurant in Dallas, Texas. It is a process because it "produces," or "generates," meals over time. That is, it services customers over time.

b. The variable the company monitored is customer waiting time, the length of time a customer waits to receive a meal after placing an order. Since the study is focusing only on the output of the process (the time to produce the output) and not the internal operations of the process (the tasks required to produce a meal for a customer), the process is being treated as a black box.

c. The sampling plan was to monitor every order over a particular 7-day period. The sample is the 2,109 orders that were processed during the 7-day period.

d. The company's immediate interest is in learning about the drive-through window in Dallas. They plan to do this by using the waiting times from the sample to make a statistical inference about the drive-through process. In particular, they might use the average waiting time for the sample to estimate the average waiting time at the Dallas facility.

e. As for inferences about populations, measures of reliability can be developed for inferences about processes. The reliability of the estimate of the average waiting time for the Dallas restaurant could be measured by a bound on the error of estimation. That is, we might find that the average waiting time is 4.2 minutes, with a bound on the error of estimation of .5 minute. The implication would be that we could be reasonably certain that the true average waiting time for the Dallas process is between 3.7 and 4.7 minutes.

Notice that there is also a population described in this example: the company's 6,289 existing outlets with drive-through facilities. In the final analysis, the company will use what it learns about the process in Dallas and, perhaps, similar studies at other locations to make an inference about the waiting times in its populations of outlets.

Note that output already generated by a process can be viewed as a population. Suppose a soft-drink canning process produced 2,000 twelve-packs yesterday, all of which were stored in a warehouse. If we were interested in learning something about those 2,000 packages—such as the percentage with defective cardboard packaging—we could treat the 2,000 packages as a population. We might draw a sample from the population in the warehouse, measure the variable of interest, and use the sample data to make a statistical inference about the 2,000 packages, as described in Sections 1.2 and 1.3.

In this optional section we have presented a brief introduction to processes and the use of statistical methods to analyze and learn about processes. In Chapter 11 we present an in-depth treatment of these subjects.

1.5 TYPES OF DATA

You have learned that statistics is the science of data and that data are obtained by measuring the values of one or more variables on the units in the sample (or population). All data (and hence the variables we measure) can be classified as one of two general types: *quantitative data* and *qualitative data.*

Quantitative data are data that are measured on a naturally occurring numerical scale.* The following are examples of quantitative data:

1. The temperature (in degrees Celsius) at which each unit in a sample of 20 pieces of heat-resistant plastic begins to melt
2. The current unemployment rate (measured as a percentage) for each of the 50 states
3. The scores of a sample of 150 MBA applicants on the GMAT, a standardized business graduate school entrance exam administered nationwide
4. The number of female executives employed in each of a sample of 75 manufacturing companies

DEFINITION 1.12

Quantitative data are measurements that are recorded on a naturally occurring numerical scale.

In contrast, qualitative data cannot be measured on a natural numerical scale; they can only be classified into categories.† Examples of qualitative data are:

1. The political party affiliation (Democrat, Republican, or Independent) in a sample of 50 chief executive officers
2. The defective status (defective or not) of each of 100 computer chips manufactured by Intel
3. The size of a car (subcompact, compact, mid-size, or full-size) rented by each of a sample of 30 business travelers
4. A taste tester's ranking (best, worst, etc.) of four brands of barbecue sauce for a panel of 10 testers

Often, we assign arbitrary numerical values to qualitative data for ease of computer entry and analysis. But these assigned numerical values are simply codes: They cannot be meaningfully added, subtracted, multiplied, or divided. For example, we might code Democrat = 1, Republican = 2, and Independent = 3. Similarly, a taste tester might rank the barbecue sauces from 1 (best) to 4 (worst). These are simply arbitrarily selected numerical codes for the categories and have no utility beyond that.

*Quantitative data can be subclassified as either *interval data* or *ratio data*. For ratio data, the origin (i.e., the value 0) is a meaningful number. But the origin has no meaning with interval data. Consequently, we can add and subtract interval data, but we can't multiply and divide them. Of the four quantitative data sets listed, (1) and (3) are interval data, while (2) and (4) are ratio data.

†Qualitative data can be subclassified as either *nominal data* or *ordinal data*. The categories of an ordinal data set can be ranked or meaningfully ordered, but the categories of a nominal data set can't be ordered. Of the four qualitative data sets listed above, (1) and (2) are nominal and (3) and (4) are ordinal.

DEFINITION 1.13

Qualitative data are measurements that cannot be measured on a natural numerical scale; they can only be classified into one of a group of categories.

EXAMPLE 1.5

Chemical and manufacturing plants sometimes discharge toxic-waste materials such as DDT into nearby rivers and streams. These toxins can adversely affect the plants and animals inhabiting the river and the river bank. The U.S. Army Corps of Engineers conducted a study of fish in the Tennessee River (in Alabama) and its three tributary creeks: Flint Creek, Limestone Creek, and Spring Creek. A total of 144 fish were captured and the following variables measured for each:

1. River/creek where fish was captured
2. Species (channel catfish, largemouth bass, or smallmouth buffalofish)
3. Length (centimeters)
4. Weight (grams)
5. DDT concentration (parts per million)

Classify each of the five variables measured as quantitative or qualitative.

Solution The variables length, weight, and DDT are quantitative because each is measured on a numerical scale: length in centimeters, weight in grams, and DDT in parts per million. In contrast, river/creek and species cannot be measured quantitatively: They can only be classified into categories (e.g., channel catfish, largemouth bass, and smallmouth buffalofish for species). Consequently, data on river/creek and species are qualitative. ✶

As you would expect, the statistical methods for describing, reporting, and analyzing data depend on the type (quantitative or qualitative) of data measured. We demonstrate many useful methods in the remaining chapters of the text. But first we discuss some important ideas on data collection.

1.6 COLLECTING DATA

Once you decide on the type of data—quantitative or qualitative—appropriate for the problem at hand, you'll need to collect the data. Generally, you can obtain the data in four different ways:

1. Data from a *published source*
2. Data from a *designed experiment*
3. Data from a *survey*
4. Data collected *observationally*

Sometimes, the data set of interest has already been collected for you and is available in a **published source,** such as a book, journal, or newspaper. For example, you may want to examine and summarize the unemployment rates (i.e., percentages of eligible workers who are unemployed) in the 50 states of the United States. You can find this data set (as well as numerous other data sets) at your library in the *Statistical Abstract of the United States,* published annually by the U.S. government. Similarly, someone who is interested in monthly mortgage applications for new home construction would find this data set in the *Survey of Current Business,* another government publication. Other examples of published data sources include *The Wall Street Journal* (financial data) and *The Sporting News* (sports information).*

A second method of collecting data involves conducting a **designed experiment,** in which the researcher exerts strict control over the units (people, objects, or events) in the study. For example, a recent medical study investigated the potential of aspirin in preventing heart attacks. Volunteer physicians were divided into two groups—the *treatment* group and the *control* group. In the treatment group, each physician took one aspirin tablet a day for one year, while each physician in the control group took an aspirin-free placebo (no drug) made to look like an aspirin tablet. The researchers, not the physicians under study, controlled who received the aspirin (the treatment) and who received the placebo. A properly designed experiment allows you to extract more information from the data than is possible with an uncontrolled study.

Surveys are a third source of data. With a **survey,** the researcher samples a group of people, asks one or more questions, and records the responses. Probably the most familiar type of survey is the political polls conducted by any one of a number of organizations (e.g., Harris, Gallup, Roper, and CNN) and designed to predict the outcome of a political election. Another familiar survey is the Nielsen survey, which provides the major television networks with information on the most watched TV programs. Surveys can be conducted through the mail, with telephone interviews, or with in-person interviews. Although in-person interviews are more expensive than mail or telephone surveys, they may be necessary when complex information must be collected.

Finally, observational studies can be employed to collect data. In an **observational study,** the researcher observes the experimental units in their natural setting and records the variable(s) of interest. For example, a company psychologist might observe and record the level of "Type A" behavior of a sample of assembly line workers. Similarly, a finance researcher may observe and record the closing stock prices of companies that are acquired by other firms on the day prior to the buyout and compare them to the closing prices on the day the acquisition is announced. Unlike a designed experiment, an observational study is one in which the researcher makes no attempt to control any aspect of the experimental units.

Regardless of the data collection method employed, it is likely that the data will be a sample from some population. And if we wish to apply inferential statistics, we must obtain a *representative sample.*

DEFINITION 1.14

A **representative sample** exhibits characteristics typical of those possessed by the population of interest.

For example, consider a political poll conducted during a presidential election year. Assume the pollster wants to estimate the percentage of all 120,000,000 registered voters in the United States who favor the incumbent president. The pollster would be unwise to base the estimate on survey data collected for a sample of voters from the incumbent's own state. Such an estimate would almost certainly be *biased* high.

*With published data, we often make a distinction between the *primary source* and *secondary source.* If the publisher is the original collector of the data, the source is primary. Otherwise, the data are secondary source data.

The most common way to satisfy the representative sample requirement is to select a random sample. A **random sample** ensures that every subset of fixed size in the population has the same chance of being included in the sample. If the pollster samples 1,500 of the 120,000,000 voters in the population so that every subset of 1,500 voters has an equal chance of being selected, he has devised a random sample. The procedure for selecting a random sample is discussed in Chapter 3. Here, however, let's look at two examples involving actual sampling studies.

EXAMPLE 1.6

What percentage of Web users are addicted to the Internet? To find out, a psychologist designed a series of 10 questions based on a widely used set of criteria for gambling addiction and distributed them through the Web site, *ABCNews.com*.(A sample question: "Do you use the Internet to escape problems?") A total of 17,251 Web users responded to the questionnaire. If participants answered "yes" to at least half of the questions, they were viewed as addicted. The findings, released at the 1999 annual meeting of the American Psychological Association, revealed that 990 respondents, or 5.7%, are addicted to the Internet (*Tampa Tribune*, Aug. 23, 1999).

a. Identify the data collection method.
b. Identify the target population.
c. Are the sample data representative of the population?

Solution

a. The data collection method is a survey: 17,251 Internet users responded to the questions posed at the *ABCNews.com* Web site.
b. Since the Web site can be accessed by anyone surfing the Internet, presumably the target population is *all* Internet users.
c. Because the 17,251 respondents clearly make up a subset of the target population, they do form a sample. Whether or not the sample is representative is unclear, since we are given no information on the 17,251 respondents. However, a survey like this one in which the respondents are *self-selected* (i.e., each Internet user who saw the survey chose whether or not to respond to it) often suffers from *nonresponse bias.* It is possible that many Internet users who chose not to respond (or who never saw the survey) would have answered the questions differently, leading to a higher (or lower) percentage of affirmative answers.

EXAMPLE 1.7

Many business decisions are made because of offered incentives that are intended to make the decision-maker "feel good." Researchers at the Ohio State University conducted a study to determine how such a positive effect influences the risk preference of decision-makers (*Organizational Behavior and Human Decision Processes,* Vol. 39, 1987). Each in a random sample of 24 undergraduate business students at the university was assigned to one of two groups. Each student assigned to the "positive affect" group was given a bag of candies as a token of appreciation for participating in the study; students assigned to the "control" group did not receive the gift. All students were then given 10 gambling chips (worth $10) to bet in the casino game of roulette. The researchers measured the win probability (i.e., chance of winning) associated with the riskiest bet each student was willing to make. The win probabilities of the bets made by two groups of students were compared.

a. Identify the data collection method.
b. Are the sample data representative of the target population?

Solution

a. The researchers controlled which group—"positive affect" or "control"—the students were assigned to. Consequently, a designed experiment was used to collect the data.

b. The sample of 24 students was randomly selected from all business students at the Ohio State University. If the target population is *all Ohio State University business students,* it is likely that the sample is representative. However, the researchers warn that the sample data should not be used to make inferences about other, more general, populations.

1.7 THE ROLE OF STATISTICS IN MANAGERIAL DECISION-MAKING

According to H. G. Wells, author of such science fiction classics as *The War of the Worlds* and *The Time Machine,* "*Statistical thinking* will one day be as necessary for efficient citizenship as the ability to read and write." Written more than a hundred years ago, Wells' prediction is proving true today.

The growth in data collection associated with scientific phenomena, business operations, and government activities (quality control, statistical auditing, forecasting, etc.) has been remarkable in the past several decades. Every day the media present us with the published results of political, economic, and social surveys. In increasing government emphasis on drug and product testing, for example, we see vivid evidence of the need to be able to evaluate data sets intelligently. Consequently, each of us has to develop a discerning sense—an ability to use rational thought to interpret and understand the meaning of data. This ability can help you make intelligent decisions, inferences, and generalizations; that is, it helps you *think critically* using statistics.

DEFINITION 1.15

Statistical thinking involves applying rational thought and the science of statistics to critically assess data and inferences. Fundamental to the thought process is that variation exists in populations and process data.

To gain some insight into the role statistics plays in critical thinking, let's look at a study evaluated by a group of 27 mathematics and statistics teachers attending an American Statistical Association course called "Chance." Consider the following excerpt from an article describing the problem.

> *There are few issues in the news that are not in some way statistical. Take one. Should motorcyclists be required by law to wear helmets?. . . In "The Case for No Helmets"* (New York Times, *June 17, 1995), Dick Teresi, editor of a magazine for Harley-Davidson bikers, argued that helmets may actually kill, since in collisions at speeds greater than 15 miles an hour the heavy helmet may protect the head but snap the spine. [Teresi] citing a "study," said "nine states without helmet laws had a lower fatality rate (3.05 deaths per 10,000 motorcycles) than those that mandated helmets (3.38)," and "in a survey of 2,500 [at a rally], 98% of the respondents opposed such laws."*
>
> *[The course instructors] asked: After reading this* [New York Times] *piece, do you think it is safer to ride a motorcycle without a helmet? Do you think 98% might be a valid estimate of bikers who oppose helmet laws? What*

STATISTICS IN Action

A *20/20* View of Survey Results: Fact or Fiction?

Did you ever notice that, no matter where you stand on popular issues of the day, you can always find statistics or surveys to back up your point of view—whether to take vitamins, whether day care harms kids, or what foods can hurt you or save you? There is an endless flow of information to help you make decisions, but is this information accurate, unbiased? John Stossel decided to check that out, and you may be surprised to learn if the picture you're getting doesn't seem quite right, maybe it isn't.

Barbara Walters gave this introduction to a March 31, 1995, segment of the popular prime-time ABC television program *20/20*. The story is titled "Facts or Fiction?—Exposés of So-Called Surveys." One of the surveys investigated by ABC correspondent John Stossel compared the discipline problems experienced by teachers in the 1940s and those experienced today. The results: In the 1940s, teachers worried most about students talking in class, chewing gum, and running in the halls. Today, they worry most about being assaulted! This information was highly publicized in the print media—in daily newspapers, weekly magazines, Ann Landers' column, the *Congressional Quarterly*, and *The Wall Street Journal*, among others—and referenced in speeches by a variety of public figures, including former first lady Barbara Bush and former Education secretary William Bennett.

"Hearing this made me yearn for the old days when life was so much simpler and gentler, but was life that simple then?" asks Stossel. "Wasn't there juvenile delinquency [in the 1940s]? Is the survey true?" With the help of a Yale School of Management professor, Stossel found the original source of the teacher survey—Texas oilman T. Colin Davis—and discovered it wasn't a survey at all! Davis had simply identified certain disciplinary problems encountered by teachers in a conservative newsletter—a list he admitted was not obtained from a statistical survey, but from Davis' personal knowledge of the problems in the 1940s ("I was in school then") and his understanding of the problems today ("I read the papers").

Stossel's critical thinking about the teacher "survey" led to the discovery of research that is misleading at best and unethical at worst. Several more misleading (and possibly unethical) surveys were presented on the ABC program. Listed here, most of these were conducted by businesses or special interest groups with specific objectives in mind.

The *20/20* segment ended with an interview of Cynthia Crossen, author of *Tainted Truth*, an exposé of misleading and biased surveys. Crossen warns: "If everybody is misusing numbers and scaring us with numbers to get us to do something, however good [that something] is, we've lost the power of numbers. Now, we know certain things from research. For example, we know that smoking cigarettes is hard on your lungs and heart, and because we know that, many people's lives have been extended or saved. We don't

further statistical information would you like? [From Cohn, V. "Chance in college curriculum," AmStat News, *Aug.–Sept. 1995, No. 223, p. 2.]*

You can use "statistical thinking" to help you critically evaluate the study. For example, before you can evaluate the validity of the 98% estimate, you would want to know how the data were collected for the study cited by the editor of the biker magazine. If a survey was conducted, it's possible that the 2,500 bikers in the sample were not selected at random from the target population of all bikers, but rather were "self-selected." (Remember, they were all attending a rally—a rally likely for bikers who oppose the law.) If the respondents were likely to have strong opinions regarding the helmet law (e.g., strongly oppose the law), the resulting estimate is probably biased high. Also, if the biased sample was intentional, with the sole purpose to mislead the public, the researchers would be guilty of **unethical statistical practice.**

You'd also want more information about the study comparing the motorcycle fatality rate of the nine states without a helmet law to those states that mandate hel-

want to lose the power of information to help us make decisions, and that's what I worry about."

Focus

a. Consider the false March of Dimes report on domestic violence and birth defects. Discuss the type of data required to investigate the impact of domestic violence on birth defects. What data collection method would you recommend?

b. Refer to the American Association of University Women (AAUW) study of self-esteem of high school girls. Explain why the results of the AAUW study are likely to be misleading. What data might be appropriate for assessing the self-esteem of high school girls?

c. Refer to the Food Research and Action Center study of hunger in America. Explain why the results of the study are likely to be misleading. What data would provide insight into the proportion of hungry American children?

Reported Information (Source)	Actual Study Information
Eating oat bran is a cheap and easy way to reduce your cholesterol count. (Quaker Oats)	Diet must consist of nothing but oat bran to achieve a slightly lower cholesterol count.
150,000 women a year die from anorexia. (Feminist group)	Approximately 1,000 women a year die from problems that were likely caused by anorexia.
Domestic violence causes more birth defects than all medical issues combined. (March of Dimes)	No study—false report.
Only 29% of high school girls are happy with themselves, compared to 66% of elementary school girls. (American Association of University Women)	Of 3,000 high school girls 29% responded "Always true" to the statement, "I am happy the way I am." Most answered, "Sort of true" and "Sometimes true."
One in four American children under age 12 is hungry or at risk of hunger. (Food Research and Action Center)	Based on responses to the questions: "Do you ever cut the size of meals?" "Do you ever eat less than you feel you should?" "Did you ever rely on limited numbers of foods to feed your children because you were running out of money to buy food for a meal?"

mets. Were the data obtained from a published source? Were all 50 states included in the study? That is, are you seeing sample data or population data? Furthermore, do the helmet laws vary among states? If so, can you really compare the fatality rates?

These questions led the Chance group to the discovery of two scientific and statistically sound studies on helmets. The first, a UCLA study of nonfatal injuries, disputed the charge that helmets shift injuries to the spine. The second study reported a dramatic *decline* in motorcycle crash deaths after California passed its helmet law.

Successful managers rely heavily on statistical thinking to help them make decisions. The role statistics can play in managerial decision-making is displayed in the flow diagram in Figure 1.5. Every managerial decision-making problem begins with a real-world problem. This problem is then formulated in managerial terms and framed as a managerial question. The next sequence of steps (proceeding counterclockwise around the flow diagram) identifies the role that statistics can play in this process. The managerial question is translated into a statistical question,

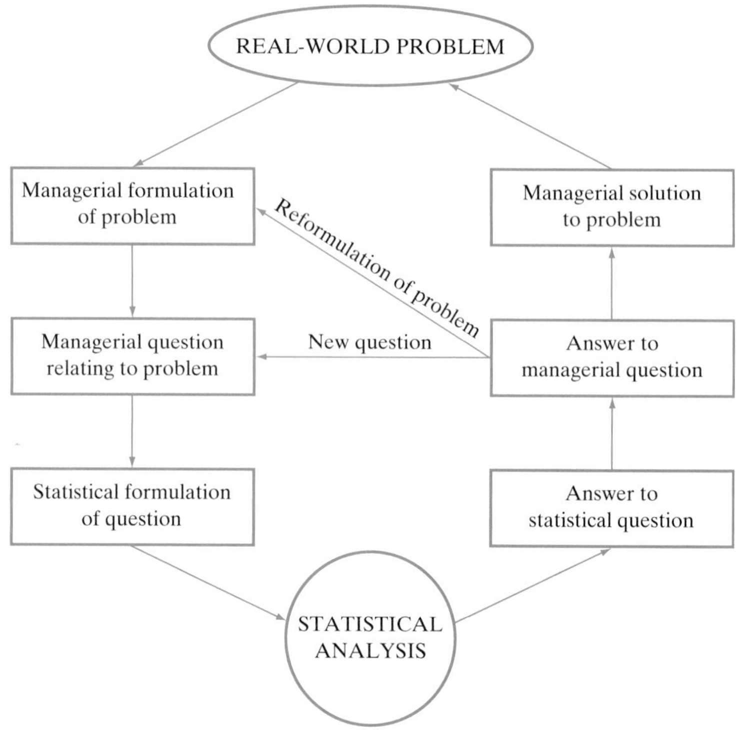

FIGURE 1.5
Flow diagram showing the role of statistics in managerial decision-making
Source: Chervany, Benson, and Iyer (1980)

the sample data are collected and analyzed, and the statistical question is answered. The next step in the process is using the answer to the statistical question to reach an answer to the managerial question. The answer to the managerial question may suggest a reformulation of the original managerial problem, suggest a new managerial question, or lead to the solution of the managerial problem.

One of the most difficult steps in the decision-making process—one that requires a cooperative effort among managers and statisticians—is the translation of the managerial question into statistical terms (for example, into a question about a population). This statistical question must be formulated so that, when answered, it will provide the key to the answer to the managerial question. Thus, as in the game of chess, you must formulate the statistical question with the end result, the solution to the managerial question, in mind.

In the remaining chapters of the text, you'll become familiar with the tools essential for building a firm foundation in statistics and statistical thinking.

QUICK REVIEW

Key Terms

Note: Starred (*) terms are from the optional section in this chapter.

Black box* 10
Census 5
Data 2
Descriptive statistics 2
Designed experiment 16
Inference 3
Inferential statistics 3
Measure of reliability 8
Measurement 5
Observational study 15
Population 5
Process* 9
Published source 14
Qualitative data 14
Quantitative data 13
Random sample 16
Reliability 8
Representative sample 15
Sample 6, 11
Statistical inference 7
Statistical thinking 17
Statistics 2
Survey 15
Unethical statistical practice 18
Variable 5

EXERCISES 1.1 – 1.28

Note: Starred (*) exercises are from the optional section in this chapter.

Learning the Mechanics

1.1 What is statistics?

1.2 Explain the difference between descriptive and inferential statistics.

1.3 List and define the four elements of a descriptive statistics problem.

1.4 List and define the five elements of an inferential statistical analysis.

1.5 List the four major methods of collecting data and explain their differences.

1.6 Explain the difference between quantitative and qualitative data.

1.7 Explain how populations and variables differ.

1.8 Explain how populations and samples differ.

1.9 What is a representative sample? What is its value?

1.10 Why would a statistician consider an inference incomplete without an accompanying measure of its reliability?

*1.11 Explain the difference between a population and a process.

1.12 Define statistical thinking.

1.13 Suppose you're given a data set that classifies each sample unit into one of four categories: A, B, C, or D. You plan to create a computer database consisting of these data, and you decide to code the data as A = 1, B = 2, C = 3, and D = 4. Are the data consisting of the classifications A, B, C, and D qualitative or quantitative? After the data are input as 1, 2, 3, or 4, are they qualitative or quantitative? Explain your answers.

Applying the Concepts

1.14 The Cutter Consortium recently surveyed 154 U.S. companies to determine the extent of their involvement in e-commerce. They found that "a stunning 65% of companies. . .do not have an overall e-commerce strategy." Four of the questions they asked are listed below. For each question, determine the variable of interest and classify it as quantitative or qualitative. (*Internet Week,* Sept. 6, 1999, *www.internetwk.com*)

a. Do you have an overall e-commerce strategy?

b. If you don't already have an e-commerce plan, when will you implement one: never, later than 2000, by the second half of 2000, by the first half of 2000, by the end of 1999?

c. Are you delivering products over the Internet?

d. What was your company's total revenue in the last fiscal year?

1.15 Pollsters regularly conduct opinion polls to determine the popularity rating of the current president. Suppose a poll is to be conducted tomorrow in which 2,000 individuals will be asked whether the president is doing a good or bad job. The 2,000 individuals will be selected by random-digit telephone dialing and asked the question over the phone.

a. What is the relevant population?

b. What is the variable of interest? Is it quantitative or qualitative?

c. What is the sample?

d. What is the inference of interest to the pollster?

e. What method of data collection is employed?

f. How likely is the sample to be representative?

1.16 Colleges and universities are requiring an increasing amount of information about applicants before making acceptance and financial aid decisions. Classify each of the following types of data required on a college application as quantitative or qualitative.

a. High school GPA

b. High school class rank

c. Applicant's score on the SAT or ACT

d. Gender of applicant

e. Parents' income

f. Age of applicant

1.17 As the 1990s came to a close, the U.S. economy was booming. One of the consequences was an ultra-tight labor market in which companies struggled to find, attract, and retain good employees. To help employers better understand what employees value, Fort Lauderdale-based Interim Services, Inc. surveyed a random sample of 1,000 employees in the U.S. One question they asked was, "If your employer provides you with mentoring opportunities are you likely to remain in your job for the next five years?" They found that 620 members of the sample said "yes." (*HRMagazine,* Sept. 1999)

a. Identify the population of interest to Interim Services, Inc.

b. Based on the question posed by Interim Services, Inc., what is the variable of interest?

c. Is the variable quantitative or qualitative? Explain.

d. Describe the sample.

e. What inference can be made from the results of the survey?

1.18 For the past 15 years, global competition has spurred U.S. companies to downsize, streamline, and cut costs through outsourcing and the use of temporary employees. In fact, the number of temporary employees has increased by more than 250% during the 1990s. The Institute of Management and Office Angels—the United Kingdom's secretarial recruitment agency—conducted a survey to study the temporary employment market. They mailed a questionnaire to a random sample of

4,000 Institute of Management members and received 684 replies. One question asked: "Do you expect an increase, no change, or decrease in the number of temporary employees in your organization by 2002?" 43% indicated the number of temporary employees would increase. (*Management Services,* Sept. 1999)

a. Identify the data collection method used by the researchers.
b. Identify the population sampled by the researchers.
c. Based on the question posed by the researchers, what is the variable of interest?
d. Is the variable quantitative or qualitative? Explain.
e. What inference can be made from the results of the study?

1.19 All highway bridges in the United States are inspected periodically for structural deficiency by the Federal Highway Administration (FHWA). Data from the FHWA inspections are compiled into the National Bridge Inventory (NBI). Several of the nearly 100 variables maintained by the NBI are listed below. Classify each variable as quantitative or qualitative.

a. Length of maximum span (feet)
b. Number of vehicle lanes
c. Toll bridge (yes or no)
d. Average daily traffic
e. Condition of deck (good, fair, or poor)
f. Bypass or detour length (miles)
g. Route type (interstate, U.S., state, county, or city)

1.20 Refer to Exercise 1.19. The most recent NBI data were analyzed and the results published in the *Journal of Infrastructure Systems* (June 1995). Using the FHWA inspection ratings, each of the 470,515 highway bridges in the United States was categorized as structurally deficient, functionally obsolete, or safe. About 26% of the bridges were found to be structurally deficient, while 19% were functionally obsolete.

a. What is the variable of interest to the researchers?
b. Is the variable of part **a** quantitative or qualitative?
c. Is the data set analyzed a population or a sample? Explain.
d. How did the researchers obtain the data for their study?

1.21 The *Journal of Retailing* (Spring 1988) published a study of the relationship between job satisfaction and the degree of *Machiavellian orientation.* Briefly, the Machiavellian orientation is one in which the executive exerts very strong control, even to the point of deception and cruelty, over the employees he or she supervises. The authors administered a questionnaire to each in a sample of 218 department store executives and obtained both a job satisfaction score and a Machiavellian rating. They concluded that those with higher job satisfaction scores are likely to have a lower "Mach" rating.

a. What is the population from which the sample was selected?
b. What variables were measured by the authors?
c. Identify the sample.
d. Identify the data collection method used.
e. What inference was made by the authors?

1.22 Media reports suggest that disgruntled shareholders are becoming more willing to put pressure on corporate management. Is this an impression caused by a few recent high-profile cases involving a few large investors, or is shareholder activism widespread? To answer this question the Wirthlin Group, an opinion research organization in McLean, Virginia, sampled and questioned 240 large investors (money managers, mutual fund managers, institutional investors, etc.) in the United States. One question they asked was: Have you written or called a corporate director to express your views? They found that a surprisingly large 40% of the sample had (*New York Times,* Oct. 31, 1995).

a. Identify the population of interest to the Wirthlin Group.
b. Based on the question the Wirthlin Group asked, what is the variable of interest?
c. Describe the sample.
d. What inference can be made from the results of the survey?

1.23 *Corporate merger* is a means through which one firm (the bidder) acquires control of the assets of another firm (the target). During 1995 there was a frenzy of bank mergers in the United States, as the banking industry consolidated into more efficient and more competitive units. The number of banks in the United States has fallen from a high of 14,496 in 1984 to just under 10,000 at the end of 1995 (*Fortune,* Oct. 2, 1995).

a. Construct a brief questionnaire (two or three questions) that could be used to query a sample of bank presidents concerning their opinions of why the industry is consolidating and whether it will consolidate further.
b. Describe the population about which inferences could be made from the results of the survey.
c. Discuss the pros and cons of sending the questionnaire to all bank presidents versus a sample of 200.

*1.24 Coca-Cola and Schweppes Beverages Limited (CCSB), which was formed in 1987, is 49% owned by the Coca-Cola Company. According to *Industrial Management and Data Systems* (Vol. 92, 1992), CCSB's Wakefield plant can produce 4,000 cans of soft drink per minute. The automated process consists of measuring and dispensing the raw ingredients into storage vessels to create the syrup, and then injecting the syrup, along with carbon dioxide, into the beverage cans. In order to monitor the subprocess that adds carbon dioxide to the cans, five filled cans are pulled off the line every 15 minutes and the amount of carbon dioxide in each of these five is measured to determine whether the amounts are within prescribed limits.

a. Describe the process studied.
b. Describe the variable of interest.
c. Describe the sample.
d. Describe the inference of interest.
e. *Brix* is a unit for measuring sugar concentration. If a technician is assigned the task of estimating the average brix level of all 240,000 cans of beverage stored in a warehouse near Wakefield, will the technician be examining a process or a population? Explain.

1.25 *Job-sharing* is an innovative employment alternative that originated in Sweden and is becoming very popular in the United States. Firms that offer job-sharing plans allow two or more persons to work part-time, sharing one full-time job. For example, two job-sharers might alternate work weeks, with one working while the other is off. Job-sharers never work at the same time and may not even know each other. Job-sharing is particularly attractive to working mothers and to people who frequently lose their jobs due to fluctuations in the economy. In a survey of 1,035 major U.S. firms, approximately 22% offer job-sharing to their employees (*Entrepreneur*, Mar. 1995).

a. Identify the population from which the sample was selected.
b. Identify the variable measured.
c. Identify the sample selected.
d. What type of inference is of interest to the government agency?

1.26 The People's Republic of China with its 1.2 billion people is emerging as the world's biggest cigarette market. In fact, China's cigarette industry is the central government's largest source of tax revenue. To better understand Chinese smokers and the potential public health disaster they represent, door-to-door interviews of 3,423 men and 3,593 women were conducted in the Minhang District, a suburb of 500,000 people near Shanghai. The study concluded that "people in China, despite their modest incomes, are willing to spend an average of 60 percent of personal income and 17 percent of household income to buy cigarettes" (*Newark Star-Ledger*, Oct. 19, 1995).

a. Identify the population that was sampled.
b. How large was the sample size?
c. The study made inferences about what population?
d. Explain why different answers to parts **a** and **c** might affect the reliability of the study's conclusions.

1.27 To assess how extensively accounting firms in New York State use sampling methods in auditing their clients, the New York Society of CPAs mailed a questionnaire to 800 New York accounting firms employing two or more professionals. They received responses from 179 firms of which four responses were unusable and 12 reported they had no audit practice. The questionnaire asked firms whether they use audit sampling methods and, if so, whether or not they use random sampling (*CPA Journal*, July 1995).

a. Identify the population, the variables, the sample, and the inferences of interest to the New York Society of CPAs.
b. Speculate as to what could have made four of the responses unusable.
c. In Chapters 6–9 you will learn that the reliability of an inference is related to the size of the sample used. In addition to sample size, what factors might affect the reliability of the inferences drawn in the mail survey described above?

1.28 The employment status (employed or unemployed) of each individual in the U.S. workforce is a set of data that is of interest to economists, businesspeople, and sociologists. These data provide information on the social and economic health of our society. To obtain information about the employment status of the workforce, the U.S. Bureau of the Census conducts what is known as the *Current Population Survey*. Each month approximately 1,500 interviewers visit about 59,000 of the 92 million households in the United States and question the occupants over 14 years of age about their employment status. Their responses enable the Bureau of the Census to *estimate* the percentage of people in the labor force who are unemployed (the *unemployment rate*).

a. Define the population of interest to the Census Bureau.
b. What variable is being measured? Is it quantitative or qualitative?
c. Is the problem of interest to the Census Bureau descriptive or inferential?
d. In order to monitor the rate of unemployment, it is essential to have a definition of "unemployed." Different economists and even different countries define it in various ways. Develop your own definition of an "unemployed person." Your definition should answer such questions as: Are students on summer vacation unemployed? Are college professors who do not teach summer school unemployed? At what age are people considered to be eligible for the workforce? Are people who are out of work but not actively seeking a job unemployed?

Chapter 2

METHODS FOR DESCRIBING SETS OF DATA

CONTENTS

STATISTICS IN ACTION

Where We've Been

In Chapter 1 we looked at some typical examples of the use of statistics and we discussed the role that statistical thinking plays in supporting managerial decision-making. We examined the difference between descriptive and inferential statistics and described the five elements of inferential statistics: a population, one or more variables, a sample, an inference, and a measure of reliability for the inference. We also learned that data can be of two types—quantitative and qualitative.

Where We're Going

Before we make an inference, we must be able to describe a data set. We can do this by using graphical and/or numerical methods, which we discuss in this chapter. As we'll see in Chapter 5, we use sample numerical descriptive measures to estimate the values of corresponding population descriptive measures. Therefore, our efforts in this chapter will ultimately lead us to statistical inference.

Suppose you wish to evaluate the managerial capabilities of a class of 400 MBA students based on their Graduate Management Aptitude Test (GMAT) scores. How would you describe these 400 measurements? Characteristics of the data set include the typical or most frequent GMAT score, the variability in the scores, the highest and lowest scores, the "shape" of the data, and whether or not the data set contains any unusual scores. Extracting this information by "eye-balling" the data isn't easy. The 400 scores may provide too many bits of information for our minds to comprehend. Clearly we need some formal methods for summarizing and characterizing the information in such a data set. Methods for describing data sets are also essential for statistical inference. Most populations are large data sets. Consequently, we need methods for describing a sample data set that let us make descriptive statements (inferences) about the population from which the sample was drawn.

Two methods for describing data are presented in this chapter, one *graphical* and the other *numerical.* Both play an important role in statistics. Section 2.1 presents both graphical and numerical methods for describing qualitative data. Graphical methods for describing quantitative data are presented in Section 2.2 and optional Sections 2.8, 2.9, and 2.10; numerical descriptive methods for quantitative data are presented in Sections 2.3–2.7. We end this chapter with a section on the *misuse* of descriptive techniques.

2.1 DESCRIBING QUALITATIVE DATA

Recall the "Executive Compensation Scoreboard" tabulated annually by *Business Week* (see Study 2 in Section 1.2). *Forbes* magazine also conducts a salary survey of chief executive officers each year. In addition to salary information, *Forbes* collects and reports personal data on the CEOs, including level of education. Do most CEOs have advanced degrees, such as masters degrees or doctorates? To answer this question, Table 2.1 gives the highest college degree obtained (bachelors, masters, doctorate, or none) for each of the 25 best-paid CEOs in 1998.

For this study, the variable of interest, highest college degree obtained, is qualitative in nature. Qualitative data are nonnumerical in nature; thus, the value of a qualitative variable can only be classified into categories called *classes.* The possible degree types—bachelors, masters, doctorate, and none—represent the classes for this qualitative variable. We can summarize such data numerically in two ways: (1) by computing the *class frequency*—the number of observations in the data set that fall into each class; or (2) by computing the *class relative frequency*—the proportion of the total number of observations falling into each class.

DEFINITION 2.1

A **class** is one of the categories into which qualitative data can be classified.

DEFINITION 2.2

The **class frequency** is the number of observations in the data set falling into a particular class.

TABLE 2.1 Data on 25 Best-Paid Executives

CEO	Company	Degree
1. Michael D. Eisner	Walt Disney	Bachelors
2. Mel Karmazin	CBS	Bachelors
3. Stephen M. Case	America Online	Bachelors
4. Stephen C. Hilbert	Conseco	None
5. Craig R. Barrett	Intel	Doctorate
6. Millard Drexler	Gap	Masters
7. John F. Welch, Jr.	General Electric	Doctorate
8. Thomas G. Stemberg	Staples	Masters
9. Henry R. Silverman	Cendant	JD(law)
10. Reuben Mark	Colgate-Palmolive	Masters
11. Philip J. Purcell	Morgan Stanley Dean Witter	Masters
12. Scott G. McNealy	Sun Microsystems	Masters
13. Margaret C. Whitman	eBay	Masters
14. Louis V. Gerstner, Jr.	IBM	Masters
15. John F. Gifford	Maxim Integrated Products	Bachelors
16. Robert L. Waltrip	Service Corp. International	Bachelors
17. M. Douglas Ivester	Coca-Cola	Bachelors
18. Gordon M. Binder	Amgen	Masters
19. Charles R. Schwab	Charles Schwab	Masters
20. William R. Steere, Jr.	Pfizer	Bachelors
21. Nolan D. Archibald	Black & Decker	Masters
22. Charles A. Heimbold, Jr.	Bristol-Myers Squibb	LLB (law)
23. William L. Larson	Network Association	JD (law)
24. Maurice R. Greenberg	American International Group	LLB (law)
25. Richard Jay Kogan	Schering-Plough	Masters

Source: *Forbes*, May 17, 1999.

DEFINITION 2.3

The **class relative frequency** is the class frequency divided by the total number of observations in the data set.

Examining Table 2.1, we observe that 1 of the 25 best-paid CEOs did not obtain a college degree, 7 obtained bachelors degrees, 11 masters degrees, and 6 doctorates or law degrees. These numbers—1, 7, 11, and 6—represent the class frequencies for the four classes and are shown in the summary table, Table 2.2.

TABLE 2.2 Summary Table for Data on 25 Best-Paid CEOs

Class	Frequency	Relative Frequency
Highest Degree Obtained	Number of CEOs	Proportion
None	1	.04
Bachelors	7	.28
Masters	11	.44
Doctorate/Law	6	.24
Totals	25	1.000

Table 2.2 also gives the relative frequency of each of the four degree classes. From Definition 2.3, we know that we calculate the relative frequency by dividing the class frequency by the total number of observations in the data set. Thus, the relative frequencies for the four degree types are

$$\text{None: } \frac{1}{25} = .04$$

$$\text{Bachelors: } \frac{7}{25} = .28$$

$$\text{Masters: } \frac{11}{25} = .44$$

$$\text{Doctorate: } \frac{6}{25} = .24$$

From these relative frequencies we observe that nearly half (44%) of the 25 best-paid CEOs obtained their masters degree.

Although the summary table of Table 2.2 adequately describes the data of Table 2.1, we often want a graphical presentation as well. Figures 2.1 and 2.2 show two of the most widely used graphical methods for describing qualitative data—**bar graphs** and **pie charts.** Figure 2.1 shows the frequencies of "highest degree obtained" in a *bar graph* created using the EXCEL software package. Note that the height of the rectangle, or "bar," over each class is equal to the class frequency. (Optionally, the bar heights can be proportional to class relative frequencies.) In contrast, Figure 2.2 (also created using EXCEL) shows the relative frequencies of the four degree types in a *pie chart.* Note that the pie is a circle (spanning 360°) and the size (angle) of the "pie slice" assigned to each class is proportional to the class relative frequency. For example, the slice assigned to masters degree is 44% of 360°, or (.44)(360°) = 158.4°.

FIGURE 2.1
EXCEL graph for data on 25 CEOs

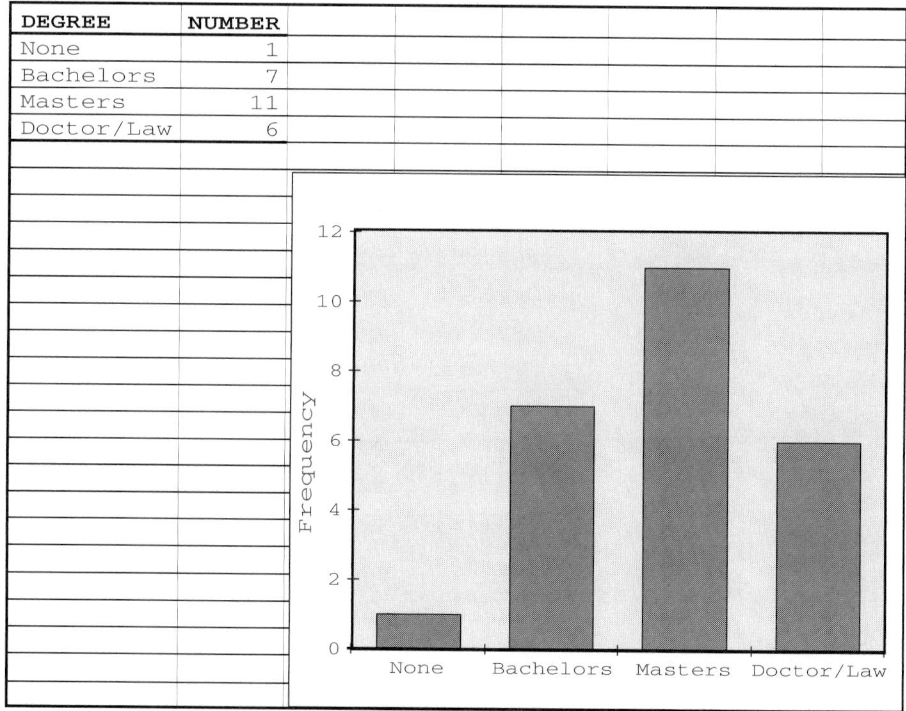

DEGREE	NUMBER
None	1
Bachelors	7
Masters	11
Doctor/Law	6

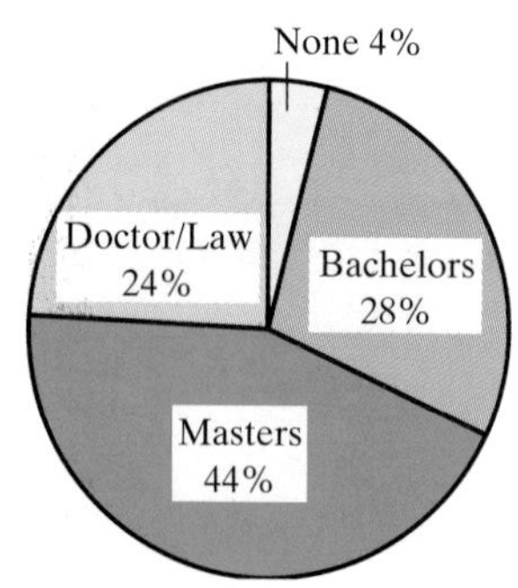

FIGURE 2.2
EXCEL pie chart for data on 25 CEOs

Let's look at two practical examples that require interpretation of the graphical results.

EXAMPLE 2.1

A group of cardiac physicians in southwest Florida have been studying a new drug designed to reduce blood loss in coronary artery bypass operations. Blood loss data for 114 coronary artery bypass patients (some who received a dosage of the drug and others who did not) were collected and are made available for analysis.* Although the drug shows promise in reducing blood loss, the physicians are concerned about possible side effects and complications. So their data set includes not only the qualitative variable, DRUG, which indicates whether or not the patient received the drug, but also the qualitative variable, COMP, which specifies the type (if any) of complication experienced by the patient. The four values of COMP recorded by the physicians are: (1) redo surgery, (2) post-op infection, (3) both, or (4) none.

a. Figure 2.3, generated using SAS computer software, shows summary tables for the two qualitative variables, DRUG and COMP. Interpret the results.
b. Interpret the SAS graph and summary tables shown in Figure 2.4.

FIGURE 2.3
SAS summary tables for DRUG and COMP

DRUG	Frequency	Percent	Cumulative Frequency	Cumulative Percent
NO	57	50.0	57	50.0
YES	57	50.0	114	100.0

COMP	Frequency	Percent	Cumulative Frequency	Cumulative Percent
1:REDO	12	10.5	12	10.5
2:INFECT	12	10.5	24	21.0
3:BOTH	4	3.5	28	24.5
4:NONE	86	75.5	114	100.0

Solution

a. The top table in Figure 2.3 is a summary frequency table for DRUG. Note that exactly half (57) of the 114 coronary artery bypass patients received the drug and half did not. The bottom table in Figure 2.4 is a summary frequency table for COMP. The class relative frequencies are given in the **Percent** column. We see that 75.5% of the 114 patients had no complications, leaving 24.5% who experienced either a redo surgery, a post-op infection, or both.
b. At the top of Figure 2.4 is a side-by-side bar graph for the data. The first four bars represent the frequencies of COMP for the 57 patients who did not receive the drug; the next four bars represent the frequencies of COMP for the 57 patients who did receive a dosage of the drug. The graph clearly shows that patients who got the drug suffered more complications. The exact percentages are displayed in the summary tables of Figure 2.4. About 30% of the patients who got the drug had complications, compared to about 17% for the patients who got no drug.

Although these results show that the drug may be effective in reducing blood loss, they also imply that patients on the drug may have a higher risk of

*The data for this study are real. For confidentiality reasons, the drug name and physician group are omitted.

complications. But before using this information to make a decision about the drug, the physicians will need to provide a measure of reliability for the inference. That is, the physicians will want to know whether the difference between the percentages of patients with complications observed in this sample of 114 patients is

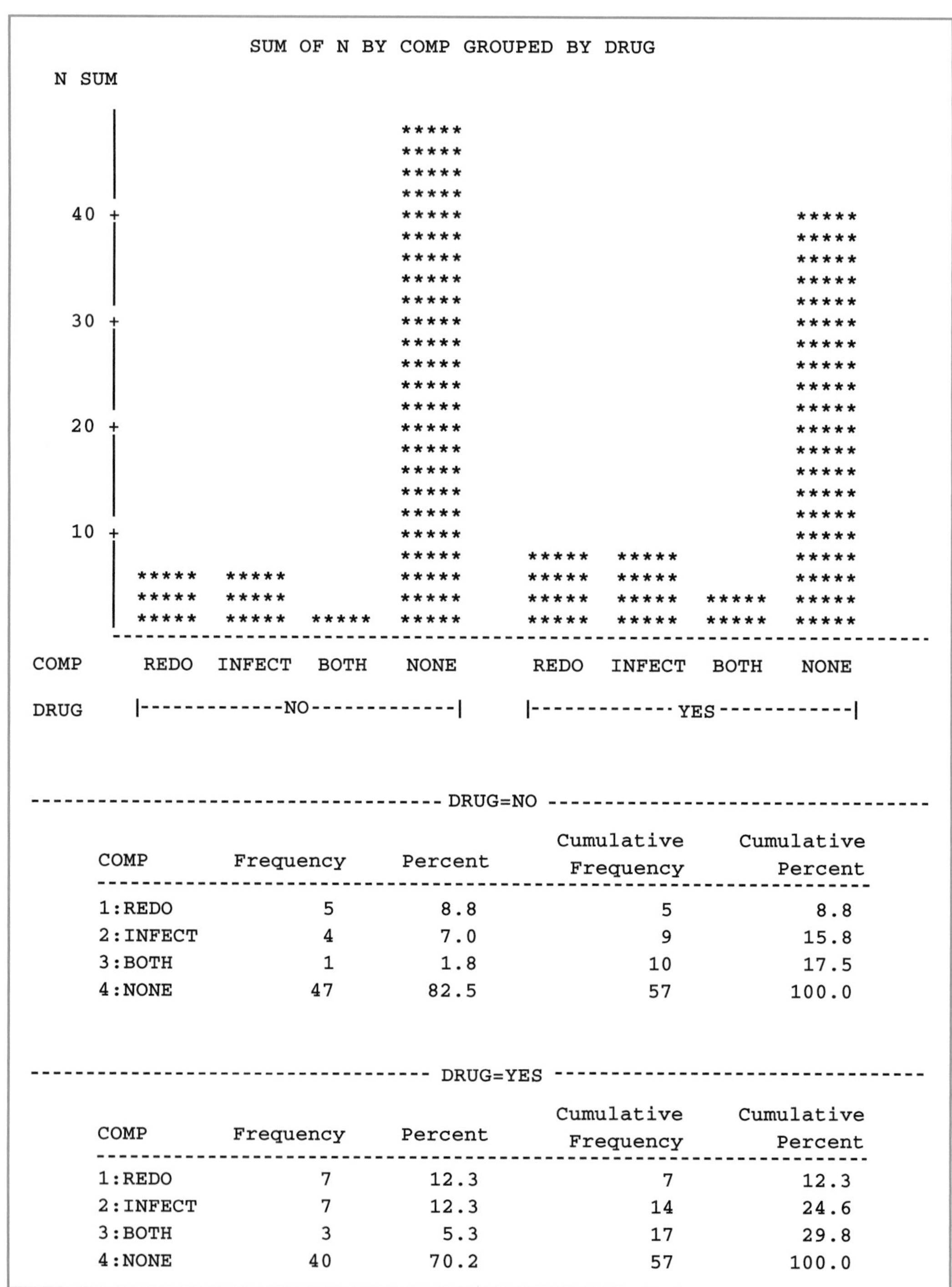

DRUG=NO

COMP	Frequency	Percent	Cumulative Frequency	Cumulative Percent
1:REDO	5	8.8	5	8.8
2:INFECT	4	7.0	9	15.8
3:BOTH	1	1.8	10	17.5
4:NONE	47	82.5	57	100.0

DRUG=YES

COMP	Frequency	Percent	Cumulative Frequency	Cumulative Percent
1:REDO	7	12.3	7	12.3
2:INFECT	7	12.3	14	24.6
3:BOTH	3	5.3	17	29.8
4:NONE	40	70.2	57	100.0

FIGURE 2.4
SAS bar graph and summary tables for COMP by DRUG

generalizable to the population of all coronary artery bypass patients. Measures of reliability will be discussed in Chapters 5–8.

EXAMPLE 2.2

Vilfredo Pareto (1843–1923), an Italian economist, discovered that approximately 80% of the wealth of a country lies with approximately 20% of the people. This discovery of "the vital few and the trivial many," called the *Pareto principle,* holds true even today. In his book *Defect Prevention* (1989), V. E. Kane reports the following: 80% of sales are attributable to 20% of the customers; 80% of customer complaints result from 20% of the components of a product; 80% of defective items produced by a process result from 20% of the types of errors that are made in production. In industry a *Pareto analysis* involves the categorization of items and the determination of which categories contain the most observations, i.e., which are the "vital few" categories. The primary tool of Pareto analysis is the **Pareto diagram.** The Pareto diagram is simply a bar graph with the bars arranged in descending order of height from left to right across the horizontal axis. This arrangement locates the most important categories—those with the largest frequencies—at the left of the graph.

a. Table 2.3a contains summary data from the automobile industry (adapted from Kane, 1989). All cars produced on a particular day were inspected for general defects. Each of the 125 defects discovered were categorized by type: accessory, body, electrical, engine, and transmission. The table gives the number of defects of each type. Construct a Pareto diagram for the data. Identify the categories that produced the most defects.

TABLE 2.3 Summary of Car Defects

a. General Defect	Number	b. Body Defect	Number
Accessory	50	Chrome	2
Body	70	Dents	25
Electrical	12	Paint	30
Engine	8	Upholstery	10
Transmission	5	Windshield	3
Total	125	Total	70

b. All 70 body defects were further classified as to whether they were chrome, dent, paint, upholstery, of windshield defects. Table 2.3b gives the number of each type. Construct a Pareto diagram for the body type defects. Interpret the results.

Solution

a. The Pareto diagram for the 125 car defects is a frequency bar graph, with the bars arranged in order of height. The diagram is displayed in Figure 2.5a. Clearly, body and accessory defects (the two categories at the far left of the graph) are the most frequently observed types of car defects. Management should focus their problem-solving efforts in these two areas.

b. A Pareto diagram for the 70 body part defects is shown in Figure 2.5b. You can see that paint and dent defects (again, the two categories at the far left of the graph) are the most frequently observed types of body defects. These defects should be targeted for special attention by managers, engineers, and assembly-line workers. [*Note:* When one or more Pareto diagrams are used to decompose the original Pareto diagram in Figure 2.5a, the resulting graph (Figure 2.5b) is called *exploding the Pareto diagram.*]

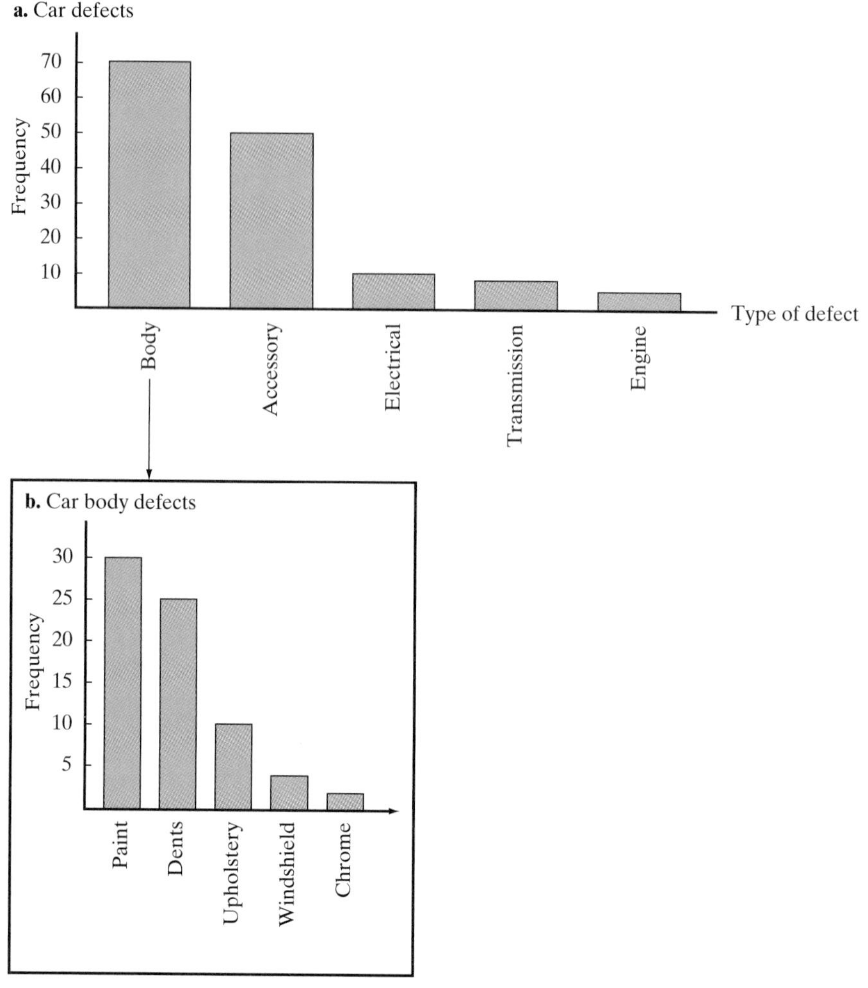

FIGURE 2.5 Pareto diagrams for Example 2.2

EXERCISES 2.1–2.11

Learning the Mechanics

2.1 Complete the following table.

Grade on Business Statistics Exam	Frequency	Relative Frequency
A: 90–100	—	.08
B: 80–89	36	—
C: 65–79	90	—
D: 50–64	30	—
F: Below 50	28	—
Total	200	1.00

2.2 A qualitative variable with three classes (X, Y, and Z) is measured for each of 20 units randomly sampled from a target population. The data (observed class for each unit) are listed below.

Y X X Z X Y Y Y X X Z X
Y Y X Z Y Y Y X

a. Compute the frequency for each of the three classes.
b. Compute the relative frequency for each of the three classes.
c. Display the results, part **a,** in a frequency bar graph.
d. Display the results, part **b,** in a pie chart.

Applying the Concepts

2.3 Until their profitability was threatened by competition from Japan and Europe in the 1970s, most U.S. firms paid relatively little attention to customer satisfaction. Today, customer satisfaction and loyalty are valued and monitored by all world-class organizations. But are satisfied customers necessarily loyal customers? Harte-Hanks Market Research surveyed customers of department stores and banks and published the results (shown on p. 33) in *American Demographics* (Aug. 1999).

a. Construct a relative frequency bar chart for each of the data sets.

	Banks	Department Stores
Totally satisfied and very loyal	27%	4%
Totally satisfied and not very loyal	18%	25%
Not totally satisfied and very loyal	13%	2%
Not totally satisfied and not very loyal	42%	69%
	100%	100%

Source: *American Demographics*, Aug. 1999.

b. Could these data have been described using pie charts? Explain.

c. Do the data indicate that customers who are totally satisfied are very loyal? Explain.

2.4 Port Canaveral (Florida) handled over 1.5 million cruise passengers in 1998. The number of passengers handled by each of the cruise ships that sail out of Port Canaveral is listed in the table.

Cruise Line (Ship)	Number of Passengers
Canaveral (Dolphin)	152,240
Carnival (Fantasy)	480,924
Disney (Magic)	73,504
Premier (Oceanic)	270,361
Royal Caribbean (Nordic Empress)	106,161
Sun Cruz Casinos	453,806
Sterling Cruises (New Yorker)	15,782
Topaz Int'l. Shipping (Topaz)	28,280
Other	10,502
Total	1,591,560

Source: Florida Trend, Vol. 41, No. 9, Jan. 1999.

a. Find the relative frequency of the number of passengers for each cruise ship.

b. Identify the cruise ship with the highest relative frequency. Interpret this number.

c. Construct a bar graph to describe the popularity of cruise ships that sailed from Port Canaveral in 1998.

2.5 Disgruntled shareholders who put pressure on corporate management to make certain financial decisions are referred to as shareholder activists. In Exercise 1.22 we described a survey of 240 large investors designed to determine how widespread shareholder activism actually is. One of several questions asked was: If the chief executive officer and the board of directors differed on company strategy, what action would you, as a large investor of the firm, take? (*New York Times,* Oct. 31, 1995) The responses are summarized in the table.

Response	Number of Investors
Seek formal explanation	154
Seek CEO performance review	49
Dismiss CEO	20
Seek no action	17
Total	240

a. Construct a relative frequency table for the data.

b. Display the relative frequencies in a graph.

c. Discuss the findings.

2.6 According to Topaz Enterprises, a Portland, Oregon-based airfare accounting firm, "more than 80% of all tickets purchased for domestic flights are discounted" (*Travel Weekly,* May 15, 1995). The results of the accounting firm's survey of domestic airline tickets are summarized in the table.

Domestic Airline Ticket Type	Proportion
Full coach	.005
Discounted coach	.206
Negotiated coach	.425
First class	.009
Business class	.002
Business class negotiated	.001
Advance purchase	.029
Capacity controlled discount	.209
Nonrefundable	.114
Total	1.000

a. Give your opinion on whether the data described in the table are from a population or a sample. Explain your reasoning.

b. Display the data with a bar graph. Arrange the bars in order of height to form a Pareto diagram. Interpret the resulting graph.

c. Do the data support the conclusion reached by Topaz Enterprises regarding the percentage of tickets purchased that are discounted?

[*Note:* Advance purchase and negotiated tickets are considered discounted.]

2.7 "Reader-response cards" are used by marketers to advertise their product and obtain sales leads. These cards are placed in magazines and trade publications. Readers detach and mail in the cards to indicate their interest in the product, expecting literature or a phone call in return. How effective are these cards (called "bingo cards" in the industry) as a marketing tool? Performark, a Minneapolis business that helps companies close on sales leads, attempted to answer this question by responding to 17,000 card-advertisements placed by industrial marketers in a wide variety of trade

Advertiser's Response Time	Percentage
Never responded	21
13–59 days	33
60–120 days	34
More than 120 days	12
Total	100

publications over a 6-year period. Performark kept track of how long it took for each advertiser to respond. A summary of the response times, reported in *Inc.* magazine (July 1995), is given in the table on p. 33.

a. Describe the variable measured by Performark.
b. *Inc.* displayed the results in the form of a pie chart. Reconstruct the pie chart from the information given in the table.
c. How many of the 17,000 advertisers never responded to the sales lead?
d. Advertisers typically spend at least a million dollars on a reader-response card marketing campaign. Many industrial marketers feel these "bingo cards" are not worth their expense. Does the information in the pie chart, part **b,** support this contention? Explain why or why not. If not, what information can be gleaned from the pie chart to help potential "bingo card" campaigns?

2.8 Many librarians rely on book reviews to determine which new books to purchase for their library. A random sample of 375 book reviews in American history, geography, and area studies was selected and the "overall opinion" of the book stated in each review was ascertained (*Library Acquisitions: Practice and Theory,* Vol. 19, 1995). Overall opinion was coded as follows: 1 = would not recommend, 2 = cautious or very little recommendation, 3 = little or no preference, 4 = favorable/recommended, 5 = outstanding/significant contribution. A summary of the data is provided in the bar graph.

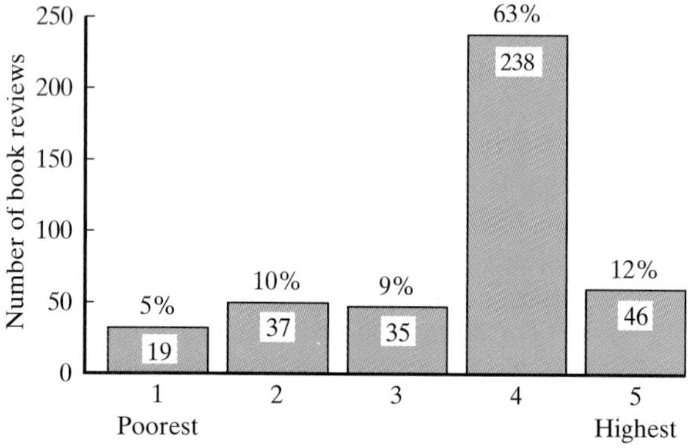

Source: Reprinted from *Library Acquisitions: Practice and Theory,* Vol. 19, No. 2, P.W. Carlo and A. Natowitz, "Choice Book Reviews in American History, Geography, and Area Studies: An Analysis for 1988–1993," p. 159. Copyright 1995, with kind permission from Elsevier Science Ltd, The Boulevard, Langford Lane, Kidlington OX5 1GB, UK.

a. Interpret the bar graph.
b. Comment on the following statement extracted from the study: "A majority (more than 75%) of books reviewed are evaluated favorably and recommended for purchase."

2.9 The Internet and its World Wide Web provide computer users with a medium for both communication and entertainment. However, many businesses are recognizing the potential of using the Internet for advertising and selling their products. *Inc. Technology* (Sept. 12, 1995) conducted a survey of 2,016 small businesses (fewer than 100 employees) regarding their weekly Internet usage. The survey found 1,855 small businesses that do not use the Internet, 121 that use the Internet from one to five hours per week, and 40 that use the Internet six or more hours per week.

a. Identify the variable measured in the survey.
b. Summarize the survey results with a graph.
c. What portion of the 2,016 small businesses use the Internet on a weekly basis?

2.10 Owing to several major ocean oil spills by tank vessels, Congress passed the 1990 Oil Pollution Act, which requires all tankers to be designed with thicker hulls. Further improvements in the structural design of a tank vessel have been implemented since then, each with the objective of reducing the likelihood of an oil spill and decreasing the amount of outflow in the event of hull puncture. To aid in this development, J. C. Daidola reported on the spillage amount and cause of puncture for 50 recent major oil spills from tankers and carriers. The data are reproduced in the table on p. 35 (*Marine Technology,* Jan. 1995).

a. Use a graphical method to describe the cause of oil spillage for the 50 tankers.
b. Does the graph, part **a,** suggest that any one cause is more likely to occur than any other? How is this information of value to the design engineers?

2.11 Since opening its doors to Western investors in 1979, the People's Republic of China has been steadily moving toward a market economy. However, because of the considerable political and economic uncertainties in China, Western investors remain uneasy about their investments in China. In 1995 an agency of the Chinese government surveyed 402 foreign investors to assess their concerns with the investment environment. Each was asked to indicate their most serious concern. The results appear below.

CHINA.DAT

Investor's Concern	Frequency
Communication infrastructure	8
Environmental protection	13
Financial services	14
Government efficiency	30
Inflation rate	233
Labor supply	11
Personal safety	2
Real estate prices	82
Security of personal property	4
Water supply	5

Source: Adapted from *China Marketing News,* No. 26, November 1995.

OILSPILL.DAT

Tanker	Spillage (metric tons, thousands)	Cause of Spillage				
		Collision	Grounding	Fire/ Explosion	Hull Failure	Unknown
Atlantic Empress	257	X				
Castillo De Bellver	239			X		
Amoco Cadiz	221				X	
Odyssey	132			X		
Torrey Canyon	124		X			
Sea Star	123	X				
Hawaiian Patriot	101				X	
Independento	95	X				
Urquiola	91		X			
Irenes Serenade	82			X		
Khark 5	76			X		
Nova	68	X				
Wafra	62		X			
Epic Colocotronis	58		X			
Sinclair Petrolore	57			X		
Yuyo Maru No 10	42	X				
Assimi	50			X		
Andros Patria	48			X		
World Glory	46				X	
British Ambassador	46				X	
Metula	45		X			
Pericles G.C.	44			X		
Mandoil II	41	X				
Jacob Maersk	41		X			
Burmah Agate	41	X				
J. Antonio Lavalleja	38		X			
Napier	37		X			
Exxon Valdez	36		X			
Corinthos	36	X				
Trader	36				X	
St. Peter	33			X		
Gino	32	X				
Golden Drake	32			X		
Ionnis Angelicoussis	32			X		
Chryssi	32				X	
Irenes Challenge	31				X	
Argo Merchant	28		X			
Heimvard	31	X				
Pegasus	25					X
Pacocean	31				X	
Texaco Oklahoma	29				X	
Scorpio	31		X			
Ellen Conway	31		X			
Caribbean Sea	30				X	
Cretan Star	27					X
Grand Zenith	26				X	
Athenian Venture	26			X		
Venoil	26	X				
Aragon	24				X	
Ocean Eagle	21		X			

Source: Daidola, J. C. "Tanker structure behavior during collision and grounding." *Marine Technology,* Vol. 32, No. 1, Jan. 1995, p. 22 (Table 1). Reprinted with permission of The Society of Naval Architects and Marine Engineers (SNAME), 601 Pavonia Ave., Jersey City, NJ 07306, USA, (201) 798-4800. Material appearing in The Society of Naval Architect and Marine Engineers (SNAME) publications cannot be reprinted without obtaining written permission.

a. Construct a Pareto diagram for the 10 categories.
b. According to your Pareto diagram, which environmental factors most concern investors?
c. In this case, are 80% of the investors concerned with 20% of the environmental factors as the Pareto principle would suggest? Justify your answer.

2.2 GRAPHICAL METHODS FOR DESCRIBING QUANTITATIVE DATA

Recall from Section 1.5 that quantitative data sets consist of data that are recorded on a meaningful numerical scale. For describing, summarizing, and detecting patterns in such data, we can use three graphical methods: dot plots, stem-and-leaf displays, and histograms.

For example, suppose a financial analyst is interested in the amount of resources spent by computer hardware and software companies on research and development (R&D). She samples 50 of these high-technology firms and calculates the amount each spent last year on R&D as a percentage of their total revenues. The results are given in Table 2.4. As numerical measurements made on the sample of 50 units (the firms), these percentages represent quantitative data. The analyst's initial objective is to summarize and describe these data in order to extract relevant information.

TABLE 2.4 Percentage of Revenues Spent on Research and Development

Company	Percentage	Company	Percentage	Company	Percentage	Company	Percentage
1	13.5	14	9.5	27	8.2	39	6.5
2	8.4	15	8.1	28	6.9	40	7.5
3	10.5	16	13.5	29	7.2	41	7.1
4	9.0	17	9.9	30	8.2	42	13.2
5	9.2	18	6.9	31	9.6	43	7.7
6	9.7	19	7.5	32	7.2	44	5.9
7	6.6	20	11.1	33	8.8	45	5.2
8	10.6	21	8.2	34	11.3	46	5.6
9	10.1	22	8.0	35	8.5	47	11.7
10	7.1	23	7.7	36	9.4	48	6.0
11	8.0	24	7.4	37	10.5	49	7.8
12	7.9	25	6.5	38	6.9	50	6.5
13	6.8	26	9.5				

A visual inspection of the data indicates some obvious facts. For example, the smallest R&D percentage is 5.2% and the largest is 13.5%. But it is difficult to provide much additional information on the 50 R&D percentages without resorting to some method of summarizing the data. One such method is a dot plot.

Dot Plots

A **dot plot** for the 50 R&D percentages, produced using MINITAB software, is shown in Figure 2.6. The horizontal axis of Figure 2.6 is a scale for the quantitative variable, percent. The numerical value of each measurement in the data set is located on the horizontal scale by a dot. When data values repeat, the dots are placed above one another, forming a pile at that particular numerical location. As you can see, this dot plot shows that almost all of the R&D percentages are between 6% and 12%, with most falling between 7% and 9%.

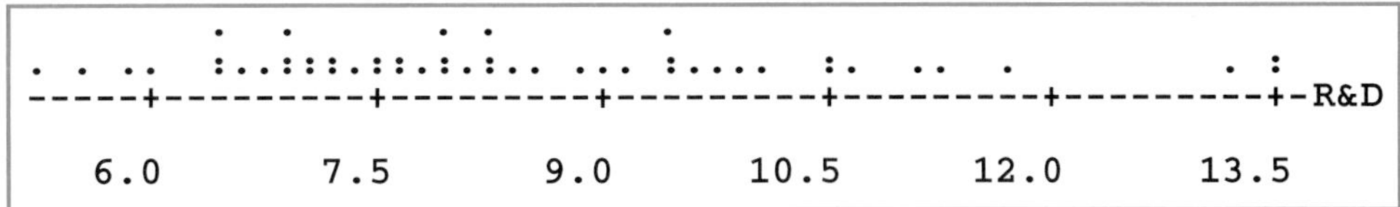

FIGURE 2.6
A MINITAB dot plot for the 50 R&D percentages

Stem-and-Leaf Display

We used STATISTIX software to generate another graphical representation of these same data, a **stem-and-leaf display,** in Figure 2.7. In this display the *stem* is the portion of the measurement (percentage) to the left of the decimal point, while the remaining portion to the right of the decimal point is the *leaf.*

The stems for the data set are listed in a column from the smallest (5) to the largest (13). Then the leaf for each observation is recorded in the row of the display corresponding to the observation's stem. For example, the leaf 5 of the first observation (13.5) in Table 2.3 is placed in the row corresponding to the stem 13. Similarly, the leaf 4 for the second observation (8.4) in Table 2.3 is recorded in the row corresponding to the stem 8, while the leaf 5 for the third observation (10.5) is recorded in the row corresponding to the stem 10. (The leaves for these first three observations are shaded in Figure 2.7.) Typically, the leaves in each row are ordered as shown in Figure 2.7.

FIGURE 2.7
A STATISTIX stem-and-leaf display for the 50 R&D percentages

```
STEM AND LEAF PLOT OF RDPCT    MINIMUM   5.2000
                               MEDIAM    8.0500
                               MAXIMUM   13.500

LEAF DIGIT UNIT = 0.1
5  2  REPRESENTS 5.2

          STEM   LEAVES
     3       5   269
    12       6   055568999
    23       7   11224557789
   (9)       8   001222458
    18       9   02455679
    10      10   1556
     6      11   137
     3      12
     3      13   255

50 CASES INCLUDED    0 MISSING CASES
```

The stem-and-leaf display presents another compact picture of the data set. You can see at a glance that most of the sampled computer companies (37 of 50) spent between 6.0% and 9.9% of their revenues on R&D, and 11 of them spent between 7.0% and 7.9%. Relative to the rest of the sampled companies, three spent a high percentage of revenues on R&D—in excess of 13%

Most statistical software packages allow you to modify the definitions of the stem and leaf to alter the graphical description. For example, suppose we had defined the stem as the tens digit for the R&D percentage data, rather than the ones and tens digits. With this definition, the stems and leaves corresponding to the measurements 13.5 and 8.4 would be as follows:

Stem	Leaf
1	3

Stem	Leaf
0	8

Note that the decimal portion of the numbers has been dropped. Generally, only one digit is displayed in the leaf.

If you look at the data, you'll see why we didn't define the stem this way. All the R&D measurements fall below 13.5, so all the leaves would fall into just two stem rows—1 and 0—in this display. The resulting picture would not be nearly as informative as Figure 2.7.

Histograms

A **relative frequency histogram** for these 50 R&D percentages is shown in Figure 2.8. The horizontal axis of Figure 2.8, which gives the percentage spent on R&D for each company, is divided into *intervals* commencing with the interval from (5.15–6.25) and proceeding in intervals of equal size to (12.85–13.95) percent. (The procedure for creating the class intervals will become clear in Example 2.3.) The vertical axis gives the proportion (or *relative frequency*) of the 50 percentages that fall in each interval. Thus, you can see that nearly a third of the companies spent between 7.35% and 8.45% of their revenues on research and development. This interval contains the highest relative frequency, and the intervals tend to contain a smaller fraction of the measurements as R&D percentage gets smaller or larger.

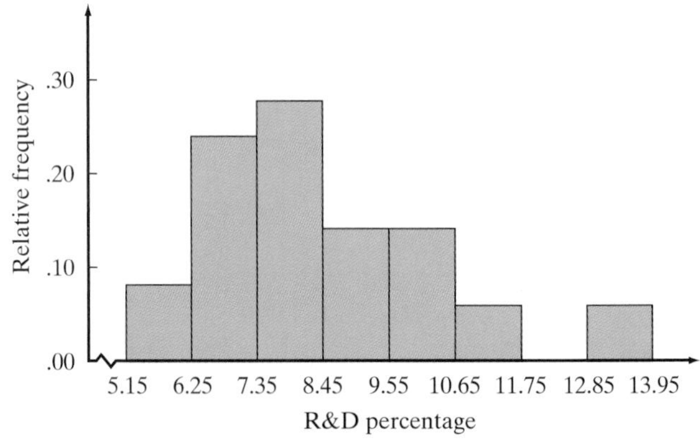

FIGURE 2.8
Histogram for the 50 computer companies' R&D percentages

By summing the relative frequencies in the intervals 6.25–7.35, 7.35–8.45, 8.45–9.55, 9.55–10.65, you can see that 80% of the R&D percentages are between 6.25 and 10.65. Similarly, only 6% of the computer companies spent over 12.85 percent of their revenues on R&D. Many other summary statements can be made by further study of the histogram.

Dot plots, stem-and-leaf displays, and histograms all provide useful graphic descriptions of quantitative data. Since most statistical software packages can be used to construct these displays, we will focus on their interpretation rather than their construction.

Histograms can be used to display either the frequency or relative frequency of the measurements falling into specified intervals known as **measurement classes.** The measurement classes, frequencies, and relative frequencies for the R&D percentage data are shown in Table 2.5.

TABLE 2.5 Measurement Classes, Frequencies, and Relative Frequencies for the R&D Percentage Data

Class	Measurement Class	Class Frequency	Class Relative Frequency
1	5.15–6.25	4	$4/50 = .08$
2	6.25–7.35	12	$12/50 = .24$
3	7.35–8.45	14	$14/50 = .28$
4	8.45–9.55	7	$7/50 = .14$
5	9.55–10.65	7	$7/50 = .14$
6	10.65–11.75	3	$3/50 = .06$
7	11.75–12.85	0	$0/50 = .00$
8	12.85–13.95	3	$3/50 = .06$
Totals		50	1.00

By looking at a histogram (say, the relative frequency histogram in Figure 2.8), you can see two important facts. First, note the total area under the histogram and then note the proportion of the total area that falls over a particular interval of the horizontal axis. You'll see that the proportion of the total area above an interval is equal to the relative frequency of measurements falling in the interval. For example, the relative frequency for the class interval 7.35–8.45 is .28. Consequently, the rectangle above the interval contains .28 of the total area under the histogram.

Second, you can imagine the appearance of the relative frequency histogram for a very large set of data (say, a population). As the number of measurements in a data set is increased, you can obtain a better description of the data by decreasing the width of the class intervals. When the class intervals become small enough, a relative frequency histogram will (for all practical purposes) appear as a smooth curve (see Figure 2.9).

FIGURE 2.9
Effect of the size of a data set on the outline of a histogram

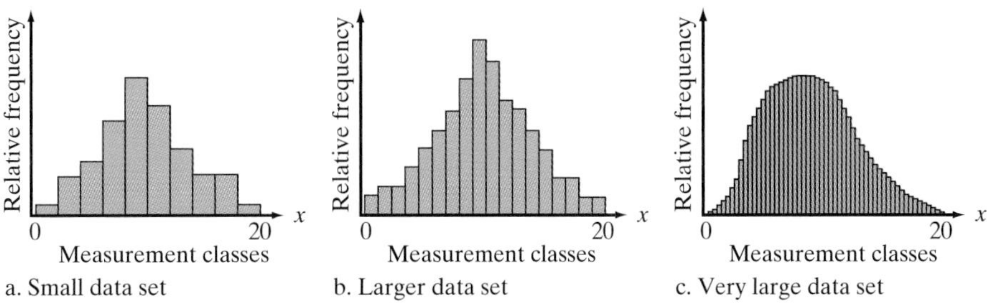

While histograms provide good visual descriptions of data sets—particularly very large ones—they do not let us identify individual measurements. In contrast, each of the original measurements is visible to some extent in a dot plot and clearly visible in a stem-and-leaf display. The stem-and-leaf display arranges the data in ascending order, so it's easy to locate the individual measurements. For example, in Figure 2.7 we can easily see that three of the R&D measurements are equal to 8.2, but we can't see that fact by inspecting the histogram in Figure 2.8. However, stem-and-leaf displays can become unwieldy for very large data sets. A very large number of stems and leaves causes the vertical and horizontal dimensions of the display to become cumbersome, diminishing the usefulness of the visual display.

EXAMPLE 2.3 A manufacturer of industrial wheels suspects that profitable orders are being lost because of the long time the firm takes to develop price quotes for potential customers. To investigate this possibility, 50 requests for price quotes were randomly selected from the set of all quotes made last year, and the processing time was determined for each quote. The processing times are displayed in Table 2.6, and each quote was classified according to whether the order was "lost" or not (i.e., whether or not the customer placed an order after receiving a price quote).

TABLE 2.6 Price Quote Processing Time (Days)

Request Number	Processing Time	Lost?	Request Number	Processing Time	Lost?
1	2.36	No	26	3.34	No
2	5.73	No	27	6.00	No
3	6.60	No	28	5.92	No
4	10.05	Yes	29	7.28	Yes
5	5.13	No	30	1.25	No
6	1.88	No	31	4.01	No
7	2.52	No	32	7.59	No
8	2.00	No	33	13.42	Yes
9	4.69	No	34	3.24	No
10	1.91	No	35	3.37	No
11	6.75	Yes	36	14.06	Yes
12	3.92	No	37	5.10	No
13	3.46	No	38	6.44	No
14	2.64	No	39	7.76	No
15	3.63	No	40	4.40	No
16	3.44	No	41	5.48	No
17	9.49	Yes	42	7.51	No
18	4.90	No	43	6.18	No
19	7.45	No	44	8.22	Yes
20	20.23	Yes	45	4.37	No
21	3.91	No	46	2.93	No
22	1.70	No	47	9.95	Yes
23	16.29	Yes	48	4.46	No
24	5.52	No	49	14.32	Yes
25	1.44	No	50	9.01	No

a. Use a statistical software package to create a frequency histogram for these data. Then shade the area under the histogram that corresponds to lost orders.

b. Use a statistical software package to create a stem-and-leaf display for these data. Then shade each leaf of the display that corresponds to a lost order.

c. Compare and interpret the two graphical displays of these data.

Solution

a. We used SAS to generate the frequency histogram in Figure 2.10. SAS, like most statistical software, offers the user the choice of accepting default class intervals and interval widths, or the user can make his or her own selections. After some experimenting with various numbers of class intervals and interval widths, we used 10 intervals. SAS then created intervals of width 2 days, beginning at 1 day, just below the smallest measurement of

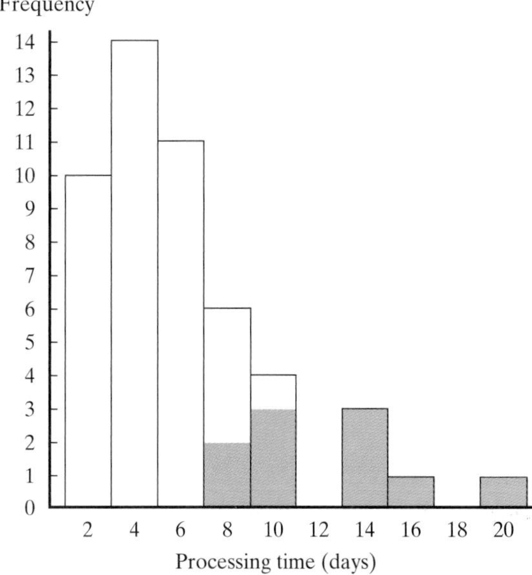

FIGURE 2.10
SAS frequency histogram for the quote processing time data

1.25 days, and ending with 21 days, just above the largest measurement of 20.2 days. Note that SAS labels the midpoint of each bar, rather than its endpoints. Thus, the bar labeled "2" represents measurements from 1.00 to 2.99, the bar labeled "4" represents measurements from 3.00 to 4.99, etc. This histogram clearly shows the clustering of the measurements in the lower end of the distribution (between approximately 1 and 7 days), and the relatively few measurements in the upper end of the distribution (greater than 12 days). The shading of the area of the frequency histogram corresponding to lost orders clearly indicates that they lie in the upper tail of the distribution.

b. We used SPSS to generate the stem-and-leaf display in Figure 2.11. Note that the stem consists of the number of whole days (units and tens digits), and the leaf is the tenths digit (first digit after the decimal) of each measurement.* The hundredths digit has been dropped to make the display more visually effective. SPSS also includes a column titled *Frequency* showing the number of measurements corresponding to each stem. Note, too, that instead of extending the stems all the way to 20 days to show the largest measurement, SPSS truncates the display after the stem corresponding to 13 days, labels the largest four measurements (shaded) as *Extremes,* and simply lists them horizontally in the last row of the display. Extreme observations that are detached from the remainder of the data are called *outliers,* and they usually receive special attention in statistical analyses. Although outliers may represent legitimate measurements, they are frequently mistakes: incorrectly recorded, miscoded during data entry, or taken from a population different from the one from which the rest of the sample was selected. Stem-and-leaf displays are useful for identifying outliers. Note that like the histogram, the stem-and-leaf display shows the shaded "lost" orders in the upper-tail of the distribution.

*In the examples in this section, the stem was formed from the digits to the left of the decimal. This is not always the case. For example, in the following data set the stems could be the tenths digit and the leaves the hundredths digit: .12, .15, .22, .25, .28, .33.

FIGURE 2.11
SPSS stem-and-leaf display for the quote processing time data

```
   Frequency      Stem & Leaf
       5.00          1 .  24789
       5.00          2 .  03569
       8.00          3 .  23344699
       6.00          4 .  034469
       6.00          5 .  114579
       5.00          6 .  01467
       5.00          7 .  24557
       1.00          8 .  2
       3.00          9 .  049
       1.00         10 .  0
        .00         11 .
        .00         12 .
       1.00         13 .  4
       4.00 Extremes      (14.1), (14.3), (16.3), (20.2)
 Stem width:         1.00
 Each leaf:             1 case(s)
```

c. As is usually the case for data sets that are not too large (say, fewer than 100 measurements), the stem-and-leaf display provides more detail than the histogram without being unwieldy. For instance, the stem-and-leaf display in Figure 2.11 clearly indicates not only that the lost orders are associated with high processing times (as does the histogram in Figure 2.10), but also exactly which of the times correspond to lost orders. Histograms are most useful for displaying very large data sets, when the overall shape of the distribution of measurements is more important than the identification of individual measurements. Nevertheless, the message of both graphical displays is clear: establishing processing time limits may well result in fewer lost orders. ✶

Most statistical software packages can be used to generate histograms, stem-and-leaf displays, and dot plots. All three are useful tools for graphically describing data sets. We recommend that you generate and compare the displays whenever you can. You'll find that histograms are generally more useful for very large data sets, while stem-and-leaf displays and dot plots provide useful detail for smaller data sets.

Histograms

USING THE TI-83 GRAPHING CALCULATOR

Making a Histogram on the TI-83

Step 1 *Enter the data*
Press **STAT 1** for **STAT edit**
Use the arrow and **ENTER** keys to enter the data set into **L1.**

Step 2 *Set up the histogram plot*
Press **2nd Y =** for **STAT PLOT**
Press **1** for **Plot 1**

(continued)

Use the arrow and **ENTER** keys to set up the screen as shown below.

Note: Press **2nd 1** for **L1**

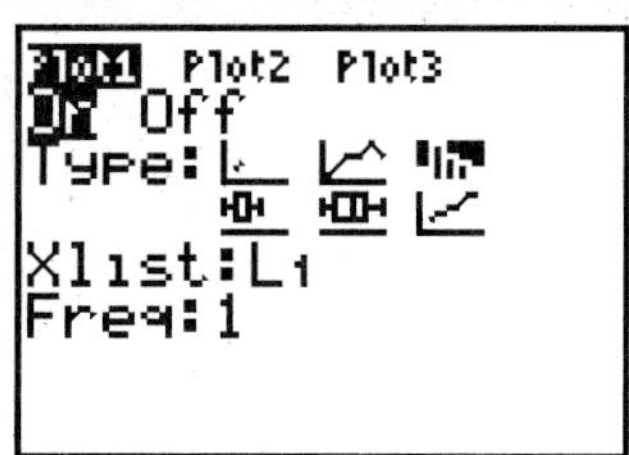

Step 3 *Select your window settings*
Press **WINDOW** and adjust the settings as follows:

Xmin = lowest class boundary
Xmax = highest class boundary
Xscl = class width
Ymin = 0
Ymax = greatest class frequency
Yscl = approximately Ymax/10
Xres = 1

Step 4 *View the graph*
Press **GRAPH**

Optional Step *Read class frequencies and class boundaries*
You can press **TRACE** to read the class frequencies and class boundaries. Use the arrow keys to move between bars.

Example The figures below show TI-83 window settings and histogram for the following sample data:

86, 70, 62, 98, 73, 56, 53, 92, 86, 37, 62, 83, 78, 49, 78, 37, 67, 79, 57

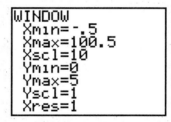

WINDOW
Xmin=-.5
Xmax=100.5
Xscl=10
Ymin=0
Ymax=5
Yscl=1
Xres=1

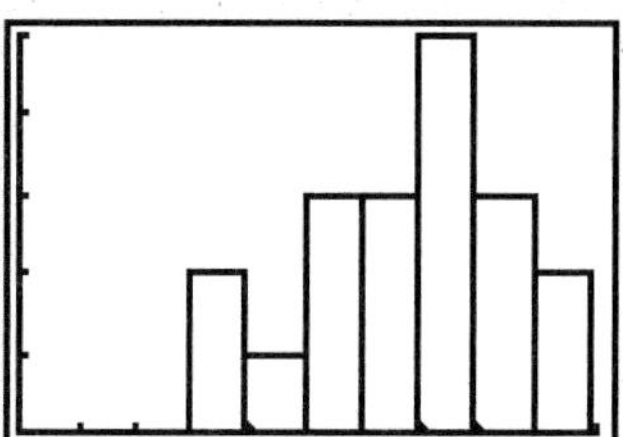

Making a Histogram From a Frequency Table

Step 1 *Enter the data*
Enter a value from the middle of each class in **L1**
Enter the class frequencies or relative frequencies in **L2**

Step 2 *Set up the histogram plot*
Press **2nd Y =** for **STAT PLOT**
Press **1** for **Plot 1**

(continued)

Use the arrow and **ENTER** keys to set up the screen as shown below.

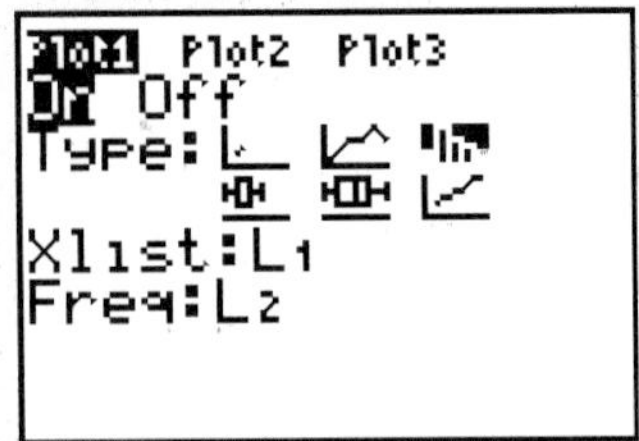

Steps 3–4 Follow steps 3–4 given above.

EXERCISES 2.12–2.25

Learning the Mechanics

2.12 Graph the relative frequency histogram for the 500 measurements summarized in the accompanying relative frequency table.

Measurement Class	Relative Frequency
.5–2.5	.10
2.5–4.5	.15
4.5–6.5	.25
6.5–8.5	.20
8.5–10.5	.05
10.5–12.5	.10
12.5–14.5	.10
14.5–16.5	.05

2.13 Refer to Exercise 2.12. Calculate the number of the 500 measurements falling into each of the measurement classes. Then graph a frequency histogram for these data.

2.14 SAS was used to generate the stem-and-leaf display shown here. Note that SAS arranges the stems in descending order.

Stem	Leaf
5	1
4	4 5 7
3	0 0 0 3 6
2	1 1 3 4 5 9 9
1	2 2 4 8
0	0 1 2

a. How many observations were in the original data set?
b. In the bottom row of the stem-and-leaf display, identify the stem, the leaves, and the numbers in the orignal data set represented by this stem and its leaves.
c. Re-create all the numbers in the data set and construct a dot plot.

2.15 MINITAB was used to generate the following histogram:
a. Is this a frequency histogram or a relative frequency histogram? Explain.
b. How many measurement classes were used in the construction of this histogram?
c. How many measurements are there in the data set described by this histogram?

MINITAB output for Exercise 2.15

```
MIDDLE OF    NUMBER OF
INTERVAL     OBSERVATIONS
   20           1   *
   22           3   ***
   24           2   **
   26           3   ***
   28           4   ****
   30           7   *******
   32          11   ***********
   34           6   ******
   36           2   **
   38           3   ***
   40           3   ***
   42           2   **
   44           1   *
   46           1   *
```

2.16 The graph on p. 45 summarizes the scores obtained by 100 students on a questionnaire designed to measure managerial ability. (Scores are integer values that range from 0 to 20. A high score indicates a high level of ability.)
a. Which measurement class contains the highest proportion of test scores?
b. What proportion of the scores lie between 3.5 and 5.5?
c. What proportion of the scores are higher than 11.5?
d. How many students scored less than 5.5?

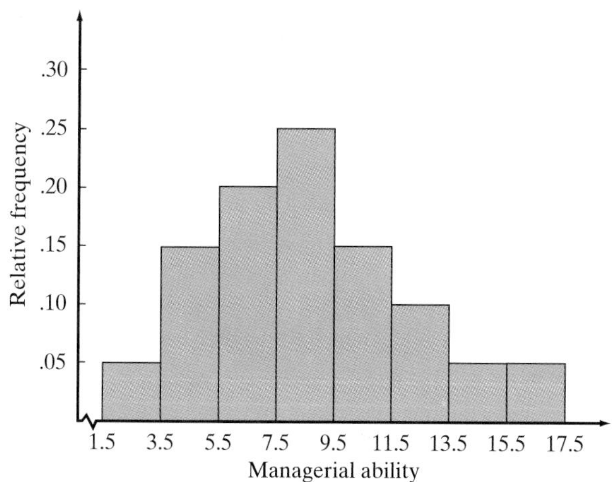

Applying the Concepts

2.17 The table (p. 46) reports the one-year percentage change in stock price for all technology companies and all industrial companies on *Fortune* (Sept. 6, 1999) magazine's ranking of the "One Hundred Fastest-Growing Companies."

a. Use a statistical software package to construct a stem-and-leaf display for the stock price changes of technology companies. Do the same for industrial companies.

b. Use the results of part **a** to compare and contrast the stock price changes of the technology and industrial companies.

c. What percentage of the technology companies in the data set had stock prices that more than doubled?

2.18 Mark McGwire of the St. Louis Cardinals and Sammy Sosa of the Chicago Cubs hit 70 and 66 home runs, respectively, during the 1998 Major League Baseball season, breaking the record held by Roger Maris (61 home runs) since 1961. J.S. Simonoff of New York University collected data on the number of runs scored by their respective teams in games in which McGwire and Sosa hit home runs (*Journal of Statistics Education*, Vol. 6, 1998). The data are reproduced in the table below. (An asterisk indicates a game in which McGwire or Sosa hit multiple home runs.)

a. Construct a stem-and-leaf display for the number of runs scored by St. Louis during games when McGwire hit a home run.

b. Repeat part **a** for Chicago and Sosa.

c. Compare and contrast the two distributions.

d. On the stem-and-leaf display, circle the games in which McGwire or Sosa hit multiple home runs. Do you detect any patterns?

2.19 Bonds can be issued by the federal government, state and local governments, and US corporations. A *mortgage bond* is a promissory note in which the issuing company pledges certain real assets as security in exchange for a specified amount of money. A *debenture* is an unsecured promissory note, backed only by the general credit of the issuer. The bond price of either a mortgage bond or debenture is negotiated between the asked price (the lowest price anyone will accept) and the bid price (the highest price anyone wants to pay) (Alexander, Sharpe, and Bailey, *Fundamentals of Investments,* 1993). The table on page 47 contains the bid prices for a sample of 30 publicly traded bonds issued by utility companies.

a. A frequency histogram (p. 47) was generated using SPSS. Note that SPSS labels the midpoint of each measurement class rather than the two endpoints. Interpret the histogram.

b. Use the histogram to determine the number of bonds in the sample that had a bid price greater than \$96.50. What proportion of the total number of bonds is this group?

c. Shade the area under the histogram that corresponds to the proportion in part **b.**

STLRUNS.DAT

St. Louis Cardinals				
6	6	3	11	13
8	1	10	6	7
5	8	9	6*	3
8	2	3	6*	6
15*	2	8*	5	6
8	6	2	3	5
5	8	4	10*	
8	9	4	4	
3	5	3	11*	
5	7	6	1	
2	3	8	4	
6	2	7*	6*	
3	7	14*	4*	

CUBSRUNS.DAT

Chicago Cubs				
3	6*	8*	6	7*
4	5	2	7	2
1	8*	6	13	
1	9*	6	8	
4	2	3*	10	
3	6	9	6*	
5	4	10	5	
5	4	4	9	
2	9	5	7	
5*	5	4	8	
5*	6	5	15	
10*	9	8	11*	
5	3	11	6	

FORT100.DAT

Technology Companies	% Change	Industrial Companies	% Change
SIEBEL SYSTEMS	120		
		MERITAGE	−32
THQ	58		
NETWORK APPLIANCE	159		
CITRIX SYSTEMS	52		
		SALTON	158
VERITAS SOFTWARE	119		
VITESSE SEMICONDUCTOR	89		
		CONSOLIDATED GRAPHICS	−32
DELL COMPUTER	45		
CREE RESEARCH	312		
QUALCOMM	392		
ARGUSS HOLDINGS	−8		
		KELLSTROM INDUSTRIES	−59
		ARMOR HOLDINGS	1
TEKELEC	−44		
LEGATO SYSTEMS	65		
		MONACO COACH	161
ASPECT DEVELOPMENT	−37		
COMPUWARE	16		
HAUPPAUGE DIGITAL	146		
ZOMAX	317		
AVT	39		
MERCURY INTERACTIVE	137		
		SUMMA INDUSTRIES	49
WHITTMAN-HART	9		
AAVID THERMAL TECH.	98		
i2 TECHNOLOGIES	50		
		TOWER AUTOMOTIVE	−6
		CADE INDUSTRIES	0
INSIGHT ENTERPRISES	37		
ANALYTICAL SURVEYS	−9		
HNC SOFTWARE	−15		
CIBER	−41		
TSR	−5		
		DYCOM INDUSTRIES	119
		MODTECH HOLDINGS	−34
		MORRISON KNUDSEN	−23
		SCHULER HOMES	−6
TECH DATA	−17		
POMEROY COMPUTERS RES.	−43		

Source: *Fortune*, Sept. 6, 1999.

2.20 Production processes may be classified as *make-to-stock processes* or *make-to-order processes.* Make-to-stock processes are designed to produce a standardized product that can be sold to customers from the firm's inventory. Make-to-order processes are designed to produce products according to customer specifications (Schroeder, *Operations Management,* 1993). In general, performance of make-to-order processes is measured by delivery time—the time from receipt of an order until the product is delivered to the customer. The following data set is a sample of delivery times (in days) for a particular make-to-order firm last year. The delivery times marked by an asterisk are associated with customers who subsequently placed additional orders with the firm.

DELTIMES.DAT

50* 64* 56* 43* 64* 82* 65* 49* 32* 63* 44* 71
54* 51* 102 49* 73* 50* 39* 86 33* 95 59* 51*
68

The MINITAB stem-and-leaf display of these data is shown at the bottom of page 47.

a. Circle the individual leaves that are associated with customers who did not place a subsequent order.

b. Concerned that they are losing potential repeat customers because of long delivery times, the management would like to establish a guideline for the maximum tolerable delivery time. Using the stem-

UTILBOND.DAT

Utility Company	Bid Price	Utility Company	Bid Price
Gulf States Utilities	$102\frac{3}{8}$	Indiana & Michigan Electric	$100\frac{1}{8}$
Northern States Power	$99\frac{1}{2}$	Toledo Edison Co.	$92\frac{7}{8}$
Indiana Gas	$102\frac{7}{8}$	Dayton Power and Light	$99\frac{1}{2}$
Appalachian Power	$97\frac{3}{8}$	Atlantic City Electric	$100\frac{3}{8}$
Empire Gas Corp.	70	Long Island Lighting	$91\frac{5}{8}$
Wisconsin Electric Power	$87\frac{1}{4}$	Portland General Electric	100
Pennsylvania Electric	$99\frac{7}{8}$	Boston Gas	$102\frac{7}{8}$
Commonwealth Edison	$89\frac{1}{8}$	Duquesne Light Co.	73
El Paso Natural Gas	$105\frac{1}{4}$	General Electric Co.	$93\frac{1}{8}$
Montana Power Co.	$100\frac{3}{8}$	Ohio Power Co.	$99\frac{7}{8}$
Elizabethtown Water	$103\frac{5}{8}$	Texas Utilities Electric	$100\frac{5}{8}$
Tennessee Gas Pipeline	$82\frac{1}{2}$	Central Power and Light	$100\frac{1}{8}$
Western Mass. Electric	$99\frac{5}{8}$	Boston Edison	$99\frac{3}{8}$
Carolina P&L	$99\frac{7}{8}$	Philadelphia Electric	99
Hartford Electric Lt.	$100\frac{1}{8}$	Colorado Interstate Gas	$114\frac{1}{4}$

Source: Bond Guide (a publication of the Standard & Poor Corporation), June 1996.

SSPS Output for Exercise 2.19

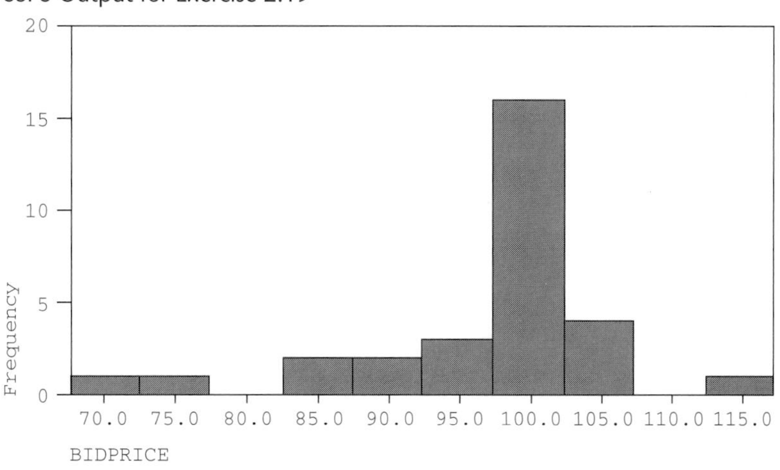

MINITAB Output for Exercise 2.20

```
Stem-and-leaf of Time          N = 25
Leaf Unit = 1.0

       3     3 239
       7     4 3499
     (7)     5 0011469
      11     6 34458
       6     7 13
       4     8 26
       2     9 5
       1    10 2
```

and-leaf display, suggest a guideline. Explain your reasoning.

2.21 Any corporation doing business in the United States must be aware of and obey both federal and state environmental regulations. Failure to do so may result in irreparable damage to the environment and costly financial penalties to guilty corporations. Of the 55 civil actions filed against corporations within the state of Arkansas by the US Department of Justice on behalf of the Environmental Protection Agency, 38 resulted in financial penalties. These penalties along with the laws that were violated are listed in the table on page 48.

CLEANAIR.DAT

Company Identification Number	Penalty	Law*	Company Identification Number	Penalty	Law*
01	$ 930,000	CERCLA	16	90,000	RCRA
02	10,000	CWA	17	20,000	CWA
03	90,600	CAA	18	40,000	CWA
04	123,549	CWA	19	20,000	CWA
05	37,500	CWA	20	40,000	CWA
06	137,500	CWA	21	850,000	CWA
07	2,500	SDWA	22	35,000	CWA
08	1,000,000	CWA	23	4,000	CAA
09	25,000	CAA	24	25,000	CWA
09	25,000	CAA	25	40,000	CWA
10	25,000	CWA	26	30,000	CAA
10	25,000	RCRA	27	15,000	CWA
11	19,100	CAA	28	15,000	CAA
12	100,000	CWA	29	105,000	CAA
12	30,000	CWA	30	20,000	CWA
13	35,000	CAA	31	400,000	CWA
13	43,000	CWA	32	85,000	CWA
14	190,000	CWA	33	300,000	CWA/RCRA/CERCLA
15	15,000	CWA	34	30,000	CWA

*CAA: Clean Air Act; CERCLA: Comprehensive Environmental Response, Compensation, and Liability Act; CWA: Clean Water Act; RCRA: Resource Conservation and Recovery Act; SDWA: Safe Drinking Water Act.

Source: Tabor, R. H., and Stanwick, S. D. "Arkansas: An environmental perspective." *Arkansas Business and Economic Review,* Vol. 28, No. 2, Summer 1995, pp. 22–32 (Table 4).

(*Note:* Some companies were involved in more than one civil action.)

a. Construct a stem-and-leaf display for all 38 penalties.

b. Circle the individual leaves that are associated with penalties imposed for violations of the Clean Air Act.

c. What does the pattern of circles in part **b** suggest about the severity of the penalties imposed for Clean Air Act violations relative to the other types of violations reported in the table? Explain.

2.22 In a manufacturing plant a *work center* is a specific production facility that consists of one or more people and/or machines and is treated as one unit for the purposes of capacity requirements planning and job scheduling. If jobs arrive at a particular work center at a

WORKCTR.DAT

Number of Items Arriving at Work Center per Hour

155	115	156	150	159	163	172	143	159	166	148	175
151	161	138	148	129	135	140	152	139			

Number of Items Departing Work Center per Hour

156	109	127	148	135	119	140	127	115	122	99	106
171	123	135	125	107	152	111	137	161			

MINITAB Output for Exercise 2.22

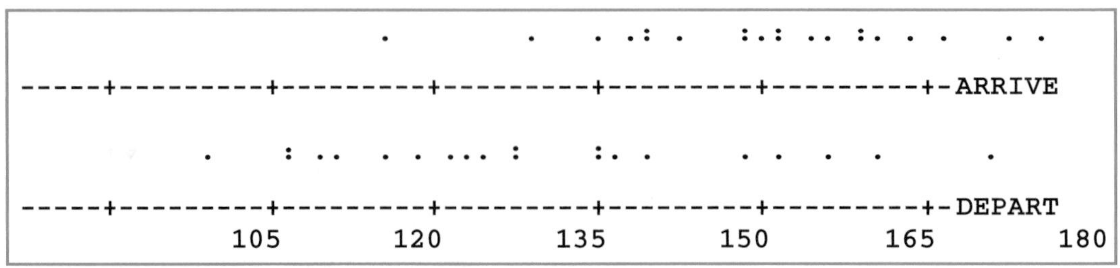

faster rate than they depart, the work center impedes the overall production process and is referred to as a *bottleneck* (Fogarty, Blackstone, and Hoffmann, *Production and Inventory Management,* 1991). The data in the table (bottom of p. 48) were collected by an operations manager for use in investigating a potential bottleneck work center. MINITAB dot plots for the two sets of data are also shown on p. 48. Do the dot plots suggest that the work center may be a bottleneck? Explain.

2.23 In order to estimate how long it will take to produce a particular product, a manufacturer will study the relationship between production time per unit and the number of units that have been produced. The line or curve characterizing this relationship is called a *learning curve* (Adler and Clark, *Management Science,* Mar. 1991). Twenty-five employees, all of whom were performing the same production task for the tenth time, were observed. Each person's task completion time (in minutes) was recorded. The same 25 employees were observed again the 30th time they performed the same task and the 50th time they performed the task. The resulting completion times are shown in the table below.

a. Use a statistical software package to construct a frequency histogram for each of the three data sets.

b. Compare the histograms. Does it appear that the relationship between task completion time and the number of times the task is performed is in agreement with the observations noted above about production processes in general? Explain.

COMPTIME.DAT

Employee	Performance 10th	30th	50th
1	15	16	10
2	21	10	5
3	30	12	7
4	17	9	9
5	18	7	8
6	22	11	11
7	33	8	12
8	41	9	9
9	10	5	7
10	14	15	6
11	18	10	8
12	25	11	14
13	23	9	9
14	19	11	8
15	20	10	10
16	22	13	8
17	20	12	7
18	19	8	8
19	18	20	6
20	17	7	5
21	16	6	6
22	20	9	4
23	22	10	15
24	19	10	7
25	24	11	20

2.24 Financially distressed firms can gain protection from their creditors while they restructure by filing for protection under US Bankruptcy Codes. In a *prepackaged bankruptcy,* a firm negotiates a reorganization plan with its creditors prior to filing for bankruptcy. This can result in a much quicker exit from bankruptcy than traditional bankruptcy filings. Brian Betker conducted a study of 49 prepackaged bankruptcies that were filed between 1986 and 1993 and reported the results in *Financial Management* (Spring 1995). The table on page 50 lists the time in bankruptcy (in months) for these 49 companies. The table also lists the results of a vote by each company's board of directors concerning their preferred reorganization plan. (*Note:* "Joint" = joint exchange offer with prepackaged bankruptcy solicitation; "Prepack" = prepackaged bankruptcy solicitation only; "None" = no pre-filing vote held.)

a. Construct a stem-and-leaf display for the length of time in bankruptcy for all 49 companies.

b. Summarize the information reflected in the stem-and-leaf display, part **a.** Make a general statement about the length of time in bankruptcy for firms using "prepacks."

c. Select a graphical technique that will permit a comparison of the time-in-bankruptcy distributions for the three types of "prepack" firms: those who held no pre-filing vote; those who voted their preference for a joint solution; and those who voted their preference for a prepack.

Histogram for Exercise 2.25

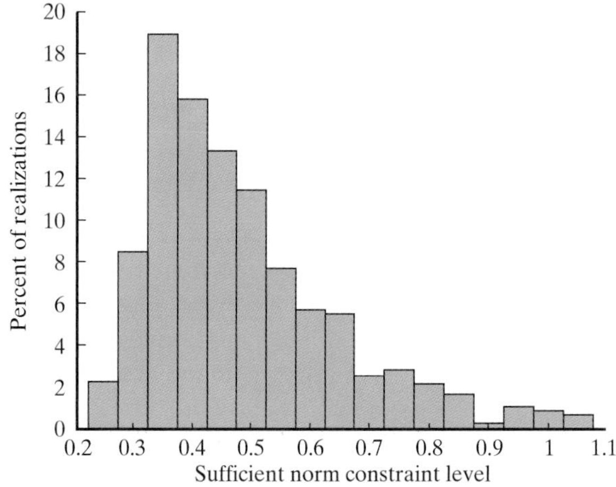

Source: Hoffman, M.W., and Buckley, K.M. "Robust time-domain processing of broadband microphone array data." *IEEE Transactions on Speech and Audio Processing,* Vol. 3, No. 3, May 1995, p. 199 (Figure 4). ©1995 IEEE.

d. The companies that were reorganized through a leveraged buyout are identified by an asterisk (*) in the table. Identify these firms on the stem-and-leaf display, part **a,** by circling their bankruptcy times. Do you observe any pattern in the graph? Explain.

2.25 It's not uncommon for hearing aids to malfunction and cancel the desired signal. *IEEE Transactions on Speech and Audio Processing* (May 1995) reported on a new audio processing system designed to limit the amount of signal cancellation that may occur. The system utilizes a mathematical equation that involves a variable, *V*, called a *sufficient norm constraint.* A histogram for realizations of *V*, produced using simulation, is shown on page 49.

a. Estimate the percentage of realizations of *V* with values ranging from .425 to .675.

b. Cancellation of the desired signal is limited by selecting a norm constraint *V*. Find the value of *V* for a company that wants to market the new hearing aid so that only 10% of the realizations have values below the selected level.

BANKRUPT.DAT

Company	Pre-filing Votes	Time in Bankruptcy (months)	Company	Pre-filing Votes	Time in Bankruptcy (months)
AM International	None	3.9	LIVE Entertainment	Joint	1.4
Anglo Energy	Prepack	1.5	Mayflower Group*	Prepack	1.4
Arizona Biltmore*	Prepack	1.0	Memorex Telex*	Prepack	1.1
Astrex	None	10.1	Munsingwear	None	2.9
Barry's Jewelers	None	4.1	Nat'l Environmental	Joint	5.2
Calton	Prepack	1.9	Petrolane Gas	Prepack	1.2
Cencor	Joint	1.4	Price Communications	None	2.4
Charter Medical*	Prepack	1.3	Republic Health*	Joint	4.5
Cherokee*	Joint	1.2	Resorts Int'l*	None	7.8
Circle Express	Prepack	4.1	Restaurant Enterprises*	Prepack	1.5
Cook Inlet Comm.	Prepack	1.1	Rymer Foods	Joint	2.1
Crystal Oil	None	3.0	SCI TV*	Prepack	2.1
Divi Hotels	None	3.2	Southland*	Joint	3.9
Edgell Comm.*	Prepack	1.0	Specialty Equipment*	None	2.6
Endevco	Prepack	3.8	SPI Holdings*	Joint	1.4
Gaylord Container	Joint	1.2	Sprouse-Reitz	Prepack	1.4
Great Amer. Comm.*	Prepack	1.0	Sunshine Metals	Joint	5.4
Hadson	Prepack	1.5	TIE/Communications	None	2.4
In-Store Advertising	Prepack	1.0	Trump Plaza	Prepack	1.7
JPS Textiles*	Prepack	1.4	Trump Taj Mahal	Prepack	1.4
Kendall*	Prepack	1.2	Trump's Castle	Prepack	2.7
Kinder-Care	None	4.2	USG	Prepack	1.2
Kroy*	Prepack	3.0	Vyquest	Prepack	4.1
Ladish*	Joint	1.5	West Point Acq.*	Prepack	2.9
LaSalle Energy*	Prepack	1.6			

*Leveraged buyout.

Source: Betker, B.L. "An empirical examination of prepackaged bankruptcy." *Financial Management,* Vol. 24, No. 1, Spring 1995, p. 6 (Table 2).

2.3 SUMMATION NOTATION

Now that we've examined some graphical techniques for summarizing and describing quantitative data sets, we turn to numerical methods for accomplishing this objective. Before giving the formulas for calculating numerical descriptive measures, let's look at some shorthand notation that will simplify our calculation instructions. Remember that such notation is used for one reason only—to avoid repeating the same verbal descriptions over and over. If you mentally substitute the verbal definition of a symbol each time you read it, you'll soon get used to it.

We denote the measurements of a quantitative data set as follows: $x_1, x_2, x_3, \dots, x_n$ where x_1 is the first measurement in the data set, x_2 is the second measurement in the data set, x_3 is the third measurement in the data set, ... , and

x_n is the nth (and last) measurement in the data set. Thus, if we have five measurements in a set of data, we will write x_1, x_2, x_3, x_4, x_5 to represent the measurements. If the actual numbers are 5, 3, 8, 5, and 4, we have $x_1 = 5$, $x_2 = 3$, $x_3 = 8$, $x_4 = 5$, and $x_5 = 4$.

Most of the formulas we use require a summation of numbers. For example, one sum we'll need to obtain is the sum of all the measurements in the data set, or $x_1 + x_2 + x_3 + \cdots + x_n$. To shorten the notation, we use the symbol Σ for the summation. That is, $x_1 + x_2 + x_3 + \cdots + x_n = \sum_{i=1}^{n} x_i$. Verbally translate $\sum_{i=1}^{n} x_i$ as follows: "The sum of the measurements, whose typical member is x_i, beginning with the member x_1 and ending with the member x_n."

Suppose, as in our earlier example, $x_1 = 5$, $x_2 = 3$, $x_3 = 8$, $x_4 = 5$, and $x_5 = 4$. Then the sum of the five measurements, denoted $\sum_{i=1}^{5} x_i$, is obtained as follows:

$$\begin{aligned}\sum_{i=1}^{5} x_i &= x_1 + x_2 + x_3 + x_4 + x_5 \\ &= 5 + 3 + 8 + 5 + 4 = 25\end{aligned}$$

Another important calculation requires that we square each measurement and then sum the squares. The notation for this sum is $\sum_{i=1}^{n} x_i^2$. For the five measurements above, we have

$$\begin{aligned}\sum_{i=1}^{5} x_i^2 &= x_1^2 + x_2^2 + x_3^2 + x_4^2 + x_5^2 \\ &= 5^2 + 3^2 + 8^2 + 5^2 + 4^2 \\ &= 25 + 9 + 64 + 25 + 16 = 139\end{aligned}$$

In general, the symbol following the summation sign Σ represents the variable (or function of the variable) that is to be summed.

The Meaning of Summation Notation $\sum_{i=1}^{n} x_i$

Sum the measurements on the variable that appears to the right of the summation symbol, beginning with the 1st measurement and ending with the nth measurement.

EXERCISES 2.26–2.29

Learning the Mechanics

Note: In all exercises, Σ represents $\sum_{i=1}^{n}$.

2.26 A data set contains the observations 5, 1, 3, 2, 1. Find:
a. Σx b. Σx^2 c. $\Sigma(x - 1)$
d. $\Sigma(x - 1)^2$ e. $(\Sigma x)^2$

2.27 Suppose a data set contains the observations 3, 8, 4, 5, 3, 4, 6. Find:
a. Σx b. Σx^2 c. $\Sigma(x - 5)^2$
d. $\Sigma(x - 2)^2$ e. $(\Sigma x)^2$

2.28 Refer to Exercise 2.26. Find:

a. $\sum x^2 - \frac{(\sum x)^2}{5}$ b. $\sum(x-2)^2$ c. $\sum x^2 - 10$

2.29 A data set contains the observations 6, 0, −2, −1, 3. Find:

a. $\sum x$ b. $\sum x^2$ c. $\sum x^2 - \frac{(\sum x)^2}{5}$

2.4 NUMERICAL MEASURES OF CENTRAL TENDENCY

When we speak of a data set, we refer to either a sample or a population. If statistical inference is our goal, we'll wish ultimately to use sample **numerical descriptive measures** to make inferences about the corresponding measures for a population.

As you'll see, a large number of numerical methods are available to describe quantitative data sets. Most of these methods measure one of two data characteristics:

1. The **central tendency** of the set of measurements—that is, the tendency of the data to cluster, or center, about certain numerical values (see Figure 2.12a).
2. The **variability** of the set of measurements—that is, the spread of the data (see Figure 2.12b).

In this section we concentrate on measures of central tendency. In the next section, we discuss measures of variability.

The most popular and best-understood measure of central tendency for a quantitative data set is the *arithmetic mean* (or simply the *mean*) of a data set.

DEFINITION 2.4

The **mean** of a set of quantitative data is the sum of the measurements divided by the number of measurements contained in the data set.

In everyday terms, the mean is the average value of the data set and is often used to represent a "typical" value. We denote the **mean of a sample** of measurements by $\bar{x}$ (read "x-bar"), and represent the formula for its calculation as shown in the box.

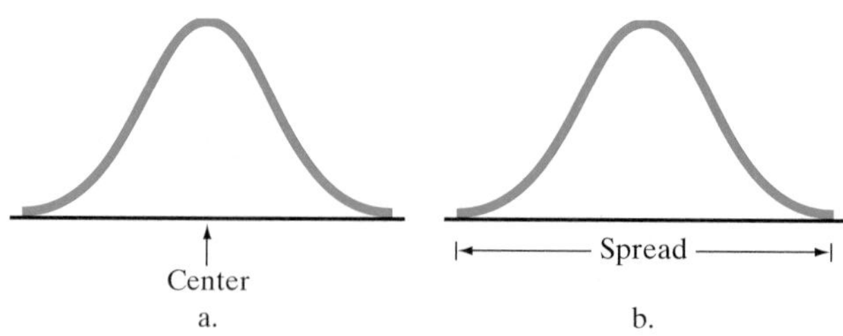

FIGURE 2.12 Numerical descriptive measures

Calculating a Sample Mean

$$\bar{x} = \frac{\sum_{i=1}^{n} x_i}{n}$$

EXAMPLE 2.4 Calculate the mean of the following five sample measurements: 5, 3, 8, 5, 6.

Solution Using the definition of sample mean and the summation notation, we find

$$\bar{x} = \frac{\sum_{i=1}^{5} x_i}{5} = \frac{5 + 3 + 8 + 5 + 6}{5} = \frac{27}{5} = 5.4$$

Thus, the mean of this sample is 5.4.*

EXAMPLE 2.5 Calculate the sample mean for the R&D expenditure percentages of the 50 companies given in Table 2.4.

Solution The mean R&D percentage for the 50 companies is denoted

$$\bar{x} = \frac{\sum_{i=1}^{50} x_i}{50}$$

Rather than compute $\bar{x}$ by hand (or calculator), we entered the data of Table 2.4 into a computer and employed SPSS statistical software to compute the mean. The SPSS printout is shown in Figure 2.13. The sample mean, highlighted on the printout, is $\bar{x} = 8.492$.

```
  RDEXP
Valid cases:          50.0   Missing cases:      .0   Percent missing:      .0

Mean       8.4920   Std Err      .2801   Min       5.2000   Skewness     .8546
Median     8.0500   Variance    3.9228   Max      13.5000   S E Skew     .3366
5% Trim    8.3833   Std Dev     1.9806   Range     8.3000   Kurtosis     .4193
                                         IQR       2.5750   S E Kurt     .6619
```

FIGURE 2.13
SPSS printout of numerical descriptive measures for 50 R&D percentages

Given this information, you can visualize a distribution of R&D percentages centered in the vicinity of $\bar{x} = 8.492$. An examination of the relative frequency histogram (Figure 2.8) confirms that $\bar{x}$ does in fact fall near the center of the distribution.

The sample mean $\bar{x}$ will play an important role in accomplishing our objective of making inferences about populations based on sample information. For this reason we need to use a different symbol for the *mean of a population*—the mean

*In the examples given here, $\bar{x}$ is sometimes rounded to the nearest tenth, sometimes the nearest hundredth, sometimes the nearest thousandth, and so on. There is no specific rule for rounding when calculating $\bar{x}$ because $\bar{x}$ is specifically defined to be the sum of all measurements divided by n; that is, it is a specific fraction. When $\bar{x}$ is used for descriptive purposes, it is often convenient to round the calculated value of $\bar{x}$ to the number of significant figures used for the original measurements. When $\bar{x}$ is to be used in other calculations, however, it may be necessary to retain more significant figures.

of the set of measurements on every unit in the population. We use the Greek letter μ (mu) for the population mean.

Symbols for the Sample and Population Mean

In this text, we adopt a general policy of using Greek letters to represent population numerical descriptive measures and Roman letters to represent corresponding descriptive measures for the sample. The symbols for the mean are:

$\bar{x}$ = Sample mean
μ = Population mean

We'll often use the sample mean, $\bar{x}$, to estimate (make an inference about) the population mean, μ. For example, the percentages of revenues spent on R&D by the population consisting of *all* US companies has a mean equal to some value, μ. Our sample of 50 companies yielded percentages with a mean of $\bar{x} = 8.492$. If, as is usually the case, we don't have access to the measurements for the entire population, we could use $\bar{x}$ as an estimator or approximator for μ. Then we'd need to know something about the reliability of our inference. That is, we'd need to know how accurately we might expect $\bar{x}$ to estimate μ. In Chapter 5, we'll find that this accuracy depends on two factors:

1. The *size of the sample.* The larger the sample, the more accurate the estimate will tend to be.
2. The *variability,* or *spread, of the data.* All other factors remaining constant, the more variable the data, the less accurate the estimate.

Another important measure of central tendency is the *median.*

DEFINITION 2.5

The **median** of a quantitative data set is the middle number when the measurements are arranged in ascending (or descending) order.

The median is of most value in describing large data sets. If the data set is characterized by a relative frequency histogram (Figure 2.14), the median is the point on the x-axis such that half the area under the histogram lies above the median and half lies below. [*Note:* In Section 2.2 we observed that the relative frequency associated with a particular interval on the horizontal axis is proportional

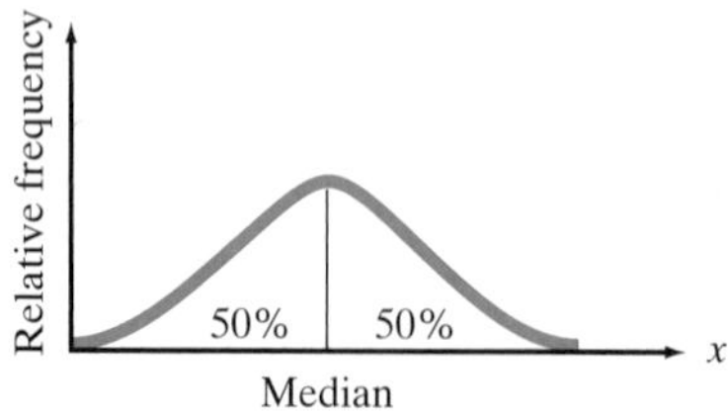

FIGURE 2.14
Location of the median

to the amount of area under the histogram that lies above the interval.] We denote the *median of a sample* by m.

Calculating a Sample Median, m

Arrange the n measurements from smallest to largest.

1. If n is odd, m is the middle number.
2. If n is even, m is the mean of the middle two numbers.

EXAMPLE 2.6 Consider the following sample of $n = 7$ measurements: 5, 7, 4, 5, 20, 6, 2.

a. Calculate the median m of this sample.
b. Eliminate the last measurement (the 2) and calculate the median of the remaining $n = 6$ measurements.

Solution

a. The seven measurements in the sample are ranked in ascending order: 2, 4, 5, 5, 6, 7, 20

   Because the number of measurements is odd, the median is the middle measurement. Thus, the median of this sample is $m = 5$ (the second 5 listed in the sequence).

b. After removing the 2 from the set of measurements (the second 5 listed in the sequence), we rank the sample measurements in ascending order as follows: 4, 5, 5, 6, 7, 20

   Now the number of measurements is even, so we average the middle two measurements. The median is $m = (5 + 6)/2 = 5.5$.

In certain situations, the median may be a better measure of central tendency than the mean. In particular, the median is less sensitive than the mean to extremely large or small measurements. Note, for instance, that all but one of the measurements in part **a** of Example 2.6 center about $x = 5$. The single relatively large measurement, $x = 20$, does not affect the value of the median, 5, but it causes the mean, $\bar{x} = 7$, to lie to the right of most of the measurements.

As another example of data from which the central tendency is better described by the median than the mean, consider the salaries of professional athletes (e.g., National Basketball Association players). The presence of just a few athletes (e.g., Shaquille O'Neal) with very high salaries will affect the mean more than the median. Thus, the median will provide a more accurate picture of the typical salary for the professional league. The mean could exceed the vast majority of the sample measurements (salaries), making it a misleading measure of central tendency.

EXAMPLE 2.7 Calculate the median for the 50 R&D percentages given in Table 2.5. Compare the median to the mean computed in Example 2.5.

Solution For this large data set, we again resort to a computer analysis. The SPSS printout is reproduced in Figure 2.15, with the median highlighted. You can see that the median is 8.05. This value implies that half of the 50 R&D percentages in the data set fall below 8.05 and half lie above 8.05.

```
     RDEXP
Valid cases:          50.0   Missing cases:      .0   Percent missing:       .0

Mean         8.4920   Std Err      .2801  Min      5.2000  Skewness      .8546
Median       8.0500   Variance    3.9228  Max     13.5000  S E Skew      .3366
5% Trim      8.3833   Std Dev     1.9806  Range    8.3000  Kurtosis      .4193
                                          IQR      2.5750  S E Kurt      .6619
```

FIGURE 2.15
SPSS printout of numerical descriptive measures for 50 R&D percentages.

Note that the mean (8.492) for these data is larger than the median. This fact indicates that the data are **skewed** to the right—that is, there are more extreme measurements in the right tail of the distribution than in the left tail (recall the histogram, Figure 2.8).

In general, extreme values (large or small) affect the mean more than the median since these values are used explicitly in the calculation of the mean. On the other hand, the median is not affected directly by extreme measurements, since only the middle measurement (or two middle measurements) is explicitly used to calculate the median. Consequently, if measurements are pulled toward one end of the distribution (as with the R&D percentages), the mean will shift toward that tail more than the median.

A comparison of the mean and median gives us a general method for detecting skewness in data sets, as shown in the next box.

Comparing the Mean and the Median

If the data set is skewed to the right, then the median is less than the mean.

If the data set is symmetric, the mean equals the median.

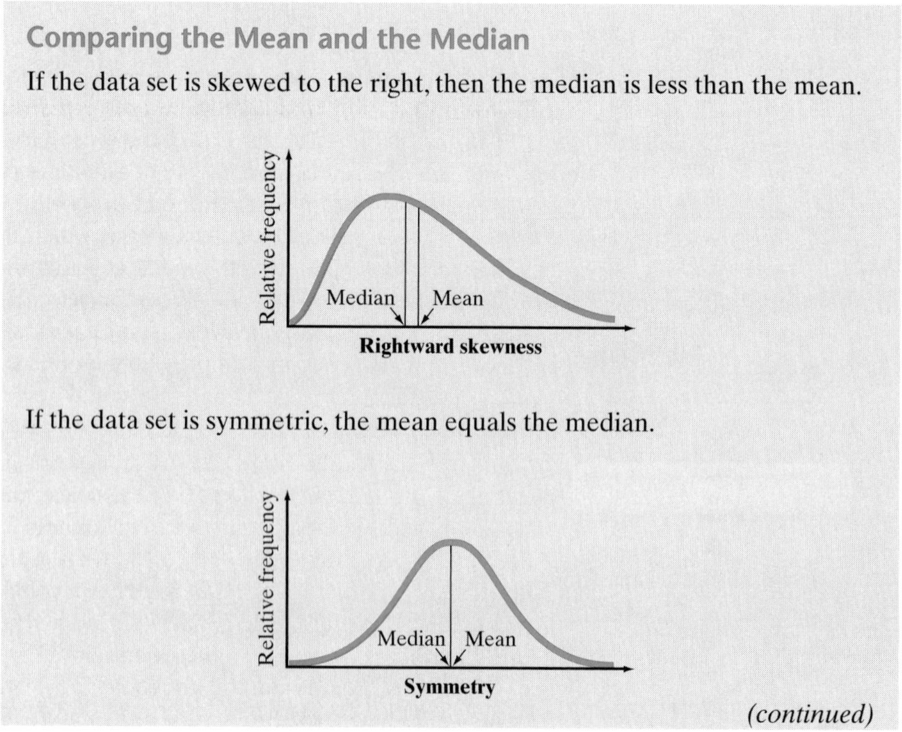

(continued)

If the data set is skewed to the left, the mean is less than (to the left of) the median.

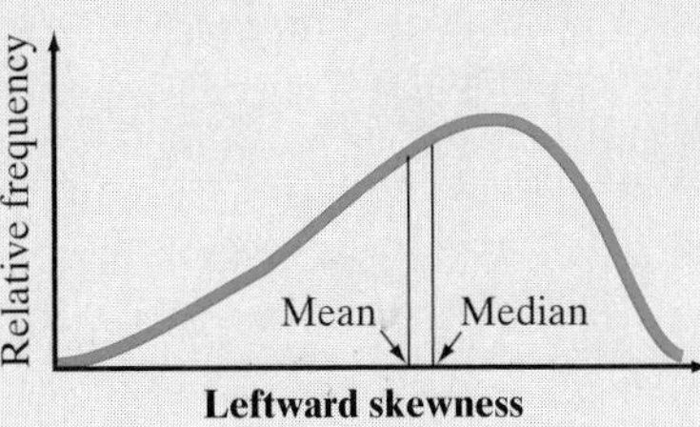

A third measure of central tendency is the *mode* of a set of measurements.

DEFINITION 2.6

The **mode** is the measurement that occurs most frequently in the data set.

EXAMPLE 2.8 Each of 10 taste testers rated a new brand of barbecue sauce on a 10 point scale, where 1 = awful and 10 = excellent. Find the mode for the 10 ratings shown below.

8 7 9 6 8 10 9 9 5 7

Solution Since 9 occurs most often, the mode of the 10 taste ratings is 9. 

Note that the data in Example 2.8 are actually qualitative in nature (e.g., "awful," "excellent"). The mode is particularly useful for describing qualitative data. The modal category is simply the category (or class) that occurs most often. Because it emphasizes data concentration, the mode is also used with quantitative data sets to locate the region in which much of the data is concentrated. A retailer of men's clothing would be interested in the modal neck size and sleeve length of potential customers. The modal income class of the laborers in the United States is of interest to the Labor Department.

For some quantitative data sets, the mode may not be very meaningful. For example, consider the percentages of revenues spent on research and development (R&D) by 50 companies, Table 2.4. A reexamination of the data reveals that three of the measurements are repeated three times: 6.5%, 6.9%, and 8.2%. Thus, there are three modes in the sample and none is particularly useful as a measure of central tendency.

A more meaningful measure can be obtained from a relative frequency histogram for quantitative data. The measurement class containing the largest relative frequency is called the **modal class.** Several definitions exist for locating the position of the mode within a modal class, but the simplest is to define the mode as the midpoint of the modal class. For example, examine the relative frequency histogram for the R&D expenditure percentages, reproduced below in Figure 2.16. You can see that the modal class is the interval 7.35—8.45. The mode (the midpoint) is 7.90. This modal class (and the mode itself) identifies the area in which the data are most concentrated, and in that sense it is a measure of central tendency. However, for most applications involving quantitative

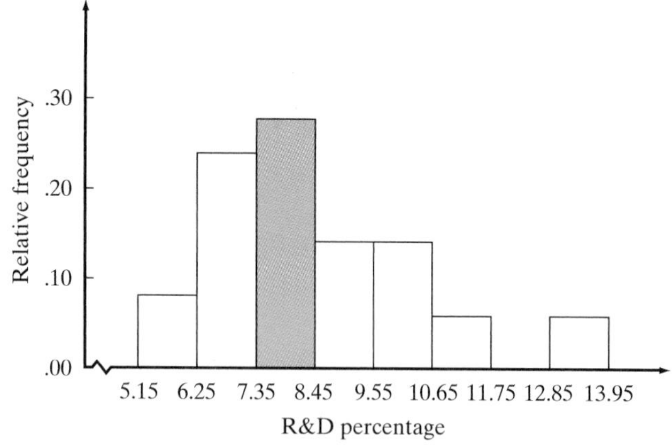

FIGURE 2.16 Relative frequency histogram for the computer companies' R&D percentages: The modal class

data, the mean and median provide more descriptive information than the mode.

Finding One-Variable Descriptive Statistics

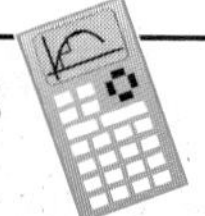

USING THE TI-83 GRAPHING CALCULATOR

Step 1 *Enter the data*
Press **STAT 1** for **STAT Edit**
Enter the data into one of the lists.

Step 2 *Calculate descriptive statistics*
Press **STAT**
Press the right arrow key to highlight **CALC**
Press **ENTER** for **1-Var Stats**

Enter the name of the list containing your data.
Press **2nd 1** for **L1** (or **2nd 2** for **L2** etc.)
Press **ENTER**

You should see the statistics on your screen. Some of the statistics are off the bottom of the screen. Use the down arrow to scroll through to see the remaining statistics. Use the up arrow to scroll back up.

Example The descriptive statistics for the sample data set

86, 70, 62, 98, 73, 56, 53, 92, 86, 37, 62, 83, 78, 49, 78, 37, 67, 79, 57

are shown below, as calculated by the TI-83.

```
1-Var Stats
 x̄=68.57894737
 Σx=1303
 Σx²=94897
 Sx=17.54142966
 σx=17.07357389
↓n=19
```

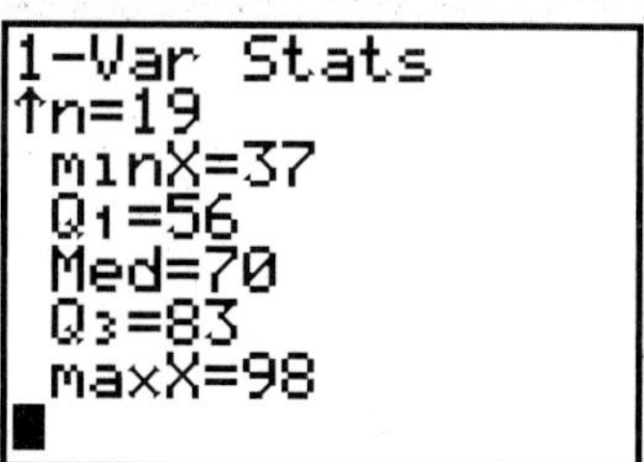

(continued)

Sorting Data The descriptive statistics do not include the mode. To find the mode, sort your data as follows:

Press **STAT**
Press **2** for **SORTA(**
Enter the name of the list your data is in. If your data is in **L1**, press **2nd 1**

Press **ENTER**
The screen will say: **DONE**
To see the sorted data, press **STAT 1** for **STAT Edit**

EXERCISES 2.30–2.42

Learning the Mechanics

2.30 Calculate the mode, mean, and median of the following data:

18 10 15 13 17 15 12 15 18 16 11

2.31 Calculate the mean and median of the following grade point averages:

3.2 2.5 2.1 3.7 2.8 2.0

2.32 Calculate the mean for samples where

a. $n = 10, \Sigma x = 85$ b. $n = 16, \Sigma x = 400$
c. $n = 45, \Sigma x = 35$ d. $n = 18, \Sigma x = 242$

2.33 Calculate the mean, median, and mode for each of the following samples:

a. 7, −2, 3, 3, 0, 4 b. 2, 3, 5, 3, 2, 3, 4, 3, 5, 1, 2, 3, 4
c. 51, 50, 47, 50, 48, 41, 59, 68, 45, 37

2.34 Describe how the mean compares to the median for a distribution as follows:

a. Skewed to the left b. Skewed to the right
c. Symmetric

Applying the Concepts

2.35 The total number of passengers handled in 1998 by eight cruise ships based in Port Canaveral (Florida) are listed in the table below. Find and interpret the mean and median of the data set.

2.36 *Fortune* (Oct. 25, 1999) magazine's second annual ranking of the 50 most powerful women in America is provided in the table on page 60. In addition to salary, position, and profile, *Fortune* based these rankings on the woman's influence within her company and her company's effect on culture in society. Consider the age (in years) distribution of these 50 women. Numerical descriptive statistics for the data are shown in the MINITAB printout below.

a. Find the mean, median, and modal age of the distribution. Interpret these values.
b. What do the mean and the median indicate about the skewness of the age distribution?
c. What percentage of these women are in their forties? Their fifties? Their sixties?

CRUISE.DAT

Cruise Line (Ship)	Number of Passengers
Canaveral (Dolphin)	152,240
Carnival (Fantasy)	480,924
Disney (Magic)	73,504
Premier (Oceanic)	270,361
Royal Caribbean (Nordic Empress)	106,161
Sun Cruz Casinos	453,806
Sterling Cruises (New Yorker)	15,782
Topaz Int'l. Shipping (Topaz)	28,280

Source: Florida Trend, Vol. 41, No. 9, Jan. 1999.

MINITAB Output for Exercise 2.36

```
Descriptive Statistics

Variable          N      Mean    Median   Tr Mean    StDev   SE Mean
Age              50    48.160    47.000    47.795    6.015     0.851

Variable        Min       Max        Q1        Q3
Age          36.000    68.000    45.000    51.250
```

WOMENPOW.DAT

Rank	Name	Age	Company	Title
1	Carly Fiorina	45	Hewlett-Packard	CEO
2	Heidi Miller	46	Citigroup	CFO
3	Mary Meeker	40	Morgan Stanley	Managing Director
4	Shelly Lazarus	52	Ogilvy & Mather	CEO
5	Meg Whitman	43	eBay	CEO
6	Debby Hopkins	44	Boeing	CFO
7	Marjorie Scardino	52	Pearson	CEO
8	Martha Stewart	58	Martha Stewart Living	CEO
9	Nancy Peretsman	45	Allen & Co.	Ex. V.P.
10	Pat Russo	47	Lucent Technologies	Ex. V.P.
11	Patricia Dunn	46	Barclays Global Investors	Chairman
12	Abby Joseph Cohen	47	Goldman Sachs	Managing Director
13	Ann Livermore	41	Hewlett-Packard	CEO
14	Andrea Jung	41	Avon Products	COO
15	Sherry Lansing	55	Paramount Pictures	Chairman
16	Karen Katen	50	Pfizer	Ex. V.P.
17	Marilyn Carlson Nelson	60	Carlson Cos.	CEO
18	Judy McGrath	47	MTV & M2	President
19	Lois Juliber	50	Colgate-Palmolive	COO
20	Gerry Laybourne	52	Oxygen Media	CEO
21	Judith Estrin	44	Cisco Systems	Sr. V.P.
22	Cathleen Black	55	Hearst Magazines	President
23	Linda Sandford	46	IBM	General Manager
24	Ann Moore	49	Time Inc.	President
25	Jill Barad	48	Mattel	CEO
26	Oprah Winfrey	45	Harpo Entertainment	Chairman
27	Judy Lewent	50	Merck	Sr. V.P.
28	Joy Covey	36	Amazon.com	COO
29	Rebecca Mark	45	Azurix	CEO
30	Deborah Willingham	43	Microsoft	V.P.
31	Dina Dubion	46	Chase Manhattan	Ex. V.P.
32	Patricia Woertz	46	Chevron	President
33	Lawton Fitt	46	Goldman Sachs	Managing Director
34	Ann Fudge	48	Kraft Foods	Ex. V.P.
35	Carolyn Ticknor	52	Hewlett-Packard	CEO
36	Dawn Lepore	45	Charles Schwab	CIO
37	Jeannine Rivet	51	UnitedHealthcare	CEO
38	Jamie Gorelick	49	Fannie Mae	Vice Chairman
39	Jan Brandt	48	America Online	Mar. President
40	Bridget Macaskill	51	OppenheimerFunds	CEO
41	Jeanne Jackson	48	Banana Republic	CEO
42	Cynthia Trudell	46	General Motors	V.P.
43	Nina DiSesa	53	McCann-Erickson	Chairman
44	Linda Wachner	53	Warnaco	Chairman
45	Darla Moore	45	Rainwater Inc.	President
46	Marion Sandler	68	Golden West	Co-CEO
47	Michelle Anthony	42	Sony Music	Ex. V.P.
48	Orit Gadlesh	48	Bain & Co.	Chairman
49	Charlotte Beers	64	J. Walter Thompson	Chairman
50	Abigail Johnson	37	Fidelity Investments	V.P.

Source: *Fortune*, October 25, 1999.

d. Use a statistical software package to construct a relative frequency histogram. What is the modal age class? Compare this to the modal age found in part **a.**

e. Locate the mean and median on the histogram, part **d.**

2.37 The Superfund Act was passed by Congress to encourage state participation in the implementation of laws relating to the release and cleanup of hazardous substances. Hazardous waste sites financed by the Superfund

Act are called Superfund sites. A total of 395 Superfund sites are operated by waste management companies in Arkansas (Tabor and Stanwick, *Arkansas Business and Economic Review,* Summer 1995). The number of these Superfund sites in each of Arkansas' 75 counties is shown in the table. Numerical descriptive measures for the data set are provided in the EXCEL printout.

ARKFUND.DAT

3	3	2	1	2	0	5	3	5	2	1	8	2
12	3	5	3	1	3	0	8	0	9	6	8	6
2	16	0	6	0	5	5	0	1	25	0	0	0
6	2	10	12	3	10	3	17	2	4	2	1	21
4	2	1	11	5	2	2	7	2	3	1	8	2
0	0	0	2	3	10	2	3	48	21			

Source: Tabor, R.H., and Stanwick, S.D. "Arkansas: An environmental perspective. "*Arkansas Business and Economic Review,* Vol. 28, No. 2, Summer 1995, pp. 22–32 (Table 1).

EXCEL Output for Exercise 2.37

SITES	
Mean	5.24
Standard Error	0.836517879
Median	3
Mode	2
Standard Deviation	7.244457341
Sample Variance	52.48216216
Kurtosis	16.41176573
Skewness	3.468289878
Range	48
Minimum	0
Maximum	48
Sum	393
Count	75
Confidence Level(95.000%)	1.639542488

a. Locate the measures of central tendency on the printout and interpret their values.

b. Note that the data set contains at least one county with an unusually large number of Superfund sites. Find the largest of these measurements, called an *outlier*.

c. Delete the outlier, part **b,** from the data set and recalculate the measures of central tendency. Which measure is most affected by the elimination of the outlier?

2.38 Platelet-activating factor (PAF) is a potent chemical that occurs in patients suffering from shock, inflammation, hypotension, and allergic responses as well as respiratory and cardiovascular disorders. Consequently, drugs that effectively inhibit PAF, keeping it from binding to human cells, may be successful in treating these disorders. A bioassay was undertaken to investigate the potential of 17 traditional Chinese herbal drugs in PAF inhibition (H. Guiqui, *Progress in Natural Science,* June 1995). The prevention of the PAF binding process, measured as a percentage, for each drug is provided in the accompanying table.

DRUGPAF.DAT

Drug	PAF Inhibition (%)
Hai-feng-teng (Fuji)	77
Hai-feng-teng (Japan)	33
Shan-ju	75
Zhang-yiz-hu-jiao	62
Shi-nan-teng	70
Huang-hua-hu-jiao	12
Hua-nan-hu-jiao	0
Xiao-yie-pa-ai-xiang	0
Mao-ju	0
Jia-ju	15
Xie-yie-ju	25
Da-yie-ju	0
Bian-yie-hu-jiao	9
Bi-bo	24
Duo-mai-hu-jiao	40
Yan-sen	0
Jiao-guo-hu-jiao	31

Source: Guiqui, H. "PAF receptor antagonistic principles from Chinese traditional drugs." *Progress in Natural Science,* Vol. 5, No. 3, June 1995, p. 301 (Table 1).

a. Construct a stem-and-leaf display for the data.

b. Compute the median inhibition percentage for the 17 herbal drugs. Interpret the result.

c. Compute the mean inhibition percentage for the 17 herbal drugs. Interpret the result.

d. Compute the mode of the 17 inhibition percentages. Interpret the result.

e. Locate the median, mean, and mode on the stem-and-leaf display, part **a.** Do these measures of central tendency appear to locate the center of the data?

2.39 The salaries of superstar professional athletes receive much attention in the media. The multimillion-dollar long-term contract is now commonplace among this elite group. Nevertheless, rarely does a season pass without negotiations between one or more of the players' associations and team owners for additional salary and fringe benefits for *all* players in their particular sports.

a. If a players' association wanted to support its argument for higher "average" salaries, which measure of central tendency do you think it should use? Why?

b. To refute the argument, which measure of central tendency should the owners apply to the players' salaries? Why?

2.40 Major conventions and conferences attract thousands of people and pump millions of dollars into the local economy of the host city. The decision as to where to hold such conferences hinges to a large extent on the availability of hotel rooms. The table, extracted from *The Wall Street Journal* (Nov. 17, 1995), lists the top ten U.S. cities ranked by the number of hotel rooms.

HOTELS.DAT

City	No. of Rooms	No. of Hotels
Las Vegas	93,719	231
Orlando	84,982	311
Los Angeles—Long Beach	78,597	617
Chicago	68,793	378
Washington, D.C.	66,505	351
New York City	61,512	230
Atlanta	58,445	370
San Diego	44,655	352
Anaheim—Santa Ana	44,374	351
San Francisco	42,531	294

Source: Smith Travel Research, September 1995.

a. Find and interpret the median for each of the data sets.
b. For each city, calculate the ratio of the number of rooms to the number of hotels. Then find the average number of rooms per hotel in each city.
c. Re-rank the cities based on your answer to part **b.**

2.41 Refer to the *Financial Management* (Spring 1995) study of prepackaged bankruptcy filings, Exercise 2.24 (p. 49). Recall that each of 49 firms that negotiated a reorganization plan with its creditors prior to filing for bankruptcy was classified in one of three categories: joint exchange offer with prepack, prepack solicitation only, and no pre-filing vote held. An SPSS printout of descriptive statistics for the length of time in bankruptcy (months), by category, is shown below.

a. Locate the measures of central tendency on the printout and interpret their values.
b. Is it reasonable to use a single number (e.g., mean or median) to describe the center of the time-in-bankruptcy distributions? Or should three "centers" be calculated, one for each of the three categories of prepack firms? Explain.

2.42 The U.S. Energy Information Association tracks the prices of regular unleaded gasoline in the United States each year. The table (p. 63) lists the average 1998 prices (in cents) in each of a sample of 20 states.

SPSS Output for Exercise 2.41

```
   TIME
By  CATEGORY  Joint

Valid cases:          11.0   Missing cases:           .0   Percent missing:        .0

Mean         2.6545   Std Err       .5185  Min       1.2000  Skewness       .7600
Median       1.5000   Variance     2.9567  Max       5.4000  S E Skew       .6607
5% Trim      2.5828   Std Dev      1.7195  Range     4.2000  Kurtosis     -1.4183
                                           IQR       3.1000  S E Kurt      1.2794

-----------------------------------------------------------------------------------

   TIME
By  CATEGORY  None

Valid cases:          11.0   Missing cases:           .0   Percent missing:        .0

Mean         4.2364   Std Err       .7448  Min       2.4000  Skewness      1.8215
Median       3.2000   Variance     6.1025  Max      10.1000  S E Skew       .6607
5% Trim      4.0126   Std Dev      2.4703  Range     7.7000  Kurtosis      2.6270
                                           IQR       1.6000  S E Kurt      1.2794

-----------------------------------------------------------------------------------

   TIME
By  CATEGORY  Prepack

Valid cases:          27.0   Missing cases:           .0   Percent missing:        .0

Mean         1.8185   Std Err       .1847  Min       1.0000  Skewness      1.4539
Median       1.4000   Variance      .9216  Max       4.1000  S E Skew       .4479
5% Trim      1.7372   Std Dev       .9600  Range     3.1000  Kurtosis       .9867
                                           IQR        .9000  S E Kurt       .8721
```

a. Calculate the mean, median, and mode of this data set.
b. Eliminate the highest price from the data set and repeat part **a.** What effect does dropping this measurement have on the measures of central tendency calculated in part **a**?
c. Arrange the 20 prices in order from lowest to highest. Next, eliminate the lowest two prices and the highest two prices from the data set and calculate the mean of the remaining prices. The result is called a 10% *trimmed mean,* since it is calculated after dropping the highest 10% and the lowest 10% of the values in the data set. An advantage of the trimmed mean is that it is not as sensitive as the arithmetic mean to extreme observations in the data set.

GASPRICE.DAT

State	Price
Arkansas	85.2
Connecticut	112.2
Delaware	94.6
Hawaii	117.9
Louisiana	85.7
Maine	90.1
Massachusetts	95.6
Michigan	84.4
Missouri	85.9
Nevada	102.1
New Hampshire	96.6
New Jersey	81.7
New York	96.4
North Dakota	90.4
Oklahoma	81.4
Oregon	100.2
Pennsylvania	91.1
Texas	83.8
Wisconsin	95.6
Wyoming	84.4

Source: Statistical Abstract of the United States: 1998. U.S. Energy Information Administration, *Petroleum Marketing Monthly.*

2.5 NUMERICAL MEASURES OF VARIABILITY

Measures of central tendency provide only a partial description of a quantitative data set. The description is incomplete without a measure of the variability, or spread, of the data set. Knowledge of the data's variability along with its center can help us visualize the shape of a data set as well as its extreme values.

For example, suppose we are comparing the profit margin per construction job (as a percentage of the total bid price) for 100 construction jobs for each of two cost estimators working for a large construction company. The histograms for the two sets of 100 profit margin measurements are shown in Figure 2.17. If you examine the two histograms, you will notice that both data sets are symmetric with equal modes, medians, and means. However, cost estimator A (Figure 2.17a) has profit margins spread with almost equal relative frequency over the measurement classes, while cost estimator B (Figure 2.17b) has profit margins clustered about the center of the distribution. Thus, estimator B's profit margins are *less variable* than estimator A's. Consequently, you can see that we need a measure of variability as well as a measure of central tendency to describe a data set.

Perhaps the simplest measure of the variability of a quantitative data set is its *range.*

DEFINITION 2.7

The **range** of a quantitative data set is equal to the largest measurement minus the smallest measurement.

The range is easy to compute and easy to understand, but it is a rather insensitive measure of data variation when the data sets are large. This is because

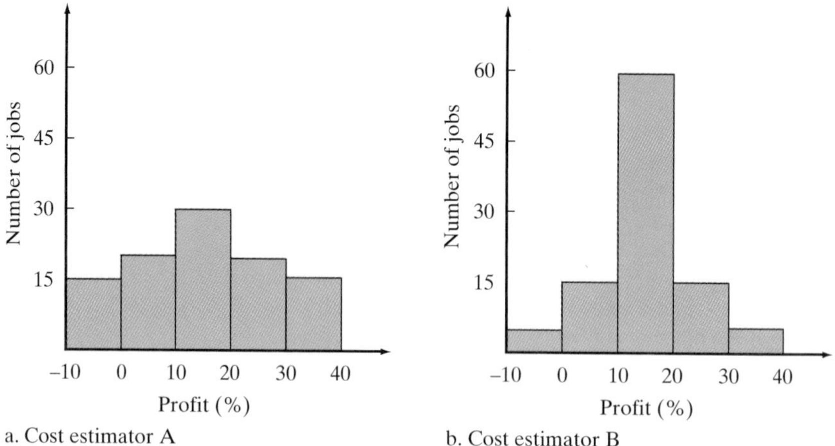

FIGURE 2.17
Profit margin histograms for two cost estimators

two data sets can have the same range and be vastly different with respect to data variation. This phenomenon is demonstrated in Figure 2.17. Although the ranges are equal and all central tendency measures are the same for these two symmetric data sets, there is an obvious difference between the two sets of measurements. The difference is that estimator B's profit margins tend to be more stable—that is, to pile up or to cluster about the center of the data set. In contrast, estimator A's profit margins are more spread out over the range, indicating a higher incidence of some high profit margins, but also a greater risk of losses. Thus, even though the ranges are equal, the profit margin record of estimator A is more variable than that of estimator B, indicating a distinct difference in their cost estimating characteristics.

Let's see if we can find a measure of data variation that is more sensitive than the range. Consider the two samples in Table 2.7: Each has five measurements. (We have ordered the numbers for convenience.)

TABLE 2.7 Two Hypothetical Data Sets

	Sample 1	**Sample 2**
Measurements	1, 2, 3, 4, 5	2, 3, 3, 3, 4
Mean	$\bar{x} = \frac{1+2+3+4+5}{5} = \frac{15}{5} = 3$	$\bar{x} = \frac{2+3+3+3+4}{5} = \frac{15}{5} = 3$
Deviations of measurement values from $\bar{x}$	$(1-3), (2-3), (3-3), (4-3), (5-3)$, or $-2, -1, 0, 1, 2$	$(2-3), (3-3), (3-3), (3-3), (4-3)$, or $-1, 0, 0, 0, 1$

Note that both samples have a mean of 3 and that we have also calculated the distance and direction, or *deviation,* between each measurement and the mean. What information do these deviations contain? If they tend to be large in magnitude, as in sample 1, the data are spread out, or highly variable. If the deviations are mostly small, as in sample 2, the data are clustered around the mean, $\bar{x}$, and therefore do not exhibit much variability. You can see that these deviations, displayed graphically in Figure 2.18, provide information about the variability of the sample measurements.

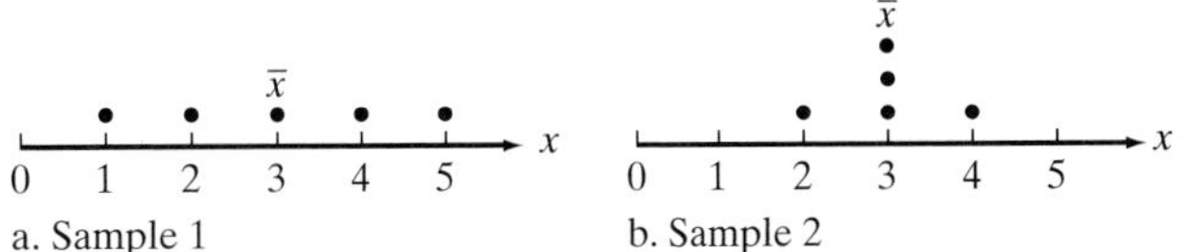

FIGURE 2.18
Dot plots for two data sets

The next step is to condense the information in these deviations into a single numerical measure of variability. Averaging the deviations from $\overline{x}$ won't help because the negative and positive deviations cancel; that is, the sum of the deviations (and thus the average deviation) is always equal to zero.

Two methods come to mind for dealing with the fact that positive and negative deviations from the mean cancel. The first is to treat all the deviations as though they were positive, ignoring the sign of the negative deviations. We won't pursue this line of thought because the resulting measure of variability (the mean of the absolute values of the deviations) presents analytical difficulties beyond the scope of this text. A second method of eliminating the minus signs associated with the deviations is to square them. The quantity we can calculate from the squared deviations will provide a meaningful description of the variability of a data set and presents fewer analytical difficulties in inference-making.

To use the squared deviations calculated from a data set, we first calculate the *sample variance.*

DEFINITION 2.8

The **sample variance** for a sample of n measurements is equal to the sum of the squared deviations from the mean divided by $(n - 1)$. In symbols, using s^2 to represent the sample variance,

$$s^2 = \frac{\sum_{i=1}^{n} (x_i - \overline{x})^2}{n - 1}$$

Note: A shortcut formula for calculating s^2 is

$$s^2 = \frac{\sum_{i=1}^{n} x_i^2 - \frac{\left(\sum_{i=1}^{n} x_i\right)^2}{n}}{n - 1}$$

Referring to the two samples in Table 2.7, you can calculate the variance for sample 1 as follows:

$$s^2 = \frac{(1 - 3)^2 + (2 - 3)^2 + (3 - 3)^2 + (4 - 3)^2 + (5 - 3)^2}{5 - 1}$$

$$= \frac{4 + 1 + 0 + 1 + 4}{4} = 2.5$$

The second step in finding a meaningful measure of data variability is to calculate the *standard deviation* of the data set.

DEFINITION 2.9

The **sample standard deviation,** s, is defined as the positive square root of the sample variance, s^2. Thus, $s = \sqrt{s^2}$.

The population variance, denoted by the symbol σ^2 (sigma squared), is the average of the squared distances of the measurements on *all* units in the population from the mean, μ, and σ (sigma) is the square root of this quantity. Since we never really compute σ^2 or σ from the population (the object of sampling is to avoid this costly procedure), we simply denote these two quantities by their respective symbols.

Symbols for Variance and Standard Deviation

s^2 = Sample variance
s = Sample standard deviation
σ^2 = Population variance
σ = Population standard deviation

Notice that, unlike the variance, the standard deviation is expressed in the original units of measurement. For example, if the original measurements are in dollars, the variance is expressed in the peculiar units "dollar squared," but the standard deviation is expressed in dollars.

You may wonder why we use the divisor $(n - 1)$ instead of n when calculating the sample variance. Wouldn't using n be more logical, so that the sample variance would be the average squared deviation from the mean? The trouble is, using n tends to produce an underestimate of the population variance, σ^2. So we use $(n - 1)$ in the denominator to provide the appropriate correction for this tendency.* Since sample statistics like s^2 are primarily used to estimate population parameters like σ^2, $(n - 1)$ is preferred to n when defining the sample variance.

EXAMPLE 2.9 Calculate the variance and standard deviation of the following sample: 2, 3, 3, 3, 4.

Solution As the number of measurements increases, calculating s^2 and s becomes very tedious. Fortunately, as we show in Example 2.10, we can use a statistical software package (or calculator) to find these values. If you must calculate these quantities by hand, it is advantageous to use the shortcut formula provided in Definition 2.8. To do this, we need two summations: Σx and Σx^2. These can easily be obtained from the following type of tabulation:

x	x^2
2	4
3	9
3	9
3	9
4	16
$\Sigma x = 15$	$\Sigma x^2 = 47$

*"Appropriate" here means that s^2 with the divisor of $(n - 1)$ is an *unbiased estimator* of σ^2. We define and discuss "unbiasedness" of estimators in Chapter 4.

Then we use*

$$s^2 = \frac{\sum_{i=1}^{n} x_i^2 - \frac{\left(\sum_{i=1}^{n} x_i\right)^2}{n}}{n-1} = \frac{47 - \frac{(15)^2}{5}}{5-1} = \frac{2}{4} = .5$$

$$s = \sqrt{.5} = .71$$

EXAMPLE 2.10 Use the computer to find the sample variance s^2 and the sample standard deviation s for the 50 companies' percentages of revenues spent on R&D.

Solution The SAS printout describing the R&D percentage data is displayed in Figure 2.19. The variance and standard deviation, highlighted on the printout, are: $s^2 = 3.922792$ and $s = 1.980604$.

FIGURE 2.19
SAS printout of numerical descriptive measures for 50 R&D percentages

```
                         UNIVARIATE PROCEDURE
Variable=RDPCT
                               Moments

            N               50   Sum Wgts          50
            Mean         8.492   Sum            424.6
            Std Dev   1.980604   Variance    3.922792
            Skewness  0.854601   Kurtosis    0.419288
            USS        3797.92   CSS         192.2168
            CV        23.32317   Std Mean      0.2801
            T:Mean=0  30.31778   Prob>|T|      0.0001
            Sgn Rank     637.5   Prob>|S|      0.0001
            Num ^= 0        50

                          Quantiles(Def=5)

             100% Max     13.5         99%       13.5
              75% Q3       9.6         95%       13.2
              50% Med     8.05         90%       11.2
              25% Q1       7.1         10%        6.5
               0% Min      5.2          5%        5.9
                                        1%        5.2

             Range         8.3
             Q3-Q1         2.5
             Mode          6.5
```

You now know that the standard deviation measures the variability of a set of data and how to calculate it. But how can we interpret and use the standard deviation? This is the topic of Section 2.6.

*When calculating s^2, how many decimal places should you carry? Although there are no rules for the rounding procedure, it's reasonable to retain twice as many decimal places in s^2 as you ultimately wish to have in s. If you wish to calculate s to the nearest hundredth (two decimal places), for example, you should calculate s^2 to the nearest ten-thousandth (four decimal places).

EXERCISES 2.43–2.53

Learning the Mechanics

2.43 Answer the following questions about variability of data sets:

a. What is the primary disadvantage of using the range to compare the variability of data sets?

b. Describe the sample variance using words rather than a formula. Do the same with the population variance.

c. Can the variance of a data set ever be negative? Explain. Can the variance ever be smaller than the standard deviation? Explain.

2.44 Calculate the variance and standard deviation for samples where

a. $n = 10$, $\Sigma x^2 = 84$, $\Sigma x = 20$

b. $n = 40$, $\Sigma x^2 = 380$, $\Sigma x = 100$

c. $n = 20$, $\Sigma x^2 = 18$, $\Sigma x = 17$

2.45 Calculate the range, variance, and standard deviation for the following samples:

a. 4, 2, 1, 0, 1 b. 1, 6, 2, 2, 3, 0, 3

c. 8, −2, 1, 3, 5, 4, 4, 1, 3, 3

d. 0, 2, 0, 0, −1, 1, −2, 1, 0, −1, 1, −1, 0, −3, −2, −1, 0, 1

2.46 Calculate the range, variance, and standard deviation for the following samples:

a. 39, 42, 40, 37, 41 b. 100, 4, 7, 96, 80, 3, 1, 10, 2

c. 100, 4, 7, 30, 80, 30, 42, 2

2.47 Compute $\bar{x}$, s^2, and s for each of the following data sets. If appropriate, specify the units in which your answer is expressed.

a. 3, 1, 10, 10, 4 b. 8 feet, 10 feet, 32 feet, 5 feet

c. −1, −4, −3, 1, −4, −4

d. $\frac{1}{5}$ ounce, $\frac{1}{5}$ ounce, $\frac{1}{5}$ ounce, $\frac{2}{5}$ ounce, $\frac{1}{5}$ ounce, $\frac{4}{5}$ ounce

2.48 Consider the following sample of five measurements: 2, 1, 1, 0, 3

a. Calculate the range, s^2, and s.

b. Add 3 to each measurement and repeat part **a.**

c. Subtract 4 from each measurement and repeat part **a.**

d. Considering your answers to parts **a, b,** and **c,** what seems to be the effect on the variability of a data set by adding the same number to or subtracting the same number from each measurement?

Applying the Concepts

2.49 The table at the bottom of the page lists the 1999 base prices for automobiles manufactured by Buick and Cadillac.

a. Calculate the range of the Buick prices and the range of the Cadillac prices.

b. The lowest and highest priced Chevrolet cars are \$9,373 (Metro) and \$45,575 (Corvette), respectively. Calculate Chevrolet's range.

c. Using only the three ranges you computed in parts **a** and **b** and no other information, is it possible to determine which manufacturer produces only luxury cars? Explain.

2.50 Refer to Exercise 2.35 (p. 59). The total number of passengers handled in 1998 by eight Port Canaveral (Florida) cruise ships are reproduced in the next table.

a. Find the range of the data.

b. Find the variance of the data.

CRUISE.DAT

Cruise Line (Ship)	Number of Passengers
Canaveral (Dolphin)	152,240
Carnival (Fantasy)	480,924
Disney (Magic)	73,504
Premier (Oceanic)	270,361
Royal Caribbean (Nordic Empress)	106,161
Sun Cruz Casinos	453,806
Sterling Cruises (New Yorker)	15,782
Topaz Int'l. shipping (Topaz)	28,280

Source: Florida Trend, Vol. 41, No. 9, Jan. 1999.

AUTO99.DAT

Buick	Price	Cadillac	Price
Century Custom	\$19,335	Catera	\$34,820
Century Limited	20,705	DeVille	39,300
Regal LS	22,255	DeVille D'Elegance	43,400
Regal GS	24,955	DeVille Concours	43,900
LeSabre Custom	23,340	Eldorado	39,905
LeSabre Limited	26,605	Eldorado Touring	44,165
Park Avenue	31,800	Seville SLS	44,025
Park Avenue Ultra	36,695	Seville STS	48,520
Riviera	34,490		

Source: *Automotive News,* Nov. 30, 1998.

c. Find the standard deviation of the data.
d. Suppose the standard deviation of the number of passengers handled by cruise ships in another Florida city is 209,000. For which of the two cities is the cruise ship passenger data more variable?

2.51 The Consumer Price Index (CPI) measures the price change of a constant market basket of goods and services. The Bureau of Labor Statistics publishes a national CPI (called the U.S. City Average Index) as well as separate indexes for each of 32 different cities in the United States. The CPI is used in cost-of-living escalator clauses of many labor contracts to adjust wages for inflation *(Bureau of Labor Statistics Handbook of Methods,* 1992). The table below lists the published values of the U.S. City Average Index and the Chicago Index during 1994 and 1995.

CITYCPI.DAT

Month	U.S. City Average Index	Chicago
January 1994	146.2	146.5
February	146.7	146.8
March	147.2	147.6
April	147.4	147.9
May	147.5	147.6
June	148.0	148.1
July	148.4	148.3
August	149.0	149.8
September	149.4	150.2
October	149.5	149.4
November	149.7	150.4
December	149.7	150.5
January 1995	150.3	151.8
February	150.9	152.3
March	151.4	152.6
April	151.9	153.1
May	152.2	153.0
June	152.5	153.5
July	152.5	153.6
August	152.9	153.8
September	153.2	154.0
October	153.7	154.3
November	153.6	154.0
December	153.5	153.8

Source: CPI Detailed Report, Bureau of Labor Statistics, Jan. 1994–Dec. 1995.

a. Calculate the mean values for the U.S. City Average Index and the Chicago Index.
b. Find the ranges of the U.S. City Average Index and the Chicago Index.
c. Calculate the standard deviation for both the U.S. City Average Index and the Chicago Index over the time period described in the table.
d. Which index displays greater variation about its mean over the time period in question? Justify your response.

2.52 A widely used technique for estimating the length of time it takes workers to produce a product is the *time study.* In a time study, the task to be studied is divided into measurable parts and each is timed with a stopwatch or filmed for later analysis. For each worker, this process is repeated many times for each subtask. Then the average and standard deviation of the time required to complete each subtask are computed for each worker. A worker's overall time to complete the task under study is then determined by adding his or her subtask-time averages (Gaither, *Production and Operations Management,* 1996). The data (in minutes) given in the table are the result of a time study of a production operation involving two subtasks.

TIMSTUDY.DAT

	Worker A		Worker B	
Repetition	Subtask 1	Subtask 2	Subtask 1	Subtask 2
1	30	2	31	7
2	28	4	30	2
3	31	3	32	6
4	38	3	30	5
5	25	2	29	4
6	29	4	30	1
7	30	3	31	4

a. Find the overall time it took each worker to complete the manufacturing operation under study.
b. For each worker, find the standard deviation of the seven times for subtask 1.
c. In the context of this problem, what are the standard deviations you computed in part **b** measuring?
d. Repeat part **b** for subtask 2.
e. If you could choose workers similar to A or workers similar to B to perform subtasks 1 and 2, which type would you assign to each subtask? Explain your decisions on the basis of your answers to parts **a–d.**

2.53 The table lists the 1995 profits (in millions of dollars) for a sample of seven airlines.

AIRLINES.DAT

Airline	Profit
Southwest	182.6
Continental	226.0
Northwest	342.1
Delta	510.0
U.S. Air	119.3
United	378.0
America West	54.8

Source: "*Business Week* 1000." *Business Week,* March 25, 1996, p. 90.

a. Calculate the range, variance, and standard deviation of the data set.

b. Specify the units in which each of your answers to part **a** is expressed.

c. Suppose America West had a loss of $50 instead of a profit of $54.8 million. Would the range of the data set increase or decrease? Why? Would the standard deviation of the data set increase or decrease? Why?

2.6 INTERPRETING THE STANDARD DEVIATION

We've seen that if we are comparing the variability of two samples selected from a population, the sample with the larger standard deviation is the more variable of the two. Thus, we know how to interpret the standard deviation on a relative or comparative basis, but we haven't explained how it provides a measure of variability for a single sample.

To understand how the standard deviation provides a measure of variability of a data set, consider a specific data set and answer the following questions: How many measurements are within 1 standard deviation of the mean? How many measurements are within 2 standard deviations? For a specific data set, we can answer these questions by counting the number of measurements in each of the intervals. However, if we are interested in obtaining a general answer to these questions, the problem is more difficult.

Tables 2.8 and 2.9 give two sets of answers to the questions of how many measurements fall within 1, 2, and 3 standard deviations of the mean. The first, which applies to *any* set of data, is derived from a theorem proved by the Russian mathematician P. L. Chebyshev (1821–1894). The second, which applies to **mound-shaped,** symmetric distributions of data (where the mean, median, and mode are all about the same), is based upon empirical evidence that has accumulated over the years. However, the percentages given for the intervals in Table 2.9 provide remarkably good approximations even when the distribution of the data is slightly skewed or asymmetric. Note that both rules apply to either population data sets or sample data sets.

TABLE 2.8 Interpreting the Standard Deviation: Chebyshev's Rule

Chebyshev's Rule applies to any data set, regardless of the shape of the frequency distribution of the data.

a. No useful information is provided on the fraction of measurements that fall within 1 standard deviation of the mean, i.e., within the interval $(\bar{x} - s, \bar{x} + s)$ for samples and $(\mu - \sigma, \mu + \sigma)$ for populations.

b. At least $\frac{3}{4}$ will fall within 2 standard deviations of the mean, i.e., within the interval $(\bar{x} - 2s, \bar{x} + 2s)$ for samples and $(\mu - 2\sigma, \mu + 2\sigma)$ for populations.

c. At least $\frac{8}{9}$ of the measurements will fall within 3 standard deviations of the mean, i.e., within the interval $(\bar{x} - 3s, \bar{x} + 3s)$ for samples and $(\mu - 3\sigma, \mu + 3\sigma)$ for populations.

d. Generally, for any number k greater than 1, at least $(1 - 1/k^2)$ of the measurements will fall within k standard deviations of the mean, i.e., within the interval $(\bar{x} - ks, \bar{x} + ks)$ for samples and $(\mu - k\sigma, \mu + k\sigma)$ for populations.

TABLE 2.9 Interpreting the Standard Deviation: The Empirical Rule

The **Empirical Rule** is a rule of thumb that applies to data sets with frequency distributions that are mound-shaped and symmetric, as shown below.

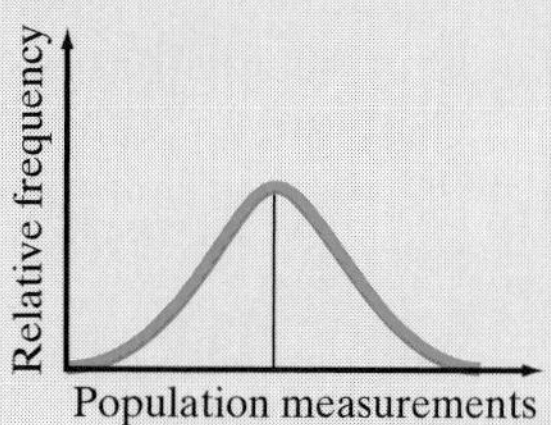

a. Approximately 68% of the measurements will fall within 1 standard deviation of the mean, i.e., within the interval $(\bar{x} - s, \bar{x} + s)$ for samples and $(\mu - \sigma, \mu + \sigma)$ for populations.
b. Approximately 95% of the measurements will fall within 2 standard deviations of the mean, i.e., within the interval $(\bar{x} - 2s, \bar{x} + 2s)$ for samples and $(\mu - 2\sigma, \mu + 2\sigma)$ for populations.
c. Approximately 99.7% (essentially all) of the measurements will fall within 3 standard deviations of the mean, i.e., within the interval $(\bar{x} - 3s, \bar{x} + 3s)$ for samples and $(\mu - 3\sigma, \mu + 3\sigma)$ for populations.

EXAMPLE 2.11 The 50 companies' percentages of revenues spent on R&D are repeated in Table 2.10.

TABLE 2.10 R&D Percentages for 50 Companies

13.5	9.5	8.2	6.5	8.4	8.1	6.9	7.5	10.5	13.5
7.2	7.1	9.0	9.9	8.2	13.2	9.2	6.9	9.6	7.7
9.7	7.5	7.2	5.9	6.6	11.1	8.8	5.2	10.6	8.2
11.3	5.6	10.1	8.0	8.5	11.7	7.1	7.7	9.4	6.0
8.0	7.4	10.5	7.8	7.9	6.5	6.9	6.5	6.8	9.5

We have previously shown (see Figure 2.13, p. 53) that the mean and standard deviation of these data (rounded) are 8.49 and 1.98, respectively. Calculate the fraction of these measurements that lie within the intervals $\bar{x} \pm s$, $\bar{x} \pm 2s$, and $\bar{x} \pm 3s$, and compare the results with those predicted in Tables 2.8 and 2.9.

Solution We first form the interval

$$(\bar{x} - s, \bar{x} + s) = (8.49 - 1.98, 8.49 + 1.98) = (6.51, 10.47)$$

A check of the measurements reveals that 34 of the 50 measurements, or 68%, are within 1 standard deviation of the mean.

The next interval of interest

$$(\bar{x} - 2s, \bar{x} + 2s) = (8.49 - 3.96, 8.49 + 3.96) = (4.53, 12.45)$$

contains 47 of the 50 measurements, or 94%.

Finally, the 3-standard-deviation interval around $\bar{x}$,

$$(\bar{x} - 3s, \bar{x} + 3s) = (8.49 - 5.94, 8.49 + 5.94) = (2.55, 14.43)$$

contains all, or 100%, of the measurements.

In spite of the fact that the distribution of these data is skewed to the right (see Figure 2.8, page 38), the percentages within 1, 2, and 3 standard deviations (68%, 94%, and 100%) agree very well with the approximations of 68%, 95%, and 99.7% given by the Empirical Rule (Table 2.9). You will find that unless the distribution is extremely skewed, the mound-shaped approximations will be reasonably accurate. Of course, no matter what the shape of the distribution, Chebyshev's Rule (Table 2.8) assures that at least 75% and at least 89% ($^8/_9$) of the measurements will lie within 2 and 3 standard deviations of the mean, respectively.

EXAMPLE 2.12

Chebyshev's Rule and the Empirical Rule are useful as a check on the calculation of the standard deviation. For example, suppose we calculated the standard deviation for the R&D percentages (Table 2.10) to be 3.92. Are there any "clues" in the data that enable us to judge whether this number is reasonable?

Solution

The range of the R&D percentages in Table 2.10 is 13.5 − 5.2 = 8.3. From Chebyshev's Rule and the Empirical Rule we know that most of the measurements (approximately 95% if the distribution is mound-shaped) will be within 2 standard deviations of the mean. And, regardless of the shape of the distribution and the number of measurements, almost all of them will fall within 3 standard deviations of the mean. Consequently, we would expect the range of the measurements to be between 4 (i.e., $\pm\, 2s$) and 6 (i.e., $\pm\, 3s$) standard deviations in length (see Figure 2.20).

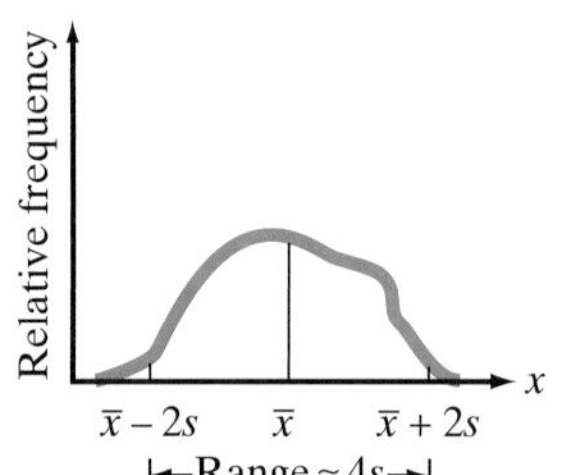

FIGURE 2.20
The relation between the range and the standard deviation

For the R&D data, this means that s should fall between

$$\frac{Range}{6} = \frac{8.3}{6} = 1.38 \quad \text{and} \quad \frac{Range}{4} = \frac{8.3}{4} = 2.08$$

In particular, the standard deviation should not be much larger than $^1/_4$ of the range, particularly for the data set with 50 measurements. Thus, we have reason to believe that the calculation of 3.92 is too large. A check of our work reveals that 3.92 is the variance s^2, not the standard deviation s (see Example 2.10). We "forgot" to take the square root (a common error); the correct value is $s = 1.98$. Note that this value is between $^1/_6$ and $^1/_4$ of the range.

In examples and exercises we'll sometimes use $s \approx$ range/4 to obtain a crude, and usually conservatively large, approximation for s. However, we stress that this is no substitute for calculating the exact value of s when possible.

Finally, and most importantly, we will use the concepts in Chebyshev's Rule and the Empirical Rule to build the foundation for statistical inference-making. The method is illustrated in Example 2.13.

EXAMPLE 2.13

A manufacturer of automobile batteries claims that the average length of life for its grade A battery is 60 months. However, the guarantee on this brand is for just 36 months. Suppose the standard deviation of the life length is known to be 10 months, and the frequency distribution of the life-length data is known to be mound-shaped.

a. Approximately what percentage of the manufacturer's grade A batteries will last more than 50 months, assuming the manufacturer's claim is true?

b. Approximately what percentage of the manufacturer's batteries will last less than 40 months, assuming the manufacturer's claim is true?

c. Suppose your battery lasts 37 months. What could you infer about the manufacturer's claim?

Solution If the distribution of life length is assumed to be mound-shaped with a mean of 60 months and a standard deviation of 10 months, it would appear as shown in Figure 2.21. Note that we can take advantage of the fact that mound-shaped distributions are (approximately) symmetric about the mean, so that the percentages given by the Empirical Rule can be split equally between the halves of the distribution on each side of the mean. The approximations given in Figure 2.21 are more dependent on the assumption of a mound-shaped distribution than those given by the Empirical Rule (Table 2.9), because the approximations in Figure 2.21 depend on the (approximate) symmetry of the mound-shaped distribution. We saw in Example 2.11 that the Empirical Rule can yield good approximations even for skewed distributions. This will *not* be true of the approximations in Figure 2.21; the distribution *must* be mound-shaped and approximately symmetric.

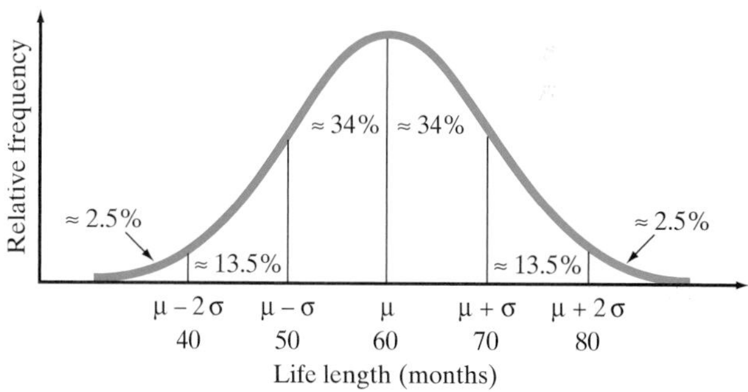

FIGURE 2.21
Battery life-length distribution: Manufacturer's claim assumed true

For example, since approximately 68% of the measurements will fall within 1 standard deviation of the mean, the distribution's symmetry implies that approximately $\frac{1}{2}(68\%) = 34\%$ of the measurements will fall between the mean and 1 standard deviation on each side. This concept is illustrated in Figure 2.21. The figure also shows that 2.5% of the measurements lie beyond 2 standard deviations in each direction from the mean. This result follows from the fact that if approximately 95% of the measurements fall within 2 standard deviations of the mean, then about 5% fall outside 2 standard deviations; if the distribution is approximately symmetric, then about 2.5% of the measurements fall beyond 2 standard deviations on each side of the mean.

a. It is easy to see in Figure 2.21 that the percentage of batteries lasting more than 50 months is approximately 34% (between 50 and 60 months) plus 50% (greater than 60 months). Thus, approximately 84% of the batteries should have life length exceeding 50 months.

b. The percentage of batteries that last less than 40 months can also be easily determined from Figure 2.21. Approximately 2.5% of the batteries should fail prior to 40 months, assuming the manufacturer's claim is true.

c. If you are so unfortunate that your grade A battery fails at 37 months, you can make one of two inferences: either your battery was one of the approximately 2.5% that fail prior to 40 months, or something about the manufacturer's claim is not true. Because the chances are so small that a battery fails before 40 months, you would have good reason to have serious doubts about the manufacturer's claim. A mean smaller than 60 months and/or a standard deviation longer than 10 months would both increase the likelihood of failure prior to 40 months.*

Example 2.13 is our initial demonstration of the statistical inference-making process. At this point you should realize that we'll use sample information (in Example 2.13, your battery's failure at 37 months) to make inferences about the population (in Example 2.13, the manufacturer's claim about the life length for the population of all batteries). We'll build on this foundation as we proceed.

*The assumption that the distribution is mound-shaped and symmetric may also be incorrect. However, if the distribution were skewed to the right, as life-length distributions often tend to be, the percentage of measurements more than 2 standard deviations *below* the mean would be even less than 2.5%.

EXERCISES 2.54–2.67

Learning the Mechanics

2.54 For any set of data, what can be said about the percentage of the measurements contained in each of the following intervals?
a. $\bar{x} - s$ to $\bar{x} + s$ b. $\bar{x} - 2s$ to $\bar{x} + 2s$
c. $\bar{x} - 3s$ to $\bar{x} + 3s$

2.55 For a set of data with a mound-shaped relative frequency distribution, what can be said about the percentage of the measurements contained in each of the intervals specified in Exercise 2.54?

2.56 Given a data set with a largest value of 760 and a smallest value of 135, what would you estimate the standard deviation to be? Explain the logic behind the procedure you used to estimate the standard deviation. Suppose the standard deviation is reported to be 25. Is this feasible? Explain.

2.57 The following is a sample of 25 measurements:

LM2_57.DAT

7	6	6	11	8	9	11	9	10	8	7	7	
5	9	10	7	7	7	7	9	12	10	10	8	6

a. Compute $\bar{x}$, s^2, and s for this sample.
b. Count the number of measurements in the intervals $\bar{x} \pm s, \bar{x} \pm 2s, \bar{x} \pm 3s$. Express each count as a percentage of the total number of measurements.
c. Compare the percentages found in part **b** to the percentages given by the Empirical Rule and Chebyshev's Rule.
d. Calculate the range and use it to obtain a rough approximation for s. Does the result compare favorably with the actual value for s found in part **a**?

Applying the Concepts

2.58 To minimize the potential for gastrointestinal disease outbreaks, all passenger cruise ships arriving at U.S. ports are subject to unannounced sanitation inspections. Ships are rated on a 100-point scale by the Centers for Disease Control. A score of 86 or higher indicates that the ship is providing an accepted standard of sanitation. The January 1999 sanitation scores for 121 cruise ships are listed in the table on p. 75. A MINITAB printout of descriptive statistics for the data is shown below.
a. Locate the mean and standard deviation on the MINITAB printout.
b. Calculate the intervals $\bar{x} \pm s$, $\bar{x} \pm 2s$, and $\bar{x} \pm 3s$.
c. Find the percentage of measurements in the data set that fall within each of the intervals, part **b**. Do these percentages agree with either Chebyshev's Rule or the Empirical Rule?

2.59 In the spring of 1998, the New Jersey State Chamber of Commerce and Rutgers Business School—with sponsorship by Arthur Andersen—conducted a survey to

MINITAB Output for Exercise 2.58

```
Descriptive Statistics

Variable          N       Mean     Median    Tr Mean     StDev   SE Mean
Sanlevel        121     90.339     92.000     91.138     6.947     0.632

Variable        Min        Max         Q1         Q3
Sanlevel     36.000     99.000     88.000     94.000
```

SANIT.DAT

Ship	Score	Ship	Score	Ship	Score
Americana	75	Hanseatic	93	Regal Voyager	88
Arcadia	93	Holiday	93	Rembrandt	78
Arkona	89	Horizon	94	Rhapsody of the Seas	93
Astor	74	Imagination	91	Rotterdam VI	96
Asuka	88	Inspiration	91	Royal Princess	93
BlackWatch	86	Island Adventure	95	Royal Viking Sun	89
C. Columbus	92	Island Dawn	86	Ryndam	93
Carnival Destiny	87	Island Princess	88	Sea Bird	89
Celebration	93	Islandbreeze	94	Sea Goddess I	89
Century	96	Jubilee	93	Sea Goddess II	90
Clipper Adventurer	93	Leeward	92	Sea Lion	97
Club Med I	92	Legacy	86	Seabourn Legend	94
Contessa I	87	Legend of the Seas	99	Seabourn Pride	88
Costa Romantica	94	Maasdam	96	Seabreeze I	86
Costa Victoria	92	Majesty of the Seas	93	Sensation	86
Crown Princess	90	Maxim Gorky	81	Silver Cloud	91
Crystal Harmony	91	Mayan Prince	94	Sky Princess	90
Crystal Symphony	88	Melody	91	Song of America	96
Dawn Princess	79	Mercury	97	Sovereign of the Seas	89
Delphin	91	Monarch of the Seas	96	Spirit of Columbia	89
Destiny	87	Nantucket Clipper	89	Splendour of the Seas	94
Discovery Sun	94	Nieuw Amsterdam	86	Starship Oceanic	94
Disney Magic	88	Nippon Maru	36	Statendam	92
Dolphin IV	90	Noordam	93	Stella Solaris	91
Dreamward	95	Nordic Princess	93	Sun Princess	86
Ecstasy	93	Norway	88	Superstar Capricorn	70
Edinburgh Castle	86	Norwegian Crown	90	Topaz	92
Elation	92	Norwegian Dynasty	95	Tropicale	95
Emerald	95	Norwegian Majesty	91	Universe Explorer	95
Enchanted Capri	95	Norwegian Sea	91	Veendam	91
Enchanted Isle	90	Norwegian Star	78	Victoria	91
Enchantment of the Seas	97	Norwegian Wind	95	Viking Serenade	91
Europa	88	Oceanbreeze	87	Vision of the Seas	96
Fantasy	93	Oriana	98	Vistafjord	92
Fascination	93	Palm Beach Princess	88	Westerdam	92
Flamenco	93	Paradise	95	Wind Spirit II	93
Galaxy	97	Paul Gauguin	86	World Discoverer	89
Grand Princess	94	Queen Elizabeth 2	87	Yorktown Clipper	91
Grande Caribe	95	Radisson Diamond	90	Zenith	93
Grande Mariner	87	Regal Empress	95		
Grandeur of the Seas	98	Regal Princess	95		

Source: Center for Environmental Health and Injury Control; *Tampa Tribune*, Feb. 7, 1999.

investigate Generation Xers' expectations of the future workplace and their careers. Telephone interviews were conducted with 662 randomly selected New Jerseyans between the ages of 21 and 28. One question asked: "What is the maximum number of years you expect to spend with any one employer over the course of your career?" The 590 useable responses to this question are summarized as follows:

$$n = 590$$
$$\bar{x} = 18.2 \text{ years}$$
$$\text{median} = 15 \text{ years}$$
$$s = 10.64$$
$$\text{min} = 2.0$$
$$\text{max} = 50$$

Sources: N.J. State Chamber of Commerce, press release, June 18, 1998 and personal communication from P. George Benson.

a. What evidence exists to suggest that the distribution of years is not mound-shaped?

b. Suppose you did not know the sample standard deviation, s. Use the range of the data set to estimate s. Compare your estimate to the actual sample standard deviation.

c. In the last decade, workers moved between companies much more frequently than in the 1980s. Consequently, the researchers were surprised by the expectations of longevity expressed by the Generation Xers. What can you say about the percentage of Generation Xers in the sample whose response was 40 years or more? 8 years or more?

2.60 As a result of government and consumer pressure, automobile manufacturers in the United States are deeply involved in research to improve their products' gasoline mileage. One manufacturer, hoping to achieve 40 miles per gallon on one of its compact models, measured the mileage obtained by 36 test versions of the model with the following results (rounded to the nearest mile for convenience):

MPG36.DAT

43	35	41	42	42	38	40	41	41	40	40	41
42	36	43	40	38	40	38	45	39	41	42	37
40	40	44	39	40	37	39	41	39	41	37	40

The mean and standard deviation of these data are shown in the SAS printout below.

a. Find the mean and standard deviation on the printout and give the units in which they are expressed.

b. If the manufacturer would be satisfied with a (population) mean of 40 miles per gallon, how would it react to the above test data?

c. Use the information in Tables 2.8–2.9 to check the reasonableness of the calculated standard deviation $s = 2.2$.

d. Construct a relative frequency histogram of the data set. Is the data set mound-shaped?

e. What percentage of the measurements would you expect to find within the intervals $\bar{x} \pm s$, $\bar{x} \pm 2s$, $\bar{x} \pm 3s$?

f. Count the number of measurements that actually fall within the intervals of part **e.** Express each interval count as a percentage of the total number of measurements. Compare these results with your answers to part **e.**

2.61 Refer to the *Marine Technology* (Jan. 1995) data on spillage amounts (in thousands of metric tons) for 50 major oil spills, Exercise 2.10 (p. 34). An SPSS histogram for the 50 spillage amounts is shown on p. 77.

a. Interpret the histogram.

b. Descriptive statistics for the 50 spillage amounts are provided in the SPSS printout. Use this information to form an interval that can be used to predict the spillage amount for the next major oil spill.

2.62 Refer to the *Arkansas Business and Economic Review* (Summer 1995) study of the number of Superfund hazardous waste sites in Arkansas counties, Exercise 2.37 (p. 60). The EXCEL numerical descriptive statistics printout is reproduced here and the data are listed on page 78. Calculate the percentage of measurements in the intervals $\bar{x} \pm s$, $\bar{x} \pm 2s$, and $\bar{x} \pm 3s$. Check the agreement of these percentages with both Chebyshev's Rule and the Empirical Rule.

EXCEL Output for Exercise 2.62

SITES	
Mean	5.24
Standard Error	0.836517879
Median	3
Mode	2
Standard Deviation	7.244457341
Sample Variance	52.48216216
Kurtosis	16.41176573
Skewness	3.468289878
Range	48
Minimum	0
Maximum	48
Sum	393
Count	75
Confidence Level(95.000%)	1.639542488

2.63 Refer to the *Financial Management* (Spring 1995) study of 49 firms filing for prepackaged bankruptcy, Exercise 2.24 (p. 49). Recall that the variable of interest was length of time (months) in bankruptcy for each firm.

a. A MINITAB histogram for the 49 bankruptcy times is displayed on p. 77. Comment on whether the Empirical Rule is applicable for describing the bankruptcy time distribution for firms filing for prepackaged bankruptcy.

b. Numerical descriptive statistics for the data set are also shown in the MINITAB printout at the bottom of p. 77. Use this information to construct an interval that captures at least 75% of the bankruptcy times for "prepack" firms.

SAS Output for Exercise 2.60

```
Analysis Variable : MPG

N Obs   N       Minimum        Maximum          Mean        Std Dev
--------------------------------------------------------------------
   36  36    35.0000000     45.0000000    40.0555556      2.1770812
--------------------------------------------------------------------
```

SPSS Output for Exercise 2.61

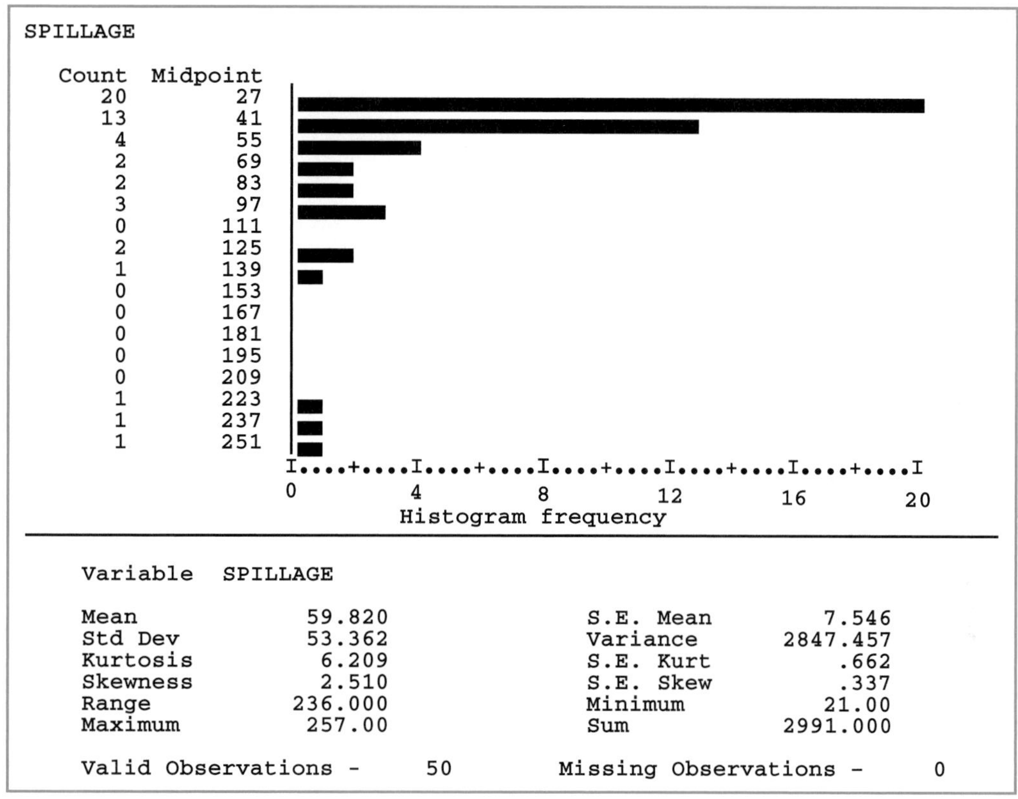

```
SPILLAGE

  Count  Midpoint
    20       27
    13       41
     4       55
     2       69
     2       83
     3       97
     0      111
     2      125
     1      139
     0      153
     0      167
     0      181
     0      195
     0      209
     1      223
     1      237
     1      251
                  I....+....I....+....I....+....I....+....I....+....I
                  0         4         8        12        16        20
                           Histogram frequency

    Variable   SPILLAGE

    Mean            59.820          S.E. Mean        7.546
    Std Dev         53.362          Variance      2847.457
    Kurtosis         6.209          S.E. Kurt         .662
    Skewness         2.510          S.E. Skew         .337
    Range          236.000          Minimum          21.00
    Maximum         257.00          Sum           2991.000

    Valid Observations -     50     Missing Observations -     0
```

MINITAB Output for Exercise 2.63

Descriptive Statistics

Variable	N	Mean	Median	Tr Mean	StDev	SE Mean
Time	49	2.549	1.700	2.333	1.828	0.261

Variable	Min	Max	Q1	Q3
Time	1.000	10.100	1.350	3.500

MINITAB Histogram for Exercise 2.63

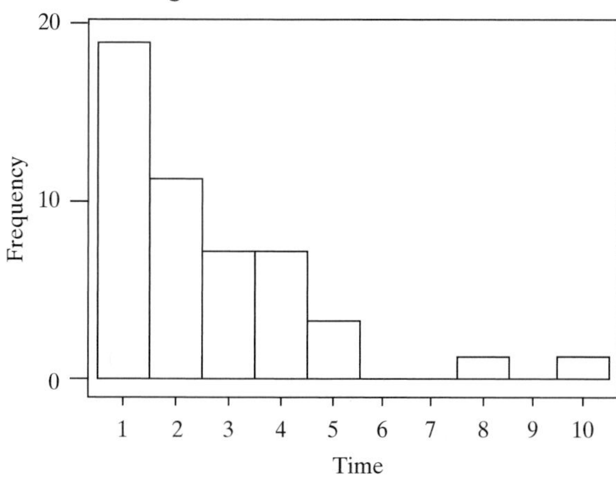

c. Refer to the data listed in Exercise 2.24. Count the number of the 49 bankruptcy times that fall within the interval, part **b,** and convert the result to a percentage. Does the result agree with Chebyshev's Rule? The Empirical Rule?

d. A firm is considering filing a prepackaged bankruptcy plan. Estimate the length of time the firm will be in bankruptcy.

2.64 The *American Rifleman* (June 1993) reported on the velocity of ammunition fired from the FEG P9R pistol, a 9mm gun manufactured in Hungary. Field tests revealed that Winchester bullets fired from the pistol had a mean velocity (at 15 feet) of 936 feet per second and a standard deviation of 10 feet per second. Tests were also conducted with Uzi and Black Hills ammunition.

a. Describe the velocity distribution of Winchester bullets fired from the FEG P9R pistol.

b. A bullet, brand unknown, is fired from the FEG P9R pistol. Suppose the velocity (at 15 feet) of the bullet is 1,000 feet per second. Is the bullet likely to be manufactured by Winchester? Explain.

2.65 A buyer for a lumber company must decide whether to buy a piece of land containing 5,000 pine trees. If 1,000 of the trees are at least 40 feet tall, the buyer will purchase the land; otherwise, he won't. The owner of the land reports that the height of the trees has a mean of 30 feet and a standard deviation of 3 feet. Based on this information, what is the buyer's decision?

2.66 A chemical company produces a substance composed of 98% cracked corn particles and 2% zinc phosphide for use in controlling rat populations in sugarcane fields. Production must be carefully controlled to maintain the 2% zinc phosphide because too much zinc phosphide will cause damage to the sugarcane and too little will be ineffective in controlling the rat population. Records from past production indicate that the distribution of the actual percentage of zinc phosphide present in the substance is approximately mound-shaped, with a mean of 2.0% and a standard deviation of .08%.

a. If the production line is operating correctly, approximately what proportion of batches from a day's production will contain less than 1.84% of zinc phosphide?

b. Suppose one batch chosen randomly actually contains 1.80% zinc phosphide. Does this indicate that there is too little zinc phosphide in today's production? Explain your reasoning.

2.67 When it is working properly, a machine that fills 25-pound bags of flour dispenses an average of 25 pounds per fill; the standard deviation of the amount of fill is .1 pound. To monitor the performance of the machine, an inspector weighs the contents of a bag coming off the machine's conveyor belt every half-hour during the day. If the contents of two consecutive bags fall more than 2 standard deviations from the mean (using the mean and standard deviation given above), the filling process is said to be out of control and the machine is shut down briefly for adjustments. The data given in the table below are the weights measured by the inspector yesterday. Assume the machine is never shut down for more than 15 minutes at a time. At what times yesterday was the process shut down for adjustment? Justify your answer.

FLOUR.DAT

Time	Weight (pounds)	Time	Weight (pounds)
8:00 A.M.	25.10	12:30 P.M.	25.06
8:30	25.15	1:00	24.95
9:00	24.81	1:30	24.80
9:30	24.75	2:00	24.95
10:00	25.00	2:30	25.21
10:30	25.05	3:00	24.90
11:00	25.23	3:30	24.71
11:30	25.25	4:00	25.31
12:00	25.01	4:30	25.15
		5:00	25.20

ARKFUND.DAT

3	3	2	1	2	0	5	3	5	2	1	8	2	12	3	5	3	1	3
0	8	0	9	6	8	6	2	16	0	6	0	5	5	0	1	25	0	0
0	6	2	10	12	3	10	3	17	2	4	2	1	21	4	2	1	11	5
2	2	7	2	3	1	8	2	0	0	0	2	3	10	2	3	48	21	

Source: Tabor, R. H., and Stanwick, S. D. "Arkansas: An environmental perspective." *Arkansas Business and Economic Review*, Vol. 28, No. 2, Summer 1995, pp. 22–32 (Table 1).

2.7 NUMERICAL MEASURES OF RELATIVE STANDING

We've seen that numerical measures of central tendency and variability describe the general nature of a quantitative data set (either a sample or a population). In addition, we may be interested in describing the *relative* quantitative location of a particular measurement within a data set. Descriptive measures of the relationship of a measurement to the rest of the data are called **measures of relative standing.**

One measure of the relative standing of a measurement is its **percentile ranking.** For example, if oil company A reports that its yearly sales are in the 90th percentile of all companies in the industry, the implication is that 90% of all oil companies have yearly sales less than company A's, and only 10% have yearly

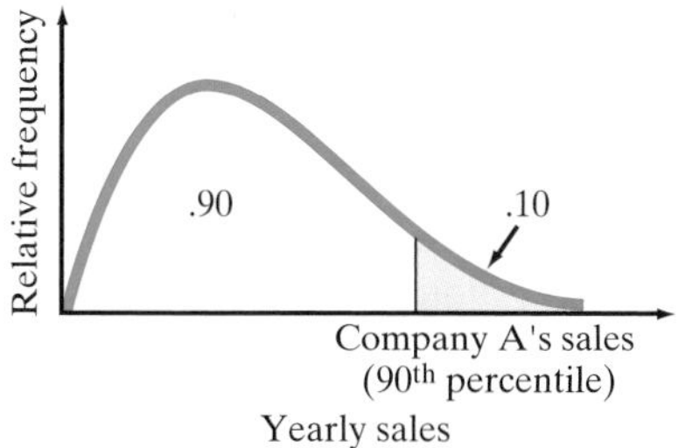

FIGURE 2.22
Location of 90th percentile for yearly sales of oil companies.

sales exceeding company A's. This is demonstrated in Figure 2.22. Similarly, if the oil company's yearly sales are in the 50th percentile (the median of the data set), 50% of all oil companies would have lower yearly sales and 50% would have higher yearly sales.

Percentile rankings are of practical value only for large data sets. Finding them involves a process similar to the one used in finding a median. The measurements are ranked in order and a rule is selected to define the location of each percentile. Since we are primarily interested in interpreting the percentile rankings of measurements (rather than finding particular percentiles for a data set), we define the *pth percentile* of a data set as shown in Definition 2.10.

DEFINITION 2.10

For any set of n measurements (arranged in ascending or descending order), the ***pth* percentile** is a number such that $p\%$ of the measurements fall below the *pth* percentile and $(100 - p)\%$ fall above it.

EXAMPLE 2.14

Refer to the percentages spent on research and development by the 50 high-technology firms listed in Table 2.10 (p. 71). An SAS printout describing the data is shown in Figure 2.23. Locate the 25th percentile and 95th percentile on the printout and interpret these values.

Solution Both the 25th percentile and 95th percentile are highlighted on the SAS printout, Figure 2.23. These values are 7.1 and 13.2, respectively. Our interpretations are as follows: 25% of the 50 R&D percentages fall below 7.1 and 95% of the R&D percentages fall below 13.2.

Another measure of relative standing in popular use is the *z-score.* As you can see in Definition 2.11, the z-score makes use of the mean and standard deviation of the data set in order to specify the relative location of a measurement. Note that the z-score is calculated by subtracting $\bar{x}$ (or μ) from the measurement x and then dividing the result by s (or σ). The final result, the z-score, represents the distance between a given measurement x and the mean, expressed in standard deviations.

EXAMPLE 2.15

Suppose 200 steelworkers are selected, and the annual income of each is determined. The mean and standard deviation are $\bar{x}$ = \$24,000 and s = \$2,000. Suppose Joe Smith's annual income is \$22,000. What is his sample z-score?

FIGURE 2.23
SAS Descriptive Statistics for 50 R&D Percentages

```
                          UNIVARIATE PROCEDURE
Variable=RDPCT
                                Moments

                N                  50  Sum Wgts          50
                Mean            8.492  Sum            424.6
                Std Dev      1.980604  Variance    3.922792
                Skewness     0.854601  Kurtosis    0.419288
                USS           3797.92  CSS         192.2168
                CV           23.32317  Std Mean      0.2801
                T:Mean=0     30.31778  Prob>|T|      0.0001
                Sgn Rank        637.5  Prob>|S|      0.0001
                Num ^=0            50

                          Quantiles(Def=5)

                 100% Max        13.5        99%       13.5
                  75% Q3          9.6        95%       13.2
                  50% Med        8.05        90%       11.2
                  25% Q1          7.1        10%        6.5
                   0% Min         5.2         5%        5.9
                                              1%        5.2

                 Range            8.3
                 Q3-Q1            2.5
                 Mode             6.5

                                Extremes

                   Lowest    Obs      Highest     Obs
                      5.2(    45)        11.3(     34)
                      5.6(    46)        11.7(     47)
                      5.9(    44)        13.2(     42)
                        6(    48)        13.5(      1)
                      6.5(    50)        13.5(     16)
```

DEFINITION 2.11

The **sample z-score** for a measurement x is

$$z = \frac{x - \bar{x}}{s}$$

The **population z-score** for a measurement x is

$$z = \frac{x - \mu}{\sigma}$$

Solution Joe Smith's annual income lies below the mean income of the 200 steelworkers (see Figure 2.24). We compute

$$z = \frac{x - \bar{x}}{s} = \frac{\$22{,}000 - \$24{,}000}{\$2{,}000} = -1.0$$

which tells us that Joe Smith's annual income is 1.0 standard deviation *below* the sample mean, or, in short, his sample z-score is -1.0.

FIGURE 2.24
Annual income of steel workers

$18,000	$22,000	$24,000	$30,000
$\bar{x} - 3s$	Joe Smith's income	$\bar{x}$	$\bar{x} + 3s$

The numerical value of the z-score reflects the relative standing of the measurement. A large positive z-score implies that the measurement is larger than almost all other measurements, whereas a large negative z-score indicates that the measurement is smaller than almost every other measurement. If a z-score is 0 or near 0, the measurement is located at or near the mean of the sample or population.

We can be more specific if we know that the frequency distribution of the measurements is mound-shaped. In this case, the following interpretation of the z-score can be given.

Interpretation of z-scores for Mound-Shaped Distributions of Data

1. Approximately 68% of the measurements will have a z-score between -1 and 1.
2. Approximately 95% of the measurements will have a z-score between -2 and 2.
3. Approximately 99.7% (almost all) of the measurements will have a z-score between -3 and 3.

Note that this interpretation of z-scores is identical to that given by the Empirical Rule for mound-shaped distributions (Table 2.9). The statement that a measurement falls in the interval $(\mu - \sigma)$ to $(\mu + \sigma)$ is equivalent to the statement that a measurement has a population z-score between -1 and 1, since all measurements between $(\mu - \sigma)$ and $(\mu + \sigma)$ are within 1 standard deviation of μ. These z-scores are displayed in Figure 2.25.

FIGURE 2.25
Population z-scores for a mound-shaped distribution

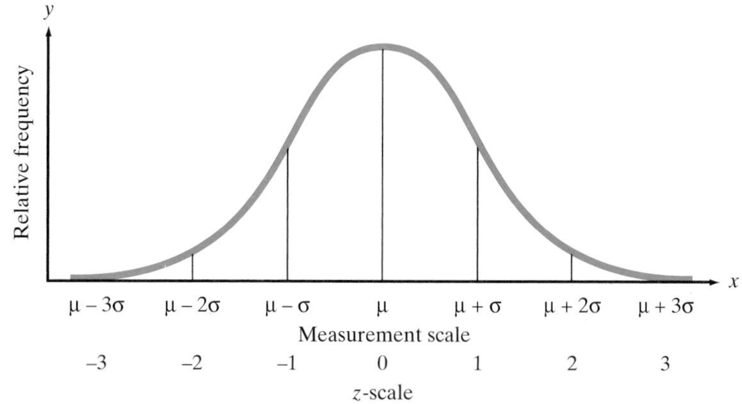

EXERCISES 2.68–2.78

Learning the Mechanics

2.68 Compute the z-score corresponding to each of the following values of x:

a. $x = 40, s = 5, \bar{x} = 30$

b. $x = 90, \mu = 89, \sigma = 2$

c. $\mu = 50, \sigma = 5, x = 50$

d. $s = 4, x = 20, \bar{x} = 30$

e. In parts **a–d,** state whether the z-score locates x within a sample or a population.

f. In parts **a–d,** state whether each value of x lies above or below the mean and by how many standard deviations.

2.69 Give the percentage of measurements in a data set that are above and below each of the following percentiles:

a. 75th percentile b. 50th percentile

c. 20th percentile d. 84th percentile

2.70 What is the 50th percentile of a quantitative data set called?

2.71 Compare the z-scores to decide which of the following x values lie the greatest distance above the mean and the greatest distance below the mean.

a. $x = 100, \mu = 50, \sigma = 25$

b. $x = 1, \mu = 4, \sigma = 1$

c. $x = 0, \mu = 200, \sigma = 100$

d. $x = 10, \mu = 5, \sigma = 3$

2.72 Suppose that 40 and 90 are two elements of a population data set and that their z-scores are -2 and 3, respectively. Using only this information, is it possible to determine the population's mean and standard deviation? If so, find them. If not, explain why it's not possible.

Applying the Concepts

2.73 The U.S. Environmental Protection Agency (EPA) sets a limit on the amount of lead permitted in drinking water. The EPA *Action Level* for lead is .015 milligrams per liter (mg/L) of water. Under EPA guidelines, if 90% of a water system's study samples have a lead concentration less than .015 mg/L, the water is considered safe for drinking. I (co-author Sincich) received a recent report on a study of lead levels in the drinking water of homes in my subdivision. The 90th percentile of the study sample had a lead concentration of .00372 mg/L. Are water customers in my subdivision at risk of drinking water with unhealthy lead levels? Explain.

2.74 Refer to the January 1999 sanitation levels of cruise ships, Exercise 2.58 (p. 74). The MINITAB descriptive statistics printout is reproduced below.

a. Give a measure of relative standing for the Dawn Princess' score of 79. Interpret the result.

b. Give a measure of relative standing for the Topaz's score of 92. Interpret the result.

c. Find the 75th percentile of the sanitation level scores and interpret its value. [*Note:* The 75th percentile is denoted Q3 on the MINITAB printout.]

2.75 In 1997 the United States imported merchandise valued at \$871 billion and exported merchandise worth \$689 billion. The difference between these two quantities (exports minus imports) is referred to as the *merchandise trade balance.* Since more goods were imported than exported in 1997, the merchandise trade balance was a *negative* \$182 billion. The accompanying table lists the U.S. exports to and imports from a sample of 10 countries in 1997 (in millions of dollars).

a. Calculate the U.S. merchandise trade balance with each of the ten countries. Express your answers in billions of dollars.

b. Use a z-score to identify the relative position of the U.S. trade balance with Japan within the data set you developed in part **a.** Do the same for the trade balance with Egypt. Write a sentence or two that describes the relative positions of these two trade balances.

EXPIMP.DAT

Country	Exports	Imports
Brazil	15,914.7	9,625.5
China	12,862.3	62,557.6
Egypt	3,835.4	657.5
France	15,964.9	20,636.4
Italy	8,994.7	19,407.5
Japan	65,548.5	121,663.2
Mexico	71,388.4	85,937.5
Panama	1,536.1	367.2
Sweden	3,314.1	7,298.9
Singapore	17,696.2	20,074.6

Source: Statistical Abstract of the United States: 1998, pp. 801–804.

2.76 In 1998, the food, drink, and tobacco sector of the U.S. economy did not fare well. *Forbes* (Jan. 11, 1999) reports

MINITAB Output for Exercise 2.74

```
Descriptive Statistics

Variable        N      Mean    Median   Tr Mean    StDev   SE Mean
Sanlevel      121    90.339    92.000    91.138    6.947     0.632

Variable      Min       Max        Q1        Q3
Sanlevel   36.000    99.000    88.000    94.000
```

the sales growth of a sample of 12 companies from that sector.

FOOD98.DAT

Company	1998 Sales Growth
Anheuser-Busch	.9%
Campbell Soup	−.1
Coca-Cola	2.4
Dole Food	7.9
Flowers Industries	120.5
General Mills	6.6
H.J. Heinz	−1.9
Hershey Foods	4.5
Philip Morris	2.3
Smithfield Foods	−5.0
Universal	−4.0
Wm Wrigley Jr.	4.7

Source: *Forbes,* Jan. 11, 1999, p. 175.

a. Find the mean and standard deviation of the sales growth data.

b. Find the z-scores for Coca-Cola, Flowers Industries, and Smithfield Foods.

c. Using the z-scores from part **b,** describe the location of each of the three companies within the sample of sales growths.

2.77 Refer to the *Arkansas Business and Economic Review* (Summer 1995) study of hazardous waste sites in Arkansas counties, Exercise 2.37 (p. 61). An SAS descriptive statistics printout for the number of Superfund waste sites in each of the 75 counties is displayed here.

a. Find the 10th percentile of the data set on the printout. Interpret the result.

b. Find the 95th percentile of the data set on the printout. Interpret the result.

c. Use the information on the SAS printout to calculate the z-score for an Arkansas county with 48 Superfund sites.

d. Based on your answer to part **c,** would you classify 48 as an extreme number of Superfund sites?

2.78 At one university, the students are given z-scores at the end of each semester rather than the traditional GPAs.

SAS Output for Exercise 2.77

```
                         UNIVARIATE PROCEDURE

Variable=NUMSITES
                               Moments

                  N              75   Sum Wgts         75
                  Mean         5.24   Sum             393
                  Std Dev  7.244457   Variance   52.48216
                  Skewness  3.46829   Kurtosis   16.41177
                  USS          5943   CSS         3883.68
                  CV        138.253   Std Mean   0.836518
                  T:Mean=0 6.264062   Prob>|T|     0.0001
                  Sgn Rank     1008   Prob>|S|     0.0001
                  Num ^=0        63

                          Quantiles(Def=5)

                   100% Max      48        99%        48
                    75% Q3        6        95%        21
                    50% Med       3        90%        12
                    25% Q1        1        10%         0
                     0% Min       0         5%         0
                                            1%         0

                   Range         48
                   Q3-Q1          5
                   Mode           2

                               Extremes

                    Lowest    Obs      Highest    Obs
                         0(    68)        17(     47)
                         0(    67)        21(     52)
                         0(    66)        21(     75)
                         0(    39)        25(     36)
                         0(    38)        48(     74)
```

The mean and standard deviation of all students' cumulative GPAs, on which the z-scores are based, are 2.7 and .5, respectively.

a. Translate each of the following z-scores to corresponding GPA: $z = 2.0$, $z = -1.0$, $z = .5$, $z = -2.5$.

b. Students with z-scores below -1.6 are put on probation. What is the corresponding probationary GPA?

c. The president of the university wishes to graduate the top 16% of the students with *cum laude* honors and the top 2.5% with *summa cum laude* honors. Where (approximately) should the limits be set in terms of z-scores? In terms of GPAs? What assumption, if any, did you make about the distribution of the GPAs at the university?

2.8 METHODS FOR DETECTING OUTLIERS (OPTIONAL)

Sometimes it is important to identify inconsistent or unusual measurements in a data set. An observation that is unusually large or small relative to the data values we want to describe is called an *outlier.*

Outliers are often attributable to one of several causes. First, the measurement associated with the outlier may be invalid. For example, the experimental procedure used to generate the measurement may have malfunctioned, the experimenter may have misrecorded the measurement, or the data might have been coded incorrectly in the computer. Second, the outlier may be the result of a misclassified measurement. That is, the measurement belongs to a population different from that from which the rest of the sample was drawn. Finally, the measurement associated with the outlier may be recorded correctly and from the same population as the rest of the sample, but represents a rare (chance) event. Such outliers occur most often when the relative frequency distribution of the sample data is extremely skewed, because such a distribution has a tendency to include extremely large or small observations relative to the others in the data set.

DEFINITION 2.12

An observation (or measurement) that is unusually large or small relative to the other values in a data set is called an **outlier.** Outliers typically are attributable to one of the following causes:

1. The measurement is observed, recorded, or entered into the computer incorrectly.
2. The measurement comes from a different population.
3. The measurement is correct, but represents a rare (chance) event.

Two useful methods for detecting outliers, one graphical and one numerical, are **box plots** and z-scores. The box plot is based on the *quartiles* of a data set. **Quartiles** are values that partition the data set into four groups, each containing 25% of the measurements. The *lower quartile* Q_L is the 25th percentile, the *middle quartile* is the median m (the 50th percentile), and the *upper quartile* Q_U is the 75th percentile (see Figure 2.26).

FIGURE 2.26
The quartiles for a data set

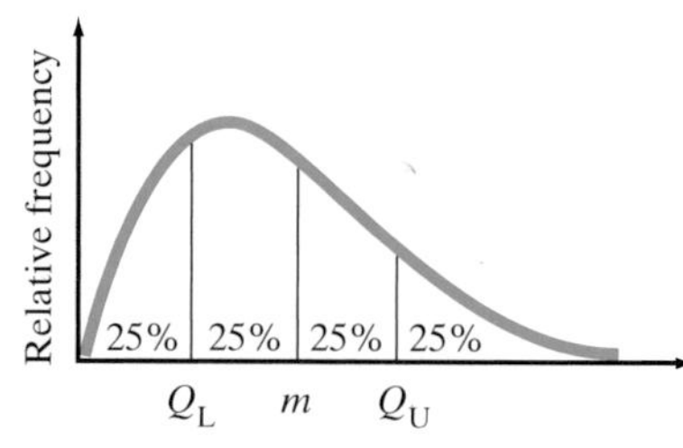

DEFINITION 2.13

The **lower quartile Q_L** is the 25th percentile of a data set. The **middle quartile *m*** is the median. The **upper quartile Q_U** is the 75th percentile.

A box plot is based on the *interquartile range* (IQR), the distance between the lower and upper quartiles:

$$\text{IQR} = Q_U - Q_L$$

DEFINITION 2.14

The **interquartile range (IQR)** is the distance between the lower and upper quartiles:

$$\text{IQR} = Q_U - Q_L$$

A vertical MINITAB box plot for the 50 companies' percentages of revenues spent on R&D (Table 2.4) is shown in Figure 2.27*. Note that a rectangle (the **box**) is drawn, with the top and bottom sides of the rectangle (the **hinges**) drawn at the quartiles Q_L and Q_U. By definition, then, the "middle" 50% of the observations—those between Q_L and Q_U—fall inside the box. For the R&D data, these quartiles appear to be at (approximately) 7.0 and 9.5. Thus,

$$\text{IQR} = 9.5 - 7.0 = 2.5 \text{ (approximately)}$$

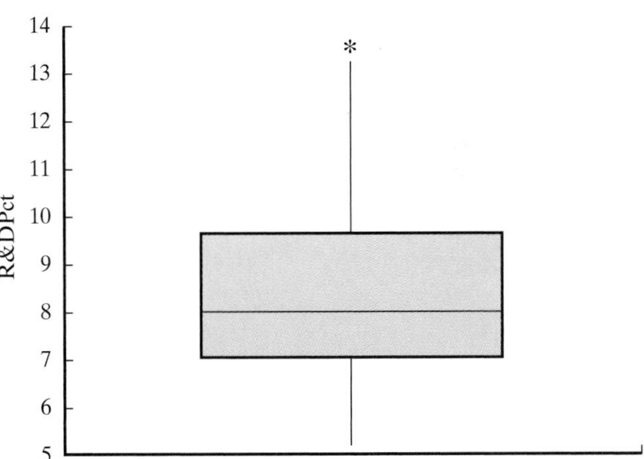

FIGURE 2.27 MINITAB box plot for R&D percentages

The median is shown at about 8.0 by a horizontal line within the box.

To guide the construction of the "tails" of the box plot, two sets of limits, called **inner fences** and **outer fences,** are used. Neither set of fences actually appears on the box plot. Inner fences are located at a distance of 1.5(IQR) from the hinges. Emanating from the hinges of the box are vertical lines called the **whiskers.** The two whiskers extend to the most extreme observation inside the inner fences. For example, the inner fence on the lower side (bottom) of the R&D percentage box plot is (approximately)

*Although box plots can be generated by hand, the amount of detail required makes them particularly well suited for computer generation. We use computer software to generate the box plots in this section.

$$\begin{aligned}\text{Lower inner fence} &= \text{Lower hinge} - 1.5(\text{IQR}) \\ &\approx 7.0 - 1.5(2.5) \\ &= 7.0 - 3.75 = 3.25\end{aligned}$$

The smallest measurement in the data set is 5.2, which is well inside this inner fence. Thus, the lower whisker extends to 5.2. Similarly, the upper whisker extends to about $(9.5 + 3.75) = 13.25$. The largest measurement inside this fence is the third largest measurement, 13.2. Note that the longer upper whisker reveals the rightward skewness of the R&D distribution.

Values that are beyond the inner fences are deemed *potential outliers* because they are extreme values that represent relatively rare occurrences. In fact, for mound-shaped distributions, fewer than 1% of the observations are expected to fall outside the inner fences. Two of the 50 R&D measurements, both at 13.5, fall outside the upper inner fence. Each of these potential outliers is represented by the asterisk (*) at 13.5.

The other two imaginary fences, the outer fences, are defined at a distance 3(IQR) from each end of the box. Measurements that fall beyond the outer fences are represented by 0s (zeros) and are very extreme measurements that require special analysis. Since less than one-hundredth of 1% (.01% or .0001) of the measurements from mound-shaped distributions are expected to fall beyond the outer fences, these measurements are considered to be *outliers*. No measurement in the R&D percentage box plot (Figure 2.27) is represented by a 0; thus there are no outliers.

Recall that outliers are extreme measurements that stand out from the rest of the sample and may be faulty: They may be incorrectly recorded observations, members of a population different from the rest of the sample, or, at the least, very unusual measurements from the same population. For example, the two R&D measurements at 13.5 (identified by an asterisk) may be considered outliers. When we analyze these measurements, we find that they are correctly recorded. However, it turns out that both represent R&D expenditures of relatively young and fast-growing companies. Thus, the outlier analysis may have revealed important factors that relate to the R&D expenditures of high-tech companies: their age and rate of growth. Outlier analysis often reveals useful information of this kind and therefore plays an important role in the statistical inference-making process.

In addition to detecting outliers, box plots provide useful information on the variation in a data set. The elements (and nomenclature) of box plots are summarized in the next box. Some aids to the interpretation of box plots are also given.

Elements of a Box Plot

1. A rectangle (the *box*) is drawn with the ends (the *hinges*) drawn at the lower and upper quartiles (Q_L and Q_U). The median of the data is shown in the box, usually by a line or a symbol (such as " + ").
2. The points at distances 1.5(IQR) from each hinge define the *inner fences* of the data set. Lines (the *whiskers*) are drawn from each hinge to the most extreme measurement inside the inner fence.
3. A second pair of fences, the *outer fences,* are defined at a distance of 3 interquartile ranges, 3(IQR), from the hinges. One symbol (usually "*") is used to represent measurements falling between the inner and outer fences, and another (usually "0") is used to represent measurements beyond the outer fences.
4. The symbols used to represent the median and the extreme data points (those beyond the fences) will vary depending on the software you use

(continued)

to construct the box plot. (You may use your own symbols if you are constructing a box plot by hand.) You should consult the program's documentation to determine exactly which symbols are used.

Aids to the Interpretation of Box Plots

1. Examine the length of the box. The IQR is a measure of the sample's variability and is especially useful for the comparison of two samples (see Example 2.17).
2. Visually compare the lengths of the whiskers. If one is clearly longer, the distribution of the data is probably skewed in the direction of the longer whisker.
3. Analyze any measurements that lie beyond the fences. Fewer than 5% should fall beyond the inner fences, even for very skewed distributions. Measurements beyond the outer fences are probably outliers, with one of the following explanations:
   a. The measurement is incorrect. It may have been observed, recorded, or entered into the computer incorrectly.
   b. The measurement belongs to a population different from the population that the rest of the sample was drawn from (see Example 2.17).
   c. The measurement is correct *and* from the same population as the rest. Generally, we accept this explanation only after carefully ruling out all others.

EXAMPLE 2.16 In Example 2.3 we analyzed 50 processing times for the development of price quotes by the manufacturer of industrial wheels. The intent was to determine whether the success or failure in obtaining the order was related to the amount of time to process the price quotes. Each quote that corresponds to "lost" business was so classified. The data are repeated in Table 2.11 (p. 88). Use a statistical software package to draw a box plot for these data.

Solution The SAS box plot printout for these data is shown in Figure 2.28. SAS uses a horizontal dashed line in the box to represent the median, and a plus sign (+) to

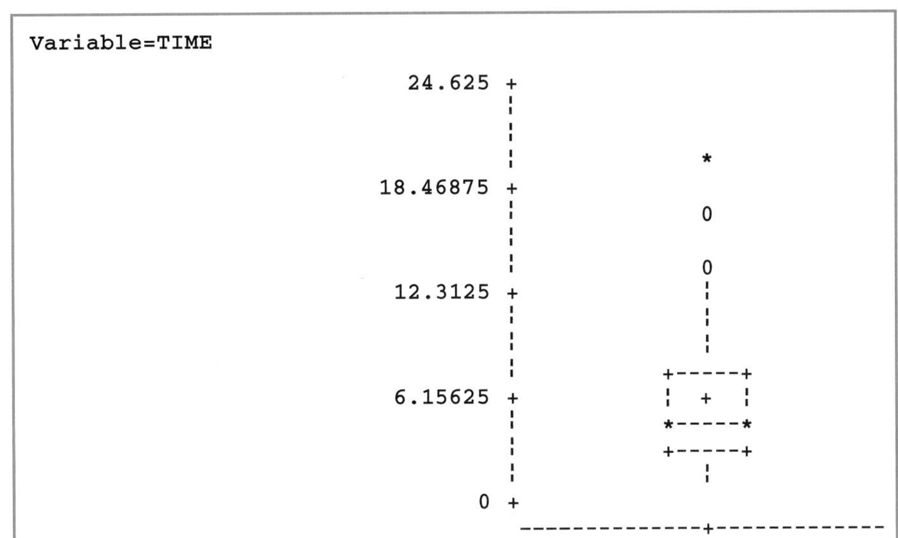

FIGURE 2.28
SAS box plot for processing time data

TABLE 2.11 Price Quote Processing Time (Days)

Request Number	Processing Time	Lost?	Request Number	Processing Time	Lost?
1	2.36	No	26	3.34	No
2	5.73	No	27	6.00	No
3	6.60	No	28	5.92	No
4	10.05	Yes	29	7.28	Yes
5	5.13	No	30	1.25	No
6	1.88	No	31	4.01	No
7	2.52	No	32	7.59	No
8	2.00	No	33	13.42	Yes
9	4.69	No	34	3.24	No
10	1.91	No	35	3.37	No
11	6.75	Yes	36	14.06	Yes
12	3.92	No	37	5.10	No
13	3.46	No	38	6.44	No
14	2.64	No	39	7.76	No
15	3.63	No	40	4.40	No
16	3.44	No	41	5.48	No
17	9.49	Yes	42	7.51	No
18	4.90	No	43	6.18	No
19	7.45	No	44	8.22	Yes
20	20.23	Yes	45	4.37	No
21	3.91	No	46	2.93	No
22	1.70	No	47	9.95	Yes
23	16.29	Yes	48	4.46	No
24	5.52	No	49	14.32	Yes
25	1.44	No	50	9.01	No

represent the mean. (SAS shows the mean in box plots, unlike many other statistical programs.) Also, SAS uses the symbol "0" to represent measurements between the inner and outer fences and "*" to represent observations beyond the outer fences (the opposite of MINITAB).

Note that the upper whisker is longer than the lower whisker and that the mean lies above the median; these characteristics reveal the rightward skewness of the data. However, the most important feature of the data is made very obvious by the box plot: There are at least two measurements between the inner and outer fences (in fact, there are three, but two are almost equal and are represented by the same "0") and at least one beyond the outer fence, all on the upper end of the distribution. Thus, the distribution is extremely skewed to the right, and several measurements need special attention in our analysis. We offer an explanation for the outliers in the following example.

EXAMPLE 2.17

The box plot for the 50 processing times (Figure 2.28) does not explicitly reveal the differences, if any, between the set of times corresponding to the success and the set of times corresponding to the failure to obtain the business. Box plots corresponding to the 39 "won" and 11 "lost" bids were generated using SAS, and are shown in Figure 2.29. Interpret them.

Solution

The division of the data set into two parts, corresponding to won and lost bids, eliminates any observations that are beyond inner or outer fences. Furthermore, the skewness in the distributions has been reduced, as evidenced by the facts that the upper whiskers are only slightly longer than the lower, and that the means are closer to the medians than for the combined sample. The box plots also reveal that the processing times corresponding to the lost bids tend to exceed those of the

FIGURE 2.29
SAS box plots of processing time data: Won and lost bids

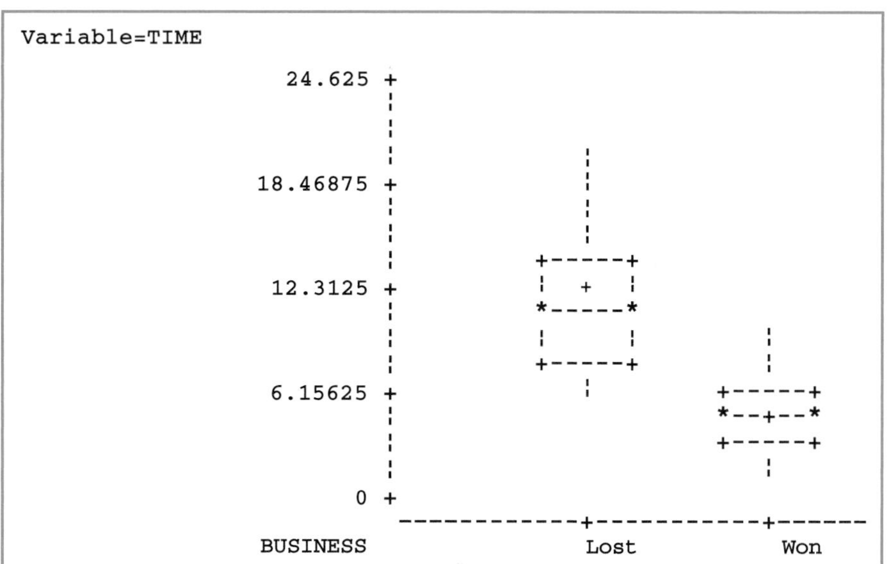

won bids. A plausible explanation for the outliers in the combined box plot (Figure 2.29) is that they are from a different population than the bulk of the times. In other words, there are two populations represented by the sample of processing times—one corresponding to lost bids, and the other to won bids.

The box plots lend support to the conclusion that the price quote processing time and the success of acquiring the business are related. However, whether the visual differences between the box plots generalize to inferences about the populations corresponding to these two samples is a matter for inferential statistics, not graphical descriptions. We'll discuss how to use samples to compare two populations using inferential statistics in Chapters 7 and 8.

The following example illustrates how z-scores can be used to detect outliers and make inferences.

EXAMPLE 2.18 Suppose a female bank employee believes that her salary is low as a result of sex discrimination. To substantiate her belief, she collects information on the salaries of her male counterparts in the banking business. She finds that their salaries have a mean of \$34,000 and a standard deviation of \$2,000. Her salary is \$27,000. Does this information support her claim of sex discrimination?

Solution The analysis might proceed as follows: First, we calculate the z-score for the woman's salary with respect to those of her male counterparts. Thus,

$$z = \frac{\$27,000 - \$34,000}{\$2,000} = -3.5$$

The implication is that the woman's salary is 3.5 standard deviations *below* the mean of the male salary distribution. Furthermore, if a check of the male salary data shows that the frequency distribution is mound-shaped, we can infer that very few salaries in this distribution should have a z-score less than -3, as shown in Figure 2.30. Clearly, a z-score of -3.5 represents an outlier—a measurement from a distribution different from the male salary distribution or a very unusual (highly improbable) measurement for the male salary distribution.

FIGURE 2.30
Male salary distribution

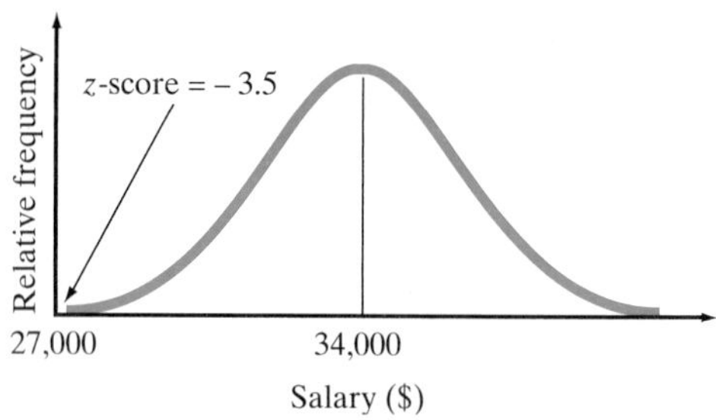

Which of the two situations do you think prevails? Do you think the woman's salary is simply unusually low in the distribution of salaries, or do you think her claim of sex discrimination is justified? Most people would probably conclude that her salary does not come from the male salary distribution. However, the careful investigator should require more information before inferring sex discrimination as the cause. We would want to know more about the data collection technique the woman used and more about her competence at her job. Also, perhaps other factors such as length of employment should be considered in the analysis.

Examples 2.17 and 2.18 exemplify an approach to statistical inference that might be called the **rare-event approach.** An experimenter hypothesizes a specific frequency distribution to describe a population of measurements. Then a sample of measurements is drawn from the population. If the experimenter finds it unlikely that the sample came from the hypothesized distribution, the hypothesis is concluded to be false. Thus, in Example 2.18 the woman believes her salary reflects discrimination. She hypothesizes that her salary should be just another measurement in the distribution of her male counterparts' salaries if no discrimination exists. However, it is so unlikely that the sample (in this case, her salary) came from the male frequency distribution that she rejects that hypothesis, concluding that the distribution from which her salary was drawn is different from the distribution for the men.

This rare-event approach to inference-making is discussed further in later chapters. Proper application of the approach requires a knowledge of probability, the subject of our next chapter.

We conclude this section with some rules of thumb for detecting outliers.

Rules of Thumb for Detecting Outliers*

Box Plots: Observations falling between the inner and outer fences are deemed *suspect outliers.* Observations falling beyond the outer fence are deemed *highly suspect outliers.*

z-scores: Observations with z-scores greater than 3 in absolute value are considered outliers. (For some highly skewed data sets, observations with z-scores greater than 1 in absolute value may be outliers).

*The z-score and box plot methods both establish rule-of-thumb limits outside of which a measurement is deemed to be an outlier. Usually, the two methods produce similar results. However, the presence of one or more outliers in a data set can inflate the computed value of s. Consequently, it will be less likely that an errant observation would have a z-score larger than 3 in absolute value. In contrast, the values of the quartiles used to calculate the intervals for a box plot are not affected by the presence of outliers.

Box Plots

USING THE TI-83 GRAPHING CALCULATOR

Making a Box Plot on the TI-83

Step 1 *Enter the data*
Press **STAT** **1** for **STAT Edit**
Enter the data set into **L1.**

Step 2 *Set up the box plot*
Press **2nd** **Y=** for **STAT PLOT**
Press **1** for **Plot 1**
Use the arrow and **ENTER** keys to set up the screen as shown below.

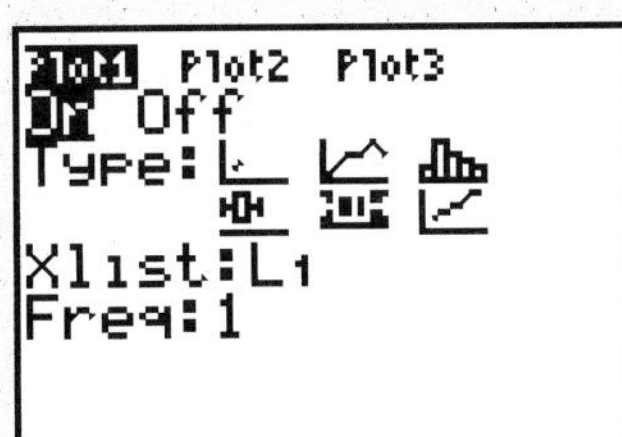

Step 3 *Select your window settings*
Press **WINDOW** and adjust the settings as follows:

Xmin = smallest data value (or smaller)
Xmax = largest data value (or larger)
Xscl = approximately (xmax − xmin)/10
Ymin = 0
Ymax = 10
Yscl = 1

Step 4 *View the graph*
Press **GRAPH**

Optional Step *Read the five number summary*
Press **TRACE**
Use the left and right arrow keys to move between minX, Q1, Med, Q3, and maxX.

Example Make a box plot for the given data,

86, 70, 62, 98, 73, 56, 53, 92, 86, 37, 62, 83, 78, 49, 78, 37, 67, 79, 57

The window settings and horizontal box plot are shown below.

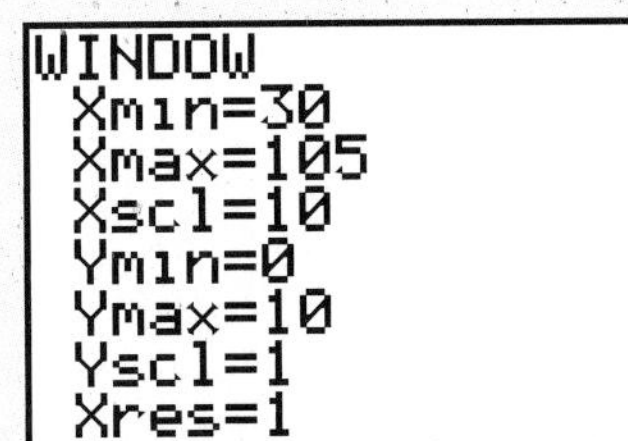

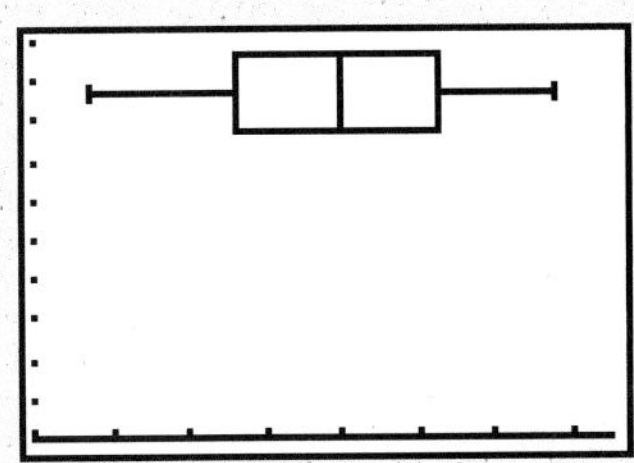

EXERCISES 2.79–2.88

Learning the Mechanics

2.79 A sample data set has a mean of 57 and a standard deviation of 11. Determine whether each of the following sample measurements are outliers.

a. 65
b. 21
c. 72
d. 98

2.80 Define the 25th, 50th, and 75th percentiles of a data set. Explain how they provide a description of the data.

2.81 Suppose a data set consisting of exam scores has a lower quartile $Q_L = 60$, a median $m = 75$, and an upper quartile $Q_U = 85$. The scores on the exam range from 18 to 100. Without having the actual scores available to you, construct as much of the box plot as possible.

2.82 MINITAB was used to generate the box plot shown here.

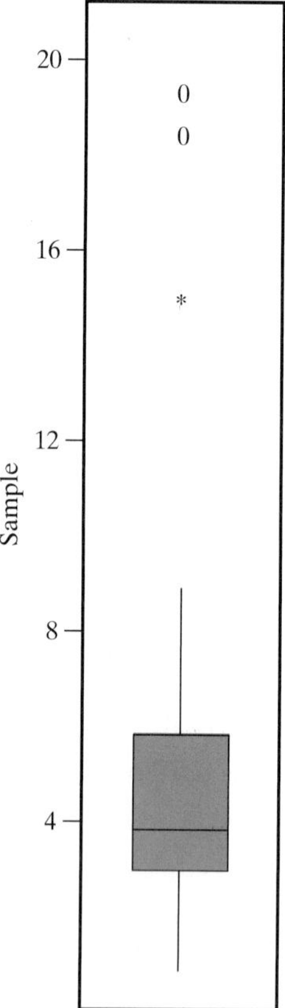

a. What is the median of the data set (approximately)?
b. What are the upper and lower quartiles of the data set (approximately)?
c. What is the interquartile range of the data set (approximately)?
d. Is the data set skewed to the left, skewed to the right, or symmetric?
e. What percentage of the measurements in the data set lie to the right of the median? To the left of the upper quartile?
f. Identify any outliers in the data.

2.83 Consider the following two sample data sets:

LM2_83.DAT

Sample A			Sample B		
121	171	158	171	152	170
173	184	163	168	169	171
157	85	145	190	183	185
165	172	196	140	173	206
170	159	172	172	174	169
161	187	100	199	151	180
142	166	171	167	170	188

a. Use a statistical software package to construct a box plot for each data set.
b. Using information reflected in your box plots, describe the similarities and differences in the two data sets.

Applying the Concepts

2.84 The table contains the top salary offer (in thousands of dollars) received by each member of a sample of 50 MBA students who recently graduated from the Graduate School of Management at Rutgers, the state university of New Jersey.

MBASAL.DAT

61.1	48.5	47.0	49.1	43.5
50.8	62.3	50.0	65.4	58.0
53.2	39.9	49.1	75.0	51.2
41.7	40.0	53.0	39.6	49.6
55.2	54.9	62.5	35.0	50.3
41.5	56.0	55.5	70.0	59.2
39.2	47.0	58.2	59.0	60.8
72.3	55.0	41.4	51.5	63.0
48.4	61.7	45.3	63.2	41.5
47.0	43.2	44.6	47.7	58.6

Source: Career Services Office, Graduate School of Management, Rutgers University.

a. The mean and standard deviation are 52.33 and 9.22, respectively. Find and interpret the z-score associated with the highest salary offer, the lowest salary offer, and the mean salary offer. Would you consider the highest offer to be unusually high? Why or why not?
b. Use a statistical software package to construct a box plot for this data set. Which salary offers (if any) are potentially faulty observations? Explain.

2.85 Refer to the *Financial Management* (Spring 1995) study of 49 firms filing for prepackaged bankruptcies, Exercise 2.24 (p. 49). Recall that three types of "prepack" firms exist: (1) those who hold no pre-filing vote; (2) those who vote their preference for a joint solution; and (3) those who vote their preference for a prepack. Box plots, constructed using MINITAB, for the time in bankruptcy (months) for each type of firm are shown below.

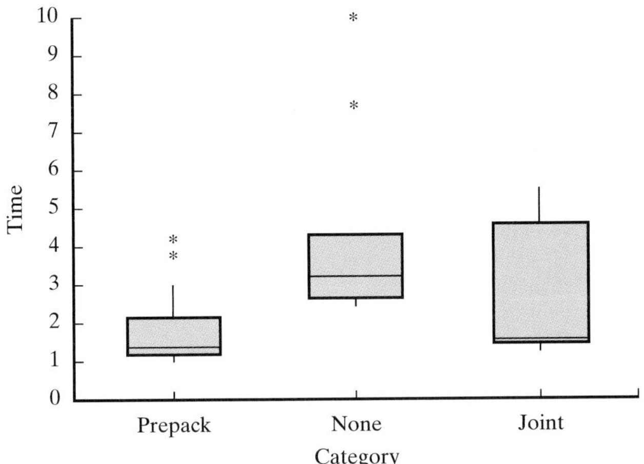

a. How do the median bankruptcy times compare for the three types? [*Hint:* Recall that MINITAB uses a horizontal line through the box to represent the median.]
b. How do the variabilities of the bankruptcy times compare for the three types?
c. The standard deviations of the bankruptcy times are 2.47 for "none," 1.72 for "joint," and 0.96 for "prepack." Do the standard deviations agree with the interquartile ranges (part **b**) with regard to the comparison of the variabilities of the bankruptcy times?
d. Is there evidence of outliers in any of the three distributions?

2.86 Refer to the *Fortune* (Oct. 25, 1999) ranking of the 50 most powerful women in America, Exercise 2.36 (p. 59). A box plot for the ages of the 50 women, produced using STATISTIX, is shown above right.
a. Use the box plot to estimate the lower quartile, median, and upper quartile of these data. (Compare your estimates to the actual values shown on the MINITAB printout, p. 59.)
b. Does the age distribution appear to be skewed? Explain.
c. Are there any outliers in these data? If so, identify them.

2.87 A manufacturer of minicomputer systems is interested in improving its customer support services. As a first step, its marketing department has been charged with the responsibility of summarizing the extent of customer problems in terms of system down time. The 40 most recent customers were surveyed to determine the amount of down time (in hours) they had experienced during the previous month. These data are listed in the table.

STATISTIX Output for Exercise 2.86

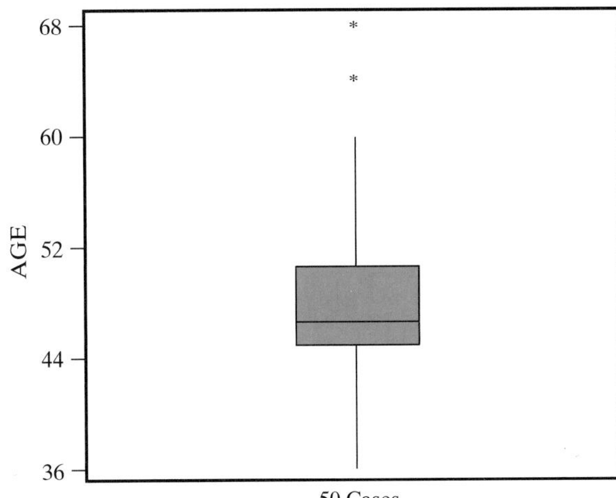

DOWNTIME.DAT

Customer Number	Down Time	Customer Number	Down Time	Customer Number	Down Time
230	12	244	2	258	28
231	16	245	11	259	19
232	5	246	22	260	34
233	16	247	17	261	26
234	21	248	31	262	17
235	29	249	10	263	11
236	38	250	4	264	64
237	14	251	10	265	19
238	47	252	15	266	18
239	0	253	7	267	24
240	24	254	20	268	49
241	15	255	9	269	50
242	13	256	22		
243	8	257	18		

a. Use a statistical software package to construct a box plot for these data. Use the information reflected in the box plot to describe the frequency distribution of the data set. Your description should address central tendency, variation, and skewness.
b. Use your box plot to determine which customers are having unusually lengthy down times.
c. Find and interpret the z-scores associated with the customers you identified in part **b**.

2.88 According to *Forbes* (Jan. 11, 1999), retailing was one of the U.S. economy's best-performing sectors in 1998. The Internet and its associated on-line sales played a significant role in the performance. The table on p. 94 lists the 1998 sales and net income (in millions of dollars) for 24 major retailers.

a. Use a statistical software package to construct a box plot for each of the two variables, sales and net income.
b. Which companies (if any) show up as outliers with respect to sales? With respect to net income?
c. Use the box plots to estimate the upper quartiles of the two data sets and interpret their values. Which companies fall above the upper quartiles?

RETAIL 98.DAT

Company	Sales	Net Income
Ames Dept Stores	2,500	42
AutoZone	3,243	228
Bed Bath & Beyond	1,201	82
Best Buy	9,084	150
BJ's Wholesale Club	3,497	77
CDW Computer Centers	1,607	61
Costco Cos	24,270	460
Dollar General	3,089	169
Family Dollar Stores	2,362	103
Gap	8,190	726
Global DirectMail	1,401	43
Goody's Family	1,062	37
Home Depot	28,692	1,503
Kohl's	3,470	171
Lowe's Cos	11,727	449
Office Depot	8,425	211
Pier 1 Imports	1,120	76
Ross Stores	2,125	129
Staples	6,596	178
Starbucks	1,309	68
Tiffany	1,094	79
Wal-Mart Stores	132,235	4,158
Walgreen	15,307	537
Williams-Sonoma	1,033	45

Source: *Forbes,* January 11, 1999, p. 196.

2.9 GRAPHING BIVARIATE RELATIONSHIPS (OPTIONAL)

The claim is often made that the crime rate and the unemployment rate are "highly correlated." Another popular belief is that the Gross Domestic Product (GDP) and the rate of inflation are "related." Some people even believe that the Dow Jones Industrial Average and the lengths of fashionable skirts are "associated." The words "correlated," "related," and "associated" imply a relationship between two variables—in the examples above, two *quantitative* variables.

One way to describe the relationship between two quantitative variables—called a **bivariate relationship**—is to plot the data in a **scattergram** (or **scatterplot**). A scattergram is a two-dimensional plot, with one variable's values plotted along the vertical axis and the other along the horizontal axis. For example, Figure 2.31 is a scattergram relating (1) the cost of mechanical work (heating, ventilating, and plumbing) to (2) the floor area of the building for a sample of 26 factory and warehouse buildings. Note that the scattergram suggests a general tendency for mechanical cost to increase as building floor area increases.

When an increase in one variable is generally associated with an increase in the second variable, we say that the two variables are "positively related" or "positively correlated."* Figure 2.31 implies that mechanical cost and floor area are positively correlated. Alternatively, if one variable has a tendency to decrease as the other increases, we say the variables are "negatively correlated." Figure 2.32 shows several hypothetical scattergrams that portray a positive bivariate rela-

*A formal definition of correlation is given in Chapter 9. We will learn that correlation measures the strength of the linear (or straight-line) relationship between two variables.

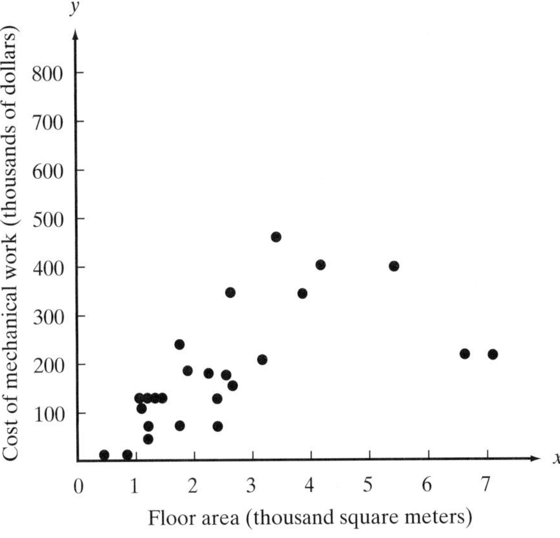

FIGURE 2.31
Scattergram of cost vs. floor area

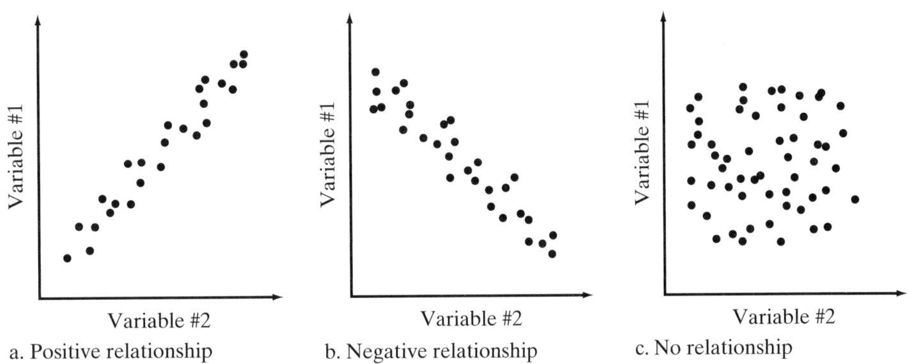

FIGURE 2.32
Hypothetical bivariate relationship

tionship (Figure 2.32a), a negative bivariate relationship (Figure 2.32b), and a situation where the two variables are unrelated (Figure 2.32c).

EXAMPLE 2.19 A medical item used to administer to a hospital patient is called a *factor.* For example, factors can be intravenous (IV) tubing, IV fluid, needles, shave kits, bedpans, diapers, dressings, medications, and even code carts. The coronary care unit at Bayonet Point Hospital (St. Petersburg, Florida) recently investigated the relationship between the number of factors administered per patient and the patient's length of stay (in days). Data on these two variables for a sample of 50 coronary care patients are given in Table 2.12. Use a scattergram to describe the relationship between the two variables of interest, number of factors and length of stay.

Solution Rather than construct the plot by hand, we resort to a statistical software package. The SPSS plot of the data in Table 2.12, with length of stay (LOS) on the vertical axis and number of factors (FACTORS) on the horizontal axis, is shown in Figure 2.33.

As plotting symbols, SPSS uses numbers. Each symbol represents the number of sample points (e.g., patients) plotted at that particular coordinate. Although the plotted points exhibit a fair amount of variation, the scattergram clearly shows

TABLE 2.12 Data on Patient's Factors and Length of Stay

Number of Factors	Length of Stay (days)	Number of Factors	Length of Stay (days)
231	9	354	11
323	7	142	7
113	8	286	9
208	5	341	10
162	4	201	5
117	4	158	11
159	6	243	6
169	9	156	6
55	6	184	7
77	3	115	4
103	4	202	6
147	6	206	5
230	6	360	6
78	3	84	3
525	9	331	9
121	7	302	7
248	5	60	2
233	8	110	2
260	4	131	5
224	7	364	4
472	12	180	7
220	8	134	6
383	6	401	15
301	9	155	4
262	7	338	8

Source: Bayonet Point Hospital, Coronary Care Unit.

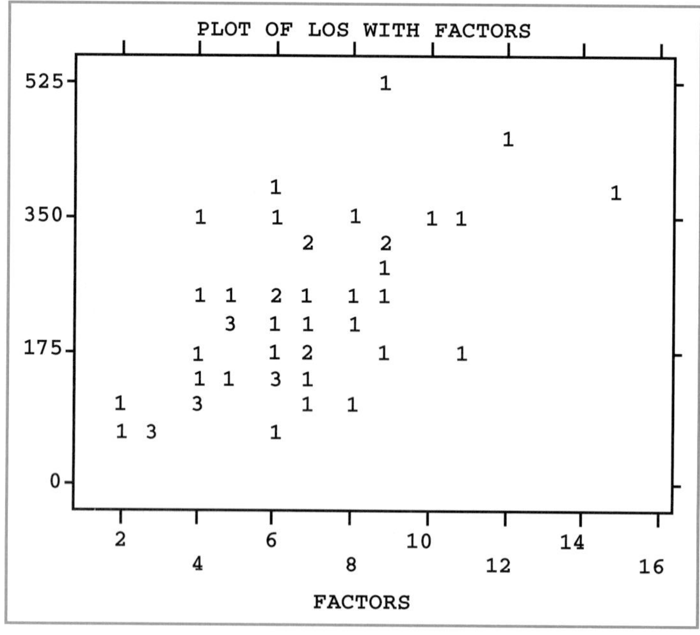

FIGURE 2.33
SPSS scatterplot of data in Table 2.12

an increasing trend. It appears that a patient's length of stay is positively correlated with the number of factors administered to the patient. Hospital administrators may use this information to improve their forecasts of lengths of stay for future patients.

Scatterplots

USING THE TI-83 GRAPHING CALCULATOR

Making Scatterplots

To make a scatterplot for paired data,

Step 1 *Enter the data*
Press **STAT 1** for **STAT Edit**
Enter your x-data in **L1** and your y-data in **L2.**

Step 2 *Set up the scatterplot*
Press **2nd Y=** for **STAT PLOT**
Press **1** for **Plot1**
Use the arrow and **ENTER** keys to set up the screen as shown below.

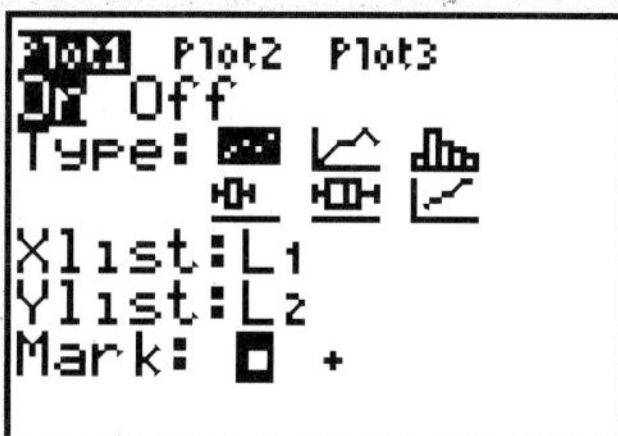

Step 3 *View the scatterplot*
Press **ZOOM 9** for **ZoomStat**

Example The figures below show a table of data entered on the TI-83 and the scatterplot of the data obtained using the steps given above.

L1	L2	L3 2
2	67	------
19	68	
23	70	
39	74	
64	78	
74	81	
68		

L2(7) =82

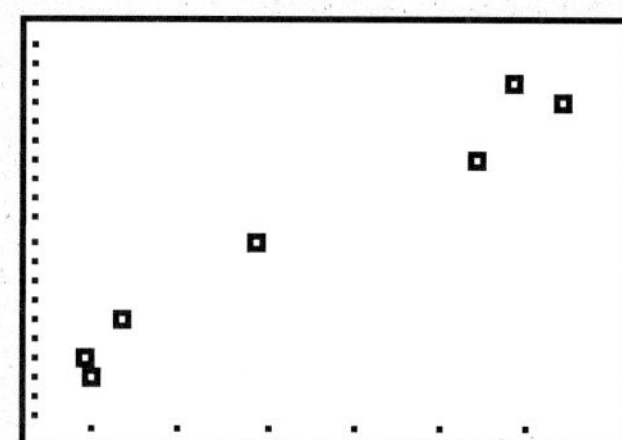

The scattergram is a simple but powerful tool for describing a bivariate relationship. However, keep in mind that it is only a graph. No measure of reliability can be attached to inferences made about bivariate populations based on scattergrams of sample data. The statistical tools that enable us to make inferences about bivariate relationships are presented in Chapter 9.

2.10 THE TIME SERIES PLOT (OPTIONAL)

Each of the previous sections has been concerned with describing the information contained in a sample or population of data. Often these data are viewed as having been produced at essentially the same point in time. Thus, time has not been a factor in any of the graphical methods described so far.

Data of interest to managers are often produced and monitored over time. Examples include the daily closing price of their company's common stock, the company's weekly sales volume and quarterly profits, and characteristics—such as weight and length—of products produced by the company.

DEFINITION 2.15

Data that are produced and monitored over time are called **time series data.**

Recall from Section 1.4 that a process is a series of actions or operations that generates output over time. Accordingly, measurements taken of a sequence of units produced by a process—such as a production process—are time series data. In general, any sequence of numbers produced over time can be thought of as being generated by a process.

When measurements are made over time, it is important to record both the numerical value and the time or the time period associated with each measurement. With this information a **time series plot**—sometimes called a **run chart**—can be constructed to describe the time series data and to learn about the process that generated the data. A time series plot is simply a scatterplot with the measurements on the vertical axis and time or the order in which the measurements were made on the horizontal axis. The plotted points are usually connected by straight lines to make it easier to see the changes and movement in the measurements over time. For example, Figure 2.34 is a time series plot of a particular company's monthly sales (number of units sold per month). And Figure 2.35 is a time series plot of the weights of 30 one-gallon paint cans that were consecutively filled by the same filling head. Notice that the weights are plotted against the order in which the cans were filled rather than some unit of time. When monitoring production processes, it is often more convenient to record the order rather than the exact time at which each measurement was made.

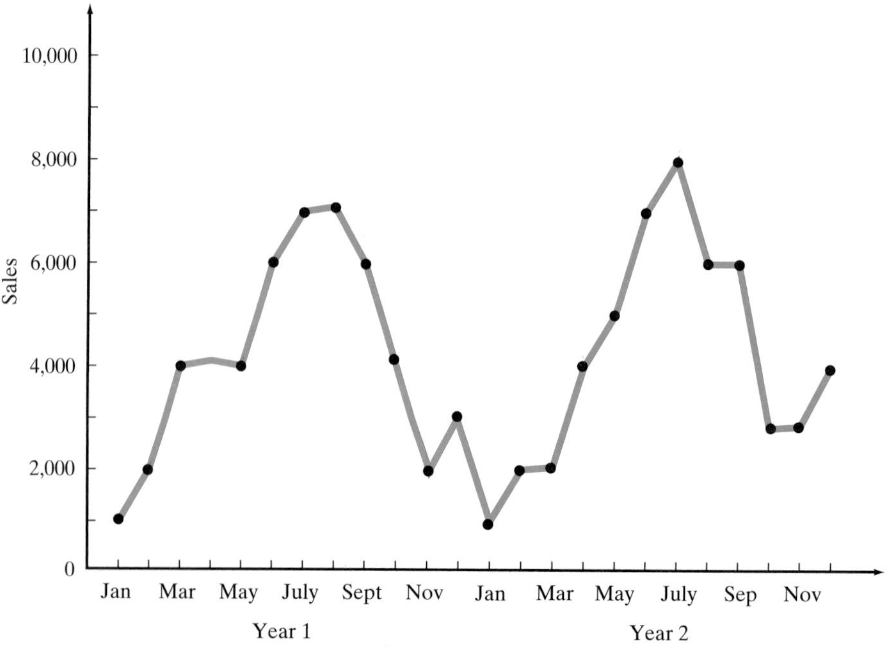

FIGURE 2.34
Time series plot of company sales

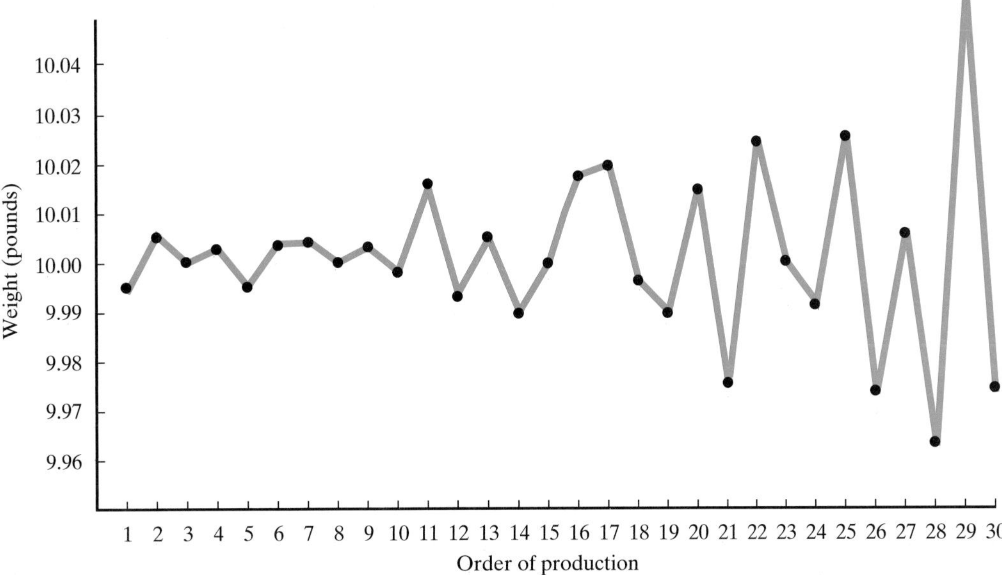

FIGURE 2.35
Time series plot of paint can weights

Time series plots reveal the movement (trend) and changes (variation) in the variable being monitored. Notice how sales trend upward in the summer and how the variation in the weights of the paint cans increases over time. This kind of information would not be revealed by stem-and-leaf displays or histograms, as the following example illustrates.

EXAMPLE 2.20 W. Edwards Deming was one of America's most famous statisticians. He was best known for the role he played after World War II in teaching the Japanese how to improve the quality of their products by monitoring and continually improving their production processes. In his book *Out of the Crisis* (1986), Deming warned against the knee-jerk (i.e., automatic) use of histograms to display and extract information from data. As evidence he offered the following example.

Fifty camera springs were tested in the order in which they were produced. The elongation of each spring was measured under the pull of 20 grams. Both a time series plot and a histogram were constructed from the measurements. They are shown in Figure 2.36, which has been reproduced from Deming's book. If you had to predict the elongation measurement of the next spring to be produced (i.e., spring 51) and could use only one of the two plots to guide your prediction, which would you use? Why?

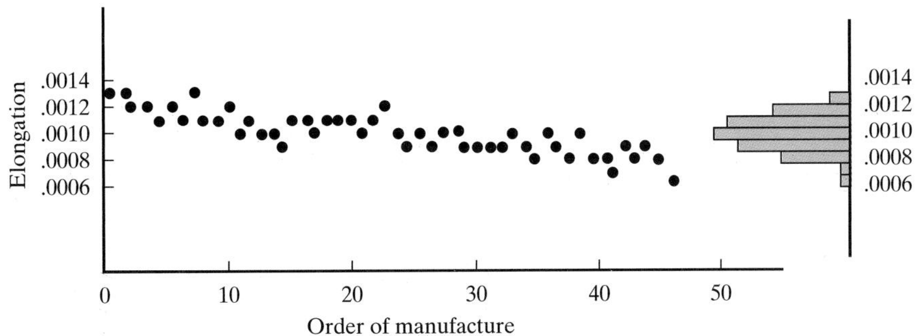

FIGURE 2.36
Deming's time series plot and histogram

Solution Only the time series plot describes the behavior *over time* of the process that produces the springs. The fact that the elongation measurements are decreasing over time can only be gleaned from the time series plot. Because the histogram does not reflect the order in which the springs were produced, it in effect represents all observations as having been produced simultaneously. Using the histogram to predict the elongation of the 51st spring would very likely lead to an overestimate.

The lesson from Deming's example is this: For displaying and analyzing data that have been generated over time by a process, the primary graphical tool is the time series plot, not the histogram.

2.11 DISTORTING THE TRUTH WITH DESCRIPTIVE TECHNIQUES

A picture may be "worth a thousand words," but pictures can also color messages or distort them. In fact, the pictures in statistics (e.g., histograms, bar charts, time series plots, etc.) are susceptible to distortion, whether unintentional or as a result of unethical statistical practices. In this section, we will mention a few of the pitfalls to watch for when interpreting a chart, graph, or numerical descriptive measure.

One common way to change the impression conveyed by a graph is to change the scale on the vertical axis, the horizontal axis, or both. For example, Figure 2.37 is a bar graph that shows the market share of sales for a company for each of the years 1995 to 2000. If you want to show that the change in firm A's market share over time is moderate, you should pack in a large number of units per inch on the vertical axis—that is, make the distance between successive units on the vertical scale small, as shown in Figure 2.37. You can see that a change in the firm's market share over time is barely apparent.

FIGURE 2.37
Firm A's market share from 1995 to 2000—packed vertical axis

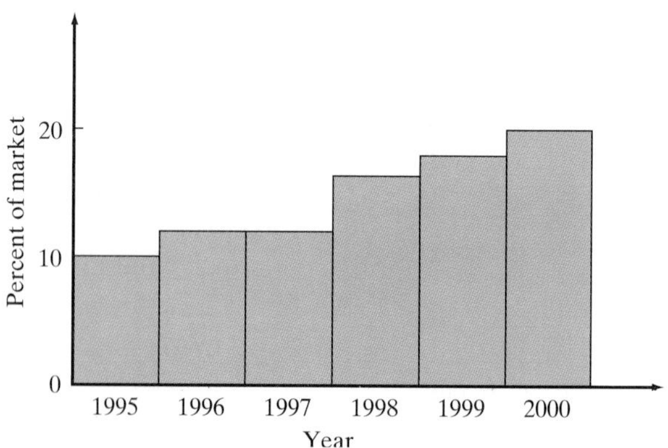

If you want to use the same data to make the changes in firm A's market share appear large, you should increase the distance between successive units on the vertical axis. That is, stretch the vertical axis by graphing only a few units per inch as in Figure 2.38. A telltale sign of stretching is a long vertical axis, but this is often hidden by starting the vertical axis at some point above 0, as shown in the

FIGURE 2.38
Firm A's market share from 1995 to 2000—stretched vertical axis

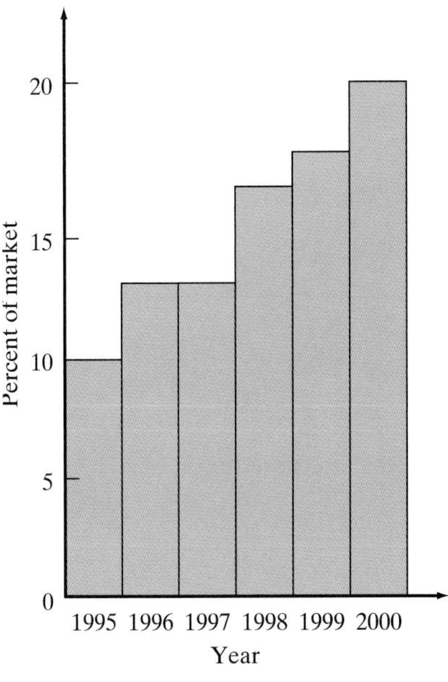

FIGURE 2.39
Changes in money supply from January to June

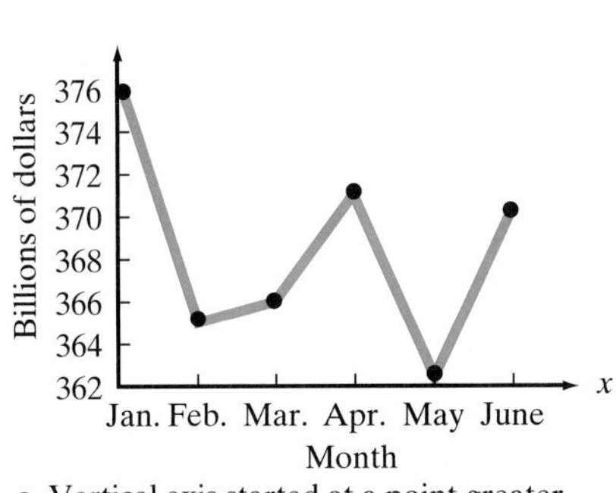

a. Vertical axis started at a point greater than zero

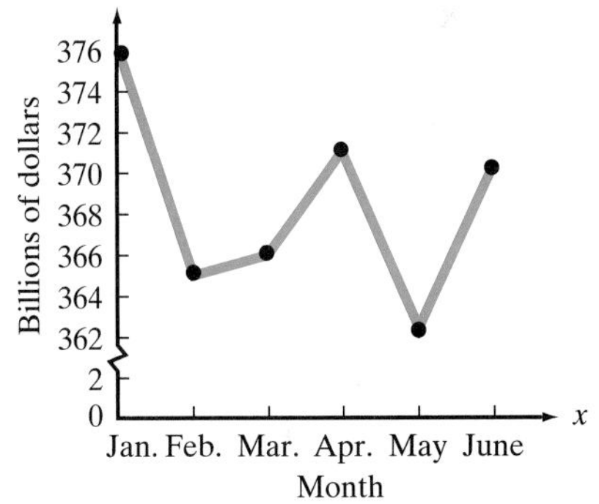

b. Gap in vertical axis

time series plot, Figure 2.39a. The same effect can be achieved by using a broken line—called a *scale break*—for the vertical axis, as shown in Figure 2.39b.

Stretching the horizontal axis (increasing the distance between successive units) may also lead you to incorrect conclusions. With bar graphs, a visual distortion can be achieved by making the width of the bars proportional to the height. For example, look at the bar chart in Figure 2.40a, which depicts the percentage of

FIGURE 2.40
Relative share of the automobile market for each of four major manufacturers

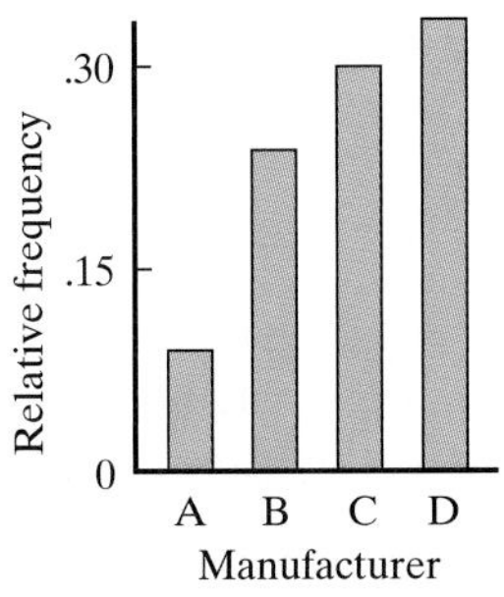

a. Bar chart

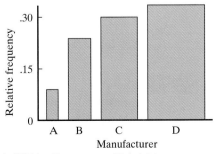

b. Width of bars grows with height

a year's total automobile sales attributable to each of the four major manufacturers. Now suppose we make both the width and the height grow as the market share grows. This change is shown in Figure 2.40b. The reader may tend to equate the *area* of the bars with the relative market share of each manufacturer. But in fact, the true relative market share is proportional only to the *height* of the bars.

Sometimes we do not need to manipulate the graph to distort the impression it creates. Modifying the verbal description that accompanies the graph can change the interpretation that will be made by the viewer. Figure 2.41 provides a good illustration of this ploy.

FIGURE 2.41
Changing the verbal description to change a viewer's interpretation

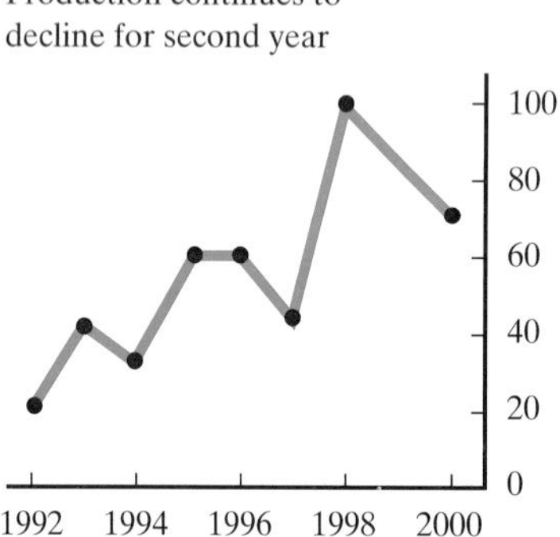

For our production, we need not even change the chart, so we can't be accused of fudging the data. Here we'll simply change the title so that for the Senate subcommittee, we'll indicate that we're not doing as well as in the past...

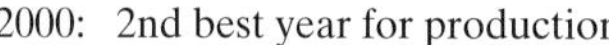

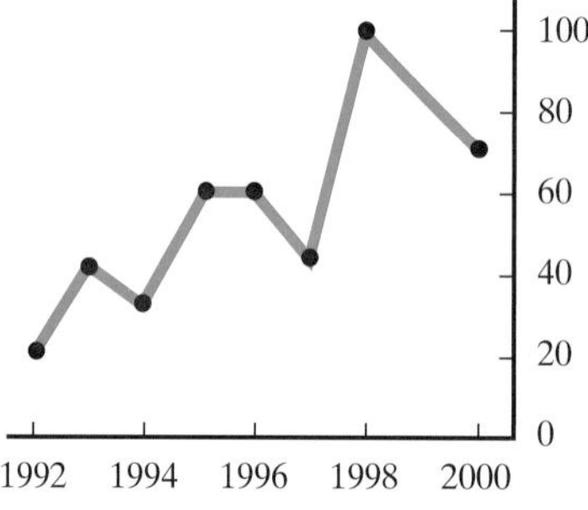

whereas for the general public, we'll tell them that we're still in the prime years.

Source: Adapted from Selazny, G. "Grappling with Graphics," *Management Review,* Oct. 1975, p. 7.

Although we've discussed only a few of the ways that graphs can be used to convey misleading pictures of phenomena, the lesson is clear. Look at all graphical descriptions of data with a critical eye. Particularly, check the axes and the size of the units on each axis. Ignore the visual changes and concentrate on the actual numerical changes indicated by the graph or chart.

The information in a data set can also be distorted by using numerical descriptive measures, as Example 2.21 indicates.

EXAMPLE 2.21

Suppose you're considering working for a small law firm—one that currently has a senior member and three junior members. You inquire about the salary you could expect to earn if you join the firm. Unfortunately, you receive two answers:

Answer A: The senior member tells you that an "average employee" earns $67,500.

Answer B: One of the junior members later tells you that an "average employee" earns \$55,000.

Which answer can you believe?

Solution The confusion exists because the phrase "average employee" has not been clearly defined. Suppose the four salaries paid are \$55,000 for each of the three junior members and \$105,000 for the senior member. Thus,

$$\text{Mean} = \frac{3(\$55{,}000) + \$105{,}000}{4} = \frac{\$270{,}000}{4} = \$67{,}500$$

$$\text{Median} = \$55{,}000$$

You can now see how the two answers were obtained. The senior member reported the mean of the four salaries, and the junior member reported the median. The information you received was distorted because neither person stated which measure of central tendency was being used.

Another distortion of information in a sample occurs when *only* a measure of central tendency is reported. Both a measure of central tendency and a measure of variability are needed to obtain an accurate mental image of a data set.

Suppose you want to buy a new car and are trying to decide which of two models to purchase. Since energy and economy are both important issues, you decide to purchase model A because its EPA mileage rating is 32 miles per gallon in the city, whereas the mileage rating for model B is only 30 miles per gallon in the city.

However, you may have acted too quickly. How much variability is associated with the ratings? As an extreme example, suppose that further investigation reveals that the standard deviation for model A mileages is 5 miles per gallon, whereas that for model B is only 1 mile per gallon. If the mileages form a mound-shaped distribution, they might appear as shown in Figure 2.42. Note that the larger amount of variability associated with model A implies that more risk is involved in purchasing model A. That is, the particular car you purchase is more likely to have a mileage rating that will greatly differ from the EPA rating of 32 miles per gallon if you purchase model A, while a model B car is not likely to vary from the 30-miles-per-gallon rating by more than 2 miles per gallon.

FIGURE 2.42
Mileage distributions for two car models

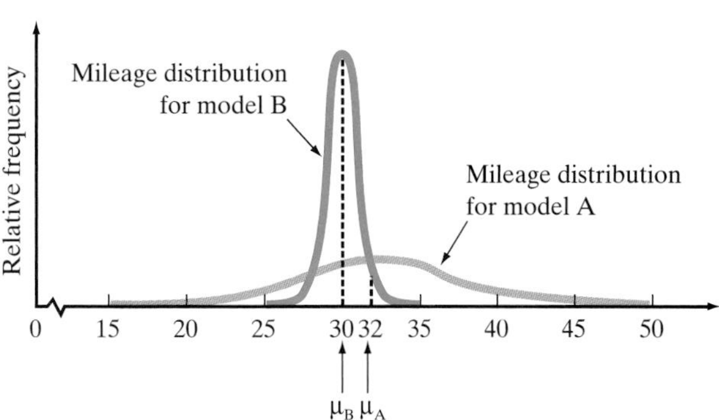

We conclude this section with another example on distorting the truth with numerical descriptive measures.

STATISTICS IN Action

Car & Driver's "Road Test Digest"

Periodically, *Car & Driver* magazine conducts comprehensive road tests on all new car models. The results of the tests are reported in *Car & Driver's* "Road Test Digest." The "Road Test Digest" includes the following variables for each new car tested:

1. Model
2. List price ($)
3. Elapsed time from 0 to 60 mph (seconds)
4. Elapsed time for $\frac{1}{4}$ mile at full throttle (seconds)
5. Maximum speed (mph)
6. Braking distance from 70 to 0 mph (feet)
7. EPA-estimated city fuel economy (mpg)
8. Road-holding (grip) during cornering (gravitational force, in g's)

Focus

The "Road Test Digest" data from the July 1998 issue of *Car & Driver* is available on the data disk that accompanies this text. The name of the file containing the data is CAR.DAT. Your assignment is to completely describe the data for *Car & Driver* magazine. Are there any trends in the data? What are typical values of these variables that a new car buyer can expect? Are there any new car models that have exceptional values of these variables? Are there any relationships among the variables? Your summary results will be reported in a future issue of the magazine.

EXAMPLE 2.22 *Children Out of School in America* is a report on delinquency of school-age children prepared by the Children's Defense Fund (CDF), a government-sponsored organization. Consider the following three reported results of the CDF survey.

- Reported result 1: 25 percent of the 16- and 17-year-olds in the Portland, Maine, Bayside East Housing Project were out of school. Fact: *Only eight children were surveyed; two were found to be out of school.*
- Reported result 2: Of all the secondary school students who had been suspended more than once in census tract 22 in Columbia, South Carolina, 33% had been suspended two times and 67% had been suspended three or more times. Fact: *CDF found only three children in that entire census tract who had been suspended; one child was suspended twice and the other two children, three or more times.*
- Reported result 3: In the Portland Bayside East Housing Project, 50% of all the secondary school children who had been suspended more than once had been suspended three or more times. Fact: *The survey found two secondary school children had been suspended in that area; one of them had been suspended three or more times.*

Identify the potential distortions in the results reported by the CDF.

Solution In each of these examples the reporting of percentages (i.e., relative frequencies) instead of the numbers themselves is misleading. No inference we might draw from the cited examples would be reliable. (We'll see how to measure the reliability of estimated percentages in Chapter 5.) In short, either the report should state the numbers alone instead of percentages, or, better yet, it should state that the numbers were too small to report by region. If several regions were combined, the numbers (and percentages) would be more meaningful. ★

QUICK REVIEW

Key Terms

Note: Starred (*) items are from the optional sections in this chapter.

Key Formulas

$$\frac{(\text{Class frequency})}{n}$$ Class relative frequency 27

$$\bar{x} = \frac{\sum_{i=1}^{n} x_i}{n}$$ Sample mean 52

$$s^2 = \frac{\sum_{i=1}^{n}(x_i - \bar{x})^2}{n-1} = \frac{\sum_{i=1}^{n} x_i^2 - \frac{\left(\sum_{i=1}^{n} x_i\right)^2}{n}}{n-1}$$ Sample variance 65

$$s = \sqrt{s^2}$$ Sample standard deviation 66

$$z = \frac{x - \bar{x}}{s}$$ Sample z-score 80

$$z = \frac{x - \mu}{\sigma}$$ Population z-score 80

$$\text{IQR} = Q_U - Q_L$$ Interquartile range 85

LANGUAGE LAB

Symbol	Pronunciation	Description
Σ	sum of	Summation notation; $\sum_{i=1}^{n} x_i$ represents the sum of the measurements $x_1, x_2, \ldots, x_n$
μ	mu	Population mean
$\bar{x}$	x-bar	Sample mean
σ^2	sigma squared	Population variance
σ	sigma	Population standard deviation
s^2		Sample variance
s		Sample standard deviation
z		z-score for a measurement
m		Median (middle quartile) of a sample data set

Q_L	Lower quartile (25th percentile)
Q_U	Upper quartile (75th percentile)
IQR	Interquartile range

SUPPLEMENTARY EXERCISES 2.89–2.113

Starred (*) exercises are from the optional sections in this chapter.

Learning the Mechanics

2.89 Construct a relative frequency histogram for the data summarized in the accompanying table.

Measurement Class	Relative Frequency	Measurement Class	Relative Frequency
.00–.75	.02	5.25–6.00	.15
.75–1.50	.01	6.00–6.75	.12
1.50–2.25	.03	6.75–7.50	.09
2.25–3.00	.05	7.50–8.25	.05
3.00–3.75	.10	8.25–9.00	.04
3.75–4.50	.14	9.00–9.75	.01
4.50–5.25	.19		

2.90 Discuss the conditions under which the median is preferred to the mean as a measure of central tendency.

2.91 Consider the following three measurements: 50, 70, 80. Find the z-score for each measurement if they are from a population with a mean and standard deviation equal to

a. $\mu = 60, \sigma = 10$ b. $\mu = 50, \sigma = 5$
c. $\mu = 40, \sigma = 10$ d. $\mu = 40, \sigma = 100$

2.92 If the range of a set of data is 20, find a rough approximation to the standard deviation of the data set.

2.93 For each of the following data sets, compute $\bar{x}$, s^2, and s:

a. 13, 1, 10, 3, 3 b. 13, 6, 6, 0
c. 1, 0, 1, 10, 11, 11, 15 d. 3, 3, 3, 3

2.94 For each of the following data sets, compute $\bar{x}$, s^2, and s. If appropriate, specify the units in which your answers are expressed.

a. 4, 6, 6, 5, 6, 7 b. −\$1, \$4, −\$3, \$0, −\$3, −\$6
c. $\frac{3}{5}\%, \frac{4}{5}\%, \frac{2}{5}\%, \frac{1}{5}\%, \frac{1}{16}\%,$
d. Calculate the range of each data set in parts **a–c.**

2.95 Explain why we generally prefer the standard deviation to the range as a measure of variability for quantitative data.

Applying the Concepts

2.96 U.S. manufacturing executives frequently complain about the high cost of labor in this country. While it may be high relative to many Pacific Rim and South American countries, the table indicates that among Western countries, U.S. labor costs are relatively low.

LABRATES.DAT

Country	Hourly Manufacturing Labor Rates (in German marks)
Germany	43.97
Switzerland	41.47
Belgium	37.35
Japan	36.01
Austria	35.19
Netherlands	34.87
Sweden	31.00
France	28.92
United States	27.97
Italy	27.21
Ireland	22.17
Britain	22.06
Spain	20.25
Portugal	9.10

Source: The New York Times, October 15, 1995, p. 10.

a. What percentage of countries listed in the table have a higher wage rate than the United States? A lower wage rate than the United States?
b. As of July 5, 1996, one German mark was worth .65 U.S. dollars (*The Wall Street Journal,* July 8, 1996). Convert the data set to U.S. dollars and use the data set to answer the remaining parts of this exercise.
c. What is the mean hourly wage for the 13 Western countries listed in the table? For all 14 countries?
d. Find s^2 and s for all 14 countries.
e. According to Chebyshev's Rule, what percentage of the measurements in the table would you expect to find in the intervals $\bar{x} \pm .75s$, $\bar{x} \pm 2.5s$, $\bar{x} \pm 4s$?
f. What percentage of measurements actually fall in the intervals of part **e?** Compare your results with those of part **e.**

2.97 Beanie Babies are toy stuffed animals that have become valuable collector's items since the introduction of Ally the Alligator in 1994. *Beanie World Magazine* provided the information (page 107) on 50 Beanie Babies.

a. Summarize the retired/current status of the 50 Beanie Babies with an appropriate graph. Interpret the graph.
b. Summarize the values of the 50 Beanie Babies with an appropriate graph. Interpret the graph.
*c. Use a graph to portray the relationship between a Beanie Baby's value and its age. Do you detect a trend?

BEANIE.DAT

Name	Age (Months) as of Sept. 1998	Retired (R) Current (C)	Value ($)
1. Ally the Alligator	52	R	55.00
2. Batty the Bat	12	C	12.00
3. Bongo the Brown Monkey	28	R	40.00
4. Blackie the Bear	52	C	10.00
5. Bucky the Beaver	40	R	45.00
6. Bumble the Bee	28	R	600.00
7. Crunch the Shark	21	C	10.00
8. Congo the Gorilla	28	C	10.00
9. Derby the Coarse Mained Horse	28	R	30.00
10. Digger the Red Crab	40	R	150.00
11. Echo the Dolphin	17	R	20.00
12. Fetch the Golden Retriever	5	C	15.00
13. Early the Robin	5	C	20.00
14. Flip the White Cat	28	R	40.00
15. Garcia the Teddy	28	R	200.00
16. Happy the Hippo	52	R	20.00
17. Grunt the Razorback	28	R	175.00
18. Gigi the Poodle	5	C	15.00
19. Goldie the Goldfish	52	R	45.00
20. Iggy the Iguana	10	C	10.00
21. Inch the Inchworm	28	R	20.00
22. Jake the Mallard Duck	5	C	20.00
23. Kiwi the Toucan	40	R	165.00
24. Kuku the Cockatoo	5	C	20.00
25. Mistic the Unicorn	11	R	45.00
26. Mel the Koala Bear	21	C	10.00
27. Nanook the Husky	17	C	15.00
28. Nuts the Squirrel	21	C	10.00
29. Peace the Tie Died Teddy	17	C	25.00
30. Patty the Platypus	64	R	800.00
31. Quacker the Duck	40	R	15.00
32. Puffer the Penguin	10	C	15.00
33. Princess the Bear	12	C	65.00
34. Scottie the Scottie	28	R	28.00
35. Rover the Dog	28	R	15.00
36. Rex the Tyrannosaurus	40	R	825.00
37. Sly the Fox	28	C	10.00
38. Slither the Snake	52	R	1,900.00
39. Skip the Siamese Cat	21	C	10.00
40. Splash the Orca Whale	52	R	150.00
41. Spooky the Ghost	28	R	40.00
42. Snowball the Snowman	12	R	40.00
43. Stinger the Scorpion	5	C	15.00
44. Spot the Dog	52	R	65.00
45. Tank the Armadillo	28	R	85.00
46. Stripes the Tiger (Gold/Black)	40	R	400.00
47. Teddy the 1997 Holiday Bear	12	R	50.00
48. Tuffy the Terrier	17	C	10.00
49. Tracker the Basset Hound	5	C	15.00
50. Zip the Black Cat	28	R	40.00

Source: Beanie World Magazine, Sept. 1998.

2.98 *Consumer Reports,* published by Consumers Union, is a magazine that contains ratings and reports for consumers on goods, services, health, and personal finances. Consumers Union reported on the testing of 46 brands of toothpaste (*Consumer Reports,* Sept. 1992). Each was rated on: package design, flavor, cleaning ability, fluoride content, and cost per month (a cost estimate based on brushing with half-inch of toothpaste twice daily). The data shown below are costs per month for the 46 brands. Costs marked by an asterisk represent those brands that carry the American Dental Association (ADA) seal verifying effective decay prevention.

a. Use a statistical software package to construct a stem-and-leaf display for the data.
b. Circle the individual leaves that represent those brands that carry the ADA seal.
c. What does the pattern of circles suggest about the costs of those brands approved by the ADA?

2.99 A manufacturer of industrial wheels is losing many profitable orders because of the long time it takes the firm's marketing, engineering, and accounting departments to develop price quotes for potential customers. To remedy this problem the firm's management would like to set guidelines for the length of time each department should spend developing price quotes. To help develop these guidelines, 50 requests for price quotes were randomly selected from the set of all price quotes made last year; the processing time (in days) was determined for each price quote for each department. These times are displayed in the table below. The price quotes are also classified by whether they were "lost" (i.e., whether or not the customer placed an order after receiving the price quote).

a. MINITAB stem-and-leaf displays for each of the departments and for the total processing time are given on pg. 109. Note that the units of the leaves for accounting and total processing times are units (1.0), while the leaf units for marketing and engineering processing times are tenths (.1). Shade the leaves that correspond to "lost" orders in each of the displays, and interpret each of the displays.
b. Using your results from part **a**, develop "maximum processing time" guidelines for each department that, if followed, will help the firm reduce the number of lost orders.

TOOTHPAS.DAT

.58	.66	1.02	1.11	1.77	1.40	.73*	.53*	.57*	1.34
1.29	.89*	.49	.53*	.52	3.90	4.73	1.26	.71*	.55*
.59*	.97	.44*	.74*	.51*	.68*	.67	1.22	.39	.55
.62	.66*	1.07	.64	1.32*	1.77*	.80*	.79	.89*	.64
.81*	.79*	.44*	1.09	1.04	1.12				

PRQUOTES.DAT

Request Number	Marketing	Engineering	Accounting	Lost?	Request Number	Marketing	Engineering	Accounting	Lost?
1	7.0	6.2	.1	No	26	.6	2.2	.5	No
2	.4	5.2	.1	No	27	6.0	1.8	.2	No
3	2.4	4.6	.6	No	28	5.8	.6	.5	No
4	6.2	13.0	.8	Yes	29	7.8	7.2	2.2	Yes
5	4.7	.9	.5	No	30	3.2	6.9	.1	No
6	1.3	.4	.1	No	31	11.0	1.7	3.3	No
7	7.3	6.1	.1	No	32	6.2	1.3	2.0	No
8	5.6	3.6	3.8	No	33	6.9	6.0	10.5	Yes
9	5.5	9.6	.5	No	34	5.4	.4	8.4	No
10	5.3	4.8	.8	No	35	6.0	7.9	.4	No
11	6.0	2.6	.1	No	36	4.0	1.8	18.2	Yes
12	2.6	11.3	1.0	No	37	4.5	1.3	.3	No
13	2.0	.6	.8	No	38	2.2	4.8	.4	No
14	.4	12.2	1.0	No	39	3.5	7.2	7.0	Yes
15	8.7	2.2	3.7	No	40	.1	.9	14.4	No
16	4.7	9.6	.1	No	41	2.9	7.7	5.8	No
17	6.9	12.3	.2	Yes	42	5.4	3.8	.3	No
18	.2	4.2	.3	No	43	6.7	1.3	.1	No
19	5.5	3.5	.4	No	44	2.0	6.3	9.9	Yes
20	2.9	5.3	22.0	No	45	.1	12.0	3.2	No
21	5.9	7.3	1.7	No	46	6.4	1.3	6.2	No
22	6.2	4.4	.1	No	47	4.0	2.4	13.5	Yes
23	4.1	2.1	30.0	Yes	48	10.0	5.3	.1	No
24	5.8	.6	.1	No	49	8.0	14.4	1.9	Yes
25	5.0	3.1	2.3	No	50	7.0	10.0	2.0	No

MINITAB Output for Exercise 2.99

```
Stem-and-leaf of MKT          N = 50
Leaf Unit = 0.10

   6    0 112446
   7    1 3
  14    2 0024699
  16    3 25
  22    4 001577
 (10)   5 0344556889
  18    6 0002224799
   8    7 0038
   4    8 07
   2    9
   2   10 0
   1   11 0
```

```
Stem-and-leaf of ENG          N = 50
Leaf Unit = 0.10

   7    0 4466699
  14    1 3333788
  19    2 12246
  23    3 1568
  (5)   4 24688
  22    5 233
  19    6 01239
  14    7 22379
   9    8
   9    9 66
   7   10 0
   6   11 3
   5   12 023
   2   13 0
   1   14 4
```

```
Stem-and-leaf of ACC          N = 50
Leaf Unit = 1.0

 (31)    0 0000000000000000000000000001111
  19     0 22223333
  11     0 5
  10     0 67
   8     0 89
   6     1 0
   5     1 3
   4     1 4
   3     1
   3     1 8
   2     2
   2     2 2
   1     2
   1     2
   1     2
   1     3 0
```

```
Stem-and-leaf of TOTAL        N = 50
Leaf Unit = 1.0

   4     0 1334
  17     0 5666677888999
 (15)    1 000033333444444
  18     1 555566778999
   6     2 0344
   2     2
   2     3 0
   1     3 6
```

2.100 Refer to Exercise 2.99. Summary statistics for the processing times are given in the MINITAB printout below.

a. Calculate the z-score corresponding to the maximum processing time guideline you developed in Exercise 2.99 for each department, and for the total processing time.

b. Calculate the maximum processing time corresponding to a z-score of 3 for each of the departments. What percentage of the orders exceed these guidelines? How does this agree with Chebyshev's Rule and the Empirical Rule?

c. Repeat part **b** using a z-score of 2.

MINITAB Output for Exercise 2.100

	N	MEAN	MEDIAN	TRMEAN	STDEV	SEMEAN
MKT	50	4.766	5.400	4.732	2.584	0.365
ENG	50	5.044	4.500	4.798	3.835	0.542
ACC	50	3.652	0.800	2.548	6.256	0.885
TOTAL	50	13.462	13.750	13.043	6.820	0.965

	MIN	MAX	Q1	Q3
MKT	0.100	11.000	2.825	6.250
ENG	0.400	14.400	1.775	7.225
ACC	0.100	30.000	0.200	3.725
TOTAL	1.800	36.200	8.075	16.600

d. Compare the percentage of "lost" quotes with corresponding times that exceed at least one of the guidelines in part **b** to the same percentage using the guidelines in part **c.** Which set of guidelines would you recommend be adopted? Why?

*2.101 A time series plot similar to the one shown here appeared in a recent advertisement for a well-known golf magazine. One person might interpret the plot's message as the longer you subscribe to the magazine, the better golfer you should become. Another person might interpret it as indicating that if you subscribe for 3 years, your game should improve dramatically.

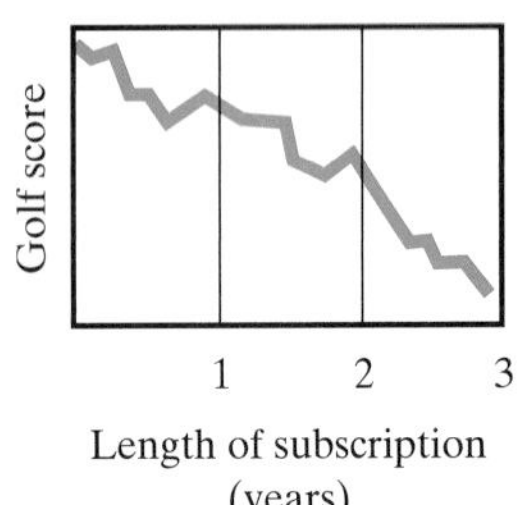

a. Explain why the plot can be interpreted in more than one way.
b. How could the plot be altered to rectify the current distortion?

2.102 A company has roughly the same number of people in each of five departments: Production, Sales, R&D, Maintenance, and Administration. The following table lists the number and type of major injuries that occurred in each department last year.

INJURY.DAT

Type of Injury	Department	Number of Injuries
Burn	Production	3
	Maintenance	6
Back strain	Production	2
	Sales	1
	R&D	1
	Maintenance	5
	Administration	2
Eye damage	Production	1
	Maintenance	2
	Administration	1
Deafness	Production	1
Cuts	Production	4
	Sales	1
	R&D	1
	Maintenance	10
Broken arm	Production	2
	Maintenance	2
Broken leg	Sales	1
	Maintenance	1
Broken finger	Administration	1
Concussion	Maintenance	3
	Administration	1
Hearing loss	Maintenance	2

a. Construct a Pareto diagram to identify which department or departments have the worst safety record.
b. Explode the Pareto diagram of part **a** to identify the most prevalent type of injury in the department with the worst safety record.

2.103 In some locations, radiation levels in homes are measured at well above normal background levels in the environment. As a result, many architects and builders are making design changes to ensure adequate air exchange so that radiation will not be "trapped" in homes. In one such location, 50 homes' levels were measured, and the mean level was 10 parts per billion (ppb), the median was 8 ppb, and the standard deviation was 3 ppb. Background levels in this location are at about 4 ppb.

a. Based on these results, is the distribution of the 50 homes' radiation levels symmetric, skewed to the left, or skewed to the right? Why?
b. Use both Chebyshev's Rule and the Empirical Rule to describe the distribution of radiation levels. Which do you think is most appropriate in this case? Why?
c. Use the results from part **b** to approximate the number of homes in this sample that have radiation levels above the background level.
d. Suppose another home is measured at a location 10 miles from the one sampled, and has a level of 20 ppb. What is the z-score for this measurement relative to the 50 homes sampled in the other location? Is it likely that this new measurement comes from the same distribution of radiation levels as the other 50? Why? How would you go about confirming your conclusion?

2.104 The accompanying table lists the unemployment rate in 1997 for a sample of nine countries.

UNEMPLOY.DAT

Country	Percent Unemployed
Australia	8.7
Canada	9.2
France	12.4
Germany	10.0
Great Britain	7.0
Italy	12.1
Japan	3.4
Sweden	9.9
United States	4.9

Source: Statistical Abstract of the United States: 1998, p. 842.

a. Find the mean and median unemployment rate in the sample. Interpret these values.
b. Find the standard deviation of the unemployment rate in the sample.
c. Calculate the z-scores of the unemployment rates of the United States and France.

d. Describe the information conveyed by the sign (positive or negative) of the z-scores you calculated in part **c.**

2.105 *Forbes* magazine (Jan. 11, 1999) reported the financial standings of each team in the National Football League (NFL). The next table lists current team value (without deduction for debt, except stadium debt) and operating income for each team in 1998.

a. Use a statistical software package to construct a stem-and-leaf plot for an NFL team's current value.
b. Does the distribution of current values appear to be skewed? Explain.
c. Use the stem-and-leaf plot of part **a** to find the median of the current values.
d. Calculate the z-scores for the Denver Broncos current value and operating income.
e. Interpret the two z-scores of part **d.**
f. Which other NFL teams have positive current value z-scores and negative operating income z-scores?
*g. Identify any outliers in the current value data set.
*h. Construct a graph to investigate a possible trend between an NFL team's current value and its operating income. What do you observe?

NFLVALUE.DAT

Team	Current Value ($ millions)	Operating Income ($ millions)
Dallas Cowboys	663	56.7
Washington Redskins	607	48.8
Tampa Bay Buccaneers	502	41.2
Carolina Panthers	488	18.8
New England Patriots	460	13.5
Miami Dolphins	446	32.9
Denver Broncos	427	5.0
Jacksonville Jaguars	419	29.3
Baltimore Ravens	408	33.2
Seattle Seahawks	399	6.4
Pittsburgh Steelers	397	15.5
Cincinnati Bengals	394	3.4
St. Louis Rams	390	33.2
New York Giants	376	25.2
San Francisco 49ers	371	12.7
Tennessee Titans	369	4.1
New York Jets	363	12.1
Kansas City Chiefs	353	31.0
Buffalo Bills	326	10.7
San Diego Chargers	323	8.2
Green Bay Packers	320	16.4
Philadelphia Eagles	318	19.1
New Orleans Saints	315	11.3
Chicago Bears	313	19.7
Minnesota Vikings	309	5.1
Atlanta Falcons	306	16.8
Indianapolis Colts	305	15.8
Arizona Cardinals	301	10.6
Oakland Raiders	299	17.3
Detroit Lions	293	16.4

Source: *Forbes*, Jan. 11, 1999.

*2.106 If not examined carefully, the graphical description of U.S. peanut production shown at the bottom of the page can be misleading.

a. Explain why the graph may mislead some readers.
b. Construct an undistorted graph of U.S. peanut production for the given years.

2.107 A study by the U.S. Public Research Interest Group found that in Massachusetts bank customers were charged lower fees than the national average for regular checking accounts, NOW accounts, and savings accounts. For regular checking accounts the Massachusetts mean was $190.06 per year, while the national mean was $201.94 (*Boston Globe*, Aug. 9, 1995). The referenced article did not explain how these averages were determined other than to say the national average was estimated from a sample of 271 banks in 25 states. Prepare a report that explains in detail how Massachusetts' mean could have been estimated. There are 245 banks in Massachusetts. Your answer should include a sampling plan, a measurement plan, and a calculation formula.

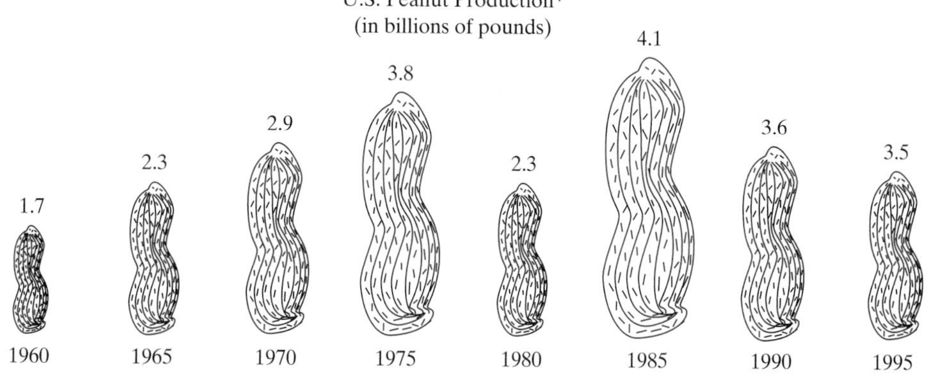

2.108 The U.S. Federal Trade Commission has recently begun assessing fines and other penalties against weight-loss clinics that make unsupported or misleading claims about the effectiveness of their programs. Brochures from two weight-loss clinics both advertise "statistical evidence" about the effectiveness of their programs. Clinic A claims that the *mean* weight loss during the first month is 15 pounds; Clinic B claims a *median* weight loss of 10 pounds.

a. Assuming the statistics are accurately calculated, which clinic would you recommend if you had no other information? Why?

b. Upon further research, the median and standard deviation for Clinic A are found to be 10 pounds and 20 pounds, respectively, while the mean and standard deviation for Clinic B are found to be 10 and 5 pounds, respectively. Both are based on samples of more than 100 clients. Describe the two clinics' weight-loss distributions as completely as possible given this additional information. What would you recommend to a prospective client now? Why?

c. Note that nothing has been said about how the sample of clients upon which the statistics are based was selected. What additional information would be important regarding the sampling techniques employed by the clinics?

2.109 The Baltimore Orioles had the highest player payroll in Major League Baseball (MLB) in 1998 while the Tampa Bay Devil Rays (an expansion team) had one of the lowest payrolls. The 1998 salaries for the rostered players on these two MLB teams were analyzed using SPSS. The SPSS histograms for each data set are displayed in the right column.

a. Compare the two histograms. Do you detect any differences in the shapes of the distributions? Skewness?

b. Interpret the descriptive statistics shown on the SPSS printouts.

2.110 The Age Discrimination in Employment Act mandates that workers 40 years of age or older be treated without regard to age in all phases of employment (hiring, promotions, firing, etc.). Age discrimination cases are of two types: *disparate treatment* and *disparate impact.* In the former, the issue is whether workers have been intentionally discriminated against. In the latter, the issue is whether employment practices adversely affect the protected class (i.e., workers 40 and over) even though no such effect was intended by the employer (Zabel, 1989). A small computer manufacturer laid off 10 of its 20 software engineers. The ages of all engineers at the time of the layoff are listed in the next table. Analyze the data to determine whether the company may be vulnerable to a disparate impact claim.

LAYOFF.DAT

Not laid off:	34	55	42	38	42	32	40	40	46	29
Laid off:	52	35	40	41	40	39	40	64	47	44

SPSS Histogram of the BALTIMORE Salaries, Ex. 2.109

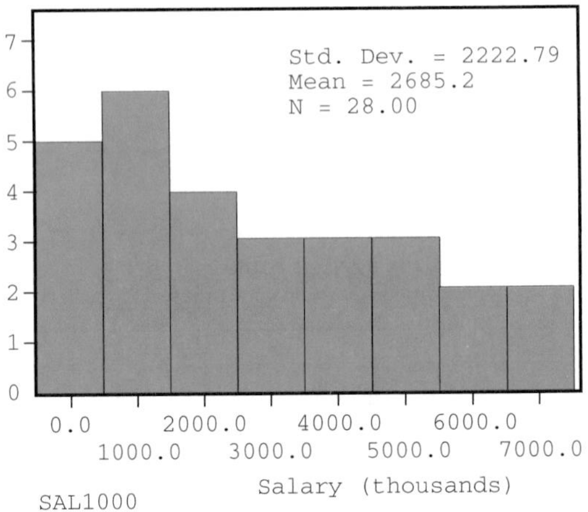

SPSS Histogram of the TAMPA BAY Salaries, Ex. 2.109

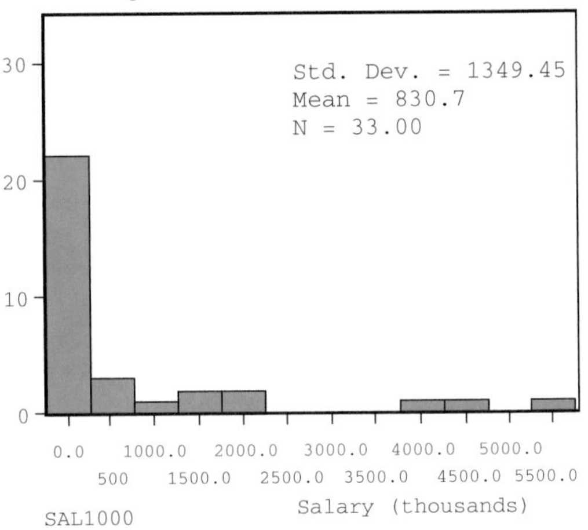

*2.111 A national chain of automobile oil-change franchises claims that "your hood will be open for less than 12 minutes when we service your car." To check their claim, an undercover consumer reporter from a local television station monitored the "hood time" of 25 consecutive customers at one of the chain's franchises. The resulting data are shown on p. 113. Construct a time series plot for these data and describe in words what it reveals.

2.112 The automobile sales in the United States (in thousands of cars) for the "Big Three" U.S. manufacturers (Ford, General Motors, and Chrysler), European manufacturers, and Japanese manufacturers for 1995 are reported in the table on p.113.

HOODTIME.DAT

Customer Number	Hood Open (Minutes)	Customer Number	Hood Open (Minutes)
1	11.50	14	12.50
2	13.50	15	13.75
3	12.25	16	12.00
4	15.00	17	11.50
5	14.50	18	14.25
6	13.75	19	15.50
7	14.00	20	13.00
8	11.00	21	18.25
9	12.75	22	11.75
10	11.50	23	12.50
11	11.00	24	11.25
12	13.00	25	14.75
13	16.25		

a. Construct a relative frequency bar graph for these data.

b. *Stacking* is the combining of all bars in a bar graph into a single bar, by drawing one on top of the other and distinguishing one from another by the use of colors or patterns. Stack the relative frequencies of the five car manufacturers' sales.

c. What information about the U.S. automobile market is reflected in your graph of part **a?**

d. What share of the U.S. automobile market has been captured by U.S. manufacturers?

CARSALES.DAT

Manufacturer	Sales
General Motors	229.7
Ford	131.2
Chrysler	58.3
Japanese	192.6
European	37.0
Total	648.8

Source: Wall Street Journal, December 6, 1995, p. B5.

2.113 Computer anxiety is defined as "the mixture of fear, apprehension, and hope that people feel when planning to interact, or when interacting with a computer." Researchers have found computer anxiety in people at all levels of society, including students, doctors, lawyers, secretaries, managers, and college professors. One profession for which little is known about the level and impact of computer anxiety is secondary technical education (STE). The extent of computer anxiety among STE teachers was investigated in the *Journal of Studies in Technical Careers* (Vol. 15, 1995). A sample of 116 teachers were administered the Computer Anxiety Scale (COMPAS) designed to measure level of computer anxiety. Scores, ranging from 10 to 50, were categorized as follows: very anxious (37–50); anxious/tense (33–36); some mild anxiety (27–32); generally relaxed/comfortable (20–26); very relaxed/confident (10–19). A summary of the COMPAS anxiety levels for the sample is provided in the table at the bottom of the page.

a. Graph and interpret the results.

b. One of the objectives of the research is to compare the computer anxiety levels of male and female STE teachers. Use the summary information in the table below to make the comparison.

	Male Teachers	Female Teachers	All Teachers
n	68	48	116
$\bar{x}$	26.4	24.5	25.6
s	10.6	11.2	10.8

Source: Gordon, H. R. D. "Analysis of the computer anxiety levels of secondary technical education teachers in West Virginia." *Journal of Studies in Technical Careers,* Vol. 15, No. 2, 1995, pp. 26–27 (Table 2).

Category	Score Range	Frequency	Relative Frequency
Very anxious	37–50	22	.19
Anxious/tense	33–36	8	.07
Some mild anxiety	27–32	23	.20
Generally relaxed/ comfortable	20–26	24	.21
Very relaxed/confident	10–19	39	.33
Totals		116	1.00

Source: Gordon, H. R. D. "Analysis of the computer anxiety levels of secondary technical education teachers in West Virginia." *Journal of Studies in Technical Careers,* Vol. 15, No. 2, 1995, pp. 26–27 (Table 1).

Real-World Case The Kentucky Milk Case–Part 1

(A Case Covering Chapters 1 and 2)

Many products and services are purchased by governments, cities, states, and businesses on the basis of sealed bids, and contracts are awarded to the lowest bidders. This process works extremely well in competitive markets, but it has the potential to increase the cost of purchasing if the markets are noncompetitive or if collusive practices are present. An investigation that began with a statistical analysis of bids in the Florida school milk market in 1986 led to the recovery of more than $33,000,000 from dairies who had conspired to rig the bids there in the 1980s. The investigation spread quickly to other states, and to date settlements and fines from dairies exceed $100,000,000 for school milk bidrigging in twenty other states. This case concerns a school milk bidrigging investigation in Kentucky.

Each year, the Commonwealth of Kentucky invites bids from dairies to supply half-pint containers of fluid milk products for its school districts. The products include whole white milk, low-fat white milk, and low-fat chocolate milk. In 13 school districts in northern Kentucky, the suppliers (dairies) were accused of "price-fixing," that is, conspiring to allocate the districts, so that the "winner" was predetermined. Since these districts are located in Boone, Campbell, and Kenton counties, the geographic market they represent is designated as the "tri-county" market. Between 1983 and 1991, two dairies—Meyer Dairy and Trauth Dairy—were the only bidders on the milk contracts in the school districts in the tri-county market. Consequently, these two companies were awarded all the milk contracts in the market. (In contrast, a large number of different dairies won the milk contracts for the school districts in the remainder of the northern Kentucky market—called the "surrounding" market.) The Commonwealth of Kentucky alleged that Meyer and Trauth conspired to allocate the districts in the tri-county market. To date, one of the dairies (Meyer) has admitted guilt, while the other (Trauth) steadfastly maintains its innocence.

The Commonwealth of Kentucky maintains a database on all bids received from the dairies competing for the milk contracts. Some of these data have been made available to you to analyze to determine whether there is empirical evidence of bid collusion in the tri-county market. The data, available in ASCII format on a 3.5" diskette, is described in detail below. Some background information on the data and important economic theory regarding bid collusion is also provided. Use this information to guide your analysis. Prepare a professional document which presents the results of your analysis and gives your opinion regarding collusion.

DATA. ASCII file name: MILK.DAT
Number of observations: 392

Variable	Column(s)	Type	Description
YEAR	1–4	QN	Year in which milk contract awarded
MARKET	6–15	QL	Northern Kentucky Market (TRI-COUNTY or SURROUND)
WINNER	17–30	QL	Name of winning dairy
WWBID	32–38	QN	Winning bid price of whole white milk (dollars per half-pint)
WWQTY	40–46	QN	Quantity of whole white milk purchased (number of half-pints)
LFWBID	48–53	QN	Winning bid price of low-fat white milk (dollars per half-pint)
LFWQTY	55–62	QN	Quantity of low-fat white milk purchased (number of half-pints)
LFCBID	64–69	QN	Winning bid price of low-fat chocolate milk (dollars per half-pint)
LFCQTY	71–78	QN	Quantity of low-fat chocolate milk purchased (number of half-pints)
DISTRICT	80–82	QL	School district number
KYFMO	84–89	QN	FMO minimum raw cost of milk (dollars per half-pint)
MILESM	91–93	QN	Distance (miles) from Meyer processing plant to school district
MILEST	95–97	QN	Distance (miles) from Trauth processing plant to school district
LETDATE	99–106	QL	Date on which bidding on milk contract began (month/day/year)

Background Information

Collusive Market Environment.

Certain economic features of a market create an environment in which collusion may be found. These basic features include:

1. *Few sellers and high concentration.* Only a few dairies control all or nearly all of the milk business in the market.

2. *Homogeneous products.* The products sold are essentially the same from the standpoint of the buyer (i.e., the school district).
3. *Inelastic demand.* Demand is relatively insensitive to price. (Note: The quantity of milk required by a school district is primarily determined by school enrollment, not price.)
4. *Similar costs.* The dairies bidding for the milk contracts face similar cost conditions. (Note: Approximately 60% of a dairy's production cost is raw milk, which is federally regulated. Meyer and Trauth are dairies of similar size and both bought their raw milk from the same supplier.)

Although these market structure characteristics create an environment which makes collusive behavior easier, they do not necessarily indicate the existence of collusion. An analysis of the actual bid prices may provide additional information about the degree of competition in the market.

Collusive Bidding Patterns. The analyses of patterns in sealed bids reveal much about the level of competition, or lack thereof, among the vendors serving the market. Consider the following bid analyses:

1. *Market shares.* A market share for a dairy is the number of milk half-pints supplied by the dairy over a given school year, divided by the total number of half-pints supplied to the entire market. One sign of potential collusive behavior is stable, nearly equal market shares over time for the dairies under investigation.
2. *Incumbency rates.* Market allocation is a common form of collusive behavior in bidrigging conspiracies. Typically, the same dairy controls the same school districts year after year. The incumbency rate for a market in a given school year is defined as the percentage of school districts that are won by the same vendor who won the previous year. An incumbency rate that exceeds 70% has been considered a sign of collusive behavior.
3. *Bid levels and dispersion.* In competitive sealed bid markets vendors do not share information about their bids. Consequently, more dispersion or variability among the bids is observed than in collusive markets, where vendors communicate about their bids and have a tendency to submit bids in close proximity to one another in an attempt to make the bidding appear competitive. Furthermore, in competitive markets the bid dispersion tends to be directly proportional to the level of the bid: When bids are submitted at relatively high levels, there is more variability among the bids than when they are submitted at or near marginal cost, which will be approximately the same among dairies in the same geographic market.
4. *Price versus cost/distance.* In competitive markets, bid prices are expected to track costs over time. Thus, if the market is competitive, the bid price of milk should be highly correlated with the raw milk cost. Lack of such a relationship is another sign of collusion. Similarly, bid price should be correlated to the distance the product must travel from the processing plant to the school (due to delivery costs) in a competitive market.
5. *Bid sequence.* School milk bids are submitted over the spring and summer months, generally at the end of one school year and before the beginning of the next. When the bids are examined in sequence in competitive markets, the level of bidding is expected to fall as the bidding season progresses. (This phenomenon is attributable to the learning process that occurs during the season, with bids adjusted accordingly. Dairies may submit relatively high bids early in the season to "test the market," confident that volume can be picked up later if the early high bids lose. But, dairies who do not win much business early in the season are likely to become more aggressive in their bidding as the season progresses, driving price levels down.) Constant or slightly increasing price patterns of sequential bids in a market where a single dairy wins year after year is considered another indication of collusive behavior.
6. *Comparison of average winning bid prices.* Consider two similar markets, one in which bids are possibly rigged and the other in which bids are competitively determined. In theory, the mean winning price in the "rigged" market will be significantly higher than the mean price in the competitive market for each year in which collusion occurs.

Chapter 3

PROBABILITY

CONTENTS

STATISTICS IN ACTION

Where We've Been

We've identified inference, from a sample to a population, as the goal of statistics. And we've seen that to reach this goal, we must be able to describe a set of measurements. Thus, we explored the use of graphical and numerical methods for describing both quantitative and qualitative data sets.

Where We're Going

We now turn to the problem of making an inference. What is it that permits us to make the inferential jump from sample to population and then to give a measure of reliability for the inference? As you'll see, the answer is *probability*. This chapter is devoted to a study of probability—what it is and some of the basic concepts of the theory behind it.

Recall that one branch of statistics is concerned with decisions about a population based on sample information. You can see how this is accomplished more easily if you understand the relationship between population and sample—a relationship that becomes clearer if we reverse the statistical procedure of making inferences from sample to population. In this chapter then, we assume that the population is *known* and calculate the chances of obtaining various samples from the population. Thus, we show that probability is the reverse of statistics: In probability, we use the population information to infer the probable nature of the sample.

Probability plays an important role in inference-making. Suppose, for example, you have an opportunity to invest in an oil exploration company. Past records show that out of 10 previous oil drillings (a sample of the company's experiences), all 10 came up dry. What do you conclude? Do you think the chances are better than 50:50 that the company will hit a gusher? Should you invest in this company? Chances are, your answer to these questions will be an emphatic No. If the company's exploratory prowess is sufficient to hit a producing well 50% of the time, a record of 10 dry wells out of 10 drilled is an event that is just too improbable.

Or suppose you're playing poker with what your opponents assure you is a well-shuffled deck of cards. In three consecutive five-card hands, the person on your right is dealt four aces. Based on this sample of three deals, do you think the cards are being adequately shuffled? Again, your answer is likely to be No because dealing three hands of four aces is just too improbable if the cards were properly shuffled.

Note that the decisions concerning the potential success of the oil drilling company and the adequacy of card shuffling both involve knowing the chance—or probability—of a certain sample result. Both situations were contrived so that you could easily conclude that the probabilities of the sample results were small. Unfortunately, the probabilities of many observed sample results aren't so easy to evaluate intuitively. For these cases we will need the assistance of a theory of probability.

3.1 EVENTS, SAMPLE SPACES, AND PROBABILITY

Let's begin our treatment of probability with simple examples that are easily described. With the aid of simple examples, we can introduce important definitions that will help us develop the notion of probability more easily.

Suppose a coin is tossed once and the up face is recorded. The result we see and record is called an *observation,* or *measurement,* and the process of making an observation is called an *experiment.* Notice that our definition of experiment is broader than the one used in the physical sciences, where you would picture test tubes, microscopes, and other laboratory equipment. Among other things, statistical experiments may include recording an Internet user's preference for a Web browser, recording a change in the Dow Jones Industrial Average from one day to the next, recording the weekly sales of a business firm, and counting the number of errors on a page of an accountant's ledger. The point is that a statistical experiment can be almost any act of observation as long as the outcome is uncertain.

DEFINITION 3.1

An **experiment** is an act or process of observation that leads to a single outcome that cannot be predicted with certainty.

Consider another simple experiment consisting of tossing a die and observing the number on the up face. The six basic possible outcomes to this experiment are:

1. Observe a 1
2. Observe a 2
3. Observe a 3
4. Observe a 4
5. Observe a 5
6. Observe a 6

Note that if this experiment is conducted once, *you can observe one and only one of these six basic outcomes, and the outcome cannot be predicted with certainty.* Also, these possibilities cannot be decomposed into more basic outcomes. Because observing the outcome of an experiment is similar to selecting a sample from a population, the basic possible outcomes to an experiment are called *sample points.**

DEFINITION 3.2

A **sample point** is the most basic outcome of an experiment.

EXAMPLE 3.1 Two coins are tossed, and their up faces are recorded. List all the sample points for this experiment.

Solution Even for a seemingly trivial experiment, we must be careful when listing the sample points. At first glance, we might expect three basic outcomes: Observe two heads, Observe two tails, or Observe one head and one tail. However, further reflection reveals that the last of these, Observe one head and one tail, can be decomposed into two outcomes: Head on coin 1, Tail on coin 2; and Tail on coin 1, Head on coin 2.† Thus, we have four sample points:

1. Observe HH
2. Observe HT
3. Observe TH
4. Observe TT

where H in the first position means "Head on coin 1," H in the second position means "Head on coin 2," and so on.

We often wish to refer to the collection of all the sample points of an experiment. This collection is called the *sample space* of the experiment. For example, there are six sample points in the sample space associated with the die-toss experiment. The sample spaces for the experiments discussed thus far are shown in Table 3.1.

DEFINITION 3.3

The **sample space** of an experiment is the collection of all its sample points.

*Alternatively, the term "simple event" can be used.

†Even if the coins are identical in appearance, there are, in fact, two distinct coins. Thus, the designation of one coin as coin 1 and the other coin as coin 2 is legitimate in any case.

TABLE 3.1 Experiments and Their Sample Spaces

Experiment: Observe the up face on a coin.
Sample space: 1. Observe a head
2. Observe a tail

This sample space can be represented in set notation as a set containing two sample points:

$$S: \{H, T\}$$

where H represents the sample point Observe a head and T represents the sample point Observe a tail.

Experiment: Observe the up face on a die.
Sample space: 1. Observe a 1
2. Observe a 2
3. Observe a 3
4. Observe a 4
5. Observe a 5
6. Observe a 6

This sample space can be represented in set notation as a set of six sample points:

$$S: \{1, 2, 3, 4, 5, 6\}$$

Experiment: Observe the up faces on two coins.
Sample space: 1. Observe HH
2. Observe HT
3. Observe TH
4. Observe TT

This sample space can be represented in set notation as a set of four sample points:

$$S: \{HH, HT, TH, TT\}$$

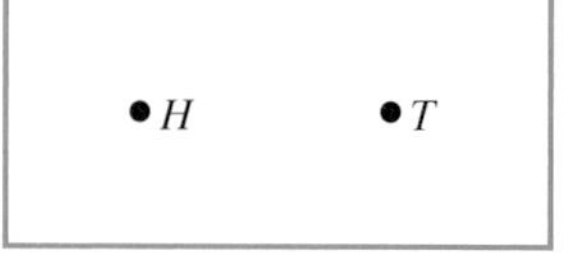

a. Experiment: Observe the up face on a coin

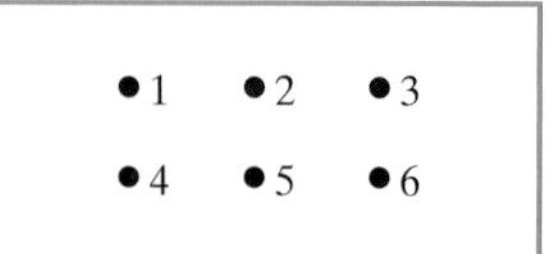

b. Experiment: Observe the up face on a die

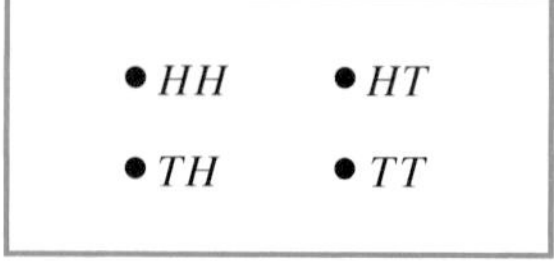

c. Experiment: Observe the up faces on two coins

FIGURE 3.1
Venn diagrams for the three experiments from Table 3.1

Just as graphs are useful in describing sets of data, a pictorial method for presenting the sample space will often be useful. Figure 3.1 shows such a representation for each of the experiments in Table 3.1. In each case, the sample space is shown as a closed figure, labeled S, containing all possible sample points. Each sample point is represented by a solid dot (i.e., a "point") and labeled accordingly. Such graphical representations are called **Venn diagrams.**

Now that we know that an experiment will result in *only one* basic outcome—called a sample point—and that the sample space is the collection of all possible sample points, we're ready to discuss the probabilities of the sample points. You've undoubtedly used the term *probability* and have some intuitive idea about its meaning. Probability is generally used synonymously with "chance," "odds," and similar concepts. For example, if a fair coin is tossed, we might reason that both the sample points, Observe a head and Observe a tail, have the same *chance* of occurring. Thus, we might state that "the probability of observing a head is 50%" or "the *odds* of seeing a head are 50:50." Both of these statements are based on an informal knowledge of probability. We'll begin our treatment of probability by using such informal concepts and then solidify what we mean later.

The probability of a sample point is a number between 0 and 1 inclusive that measures the likelihood that the outcome will occur when the experiment is performed. This number is usually taken to be the relative frequency of the occurrence of a sample point in a very long series of repetitions of an experiment.* For

*The result derives from an axiom in probability theory called the **Law of Large Numbers.** Phrased informally, this law states that the relative frequency of the number of times that an outcome occurs when an experiment is replicated over and over again (i.e., a large number of times) approaches the theoretical probability of the outcome.

example, if we are assigning probabilities to the two sample points (Observe a head and Observe a tail) in the coin-toss experiment, we might reason that if we toss a balanced coin a very large number of times, the sample points Observe a head and Observe a tail will occur with the same relative frequency of .5.

Our reasoning is supported by Figure 3.2. The figure plots the relative frequency of the number of times that a head occurs when simulating (by computer) the toss of a coin N times, where N ranges from as few as 25 tosses to as many as 1,500 tosses of the coin. You can see that when N is large (i.e., $N = 1{,}500$), the relative frequency is converging to .5. Thus, the probability of each sample point in the coin-tossing experiment is .5.

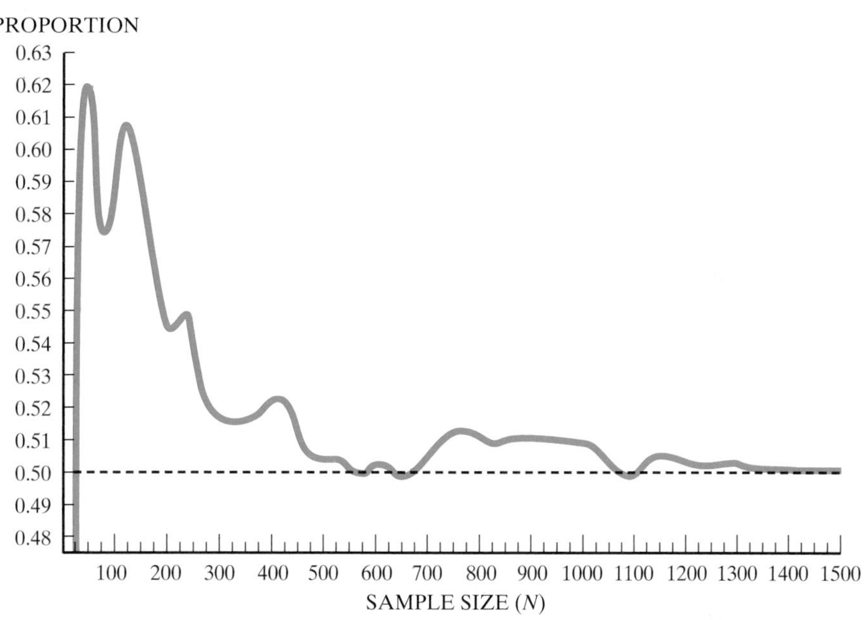

FIGURE 3.2
The proportion of heads in N tosses of a coin

For some experiments, we may have little or no information on the relative frequency of occurrence of the sample points; consequently, we must assign probabilities to the sample points based on general information about the experiment. For example, if the experiment is to invest in a business venture and to observe whether it succeeds or fails, the sample space would appear as in Figure 3.3. We are unlikely to be able to assign probabilities to the sample points of this experiment based on a long series of repetitions since unique factors govern each performance of this kind of experiment. Instead, we may consider factors such as the personnel managing the venture, the general state of the economy at the time, the rate of success of similar ventures, and any other pertinent information. If we finally decide that the venture has an 80% chance of succeeding, we assign a probability of .8 to the sample point Success. This probability can be interpreted as a measure of our degree of belief in the outcome of the business venture; that is, it is a subjective probability. Notice, however, that such probabilities should be based on expert information that is carefully assessed. If not, we may be misled on any decisions based on these probabilities or based on any calculations in which they appear. [*Note:* For a text that deals in detail with the subjective evaluation of probabilities, see Winkler (1972) or Lindley (1985).]

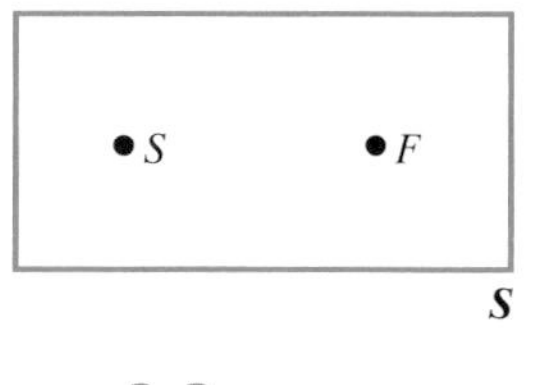

FIGURE 3.3
Experiment: Invest in a business venture and observe whether it succeeds (S) or fails (F)

No matter how you assign the probabilities to sample points, the probabilities assigned must obey two rules:

Probability Rules for Sample Points

1. All sample point probabilities *must* lie between 0 and 1 inclusive.
2. The probabilities of all the sample points within a sample space *must* sum to 1.

Assigning probabilities to sample points is easy for some experiments. For example, if the experiment is to toss a fair coin and observe the face, we would probably all agree to assign a probability of $\frac{1}{2}$ to the two sample points, Observe a head and Observe a tail. However, many experiments have sample points whose probabilities are more difficult to assign.

EXAMPLE 3.2

A retail computer store sells two basic types of personal computers (PCs): standard desktop units and laptop units. Thus the owner must decide how many of each type of PC to stock. An important factor affecting the solution is the proportion of customers who purchase each type of PC. Show how this problem might be formulated in the framework of an experiment with sample points and a sample space. Indicate how probabilities might be assigned to the sample points.

Solution If we use the term *customer* to refer to a person who purchases one of the two types of PCs, the experiment can be defined as the entrance of a customer and the observation of which type of PC is purchased. There are two sample points in the sample space corresponding to this experiment:

D: {The customer purchases a standard desktop unit}

L: {The customer purchases a laptop unit}

The difference between this and the coin-toss experiment becomes apparent when we attempt to assign probabilities to the two sample points. What probability should we assign to the sample point D? If you answer .5, you are assuming that the events D and L should occur with equal likelihood, just like the sample points Heads and Tails in the coin-toss experiment. But assignment of sample point probabilities for the PC purchase experiment is not so easy. Suppose a check of the store's records indicates that 80% of its customers purchase desktop units. Then it might be reasonable to approximate the probability of the sample point D as .8 and that of the sample point L as .2. Here we see that sample points are not always equally likely, so assigning probabilities to them can be complicated—particularly for experiments that represent real applications (as opposed to coin- and die-toss experiments).

Although the probabilities of sample points are often of interest in their own right, it is usually probabilities of collections of sample points that are important. Example 3.3 demonstrates this point.

EXAMPLE 3.3

A fair die is tossed, and the up face is observed. If the face is even, you win $1. Otherwise, you lose $1. What is the probability that you win?

Solution Recall that the sample space for this experiment contains six sample points:

$$S:\{1, 2, 3, 4, 5, 6\}$$

Since the die is balanced, we assign a probability of $1/6$ to each of the sample points in this sample space. An even number will occur if one of the sample points, Observe a 2, Observe a 4, or Observe a 6, occurs. A collection of sample points such as this is called an *event,* which we denote by the letter A. Since the event A contains three sample points—each with probability $1/6$—and since no sample points can occur simultaneously, we reason that the probability of A is the sum of the probabilities of the sample points in A. Thus, the probability of A is $1/6 + 1/6 + 1/6 = 1/2$. This implies that, *in the long run,* you will win \$1 half the time and lose \$1 half the time.

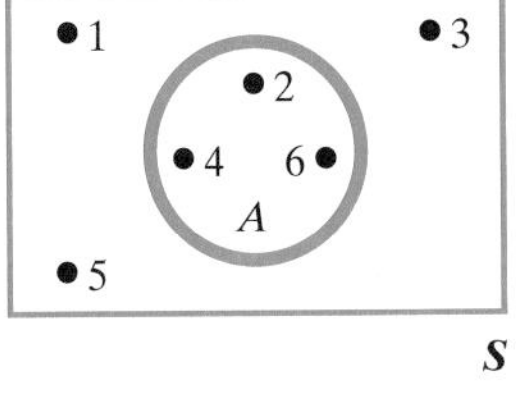

FIGURE 3.4
Die-toss experiment with event *A:* Observe an even number

Figure 3.4 is a Venn diagram depicting the sample space associated with a die-toss experiment and the event A, Observe an even number. The event A is represented by the closed figure inside the sample space S. This closed figure A contains all the sample points that comprise it.

To decide which sample points belong to the set associated with an event A, test each sample point in the sample space S. If event A occurs, then that sample point is in the event A. For example, the event A, Observe an even number, in the die-toss experiment will occur if the sample point Observe a 2 occurs. By the same reasoning, the sample points Observe a 4 and Observe a 6 are also in event A.

To summarize, we have demonstrated that an event can be defined in words or it can be defined as a specific set of sample points. This leads us to the following general definition of an event:

DEFINITION 3.4

An **event** is a specific collection of sample points.

EXAMPLE 3.4

Consider the experiment of tossing two *unbalanced* coins. Because the coins are *not* balanced, their outcomes (H or T) are not equiprobable. Suppose the correct probabilities associated with the sample points are given in the table. [*Note:* The necessary properties for assigning probabilities to sample points are satisfied.]

Consider the events

A: {Observe exactly one head}

B: {Observe at least one head}

Calculate the probability of A and the probability of B.

Sample Point	Probability
HH	$4/9$
HT	$2/9$
TH	$2/9$
TT	$1/9$

Solution Event A contains the sample points HT and TH. Since two or more sample points cannot occur at the same time, we can easily calculate the probability of event A by summing the probabilities of the two sample points. Thus, the probability of observing exactly one head (event A), denoted by the symbol $P(A)$, is

$$P(A) = P(\text{Observe } HT) + P(\text{Observe } TH) = \tfrac{2}{9} + \tfrac{2}{9} = \tfrac{4}{9}$$

Similarly, since B contains the sample points HH, HT, and TH,

$$P(B) = \tfrac{4}{9} + \tfrac{2}{9} + \tfrac{2}{9} = \tfrac{8}{9}$$

The preceding example leads us to a general procedure for finding the probability of an event A:

Probability of an Event

The probability of an event A is calculated by summing the probabilities of the sample points in the sample space for A.

Thus, we can summarize the steps for calculating the probability of any event, as indicated in the next box.

Steps for Calculating Probabilities of Events

1. Define the experiment; that is, describe the process used to make an observation and the type of observation that will be recorded.
2. List the sample points.
3. Assign probabilities to the sample points.
4. Determine the collection of sample points contained in the event of interest.
5. Sum the sample point probabilities to get the event probability.

EXAMPLE 3.5 Diversity training of employees is the latest trend in U.S. business. *USA Today* (Aug. 15, 1995) reported on the primary reasons businesses give for making diversity training part of their strategic planning process. The reasons are summarized in Table 3.2. Assume that one business is selected at random from all U.S. businesses that use diversity training and the primary reason is determined.

a. Define the experiment that generated the data in Table 3.2, and list the sample points.

TABLE 3.2 Primary Reasons for Diversity Training

Reason	Percentage
Comply with personnel policies (CPP)	7
Increase productivity (IP)	47
Stay competitive (SC)	38
Social responsibility (SR)	4
Other (O)	4
Total	100%

Source: USA Today, August 15, 1995.

b. Assign probabilities to the sample points.

c. What is the probability that the primary reason for diversity training is business related; that is, related to competition or productivity?

d. What is the probability that social responsibility is not a primary reason for diversity training?

Solution

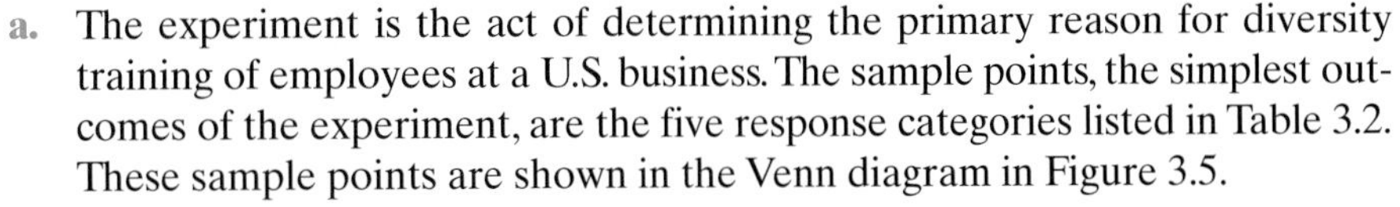

a. The experiment is the act of determining the primary reason for diversity training of employees at a U.S. business. The sample points, the simplest outcomes of the experiment, are the five response categories listed in Table 3.2. These sample points are shown in the Venn diagram in Figure 3.5.

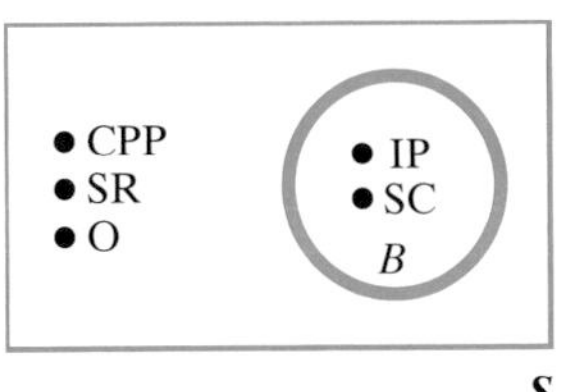

FIGURE 3.5
Venn diagram for diversity training survey

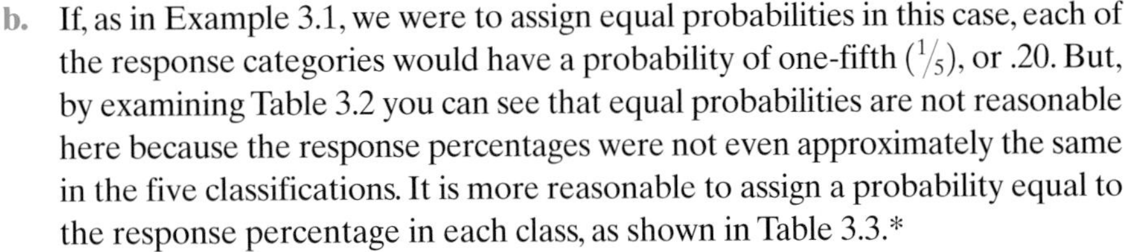

b. If, as in Example 3.1, we were to assign equal probabilities in this case, each of the response categories would have a probability of one-fifth ($^1/_5$), or .20. But, by examining Table 3.2 you can see that equal probabilities are not reasonable here because the response percentages were not even approximately the same in the five classifications. It is more reasonable to assign a probability equal to the response percentage in each class, as shown in Table 3.3.*

c. Let the symbol B represent the event that the primary reason for diversity training is business related. B is not a sample point because it consists of more than one of the response classifications (the sample points). In fact, as shown in Figure 3.5, B consists of two sample points, IP and SC. The probability of B is defined to be the sum of the probabilities of the sample points in B.

$$P(B) = P(\text{IP}) + P(\text{SC}) = .47 + .38 = .85$$

TABLE 3.3 Sample Point Probabilities for Diversity Training Survey

Sample Point	Probability
CPP	.07
IP	.47
SC	.38
SR	.04
O	.04

d. Let NSR represent the event that social responsibility is not a primary reason for diversity training. Then NSR consists of all sample points except SR, and the probability is the sum of the corresponding sample point probabilities:

$$P(NSR) = P(\text{CPP}) + P(\text{IP}) + P(\text{SC}) + P(\text{O})$$
$$= .07 + .47 + .38 + .04 = .96$$

EXAMPLE 3.6

You have the capital to invest in two of four ventures, each of which requires approximately the same amount of investment capital. Unknown to you, two of the investments will eventually fail and two will be successful. You research the four ventures because you think that your research will increase your probability of a successful choice over a purely random selection, and you eventually decide on two. What is the lower limit of your probability of selecting the two best out of four? That is, if you used none of the information generated by your research, and selected two ventures at random, what is the probability that you would select the two successful ventures? At least one?

Solution

Denote the two successful enterprises as S_1 and S_2 and the two failing enterprises as F_1 and F_2. The experiment involves a random selection of two out of the four ventures, and each possible pair of ventures represents a sample point. The six sample points that make up the sample space are

*The response percentages were based on a sample of U.S. businesses; consequently, these assigned probabilities are estimates of the true population-response percentages. You'll learn how to measure the reliability of probability estimates in Chapter 5.

1. (S_1, S_2)
2. (S_1, F_1)
3. (S_1, F_2)
4. (S_2, F_1)
5. (S_2, F_2)
6. (F_1, F_2)

The next step is to assign probabilities to the sample points. If we assume that the choice of any one pair is as likely as any other, then the probability of each sample point is $1/6$. Now check to see which sample points result in the choice of two successful ventures. Only one such sample point exists—namely, (S_1, S_2). Therefore, the probability of choosing two successful ventures out of the four is

$$P(S_1, S_2) = 1/6$$

The event of selecting at least one of the two successful ventures includes all the sample points except (F_1, F_2).

$$\begin{aligned} P(\text{Select at least one success}) &= P(S_1, S_2) + P(S_1, F_1) + P(S_1, F_2) + P(S_2, F_1) \\ &\quad + P(S_2, F_2) \\ &= 1/6 + 1/6 + 1/6 + 1/6 + 1/6 = 5/6 \end{aligned}$$

Therefore, the worst that you could do in selecting two ventures out of four may not be too bad. With a random selection, the probability of selecting two successful ventures will be $1/6$ and the probability of selecting at least one successful venture out of two is $5/6$. ✶

The preceding examples have one thing in common: The number of sample points in each of the sample spaces was small; hence, the sample points were easy to identify and list. How can we manage this when the sample points run into the thousands or millions? For example, suppose you wish to select five business ventures from a group of 1,000. Then each different group of five ventures would represent a sample point. How can you determine the number of sample points associated with this experiment?

One method of determining the number of sample points for a complex experiment is to develop a counting system. Start by examining a simple version of the experiment. For example, see if you can develop a system for counting the number of ways to select two ventures from a total of four (this is exactly what was done in Example 3.6). If the ventures are represented by the symbols V_1, V_2, V_3, and V_4, the sample points could be listed in the following pattern:

$$\begin{array}{lll} (V_1, V_2) & (V_2, V_3) & (V_3, V_4) \\ (V_1, V_3) & (V_2, V_4) & \\ (V_1, V_4) & & \end{array}$$

Note the pattern and now try a more complex situation—say, sampling three ventures out of five. List the sample points and observe the pattern. Finally, see if you can deduce the pattern for the general case. Perhaps you can program a computer to produce the matching and counting for the number of samples of 5 selected from a total of 1,000.

A second method of determining the number of sample points for an experiment is to use **combinatorial mathematics.** This branch of mathematics is concerned with developing counting rules for given situations. For example, there is a simple rule for finding the number of different samples of five ventures selected from 1,000. This rule, called the **combinatorial rule,** is given by the formula

$$\binom{N}{n} = \frac{N!}{n!(N-n)!}$$

where N is the number of elements in the population; n is the number of elements in the sample; and the factorial symbol (!) means that, say,

$$n! = n(n-1)(n-2)\cdots(3)(2)(1)$$

Thus, $5! = 5 \cdot 4 \cdot 3 \cdot 2 \cdot 1$. (The quantity 0! is defined to be equal to 1.)

EXAMPLE 3.7

Refer to Example 3.6 in which we selected two ventures from four in which to invest. Use the combinatorial counting rule to determine how many different selections can be made.

Solution

For this example, $N = 4$, $n = 2$, and

$$\binom{4}{2} = \frac{4!}{2!2!} = \frac{4 \cdot 3 \cdot 2 \cdot 1}{(2 \cdot 1)(2 \cdot 1)} = 6$$

You can see that this agrees with the number of sample points obtained in Example 3.6.

EXAMPLE 3.8

Suppose you plan to invest equal amounts of money in each of five business ventures. If you have 20 ventures from which to make the selection, how many different samples of five ventures can be selected from the 20?

Solution

For this example, $N = 20$ and $n = 5$. Then the number of different samples of 5 that can be selected from the 20 ventures is

$$\binom{20}{5} = \frac{20!}{5!(20-5)!} = \frac{20!}{5!15!}$$

$$= \frac{20 \cdot 19 \cdot 18 \cdot \cdots \cdot 3 \cdot 2 \cdot 1}{(5 \cdot 4 \cdot 3 \cdot 2 \cdot 1)(15 \cdot 14 \cdot 13 \cdot \cdots \cdot 3 \cdot 2 \cdot 1)} = 15{,}504$$

The symbol $\binom{N}{n}$, meaning the **number of combinations of N elements taken n at a time,** is just one of a large number of counting rules that have been developed by combinatorial mathematicians. This counting rule applies to situations in which the experiment calls for selecting n elements from a total of N elements, without replacing each element before the next is selected. If you are interested in learning other methods for counting sample points for various types of experiments, you will find a few of the basic counting rules in Appendix A. Others can be found in the chapter references.

EXERCISES 3.1–3.15

Learning the Mechanics

3.1 An experiment results in one of the following sample points: E_1, E_2, E_3, E_4, or E_5.

a. Find $P(E_3)$ if $P(E_1) = .1$, $P(E_2) = .2$, $P(E_4) = .1$, and $P(E_5) = .1$.

b. Find $P(E_3)$ if $P(E_1) = P(E_3)$, $P(E_2) = .1$, $P(E_4) = .2$, and $P(E_5) = .1$.

c. Find $P(E_3)$ if $P(E_1) = P(E_2) = P(E_4) = P(E_5) = .1$.

3.2 The accompanying diagram describes the sample space of a particular experiment and events A and B.

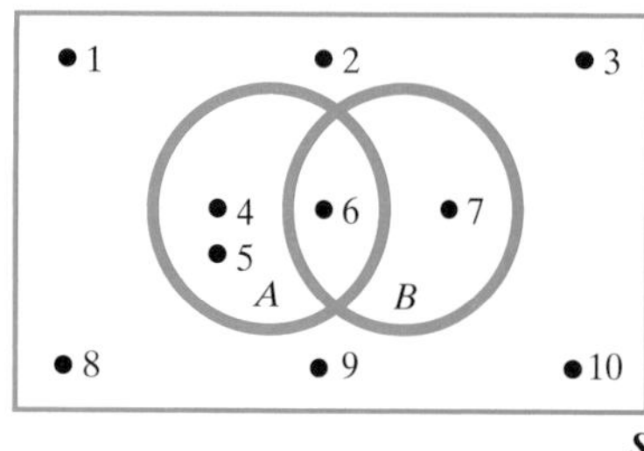

a. What is this type of diagram called?

b. Suppose the sample points are equally likely. Find $P(A)$ and $P(B)$.

c. Suppose $P(1) = P(2) = P(3) = P(4) = P(5) = 1/20$ and $P(6) = P(7) = P(8) = P(9) = P(10) = 3/20$. Find $P(A)$ and $P(B)$.

3.3 The sample space for an experiment contains five sample points with probabilities as shown in the table. Find the probability of each of the following events:

Sample Points	Probabilities
1	.05
2	.20
3	.30
4	.30
5	.15

A: {Either 1, 2, or 3 occurs}
B: {Either 1, 3, or 5 occurs}
C: {4 does not occur}

3.4 Compute each of the following:

a. $\binom{9}{4}$ b. $\binom{7}{2}$ c. $\binom{4}{4}$ d. $\binom{5}{0}$ e. $\binom{6}{5}$

3.5 Two marbles are drawn at random and without replacement from a box containing two blue marbles and three red marbles. Determine the probability of observing each of the following events:

A: {Two blue marbles are drawn}
B: {A red and a blue marble are drawn}
C: {Two red marbles are drawn}

3.6 Simulate the experiment described in Exercise 3.5 using any five identically shaped objects, two of which are one color and three, another. Mix the objects, draw two, record the results, and then replace the objects. Repeat the experiment a large number of times (at least 100). Calculate the proportion of time events A, B, and C occur. How do these proportions compare with the probabilities you calculated in Exercise 3.5? Should these proportions equal the probabilities? Explain.

Applying the Concepts

3.7 *Total Quality Management* (TQM) has been defined as responsive customer service through continuously improved and redesigned work processes (*Quality Progress*, July 1995). In evaluating perceptions of TQM, a University of North Carolina in Charlotte study asked 159 employees to indicate how strongly they agreed or disagreed with a series of statements including: "I believe that management is committed to TQM." The following responses were received:

Strongly Agree	Agree	Neither Agree nor Disagree	Disagree	Strongly Disagree
30	64	41	18	6

Source: Buch, K., and Shelnut, J.W. "UNC Charlotte measures the effects of its quality initiative." *Quality Progress*, July 1995, p. 75 (Table 2).

a. Define the experiment and list the sample points.

b. Assign probabilities to the sample points.

c. What is the probability that an employee agrees or strongly agrees with the above statement?

d. What is the probability that an employee does not strongly agree with the above statement?

3.8 The table on page 128, extracted from *Railway Age* (May 1999), lists the number of carloads of different types of commodities that were shipped by the major U.S. railroads during the week of April 10, 1999. Suppose the computer record for a carload shipped during the week of April 10th is randomly selected from a masterfile of all carloads shipped that week and the commodity type shipped is identified.

a. List or describe the sample points in this experiment.

b. Find the probability of each sample point.

c. What is the probability that the rail car was transporting automobiles? Nonagricultural products?

d. What is the probability that the rail car contained chemicals or coal?

Table for Exercise 3.8

Type of Commodity	Number of Carloads
Agricultural products	41,690
Chemicals	38,331
Coal	124,595
Forest products	21,929
Metallic ores and minerals	34,521
Motor vehicles and equipment	22,906
Nonmetallic minerals and products	37,416
Other carloads	14,382
Total	335,770

Source: *Railway Age*, May 1999, p. 1.

e. One of the carloads shipped that week was in a boxcar with serial number 1003642. What is the probability that that particular carload would be the one randomly selected from the computer file? Justify your answer.

3.9 Of six cars produced at a particular factory between 8 and 10 A.M. last Monday morning, test runs revealed three of them to be "lemons." Nevertheless, three of the six cars were shipped to dealer A and the other three to dealer B. Dealer A received all three lemons. What is the probability of this event occurring if, in fact, the three cars shipped to dealer A were selected at random from the six produced?

3.10 *The American Journal of Public Health* (July 1995) published a study on unintentional carbon monoxide (CO) poisoning of Colorado residents. A total of 981 cases of CO poisoning were reported during a six-year period. Each case was classified as fatal or nonfatal and by source of exposure. The number of cases occurring in each of the categories is shown in the next table. Assume that one of the 981 cases of unintentional CO poisoning is randomly selected.

a. List all sample points for this experiment.

b. What is the set of all sample points called?

Source of Exposure	Fatal	Nonfatal	Total
Fire	63	53	116
Auto exhaust	60	178	238
Furnace	18	345	363
Kerosene or spaceheater	9	18	27
Appliance	9	63	72
Other gas-powered motor	3	73	76
Fireplace	0	16	16
Other	3	19	22
Unknown	9	42	51
Total	174	807	981

Source: Cook, M. C., Simon, P. A., and Hoffman, R. E. "Unintentional carbon monoxide poisoning in Colorado, 1986 through 1991." *American Journal of Public Health,* Vol. 85, No. 7, July 1995, p. 989 (Table 1). American Public Health Association.

c. Let A be the event that the CO poisoning is caused by fire. Find $P(A)$.

d. Let B be the event that the CO poisoning is fatal. Find $P(B)$.

e. Let C be the event that the CO poisoning is caused by auto exhaust. Find $P(C)$.

f. Let D be the event that the CO poisoning is caused by auto exhaust and is fatal. Find $P(D)$.

g. Let E be the event that the CO poisoning is caused by fire but is nonfatal. Find $P(E)$.

3.11 Of 11,855 news stories broadcast on network television (ABC, NBC, or CBS) in 1998, only 118 focused on Hispanics or Hispanic-related issues. Since Hispanics comprise 11% of the U.S. population, some argue that a serious imbalance exists in news coverage of Hispanics. The National Association of Hispanic Journalists compiled the topics of the 118 Hispanic-related stories and reported them in the following table.

a. If a network news story were randomly selected from all that were broadcast in 1998, what is the probability that its topic was not related to Hispanics? Was related to Hispanics?

b. If a news story were randomly selected from the 118 Hispanic-related stories, what is the probability that it focused on crime? On crime or drugs? Not on politics or crime?

News Story Topic	Frequency	Percentage
Bilingual education	10	8.5
Crime	23	19.5
Immigration	10	8.5
Drugs	1	.8
Affirmative action	5	4.2
Environment	1	.8
Employment	3	2.5
Politics	27	22.9
Honors	3	2.5
Arts and culture	3	2.5
Health and safety	11	9.3
Disasters	5	4.2
Business	5	4.2
Sports	10	8.5
Religion	1	.8
Total	118	100

Source: *Hispanic Business,* September 1999, p. 68.

3.12 *Consumer Reports* magazine annually asks readers to evaluate their experiences in buying a new car during the previous year. Analysis of the questionnaires for a recent year revealed that readers' were most satisfied with the following three dealers (in no particular order): Infiniti, Saturn, and Saab (*Consumer Reports,* Apr. 1995).

a. List all possible sets of rankings for these top three dealers.

b. Assuming that each set of rankings in part **a** is equally likely, what is the probability that readers ranked

Saturn first? That readers ranked Saturn third? That readers ranked Saturn first and Infiniti second (which is, in fact, what they did)?

3.13 Handicappers for greyhound races express their belief about the probabilities that each greyhound will win a race in terms of **odds.** If the probability of event E is $P(E)$, then the *odds in favor of* E are $P(E)$ to $1 - P(E)$. Thus, if a handicapper assesses a probability of .25 that Oxford Shoes will win its next race, the odds in favor of Oxford Shoes are $^{25}/_{100}$ to $^{75}/_{100}$, or 1 to 3. It follows that the *odds against* E are $1 - P(E)$ to $P(E)$, or 3 to 1 against a win by Oxford Shoes. In general, if the odds in favor of event E are a to b, then $P(E) = a/(a + b)$.

a. A second handicapper assesses the probability of a win by Oxford Shoes to be $\frac{1}{3}$. According to the second handicapper, what are the odds in favor of Oxford Shoes winning?

b. A third handicapper assesses the odds in favor of Oxford Shoes to be 1 to 1. According to the third handicapper, what is the probability of Oxford Shoes winning?

c. A fourth handicapper assesses the odds against Oxford Shoes winning to be 3 to 2. Find this handicapper's assessment of the probability that Oxford Shoes will win.

3.14 In her September 9, 1990, *Parade Magazine* column, "Ask Marilyn," which is devoted to games of skill, puzzles, and mind-bending riddles, Marilyn vos Savant posed the following question:

Suppose you're on a game show, and you're given a choice of three doors. Behind one door is a car; behind the others, goats. You pick a door—say, #1—and the host, who knows what's behind the doors, opens another door—say #3—which has a goat. He then says to you, "Do you want to pick door #2?" Is it to your advantage to switch your choice?

Vos Savant's answer: "Yes, you should switch. The first door has a $\frac{1}{3}$ chance of winning [the car], but the second has a $\frac{2}{3}$ chance [of winning the car]." Vos Savant's answer elicited thousands of critical letters, many of them from Ph.D. mathematicians, who disagreed with her. Those who disagreed felt strongly that there is no advantage to switching. Who is correct, the Ph.D.s or vos Savant? By answering the following series of questions, you'll arrive at the correct solution.

a. Before the show is taped, the host randomly decides the door behind which to put the car; then the goats go behind the remaining two doors. List the sample points for this experiment.

b. Suppose you choose at random door #1. Now, form a new sample space for this event as follows: For each sample point in part **a** eliminate one of the remaining two doors that hides a goat. (This is the door that the host shows—always a goat.)

c. Refer to the altered sample points in part **b.** Assume your strategy is to keep door #1. Count the number of sample points for which this is a "winning" strategy (i.e., you win the car). Assuming equally likely sample points, what is the probability that you win the car?

d. Repeat part **c,** but assume your strategy is to always switch doors.

e. Based on the probabilities of parts **c** and **d,** is it to your advantage to switch your choice?

f. Repeat parts **b–e**, but assume you select door #2 at random.

g. Repeat parts **b–e**, but assume you select door #3 at random.

h. Demonstrate that your choice of doors does not impact your *long-run* strategy.

3.15 *Sustainable development* or *sustainable farming* means "finding ways to live and work the Earth without jeopardizing the future" (*Minneapolis Star Tribune,* June 20, 1992). Studies were conducted in five midwestern states to develop a profile of a sustainable farmer. The results revealed that farmers can be classified along a sustainability scale, depending on whether they are likely or unlikely to engage in the following practices: (1) Raise a broad mix of crops; (2) Raise livestock; (3) Use chemicals sparingly; (4) Use techniques for regenerating the soil, such as crop rotation.

a. List the different sets of classifications that are possible.

b. Suppose you are planning to interview farmers across the country to determine the frequency with which they fall into the classification sets you listed for part **a.** Since no information is yet available, assume initially that there is an equal chance of a farmer falling into any single classification set. Using that assumption, what is the probability that a farmer will be classified as unlikely on all four criteria (i.e., classified as a nonsustainable farmer)?

c. Using the same assumption as in part **b,** what is the probability that a farmer will be classified as likely on at least three of the criteria (i.e., classified as a near-sustainable farmer)?

3.2 UNIONS AND INTERSECTIONS

An event can often be viewed as a composition of two or more other events. Such events, which are called **compound events,** can be formed (composed) in two ways, as defined and illustrated here.

DEFINITION 3.5

The **union** of two events A and B is the event that occurs if either A or B or both occur on a single performance of the experiment. We denote the union of events A and B by the symbol $A \cup B$. $A \cup B$ consists of all the sample points that belong to *A or B or both.* (See Figure 3.6a.)

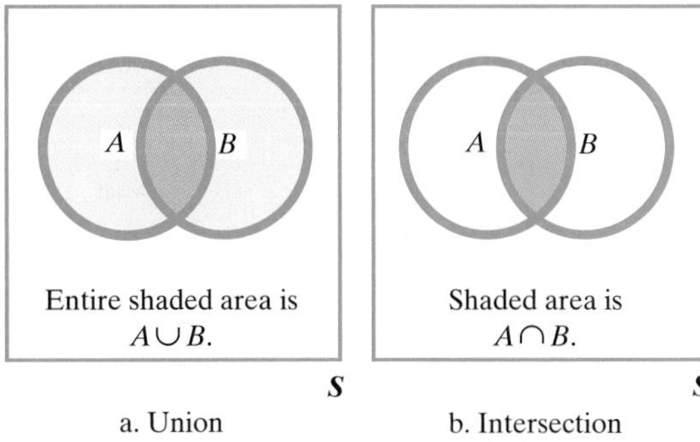

FIGURE 3.6
Venn diagrams for union and intersection

DEFINITION 3.6

The **intersection** of two events A and B is the event that occurs if both A and B occur on a single performance of the experiment. We write $A \cap B$ for the intersection of A and B. $A \cap B$ consists of all the sample points belonging to *both A and B.* (See Figure 3.6b.)

EXAMPLE 3.9 Consider the die-toss experiment. Define the following events:

A: {Toss an even number}
B: {Toss a number less than or equal to 3}

a. Describe $A \cup B$ for this experiment.
b. Describe $A \cap B$ for this experiment.
c. Calculate $P(A \cup B)$ and $P(A \cap B)$ assuming the die is fair.

Solution Draw the Venn diagram as shown in Figure 3.7.

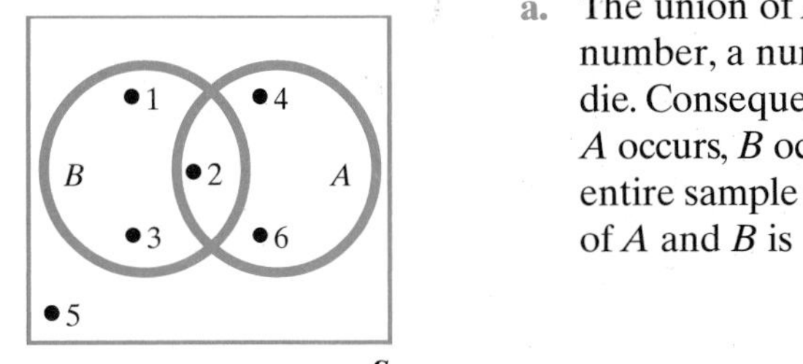

FIGURE 3.7
Venn diagram for die toss

a. The union of A and B is the event that occurs if we observe either an even number, a number less than or equal to 3, or both on a single throw of the die. Consequently, the sample points in the event $A \cup B$ are those for which A occurs, B occurs, or both A and B occur. Checking the sample points in the entire sample space, we find that the collection of sample points in the union of A and B is

$$A \cup B = \{1, 2, 3, 4, 6\}$$

b. The intersection of A and B is the event that occurs if we observe *both* an even number and a number less than or equal to 3 on a single throw of the die. Checking the sample points to see which imply the occurrence of *both* events A and B, we see that the intersection contains only one sample point:

$$A \cap B = \{2\}$$

In other words, the intersection of A and B is the sample point Observe a 2.

c. Recalling that the probability of an event is the sum of the probabilities of the sample points of which the event is composed, we have

$$\begin{aligned} P(A \cup B) &= P(1) + P(2) + P(3) + P(4) + P(6) \\ &= \tfrac{1}{6} + \tfrac{1}{6} + \tfrac{1}{6} + \tfrac{1}{6} + \tfrac{1}{6} = \tfrac{5}{6} \end{aligned}$$

and

$$P(A \cap B) = P(2) = \tfrac{1}{6}$$

EXAMPLE 3.10 Many firms undertake direct marketing campaigns to promote their products. The campaigns typically involve mailing information to millions of households. The response rates are carefully monitored to determine the demographic characteristics of respondents. By studying tendencies to respond, the firms can better target future mailings to those segments of the population most likely to purchase their products.

Suppose a distributor of mail-order tools is analyzing the results of a recent mailing. The probability of response is believed to be related to income and age. The percentages of the total number of respondents to the mailing are given by income and age classification in Table 3.4.

TABLE 3.4 Percentage of Respondents in Age-Income Classes

	Income		
Age	**<\$25,000**	**\$25,000–\$50,000**	**>\$50,000**
< 30 yrs	5%	12%	10%
30–50 yrs	14%	22%	16%
> 50 yrs	8%	10%	3%

Define the following events:

A: {A respondent's income is more than \$50,000}

B: {A respondent's age is 30 or more}

a. Find $P(A)$ and $P(B)$.

b. Find $P(A \cup B)$.

c. Find $P(A \cap B)$.

Solution Following the steps for calculating probabilities of events, we first note that the objective is to characterize the income and age distribution of respondents to the mailing. To accomplish this, we define the experiment to consist of selecting a respondent from the collection of all respondents and observing which income and age class he or she occupies. The sample points are the nine different age-income classifications:

E_1: {<30 yrs, <\$25,000} E_4: {<30 yrs, \$25,000–\$50,000} E_7: {<30 yrs, >\$50,000}
E_2: {30–50 yrs, <\$25,000} E_5: {30–50 yrs, \$25,000–\$50,000} E_8: {30–50 yrs, >\$50,000}
E_3: {>50 yrs, <\$25,000} E_6: {>50 yrs, \$25,000–\$50,000} E_9: {>50 yrs, >\$50,000}

Next, we assign probabilities to the sample points. If we blindly select one of the respondents, the probability that he or she will occupy a particular age-income classification is just the proportion, or relative frequency, of respondents in the classification. These proportions are given (as percentages) in Table 3.4. Thus,

$$P(E_1) = \text{Relative frequency of respondents in age-income class } \{<30 \text{ yrs}, <\$25{,}000\} = .05$$

$$P(E_2) = .14$$
$$P(E_3) = .08$$
$$P(E_4) = .12$$
$$P(E_5) = .22$$
$$P(E_6) = .10$$
$$P(E_7) = .10$$
$$P(E_8) = .16$$
$$P(E_9) = .03$$

You may verify that the sample points probabilities add to 1.

a. To find $P(A)$, we first determine the collection of sample points contained in event A. Since A is defined as {>\$50,000}, we see from Table 3.4 that A contains the three sample points represented by the last column of the table. In words, the event A consists of the income classification {>\$50,000} in all three age classifications. The probability of A is the sum of the probabilities of the sample points in A:

$$P(A) = P(E_7) + P(E_8) + P(E_9) = .10 + .16 + .03 = .29$$

Similarly, $B = \{\geq 30 \text{ yrs}\}$ consists of the six sample points in the second and third rows of Table 3.4:

$$P(B) = P(E_2) + P(E_3) + P(E_5) + P(E_6) + P(E_8) + P(E_9)$$
$$= .14 + .08 + .22 + .10 + .16 + .03 = .73$$

b. The union of events A and B, $A \cup B$, consists of all the sample points in *either A or B or both.* That is, the union of A and B consists of all respondents whose income exceeds \$50,000 *or* whose age is 30 or more. In Table 3.4 this is any sample point found in the third column *or* the last two rows. Thus,

$$P(A \cup B) = .10 + .14 + .22 + .16 + .08 + .10 + .03 = .83$$

c. The intersection of events A and B, $A \cap B$, consists of all sample points in *both A and B.* That is, the intersection of A and B consists of all respondents whose income exceeds \$50,000 *and* whose age is 30 or more. In Table 3.4 this is any sample point found in the third column *and* the last two rows. Thus,

$$P(A \cap B) = .16 + .03 = .19$$

✶

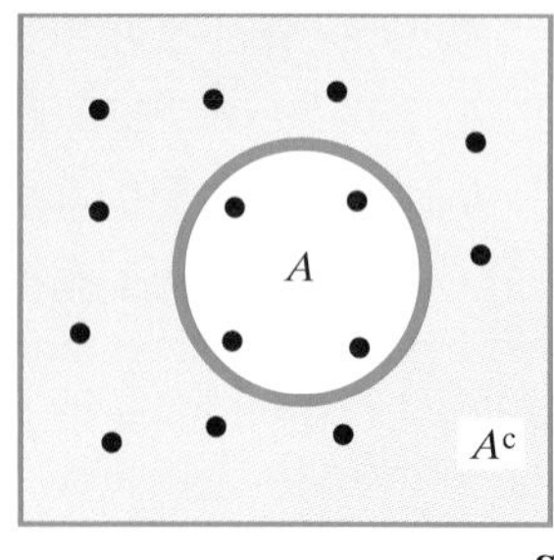

FIGURE 3.8
Venn diagram of complementary events

3.3 COMPLEMENTARY EVENTS

A very useful concept in the calculation of event probabilities is the notion of *complementary events:*

> **DEFINITION 3.7**
>
> The **complement** of an event A is the event that A does *not* occur—that is, the event consisting of all sample points that are not in event A. We denote the complement of A by A^c.

An event A is a collection of sample points, and the sample points included in A^c are those not in A. Figure 3.8 demonstrates this idea. Note from the figure that all sample points in S are included in *either* A or A^c and that *no* sample point is in both A and A^c. This leads us to conclude that the probabilities of an event and its complement *must sum to 1:*

> **Summing Probabilities of Complementary Events**
>
> The sum of the probabilities of complementary events equals 1; i.e., $P(A) + P(A^c) = 1$.

In many probability problems, calculating the probability of the complement of the event of interest is easier than calculating the event itself. Then, because

$$P(A) + P(A^c) = 1$$

we can calculate $P(A)$ by using the relationship

$$P(A) = 1 - P(A^c).$$

EXAMPLE 3.11 Consider the experiment of tossing two fair coins. Use the complementary relationship to calculate the probability of event A: {Observing at least one head}.

Solution We know that the event A: {Observing at least one head} consists of the sample points

$A: \{HH, HT, TH\}$

The complement of A is defined as the event that occurs when A does not occur. Therefore,

A^c: {Observe no heads} = {TT}

This complementary relationship is shown in Figure 3.9. Assuming the coins are balanced,

$$P(A^c) = P(TT) = 1/4$$

and

$$P(A) = 1 - P(A^c) = 1 - 1/4 = 3/4.$$

FIGURE 3.9
Complementary events in the toss of two coins

3.4 THE ADDITIVE RULE AND MUTUALLY EXCLUSIVE EVENTS

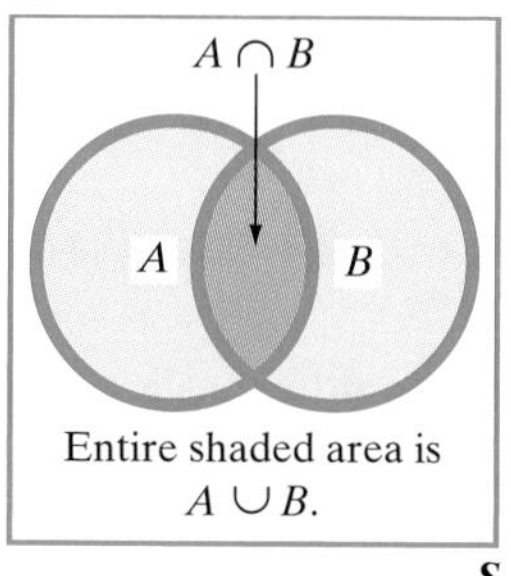

FIGURE 3.10
Venn diagram of union

In Section 3.2 we saw how to determine which sample points are contained in a union and how to calculate the probability of the union by adding the probabilities of the sample points in the union. It is also possible to obtain the probability of the union of two events by using the **additive rule of probability.**

The union of two events will often contain many sample points, since the union occurs if either one or both of the events occur. By studying the Venn diagram in Figure 3.10, you can see that the probability of the union of two events, A and B, can be obtained by summing $P(A)$ and $P(B)$ and subtracting the probability corresponding to $A \cap B$. Therefore, the formula for calculating the probability of the union of two events is given in the next box.

Additive Rule of Probability

The probability of the union of events A and B is the sum of the probabilities of events A and B minus the probability of the intersection of events A and B, that is,

$$P(A \cup B) = P(A) + P(B) - P(A \cap B)$$

EXAMPLE 3.12 Hospital records show that 12% of all patients are admitted for surgical treatment, 16% are admitted for obstetrics, and 2% receive both obstetrics and surgical treatment. If a new patient is admitted to the hospital, what is the probability that the patient will be admitted either for surgery, obstetrics, or both? Use the additive rule of probability to arrive at the answer.

Solution Consider the following events:

A: {A patient admitted to the hospital receives surgical treatment}

B: {A patient admitted to the hospital receives obstetrics treatment}

Then, from the given information,

$$P(A) = .12$$
$$P(B) = .16$$

and the probability of the event that a patient receives both obstetrics and surgical treatment is

$$P(A \cap B) = .02$$

The event that a patient admitted to the hospital receives either surgical treatment, obstetrics treatment, or both is the union $A \cup B$. The probability of $A \cup B$ is given by the additive rule of probability:

$$P(A \cup B) = P(A) + P(B) - P(A \cap B) = .12 + .16 - .02 = .26$$

Thus, 26% of all patients admitted to the hospital receive either surgical treatment, obstetrics treatment, or both.

A very special relationship exists between events A and B when $A \cap B$ contains no sample points. In this case we call the events A and B *mutually exclusive events.*

DEFINITION 3.8

Events A and B are **mutually exclusive** if $A \cap B$ contains no sample points, that is, if A and B have no sample points in common.

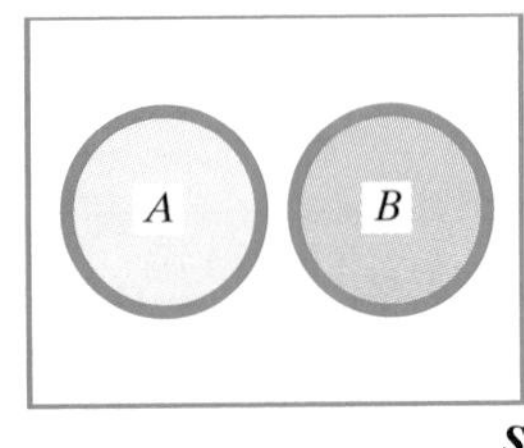

FIGURE 3.11
Venn diagram of mutually exclusive events

Figure 3.11 shows a Venn diagram of two mutually exclusive events. The events A and B have no sample points in common, that is, A and B cannot occur simultaneously, and $P(A \cap B) = 0$. Thus, we have the important relationship given in the box.

Probability of Union of Two Mutually Exclusive Events

If two events A and B are *mutually exclusive,* the probability of the union of A and B equals the sum of the probabilities of A and B; that is, $P(A \cup B) = P(A) + P(B)$.

Caution: The formula shown above is *false* if the events are *not* mutually exclusive. In this case (i.e., two nonmutually exclusive events), you must apply the general additive rule of probability.

EXAMPLE 3.13 Consider the experiment of tossing two balanced coins. Find the probability of observing at *least* one head.

Solution Define the events

A: {Observe at least one head}
B: {Observe exactly one head}
C: {Observe exactly two heads}

Note that

$$A = B \cup C$$

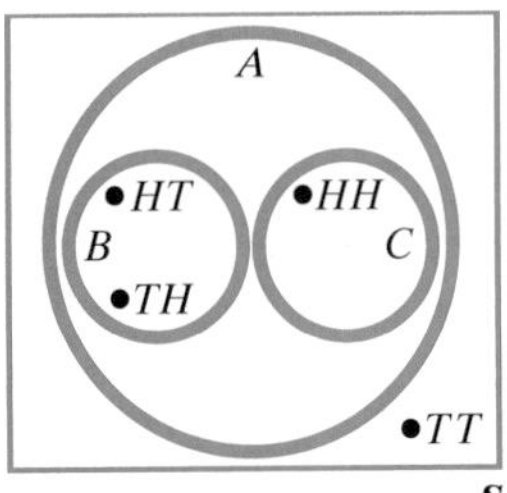

FIGURE 3.12
Venn diagram for coin-toss experiment

and that $B \cap C$ contains no sample points (see Figure 3.12). Thus, B and C are mutually exclusive, so that

$$P(A) = P(B \cup C) = P(B) + P(C) = 1/2 + 1/4 = 3/4$$

Although Example 3.13 is very simple, it shows us that writing events with verbal descriptions that include the phrases "at least" or "at most" as unions of mutually exclusive events is very useful. This practice enables us to find the probability of the event by adding the probabilities of the mutually exclusive events.

EXERCISES 3.16–3.31

Learning the Mechanics

3.16 A fair coin is tossed three times and the events A and B are defined as follows:

A: {At least one head is observed}
B: {The number of heads observed is odd}

a. Identify the sample points in the events A, B, $A \cup B$, A^c and $A \cap B$.
b. Find $P(A)$, $P(B)$, $P(A \cup B)$, $P(A^c)$, and $P(A \cap B)$ by summing the probabilities of the appropriate sample points.
c. Find $P(A \cup B)$ using the additive rule. Compare your answer to the one you obtained in part **b.**
d. Are the events A and B mutually exclusive? Why?

3.17 What are mutually exclusive events? Give a verbal description, then draw a Venn diagram.

3.18 A pair of fair dice is tossed. Define the following events:

A: {You will roll a 7} (i.e., the sum of the dots on the up faces of the two dice is equal to 7)
B: {At least one of the two dice shows a 4}

a. Identify the sample points in the events A, B, $A \cap B$, $A \cup B$, and A^c.
b. Find $P(A)$, $P(B)$, $P(A \cap B)$, $P(A \cup B)$, and $P(A^c)$ by summing the probabilities of the appropriate sample points.
c. Find $P(A \cup B)$ using the additive rule. Compare your answer to that for the same event in part **b.**
d. Are A and B mutually exclusive? Why?

3.19 Consider the accompanying Venn diagram, where $P(E_1) = P(E_2) = P(E_3) = \frac{1}{5}$, $P(E_4) = P(E_5) = \frac{1}{20}$, $P(E_6) = \frac{1}{10}$, and $P(E_7) = \frac{1}{5}$. Find each of the following probabilities:

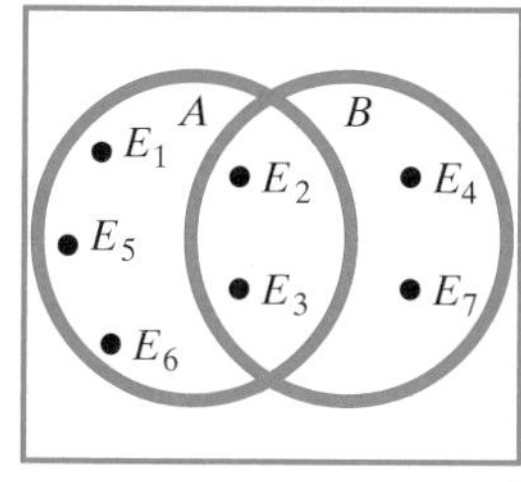

a. $P(A)$ b. $P(B)$ c. $P(A \cup B)$ d. $P(A \cap B)$
e. $P(A^c)$ f. $P(B^c)$ g. $P(A \cup A^c)$ h. $P(A^c \cap B)$

3.20 Consider the next Venn diagram, where $P(E_1) = .10$, $P(E_2) = .05$, $P(E_3) = P(E_4) = .2$, $P(E_5) = .06$, $P(E_6) = .3$, $P(E_7) = .06$, and $P(E_8) = .03$. Find the following probabilities:

a. $P(A^c)$ b. $P(B^c)$ c. $P(A^c \cap B)$ d. $P(A \cup B)$
e. $P(A \cap B)$ f. $P(A^c \cup B^c)$
g. Are events A and B mutually exclusive? Why?

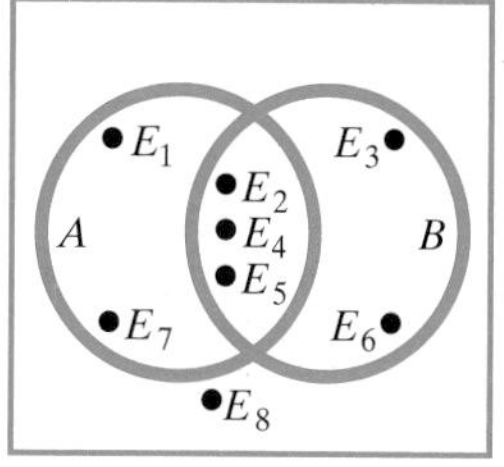

3.21 The outcomes of two variables are (Low, Medium, High) and (On, Off), respectively. An experiment is conducted in which the outcomes of each of the two variables are observed. The probabilities associated with each of the six possible outcome pairs are given in the accompanying table.

	Low	Medium	High
On	.50	.10	.05
Off	.25	.07	.03

Consider the following events:

A: {On}
B: {Medium or On}
C: {Off and Low}
D: {High}

a. Find $P(A)$.
b. Find $P(B)$.
c. Find $P(C)$.
d. Find $P(D)$.
e. Find $P(A^c)$.
f. Find $P(A \cup B)$.
g. Find $P(A \cap C)$.
h. Consider each pair of events (A and B, A and C, A and D, B and C, B and D, C and D). List the pairs of events that are mutually exclusive. Justify your choices.

3.22 Refer to Exercise 3.21. Use the same event definitions to do the following exercises.

a. Write the event that the outcome is "On" and "High" as an intersection of two events.
b. Write the event that the outcome is "Low" or "Medium" as the complement of an event.

Applying the Concepts

3.23 A state energy agency mailed questionnaires on energy conservation to 1,000 homeowners in the state capital. Five hundred questionnaires were returned.

Suppose an experiment consists of randomly selecting and reviewing one of the returned questionnaires. Consider the events:

A: {The home is constructed of brick}
B: {The home is more than 30 years old}
C: {The home is heated with oil}

Describe each of the following events in terms of unions, intersections, and complements (i.e., $A \cup B$, $A \cap B$, A^c, etc.):

a. The home is more than 30 years old and is heated with oil.
b. The home is not constructed of brick.
c. The home is heated with oil or is more than 30 years old.
d. The home is constructed of brick and is not heated with oil.

3.24 Corporate downsizing in Japan has caused a significant increase in the demand for temporary and part-time workers. The distribution (in percent) of nonregular workers in Japan (by age) is provided in the table (adapted from *Monthly Labor Review*, Oct. 1995). Column headings are defined below the table.

Suppose a nonregular worker is to be chosen at random from this population. Define the following events:

A: {The worker is 40 or over}
B: {The worker is a teenager and part-time}
C: {The worker is under 40 and either arubaito or dispatched}
D: {The worker is part-time}

a. Find the probability of each of the above events.
b. Find $P(A \cap D)$ and $P(A \cup D)$.
c. Describe in words the following events: A^c, B^c, and D^c.
d. Find the probability of each of the events you described in part **c**.

3.25 A few years ago, E* Trade Group Inc. began providing on-line securities trading for its clients, offering an alternative to traditional investment firms. According to *Business Week*, on-line securities trading now accounts for a significant share of the brokerage business. The table below reports the number of on-line and traditional accounts for five leading brokerages.

Suppose a customer account is to be drawn at random from the population of accounts described in the table. Consider the following events:

A: {The account is with Merrill Lynch}
B: {The account is an on-line account}
C: {The account is with E* Trade and is an on-line account}
D: {The account is either with TD Waterhouse or E* Trade, and is an on-line account}
E: {The account is with E* Trade}

a. Find the probability of each of the above events.

Table for Exercise 3.24

Age	Part-Time	Arubaito	Temporary and Day	Dispatched	Totals
15–19	.3	3.7	2.3	.2	6.5
20–29	3.4	7.8	6.1	4.7	22.0
30–39	8.4	1.6	4.5	2.7	17.2
40–49	15.6	1.6	7.3	1.4	25.9
50–59	9.4	1.1	5.8	.6	16.9
60 and over	4.3	1.8	4.8	.6	11.5
Totals	41.4	17.6	30.8	10.2	100.0

Part-time: Work fewer hours per day or days per week than regular workers; *arubaito:* someone with a "side" job who is in school or has regular employment elsewhere; *temporary:* employed on a contract lasting more than one month but less than one year; *day:* employed on a contract of less than one month's duration; *dispatched:* hired from a temporary-help agency.

Source: Houseman, S., and Osawa, M. "Part-time and temporary employment in Japan. "*Monthly Labor Review,* October 1995, pp. 12–13 (Tables 1 and 2).

Table for Exercise 3.25

Brokerage Firms	On-line Accounts	Traditional Accounts	Total Accounts
Fidelity Investments	2.8 million	8 million	10.8 million
Merrill Lynch & Co.	0	8 million	8 million
Charles Schwab & Co.	2.8 million	3.5 million	6.3 million
TD Waterhouse Group Inc.	1.0 million	1.1 million	2.1 million
E* Trade Group Inc.	1.24 million	0	1.24 million
Totals	7.84 million	20.6 million	28.44 million

Source: *Business Week,* October 18, 1999, pp. 185–186.

b. Find $P(A \cap B)$.
c. Find $P(A \cup B)$.
d. Find $P(B^c \cap E)$.
e. Find $P(A \cup E)$.
f. Which pairs of events are mutually exclusive?

3.26 *Roulette* is a very popular game in many American casinos. In roulette, a ball spins on a circular wheel that is divided into 38 arcs of equal length, bearing the numbers 00, 0, 1, 2, . . ., 35, 36. The number of the arc on which the ball stops is the outcome of one play of the game. The numbers are also colored in the following manner:

Red: 1, 3, 5, 7, 9, 12, 14, 16, 18, 19, 21, 23, 25, 27, 30, 32, 34, 36
Black: 2, 4, 6, 8, 10, 11, 13, 15, 17, 20, 22, 24, 26, 28, 29, 31, 33, 35
Green: 00, 0

Players may place bets on the table in a variety of ways, including bets on odd, even, red, black, high, low, etc. Define the following events:

A: {Outcome is an odd number (00 and 0 are considered neither odd nor even)}
B: {Outcome is a black number}
C: {Outcome is a low number (1–18)}

a. Define the event $A \cap B$ as a specific set of sample points.
b. Define the event $A \cup B$ as a specific set of sample points.
c. Find $P(A)$, $P(B)$, $P(A \cap B)$, $P(A \cup B)$, and $P(C)$ by summing the probabilities of the appropriate sample points.
d. Define the event $A \cap B \cap C$ as a specific set of sample points.
e. Find $P(A \cup B)$ using the additive rule. Are events A and B mutually exclusive? Why?
f. Find $P(A \cap B \cap C)$ by summing the probabilities of the sample points given in part **d.**
g. Define the event $(A \cup B \cup C)$ as a specific set of sample points.
h. Find $P(A \cup B \cup C)$ by summing the probabilities of the sample points given in part **g.**

3.27 After completing an inventory of three warehouses, a manufacturer of golf club shafts described its stock of 20,125 shafts with the percentages given in the table. Suppose a shaft is selected at random from the 20,125 currently in stock and the warehouse number and type of shaft are observed.

		Type of Shaft		
		Regular	Stiff	Extra Stiff
Warehouse	1	41%	6%	0%
	2	10%	15%	4%
	3	11%	7%	6%

a. List all the sample points for this experiment.
b. What is the set of all sample points called?
c. Let C be the event that the shaft selected is from warehouse 3. Find $P(C)$ by summing the probabilities of the sample points in C.
d. Let F be the event that the shaft chosen is an extra-stiff type. Find $P(F)$.
e. Let A be the event that the shaft selected is from warehouse 1. Find $P(A)$.
f. Let D be the event that the shaft selected is a regular type. Find $P(D)$.
g. Let E be the event that the shaft selected is a stiff type. Find $P(E)$.

3.28 Refer to Exercise 3.27. Define the characteristics of a golf club shaft portrayed by the following events, and then find the probability of each. For each union, use the additive rule to find the probability. Also, determine whether the events are mutually exclusive.

a. $A \cap F$ b. $C \cup E$ c. $C \cap D$
d. $A \cup F$ e. $A \cup D$

3.29 *Automotive News* tracks and reports monthly inventories for both domestic and foreign auto manufacturers. The table presents the inventories for the Big Three U.S. auto manufacturers for November 1998.

Manufacturer	Cars	Trucks	Totals
DaimlerChrysler	178,300	381,900	560,200
Ford	321,300	467,300	788,600
General Motors	550,500	433,900	984,400
Totals	1,050,100	1,283,100	2,333,200

Source: *Automotive News*, December 14, 1998, p. 38.

Suppose a vehicle is to be drawn at random from this population and the manufacturer and type of vehicle are observed.

a. List the sample points for this experiment.
b. Find the probability that the vehicle is a car. A truck. A Ford.
c. Find the probability that the vehicle is a DaimlerChrysler or a Ford. A DaimlerChrysler and a Ford.
d. Find the probability that the vehicle is a car and is manufactured by General Motors. A truck and is manufactured by General Motors.

3.30 The long-run success of a business depends on its ability to market products with superior characteristics that maximize consumer satisfaction and that give the firm a competitive advantage (Kotler, *Marketing Management*, 1994). Ten new products have been developed by a food-products firm. Market research has indicated that the 10 products have the characteristics described by the Venn diagram shown on page 140.

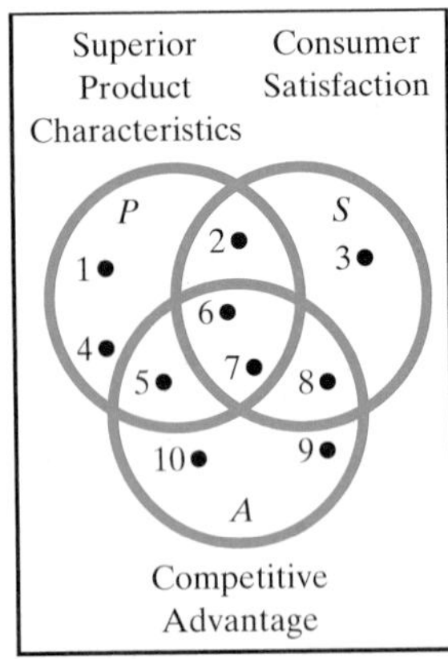

a. Write the event that a product possesses all the desired characteristics as an intersection of the events defined in the Venn diagram. Which products are contained in this intersection?
b. If one of the 10 products were selected at random to be marketed, what is the probability that it would possess all the desired characteristics?
c. Write the event that the randomly selected product would give the firm a competitive advantage or would satisfy consumers as a union of the events defined in the Venn diagram. Find the probability of this union.
d. Write the event that the randomly selected product would possess superior product characteristics and satisfy consumers. Find the probability of this intersection.

3.31 Identifying managerial prospects who are both talented and motivated is difficult. A human resources director constructed the following two-way table to define nine combinations of talent-motivation levels. The number in a cell is the director's estimate of the probability that a managerial prospect will fall in that category. Suppose the director has decided to hire a new manager. Define the following events:

A: {Prospect places in high-motivation category}
B: {Prospect places in high-talent category}
C: {Prospect is medium or better in both categories}
D: {Prospect places low in at least one category}
E: {Prospect places highest in both categories}

	Talent		
Motivation	High	Medium	Low
High	.05	.16	.05
Medium	.19	.32	.05
Low	.11	.05	.02

a. Does the sum of the cell probabilities equal 1?
b. List the sample points in each of the events described above and find their probabilities.
c. Find $P(A \cup B)$, $P(A \cap B)$, and $P(A \cup C)$.
d. Find $P(A^c)$ and explain what this means from a practical point of view.
e. Consider each pair of events (A and B, A and C, etc.). Which of the pairs are mutually exclusive? Why?

3.5 CONDITIONAL PROBABILITY

The event probabilities we've been discussing give the relative frequencies of the occurrences of the events when the experiment is repeated a very large number of times. Such probabilities are often called **unconditional probabilities** because no special conditions are assumed, other than those that define the experiment.

Often, however, we have additional knowledge that might affect the likelihood of the outcome of an experiment, so we need to alter the probability of an event of interest. A probability that reflects such additional knowledge is called the **conditional probability** of the event. For example, we've seen that the probability of observing an even number (event A) on a toss of a fair die is $\frac{1}{2}$. But suppose we're given the information that on a particular throw of the die the result was a number less than or equal to 3 (event B). Would the probability of observing an even number on that throw of the die still be equal to $\frac{1}{2}$? It can't be, because making the assumption that B has occurred reduces the sample space from six sample points to three sample points (namely, those contained in event B). This reduced sample space is as shown in Figure 3.13.

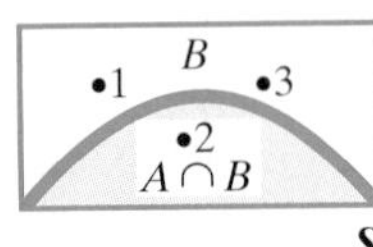

FIGURE 3.13
Reduced sample space for the die-toss experiment given that event B has occurred

Because the sample points for the die-toss experiment are equally likely, each of the three sample points in the reduced sample space is assigned an equal *conditional probability* of $\frac{1}{3}$. Since the only even number of the three in the reduced sample space B is the number 2 and the die is fair, we conclude that the probability that A occurs *given that B occurs* is $\frac{1}{3}$. We use the symbol $P(A|B)$ to represent the probability of event A given that event B occurs. For the die-toss example $P(A|B) = \frac{1}{3}$.

To get the probability of event A given that event B occurs, we proceed as follows. We divide the probability of the part of A that falls within the reduced sample space B, namely $P(A \cap B)$, by the total probability of the reduced sample space, namely, $P(B)$. Thus, for the die-toss example with event A: {Observe an even number} and event B: {Observe a number less than or equal to 3}, we find

$$P(A|B) = \frac{P(A \cap B)}{P(B)} = \frac{P(2)}{P(1) + P(2) + P(3)} = \frac{\frac{1}{6}}{\frac{3}{6}} = \frac{1}{3}$$

The formula for $P(A|B)$ is true in general:

Conditional Probability Formula

To find the *conditional probability that event A occurs given that event B occurs,* divide the probability that *both* A and B occur by the probability that B occurs, that is,

$$P(A|B) = \frac{P(A \cap B)}{P(B)} \quad \text{[We assume that } P(B) \neq 0.]$$

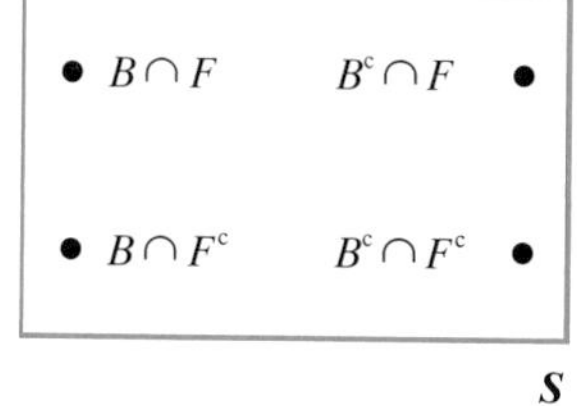

FIGURE 3.14
Sample space for contacting a sales prospect

This formula adjusts the probability of $A \cap B$ from its original value in the complete sample space S to a conditional probability in the reduced sample space B. If the sample points in the complete sample space are equally likely, then the formula will assign equal probabilities to the sample points in the reduced sample space, as in the die-toss experiment. If, on the other hand, the sample points have unequal probabilities, the formula will assign conditional probabilities proportional to the probabilities in the complete sample space. This is illustrated by the following examples.

EXAMPLE 3.14

Suppose you are interested in the probability of the sale of a large piece of earth-moving equipment. A single prospect is contacted. Let F be the event that the buyer has sufficient money (or credit) to buy the product and let F^c denote the complement of F (the event that the prospect does not have the financial capability to buy the product). Similarly, let B be the event that the buyer wishes to buy the product and let B^c be the complement of that event. Then the four sample points associated with the experiment are shown in Figure 3.14, and their probabilities are given in Table 3.5. Use the sample point probabilities to find the probability that a single prospect will buy, given that the prospect is able to finance the purchase.

Solution Suppose you consider the large collection of prospects for the sale of your product and randomly select one person from this collection. What is the probability that the person selected will buy the product? In order to buy the product, the customer must be financially able *and* have the desire to buy, so this probability would correspond to the entry in Table 3.5 below {To buy, B} and next to {Yes, F}, or $P(B \cap F) = .2$. This is called the **unconditional probability** of the event $B \cap F$.

TABLE 3.5 Probabilities of Customer Desire to Buy and Ability to Finance

		Desire	
		To Buy, B	Not to Buy, B^c
Able to Finance	Yes, F	.2	.1
	No, F^c	.4	.3

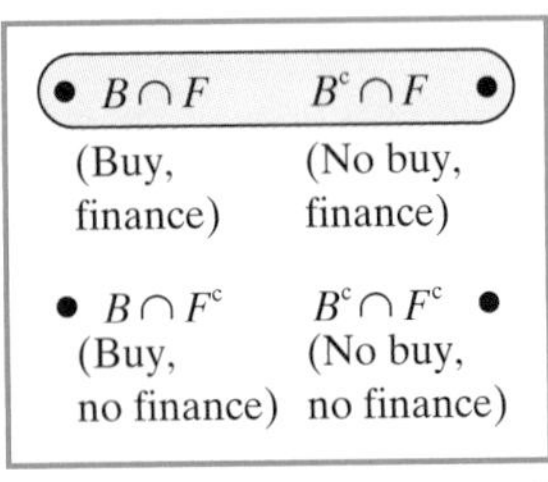

FIGURE 3.15
Subspace (shaded) containing sample points implying a financially able prospect

In contrast, suppose you know that the prospect selected has the financial capability for purchasing the product. Now you are seeking the probability that the customer will buy given (the condition) that the customer has the financial ability to pay. This probability, the **conditional probability** of B given that F has occurred and denoted by the symbol $P(B|F)$, would be determined by considering only the sample points in the reduced sample space containing the sample points $B \cap F$ and $B^c \cap F$—i.e., sample points that imply the prospect is financially able to buy. (This subspace is shaded in Figure 3.15.) From our definition of conditional probability,

$$P(B|F) = \frac{P(B \cap F)}{P(F)}$$

where $P(F)$ is the sum of the probabilities of the two sample points corresponding to $B \cap F$ and $B^c \cap F$ (given in Table 3.5). Then

$$P(F) = P(B \cap F) + P(B^c \cap F) = .2 + .1 = .3$$

and the conditional probability that a prospect buys, given that the prospect is financially able, is

$$P(B|F) = \frac{P(B \cap F)}{P(F)} = \frac{.2}{.3} = .667$$

As we would expect, the probability that the prospect will buy, given that he or she is financially able, is higher than the unconditional probability of selecting a prospect who will buy.

Note in Example 3.14 that the conditional probability formula assigns a probability to the event $(B \cap F)$ in the reduced sample space that is proportional to the probability of the event in the complete sample space. To see this, note that the two sample points in the reduced sample space, $(B \cap F)$ and $(B^c \cap F)$, have probabilities of .2 and .1, respectively, in the complete sample space S. The formula assigns conditional probabilities $^2/_3$ and $^1/_3$ (use the formula to check the second one) to these sample points in the reduced sample space F, so that the conditional probabilities retain the 2 to 1 proportionality of the original sample point probabilities.

EXAMPLE 3.15 The investigation of consumer product complaints by the Federal Trade Commission (FTC) has generated much interest by manufacturers in the quality of their products. A manufacturer of an electromechanical kitchen utensil conducted an analysis of a large number of consumer complaints and found that they fell into the six categories shown in Table 3.6. If a consumer complaint is received, what is the probability that the cause of the complaint was product appearance given that the complaint originated during the guarantee period?

Solution Let A represent the event that the cause of a particular complaint is product appearance, and let B represent the event that the complaint occurred during the guarantee period. Checking Table 3.6, you can see that $(18 + 13 + 32)\% = 63\%$ of the complaints occur during the guarantee period. Hence, $P(B) = .63$. The percentage of complaints that were caused by the appearance and occurred during the guarantee period (the event $A \cap B$) is 32%. Therefore, $P(A \cap B) = .32$.

TABLE 3.6 Distribution of Product Complaints

	Reason for Complaint			
Complaint Origin	**Electrical**	**Mechanical**	**Appearance**	**Totals**
During Guarantee Period	18%	13%	32%	63%
After Guarantee Period	12%	22%	3%	37%
Totals	30%	35%	35%	100%

Using these probability values, we can calculate the conditional probability $P(A|B)$ that the cause of a complaint is appearance given that the complaint occurred during the guarantee time:

$$P(A|B) = \frac{P(A \cap B)}{P(B)} = \frac{.32}{.63} = .51$$

Consequently, we can see that slightly more than half the complaints that occurred during the guarantee period were due to scratches, dents, or other imperfections in the surface of the kitchen devices.

You will see in later chapters that conditional probability plays a key role in many applications of statistics. For example, we may be interested in the probability that a particular stock gains 10% during the next year. We may assess this probability using information such as the past performance of the stock or the general state of the economy at present. However, our probability may change drastically if we assume that the Gross Domestic Product (GDP) will increase by 10% in the next year. We would then be assessing the *conditional probability* that our stock gains 10% in the next year given that the GDP gains 10% in the same year. Thus, the probability of any event that is calculated or assessed based on an assumption that some other event occurs concurrently is a conditional probability.

3.6 THE MULTIPLICATIVE RULE AND INDEPENDENT EVENTS

The probability of an intersection of two events can be calculated using the multiplicative rule, which employs the conditional probabilities we defined in the previous section. Actually, we have already developed the formula in another context (page 141). You will recall that the formula for calculating the conditional probability of A given B is

$$P(A|B) = \frac{P(A \cap B)}{P(B)}$$

Multiplying both sides of this equation by $P(B)$, we obtain a formula for the probability of the intersection of events A and B. This is often called the **multiplicative rule of probability.**

Multiplicative Rule of Probability

$$P(A \cap B) = P(A)P(B|A) \text{ or, equivalently, } P(A \cap B) = P(B)P(A|B)$$

EXAMPLE 3.16 An investor in wheat futures is concerned with the following events:

B: {U.S. production of wheat will be profitable next year}

A: {A serious drought will occur next year}

Based on available information, the investor believes that the probability is .01 that production of wheat will be profitable *assuming* a serious drought will occur in the same year and that the probability is .05 that a serious drought will occur. That is,

$$P(B|A) = .01 \text{ and } P(A) = .05$$

Based on the information provided, what is the probability that a serious drought will occur *and* that a profit will be made? That is, find $P(A \cap B)$, the probability of the intersection of events A and B.

Solution We want to calculate $P(A \cap B)$. Using the formula for the multiplicative rule, we obtain:

$$P(A \cap B) = P(A)P(B|A) = (.05)(.01) = .0005$$

The probability that a serious drought occurs *and* the production of wheat is profitable is only .0005. As we might expect, this intersection is a very rare event.

Intersections often contain only a few sample points. In this case, the probability of an intersection is easy to calculate by summing the appropriate sample point probabilities. However, the formula for calculating intersection probabilities is invaluable when the intersection contains numerous sample points, as the next example illustrates.

EXAMPLE 3.17 A county welfare agency employs 10 welfare workers who interview prospective food stamp recipients. Periodically the supervisor selects, at random, the forms completed by two workers to audit for illegal deductions. Unknown to the supervisor, three of the workers have regularly been giving illegal deductions to applicants. What is the probability that both of the two workers chosen have been giving illegal deductions?

Solution Define the following two events:

A: {First worker selected gives illegal deductions}
B: {Second worker selected gives illegal deductions}

We want to find the probability of the event that both selected workers have been giving illegal deductions. This event can be restated as: {First worker gives illegal deductions *and* second worker gives illegal deductions}. Thus, we want to find the probability of the intersection, $A \cap B$. Applying the multiplicative rule, we have

$$P(A \cap B) = P(A)P(B|A)$$

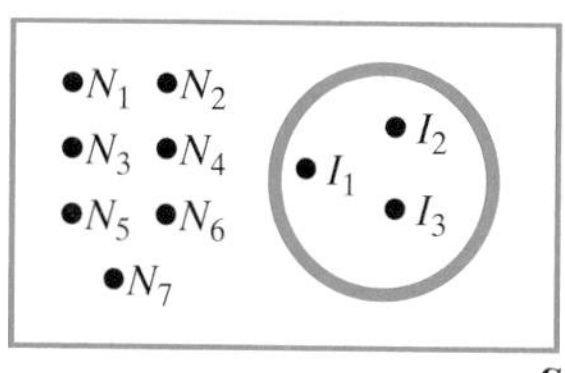

FIGURE 3.16
Venn diagram for finding $P(A)$

To find $P(A)$ it is helpful to consider the experiment as selecting one worker from the 10. Then the sample space for the experiment contains 10 sample points (representing the 10 welfare workers), where the three workers giving illegal deductions are denoted by the symbol I (I_1, I_2, I_3), and the seven workers not giving illegal deductions are denoted by the symbol N ($N_1, \ldots, N_7$). The resulting Venn diagram is illustrated in Figure 3.16.

Since the first worker is selected at random from the 10, it is reasonable to assign equal probabilities to the 10 sample points. Thus, each sample point has a probability of $^1/_{10}$. The sample points in event A are $\{I_1, I_2, I_3\}$—the three workers who are giving illegal deductions. Thus,

$$P(A) = P(I_1) + P(I_2) + P(I_3) = {}^1/_{10} + {}^1/_{10} + {}^1/_{10} = {}^3/_{10}$$

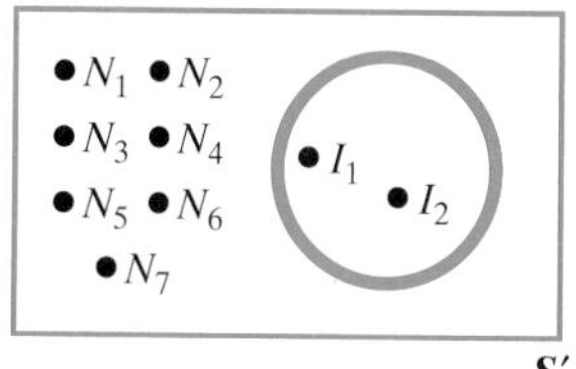

FIGURE 3.17
Venn diagram for finding $P(B|A)$

To find the conditional probability, $P(B|A)$, we need to alter the sample space S. Since we know A has occurred, i.e., the first worker selected is giving illegal deductions (say I_3), only two of the nine remaining workers in the sample space are giving illegal deductions. The Venn diagram for this new sample space (S') is shown in Figure 3.17. Each of these nine sample points are equally likely, so each is assigned a probability of $^1/_9$. Since the event $(B|A)$ contains the sample points $\{I_1, I_2\}$, we have

$$P(B|A) = P(I_1) + P(I_2) = {}^1/_9 + {}^1/_9 = {}^2/_9$$

Substituting $P(A) = {}^3/_{10}$ and $P(B|A) = {}^2/_9$ into the formula for the multiplicative rule, we find

$$P(A \cap B) = P(A)P(B|A) = ({}^3/_{10})({}^2/_9) = {}^6/_{90} = {}^1/_{15}$$

Thus, there is a 1 in 15 chance that both workers chosen by the supervisor have been giving illegal deductions to food stamp recipients.

The sample space approach is only one way to solve the problem posed in Example 3.17. An alternative method employs the concept of a **tree diagram.** Tree diagrams are helpful for calculating the probability of an intersection.

To illustrate, a tree diagram for Example 3.17 is displayed in Figure 3.18. The tree begins at the far left with two branches. These branches represent the two possible outcomes N (no illegal deductions) and I (illegal deductions) for the first worker selected. The unconditional probability of each outcome is given (in parentheses) on the appropriate branch. That is, for the first worker selected, $P(N) = 7/10$ and $P(I) = 3/10$. (These can be obtained by summing sample point probabilities as in Example 3.17.)

The next level of the tree diagram (moving to the right) represents the outcomes for the second worker selected. The probabilities shown here are conditional probabilities since the outcome for the first worker is assumed to be known. For example, if the first worker is giving illegal deductions *(I)*, the probability that the second worker is also giving illegal deductions *(I)* is $2/9$ since of the nine workers left to be selected, only two remain who are giving illegal deductions. This conditional probability, $2/9$, is shown in parentheses on the bottom branch of Figure 3.18.

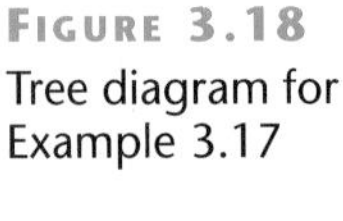

FIGURE 3.18
Tree diagram for Example 3.17

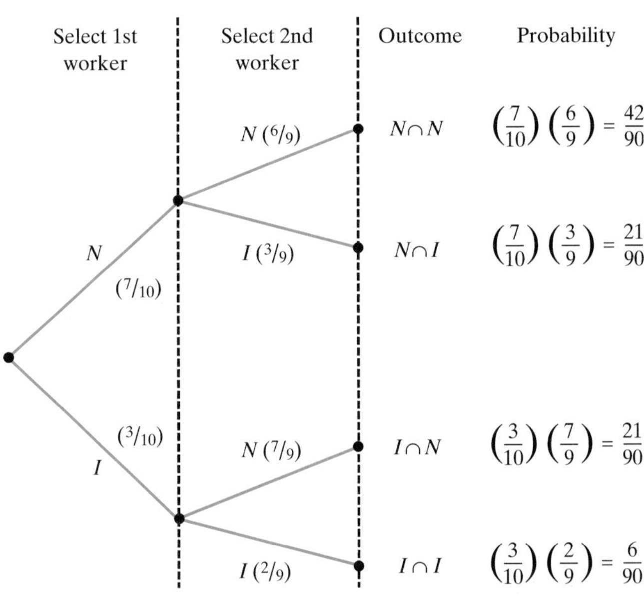

Finally, the four possible outcomes of the experiment are shown at the end of each of the four tree branches. These events are intersections of two events (outcome of first worker *and* outcome of second worker). Consequently, the multiplicative rule is applied to calculate each probability, as shown in Figure 3.18. You can see that the intersection $\{I \cap I\}$, i.e., the event that both workers selected are giving illegal deductions, has probability $6/90 = 1/15$—the same value obtained in Example 3.17.

In Section 3.5 we showed that the probability of an event A may be substantially altered by the knowledge that an event B has occurred. However, this will not always be the case. In some instances, the assumption that event B has occurred will *not* alter the probability of event A at all. When this is true, we say that the two events A and B are *independent events.*

DEFINITION 3.9

Events A and B are **independent events** if the occurrence of B does not alter the probability that A has occurred; that is, events A and B are independent if

$$P(A|B) = P(A)$$

When events A and B are independent, it is also true that

$$P(B|A) = P(B)$$

Events that are not independent are said to be **dependent.**

EXAMPLE 3.18 Consider the experiment of tossing a fair die and let

A: {Observe an even number}

B: {Observe a number less than or equal to 4}

Are events A and B independent?

Solution The Venn diagram for this experiment is shown in Figure 3.19. We first calculate

$$P(A) = P(2) + P(4) + P(6) = \tfrac{1}{2}$$
$$P(B) = P(1) + P(2) + P(3) + P(4) = \tfrac{2}{3}$$
$$P(A \cap B) = P(2) + P(4) = \tfrac{1}{3}$$

Now assuming B has occurred, the conditional probability of A given B is

$$P(A|B) = \frac{P(A \cap B)}{P(B)} = \frac{\frac{1}{3}}{\frac{2}{3}} = \frac{1}{2} = P(A)$$

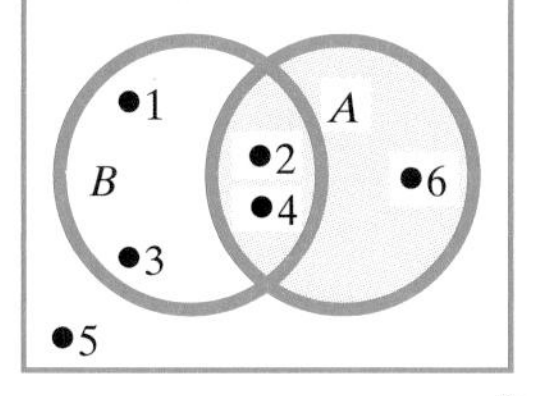

FIGURE 3.19
Venn diagram for die-toss experiment

Thus, assuming that event B does not alter the probability of observing an even number, $P(A)$ remains $\tfrac{1}{2}$. Therefore, the events A and B are independent. Note that if we calculate the conditional probability of B given A, our conclusion is the same:

$$P(B|A) = \frac{P(A \cap B)}{P(A)} = \frac{\frac{1}{3}}{\frac{1}{2}} = \frac{2}{3} = P(B)$$

EXAMPLE 3.19 Refer to the consumer product complaint study in Example 3.15. The percentages of complaints of various types during and after the guarantee period are shown in Table 3.6. Define the following events:

A: {Cause of complaint is product appearance}

B: {Complaint occurred during the guarantee term}

Are A and B independent events?

Solution Events A and B are independent if $P(A|B) = P(A)$. We calculated $P(A|B)$ in Example 3.15 to be .51, and from Table 3.6 we see that

$$P(A) = .32 + .03 = .35$$

Therefore, $P(A|B)$ is not equal to $P(A)$, and A and B are dependent events. ✶

To gain an intuitive understanding of independence, think of situations in which the occurrence of one event does not alter the probability that a second event will occur. For example, suppose two small companies are being monitored by a financier for possible investment. If the businesses are in different industries and they are otherwise unrelated, then the success or failure of one company may be *independent* of the success or failure of the other. That is, the event that company A fails may not alter the probability that company B will fail.

As a second example, consider an election poll in which 1,000 registered voters are asked their preference between two candidates. Pollsters try to use procedures for selecting a sample of voters so that the responses are independent. That is, the objective of the pollster is to select the sample so the event that one polled voter prefers candidate A does not alter the probability that a second polled voter prefers candidate A.

We will make three final points about independence. The first is that the property of independence, unlike the mutually exclusive property, cannot be shown on or gleaned from a Venn diagram. This means *you can't trust your intuition.* In general, the only way to check for independence is by performing the calculations of the probabilities in the definition.

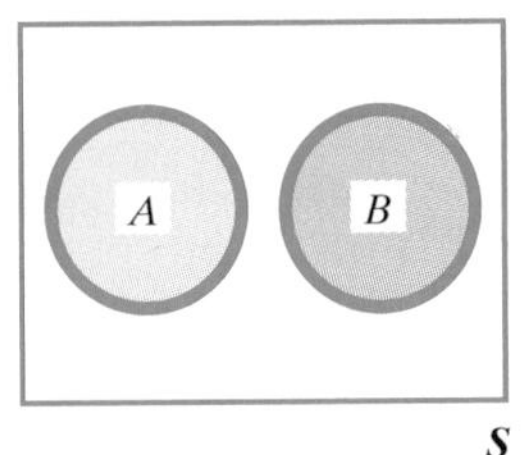

FIGURE 3.20
Mutually exclusive events are dependent events

The second point concerns the relationship between the mutually exclusive and independence properties. Suppose that events A and B are mutually exclusive, as shown in Figure 3.20, and both events have nonzero probabilities. Are these events independent or dependent? That is, does the assumption that B occurs alter the probability of the occurrence of A? It certainly does, because if we assume that B has occurred, it is impossible for A to have occurred simultaneously. That is, $P(A|B) = 0$. Thus, *mutually exclusive events are dependent events* since $P(A) \neq P(A|B)$.

The third point is that the probability of the intersection of independent events is very easy to calculate. Referring to the formula for calculating the probability of an intersection, we find

$$P(A \cap B) = P(A)P(B|A)$$

Thus, since $P(B|A) = P(B)$ when A and B are independent, we have the following useful rule:

Probability of Intersection of Two Independent Events

If events A and B are independent, the probability of the intersection of A and B equals the product of the probabilities of A and B; that is,

$$P(A \cap B) = P(A)P(B)$$

The converse is also true: If $P(A \cap B) = P(A)P(B)$, then events A and B are independent.

In the die-toss experiment, we showed in Example 3.18 that the events A: {Observe an even number} and B: {Observe a number less than or equal to 4} are independent if the die is fair. Thus,

$$P(A \cap B) = P(A)P(B) = (\tfrac{1}{2})(\tfrac{2}{3}) = \tfrac{1}{3}$$

This agrees with the result that we obtained in the example:

$$P(A \cap B) = P(2) + P(4) = \tfrac{2}{6} = \tfrac{1}{3}$$

EXAMPLE 3.20

Almost every retail business has the problem of determining how much inventory to purchase. Insufficient inventory may result in lost business, and excess inventory may have a detrimental effect on profits. Suppose a retail computer store owner is planning to place an order for personal computers (PCs). She is trying to decide how many desktop PCs and how many laptop PCs to order.

The owner's records indicate that 80% of the previous PC customers purchased desktop models and 20% purchased laptops.

a. What is the probability that the next two customers will purchase laptops?
b. What is the probability that the next 10 customers will purchase laptops?

Solution

a. Let L_1 represent the event that customer 1 will purchase a laptop and L_2 represent the event that customer 2 will purchase a laptop. The event that *both* customers purchase laptops is the intersection of the two events, $L_1 \cap L_2$. From the records the store owner could reasonably conclude that $P(L_1) = .2$ (based on the fact that 20% of past customers have purchased laptops), and the same reasoning would apply to $P(L_2)$. However, in order to compute the probability of $L_1 \cap L_2$, we need more information. Either the records must be examined for the occurrence of consecutive purchases of laptops, or some assumption must be made to allow the calculation of $P(L_1 \cap L_2)$ from the multiplicative rule. It seems reasonable to make the assumption that the two events are independent, since the decision of the first customer is not likely to affect the decision of the second customer. Assuming independence, we have

$$P(L_1 \cap L_2) = P(L_1)P(L_2) = (.2)(.2) = .04$$

b. To see how to compute the probability that 10 consecutive purchases will be laptops, first consider the event that three consecutive customers purchase laptops. If L_3 represents the event that the third customer purchases a laptop, then we want to compute the probability of the intersection $L_1 \cap L_2$ with L_3. Again assuming independence of the purchasing decisions, we have

$$P(L_1 \cap L_2 \cap L_3) = P(L_1 \cap L_2)P(L_3) = (.2)^2(.2) = .008$$

Similar reasoning leads to the conclusion that the intersection of 10 such events can be calculated as follows:

$$P(L_1 \cap L_2 \cap \cdots \cap L_{10}) = P(L_1)P(L_2)\cdots P(L_{10}) = (.2)^{10} = .0000001024$$

Thus, the probability that 10 consecutive customers purchase laptop computers is about 1 in 10 million, assuming the probability of each customer's purchase of a laptop is .2 and the purchase decisions are independent.

EXERCISES 3.32–3.51

Learning the Mechanics

3.32 An experiment results in one of three mutually exclusive events, A, B, or C. It is known that $P(A) = .30$, $P(B) = .55$, and $P(C) = .15$. Find each of the following probabilities:

a. $P(A \cup B)$ b. $P(A \cap C)$
c. $P(A|B)$ d. $P(B \cup C)$
e. Are B and C independent events? Explain.

3.33 Consider the experiment depicted by the Venn diagram, with the sample space S containing five sample points. The sample points are assigned the following probabilities: $P(E_1) = .20$, $P(E_2) = .30$, $P(E_3) = .30$, $P(E_4) = .10$, $P(E_5) = .10$.

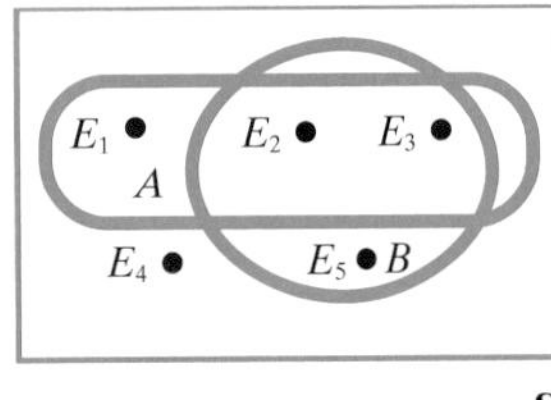

a. Calculate $P(A)$, $P(B)$, and $P(A \cap B)$.
b. Suppose we know that event A has occurred, so that the reduced sample space consists of the three sample points in A—namely, E_1, E_2, and E_3. Use the formula for conditional probability to adjust the probabilities of these three sample points for the knowledge that A has occurred [i.e., $P(E_i|A)$.] Verify that the conditional probabilities are in the same proportion to one another as the original sample point probabilities.
c. Calculate the conditional probability $P(B|A)$ in two ways: (1) Add the adjusted (conditional) probabilities of the sample points in the intersection $A \cap B$ since these represent the event that B occurs given that A has occurred; (2) Use the formula for conditional probability:

$$P(B|A) = \frac{P(A \cap B)}{P(A)}$$

Verify that the two methods yield the same result.
d. Are events A and B independent? Why or why not?

3.34 Three fair coins are tossed and the following events are defined:

A: {Observe at least one head}
B: {Observe exactly two heads}
C: {Observe exactly two tails}
D: {Observe at most one head}

a. Sum the probabilities of the appropriate sample points to find: $P(A)$, $P(B)$, $P(C)$, $P(D)$, $P(A \cap B)$, $P(A \cap D)$, $P(B \cap C)$, and $P(B \cap D)$.
b. Use your answers to part **a** to calculate $P(B|A)$, $P(A|D)$, and $P(C|B)$.
c. Which pairs of events, if any, are independent? Why?

3.35 An experiment results in one of five sample points with the following probabilities: $P(E_1) = .22$, $P(E_2) = .31$, $P(E_3) = .15$, $P(E_4) = .22$, and $P(E_5) = .1$. The following events have been defined:

$A: \{E_1, E_3\}$
$B: \{E_2, E_3, E_4\}$
$C: \{E_1, E_5\}$

Find each of the following probabilities:

a. $P(A)$ b. $P(B)$ c. $P(A \cap B)$
d. $P(A|B)$ e. $P(B \cap C)$ f. $P(C|B)$
g. Consider each pair of events: A and B, A and C, and B and C. Are any of the pairs of events independent? Why?

3.36 Two fair dice are tossed, and the following events are defined:

A: {Sum of the numbers showing is odd}
B: {Sum of the numbers showing is 9, 11, or 12}

Are events A and B independent? Why?

3.37 A sample space contains six sample points and events A, B, and C as shown in the Venn diagram. The probabilities of the sample points are

$$P(1) = .20, P(2) = .05, P(3) = .30, P(4) = .10,$$
$$P(5) = .10, P(6) = .25.$$

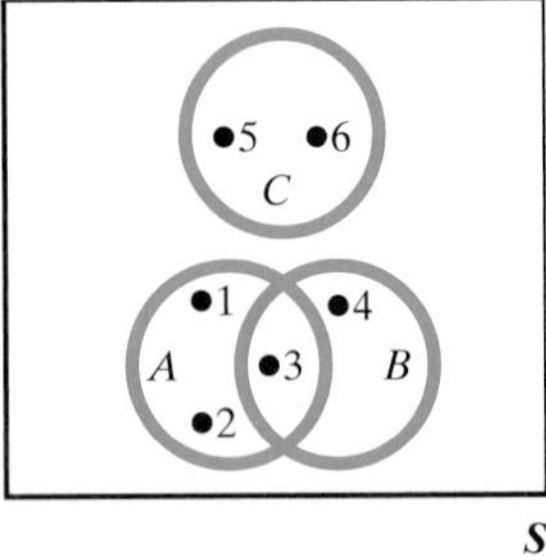

a. Which pairs of events, if any, are mutually exclusive? Why?
b. Which pairs of events, if any, are independent? Why?
c. Find $P(A \cup B)$ by adding the probabilities of the sample points and then by using the additive rule. Verify that the answers agree. Repeat for $P(A \cup C)$.

3.38 Defend or refute each of the following statements:

a. Dependent events are always mutually exclusive.
b. Mutually exclusive events are always dependent.
c. Independent events are always mutually exclusive.

3.39 For two events, A and B, $P(A) = .4$ and $P(B) = .2$.

a. If A and B are independent, find $P(A \cap B)$, $P(A|B)$, and $P(A \cup B)$.

b. If A and B are dependent, with $P(A|B) = .6$, find $P(A \cap B)$ and $P(B|A)$.

Applying the Concepts

3.40 *Forbes* (July 26, 1999) featured a story on the 20 largest public companies (determined by sales revenues) based outside the United States. For each company, the accompanying table lists the country of origin and type of business. One of these 20 firms is to be chosen at random and the country and business type observed.

a. Form a frequency table for the data, with country as the row variable and business type as the column variable.
b. Find the probability that a Japanese firm is selected.
c. Find the probability that an automobile manufacturer is selected.
d. Find the probability that an insurance or an electronics firm is selected.
e. Find the probability that a Japanese automobile manufacturer is selected.
f. Find the probability that either a German firm or an electronics firm is selected.
g. If a Japanese firm is selected, what is the probability that the company is also an automobile manufacturer?
h. If an automobile manufacturer is selected, what is the probability that a Japanese firm is also selected?
i. Are the events described in parts **b** and **c** independent? Justify your answer.

3.41 During the 1990s Major League Baseball's World Series was played nine times. There was no World Series in 1994 due to a players' strike. The next table lists the league and the division of each of the nine World Series winners. A 1990s World Series winner is to be chosen at random.

		League	
		National	American
Division	Eastern	2	5
	Central	1	1
	Western	0	0

Source: Major League Baseball, 1990.

a. Given that the winner is a member of the American League, what is the probability that the winner plays in the Eastern Division?
b. If the winner plays in the Central Division, what is the probability that the winner is a member of the National League?
c. If the winner is a member of the National League, what is the probability that the winner plays in either the Central or Western Division?

3.42 "Go" is one of the oldest and most popular strategic board games in the world, especially in Japan and Korea. This two-player game is played on a flat surface marked with 19 vertical and 19 horizontal lines. The objective is to control territory by placing pieces called "stones" on vacant points on the board. Players alternate placing their stones. The player using black stones goes first, followed by the player using white stones.

PUBLIC.DAT

Company	Country	Business
DaimlerChrysler	Germany	Automobiles
Mitsui & Co.	Japan	Trading
Itochu	Japan	Trading
Mitsubishi	Japan	Trading
Toyota Motor	Japan	Automobiles
Royal Dutch/Shell Group	Netherlands	Energy
Marubeni	Japan	Trading
Sumitomo	Japan	Trading
AXA Group	France	Insurance
Volkswagen Group	Germany	Automobiles
Nippon Tei & Tel	Japan	Telecommunications
BP Amoco	United Kingdom	Energy
Nissho Iwai	Japan	Trading
Siemens Group	Germany	Electronics
Allianz Worldwide	Germany	Insurance
Hitachi	Japan	Electronics
Matsushita Electric	Japan	Appliances
ING Group	Netherlands	Financial Services
Sony	Japan	Appliances
Metro	Germany	Retailing

Source: *Forbes,* July 26, 1999, p. 160.

GO.DAT

Black Player Level	Opponent Level	Number of Wins	Number of Games
C	A	34	34
C	B	69	79
C	C	66	118
B	A	40	54
B	B	52	95
B	C	27	79
A	A	15	28
A	B	11	51
A	C	5	39
	Totals	319	577

Source: J. Kim, and H. J. Kim. "The advantage of playing first in Go." *Chance*, Vol. 8, No. 3, Summer 1995, p. 26 (Table 3).

[*Note:* The University of Virginia requires MBA students to learn Go to understand how the Japanese conduct business.] *Chance* (Summer 1995) published an article that investigated the advantage of playing first (i.e., using the black stones) in Go. The results of 577 games recently played by professional Go players were analyzed.

a. In the 577 games, the player with the black stones won 319 times and the player with the white stones won 258 times. Use this information to assess the probability of winning when you play first in Go.

b. Professional Go players are classified by level. Group C includes the top-level players followed by Group B (middle-level) and Group A (low-level) players. The table above describes the number of games won by the player with the black stones, categorized by level of the black player and level of the opponent. Assess the probability of winning when you play first in Go for each combination of player and opponent level.

c. If the player with the black stones is ranked higher than the player with the white stones, what is the probability that black wins?

d. Given the players are of the same level, what is the probability that the player with the black stones wins?

3.43 A new type of lie detector—called the Computerized Voice Stress Analyzer (CVSA)—has been developed. The manufacturer claims that the CVSA is 98% accurate, and, unlike a polygraph machine, will not be thrown off by drugs and medical factors. However, laboratory studies by the U.S. Defense Department found that the CVSA had an accuracy rate of 49.8%—slightly less than pure chance (*Tampa Tribune*, Jan. 10, 1999). Suppose the CVSA is used to test the veracity of four suspects. Assume the suspects' responses are independent.

a. If the manufacturer's claim is true, what is the probability that the CVSA will correctly determine the veracity of all four suspects?

b. If the manufacturer's claim is true, what is the probability that the CVSA will yield an incorrect result for at least one of the four suspects?

c. Suppose that in a laboratory experiment conducted by the U.S. Defense Department on four suspects, the CVSA yielded incorrect results for two of the suspects. Use this result to make an inference about the true accuracy rate of the new lie detector.

3.44 Most companies offer their employees a variety of health care plans to choose from, e.g., preferred provider organizations (PPOs) and health maintenance organizations (HMOs) (*Monthly Labor Review*, Oct. 1995). A survey of 100 large, 100 medium, and 100 small companies that offer their employees HMOs, PPOs, and fee-for-service plans was conducted; each firm provided information on the plans chosen by their employees. These companies had a total employment of 833,303 people. A breakdown of the number of employees in each category by firm size and plan is provided in the table.

Company Size	Fee-for-Service	PPO	HMO	Totals
Small	1,808	1,757	1,456	5,021
Medium	8,953	6,491	6,983	22,382
Large	330,419	241,770	233,711	805,900
Totals	341,180	250,018	242,105	833,303

Source: Adapted from Bucci, M., and Grant, R. "Employer-sponsored health insurance: What's offered; what's chosen?" *Monthly Labor Review*, October 1995, pp. 38–43.

One employee from the 833,303 total employees is to be chosen at random for further analysis. Define the events A and B as follows:

A: {Observe an employee that chose fee-for-service}
B: {Observe an employee from a small company}

a. Find $P(B)$. b. Find $P(A \cap B)$.
c. Find $P(A \cup B)$. d. Find $P(A|B)$.
e. Are A and B independent? Justify your answer.

3.45 Refer to the *American Journal of Public Health* study of unintentional carbon monoxide (CO) poisonings in

Colorado, Exercise 3.10 (p. 129). The 981 cases were classified in a table, which is reproduced below. A case of unintentional CO poisoning is chosen at random from the 981 cases.

Source of Exposure	Fatal	Nonfatal	Total
Fire	63	53	116
Auto exhaust	60	178	238
Furnace	18	345	363
Kerosene or spaceheater	9	18	27
Appliance	9	63	72
Other gas-powered motor	3	73	76
Fireplace	0	16	16
Other	3	19	22
Unknown	9	42	51
Total	174	807	981

Source: Cook, M. C., Simon, P. A., and Hoffman, R. E. "Unintentional carbon monoxide poisoning in Colorado, 1986 through 1991." *American Journal of Public Health,* Vol. 85, No. 7, July 1995, p. 989 (Table 1). © 1995 American Public Health Association.

a. Given that the source of the poisoning is fire, what is the probability that the case is fatal?
b. Given that the case is nonfatal, what is the probability that it is caused by auto exhaust?
c. If the case is fatal, what is the probability that the source is unknown?
d. If the case is nonfatal, what is the probability that the source is not fire or a fireplace?

3.46 Physicians and pharmacists sometimes fail to inform patients adequately about the proper application of prescription drugs and about the precautions to take in order to avoid potential side effects. One method of increasing patients' awareness of the problem is for physicians to provide Patient Medication Instruction (PMI) sheets. The American Medical Association, however, has found that only 20% of the doctors who prescribe drugs frequently distribute PMI sheets to their patients. Assume that 20% of all patients receive the PMI sheet with their prescriptions and that 12% receive the PMI sheet and are hospitalized because of a drug-related problem. What is the probability that a person will be hospitalized for a drug-related problem given that the person has received the PMI sheet?

3.47 "Channel One" is an education television network that is available to all secondary schools in the United States. Participating schools are equipped with TV sets in every classroom in order to receive the Channel One broadcasts. According to *Educational Technology* (May–June 1995), 40% of all U.S. secondary schools subscribe to the Channel One Communications Network (CCN). Of these subscribers, only 5% never use the CCN broadcasts, while 20% use CCN more than five times per week.

a. Find the probability that a randomly selected U.S. secondary school subscribes to CCN but never uses the CCN broadcasts.
b. Find the probability that a randomly selected U.S. secondary school subscribes to CCN and uses the broadcasts more than five times per week.

3.48 The table describes the 62 million long-form federal tax returns filed with the Internal Revenue Service (IRS) in 1996 and the percentage of those returns that were audited by the IRS.

Income	Number of Tax Filers (millions)	Percentage Audited
Under \$25,000	13.2	1.17
\$25,000–\$49,999	27.3	0.95
\$50,000–\$99,999	17.0	1.16
\$100,000 or more	4.5	2.85

Source: Statistical Abstract of the United States: 1998, p. 347.

a. If a tax filer is randomly selected from this population of tax filers (i.e., each tax filer has an equal probability of being selected), what is the probability that the tax filer was audited?
b. If a tax filer is randomly selected from this population of tax filers, what is the probability that the tax filer had an income of \$25,000–\$49,999 *and* was audited? What is the probability that the tax filer had an income of \$50,000 or more *or* was not audited?

3.49 The genetic origin and properties of maize (modern-day corn), a domestic plant developed 8,000 years ago in Mexico, was investigated in *Economic Botany* (Jan.–Mar. 1995). Seeds from maize ears carry either single spikelets or paired spikelets, but not both. Progeny tests on approximately 600 maize ears revealed the following information. Forty percent of all seeds carry single spikelets, while 60% carry paired spikelets. A seed with single spikelets will produce maize ears with single spikelets 29% of the time and paired spikelets 71% of the time. A seed with paired spikelets will produce maize ears with single spikelets 26% of the time and paired spikelets 74% of the time.

a. Find the probability that a randomly selected maize ear seed carries a single spikelet and produces ears with single spikelets.
b. Find the probability that a randomly selected maize ear seed produces ears with paired spikelets.

3.50 In October 1994, a flaw was discovered in the Pentium chip installed in many new personal computers. The chip produced an incorrect result when dividing two numbers. Intel, the manufacturer of the Pentium chip, initially announced that such an error would occur only once in 9 billion divides, or "once in every 27,000 years" for a typical user; consequently, it did not immediately replace the chip. Assume the probability of a divide error with the Pentium chip is, in fact, $^1/_{9,000,000,000}$.

a. For a division performed using the flawed Pentium chip, what is the probability that no error will occur?

b. Consider two successive divisions performed using the flawed chip. What is the probability that neither result will be in error? (Assume that any one division has no impact on the result of any other division performed by the chip.)

c. Depending on the procedure, statistical software packages may perform an extremely large number of divisions to produce the required output. For heavy users of the software, 1 billion divisions over a short time frame is not unusual. Calculate the probability that 1 billion divisions performed using the flawed Pentium chip will result in no errors.

d. Use the result, part **c**, to compute the probability of at least one error in the 1 billion divisions. [*Note:* Two months after the flaw was discovered, Intel agreed to replace all Pentium chips free of charge.]

3.51 One definition of *Total Quality Management* (TQM) was given in Exercise 3.7. Another definition is a "management philosophy and a system of management techniques to improve product and service quality and worker productivity" (Benson, *Minnesota Management Review,* Fall 1992). One hundred U.S. companies were surveyed and it was found that 30 had implemented TQM. Among the 100 companies surveyed, 60 reported an increase in sales last year. Of those 60, 20 had implemented TQM. Suppose one of the 100 surveyed companies is to be selected at random for additional analysis.

a. What is the probability that a firm that implemented TQM is selected? That a firm whose sales increased is selected?

b. Are the two events {TQM implemented} and {Sales increased} independent or dependent? Explain.

c. Suppose that instead of 20 TQM implementers among the 60 firms reporting sales increases, there were 18. Now are the events {TQM implemented} and {Sales increased} independent or dependent? Explain.

3.7 RANDOM SAMPLING

How a sample is selected from a population is of vital importance in statistical inference because the probability of an observed sample will be used to infer the characteristics of the sampled population. To illustrate, suppose you deal yourself four cards from a deck of 52 cards and all four cards are aces. Do you conclude that your deck is an ordinary bridge deck, containing only four aces, or do you conclude that the deck is stacked with more than four aces? It depends on how the cards were drawn. If the four aces were always placed at the top of a standard bridge deck, drawing four aces is not unusual—it is certain. On the other hand, if the cards are thoroughly mixed, drawing four aces in a sample of four cards is highly improbable. The point, of course, is that in order to use the observed sample of four cards to draw inferences about the population (the deck of 52 cards), you need to know how the sample was selected from the deck.

One of the simplest and most frequently employed sampling procedures is implied in many of the previous examples and exercises. It is called *random sampling* and produces what is known as a *random sample.*

DEFINITION 3.10

If n elements are selected from a population in such a way that every set of n elements in the population has an equal probability of being selected, the n elements are said to be a **random sample.***

If a population is not too large and the elements can be numbered on slips of paper, poker chips, etc., you can physically mix the slips of paper or chips and remove n elements from the total. The numbers that appear on the chips selected would indicate the population elements to be included in the sample. Since it is often difficult to achieve a thorough mix, such a procedure only provides an approximation to

*Strictly speaking, this is a **simple random sample.** There are many different types of random samples. The simple random sample is the most common.

random sampling. Most researchers rely on **random number generators** to automatically generate the random sample. Random number generators are available in table form and they are built into most statistical software packages.

EXAMPLE 3.21

Suppose you wish to randomly sample five households from a population of 100,000 households to participate in a study.

a. How many different samples can be selected?
b. Use a random number generator to select a random sample.

Solution

a. To determine the number of samples, we'll apply the combinatorial rule of Section 3.1. In this case, $N = 100{,}000$ and $n = 5$. Then,

$$\binom{N}{n} = \binom{100{,}000}{5} = \frac{100{,}000!}{5!99{,}995!}$$

$$= \frac{100{,}000 \cdot 99{,}999 \cdot 99{,}998 \cdot 99{,}997 \cdot 99{,}996}{5 \cdot 4 \cdot 3 \cdot 2 \cdot 1}$$

$$= 8.33 \times 10^{22}$$

Thus, there are 83.3 billion trillion different samples of five households that can be selected from 100,000.

b. To ensure that each of the possible samples has an equal chance of being selected, as required for random sampling, we can employ a **random number table,** as provided in Table I of Appendix B. Random number tables are constructed in such a way that every number occurs with (approximately) equal probability. Furthermore, the occurrence of any one number in a position is independent of any of the other numbers that appear in the table. To use a table of random numbers, number the N elements in the population from 1 to N. Then turn to Table I and select a starting number in the table. Proceeding from this number either across the row or down the column, remove and record n numbers from the table.

To illustrate, first we number the households in the population from 1 to 100,000. Then, we turn to a page of Table I, say the first page. (A partial reproduction of the first page of Table I is shown in Table 3.7.) Now, we arbitrarily select a starting number, say the random number appearing in the third row, second column. This number is 48,360. Then we proceed down the second column to obtain the remaining four random numbers. In this case we have selected five random numbers, which are shaded in Table 3.7. Using the first five digits to represent households from 1 to 99,999 and the number 00000 to represent household 100,000, we can see that the households numbered

48,360
93,093
39,975
6,907
72,905

should be included in our sample. *Note:* Use only the necessary number of digits in each random number to identify the element to be included in the sample. If, in the course of recording the n numbers from the table, you select a number that has already been selected, simply discard the duplicate and select a replacement at the end of the sequence. Thus, you may have to record more than n numbers from the table to obtain a sample of n unique numbers.

TABLE 3.7 Partial Reproduction of Table I in Appendix B

Row \ Column	1	2	3	4	5	6
1	10480	15011	01536	02011	81647	91646
2	22368	46573	25595	85393	30995	89198
3	24130	48360	22527	97265	76393	64809
4	42167	93093	06243	61680	07856	16376
5	37570	39975	81837	16656	06121	91782
6	77921	06907	11008	42751	27756	53498
7	99562	72905	56420	69994	98872	31016
8	96301	91977	05463	07972	18876	20922
9	89579	14342	63661	10281	17453	18103
10	85475	36857	53342	53988	53060	59533
11	28918	69578	88231	33276	70997	79936
12	63553	40961	48235	03427	49626	69445
13	09429	93969	52636	92737	88974	33488

Can we be perfectly sure that all 83.3 billion trillion samples have an equal chance of being selected? That fact is, we can't; but to the extent that the random number table contains truly random sequences of digits, the sample should be very close to random.

Table I in Appendix B is just one example of a random number generator. For most scientific studies that require a large random sample, computers are used to generate the random sample. The SAS, MINITAB, and SPSS statistical software packages all have easy-to-use random number generators.

For example, suppose we required a random sample of $n = 50$ households from the population of 100,000 households in Example 3.21. Here, we might employ the SAS random number generator. Figure 3.21 shows a SAS printout listing 50 random numbers (from a population of 100,000). The households with these identification numbers would be included in the random sample.

FIGURE 3.21
SAS-generated random sample of 50 households

OBS	HOUSENUM	OBS	HOUSENUM	OBS	HOUSENUM	OBS	HOUSENUM
1	47122	14	47271	27	17098	40	4260
2	94231	15	3642	28	23259	41	58140
3	95531	16	7611	29	30512	42	22903
4	41445	17	81646	30	91548	43	65959
5	80287	18	92158	31	7673	44	13962
6	11731	19	36667	32	68549	45	25819
7	47523	20	71811	33	85433	46	66497
8	84847	21	78988	34	5231	47	79559
9	69822	22	3819	35	13455	48	87017
10	18270	23	21873	36	71666	49	28483
11	52636	24	74938	37	66280	50	91806
12	21750	25	23635	38	66210		
13	63363	26	35807	39	21998		

EXERCISES 3.52–3.58

Learning the Mechanics

3.52 Suppose you wish to sample $n = 2$ elements from a total of $N = 10$ elements.

a. Count the number of different samples that can be drawn, first by listing them, and then by using combinatorial mathematics. (See Section 3.1.)

b. If random sampling is to be employed, what is the probability that any particular sample will be selected?

c. Show how to use the random number table, Table I in Appendix B, to select a random sample of 2 elements from a population of 10 elements. Perform the sampling procedure 20 times. Do any two of the samples contain the same 2 elements? Given your answer to part **b,** did you expect repeated samples?

3.53 Suppose you wish to sample $n = 3$ elements from a total of $N = 600$ elements.

a. Count the number of different samples by using combinatorial mathematics (see Section 3.1).

b. If random sampling is to be employed, what is the probability that any particular sample will be selected?

c. Show how to use the random number table, Table I in Appendix B, to select a random sample of 3 elements from a population of 600 elements. Perform the sampling procedure 20 times. Do any two of the samples contain the same three elements? Given your answer to part **b,** did you expect repeated samples?

d. Use a computer to generate a random sample of 3 from the population of 600 elements.

3.54 Suppose that a population contains $N = 200{,}000$ elements. Use a computer or Table I of Appendix B to select a random sample of $n = 10$ elements from the population. Explain how you selected your sample.

Applying the Concepts

3.55 In auditing a firm's financial statements, an auditor will (1) assess the capability of the firm's accounting system to accumulate, measure, and synthesize transactional data properly, and (2) assess the operational effectiveness of the accounting system. In performing the second assessment, the auditor frequently relies on a random sample of actual transactions (Stickney and Weil, *Financial Accounting: An Introduction to Concepts, Methods, and Uses,* 1994). A particular firm has 5,382 customer accounts that are numbered from 0001 to 5382.

a. One account is to be selected at random for audit. What is the probability that account number 3,241 is selected?

b. Draw a random sample of 10 accounts and explain in detail the procedure you used.

c. Refer to part **b.** The following are two possible random samples of size 10. Is one more likely to be selected than the other? Explain.

Sample Number 1				
5011	0082	0963	0772	3415
2663	1126	0008	0026	4189
Sample Number 2				
0001	0003	0005	0007	0009
0002	0004	0006	0008	0010

3.56 To ascertain the effectiveness of their advertising campaigns, firms frequently conduct telephone interviews with consumers using *random-digit dialing.* With this approach, a random number generator mechanically creates the sample of phone numbers to be called.

a. Explain how the random number table (Table I of Appendix B, or a computer) could be used to generate a sample of seven-digit telephone numbers.

b. Use the procedure you described in part **a** to generate a sample of 10 seven-digit telephone numbers.

c. Use the procedure you described in part **a** to generate five seven-digit telephone numbers whose first three digits are 373.

3.57 The results of the previous business day's transactions for stocks traded on the New York Stock Exchange (NYSE) and five regional exchanges—the Chicago, Pacific, Philadelphia, Boston, and Cincinnati stock exchanges—are summarized each business day in the NYSE–Composite Transactions table in *The Wall Street Journal.*

a. Examine the NYSE–Composite Transactions table in a recent issue of *The Wall Street Journal* and explain how to draw a random sample of stocks from the table.

b. Use the procedure you described in part **a** to draw a random sample of 20 stocks from a recent NYSE–Composite Transactions table. For each stock in the sample, list its name (i.e., the abbreviation given in the table), its sales volume, and its closing price.

3.58 In addition to its decennial enumeration of the population, the U.S. Bureau of the Census regularly samples the population to estimate level of and changes in a number of other attributes, such as income, family size, employment, and marital status. Suppose the bureau plans to sample 1,000 households in a city that has a total of 534,322 households. Show how the bureau could use the random number table in Appendix B or a computer to generate the sample. Select the first 10 households to be included in the sample.

STATISTICS IN Action

Lottery Buster

Welcome to the Wonderful World of Lottery Bu$ters. So begins the premier issue of *Lottery Buster,* a monthly publication for players of the state lottery games. *Lottery Buster* provides interesting facts and figures on the over 40 state lotteries currently operating in the United States and purported "tips" on how to increase a player's odds of winning the lottery.

New Hampshire, in 1963, was the first state in modern times to authorize a state lottery as an alternative to increasing taxes. (Prior to this time, beginning in 1895, lotteries were banned in America for fear of corruption.) Since then, lotteries have become immensely popular for two reasons. First, they lure you with the opportunity to win millions of dollars with a $1 investment; second, when you lose, at least you know your money is going to a good cause.

The popularity of the state lottery has brought with it an avalanche of self-proclaimed "experts" and "mathematical wizards" (such as the editors of *Lottery Buster*) who provide advice on how to win the lottery—for a fee, of course! These experts—the legitimate ones, anyway—base their "systems" of winning on their knowledge of probability and statistics.

For example, more experts would agree that the "golden rule" or "first rule" in winning lotteries is *game selection.* State lotteries generally offer three types of games: Instant (scratch-off) tickets, Daily Numbers (Pick-3 and Pick-4), and the weekly Pick-6 Lotto game.

The Instant game involves scratching off the thin, opaque covering on a ticket to determine whether you have won or lost. The cost of a ticket is 50¢, and the amount to be won ranges from $1 to $100,000 in most states, while it reaches $1 million in others. *Lottery Buster* advises against playing the Instant game because it is "a pure chance play, and you can win only by dumb luck. No skill can be applied to this game."

The Daily Numbers game permits you to choose either a three-digit (Pick-3) or four-digit (Pick-4) number at a cost of $1 per ticket. Each night, the winning number is drawn. If your number matches the winning number, you win a large sum of money, usually $100,000. You do have some control over the Daily Numbers game (since you pick the numbers that you play) and, consequently, there are strategies available to increase your chances of winning. However, the Daily Numbers game, like the Instant game, is not available for out-of-state play. For this reason, and because the payoffs are relatively small, lottery experts prefer the weekly Pick-6 Lotto game.

To play Pick-6 Lotto, you select six numbers of your choice from a field of numbers ranging from 1 to *N,* where *N* depends on which state's game you are playing. For example, Florida's Lotto game involves picking six numbers ranging from 1 to 53 (denoted 6/53) as shown on the Florida Lotto ticket, Figure 3.22. Delaware's Lotto is a 6/30 game, and Pennsylvania's is a 6/40 game. The cost of a ticket is $1 and the payoff, if your six numbers match the winning numbers drawn at the end of each week, is $6 million or more, depending on the number of tickets purchased. In addition to the grand prize, you can win second-, third-, and fourth-

QUICK REVIEW

Key Terms

Additive rule of probability 135
Combinations rule 127
Combinatorial mathematics 127
Complementary events 134
Compound event 130
Conditional probability 140
Dependent events 147
Event 123
Experiment 118
Independent events 147
Intersection 131
Multiplicative rule of probability 144
Mutually exclusive events 136
Odds 130
Probability rules 122
Random number generator 155
Random number table 155
Random sample 154
Sample point 119
Sample space 119
Tree diagram 146
Unconditional probabilities 140
Union 131
Venn diagram 120

Key Formulas

$$\binom{N}{n} = \frac{N!}{n!(N-n)!}$$

where $N! = N(N-1)(N-2)\cdots(2)(1)$ Combinatorial rule 127

prize payoffs by matching five, four, and three of the six numbers drawn, respectively. And you don't have to be a resident of the state to play the state's Lotto game. Anyone can play by calling a toll-free "hotline" number.

Focus

a. Consider Florida's 6/53 Lotto game. Calculate the number of possible ways in which you can choose the six numbers from the 53 available. If you purchase a single $1 ticket, what is the probability that you win the grand prize (i.e., match all six numbers)?

b. Repeat part **a** for Delaware's 6/30 game.

c. Repeat part **a** for Pennsylvania's 6/40 game.

d. Since you can play any state's Lotto game, which of the three, Florida, Delaware, or Pennsylvania, would you choose to play? Why?

e. One strategy used to increase your odds of winning a Lotto is to employ a *wheeling system*. In a complete wheeling system, you select more than six numbers, say, seven, and play every combination of six of those seven numbers. Suppose you choose to "wheel" the following seven numbers in a 6/40 game: 2, 7, 18, 23, 30, 32, 39. How many tickets would you need to purchase to have every possible combination of the seven numbers? List the six numbers on each of these tickets.

f. Refer to part **e.** What is the probability of winning the 6/40 Lotto when you wheel seven numbers? Does the strategy, in fact, increase your odds of winning?

g. Consider the strategy of playing *neighboring pairs*. Neighboring pairs are two consecutive numbers that come up together on the winning ticket. In one state lottery, for example, 79% of the winning tickets had at least one neighboring pair. Thus, some "experts" feel that you have a better chance of winning if you include at least one neighboring pair in your number selection. Calculate the probability of winning the $^6/_{40}$ Lotto with the six numbers: 2, 15, 19, 20, 27, 37. [*Note:* 19, 20 is a neighboring pair.] Compare this probability to the one in part **c.** Comment on the neighboring pairs strategy.

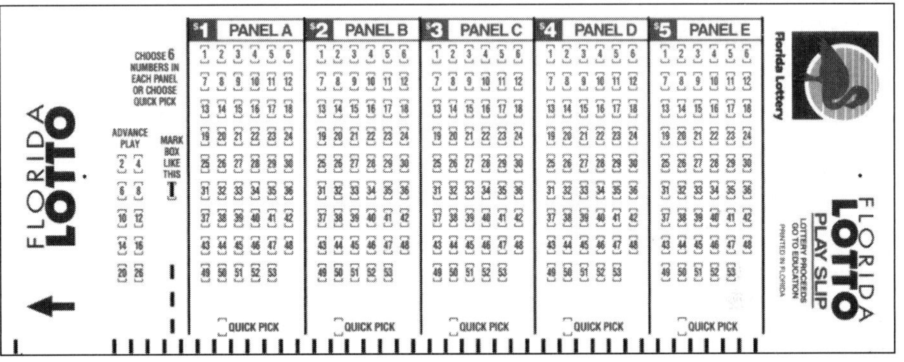

FIGURE 3.22 Reproduction of Florida's 6/53 Lotto ticket

$P(A) + P(A^c) = 1$	Complementary events 134
$P(A \cup B) = P(A) + P(B) - P(A \cap B)$	Additive rule 135
$P(A \cap B) = 0$	Mutually exclusive events 136
$P(A \cup B) = P(A) + P(B)$	Additive rule for mutually exclusive events 136
$P(A\|B) = \frac{P(A \cap B)}{P(B)}$	Conditional probability 141
$P(A \cap B) = P(A)P(B\|A) = P(B)P(A\|B)$	Multiplicative rule 144
$P(A\|B) = P(A)$	Independent events 147
$P(A \cap B) = P(A)P(B)$	Multiplicative rule for independent events 148

LANGUAGE LAB

Symbol	Pronunciation	Description
S		Sample space
S: {1, 2, 3, 4, 5}		Set of sample points, 1, 2, 3, 4, 5, in sample space

A: {1, 2}		Set of sample points, 1, 2, in event A
$P(A)$	Probability of A	Probability that event A occurs
$A \cup B$	A union B	Union of events A and B (either A or B or both occur)
$A \cap B$	A intersect B	Intersection of events A and B (both A and B occur)
A^c	A complement	Complement of event A (the event that A does not occur)
$P(A\|B)$	Probability of A given B	Conditional probability that event A occurs given that event B occurs
$\binom{N}{n}$	N chose n	Number of combinations of N elements taken n at a time
$N!$	N factorial	Multiply $N(N-1)(N-2)\cdots(2)(1)$

SUPPLEMENTARY EXERCISES 3.59–3.88

Learning the Mechanics

3.59 What are the two rules that probabilities assigned to sample points must obey?

3.60 Are mutually exclusive events also dependent events? Explain.

3.61 Given that $P(A \cap B) = .4$ and $P(A|B) = .8$, find $P(B)$.

3.62 Which of the following pairs of events are mutually exclusive? Justify your response.

a. {The Dow Jones Industrial Average increases on Monday}, {A large New York bank decreases its prime interest rate on Monday}

b. {The next sale by a PC retailer is an IBM compatible microcomputer}, {The next sale by a PC retailer is an Apple microcomputer}

c. {You reinvest all your dividend income for 1997 in a limited partnership}, {You reinvest all your dividend income for 1997 in a money market fund}

3.63 The accompanying Venn diagram illustrates a sample space containing six sample points and three events, A, B, and C. The probabilities of the sample points are: $P(1) = .3$, $P(2) = .2$, $P(3) = .1$, $P(4) = .1$, $P(5) = .1$, and $P(6) = .2$.

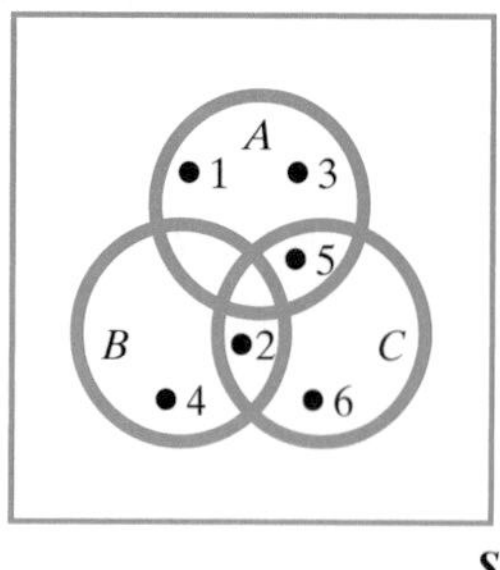

a. Find $P(A \cap B)$, $P(B \cap C)$, $P(A \cup C)$, $P(A \cup B \cup C)$, $P(B^c)$, $P(A^c \cap B)$, $P(B|C)$, and $P(B|A)$.

b. Are A and B independent? Mutually exclusive? Why?

c. Are B and C independent? Mutually exclusive? Why?

3.64 Two events, A and B, are independent, with $P(A) = .3$ and $P(B) = .1$.

a. Are A and B mutually exclusive? Why?

b. Find $P(A|B)$ and $P(B|A)$.

c. Find $P(A \cup B)$.

3.65 Find the numerical value of:

a. $6!$ b. $\binom{10}{9}$ c. $\binom{10}{1}$ d. $\binom{6}{3}$ e. $0!$

3.66 A random sample of five graduate students is to be selected from 50 MBA majors for participation in a case competition.

a. In how many different ways can the sample be drawn?

b. Show how the random number table, Table I of Appendix B, can be used to select the sample of students.

Applying the Concepts

3.67 According to a 1998 national survey conducted for CACI Marketing Systems, 25% of American adults smoke cigarettes. Of these smokers, 13% attempted (but failed) to quit smoking during the past year. Define the following events:

A: {An American adult smokes}

B: {A smoker attempted to quit smoking last year}

a. Find $P(A)$.

b. Find $P(B|A)$.

c. Find $P(A^c)$. State this probability in the words of the problem.

d. Find $P(A \cap B)$. State this probability in the words of the problem.

3.68 The types of occupations of the 106,757,000 employed workers (age 16 years and older) in the United States in 1997 are described in the table on page 161, and their relative frequencies are listed. A worker is to be selected at random from this population and his or her occupation is to be determined. (Assume that each worker in the population has only one occupation.)

a. What is the probability that the worker will be a male service worker?

b. What is the probability that the worker will be a manager or a professional?

Table for Exercise 3.68

Occupation	Relative Frequency	
Male Worker	.54	
Managerial/professional		.16
Technical/sales/administrative		.10
Service		.05
Precision production, craft, and repair		.11
Operators/fabricators/laborers		.10
Farming, forestry, and fishing		.02
Female Worker	.46	
Managerial/professional		.16
Technical/sales/administrative		.18
Service		.07
Precision production, craft, and repair		.01
Operators/fabricators/laborers		.03
Farming, forestry, and fishing		.01

Source: Statistical Abstract of the United States: 1998. p. 421.

c. What is the probability that the worker will be a female professional or a female operator/fabricator/laborer?

d. What is the probability that the worker will not be in a technical/sales administrative occupation?

3.69 A research and development company surveyed all 200 of its employees over the age of 60 and obtained the information given in the table below. One of these 200 employees is selected at random.

a. What is the probability that the person selected is on the technical staff?

b. If the person selected has over 20 years of service with the company, what is the probability that the person plans to retire at age 68?

c. If the person selected is on the technical staff, what is the probability that the person has been with the company less than 20 years?

d. What is the probability that the person selected has over 20 years with the company, is on the nontechnical staff, and plans to retire at age 65?

e. Consider the events *A:* {Plan to retire at age 68} and *B:* {On the technical staff}. Are events *A* and *B* independent? Explain.

f. Consider the event *D:* {Plan to retire at age 68 *and* on the technical staff}. Describe the complement of event *D.*

g. Consider the event *E:* {On the nontechnical staff}. Are events *B* and *E* mutually exclusive? Explain.

3.70 Many U.S. manufacturers are adopting the ISO 9000 series of standards for setting up and documenting quality systems, processes, and procedures. However, it is not generally known how managers who have led or participated in the implementation of the standards view them or how the standards were achieved. A sample of 40 ISO 9000–registered companies in Colorado was selected and the manager most responsible for ISO 9000 implementation was interviewed (*Quality Progress,* 1995). The following are some of the data obtained by the study:

Level of Top Management Involvement in the ISO 9000 Registration Process	Frequency
Very involved	9
Moderate involvement	16
Minimal involvement	12
Not involved	3

Length of Time to Achieve ISO 9000 Registration	Frequency
Less than 1 year	5
1–1.5 years	21
1.6–2 years	9
2.1–2.5 years	2
More than 2.5 years	3

Source: Weston, F.C., "What do managers really think of the ISO 9000 registration process?" *Quality Progress,* October 1995, p. 68–69 (Tables 3 and 4).

Suppose one of the 40 managers who were interviewed is to be randomly selected for additional questioning. Consider the events defined below:

A: {The manager was involved in the ISO 9000 registration}

B: {The length of time to achieve ISO 9000 registration was more than 2 years}

a. Find $P(A)$.

b. Find $P(B)$.

c. Explain why the above data are not sufficient to determine whether events *A* and *B* are independent.

3.71 The table on page 162 lists the overall percentage of domestic flights of major U.S. airlines that arrive on time.

a. One of these 10 airlines is to be selected at random. What is the probability that Southwest is selected? That Continental is selected?

b. If one of Continental's domestic flights were randomly selected, what is the probability that the flight arrived on time? Was late?

c. These data are reported each month by the airlines to the U.S. Department of Transportation. Consequently,

Table for Exercise 3.69

	UNDER 20 YEARS WITH COMPANY		OVER 20 YEARS WITH COMPANY	
	Technical Staff	Nontechnical Staff	Technical Staff	Nontechnical Staff
Plan to Retire at Age 65	31	5	45	12
Plan to Retire at Age 68	59	25	15	8

Table for Exercise 3.71

Carrier	Percent Arriving on Time
Southwest	82.9
American	78.5
Northwest	78.4
USAir	77.0
America West	75.8
United	75.4
Delta	74.3
TWA	72.9
Alaska	70.0
Continental	64.1

Source: Aviation Daily, August 7, 1995.

some experts question their accuracy. With this in mind, would you recommend that these percentages be treated as upper or lower bounds for the actual on-time percentages? Explain.

3.72 The state legislature has appropriated $1 million to be distributed in the form of grants to individuals and organizations engaged in the research and development of alternative energy sources. You have been hired by the state's energy agency to assemble a panel of five energy experts whose task it will be to determine which individuals and organizations should receive the grant money. You have identified 11 equally qualified individuals who are willing to serve on the panel. How many different panels of five experts could be formed from these 11 individuals?

3.73 A manufacturer of electronic digital watches claims that the probability of its watch running more than 1 minute slow or 1 minute fast after 1 year of use is .05. A consumer protection agency has purchased four of the manufacturer's watches with the intention of testing the claim.

a. Assuming that the manufacturer's claim is correct, what is the probability that none of the watches are as accurate as claimed?

b. Assuming that the manufacturer's claim is correct, what is the probability that exactly two of the four watches are as accurate as claimed?

c. Suppose that only one of the four tested watches is as accurate as claimed. What inference can be made about the manufacturer's claim? Explain.

d. Suppose that none of the watches tested are as accurate as claimed. Is it necessarily true that the manufacturer's claim is false? Explain.

3.74 The corporations in the highly competitive razor blade industry do a tremendous amount of advertising each year. Corporation G gave a supply of three top name brands, G, S, and W, to a consumer and asked her to use them and rank them in order of preference. The corporation was, of course, hoping the consumer would prefer its brand and rank it first, thereby giving them some material for a consumer interview advertising campaign. If the consumer did not prefer one blade over any other, but was still required to rank the blades, what is the probability that:

a. The consumer ranked brand G first?

b. The consumer ranked brand G last?

c. The consumer ranked brand G last and brand W second?

d. The consumer ranked brand W first, brand G second, and brand S third?

3.75 Acupoll is a consumer preference poll used to predict whether newly developed products will succeed if they are brought to market. The reliability of the Acupoll has been described as follows: The probability that Acupoll predicts the success of a particular product, given that later the product actually is successful, is .89 (*Minneapolis Star Tribune,* Dec. 16, 1992). A company is considering the introduction of a new product and assesses the product's probability of success to be .90. If this company were to have its product evaluated through Acupoll, what is the probability that Acupoll predicts success for the product and the product actually turns out to be successful?

3.76 Use your intuitive understanding of independence to form an opinion about whether each of the following scenarios represents an independent event.

a. The results of consecutive tosses of a coin

b. The opinions of randomly selected individuals in a preelection poll

c. A major league baseball player's results in two consecutive at-bats

d. The amount of gain or loss associated with investments in different stocks if these stocks are bought on the same day and sold on the same day one month later

e. The amount of gain or loss associated with investments in different stocks that are bought and sold in different time periods, five years apart

f. The prices bid by two different development firms in response to a building construction proposal

3.77 A local country club has a membership of 600 and operates facilities that include an 18-hole championship golf course and 12 tennis courts. Before deciding whether to accept new members, the club president would like to know how many members regularly use each facility. A survey of the membership indicates that 70% regularly use the golf course, 50% regularly use the tennis courts, and 5% use neither of these facilities regularly.

a. Construct a Venn diagram to describe the results of the survey.

b. If one club member is chosen at random, what is the probability that the member uses either the golf course or the tennis courts or both?

c. If one member is chosen at random, what is the probability that the member uses both the golf and the tennis facilities?

d. A member is chosen at random from among those known to use the tennis courts regularly. What is the probability that the member also uses the golf course regularly?

3.78 A particular automatic sprinkler system for high-rise apartment buildings, office buildings, and hotels has two different types of activation devices for each sprinkler head. One type has a reliability of .91 (i.e., the probability that it will activate the sprinkler when it should is .91). The other type, which operates independently of the first type, has a reliability of .87. Suppose a serious fire starts near a particular sprinkler head.

a. What is the probability that the sprinkler head will be activated?

b. What is the probability that the sprinkler head will not be activated?

c. What is the probability that both activation devices will work properly?

d. What is the probability that only the device with reliability .91 will work properly?

3.79 "What are the characteristics of families with young children (under age 6)?" This was one of several questions posed by a University of Michigan researcher in *Children and Youth Services Review* (Vol. 17, 1995). Using data obtained from the National Child Care Survey, the income distribution and employment status of these families are summarized in the table below.

a. Find the probability that a randomly selected family with young children has an income above the poverty line, but less than $25,000.

b. Find the probability that a randomly selected family with young children has unemployed parents or no parents.

c. Find the probability that a randomly selected family with young children has an income below the poverty line.

3.80 The *Journal of Risk and Uncertainty* (May 1992) published an article investigating the relationship of injury rate of drivers of all-terrain vehicles (ATVs) to a variety of factors. One of the more interesting factors studied, age of the driver, was found to have a strong relationship to injury rate. The article reports that prior to a safety-awareness program, 14% of the ATV drivers were under age 12; another 13% were 12–15, and 48% were under age 25. Suppose an ATV driver is selected at random prior to the installation of the safety-awareness program.

a. Find the probability that the ATV driver is 15 years old or younger.

b. Find the probability that the ATV driver is 25 years old or older.

c. Given that the ATV driver is under age 25, what is the probability the driver is under age 12?

d. Are the events Under age 25 and Under age 12 mutually exclusive? Why or why not?

e. Are the events Under age 25 and Under age 12 independent? Why or why not?

3.81 The probability that an Avon salesperson sells beauty products to a prospective customer on the first visit to the customer is .4. If the salesperson fails to make the sale on the first visit, the probability that the sale will be made on the second visit is .65. The salesperson never visits a prospective customer more than twice. What is the probability that the salesperson will make a sale to a particular customer?

3.82 The performance of quality inspectors affects both the quality of outgoing products and the cost of the products. A product that passes inspection is assumed to meet quality standards; a product that fails inspection may be reworked, scrapped, or reinspected. Quality engineers at Westinghouse Electric Corporation evaluated performances of inspectors in judging the quality of solder joints by comparing each inspector's classifications of a set of 153 joints with the consensus evaluation of a panel of experts. The results for a particular inspector are shown in the accompanying table.

	Inspector's Judgment	
Committee's Judgment	**Joint Acceptable**	**Joint Rejectable**
Joint acceptable	101	10
Joint rejectable	23	19

Source: Meagher, J.J., and Scazzero, J.A. "Measuring inspector variability." *39th Annual Quality Congress Transactions,* May 1985, pp. 75–81, American Society for Quality Control

One of the 153 solder joints is to be selected at random.

Table for Exercise 3.79

Income Characteristic	Percentage
No parent	1
Below poverty line; not employed	7
Below poverty line; employed	7
Above poverty line, but less than $25,000; not employed	2
Above poverty line, but less than $25,000; employed	22
$25,000 or more	61
Total	100

a. What is the probability that the inspector judges the joint to be acceptable? That the committee judges the joint to be acceptable?
b. What is the probability that both the inspector and the committee judge the joint to be acceptable? That neither judge the joint to be acceptable?
c. What is the probability that the inspector and the committee disagree? Agree?

3.83 The first figure shown below is a schematic representation of a system comprised of three components. The system operates properly only if all three components operate properly. The three components are said to operate *in series*. The components could be mechanical or electrical; they could be work stations in an assembly process; or they could represent the functions of three different departments in an organization. The probability of failure for each component is listed in the table. Assume the components operate independently of each other.

Component	Probability of Failure
1	.12
2	.09
3	.11

a. Find the probability that the system operates properly.
b. What is the probability that at least one of the components will fail and therefore that the system will fail?

3.84 The second figure shown below is a representation of a system comprised of two subsystems that are said to operate *in parallel*. Each subsystem has two components that operate in series (refer to Exercise 3.83). The system will operate properly as long as at least one of the subsystems functions properly. The probability of failure for each component in the system is .1. Assume the components operate independently of each other.

a. Find the probability that the system operates properly.
b. Find the probability that exactly one subsystem fails.
c. Find the probability that the system fails to operate properly.
d. How many parallel subsystems like the two shown here would be required to guarantee that the system would operate properly at least 99% of the time?

3.85 Consider the population of new savings accounts opened in one business day at a bank, as shown in the table. Suppose you wish to draw a random sample of two accounts from this population.

Account Number	0001	0002	0003	0004	0005
Account Balance	\$1,000	\$12,500	\$850	\$1,000	\$3,450

a. List all possible different pairs of accounts that could be obtained.
b. What is the probability of selecting accounts 0001 and 0004?
c. What is the probability of selecting two accounts that each have a balance of \$1,000? That each have a balance other than \$1,000?

3.86 A small brewery has two bottling machines. Machine A produces 75% of the bottles and machine B produces 25%. One out of every 20 bottles filled by A is rejected for some reason, while one out of every 30 bottles from B is rejected. What proportion of bottles is rejected? What is the probability that a randomly selected bottle comes from machine A, given that it is accepted?

3.87 Businesses that offer credit to their customers are inevitably faced with the task of collecting unpaid bills. A study of collection remedies used by creditors was published in the *Journal of Financial Research* (Spring 1986). As part of the study, creditors in four states were asked about how they deal with past-due bills. Their responses are tallied in the table on page 165. "Tough actions" included filing a legal action, turning the debt over to a

Figure for Exercise 3.83

A System Comprised of Three Components in Series

Figure for Exercise 3.84

A System Comprised of Two Parallel Subsystems

Subsystem A
#1
#2
Input
Output
Subsystem B
#3
#4

	Wisconsin	Illinois	Arkansas	Louisiana
Take tough action early	0	1	5	1
Take tough action later	37	23	22	21
Never take tough action	9	11	6	15

third party such as an attorney or collection agency, garnishing wages, and repossessing secured property. Suppose one of the creditors questioned is selected at random.

a. What is the probability that the creditor is from Wisconsin or Louisiana?

b. What is the probability that the creditor is not from Wisconsin or Louisiana?

c. What is the probability that the creditor never takes tough action?

d. What is the probability that the creditor is from Arkansas and never takes tough action?

e. What is the probability that the creditor never takes tough action, given that the creditor is from Arkansas?

f. If the creditor takes tough action early, what is the probability that the creditor is from Arkansas or Louisiana?

g. What is the probability that a creditor from Arkansas never takes tough action?

3.88 A fair coin is flipped 20 times and 20 heads are observed. In such cases it is often said that a tail is due on the next flip. Is this statement true or false? Explain.

Chapter 4

RANDOM VARIABLES AND PROBABILITY DISTRIBUTIONS

CONTENTS

STATISTICS IN ACTION

Where We've Been

We saw by illustration in Chapter 3 how probability would be used to make an inference about a population from data contained in an observed sample. We also noted that probability would be used to measure the reliability of the inference.

Where We're Going

Most of the experimental events we encountered in Chapter 3 were events described in words and denoted by capital letters. In real life, most sample observations are numerical—in other words, they are numerical data. In this chapter, we learn that data are observed values of random variables. We study several important random variables and learn how to find the probabilities of specific numerical outcomes.

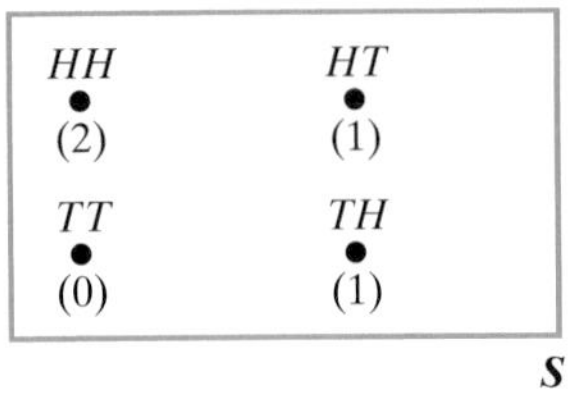

HH ● (2)	*HT* ● (1)
TT ● (0)	*TH* ● (1)

S

FIGURE 4.1
Venn diagram for coin-tossing experiment

You may have noticed that many of the examples of experiments in Chapter 3 generated quantitative (numerical) observations. The Consumer Price Index, the unemployment rate, the number of sales made in a week, and the yearly profit of a company are all examples of numerical measurements of some phenomenon. Thus, most experiments have sample points that correspond to values of some numerical variable.

To illustrate, consider the coin-tossing experiment of Chapter 3. Figure 4.1 is a Venn diagram showing the sample points when two coins are tossed and the up faces (heads or tails) of the coins are observed. One possible numerical outcome is the total number of heads observed. These values (0, 1, or 2) are shown in parentheses on the Venn diagram, one numerical value associated with each sample point. In the jargon of probability, the variable "total number of heads observed when two coins are tossed" is called a *random variable.*

DEFINITION 4.1

A **random variable** is a variable that assumes numerical values associated with the random outcomes of an experiment, where one (and only one) numerical value is assigned to each sample point.

The term *random variable* is more meaningful than the term *variable* because the adjective *random* indicates that the coin-tossing experiment may result in one of the several possible values of the variable—0, 1, and 2—according to the *random* outcome of the experiment, *HH*, *HT*, *TH*, and *TT*. Similarly, if the experiment is to count the number of customers who use the drive-up window of a bank each day, the random variable (the number of customers) will vary from day to day, partly because of the random phenomena that influence whether customers use the drive-up window. Thus, the possible values of this random variable range from 0 to the maximum number of customers the window could possibly serve in a day.

We define two different types of random variables, *discrete* and *continuous*, in Section 4.1. Then we spend the remainder of this chapter discussing specific types of random variables and the aspects that make them important in business applications.

4.1 TWO TYPES OF RANDOM VARIABLES

Recall that the sample point probabilities corresponding to an experiment must sum to 1. Dividing one unit of probability among the sample points in a sample space and consequently assigning probabilities to the values of a random variable is not always as easy as the examples in Chapter 3 might lead you to believe. If the number of sample points can be completely listed, the job is straightforward. But if the experiment results in an infinite number of numerical sample points that are impossible to list, the task of assigning probabilities to the sample points is impossible without the aid of a probability model. The next three examples demonstrate the need for different probability models depending on the number of values that a random variable can assume.

EXAMPLE 4.1

A panel of 10 experts for the *Wine Spectator* (a national publication) is asked to taste a new white wine and assign a rating of 0, 1, 2, or 3. A score is then obtained by adding together the ratings of the 10 experts. How many values can this random variable assume?

Solution A sample point is a sequence of 10 numbers associated with the rating of each expert. For example, one sample point is

$$\{1, 0, 0, 1, 2, 0, 0, 3, 1, 0\}$$

The random variable assigns a score to each one of these sample points by adding the 10 numbers together. Thus, the smallest score is 0 (if all 10 ratings are 0) and the largest score is 30 (if all 10 ratings are 3). Since every integer between 0 and 30 is a possible score, the random variable denoted by the symbol x can assume 31 values. Note that the value of the random variable for the sample point above is $x = 8$.*

This is an example of a *discrete random variable,* since there is a finite number of distinct possible values. Whenever all the possible values a random variable can assume can be listed (or counted), the random variable is discrete. ✶

EXAMPLE 4.2 Suppose the Environmental Protection Agency (EPA) takes readings once a month on the amount of pesticide in the discharge water of a chemical company. If the amount of pesticide exceeds the maximum level set by the EPA, the company is forced to take corrective action and may be subject to penalty. Consider the following random variable:

Number, x, of months before the company's discharge exceeds the EPA's maximum level

What values can x assume?

Solution The company's discharge of pesticide may exceed the maximum allowable level on the first month of testing, the second month of testing, etc. It is possible that the company's discharge will *never* exceed the maximum level. Thus, the set of possible values for the number of months until the level is first exceeded is the set of all positive integers

$$1, 2, 3, 4, \ldots$$

If we can list the values of a random variable x, even though the list is never-ending, we call the list **countable** and the corresponding random variable *discrete*. Thus, the number of months until the company's discharge first exceeds the limit is a *discrete random variable.* ✶

EXAMPLE 4.3 Refer to Example 4.2. A second random variable of interest is the amount x of pesticide (in milligrams per liter) found in the monthly sample of discharge waters from the chemical company. What values can this random variable assume?

*The standard mathematical convention is to use a capital letter (e.g., X) to denote the theoretical random variable. The possible values (or realizations) of the random variable are typically denoted with a lowercase letter (e.g., x). Thus, in Example 4.1, the random variable X can take on the values $x = 0, 1, 2, \ldots, 30$. Since this notation can be confusing for introductory statistics students, we simplify the notation by using the lowercase x to represent the random variable throughout.

Solution Unlike the *number* of months before the company's discharge exceeds the EPA's maximum level, the set of all possible values for the *amount* of discharge *cannot* be listed—i.e., is not countable. The possible values for the amounts of pesticide would correspond to the points on the interval between 0 and the largest possible value the amount of the discharge could attain, the maximum number of milligrams that could occupy 1 liter of volume. (Practically, the interval would be much smaller, say, between 0 and 500 milligrams per liter.) When the values of a random variable are not countable but instead correspond to the points on some interval, we call it a *continuous random variable.* Thus, the *amount* of pesticide in the chemical plant's discharge waters is a *continuous random variable.* ✶

DEFINITION 4.2

Random variables that can assume a *countable* number of values are called **discrete.**

DEFINITION 4.3

Random variables that can assume values corresponding to any of the points contained in one or more intervals are called **continuous.**

Several more examples of discrete random variables follow:

1. The number of sales made by a salesperson in a given week: $x = 0, 1, 2, \ldots$
2. The number of consumers in a sample of 500 who favor a particular product over all competitors: $x = 0, 1, 2, \ldots, 500$
3. The number of bids received in a bond offering: $x = 0, 1, 2, \ldots$
4. The number of errors on a page of an accountant's ledger: $x = 0, 1, 2, \ldots$
5. The number of customers waiting to be served in a restaurant at a particular time: $x = 0, 1, 2, \ldots$

Note that each of the examples of discrete random variables begins with the words "The number of . . ." This wording is very common, since the discrete random variables most frequently observed are counts.

We conclude this section with some more examples of continuous random variables:

1. The length of time between arrivals at a hospital clinic: $0 \le x < \infty$ (infinity)
2. For a new apartment complex, the length of time from completion until a specified number of apartments are rented: $0 \le x < \infty$
3. The amount of carbonated beverage loaded into a 12-ounce can in a can-filling operation: $0 \le x \le 12$
4. The depth at which a successful oil drilling venture first strikes oil: $0 \le x \le c$, where c is the maximum depth obtainable
5. The weight of a food item bought in a supermarket: $0 \le x \le 500$ [*Note*: Theoretically, there is no upper limit on x, but it is unlikely that it would exceed 500 pounds.]

Discrete random variables and their probability distributions are discussed in Sections 4.2-4.4. Continuous random variables and their probability distributions are the topic of Sections 4.5-4.12.

EXERCISES 4.1–4.10

Applying the Concepts

4.1 What is a random variable?

4.2 How do discrete and continuous random variables differ?

4.3 Security analysts are professionals who devote full-time efforts to evaluating the investment worth of a narrow list of stocks. For example, one security analyst might specialize in bank stocks while another specializes in evaluating firms in the computer or pharmaceutical industries. The following variables are of interest to security analysts (Radcliffe, *Investments: Concepts, Analysis and Strategy,* 1994). Which are discrete and which are continuous random variables?

a. The closing price of a particular stock on the New York Stock Exchange
b. The number of shares of a particular stock that are traded each business day
c. The quarterly earnings of a particular firm
d. The percentage change in yearly earnings between 1999 and 2000 for a particular firm
e. The number of new products introduced per year by a firm
f. The time until a pharmaceutical company gains approval from the U.S. Food and Drug Administration to market a new drug

4.4 Which of the following describe continuous random variables, and which describe discrete random variables?

a. The number of newspapers sold by the *New York Times* each month
b. The amount of ink used in printing a Sunday edition of the *New York Times*
c. The actual number of ounces in a one-gallon bottle of laundry detergent
d. The number of defective parts in a shipment of nuts and bolts
e. The number of people collecting unemployment insurance each month

4.5 Give two examples of a business-oriented discrete random variable. Do the same for a continuous random variable.

4.6 Give an example of a discrete random variable that would be of interest to a banker.

4.7 Give an example of a continuous random variable that would be of interest to an economist.

4.8 Give an example of a discrete random variable that would be of interest to the manager of a hotel.

4.9 Give two examples of discrete random variables that would be of interest to the manager of a clothing store.

4.10 Give an example of a continuous random variable that would be of interest to a stockbroker.

4.2 PROBABILITY DISTRIBUTIONS FOR DISCRETE RANDOM VARIABLES

A complete description of a discrete random variable requires that we *specify the possible values the random variable can assume and the probability associated with each value.* To illustrate, consider Example 4.4.

EXAMPLE 4.4 Recall the experiment of tossing two coins (Section 4.1), and let x be the number of heads observed. Find the probability associated with each value of the random variable x, assuming the two coins are fair.

Solution The sample space and sample points for this experiment are reproduced in Figure 4.2. Note that the random variable x can assume values 0, 1, 2. Recall (from Chapter 3) that the probability associated with each of the four sample points is $\frac{1}{4}$. Then, identifying the probabilities of the sample points associated with each of these values of x, we have

$$P(x = 0) = P(TT) = \tfrac{1}{4}$$
$$P(x = 1) = P(TH) + P(HT) = \tfrac{1}{4} + \tfrac{1}{4} = \tfrac{1}{2}$$
$$P(x = 2) = P(HH) = \tfrac{1}{4}$$

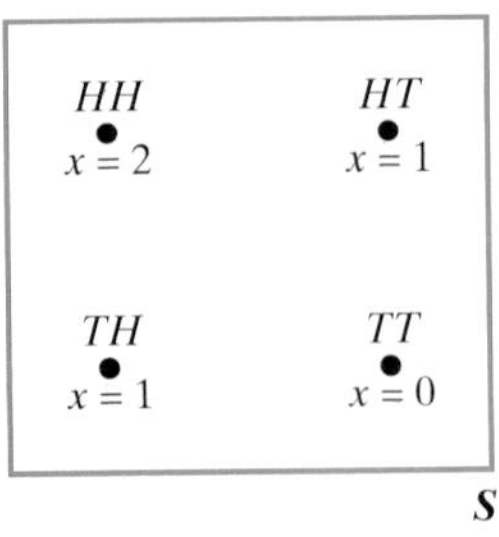
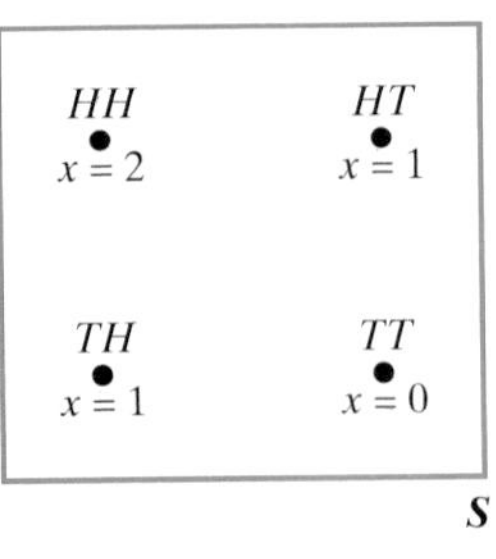

FIGURE 4.2
Venn diagram for the two-coin-toss experiment

TABLE 4.1 Probability Distribution for Coin-Toss Experiment: Tabular Form

x	$p(x)$
0	$\frac{1}{4}$
1	$\frac{1}{2}$
2	$\frac{1}{4}$

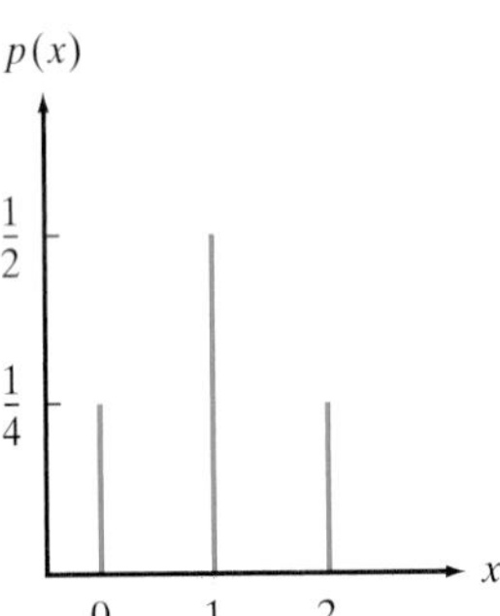

a. Point representation of $p(x)$

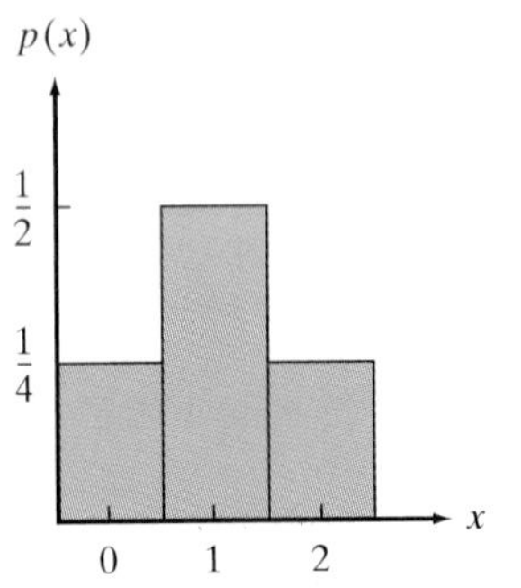

b. Histogram representation of $p(x)$

FIGURE 4.3
Probability distribution for coin-toss experiment: Graphical form

Thus, we now know the values the random variable can assume (0, 1, 2) and how the probability is *distributed over* these values ($^1\!/_4$, $^1\!/_2$, $^1\!/_4$). This completely describes the random variable and is referred to as the *probability distribution*, denoted by the symbol $p(x)$.* The probability distribution for the coin-toss example is shown in tabular form in Table 4.1 and in graphical form in Figure 4.3. Since the probability distribution for a discrete random variable is concentrated at specific points (values of x), the graph in Figure 4.3a represents the probabilities as the heights of vertical lines over the corresponding values of x. Although the representation of the probability distribution as a histogram, as in Figure 4.3b, is less precise (since the probability is spread over a unit interval), the histogram representation will prove useful when we approximate probabilities of certain discrete random variables in Section 4.4.

We could also present the probability distribution for x as a formula, but this would unnecessarily complicate a very simple example. We give the formulas for the probability distributions of some common discrete random variables later in this chapter.

DEFINITION 4.4

The **probability distribution** of a discrete random variable is a graph, table, or formula that specifies the probability associated with each possible value the random variable can assume.

Two requirements must be satisfied by all probability distributions for discrete random variables.

*In standard mathematical notation, the probability that a random variable X takes on a value x is denoted $P(X = x) = p(x)$. Thus, $P(X = 0) = p(0)$, $P(X = 1) = p(1)$, etc. In this introductory text, we adopt the simpler $p(x)$ notation.

Requirements for the Probability Distribution of a Discrete Random Variable, x

1. $p(x) \geq 0$ for all values of x
2. $\sum p(x) = 1$

where the summation of $p(x)$ is over all possible values of x.*

Example 4.4 illustrates how the probability distribution for a discrete random variable can be derived, but for many practical situations the task is much more difficult. Fortunately, many experiments and associated discrete random variables observed in business possess identical characteristics. Thus, you might observe a random variable in a marketing experiment that would possess the same characteristics as a random variable observed in accounting, economics, or management. We classify random variables according to type of experiment, derive the probability distribution for each of the different types, and then use the appropriate probability distribution when a particular type of random variable is observed in a practical situation. The probability distributions for most commonly occurring discrete random variables have already been derived. (We describe two of these in Sections 4.3 and 4.4.) This fact simplifies the problem of finding the appropriate probability distributions for the business analyst.

Since probability distributions are analogous to the relative frequency distributions of Chapter 2, it should be no surprise that the mean and standard deviation are useful descriptive measures. For example, if a discrete random variable x were observed a very large number of times and the data generated were arranged in a relative frequency distribution, the relative frequency distribution would be indistinguishable from the probability distribution for the random variable. Thus, the probability distribution for a random variable is a theoretical model for the relative frequency distribution of a population. To the extent that the two distributions are equivalent (and we will assume they are), the probability distribution for x possesses a mean μ and a variance σ^2 that are identical to the corresponding descriptive measures for the population. This section explains how you can find the mean value for a random variable. We illustrate the procedure with an example.

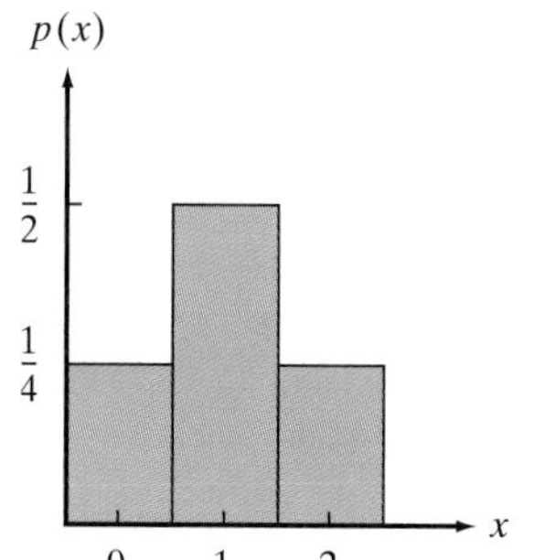

FIGURE 4.4
Probability distribution for a two-coin toss

Examine the probability distribution for x (the number of heads observed in the toss of two fair coins) in Figure 4.4. Try to locate the mean of the distribution intuitively. We may reason that the mean μ of this distribution is equal to 1 as follows: In a large number of experiments, $\frac{1}{4}$ should result in $x = 0$, $\frac{1}{2}$ in $x = 1$, and $\frac{1}{4}$ in $x = 2$ heads. Therefore, the average number of heads is

$$\mu = 0(\tfrac{1}{4}) + 1(\tfrac{1}{2}) + 2(\tfrac{1}{4}) = 0 + \tfrac{1}{2} + \tfrac{1}{2} = 1$$

Note that to get the population mean of the random variable x, we multiply each possible value of x by its probability $p(x)$, and then sum this product over all possible values of x. The *mean of x* is also referred to as the *expected value of x*, denoted $E(x)$.

*Unless otherwise indicated, summations will always be over all possible values of x.

DEFINITION 4.5

The **mean,** or **expected value,** of a discrete random variable x is

$$\mu = E(x) = \sum xp(x)$$

The term *expected* is a mathematical term and should not be interpreted as it is typically used. Specifically, a random variable might never be equal to its "expected value." Rather, the expected value is the mean of the probability distribution or a measure of its central tendency. You can think of μ as the mean value of x in a *very large* (actually, *infinite*) number of repetitions of the experiment.

EXAMPLE 4.5 Suppose you work for an insurance company, and you sell a $10,000 one-year term insurance policy at an annual premium of $290. Actuarial tables show that the probability of death during the next year for a person of your customer's age, sex, health, etc., is .001. What is the expected gain (amount of money made by the company) for a policy of this type?

Solution The experiment is to observe whether the customer survives the upcoming year. The probabilities associated with the two sample points, Live and Die, are .999 and .001, respectively. The random variable you are interested in is the gain x, which can assume the values shown in the following table.

Gain, x	Sample Point	Probability
$290	Customer lives	.999
−$9,710	Customer dies	.001

If the customer lives, the company gains the $290 premium as profit. If the customer dies, the gain is negative because the company must pay $10,000, for a net "gain" of $(290 − 10,000) = −$9,710. The expected gain is therefore

$$\begin{aligned}\mu = E(x) &= \sum_{\text{all } x} xp(x) \\ &= (290)(.999) + (-9{,}710)(.001) = \$280\end{aligned}$$

In other words, if the company were to sell a very large number of one-year $10,000 policies to customers possessing the characteristics described above, it would (on the average) net $280 per sale in the next year.

Example 4.5 illustrates that the expected value of a random variable x need not equal a possible value of x. That is, the expected value is $280, but x will equal either $290 or −$9,710 each time the experiment is performed (a policy is sold and a year elapses). The expected value is a measure of central tendency—and in this case represents the average over a very large number of one-year policies—but is not a possible value of x.

We learned in Chapter 2 that the mean and other measures of central tendency tell only part of the story about a set of data. The same is true about probability distributions. We need to measure variability as well. Since a probability distribution can be viewed as a representation of a population, we will use the population variance to measure its variability.

The *population variance* σ^2 is defined as the average of the squared distance of x from the population mean μ. Since x is a random variable, the squared distance, $(x - \mu)^2$, is also a random variable. Using the same logic used to find the mean value of x, we find the mean value of $(x - \mu)^2$ by multiplying all possible values of $(x - \mu)^2$ by $p(x)$ and then summing over all possible x values.* This quantity,

$$E[(x - \mu)^2] = \sum_{\text{all } x} (x - \mu)^2 p(x)$$

is also called the *expected value of the squared distance from the mean;* that is, $\sigma^2 = E[(x - \mu)^2]$. The standard deviation of x is defined as the square root of the variance σ^2.

DEFINITION 4.6

The **variance** of a discrete random variable x is

$$\sigma^2 = E[(x - \mu)^2] = \sum (x - \mu)^2 p(x)$$

DEFINITION 4.7

The **standard deviation** of a discrete random variable is equal to the square root of the variance, i.e., $\sigma = \sqrt{\sigma^2}$.

Knowing the mean μ and standard deviation σ of the probability distribution of x, in conjunction with Chebyshev's Rule (Table 2.8) and the Empirical Rule (Table 2.9), we can make statements about the likelihood that values of x will fall within the intervals $\mu \pm \sigma$, $\mu \pm 2\sigma$, and $\mu \pm 3\sigma$. These probabilities are given in the box.

Chebyshev's Rule and Empirical Rule for a Discrete Random Variable

Let x be a discrete random variable with probability distribution $p(x)$, mean μ, and standard deviation σ. Then, depending on the shape of $p(x)$, the following probability statements can be made:

	Chebyshev's Rule	**Empirical Rule**
	Applies to any probability distribution (see Figure 4.5a)	Applies to probability distributions that are mound-shaped and symmetric (see Figure 4.5b)
$P(\mu - \sigma < x < \mu + \sigma)$	≥ 0	$\approx .68$
$P(\mu - 2\sigma < x < \mu + 2\sigma)$	$\geq \frac{3}{4}$	$\approx .95$
$P(\mu - 3\sigma < x < \mu + 3\sigma)$	$\geq \frac{8}{9}$	≈ 1.00

*It can be shown that $E[(x - \mu)^2] = E(x^2) - \mu^2$ where $E(x^2) = \sum x^2 p(x)$. Note the similarity between this expression and the shortcut formula $\sum (x - \bar{x})^2 = \sum x^2 - \left(\sum x\right)^2 / n$ given in Chapter 2.

FIGURE 4.5
Shapes of two probability distributions for a discrete random variable x

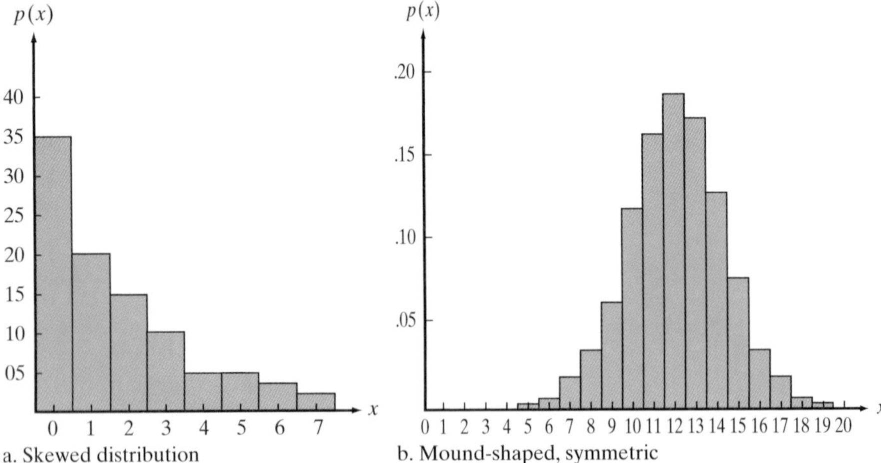

EXAMPLE 4.6

Suppose you invest a fixed sum of money in each of five Internet business ventures. Assume you know that 70% of such ventures are successful, the outcomes of the ventures are independent of one another, and the probability distribution for the number, x, of successful ventures out of five is:

x	0	1	2	3	4	5
$p(x)$	.002	.029	.132	.309	.360	.168

a. Find $\mu = E(x)$. Interpret the result.

b. Find $\sigma = \sqrt{E[(x - \mu)^2]}$. Interpret the result.

c. Graph $p(x)$. Locate μ and the interval $\mu \pm 2\sigma$ on the graph. Use either Chebyshev's Rule or the Empirical Rule to approximate the probability that x falls in this interval. Compare this result with the actual probability.

d. Would you expect to observe fewer than two successful ventures out of five?

Solution

a. Applying the formula,

$$\mu = E(x) = \sum xp(x) = 0(.002) + 1(.029) + 2(.132) + 3(.309) + 4(.360) + 5(.168) = 3.50$$

On average, the number of successful ventures out of five will equal 3.5. Remember that this expected value only has meaning when the experiment—investing in five Internet business ventures—is repeated a large number of times.

b. Now we calculate the variance of x:

$$\begin{aligned}\sigma^2 = E[(x - \mu)^2] &= \sum (x - \mu)^2 p(x) \\ &= (0 - 3.5)^2(.002) + (1 - 3.5)^2(.029) + (2 - 3.5)^2(.132) \\ &\quad + (3 - 3.5)^2(.309) + (4 - 3.5)^2(.360) + (5 - 3.5)^2(.168) \\ &= 1.05\end{aligned}$$

Thus, the standard deviation is

$$\sigma = \sqrt{\sigma^2} = \sqrt{1.05} = 1.02$$

This value measures the spread of the probability distribution of x, the number of successful ventures out of five. A more useful interpretation is obtained by answering parts **c** and **d.**

c. The graph of $p(x)$ is shown in Figure 4.6 with the mean μ and the interval $\mu \pm 2\sigma = 3.50 \pm 2(1.02) = 3.50 \pm 2.04 = (1.46, 5.54)$ shown on the graph. Note particularly that $\mu = 3.5$ locates the center of the probability distribution. Since this distribution is a theoretical relative frequency distribution that is moderately mound-shaped (see Figure 4.6), we expect (from Chebyshev's Rule) at least 75% and, more likely (from the Empirical Rule), approximately 95% of observed x values to fall in the interval $\mu \pm 2\sigma$—that is, between 1.46 and 5.54. You can see from Figure 4.6 that the actual probability that x falls in the interval $\mu \pm 2\sigma$ includes the sum of $p(x)$ for the values $x = 2$, $x = 3$, $x = 4$, and $x = 5$. This probability is $p(2) + p(3) + p(4) + p(5) = .132 + .309 + .360 + .168 = .969$. Therefore, 96.9% of the probability distribution lies within 2 standard deviations of the mean. This percentage is consistent with both Chebyshev's Rule and the Empirical Rule.

FIGURE 4.6
Graph of $p(x)$ for Example 4.6

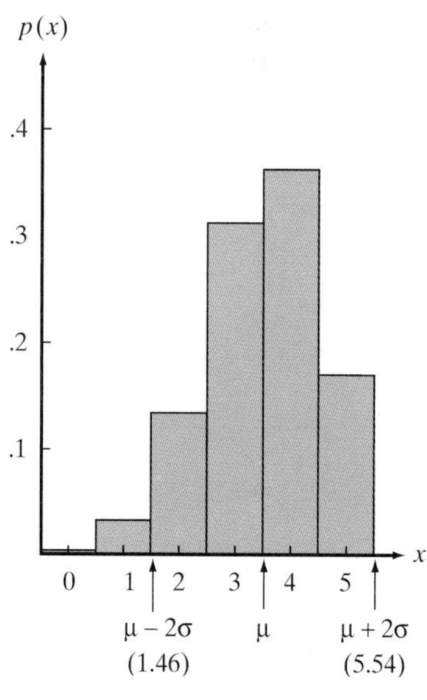

d. Fewer than two successful ventures out of five implies that $x = 0$ or $x = 1$. Since both these values of x lie outside the interval $\mu \pm 2\sigma$, we know from the Empirical Rule that such a result is unlikely (approximate probability of .05). The exact probability, $P(x \leq 1)$, is $p(0) + p(1) = .002 + .029 = .031$. Consequently, in a single experiment where we invest in five Internet business ventures, we would not expect to observe fewer than two successful ones.

EXERCISES 4.11–4.24

Learning the Mechanics

4.11 A discrete random variable x can assume five possible values: 2, 3, 5, 8, and 10. Its probability distribution is shown here:

x	2	3	5	8	10
$p(x)$	.15	.10	—	.25	.25

a. What is $p(5)$?
b. What is the probability that x equals 2 or 10?
c. What is $P(x \le 8)$?

4.12 Explain why each of the following is or is not a valid probability distribution for a discrete random variable x:

a.

x	0	1	2	3
$p(x)$	.1	.3	.3	.2

b.

x	−2	−1	0
$p(x)$	.25	.50	.25

c.

x	4	9	20
$p(x)$	−.3	.4	.3

d.

x	2	3	5	6
$p(x)$	.15	.15	.45	.35

4.13 The random variable x has the following discrete probability distribution:

x	1	3	5	7	9
$p(x)$	.1	.2	.4	.2	.1

a. Find $P(x \le 3)$.
b. Find $P(x < 3)$.
c. Find $P(x = 7)$.
d. Find $P(x \ge 5)$.
e. Find $P(x > 2)$.
f. Find $P(3 \le x \le 9)$.

4.14 Consider the probability distribution shown here.

x	1	2	4	10
$p(x)$	.2	.4	.2	.2

a. Find $\mu = E(x)$.
b. Find $\sigma^2 = E[(x - \mu)^2]$.
c. Find σ.
d. Interpret the value you obtained for μ.
e. In this case, can the random variable x ever assume the value μ? Explain.
f. In general, can a random variable ever assume a value equal to its expected value? Explain.

4.15 Consider the probability distribution for the random variable x shown at the top of the next column.

x	10	20	30	40	50	60
$p(x)$	.05	.20	.30	.25	.10	.10

a. Find μ, σ^2, and σ.
b. Graph $p(x)$.
c. Locate μ and the interval $\mu \pm 2\sigma$ on your graph. What is the probability that x will fall within the interval $\mu \pm 2\sigma$?

Applying the Concepts

4.16 The age distribution as of July 1, 1999 for the 55 employees of a highly successful two-year old "dot-com" company headquartered in Atlanta is shown at the bottom of the page. An employee is to be randomly selected from this population.
a. Can the relative frequency distribution in the table be interpreted as a probability distribution? Explain.
b. Graph the probability distribution.
c. What is the probability that the randomly selected employee is over 30 years of age? Over 40 years of age? Under 30 years of age?
d. What is the probability that the randomly selected employee will be 25 or 26 years old?

4.17 Nitrous oxide, more commonly known as "laughing gas," is used extensively in dental procedures. According to the American Dental Association, 60% of all dentists use nitrous oxide in their practice (*New York Times*, June 20, 1995). Suppose x equals the number of dentists in a random sample of five dentists who use laughing gas in practice. If $p = .60$ is the probability of any one dentist using laughing gas (and the dentists operate independently), then the probability distribution of x (we show how to calculate these probabilities in Section 4.3) is:

x	0	1	2	3	4	5
$p(x)$	.0102	.0768	.2304	.3456	.2592	.0778

Find the probability that the number of dentists using laughing gas in the sample of five is
a. 4
b. less than 2
c. greater than or equal to 3

4.18 A team of consultants studied the service operation at the Wendy's Restaurant in the Woodbridge Mall in Woodbridge, New Jersey. They measured the time between customer arrivals to the restaurant over the course of a day and used those data to develop a probability distribution to characterize x, the number of

Age	20	21	22	23	24	25	26	27	28	29	30	31	32	33
% of employees	1.82	3.64	5.45	7.27	3.64	1.82	7.27	1.82	10.9	7.27	9.09	12.73	14.55	12.73

Source: Personal communication from P. George Benson.

Probability Distribution for Exercise 4.18

x	5	6	7	8	9	10	11	12	13	14	15
$p(x)$	.01	.02	.03	.05	.08	.09	.11	.13	.12	.10	.08

x	16	17	18	19	20	21
$p(x)$	.06	.05	.03	.02	.01	.01

Source: Ford, R., Roberts, D., and Saxton, P. *Queuing Models.* Graduate School of Management, Rutgers University, 1992.

customer arrivals per 15-minute period. The distribution is shown in the table at the top of this page.

a. Does this distribution meet the two requirements for the probability distribution of a discrete random variable? Justify your answer.
b. What is the probability that exactly 16 customers enter the restaurant in the next 15 minutes?
c. Find $p(x \leq 10)$.
d. Find $p(5 \leq x \leq 15)$.

4.19 In a study of tax write-offs by the affluent, Peter Dreier of Occidental College (Los Angeles) compiled the relative frequency distribution shown on the right. The distribution describes the incomes of all households in the United States that filed tax returns in 1995. A household is to be randomly sampled from this population.

a. Explain why the percentages in the table can be interpreted as probabilities. For example, the probability of selecting a household with income under $10,000 is .185.
b. Find the probability that the selected household has income over $200,000; over $100,000; less than $100,000; between $30,000 and $49,999.
c. Together, the income categories (1, 2, 3, ...) and the percentages form a discrete probability distribution. Graph this distribution.
d. What is the probability that the randomly selected household will fall in income category 6? In income category 1 or 9?

Income Category	Household Income	Percentage of Households
1	Under $10,000	18.5
2	$10,000 to $19,999	19.0
3	$20,000 to $29,999	15.9
4	$30,000 to $39,999	12.8
5	$40,000 to $49,999	9.1
6	$50,000 to $74,999	13.8
7	$75,000 to $99,999	5.7
8	$100,000 to $199,999	4.1
9	$200,000 and over	1.1

Source: Johnston, D.C. "The Divine Write-off." *New York Times,* January 12, 1996, p.D1.

4.20 Many real-world systems (e.g., electric power transmission, transportation, telecommunications, and manufacturing systems) can be regarded as capacitated-flow networks, whose arcs have independent but random capacities. A team of Chinese university professors investigated the reliability of several flow networks in the journal *Networks* (May 1995). One network examined in the article, and illustrated below, is a bridge network with arcs a_1, a_2, a_3, a_4, a_5, and a_6. The probability distribution of the capacity x for each of the six arcs is provided in the table on p. 180.

a. Verify that the properties of discrete probability distributions are satisfied for each arc capacity distribution.

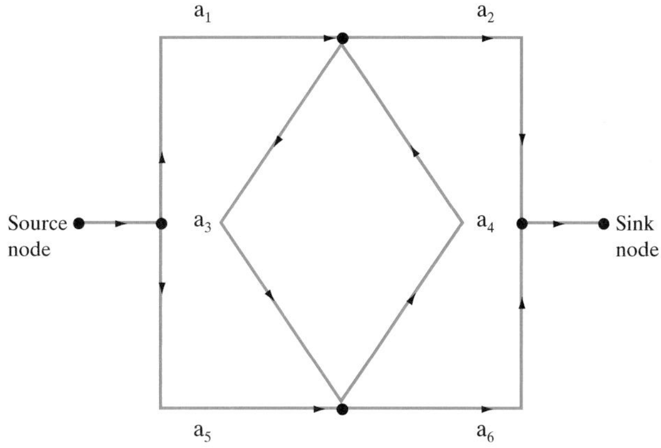

b. Find the probability that the capacity for arc a_1 will exceed 1.
c. Repeat part **b** for each of the remaining five arcs.
d. One path from the source node to the sink node is through arcs a_1 and a_2. Find the probability that the system maintains a capacity of more than 1 through the a_1–a_2 path. (Recall that the arc capacities are independent.)

Probability Distribution for Exercise 4.20

Arc	Capacity (x)	$p(x)$	Arc	Capacity (x)	$p(x)$
a_1	3	.60	a_4	1	.90
	2	.25		0	.10
	1	.10			
	0	.05			
a_2	2	.60	a_5	1	.90
	1	.30		0	.10
	0	.10			
a_3	1	.90	a_6	2	.70
	0	.10		1	.25
				0	.05

Source: Lin, J., *et al.* "On reliability evaluation of capacitated-flow network in terms of minimal pathsets." *Networks,* Vol. 25, No. 3, May 1995, p. 135 (Table 1), 1995, John Wiley and Sons.

4.21 Refer to Exercise 4.20. Compute the mean capacity of each of the six arcs. Interpret the results.

4.22 The risk of a portfolio of financial assets is sometimes called *investment risk* (Radcliffe, 1994). In general, investment risk is typically measured by computing the variance or standard deviation of the probability distribution that describes the decision-maker's potential outcomes (gains or losses). The greater the variation in potential outcomes, the greater the uncertainty faced by the decision-maker; the smaller the variation in potential outcomes, the more predictable the decision-maker's gains or losses. The two discrete probability distributions given in the table (upper right) were developed from historical data. They describe the potential total physical damage losses next year to the fleets of delivery trucks of two different firms.

a. Verify that both firms have the same expected total physical damage loss.
b. Compute the standard deviation of each probability distribution, and determine which firm faces the greater risk of physical damage to its fleet next year.

Firm A		Firm B	
Loss next year	Probability	Loss next year	Probability
$ 0	.01	$ 0	.00
500	.01	200	.01
1,000	.01	700	.02
1,500	.02	1,200	.02
2,000	.35	1,700	.15
2,500	.30	2,200	.30
3,000	.25	2,700	.30
3,500	.02	3,200	.15
4,000	.01	3,700	.02
4,500	.01	4,200	.02
5,000	.01	4,700	.01

4.23 A team of consultants working for a large national supermarket chain based in the New York metropolitan area developed a statistical model for predicting the annual sales of potential new store locations. Part of their analysis involved identifying variables that influence store sales, such as the size of the store (in square feet), the size of the surrounding population, and the number of checkout lanes. They surveyed 52 supermarkets in a particular region of the country and constructed the relative frequency distribution shown at the bottom of the page to describe the number of checkout lanes per store, x.

a. Why do the relative frequencies in the table represent the approximate probabilities of a randomly selected supermarket having x number of checkout lanes?
b. Find $E(x)$ and interpret its value in the context of the problem.
c. Find the standard deviation of x.
d. According to Chebyshev's Rule (Chapter 2), what percentage of supermarkets would be expected to fall within $\mu \pm \sigma$? Within $\mu \pm 2\sigma$?
e. What is the actual number of supermarkets that fall within $\mu \pm \sigma$? $\mu \pm 2\sigma$? Compare your answers to those of part **d.** Are the answers consistent?

4.24 Most states offer weekly lotteries to generate revenue for the state. Despite the long odds of winning, residents continue to gamble on the lottery each week (see Chapter 3's Statistics in Action). The chance of winning Florida's Pick-6 Lotto game is 1 in approximately 23 million. Suppose you buy a $1 Lotto ticket in anticipation of winning the $7 million grand prize. Calculate your expected net winnings. Interpret the result.

x	1	2	3	4	5	6	7	8	9	10
Relative Frequency	.01	.04	.04	.08	.10	.15	.25	.20	.08	.05

Source: Adapted from Chow, W., *et. al.* "A model for predicting a supermarket's annual sales per square foot." Graduate School of Management, Rutgers University, 1994.

4.3 THE BINOMIAL DISTRIBUTION

Many experiments result in *dichotomous* responses—i.e., responses for which there exist two possible alternatives, such as Yes-No, Pass-Fail, Defective-Nondefective, or Male-Female. A simple example of such an experiment is the coin-toss experiment. A coin is tossed a number of times, say 10. Each toss results in one of two outcomes, Head or Tail. Ultimately, we are interested in the probability distribution of x, the number of heads observed. Many other experiments are equivalent to tossing a coin (either balanced or unbalanced) a fixed number n of times and observing the number x of times that one of the two possible outcomes occurs. Random variables that possess these characteristics are called **binomial random variables.**

Public opinion and consumer preference polls (e.g., the CNN, Gallup, and Harris polls) frequently yield observations on binomial random variables. For example, suppose a sample of 100 current customers is selected from a firm's data base and each person is asked whether he or she prefers the firm's product (a Head) or prefers a competitor's product (a Tail). Suppose we are interested in x, the number of customers in the sample who prefer the firm's product. Sampling 100 customers is analogous to tossing the coin 100 times. Thus, you can see that consumer preference polls like the one described here are real-life equivalents of coin-toss experiments. We have been describing a **binomial experiment;** it is identified by the following characteristics.

Characteristics of a Binomial Random Variable

1. The experiment consists of n identical trials.
2. There are only two possible outcomes on each trial. We will denote one outcome by S (for Success) and the other by F (for Failure).
3. The probability of S remains the same from trial to trial. This probability is denoted by p, and the probability of F is denoted by q. Note that $q = 1 - p$.
4. The trials are independent.
5. The binomial random variable x is the number of S's in n trials.

EXAMPLE 4.7

For the following examples, decide whether x is a binomial random variable.

a. You randomly select three bonds out of a possible 10 for an investment portfolio. Unknown to you, eight of the 10 will maintain their present value, and the other two will lose value due to a change in their ratings. Let x be the number of the three bonds you select that lose value.

b. Before marketing a new product on a large scale, many companies will conduct a consumer preference survey to determine whether the product is likely to be successful. Suppose a company develops a new diet soda and then conducts a taste preference survey in which 100 randomly chosen consumers state their preferences among the new soda and the two leading sellers. Let x be the number of the 100 who choose the new brand over the two others.

c. Some surveys are conducted by using a method of sampling other than simple random sampling (defined in Chapter 3). For example, suppose a television cable company plans to conduct a survey to determine the fraction of households in the city that would use the cable television service. The sampling method is to choose a city block at random and then survey every household on that block. This sampling technique is called *cluster sampling.* Suppose 10 blocks are so sampled, producing a total of 124 household responses. Let x be the number of the 124 households that would use the television cable service.

Solution

a. In checking the binomial characteristics in the box, a problem arises with both characteristic 3 (probabilities remaining the same from trial to trial) and characteristic 4 (independence). The probability that the first bond you pick loses value is clearly $^2/_{10}$. Now suppose the first bond you picked was one of the two that will lose value. This reduces the chance that the second bond you pick will lose value to $^1/_9$, since now only one of the nine remaining bonds are in that category. Thus, the choices you make are dependent, and therefore x, the number of three bonds you select that lose value, is *not* a binomial random variable.

b. Surveys that produce dichotomous responses and use random sampling techniques are classic examples of binomial experiments. In our example, each randomly selected consumer either states a preference for the new diet soda or does not. The sample of 100 consumers is a very small proportion of the totality of potential consumers, so the response of one would be, for all practical purposes, independent of another.* Thus, x is a binomial random variable.

c. This example is a survey with dichotomous responses (Yes or No to the cable service), but the sampling method is not simple random sampling. Again, the binomial characteristic of independent trials would probably not be satisfied. The responses of households within a particular block would be dependent, since the households within a block tend to be similar with respect to income, level of education, and general interests. Thus, the binomial model would not be satisfactory for x if the cluster sampling technique were employed.

EXAMPLE 4.8

A computer retailer sells both desktop and laptop personal computers (PCs) on-line. Assume that 80% of the PCs that the retailer sells on-line are desktops, and 20% are laptops.

a. Use the steps given in Chapter 3 (box on page 124) to find the probability that all of the next four on-line PC purchases are laptops.

b. Find the probability that three of the next four on-line PC purchases are laptops.

c. Let x represent the number of the next four on-line PC purchases that are laptops. Explain why x is a binomial random variable.

d. Use the answers to parts **a** and **b** to derive a formula for $p(x)$, the probability distribution of the binomial random variable x.

*In most real-life applications of the binomial distribution, the population of interest has a finite number of elements (trials), denoted N. When N is large and the sample size n is small relative to N, say $n/N \leq .05$, the sampling procedure, for all practical purposes, satisfies the conditions of a binomial experiment.

Solution a. 1. The first step is to define the experiment. Here we are interested in observing the type of PC purchased on-line by each of the next four (buying) customers: desktop (D) or laptop (L).

2. Next, we list the sample points associated with the experiment. Each sample point consists of the purchase decisions made by the four on-line customers. For example, $DDDD$ represents the sample point that all four purchase desktop PCs, while $LDDD$ represents the sample point that customer 1 purchases a laptop, while customers 2, 3, and 4 purchase desktops. The 16 sample points are listed in Table 4.2.

TABLE 4.2 Sample Points for PC Experiment of Example 4.8

$DDDD$	$LDDD$	$LLDD$	$DLLL$	LLLL
	$DLDD$	$LDLD$	$LDLL$	
	$DDLD$	$LDDL$	$LLDL$	
	$DDDL$	$DLLD$	$LLLD$	
		$DLDL$		
		$DDLL$		

3. We now assign probabilities to the sample points. Note that each sample point can be viewed as the intersection of four customers' decisions and, assuming the decisions are made independently, the probability of each sample point can be obtained using the multiplicative rule, as follows:

$$\begin{aligned} P(DDDD) &= P[(\text{customer 1 chooses desktop}) \cap (\text{customer 2 chooses desktop}) \\ &\quad \cap (\text{customer 3 chooses desktop}) \cap (\text{customer 4 chooses desktop})] \\ &= P(\text{customer 1 chooses desktop}) \times P(\text{customer 2 chooses} \\ &\quad \text{desktop}) \times P(\text{customer 3 chooses desktop}) \\ &\quad \times P(\text{customer 4 chooses desktop}) \\ &= (.8)(.8)(.8)(.8) = (.8)^4 = .4096 \end{aligned}$$

All other sample point probabilities are calculated using similar reasoning. For example,

$$P(LDDD) = (.2)(.8)(.8)(.8) = (.2)(.8)^3 = .1024$$

You can check that this reasoning results in sample point probabilities that add to 1 over the 16 points in the sample space.

4. Finally, we add the appropriate sample point probabilities to obtain the desired event probability. The event of interest is that all four on-line customers purchase laptops. In Table 4.2 we find only one sample point, LLLL, contained in this event. All other sample points imply that at least one desktop is purchased. Thus,

$$P(\text{All four purchase laptops}) = P(LLLL) = (.2)^4 = .0016$$

That is, the probability is only 16 in 10,000 that all four customers purchase laptop PCs.

b. The event that three of the next four on-line buyers purchase laptops consists of the four sample points in the fourth column of Table 4.2: *DLLL, LDLL, LLDL,* and *LLLD*. To obtain the event probability we add the sample point probabilities:

$$\begin{aligned}&P(\text{3 of next 4 customers purchase laptops})\\&= P(DLLL) + P(LDLL) + P(LLDL) + P(LLLD)\\&= (.2)^3(.8) + (.2)^3(.8) + (.2)^3(.8) + (.2)^3(.8)\\&= 4(.2)^3(.8) = .0256\end{aligned}$$

Note that each of the four sample point probabilities is the same, because each sample point consists of three L's and one D; the order does not affect the probability because the customers' decisions are (assumed) independent.

c. We can characterize the experiment as consisting of four identical trials—the four customers' purchase decisions. There are two possible outcomes to each trial, D or L, and the probability of L, $p = .2$, is the same for each trial. Finally, we are assuming that each customer's purchase decision is independent of all others, so that the four trials are independent. Then it follows that x, the number of the next four purchases that are laptops, is a binomial random variable.

d. The event probabilities in parts **a** and **b** provide insight into the formula for the probability distribution $p(x)$. First, consider the event that three purchases are laptops (part **b**). We found that

$$\begin{aligned}P(x = 3) &= (\text{Number of sample points for which } x = 3) \times\\&\quad (.2)^{\text{Number of laptops purchased}} \times (.8)^{\text{Number of desktops purchased}}\\&= 4(.2)^3(.8)^1\end{aligned}$$

In general, we can use combinatorial mathematics to count the number of sample points. For example,

$$\begin{aligned}&\text{Number of sample points for which } (x = 3)\\&= \text{Number of different ways of selecting 3 of the 4 trials for } L \text{ purchases}\\&= \binom{4}{3} = \frac{4!}{3!(4-3)!} = \frac{4\cdot 3\cdot 2\cdot 1}{(3\cdot 2\cdot 1)\cdot 1} = 4\end{aligned}$$

The formula that works for any value of x can be deduced as follows. Since

$$P(x = 3) = \binom{4}{3}(.2)^3(.8)^1, \text{ the } p(x) = \binom{4}{x}(.2)^x(.8)^{4-x}$$

The component $\binom{4}{x}$ counts the number of sample points with x laptops and the component $(.2)^x(.8)^{4-x}$ is the probability associated with each sample point having x laptops.

For the general binomial experiment, with n trials and probability of Success p on each trial, the probability of x Successes is

$$p(x) = \binom{n}{x} \cdot p^x(1 - p)^{n-x}$$

↑	↑
No. of simple events with x S's	Probability of x S's and $(n - x)$ F's in any simple event

In theory, you could always resort to the principles developed in Example 4.8 to calculate binomial probabilities; list the sample points and sum their probabilities. However, as the number of trials (n) increases, the number of sample points grows very rapidly (the number of sample points is 2^n). Thus, we prefer the formula for calculating binomial probabilities, since its use avoids listing sample points.

The binomial distribution is summarized in the box.

The Binomial Probability Distribution

$$p(x) = \binom{n}{x} p^x q^{n-x} \qquad (x = 0, 1, 2, \ldots, n)$$

where

p = Probability of a success on a single trial
$q = 1 - p$
n = Number of trials
x = Number of successes in n trials

$$\binom{n}{x} = \frac{n!}{x!(n - x)!}$$

As noted in Chapter 3, the symbol 5! means $5 \cdot 4 \cdot 3 \cdot 2 \cdot 1 = 120$. Similarly, $n! = n(n - 1)(n - 2) \cdots 3 \cdot 2 \cdot 1$; remember, $0! = 1$.

The mean, variance, and standard deviation for the binomial random variable x are shown in the box.

Mean, Variance, and Standard Deviation for a Binomial Random Variable

Mean: $\mu = np$

Variance: $\sigma^2 = npq$

Standard deviation: $\sigma = \sqrt{npq}$

As we demonstrated in Chapter 2, the mean and standard deviation provide measures of the central tendency and variability, respectively, of a distribution. Thus, we can use μ and σ to obtain a rough visualization of the probability distribution for

x when the calculation of the probabilities is too tedious. To illustrate the use of the binomial probability distribution, consider Examples 4.9 and 4.10.

EXAMPLE 4.9 A machine that produces stampings for automobile engines is malfunctioning and producing 10% defectives. The defective and nondefective stampings proceed from the machine in a random manner. If the next five stampings are tested, find the probability that three of them are defective.

Solution Let x equal the number of defectives in $n = 5$ trials. Then x is a binomial random variable with p, the probability that a single stamping will be defective, equal to .1, and $q = 1 - p = 1 - .1 = .9$. The probability distribution for x is given by the expression

$$p(x) = \binom{n}{x} p^x q^{n-x} = \binom{5}{x}(.1)^x(.9)^{5-x}$$

$$= \frac{5!}{x!(5-x)!}(.1)^x(.9)^{5-x} \qquad (x = 0, 1, 2, 3, 4, 5)$$

To find the probability of observing $x = 3$ defectives in a sample of $n = 5$, substitute $x = 3$ into the formula for $p(x)$ to obtain

$$p(3) = \frac{5!}{3!(5-3)!}(.1)^3(.9)^{5-3} = \frac{5!}{3!2!}(.1)^3(.9)^2$$

$$= \frac{5 \cdot 4 \cdot 3 \cdot 2 \cdot 1}{(3 \cdot 2 \cdot 1)(2 \cdot 1)}(.1)^3(.9)^2 = 10(.1)^3(.9)^2$$

$$= .0081$$

Note that the binomial formula tells us that there are 10 sample points having 3 defectives (check this by listing them), each with probability $(.1)^3(.9)^2$.

EXAMPLE 4.10 Refer to Example 4.9 and find the values of $p(0), p(1), p(2), p(4)$, and $p(5)$. Graph $p(x)$. Calculate the mean μ and standard deviation σ. Locate μ and the interval $\mu - 2\sigma$ to $\mu + 2\sigma$ on the graph. If the experiment were to be repeated many times, what proportion of the x observations would fall within the interval $\mu - 2\sigma$ to $\mu + 2\sigma$?

Solution Again, $n = 5$, $p = .1$, and $q = .9$. Then, substituting into the formula for $p(x)$:

$$p(0) = \frac{5!}{0!(5-0)!}(.1)^0(.9)^{5-0} = \frac{5 \cdot 4 \cdot 3 \cdot 2 \cdot 1}{(1)(5 \cdot 4 \cdot 3 \cdot 2 \cdot 1)}(1)(.9)^5 = .59049$$

$$p(1) = \frac{5!}{1!(5-1)!}(.1)^1(.9)^{5-1} = 5(.1)(.9)^4 = .32805$$

$$p(2) = \frac{5!}{2!(5-2)!}(.1)^2(.9)^{5-2} = (10)(.1)^2(.9)^3 = .07290$$

$$p(4) = \frac{5!}{4!(5-4)!}(.1)^4(.9)^{5-4} = 5(.1)^4(.9) = .00045$$

$$p(5) = \frac{5!}{5!(5-5)!}(.1)^5(.9)^{5-5} = (.1)^5 = .00001$$

The graph of $p(x)$ is shown as a probability histogram in Figure 4.7. [$p(3)$ is taken from Example 4.9 to be .0081.]

FIGURE 4.7
The binomial distribution: $n = 5$, $p = .1$

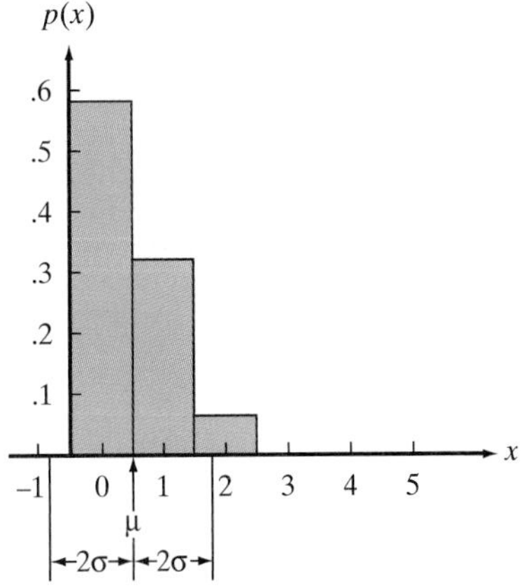

To calculate the values of μ and σ, substitute $n = 5$ and $p = .1$ into the following formulas:

$$\mu = np = (5)(.1) = .5$$

$$\sigma = \sqrt{npq} = \sqrt{(5)(.1)(.9)} = \sqrt{.45} = .67$$

To find the interval $\mu - 2\sigma$ to $\mu + 2\sigma$, we calculate

$$\mu - 2\sigma = .5 - 2(.67) = -.84$$

$$\mu + 2\sigma = .5 + 2(.67) = 1.84$$

If the experiment were to be repeated a large number of times, what proportion of the x observations would fall within the interval $\mu - 2\sigma$ to $\mu + 2\sigma$? You can see from Figure 4.7 that all observations equal to 0 or 1 will fall within the interval. The probabilities corresponding to these values are .5905 and .3280, respectively. Consequently, you would expect $.5905 + .3280 = .9185$, or approximately 91.9%, of the observations to fall within the interval $\mu - 2\sigma$ to $\mu + 2\sigma$. This again emphasizes that for most probability distributions, observations rarely fall more than 2 standard deviations from μ.

Using Binomial Tables

Calculating binomial probabilities becomes tedious when n is large. For some values of n and p the binomial probabilities have been tabulated in Table II of Appendix B. Part of Table II is shown in Table 4.3; a graph of the binomial probability distribution for $n = 10$ and $p = .10$ is shown in Figure 4.8. Table II actually contains a total of nine tables, labeled (**a**) through (**i**), one each corresponding to $n = 5, 6, 7, 8, 9, 10, 15, 20$, and 25. In each of these tables the columns correspond to values of p, and the rows correspond to values (k) of the random variable x. The entries in the table represent **cumulative binomial probabilities,** $P(x \leq k)$.

TABLE 4.3 Reproduction of Part of Table II of Appendix B: Binomial Probabilities for $n = 10$

k \ p	.01	.05	.10	.20	.30	.40	.50	.60	.70	.80	.90	.95	.99
0	.904	.599	.349	.107	.028	.006	.001	.000	.000	.000	.000	.000	.000
1	.996	.914	.736	.376	.149	.046	.011	.002	.000	.000	.000	.000	.000
2	1.000	.988	.930	.678	.383	.167	.055	.012	.002	.000	.000	.000	.000
3	1.000	.999	.987	.879	.650	.382	.172	.055	.011	.001	.000	.000	.000
4	1.000	1.000	.998	.967	.850	.633	.377	.166	.047	.006	.000	.000	.000
5	1.000	1.000	1.000	.994	.953	.834	.623	.367	.150	.033	.002	.000	.000
6	1.000	1.000	1.000	.999	.989	.945	.828	.618	.350	.121	.013	.001	.000
7	1.000	1.000	1.000	1.000	.998	.988	.945	.833	.617	.322	.070	.012	.000
8	1.000	1.000	1.000	1.000	1.000	.998	.989	.954	.851	.624	.264	.086	.004
9	1.000	1.000	1.000	1.000	1.000	1.000	.999	.994	.972	.893	.651	.401	.096

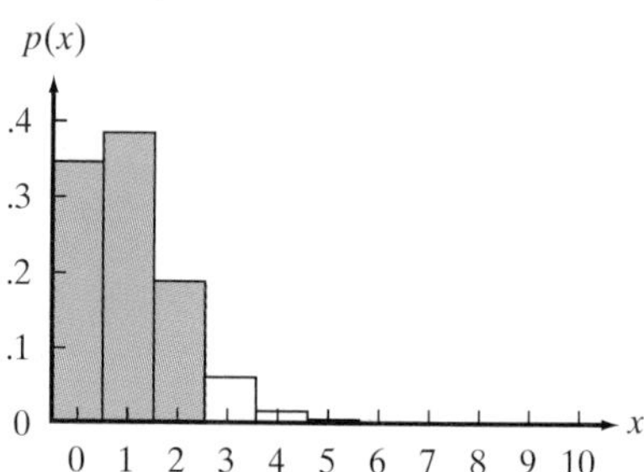

FIGURE 4.8
Binomial probability distribution for $n = 10$ and $p = .10$; $P(x \le 2)$ shaded

Thus, for example, the entry in the column corresponding to $p = .10$ and the row corresponding to $k = 2$ is .930 (shaded), and its interpretation is

$$P(x \le 2) = P(x = 0) + P(x = 1) + P(x = 2) = .930$$

This probability is also shaded in the graphical representation of the binomial distribution with $n = 10$ and $p = .10$ in Figure 4.8.

You can also use Table II to find the probability that x equals a specific value. For example, suppose you want to find the probability that $x = 2$ in the binomial distribution with $n = 10$ and $p = .10$. This is found by subtraction as follows:

$$P(x = 2) = [P(x = 0) + P(x = 1) + P(x = 2)] - [P(x = 0) + P(x = 1)]$$
$$= P(x \le 2) - P(x \le 1) = .930 - .736 = .194$$

The probability that a binomial random variable exceeds a specified value can be found using Table II and the notion of complementary events. For example, to find the probability that x exceeds 2 when $n = 10$ and $p = .10$, we use

$$P(x > 2) = 1 - P(x \le 2) = .930 = .070$$

Note that this probability is represented by the unshaded portion of the graph in Figure 4.8.

All probabilities in Table II are rounded to three decimal places. Thus, although none of the binomial probabilities in the table is exactly zero, some are small enough (less than .0005) to round to .000. For example, using the formula to find $P(x = 0)$ when $n = 10$ and $p = .6$, we obtain

$$P(x = 0) = \binom{10}{0}(.6)^0(.4)^{10-0} = .4^{10} = .00010486$$

but this is rounded to .000 in Table II of Appendix B (see Table 4.3).

Similarly, none of the table entries is exactly 1.0, but when the cumulative probabilities exceed .9995, they are rounded to 1.000. The row corresponding to the largest possible value for x, $x = n$, is omitted, because all the cumulative probabilities in that row are equal to 1.0 (exactly). For example, in Table 4.3 with $n = 10$, $P(x \leq 10) = 1.0$, no matter what the value of p.

The following example further illustrates the use of Table II.

EXAMPLE 4.11

Suppose a poll of 20 employees is taken in a large company. The purpose is to determine x, the number who favor unionization. Suppose that 60% of all the company's employees favor unionization.

a. Find the mean and standard deviation of x.

b. Use Table II of Appendix B to find the probability that $x \leq 10$.

c. Use Table II to find the probability that $x > 12$.

d. Use Table II to find the probability that $x = 11$.

e. Graph the probability distribution of x and locate the interval $\mu \pm 2\sigma$ on the graph.

Solution

a. The number of employees polled is presumably small compared with the total number of employees in this company. Thus, we may treat x, the number of the 20 who favor unionization, as a binomial random variable. The value of p is the fraction of the total employees who favor unionization; i.e., $p = .6$. Therefore, we calculate the mean and variance:

$$\mu = np = 20(.6) = 12$$

$$\sigma^2 = npq = 20(.6)(.4) = 4.8$$

$$\sigma = \sqrt{4.8} = 2.19$$

b. Looking in the $k = 10$ row and the $p = .6$ column of Table II (Appendix B) for $n = 20$, we find the value of .245. Thus,

$$P(x \leq 10) = .245$$

c. To find the probability

$$P(x > 12) = \sum_{x=13}^{20} p(x)$$

we use the fact that for all probability distributions, $\sum_{\text{All } x} p(x) = 1$. Therefore,

$$P(x > 12) = 1 - P(x \leq 12) = 1 - \sum_{x=0}^{12} p(x)$$

Consulting Table II, we find the entry in row $k = 12$, column $p = .6$ to be .584. Thus,

$$P(x > 12) = 1 - .584 = .416$$

d. To find the probability that exactly 11 employees favor unionization, recall that the entries in Table II are cumulative probabilities and use the relationship

$$P(x = 11) = [p(0) + p(1) + \cdots + p(11)] - [p(0) + p(1) + \cdots + p(10)]$$
$$= P(x \le 11) - P(x \le 10)$$

Then

$$P(x = 11) = .404 - .245 = .159$$

e. The probability distribution for x in this example is shown in Figure 4.9. Note that

$$\mu - 2\sigma = 12 - 2(2.2) = 7.6 \qquad \mu + 2\sigma = 12 + 2(2.2) = 16.4$$

The interval (7.6, 16.4) is also shown on Figure 4.9. The probability that x falls in this interval is $P(x = 8, 9, 10, \ldots, 16) = P(x \le 16) - P(x \le 7) = .984 - .021 = .963$. This probability is very close to the .95 given by the Empirical Rule. Thus, we expect the number of employees in the sample of 20 who favor unionization to be between 8 and 16.

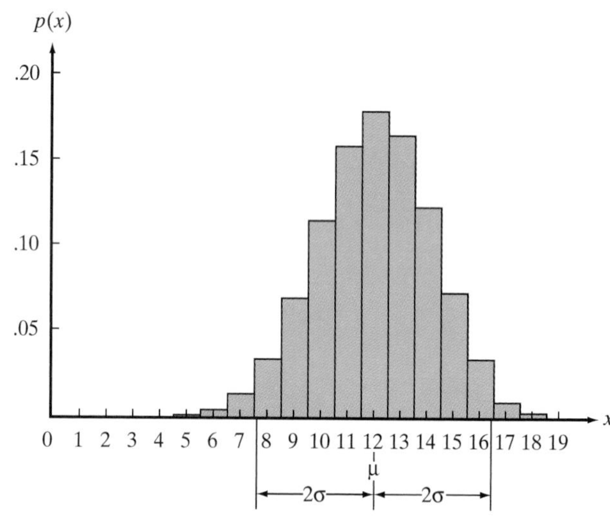

FIGURE 4.9 The binomial probability distribution for x in Example 4.11: $n = 20$, $p = .6$

Binomial Probabilities

USING THE TI-83 GRAPHING CALCULATOR

Binomial Probabilities on the TI-83

$P(x = k)$

To compute $P(x = k)$, the probability of k successes in n trials, where the p is probability of success for each trial, use the **binompdf(** command. Binompdf stands for "bi-

(continued)

nomial probability density function." This command is under the **DISTR**ibution menu and has the format **binompdf(*n*, *p*, *k*)**.

EXAMPLE:

Compute the probability of 5 successes in 8 trials where the probability of success for a single trial is 40%

In this example, $n = 8$, $p = .4$, and $k = 5$

Press **2nd** **VARS** for **DISTR**
Press the down arrow key until **0:binompdf** is highlighted
Press **ENTER**
After **binompdf(**, type **8, .4, 5)**
Press **ENTER**

You should see

```
binompdf(8,.4,5)
          .12386304
```

Thus, $P(x = 5)$ is about 12.4%.

***P*(*x* ≤ *k*)**

To compute $P(x \leq k)$, the probability of k or fewer successes in n trials, where the p is probability of success for each trial, use the **binomcdf(** command. Binomcdf stands for "binomial ***cumulative*** probability density function." This command is under the **DISTR**ibution menu and has the format **binomcdf(*n*, *p*, *k*).**

EXAMPLE:

Compute the probability of less than 5 successes in 8 trials where the probability of success for a single trial is 40%.

In this example, $n = 8$, $p = .4$, and $k = 5$.

Press **2nd** **VARS** for **DISTR**
Press down the arrow key until **A:binomcdf** is highlighted
Press **ENTER**
After **binomcdf(**, type **8, .4, 5)**
Press **ENTER**

You should see

```
binomcdf(8,.4,5)
          .95019264
```

(continued)

Thus, $P(x < 5)$is about 95%.

$P(x < k)$, $P(x > k)$, $P(x \geq k)$

To find the probability of less than k successes $P(x < k)$, more than k successes $P(x > k)$, or at least k successes $P(x \geq k)$, variations of the **binomcdf(** command must be used as shown below.

$P(x < k)$	use	**binomcdf(n, p, $k - 1$)**
$P(x > k)$	use	**1-binomcdf(n, p, k)**
$P(x \geq k)$	use	**1-binomcdf(n, p, $k - 1$)**

where n = number of trials and p = probability of success in each trial.

EXERCISES 4.25–4.38

Learning the Mechanics

4.25 Compute the following:

a. $\frac{6!}{2!(6-2)!}$ b. $\binom{5}{2}$ c. $\binom{7}{0}$ d. $\binom{6}{6}$ e. $\binom{4}{3}$

4.26 Consider the following probability distribution:

$$p(x) = \binom{5}{x}(.7)^x(.3)^{5-x} \qquad (x = 0, 1, 2, \ldots, 5)$$

a. Is x a discrete or a continuous random variable?
b. What is the name of this probability distribution?
c. Graph the probability distribution.
d. Find the mean and standard deviation of x.
e. Show the mean and the 2-standard-deviation interval on each side of the mean on the graph you drew in part **c**.

4.27 If x is a binomial random variable, compute $p(x)$ for each of the following cases:

a. $n = 5, x = 1, p = .2$
b. $n = 4, x = 2, q = .4$
c. $n = 3, x = 0, p = .7$
d. $n = 5, x = 3, p = .1$
e. $n = 4, x = 2, q = .6$
f. $n = 3, x = 1, p = .9$

4.28 If x is a binomial random variable, use Table II in Appendix B to find the following probabilities:

a. $P(x = 2)$ for $n = 10, p = .4$
b. $P(x \leq 5)$ for $n = 15, p = .6$
c. $P(x > 1)$ for $n = 5, p = .1$
d. $P(x < 10)$ for $n = 25, p = .7$
e. $P(x \geq 10)$ for $n = 15, p = .9$
f. $P(x = 2)$ for $n = 20, p = .2$

4.29 If x is a binomial random variable, calculate μ, σ^2, and σ for each of the following:

a. $n = 25, p = .5$
b. $n = 80, p = .2$
c. $n = 100, p = .6$
d. $n = 70, p = .9$
e. $n = 60, p = .8$
f. $n = 1{,}000, p = .04$

Applying the Concepts

4.30 Periodically, the Federal Trade Commission (FTC) monitors the pricing accuracy of electronic checkout scanners at stores to ensure consumers are charged the correct price at checkout. A 1998 study of over 100,000 items found that one of every 30 items is priced incorrectly by the scanners (*Price Check II: A Follow-Up Report on the Accuracy of Checkout Scanner Prices*, Dec. 16, 1998). Suppose the FTC randomly selects five items at a retail store and checks the accuracy of the scanner price of each. Let x represent the number of the five items that is priced incorrectly.

a. Show that x is (approximately) a binomial random variable.
b. Use the information in the FTC study to estimate p for the binomial experiment.
c. What is the probability that exactly one of the five items is priced incorrectly by the scanner?
d. What is the probability that at least one of the five items is priced incorrectly by the scanner?

4.31 According to the Internal Revenue Service (IRS), the chances of your tax return being audited are about 15 in 1,000 if your income is less than \$100,000 and 30 in 1,000 if your income is \$100,000 or more (*Statistical Abstract of the United States: 1998*).

a. What is the probability that a taxpayer with income less than \$100,000 will be audited by the IRS? With income \$100,000 or more?
b. If five taxpayers with incomes under \$100,000 are randomly selected, what is the probability that exactly one will be audited? That more than one will be audited?
c. Repeat part **b** assuming that five taxpayers with incomes of \$100,000 or more are randomly selected.

d. If two taxpayers with incomes under \$100,000 are randomly selected and two with incomes more than \$100,000 are randomly selected, what is the probability that none of these taxpayers will be audited by the IRS?

e. What assumptions did you have to make in order to answer these questions using the methodology presented in this section?

4.32 As the baby boom generation ages, the number of employees injured on the job will continue to increase. A recent poll by the Gallup Organization sponsored by Philadelphia-based CIGNA Integrated Care found that about 40% of employees have missed work due to a musculoskeletal (back) injury of some kind (*National Underwriter,* Apr. 5, 1999). Let x be the number of sampled workers who have missed work due to a back injury.

a. Explain why x is approximately a binomial random variable.

b. Use the Gallup poll data to estimate p for the binomial random variable of part **a**.

c. A random sample of 10 workers is to be drawn from a particular manufacturing plant. Use the p from part **b** to find the mean and standard deviation of x, the number of workers that missed work due to back injuries.

d. For the sample in part **c**, find the probability that exactly one worker missed work due to a back injury. That more than one worker missed work due to a back injury.

4.33 "Do you believe your children will have a higher standard of living than you have?" This question was asked of a national sample of American adults with children in a *Time/CNN* poll (Jan. 29, 1996). Sixty-three percent answered in the affirmative, with a margin of error of plus or minus 3%. Assume that the true percentage of all American adults who believe their children will have a higher standard of living is .60. Let x represent the number in a random sample of five American adults who believe their children will have a higher standard of living.

a. Demonstrate that x is (approximately) a binomial random variable.

b. What is the value of p for the binomial experiment?

c. Find $P(x = 3)$.

d. Find $P(x \leq 2)$.

4.34 According to Catalyst, a New York–based women's advocacy and research group, 12% of all corporate officers at the 500 largest U.S. corporations in 1999 were women, compared to 8% in 1995. (*Atlanta Journal Constitution,* Nov. 12, 1999).

a. According to Catalyst's data, in a sample of 1,000 corporate officers at the 500 largest U.S. firms, how many would you expect to be women?

b. If eight corporate officers were randomly selected from the 500 largest U.S. firms, what is the probability that none would be women? That half would be women?

c. What assumptions did you have to make in order to answer part **b** using the binomial distribution?

4.35 On January 28, 1986, the space shuttle *Challenger* was totally enveloped in an explosive burn that destroyed the shuttle and resulted in the deaths of all seven astronauts aboard. A presidential commission assigned to investigate the accident concluded that the explosion was caused by the failure of the O-ring seal in the joint between the two lower segments of the right solid-fuel rocket booster. In a report made one year prior to the catastrophe, the National Aeronautics and Space Administration (NASA) claimed that the probability of such a failure was about $^1/_{60,000}$, or about once in every 60,000 flights. But a risk assessment study conducted for the Air Force at about the same time assessed the probability of shuttle catastrophe due to booster rocket "burn-through" to be $^1/_{35}$, or about once in every 35 missions.

a. The catastrophe occurred on the twenty-fifth shuttle mission. Assuming NASA's failure-rate estimate was accurate, compute the probability that no disasters would have occurred during 25 shuttle missions.

b. Repeat part **a,** but use the Air Force's failure-rate estimate.

c. What conditions must exist for the probabilities, parts **a** and **b,** to be valid?

d. Given the events of January 28, 1986, which risk assessment—NASA's or the Air Force's—appears to be more appropriate? [Hint: Consider the complement of the events, parts **a** and **b.**]

e. After making improvements in the shuttle's systems over the late 1980s and early 1990s, NASA issued a report in 1993 in which the risk of catastrophic failure of the shuttle's main engine was assessed for each mission at 1 in 120. ("Laying Odds on Shuttle Disaster," *Chance,* Fall 1993.) Use this risk assessment and the binomial probability distribution to find the probability of at least one catastrophic failure in the next 10 missions.

4.36 The number of bank mergers in the 1990s far exceeded any previous 10-year period in U.S. history. As mergers created larger and larger banks, many customers charged the mega-banks with becoming more and more impersonal in dealing with customers. A recent poll by the Gallup Organization found 20% of retail customers switched banks after their banks merged with another (*Bank Marketing,* Feb. 1999). One year after the acquisition of First Fidelity by First Union, a random sample of 25 retail customers who had banked with First Fidelity were questioned. Let x be the number of those customers who switched their business from First Union to a different bank.

a. What assumptions must hold in order for x to be a binomial random variable? In the remainder of this exercise, use the data from the Gallop Poll to estimate p.

b. What is the probability that $x \leq 10$?

c. Find $E(x)$ and the standard deviation of x.
d. Calculate the interval $\mu \pm 2\sigma$.
e. If samples of size 25 were drawn repeatedly a large number of times and x determined for each sample, what proportion of the x values would fall within the interval you calculated in part **d**?

4.37 Every quarter the Food and Drug Administration (FDA) produces a report called the *Total Diet Study.* The FDA's report covers more than 200 food items, each of which is analyzed for potentially harmful chemical compounds. A recent *Total Diet Study* reported that no pesticides at all were found in 65% of the domestically produced food samples (*Consumer's Research,* June 1995). Consider a random sample of 800 food items analyzed for the presence of pesticides.
a. Compute μ and σ for the random variable x, the number of food items found that showed no trace of pesticide.
b. Based on a sample of 800 food items, is it likely you would observe less than half without any traces of pesticide? Explain.

4.38 A study conducted in New Jersey by the Governor's Council for a Drug Free Workplace concluded that 70% of New Jersey's businesses have employees whose performance is affected by drugs and/or alcohol. In those businesses, it was estimated that 8.5% of their workforces have alcohol problems and 5.2% have drug problems. These last two numbers are slightly lower than the national statistics of 10% and 7%, respectively (*Report: The Governor's Council for a Drug Free Workplace,* Spring/Summer 1995).
a. In a New Jersey company that acknowledges it has performance problems caused by substance abuse, out of every 1,000 employees, approximately how many have drug problems?
b. In the company referred to in part **a,** if 10 employees are randomly selected to form a committee to address alcohol abuse problems, what is the probability that at least one member of the committee is an alcohol abuser? That exactly two are alcohol abusers?
c. What assumptions did you have to make in order to answer part **b** using the methodology of this section?

4.4 THE POISSON DISTRIBUTION (OPTIONAL)

A type of probability distribution that is often useful in describing the number of events that will occur in a specific period of time or in a specific area or volume is the **Poisson distribution** (named after the 18th-century physicist and mathematician, Siméon Poisson). Typical examples of random variables for which the Poisson probability distribution provides a good model are

1. The number of industrial accidents per month at a manufacturing plant
2. The number of noticeable surface defects (scratches, dents, etc.) found by quality inspectors on a new automobile
3. The parts per million of some toxin found in the water or air emission from a manufacturing plant
4. The number of customer arrivals per unit of time at a supermarket checkout counter
5. The number of death claims received per day by an insurance company
6. The number of errors per 100 invoices in the accounting records of a company

Characteristics of a Poisson Random Variable

1. The experiment consists of counting the number of times a certain event occurs during a given unit of time or in a given area or volume (or weight, distance, or any other unit of measurement).
2. The probability that an event occurs in a given unit of time, area, or volume is the same for all the units.
3. The number of events that occur in one unit of time, area, or volume is independent of the number that occur in other units.
4. The mean (or expected) number of events in each unit is denoted by the Greek letter lambda, λ.

The characteristics of the Poisson random variable are usually difficult to verify for practical examples. The examples given satisfy them well enough that the Poisson distribution provides a good model in many instances. As with all probability models, the real test of the adequacy of the Poisson model is in whether it provides a reasonable approximation to reality—that is, whether empirical data support it.

The probability distribution, mean, and variance for a Poisson random variable are shown in the next box.

Probability Distribution, Mean, and Variance for a Poisson Random Variable*

$$p(x) = \frac{\lambda^x e^{-\lambda}}{x!} \quad (x = 0, 1, 2, \ldots)$$

$$\mu = \lambda$$

$$\sigma^2 = \lambda$$

where

$\lambda =$ Mean number of events during given unit of time, area, volume, etc.

$e = 2.71828\ldots$

The calculation of Poisson probabilities is made easier by the use of Table III in Appendix B, which gives the cumulative probabilities $P(x \leq k)$ for various values of λ. The use of Table III is illustrated in Example 4.12.

EXAMPLE 4.12

Suppose the number, x, of a company's employees who are absent on Mondays has (approximately) a Poisson probability distribution. Furthermore, assume that the average number of Monday absentees is 2.6.

a. Find the mean and standard deviation of x, the number of employees absent on Monday.

b. Use Table III to find the probability that fewer than two employees are absent on a given Monday.

c. Use Table III to find the probability that more than five employees are absent on a given Monday.

d. Use Table III to find the probability that exactly five employees are absent on a given Monday.

Solution

a. The mean and variance of a Poisson random variable are both equal to λ. Thus, for this example,

$$\mu = \lambda = 2.6$$

$$\sigma^2 = \lambda = 2.6$$

*The Poisson probability distribution also provides a good approximation to a binomial distribution with mean $\lambda = np$ when n is large and p is small (say, $np \leq 7$).

Then the standard deviation of x is

$$\sigma = \sqrt{2.6} = 1.61$$

Remember that the mean measures the central tendency of the distribution and does not necessarily equal a possible value of x. In this example, the mean is 2.6 absences, and although there cannot be 2.6 absences on a given Monday, the average number of Monday absences is 2.6. Similarly, the standard deviation of 1.61 measures the variability of the number of absences per week. Perhaps a more helpful measure is the interval $\mu \pm 2\sigma$, which in this case stretches from $-.62$ to 5.82. We expect the number of absences to fall in this interval most of the time—with at least 75% relative frequency (according to Chebyshev's Rule) and probably with approximately 95% relative frequency (the Empirical Rule). The mean and the 2-standard-deviation interval around it are shown in Figure 4.10.

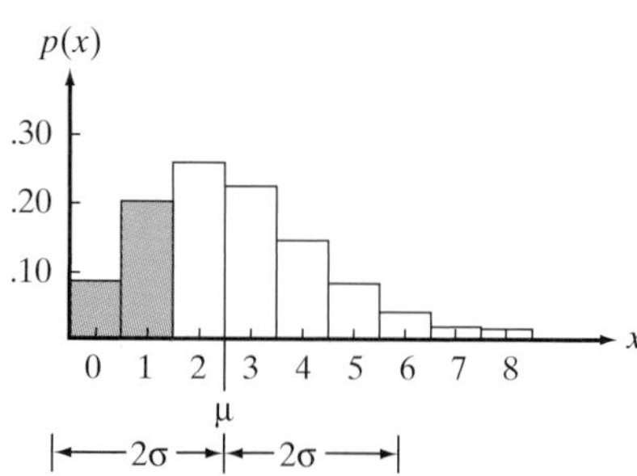

FIGURE 4.10
Probability distribution for number of Monday absences

b. A partial reproduction of Table III is shown in Table 4.4. The rows of the table correspond to different values of λ, and the columns correspond to different values (k) of the Poisson random variable x. The entries in the table

TABLE 4.4 Reproduction of Part of Table III in Appendix B

λ \ k	0	1	2	3	4	5	6	7	8	9
2.2	.111	.355	.623	.819	.928	.975	.993	.998	1.000	1.000
2.4	.091	.308	.570	.779	.904	.964	.988	.997	.999	1.000
2.6	.074	.267	.518	.736	.877	.951	.983	.995	.999	1.000
2.8	.061	.231	.469	.692	.848	.935	.976	.992	.998	.999
3.0	.050	.199	.423	.647	.815	.916	.966	.988	.996	.999
3.2	.041	.171	.380	.603	.781	.895	.955	.983	.994	.998
3.4	.033	.147	.340	.558	.744	.871	.942	.977	.992	.997
3.6	.027	.126	.303	.515	.706	.844	.927	.969	.988	.996
3.8	.022	.107	.269	.473	.668	.816	.909	.960	.984	.994
4.0	.018	.092	.238	.433	.629	.785	.889	.949	.979	.992
4.2	.015	.078	.210	.395	.590	.753	.867	.936	.972	.989
4.4	.012	.066	.185	.359	.551	.720	.844	.921	.964	.985
4.6	.010	.056	.163	.326	.513	.686	.818	.905	.955	.980
4.8	.008	.048	.143	.294	.476	.651	.791	.887	.944	.975
5.0	.007	.040	.125	.265	.440	.616	.762	.867	.932	.968
5.2	.006	.034	.109	.238	.406	.581	.732	.845	.918	.960
5.4	.005	.029	.095	.213	.373	.546	.702	.822	.903	.951
5.6	.004	.024	.082	.191	.342	.512	.670	.797	.886	.941
5.8	.003	.021	.072	.170	.313	.478	.638	.771	.867	.929
6.0	.002	.017	.062	.151	.285	.446	.606	.744	.847	.916

(like the binomial probabilities in Table II) give the cumulative probability $P(x \leq k)$. To find the probability that fewer than two employees are absent on Monday, we first note that

$$P(x < 2) = P(x \leq 1)$$

This probability is a cumulative probability and therefore is the entry in Table III in the row corresponding to $\lambda = 2.6$ and the column corresponding to $k = 1$. The entry is .267, shown shaded in Table 4.4. This probability corresponds to the shaded area in Figure 4.10 and may be interpreted as meaning that there is a 26.7% chance that fewer than two employees will be absent on a given Monday.

c. To find the probability that more than five employees are absent on a given Monday, we consider the complementary event

$$P(x > 5) = 1 - P(x \leq 5) = 1 - .951 = .049$$

where .951 is the entry in Table III corresponding to $\lambda = 2.6$ and $k = 5$ (see Table 4.4). Note from Figure 4.10 that this is the area in the interval $\mu \pm 2\sigma$, or $-.62$ to 5.82. Then the number of absences should exceed 5—or, equivalently, should be more than 2 standard deviations from the mean—during only about 4.9% of all Mondays. Note that this percentage agrees remarkably well with that given by the Empirical Rule for mound-shaped distributions, which tells us to expect approximately 5% of the measurements (values of the random variable) to lie farther than 2 standard deviations from the mean.

d. To use Table III to find the probability that *exactly* five employees are absent on a Monday, we must write the probability as the difference between two cumulative probabilities:

$$P(x = 5) = P(x \leq 5) - P(x \leq 4) = .951 - .877 = .074$$

Note that the probabilities in Table III are all rounded to three decimal places. Thus, although in theory a Poisson random variable can assume infinitely large values, the values of k in Table III are extended only until the cumulative probability is 1.000. This does not mean that x *cannot* assume larger values, but only that the likelihood is less than .001 (in fact, less than .0005) that it will do so.

Finally, you may need to calculate Poisson probabilities for values of λ not found in Table III. You may be able to obtain an adequate approximation by interpolation, but if not, consult more extensive tables for the Poisson distribution.

EXERCISES 4.39–4.49

Learning the Mechanics

4.39 Consider the probability distribution shown here:

$$p(x) = \frac{3^x e^{-3}}{x!} \quad (x = 0, 1, 2, \ldots)$$

a. Is x a discrete or continuous random variable? Explain.

b. What is the name of this probability distribution?

c. Graph the probability distribution.

d. Find the mean and standard deviation of x.

e. Find the mean and standard deviation of the probability distribution.

4.40 Given that x is a random variable for which a Poisson probability distribution provides a good approximation, use Table III to compute the following:

Poisson Probabilities

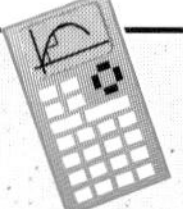

USING THE TI-83 GRAPHING CALCULATOR

Poisson Probabilities on the TI-83

$P(x = k)$

To compute $P(x = k)$, the probability of exactly k successes in a specified interval where λ is the mean number of successes in the interval, use the **poissonpdf(** command. Poisson**p**df stands for "Poisson probability density function." This command is under the **DISTR**ibution menu and has the format **poissonpdf(λ, k).**

EXAMPLE:

Suppose that the number, x, of reported sightings per week of blue whales is recorded. Assume that x has approximately a Poisson probability distribution, and that the average number of weekly sightings is 2.6.

Compute the probability that exactly five sightings are made during a given week.

In this example, $\lambda = 2.6$ and $k = 5$.

Press **2nd** **VARS** for **DISTR**
Press the down arrow key until **B:poissonpdf** is highlighted
Press **ENTER**
After **poissonpdf(**, type **2.6, 5)**
Press **ENTER**

You should see

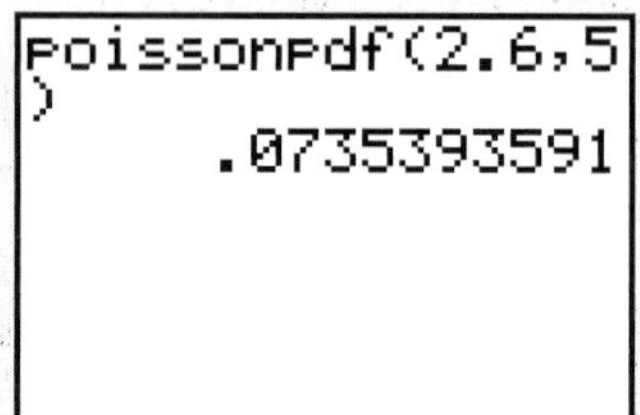

Thus, the $P(x = 5)$ is about 7.4%.

$P(x \le k)$

To compute $P(x \le k)$, the probability of k or fewer successes in a specified interval, where λ is the mean number of successes in the interval, use the **poissoncdf(** command. Poisson**c**df stands for "Poisson *cumulative* probability density function." This command is under the **DISTR**ibution menu and has the format **poissoncdf(λ, k).**

EXAMPLE:

In the example given above, compute the probability that five or fewer sightings are made during a given week.

(continued)

In this example, $\lambda = 2.6$ and $k = 5$
Press **2nd** **VARS** for **DISTR**
Press the down arrow key until **C:poissoncdf** is highlighted
Press **ENTER**
After **poissoncdf(**, type **2.6, 5)**
Press **ENTER**

You should see:

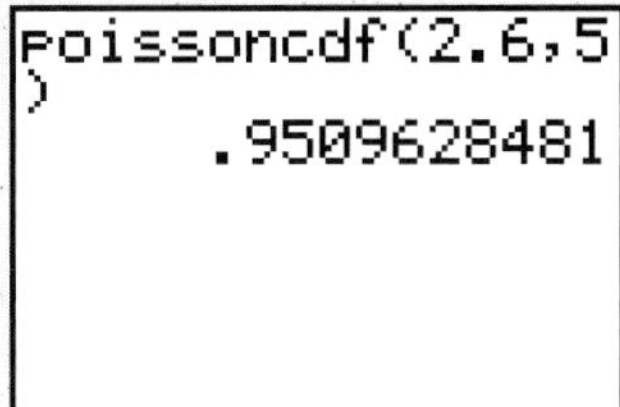

Thus, the $P(x \leq 5)$ is about 95.1%.

$P(x < k)$, $P(x > k)$, $P(x \geq k)$

To find the probability of less than k successes $P(x < k)$, more than k successes $P(x > k)$, or at least k successes $P(x \geq k)$, variations of **poissoncdf(** command must be used as shown below.

$P(x < k)$ use **poissoncdf(λ, $k - 1$)**

$P(x > k)$ use **1 − poissoncdf(λ, k)**

$P(x \geq k)$ use **1 − poissoncdf(λ, $k - 1$)**

where λ is the mean number of successes in the specified interval.

a. $P(x \leq 2)$ when $\lambda = 1$
b. $P(x \leq 2)$ when $\lambda = 2$
c. $P(x \leq 2)$ when $\lambda = 3$
d. What happens to the probability of the event $\{x \leq 2\}$ as λ increases from 1 to 3? Is this intuitively reasonable?

4.41 Assume that x is a random variable having a Poisson probability distribution with a mean of 1.5. Use Table III to find the following probabilities:
a. $P(x \leq 3)$ b. $P(x \geq 3)$ c. $P(x = 3)$
d. $P(x = 0)$ e. $P(x > 0)$ f. $P(x > 6)$

4.42 Suppose x is a random variable for which a Poisson probability distribution with $\lambda = 5$ provides a good characterization.
a. Graph $p(x)$ for $x = 0, 1, 2, \ldots, 15$.
b. Find μ and σ for x, and locate μ and the interval $\mu \pm 2\sigma$ on the graph.
c. What is the probability that x will fall within the interval $\mu \pm 2\sigma$?

Applying the Concepts

4.43 The Federal Deposit Insurance Corporation (FDIC), insures deposits of up to $100,000 in banks that are members of the Federal Reserve System against losses due to bank failure or theft. Over the last 5 years, the average number of bank failures per year among insured banks was 4.4 (FDIC, Nov. 1999). Assume that x, the number of bank failures per year among insured banks, can be adequately characterized by a Poisson probability distribution with mean 4.
a. Find the expected value and standard deviation of x.
b. In 1997, only one insured bank failed. How far (in standard deviations) does $x = 1$ lie below the mean of the Poisson distribution? That is, find the z-score for $x = 1$.

c. In 1999, six insured banks failed. Find $P(x \leq 6)$.
d. Discuss conditions that would make the Poisson assumption plausible.

4.44 As part of a project targeted at improving the services of a local bakery, a management consultant (L. Lei of Rutgers University) monitored customer arrivals for several Saturdays and Sundays. Using the arrival data, she estimated the average number of customer arrivals per 10-minute period on Saturdays to be 6.2. She assumed that arrivals per 10-minute interval followed the Poisson distribution (some of whose values are missing) shown at the bottom of the page.
a. Compute the missing probabilities.
b. Plot the distribution.
c. Find μ and σ and plot the intervals $\mu \pm \sigma$, $\mu \pm 2\sigma$, and $\mu \pm 3\sigma$ on your plot of part **b.**
d. The owner of the bakery claims that more than 75 customers per hour enter the store on Saturdays. Based on the consultant's data, is this likely? Explain.

4.45 The Environmental Protection Agency (EPA) issues pollution standards that vitally affect the safety of consumers and the operations of industry (*The United States Government Manual 1998–1999*). For example, the EPA states that manufacturers of vinyl chloride and similar compounds must limit the amount of these chemicals in plant air emissions to no more than 10 parts per million. Suppose the mean emission of vinyl chloride for a particular plant is 4 parts per million. Assume that the number of parts per million of vinyl chloride in air samples, x, follows a Poisson probability distribution.
a. What is the standard deviation of x for the plant?
b. Is it likely that a sample of air from the plant would yield a value of x that would exceed the EPA limit? Explain.
c. Discuss conditions that would make the Poisson assumption plausible.

4.46 U.S. airlines fly approximately 48 billion passenger-miles per month and average about 2.63 fatalities per month (*Statistical Abstract of the United States: 1998*). Assume the probability distribution for x, the number of fatalities per month, can be approximated by a Poisson probability distribution.
a. What is the probability that no fatalities will occur during any given month? [*Hint:* Either use Table III of Appendix B and interpolate to approximate the probability, or use a calculator or computer to calculate the probability exactly.]
b. Find $E(x)$ and the standard deviation of x.
c. Use your answers to part **b** to describe the probability that as many as 10 fatalities will occur in any given month.
d. Discuss conditions that would make the Poisson assumption plausible.

4.47 University of New Mexico economists Kishore Gawande and Timothy Wheeler studied the effectiveness of the Maritime Safety Program of the U.S. Coast Guard by examining the records of 951 deep-draft U.S. Flag vessels. They modeled the number of casualties experienced by a vessel over a three-year period as a Poisson random variable, x. Casualties were defined as the number of deaths or missing persons in a three-year interval. Using the data on the 951 vessels, they estimated $E(x)$ to be .03 (*Management Science,* January 1999).
a. Find the variance x.
b. Discuss the conditions that would make the researchers' Poisson assumption plausible.
c. What is the probability that a deep-draft U.S. flag vessel will have exactly one casualty in a three-year time period? No casualties in a three-year period?

4.48 The number x of people who arrive at a cashier's counter in a bank during a specified period of time often exhibits (approximately) a Poisson probability distribution. If we know the mean arrival rate λ, the Poisson probability distribution can be used to aid in the design of the customer service facility. Suppose you estimate that the mean number of arrivals per minute for cashier service at a bank is one person per minute.
a. What is the probability that in a given minute the number of arrivals will equal three or more?
b. Can you tell the bank manager that the number of arrivals will rarely exceed two per minute?

4.49 In studying the product life cycle in the commercial mainframe computer market over the period 1968 to 1982, Shane Greenstein (Northwestern University) and James Wade (University of Illinois) found that the number of new product introductions per year per firm, x, could be approximated by a Poisson random variable with mean equal to .37 (*Rand Journal of Economics,* Winter 1998).
a. Find the standard deviation of x.
b. Plot $p(x)$, the probability distribution for x.
c. Is it likely that the mainframe manufacturer would introduce more than two new products per year? Less than one new product per year? Justify your answers.

Probability Distribution for Exercise 4.44

x	0	1	2	3	4	5	6	7	8	9	10	11	12	13
$p(x)$	.002	.013	—	.081	.125	.155	—	.142	.110	.076	—	.026	.014	.007

Source: Lei, L. *Dorsi's Bakery: Modeling Service Operations.* Graduate School of Management, Rutgers University, 1993.

4.5 PROBABILITY DISTRIBUTIONS FOR CONTINUOUS RANDOM VARIABLES

Recall that a continuous random variable is one that can assume any value within some interval or intervals. For example, the length of time between a customer's purchase of new automobiles, the thickness of sheets of steel produced in a rolling mill, and the yield of wheat per acre of farmland are all continuous random variables.

The graphical form of the probability distribution for a **continuous random variable** x is a smooth curve that might appear as shown in Figure 4.11. This curve, a function of x, is denoted by the symbol $f(x)$ and is variously called a **probability density function (pdf),** a **frequency function,** or a **probability distribution.**

The areas under a probability distribution correspond to probabilities for x. For example, the area A beneath the curve between the two points a and b, as shown in Figure 4.11, is the probability that x assumes a value between a and b $(a < x < b)$. Because there is no area over a point, say $x = a$, it follows that (according to our model) the probability associated with a particular value of x is equal to 0; that is, $P(x = a) = 0$ and hence $P(a < x < b) = P(a \leq x \leq b)$. In other words, the probability is the same whether or not you include the endpoints of the interval. Also, because areas over intervals represent probabilities, it follows that the total area under a probability distribution, the probability assigned to all values of x, should equal 1. Note that probability distributions for continuous random variables possess different shapes depending on the relative frequency distributions of real data that the probability distributions are supposed to model.

FIGURE 4.11
A probability distribution $f(x)$ for a continuous random variable x

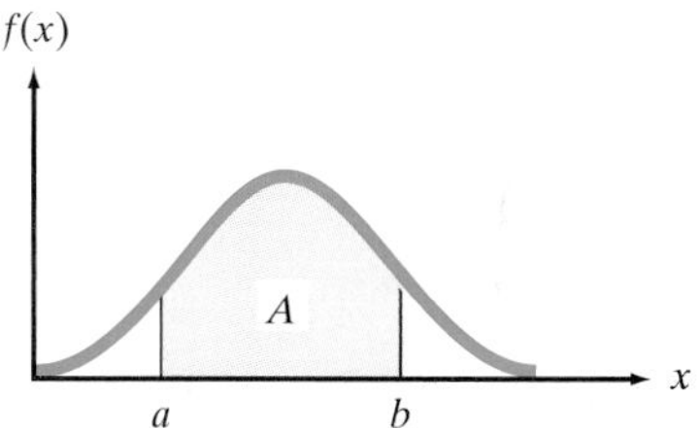

The areas under most probability distributions are obtained by using calculus or numerical methods.* Because these methods often involve difficult procedures, we will give the areas for some of the most common probability distributions in tabular form in Appendix B. Then, to find the area between two values of x, say $x = a$ and $x = b$, you simply have to consult the appropriate table.

For each of the continuous random variables presented in this chapter, we will give the formula for the probability distribution along with its mean μ and standard deviation σ. These two numbers will enable you to make some approximate probability statements about a random variable even when you do not have access to a table of areas under the probability distribution.

*Students with knowledge of calculus should note that the probability that x assumes a value in the interval $a < x < b$ is $P(a < x < b) = \int_a^b f(x)\,dx$, assuming the integral exists. Similar to the requirement for a discrete probability distribution, we require $f(x) \geq 0$ and $\int_{-\infty}^{\infty} f(x)\,dx = 1$.

4.6 THE UNIFORM DISTRIBUTION (OPTIONAL)

All the probability problems discussed in Chapter 3 had sample spaces that contained a finite number of sample points. In many of these problems, the sample points were assigned equal probabilities—for example, the die toss or the coin toss. For continuous random variables, there is an infinite number of values in the sample space, but in some cases the values may appear to be equally likely. For example, if a short exists in a 5-meter stretch of electrical wire, it may have an equal probability of being in any particular 1-centimeter segment along the line. Or if a safety inspector plans to choose a time at random during the four afternoon work hours to pay a surprise visit to a certain area of a plant, then each 1-minute time interval in this 4-work-hour period will have an equally likely chance of being selected for the visit.

Continuous random variables that appear to have equally likely outcomes over their range of possible values possess a **uniform probability distribution,** perhaps the simplest of all continuous probability distributions. Suppose the random variable x can assume values only in an interval $c \leq x \leq d$. Then the uniform frequency function has a rectangular shape, as shown in Figure 4.12. Note that the possible values of x consist of all points in the interval between point c and point d. The height of $f(x)$ is constant in that interval and equals $1/(d - c)$. Therefore, the total area under $f(x)$ is given by

$$\text{Total area of rectangle} = (\text{Base})(\text{Height}) = (d - c)\left(\frac{1}{d - c}\right) = 1$$

FIGURE 4.12
The uniform probability distribution

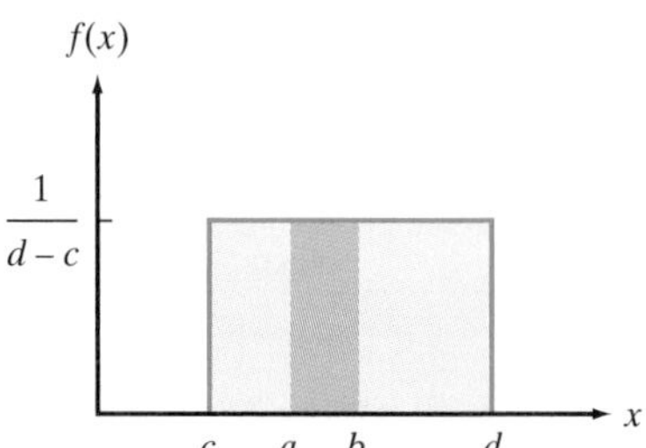

The uniform probability distribution provides a model for continuous random variables that are *evenly distributed* over a certain interval. That is, a uniform random variable is one that is just as likely to assume a value in one interval as it is to assume a value in any other interval of equal size. There is no clustering of values around any value; instead, there is an even spread over the entire region of possible values.

The uniform distribution is sometimes referred to as the *randomness distribution,* since one way of generating a uniform random variable is to perform an experiment in which a point is *randomly selected* on the horizontal axis between the points c and d. If we were to repeat this experiment infinitely often, we would create a uniform probability distribution like that shown in Figure 4.12. The random selection of points in an interval can also be used to generate random numbers such as those in Table I of Appendix B. Recall that random numbers are selected in such a way that every number would have an equal probability of selection. Therefore, random numbers are realizations of a uniform random variable. (Random numbers were used to draw random samples in Section 3.7.) The formulas for the uniform probability distribution, its mean, and standard deviation are shown in the box.

Probability Distribution, Mean, and Standard Deviation of a Uniform Random Variable *x*

$$f(x) = \frac{1}{d - c} \qquad c \le x \le d$$

$$\mu = \frac{c + d}{2} \qquad \sigma = \frac{d - c}{\sqrt{12}}$$

Suppose the interval $a < x < b$ lies within the domain of x; that is, it falls within the larger interval $c \le x \le d$. Then the probability that x assumes a value within the interval $a < x < b$ is equal to the area of the rectangle over the interval, namely, $(b - a)/(d - c)$. * (See the shaded area in Figure 4.12).

EXAMPLE 4.13 Suppose the research department of a steel manufacturer believes that one of the company's rolling machines is producing sheets of steel of varying thickness. The thickness is a uniform random variable with values between 150 and 200 millimeters. Any sheets less than 160 millimeters must be scrapped because they are unacceptable to buyers.

a. Calculate and interpret the mean and standard deviation of x, the thickness of the sheets produced by this machine.
b. Graph the probability distribution of x, and show the mean on the horizontal axis. Also show 1- and 2-standard-deviation intervals around the mean.
c. Calculate the fraction of steel sheets produced by this machine that have to be scrapped.

Solution

a. To calculate the mean and standard deviation for x, we substitute 150 and 200 millimeters for c and d, respectively, in the formulas for uniform random variables. Thus,

$$\mu = \frac{c + d}{2} = \frac{150 + 200}{2} = 175 \text{ millimeters}$$

and

$$\sigma = \frac{d - c}{\sqrt{12}} = \frac{200 - 150}{\sqrt{12}} = \frac{50}{3.464} = 14.43 \text{ millimeters}$$

*The student with knowledge of calculus should note that

$$P(a < x < b) = \int_a^b f(x)d(x) = \int_a^b 1/(d - c)dx = (b - a)/(d - c)$$

Our interpretations follow:

The average thickness of all manufactured steel sheets is $\mu = 175$ millimeters. From Chebyshev's Theorem (Table 2.8, p. 70), we know that at least 75% of the thickness values, x, in the distribution will fall in the interval

$$\mu \pm 2\sigma = 175 \pm 2(14.43)$$
$$= 175 \pm 28.86$$

or, between 146.14 and 203.86 millimeters. (This demonstrates, once again, the conservativeness of Chebyshev's Theorem since we know that all values of x fall between 150 and 200 millimeters.)

b. The uniform probability distribution is

$$f(x) = \frac{1}{d - c} = \frac{1}{200 - 150} = \frac{1}{50} \quad (150 \le x \le 200)$$

The graph of this function is shown in Figure 4.13. The mean and 1- and 2-standard-deviation intervals around the mean are shown on the horizontal axis.

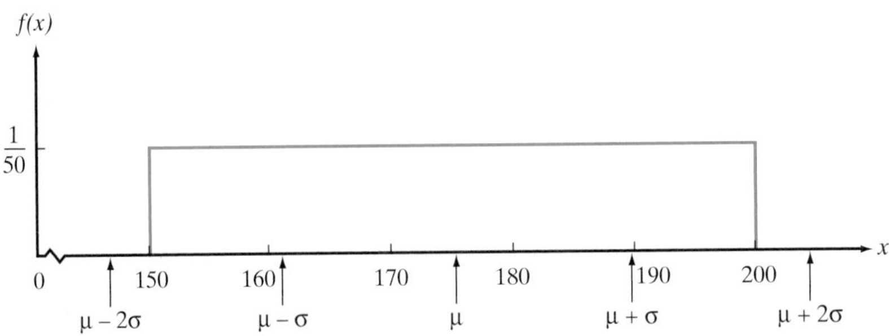

FIGURE 4.13 Distribution for x in Example 4.13

c. To find the fraction of steel sheets produced by the machine that have to be scrapped, we must find the probability that x, the thickness, is less than 160 millimeters. As indicated in Figure 4.14, we need to calculate the area under the frequency function $f(x)$ between the points $x = 150$ and $x = 160$. This is the area of a rectangle with base $160 - 150 = 10$ and height $1/50$. The fraction that has to be scrapped is then

$$P(x < 160) = (\text{Base})(\text{Height}) = (10)\left(\frac{1}{50}\right) = \frac{1}{5}$$

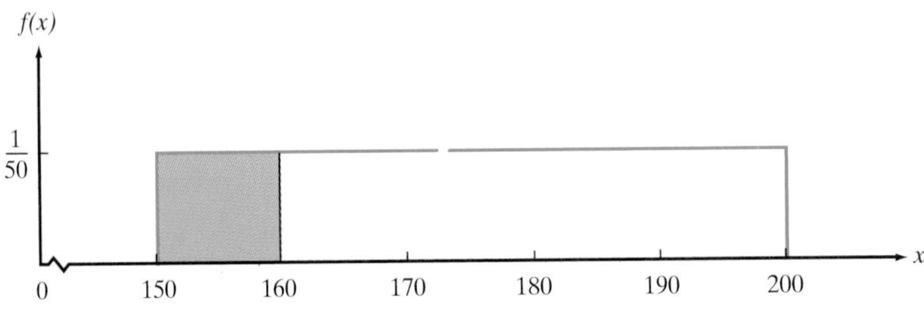

FIGURE 4.14 Probability that sheet thickness, x, is between 150 and 160 millimeters

That is, 20% of all the sheets made by this machine must be scrapped. 

EXERCISES 4.50–4.60

Learning the Mechanics

4.50 Suppose x is a random variable best described by a uniform probability distribution with $c = 20$ and $d = 45$. Find the following probabilities:
a. $P(20 \le x \le 30)$ b. $P(20 < x \le 30)$
c. $P(x \ge 30)$ d. $P(x \ge 45)$ e. $P(x \le 40)$
f. $P(x < 40)$ g. $P(15 \le x \le 35)$
h. $P(21.5 \le x \le 31.5)$

4.51 Suppose x is a random variable best described by a uniform probability distribution with $c = 3$ and $d = 7$.
a. Find $f(x)$.
b. Find the mean and standard deviation of x.
c. Find $P(\mu - \sigma \le x \le \mu + \sigma)$.

4.52 Refer to Exercise 4.51. Find the value of a that makes each of the following probability statements true.
a. $P(x \ge a) = .6$ b. $P(x \le a) = .25$
c. $P(x \le a) = 1$ d. $P(4 \le x \le a) = .5$

4.53 The random variable x is best described by a uniform probability distribution with $c = 100$ and $d = 200$. Find the probability that x assumes a value
a. More than 2 standard deviations from μ.
b. Less than 3 standard deviations from μ.
c. Within 2 standard deviations of μ.

4.54 The random variable x is best described by a uniform probability distribution with mean 10 and standard deviation 1. Find c, d, and $f(x)$. Graph the probability distribution.

Applying the Concepts

4.55 The frequency distribution shown in the next table depicts the property and marine losses incurred by a large oil company over the last two years. This distribution can be used by the company to predict future losses and to help determine an appropriate level of insurance coverage. In analyzing the losses within an interval of the distribution, for simplification, analysts may treat the interval as a uniform probability distribution (*Research Review*, Summer 1998). In the insurance business, intervals like these are often called *layers.*
a. Use a uniform distribution to model the loss amount in layer 2. Graph the distribution. Calculate and interpret its mean and variance.
b. Repeat part **a** for layer 6.
c. If a loss occurs in layer 2, what is the probability that it exceeds \$10,000? That it is under \$25,000?
d. If a layer-6 loss occurs, what is the probability that it is between \$750,000 and \$1,000,000? That it exceeds \$900,000? That it is exactly \$900,000?

Layer	Property and Marine Losses (millions of \$)	Frequency
1	0.00–0.01	668
2	0.01–0.05	38
3	0.05–0.10	7
4	0.10–0.25	4
5	0.25–0.50	2
6	0.50–1.00	1
7	1.00–2.50	0
		720

Source: Cozzolino, John M., and Perter J. Mikola, "Applications of the Piecewise Constant Pareto Distribution," *Research Review*, Summer 1998.

4.56 Researchers at the University of California–Berkeley have designed, built, and tested a switched-capacitor circuit for generating random signals (*International Journal of Circuit Theory and Applications*, May–June 1990). The circuit's trajectory was shown to be uniformly distributed on the interval (0, 1).
a. Give the mean and variance of the circuit's trajectory.
b. Compute the probability that the trajectory falls between .2 and .4.
c. Would you expect to observe a trajectory that exceeds .995? Explain.

4.57 The data set listed in the table was created using the MINITAB random number generator. Construct a relative frequency histogram for the data. Except for the expected variation in relative frequencies among the class intervals, does your histogram suggest that the data are observations on a uniform random variable with $c = 0$ and $d = 100$? Explain.

RANUNI.DAT

38.8759	98.0716	64.5788	60.8422	.8413
88.3734	31.8792	32.9847	.7434	93.3017
12.4337	11.7828	87.4506	94.1727	23.0892
47.0121	43.3629	50.7119	88.2612	69.2875
62.6626	55.6267	78.3936	28.6777	71.6829
44.0466	57.8870	71.8318	28.9622	23.0278
35.6438	38.6584	46.7404	11.2159	96.1009
95.3660	21.5478	87.7819	12.0605	75.1015

4.58 During the recession of the late 1980s and early 1990s, many companies began tightening their reimbursement expense policies. For example, a survey of 550 companies by the Dartnell Corporation found that in 1992 about half reimbursed their salespeople for home fax machines, but by 1994 only one-fourth continued to do so (*Inc.*, Sept. 1995). One company found that monthly reimbursements to their employees, x, could be adequately modeled by a uniform distribution over the interval $\$10,000 \le x \le \$15,000$.

a. Find $E(x)$ and interpret it in the context of the exercise.
b. What is the probability of employee reimbursements exceeding \$12,000 next month?
c. For budgeting purposes, the company needs to estimate next month's employee reimbursement expenses. How much should the company budget for employee reimbursements if they want the probability of exceeding the budgeted amount to be only .20?

4.59 The manager of a local soft-drink bottling company believes that when a new beverage-dispensing machine is set to dispense 7 ounces, it in fact dispenses an amount x at random anywhere between 6.5 and 7.5 ounces inclusive. Suppose x has a uniform probability distribution.
a. Is the amount dispensed by the beverage machine a discrete or a continuous random variable? Explain.
b. Graph the frequency function for x, the amount of beverage the manager believes is dispensed by the new machine when it is set to dispense 7 ounces.
c. Find the mean and standard deviation for the distribution graphed in part **b,** and locate the mean and the interval $\mu \pm 2\sigma$ on the graph.
d. Find $P(x \geq 7)$.
e. Find $P(x < 6)$.
f. Find $P(6.5 \leq x \leq 7.25)$.
g. What is the probability that each of the next six bottles filled by the new machine will contain more than 7.25 ounces of beverage? Assume that the amount of beverage dispensed in one bottle is independent of the amount dispensed in another bottle.

4.60 The *reliability* of a piece of equipment is frequently defined to be the probability, p, that the equipment performs its intended function successfully for a given period of time under specific conditions (Render and Heizer, *Principles of Operations Management,* 1995). Because p varies from one point in time to another, some reliability analysts treat p as if it were a random variable. Suppose an analyst characterizes the uncertainty about the reliability of a particular robotic device used in an automobile assembly line using the following distribution:

$$f(p) = \begin{cases} 1 & 0 \leq p \leq 1 \\ 0 & \text{otherwise} \end{cases}$$

a. Graph the analyst's probability distribution for p.
b. Find the mean and variance of p.
c. According to the analyst's probability distribution for p, what is the probability that p is greater than .95? Less than .95?
d. Suppose the analyst receives the additional information that p is definitely between .90 and .95, but that there is complete uncertainty about where it lies between these values. Describe the probability distribution the analyst should now use to describe p.

4.7 THE NORMAL DISTRIBUTION

One of the most commonly observed continuous random variables has a **bell-shaped** probability distribution (or **bell curve**) as shown in Figure 4.15. It is known as a **normal random variable** and its probability distribution is called a **normal distribution.**

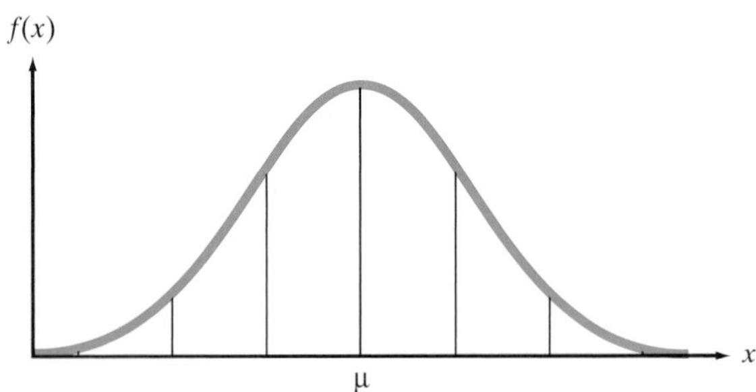

FIGURE 4.15
A normal probability distribution

The normal distribution plays a very important role in the science of statistical inference. Moreover, many business phenomena generate random variables with probability distributions that are very well approximated by a normal distribution. For example, the monthly rate of return for a particular stock is approximately a normal random variable, and the probability distribution for the weekly sales of a corporation might be approximated by a normal probability distribution. The normal distribution might also provide an accurate model for the distribution of scores on an employment aptitude test. You can determine the adequacy of the normal approximation to an existing population by comparing the relative frequency distribution of a large sample of the data to the normal probability distribution. Methods to detect disagreement between a set of data and the assumption of normality are presented in Section 4.8.

The normal distribution is perfectly symmetric about its mean μ, as can be seen in the examples in Figure 4.16. Its spread is determined by the value of its standard deviation σ.

FIGURE 4.16
Several normal distributions with different means and standard deviations

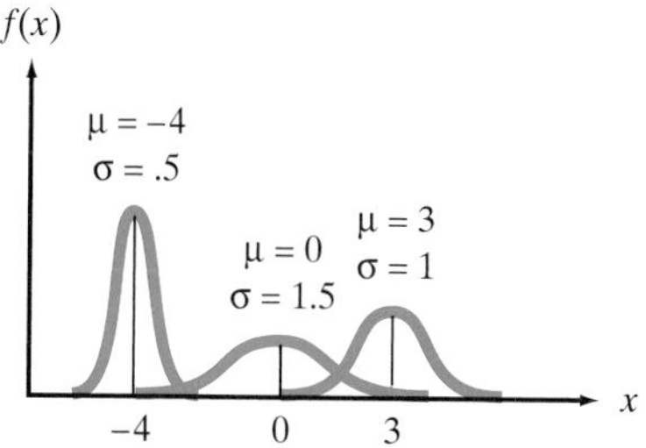

The formula for the normal probability distribution is shown in the box. When plotted, this formula yields a curve like that shown in Figure 4.15.

Probability Distribution for a Normal Random Variable x

$$f(x) = \frac{1}{\sigma\sqrt{2\pi}} e^{-(1/2)[(x-\mu)/\sigma]^2}$$

where μ = Mean of the normal random variable x
σ = Standard deviation
π = 3.1416...
e = 2.71828...

Note that the mean μ and standard deviation σ appear in this formula, so that no separate formulas for μ and σ are necessary. To graph the normal curve we have to know the numerical values of μ and σ.

Computing the area over intervals under the normal probability distribution is a difficult task.* Consequently, we will use the computed areas listed in Table IV of Appendix B. Although there are an infinitely large number of normal curves—one for each pair of values for μ and σ—we have formed a single table that will apply to any normal curve.

Table IV is based on a normal distribution with mean $\mu = 0$ and standard deviation $\sigma = 1$, called a *standard normal distribution.* A random variable with a standard normal distribution is typically denoted by the symbol z. The formula for the probability distribution of z is given by

$$f(z) = \frac{1}{\sqrt{2\pi}} e^{-(1/2)z^2}$$

*The student with knowledge of calculus should note that there is not a closed-form expression for $P(a < x < b) = \int_a^b f(x)\,dx$ for the normal probability distribution. The value of this definite integral can be obtained to any desired degree of accuracy by numerical approximation procedures. For this reason, it is tabulated for the user.

Figure 4.17 shows the graph of a standard normal distribution.

FIGURE 4.17
Standard normal distribution: $\mu = 0, \sigma = 1$

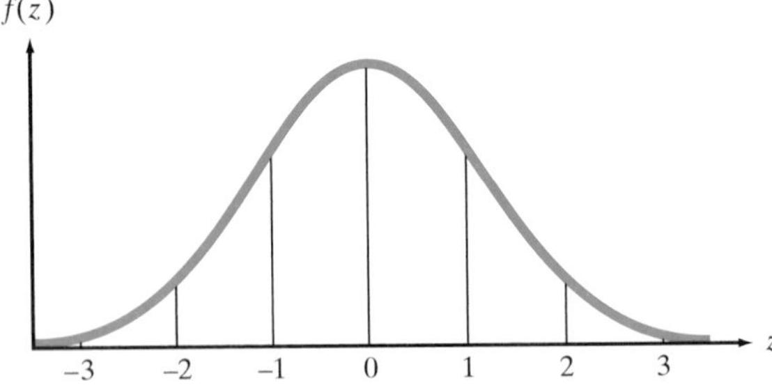

DEFINITION 4.8

The **standard normal distribution** is a normal distribution with $\mu = 0$ and $\sigma = 1$. A random variable with a standard normal distribution, denoted by the symbol z, is called a *standard normal random variable.*

Since we will ultimately convert all normal random variables to standard normal in order to use Table IV to find probabilities, it is important that you learn to use Table IV well. A partial reproduction of Table IV is shown in Table 4.5. Note that the values of the standard normal random variable z are listed in the left-hand column. The entries in the body of the table give the area (probability) between 0 and z. Examples 4.14–4.17 illustrate the use of the table.

TABLE 4.5 Reproduction of Part of Table IV in Appendix B

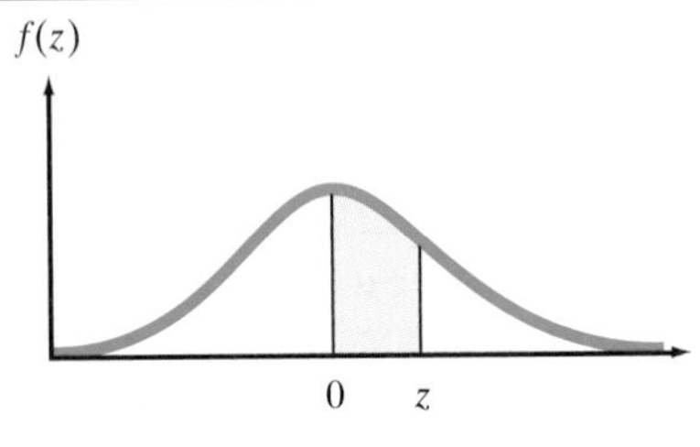

z	.00	.01	.02	.03	.04	.05	.06	.07	.08	.09
.0	.0000	.0040	.0080	.0120	.0160	.0199	.0239	.0279	.0319	.0359
.1	.0398	.0438	.0478	.0517	.0557	.0596	.0636	.0675	.0714	.0753
.2	.0793	.0832	.0871	.0910	.0948	.0987	.1026	.1064	.1103	.1141
.3	.1179	.1217	.1255	.1293	.1331	.1368	.1406	.1443	.1480	.1517
.4	.1554	.1591	.1628	.1664	.1700	.1736	.1772	.1808	.1844	.1879
.5	.1915	.1950	.1985	.2019	.2054	.2088	.2123	.2157	.2190	.2224
.6	.2257	.2291	.2324	.2357	.2389	.2422	.2454	.2486	.2517	.2549
.7	.2580	.2611	.2642	.2673	.2704	.2734	.2764	.2794	.2823	.2852
.8	.2881	.2910	.2939	.2967	.2995	.3023	.3051	.3078	.3106	.3133
.9	.3159	.3186	.3212	.3238	.3264	.3289	.3315	.3340	.3365	.3389
1.0	.3413	.3438	.3461	.3485	.3508	.3531	.3554	.3577	.3599	.3621
1.1	.3643	.3665	.3686	.3708	.3729	.3749	.3770	.3790	.3810	.3830
1.2	.3849	.3869	.3888	.3907	.3925	.3944	.3962	.3980	.3997	.4015
1.3	.4032	.4049	.4066	.4082	.4099	.4115	.4131	.4147	.4162	.4177
1.4	.4192	.4207	.4222	.4236	.4251	.4265	.4279	.4292	.4306	.4319
1.5	.4332	.4345	.4357	.4370	.4382	.4394	.4406	.4418	.4429	.4441

EXAMPLE 4.14 Find the probability that the standard normal random variable z falls between -1.33 and $+1.33$.

Solution The standard normal distribution is shown again in Figure 4.18. Since all probabilities associated with standard normal random variables can be depicted as areas under the standard normal curve, you should always draw the curve and then equate the desired probability to an area.

In this example we want to find the probability that z falls between -1.33 and $+1.33$, which is equivalent to the area between -1.33 and $+1.33$, shown shaded in Figure 4.18. Table IV provides the area between $z = 0$ and any value of z, so that if we look up $z = 1.33$, we find that the area between $z = 0$ and $z = 1.33$ is .4082. This is the area labeled A_1 in Figure 4.18. To find the area A_2 located between $z = 0$ and $z = -1.33$, we note that the symmetry of the normal distribution implies that the area between $z = 0$ and any point to the left is equal to the area between $z = 0$ and the point equidistant to the right. Thus, in this example the area between $z = 0$ and $z = -1.33$ is equal to the area between $z = 0$ and $z = +1.33$. That is,

$$A_1 = A_2 = .4082$$

FIGURE 4.18
Areas under the standard normal curve for Example 4.14

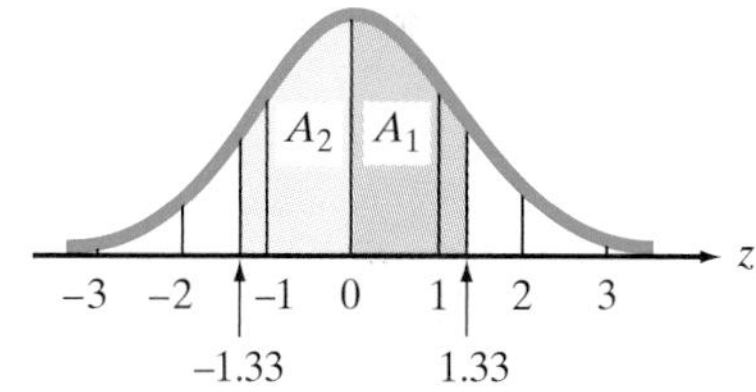

The probability that z falls between -1.33 and $+1.33$ is the sum of the areas of A_1 and A_2. We summarize in probabilistic notation:

$$P(-1.33 < z < 1.33) = P(-1.33 < z < 0) + P(0 < z < 1.33)$$
$$= A_1 + A_2 = .4082 + .4082 = .8164$$

Remember that "$<$" and "$\leq$" are equivalent in events involving z, because the inclusion (or exclusion) of a single point does not alter the probability of an event involving a continuous random variable.

EXAMPLE 4.15 Find the probability that a standard normal random variable exceeds 1.64; that is, find $P(z > 1.64)$.

Solution The area under the standard normal distribution to the right of 1.64 is the shaded area labeled A_1 in Figure 4.19. This area represents the desired probability that z exceeds 1.64. However, when we look up $z = 1.64$ in Table IV, we must remember that the probability given in the table corresponds to the area between $z = 0$ and $z = 1.64$ (the area labeled A_2 in Figure 4.19). From Table IV we find that $A_2 = .4495$. To find the area A_1 to the right of 1.64, we make use of two facts:

1. The standard normal distribution is symmetric about its mean, $z = 0$.
2. The total area under the standard normal probability distribution equals 1.

Taken together, these two facts imply that the areas on either side of the mean $z = 0$ equal .5; thus, the area to the right of $z = 0$ in Figure 4.19 is $A_1 + A_2 = .5$. Then

$$P(z > 1.64) = A_1 = .5 - A_2 = .5 - .4495 = .0505$$

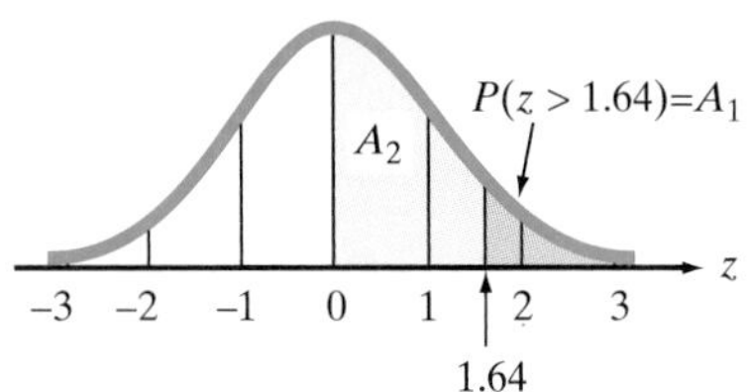

FIGURE 4.19
Areas under the standard normal curve for Example 4.15

To attach some practical significance to this probability, note that the implication is that the chance of a standard normal random variable exceeding 1.64 is approximately .05.

EXAMPLE 4.16 Find the probability that a standard normal random variable lies to the left of .67.

Solution The event is shown as the highlighted area in Figure 4.20. We want to find $P(z < .67)$. We divide the highlighted area into two parts: the area A_1 between $z = 0$ and $z = .67$, and the area A_2 to the left of $z = 0$. We must always make such a division when the desired area lies on both sides of the mean $(z = 0)$ because Table IV contains areas between $z = 0$ and the point you look up. We look up $z = .67$ in Table IV to find that $A_1 = .2486$. The symmetry of the standard normal distribution also implies that half the distribution lies on each side of the mean, so the area A_2 to the left of $z = 0$ is .5. Then,

$$P(z < .67) = A_1 + A_2 = .2486 + .5 = .7486$$

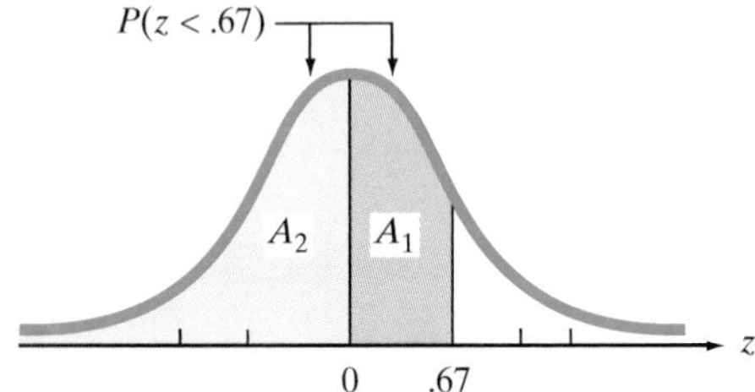

FIGURE 4.20
Areas under the standard normal curve for Example 4.16

Note that this probability is approximately .75. Thus, about 75% of the time the standard normal random variable z will fall below .67. This implies that $z = .67$ represents the approximate 75th percentile for the distribution.

EXAMPLE 4.17 Find the probability that a standard normal random variable exceeds 1.96 in absolute value.

Solution We want to find

$$P(|z| > 1.96) = P(z < -1.96 \text{ or } z > 1.96)$$

This probability is the shaded area in Figure 4.21. Note that the total shaded area is the sum of two areas, A_1 and A_2—areas that are equal because of the symmetry of the normal distribution.

We look up $z = 1.96$ and find the area between $z = 0$ and $z = 1.96$ to be .4750. Then the area to the right of 1.96, A_2, is $.5 - .4750 = .0250$, so that

$$P(|z| > 1.96) = A_1 + A_2 = .0250 + .0250 = .05$$

FIGURE 4.21
Areas under the standard normal curve for Example 4.17

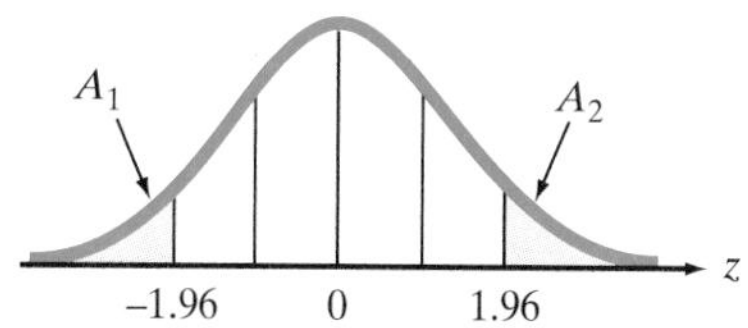

To apply Table IV to a normal random variable x with any mean μ and any standard deviation σ, we must first convert the value of x to a z-score. The population z-score for a measurement was defined (in Section 2.6) as the *distance* between the measurement and the population mean, divided by the population standard deviation. Thus, the z-score gives the distance between a measurement and the mean in units equal to the standard deviation. In symbolic form, the z-score for the measurement x is

$$z = \frac{x - \mu}{\sigma}$$

Note that when $x = \mu$, we obtain $z = 0$.

An important property of the normal distribution is that if x is normally distributed with any mean and any standard deviation, z is *always* normally distributed with mean 0 and standard deviation 1. That is, z is a standard normal random variable.

Property of Normal Distributions

If x is a normal random variable with mean μ and standard deviation σ, then the random variable z, defined by the formula

$$z = \frac{x - \mu}{\sigma}$$

has a standard normal distribution. The value z describes the number of standard deviations between x and μ.

Recall from Example 4.17 that $P(|z| > 1.96) = .05$. This probability coupled with our interpretation of z implies that any normal random variable lies more than 1.96 standard deviations from its mean only 5% of the time. Compare this to the Empirical Rule (Chapter 2) which tells us that about 5% of the measurements in mound-shaped distributions will lie beyond 2 standard deviations from the mean. The normal distribution actually provides the model on which the Empirical Rule is based, along with much "empirical" experience with real data that often approximately obey the rule, whether drawn from a normal distribution or not.

EXAMPLE 4.18

Assume that the length of time, x, between charges of a cellular phone is normally distributed with a mean of 10 hours and a standard deviation of 1.5 hours. Find the probability that the cell phone will last between 8 and 12 hours between charges.

Solution The normal distribution with mean $\mu = 10$ and $\sigma = 1.5$ is shown in Figure 4.22. The desired probability that the charge lasts between 8 and 12 hours is shaded. In order to find the probability, we must first convert the distribution to standard normal, which we do by calculating the z-score:

$$z = \frac{x - \mu}{\sigma}$$

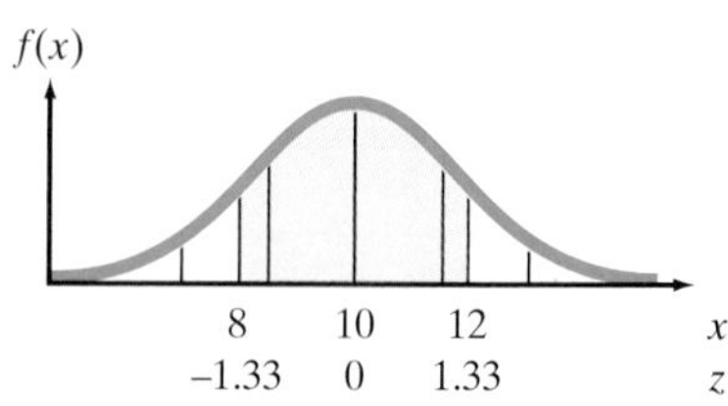

FIGURE 4.22
Areas under the normal curve for Example 4.18

The z-scores corresponding to the important values of x are shown beneath the x values on the horizontal axis in Figure 4.22. Note that $z = 0$ corresponds to the mean of $\mu = 10$ hours, whereas the x values 8 and 12 yield z-scores of -1.33 and $+1.33$, respectively. Thus, the event that the cell phone charge lasts between 8 and 12 hours is equivalent to the event that a standard normal random variable lies between -1.33 and $+1.33$. We found this probability in Example 4.14 (see Figure 4.18) by doubling the area corresponding to $z = 1.33$ in Table IV. That is,

$$P(8 \leq x \leq 12) = P(-1.33 \leq z \leq 1.33) = 2(.4082) = .8164$$

The steps to follow when calculating a probability corresponding to a normal random variable are shown in the box.

Steps for Finding a Probability Corresponding to a Normal Random Variable

1. Sketch the normal distribution and indicate the mean of the random variable x. Then shade the area corresponding to the probability you want to find.
2. Convert the boundaries of the shaded area from x values to standard normal random variable z values using the formula

$$z = \frac{x - \mu}{\sigma}$$

   Show the z values under the corresponding x values on your sketch.
3. Use Table IV in Appendix B to find the areas corresponding to the z values. If necessary, use the symmetry of the normal distribution to find areas corresponding to negative z values and the fact that the total area on each side of the mean equals .5 to convert the areas from Table IV to the probabilities of the event you have shaded.

Normal Probabilities

USING THE TI-83 GRAPHING CALCULATOR

How to Graph the Area under the Standard Normal

Start from the home screen.

Step 1 Set the viewing window. (*Recall Standard Normal uses z-values, not the actual data.*)

Press **WINDOW**
Set **Xmin** = −5
Xmax = 5
Xscl = 1
Ymin = 0
Ymax = .5
Yscl = 0
Xres = 1

Recall, the negative sign is the gray key not the blue key

Step 2 Access the Distributions Menu.

Press **2nd VARS**
Arrow right to **DRAW**
Press **ENTER**
Enter your lower limit
Press **comma**
Enter your upper limit
Press **)** Press **ENTER**

Step 3 View graph.
The graph will be displayed along with the area, lower limit, and upper limit.

Example What is the probability that z is less than 1.5 under the Standard Normal curve?

Step 1 Set your window. (See screen below.)

```
WINDOW
 Xmin=-5
 Xmax=5
 Xscl=1
 Ymin=0
 Ymax=.5
 Yscl=0
 Xres=1
```

Step 2 Enter your values (see lower left screen). Press **ENTER.**

Step 3 You will see display (see lower right screen).

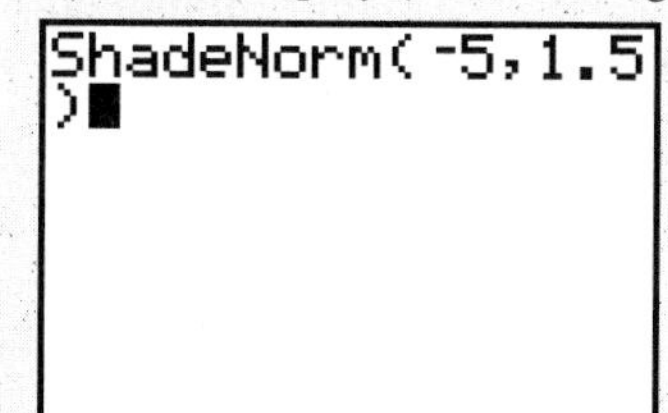

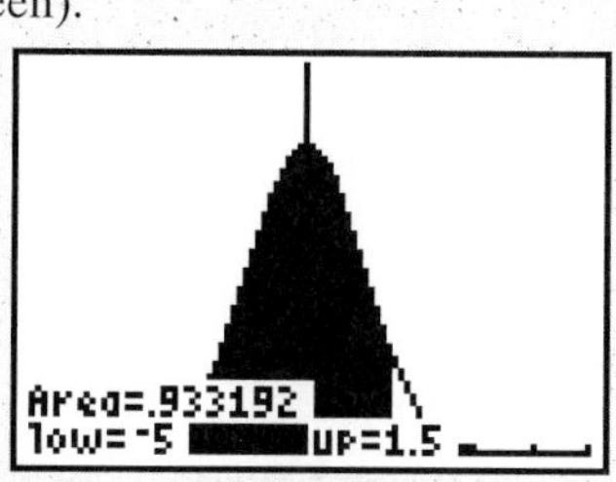

Step 4 Clear the screen for the next problem. Return to the home screen.
Press **2nd PRGM ENTER CLEAR CLEAR.**

EXAMPLE 4.19 Suppose an automobile manufacturer introduces a new model that has an advertised mean in-city mileage of 27 miles per gallon. Although such advertisements seldom report any measure of variability, suppose you write the manufacturer for the details of the tests, and you find that the standard deviation is 3 miles per gallon. This information leads you to formulate a probability model for the random variable x, the in-city mileage for this car model. You believe that the probability distribution of x can be approximated by a normal distribution with a mean of 27 and a standard deviation of 3.

a. If you were to buy this model of automobile, what is the probability that you would purchase one that averages less than 20 miles per gallon for in-city driving? In other words, find $P(x < 20)$.

b. Suppose you purchase one of these new models and it does get less than 20 miles per gallon for in-city driving. Should you conclude that your probability model is incorrect?

Solution a. The probability model proposed for x, the in-city mileage, is shown in Figure 4.23.

FIGURE 4.23
Areas under the normal curve for Example 4.19

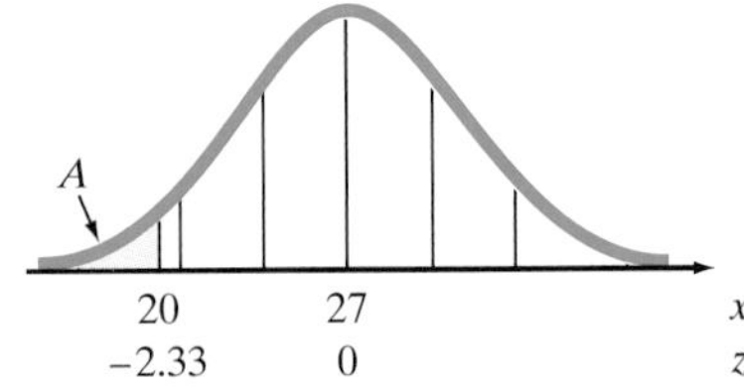

We are interested in finding the area A to the left of 20 since this area corresponds to the probability that a measurement chosen from this distribution falls below 20. In other words, if this model is correct, the area A represents the fraction of cars that can be expected to get less than 20 miles per gallon for in-city driving. To find A, we first calculate the z value corresponding to $x = 20$. That is,

$$z = \frac{x - \mu}{\sigma} = \frac{20 - 27}{3} = -\frac{7}{3} = -2.33$$

Then

$$P(x < 20) = P(z < -2.33)$$

as indicated by the shaded area in Figure 4.23. Since Table IV gives only areas to the right of the mean (and because the normal distribution is symmetric about its mean), we look up 2.33 in Table IV and find that the corresponding area is .4901. This is equal to the area between $z = 0$ and $z = -2.331$, so we find

$$P(x < 20) = A = .5 - .4901 = .0099 \approx .01$$

According to this probability model, you should have only about a 1% chance of purchasing a car of this make with an in-city mileage under 20 miles per gallon.

b. Now you are asked to make an inference based on a sample—the car you purchased. You are getting less than 20 miles per gallon for in-city driving. What do you infer? We think you will agree that one of two possibilities is true:

1. The probability model is correct. You simply were unfortunate to have purchased one of the cars in the 1% that get less than 20 miles per gallon in the city.
2. The probability model is incorrect. Perhaps the assumption of a normal distribution is unwarranted or the mean of 27 is an overestimate, or the standard deviation of 3 is an underestimate, or some combination of these errors was made. At any rate, the form of the actual probability model certainly merits further investigation.

You have no way of knowing with certainty which possibility is correct, but the evidence points to the second one. We are again relying on the rare-event approach to statistical inference that we introduced earlier. The sample (one measurement in this case) was so unlikely to have been drawn from the proposed probability model that it casts serious doubt on the model. We would be inclined to believe that the model is somehow in error. ✶

Occasionally you will be given a probability and will want to find the values of the normal random variable that correspond to the probability. For example, suppose the scores on a college entrance examination are known to be normally distributed, and a certain prestigious university will consider for admission only those applicants whose scores exceed the 90th percentile of the test score distribution. To determine the minimum score for admission consideration, you will need to be able to use Table IV in reverse, as demonstrated in the following example.

EXAMPLE 4.20

Find the value of z, call it z_0, in the standard normal distribution that will be exceeded only 10% of the time. That is, find z_0 such that $P(z \geq z_0) = .10$.

Solution

In this case we are given a probability, or an area, and asked to find the value of the standard normal random variable that corresponds to the area. Specifically, we want to find the value z_0 such that only 10% of the standard normal distribution exceeds z_0 (see Figure 4.24).

FIGURE 4.24
Area under the standard normal curve for Example 4.20

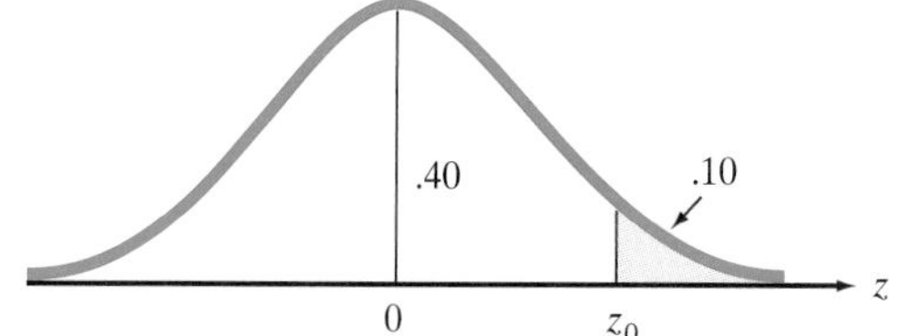

We know that the total area to the right of the mean $z = 0$ is .5, which implies that z_0 must lie to the right of (above) 0. To pinpoint the value, we use the fact that the area to the right of z_0 is .10, which implies that the area between $z = 0$ and z_0 is $.5 - .1 = .4$. But areas between $z = 0$ and some other z value are exactly the types given in Table IV. Therefore, we look up the area .4000 in the body of Table IV and find that the corresponding z value is (to the closest approximation) $z_0 = 1.28$. The implication is that the point 1.28 standard deviations above the mean is the 90th percentile of a normal distribution. ✶

EXAMPLE 4.21 Find the value of z_0 such that 95% of the standard normal z values lie between $-z_0$ and $+z_0$, i.e., $P(-z_0 \leq z \leq z_0) = .95$.

Solution Here we wish to move an equal distance z_0 in the positive and negative directions from the mean $z = 0$ until 95% of the standard normal distribution is enclosed. This means that the area on each side of the mean will be equal to $\frac{1}{2}(.95) = .475$, as shown in Figure 4.25. Since the area between $z = 0$ and z_0 is .475, we look up .475 in the body of Table IV to find the value $z_0 = 1.96$. Thus, as we found in the reverse order in Example 4.17, 95% of a normal distribution lies between +1.96 and −1.96 standard deviations of the mean.

FIGURE 4.25
Areas under the standard normal curve for Example 4.21

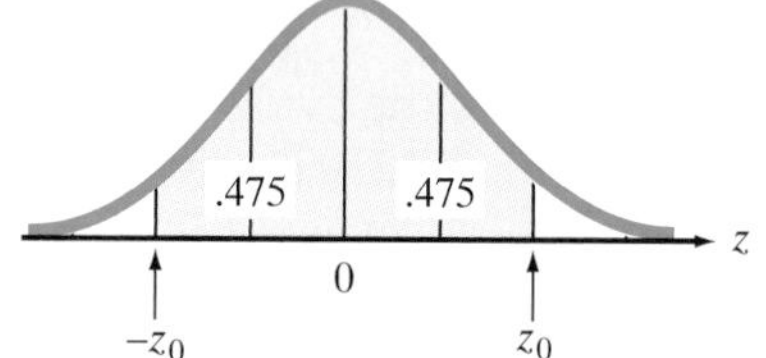

Now that you have learned to use Table IV to find a standard normal z value that corresponds to a specified probability, we demonstrate a practical application in Example 4.22.

EXAMPLE 4.22 Suppose a paint manufacturer has a daily production, x, that is normally distributed with a mean of 100,000 gallons and a standard deviation of 10,000 gallons. Management wants to create an incentive bonus for the production crew when the daily production exceeds the 90th percentile of the distribution, in hopes that the crew will, in turn, become more productive. At what level of production should management pay the incentive bonus?

Solution In this example, we want to find a production level, x_0, such that 90% of the daily levels (x values) in the distribution fall below x_0 and only 10% fall above x_0. That is,

$$P(x \leq x_0) = .90$$

Converting x to a standard normal random variable, where $\mu = 100{,}000$ and $\sigma = 10{,}000$, we have

$$\begin{aligned} P(x \leq x_0) &= P\left(z \leq \frac{x_0 - \mu}{\sigma}\right) \\ &= P\left(z \leq \frac{x_0 - 100{,}000}{10{,}000}\right) = .90 \end{aligned}$$

In Example 4.20 (see Figure 4.24) we found the 90th percentile of the standard normal distribution to be $z_0 = 1.28$. That is, we found $P(z \leq 1.28) = .90$. Consequently, we know the production level x_0 at which the incentive bonus is paid corresponds to a z-score of 1.28; that is,

$$\frac{x_0 - 100{,}000}{10{,}000} = 1.28$$

If we solve this equation for x_0, we find

$$x_0 = 100{,}000 + 1.28(10{,}000) = 100{,}000 + 12{,}800 = 112{,}800$$

This x value is shown in Figure 4.26. Thus, the 90th percentile of the production distribution is 112,800 gallons. Management should pay an incentive bonus when a day's production exceeds this level if its objective is to pay only when production is in the top 10% of the current daily production distribution.

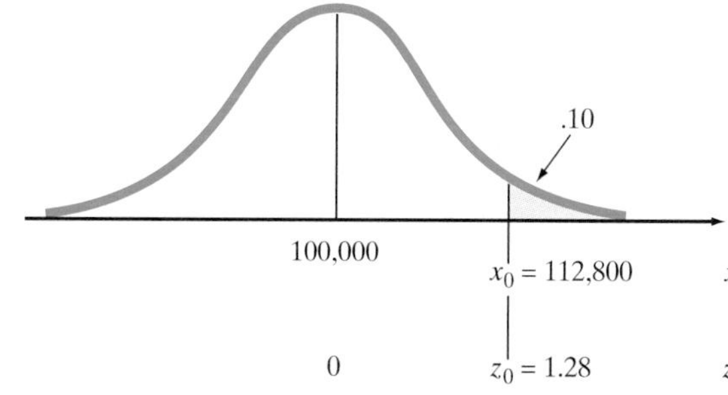

FIGURE 4.26
Area under the normal curve for Example 4.22

EXERCISES 4.61–4.75

Learning the Mechanics

4.61 Find the area under the standard normal probability distribution between the following pairs of z-scores:
a. $z = 0$ and $z = 2.00$ b. $z = 0$ and $z = 3$
c. $z = 0$ and $z = 1.5$ d. $z = 0$ and $z = .80$

4.62 Find the following probabilities for the standard normal random variable z:
a. $P(-1 \le z \le 1)$ b. $P(-2 \le z \le 2)$
c. $P(-2.16 \le z \le .55)$ d. $P(-.42 < z < 1.96)$
e. $P(z \ge -2.33)$ f. $P(z < 2.33)$

4.63 Find a value of the standard normal random variable z, call it z_0, such that
a. $P(z \le z_0) = .2090$
b. $P(z \le z_0) = .7090$
c. $P(-z_0 \le z < z_0) = .8472$
d. $P(-z_0 \le z \le z_0) = .1664$
e. $P(z_0 \le z \le 0) = .4798$
f. $P(-1 < z < z_0) = .5328$

4.64 The random variable x has a normal distribution with $\mu = 1{,}000$ and $\sigma = 10$.
a. Find the probability that x assumes a value more than 2 standard deviations from its mean. More than 3 standard deviations from μ.
b. Find the probability that x assumes a value within 1 standard deviation of its mean. Within 2 standard deviations of μ.
c. Find the value of x that represents the 80th percentile of this distribution. The 10th percentile.

4.65 Suppose x is a normally distributed random variable with $\mu = 11$ and $\sigma = 2$. Find each of the following:
a. $P(10 \le x \le 12)$ b. $P(6 \le x \le 10)$
c. $P(13 \le x \le 16)$ d. $P(7.8 \le x \le 12.6)$
e. $P(x \ge 13.24)$ f. $P(x \ge 7.62)$

4.66 Suppose x is a normally distributed random variable with $\mu = 50$ and $\sigma = 3$. Find a value of the random variable, call it x_0, such that
a. $P(x \le x_0) = .8413$ b. $P(x > x_0) = .025$
c. $P(x > x_0) = .95$ d. $P(41 \le x < x_0) = .8630$
e. 10% of the values of x are less than x_0.
f. 1% of the values of x are greater than x_0.

Applying the Concepts

4.67 The crop yield for a particular farm in a particular year is typically measured as the amount of the crop produced per acre. For example, cotton is measured in pounds per acre. It has been demonstrated that the normal distribution can be used to characterize crop yields over time (*American Journal of Agricultural Economics*, May 1999). Historical data indicate that next summer's cotton yield for a particular Georgia farmer can be characterized by a normal distribution with mean 1,500 pounds per acre and standard deviation 250. The farm in question will be profitable if it produces at least 1,600 pounds per acre.
a. What is the probability that the farm will lose money next summer?
b. Assume the same normal distribution is appropriate for describing cotton yield in each of the next two summers. Also assume that the two yields are statistically independent. What is the probability that the farm will lose money for two straight years?
c. What is the probability that the cotton yield falls within 2 standard deviations of 1,500 pounds per acre next summer?

4.68 The characteristics of an industrial filling process in which an expensive liquid is injected into a container was investigated in *Journal of Quality Technology* (July 1999). The quantity injected per container is approximately normally distributed with mean 10 units and standard deviation .2 units. Each unit of fill costs \$20 per unit. If a container contains less than 10 units (i.e., is underfilled) it must be reprocessed at a cost of \$10. A properly filled container sells for \$230.

a. Find the probability that a container is underfilled. Not underfilled.

b. A container is initially underfilled and must be reprocessed. Upon refilling it contains 10.60 units. How much profit will the company make on this container?

c. The operations manager adjusts the mean of the filling process upward to 10.10 units in order to make the probability of underfilling approximately zero. Under these conditions, what is the expected profit per container?

4.69 The problem of matching aircraft to passenger demand on each flight leg is called the *flight assignment problem* in the airline industry. *Spill* is defined as the number of passengers not carried because the aircraft's capacity is insufficient. A solution to the flight assignment problem at Delta Airlines was published in *Interfaces* (Jan.–Feb. 1994). The authors—four Delta Airlines researchers and a Georgia Tech professor (Roy Marsten)—demonstrated their approach with an example in which passenger demand for a particular flight leg is normally distributed with a mean of 125 passengers and a standard deviation of 45. Consider a Boeing 727 with a capacity of 148 passengers and a Boeing 757 with a capacity of 182.

a. What is the probability that passenger demand will exceed the capacity of the Boeing 727? The Boeing 757?

b. If the 727 is assigned to the flight leg, what is the probability that the flight will depart with one or more empty seats? Answer the same question for the Boeing 757.

c. If the 727 is assigned to the flight, what is the probability that the spill will be more than 100 passengers?

4.70 Government data indicate that the mean hourly wage for manufacturing workers in the United States is \$14 (*Statistical Abstract of the United States: 1999*). Suppose the distribution of manufacturing wage rates nationwide can be approximated by a normal distribution with standard deviation \$1.25 per hour. The first manufacturing firm contacted by a particular worker seeking a new job pays \$15.30 per hour.

a. If the worker were to undertake a nationwide job search, approximately what proportion of the wage rates would be greater than \$15.30 per hour?

b. If the worker were to randomly select a U.S. manufacturing firm, what is the probability the firm would pay more than \$15.30 per hour?

c. The population median, call it η, of a continuous random variable x is the value such that $P(x \geq \eta) = P(x \leq \eta) = .5$. That is, the median is the value η such that half the area under the probability distribution lies above η and half lies below it. Find the median of the random variable corresponding to the wage rate and compare it to the mean wage rate.

4.71 In studying the dynamics of fish populations, knowing the length of a species at different ages is critical, especially for commercial fishermen. *Fisheries Science* (Feb. 1995) published a study of the length distributions of sardines inhabiting Japanese waters. At two years of age, fish have a length distribution that is approximately normal with $\mu = 20.20$ centimeters (cm) and $\sigma = .65$ cm.

a. Find the probability that a two-year-old sardine inhabiting Japanese waters is between 20 and 21 cm long.

b. A sardine captured in Japanese waters has a length of 19.84 cm. Is this sardine likely to be two years old?

c. Repeat part **b** for a sardine with a length of 22.01 cm.

4.72 Personnel tests are designed to test a job applicant's cognitive and/or physical abilities. An IQ test is an example of the former; a speed test involving the arrangement of pegs on a peg board is an example of the latter (Cowling and James, *The Essence of Personnel Management and Industrial Relations*, 1994). A particular dexterity test is administered nationwide by a private testing service. It is known that for all tests administered last year the distribution of scores was approximately normal with mean 75 and standard deviation 7.5.

a. A particular employer requires job candidates to score at least 80 on the dexterity test. Approximately what percentage of the test scores during the past year exceeded 80?

b. The testing service reported to a particular employer that one of its job candidate's scores fell at the 98th percentile of the distribution (i.e., approximately 98% of the scores were lower than the candidate's, and only 2% were higher). What was the candidate's score?

4.73 In baseball, a "no-hitter" is a regulation 9-inning game in which the pitcher yields no hits to the opposing batters. *Chance* (Summer 1994) reported on a study of no-hitters in Major League Baseball (MLB). The initial analysis focused on the total number of hits yielded per game per team for all 9-inning MLB games played between 1989 and 1993. The distribution of hits/9-innings is approximately normal with mean 8.72 and standard deviation 1.10.

a. What percentage of 9-inning MLB games result in fewer than 6 hits?

b. Demonstrate, statistically, why a no-hitter is considered an extremely rare occurrence in MLB.

4.74 Before negotiating a long-term construction contract, building contractors must carefully estimate the total cost of completing the project. The process is complicated by the fact that total cost cannot be known with certainty ahead of time. Benzion Barlev of New York University proposed a model for total cost of a long-term contract based on the normal distribution (*Journal of Business Finance and Accounting*, July 1995). For one particular construction contract, Barlev assumed total cost, x, to be normally distributed with mean \$850,000 and standard deviation \$170,000. The revenue, R, promised to the contractor is \$1,000,000.

a. The contract will be profitable if revenue exceeds total cost. What is the probability that the contract will be profitable for the contractor?

b. What is the probability that the project will result in a loss for the contractor?

c. Suppose the contractor has the opportunity to renegotiate the contract. What value of R should the contractor strive for in order to have a .99 probability of making a profit?

4.75 A machine used to regulate the amount of dye dispensed for mixing shades of paint can be set so that it discharges an average of μ milliliters (mL) of dye per can of paint. The amount of dye discharged is known to have a normal distribution with a standard deviation of .4 mL. If more than 6 mL of dye are discharged when making a certain shade of blue paint, the shade is unacceptable. Determine the setting for μ so that only 1% of the cans of paint will be unacceptable.

4.8 DESCRIPTIVE METHODS FOR ASSESSING NORMALITY

In the chapters that follow, we learn how to make inferences about the population based on information in the sample. Several of these techniques are based on the assumption that the population is approximately normally distributed. Consequently, it will be important to determine whether the sample data come from a normal population before we can properly apply these techniques.

Several descriptive methods can be used to check for normality. In this section, we consider the four methods summarized in the box.

The first two methods come directly from the properties of a normal distribution established in Section 4.7. Method 3 is based on the fact that for normal distributions, the z values corresponding to the 25th and 75th percentiles are $-.67$ and $.67$, respectively (see Example 4.16). Since $\sigma = 1$ for a standard normal distribution,

$$\frac{\text{IQR}}{\sigma} = \frac{Q_U - Q_L}{\sigma} = \frac{.67 - (-.67)}{1} = 1.34$$

The final descriptive method for checking normality is based on a *normal probability plot*. In such a plot, the observations in a data set are ordered from smallest to largest and then plotted against the expected z-scores of observations calculated under the assumption that the data come from a normal distribution. When the data are, in fact, normally distributed, a linear (straight-line) trend will result. A nonlinear trend in the plot suggest that the data are nonnormal.

Determining Whether the Data Are From an Approximately Normal Distribution

1. Construct either a histogram or stem-and-leaf display for the data and note the shape of the graph. If the data are approximately normal, the shape of the histogram or stem-and-leaf display will be similar to the normal curve, Figure 4.15 (i.e., mound-shaped and symmetric about the mean).
2. Compute the intervals $\bar{x} \pm s$, $\bar{x} \pm 2s$, and $\bar{x} \pm 3s$, and determine the percentage of measurements falling in each. If the data are approximately normal, the percentages will be approximately equal to 68%, 95%, and 100%, respectively.
3. Find the interquartile range, IQR, and standard deviation, s, for the sample, then calculate the ratio IQR/s. If the data are approximately normal, then IQR/$s \approx 1.3$.

(continued)

4. Construct a *normal probability plot* for the data. If the data are approximately normal, the points will fall (approximately) on a straight line.

DEFINITION 4.9

A **normal probability plot** for a data set is a scatterplot with the ranked data values on one axis and their corresponding expected z-scores from a standard normal distribution on the other axis. [*Note:* Computation of the expected standard normal z-scores are beyond the scope of this text. Therefore, we will rely on available statistical software packages to generate a normal probability plot.]

EXAMPLE 4.23

The Environmental Protection Agency (EPA) performs extensive tests on all new car models to determine their mileage ratings. The results of 100 EPA tests on a certain new car model are displayed in Table 4.6. Numerical and graphical descriptive measures for the data are shown on the MINITAB and SPSS printouts, Figures 4.27a-c. Determine whether the EPA mileage ratings are from an approximate normal distribution.

TABLE 4.6 EPA Gas Mileage Ratings for 100 Cars (miles per gallon)

36.3	41.0	36.9	37.1	44.9	36.8	30.0	37.2	42.1	36.7
32.7	37.3	41.2	36.6	32.9	36.5	33.2	37.4	37.5	33.6
40.5	36.5	37.6	33.9	40.2	36.4	37.7	37.7	40.0	34.2
36.2	37.9	36.0	37.9	35.9	38.2	38.3	35.7	35.6	35.1
38.5	39.0	35.5	34.8	38.6	39.4	35.3	34.4	38.8	39.7
36.3	36.8	32.5	36.4	40.5	36.6	36.1	38.2	38.4	39.3
41.0	31.8	37.3	33.1	37.0	37.6	37.0	38.7	39.0	35.8
37.0	37.2	40.7	37.4	37.1	37.8	35.9	35.6	36.7	34.5
37.1	40.3	36.7	37.0	33.9	40.1	38.0	35.2	34.8	39.5
39.9	36.9	32.9	33.8	39.8	34.0	36.8	35.0	38.1	36.9

Solution As a first check, we examine the MINITAB histogram of the data shown in Figure 4.27a. Clearly, the mileages fall in an approximately mound-shaped, symmetric distribution centered around the mean of approximately 37 mpg. Note that a normal curve is superimposed on the figure. Therefore, using check #1 in the box, the data appear to be approximately normal.

FIGURE 4.27a MINITAB histogram for mileage data

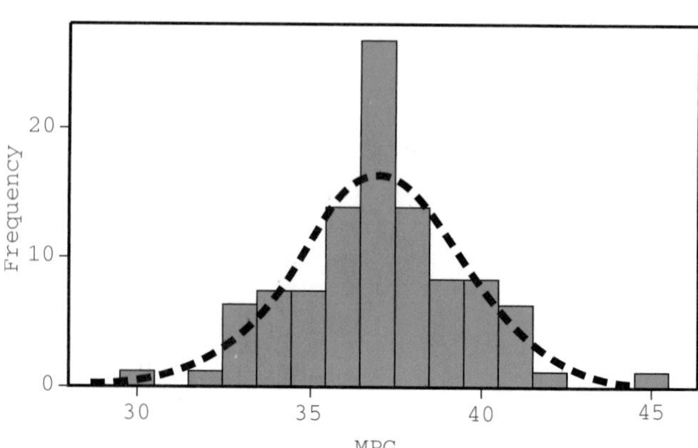

To apply check #2, we obtain $\bar{x} = 37$ and $s = 2.4$ from the MINITAB printout, Figure 4.27b. The intervals $\bar{x} \pm s$, $\bar{x} \pm 2s$, and $\bar{x} \pm 3s$, are shown in Table 4.7, as well as the percentage of mileage ratings that fall in each interval. These percentages agree almost exactly with those from a normal distribution.

FIGURE 4.27b MINITAB descriptive statistics for mileage data

```
Descriptive Statistics

Variable        N       Mean     Median    Tr Mean     StDev   Se Mean
MPG           100     36.994     37.000     36.992     2.418     0.242

Variable      Min        Max         Q1         Q3
MPG        30.000     44.900     35.625     38.375
```

TABLE 4.7 Describing the 100 EPA Mileage Ratings

Interval	Percentage in Interval
$\bar{x} \pm s = (34.6, 39.4)$	68
$\bar{x} \pm 2s = (32.2, 41.8)$	96
$\bar{x} \pm 3s = (29.8, 44.2)$	99

Check #3 in the box requires that we find the ratio IQR/s. From Figure 4.27b, the 25th percentile (called Q_1 by MINITAB) is $Q_L = 35.625$ and the 75th percentile (labeled Q_3 by MINITAB) is $Q_U = 38.375$. Then, IQR $= Q_U - Q_L = 2.75$ and the ratio is

$$\frac{\text{IRQ}}{s} = \frac{2.75}{2.4} = 1.15$$

Since this value is approximately equal to 1.3, we have further confirmation that the data are approximately normal.

A fourth descriptive method is to interpret a normal probability plot. An SPSS normal probability plot for the mileage data is shown in Figure 4.27c. Notice that the (standardized) ordered mileage values (shown on the horizontal axis) fall reasonably close to a straight line when plotted against the expected z-scores from a normal distribution. Thus, check #4 also suggests that the EPA mileage data are likely to be approximately normally distributed.

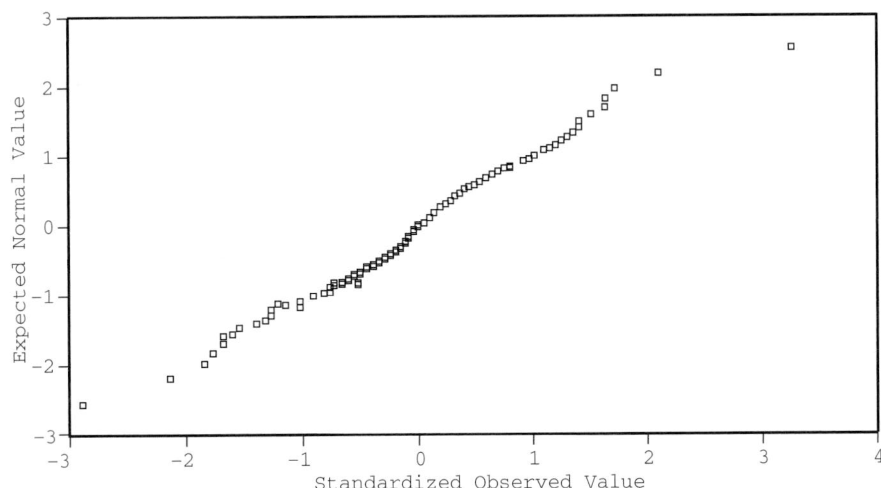

FIGURE 4.27c SPSS normal probability plot for mileage data

The checks for normality given in the box are simple, yet powerful, techniques to apply, but they are only descriptive in nature. It is possible (although unlikely) that the data are nonnormal even when the checks are reasonably satisfied. Thus, we should be careful not to claim that the 100 EPA mileage ratings of Example 4.23 are, in fact, normally distributed. We can only state that it is reasonable to believe that the data are from a normal distribution.*

As we will learn in the next chapter, several inferential methods of analysis require the data to be approximately normal. If the data are clearly nonnormal, inferences derived from the method may be invalid. Therefore, it is advisable to check the normality of the data prior to conducting the analysis.

Normal Probability Plot

USING THE TI-83 GRAPHING CALCULATOR

How to Graph a Normal Probability Plot

Start from the home screen

Step 1 Enter your data into **List 1** (Recall the List are accessed by pressing **STAT ENTER**. Always begin from a "clear" List).

Step 2 Access the "Stat Plot" menu.

Press **2nd ENTER**
Press **ENTER**
Press **ENTER**
Arrow down and right to last graph.
Press **ENTER**
Set Data List: **L1**
Data Axis: **X**

Step 3 Press **ZOOM 9**
Your data will be displayed against the residuals. If you see a "generally" linear relationship your data are near normal.

Example Using a Normal Probability Plot, test whether or not the data are normally distributed.

9.7	93.1	33.0	21.2	81.4	51.1
43.5	10.6	12.8	7.8	18.1	12.7

(continued)

*Statistical tests of normality that provide a measure of reliability for the inference are available. However, these tests tend to be very sensitive to slight departures from normality, i.e., they tend to reject the hypothesis of normality for any distribution that is not perfectly symmetrical and mound-shaped. Consult the references (see Ramsey & Ramsey, 1990) if you want to learn more about these tests.

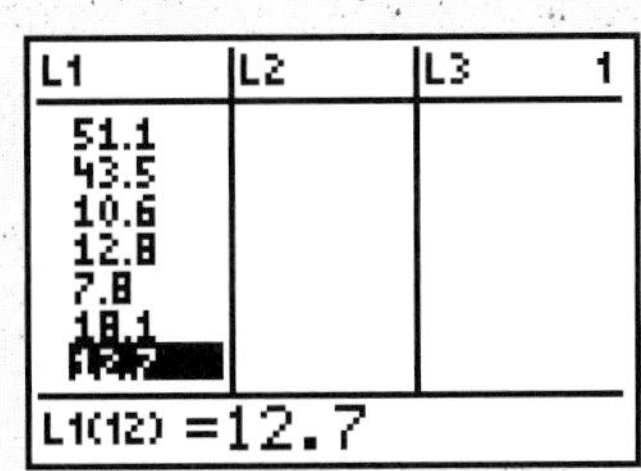

Step 1 Enter Data into List1 (see screen above).

Step 2 Access the STAT PLOT Menu. Press **2nd Y = ENTER ENTER.** (You will see the screen below after you change your setting to match.)

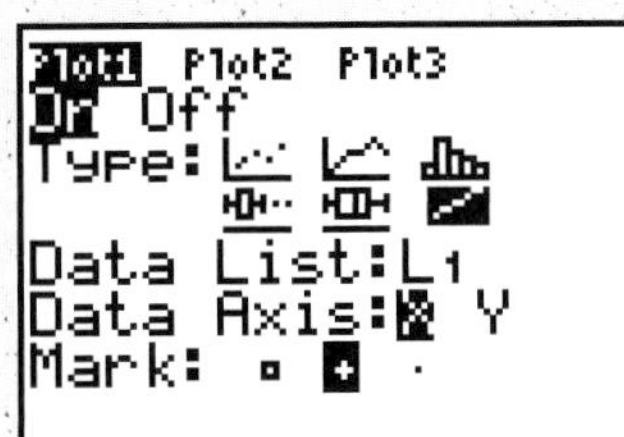

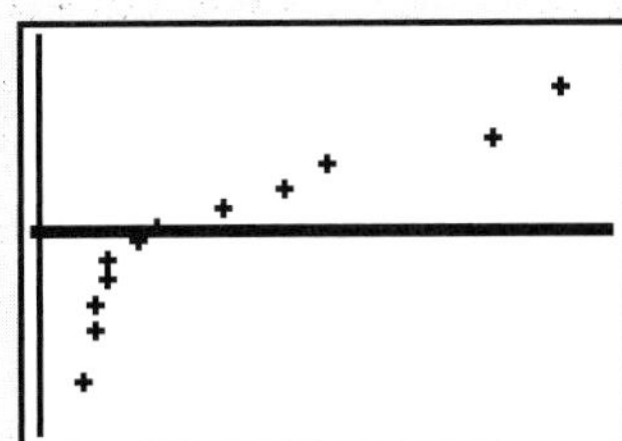

Step 3 View Display. Press **ZOOM 9** (see screen above right). There is a noticeable curve. The data are not Normally Distributed.

Step 4 Clear the screen for the next problem. Return to the home screen. Press **2nd Y = ENTER.** Arrow right. Press **ENTER CLEAR**.

EXERCISES 4.76–4.83

Learning the Mechanics

4.76 If a population data set is normally distributed, what is the proportion of measurements you would expect to fall within the following intervals?

a. $\mu \pm \sigma$

b. $\mu \pm 2\sigma$

c. $\mu \pm 3\sigma$

4.77 Consider a sample data set with the following summary statistics: $s = 95$, $Q_L = 72$, $Q_U = 195$.

a. Calculate IQR.

b. Calculate IQR/s.

c. Is the value of IQR/s approximately equal to 1.3? What does this imply?

4.78 Normal probability plots for three data sets are shown below. Which plot indicates that the data are approximately normally distributed?

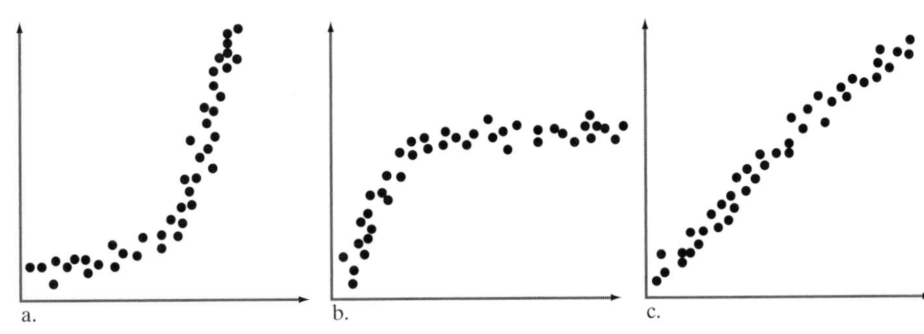

4.79 Examine the sample data below.

LM4_79.DAT

5.9	5.3	1.6	7.4	8.6	1.2	2.1
4.0	7.3	8.4	8.9	6.7	4.5	6.3
7.6	9.7	3.5	1.1	4.3	3.3	8.4
1.6	8.2	6.5	1.1	5.0	9.4	6.4

a. Construct a stem-and-leaf plot to assess whether the data are from an approximately normal distribution.

b. Compute s for the sample data.

c. Find the values of Q_L and Q_U and the value of s from part **b** to assess whether the data come from an approximately normal distribution.

d. Generate a normal probability plot for the data and use it to assess whether the data are approximately normal.

Applying the Concepts

4.80 In Exercise 2.18 (p. 45) you read about a *Journal of Statistics Education* study of team performance on games in which Mark McGwire (of the St. Louis Cardinals) and Sammy Sosa (of the Chicago Cubs) hit home runs during their record-breaking 1998 Major League Baseball season. The data on number of runs scored by their respective teams in these games are reproduced in the table on the right.

a. Determine whether the data on number of runs scored by the St. Louis Cardinals are approximately normal.

b. Repeat part **a** for the Chicago Cubs.

STLRUNS.DAT **CUBSRUNS.DAT**

St. Louis Cardinals				Chicago Cubs		
6	6	3	11	3	6	8
8	1	10	6	4	5	2
5	8	9	6	1	8	6
8	2	3	6	1	9	6
15	2	8		4	2	3
8	6	2		3	6	9
5	8	4		5	4	10
8	9	4		5	4	4
3	5	3		2	9	5
5	7	6		5	5	4
2	3	8		5	6	5
6	2	7		10	9	8
3	7	14		5	3	11
5	1	7		6	6	15
3	4	3		7	5	11
10	6	6		13	9	6
4	4	6		8	7	7
11	13	5		10	8	2

4.81 The data on January 1999 sanitation scores for 121 cruise ships, first presented in Exercise 2.58 (p. 74), are reproduced on page 225. Assess whether the sanitation scores are approximately normally distributed.

4.82 Refer to Exercise 2.36 (p. 59) and the ages of the 50 most powerful women in corporate America as determined by *Fortune* (Oct. 25, 1999). A MINITAB printout with summary statistics for the age distribution is reproduced below.

a. Use the relevant statistics on the printout to determine whether the age distribution is approximately normal.

b. In Exercise 2.36d you constructed a relative frequency histogram for the age data. Use this graph to support your conclusion in part **a.**

4.83 Refer to the New Jersey Chamber of Commerce/Rutgers Business School/Arthur Andersen 1998 study of Generation Xers' expectations of their future careers, Exercise 2.59 (p. 75). Recall that a total of 590 GenXers responded to the question: "What is the maximum number of years you expect to spend with any one employer?" The mean response was 18.2 years with a standard deviation of 10.64 years. Demonstrate why the distribution of years for all GenXers who respond is unlikely to be normally distributed.

MINITAB Output for Exercise 4.82

```
Descriptive Statistics

Variable          N       Mean     Median    Tr Mean     StDev   SE Mean
Age              50     48.160     47.000     47.795     6.015     0.851

Variable        Min        Max         Q1         Q3
Age          36.000     68.000     45.000     51.250
```

SANIT.DAT (Data for Exercise 4.81)

Ship	Score	Ship	Score	Ship	Score
Americana	75	Hanseatic	93	Regal Voyager	88
Arcadia	93	Holiday	93	Rembrandt	78
Arkona	89	Horizon	94	Rhapsody of the Seas	93
Astor	74	Imagination	91	Rotterdam VI	96
Asuka	88	Inspiration	91	Royal Princess	93
Black Watch	86	Island Adventure	95	Royal Viking Sun	89
C. Columbus	92	Island Dawn	86	Ryndam	93
Carnival Destiny	87	Island Princess	88	Sea Bird	89
Celebration	93	Islandbreeze	94	Sea Goddess I	89
Century	96	Jubilee	93	Sea Goddess II	90
Clipper Adventurer	93	Leeward	92	Sea Lion	97
Club Med I	92	Legacy	86	Seabourn Legend	94
Contessa I	87	Legend of the Seas	99	Seabourn Pride	88
Costa Romantica	94	Maasdam	96	Seabreeze I	86
Costa Victoria	92	Majesty of the Seas	93	Sensation	86
Crown Princess	90	Maxim Gorky	81	Silver Cloud	91
Crystal Harmony	91	Mayan Prince	94	Sky Princess	90
Crystal Symphony	88	Melody	91	Song of America	96
Dawn Princess	79	Mercury	97	Sovereign of the Seas	89
Delphin	91	Monarch of the Seas	96	Spirit of Columbia	89
Destiny	87	Nantucket Clipper	89	Splendour of the Seas	94
Discovery Sun	94	Nieuw Amsterdam	86	Starship Oceanic	94
Disney Magic	88	Nippon Maru	36	Statendam	92
Dolphin IV	90	Noordam	93	Stella Solaris	91
Dreamward	95	Nordic Princess	93	Sun Princess	86
Ecstasy	93	Norway	88	Superstar Capricorn	70
Edinburgh Castle	86	Norwegian Crown	90	Topaz	92
Elation	92	Norwegian Dynasty	95	Tropicale	95
Emerald	95	Norwegian Majesty	91	Universe Explorer	95
Enchanted Capri	95	Norwegian Sea	91	Veendam	91
Enchanted Isle	90	Norwegian Star	78	Victoria	91
Enchantment of the Seas	97	Norwegian Wind	95	Viking Serenade	91
Europa	88	Oceanbreeze	87	Vision of the Seas	96
Fantasy	93	Oriana	98	Vistafjord	92
Fascination	93	Palm Beach Princess	88	Westerdam	92
Flamenco	93	Paradise	95	Wind Spirit II	93
Galaxy	97	Paul Gauguin	86	World Discoverer	89
Grand Princess	94	Queen Elizabeth 2	87	Yorktown Clipper	91
Grande Caribe	95	Radisson Diamond	90	Zenith	93
Grande Mariner	87	Regal Empress	95		
Grandeur of the Seas	98	Regal Princess	95		

Source: Center for Environmental Health and Injury Control; *Tampa Tribune*, Feb. 7, 1999.

4.9 APPROXIMATING A BINOMIAL DISTRIBUTION WITH A NORMAL DISTRIBUTION (OPTIONAL)

When the discrete binomial random variable (Section 4.3) can assume a large number of values, the calculation of its probabilities may become very tedious. To contend with this problem, we provide tables in Appendix B to give the probabilities for some values of n and p, but these tables are by necessity incomplete. Recall that the binomial probability table (Table II) can be used only for $n = 5, 6, 7, 8, 9, 10, 15, 20$, or 25. To deal with this limitation, we seek approximation procedures for calculating the probabilities associated with a binomial probability distribution.

When n is large, a normal probability distribution may be used to provide a good approximation to the probability distribution of a binomial random variable. To show how this approximation works, we refer to Example 4.11, in which we used the binomial distribution to model the number x of 20 employees who favor unionization. We assumed that 60% of all the company's employees favored unionization. The mean and standard deviation of x were found to be $\mu = 12$ and $\sigma = 2.2$. The binomial distribution for $n = 20$ and $p = .6$ is shown in Figure 4.28, and the approximating normal distribution with mean $\mu = 12$ and standard deviation $\sigma = 2.2$ is superimposed.

As part of Example 4.11, we used Table II to find the probability that $x \leq 10$. This probability, which is equal to the sum of the areas contained in the rectangles (shown in Figure 4.28) that correspond to $p(0), p(1), p(2), \ldots, p(10)$, was found to equal .245. The portion of the approximating normal curve that would be used to approximate the area $p(0) + p(1) + p(2) + \cdots + p(10)$ is shaded in Figure 4.28. Note that this shaded area lies to the left of 10.5 (not 10), so we may include all of the probability in the rectangle corresponding to $p(10)$. Because we are approximating a discrete distribution (the binomial) with a continuous distribution (the normal), we call the use of 10.5 (instead of 10 or 11) a **correction for continuity.** That is, we are correcting the discrete distribution so that it can be approximated by the continuous one. The use of the correction for continuity leads to the calculation of the following standard normal z value:

$$z = \frac{x - \mu}{\sigma} = \frac{10.5 - 12}{2.2} = -.68$$

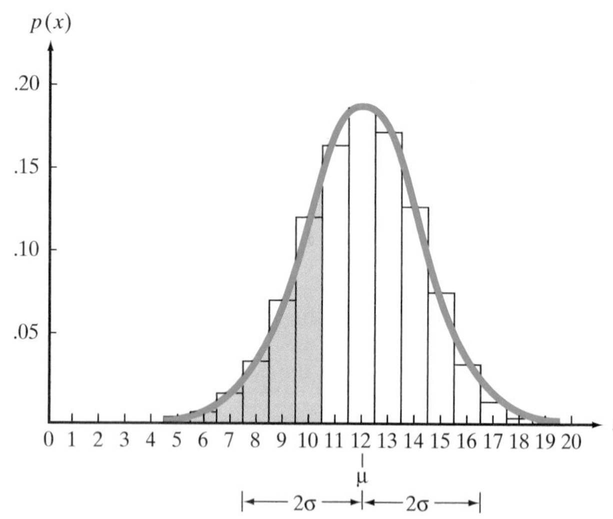

FIGURE 4.28 Binomial distribution for $n = 20$, $p = .6$ and normal distribution with $\mu = 12$, $\sigma = 2.2$

Using Table IV, we find the area between $z = 0$ and $z = .68$ to be .2517. Then the probability that x is less than or equal to 10 is approximated by the area under the normal distribution to the left of 10.5, shown shaded in Figure 4.28. That is,

$$P(x \leq 10) \approx P(z \leq -.68) = .5 - P(-.68 < z \leq 0) = .5 - .2517 = .2438$$

The approximation differs only slightly from the exact binomial probability, .245. Of course, when tables of exact binomial probabilities are available, we will use the exact value rather than a normal approximation.

Use of the normal distribution will not always provide a good approximation for binomial probabilities. The following is a useful rule of thumb to determine when n is large enough for the approximation to be effective: *The interval $\mu \pm 3\sigma$ should lie within the range of the binomial random variable* x *(i.e., 0 to* n*) in order for the normal approximation to be adequate.* The rule works well because almost all of the normal distribution falls within 3 standard deviations of the mean, so if this interval is contained within the range of x values, there is "room" for the normal approximation to work.

As shown in Figure 4.29a for the preceding example with $n = 20$ and $p = .6$, the interval $\mu \pm 3\sigma = 12 \pm 3(2.19) = (5.43, 18.57)$ lies within the range 0 to 20. However, if we were to try to use the normal approximation with $n = 10$ and $p = .1$, the interval $\mu \pm 3\sigma$ is $1 \pm 3(.95)$, or $(-1.85, 3.85)$. As shown in Figure 4.29b, this interval is not contained within the range of x since $x = 0$ is the lower bound for a binomial random variable. Note in Figure 4.29b that the normal distribution will not "fit" in the range of x, and therefore it will not provide a good approximation to the binomial probabilities.

FIGURE 4.29
Rule of thumb for normal approximation to binomial probabilities

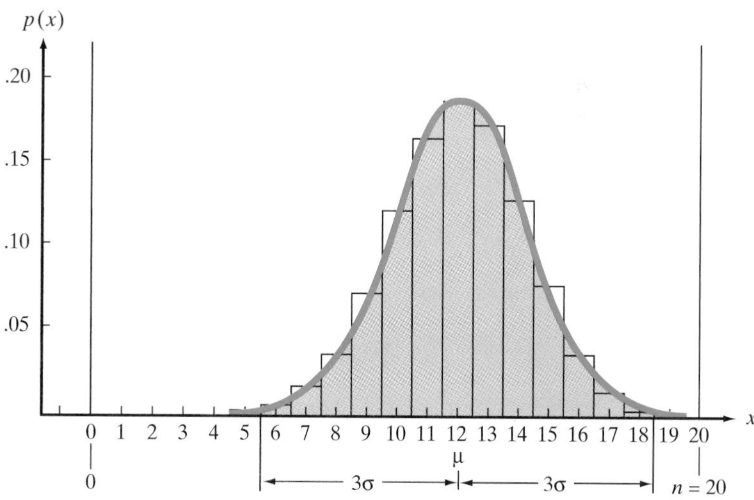

a. $n = 20, p = .6$: Normal approximation is good

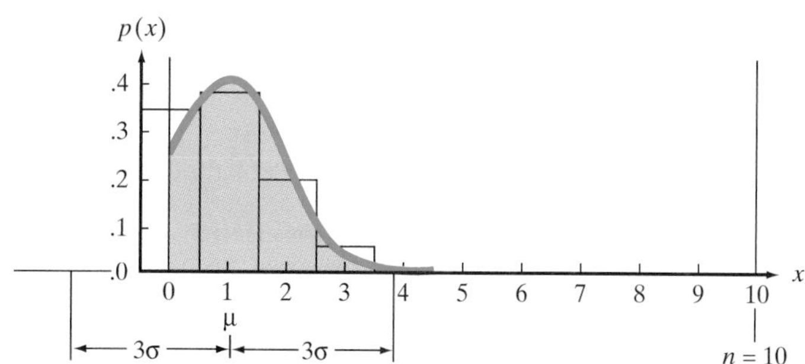

b. $n = 10, p = .1$: Normal approximation is poor

EXAMPLE 4.24

One problem with any product (e.g., a graphing calculator) that is mass-produced is quality control. The process must somehow be monitored or audited to be sure the output of the process conforms to requirements. One method of dealing with this problem is *lot acceptance sampling,* in which items being produced are sampled at various stages of the production process and are carefully inspected. The lot of items from which the sample is drawn is then accepted or rejected, based on the number of defectives in the sample. Lots that are accepted may be sent forward for further processing or may be shipped to customers; lots that are rejected may be reworked or scrapped.

For example, suppose a manufacturer of calculators chooses 200 stamped circuits from the day's production and determines x, the number of defective circuits in the sample. Suppose that up to a 6% rate of defectives is considered acceptable for the process.

a. Find the mean and standard deviation of x, assuming the defective rate is 6%.
b. Use the normal approximation to determine the probability that 20 or more defectives are observed in the sample of 200 circuits (i.e., find the approximate probability that $x \geq 20$).

Solution

a. The random variable x is binomial with $n = 200$ and the fraction defective $p = .06$. Thus,

$$\mu = np = 200(.06) = 12$$

$$\sigma = \sqrt{npq} = \sqrt{200(.06)(.94)} = \sqrt{11.28} = 3.36$$

We first note that

$$\mu \pm 3\sigma = 12 \pm 3(3.36) = 12 \pm 10.08 = (1.92, 22.08)$$

lies completely within the range from 0 to 200. Therefore, a normal probability distribution should provide an adequate approximation to this binomial distribution.

b. Use the rule of complements, $P(x \geq 20) = 1 - P(x \leq 19)$. To find the approximating area corresponding to $x \leq 19$, refer to Figure 4.30. Note that we want to include all the binomial probability histogram from 0 to 19, inclusive. Since the event is of the form $x \leq a$, the proper correction for continuity is $a + .5 = 19 + .5 = 19.5$. Thus, the z value of interest is

$$z = \frac{(a + .5) - \mu}{\sigma} = \frac{19.5 - 12}{3.36} = \frac{7.5}{3.36} = 2.23$$

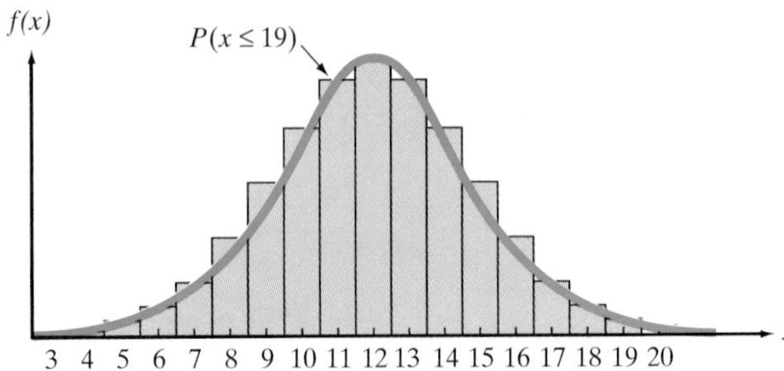

FIGURE 4.30 Normal approximation to the binomial distribution with $n = 200$, $p = .06$

Referring to Table IV in Appendix B, we find that the area to the right of the mean 0 corresponding to $z = 2.23$ (see Figure 4.31) is .4871. So the area $A = P(z \leq 2.23)$ is:

$$A = .5 + .4871 = .9871$$

FIGURE 4.31
Standard normal distribution

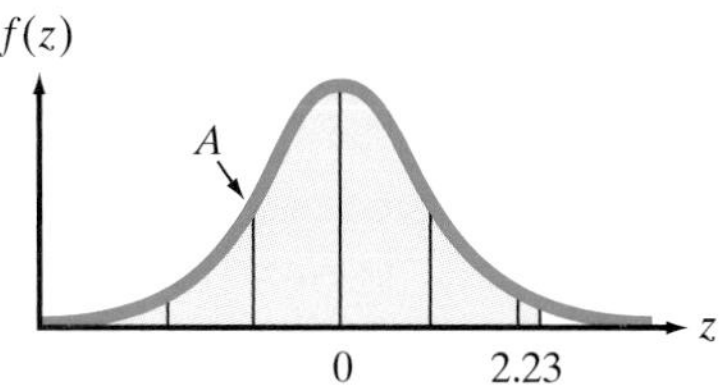

Thus, the normal approximation to the binomial probability we seek is

$$P(x \geq 20) = 1 - P(x \leq 19) \approx 1 - .9871 = .0129$$

In other words, the probability is extremely small that 20 or more defectives will be observed in a sample of 200 circuits—*if in fact the true fraction of defectives is .06.* If the manufacturer observes $x \geq 20$, the likely reason is that the process is producing more than the acceptable 6% defectives. The lot acceptance sampling procedure is another example of using the rare-event approach to make inferences.

The steps for approximating a binomial probability by a normal probability are given in the accompanying box.

Using a Normal Distribution to Approximate Binomial Probabilities

1. After you have determined n and p for the binomial distribution, calculate the interval

$$\mu \pm 3\sigma = np \pm 3\sqrt{npq}$$

If the interval lies in the range 0 to n, the normal distribution will provide a reasonable approximation to the probabilities of most binomial events.

2. Express the binomial probability to be approximated in the form $P(x \leq a)$ or $P(x \leq b) - P(x \leq a)$. For example,

$$P(x < 3) = P(x \leq 2)$$
$$P(x \geq 5) = 1 - P(x \leq 4)$$
$$P(7 \leq x \leq 10) = P(x \leq 10) - P(x \leq 6)$$

3. For each value of interest a, the correction for continuity is $(a + .5)$, and the corresponding standard normal z value is

$$z = \frac{(a + .5) - \mu}{\sigma} \quad \text{(See Figure 4.32)}$$

4. Sketch the approximating normal distribution and shade the area corresponding to the probability of the event of interest, as in Figure 4.32. Verify that the rectangles you have included in the shaded area correspond to the event probability you wish to approximate. Using Table IV and the z value(s) you calculated in step 3, find the shaded area. This is the approximate probability of the binomial event.

(continued)

FIGURE 4.32
Approximating binomial probabilities by normal probabilities

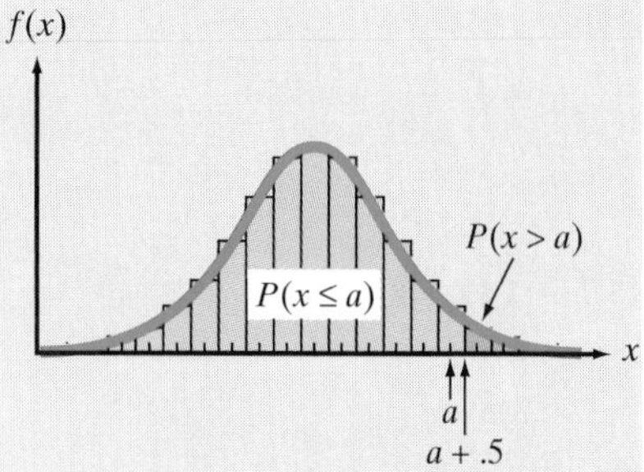

EXERCISES 4.84–4.93

Learning the Mechanics

4.84 Assume that x is a binomial random variable with n and p as specified in parts **a–f.** For which cases would it be appropriate to use a normal distribution to approximate the binomial distribution?

a. $n = 100, p = .01$
b. $n = 20, p = .6$
c. $n = 10, p = .4$
d. $n = 1{,}000, p = .05$
e. $n = 100, p = .8$
f. $n = 35, p = .7$

4.85 Assume that x is a binomial random variable with $n = 25$ and $p = .5$. Use Table II of Appendix B and the normal approximation to find the exact and approximate values, respectively, for the following probabilities:

a. $P(x \leq 11)$
b. $P(x \geq 16)$
c. $P(8 \leq x \leq 16)$

4.86 Assume that x is a binomial random variable with $n = 100$ and $p = .40$. Use a normal approximation to find the following:

a. $P(x \leq 35)$
b. $P(40 \leq x \leq 50)$
c. $P(x \geq 38)$

Applying the Concepts

4.87 Refer to the FTC study of the pricing accuracy of supermarket electronic scanners, Exercise 4.30 (p. 192). Recall that the probability that a scanned item is priced incorrectly is $^1/_{30} = .033$.

a. Suppose 10,000 supermarket items are scanned. What is the approximate probability that you observe at least 100 items with incorrect prices?
b. Suppose 100 items are scanned and you are interested in the probability that fewer than five are incorrectly priced. Explain why the approximate method of part **a** may not yield an accurate estimate of the probability.

4.88 The computer chips in today's notebook and laptop computers are produced from semiconductor wafers. Certain semiconductor wafers are exposed to an environment that generates up to 100 possible defects per wafer. The number of defects per wafer, x, was found to follow a binomial distribution if the manufacturing process is stable and generates defects that are randomly distributed on the wafers (*IEEE Transactions on Semiconductor Manufacturing,* May 1995). Let p represent the probability that a defect occurs at any one of the 100 points of the wafer. For each of the following cases, determine whether the normal approximation can be used to characterize x.

a. $p = .01$
b. $p = .50$
c. $p = .90$

4.89 In 1999, nearly 500,000 Americans underwent laser surgery to correct their vision. While the majority of patients were pleased with the results, it is estimated that 1% of patients of corneal specialists and 5% of patients of less experienced ophthalmologists have serious post-laser vision problems (*Time,* Oct. 11, 1999).

a. If all 500,000 patients were operated on by corneal specialists, what is the expected number of patients who will experience serious post-laser vision problems? Answer the same question assuming all patients are operated on by ophthalmologists.
b. If 400 employees of a particular company choose to undergo laser surgery with ophthalmologists, what is the approximate probability that 20 or more of these employees will suffer serious vision problems? Justify the methodology you used to answer the question.
c. Refer to part **b.** Can the same methodology be used to answer the same question assuming all 400 employees had chosen a corneal specialist? Explain.

4.90 In recent years, American consumers have come to regard credit cards as commodities. As a result, the credit card industry has become increasingly competitive. The table on p. 231 reports the industry's market share data for mid-1999. A random sample of 100 credit card users is to be questioned regarding their satisfaction with their credit card company. For simplification, assume that each credit card user carries just one credit card and that the market share percentages are the percentages of all credit card customers that carry each brand.

Credit Card	Market Share %
Visa	47.0
MasterCard	25.5
American Express	20.2
Discover	6.0
Diners Club	1.3

Source: *Newsweek,* Oct. 4, 1999, p. 55.

a. Propose a procedure for randomly selecting the 100 credit card users.
b. For random samples of 100 credit card users, what is the expected number of customers who carry Visa? Discover?
c. What is the probability that half or more of the sample of credit card users carry Visa? American Express?
d. Justify the use of the normal approximation to the binomial in answering the question in part **c.**

4.91 Refer to Exercise 4.35 (p. 193), where the number of shuttle catastrophes caused by booster failure in n missions was treated as a binomial random variable. Using the binomial distribution and the probability of catastrophe determined by the Air Force's risk assessment study ($^1/_{35}$), you determined the probability of at least one shuttle catastrophe in 25 missions to be .5155.
a. Based on the guidelines presented in this section, would it have been advisable to approximate this probability using the normal approximation to the binomial distribution? Explain.
b. Regardless of your answer to part **a,** use the normal distribution to approximate the binomial probability. Comment on the difference between the exact and approximate probabilities.
c. Refer to part **a.** Would the normal approximation be advisable if $n = 100$? If $n = 500$? If $n = 1{,}000$?
d. Approximate the probability that more than 25 catastrophes occur in 1,000 flights, assuming that the probability of a catastrophe in any given flight remains $^1/_{35}$.

4.92 The *Chronicle of Higher Education Almanac* (Aug. 27, 1999) reports that the percentage of undergraduates in the United States receiving federal financial aid is 45% at public four-year institutions and 52% at private four-year institutions. The U.S. Department of Education is interested in questioning a random sample of 100 U.S. undergraduate students to assess their satisfaction with federal financial aid procedures and policies.
a. Explain the difficulties of obtaining the desired random sample.
b. Assume the appropriate percentage above applies to your institution. If a random sample of 100 students from your institution were contacted, what is the approximate probability that 50 or more receive financial aid? Less than 25?
c. What assumptions must be made in order to answer part **b** using the normal approximation to the binomial?

4.93 According to *New Jersey Business* (Feb. 1996), Newark International Airport's new terminal handles an average of 3,000 international passengers an hour, but is capable of handling twice that number. Also, 80% of arriving international passengers pass through without their luggage being inspected and the remainder are detained for inspection. The inspection facility can handle 600 passengers an hour without unreasonable delays for the travelers.
a. When international passengers arrive at the rate of 1,500 per hour, what is the expected number of passengers who will be detained for luggage inspection?
b. In the future, it is expected that as many as 4,000 international passengers will arrive per hour. When that occurs, what is the expected number of passengers who will be detained for luggage inspection?
c. Refer to part **b.** Find the approximate probability that more than 600 international passengers will be detained for luggage inspection. (This is also the probability that travelers will experience unreasonable luggage inspection delays.)

4.10 THE EXPONENTIAL DISTRIBUTION (OPTIONAL)

The length of time between arrivals at a fast-food drive-through restaurant, the length of time between breakdowns of manufacturing equipment, and the length of time between filings of claims in a small insurance office are all business phenomena that we might want to describe probabilistically. The amount of time between occurrences of random events like these can often be described by the **exponential probability distribution.** For this reason, the exponential distribution is sometimes called the **waiting time distribution.** The formula for the exponential probability distribution is shown in the box along with its mean and standard deviation.

Probability Distribution, Mean, and Standard Deviation for an Exponential Random Variable *x*

$$f(x) = \lambda e^{-\lambda x} \qquad (x > 0)$$

$$\mu = \frac{1}{\lambda}$$

$$\sigma = \frac{1}{\lambda}$$

Unlike the normal distribution which has a shape and location determined by the values of the two quantities μ and σ, the shape of the exponential distribution is governed by a single quantity, λ. Further, it is a probability distribution with the property that its mean equals its standard deviation. Exponential distributions corresponding to $\lambda = .5, 1,$ and 2 are shown in Figure 4.33.

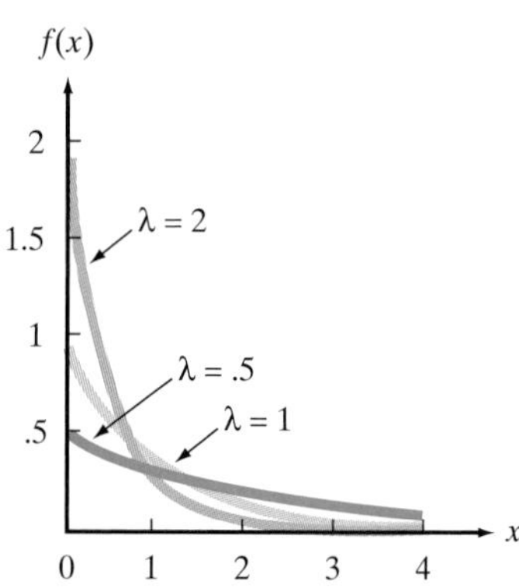

FIGURE 4.33
Exponential distributions

To calculate probabilities for exponential random variables, we need to be able to find areas under the exponential probability distribution. Suppose we want to find the area A to the right of some number a, as shown in Figure 4.34. This area can be calculated by using the formula in the box.

Finding the Area *A* to the Right of a Number *a* for an Exponential Distribution*

$$A = P(x \geq a) = e^{-\lambda a}$$

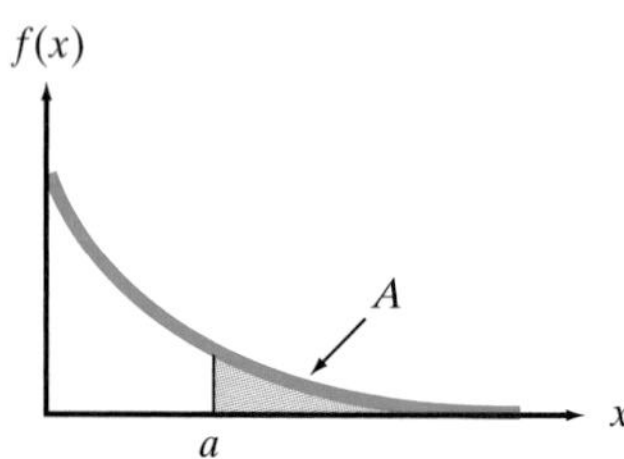

FIGURE 4.34
The area A to the right of a number a for an exponential distribution

*For students with a knowledge of calculus, the shaded area in Figure 4.34 corresponds to the integral

$$\int_a^{\infty} \lambda e^{-\lambda x} dx = -e^{-\lambda x}\Big|_a^{\infty} = e^{-\lambda a}$$

Use Table V in Appendix B or a pocket calculator with an exponential function to find the value of $e^{-\lambda a}$ after substituting the appropriate numerical values for λ and a.

EXAMPLE 4.25 Suppose the length of time (in days) between sales for an automobile salesperson is modeled as an exponential distribution with $\lambda = .5$. What is the probability the salesperson goes more than 5 days without a sale?

Solution The probability we want is the area A to the right of $a = 5$ in Figure 4.35. To find this probability, use the formula given for area:

$$A = e^{-\lambda a} = e^{-(.5)5} = e^{-2.5}$$

FIGURE 4.35
Area to the right of $a = 5$ for Example 4.25

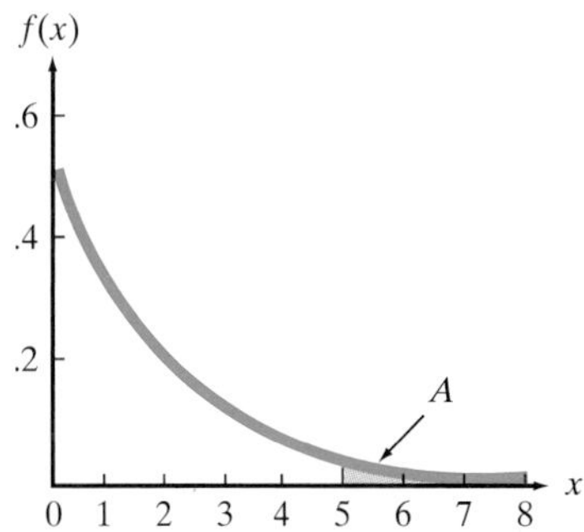

Referring to Table V, we find

$$A = e^{-2.5} = .082085$$

Our exponential model indicates that the probability of going more than 5 days without a sale is about .08 for this automobile salesperson.

EXAMPLE 4.26 A microwave oven manufacturer is trying to determine the length of warranty period it should attach to its magnetron tube, the most critical component in the oven. Preliminary testing has shown that the length of life (in years), x, of a magnetron tube has an exponential probability distribution with $\lambda = .16$.

a. Find the mean and standard deviation of x.
b. Suppose a warranty period of 5 years is attached to the magnetron tube. What fraction of tubes must the manufacturer plan to replace, assuming that the exponential model with $\lambda = .16$ is correct?
c. Find the probability that the length of life of a magnetron tube will fall within the interval $\mu - 2\sigma$ to $\mu + 2\sigma$.

Solution

a. For this exponential random variable, $\mu = 1/\lambda = {}^{1}/_{.16} = 6.25$ years. Also, since $\mu = \sigma$, $\sigma = 6.25$ years.
b. To find the fraction of tubes that will have to be replaced before the 5-year warranty period expires, we need to find the area between 0 and 5 under the distribution. This area, A, is shown in Figure 4.36.

FIGURE 4.36
Area to the left of $a = 5$ for Example 4.26

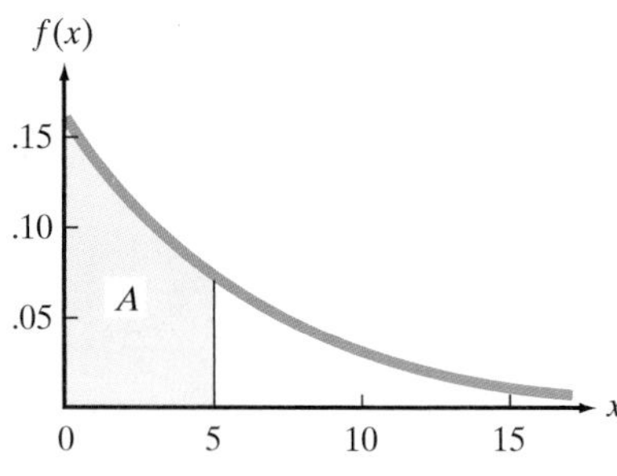

To find the required probability, we recall the formula

$$P(x > a) = e^{-\lambda a}$$

Using this formula, we can find

$$P(x > 5) = e^{-\lambda(5)} = e^{-(.16)(5)} = e^{-.80} = .449329$$

(see Table V). To find the area A, we use the complementary relationship:

$$P(x \le 5) = 1 - P(x > 5) = 1 - .449329 = .550671$$

So approximately 55% of the magnetron tubes will have to be replaced during the 5-year warranty period.

c. We would expect the probability that the life of a magnetron tube, x, falls within the interval $\mu - 2\sigma$ to $\mu + 2\sigma$ to be quite large. A graph of the exponential distribution showing the interval $\mu - 2\sigma$ to $\mu + 2\sigma$ is given in Figure 4.37. Since the point $\mu - 2\sigma$ lies below $x = 0$, we need to find only the area between $x = 0$ and $x = \mu + 2\sigma = 6.25 + 2(6.25) = 18.75$.

This area, P, which is shaded in Figure 4.37, is

$$P = 1 - P(x > 18.75) = 1 - e^{-\lambda(18.75)} = 1 - e^{-(.16)(18.75)} = 1 - e^{-3}$$

FIGURE 4.37
Area in the interval $\mu \pm 2\sigma$ for Example 4.26

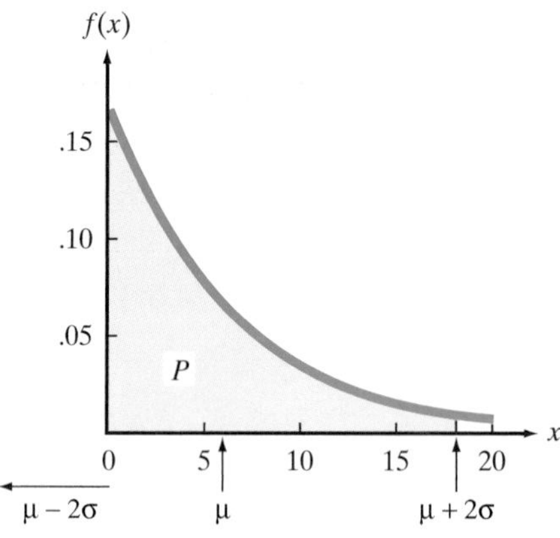

Using Table V or a calculator, we find $e^{-3} = .049787$. Therefore, the probability that the life x of a magnetron tube will fall within the interval $\mu - 2\sigma$ to $\mu + 2\sigma$ is

$$P = 1 - e^{-3} = 1 - .049787 = .950213$$

You can see that this probability agrees very well with the Empirical Rule (Table 2.9, p. 71) even though this probability distribution is not mound-shaped. (It is strongly skewed to the right.)

EXERCISES 4.94–4.104

Learning the Mechanics

4.94 The random variables x and y have exponential distributions with $\lambda = 3$ and $\lambda = .75$, respectively. Using Table V in Appendix B, carefully plot both distributions on the same set of axes.

4.95 Use Table V in Appendix B to determine the value of $e^{-\lambda a}$ for each of the following cases.
a. $\lambda = 1, a = 1$ b. $\lambda = 1, a = 2.5$
c. $\lambda = 2.5, a = 3$ d. $\lambda = 5, a = .3$

4.96 Suppose x has an exponential distribution with $\lambda = 3$. Find the following probabilities:
a. $P(x > 2)$ b. $P(x > 1.5)$ c. $P(x > 3)$
d. $P(x > .45)$

4.97 Suppose x has an exponential distribution with $\lambda = 2.5$. Find the following probabilities:
a. $P(x \leq 3)$ b. $P(x \leq 4)$ c. $P(x \leq 1.6)$
d. $P(x \leq .4)$

4.98 Suppose the random variable x has an exponential probability distribution with $\lambda = 2$. Find the mean and standard deviation of x. Find the probability that x will assume a value within the interval $\mu \pm 2\sigma$.

Applying the Concepts

4.99 University of Michigan researchers B. Wilkinson, N. Diedrich and E. Rothman, and C. Drummond of Indiana-Purdue University in Fort Wayne studied the duration between goals scored by the University of Michigan hockey team during its 40-game, 1996 national championship season. They found that the time-between-scores could be characterized with an exponential distribution with a mean of 10.54 minutes (*Geological Society of America Bulletin,* August 1998).
a. Find the value of λ for this exponential distribution.
b. Find the mean and standard deviation for this distribution and interpret each in the context of the problem.
c. Graph this exponential distribution. Locate the mean on the graph.
d. If Michigan scores with exactly two minutes left in the game, what is the probability they will score again before time runs out?

4.100 Lack of port facilities or shallow water may require cargo on a large ship to be transferred to a pier using smaller craft. This process may require the smaller craft to cycle back and forth from ship to shore many times. Researchers G. Horne (Center for Naval Analysis) and T. Irony (George Washington University) developed models of this transfer process that provide estimates of ship-to-shore transfer times (*Naval Research Logistics,* Vol. 41, 1994). They modeled the time between arrivals of the smaller craft at the pier using an exponential distribution.
a. Assume the mean time between arrivals at the pier is 17 minutes. Give the value of λ for this exponential distribution. Graph the distribution.
b. Suppose there is only one unloading zone at the pier available for the small craft to use. If the first craft docks at 10:00 A.M. and doesn't finish unloading until 10:15 A.M., what is the probability that the second craft will arrive at the unloading zone and have to wait before docking?

4.101 *Product reliability* has been defined as the probability that a product will perform its intended function satisfactorily for its intended life when operating under specified conditions. The *reliability function*, $R(x)$, for a product indicates the probability of the product's life exceeding x time periods. When the time until failure of a product can be adequately modeled by an exponential distribution, the product's reliability function is $R(x) = e^{-\lambda x}$ (Ross, *Stochastic Processes,* 1996). Suppose that the time to failure (in years) of a particular product is modeled by an exponential distribution with $\lambda = .5$.
a. What is the product's reliability function?
b. What is the probability that the product will perform satisfactorily for at least four years?
c. What is the probability that a particular product will survive longer than the mean life of the product?
d. If λ changes, will the probability that you calculated in part **c** change? Explain.
e. If 10,000 units of the product are sold, approximately how many will perform satisfactorily for more than five years? About how many will fail within one year?
f. How long should the length of the warranty period be for the product if the manufacturer wants to replace no more than 5% of the units sold while under warranty?

4.102 A part processed in a flexible manufacturing system (FMS) is routed through a set of operations, some of which are sequential and some of which are parallel. In addition, an FMS operation can be processed by alternative machines. An article in *IEEE Transactions* (Mar. 1990) gave an example of an FMS with four machines operating independently. The repair rates for the machines (i.e., the time, in hours, it takes to repair a failed machine) are exponentially distributed with means $\mu_1 = 1, \mu_2 = 2, \mu_3 = .5$, and $\mu_4 = .5$, respectively.

a. Find the probability that the repair time for machine 1 exceeds one hour.

b. Repeat part **a** for machine 2.

c. Repeat part **a** for machines 3 and 4.

d. If all four machines fail simultaneously, find the probability that the repair time for the entire system exceeds one hour.

4.103 The importance of modeling machine downtime correctly in simulation studies was discussed in *Industrial Engineering* (Aug. 1990). The paper presented simulation results for a single-machine-tool system with the following properties:

- The interarrival times of jobs are exponentially distributed with a mean of 1.25 minutes
- The amount of time the machine operates before breaking down is exponentially distributed with a mean of 540 minutes

a. Find the probability that two jobs arrive for processing at most one minute apart.

b. Find the probability that the machine operates for at least 720 minutes (12 hours) before breaking down.

4.104 In an article published in the *European Journal of Operational Research* (Vol. 21, 1985) the vehicle-dispatching decisions of an airport-based taxi service were investigated. In modeling the system, the authors assumed travel times of successive trips to be independent exponential random variables. Assume $\lambda = .05$.

a. What is the mean trip time for the taxi service?

b. What is the probability that a particular trip will take more than 30 minutes?

c. Two taxis have just been dispatched. What is the probability that both will be gone for more than 30 minutes? That at least one of the taxis will return within 30 minutes?

4.11 SAMPLING DISTRIBUTIONS

In previous sections we assumed that we knew the probability distribution of a random variable, and using this knowledge we were able to compute the mean, variance, and probabilities associated with the random variable. However, in most practical applications, the true mean and standard deviation are unknown quantities that would have to be estimated. Numerical quantities that describe probability distributions are called *parameters*. Thus, *p*, the probability of a success in a binomial experiment, and μ and σ, the mean and standard deviation of a normal distribution, are examples of parameters.

DEFINITION 4.10

A **parameter** is a numerical descriptive measure of a population. Because it is based on the observations in the population, its value is almost always unknown.

We have also discussed the sample mean $\bar{x}$, sample variance s^2, sample standard deviation *s*, etc., which are numerical descriptive measures calculated from the sample. We will often use the information contained in these *sample statistics* to make inferences about the parameters of a population.

DEFINITION 4.11

A **sample statistic** is a numerical descriptive measure of a sample. It is calculated from the observations in the sample.

Note that the term *statistic* refers to a *sample* quantity and the term *parameter* refers to a *population* quantity.

In order to use sample statistics to make inferences about population parameters, we need to be able to evaluate their properties. Does one sample statistic contain more information than another about a population parameter? On what basis should we choose the "best" statistic for making inferences about a parameter? If we want to estimate, for example, the population mean μ, we could use a number of sample statistics for our estimate. Two possibilities are the sample mean $\bar{x}$ and the sample median m. Which of these do you think will provide a better estimate of μ?

Before answering this question, consider the following example: Toss a fair die, and let x equal the number of dots showing on the up face. Suppose the die is tossed three times, producing the sample measurements 2, 2, 6. The sample mean is $\bar{x} = 3.33$ and the sample median is $m = 2$. Since the population mean of x is $\mu = 3.5$, you can see that for this sample of three measurements, the sample mean $\bar{x}$ provides an estimate that falls closer to μ than does the sample median (see Figure 4.38a). Now suppose we toss the die three more times and obtain the sample measurements 3, 4, 6. The mean and median of this sample are $\bar{x} = 4.33$ and $m = 4$, respectively. This time m is closer to μ (see Figure 4.38b).

FIGURE 4.38
Comparing the sample mean ($\bar{x}$) and sample median (m) as estimators of the population mean (μ)

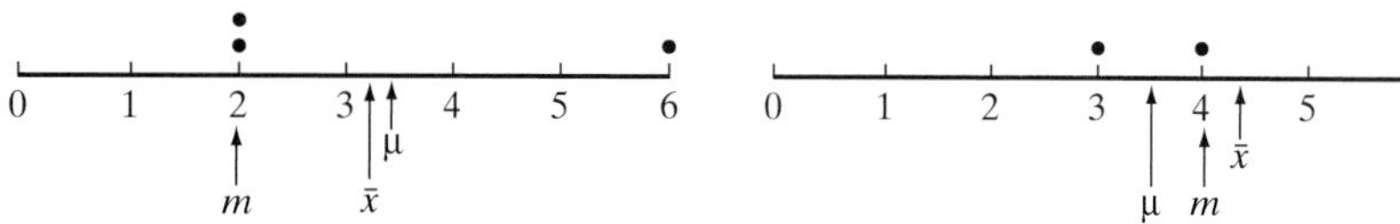

This simple example illustrates an important point: Neither the sample mean nor the sample median will *always* fall closer to the population mean. Consequently, we cannot compare these two sample statistics, or, in general, any two sample statistics, on the basis of their performance for a single sample. Instead, we need to recognize that sample statistics are themselves random variables, because different samples can lead to different values for the sample statistics. As random variables, sample statistics must be judged and compared on the basis of their probability distributions, i.e., the *collection* of values and associated probabilities of each statistic that would be obtained if the sampling experiment were repeated a *very large number of times.* We will illustrate this concept with another example.

Suppose it is known that the connector module manufactured for a certain brand of pacemaker has a mean length of $\mu = .3$ inch and a standard deviation of .005 inch. Consider an experiment consisting of randomly selecting 25 recently manufactured connector modules, measuring the length of each, and calculating the sample mean length $\bar{x}$. If this experiment were repeated a very large number of times, the value of $\bar{x}$ would vary from sample to sample. For example, the first sample of 25 length measurements might have a mean $\bar{x} = .301$, the second sample a mean $\bar{x} = .298$, the third sample a mean $\bar{x} = .303$, etc. If the sampling experiment were repeated a very large number of times, the resulting histogram of sample means would be approximately the probability distribution of $\bar{x}$. If $\bar{x}$ is a good estimator of μ, we would expect the values of $\bar{x}$ to cluster around μ as shown in Figure 4.39. This probability distribution is called a *sampling distribution* because it is generated by repeating a sampling experiment a very large number of times.

FIGURE 4.39
Sampling distribution for $\bar{x}$ based on a sample of $n = 25$ length measurements

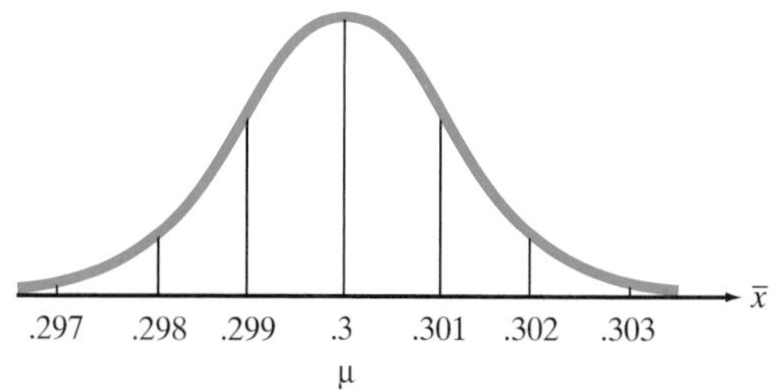

DEFINITION 4.12

The **sampling distribution** of a sample statistic calculated from a sample of n measurements is the probability distribution of the statistic.

In actual practice, the sampling distribution of a statistic is obtained mathematically or (at least approximately) by simulating the sample on a computer using a procedure similar to that just described.

If $\bar{x}$ has been calculated from a sample of $n = 25$ measurements selected from a population with mean $\mu = .3$ and standard deviation $\sigma = .005$, the sampling distribution (Figure 4.39) provides information about the behavior of $\bar{x}$ in repeated sampling. For example, the probability that you will draw a sample of 25 length measurements and obtain a value of $\bar{x}$ in the interval $.299 \le \bar{x} \le .3$ will be the area under the sampling distribution over that interval.

Since the properties of a statistic are typified by its sampling distribution, it follows that to compare two sample statistics you compare their sampling distributions. For example, if you have two statistics, A and B, for estimating the same parameter (for purposes of illustration, suppose the parameter is the population variance σ^2) and if their sampling distributions are as shown in Figure 4.40, you would choose statistic A in preference to statistic B. You would make this choice because the sampling distribution for statistic A centers over σ^2 and has less spread (variation) than the sampling distribution for statistic B. When you draw a single sample in a practical sampling situation, the probability is higher that statistic A will fall nearer σ^2.

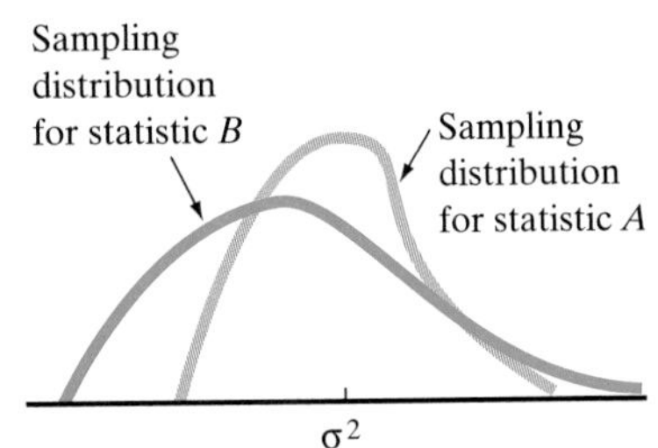

FIGURE 4.40
Two sampling distributions for estimating the population variance, σ^2

Remember that in practice we will not know the numerical value of the unknown parameter σ^2, so we will not know whether statistic A or statistic B is closer to σ^2 for a sample. We have to rely on our knowledge of the theoretical sampling distributions to choose the best sample statistic and then use it sample after sample. The procedure for finding the sampling distribution for a statistic is demonstrated in Example 4.27.

EXAMPLE 4.27

Consider a population consisting of the measurements 0, 3, and 12 and described by the probability distribution shown here. A random sample of $n = 3$ measurements is selected from the population.

a. Find the sampling distribution of the sample mean $\bar{x}$.

b. Find the sampling distribution of the sample median m.

x	0	3	12
$p(x)$	$1/3$	$1/3$	$1/3$

TABLE 4.8 All Possible Samples of $n = 3$ Measurements, Example 4.27

Possible Samples	$\bar{x}$	m	Probability
0, 0, 0	0	0	$1/27$
0, 0, 3	1	0	$1/27$
0, 0, 12	4	0	$1/27$
0, 3, 0	1	0	$1/27$
0, 3, 3	2	3	$1/27$
0, 3, 12	5	3	$1/27$
0, 12, 0	4	0	$1/27$
0, 12, 3	5	3	$1/27$
0, 12, 12	8	12	$1/27$
3, 0, 0	1	0	$1/27$
3, 0, 3	2	3	$1/27$
3, 0, 12	5	3	$1/27$
3, 3, 0	2	3	$1/27$
3, 3, 3	3	3	$1/27$
3, 3, 12	6	3	$1/27$
3, 12, 0	5	3	$1/27$
3, 12, 3	6	3	$1/27$
3, 12, 12	9	12	$1/27$
12, 0, 0	4	0	$1/27$
12, 0, 3	5	3	$1/27$
12, 0, 12	8	12	$1/27$
12, 3, 0	5	3	$1/27$
12, 3, 3	6	3	$1/27$
12, 3, 12	9	12	$1/27$
12, 12, 0	8	12	$1/27$
12, 12, 3	9	12	$1/27$
12, 12, 12	12	12	$1/27$

Solution Every possible sample of $n = 3$ measurements is listed in Table 4.8 along with the sample mean and median. Also, because any one sample is as likely to be selected as any other (random sampling), the probability of observing any particular sample is $1/27$. The probability is also listed in Table 4.8.

a. From Table 4.8 you can see that $\bar{x}$ can assume the values 0, 1, 2, 3, 4, 5, 6, 8, 9, and 12. Because $\bar{x} = 0$ occurs in only one sample, $P(\bar{x} = 0) = 1/27$. Similarly, $\bar{x} = 1$ occurs in three samples: (0, 0, 3), (0, 3, 0), and (3, 0, 0). Therefore, $P(\bar{x} = 1) = 3/27 = 1/9$. Calculating the probabilities of the remaining values of $\bar{x}$ and arranging them in a table, we obtain the probability distribution shown here.

$\bar{x}$	0	1	2	3	4	5	6	8	9	12
$p(\bar{x})$	$1/27$	$3/27$	$3/27$	$1/27$	$3/27$	$6/27$	$3/27$	$3/27$	$3/27$	$1/27$

This is the sampling distribution for $\bar{x}$ because it specifies the probability associated with each possible value of $\bar{x}$.

b. In Table 4.8 you can see that the median m can assume one of the three values 0, 3, or 12. The value $m = 0$ occurs in seven different samples. Therefore, $P(m = 0) = 7/27$. Similarly, $m = 3$ occurs in 13 samples and $m = 12$ occurs in seven samples. Therefore, the probability distribution (i.e., the sampling distribution) for the median m is as shown below.

m	0	3	12
$p(m)$	$7/27$	$13/27$	$7/27$

Example 4.27 demonstrates the procedure for finding the exact sampling distribution of a statistic when the number of different samples that could be selected from the population is relatively small. In the real world, populations often consist of a large number of different values, making samples difficult (or impossible) to enumerate. When this situation occurs, we may choose to obtain the approximate sampling distribution for a statistic by simulating the sampling over and over again and recording the proportion of times different values of the statistic occur. Example 4.28 illustrates this procedure.

EXAMPLE 4.28

Suppose we perform the following experiment over and over again: Take a sample of 11 measurements from the uniform distribution shown in Figure 4.41. This distribution, known as the *uniform distribution,* was discussed in optional Section 4.6. Calculate the two sample statistics

$$\bar{x} = \text{Sample mean} = \frac{\sum x}{11}$$

$$m = \text{Median} = \text{Sixth sample measurement when the 11 measurements are arranged in ascending order}$$

Obtain approximations to the sampling distributions of $\bar{x}$ and m.

Solution We use a computer to generate 1,000 samples, each with $n = 11$ observations. Then we compute $\bar{x}$ and m for each sample. Our goal is to obtain approximations to the sampling distributions of $\bar{x}$ and m to find out which sample statistic ($\bar{x}$ or m) contains more information about μ. [*Note:* In this particular example, we *know* the population mean is $\mu = .5$. (See optional Section 4.6)] The first 10 of the 1,000 samples generated are presented in Table 4.9. For instance, the first computer-generated sample from the uniform distribution (arranged in ascending order) contained the following measurements: .125, .138, .139, .217, .419, .506, .516, .757, .771, .786, and .919. The sample mean $\bar{x}$ and median m computed for this sample are

$$\bar{x} = \frac{.125 + .138 + \cdots + .919}{11} = .481$$

$$m = \text{Sixth ordered measurement} = .506$$

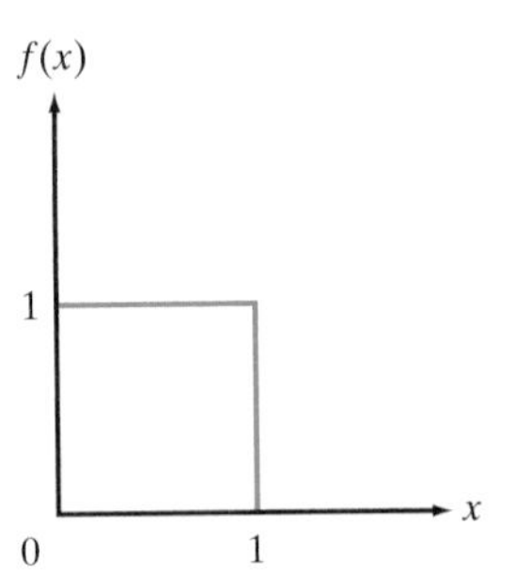

FIGURE 4.41
Uniform distribution from 0 to 1

The relative frequency histograms for $\bar{x}$ and m for the 1,000 samples of size $n = 11$ are shown in Figure 4.42.

You can see that the values of $\bar{x}$ tend to cluster around μ to a greater extent than do the values of m. Thus, on the basis of the observed sampling distributions, we

TABLE 4.9 First 10 Samples of $n = 11$ Measurements from a Uniform Distribution

Sample	Measurements										
1	.217	.786	.757	.125	.139	.919	.506	.771	.138	.516	.419
2	.303	.703	.812	.650	.848	.392	.988	.469	.632	.012	.065
3	.383	.547	.383	.584	.098	.676	.091	.535	.256	.163	.390
4	.218	.376	.248	.606	.610	.055	.095	.311	.086	.165	.665
5	.144	.069	.485	.739	.491	.054	.953	.179	.865	.429	.648
6	.426	.563	.186	.896	.628	.075	.283	.549	.295	.522	.674
7	.643	.828	.465	.672	.074	.300	.319	.254	.708	.384	.534
8	.616	.049	.324	.700	.803	.399	.557	.975	.569	.023	.072
9	.093	.835	.534	.212	.201	.041	.889	.728	.466	.142	.574
10	.957	.253	.983	.904	.696	.766	.880	.485	.035	.881	.732

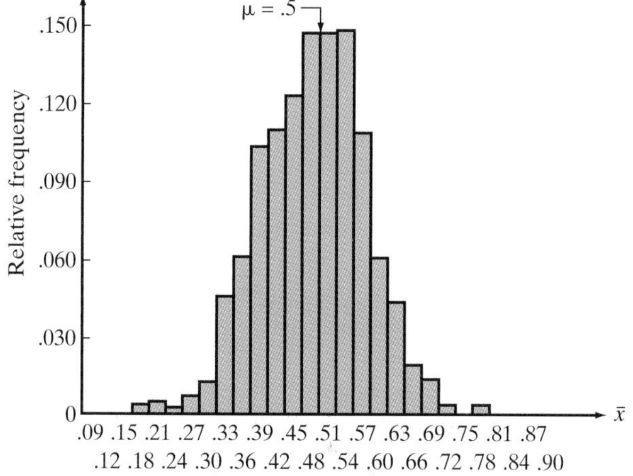

a. Sampling distribution for $\bar{x}$ (based on 1,000 samples of $n = 11$ measurements)

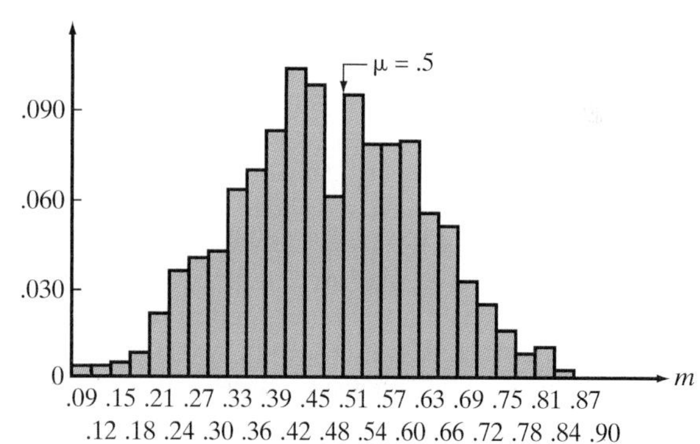

b. Sampling distribution for m (based on 1,000 samples of $n = 11$ measurements)

FIGURE 4.42
Relative frequency histograms for $\bar{x}$ and m, Example 4.28

conclude that $\bar{x}$ contains more information about μ than m does—at least for samples of $n = 11$ measurements from the uniform distribution.

As noted earlier, many sampling distributions can be derived mathematically, but the theory necessary to do this is beyond the scope of this text. Consequently, when we need to know the properties of a statistic, we will present its sampling distribution and simply describe its properties. An important sampling distribution, the sampling distribution of $\bar{x}$, is described in the next section.

EXERCISES 4.105–4.110

Learning the Mechanics

4.105 The probability distribution shown here describes a population of measurements that can assume values of 0, 2, 4, and 6, each of which occurs with the same relative frequency:

x	0	2	4	6
$p(x)$	$1/4$	$1/4$	$1/4$	$1/4$

a. List all the different samples of $n = 2$ measurements that can be selected from this population.

b. Calculate the mean of each different sample listed in part **a.**

c. If a sample of $n = 2$ measurements is randomly selected from the population, what is the probability that a specific sample will be selected?

d. Assume that a random sample of $n = 2$ measurements is selected from the population. List the different values of $\bar{x}$ found in part **b**, and find the probability of each. Then give the sampling distribution of the sample mean $\bar{x}$ in tabular form.

e. Construct a probability histogram for the sampling distribution of $\bar{x}$.

4.106 Simulate sampling from the population described in Exercise 4.105 by marking the values of x, one on each of four identical coins (or poker chips, etc.). Place the coins (marked 0, 2, 4, and 6) into a bag, randomly select one, and observe its value. Replace this coin, draw a second coin, and observe its value. Finally, calculate the mean $\bar{x}$ for this sample of $n = 2$ observations randomly selected from the population (Exercise 4.105, part **b**). Replace the coins, mix, and using the same procedure, select a sample of $n = 2$ observations from the population. Record the numbers and calculate $\bar{x}$ for this sample. Repeat this sampling process until you acquire 100 values of $\bar{x}$. Construct a relative frequency distribution for these 100 sample means. Compare this distribution to the exact sampling distribution of $\bar{x}$ found in part **e** of Exercise 4.105. [*Note:* the distribution obtained in this exercise is an approximation to the exact sampling distribution. But, if you were to repeat the sampling procedure, drawing two coins not 100 times but 10,000 times, the relative frequency distribution for the 10,000 sample means would be almost identical to the sampling distribution of $\bar{x}$ found in Exercise 4.105, part **e.**]

4.107 Consider the population described by the probability distribution shown below.

x	1	2	3	4	5
$p(x)$	.2	.3	.2	.2	.1

The random variable x is observed twice. If these observations are independent, verify that the different samples of size 2 and their probabilities are as shown at the top of the next column.

a. Find the sampling distribution of the sample mean $\bar{x}$.

Sample	Probability	Sample	Probability
1, 1	.04	3, 4	.04
1, 2	.06	3, 5	.02
1, 3	.04	4, 1	.04
1, 4	.04	4, 2	.06
1, 5	.02	4, 3	.04
2, 1	.06	4, 4	.04
2, 2	.09	4, 5	.02
2, 3	.06	5, 1	.02
2, 4	.06	5, 2	.03
2, 5	.03	5, 3	.02
3, 1	.04	5, 4	.02
3, 2	.06	5, 5	.01
3, 3	.04		

b. Construct a probability histogram for the sampling distribution of $\bar{x}$.

c. What is the probability that $\bar{x}$ is 4.5 or larger?

d. Would you expect to observe a value of $\bar{x}$ equal to 4.5 or larger? Explain.

4.108 Refer to Exercise 4.107 and find $E(x) = \mu$. Then use the sampling distribution of $\bar{x}$ found in Exercise 4.107 to find the expected value of $\bar{x}$. Note that $E(\bar{x}) = \mu$.

4.109 Refer to Exercise 4.107. Assume that a random sample of $n = 2$ measurements is randomly selected from the population.

a. List the different values that the sample median m may assume and find the probability of each. Then give the sampling distribution of the sample median.

b. Construct a probability histogram for the sampling distribution of the sample median and compare it with the probability histogram for the sample mean (Exercise 4.107, part **b**).

4.110 Consider a population that contains values of x equal to 00, 01, 02, 03, . . . , 96, 97, 98, 99. Assume that these values of x occur with equal probability. Use the computer to generate 500 samples, each containing $n = 25$ measurements, from this population. Calculate the sample mean $\bar{x}$ and sample variance s^2 for each of the 500 samples.

a. To approximate the sampling distribution of $\bar{x}$, construct a relative frequency histogram for the 500 values of $\bar{x}$.

b. Repeat part **a** for the 500 values of s^2.

4.12 THE CENTRAL LIMIT THEOREM

Estimating the mean useful life of automobiles, the mean monthly sales for all computer dealers in a large city, and the mean breaking strength of new plastic are practical problems with something in common. In each case we are interested in making an inference about the mean μ of some population. As we mentioned in Chapter 2, the sample mean $\bar{x}$ is, in general, a good estimator of μ. We now develop pertinent information about the sampling distribution for this useful statistic.

EXAMPLE 4.29 Suppose a population has the uniform probability distribution given in Figure 4.43. The mean and standard deviation of this probability distribution are $\mu = .5$ and $\sigma = .29$. (See optional Section 4.6 for the formulas for μ and σ.) Now suppose a sample of 11 measurements is selected from this population. Describe the sampling distribution of the sample mean $\bar{x}$ based on the 1,000 sampling experiments discussed in Example 4.28.

FIGURE 4.43
Sampled uniform population

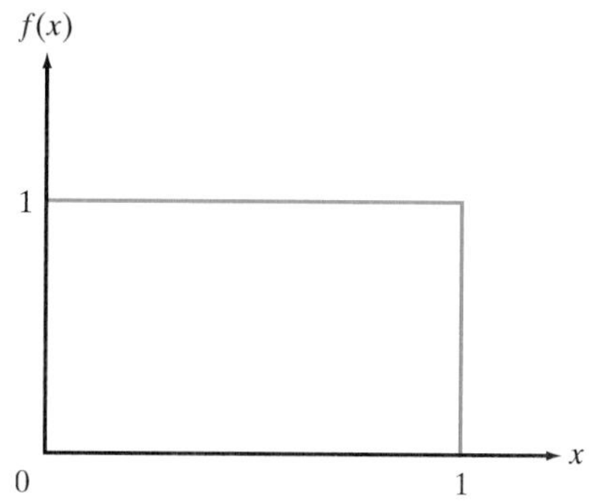

Solution You will recall that in Example 4.28 we generated 1,000 samples of $n = 11$ measurements each. The relative frequency histogram for the 1,000 sample means is shown in Figure 4.44 with a normal probability distribution superimposed. You can see that this normal probability distribution approximates the computer-generated sampling distribution very well.

FIGURE 4.44
Relative frequency histogram for $\bar{x}$ in 1,000 samples of $n = 11$ measurements with normal distribution superimposed

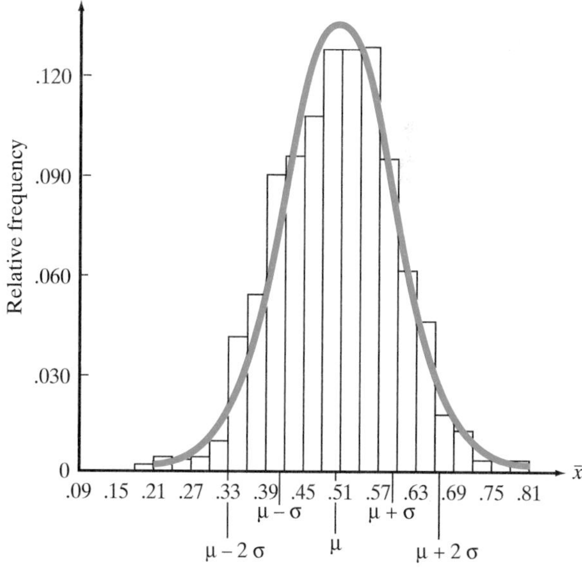

To fully describe a normal probability distribution, it is necessary to know its mean and standard deviation. Inspection of Figure 4.44 indicates that the mean of the distribution of $\bar{x}$, $\mu_{\bar{x}}$, appears to be very close to .5, the mean of the sampled uniform population. Furthermore, for a mound-shaped distribution such as that shown in Figure 4.44, almost all the measurements should fall within 3 standard deviations of the mean. Since the number of values of $\bar{x}$ is very large (1,000), the range of the observed $\bar{x}$'s divided by 6 (rather than 4) should give a reasonable approximation to the standard deviation of the sample mean, $\sigma_{\bar{x}}$. The values of $\bar{x}$ range from about .2 to .8, so we calculate

$$\sigma_{\bar{x}} \approx \frac{\text{Range of } \bar{x}\text{'s}}{6} = \frac{.8 - .2}{6} = .1$$

To summarize our findings based on 1,000 samples, each consisting of 11 measurements from a uniform population, the sampling distribution of $\bar{x}$ appears to be approximately normal with a mean of about .5 and a standard deviation of about .1.

The sampling distribution of $\bar{x}$ has the properties given in the next box, assuming only that a random sample of n observations has been selected from *any* population.

Properties of the Sampling Distribution of $\bar{x}$

1. Mean of sampling distribution equals mean of sampled population. That is, $\mu_{\bar{x}} = E(\bar{x}) = \mu$.*
2. Standard deviation of sampling distribution equals

$$\frac{\text{Standard deviation of sampled population}}{\text{Square root of sample size}}$$

That is, $\sigma_{\bar{x}} = \sigma/\sqrt{n}$.†
The standard deviation $\sigma_{\bar{x}}$ is often referred to as the **standard error of the mean.**††

You can see that our approximation to $\mu_{\bar{x}}$ in Example 4.29 was precise, since property 1 assures us that the mean is the same as that of the sampled population: .5. Property 2 tells us how to calculate the standard deviation of the sampling distribution of $\bar{x}$. Substituting $\sigma = .29$, the standard deviation of the sampled uniform distribution, and the sample size $n = 11$ into the formula for $\sigma_{\bar{x}}$, we find

$$\sigma_{\bar{x}} = \frac{\sigma}{\sqrt{n}} = \frac{.29}{\sqrt{11}} = .09$$

Thus, the approximation we obtained in Example 4.29, $\sigma_{\bar{x}} \approx .1$, is very close to the exact value, $\sigma_{\bar{x}} = .09$.

What can be said about the shape of the sampling distribution of $\bar{x}$? Two important theorems provide this information.

*When a sample statistic has a mean equal to the parameter estimated, the statistic is said to be an *unbiased estimate* of the parameter. From property 1, you can see that $\bar{x}$ is an unbiased estimate of μ.

†If the sample size, n, is large relative to the number, N, of elements in the population, (e.g., 5% or more), $\sigma/\sqrt{n}$ must be multiplied by a finite population correction factor, $\sqrt{(N - n)/(N - 1)}$. For most sampling situations, this correction factor will be close to 1 and can be ignored.

††The variance of $\bar{x}$ is the smallest among all unbiased estimators of μ. Thus $\bar{x}$ is deemed the MVUE (i.e., minimum variance, unbiased estimator) for μ.

Theorem 4.1

If a random sample of n observations is selected from a population with a normal distribution, the sampling distribution of $\bar{x}$ will be a normal distribution.

Theorem 4.2 (Central Limit Theorem)

Consider a random sample of n observations selected from a population (*any* population) with mean μ and standard deviation σ. Then, when n is sufficiently large, the sampling distribution of $\bar{x}$ will be approximately a normal distribution with mean $\mu_{\bar{x}} = \mu$ and standard deviation $\sigma_{\bar{x}} = \sigma/\sqrt{n}$. The larger the sample size, the better will be the normal approximation to the sampling distribution of $\bar{x}$.*

Thus, for sufficiently large samples the sampling distribution of $\bar{x}$ is approximately normal. How large must the sample size n be so that the normal distribution provides a good approximation for the sampling distribution of $\bar{x}$? The answer depends on the shape of the distribution of the sampled population, as shown by Figure 4.45. Generally speaking, the greater the skewness of the sampled population distribution, the larger the sample size must be before the normal distribution is an adequate approximation for the sampling distribution of $\bar{x}$. For most sampled populations, sample sizes of $n \geq 25$ will suffice for the normal approximation to be reasonable. We will use the normal approximation for the sampling distribution of $\bar{x}$ when the sample size is at least 25.

EXAMPLE 4.30

Suppose we have selected a random sample of $n = 25$ observations from a population with mean equal to 80 and standard deviation equal to 5. It is known that the population is not extremely skewed.

a. Sketch the relative frequency distributions for the population and for the sampling distribution of the sample mean, $\bar{x}$.

b. Find the probability that $\bar{x}$ will be larger than 82.

Solution

a. We do not know the exact shape of the population relative frequency distribution, but we do know that it should be centered about $\mu = 80$, its spread should be measured by $\sigma = 5$, and it is not highly skewed. One possibility is shown in Figure 4.46a. From the Central Limit Theorem, we know that the sampling distribution of $\bar{x}$ will be approximately normal since the sampled population distribution is not extremely skewed. We also know that the sampling distribution will have mean and standard deviation

$$\mu_{\bar{x}} = \mu = 80 \qquad \text{and} \qquad \sigma_{\bar{x}} = \frac{\sigma}{\sqrt{n}} = \frac{5}{\sqrt{25}} = 1$$

The sampling distribution of $\bar{x}$ is shown in Figure 4.46b.

*Moreover, because of the Central Limit Theorem, the sum of a random sample of n observations, $\sum x$, will possess a sampling distribution that is approximately normal for large samples. This distribution will have a mean equal to $n\mu$ and a variance equal to $n\sigma^2$. Proof of the Central Limit Theorem is beyond the scope of this book, but it can be found in many mathematical statistics texts.

FIGURE 4.45

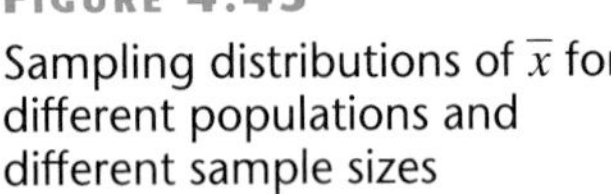

Sampling distributions of $\bar{x}$ for different populations and different sample sizes

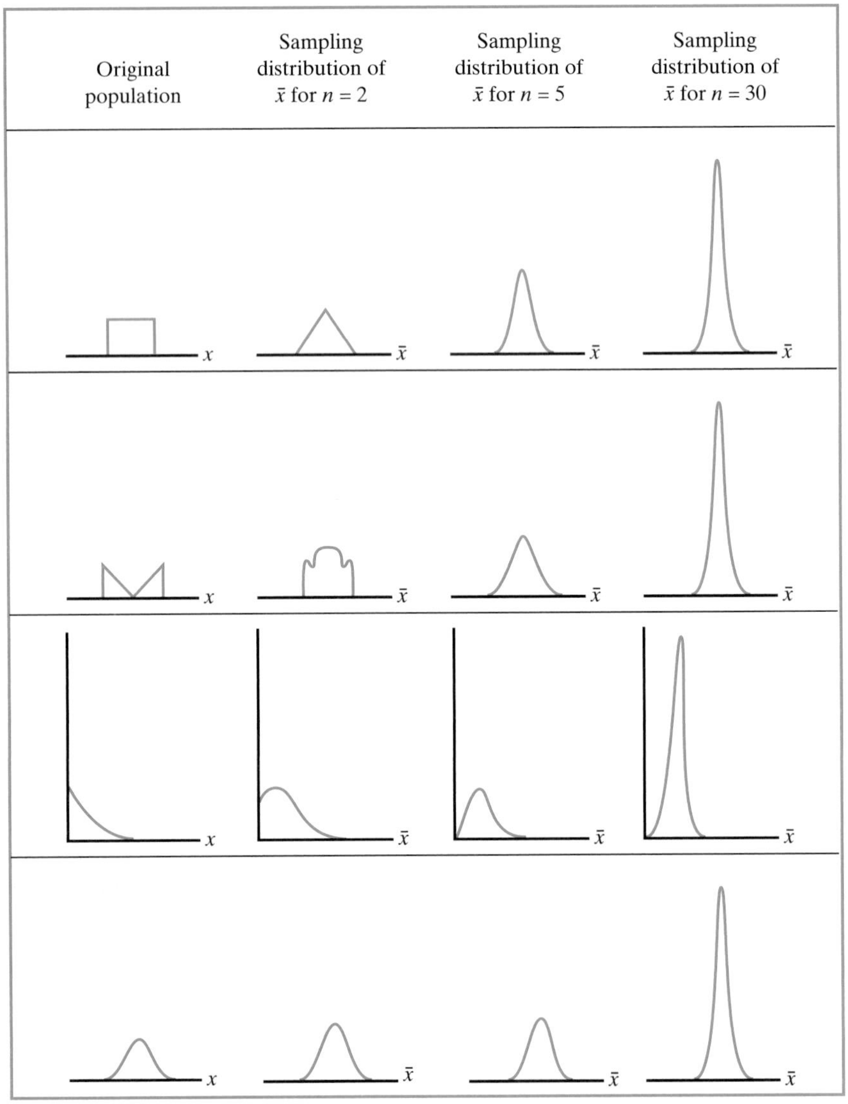

Original population	Sampling distribution of $\bar{x}$ for $n = 2$	Sampling distribution of $\bar{x}$ for $n = 5$	Sampling distribution of $\bar{x}$ for $n = 30$

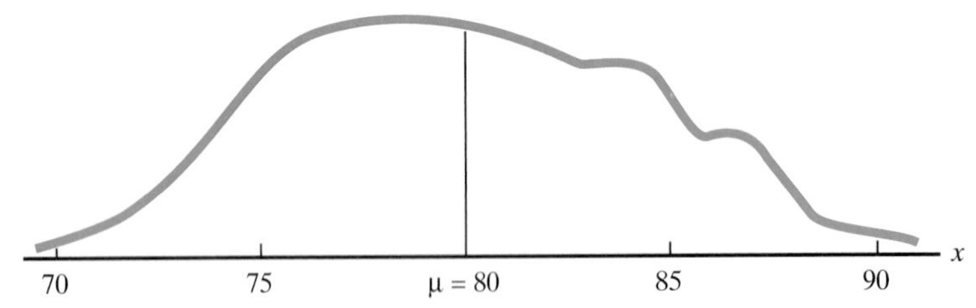

a. Population relative frequency distribution

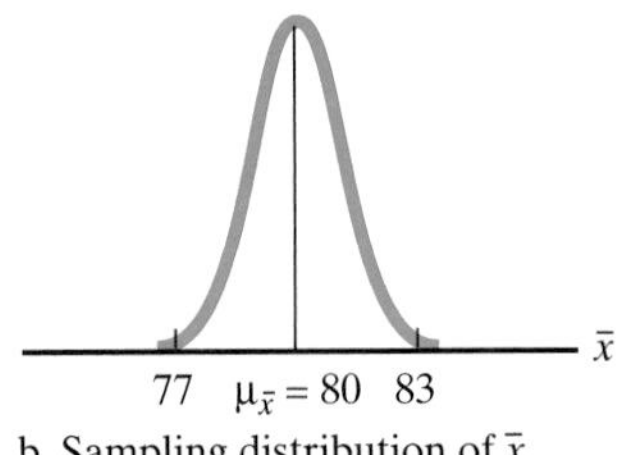

b. Sampling distribution of $\bar{x}$

FIGURE 4.46

A population relative frequency distribution and the sampling distribution for $\bar{x}$

b. The probability that $\bar{x}$ will exceed 82 is equal to the darker shaded area in Figure 4.47. To find this area, we need to find the z value corresponding to $\bar{x} = 82$. Recall that the standard normal random variable z is the difference between any normally distributed random variable and its mean, expressed in units of its standard deviation. Since $\bar{x}$ is approximately a normally distributed random variable with mean $\mu_{\bar{x}} = \mu$ and $\sigma_{\bar{x}} = \sigma/\sqrt{n}$, it follows that the standard normal z value corresponding to the sample mean, $\bar{x}$, is

$$z = \frac{\text{(Normal random variable)} - \text{(Mean)}}{\text{Standard deviation}} = \frac{\bar{x} - \mu_{\bar{x}}}{\sigma_{\bar{x}}}$$

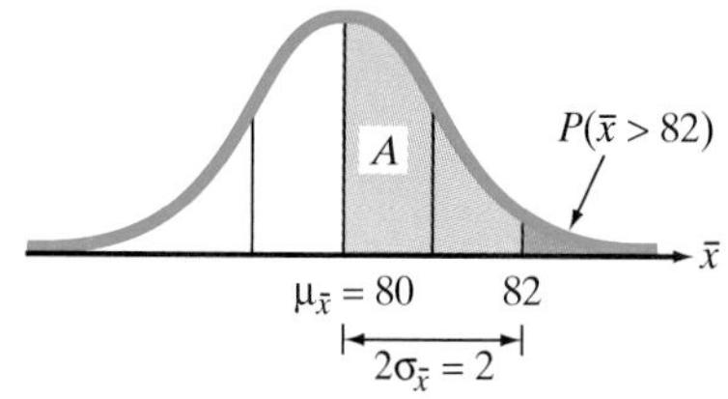

FIGURE 4.47
The sampling distribution of $\bar{x}$

Therefore, for $\bar{x} = 82$, we have

$$z = \frac{\bar{x} - \mu_{\bar{x}}}{\sigma_{\bar{x}}} = \frac{82 - 80}{1} = 2$$

The area A in Figure 4.47 corresponding to $z = 2$ is given in the table of areas under the normal curve (see Table IV of Appendix B) as .4772. Therefore, the tail area corresponding to the probability that $\bar{x}$ exceeds 82 is

$$P(\bar{x} > 82) = P(z > 2) = .5 - .4772 = .0228.$$

EXAMPLE 4.31

A manufacturer of automobile batteries claims that the distribution of the lengths of life of its best battery has a mean of 54 months and a standard deviation of 6 months. Suppose a consumer group decides to check the claim by purchasing a sample of 50 of these batteries and subjecting them to tests that determine battery life.

a. Assuming that the manufacturer's claim is true, describe the sampling distribution of the mean lifetime of a sample of 50 batteries.

b. Assuming that the manufacturer's claim is true, what is the probability the consumer group's sample has a mean life of 52 or fewer months?

Solution

a. Even though we have no information about the shape of the probability distribution of the lives of the batteries, we can use the Central Limit Theorem to deduce that the sampling distribution for a sample mean lifetime of 50 batteries is approximately normally distributed. Furthermore, the mean of this sampling distribution is the same as the mean of the sampled population, which is $\mu = 54$ months according to the manufacturer's claim. Finally, the standard deviation of the sampling distribution is given by

$$\sigma_{\bar{x}} = \frac{\sigma}{\sqrt{n}} = \frac{6}{\sqrt{50}} = .85 \text{ month}$$

FIGURE 4.48
Sampling distribution of $\bar{x}$ in Example 4.31 for $n = 50$

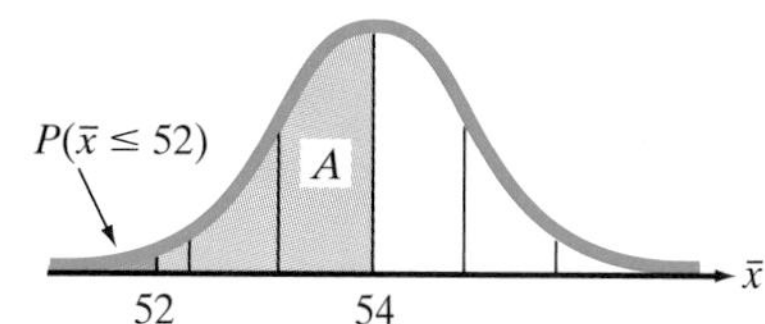

Note that we used the claimed standard deviation of the sampled population, $\sigma = 6$ months. Thus, if we assume that the claim is true, the sampling distribution for the mean life of the 50 batteries sampled is as shown in Figure 4.48.

b. If the manufacturer's claim is true, the probability that the consumer group observes a mean battery life of 52 or fewer months for their sample of 50 batteries, $P(\bar{x} \le 52)$, is equivalent to the darker shaded area in Figure 4.48. Since the sampling distribution is approximately normal, we can find this area by computing the standard normal z value:

$$z = \frac{\bar{x} - \mu_{\bar{x}}}{\sigma_{\bar{x}}} = \frac{\bar{x} - \mu}{\sigma_{\bar{x}}} = \frac{52 - 54}{.85} = -2.35$$

where $\mu_{\bar{x}}$, the mean of the sampling distribution of $\bar{x}$, is equal to μ, the mean of the lives of the sampled population, and $\sigma_{\bar{x}}$ is the standard deviation of the sampling distribution of $\bar{x}$. Note that z is the familiar standardized distance (z-score) of Section 2.7 and, since $\bar{x}$ is approximately normally distributed, it will possess (approximately) the standard normal distribution of Section 5.3.

The area A shown in Figure 4.48 between $\bar{x} = 52$ and $\bar{x} = 54$ (corresponding to $z = -2.35$) is found in Table IV of Appendix B to be .4906. Therefore, the area to the left of $\bar{x} = 52$ is

$$P(\bar{x} \le 52) = .5 - A = .5 - .4906 = .0094$$

Thus, the probability the consumer group will observe a sample mean of 52 or less is only .0094 if the manufacturer's claim is true. If the 50 tested batteries do exhibit a mean of 52 or fewer months, the consumer group will have strong evidence that the manufacturer's claim is untrue, because such an event is very unlikely to occur if the claim is true. (This is still another application of the *rare-event approach to statistical inference.*)

We conclude this section with two final comments on the sampling distribution of $\bar{x}$. First, from the formula $\sigma_{\bar{x}} = \sigma/\sqrt{n}$, we see that the standard deviation of the sampling distribution of $\bar{x}$ gets smaller as the sample size n gets larger. For example, we computed $\sigma_{\bar{x}} = .85$ when $n = 50$ in Example 4.31. However, for $n = 100$ we obtain $\sigma_{\bar{x}} = \sigma/\sqrt{n} = 6/\sqrt{100} = .60$. This relationship will hold true for most of the sample statistics encountered in this text. That is: *The standard deviation of the sampling distribution decreases as the sample size increases.* Consequently, the larger the sample size, the more accurate the sample statistic (e.g., $\bar{x}$) is in estimating a population parameter (e.g., μ). We will use this result in Chapter 5 to help us determine the sample size needed to obtain a specified accuracy of estimation.

Our second comment concerns the Central Limit Theorem. In addition to providing a very useful approximation for the sampling distribution of a sample mean, the Central Limit Theorem offers an explanation for the fact that many relative frequency distributions of data possess mound-shaped distributions. Many of the measurements we take in business are really means or sums of a large number of small phenomena. For example, a company's sales for one year are the total of the many individual sales the company made during the year. Similarly, we can view the length of time a construction company takes to build a house as the total of the times taken to complete a multitude of distinct jobs, and we can regard the monthly demand for blood at a hospital as the total of the many individual patients' needs. Whether or not the observations entering into these sums satisfy the assumptions basic to the Central Limit Theorem is open to question. However, it is a fact that many distributions of data in nature are mound-shaped and possess the appearance of normal distributions.

EXERCISES 4.111–4.122

Learning the Mechanics

4.111 Suppose a random sample of n measurements is selected from a population with mean $\mu = 100$ and variance $\sigma^2 = 100$. For each of the following values of n, give the mean and standard deviation of the sampling distribution of the sample mean $\bar{x}$.

a. $n = 4$ b. $n = 25$ c. $n = 100$
d. $n = 50$ e. $n = 500$ f. $n = 1{,}000$

4.112 Suppose a random sample of $n = 25$ measurements is selected from a population with mean μ and standard deviation σ. For each of the following values of μ and σ, give the values of $\mu_{\bar{x}}$ and $\sigma_{\bar{x}}$.

a. $\mu = 10, \sigma = 3$ b. $\mu = 100, \sigma = 25$
c. $\mu = 20, \sigma = 40$ d. $\mu = 10, \sigma = 100$

4.113 Consider the probability distribution shown here.

x	1	2	3	8
$p(x)$	.1	.4	.4	.1

a. Find μ, σ^2, and σ.
b. Find the sampling distribution of $\bar{x}$ for random samples of $n = 2$ measurements from this distribution by listing all possible values of $\bar{x}$, and find the probability associated with each.
c. Use the results of part **b** to calculate $\mu_{\bar{x}}$ and $\sigma_{\bar{x}}$. Confirm that $\mu_{\bar{x}} = \mu$ and $\sigma_{\bar{x}} = \sigma/\sqrt{n} = \sigma/\sqrt{2}$.

4.114 A random sample of $n = 64$ observations is drawn from a population with a mean equal to 20 and standard deviation equal to 16.

a. Give the mean and standard deviation of the (repeated) sampling distribution of $\bar{x}$.
b. Describe the shape of the sampling distribution of $\bar{x}$. Does your answer depend on the sample size?
c. Calculate the standard normal z-score corresponding to a value of $\bar{x} = 15.5$.
d. Calculate the standard normal z-score corresponding to $\bar{x} = 23$.

4.115 Refer to Exercise 4.114. Find the probability that

a. $\bar{x}$ is less than 16 b. $\bar{x}$ is greater than 23
c. $\bar{x}$ is greater than 25
d. $\bar{x}$ falls between 16 and 22 e. $\bar{x}$ is less than 14

Applying the Concepts

4.116 The American Automobile Association (AAA) is a not-for-profit federation of 90 clubs that provides it members with travel, financial, insurance, and auto-related services. In May 1999, AAA advised its members that the average daily meal and lodging costs for a family of four was \$213 (*Travel News,* May 11, 1999). Assume the standard deviation of such costs was \$15 and that the average daily cost reported by AAA is the population mean. Suppose 49 families of four were selected and their travel expenses during June 1999 were monitored.

a. Describe the sampling distribution of $\bar{x}$, the average daily meal and lodging costs for the sample of families. In particular, how is $\bar{x}$ distributed and what are the mean and variance of $\bar{x}$? Justify your answers.
b. What is the probability that the average daily expenses for the sample of families was greater than \$213? Greater than \$217? Between \$209 and \$217?

4.117 At the end of the twentieth century, workers were much less likely to remain with one employer for many years than their parents a generation before. (*Georgia Trend,* December 1999) Do today's college students understand that the workplace they are about to enter is vastly different than the one their parents entered? To help answer this question, researchers at the Terry College of Business at the University of Georgia sampled 344 business students and asked them this question: Over the course of your lifetime, what is the maximum number of years you expect to work for any one employer? The resulting sample had $\bar{x} = 19.1$ years and $s = 6$ years. Assume the sample of students was randomly selected from the 5,800 undergraduate students in the Terry College.

a. Describe the sampling distribution of $\bar{x}$.
b. If the population mean were 18.5 years, what is $P(\bar{x} \geq 19.1 \text{ years})$?
c. If the population mean were 19.5 years, what is $P(\bar{x} \geq 19.1 \text{ years})$?
d. If $P(\bar{x} \geq 19.1) = .5$, what is the population mean?
e. If $P(\bar{x} \geq 19.1) = .2$, is the population mean greater or less than 19.1 years? Justify your answer.

4.118 The *College Student Journal* (Dec. 1992) investigated differences in traditional and nontraditional students, where nontraditional students are generally defined as those 25 years or older and who are working full or part-time. Based on the study results, we can assume that the population mean and standard deviation for the GPA of all nontraditional students is $\mu = 3.5$ and $\sigma = .5$. Suppose that a random sample of $n = 100$ nontraditional students is selected from the population of all nontraditional students, and the GPA of each student is determined. Then $\bar{x}$, the sample mean, will be approximately normally distributed (because of the Central Limit Theorem).

a. Calculate $\mu_{\bar{x}}$ and $\sigma_{\bar{x}}$.
b. What is the approximate probability that the nontraditional student sample has a mean GPA between 3.40 and 3.60?
c. What is the approximate probability that the sample of 100 nontraditional students has a mean GPA that exceeds 3.62?

d. How would the sampling distribution of $\bar{x}$ change if the sample size n were doubled from 100 to 200? How do your answers to parts **b** and **c** change when the sample size is doubled?

4.119 University of Louisville researchers J. Usher, S. Alexander, and D. Duggins examined the process of filling plastic pouches of dry blended biscuit mix (*Quality Engineering,* Vol. 91, 1996). The current fill mean of the process is set at $\mu = 406$ grams and the process fill standard deviation is $\sigma = 10.1$ grams. (According to the researchers, "The high level of variation is due to the fact that the product has poor flow properties and is, therefore, difficult to fill consistently from pouch to pouch.") Operators monitor the process by randomly sampling 36 pouches each day and measuring the amount of biscuit mix in each. Consider $\bar{x}$, the main fill amount of the sample of 36 products.

a. Describe the sampling distribution of $\bar{x}$. (Give the values of $\mu_{\bar{x}}$ and $\sigma_{\bar{x}}$, and the shape of the probability distribution.)
b. Find $P(\bar{x} \le 400.8)$.
c. Suppose that on one particular day, the operators observe $\bar{x} = 400.8$. One of the operators believes that this indicates that the true process fill mean μ for that day is less than 406 grams. Another operator argues that $\mu = 406$ and the small value of $\bar{x}$ observed is due to random variation in the fill process. Which operator do you agree with? Why?

4.120 The ocean quahog is a type of clam found in the coastal waters of New England and the mid-Atlantic states. Extensive beds of ocean quahogs along the New Jersey shore gave rise to the development of the largest U.S. shellfish harvesting program. A federal survey of offshore ocean quahog harvesting in New Jersey, conducted from 1980 to 1992, revealed an average catch per unit effort (CPUE) of 89.34 clams. The CPUE standard deviation was 7.74 (*Journal of Shellfish Research,* June 1995). Let $\bar{x}$ represent the mean CPUE for a sample of 35 attempts to catch ocean quahogs off the New Jersey shore.

a. Compute $\mu_{\bar{x}}$ and $\sigma_{\bar{x}}$. Interpret their values.
b. Sketch the sampling distribution of $\bar{x}$.
c. Find $P(\bar{x} > 88)$. d. Find $P(\bar{x} < 87)$.

4.121 Neuroscientists at the Massachusetts Institute of Technology (MIT) have been experimenting with melatonin—a hormone secreted by the pineal gland in the brain—as a sleep-inducing hormone. Since the hormone is naturally produced, it is nonaddictive. (*Proceedings of the National Academy of Sciences,* Mar. 1994.) In the MIT study, young male volunteers were given various doses of melatonin or a placebo (a dummy medication containing no melatonin). Then they were placed in a dark room at midday and told to close their eyes for 30 minutes. The variable of interest was the time x (in minutes) elapsed before each volunteer fell asleep.

a. With the placebo (i.e., no hormone) the researchers found that the mean time to fall asleep was 15 minutes. Assume that with the placebo treatment $\mu = 15$ and $\sigma = 5$. Now, consider a random sample of 40 young males, each of whom is given a dosage of the sleep-inducing hormone, melatonin. Find $P(\bar{x} < 6)$ if melatonin is not effective against insomnia.
b. The times (in minutes) to fall asleep for these 40 males are listed in the table* below. Use the data to make an inference about the true value of μ for those taking the melatonin. Does melatonin appear to be an effective drug against insomnia?

INSOMNIA.DAT

6.4	6.0	3.2	4.4	6.2	1.7	5.1
5.9	1.6	4.4	16.2	4.8	8.3	7.5
4.8	3.3	4.0	6.2	6.3	5.0	6.3
5.1	6.4	15.6	3.4	3.1	6.1	6.0
5.0	1.8	6.1	4.5	4.5	1.5	4.7
7.6	8.2	4.9	6.1	3.9		

*These are simulated sleep times based on summary information provided in the MIT study.

4.122 National Car Rental Systems, Inc., commissioned the United States Automobile Club (USAC) to conduct a survey of the general condition of the cars rented to the public by Hertz, Avis, National, and Budget Rent-a-Car.† USAC officials evaluate each company's cars using a demerit point system. Each car starts with a perfect score of 0 points and incurs demerit points for each discrepancy noted by the inspectors. One measure of the overall condition of a company's cars is the mean of all scores received by the company, i.e., the company's *fleet mean score.* To estimate the fleet mean score of each rental car company, 10 major airports were randomly selected, and 10 cars from each company were randomly rented for inspection from each airport by USAC officials; i.e., a sample of size $n = 100$ cars from each company's fleet was drawn and inspected.

a. Describe the sampling distribution of $\bar{x}$, the mean score of a sample of $n = 100$ rental cars.
b. Interpret the mean of $\bar{x}$ in the context of this problem.
c. Assume $\mu = 30$ and $\sigma = 60$ for one rental car company. For this company, find $P(\bar{x} \ge 45)$.
d. Refer to part **c.** The company claims that their true fleet mean score "couldn't possibly be as high as 30." The sample mean score tabulated by USAC for this company was $\bar{x} = 45$. Does this result tend to support or refute the claim? Explain.

†Information by personal communication with Rajiv Tandon, Corporate Vice President and General Manager of the Car Rental Division, National Car Rental Systems, Inc., Minneapolis, Minnesota.

STATISTICS IN *Action*

IQ, Economic Mobility, and the Bell Curve

In their controversial book *The Bell Curve* (Free Press, 1994), Professors Richard J. Herrnstein (a Harvard psychologist who died while the book was in production) and Charles Murray (a political scientist at MIT) explore, as the subtitle states, "intelligence and class structure in American life." *The Bell Curve* heavily employs statistical analyses in an attempt to support the authors' positions. Since the book's publication, many expert statisticians have raised doubts about the authors' statistical methods and the inferences drawn from them. (See, for example, "Wringing *The Bell Curve:* A cautionary tale about the relationships among race, genes, and IQ," *Chance,* Summer 1995.) In Chapter 10's Statistics in Action, we explore a few of these problems.

One of the many controversies sparked by the book is the authors' tenet that level of intelligence (or lack thereof) is a cause of a wide range of intractable social problems, including constrained economic mobility. "America has taken great pride in the mobility of generations," state Herrnstein and Murray, "but this mobility has its limits . . . . The son of a father whose earnings are in the bottom five percent of the [income] distribution has something like one chance in twenty (or less) of rising to the top fifth of the income distribution and almost a fifty-fifty chance of staying in the bottom fifth. He has less than one chance in four of rising above even the median income . . . . Most people at present are stuck near where their parents were on the income distribution in part because [intelligence], which has become a major predictor of income, passes on sufficiently from one generation to the next to constrain economic mobility."

The measure of intelligence chosen by the authors is the well known Intelligent Quotient (IQ). Numerous tests have been developed to measure IQ; Herrnstein and Murray use the Armed Forces Qualification Test (AFQT), originally designed to measure the cognitive ability of military recruits. Psychologists traditionally treat IQ as a random variable having a normal distribution with mean $\mu = 100$ and standard deviation $\sigma = 15$. This distribution, or *bell curve,* is shown in Figure 4.49.

In their book, Herrnstein and Murray refer to five cognitive classes of people defined by percentiles of the normal distribution. Class I ("very bright") consists of those with IQs above the 95th percentile; Class II ("bright") are those with IQs between the 75th and 95th percentiles; Class III ("normal") includes IQs between the 25th and 75th percentiles; Class IV ("dull") are those with IQs between the 5th and 25th percentiles; and Class V ("very dull") are IQs below the 5th percentile. These classes are also illustrated in Figure 4.49.

Focus

a. Assuming that the distribution of IQ is accurately represented by the bell curve in Figure 4.49, determine the proportion of people with IQs in each of the five cognitive classes defined by Herrnstein and Murray.

b. Although the cognitive classes above are defined in terms of percentiles, the authors stress that IQ scores should be compared with z-scores, not percentiles. In other words, it is more informative to give the difference in z-scores for two IQ scores than it is to give the difference in percentiles. To demonstrate this point, calculate the difference in z-scores for IQs at the 50th and 55th percentiles. Do the same for IQs at the 94th and 99th percentiles. What do you observe?

c. Researchers have found that scores on many intelligence tests are decidedly nonnormal. Some distributions are skewed toward higher scores, others toward lower scores. How would the proportions in the five cognitive classes differ for an IQ distribution that is skewed right? Skewed left?

FIGURE 4.49
The distribution of IQ

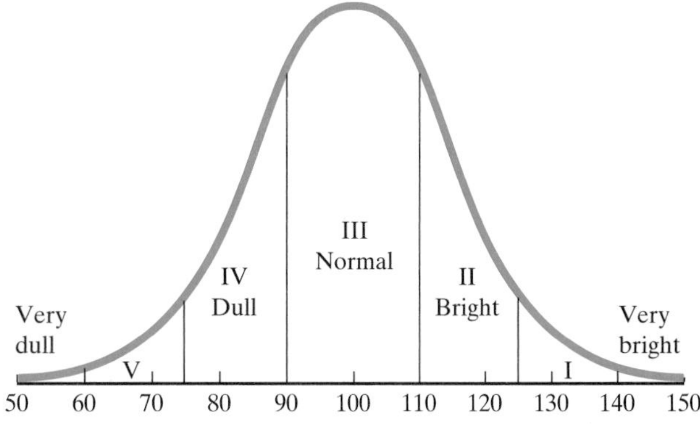

QUICK REVIEW

Key Terms

Note: Starred (*) terms refer to the optional sections in this chapter.

Key Formulas

Note: Starred (*) formulas refer to the optional sections in this chapter.

Random Variable	Probability Distribution or Density Function	Mean	Standard Deviation	
General discrete, x	$p(x)$	$\sum_{\text{all } x} xp(x)$	$\sqrt{\sum (x-\mu)^2 p(x)}$	174, 175
Binomial, x	$\binom{n}{x} p^x q^{n-x}$	np	$\sqrt{npq}$	185
Poisson,* x	$\frac{\lambda^x e^{-\lambda}}{x!}$	λ	$\sqrt{\lambda}$	195
Uniform,* x	$\frac{1}{d-c}, (c \le x \le d)$	$\frac{c+d}{2}$	$\frac{d-c}{\sqrt{12}}$	203
Normal, x	$\frac{1}{\sigma\sqrt{2\pi}} e^{-(1/2)[(x-\mu)/\sigma]^2}$	μ	σ	207
Standard Normal, $z = \left(\frac{x-\mu}{\sigma}\right)$	$\frac{1}{\sqrt{2\pi}} e^{-(1/2)z^2}$	0	1	208
Exponential,* x	$\lambda e^{-\lambda x}, (x > 0)$	$\frac{1}{\lambda}$	$\frac{1}{\lambda}$	232
Sample Mean, $\bar{x}$	Normal (for large n)	μ	$\sigma/\sqrt{n}$	245

Normal Approximation to Binomial* $P(x \le a) = P\left[z \le \frac{(a+.5)-\mu}{\sigma}\right]$ 229

LANGUAGE LAB

Symbol	Pronunciation	Description
$p(x)$		Probability distribution of the random variable x
S		The outcome of a binomial trial denoted a "success"
F		The outcome of a binomial trial denoted a "failure"
p		The probability of success (S) in a binomial trial
q		The probability of failure (F) in a binomial trial, where $q = 1 - p$
λ	lambda	The mean (or expected) number of events for a Poisson random variable; parameter for an exponential random variable
e		A constant used in the Poisson probability distribution, where $e = 2.71828\ldots$

$f(x)$	f of x	Probability density function for a continuous random variable x
θ	theta	Population parameter (general)
$\mu_{\bar{x}}$	mu of x-bar	True mean of sampling distribution of $\bar{x}$
$\sigma_{\bar{x}}$	sigma of x-bar	True standard deviation of sampling distribution of $\bar{x}$

SUPPLEMENTARY EXERCISES 4.123–4.148

Note: Starred (*) exercises refer to the optional sections in this chapter.

Learning the Mechanics

4.123 Which of the following describe discrete random variables, and which describe continuous random variables?

a. The number of damaged inventory items

b. The average monthly sales revenue generated by a salesperson over the past year

c. The number of square feet of warehouse space a company rents

d. The length of time a firm must wait before its copying machine is fixed

4.124 For each of the following examples, decide whether x is a binomial random variable and explain your decision:

a. A manufacturer of computer chips randomly selects 100 chips from each hour's production in order to estimate the proportion defective. Let x represent the number of defectives in the 100 sampled chips.

b. Of five applicants for a job, two will be selected. Although all applicants appear to be equally qualified, only three have the ability to fulfill the expectations of the company. Suppose that the two selections are made at random from the five applicants, and let x be the number of qualified applicants selected.

c. A software developer establishes a support hotline for customers to call in with questions regarding use of the software. Let x represent the number of calls received on the support hotline during a specified workday.

d. Florida is one of a minority of states with no state income tax. A poll of 1,000 registered voters is conducted to determine how many would favor a state income tax in light of the state's current fiscal condition. Let x be the number in the sample who would favor the tax.

4.125 Given that x is a binomial random variable, compute $p(x)$ for each of the following cases:

a. $n = 7, x = 3, p = .5$

b. $n = 4, x = 3, p = .8$

c. $n = 15, x = 1, p = .1$

4.126 Consider the discrete probability distribution shown here.

x	10	12	18	20
$p(x)$	.2	.3	.1	.4

a. Calculate μ, σ^2, and σ.

b. What is $P(x < 15)$?

c. Calculate $\mu \pm 2\sigma$.

d. What is the probability that x is in the interval $\mu \pm 2\sigma$?

4.127 Suppose x is a binomial random variable with $n = 20$ and $p = .7$.

a. Find $P(x = 14)$.

b. Find $P(x \leq 12)$.

c. Find $P(x > 12)$.

d. Find $P(9 \leq x \leq 18)$.

e. Find $P(8 < x < 18)$.

f. Find μ, σ^2, and σ.

g. What is the probability that x is in the interval $\mu \pm 2\sigma$

*4.128 Suppose x is a Poisson random variable. Compute $p(x)$ for each of the following cases:

a. $\lambda = 2, x = 3$

b. $\lambda = 1, x = 4$

c. $\lambda = .5, x = 2$

*4.129 Assume that x is a random variable best described by a uniform distribution with $c = 10$ and $d = 90$.

a. Find $f(x)$.

b. Find the mean and standard deviation of x.

c. Graph the probability distribution for x and locate its mean and the interval $\mu \pm 2\sigma$ on the graph.

d. Find $P(x \leq 60)$. e. Find $P(x \geq 90)$.

f. Find $P(x \leq 80)$.

g. Find $P(\mu - \sigma \leq x \leq \mu + \sigma)$.

h. Find $P(x > 75)$.

4.130 The random variable x has a normal distribution with $\mu = 75$ and $\sigma = 10$. Find the following probabilities:

a. $P(x \leq 80)$ b. $P(x \geq 85)$

c. $P(70 \leq x \leq 75)$ d. $P(x > 80)$

e. $P(x = 78)$ f. $P(x \leq 110)$

*4.131 Assume that x is a binomial random variable with $n = 100$ and $p = .5$. Use the normal probability distribution to approximate the following probabilities:

a. $P(x \leq 48)$ b. $P(50 \leq x \leq 65)$

c. $P(x \geq 70)$ d. $P(55 \leq x \leq 58)$

e. $P(x = 62)$ f. $P(x \leq 49 \text{ or } x \geq 72)$

4.132 The random variable x has a normal distribution with $\mu = 40$ and $\sigma^2 = 36$. Find a value of x, call it x_0, such that

a. $P(x \geq x_0) = .10$ b. $P(\mu \leq x < x_0) = .40$

c. $P(x < x_0) = .05$ d. $P(x \geq x_0) = .40$
e. $P(x_0 \leq x < \mu) = .45$

*4.133 Assume that x has an exponential distribution with $\lambda = 3.0$. Find
a. $P(x \leq 2)$ b. $P(x > 3)$ c. $P(x = 1)$
d. $P(x \leq 7)$ e. $P(4 \leq x \leq 12)$

4.134 A random sample of $n = 68$ observations is selected from a population with $\mu = 19.6$ and $\sigma = 3.2$. Approximate each of the following probabilities.
a. $P(\bar{x} \leq 19.6)$ b. $P(\bar{x} \leq 19)$
c. $P(\bar{x} \geq 20.1)$ d. $P(19.2 \leq \bar{x} \leq 20.6)$

4.135 A random sample of size n is to be drawn from a large population with mean 100 and standard deviation 10, and the sample mean $\bar{x}$ is to be calculated. To see the effect of different sample sizes on the standard deviation of the sampling distribution of $\bar{x}$, plot $\sigma/\sqrt{n}$ against n for $n = 1, 5, 10, 20, 30, 40$, and 50.

Applying the Concepts

4.136 A national study conducted by Geoffrey Alpert (University of South Carolina) found that 40% of all high-speed police chases end in accidents. As a result, many police departments have moved to restrict high-speed chases. One exception is the Tampa Police Department. After restricting chases for three years, management changed their policy and eased the restrictions. Although overall crime dropped by 25%, high-speed chases increased from 10 in the previous 5 months to 85 in the succeeding 5 months, with 29 of those resulting in accidents (*New York Times,* Dec. 17, 1995). Consider a random sample of five high-speed chases.
a. Demonstrate that x, the number of chases resulting in an accident, is an approximate binomial random variable.
b. Using the Alpert statistics, what is the probability that the five high-speed chases result in at least one accident?
c. Use the Tampa data to estimate the probability of part **b.**
d. Which probability, part **b** or part **c,** best describes high-speed chases in your state? Explain.

*4.137 Millions of suburban commuters are finding railroads to be a convenient, time-saving, less stressful alternative to the automobile. While generally perceived as a safe mode of transportation, the average number of deaths per week due to railroad accidents is a surprisingly high 20 (U.S. National Center for Health Statistics, *Vital Statistics of the United States, 1998*).
a. Construct arguments both for and against the use of the Poisson distribution to characterize the number of deaths per week due to railroad accidents.
b. For the remainder of this exercise, assume the Poisson distribution is an adequate approximation for x, the number of deaths per week due to railroad accidents. Find $E(x)$ and the standard deviation of x.
c. Based strictly on your answers to part **b,** is it likely that only four or fewer deaths occur next week? Explain.
d. Find $P(x \leq 4)$. Is this probability consistent with your answer to part **c**? Explain.

4.138 A large number of preventable errors (e.g., overdoses, botched operations, misdiagnoses) are being made by doctors and nurses in U.S. hospitals (*New York Times,* July 18, 1995). A study of a major metropolitan hospital revealed that of every 100 medications prescribed or dispensed, one was in error; but, only one in 500 resulted in an error that caused significant problems for the patient. It is known that the hospital prescribes and dispenses 60,000 medications per year.
a. What is the expected number of errors per year at this hospital? The expected number of significant errors per year?
b. Within what limits would you expect the number of significant errors per year to fall?
c. What assumptions did you need to make in order to answer these questions?

4.139 The *tolerance limits* for a particular quality characteristic (e.g., length, weight, or strength) of a product are the minimum and/or maximum values at which the product will operate properly. Tolerance limits are set by the engineering design function of the manufacturing operation (Moss, *Applying TQM to Product Design and Development,* 1996). The tensile strength of a particular metal part can be characterized as being normally distributed with a mean of 25 pounds and a standard deviation of 2 pounds. The upper and lower tolerance limits for the part are 30 pounds and 21 pounds, respectively. A part that falls within the tolerance limits results in a profit of \$10. A part that falls below the lower tolerance limit costs the company \$2; a part that falls above the upper tolerance limit costs the company \$1. Find the company's expected profit per metal part produced.

4.140 The distribution of the demand (in number of units per unit time) for a product can often be approximated by a normal probability distribution. For example, a bakery has determined that the number of loaves of its white bread demanded daily has a normal distribution with mean 7,200 loaves and standard deviation 300 loaves. Based on cost considerations, the company has decided that its best strategy is to produce a sufficient number of loaves so that it will fully supply demand on 94% of all days.
a. How many loaves of bread should the company produce?
b. Based on the production in part **a,** on what percentage of days will the company be left with more than 500 loaves of unsold bread?

4.141 The metropolitan airport commission is considering the establishment of limitations on noise pollution around a local airport. At the present time, the noise level per jet takeoff in one neighborhood near the airport is approximately normally distributed with a mean of 100 decibels and a standard deviation of 6 decibels.

a. What is the probability that a randomly selected jet will generate a noise level greater than 108 decibels in this neighborhood?

b. What is the probability that a randomly selected jet will generate a noise level of exactly 100 decibels?

c. Suppose a regulation is passed that requires jet noise in this neighborhood to be lower than 105 decibels 95% of the time. Assuming the standard deviation of the noise distribution remains the same, how much will the mean level of noise have to be lowered to comply with the regulation?

*4.142 A tool-and-die machine shop produces extremely high-tolerance spindles. The spindles are 18-inch slender rods used in a variety of military equipment. A piece of equipment used in the manufacture of the spindles malfunctions on occasion and places a single gouge somewhere on the spindle. However, if the spindle can be cut so that it has 14 consecutive inches without a gouge, then the spindle can be salvaged for other purposes. Assuming that the location of the gouge along the spindle is random, what is the probability that a defective spindle can be salvaged?

*4.143 The length of time between arrivals at a hospital clinic and the length of clinical service time are two random variables that play important roles in designing a clinic and deciding how many physicians and nurses are needed for its operation. The probability distributions of both the length of time between arrivals and the length of service time are often approximately exponential. Suppose the mean time between arrivals for patients at a clinic is 4 minutes.

a. What is the probability that a particular interarrival time (the time between the arrival of two patients) is less than 1 minute?

b. What is the probability that the next four interarrival times are all less than 1 minute?

c. What is the probability that an interarrival time will exceed 10 minutes?

*4.144 The net weight per package of a certain brand of corn chips is listed as 10 ounces. The weight actually delivered to each package by an automated machine is a normal random variable with mean 10.5 ounces and standard deviation .2 ounce. Suppose 1,500 packages are chosen at random and the net weights are ascertained. Let x be the number of the 1,500 selected packages that contain at least 10 ounces of corn chips. Then x is a binomial random variable with $n = 1{,}500$ and $p =$ probability that a randomly selected package contains at least 10 ounces. What is the approximate probability that they all contain at least 10 ounces of corn chips? What is the approximate probability that at least 90% of the packages contain 10 ounces or more?

4.145 Refer to the *Financial Management* (Spring 1995) study of 49 companies that filed for a prepackaged bankruptcy, Exercise 2.24 (p. 49). The time in bankruptcy (measured in months) for each company is repeated in the table on page 256. Determine whether the bankruptcy times are approximately normally distributed.

4.146 In Lee County, Georgia, the distribution of weekly wages for workers in the construction industry in 1997 was skewed to the right with mean equal to $473 (Georgia Department of Labor, *Labor Market Information,* 1999). Assume the standard deviation of the distribution was $25. An economist plans to randomly sample 40 workers in Lee County and question them regarding their weekly wages, their age, and the length of their employment.

a. Describe what is known about the distribution of x, the weekly wages of workers in the construction industry.

b. Describe what is known about the distribution of y, the age of the construction workers.

c. Describe the distributions of $\bar{x}$ and $\bar{y}$.

d. Find $P(\bar{x} \geq \$465)$.

e. What additional information is needed to be able to calculate $P(\bar{y} \geq 30)$?

4.147 One measure of elevator performance is cycle time. Elevator cycle time is the time between successive elevator starts, which includes the time when the car is moving and the time when it is standing at a floor. Researchers have found that simulation is necessary to determine the average cycle time of a system of elevators in complex traffic situations. *Simulation* (Oct. 1993) published a study on the use of a microcomputer-based simulator for elevators. The simulator produced an average cycle time μ of 26 seconds when traffic intensity was set at 50 persons every five minutes. Consider a sample of 200 simulated elevator runs and let $\bar{x}$ represent the mean cycle time of this sample.

a. What do you know about the distribution of x, the time between successive elevator starts? (Give the value of the mean and standard deviation of x and the shape of the distribution, if possible.)

b. What do you know about the distribution of $\bar{x}$? (Give the value of the mean and standard deviation of $\bar{x}$ and the shape of the distribution, if possible.)

c. Assume σ, the standard deviation of cycle time x, is 20 seconds. Use this information to calculate $P(\bar{x} > 26.8)$.

d. Repeat part **c** but assume $\sigma = 10$.

4.148 Refer to the *Simulation* (Oct. 1993) study of elevator cycle times, Exercise 4.147. Cycle time is related to the distance (measured by number of floors) the elevator covers on a particular run, called *running distance.* The simulated distribution of running distance, x, during a down-peak period in elevator traffic intensity is shown in the figure on p. 256. The distribution has mean $\mu = 5.5$ floors and standard deviation $\sigma = 7$ floors. Consider a random sample of 80 simulated elevator runs during a down-peak in traffic intensity. Of interest is the sample mean running distance, $\bar{x}$.

BANKRUPT.DAT

Company	Pre-Filing Votes	Time in Bankruptcy (months)	Company	Pre-Filing Votes	Time in Bankruptcy (months)
AM International	None	3.9	LIVE Entertainment	Joint	1.4
Anglo Energy	Prepack	1.5	Mayflower Group*	Prepack	1.4
Arizona Biltmore*	Prepack	1.0	Memorex Telex*	Prepack	1.1
Astrex	None	10.1	Munsingwear	None	2.9
Barry's Jewelers	None	1.4	Nat'l Environmental	Joint	5.2
Calton	None	1.9	Petrolane Gas	Prepack	1.2
Cencor	Joint	4.1	Price Communications	None	2.4
Charter Medical*	Prepack	1.3	Republic Health*	Joint	4.5
Cherokee*	Joint	1.2	Resorts Int'l*	None	7.8
Circle Express	Prepack	4.1	Restaurant Enterprises*	Prepack	1.5
Cook Inlet Comm.	Prepack	1.1	Rymer Foods	Joint	2.1
Crystal Oil	None	3.0	SCI TV*	Prepack	2.1
Divi Hotels	None	3.2	Southland*	Joint	3.9
Edgell Comm.*	Prepack	1.0	Specialty Equipment*	None	2.6
Endevco	Prepack	3.8	SPI Holdings*	Joint	1.4
Gaylord Container	Joint	1.2	Sprouse-Reitz	Prepack	1.4
Great Amer. Comm.*	Prepack	1.0	Sunshine Metals	Joint	5.4
Hadson	Prepack	1.5	TIE/Communications	None	2.4
In-Store Advertising	Prepack	1.0	Trump Plaza	Prepack	1.7
JPS Textiles*	Prepack	1.4	Trump Taj Mahal	Prepack	1.4
Kendall*	Prepack	1.2	Trump's Castle	Prepack	2.7
Kinder-Care	None	4.2	USG	Prepack	1.2
Kroy*	Prepack	3.0	Vyquest	Prepack	4.1
Ladish*	Joint	1.5	West Point Acq.*	Prepack	2.9
LaSalle Energy*	Prepack	1.6			

Source: Betker, Brian L. "An empirical examination of prepackaged bankruptcy." *Financial Management,* Vol. 24, No. 1, Spring 1995, p. 6 (Table 2).

*Leveraged buyout.

a. Find $\mu_{\bar{x}}$ and $\sigma_{\bar{x}}$.

b. Is the shape of the distribution of $\bar{x}$ similar to the figure? If not, sketch the distribution.

c. During a down-peak in traffic intensity, is it likely to observe a sample mean running distance of $\bar{x} = 5.3$ floors? Explain.

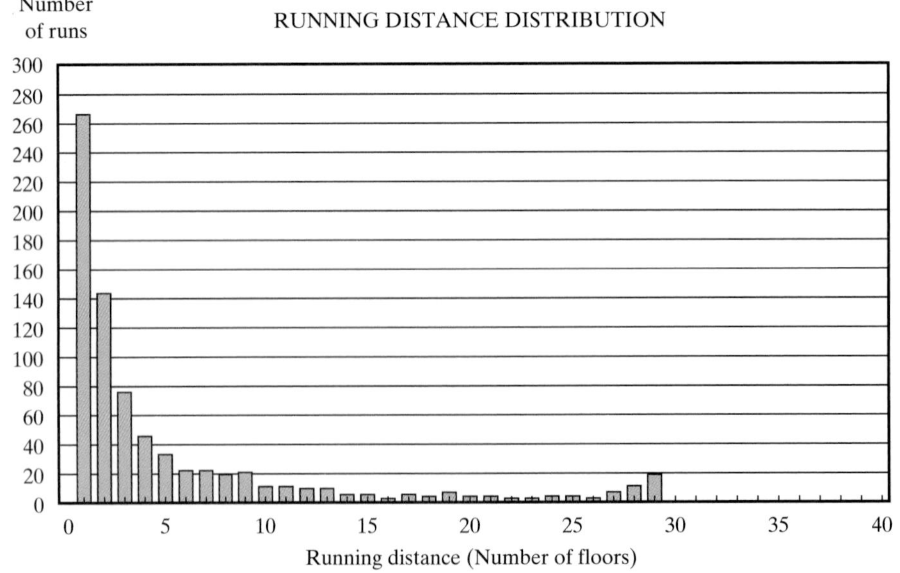

Source: Siikonen, M. L. "Elevator traffic simulation." *Simulation,* Vol. 61, No. 4, Oct. 1993, p. 266 (Figure 8). Copyright © 1993 by Simulation Councils, Inc. Reprinted by permission.

Real-World Case The Furniture Fire Case

(A Case Covering Chapters 3-4)

A wholesale furniture retailer stores in-stock items at a large warehouse located in Tampa, Florida. In early 1992, a fire destroyed the warehouse and all the furniture in it. After determining the fire was an accident, the retailer sought to recover costs by submitting a claim to its insurance company.

As is typical in a fire insurance policy of this type, the furniture retailer must provide the insurance company with an estimate of "lost" profit for the destroyed items. Retailers calculate profit margin in percentage form using the Gross Profit Factor (GPF). By definition, the GPF for a single sold item is the ratio of the profit to the item's selling price measured as a percentage, i.e.,

$$\text{Item GPF} = (\text{Profit/Sales price}) \times 100\%$$

Of interest to both the retailer and the insurance company is the average GPF for all of the items in the warehouse. Since these furniture pieces were all destroyed, their eventual selling prices and profit values are obviously unknown. Consequently, the average GPF for all the warehouse items is unknown.

One way to estimate the mean GPF of the destroyed items is to use the mean GPF of similar, recently sold items. The retailer sold 3,005 furniture items in 1991 (the year prior to the fire) and kept paper invoices on all sales. Rather than calculate the mean GPF for all 3,005 items (the data were not computerized), the retailer sampled a total of 253 of the invoices and computed the mean GPF for these items. The 253 items were obtained by first selecting a sample of 134 items and then augmenting this sample with a second sample of 119 items. The mean GPFs for the two subsamples were calculated to be 50.6% and 51.0%, respectively, yielding an overall average GPF of 50.8%. This average GPF can be applied to the costs of the furniture items destroyed in the fire to obtain an estimate of the "lost" profit.

According to experienced claims adjusters at the insurance company, the GPF for sale items of the type destroyed in the fire rarely exceeds 48%. Consequently, the estimate of 50.8% appeared to be unusually high. (A 1% increase in GPF for items of this type equates to, approximately, an additional $16,000 in profit.) When the insurance company questioned the retailer on this issue, the retailer responded, "Our estimate was based on selecting two independent, random samples from the population of 3,005 invoices in 1991. Since the samples were selected randomly and the total sample size is large, the mean GPF estimate of 50.8% is valid."

A dispute arose between the furniture retailer and the insurance company, and a lawsuit was filed. In one portion of the suit, the insurance company accused the retailer of fraudulently representing their sampling methodology. Rather than selecting the samples randomly, the retailer was accused of selecting an unusual number of "high profit" items from the population in order to increase the average GPF of the overall sample.

To support their claim of fraud, the insurance company hired a CPA firm to independently assess the retailer's 1991 Gross Profit Factor. Through the discovery process, the CPA firm legally obtained the paper invoices for the entire population of 3,005 items sold and input the information into a computer. The selling price, profit, profit margin, and month sold for these 3,005 furniture items are available on the data disk that accompanies this text, as described below.

Your objective in this case is to use these data to determine the likelihood of fraud. Is it likely that a random sample of 253 items selected from the population of 3,005 items would yield a mean GPF of at least 50.8%? Or, is it likely that two independent, random samples of size 134 and 119 will yield mean GPFs of at least 50.6% and 51.0%, respectively? (These were the questions posed to a statistician retained by the CPA firm.) Use the ideas of probability and sampling distributions to guide your analysis.

Prepare a professional document that presents the results of your analysis and gives your opinion regarding fraud. Be sure to describe the assumptions and methodology used to arrive at your findings.

FIRE.DAT

Variable	Column(s)	Type	Description
MONTH	17–19	QL	Month in which item was sold in 1991
INVOICE	25–29	QN	Invoice number
SALES	35–42	QN	Sales price of item in dollars
PROFIT	47–54	QN	Profit amount of item in dollars
MARGIN	59–64	QN	Profit margin of item = (Profit/Sales) × 100%

Chapter 5

INFERENCES BASED ON A SINGLE SAMPLE:

Estimation with Confidence Intervals

CONTENTS

STATISTICS IN ACTION

Where We've Been

We've learned that populations are characterized by numerical descriptive measures (called *parameters*) and that decisions about their values are based on sample statistics computed from sample data. Since statistics vary in a random manner from sample to sample, inferences based on them will be subject to uncertainty. This property is reflected in the sampling (probability) distribution of a statistic.

Where We're Going

In this chapter, we'll put all the preceding material into practice; that is, we'll estimate population means and proportions based on a single sample selected from the population of interest. Most importantly, we use the sampling distribution of a sample statistic to assess the reliability of an estimate.

The estimation of the mean gas mileage for a new car model, the estimation of the expected life of a computer monitor, and the estimation of the mean yearly sales for companies in the steel industry are problems with a common element. In each case, we're interested in estimating the mean of a population of quantitative measurements. This important problem constitutes the primary topic of this chapter.

You'll see that different techniques are used for estimating a mean, depending on whether a sample contains a large or small number of measurements. Nevertheless, our objectives remain the same: We want to use the sample information to estimate the mean and to assess the reliability of the estimate.

First, we consider a method of estimating a population mean using a large random sample (Section 5.1) and a small random sample (Section 5.2). Then, we consider estimation of population proportions (Section 5.3). Finally, we see how to determine the sample sizes necessary for reliable estimates based on random sampling (Section 5.4).

5.1 LARGE-SAMPLE CONFIDENCE INTERVAL FOR A POPULATION MEAN

We illustrate the *large-sample method* of estimating a population mean with an example. Suppose a large bank wants to estimate the average amount of money owed by its delinquent debtors—i.e., debtors who are more than two months behind in payment. To accomplish this objective, the bank plans to randomly sample 100 of its delinquent accounts and to use the sample mean, $\bar{x}$, of the amounts overdue to estimate μ, the mean for *all* delinquent accounts. The sample mean $\bar{x}$ represents a *point estimator* of the population mean μ. How can we assess the accuracy of this point estimator?

DEFINITION 5.1:

A **point estimator** of a population parameter is a rule or formula that tells us how to use the sample data to calculate a single number that can be used as an *estimate* of the population parameter.

According to the Central Limit Theorem, the sampling distribution of the sample mean is approximately normal for large samples, as shown in Figure 5.1. Let us calculate the interval

$$\bar{x} \pm 2\sigma_{\bar{x}} = \bar{x} \pm \frac{2\sigma}{\sqrt{n}}$$

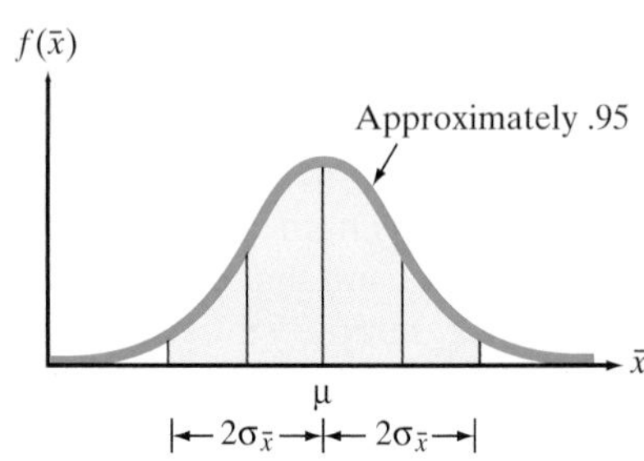

FIGURE 5.1
Sampling distribution of $\bar{x}$

That is, we form an interval 4 standard deviations wide—from 2 standard deviations below the sample mean to 2 standard deviations above the mean. *Prior to drawing the sample,* what are the chances that this interval will enclose μ, the population mean?

To answer this question, refer to Figure 5.1. If the 100 measurements yield a value of $\overline{x}$ that falls between the two lines on either side of μ—i.e., within 2 standard deviations of μ—then the interval $\overline{x} \pm 2\sigma_{\overline{x}}$ will contain μ; if $\overline{x}$ falls outside these boundaries, the interval $\overline{x} \pm 2\sigma_{\overline{x}}$ will not contain μ. Since the area under the normal curve (the sampling distribution of $\overline{x}$) between these boundaries is about .95 (more precisely, from Table IV in Appendix B the area is .9544), we know that the interval $\overline{x} \pm 2\sigma_{\overline{x}}$ will contain μ with a probability approximately equal to .95.

For instance, consider the overdue amounts for 100 delinquent accounts shown in Table 5.1. A SAS printout of summary statistics for the sample of 100 overdue amounts is shown in Figure 5.2. From the printout, we find $\overline{x} = \$233.28$ and $s = \$90.34$. To achieve our objective, we must construct the interval

$$\overline{x} \pm 2\sigma_{\overline{x}} = 233.28 \pm 2\frac{\sigma}{\sqrt{100}}$$

TABLE 5.1 Overdue Amounts (in Dollars) for 100 Delinquent Accounts

195	243	132	133	209	400	142	312	221	289
221	162	134	275	355	293	242	458	378	148
278	222	236	178	202	222	334	208	194	135
363	221	449	265	146	215	113	229	221	243
512	193	134	138	209	207	206	310	293	310
237	135	252	365	371	238	232	271	121	134
203	178	180	148	162	160	86	234	244	266
119	259	108	289	328	331	330	227	162	354
304	141	158	240	82	17	357	187	364	268
368	274	278	190	344	157	219	77	171	280

```
Analysis Variable : AMOUNT

N Obs    N        Minimum         Maximum            Mean         Std Dev
--------------------------------------------------------------------------
  100  100     17.0000000     512.0000000     233.2800000      90.3398835
--------------------------------------------------------------------------
```

FIGURE 5.2
SAS summary statistics for the overdue amounts of 100 delinquent accounts

But now we face a problem. You can see that without knowing the standard deviation σ of the original population—that is, the standard deviation of the overdue amounts of *all* delinquent accounts—we cannot calculate this interval. However, since we have a large sample ($n = 100$ measurements), we can approximate the interval by using the sample standard deviation s to approximate σ. Thus,

$$\overline{x} \pm 2\frac{\sigma}{\sqrt{100}} \approx \overline{x} \pm 2\frac{s}{\sqrt{100}} = 233.28 \pm 2\left(\frac{90.34}{10}\right) = 233.28 \pm 18.07$$

That is, we estimate the mean amount of delinquency for all accounts to fall within the interval \$215.21 to \$251.35.

Can we be sure that μ, the true mean, is in the interval (215.21, 251.35)? We cannot be certain, but we can be reasonably confident that it is. This confidence is derived from the knowledge that if we were to draw repeated random samples of 100 measurements from this population and form the interval $\overline{x} \pm 2\sigma_{\overline{x}}$ each time, approximately 95% of the intervals would contain μ. We have no way of knowing (without looking at all the delinquent accounts) whether our sample interval is one of the 95% that contains μ or one of the 5% that does not, but the odds certainly favor its containing μ. Consequently, the interval \$215.21 to \$251.35 provides a reliable estimate of the mean delinquency per account.

The formula that tells us how to calculate an interval estimate based on sample data is called an *interval estimator,* or *confidence interval.* The probability, .95, that measures the confidence we can place in the interval estimate is called a *confidence coefficient.* The percentage, 95%, is called the *confidence level* for the interval estimate. It is not usually possible to assess precisely the reliability of point estimators because they are single points rather than intervals. So, because we prefer to use estimators for which a measure of reliability can be calculated, we will generally use interval estimators.

DEFINITION 5.2

An **interval estimator** (or **confidence interval**) is a formula that tells us how to use sample data to calculate an interval that estimates a population parameter.

DEFINITION 5.3

The **confidence coefficient** is the probability that a randomly selected confidence interval encloses the population parameter—that is, the relative frequency with which similarly constructed intervals enclose the population parameter when the estimator is used repeatedly a very large number of times. The **confidence level** is the confidence coefficient expressed as a percentage.

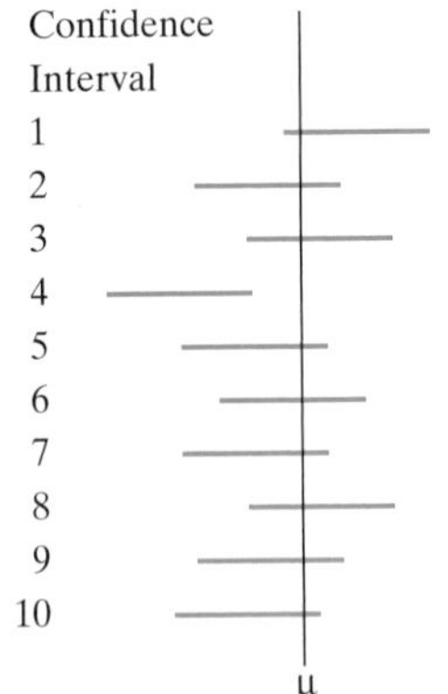

FIGURE 5.3
Confidence intervals for μ: 10 samples

Now we have seen how an interval can be used to estimate a population mean. When we use an interval estimator, we can usually calculate the probability that the estimation *process* will result in an interval that contains the true value of the population mean. That is, the probability that the interval contains the parameter in repeated usage is usually known. Figure 5.3 shows what happens when 10 different samples are drawn from a population, and a confidence interval for μ is calculated from each. The location of μ is indicated by the vertical line in the figure. Ten confidence intervals, each based on one of 10 samples, are shown as horizontal line segments. Note that the confidence intervals move from sample to sample—sometimes containing μ and other times missing μ. *If our confidence level is 95%, then in the long run, 95% of our confidence intervals will contain μ and 5% will not.*

Suppose you wish to choose a confidence coefficient other than .95. Notice in Figure 5.1 that the confidence coefficient .95 is equal to the total area under the sampling distribution, less .05 of the area, which is divided equally between the two tails. Using this idea, we can construct a confidence interval with any desired confidence coefficient by increasing or decreasing the area (call it α) assigned to the tails of the sampling distribution (see Figure 5.4). For example, if we place area $\alpha/2$ in each tail and if $z_{\alpha/2}$ is the z value such that the area $\alpha/2$ lies to its right, then the confidence interval with confidence coefficient $(1 - \alpha)$ is

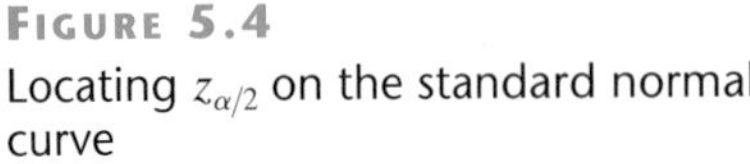

FIGURE 5.4
Locating $z_{\alpha/2}$ on the standard normal curve

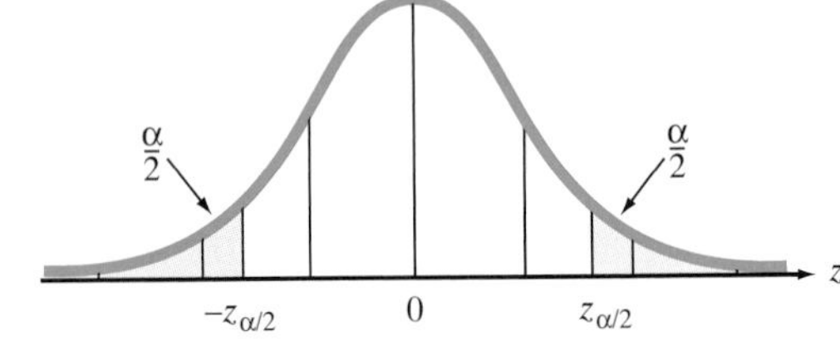

$$\bar{x} \pm z_{\alpha/2}\sigma_{\bar{x}}$$

To illustrate, for a confidence coefficient of .90 we have $(1 - \alpha) = .90$, $\alpha = .10$, and $\alpha/2 = .05$; $z_{.05}$ is the z value that locates area .05 in the upper tail of the sampling distribution. Recall that Table IV in Appendix B gives the areas between the mean and a specified z value. Since the total area to the right of the mean is .5, we find that $z_{.05}$ will be the z value corresponding to an area of $.5 - .05 = .45$ to the right of the mean (see Figure 5.5). This z value is $z_{.05} = 1.645$.

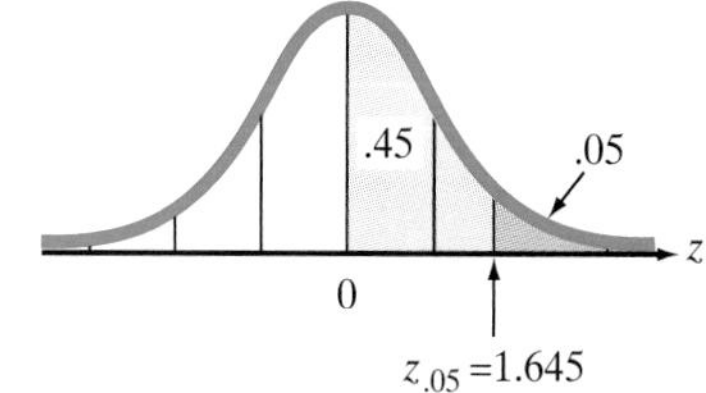

FIGURE 5.5
The z value ($z_{.05}$) corresponding to an area equal to .05 in the upper tail of the z-distribution

Confidence coefficients used in practice usually range from .90 to .99. The most commonly used confidence coefficients with corresponding values of α and $z_{\alpha/2}$ are shown in Table 5.2.

TABLE 5.2 Commonly Used Values of $z_{\alpha/2}$

Confidence Level $100(1 - \alpha)$	α	$\alpha/2$	$z_{\alpha/2}$
90%	.10	.05	1.645
95%	.05	.025	1.96
99%	.01	.005	2.575

Large-Sample $100(1 - \alpha)\%$ Confidence Interval for μ

$$\bar{x} \pm z_{\alpha/2}\sigma_{\bar{x}} = \bar{x} \pm z_{\alpha/2}\frac{\sigma}{\sqrt{n}}$$

where $z_{\alpha/2}$ is the z value with an area $\alpha/2$ to its right (see Figure 5.4) and $\sigma_{\bar{x}} = \sigma/\sqrt{n}$. The parameter σ is the standard deviation of the sampled population and n is the sample size.

Note: When σ is unknown (as is almost always the case) and n is large (say, $n \geq 30$), the confidence interval is approximately equal to

$$\bar{x} \pm z_{\alpha/2}\left(\frac{s}{\sqrt{n}}\right)$$

where s is the sample standard deviation.

Assumptions: None, since the Central Limit Theorem guarantees that the sampling distribution of $\bar{x}$ is approximately normal.

EXAMPLE 5.1 Unoccupied seats on flights cause airlines to lose revenue. Suppose a large airline wants to estimate its average number of unoccupied seats per flight over the past year. To accomplish this, the records of 225 flights are randomly selected, and the number of unoccupied seats is noted for each of the sampled flights. The sample mean and standard deviation are

$$\bar{x} = 11.6 \text{ seats} \qquad s = 4.1 \text{ seats}$$

Estimate μ, the mean number of unoccupied seats per flight during the past year, using a 90% confidence interval.

Solution The general form of the 90% confidence interval for a population mean is

$$\bar{x} \pm z_{\alpha/2}\sigma_{\bar{x}} = \bar{x} \pm z_{.05}\sigma_{\bar{x}} = \bar{x} \pm 1.645\left(\frac{\sigma}{\sqrt{n}}\right)$$

For the 225 records sampled, we have

$$11.6 \pm 1.645\left(\frac{\sigma}{\sqrt{225}}\right)$$

Since we do not know the value of σ (the standard deviation of the number of unoccupied seats per flight for all flights of the year), we use our best approximation—the sample standard deviation s. Then the 90% confidence interval is, approximately,

$$11.6 \pm 1.645\left(\frac{4.1}{\sqrt{225}}\right) = 11.6 \pm .45$$

or from 11.15 to 12.05. That is, at the 90% confidence level, we estimate the mean number of unoccupied seats per flight to be between 11.15 and 12.05 during the sampled year. This result is verified on the MINITAB printout of the analysis shown in Figure 5.6.

FIGURE 5.6 MINITAB printout for the confidence intervals in Example 5.1

```
           N     MEAN   STDEV  SE MEAN    90.0 PERCENT C.I.
NoSeats  225     11.6     4.1    0.273   (   11.15,    12.05)
```

We stress that the confidence level for this example, 90%, refers to the procedure used. If we were to apply this procedure repeatedly to different samples, approximately 90% of the intervals would contain μ. We do not know whether this particular interval (11.15, 12.05) is one of the 90% that contain μ or one of the 10% that do not—but the odds are that it does.

The interpretation of confidence intervals for a population mean is summarized in the box on page 265.

Sometimes, the estimation procedure yields a confidence interval that is too wide for our purposes. In this case, we will want to reduce the width of the interval to obtain a more precise estimate of μ. One way to accomplish this is to decrease the confidence coefficient, $1 - \alpha$. For example, reconsider the problem of estimating the mean amount owed, μ, for all delinquent accounts. Recall that for a sample of 100 accounts, $\bar{x} = \$233.28$ and $s = \$90.34$. A 90% confidence interval for μ is

Interpretation of a Confidence Interval for a Population Mean

When we form a $100(1 - \alpha)\%$ confidence interval for μ, we usually express our confidence in the interval with a statement such as, "We can be $100(1 - \alpha)\%$ confident that μ lies between the lower and upper bounds of the confidence interval," where for a particular application, we substitute the appropriate numerical values for the confidence and for the lower and upper bounds. *The statement reflects our confidence in the estimation process rather than in the particular interval that is calculated from the sample data.* We know that repeated application of the same procedure will result in different lower and upper bounds on the interval. Furthermore, we know that $100(1 - \alpha)\%$ of the resulting intervals will contain μ. There is (usually) no way to determine whether any particular interval is one of those that contain μ, or one that does not. However, unlike point estimators, confidence intervals have some measure of reliability, the confidence coefficient, associated with them. For that reason they are generally preferred to point estimators.

$$\bar{x} \pm 1.645\sigma/\sqrt{n} \approx 233.28 \pm (1.645)(90.34/\sqrt{100}) = 233.28 \pm 14.86$$

or ($218.42, $248.14). You can see that this interval is narrower than the previously calculated 95% confidence interval, ($215.21, $251.35). Unfortunately, we also have "less confidence" in the 90% confidence interval. An alternative method used to decrease the width of an interval without sacrificing "confidence" is to increase the sample size n. We demonstrate this method in Section 5.4.

EXERCISES 5.1–5.11

Learning the Mechanics

5.1 Find $z_{\alpha/2}$ for each of the following:
a. $\alpha = .10$ b. $\alpha = .01$ c. $\alpha = .05$ d. $\alpha = .20$

5.2 What is the confidence level of each of the following confidence intervals for μ?

a. $\bar{x} \pm 1.96\left(\frac{\sigma}{\sqrt{n}}\right)$ b. $\bar{x} \pm 1.645\left(\frac{\sigma}{\sqrt{n}}\right)$

c. $\bar{x} \pm 2.575\left(\frac{\sigma}{\sqrt{n}}\right)$ d. $\bar{x} \pm 1.282\left(\frac{\sigma}{\sqrt{n}}\right)$

e. $\bar{x} \pm .99\left(\frac{\sigma}{\sqrt{n}}\right)$

5.3 A random sample of n measurements was selected from a population with unknown mean μ and standard deviation σ. Calculate a 95% confidence interval for μ for each of the following situations:
a. $n = 75, \bar{x} = 28, s^2 = 12$
b. $n = 200, \bar{x} = 102, s^2 = 22$
c. $n = 100, \bar{x} = 15, s = .3$
d. $n = 100, \bar{x} = 4.05, s = .83$
e. Is the assumption that the underlying population of measurements is normally distributed necessary to ensure the validity of the confidence intervals in parts **a–d?** Explain.

5.4 A random sample of 90 observations produced a mean $\bar{x} = 25.9$ and a standard deviation $s = 2.7$.
a. Find a 95% confidence interval for the population mean μ.
b. Find a 90% confidence interval for μ.
c. Find a 99% confidence interval for μ.
d. What happens to the width of a confidence interval as the value of the confidence coefficient is increased while the sample size is held fixed?
e. Would your confidence intervals of parts **a–c** be valid if the distribution of the original population was not normal? Explain.

5.5 The mean and standard deviation of a random sample of n measurements are equal to 33.9 and 3.3, respectively.
a. Find a 95% confidence interval for μ if $n = 100$.
b. Find a 95% confidence interval for μ if $n = 400$.

c. Find the widths of the confidence intervals found in parts **a** and **b.** What is the effect on the width of a confidence interval of quadrupling the sample size while holding the confidence coefficient fixed?

Applying the Concepts

5.6 The U.S. has 1.4 million tax-exempt organizations. These include most schools and universities, foundations, and social services organizations such as the Red Cross, the Salvation Army, the YMCA, and the American Cancer Society. Donations to these organizations not only go to the stated charitable purpose, but are used to cover fundraising expenses and overhead. For a sample of 30 charities, the table below lists their *charitable commitment,* the percentage of their expenses that go toward the stated charitable purpose.

a. Give a point estimate for the mean charitable commitment of tax-exempt organizations.

b. Construct a 98% confidence interval for the true mean charitable commitment of tax-exempt organizations. Interpret the result.

c. Why is the confidence interval of part **b** a better estimator of the mean charitable commitment than the point estimator of part **a?** Explain.

5.7 The *Journal of the American Medical Association* (Apr. 21, 1993) reported on the results of a National Health Interview Survey designed to determine the prevalence of smoking among U.S. adults. More than 40,000 adults responded to questions such as "Have you smoked at least 100 cigarettes in your lifetime?" and "Do you smoke cigarettes now?" Current smokers (more than 11,000 adults in the survey) were also asked: "On the average, how many cigarettes do you now smoke a day?" The results yielded a mean of 20.0 cigarettes per day with an associated 95% confidence interval of (19.7, 20.3).

a. Carefully describe the population from which the sample was drawn.

b. Interpret the 95% confidence interval.

c. State any assumptions about the target population of current cigarette smokers that must be satisfied for inferences derived from the interval to be valid.

d. A tobacco industry researcher claims that the mean number of cigarettes smoked per day by regular cigarette smokers is less than 15. Comment on this claim.

5.8 Research indicates that bicycle helmets save lives. A study reported in *Public Health Reports* (May–June 1992) was intended to identify ways of encouraging

CHARITY.DAT

Organization	Charitable Commitment
American Cancer Society	62%
American National Red Cross	91
Big Brothers Big Sisters of America	77
Boy Scouts of America National Council	81
Boys & Girls Clubs of America	81
CARE	91
Covenant House	15
Disabled American Veterans	65
Ducks Unlimited	78
Feed the Children	90
Girl Scouts of the USA	83
Goodwill Industries International	89
Habitat for Humanity International	81
Mayo Foundation	26
Mothers Against Drunk Drivers	71
Multiple Sclerosis Association of America	56
Museum of Modern Art	79
Nature Conservancy	77
Paralyzed Veterans of America	50
Planned Parenthood Federation	81
Salvation Army	84
Shriners Hospital for Children	95
Smithsonian Institution	87
Special Olympics	72
Trust for Public Land	88
United Jewish Appeal/Federation-NY	75
United States Olympic Committee	78
United Way of New York City	85
WGBH Educational Foundation	81
YMCA of the USA	80

Source: "Look Before You Give," *Forbes,* Dec. 27, 1999, pp. 206–216.

helmet use in children. One of the variables measured was the children's perception of the risk involved in bicycling. A four-point scale was used, with scores ranging from 1 (no risk) to 4 (very high risk). A sample of 797 children in grades 4–6 yielded the following results on the perception of risk variable: $\bar{x} = 3.39$, $s = .80$.

a. Calculate a 90% confidence interval for the average perception of risk for all students in grades 4–6. What assumptions did you make to ensure the validity of the confidence interval?
b. If the population mean perception of risk exceeds 2.50, the researchers will conclude that students in these grades exhibit an awareness of the risk involved with bicycling. Interpret the confidence interval constructed in part **a** in this context.

5.9 The relationship between an employee's participation in the performance appraisal process and subsequent subordinate reactions toward the appraisal was investigated in the *Journal of Applied Psychology* (Aug. 1998). In Chapter 9 we will discuss a quantitative measure of the relationship between two variables, called the coefficient of correlation *r*. The researchers obtained *r* for a sample of 34 studies that examined the relationship between appraisal participation and a subordinate's satisfaction with the appraisal. These correlations are listed in the table. (Values of *r* near +1 reflect a strong positive relationship between the variables.) A MINITAB printout showing a 95% confidence interval for the mean of the data is provided below. Locate the 95% confidence interval on the printout and interpret it in the words of the problem.

CORR34.DAT

.50	.58	.71	.46	.63	.66	.31	.35	.51	.06	.35	.19
.40	.63	.43	.16	−.08	.51	.59	.43	.30	.69	.25	.20
.39	.20	.51	.68	.74	.65	.34	.45	.31	.27		

Source: Cawley, B. D., Keeping, L. M., and Levy, P. E. "Participation in the performance appraisal process and employee reactions: A meta-analytic review of field investigations." *Journal of Applied Psychology*, Vol. 83, No. 4, Aug. 1998, pp. 632–633 (Appendix).

5.10 Named for the section of the 1978 Internal Revenue Code that authorized them, 401(k) plans permit employees to shift part of their before-tax salaries into investments such as mutual funds. Employers typically match 50% of the employee's contribution up to about 6% of salary (*Fortune,* Dec. 28, 1992). One company, concerned with what it believed was a low employee participation rate in its 401(k) plan, sampled 30 other companies with similar plans and asked for their 401(k) participation rates. The following rates (in percentages) were obtained:

RATE401K.DAT

80	76	81	77	82	80	85	60	80	79	82	70
88	85	80	79	83	75	87	78	80	84	72	75
90	84	82	77	75	86						

Descriptive statistics for the data are given in the SPSS printout at the bottom of the page.

a. Use the information on the SPSS printout to construct a 95% confidence interval for the mean participation rate for all companies that have 401(k) plans.
b. Interpret the interval in the context of this problem.
c. What assumption is necessary to ensure the validity of this confidence interval?
d. If the company that conducted the sample has a 71% participation rate, can it safely conclude that its rate is below the population mean rate for all companies with 401(k) plans? Explain.
e. If in the data set the 60% had been 80%, how would the center and width of the confidence interval you constructed in part **a** be affected?

5.11 The 1967 Age Discrimination in Employment Act (ADEA) made it illegal to discriminate against workers 40 years of age and older. Opponents of the law argue that there are sound economic reasons why employers would not want to hire and train workers who are very close to retirement. They also argue that people's abilities tend to deteriorate with age. In fact, *Forbes* (Dec. 13, 1999) reported that 25-year-olds did significantly better than 60-year-olds on the Wechsler Adult Intelligence Scale, the most popular IQ test. The data on p. 268 are raw test scores (i.e., not the familiar normalized IQ scores) for a sample of 36 25-year-olds and 36 60-year-olds.

MINITAB Output for Exercise 5.9

```
Variable     N     Mean    StDev   SE Mean        95.0 % CI
corr        34   0.4224   0.1998    0.0343   ( 0.3526, 0.4921)
```

SPSS Output for Exercise 5.10

```
Number of Valid Observations (Listwise) =          30.00
Variable         Mean    Std Dev    Minimum    Maximum      N Label
PARTRATE        79.73       5.96      60.00      90.00     30
```

STATISTIX Output for Exercise 5.11

```
DESCRIPTIVE STATISTICS

VARIABLE        N    LO 95% CI        MEAN     UP 95% CI        SD
RAWIQ60        36       41.009      45.306        49.602    12.698
```

a. Estimate the mean raw test score for all 25-year-olds using a 95% confidence interval. Give a practical interpretation of the confidence interval.
b. What assumption(s) must hold for the method of estimation used in part **a** to be appropriate?
c. The STATISTIX printout above provides an analysis of the sample raw test scores of 60-year-olds. Find a 95% confidence interval for the mean raw score of all 60-year-olds and interpret your result. [*Note:* In Chapter 9 we will present a method for directly comparing the means of 25-year-olds and 60-year-olds.]

IQ25.DAT

25-Year-Olds

54	61	80	92	41	63
59	68	66	76	82	80
82	47	81	77	88	94
49	86	55	82	45	51
70	72	63	50	52	67
75	60	58	49	63	68

IQ60.DAT

60-Year-Olds

42	54	38	22	58	37
60	49	51	60	45	42
73	28	65	65	60	34
34	33	40	28	36	60
45	61	47	30	45	45
45	37	27	40	37	58

Source: Adapted from "The Case for Age Discrimination," *Forbes*, Dec. 13, 1999, p. 13.

5.2 SMALL-SAMPLE CONFIDENCE INTERVAL FOR A POPULATION MEAN

Federal legislation requires pharmaceutical companies to perform extensive tests on new drugs before they can be marketed. Initially, a new drug is tested on animals. If the drug is deemed safe after this first phase of testing, the pharmaceutical company is then permitted to begin human testing on a limited basis. During this second phase, inferences must be made about the safety of the drug based on information in very small samples.

Suppose a pharmaceutical company must estimate the average increase in blood pressure of patients who take a certain new drug. Assume that only six patients (randomly selected from the population of all patients) can be used in the initial phase of human testing. The use of a *small sample* in making an inference about μ presents two immediate problems when we attempt to use the standard normal z as a test statistic.

Problem 1. The shape of the sampling distribution of the sample mean $\bar{x}$ (and the z statistic) now depends on the shape of the population that is sampled. We can no longer assume that the sampling distribution of $\bar{x}$ is approximately normal, because the Central Limit Theorem ensures normality only for samples that are sufficiently large.

Solution to Problem 1. According to Theorem 4.1, the sampling distribution of $\bar{x}$ (and z) is exactly normal even for relatively small samples if the sampled population is normal. It is approximately normal if the sampled population is approximately normal.

Problem 2. The population standard deviation σ is almost always unknown. Although it is still true that $\sigma_{\bar{x}} = \sigma/\sqrt{n}$, the sample standard deviation s may provide a poor approximation for σ when the sample size is small.

Solution to Problem 2. Instead of using the standard normal statistic

$$z = \frac{\bar{x} - \mu}{\sigma_{\bar{x}}} = \frac{\bar{x} - \mu}{\sigma/\sqrt{n}}$$

which requires knowledge of or a good approximation to σ, we define and use the statistic

$$t = \frac{\bar{x} - \mu}{s/\sqrt{n}}$$

in which the sample standard deviation, s, replaces the population standard deviation, σ.

The distribution of the **t statistic** in repeated sampling was discovered by W. S. Gosset, a chemist in the Guinness brewery in Ireland, who published his discovery in 1908 under the pen name of Student. The main result of Gosset's work is that if we are sampling from a normal distribution, the t statistic has a sampling distribution very much like that of the z statistic: mound-shaped, symmetric, with mean 0. The primary difference between the sampling distributions of t and z is that the t statistic is more variable than the z, which follows intuitively when you realize that t contains two random quantities ($\bar{x}$ and s), whereas z contains only one ($\bar{x}$).

The actual amount of variability in the sampling distribution of t depends on the sample size n. A convenient way of expressing this dependence is to say that the t statistic has $(n - 1)$ **degrees of freedom (df).** Recall that the quantity $(n - 1)$ is the divisor that appears in the formula for s^2. This number plays a key role in the sampling distribution of s^2 and appears in discussions of other statistics in later chapters. In particular, the smaller the number of degrees of freedom associated with the t statistic, the more variable will be its sampling distribution.

In Figure 5.7 we show both the sampling distribution of z and the sampling distribution of a t statistic with 4 df. You can see that the increased variability of the t statistic means that the t value, t_α, that locates an area α in the upper tail of the t-distribution is larger than the corresponding value z_α. For any given value of α, the t value t_α increases as the number of degrees of freedom (df) decreases. Values of t that will be used in forming small-sample confidence intervals of μ are given in Table VI of Appendix B. A partial reproduction of this table is shown in Table 5.3.

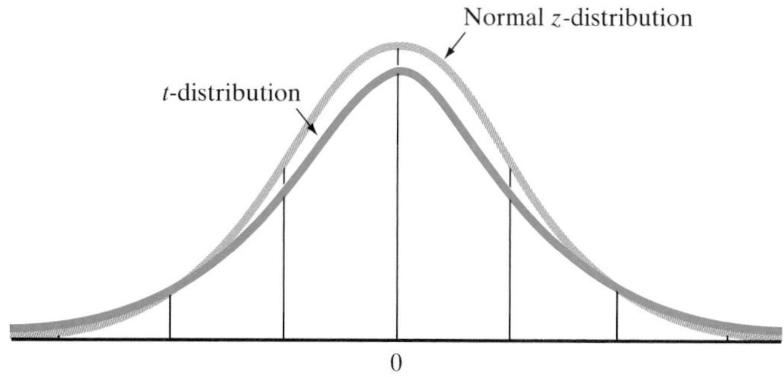

FIGURE 5.7 Standard normal (z) distribution and t-distribution with 4 df

Note that t_α values are listed for degrees of freedom from 1 to 29, where α refers to the tail area under the t-distribution to the right of t_α. For example, if we want the t value with an area of .025 to its right and 4 df, we look in the table under the column $t_{.025}$ for the entry in the row corresponding to 4 df. This entry is $t_{.025} = 2.776$, as shown in Figure 5.8. The corresponding standard normal z-score is $z_{.025} = 1.96$.

TABLE 5.3 Reproduction of Part of Table VI in Appendix B

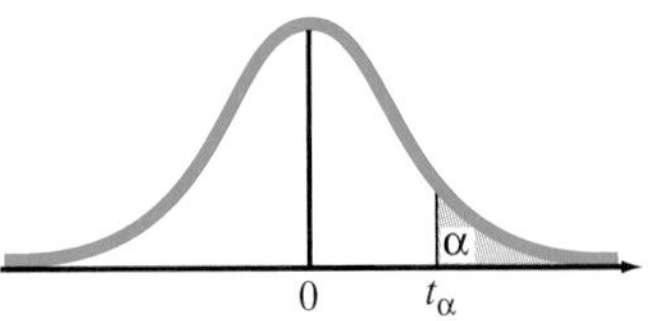

Degrees of Freedom	$t_{.100}$	$t_{.050}$	$t_{.025}$	$t_{.010}$	$t_{.005}$	$t_{.001}$	$t_{.0005}$
1	3.078	6.314	12.706	31.821	63.657	318.13	636.62
2	1.886	2.920	4.303	6.965	9.925	22.326	21.598
3	1.638	2.353	3.182	4.541	5.841	10.213	12.924
4	1.533	2.132	2.776	3.747	4.604	7.173	8.610
5	1.476	2.015	2.571	3.365	4.032	5.893	6.869
6	1.440	1.943	2.447	3.132	3.707	5.208	5.959
7	1.415	1.895	2.365	2.998	3.499	4.785	5.408
8	1.397	1.860	2.306	2.896	3.355	4.501	5.041
9	1.383	1.833	2.262	2.821	3.250	4.297	4.781
10	1.372	1.812	2.228	2.764	3.169	4.144	4.587
11	1.363	1.796	2.201	2.718	3.106	4.025	4.437
12	1.356	1.782	2.179	2.681	3.055	3.930	4.318
13	1.350	1.771	2.160	2.650	3.012	3.852	4.221
14	1.345	1.761	2.145	2.624	2.977	3.787	4.140
15	1.341	1.753	2.131	2.602	2.947	3.733	4.073
⋮	⋮	⋮	⋮	⋮	⋮	⋮	⋮
∞	1.282	1.645	1.960	2.326	2.576	3.090	3.291

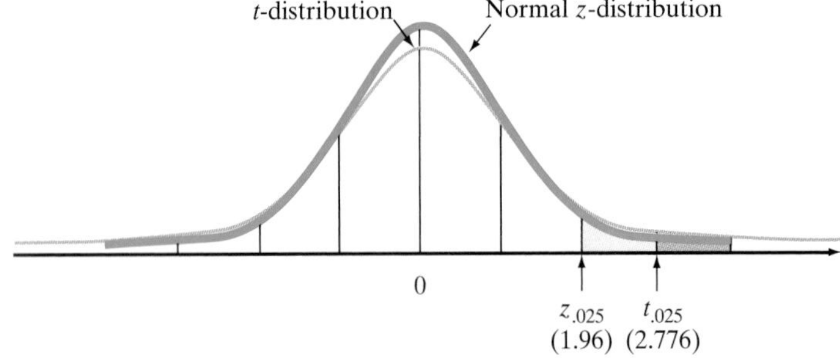

FIGURE 5.8
The $t_{.025}$ value in a t-distribution with 4 df and the corresponding $z_{.025}$ value

Note that the last row of Table VI, where df $= \infty$ (infinity), contains the standard normal z values. This follows from the fact that as the sample size n grows very large, s becomes closer to σ and thus t becomes closer in distribution to z. In fact, when df $= 29$, there is little difference between corresponding tabulated values of z and t. Thus, researchers often choose the arbitrary cutoff of $n = 30$ (df $= 29$) to distinguish between the large-sample and small-sample inferential techniques.

Returning to the example of testing a new drug, suppose that the six test patients have blood pressure increases of 1.7, 3.0, .8, 3.4, 2.7, and 2.1 points. How can we use this information to construct a 95% confidence interval for μ, the mean increase in blood pressure associated with the new drug for all patients in the population?

First, we know that we are dealing with a sample too small to assume that the sample mean $\bar{x}$ is approximately normally distributed by the Central Limit Theorem. That is, we do not get the normal distribution of $\bar{x}$ "automatically" from the Central Limit Theorem when the sample size is small. Instead, the measured variable, in this case the increase in blood pressure, must be normally distributed in order for the distribution of $\bar{x}$ to be normal.

Second, unless we are fortunate enough to know the population standard deviation σ, which in this case represents the standard deviation of *all* the patients' increases in blood pressure when they take the new drug, we cannot use the standard normal z statistic to form our confidence interval for μ. Instead, we must use the t-distribution, with $(n - 1)$ degrees of freedom.

In this case, $n - 1 = 5$ df, and the t value is found in Table 5.3 to be $t_{.025} = 2.571$ with 5 df. Recall that the large-sample confidence interval would have been of the form

$$\bar{x} \pm z_{\alpha/2}\sigma_{\bar{x}} = \bar{x} \pm z_{\alpha/2}\frac{\sigma}{\sqrt{n}} = \bar{x} \pm z_{.025}\frac{\sigma}{\sqrt{n}}$$

where 95% is the desired confidence level. To form the interval for a small sample from *a normal distribution, we simply substitute* t *for* z *and* s *for σ in the preceding formula:*

$$\bar{x} \pm t_{\alpha/2}\frac{s}{\sqrt{n}}$$

A MINITAB printout showing descriptive statistics for the six blood pressure increases is displayed in Figure 5.9. Note that $\bar{x} = 2.283$ and $s = .950$. Substituting these numerical values into the confidence interval formula, we get

$$2.283 \pm (2.571)\left(\frac{.950}{\sqrt{6}}\right) = 2.283 \pm .997$$

or 1.286 to 3.280 points. Note that this interval agrees (except for rounding) with the confidence interval generated by MINITAB in Figure 5.9.

FIGURE 5.9
MINITAB analysis of six blood pressure increases

```
              N      MEAN     STDEV   SE MEAN      95.0 PERCENT C.I.
BPIncr        6     2.283     0.950     0.388    (    1.287,    3.280)
```

We interpret the interval as follows: We can be 95% confident that the mean increase in blood pressure associated with taking this new drug is between 1.286 and 3.28 points. As with our large-sample interval estimates, our confidence is in the process, not in this particular interval. We know that if we were to repeatedly use this estimation procedure, 95% of the confidence intervals produced would contain the true mean μ, *assuming that the probability distribution of changes in blood pressure from which our sample was selected is normal.* The latter assumption is necessary for the small-sample interval to be valid.

What price did we pay for having to utilize a small sample to make the inference? First, we had to assume the underlying population is normally distributed, and if the assumption is invalid, our interval might also be invalid.* Second, we had to form the interval using a t value of 2.571 rather than a z value of 1.96, resulting in a wider interval to achieve the same 95% level of confidence. If the interval from 1.286 to 3.28 is too wide to be of use, then we know how to remedy the situation: increase the number of patients sampled to decrease the interval width (on average).

The procedure for forming a small-sample confidence interval is summarized in the next box.

*By *invalid,* we mean that the probability that the procedure will yield an interval that contains μ is not equal to $(1 - \alpha)$. Generally, if the underlying population is approximately normal, then the confidence coefficient will approximate the probability that a randomly selected interval contains μ.

Small-Sample Confidence Interval* for μ

$$\bar{x} \pm t_{\alpha/2}\left(\frac{s}{\sqrt{n}}\right)$$

where $t_{\alpha/2}$ is based on $(n - 1)$ degrees of freedom

Assumptions: A random sample is selected from a population with a relative frequency distribution that is approximately normal.

EXAMPLE 5.2

Some quality control experiments require *destructive sampling* (i.e., the test to determine whether the item is defective destroys the item) in order to measure some particular characteristic of the product. The cost of destructive sampling often dictates small samples. For example, suppose a manufacturer of printers for personal computers wishes to estimate the mean number of characters printed before the printhead fails. Suppose the printer manufacturer tests $n = 15$ randomly selected printheads and records the number of characters printed until failure for each. These 15 measurements (in millions of characters) are listed in Table 5.4, followed by an EXCEL summary statistics printout in Figure 5.10.

TABLE 5.4 Number of Characters (in Millions) for $n = 15$ Printhead Tests

1.13	1.55	1.43	.92	1.25
1.36	1.32	.85	1.07	1.48
1.20	1.33	1.18	1.22	1.29

a. Form a 99% confidence interval for the mean number of characters printed before the printhead fails. Interpret the result.

b. What assumption is required for the interval, part **a,** to be valid? Is it reasonably satisfied?

FIGURE 5.10
EXCEL summary statistics printout for data in Table 5.4

Number	
Mean	1.238667
Standard Error	0.049875
Median	1.25
Mode	#N/A
Standard Deviation	0.193164
Sample Variance	0.037312
Kurtosis	0.063636
Skewness	-0.49126
Range	0.7
Minimum	0.85
Maximum	1.55
Sum	18.58
Count	15
Confidence Level(95.000%)	0.097753

*The procedure given in the box assumes that the population standard deviation σ is unknown, which is almost always the case. If σ is known, we can form the small-sample confidence interval just as we would a large-sample confidence interval using a standard normal z value instead of t. However, we must still assume that the underlying population is approximately normal.

Solution

a. For this small sample ($n = 15$), we use the t statistic to form the confidence interval. We use a confidence coefficient of .99 and $n - 1 = 14$ degrees of freedom to find $t_{\alpha/2}$ in Table VI:

$$t_{\alpha/2} = t_{.005} = 2.977$$

[*Note:* The small sample forces us to extend the interval almost 3 standard deviations (of $\bar{x}$) on each side of the sample mean in order to form the 99% confidence interval.] From the EXCEL printout, Figure 5.10, we find $\bar{x} = 1.239$ and $s = .193$. Substituting these values into the confidence interval formula, we obtain:

$$\bar{x} \pm t_{.005}\left(\frac{s}{\sqrt{n}}\right) = 1.239 \pm 2.977\left(\frac{.193}{\sqrt{15}}\right)$$

$$= 1.239 \pm .148 \quad \text{or} \quad (1.091, 1.387)$$

Thus, the manufacturer can be 99% confident that the printhead has a mean life of between 1.091 and 1.387 million characters. If the manufacturer were to advertise that the mean life of its printheads is (at least) 1 million characters, the interval would support such a claim. Our confidence is derived from the fact that 99% of the intervals formed in repeated applications of this procedure would contain μ.

b. Since n is small, we must assume that the number of characters printed before printhead failure is a random variable from a normal distribution. That is, we assume that the population from which the sample of 15 measurements is selected is distributed normally. One way to check this assumption is to graph the distribution of data in Table 5.4. If the sample data are approximately normal, then the population from which the sample is selected is very likely to be normal. A MINITAB stem-and-leaf plot for the sample data is displayed in Figure 5.11. The distribution is mound-shaped and nearly symmetric. Therefore, the assumption of normality appears to be reasonably satisfied.

FIGURE 5.11
MINITAB stem-and-leaf display of data in Table 5.4

```
Stem-and-leaf of NUMBER    N = 15
Leaf Unit = 0.010

    1     8 5
    2     9 2
    3    10 7
    5    11 38
  (4)    12 0259
    6    13 236
    3    14 38
    1    15 5
```

We have emphasized throughout this section that an assumption that the population is approximately normally distributed is necessary for making small-sample inferences about μ when using the t statistic. Although many phenomena do have approximately normal distributions, it is also true that many random phenomena have distributions that are not normal or even mound-shaped. Empirical evidence acquired over the years has shown that the t-distribution is rather insensitive to moderate departures from normality. That is, use of the t statistic when sampling from mound-shaped populations generally produces credible results; however, for cases in which the distribution is distinctly nonnormal, we must either take a large sample or use a *nonparametric method.* (A nonparametric method for making inferences from a single sample is presented in optional Section 6.6.)

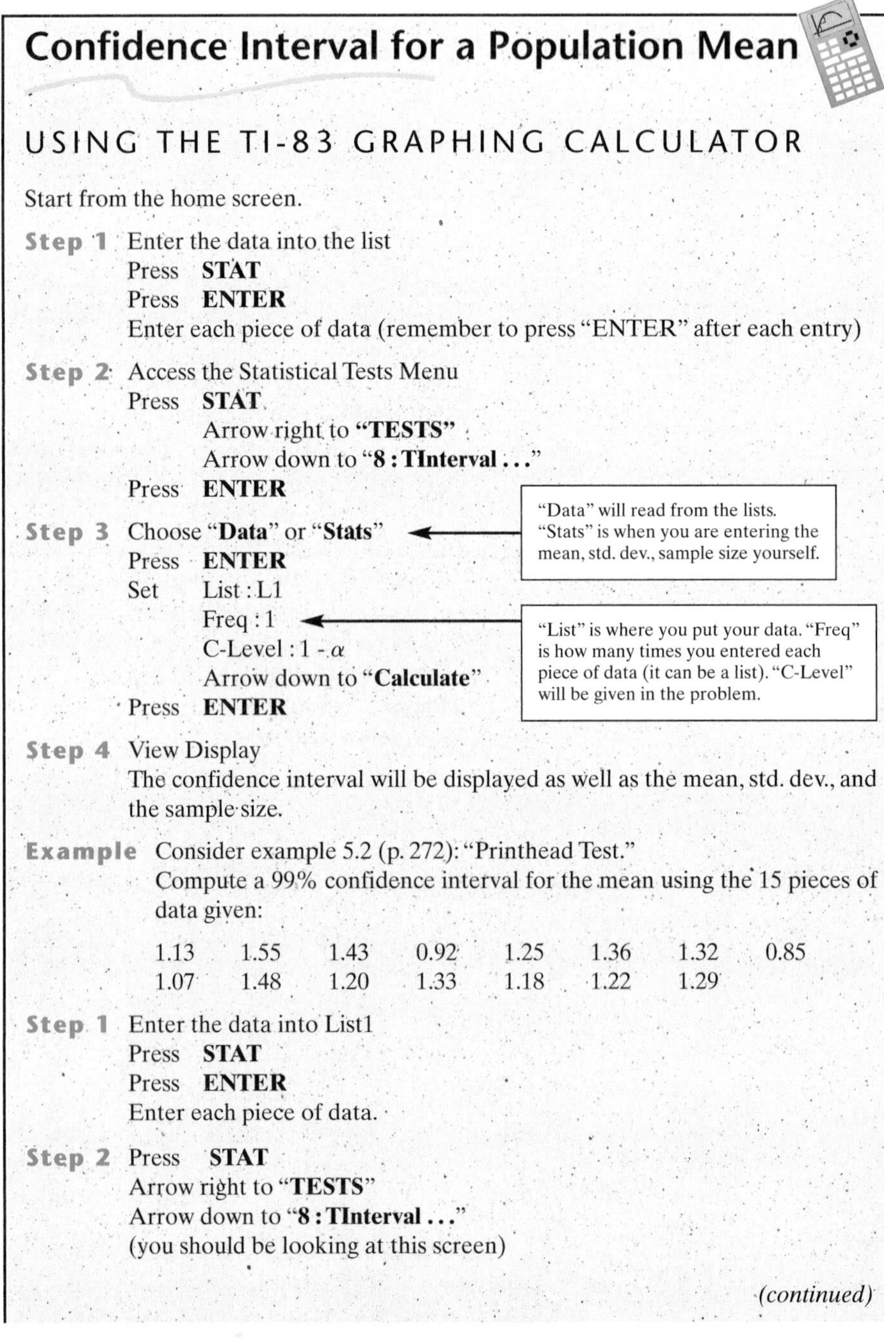

Confidence Interval for a Population Mean

USING THE TI-83 GRAPHING CALCULATOR

Start from the home screen.

Step 1 Enter the data into the list
Press **STAT**
Press **ENTER**
Enter each piece of data (remember to press "ENTER" after each entry)

Step 2 Access the Statistical Tests Menu
Press **STAT**
Arrow right to **"TESTS"**
Arrow down to "**8 : TInterval . . .**"
Press **ENTER**

Step 3 Choose "**Data**" or "**Stats**"
Press **ENTER**
Set List : L1
Freq : 1
C-Level : 1 - α
Arrow down to "**Calculate**"
Press **ENTER**

"Data" will read from the lists. "Stats" is when you are entering the mean, std. dev., sample size yourself.

"List" is where you put your data. "Freq" is how many times you entered each piece of data (it can be a list). "C-Level" will be given in the problem.

Step 4 View Display
The confidence interval will be displayed as well as the mean, std. dev., and the sample size.

Example Consider example 5.2 (p. 272): "Printhead Test."
Compute a 99% confidence interval for the mean using the 15 pieces of data given:

1.13	1.55	1.43	0.92	1.25	1.36	1.32	0.85
1.07	1.48	1.20	1.33	1.18	1.22	1.29	

Step 1 Enter the data into List1
Press **STAT**
Press **ENTER**
Enter each piece of data.

Step 2 Press **STAT**
Arrow right to "**TESTS**"
Arrow down to "**8 : TInterval . . .**"
(you should be looking at this screen)

(continued)

Press **ENTER**

Step 3 Highlight "**Data**" then press **ENTER** (you will see this screen)

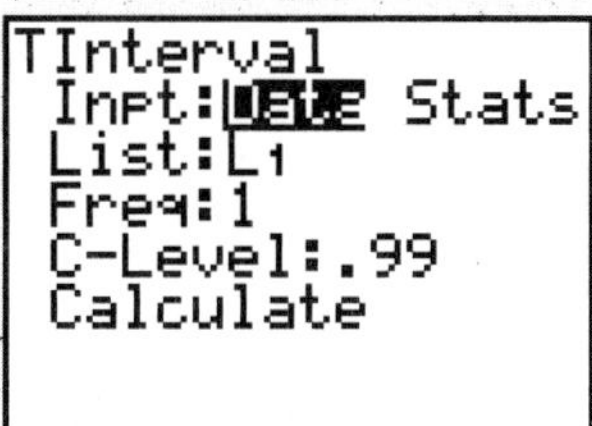

Match the settings on this screen then arrow down, highlight "**Calculate**," and press **ENTER** (you will see this screen)

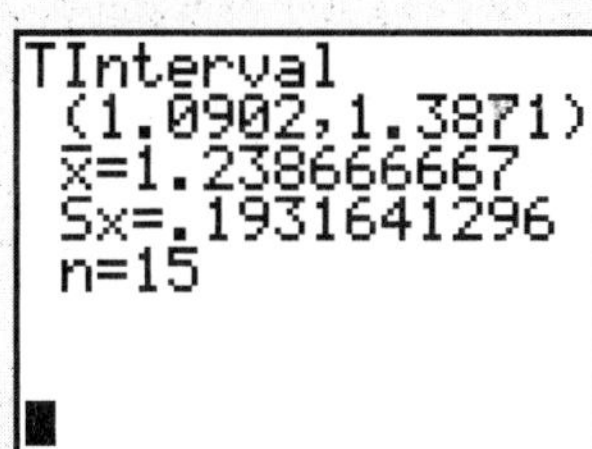

Step 4 As you can see from the screen our 99% confidence interval is (**1.0902, 1.3871**). You will also notice it gives the mean, std. dev., and the sample size.

Step 5 Return to the home screen
Press **CLEAR ENTER**

EXERCISES 5.12–5.23

Learning the Mechanics

5.12 Suppose you have selected a random sample of $n = 5$ measurements from a normal distribution. Compare the standard normal z values with the corresponding t values if you were forming the following confidence intervals.

a. 80% confidence interval
b. 90% confidence interval
c. 95% confidence interval
d. 98% confidence interval
e. 99% confidence interval
f. Use the table values you obtained in parts **a–e** to sketch the z- and t-distributions. What are the similarities and differences?

5.13 Let t_0 be a particular value of t. Use Table VI of Appendix B to find t_0 values such that the following statements are true.

a. $P(-t_0 < t < t_0) = .95$ where df $= 10$
b. $P(t \leq -t_0$ or $t \geq t_0) = .05$ where df $= 10$
c. $P(t \leq t_0) = .05$ where df $= 10$
d. $P(t \leq -t_0$ or $t \geq t_0) = .10$ where df $= 20$
e. $P(t \leq -t_0$ or $t \geq t_0) = .01$ where df $= 5$

5.14 The following random sample was selected from a normal distribution: 4, 6, 3, 5, 9, 3.

a. Construct a 90% confidence interval for the population mean μ.
b. Construct a 95% confidence interval for the population mean μ.

c. Construct a 99% confidence interval for the population mean μ.

d. Assume that the sample mean $\bar{x}$ and sample standard deviation s remain exactly the same as those you just calculated but that they are based on a sample of $n = 25$ observations rather than $n = 6$ observations. Repeat parts **a–c.** What is the effect of increasing the sample size on the width of the confidence intervals?

5.15 The following sample of 16 measurements was selected from a population that is approximately normally distributed:

LM5_15.DAT

91	80	99	110	95	106	78	121	106	100	97	82
100	83	115	104								

a. Construct an 80% confidence interval for the population mean.

b. Construct a 95% confidence interval for the population mean and compare the width of this interval with that of part **a.**

c. Carefully interpret each of the confidence intervals and explain why the 80% confidence interval is narrower.

Applying the Concepts

5.16 Health insurers and the federal government are both putting pressure on hospitals to shorten the average length of stay (LOS) of their patients. In 1996, the average LOS for men in the United States was 5.7 days and the average for women was 4.6 days (*Statistical Abstract of the United States: 1998*). A random sample of 20 hospitals in one state had a mean LOS for women in 2000 of 3.8 days and a standard deviation of 1.2 days.

a. Use a 90% confidence interval to estimate the population mean LOS for women for the state's hospitals in 2000.

b. Interpret the interval in terms of this application.

c. What is meant by the phrase "90% confidence interval"?

5.17 Periodically, the Hillsborough County (Florida) Water Department tests the drinking water of homeowners for contaminants such as lead and copper. The lead and copper levels in water specimens collected in 1998 for a sample of 10 residents of the Crystal Lakes Manors subdivision are shown in the next column.

a. Construct a 99% confidence interval for the mean lead level in water specimens from Crystal Lake Manors.

b. Construct a 99% confidence interval for the mean copper level in water specimens from Crystal Lake Manors.

c. Interpret the intervals, parts **a** and **b,** in the words of the problem.

d. Discuss the meaning of the phrase, "99% confident."

LEADCOPP.DAT

Lead (μg/L)	Copper (mg/L)
1.32	.508
0	.279
13.1	.320
.919	.904
.657	.221
3.0	.283
1.32	.475
4.09	.130
4.45	.220
0	.743

Source: Hillsborough County Water Department Environmental Laboratory, Tampa, Florida.

5.18 Deloitte & Touche rank the 500 fastest growing technology companies in the United States based on percentage growth over a five-year period. Their rankings are called the *Technology Fast 500.* A random sample of 12 companies from the 1999 *Technology Fast 500* and their growth rates are shown in the table (page 277), followed by a MINITAB analysis of the data.

a. Find a 95% confidence interval for the true mean five-year revenue growth rate for the 1999 *Technology Fast 500.* Interpret the result.

b. In order to estimate the mean described in part **a** with a small-sample confidence interval, what characteristic must the population possess?

c. Explain why the required population characteristics may not hold in this case.

5.19 Accidental spillage and misguided disposal of petroleum wastes have resulted in extensive contamination of soils across the country. A common hazardous compound found in the contaminated soil is benzo(a)pyrene [B(a)p]. An experiment was conducted to determine the effectiveness of a method designed to remove B(a)p from soil (*Journal of Hazardous Materials,* June 1995). Three soil specimens contaminated with a known amount of B(a)p were treated with a toxin that inhibits microbial growth. After 95 days of incubation, the percentage of B(a)p removed from each soil specimen was measured. The experiment produced the following summary statistics: $\bar{x} = 49.3$ and $s = 1.5$.

a. Use a 99% confidence interval to estimate the mean percentage of B(a)p removed from a soil specimen in which the toxin was used.

b. Interpret the interval in terms of this application.

c. What assumption is necessary to ensure the validity of this confidence interval?

5.20 It is customary practice in the United States to base roadway design on the 30th highest hourly volume in a year. Thus, all roadway facilities are expected to operate

FAST500.DAT

Rank	Company	1994–1999 Revenue Growth Rate
4	Netscape Communications	64,240%
22	Primary Network	10,789
89	WebTrends	3,378
160	CTX	1,864
193	ARIS	1,543
268	Iomega	1,098
274	Medarex	1,075
322	World Access	895
359	Force 3	808
396	Theragenics	704
441	Ascent Solutions	630
485	3 Com	555

Source: *Forbes ASAP,* Nov. 29, 1999, pp. 97–111.

MINITAB Output for Exercise 5.18

```
Variable      N      Mean     StDev     SE Mean          95.0% CI
grwthrate    12      7298     18157        5241   (  -4238,   18834)

Stem-and-leaf of grwthrat  N  =  12
Leaf Unit = 1000
  (10)    0 0000011113
   2      1 0
   1      2
   1      3
   1      4
   1      5
   1      6 4
```

at acceptable levels of service for all but 29 hours of the year. The Florida Department of Transportation (DOT), however, has shifted from the 30th highest hour to the 100th highest hour as the basis for level-of-service determinators. Florida Atlantic University researcher Reid Ewing investigated whether this shift was warranted in the *Journal of STAR Research* (July 1994). The table on page 276 gives the traffic counts at the 30th highest hour and the 100th highest hour of a recent year for 20 randomly selected DOT permanent count stations. MINITAB stem-and-leaf plots for the two variables are provided on p. 278 as well as summary statistics and 95% confidence interval printouts.

a. Describe the population from which the sample data is selected.
b. Does the sample appear to be representative of the population? Explain.
c. Locate and interpret the 95% confidence interval for the mean traffic count at the 30th highest hour.
d. What assumption is necessary for the confidence interval to be valid? Does it appear to be satisfied? Explain.
e. Repeat parts **c** and **d** for the 100th highest hour.

5.21 Private and public colleges and universities rely on money contributed by individuals, corporations, and foundations for both salaries and operating expenses. Much of this money is put into a fund called an *endowment,* and the college spends only the interest earned by the fund. A random sample of eight college endowments drawn from the list of endowments in the *Chronicle of Higher Education Almanac* (Sept. 2, 1996) yielded the following endowments (in millions of dollars).

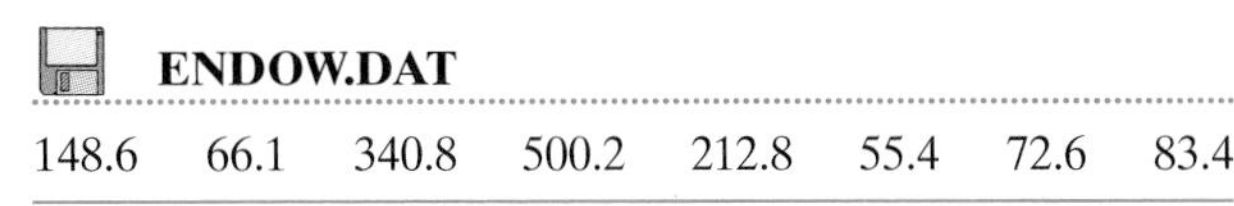

ENDOW.DAT

148.6	66.1	340.8	500.2	212.8	55.4	72.6	83.4

Estimate the mean endowment for this population of colleges and universities using a 95% confidence interval. List any assumptions you make.

5.22 In the late 1990s, the hot market for IPOs—initial public offerings of stock—created billions of dollars of new wealth for owners, managers, and employees of companies that were previously privately owned. Nevertheless,

TRAFFIC.DAT

Station	Type of Route	30th Highest Hour	100th Highest Hour
0117	small city	1,890	1,736
0087	recreational	2,217	2,069
0166	small city	1,444	1,345
0013	rural	2,105	2,049
0161	urban	4,905	4,815
0096	urban	2,022	1,958
0145	rural	594	548
0149	rural	252	229
0038	urban	2,162	2,048
0118	rural	1,938	1,748
0047	rural	879	811
0066	urban	1,913	1,772
0094	rural	3,494	3,403
0105	small city	1,424	1,309
0113	small city	4,571	4,425
0151	urban	3,494	3,359
0159	rural	2,222	2,137
0160	small city	1,076	989
0164	recreational	2,167	2,039
0165	recreational	3,350	3,123

Source: Ewing, R. "Roadway levels of service in an era of growth management." *Journal of STAR Research,* Vol. 3, July 1994, p. 103 (Table 2).

MINITAB Output for Exercise 5.20

```
Stem-and-leaf of Hour30    N = 20
Leaf Unit = 100

    1     0 2
    3     0 58
    6     1 044
    9     1 899
   (6)    2 011122
    5     2
    5     3 344
    2     3
    2     4
    2     4 59

Stem-and-leaf of Hour100   N = 20
Leaf Unit = 100
    1     0 2
    4     0 589
    6     1 33
   10     1 7779
   10     2 00001
    5     2
    5     3 134
    2     3
    2     4 4
    1     4 8

              N     MEAN     STDEV  SE MEAN    95.0 PERCENT C.I.
Hour30       20  2205.95   1223.81   273.65  ( 1633.05, 2778.85)
Hour100      20  2095.60   1203.12   269.02  ( 1532.39, 2658.81)
```

hundreds of large and thousands of small companies remain privately owned. The operating incomes (earnings before interest, taxes, and depreciation) of a random sample of 15 firms from *Forbes* 500 Biggest Private Companies list is given in the table to the right.

a. Describe the population from which the random sample was drawn.
b. Use a 98% confidence interval to estimate the mean operating income of the population of companies in question.
c. Interpret your confidence interval in the context of the problem.
d. What characteristic must the population possess to ensure the appropriateness of the estimation procedure used in part **b?**

BIGCOM.DAT

Company	Operating Income (in millions)
Pacific Coast Building Products	$52
Chef America	72
Brookshire Grocery	45
Penske Truck Leasing	700
E & J Gallo Winery	175
LDI	28
Asplundh Tree Expert	165
Ty	750
American Foods Group	11
Hobby Lobby Creative Centers	73
Weitz	14
Science Applications International	487
Findlay Industries	37
Carlson Companies	250
Quality Stores	55

Source: "Staying Private," *Forbes,* Dec. 13, 1999, pp. 182–240.

5.23 The table at the lower right lists the number of full-time employees at each of 22 office furniture dealers serving Tampa, Florida, and its surrounding communities. Summary statistics for the data are provided in the SAS printout below.

a. Construct a 99% confidence interval for the true mean number of full-time employees at office furniture dealers in Tampa.
b. Interpret the interval, part **a.**
c. Comment on the assumption required for the interval to be valid.
d. The 22 dealers in the sample were the top-ranked furniture dealers in Tampa based on sales volume in 1995. How does this fact impact the validity of the confidence interval? Explain.

OFFURN.DAT

50	78	41	32	35	12	12	15	5	3	5
23	16	24	24	15	12	11	30	43	4	4

Source: Tampa Bay Business Journal, June 21–27, 1996, p. 27.

SAS Output for Exercise 5.23

```
Analysis Variable : NUMEMPLY

N Obs    N        Minimum          Maximum           Mean          Std Dev
---------------------------------------------------------------------------
   22   22      3.0000000       78.0000000     22.4545455       18.5182722
---------------------------------------------------------------------------
```

5.3 LARGE-SAMPLE CONFIDENCE INTERVAL FOR A POPULATION PROPORTION

The number of public opinion polls has grown at an astounding rate in recent years. Almost daily, the news media report the results of some poll. Pollsters regularly determine the percentage of people who approve of the president's on-the-job performance, the fraction of voters in favor of a certain candidate, the fraction of customers who prefer a particular product, and the proportion of households that watch a particular TV program. In each case, we are interested in estimating the percentage (or proportion) of some group with a certain characteristic. In this section we consider methods for making inferences about population proportions when the sample is large.

EXAMPLE 5.3

A food-products company conducted a market study by randomly sampling and interviewing 1,000 consumers to determine which brand of breakfast cereal they prefer. Suppose 313 consumers were found to prefer the company's brand. How would you estimate the true fraction of *all* consumers who prefer the company's cereal brand?

Solution

What we have really asked is how you would estimate the probability p of success in a binomial experiment, where p is the probability that a chosen consumer prefers the company's brand. One logical method of estimating p for the population is to use the proportion of successes in the sample. That is, we can estimate p by calculating

$$\hat{p} = \frac{\text{Number of consumers sampled who prefer the company's brand}}{\text{Number of consumers sampled}}$$

where $\hat{p}$ is read "p hat." Thus, in this case,

$$\hat{p} = \frac{313}{1{,}000} = .313$$

To determine the reliability of the estimator $\hat{p}$, we need to know its sampling distribution. That is, if we were to draw samples of 1,000 consumers over and over again, each time calculating a new estimate $\hat{p}$, what would be the frequency distribution of all the $\hat{p}$ values? The answer lies in viewing $\hat{p}$ as the average, or mean, number of successes per trial over the n trials. If each success is assigned a value equal to 1 and a failure is assigned a value of 0, then the sum of all n sample observations is x, the total number of successes, and $\hat{p} = x/n$ is the average, or mean, number of successes per trial in the n trials. The Central Limit Theorem tells us that the relative frequency distribution of the sample mean for any population is approximately normal for sufficiently large samples. ✶

The repeated sampling distribution of $\hat{p}$ has the characteristics listed in the next box and shown in Figure 5.12.

Sampling Distribution of $\hat{p}$

1. The mean of the sampling distribution of $\hat{p}$ is p; that is, $\hat{p}$ is an unbiased estimator of p.
2. The standard deviation of the sampling distribution of $\hat{p}$ is $\sqrt{pq/n}$; that is, $\sigma_{\hat{p}} = \sqrt{pq/n}$, where $q = 1 - p$.
3. For large samples, the sampling distribution of $\hat{p}$ is approximately normal. A sample size is considered large if the interval $\hat{p} \pm 3\sigma_{\hat{p}}$ does not include 0 or 1. [*Note*: This requirement is almost equivalent to that given in optional Section 4.9 for approximating a binomial distribution with a normal one. The difference is that we assumed p to be known in optional Section 4.9; now we are trying to make inferences about an unknown p, so we use $\hat{p}$ to estimate p in checking the adequacy of the normal approximation.]

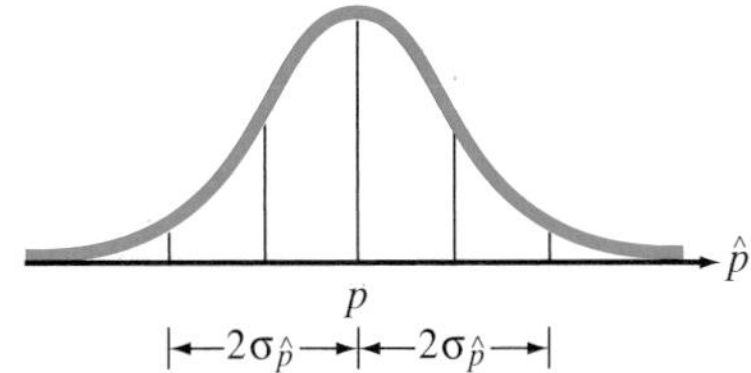

FIGURE 5.12
Sampling distribution of $\hat{p}$

The fact that $\hat{p}$ is a "sample mean number of successes per trial" allows us to form confidence intervals about p in a manner that is completely analogous to that used for large-sample estimation of μ.

Large-Sample Confidence Interval for p

$$\hat{p} \pm z_{\alpha/2}\sigma_{\hat{p}} = \hat{p} \pm z_{\alpha/2}\sqrt{\frac{pq}{n}} \approx \hat{p} \pm z_{\alpha/2}\sqrt{\frac{\hat{p}\hat{q}}{n}}$$

where $\hat{p} = \frac{x}{n}$ and $\hat{q} = 1 - \hat{p}$

Note: When n is large, $\hat{p}$ can approximate the value of p in the formula for $\sigma_{\hat{p}}$.

Thus, if 313 of 1,000 consumers prefer the company's cereal brand, a 95% confidence interval for the proportion of *all* consumers who prefer the company's brand is

$$\hat{p} \pm z_{\alpha/2}\sigma_{\hat{p}} = .313 \pm \sqrt{\frac{pq}{1{,}000}}$$

where $q = 1 - p$. Just as we needed an approximation for σ in calculating a large-sample confidence interval for μ, we now need an approximation for p. As Table 5.5 shows, the approximation for p does not have to be especially accurate, because the value of $\sqrt{pq}$ needed for the confidence interval is relatively insensitive to changes in p. Therefore, we can use $\hat{p}$ to approximate p. Keeping in mind that $\hat{q} = 1 - \hat{p}$, we substitute these values into the formula for the confidence interval:

TABLE 5.5 Values of pq for Several Different Values of p

p	pq	$\sqrt{pq}$
.5	.25	.50
.6 or .4	.24	.49
.7 or .3	.21	.46
.8 or .2	.16	.40
.9 or .1	.09	.30

$$\hat{p} \pm 1.96\sqrt{\frac{pq}{1{,}000}} \approx \hat{p} \pm 1.96\sqrt{\frac{\hat{p}\hat{q}}{1{,}000}}$$

$$= .313 \pm 1.96\sqrt{\frac{(.313)(.687)}{1{,}000}}$$

$$= .313 \pm .029$$

$$= (.284, .342)$$

The company can be 95% confident that the interval from 28.4% to 34.2% contains the true percentage of *all* consumers who prefer its brand. That is, in repeated construction of confidence intervals, approximately 95% of all samples would produce confidence intervals that enclose p. Note that the guidelines for interpreting a confidence interval about μ also apply to interpreting a confidence interval for p because p is the "population fraction of successes" in a binomial experiment.

EXAMPLE 5.4 Many public polling agencies conduct surveys to determine the current consumer sentiment concerning the state of the economy. For example, the Bureau of Economic and Business Research (BEBR) at the University of Florida conducts quarterly surveys to gauge consumer sentiment in the Sunshine State. Suppose that BEBR randomly samples 484 consumers and finds that 257 are optimistic about the state of the economy. Use a 90% confidence interval to estimate the proportion of all consumers in Florida who are optimistic about the state of the economy. Based on the confidence interval, can BEBR infer that the majority of Florida consumers are optimistic about the economy?

Solution The number, x, of the 484 sampled consumers who are optimistic about the Florida economy is a binomial random variable if we can assume that the sample was randomly selected from the population of Florida consumers and that the poll was conducted identically for each sampled consumer.

The point estimate of the proportion of Florida consumers who are optimistic about the economy is

$$\hat{p} = \frac{x}{n} = \frac{257}{484} = .531$$

We first check to be sure that the sample size is sufficiently large that the normal distribution provides a reasonable approximation for the sampling distribution of $\hat{p}$. We check the 3-standard-deviation interval around $\hat{p}$:

$$\hat{p} \pm 3\sigma_{\hat{p}} \approx \hat{p} \pm 3\sqrt{\frac{\hat{p}\hat{q}}{n}}$$

$$= .531 \pm 3\sqrt{\frac{(.531)(.469)}{484}} = .531 \pm .068 = (.463, .599)$$

Since this interval is wholly contained in the interval (0, 1), we may conclude that the normal approximation is reasonable.

We now proceed to form the 90% confidence interval for p, the true proportion of Florida consumers who are optimistic about the state of the economy:

$$\hat{p} \pm z_{\alpha/2}\sigma_{\hat{p}} = \hat{p} \pm z_{\alpha/2}\sqrt{\frac{pq}{n}} \approx \hat{p} \pm z_{\alpha/2}\sqrt{\frac{\hat{p}\hat{q}}{n}}$$

$$= .531 \pm 1.645\sqrt{\frac{(.531)(.469)}{484}} = .531 \pm .037 = (.494, .568)$$

Thus, we can be 90% confident that the proportion of all Florida consumers who are confident about the economy is between .494 and .568. As always, our confidence stems from the fact that 90% of all similarly formed intervals will contain the true proportion p and not from any knowledge about whether this particular interval does.

Can we conclude that the majority of Florida consumers are optimistic about the economy based on this interval? If we wished to use this interval to infer that a majority is optimistic, the interval would have to support the inference that p exceeds .5—that is, that more than 50% of the Florida consumers are optimistic about the economy. Note that the interval contains some values below .5 (as low as .494) as well as some above .5 (as high as .568). Therefore, we cannot conclude that the true value of p exceeds .5 based on this 90% confidence interval. ✶

Caution: Unless n is extremely large, the large-sample procedure presented in this section performs poorly when p is near 0 or 1. For example, suppose you want to estimate the proportion of executives who die from a work-related injury. This proportion is likely to be near 0 (say, $p \approx .001$). Confidence intervals for p based on a sample of size $n = 50$ will probably be misleading.

To overcome this potential problem, an *extremely* large sample size is required. Since the value of n required to satisfy "extremely large" is difficult to determine, statisticians (see Agresti & Coull, 1998) have proposed an alternative method, based on the Wilson (1927) point estimator of p. The procedure is outlined in the box. Researchers have shown that this confidence interval works well for any p even when the sample size n is very small.

Adjusted 100(1 − α)% Confidence Interval for a Population Proportion, *p*

$$\tilde{p} \pm z_{\alpha/2}\sqrt{\frac{\tilde{p}(1-\tilde{p})}{n+4}}$$

where $\tilde{p} = \frac{x+2}{n+4}$ is the adjusted sample proportion of observations with the characteristic of interest, x is the number of successes in the sample, and n is the sample size.

EXAMPLE 5.5

According to *True Odds: How Risk Affects Your Everyday Life* (Walsh, 1997), the probability of being the victim of a violent crime is less than .01. Suppose that in a random sample of 200 Americans, 3 were victims of a violent crime. Estimate the true proportion of Americans who were victims of a violent crime using a 95% confidence interval.

Solution

Let p represent the true proportion of Americans who were victims of a violent crime. Since p is near 0, an "extremely large" sample is required to estimate its value using the usual large-sample method. Since we are unsure whether the sample size of 200 is large enough, we will apply the adjustment outlined in the box.

The number of "successes" (i.e., number of violent crime victims) in the sample is $x = 3$. Therefore, the adjusted sample proportion is

$$\tilde{p} = \frac{x+2}{n+4} = \frac{3+2}{200+4} = \frac{5}{204} = .025$$

Note that this adjusted sample proportion is obtained by adding a total of four observations—two "successes" and two "failures"—to the sample data. Substituting $\tilde{p} = .025$ into the equation for a 95% confidence interval, we obtain

$$\tilde{p} \pm 1.96\sqrt{\frac{\tilde{p}(1-\tilde{p})}{n+4}} = .025 \pm 1.96\sqrt{\frac{(.025)(.975)}{204}}$$

$$= .025 \pm .021$$

or (.004, .046). Consequently, we are 95% confident that the true proportion of Americans who are victims of a violent crime falls between .004 and .046.

Confidence Interval for a Population Proportion

USING THE TI-83 GRAPHING CALCULATOR

Confidence Intervals for Proportions on the TI-83

You can find confidence intervals for proportions using the **1-PropZInt** command in the **STAT TESTS** Menu.

Step 1 Select the appropriate type of confidence interval
Press **STAT** and highlight **TESTS**
Use the arrow keys to highlight **A:1-PropZInt**
Press **ENTER**

Step 2 Determine your values for x, n and confidence level
Enter these values for $\boldsymbol{x}$, $\boldsymbol{n}$ and **C-Level**
where $\boldsymbol{x}$ = number of successes
$\boldsymbol{n}$ = sample size
C-Level = level of confidence

Step 3 Calculate the confidence interval
Highlight **Calculate**
Press **ENTER**

Example Suppose that 1,100 U.S. citizens are randomly chosen and 532 answer that they favor a flat income tax rate. Use a 95% confidence interval to estimate the true proportion of citizens who favor a flat income tax rate. In this example, $x = 532$, $n = 1{,}100$ and C-Level = .95
The TI-83 screens for this example are shown below.

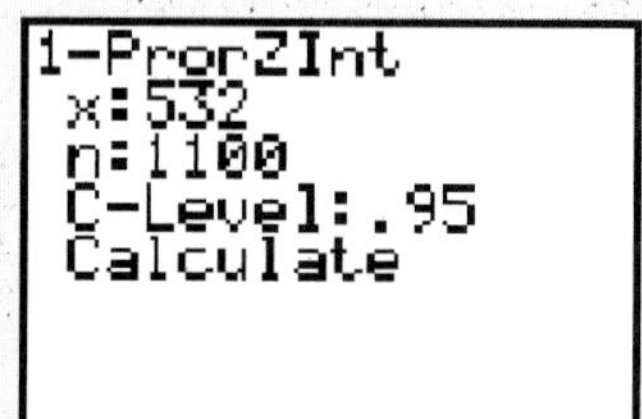

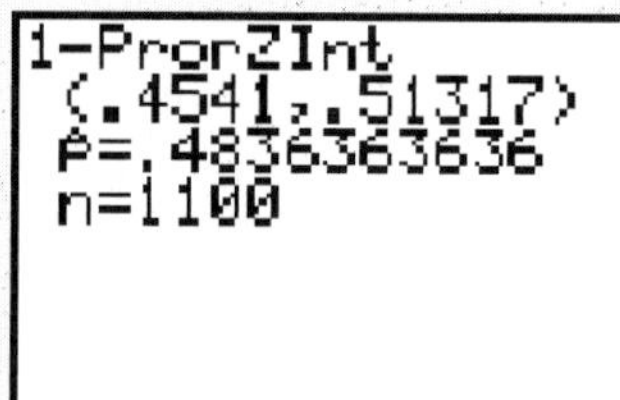

Thus, we can be 95% confident that the interval from 45.4% to 51.3% contains the true percentage of all U.S. citizens who favor a flat income tax rate.

EXERCISES 5.24–5.34

Learning the Mechanics

5.24 A random sample of size $n = 121$ yielded $\hat{p} = .88$.

a. Is the sample size large enough to use the methods of this section to construct a confidence interval for p? Explain.

b. Construct a 90% confidence interval for p.

c. What assumption is necessary to ensure the validity of this confidence interval?

5.25 For the binomial sample information summarized in each part, indicate whether the sample size is large enough to use the methods of this chapter to construct a confidence interval for p.

a. $n = 400, \hat{p} = .10$ b. $n = 50, \hat{p} = .10$
c. $n = 20, \hat{p} = .5$ d. $n = 20, \hat{p} = .3$

5.26 A random sample of 50 consumers taste tested a new snack food. Their responses were coded (0: do not like; 1: like; 2: indifferent) and recorded as follows:

SNACK.DAT

1	0	0	1	2	0	1	1	0	0
0	1	0	2	0	2	2	0	0	1
1	0	0	0	0	1	0	2	0	0
0	1	0	0	1	0	0	1	0	1
0	2	0	0	1	1	0	0	0	1

a. Use an 80% confidence interval to estimate the proportion of consumers who like the snack food.
b. Provide a statistical interpretation for the confidence interval you constructed in part **a.**

5.27 A random sample of size $n = 225$ yielded $\hat{p} = .46$.
a. Is the sample size large enough to use the methods of this section to construct a confidence interval for p? Explain.
b. Construct a 95% confidence interval for p.
c. Interpret the 95% confidence interval.
d. Explain what is meant by the phrase "95% confidence interval."

Applying the Concepts

5.28 The Gallup Organization surveyed 1,252 debit cardholders in the United States and found that 180 had used the debit card to purchase a product or service on the Internet (*Card Fax,* November 12, 1999).
a. Describe the population of interest to the Gallup Organization.
b. If you personally were charged with drawing a random sample from this population, what difficulties would you encounter? Assume in the remainder of the exercise that the 1,252 debit cardholders were randomly selected.
c. Is the sample size large enough to construct a valid confidence interval for the proportion of debit cardholders who have used their card in making purchases over the Internet? Justify your answer.
d. Estimate the proportion referred to in part **c** using a 98% confidence interval. Interpret your result in the context of the problem.
e. If you had constructed a 90% confidence interval instead, would it be wider or narrower?

5.29 As Internet usage proliferates, so do questions of security and confidentiality of personal information, including such things as social security and credit card numbers. NCR Corporation surveyed 1,000 U.S. adults and asked them under what circumstances they would give personal information to a company. Twenty-nine percent said they would never give personal data to a company, while 51% said they would if the company had strict privacy guidelines in place (*Precision Marketing,* Oct. 4, 1999).
a. Verify that the sample size is large enough to construct a valid confidence interval for p, the proportion of all U.S. adults who would never give personal information to a company.
b. Construct a 95% confidence interval for p and interpret your result in the context of the problem.
c. Other than the size of the sample, what assumption must be made about the sample in order for the estimation procedure of part **b** to be valid?

5.30 By law, all new cars must be equipped with both driver-side and passenger-side safety air bags. There is concern, however, over whether air bags pose a danger for children sitting on the passenger side. In a National Highway Traffic Safety Administration (NHTSA) study of 55 people killed by the explosive force of air bags, 35 were children seated on the front-passenger side (*Wall Street Journal,* Jan. 22, 1997). This study led some car owners with children to disconnect the passenger-side air bag. Consider all fatal automobile accidents in which it is determined that air bags were the cause of death. Let p represent the true proportion of these accidents involving children seated on the front-passenger side.
a. Use the data from the NHTSA study to estimate p.
b. Construct a 99% confidence interval for p.
c. Interpret the interval, part **b,** in the words of the problem.
d. NHTSA investigators determined that 24 of 35 children killed by the air bags were not wearing seat belts or were improperly restrained. How does this information impact your assessment of the risk of an air bag fatality?

5.31 Refer to the *Marine Technology* (Jan. 1995) study of the causes of fifty recent major oil spills from tankers and carriers, Exercise 2.10 (p. 34). Recall that 12 of the spills were caused by hull failure.
a. Give a point estimate for the proportion of major oil spills that are caused by hull failure.
b. Form a 95% confidence interval for the estimate, part **a.** Interpret the result.

5.32 Refer to the Federal Trade Commission (FTC) 1998 "Price Check" study of electronic checkout scanners, Exercise 4.30 (p. 192). The FTC inspected 1,669 scanners at retail stores and supermarkets by scanning a sample of items at each store and determining if the scanned price was accurate. The FTC gives a store a "passing" grade if 98% or more of the items are priced accurately. Of the 1,669 stores in the study, 1,185 passed inspection.
a. Find a 90% confidence interval for the true proportion of retail stores and supermarkets with electronic scanners that pass the FTC price-check test. Interpret the result.
b. In 1996, the FTC found that 45% of the stores passed inspection. Use the interval from part **a** to determine whether the proportion of stores that pass inspection in 1998 exceeds .45.

5.33 The accounting firm of Price Waterhouse annually monitors the U.S. Postal Service's performance. One parameter of interest is the percentage of mail delivered on time. In a sample of 332,000 items mailed between Dec. 10 and Mar. 3—the most difficult delivery season due to bad weather and holidays—Price Waterhouse determined that 282,200 items were delivered on time (*Tampa Tribune,* Mar. 26, 1995). Use this information to estimate with 99% confidence the true percentage of items delivered on time by the U.S. Postal Service. Interpret the result.

5.34 Family-owned companies are notorious for having difficulties in transferring control from one generation to the next. Part of this problem can be traced to lack of a well-documented strategic business plan. In a survey of 3,900 privately held family firms with revenues exceeding $1,000,000 a year, Arthur Andersen, the international accounting and consulting firm, found that 1,911 had no strategic business plan (*Minneapolis Star Tribune,* Sept. 4, 1995).

a. Describe the population studied by Arthur Andersen.

b. Assume the 3,900 firms were randomly sampled from the population. Use a 90% confidence interval to estimate the proportion of family-owned companies without strategic business plans.

c. How wide is the 90% confidence interval you constructed in part **b?** Would an 80% confidence interval be wider or narrower? Justify your answer.

5.4 DETERMINING THE SAMPLE SIZE

Recall (Section 1.5) that one way to collect the relevant data for a study used to make inferences about the population is to implement a designed (planned) experiment. Perhaps the most important design decision faced by the analyst is to determine the size of the sample. We show in this section that the appropriate sample size for making an inference about a population mean or proportion depends on the desired reliability.

Estimating a Population Mean

Consider the example from Section 5.1 in which we estimated the mean overdue amount for all delinquent accounts in a large credit corporation. A sample of 100 delinquent accounts produced the 95% confidence interval: $\bar{x} \pm 2\sigma_{\bar{x}} \approx 233.28 \pm 18.07$. Consequently, our estimate $\bar{x}$ was within $18.07 of the true mean amount due, μ, for all the delinquent accounts at the 95% confidence level. That is, the 95% confidence interval for μ was $2(18.07) = \$36.14$ wide when 100 accounts were sampled. This is illustrated in Figure 5.13a.

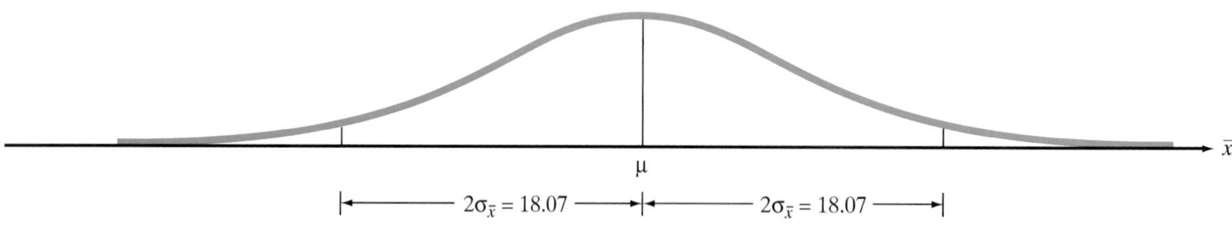

a. $n = 100$

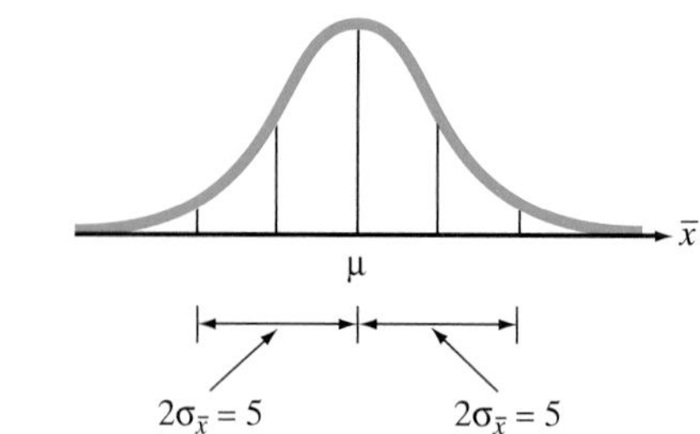

b. $n = 1{,}306$

FIGURE 5.13
Relationship between sample size and width of confidence interval: Delinquent debtors example

Now suppose we want to estimate μ to within \$5 with 95% confidence. That is, we want to narrow the width of the confidence interval from \$36.14 to \$5, as shown in Figure 5.13b. How much will the sample size have to be increased to accomplish this? If we want the estimator $\bar{x}$ to be within \$5 of μ, we must have

$$2\sigma_{\bar{x}} = 5 \qquad \text{or, equivalently,} \qquad 2\left(\frac{\sigma}{\sqrt{n}}\right) = 5$$

The necessary sample size is obtained by solving this equation for n. To do this we need an approximation for σ. We have an approximation from the initial sample of 100 accounts—namely, the sample standard deviation, $s = 90.34$. Thus,

$$2\left(\frac{\sigma}{\sqrt{n}}\right) \approx 2\left(\frac{s}{\sqrt{n}}\right) = 2\left(\frac{90.34}{\sqrt{n}}\right) = 5$$

$$\sqrt{n} = \frac{2(90.34)}{5} = 36.136$$

$$n = (36.136)^2 = 1{,}305.81 \approx 1{,}306$$

Approximately 1,306 accounts will have to be randomly sampled to estimate the mean overdue amount μ to within \$5 with (approximately) 95% confidence. The confidence interval resulting from a sample of this size will be approximately \$10 wide (see Figure 5.13b).

In general, we express the reliability associated with a confidence interval for the population mean μ by specifying the **bound, B,** within which we want to estimate μ with $100(1 - \alpha)\%$ confidence. The bound B then is equal to the half-width of the confidence interval, as shown in Figure 5.14.

FIGURE 5.14
Specifying the bound B as the half-width of a confidence interval

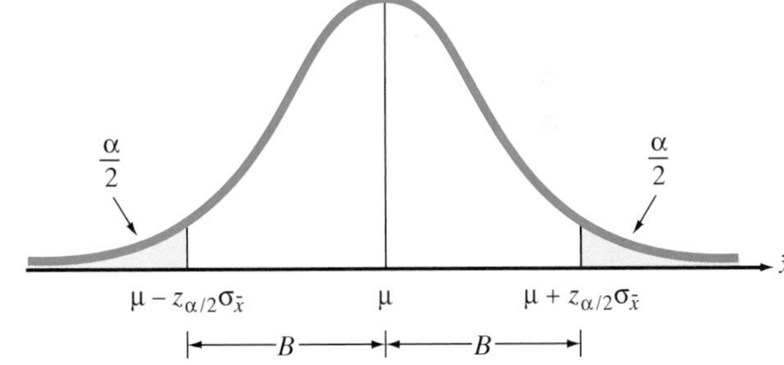

The procedure for finding the sample size necessary to estimate μ to within a given bound B is given in the box.

Sample Size Determination for $100(1 - \alpha)\%$ Confidence Interval for μ

In order to estimate μ to within a bound B with $100(1 - \alpha)\%$ confidence, the required sample size is found as follows:

$$z_{\alpha/2}\left(\frac{\sigma}{\sqrt{n}}\right) = B$$

(continued)

The solution can be written in terms of B as follows:

$$n = \frac{(z_{\alpha/2})^2\sigma^2}{B^2}$$

The value of σ is usually unknown. It can be estimated by the standard deviation, s, from a prior sample. Alternatively, we may approximate the range R of observations in the population, and (conservatively) estimate $\sigma \approx R/4$. In any case, you should round the value of n obtained *upward* to ensure that the sample size will be sufficient to achieve the specified reliability.

EXAMPLE 5.6

The manufacturer of official NFL footballs uses a machine to inflate its new balls to a pressure of 13.5 pounds. When the machine is properly calibrated, the mean inflation pressure is 13.5 pounds, but uncontrollable factors cause the pressures of individual footballs to vary randomly from about 13.3 to 13.7 pounds. For quality control purposes, the manufacturer wishes to estimate the mean inflation pressure to within .025 pound of its true value with a 99% confidence interval. What sample size should be used?

Solution We desire a 99% confidence interval that estimates μ to within $B = .025$ pound of its true value. For a 99% confidence interval, we have $z_{\alpha/2} = z_{.005} = 2.575$. To estimate σ, we note that the range of observations is $R = 13.7 - 13.3 = .4$ and use $\sigma \approx R/4 = .1$. Now we use the formula derived in the box to find the sample size n:

$$n = \frac{(z_{\alpha/2})^2\sigma^2}{B^2} \approx \frac{(2.575)^2(.1)^2}{(.025)^2} = 106.09$$

We round this up to $n = 107$. Realizing that σ was approximated by $R/4$, we might even advise that the sample size be specified as $n = 110$ to be more certain of attaining the objective of a 99% confidence interval with bound $B = .025$ pound or less.

Sometimes the formula will yield a small sample size ($n < 25$). Unfortunately, this solution is invalid because the procedures and assumptions for small samples differ from those for large samples, as we discovered in Section 5.2. Therefore, if the formulas yield a small sample size, one simple strategy is to select a sample size $n = 30$.

Estimating a Population Proportion

The method outlined above is easily applied to a population proportion p. For example, in Section 5.3 a company used a sample of 1,000 consumers to calculate a 95% confidence interval for the proportion of consumers who preferred its cereal brand, obtaining the interval $.313 \pm .029$. Suppose the company wishes to estimate its market share more precisely, say to within .015 with a 95% confidence interval.

The company wants a confidence interval with a bound B on the estimate of p of $B = .015$. The sample size required to generate such an interval is found by solving the following equation for n:

$$z_{\alpha/2}\sigma_{\hat{p}} = B \qquad \text{or} \qquad z_{\alpha/2}\sqrt{\frac{pq}{n}} = .015 \qquad \text{(see Figure 5.15)}$$

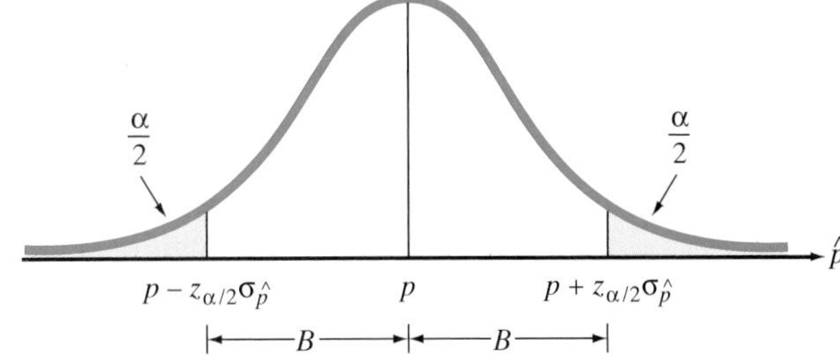

FIGURE 5.15 Specifying the bound B of a confidence interval for a population proportion p

Since a 95% confidence interval is desired, the appropriate z value is $z_{\alpha/2} = z_{.025} = 1.96 \approx 2$. We must approximate the value of the product pq before we can solve the equation for n. As shown in Table 5.5, the closer the values of p and q to .5, the larger the product pq. Thus, to find a conservatively large sample size that will generate a confidence interval with the specified reliability, we generally choose an approximation of p close to .5. In the case of the food-products company, however, we have an initial sample estimate of $\hat{p} = .313$. A conservatively large estimate of pq can therefore be obtained by using, say, $p = .35$. We now substitute into the equation and solve for n:

$$2\sqrt{\frac{(.35)(.65)}{n}} = .015$$

$$n = \frac{(2)^2(.35)(.65)}{(.015)^2}$$

$$= 4{,}044.44 \approx 4{,}045$$

The company must sample about 4,045 consumers to estimate the percentage who prefer its brand to within .015 with a 95% confidence interval.

The procedure for finding the sample size necessary to estimate a population proportion p to within a given bound B is given in the box.

Sample Size Determination for 100 $(1 - \alpha)$% Confidence Interval for p

In order to estimate a binomial probability p to within a bound B with $100(1 - \alpha)$% confidence, the required sample size is found by solving the following equation for n:

$$z_{\alpha/2}\sqrt{\frac{pq}{n}} = B$$

The solution can be written in terms of B:

$$n = \frac{(z_{\alpha/2})^2(pq)}{B^2}$$

Since the value of the product pq is unknown, it can be estimated by using the sample fraction of successes, $\hat{p}$, from a prior sample. Remember (Table 5.5) that the value of pq is at its maximum when p equals .5, so that you can obtain conservatively large values of n by approximating p by .5 or values close to .5. In any case, you should round the value of n obtained *upward* to ensure that the sample size will be sufficient to achieve the specified reliability.

EXAMPLE 5.7

A cellular telephone manufacturer that entered the postregulation market too quickly has an initial problem with excessive customer complaints and consequent returns of the cell phones for repair or replacement. The manufacturer wants to determine the magnitude of the problem in order to estimate its warranty liability. How many cellular telephones should the company randomly sample from its warehouse and check in order to estimate the fraction defective, p, to within .01 with 90% confidence?

Solution

In order to estimate p to within a bound of .01, we set the half-width of the confidence interval equal to $B = .01$, as shown in Figure 5.16.

The equation for the sample size n requires an estimate of the product pq. We could most conservatively estimate $pq = .25$ (i.e., use $p = .5$), but this may be overly conservative when estimating a fraction defective. A value of .1, corresponding to 10% defective, will probably be conservatively large for this application. The solution is therefore

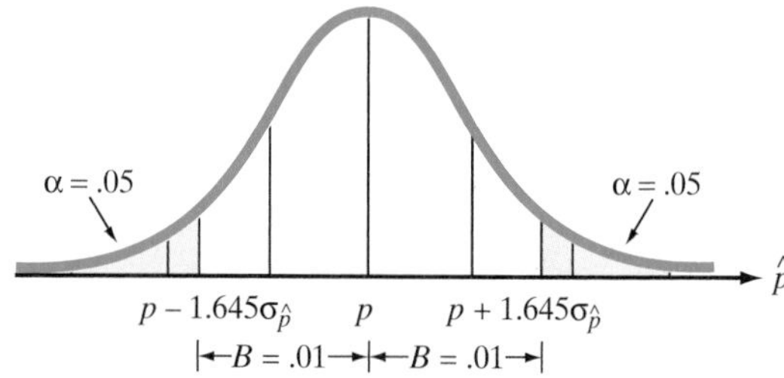

FIGURE 5.16
Specified reliability for estimate of fraction defective in Example 5.7

$$n = \frac{(z_{\alpha/2})^2(pq)}{B^2} = \frac{(1.645)^2(.1)(.9)}{(.01)^2} = 2{,}435.4 \approx 2{,}436$$

Thus, the manufacturer should sample 2,436 cellular telephones in order to estimate the fraction defective, p, to within .01 with 90% confidence. Remember that this answer depends on our approximation for pq, where we used .09. If the fraction defective is closer to .05 than .10, we can use a sample of 1,286 cell phones (check this) to estimate p to within .01 with 90% confidence.

The cost of sampling will also play an important role in the final determination of the sample size to be selected to estimate either μ or p. Although more complex formulas can be derived to balance the reliability and cost considerations, we will solve for the necessary sample size and note that the sampling budget may be a limiting factor. Consult the references for a more complete treatment of this problem.

EXERCISES 5.35–5.48

Learning the Mechanics

5.35 If you wish to estimate a population mean to within a bound $B = .3$ using a 95% confidence interval and you know from prior sampling that σ^2 is approximately equal to 7.2, how many observations would have to be included in your sample?

5.36 If nothing is known about p, .5 can be substituted for p in the sample-size formula for a population proportion. But when this is done, the resulting sample size may be larger than needed. Under what circumstances will using $p = .5$ in the sample-size formula yield a sample size larger than needed to construct a confidence interval for p with a specified bound and a specified confidence level?

5.37 Suppose you wish to estimate a population mean correct to within a bound $B = .20$ with probability equal to .90. You do not know σ^2, but you know that the observations will range in value between 30 and 34.

a. Find the approximate sample size that will produce the desired accuracy of the estimate. You wish to be conservative to ensure that the sample size will be ample to achieve the desired accuracy of the estimate. [*Hint:* Using your knowledge of data variation from Section 2.6, assume that the range of the observations will equal 4σ.]

b. Calculate the approximate sample size making the less conservative assumption that the range of the observations is equal to 6σ.

5.38 In each case, find the approximate sample size required to construct a 95% confidence interval for p that has bound $B = .08$.

a. Assume p is near .2.

b. Assume you have no prior knowledge about p, but you wish to be certain that your sample is large enough to achieve the specified accuracy for the estimate.

5.39 The following is a 90% confidence interval for p: (.26, .54). How large was the sample used to construct this interval?

5.40 Suppose you wish to estimate the mean of a normal population using a 95% confidence interval, and you know from prior information that $\sigma^2 \approx 1$.

a. To see the effect of the sample size on the width of the confidence interval, calculate the width of the confidence interval for $n = 16, 25, 49, 100$, and 400.

b. Plot the width as a function of sample size n on graph paper. Connect the points by a smooth curve and note how the width decreases as n increases.

Applying the Concepts

5.41 Do you pay for certain Web services? Georgia Institute of Technology's Graphics Visualization and Usability Center surveyed 13,000 Internet users and asked them about their willingness to pay fees for access to Web sites. Of these, 2,938 were definitely not willing to pay such fees (*Inc. Technology,* No. 3, 1995).

a. Assume the 13,000 users were randomly selected. Construct a 95% confidence interval for the proportion definitely unwilling to pay fees.

b. What is the width of the interval you constructed in part **a?** For most applications, this width is unnecessarily narrow. What does that suggest about the survey's sample size?

c. How large a sample size is necessary to estimate the proportion of interest to within 2% with 95% confidence?

5.42 The EPA wants to test a randomly selected sample of n water specimens and estimate the mean daily rate of pollution produced by a mining operation. If the EPA wants a 95% confidence interval estimate with a bound on the error of 1 milligram per liter (mg/L), how many water specimens are required in the sample? Assume prior knowledge indicates that pollution readings in water samples taken during a day are approximately normally distributed with a standard deviation equal to 5 mg/L.

5.43 A gigantic warehouse located in Tampa, Florida, stores approximately 60 million empty aluminum beer and soda cans. Recently, a fire occurred at the warehouse. The smoke from the fire contaminated many of the cans with blackspot, rendering them unusable. A University of South Florida statistician was hired by the insurance company to estimate the true proportion of cans in the warehouse that were contaminated by the fire. How many aluminum cans should be randomly sampled to estimate the true proportion to within .02 with 90% confidence?

5.44 In a survey conducted for *Money* magazine by the ICR Survey Research Group, 26% of parents with college-bound high school children reported not having saved any money for college. The poll had a "... margin of error of plus or minus 4 percentage points" (*Newark Star-Ledger,* Aug. 16, 1996).

a. Assume that random sampling was used in conducting the survey and that the researchers wanted to have 95% confidence in their results. Estimate the sample size used in the survey.

b. Repeat part **a,** but this time assume the researchers wanted to be 99% confident.

5.45 A large food-products company receives about 100,000 phone calls a year from consumers on its toll-free number. A computer monitors and records how many rings it takes for an operator to answer, how much time each caller spends "on hold," and other data. However, the reliability of the monitoring system has been called into question by the operators and their labor union. As a check on the computer system, approximately how many calls should be manually monitored during the next year to estimate the true mean time that callers spend on hold to within 3 seconds with 95% confidence? Answer this question for the following values of the standard deviation of waiting times (in seconds): 10, 20, and 30.

5.46 The United States Golf Association (USGA) tests all new brands of golf balls to ensure that they meet USGA specifications. One test conducted is intended to measure the average distance traveled when the ball is hit by a machine called "Iron Byron," a name inspired by the swing of the famous golfer Byron Nelson. Suppose the USGA wishes to estimate the mean distance for a new brand to within 1 yard with 90% confidence. Assume that past tests have indicated that the standard deviation of the distances Iron Byron hits golf balls is approximately 10 yards. How many golf balls should be hit by Iron Byron to achieve the desired accuracy in estimating the mean?

STATISTICS IN Action

Scallops, Sampling, and the Law

Arnold Bennett, a Sloan School of Management professor at the Massachusetts Institute of Technology (MIT), describes a recent legal case in which he served as a statistical "expert" in *Interfaces* (Mar.–Apr. 1995). The case involved a ship that fishes for scallops off the coast of New England. In order to protect baby scallops from being harvested, the U.S. Fisheries and Wildlife Service requires that "the average meat per scallop weigh at least $\frac{1}{36}$ of a pound." The ship was accused of violating this weight standard. Bennett lays out the scenario:

> *The vessel arrived at a Massachusetts port with 11,000 bags of scallops, from which the harbormaster randomly selected 18 bags for weighing. From each such bag, his agents took a large scoopful of scallops; then, to estimate the bag's average meat per scallop, they divided the total weight of meat in the scoopful by the number of scallops it contained. Based on the 18 [numbers] thus generated, the harbormaster estimated that each of the ship's scallops possessed an average $\frac{1}{39}$ of a pound of meat (that is, they were about seven percent lighter than the minimum requirement). Viewing this outcome as conclusive evidence that the weight standard had been violated, federal authorities at once confiscated* 95 percent *of the catch (which they then sold at auction). The fishing voyage was thus transformed into a financial catastrophe for its participants.*

Bennett provided the actual scallop weight measurements for each of the 18 sampled bags in the article. The data are listed in Table 5.6. For ease of exposition, Bennett expressed each number as a multiple of $\frac{1}{36}$ of a pound, the minimum permissible average weight per scallop. Consequently, numbers below one indicate individual bags that do not meet the standard.

 SCALLOPS.DAT

TABLE 5.6 Scallop Weight Measurements for 18 Bags Sampled

.93	.88	.85	.91	.91	.84	.90	.98	.88
.89	.98	.87	.91	.92	.99	1.14	1.06	.93

Source: Bennett, A. "Misapplications review: Jail terms." *Interfaces*, Vol. 25, No. 2, March–April 1995, p. 20.

The ship's owner filed a lawsuit against the federal government, declaring that his vessel had fully complied with the weight standard. A Boston law firm was hired to represent the owner in legal proceedings and Bennett was retained by the firm to provide statistical litigation support and, if necessary, expert witness testimony.

Focus

a. Recall that the harbormaster sampled only 18 of the ship's 11,000 bags of scallops. One of the questions the lawyers asked Bennett was: "Can a reliable estimate of the mean weight of all the scallops be obtained from a sample of size 18?" Give your opinion on this issue.

b. As stated in the article, the government's decision rule is to confiscate a scallop catch if the sample mean weight of the scallops is less than $\frac{1}{36}$ of a pound. Do you see any flaws in this rule?

c. Develop your own procedure for determining whether a ship is in violation of the minimum weight restriction. Apply your rule to the data in Table 5.6. Draw a conclusion about the ship in question.

5.47 Does the caffeine in coffee, tea, and cola induce an addiction similar to that induced by alcohol, tobacco, heroine, and cocaine? In an attempt to answer this question, researchers at Johns Hopkins University examined 27 caffeine drinkers and found 25 who displayed some type of withdrawal symptoms when abstaining from caffeine. [*Note:* The 27 caffeine drinkers volunteered for the study.] Furthermore, of 11 caffeine drinkers who were diagnosed as caffeine dependent, 8 displayed dramatic withdrawal symptoms (including impairment in normal functioning) when they consumed a caffeine-free diet in a controlled setting. The National Coffee Association claimed, however, that the study group was too small to draw conclusions (*Los Angeles Times*, Oct. 5, 1994). Is the sample large enough to estimate the true proportion of caffeine drinkers who are caffeine dependent to within .05 of the true value with 99% confidence? Explain.

5.48 It costs more to produce defective items—since they must be scrapped or reworked—than it does to produce nondefective items. This simple fact suggests that manufacturers should ensure the quality of their products by perfecting their production processes rather than through inspection of finished products (Deming, 1986). In order to better understand a particular metal-stamping process, a manufacturer wishes to estimate the mean length of items produced by the process during the past 24 hours.

a. How many parts should be sampled in order to estimate the population mean to within .1 millimeter (mm) with 90% confidence? Previous studies of this machine have indicated that the standard deviation of lengths produced by the stamping operation is about 2 mm.

b. Time permits the use of a sample size no larger than 100. If a 90% confidence interval for μ is constructed using $n = 100$, will it be wider or narrower than would have been obtained using the sample size determined in part **a?** Explain.

c. If management requires that μ be estimated to within .1 mm and that a sample size of no more than 100 be used, what is (approximately) the maximum confidence level that could be attained for a confidence interval that meets management's specifications?

QUICK REVIEW

Key Terms

Bound on the error of estimation 287
Confidence coefficient 262
Confidence interval 262
Confidence level 262
Degrees of freedom 269
Interval estimator 262
Point estimator 260
t statistic 269

Key Formulas

$\hat{\theta} \pm (z_{\alpha/2})\sigma_{\hat{\theta}}$ — Large-sample confidence interval for population parameter θ where $\hat{\theta}$ and $\sigma_{\hat{\theta}}$ are obtained from the table below

Parameter θ	Estimator $\hat{\theta}$	Standard Error $\sigma_{\hat{\theta}}$	
Mean, μ	$\bar{x}$	$\frac{\sigma}{\sqrt{n}}$	263
Proportion, p	$\hat{p}$	$\sqrt{\frac{pq}{n}}$	281

$\bar{x} \pm t_{\alpha/2}\left(\frac{s}{\sqrt{n}}\right)$ — Small-sample confidence interval for population mean μ 272

$\tilde{p} = \frac{x + 2}{n + 4}$ — Adjusted estimator of p 283

$n = \frac{(z_{\alpha/2})^2\sigma^2}{B^2}$ — Determining the sample size n for estimating μ 288

$n = \frac{(z_{\alpha/2})^2(pq)}{B^2}$ — Determining the sample size n for estimating p 289

LANGUAGE LAB

Symbol	Pronunciation	Description
θ	theta	General population parameter
μ	mu	Population mean
p		Population proportion
B		Bound on error of estimation
α	alpha	$(1 - \alpha)$ represents the confidence coefficient
$z_{\alpha/2}$	*z* of alpha over 2	*z* value used in a $100(1 - \alpha)\%$ large-sample confidence interval
$t_{\alpha/2}$	*t* of alpha over 2	*t* value used in a $100(1 - \alpha)\%$ small-sample confidence interval
$\bar{x}$	*x*-bar	Sample mean; point estimate of μ
$\hat{p}$	*p*-hat	Sample proportion; point estimate of *p*
$\tilde{p}$	*p*-curl	Adjusted sample proportion

Symbol	Pronunciation	Description
σ	sigma	Population standard deviation
s		Sample standard deviation; point estimate of σ
$\sigma_{\bar{x}}$	sigma of $\bar{x}$	Standard deviation of sampling distribution of $\bar{x}$
$\sigma_{\hat{p}}$	sigma of $\hat{p}$	Standard deviation of sampling distribution of $\hat{p}$

SUPPLEMENTARY EXERCISES 5.49–5.65

Note: List the assumptions necessary for the valid implementation of the statistical procedures you use in solving all these exercises.

Learning the Mechanics

5.49 Let t_0 represent a particular value of t from Table VI of Appendix B. Find the table values such that the following statements are true.

a. $P(t \leq t_0) = .05$ where df $= 20$
b. $P(t \geq t_0) = .005$ where df $= 9$
c. $P(t \leq -t_0$ or $t \geq t_0) = .10$ where df $= 8$
d. $P(t \leq -t_0$ or $t \geq t_0) = .01$ where df $= 17$

5.50 In each of the following instances, determine whether you would use a z or t statistic (or neither) to form a 95% confidence interval, and then look up the appropriate z or t value.

a. Random sample of size $n = 23$ from a normal distribution with unknown mean μ and standard deviation σ
b. Random sample of size $n = 135$ from a normal distribution with unknown mean μ and standard deviation σ
c. Random sample of size $n = 10$ from a normal distribution with unknown mean μ and standard deviation $\sigma = 5$
d. Random sample of size $n = 73$ from a distribution about which nothing is known
e. Random sample of size $n = 12$ from a distribution about which nothing is known

5.51 A random sample of 225 measurements is selected from a population, and the sample mean and standard deviation are $\bar{x} = 32.5$ and $s = 30.0$, respectively.

a. Use a 99% confidence interval to estimate the mean of the population, μ.
b. How large a sample would be needed to estimate μ to within .5 with 99% confidence?
c. What is meant by the phrase "99% confidence" as it is used in this exercise?

5.52 In a random sample of 400 measurements, 227 of the measurements possess the characteristic of interest, A.

a. Use a 95% confidence interval to estimate the true proportion p of measurements in the population with characteristic A.
b. How large a sample would be needed to estimate p to within .02 with 95% confidence?

Applying the Concepts

5.53 As part of a study of residential property values in Cedar Grove, New Jersey, the county tax assessor sampled 20 single-family homes that sold during 1996 and recorded their sales prices (in thousands of dollars; see table below). A stem-and-leaf display and descriptive statistics for these data are shown in the MINITAB printout on p. 295.

a. On the MINITAB printout, locate a 95% confidence interval for the mean sale price of all single-family homes in Cedar Grove, New Jersey.
b. Give a practical interpretation of the interval, part **a.**
c. What is meant by the phrase "95% confidence" as it is used in this exercise?
d. Comment on the validity of any assumptions required to properly apply the estimation procedure.

5.54 The Centers for Disease Control and Prevention (CDCP) in Atlanta, Georgia, conducts an annual survey of the general health of the U.S. population as part of its Behavioral Risk Factor Surveillance System (*New York Times,* Mar. 29, 1995). Using random-digit dialing, the CDCP telephones U.S. citizens over 18 years of age and asks them the following four questions:

(1) Is your health generally excellent, very good, good, fair, or poor?
(2) How many days during the previous 30 days was your physical health not good because of injury or illness?

NJVALUES.DAT

189.9	235.0	159.0	190.9	239.0	559.0	875.0	635.0
265.0	330.0	669.0	935.0	210.0	179.9	334.9	219.0
1,190.0	739.0	424.7	229.0				

Source: Multiple Listing Service of Suburban Essex County, New Jersey.

MINITAB Output for Exercise 5.53

```
Stem-and-leaf of SalePric   N = 20
Leaf Unit = 10

    4     1 5789
   10     2 112336
   10     3 33
    8     4 2
    7     5 5
    6     6 36
    4     7 3
    3     8 7
    2     9 3
    1    10
    1    11 9


                 N      MEAN     STDEV  SE MEAN   95.0 PERCENT C.I.
SalePric        20     440.4     303.0     67.8  (   298.6,    582.3)
```

(3) How many days during the previous 30 days was your mental health not good because of stress, depression, or emotional problems?

(4) How many days during the previous 30 days did your physical or mental health prevent you from performing your usual activities?

Identify the parameter of interest for each question.

5.55 Refer to Exercise 5.54. According to the CDCP, 89,582 of 102,263 adults interviewed stated their health was good, very good, or excellent.

a. Use a 99% confidence interval to estimate the true proportion of U.S. adults who believe their health to be good to excellent. Interpret the interval.

b. Why might the estimate, part **a**, be overly optimistic (i.e., biased high)?

5.56 Substance abuse problems are widespread at New Jersey businesses, according to the *Governor's Council for a Drug Free Workplace Report* (Spring/Summer 1995). A questionnaire on the issue was mailed to all New Jersey businesses that were members of the Governor's Council. Of the 72 companies that responded to the survey, 50 admitted that they had employees whose performance was affected by drugs or alcohol.

a. Use a 95% confidence interval to estimate the proportion of all New Jersey companies with substance abuse problems.

b. What assumptions are necessary to ensure the validity of the confidence interval?

c. Interpret the interval in the context of the problem.

d. In interpreting the confidence interval, what does it mean to say you are "95% confident"?

e. Would you use the interval of part **a** to estimate the proportion of all U.S. companies with substance abuse problems? Why or why not?

5.57 Research reported in the *Professional Geographer* (May 1992) investigates the hypothesis that the disproportionate housework responsibility of women in two-income households is a major factor in determining the proximity of a woman's place of employment. The researcher studied the distance (in miles) to work for both men and women in two-income households. Random samples of men and women yielded the following results:

	Central City Residence		Suburban Residence	
	Men	Women	Men	Women
Sample Size	159	119	138	93
Mean	7.4	4.5	9.3	6.6
Std. Deviation	6.3	4.2	7.1	5.6

a. For central city residences, calculate a 95% confidence interval for the average distance to work for men and women in two-income households. Interpret the intervals.

b. Repeat part **a** for suburban residences.

[*Note:* We will show how to use statistical techniques to compare two population means in Chapter 7.]

5.58 Refer to the *Journal of the American Medical Association* (Apr. 21, 1993) report on the prevalence of cigarette smoking among U.S. adults, Exercise 5.7 (p. 266). Of the 43,732 survey respondents, 11,239 indicated that they were current smokers and 10,539 indicated they were former smokers.

a. Construct and interpret a 90% confidence interval for the percentage of U.S. adults who currently smoke cigarettes.

b. Construct and interpret a 90% confidence interval for the percentage of U.S. adults who are former cigarette smokers.

5.59 A company is interested in estimating μ, the mean number of days of sick leave taken by all its employees. The firm's statistician selects at random 100 personnel files and notes the number of sick days taken by each employee. The following sample statistics are computed: $\bar{x} = 12.2$ days, $s = 10$ days.

a. Estimate μ using a 90% confidence interval.
b. How many personnel files would the statistician have to select in order to estimate μ to within 2 days with a 99% confidence interval?

5.60 The primary determinant of the amount of vacation time U.S. employees receive is their length of service. According to data released by Hewitt Associates (*Management Review,* Nov. 1995), more than 8 of 10 employers provide two weeks of vacation after the first year. After five years, 75% of employers provide three weeks and after 15 years most provide four-week vacations. To more accurately estimate p, the proportion of U.S. employers who provide only two weeks of vacation to new hires, a random sample of 24 major U.S. companies was contacted. The following vacation times were reported (in days):

VACTIMES.DAT

10	12	10	10	10	10
15	10	10	10	10	10
10	10	10	10	10	15
10	10	15	10	10	10

a. Is the sample size large enough to ensure that the normal distribution provides a reasonable approximation to the sampling distribution of $\hat{p}$? Justify your answer.
b. How large a sample would be required to estimate p to within .02 with 95% confidence?

5.61 *Management Accounting* (June 1995) reported the results of its sixth annual salary survey of the members of the Institute of Management Accountants (IMA). The 2,112 members responding had a salary distribution with a 20th percentile of $35,100; a median of $50,000; and an 80th percentile of $73,000.

a. Use this information to determine the minimum sample size that could be used in next year's survey to estimate the mean salary of IMA members to within $2,000 with 98% confidence.
b. Explain how you estimated the standard deviation required for the sample size calculation.
c. List any assumptions you make.

5.62 According to the U.S. Bureau of Labor Statistics, one of every 80 American workers (i.e., 1.3%) is fired or laid off. Are employees with cancer fired or laid off at the same rate? To answer this question, *Working Women* magazine and Amgen—a company that makes drugs to lessen chemotherapy side effects—conducted a telephone survey of 100 cancer survivors who worked while undergoing treatment (*Tampa Tribune,* Sept. 25, 1996). Of these 100 cancer patients, 7 were fired or laid off due to their illness.

a. Construct a 90% confidence interval for the true percentage of all cancer patients who are fired or laid off due to their illness.
b. Give a practical interpretation of the interval, part **a.**
c. Are employees with cancer fired or laid off at the same rate as all U.S. workers? Explain.

5.63 In 1989, the American Society for Quality Control began publishing a journal called *Quality Engineering.* In 1994, the journal distributed a questionnaire to its 8,521 subscribers. A total of 202 replies were received. To the question "How long have you been a subscriber?" they got the responses shown in the table below.

a. What assumption(s) would need to be made in order to apply the confidence interval methodology described in this chapter to the problem of estimating the mean subscription length for the population of 8,521 journal subscribers?
b. Use a 98% confidence interval to estimate the population mean referred to in part **a.**

5.64 Recently, a case of salmonella (bacterial) poisoning was traced to a particular brand of ice cream bar, and the manufacturer removed the bars from the market. Despite this response, many consumers refused to purchase *any* brand of ice cream bars for some period of time after the event (McClave, personal consulting). One manufacturer conducted a survey of consumers six months after the outbreak. A sample of 244 ice cream bar consumers was contacted, and 23 respondents indicated that they would not purchase ice cream bars because of the potential for food poisoning.

a. What is the point estimate of the true fraction of the entire market who refuse to purchase bars six months after the outbreak?
b. Is the sample size large enough to use the normal approximation for the sampling distribution of the

SUBSCRIB.DAT

Years	1	2	3	4	5	6	7	8	9	10	11	12	No reply
No. of Responses	44	39	27	17	12	38	1	1	0	0	0	1	22

Source: Adapted from "Quality engineering reader survey." *Quality Engineering,* Vol. 7, No. 4, 1995, p. ix.

estimator of the binomial probability? Justify your response.

c. Construct a 95% confidence interval for the true proportion of the market who still refuse to purchase ice cream bars six months after the event.

d. Interpret both the point estimate and confidence interval in terms of this application.

e. Suppose it is now one year after the outbreak of food poisoning was traced to ice cream bars. The manufacturer wishes to estimate the proportion who still will not purchase bars to within .02 using a 95% confidence interval. How many consumers should be sampled?

5.65 Refer to the National Highway Traffic Safety Administration (NHTSA) study of fatal auto accidents caused by air bags, Exercise 5.30 (p. 285). Recall that the NHTSA wants to estimate the proportion of such accidents in which children seated on the front passenger side were killed. How many fatal accidents should the NHTSA sample in order to estimate the proportion to within .1 of its true value using a 99% confidence interval?

Chapter 6

INFERENCES BASED ON A SINGLE SAMPLE:

Tests of Hypothesis

CONTENTS

STATISTICS IN ACTION

Where We've Been

We saw how to use sample information to estimate population parameters in Chapter 5. The sampling distribution of a statistic is used to assess the reliability of an estimate, which we express in terms of a confidence interval.

Where We're Going

We'll see how to utilize sample information to test what the value of a population parameter may be. This type of inference is called a *test of hypothesis.* We'll also see how to conduct a test of hypothesis about a population mean μ and a population proportion p. And, just as with estimation, we'll stress the measurement of the reliability of the inference. An inference without a measure of reliability is little more than a guess.

Suppose you wanted to determine whether the mean waiting time in the drive-through line of a fast-food restaurant is less than five minutes, or whether the majority of consumers are optimistic about the economy. In both cases you are interested in making an inference about how the value of a parameter relates to a specific numerical value. Is it less than, equal to, or greater than the specified number? This type of inference, called a **test of hypothesis,** is the subject of this chapter.

We introduce the elements of a test of hypothesis in Section 6.1. We then show how to conduct a large-sample test of hypothesis about a population mean in Sections 6.2 and 6.3. In Section 6.4 we utilize small samples to conduct tests about means, and in optional Section 6.6 we consider an alternative nonparametric test. Large-sample tests about binomial probabilities are the subject of Section 6.5.

6.1 THE ELEMENTS OF A TEST OF HYPOTHESIS

Suppose building specifications in a certain city require that the average breaking strength of residential sewer pipe be more than 2,400 pounds per foot of length (i.e., per linear foot). Each manufacturer who wants to sell pipe in this city must demonstrate that its product meets the specification. Note that we are again interested in making an inference about the mean μ of a population. However, in this example we are less interested in estimating the value of μ than we are in testing a *hypothesis* about its value. That is, *we want to decide whether the mean breaking strength of the pipe exceeds 2,400 pounds per linear foot.*

The method used to reach a decision is based on the rare-event concept explained in earlier chapters. We define two hypotheses: (1) The **null hypothesis** is that which represents the status quo to the party performing the sampling experiment—the hypothesis that will be accepted unless the data provide convincing evidence that it is false. (2) The **alternative,** or **research, hypothesis** is that which will be accepted only if the data provide convincing evidence of its truth. From the point of view of the city conducting the tests, the null hypothesis is that the manufacturer's pipe does *not* meet specifications unless the tests provide convincing evidence otherwise. The null and alternative hypotheses are therefore

Null hypothesis (H_0): $\mu \leq 2{,}400$
(i.e., the manufacturer's pipe does not meet specifications)

Alternative (research) hypothesis (H_a): $\mu > 2{,}400$
(i.e., the manufacturer's pipe meets specifications)

How can the city decide when enough evidence exists to conclude that the manufacturer's pipe meets specifications? Since the hypotheses concern the value of the population mean μ, it is reasonable to use the sample mean $\bar{x}$ to make the inference, just as we did when forming confidence intervals for μ in Sections 5.1 and 5.2. The city will conclude that the pipe meets specifications only when the sample mean $\bar{x}$ convincingly indicates that the population mean exceeds 2,400 pounds per linear foot.

"Convincing" evidence in favor of the alternative hypothesis will exist when the value of $\bar{x}$ exceeds 2,400 by an amount that cannot be readily attributed to sampling variability. To decide, we compute a **test statistic,** which is the z value that measures the distance between the value of $\bar{x}$ and the value of μ specified in the null hypothesis. When the null hypothesis contains more than one value of μ, as in this case (H_0: $\mu \leq 2{,}400$), we use the value of μ closest to the values specified in the alternative hypothesis. The idea is that if the hypothesis that μ *equals* 2,400 can be rejected in favor of $\mu > 2{,}400$, then μ *less than or equal to* 2,400 can certainly be rejected. Thus, the test statistic is

$$z = \frac{\bar{x} - 2{,}400}{\sigma_{\bar{x}}} = \frac{\bar{x} - 2{,}400}{\sigma/\sqrt{n}}$$

Note that a value of $z = 1$ means that $\bar{x}$ is 1 standard deviation above $\mu = 2{,}400$; a value of $z = 1.5$ means that $\bar{x}$ is 1.5 standard deviations above $\mu = 2{,}400$, etc. How large must z be before the city can be convinced that the null hypothesis can be rejected in favor of the alternative and conclude that the pipe meets specifications?

If you examine Figure 6.1, you will note that the chance of observing $\bar{x}$ more than 1.645 standard deviations above 2,400 is only .05—*if in fact the true mean μ is 2,400.* Thus, if the sample mean is more than 1.645 standard deviations above 2,400, either H_0 is true and a relatively rare event has occurred (.05 probability) or H_a is true and the population mean exceeds 2,400. Since we would most likely reject the notion that a rare event has occurred, we would reject the null hypothesis ($\mu \leq 2{,}400$) and conclude that the alternative hypothesis ($\mu > 2{,}400$) is true. What is the probability that this procedure will lead us to an incorrect decision?

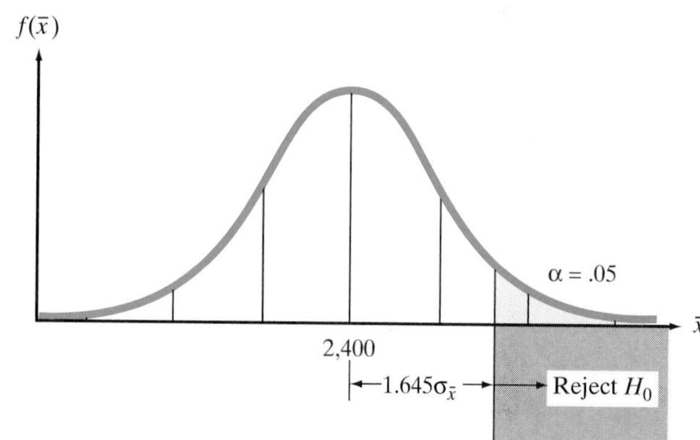

FIGURE 6.1
The sampling distribution of $\bar{x}$, assuming $\mu = 2{,}400$

Such an incorrect decision—deciding that the null hypothesis is false when in fact it is true—is called a **Type I error.** As indicated in Figure 6.1, the risk of making a Type I error is denoted by the symbol α. That is,

$$\begin{aligned} \alpha &= P(\text{Type I error}) \\ &= P(\text{Rejecting the null hypothesis when in fact the null hypothesis is true}) \end{aligned}$$

In our example

$$\alpha = P(z > 1.645 \text{ when in fact } \mu = 2{,}400) = .05$$

We now summarize the elements of the test:

H_0: $\mu \leq 2{,}400$
H_a: $\mu > 2{,}400$

Test statistic: $z = \dfrac{\bar{x} - 2{,}400}{\sigma_{\bar{x}}}$

Rejection region: $z > 1.645$, which corresponds to $\alpha = .05$

Note that the **rejection region** refers to the values of the test statistic for which we will *reject the null hypothesis.*

To illustrate the use of the test, suppose we test 50 sections of sewer pipe and find the mean and standard deviation for these 50 measurements to be

$$\bar{x} = 2{,}460 \text{ pounds per linear foot}$$
$$s = 200 \text{ pounds per linear foot}$$

As in the case of estimation, we can use s to approximate σ when s is calculated from a large set of sample measurements.

The test statistic is

$$z = \frac{\bar{x} - 2{,}400}{\sigma_{\bar{x}}} = \frac{\bar{x} - 2{,}400}{\sigma/\sqrt{n}} \approx \frac{\bar{x} - 2{,}400}{s/\sqrt{n}}$$

Substituting $\bar{x} = 2{,}460$, $n = 50$, and $s = 200$, we have

$$z \approx \frac{2{,}460 - 2{,}400}{200/\sqrt{50}} = \frac{60}{28.28} = 2.12$$

Therefore, the sample mean lies $2.12\sigma_{\bar{x}}$ above the hypothesized value of μ, 2,400, as shown in Figure 6.2. Since this value of z exceeds 1.645, it falls in the rejection region. That is, we reject the null hypothesis that $\mu = 2{,}400$ and conclude that $\mu > 2{,}400$. Thus, it appears that the company's pipe has a mean strength that exceeds 2,400 pounds per linear foot.

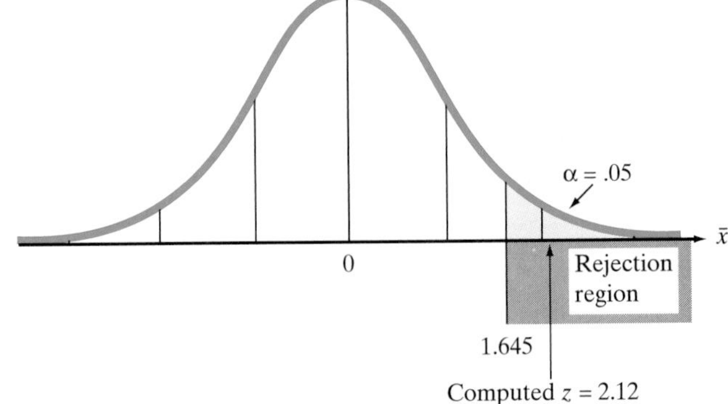

FIGURE 6.2 Location of the test statistic for a test of the hypothesis H_0: $\mu = 2{,}400$

How much faith can be placed in this conclusion? What is the probability that our statistical test could lead us to reject the null hypothesis (and conclude that the company's pipe meets the city's specifications) when in fact the null hypothesis is true? The answer is $\alpha = .05$. That is, we selected the level of risk, α, of making a Type I error when we constructed the test. Thus, the chance is only 1 in 20 that our test would lead us to conclude the manufacturer's pipe satisfies the city's specifications when in fact the pipe does *not* meet specifications.

Now, suppose the sample mean breaking strength for the 50 sections of sewer pipe turned out to be $\bar{x} = 2{,}430$ pounds per linear foot. Assuming that the sample standard deviation is still $s = 200$, the test statistic is

$$z = \frac{2{,}430 - 2{,}400}{200/\sqrt{50}} = \frac{30}{28.28} = 1.06$$

Therefore, the sample mean $\bar{x} = 2{,}430$ is only 1.06 standard deviations above the null hypothesized value of $\mu = 2{,}400$. As shown in Figure 6.3, this value does not fall into the rejection region $(z > 1.645)$. Therefore, we know that we cannot reject H_0 using $\alpha = .05$. Even though the sample mean exceeds the city's specification of 2,400 by 30 pounds per linear foot, it does not exceed the specification by enough to provide *convincing* evidence that the *population mean* exceeds 2,400.

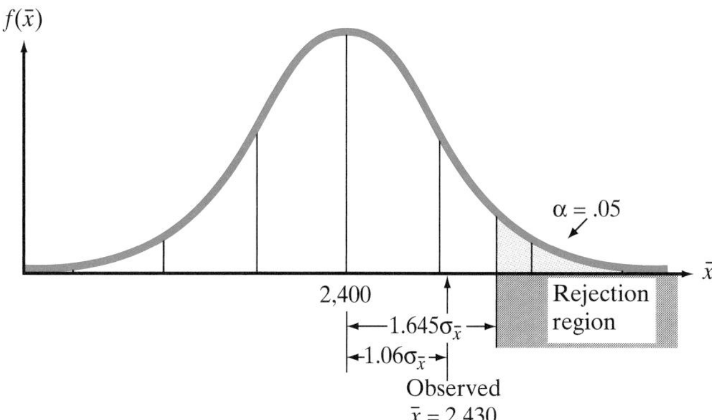

FIGURE 6.3 Location of test statistic when $\bar{x} = 2{,}430$

Should we accept the null hypothesis H_0: $\mu \leq 2{,}400$ and conclude that the manufacturer's pipe does not meet specifications? To do so would be to risk a **Type II error**—that of concluding that the null hypothesis is true (the pipe does not meet specifications) when in fact it is false (the pipe does meet specifications). We denote the probability of committing a Type II error by β. Unfortunately, β is often difficult to determine precisely. Rather than make a decision (accept H_0) for which the probability of error (β) is unknown, we avoid the potential Type II error by avoiding the conclusion that the null hypothesis is true. Instead, we will simply state that *the sample evidence is insufficient to reject H_0 at $\alpha = .05$*. Since the null hypothesis is the "status-quo" hypothesis, the effect of not rejecting H_0 is to maintain the status quo. In our pipe-testing example, the effect of having insufficient evidence to reject the null hypothesis that the pipe does not meet specifications is probably to prohibit the utilization of the manufacturer's pipe unless and until there is sufficient evidence that the pipe does meet specifications. That is, until the data indicate convincingly that the null hypothesis is false, we usually maintain the status quo implied by its truth.

Table 6.1 summarizes the four possible outcomes of a test of hypothesis. The "true state of nature" columns in Table 6.1 refer to the fact that either the null hypothesis H_0 is true or the alternative hypothesis H_a is true. Note that the true state of nature is unknown to the researcher conducting the test. The "decision" rows in Table 6.1 refer to the action of the researcher, assuming that he or she will either conclude that H_0 is true or that H_a is true, based on the results of the sampling experiment. Note that a Type I error can be made *only* when the null hypothesis is rejected in favor of the alternative hypothesis, and a Type II error can be made *only* when the null hypothesis is accepted. Our policy will be to make a decision only when we know the probability of making the error that corresponds to that decision. Since α is usually specified by the analyst, we will generally be able to reject H_0 (accept H_a) when the sample evidence supports that decision. However, since β is usually not specified, *we will generally avoid the decision to accept H_0, preferring instead to state that the sample evidence is insufficient to reject H_0 when the test statistic is not in the rejection region.*

TABLE 6.1 Conclusions and Consequences for a Test of Hypothesis

	True State of Nature	
Conclusion	**H_0 True**	**H_a True**
Accept H_0 (Assume H_0 True)	Correct decision	Type II error (probability β)
Reject H_0 (Assume H_a True)	Type I error (probability α)	Correct decision

The elements of a test of hypothesis are summarized in the following box. Note that the first four elements are all specified *before* the sampling experiment is performed. In no case will the results of the sample be used to determine the hypotheses—the data are collected to test the predetermined hypotheses, not to formulate them.

Elements of a Test of Hypothesis

1. *Null hypothesis* (H_0): A theory about the values of one or more population parameters. The theory generally represents the status quo, which we adopt until it is proven false.
2. *Alternative (research) hypothesis* (H_a): A theory that contradicts the null hypothesis. The theory generally represents that which we will adopt only when sufficient evidence exists to establish its truth.
3. *Test statistic:* A sample statistic used to decide whether to reject the null hypothesis.
4. *Rejection region:* The numerical values of the test statistic for which the null hypothesis will be rejected. The rejection region is chosen so that the probability is α that it will contain the test statistic when the null hypothesis is true, thereby leading to a Type I error. The value of α is usually chosen to be small (e.g., .01, .05, or .10), and is referred to as the **level of significance** of the test.
5. *Assumptions:* Clear statement(s) of any assumptions made about the population(s) being sampled.
6. *Experiment and calculation of test statistic:* Performance of the sampling experiment and determination of the numerical value of the test statistic.
7. *Conclusion:*
   a. If the numerical value of the test statistic falls in the rejection region, we reject the null hypothesis and conclude that the alternative hypothesis is true. We know that the hypothesis-testing process will lead to this conclusion incorrectly (Type I error) only $100\alpha\%$ of the time when H_0 is true.
   b. If the test statistic does not fall in the rejection region, we do not reject H_0. Thus, we reserve judgment about which hypothesis is true. We do not conclude that the null hypothesis is true because we do not (in general) know the probability β that our test procedure will lead to an incorrect acceptance of H_0 (Type II error).*

*In many practical business applications of hypothesis testing, nonrejection leads management to behave as if the null hypothesis were accepted. Accordingly, the distinction between acceptance and nonrejection is frequently blurred in practice.

EXERCISES 6.1–6.14

Learning the Mechanics

6.1 Which hypothesis, the null or the alternative, is the status-quo hypothesis? Which is the research hypothesis?

6.2 Which element of a test of hypothesis is used to decide whether to reject the null hypothesis in favor of the alternative hypothesis?

6.3 What is the level of significance of a test of hypothesis?

6.4 What is the difference between Type I and Type II errors in hypothesis testing? How do α and β relate to Type I and Type II errors?

6.5 List the four possible results of the combinations of decisions and true states of nature for a test of hypothesis.

6.6 We (generally) reject the null hypothesis when the test statistic falls in the rejection region, but we do not accept the null hypothesis when the test statistic does not fall in the rejection region. Why?

6.7 If you test a hypothesis and reject the null hypothesis in favor of the alternative hypothesis, does your test prove that the alternative hypothesis is correct? Explain.

Applying the Concepts

6.8 The interest rate at which London banks lend money to one another is called the *London interbank offered rate,* or *Libor.* According to *The Wall Street Journal* (Nov. 11, 1998), the British Bankers Association regularly surveys international banks for the Libor rate. One recent report had the average Libor rate at .39 percent for 3-month loans—a value considered high by many Western banks. Set up the null and alternative hypothesis for testing the reported value.

6.9 The national student loan default rate has dropped steadily over the last decade. *USF Magazine* (Spring 1999) reported the default rate (i.e., the proportion of college students who default on their loans) at .10 in fiscal year 1996. Set up the null and alternative hypotheses if you want to determine if the student loan default rate in 2000 is less than .10.

6.10 According to the *Journal of Psychology and Aging* (May 1992), older workers (i.e., workers 45 years old or older) have a mean job satisfaction rating of 4.3 on a 5-point scale. (Higher scores indicate higher levels of satisfaction.)

a. Set up H_0 and H_a to test the journal's claim.
b. Describe a Type I error for this test.
c. Describe a Type II error for this test.

6.11 Sometimes, the outcome of a jury trial defies the "commonsense" expectations of the general public (e.g., the O. J. Simpson verdict in the "Trial of the Century"). Such a verdict is more acceptable if we understand that the jury trial of an accused murderer is analogous to the statistical hypothesis-testing process. The null hypothesis in a jury trial is that the accused is innocent. (The status-quo hypothesis in the U.S. system of justice is innocence, which is assumed to be true until proven *beyond a reasonable doubt.*) The alternative hypothesis is guilt, which is accepted only when sufficient evidence exists to establish its truth. If the vote of the jury is unanimous in favor of guilt, the null hypothesis of innocence is rejected and the court concludes that the accused murderer is guilty. Any vote other than a unanimous one for guilt results in a "not guilty" verdict. The court never accepts the null hypothesis; that is, the court never declares the accused "innocent." A "not guilty" verdict (as in the O. J. Simpson case) implies that the court could not find the defendant guilty *beyond a reasonable doubt.*

a. Define Type I and Type II errors in a murder trial.
b. Which of the two errors is the more serious? Explain.
c. The court does not, in general, know the values of α and β; but ideally, both should be small. One of these probabilities is assumed to be smaller than the other in a jury trial. Which one, and why?
d. The court system relies on the belief that the value of α is made very small by requiring a unanimous vote before guilt is concluded. Explain why this is so.
e. For a jury prejudiced against a guilty verdict as the trial begins, will the value of α increase or decrease? Explain.
f. For a jury prejudiced against a guilty verdict as the trial begins, will the value of β increase or decrease? Explain.

6.12 A group of physicians subjected the *polygraph* (or *lie detector*) to the same careful testing given to medical diagnostic tests. They found that if 1,000 people were subjected to the polygraph and 500 told the truth and 500 lied, the polygraph would indicate that approximately 185 of the truth-tellers were liars and that approximately 120 of the liars were truth-tellers (*Discover,* 1986).

a. In the application of a polygraph test, an individual is presumed to be a truth-teller (H_0) until "proven" a liar (H_a). In this context, what is a Type I error? A Type II error?
b. According to the study, what is the probability (approximately) that a polygraph test will result in a Type I error? A Type II error?

6.13 According to *Chemical Marketing Reporter* (Feb. 20, 1995), pharmaceutical companies spend \$15 billion per year on research and development of new drugs. The pharmaceutical company must subject each new drug to lengthy and involved testing before receiving the necessary permission from the Food and Drug Administration (FDA) to market the drug. The FDA's policy is that the pharmaceutical company must provide substantial evidence that a new drug is safe prior to receiving FDA approval, so that the FDA can confidently certify the safety of the drug to potential consumers.

a. If the new drug testing were to be placed in a test of hypothesis framework, would the null hypothesis be that the drug is safe or unsafe? The alternative hypothesis?

b. Given the choice of null and alternative hypotheses in part **a,** describe Type I and Type II errors in terms of this application. Define α and β in terms of this application.

c. If the FDA wants to be very confident that the drug is safe before permitting it to be marketed, is it more important that α or β be small? Explain.

6.14 One of the most pressing problems in high-technology industries is computer security. Computer security is typically achieved by use of a *password*—a collection of symbols (usually letters and numbers) that must be supplied by the user before the computer permits access to the account. The problem is that persistent hackers can create programs that enter millions of combinations of symbols into a target system until the correct password is found. The newest systems solve this problem by requiring authorized users to identify themselves by unique body characteristics. For example, a system developed by Palmguard, Inc. tests the hypothesis

H_0: The proposed user is authorized

versus

H_a: The proposed user is unauthorized

by checking characteristics of the proposed user's palm against those stored in the authorized users' data bank (*Omni,* 1984).

a. Define a Type I error and Type II error for this test. Which is the more serious error? Why?

b. Palmguard reports that the Type I error rate for its system is less than 1%, whereas the Type II error rate is .00025%. Interpret these error rates.

c. Another successful security system, the EyeDentifyer, "spots authorized computer users by reading the one-of-a-kind patterns formed by the network of minute blood vessels across the retina at the back of the eye." The EyeDentifyer reports Type I and II error rates of .01% (1 in 10,000) and .005% (5 in 100,000), respectively. Interpret these rates.

6.2 LARGE-SAMPLE TEST OF HYPOTHESIS ABOUT A POPULATION MEAN

In Section 6.1 we learned that the null and alternative hypotheses form the basis for a test of hypothesis inference. The null and alternative hypotheses may take one of several forms. In the sewer pipe example we tested the null hypothesis that the population mean strength of the pipe is less than or equal to 2,400 pounds per linear foot against the alternative hypothesis that the mean strength exceeds 2,400. That is, we tested

$$H_0: \mu \leq 2{,}400$$
$$H_a: \mu > 2{,}400$$

This is a **one-tailed** (or **one-sided**) **statistical test** because the alternative hypothesis specifies that the population parameter (the population mean μ, in this example) is strictly greater than a specified value (2,400, in this example). If the null hypothesis had been H_0: $\mu \geq 2{,}400$ and the alternative hypothesis had been H_a: $\mu < 2{,}400$, the test would still be one-sided, because the parameter is still specified to be on "one side" of the null hypothesis value. Some statistical investigations seek to show that the population parameter is *either larger or smaller* than some specified value. Such an alternative hypothesis is called a **two-tailed** (or **two-sided**) **hypothesis.**

While alternative hypotheses are always specified as strict inequalities, such as $\mu < 2{,}400$, $\mu > 2{,}400$, or $\mu \neq 2{,}400$, null hypotheses are usually specified as equalities, such as $\mu = 2{,}400$. Even when the null hypothesis is an inequality, such as $\mu \leq 2{,}400$, we specify H_0: $\mu = 2{,}400$, reasoning that if sufficient evidence exists to show that H_a: $\mu > 2{,}400$ is true when tested against H_0: $\mu = 2{,}400$, then surely sufficient evidence exists to reject $\mu < 2{,}400$ as well. Therefore, the null hypothesis is specified as the value of μ closest to a one-sided alternative hypothesis and as the only value *not* specified in a two-tailed alternative hypothesis. The steps for selecting the null and alternative hypotheses are summarized in the accompanying box.

Steps for Selecting the Null and Alternative Hypotheses

1. Select the *alternative hypothesis* as that which the sampling experiment is intended to establish. The alternative hypothesis will assume one of three forms:
   a. One-tailed, upper-tailed — *Example:* H_a: $\mu > 2{,}400$
   b. One-tailed, lower-tailed — *Example:* H_a: $\mu < 2{,}400$
   c. Two-tailed — *Example:* H_a: $\mu \neq 2{,}400$
2. Select the *null hypothesis* as the status quo, that which will be presumed true unless the sampling experiment conclusively establishes the alternative hypothesis. The null hypothesis will be specified as that parameter value closest to the alternative in one-tailed tests, and as the complementary (or only unspecified) value in two-tailed tests.

Example: H_0: $\mu = 2{,}400$

The rejection region for a two-tailed test differs from that for a one-tailed test. When we are trying to detect departure from the null hypothesis in *either* direction, we must establish a rejection region in both tails of the sampling distribution of the test statistic. Figures 6.4a and 6.4b show the one-tailed rejection regions for lower- and upper-tailed tests, respectively. The two-tailed rejection region is illustrated in Figure 6.4c. Note that a rejection region is established in each tail of the sampling distribution for a two-tailed test.

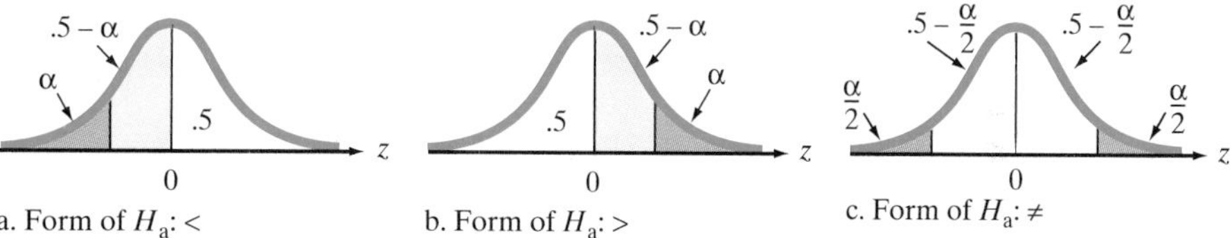

FIGURE 6.4 Rejection regions corresponding to one- and two-tailed tests

The rejection regions corresponding to typical values selected for α are shown in Table 6.2 for one- and two-tailed tests. Note that the smaller α you select, the more evidence (the larger z) you will need before you can reject H_0.

TABLE 6.2 Rejection Regions for Common Values of α

	Alternative Hypotheses		
	Lower-Tailed	Upper-Tailed	Two-Tailed
$\alpha = .10$	$z < -1.28$	$z > 1.28$	$z < -1.645$ or $z > 1.645$
$\alpha = .05$	$z < -1.645$	$z > 1.645$	$z < -1.96$ or $z > 1.96$
$\alpha = .01$	$z < -2.33$	$z > 2.33$	$z < -2.575$ or $z > 2.575$

EXAMPLE 6.1

A manufacturer of cereal wants to test the performance of one of its filling machines. The machine is designed to discharge a mean amount of $\mu = 12$ ounces per box, and the manufacturer wants to detect any departure from this setting.

This quality study calls for randomly sampling 100 boxes from today's production run and determining whether the mean fill for the run is 12 ounces per box. Set up a test of hypothesis for this study, using $\alpha = .01$. (In Chapter 11, we describe how this problem can be addresed using control charts.)

Solution Since the manufacturer wishes to detect a departure from the setting of $\mu = 12$ in either direction, $\mu < 12$ or $\mu > 12$, we conduct a two-tailed statistical test. Following the procedure for selecting the null and alternative hypotheses, we specify as the alternative hypothesis that the mean differs from 12 ounces, since detecting the machine's departure from specifications is the purpose of the quality control study. The null hypothesis is the presumption that the fill machine is operating properly unless the sample data indicate otherwise. Thus,

H_0: $\mu = 12$

H_a: $\mu \neq 12$ (i.e., $\mu < 12$ or $\mu > 12$)

The test statistic measures the number of standard deviations between the observed value of $\bar{x}$ and the null hypothesized value $\mu = 12$:

Test statistic: $\dfrac{\bar{x} - 12}{\sigma_{\bar{x}}}$

The rejection region must be designated to detect a departure from $\mu = 12$ in *either* direction, so we will reject H_0 for values of z that are either too small (negative) or too large (positive). To determine the precise values of z that comprise the rejection region, we first select α, the probability that the test will lead to incorrect rejection of the null hypothesis. Then we divide α equally between the lower and upper tail of the distribution of z, as shown in Figure 6.5. In this example, $\alpha = 0.1$, so $\alpha/2 = .005$ is placed in each tail. The areas in the tails correspond to $z = -2.575$ and $z = 2.575$, respectively (from Table 6.2):

Rejection region: $z < -2.575$ or $z > 2.575$, (see Figure 6.5)

FIGURE 6.5
Two-tailed rejection region: $\alpha = .01$

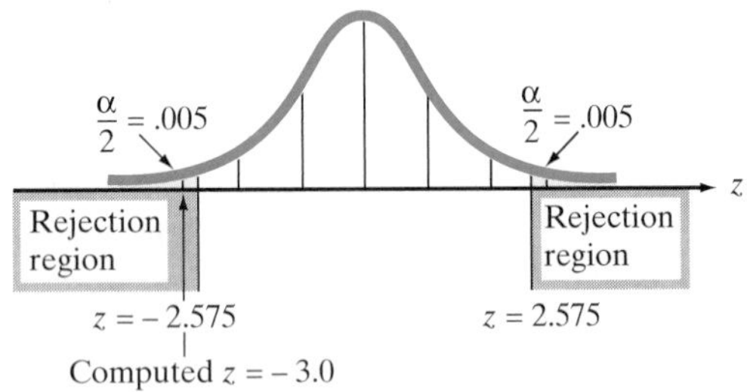

Assumptions: Since the sample size of the experiment is large enough ($n > 30$), the Central Limit Theorem will apply, and no assumptions need be made about the population of fill measurements. The sampling distribution of the sample mean fill of 100 boxes will be approximately normal regardless of the distribution of the individual boxes' fills.

Note that the test in Example 6.1 is set up *before* the sampling experiment is conducted. The data are not used to develop the test. Evidently, the manufacturer does not want to disrupt the filling process to adjust the machine unless the sample data provide very convincing evidence that it is not meeting specifications, because the value of α has been set quite low at .01. If the sample evidence results in the rejection of H_0, the manufacturer can be 99% confident that the machine needs adjustment.

Once the test is set up, the manufacturer is ready to perform the sampling experiment and conduct the test. The test is performed in Example 6.2.

EXAMPLE 6.2

Refer to the quality control test set up in Example 6.1. Suppose the sample yields the following results:

$$n = 100 \text{ observations} \qquad \bar{x} = 11.85 \text{ ounces} \qquad s = .5 \text{ ounce}$$

Use these data to conduct the test of hypothesis.

Solution Since the test is completely specified in Example 6.1, we simply substitute the sample statistics into the test statistic:

$$z = \frac{\bar{x} - 12}{\sigma_{\bar{x}}} = \frac{\bar{x} - 12}{\sigma/\sqrt{n}} = \frac{11.85 - 12}{\sigma/\sqrt{100}}$$

$$\approx \frac{11.85 - 12}{s/10} = \frac{-.15}{.5/10} = -3.0$$

The implication is that the sample mean, 11.85, is (approximately) 3 standard deviations below the null hypothesized value of 12.0 in the sampling distribution of $\bar{x}$. You can see in Figure 6.5 that this value of z is in the lower-tail rejection region, which consists of all values of $z < -2.575$. These sample data provide sufficient evidence to reject H_0 and conclude, at the $\alpha = .01$ level of significance, that the mean fill differs from the specification of $\mu = 12$ ounces. It appears that the machine is, on average, underfilling the boxes. ✶

Two final points about the test of hypothesis in Example 6.2 apply to all statistical tests:

1. Since z is less than -2.575, it is tempting to state our conclusion at a significance level lower than $\alpha = .01$. We resist the temptation because the level of α is determined *before* the sampling experiment is performed. If we decide that we are willing to tolerate a 1% Type I error rate, the result of the sampling experiment should have no effect on that decision. *In general, the same data should not be used both to set up and to conduct the test.*
2. When we state our conclusion at the .01 level of significance, we are referring to the failure rate of the *procedure*, not the result of this particular test. We know that the test procedure will lead to the rejection of the null hypothesis only 1% of the time when in fact $\mu = 12$. *Therefore, when the test statistic falls in the rejection region, we infer that the alternative* $\mu \neq 12$ *is true and express our confidence in the procedure by quoting the* α *level of significance, or the* $100(1 - \alpha)\%$ *confidence level.*

The setup of a large-sample test of hypothesis about a population mean is summarized in the following box. Both the one- and two-tailed tests are shown.

Large-Sample Test of Hypothesis About μ

One-Tailed Test	Two-Tailed Test
H_0: $\mu = \mu_0$ H_a: $\mu < \mu_0$ (or H_a: $\mu > \mu_0$)	H_0: $\mu = \mu_0$ H_a: $\mu \neq \mu_0$
Test statistic: $z = \dfrac{\bar{x} - \mu_0}{\sigma_{\bar{x}}}$	*Test statistic:* $z = \dfrac{\bar{x} - \mu_0}{\sigma_{\bar{x}}}$
Rejection region: $z < -z_\alpha$ (or $z > z_\alpha$ when H_a: $\mu > \mu_0$)	*Rejection region:* $\lvert z \rvert > z_{\alpha/2}$
where z_α is chosen so that $P(z > z_\alpha) = \alpha$	where $z_{\alpha/2}$ is chosen so that $P(z > z_{\alpha/2}) = \alpha/2$

Assumptions: No assumptions need to be made about the probability distribution of the population because the Central Limit Theorem assures us that, for large samples, the test statistic will be approximately normally distributed regardless of the shape of the underlying probability distribution of the population.

Note: μ_0 is the symbol for the numerical value assigned to μ under the null hypothesis.

Once the test has been set up, the sampling experiment is performed and the test statistic calculated. The next box contains possible conclusions for a test of hypothesis, depending on the result of the sampling experiment.

Possible Conclusions for a Test of Hypothesis

1. If the calculated test statistic falls in the rejection region, reject H_0 and conclude that the alternative hypothesis H_a is true. State that you are rejecting H_0 at the α level of significance. Remember that the confidence is in the testing *process,* not the particular result of a single test.
2. If the test statistic does not fall in the rejection region, conclude that the sampling experiment does not provide sufficient evidence to reject H_0 at the α level of significance. [Generally, we will not "accept" the null hypothesis unless the probability β of a Type II error has been calculated. Consult the chapter references for some advanced methods of calculating β.]

EXERCISES 6.15–6.27

Learning the Mechanics

6.15 For each of the following rejection regions, sketch the sampling distribution for z and indicate the location of the rejection region.

a. $z > 1.96$ **b.** $z > 1.645$ **c.** $z > 2.575$
d. $z < -1.28$ **e.** $z < -1.645$ or $z > 1.645$
f. $z < -2.575$ or $z > 2.575$
g. For each of the rejection regions specified in parts **a–f,** what is the probability that a Type I error will be made?

6.16 Suppose you are interested in conducting the statistical test of H_0: $\mu = 255$ against H_a: $\mu > 255$, and you have decided to use the following decision rule: Reject H_0 if the sample mean of a random sample of 81 items is more than 270. Assume that the standard deviation of the population is 63.

a. Express the decision rule in terms of z.
b. Find α, the probability of making a Type I error, by using this decision rule.

6.17 A random sample of 100 observations from a population with standard deviation 60 yielded a sample mean of 110.

a. Test the null hypothesis that $\mu = 100$ against the alternative hypothesis that $\mu > 100$ using $\alpha = .05$. Interpret the results of the test.

b. Test the null hypothesis that $\mu = 100$ against the alternative hypothesis that $\mu \neq 100$ using $\alpha = .05$. Interpret the results of the test.

c. Compare the results of the two tests you conducted. Explain why the results differ.

6.18 A random sample of 64 observations produced the following summary statistics: $\bar{x} = .323$ and $s^2 = .034$.

a. Test the null hypothesis that $\mu = .36$ against the alternative hypothesis that $\mu < .36$ using $\alpha = .10$.

b. Test the null hypothesis that $\mu = .36$ against the alternative hypothesis that $\mu \neq .36$ using $\alpha = .10$. Interpret the result.

Applying the Concepts

6.19 During the National Football League (NFL) season, Las Vegas oddsmakers establish a point spread on each game for betting purposes. For example, the St. Louis Rams were established as 7-point favorites over the Tennessee Titans in the 2000 Super Bowl. The final scores of NFL games were compared against the final point spreads established by the oddsmakers in *Chance* (Fall 1998). The difference between the game outcome and point spread (called a point-spread error) was calculated for 240 NFL games. The mean and standard deviation of the point-spread errors are $\bar{x} = -1.6$ and $s = 13.3$. Use this information to test the hypothesis that the true mean point-spread error for all NFL games is 0. Conduct the test at $\alpha = .01$ and interpret the result.

6.20 According to the National Funeral Directors Association, the nation's 22,000 funeral homes collected an average $5,020 per full-service funeral in 1998, up from $4,780 in 1996 (*Wall Street Journal Interactive Edition,* Jan. 7, 2000). In early 2000, a random sample of 36 funeral homes reported revenue data for 1999. Among other measures, each reported its average fee for a full-service funeral during 1999. These data (in thousands of dollars) are shown in the table below, rounded to the nearest hundred.

FUNERAL.DAT

6.1	8.1	4.0	7.1	6.2	5.2
4.9	7.0	5.4	10.3	5.0	4.6
5.4	4.5	3.9	5.1	4.7	6.1
5.9	5.3	5.0	4.0	5.3	4.3
7.1	5.9	6.1	4.5	5.0	4.8
5.7	5.9	4.8	4.1	6.1	5.3

a. What are the appropriate null and alternative hypotheses to test whether the average full-service fee of U. S. funeral homes in 1999 exceeds $5,020?

b. Conduct the test at $\alpha = .05$ using a statistical software package. Do the sample data provide sufficient evidence to conclude that the average fee in 1999 was higher than in 1998?

c. In conducting the test, was it necessary to assume that population of average full-service fees was normally distributed? Justify your answer.

6.21 Most major corporations have psychologists available to help employees who suffer from stress. One problem that is difficult to diagnose is post-traumatic stress disorder (PTSD). Researchers studying PTSD often use as subjects former prisoners of war (POWs). *Psychological Assessment* (Mar. 1995) published the results of a study of World War II aviators who were captured by German forces after they were shot down. Having located a total of 239 World War II aviator POW survivors, the researchers asked each veteran to participate in the study; 33 responded to the letter of invitation. Each of the 33 POW survivors was administered the Minnesota Multiphasic Personality Inventory, one component of which measures level of PTSD. [*Note:* The higher the score, the higher the level of PTSD.] The aviators produced a mean PTSD score of $\bar{x} = 9.00$ and a standard deviation of $s = 9.32$.

a. Set up the null and alternative hypotheses for determining whether the true mean PTSD score of all World War II aviator POWs is less than 16. [*Note:* The value, 16, represents the mean PTSD score established for Vietnam POWs.]

b. Conduct the test, part **a,** using $\alpha = .10$. What are the practical implications of the test?

c. Discuss the representativeness of the sample used in the study and its ramifications.

6.22 A study reported in the *Journal of Occupational and Organizational Psychology* (Dec. 1992) investigated the relationship of employment status to mental health. A sample of 49 unemployed men was given a mental health examination using the General Health Questionnaire (GHQ). The GHQ is a widely recognized measure of present mental health, with lower values indicating better mental health. The mean and standard deviation of the GHQ scores were $\bar{x} = 10.94$ and $s = 5.10$, respectively.

a. Specify the appropriate null and alternative hypotheses if we wish to test the research hypothesis that the mean GHQ score for all unemployed men exceeds 10. Is the test one-tailed or two-tailed? Why?

b. If we specify $\alpha = .05$, what is the appropriate rejection region for this test?

c. Conduct the test, and state your conclusion clearly in the language of this exercise.

6.23 In quality control applications of hypothesis testing, the null and alternative hypotheses are frequently specified as

H_0: The production process is performing satisfactorily

SAS Output for Exercise 6.23

```
Analysis Variable : WEIGHT

N Obs    N          Minimum          Maximum            Mean         Std Dev
------------------------------------------------------------------------------
   40   40        0.2470000        0.2560000       0.2524750       0.0022302
------------------------------------------------------------------------------
```

TEES.DAT

.247	.251	.254	.253	.253	.248	.253	.255	.256	.252
.253	.252	.253	.256	.254	.256	.252	.251	.253	.251
.253	.253	.248	.251	.253	.256	.254	.250	.254	.255
.249	.250	.254	.251	.251	.255	.251	.253	.252	.253

H_a: The process is performing in an unsatisfactory manner

Accordingly, α is sometimes referred to as the *producer's risk,* while β is called the *consumer's risk* (Stevenson, *Production/Operations Management,* 1996). An injection molder produces plastic golf tees. The process is designed to produce tees with a mean weight of .250 ounce. To investigate whether the injection molder is operating satisfactorily, 40 tees were randomly sampled from the last hour's production. Their weights (in ounces) are listed in the table above. Summary statistics for the data are shown in the SAS printout at the top of this page.

a. Do the data provide sufficient evidence to conclude that the process is not operating satisfactorily? Test using $\alpha = .01$

b. In the context of this problem, explain why it makes sense to call α the producer's risk and β the consumer's risk.

6.24 What factors inhibit the learning process in the classroom? To answer this question, researchers at Murray State University surveyed 40 students from a senior-level marketing class (*Marketing Education Review,* Fall 1994). Each student was given a list of factors and asked to rate the extent to which each factor inhibited the learning process in courses offered in their department. A 7-point rating scale was used, where 1 = "not at all" and 7 = "to a great extent." The factor with the highest rating was instructor-related: "Professors who place too much emphasis on a single right answer rather than overall thinking and creative ideas." Summary statistics for the student ratings of this factor are: $\bar{x} = 4.70$, $s = 1.62$.

a. Conduct a test to determine if the true mean rating for this instructor-related factor exceeds 4. Use $\alpha = .05$. Interpret the test results.

b. Because the variable of interest, rating, is measured on a 7-point scale, it is unlikely that the population of ratings will be normally distributed. Consequently, some analysts may perceive the test, part **a,** to be invalid and search for alternative methods of analysis. Defend or refute this argument.

6.25 Current technology uses X-rays and lasers for inspection of solder-joint defects on printed circuit boards (PCBs) (*Quality Congress Transactions,* 1986). A particular manufacturer of laser-based inspection equipment claims that its product can inspect on average at least 10 solder joints per second when the joints are spaced .1 inch apart. The equipment was tested by a potential buyer on 48 different PCBs. In each case, the equipment was operated for exactly 1 second. The number of solder joints inspected on each run follows:

PCB.DAT

10	9	10	10	11	9	12	8	8	9	6	10
7	10	11	9	9	13	9	10	11	10	12	8
9	9	9	7	12	6	9	10	10	8	7	9
11	12	10	0	10	11	12	9	7	9	9	10

a. The potential buyer wants to know whether the sample data refute the manufacturer's claim. Specify the null and alternative hypotheses that the buyer should test.

b. In the context of this exercise, what is a Type I error? A Type II error?

c. Conduct the hypothesis test you described in part **a,** and interpret the test's results in the context of this exercise. Use $\alpha = .05$ and the SPSS descriptive statistics printout at the bottom of the page.

6.26 A company has devised a new ink-jet cartridge for its plain-paper fax machine that it believes has a longer lifetime (on average) than the one currently being produced. To investigate its length of life, 225 of the new cartridges were tested by counting the number of high-quality printed pages each was able to produce. The sample mean and standard deviation were determined to be 1,511.4 pages and 35.7 pages, respectively. The his-

SPSS Output for Exercise 6.25

```
Variable   Mean   Std Dev   Minimum   Maximum    N Label
NUMBER     9.29      2.10       .00     13.00   48
```

torical average lifetime for cartridges produced by the current process is 1,502.5 pages; the historical standard deviation is 97.3 pages.

a. What are the appropriate null and alternative hypotheses to test whether the mean lifetime of the new cartridges exceeds that of the old cartridges?

b. Use $\alpha = .005$ to conduct the test in part **a.** Do the new cartridges have an average lifetime that is statistically significantly longer than the cartridges currently in production?

c. Does the difference in average lifetimes appear to be of practical significance from the perspective of the consumer? Explain.

d. Should the apparent decrease in the standard deviation in lifetimes associated with the new cartridges be viewed as an improvement over the old cartridges? Explain.

6.27 Nutritionists stress that weight control generally requires significant reductions in the intake of fat. A random sample of 64 middle-aged men on weight control programs is selected to determine whether their mean intake of fat exceeds the recommended 30 grams per day. The sample mean and standard deviation are $\bar{x} = 37$ and $s = 32$, respectively.

a. Considering the sample mean and standard deviation, would you expect the distribution for fat intake per day to be symmetric or skewed? Explain.

b. Do the sample results indicate that the mean intake for middle-aged men on weight control programs exceeds 30 grams? Test using $\alpha = .10$.

c. Would you reach the same conclusion as in part **b** using $\alpha = .05$? Using $\alpha = .01$? Why can the conclusion of a test change when the value of α is changed?

6.3 OBSERVED SIGNIFICANCE LEVELS: p-VALUES

According to the statistical test procedure described in Section 6.2, the rejection region and, correspondingly, the value of α are selected prior to conducting the test, and the conclusions are stated in terms of rejecting or not rejecting the null hypothesis. A second method of presenting the results of a statistical test is one that reports the extent to which the test statistic disagrees with the null hypothesis and leaves to the reader the task of deciding whether to reject the null hypothesis. This measure of disagreement is called the *observed significance level* (or *p-value*) for the test.

DEFINITION 6.1

The **observed significance level,** or ***p*-value,** for a specific statistical test is the probability (assuming H_0 is true) of observing a value of the test statistic that is at least as contradictory to the null hypothesis, and supportive of the alternative hypothesis, as the actual one computed from the sample data.

For example, the value of the test statistic computed for the sample of $n = 50$ sections of sewer pipe was $z = 2.12$. Since the test is one-tailed—i.e., the alternative (research) hypothesis of interest is H_a: $\mu > 2{,}400$—values of the test statistic even more contradictory to H_0 than the one observed would be values larger than $z = 2.12$. Therefore, the observed significance level (p-value) for this test is

$$p\text{-value} = P(z > 2.12)$$

or, equivalently, the area under the standard normal curve to the right of $z = 2.12$ (see Figure 6.6).

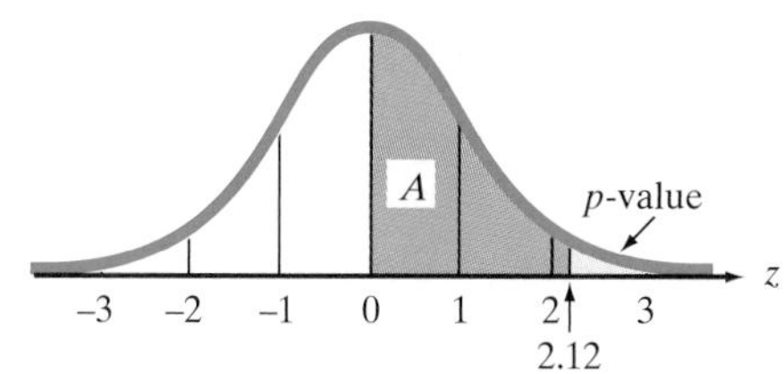

FIGURE 6.6
Finding the p-value for an upper-tailed test when $z = 2.12$

The area A in Figure 6.6 is given in Table IV in Appendix B as .4830. Therefore, the upper-tail area corresponding to $z = 2.12$ is

$$p\text{-value} = .5 - .4830 = .0170$$

Consequently, we say that these test results are "very significant"; i.e., they disagree rather strongly with the null hypothesis, H_0: $\mu = 2{,}400$, and favor H_a: $\mu > 2{,}400$. The probability of observing a z value as large as 2.12 is only .0170, if in fact the true value of μ is 2,400.

If you are inclined to select $\alpha = .05$ for this test, then you would reject the null hypothesis because the p-value for the test, .0170, is less than .05. In contrast, if you choose $\alpha = .01$, you would not reject the null hypothesis because the p-value for the test is larger than .01. Thus, the use of the observed significance level is identical to the test procedure described in the preceding sections except that the choice of α is left to you.

The steps for calculating the p-value corresponding to a test statistic for a population mean are given in the next box.

Steps for Calculating the p-value for a Test of Hypothesis

1. Determine the value of the test statistic z corresponding to the result of the sampling experiment.
2. a. If the test is one-tailed, the p-value is equal to the tail area beyond z in the same direction as the alternative hypothesis. Thus, if the alternative hypothesis is of the form $>$, the p-value is the area to the right of, or above, the observed z value. Conversely, if the alternative is of the form $<$, the p-value is the area to the left of, or below, the observed z value. (See Figure 6.7.)

   b. If the test is two-tailed, the p-value is equal to twice the tail area beyond the observed z value in the direction of the sign of z. That is, if z is positive, the p-value is twice the area to the right of, or above, the observed z value. Conversely, if z is negative, the p-value is twice the area to the left of, or below, the observed z value. (See Figure 6.8.)

FIGURE 6.7
Finding the p-value for a one-tailed test

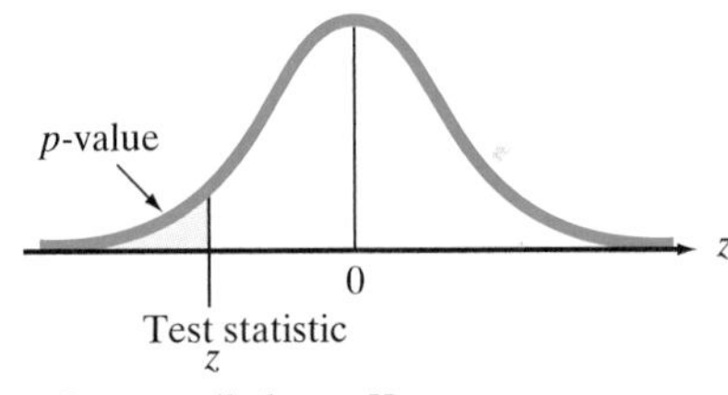

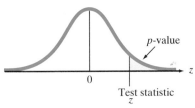

a. Lower–tailed test, H_a: $\mu < \mu_0$

p-value
0
z
Test statistic
z

b. Upper–tailed test, H_a: $\mu > \mu_0$

FIGURE 6.8
Finding the p-value for a two-tailed test: p-value $= 2(p/2)$

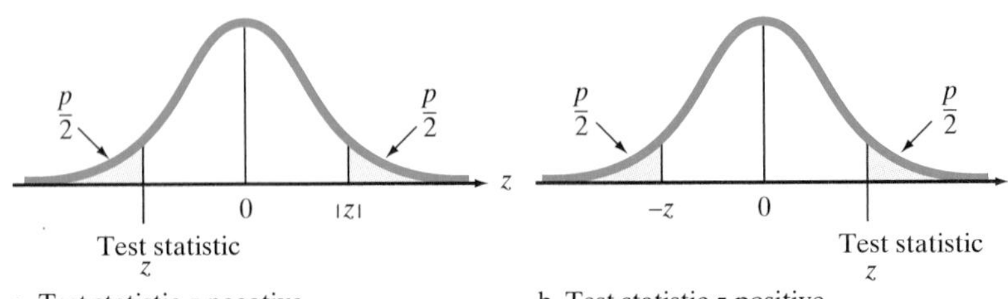

a. Test statistic z negative

b. Test statistic z positive

EXAMPLE 6.3 Find the observed significance level for the test of the mean filling weight in Examples 6.1 and 6.2.

Solution Example 6.1 presented a two-tailed test of the hypothesis

$$H_0: \mu = 12 \text{ ounces}$$

against the alternative hypothesis

$$H_a: \mu \neq 12 \text{ ounces}$$

The observed value of the test statistic in Example 6.2 was $z = -3.0$, and any value of z less than -3.0 or greater than $+3.0$ (because this is a two-tailed test) would be even more contradictory to H_0. Therefore, the observed significance level for the test is

$$p\text{-value} = P(z < -3.0 \text{ or } z > +3.0) = P(|z| > 3.0)$$

Thus, we calculate the area below the observed z value, $z = -3.0$, and double it. Consulting Table IV in Appendix B, we find that $P(z < -3.0) = .5 - .4987 = .0013$. Therefore, the p-value for this two-tailed test is

$$2P(z < -3.0) = 2(.0013) = .0026$$

We can interpret this p-value as a strong indication that the machine is not filling the boxes according to specifications, since we would observe a test statistic this extreme or more extreme only 26 in 10,000 times if the machine were meeting specifications ($\mu = 12$). The extent to which the mean differs from 12 could be better determined by calculating a confidence interval for μ.

When publishing the results of a statistical test of hypothesis in journals, case studies, reports, etc., many researchers make use of p-values. Instead of selecting α beforehand and then conducting a test, as outlined in this chapter, the researcher computes (usually with the aid of a statistical software package) and reports the value of the appropriate test statistic and its associated p-value. It is left to the reader of the report to judge the significance of the result—i.e., the reader must determine whether to reject the null hypothesis in favor of the alternative hypothesis, based on the reported p-value. Usually, the null hypothesis is rejected if the observed significance level is *less than* the fixed significance level, α, chosen by the reader. The inherent advantage of reporting test results in this manner are twofold: (1) Readers are permitted to select the maximum value of α that they would be willing to tolerate if they actually carried out a standard test of hypothesis in the manner outlined in this chapter, and (2) a measure of the degree of significance of the result (i.e., the p-value) is provided.

Reporting Test Results as *p*-values: How to Decide Whether to Reject H_0

1. Choose the maximum value of α that you are willing to tolerate.
2. If the observed significance level (p-value) of the test is less than the chosen value of α, reject the null hypothesis. Otherwise, do not reject the null hypothesis.

EXAMPLE 6.4

Knowledge of the amount of time a patient occupies a hospital bed—called length of stay (LOS)—is important for allocating resources. At one hospital, the mean length of stay was determined to be 5 days. A hospital administrator believes that the mean LOS may now be less than 5 days due to a newly adopted managed care system. To check this, the LOSs (in days) for 100 randomly selected hospital patients were recorded; these are listed in Table 6.3. Test the hypothesis that the true mean LOS at the hospital is less than 5 days, i.e.,

$$H_0: \mu = 5$$
$$H_a: \mu < 5$$

Use the data in the table to conduct the test at $\alpha = .05$.

TABLE 6.3 Lengths of Stay for 100 Hospital Patients

2	3	8	6	4	4	6	4	2	5
8	10	4	4	4	2	1	3	2	10
1	3	2	3	4	3	5	2	4	1
2	9	1	7	17	9	9	9	4	4
1	1	1	3	1	6	3	3	2	5
1	3	3	14	2	3	9	6	6	3
5	1	4	6	11	22	1	9	6	5
2	2	5	4	3	6	1	5	1	6
17	1	2	4	5	4	4	3	2	3
3	5	2	3	3	2	10	2	4	2

FIGURE 6.9
MINITAB printout for the lower-tailed test in Example 6.4

```
TEST OF MU = 5.000 VS MU L.T. 5.000
THE ASSUMED SIGMA = 3.68

              N      MEAN     STDEV   SE MEAN        Z   P VALUE
LOS         100     4.530     3.678     0.368    -1.28      0.10
```

Solution Instead of performing the computations by hand, we will use a statistical software package. The data were entered into a computer and MINITAB was used to conduct the analysis. The MINITAB printout for the lower-tailed test is displayed in Figure 6.9. Both the test statistic, $z = -1.28$, and p-value of the test, $p = .10$, are highlighted on the MINITAB printout. Since the p-value exceeds our selected α value, $\alpha = .05$, we cannot reject the null hypothesis. Hence, there is insufficient evidence (at $\alpha = .05$) to conclude that the true mean LOS at the hospital is less than 5 days.

Note: Some statistical software packages (e.g., SAS and SPSS) will conduct only two-tailed tests of hypothesis. For these packages, you obtain the p-value for a one-tailed test as shown in the box:

Converting a Two-tailed *p*-value From a Printout to a One-tailed *p*-value

$$p = \frac{\text{Reported } p\text{-value}}{2} \quad \text{if } \begin{cases} H_a \text{ is of form} > \text{and } z \text{ is positive} \\ H_a \text{ is of form} < \text{and } z \text{ is negative} \end{cases}$$

$$p = 1 - \left(\frac{\text{Reported } p\text{-value}}{2}\right) \quad \text{if } \begin{cases} H_a \text{ is of form} > \text{and } z \text{ is negative} \\ H_a \text{ is of form} < \text{and } z \text{ is positive} \end{cases}$$

Hypothesis Testing

USING THE TI-83 GRAPHING CALCULATOR

Computing the p-value for a z-Test.

Start from the home screen.

Step 1 Access the "Statistical Test" Menu.

Press **STAT**
Arrow right to **TESTS**
Press **ENTER**
Arrow right to **STATS**
Press **ENTER**
Set μ_0: **See Note I**
σ: " "
$\bar{x}$: " "
n: " "
μ: **See Note II**
Press **ENTER**
Arrow down to **Calculate**
Press **ENTER**

Note I: *μ_0 is the assumed population mean, σ is the population standard deviation, $\bar{x}$ is the sample mean, and n is the sample size.*

Note II: *Recall: you always test H_a! Arrow to highlight the appropriate test.*

Step 2 View Display
The chosen test will be displayed as well as the z-test statistic, the p-value, the sample mean, and the sample size.

Example: A manufacturer claims the average life expectancy of this particular model light bulb is 10,000 hours with $\sigma = 1{,}000$ hours. A simple random sample of 40 light bulbs shows $\bar{x} = 9{,}755$ hours. Using $\alpha = .05$ test the manufacturer's claim.

For this problem the hypotheses will be: H_0: $\mu > =10{,}000$
H_a: $\mu < 10{,}000$

Step 1 Access the Statistical Test Menu. Enter your setting for this problem (see the screen below left).

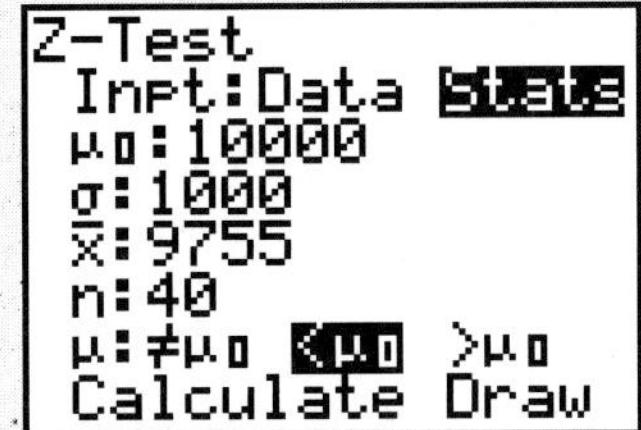

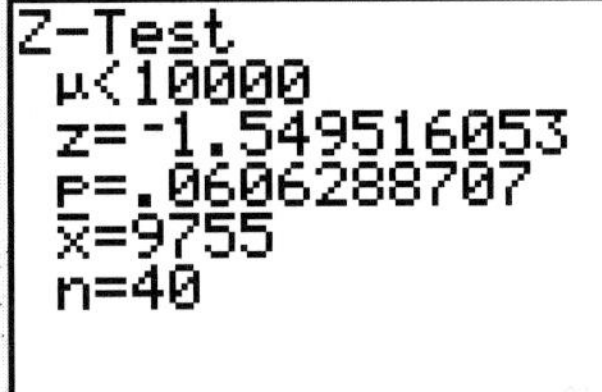

Arrow down to Calculate and press **ENTER** (screen above right will be displayed).

Step 2 View Display. As you can see the p-value is 0.061. Recall, we reject H_0 only if $p < \alpha$. Therefore *do not* reject H_0.

Step 3 Clear the screen for the next problem. Return to the home screen. Press **CLEAR.**

EXERCISES 6.28–6.40

Learning the Mechanics

6.28 If a hypothesis test were conducted using $\alpha = .05$, for which of the following p-values would the null hypothesis be rejected?
a. .06 b. .10 c. .01 d. .001 e. .251 f. .042

6.29 For each α and observed significance level (p-value) pair, indicate whether the null hypothesis would be rejected.
a. $\alpha = .05$, p-value $= .10$
b. $\alpha = .10$, p-value $= .05$
c. $\alpha = .01$, p-value $= .001$
d. $\alpha = .025$, p-value $= .05$
e. $\alpha = .10$, p-value $= .45$

6.30 An analyst tested the null hypothesis $\mu \geq 20$ against the alternative hypothesis that $\mu < 20$. The analyst reported a p-value of .06. What is the smallest value of α for which the null hypothesis would be rejected?

6.31 In a test of H_0: $\mu = 100$ against H_a: $\mu > 100$, the sample data yielded the test statistic $z = 2.17$. Find the p-value for the test.

6.32 In a test of the hypothesis H_0: $\mu = 10$ versus H_a: $\mu \neq 10$, a sample of $n = 50$ observations possessed mean $\bar{x} = 10.7$ and standard deviation $s = 3.1$. Find and interpret the p-value for this test.

6.33 Consider a test of H_0: $\mu = 75$ performed using the computer. SAS reports a two-tailed p-value of .1032. Make the appropriate conclusion for each of the following situations:
a. H_a: $\mu < 75$, $z = -1.63$, $\alpha = .05$
b. H_a: $\mu < 75$, $z = 1.63$, $\alpha = .10$
c. H_a: $\mu > 75$, $z = 1.63$, $\alpha = .10$
d. H_a: $\mu \neq 75$, $z = -1.63$, $\alpha = .01$

Applying the Concepts

6.34 According to *USA Today* (Dec. 30, 1999), the average age of viewers of MSNBC cable television news programming is 50 years. A random sample of 50 U. S. households that receive cable television programming yielded the following additional information about the ages of MSNBC news viewers:

$$\bar{x} = 51.3 \text{ years} \quad \text{and} \quad s = 7.1 \text{ years}$$

Do the sample data provide sufficient evidence to conclude that the average age of MSNBC's viewers is greater than 50 years?
a. Conduct the appropriate hypothesis test.
b. Calculate the observed significance level of the test and interpret its value in the context of the problem.
c. Would the p-value have been larger or smaller if $\bar{x}$ had been larger? Explain.

6.35 Television commercials most often employ females, or "feminized" males, to pitch a company's product. Research published in *Nature* (Aug. 27, 1998) revealed that people are, in fact, more attracted to "feminized" faces, regardless of gender. In one experiment, 50 human subjects viewed both a Japanese female and a Caucasian male face on a computer. Using special computer graphics, each subject could morph the faces (by making them more feminine or more masculine) until they attained the "most attractive" face. The level of feminization x (measured as a percentage) was measured.
a. For the Japanese female face, $\bar{x} = 10.2\%$ and $s = 31.3\%$. The researchers used this sample information to test the null hypothesis of a mean level of feminization equal to 0%. Verify that the test statistic is equal to 2.3.
b. Refer to part **a.** The researchers reported the p-value of the test as $p = .027$. Verify and interpret this result.
c. For the Caucasian male face, $\bar{x} = 15.0\%$ and $s = 25.1\%$. The researchers reported the test statistic (for the test of the null hypothesis stated in part **a**) as 4.23 with an associated p-value of approximately 0. Verify and interpret these results.

6.36 Refer to the *Wall Street Journal*/National Funeral Directors Association study of the average fee charged for a full-service funeral during 1999, Exercise 6.20 (p. 311). Recall that a test was conducted to determine if the true mean fee charged exceeds $5,020. The data (recorded in thousands of dollars) for the sample of 36 funeral homes were analyzed using STATISTIX. The resulting printout of the test of hypothesis is shown here.

STATISTIX Output for Exercise 6.36

```
ONE-SAMPLE T TEST FOR REVENUE

NULL HYPOTHESIS: MU = 5.02
ALTERNATIVE HYP: MU > 5.02

MEAN          5.5194
STD ERROR     0.2108
MEAN - H0     0.4994
LO 95% CI     0.0715
UP 95% CI     0.9274
T               2.37
DF                35
P             0.0117

CASES INCLUDED 36    MISSING CASES 0
```

a. Locate the p-value for this upper-tailed test of hypothesis.

b. Use the p-value to make a decision regarding the null hypothesis tested. Does the decision agree with your decision in Exercise 6.20?

6.37 In Exercise 5.8 (p. 266) we examined research about bicycle helmets reported in *Public Health Reports* (May–June 1992). One of the variables measured was the children's perception of the risk involved in bicycling. A random sample of 797 children in grades 4–6 were asked to rate their perception of bicycle risk without wearing a helmet, ranging from 1 (no risk) to 4 (very high risk). The mean and standard deviation of the sample were $\bar{x} = 3.39$, $s = 80$, respectively.

a. Assume that a mean score, μ, of 2.5 is indicative of indifference to risk, and values of μ exceeding 2.5 indicate a perception that a risk exists. What are the appropriate null and alternative hypotheses for testing the research hypothesis that children in this age group perceive a risk associated with failure to wear helmets?

b. Calculate the p-value for the data collected in this study.

c. Interpret the p-value in the context of this research.

6.38 Refer to Exercise 6.22 (p. 311), in which a random sample of 49 unemployed men were administered the General Health Questionnaire (GHQ). The sample mean and standard deviation were 10.94 and 5.10, respectively. Denoting the population mean GHQ for unemployed workers by μ, we wish to test the null hypothesis H_0: $\mu = 10$ versus the one-tailed alternative H_a: $\mu > 10$.

a. When the data are run through MINITAB, the results (in part) are as shown in the printout below. Check the program's results for accuracy.

b. What conclusion would you reach about the test based on the computer analysis?

6.39 An article published in the *Journal of the American Medical Association* (Oct. 16, 1995) calls smoking in China "a public health emergency." The researchers found that smokers in China smoke an average of 16.5 cigarettes a day. The high smoking rate is one reason why the tobacco industry is the central government's largest source of tax revenue. Has the average number of cigarettes smoked per day by Chinese smokers increased over the past two years? Consider that in a random sample of 200 Chinese smokers in 1997, the number of cigarettes smoked per day had a mean of 17.05 and a standard deviation of 5.21.

a. Set up the null and alternative hypotheses for testing whether Chinese smokers smoke, on average, more cigarettes a day in 1997 than in 1995. (Assume that the population mean for 1995 is $\mu = 16.5$.)

b. Compute and interpret the observed significance level of the test.

c. Why is a two-tailed test inappropriate for this problem?

6.40 In Exercise 6.23 (p. 311) you tested H_0: $\mu = .250$ versus H_a: $\mu \neq .250$, where μ is the population mean weight of plastic golf tees. A SAS printout for the hypothesis test is shown below. Locate the p-value on the printout and interpret its value.

MINITAB Output for Exercise 6.38

```
TEST OF MU = 10.00 VS MU G.T. 10.00
THE ASSUMED SIGMA = 5.10

         N    MEAN   STDEV   SE MEAN      Z   P VALUE
GHQ     49   10.94    5.10      0.73   1.29     .0985
```

SAS Output for Exercise 6.40

```
Analysis Variable : WT_250 (Test Mean Weight=.250)

N Obs          Mean        Std Dev            T   Prob>|T|
-----------------------------------------------------------
   40     0.0024750      0.0022302    7.0188284     0.0001
-----------------------------------------------------------
```

6.4 SMALL-SAMPLE TEST OF HYPOTHESIS ABOUT A POPULATION MEAN

A manufacturing operation consists of a single-machine-tool system that produces an average of 15.5 transformer parts every hour. After undergoing a complete overhaul, the system was monitored by observing the number of parts produced in each of seventeen randomly selected one-hour periods. The mean and standard deviation for the 17 production runs are:

$$\bar{x} = 15.42 \qquad s = .16$$

Does this sample provide sufficient evidence to conclude that the true mean number of parts produced every hour by the overhauled system differs from 15.5?

This inference can be placed in a test of hypothesis framework. We establish the preoverhaul mean as the null hypothesized value and utilize a two-tailed alternative that the true mean of the overhauled system differs from the preoverhaul mean:

$$H_0: \mu = 15.5$$
$$H_a: \mu \neq 15.5$$

Recall from Section 5.3 that when we are faced with making inferences about a population mean using the information in a small sample, two problems emerge:

1. The normality of the sampling distribution for $\bar{x}$ does not follow from the Central Limit Theorem when the sample size is small. We must assume that the distribution of measurements from which the sample was selected is approximately normally distributed in order to ensure the approximate normality of the sampling distribution of $\bar{x}$.
2. If the population standard deviation σ is unknown, as is usually the case, then we cannot assume that s will provide a good approximation for σ when the sample size is small. Instead, we must use the t-distribution rather than the standard normal z-distribution to make inferences about the population mean μ.

Therefore, as the test statistic of a small-sample test of a population mean, we use the t statistic:

$$\textit{Test statistic: } t = \frac{\bar{x} - \mu_0}{s/\sqrt{n}} = \frac{\bar{x} - 15.5}{s/\sqrt{n}}$$

where μ_0 is the null hypothesized value of the population mean, μ. In our example, $\mu_0 = 15.5$.

To find the rejection region, we must specify the value of α, the probability that the test will lead to rejection of the null hypothesis when it is true, and then consult the t-table (Table VI of Appendix B). Using $\alpha = .05$, the two-tailed rejection region is

Rejection region: $t_{\alpha/2} = t_{.025} = 2.120$ with $n - 1 = 16$ degrees of freedom

Reject H_0 if $t < -2.120$ or $t > 2.120$

The rejection region is shown in Figure 6.10.

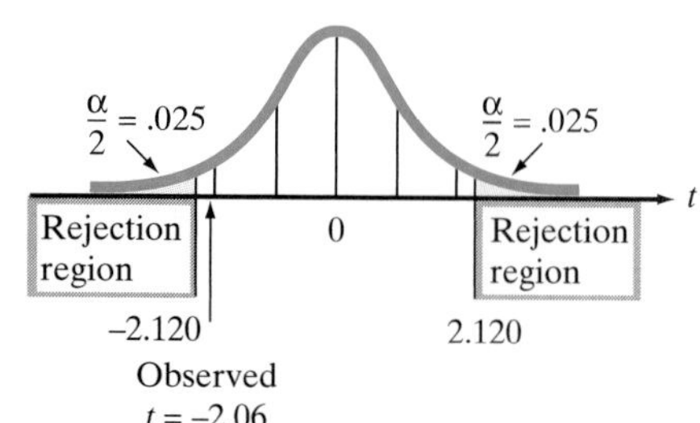

FIGURE 6.10
Two-tailed rejection region for small-sample t-test

We are now prepared to calculate the test statistic and reach a conclusion:

$$t = \frac{\bar{x} - \mu_0}{s/\sqrt{n}} = \frac{15.42 - 15.50}{.16/\sqrt{17}} = \frac{-.08}{.0388} = -2.06$$

Since the calculated value of t does not fall in the rejection region (Figure 6.10), we cannot reject H_0 at the $\alpha = .05$ level of significance. Based on the sample evidence, we should not conclude that the mean number of parts produced per hour by the overhauled system differs from 15.5.

It is interesting to note that the calculated t value, -2.06, is *less than* the .05 level z value, -1.96. The implication is that if we had *incorrectly* used a z statistic for this test, we would have rejected the null hypothesis at the .05 level, concluding that the mean production per hour of the overhauled system differs from 15.5 parts. The important point is that the statistical procedure to be used must always be closely scrutinized and all the assumptions understood. Many statistical distortions are the result of misapplications of otherwise valid procedures.

The technique for conducting a small-sample test of hypothesis about a population mean is summarized in the following box.

Small-Sample Test of Hypothesis About μ

One-Tailed Test	**Two-Tailed Test**
$H_0: \mu = \mu_0$	$H_0: \mu = \mu_0$
$H_a: \mu < \mu_0$ (or $H_a: \mu > \mu_0$)	$H_a: \mu \neq \mu_0$
Test statistic: $t = \dfrac{\bar{x} - \mu_0}{s/\sqrt{n}}$	*Test statistic:* $t = \dfrac{\bar{x} - \mu_0}{s/\sqrt{n}}$
Rejection region: $t < -t_\alpha$ (or $t > t_\alpha$ when $H_a: \mu > \mu_0$)	*Rejection region:* $\|t\| > t_{\alpha/2}$

where t_α and $t_{\alpha/2}$ are based on $(n - 1)$ degrees of freedom

Assumption: A random sample is selected from a population with a relative frequency distribution that is approximately normal.

EXAMPLE 6.5 A major car manufacturer wants to test a new engine to determine whether it meets new air pollution standards. The mean emission μ of all engines of this type must be less than 20 parts per million of carbon. Ten engines are manufactured for testing purposes, and the emission level of each is determined. The data (in parts per million) are listed below:

15.6 16.2 22.5 20.5 16.4 19.4 16.6 17.9 12.7 13.9

Do the data supply sufficient evidence to allow the manufacturer to conclude that this type of engine meets the pollution standard? Assume that the production process is stable and the manufacturer is willing to risk a Type I error with probability $\alpha = .01$.

Solution The manufacturer wants to support the research hypothesis that the mean emission level μ for all engines of this type is less than 20 parts per million. The elements of this small-sample one-tailed test are

H_0: $\mu = 20$
H_a: $\mu < 20$

Test statistic: $t = \dfrac{\bar{x} - 20}{s/\sqrt{n}}$

Assumption: The relative frequency distribution of the population of emission levels for all engines of this type is approximately normal.

Rejection region: For $\alpha = .01$ and df $= n - 1 = 9$, the one-tailed rejection region (see Figure 6.11) is $t < -t_{.01} = -2.821$.

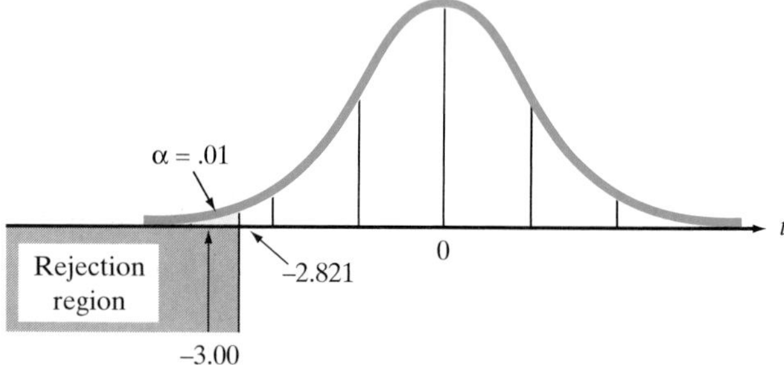

FIGURE 6.11
A *t*-distribution with 9 df and the rejection region for Example 6.5

To calculate the test statistic, we entered the data into a computer and analyzed it using SAS. The SAS descriptive statistics printout is shown in Figure 6.12. From the printout, we obtain $\bar{x} = 17.17$, $s = 2.98$. Substituting these values into the test statistic formula, we get

$$t = \frac{\bar{x} - 20}{s/\sqrt{n}} = \frac{17.17 - 20}{2.98/\sqrt{10}} = -3.00$$

FIGURE 6.12
SAS descriptive statistics for 10 emission levels

```
Analysis Variable : EMIT

N Obs    N        Minimum        Maximum            Mean          Std Dev
--------------------------------------------------------------------------
   10   10     12.7000000     22.5000000      17.1700000        2.9814426
--------------------------------------------------------------------------
```

Since the calculated t falls in the rejection region (see Figure 6.11), the manufacturer concludes that $\mu < 20$ parts per million and the new engine type meets the pollution standard. Are you satisfied with the reliability associated with this inference? The probability is only $\alpha = .01$ that the test would support the research hypothesis if in fact it were false.

EXAMPLE 6.6 Find the observed significance level for the test described in Example 6.5. Interpret the result.

Solution The test of Example 6.5 was a lower-tailed test: H_0: $\mu = 20$ versus H_a: $\mu < 20$. Since the value of t computed from the sample data was $t = -3.00$, the observed significance level (or p-value) for the test is equal to the probability that t would assume a value less than or equal to -3.00 if in fact H_0 were true. This is equal to the area in the lower tail of the t-distribution (shaded in Figure 6.13).

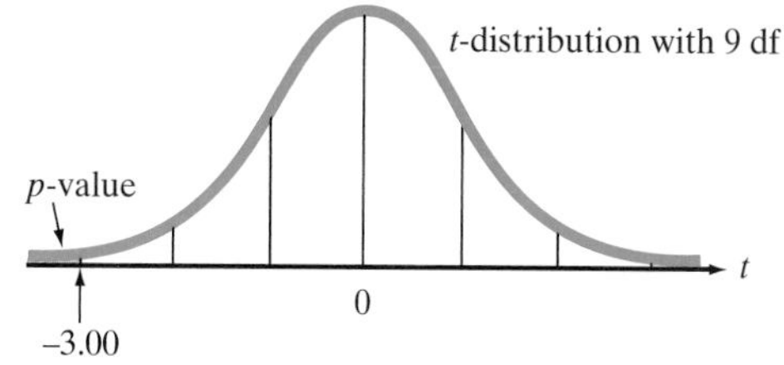

Figure 6.13
The observed significance level for the test of Example 6.5

One way to find this area—i.e., the p-value for the test—is to consult the t-table (Table VI in Appendix B). Unlike the table of areas under the normal curve, Table VI gives only the t values corresponding to the areas .100, .050, .025, .010, .005, .001, and .0005. Therefore, we can only approximate the p-value for the test. Since the observed t value was based on 9 degrees of freedom, we use the df = 9 row in Table VI and move across the row until we reach the t values that are closest to the observed $t = -3.00$. [*Note:* We ignore the minus sign.] The t values corresponding to p-values of .010 and .005 are 2.821 and 3.250, respectively. Since the observed t value falls between $t_{.010}$ and $t_{.005}$, the p-value for the test lies between .005 and .010. In other words, $.005 < p\text{-value} < .01$. Thus, we would reject the null hypothesis, H_0: $\mu = 20$ parts per million, for any value of α larger than .01 (the upper bound of the p-value).

A second, more accurate, way to obtain the p-value is to use a statistical software package to conduct the test of hypothesis. The SAS printout for the test of H_0: $\mu = 20$ is displayed in Figure 6.14. Both the test statistic (-3.00) and p-value (.0149) are highlighted in Figure 6.14. Recall (from Section 6.3) that SAS conducts, by default, a two-tailed test. That is, SAS tests the alternative H_a: $\mu \neq 20$. Thus, the p-value reported on the printout must be adjusted to obtain the appropriate p-value for our lower-tailed test. Since the value of the test statistic is negative and H_a is of the form $<$ (i.e., the value of t agrees with the direction specified in H_a), the p-value is obtained by dividing the printout value in half:

$$\text{One-tailed } p\text{-value} = \frac{\text{Reported } p\text{-value}}{2} = \frac{.0149}{2} = .00745$$

Figure 6.14
SAS test of $H_0 \mu = 20$ for Example 6.16

```
Analysis Variable : EMIT_20

N Obs         Mean        Std Dev              T   Prob>|T|
------------------------------------------------------------
   10   -2.8300000    2.9814426     -3.0016495     0.0149
------------------------------------------------------------
```

You can see that the actual p-value of the test falls within the bounds obtained from Table VI. Thus, the two methods agree; we will reject H_0: $\mu = 20$ in favor of H_a: $\mu < 20$ for any α level larger than .01.

Small-sample inferences typically require more assumptions and provide less information about the population parameter than do large-sample inferences. Nevertheless, the t-test is a method of testing a hypothesis about a population mean of a normal distribution when only a small number of observations are available. What can be done if you know that the population relative frequency distribution is decidedly nonnormal, say highly skewed? A nonparametric statistical method is described in optional Section 6.6.

EXERCISES 6.41–6.52

Learning the Mechanics

6.41 For each of the following rejection regions, sketch the sampling distribution of t, and indicate the location of the rejection region on your sketch:

a. $t > 1.440$ where df $= 6$
b. $t < -1.782$ where df $= 12$
c. $t < -2.060$ or $t > 2.060$ where df $= 25$

6.42 For each of the rejection regions defined in Exercise 6.41, what is the probability that a Type I error will be made?

6.43 A random sample of n observations is selected from a normal population to test the null hypothesis that $\mu = 10$. Specify the rejection region for each of the following combinations of H_a, α, and n:

a. H_a: $\mu \neq 10$; $\alpha = .05$; $n = 14$
b. H_a: $\mu > 10$; $\alpha = .01$; $n = 24$
c. H_a: $\mu > 10$; $\alpha = .10$; $n = 9$
d. H_a: $\mu < 10$; $\alpha = .01$; $n = 12$
e. H_a: $\mu \neq 10$; $\alpha = .10$; $n = 20$
f. H_a: $\mu < 10$; $\alpha = .05$; $n = 4$

6.44 A sample of five measurements, randomly selected from a normally distributed population, resulted in the following summary statistics: $\bar{x} = 4.8$, $s = 1.3$.

a. Test the null hypothesis that the mean of the population is 6 against the alternative hypothesis, $\mu < 6$. Use $\alpha = .05$.
b. Test the null hypothesis that the mean of the population is 6 against the alternative hypothesis, $\mu \neq 6$. Use $\alpha = .05$.
c. Find the observed significance level for each test.

6.45 MINITAB is used to conduct a t-test for the null hypothesis H_0: $\mu = 1{,}000$ versus the alternative hypothesis H_a: $\mu > 1{,}000$ based on a sample of 17 observations. The software's output is shown below.

a. What assumptions are necessary for the validity of this procedure?
b. Interpret the results of the test.
c. Suppose the alternative hypothesis had been the two-tailed H_a: $\mu \neq 1{,}000$. If the t statistic were unchanged, then what would the p-value be for this test? Interpret the p-value for the two-tailed test.

Applying the Concepts

6.46 Information Resources Inc., a Chicago-based research organization, tracks supermarket sales in 28 metropolitan markets in the United States. They convert their data for specific products to an index that measures product usage relative to the national average usage. For example, Green Bay, Wisconsin's ketchup index is 143, the highest in the nation. This means that Green Bay residents consume 43% more ketchup, on average, than the mean national consumption rate. The table lists the salad dressings index for each in a sample of seven Southeastern cities.

SALAD.DAT

Salad Dressings Index (U. S. mean = 100)	
Charlotte, N. C.	124
Birmingham. Al.	99
Raleigh, N. C.	124
Knoxville, Tenn.	99
Memphis, Tenn.	90
Atlanta, Ga.	111
Nashville, Tenn.	89

Source: *Wall Street Journal Interactive Edition,* Jan. 5, 2000.

a. Specify the appropriate null and alternative hypotheses for testing whether the true mean consumption rate of salad dressings in the Southeastern United States is different than the mean national consumption rate of 100.
b. What assumptions about the sample and population must hold in order for it to be appropriate to use a t statistic in conducting the hypothesis test?
c. Conduct the hypothesis test using $\alpha = .05$.
d. Is the observed significance level of the test greater or less than .05? Justify your answer.

6.47 A study was conducted to evaluate the effectiveness of a new mosquito repellent designed by the U.S. Army to be applied as camouflage face paint (*Journal of the Mosquito Control Association,* June 1995). The repellent was applied to the forearms of five volunteers and then the arms were exposed to fifteen active mosquitoes for a 10-hour period. Based on the number and location of the mosquito bites, the percentage of the forearm surface area protected from bites (called percent repellency) was calculated for each of the five volunteers. For one color of paint (loam), the following summary statistics were obtained:

$$\bar{x} = 83\% \qquad s = 15\%$$

MINITAB Output for Exercise 6.45

```
TEST OF MU = 1,000 VS MU G.T. 1,000

            N      MEAN     STDEV   SE MEAN        T   P VALUE
X          17      1020     43.54     10.56    1.894     .0382
```

a. The new repellent is considered effective if it provides a percent repellency of at least 95. Conduct a test to determine whether the mean repellency percentage of the new mosquito repellent is less than 95. Test using $\alpha = .10$

b. What assumptions are required for the hypothesis test in part **a** to be valid?

6.48 The Cleveland Casting Plant is a large, highly automated producer of gray and nodular iron automotive castings for Ford Motor Company (*Quality Engineering,* Vol. 7, 1995). One process variable of interest to Cleveland Casting is the pouring temperature of the molten iron. The pouring temperatures (in degrees Fahrenheit) for a sample of 10 crankshafts are listed in the table. The target setting for the pouring temperature is set at 2,550 degrees. Assuming the process is stable, conduct a test to determine whether the true mean pouring temperature differs from the target setting. Test using $\alpha = .01$.

IRONTEMP.DAT

2,543	2,541	2,544	2,620	2,560	2,559	2,562
2,553	2,552	2,553				

Source: Price, B., and Barth, B. "A structural model relating process inputs and final product characteristics." *Quality Engineering,* Vol. 7, No. 4, 1995, p. 696 (Table 2).

6.49 By law, the levels of toxic organic compounds in fish are constantly monitored. A technique, called matrix solid-phase dispersion (MSPD), has been developed for chemically extracting trace organic compounds from fish specimens (*Chromatographia,* Mar. 1995). The MSPD method was tested as follows. Uncontaminated fish fillets were injected with a known amount of toxin. The MSPD method was then used to extract the contaminant and the percentage of the toxic compound recovered was measured. The recovery percentages for $n = 5$ fish fillets are listed below:

RECPCT.DAT

99	102	94	99	95

Do the data provide sufficient evidence to indicate that the mean recovery percentage of the toxic compound exceeds 85% using the new MSPD method? Test using $\alpha = .05$.

6.50 To instill customer loyalty, airlines, hotels, rental car companies, and credit card companies (among others) have initiated *frequency marketing programs* that reward their regular customers. In the United States alone, 30 million people are members of the frequent flier programs of the airline industry (*Fortune,* Feb. 22, 1993). A large fast-food restaurant chain wished to explore the profitability of such a program. They randomly selected 12 of their 1,200 restaurants nationwide and instituted a frequency program that rewarded customers with a $5.00 gift certificate after every 10 meals purchased at full price. They ran the trial program for three months. The restaurants not in the sample had an average increase in profits of $1,047.34 over the previous three months, whereas the restaurants in the sample had the following changes in profit:

PROFIT.DAT

$2,232.90	$545.47	$3,440.70	$1,809.10
$6,552.70	$4,798.70	$2,965.00	$2,610.70
$3,381.30	$1,591.40	$2,376.20	−$2,191.00

Note that the last number is negative, representing a decrease in profits. Summary statistics and graphs for the data are given in the SPSS printout on page 326.

a. Specify the appropriate null and alternative hypotheses for determining whether the mean profit change for restaurants with frequency programs is significantly greater (in a statistical sense) than $1,047.34.

b. Conduct the test of part **b** using $\alpha = .05$. Does it appear that the frequency program would be profitable for the company if adopted nationwide?

6.51 The Occupational Safety and Health Act (OSHA) allows issuance of engineering standards to ensure safe workplaces for all Americans. The maximum allowable mean level of arsenic in smelters, herbicide production facilities, and other places where arsenic is used is .004 milligram per cubic meter of air. Suppose smelters at two plants are being investigated to determine whether they are meeting OSHA standards. Two analyses of the air are made at each plant, and the results (in milligrams per cubic meter of air) are shown in the table.

Plant 1		Plant 2	
Observation	**Arsenic Level**	**Observation**	**Arsenic Level**
1	.01	1	.05
2	.005	2	.09

a. What are the appropriate null and alternative hypotheses if we wish to test whether the plants meet the current OSHA standard?

b. These data are analyzed by MINITAB, with the results as shown on p. 326. Check the calculations of the t statistics and p-values.

c. Interpret the results of the two tests.

6.52 Periodic assessment of stress in paved highways is important to maintaining safe roads. The Mississippi Department of Transportation recently collected data on number of cracks (called *crack intensity*) in an

SPSS Output for Exercise 6.50

```
     PROFIT

 Valid cases:          12.0    Missing cases:         .0    Percent missing:        .0

 Mean       2509.431  Std Err    620.4388  Min       -2191.00   Skewness      -.3616
 Median     2493.450  Variance    4619332  Max        6552.700   S E Skew       .6373
 5% Trim    2545.940  Std Dev    2149.263  Range     8743.700   Kurtosis      1.8750
                                            IQR       1780.025   S E Kurt      1.2322
------------------------------------------------------------------------------------
 Frequency      Stem &   Leaf

     1.00 Extremes       (-2191)
     1.00         0  .   5
     2.00         1  .   58
     4.00         2  .   2369
     2.00         3  .   34
     1.00         4  .   7
     1.00 Extremes       (6553)

 Stem width:    1000.00
 Each leaf:         1 case(s)
------------------------------------------------------------------------------------
```

MINITAB Output for Exercise 6.51

```
TEST OF MU = 0.00400 VS MU G.T. 0.00400

             N      MEAN     STDEV   SE MEAN        T   P VALUE
Plant1       2   0.00750   0.00354   0.00250     1.40      0.20
Plant2       2   0.07000   0.02828   0.02000     3.30     0.094
```

undivided two-lane highway using van-mounted state-of-the-art video technology (*Journal of Infrastructure Systems,* Mar. 1995). The mean number of cracks found in a sample of eight 50-meter sections of the highway was $\bar{x} = .210$, with a variance of $s^2 = .011$. Suppose the American Association of State Highway and Transportation Officials (AASHTO) recommends a maximum mean crack intensity of .100 for safety purposes. Test the hypothesis that the true mean crack intensity of the Mississippi highway exceeds the AASHTO recommended maximum. Use $\alpha = .01$.

6.5 LARGE-SAMPLE TEST OF HYPOTHESIS ABOUT A POPULATION PROPORTION

Inferences about population proportions (or percentages) are often made in the context of the probability, p, of "success" for a binomial distribution. We saw how to use large samples from binomial distributions to form confidence intervals for p in Section 5.3. We now consider tests of hypotheses about p.

For example, consider the problem of *insider trading* in the stock market. Insider trading is the buying and selling of stock by an individual privy to inside information in a company, usually a high-level executive in the firm. The Securities and Exchange Commission (SEC) imposes strict guidelines about insider trading so that all investors can have equal access to information that may affect the stock's price. An investor wishing to test the effectiveness of the SEC guidelines monitors the market for a period of a year and records the number of times a stock price increases the day following a significant purchase of stock by an insider. For a total of 576 such transactions, the stock increased the following day 327 times. Does this sample provide evidence that the stock price may be affected by insider trading?

We first view this as a binomial experiment, with the 576 transactions as the trials, and success representing an increase in the stock's price the following day. Let p represent the probability that the stock price will increase following a large insider purchase. If the insider purchase has no effect on the stock price (that is, if the information available to the insider is identical to that available to the general market), then the investor expects the probability of a stock increase to be the same as that of a decrease, or $p = .5$. On the other hand, if insider trading affects the stock price (indicating that the market has not fully accounted for the information known to the insiders), then the investor expects the stock either to decrease or to increase more than half the time following significant insider transactions; that is, $p \neq .5$.

We can now place the problem in the context of a test of hypothesis:

H_0: $p = .5$

H_a: $p \neq .5$

Recall that the sample proportion, $\hat{p}$, is really just the sample mean of the outcomes of the individual binomial trials and, as such, is approximately normally distributed (for large samples) according to the Central Limit Theorem. Thus, for large samples we can use the standard normal z as the test statistic:

$$\textit{Test statistic: } z = \frac{\text{Sample proportion} - \text{Null hypothesized proportion}}{\text{Standard deviation of sample proportion}}$$

$$= \frac{\hat{p} - p_0}{\sigma_{\hat{p}}}$$

where we use the symbol p_0 to represent the null hypothesized value of p.

Rejection region: We use the standard normal distribution to find the appropriate rejection region for the specified value of α. Using $\alpha = .05$, the two-tailed rejection region is

$$z < -z_{\alpha/2} = -z_{.025} = -1.96 \quad \text{or} \quad z > z_{\alpha/2} = z_{.025} = 1.96$$

See Figure 6.15.

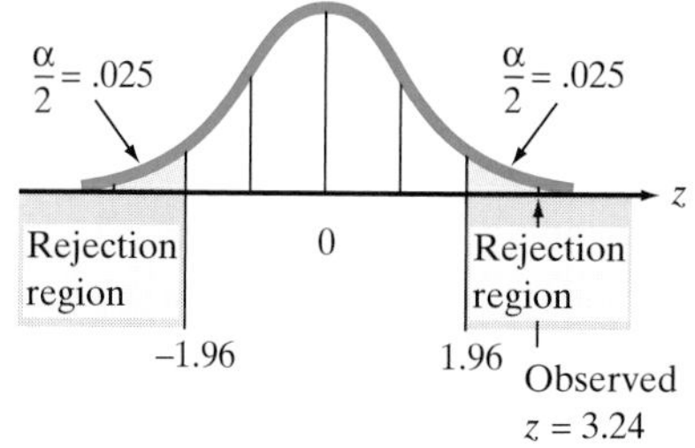

FIGURE 6.15
Rejection region for insider trading example

We are now prepared to calculate the value of the test statistic. Before doing so, we want to be sure that the sample size is large enough to ensure that the normal approximation for the sampling distribution of $\hat{p}$ is reasonable. To check this, we calculate a 3-standard-deviation interval around the null hypothesized value, p_0, which is assumed to be the true value of p until our test procedure indicates otherwise. Recall that $\sigma_{\hat{p}} = \sqrt{pq/n}$ and that we need an estimate of the product pq in order to calculate a numerical value of the test statistic z. Since the null hypothesized value is generally the accepted-until-proven-otherwise value, we use the value of p_0q_0 (where $q_0 = 1 - p_0$) to estimate pq in the calculation of z. Thus,

$$\sigma_{\hat{p}} = \sqrt{\frac{pq}{n}} = \sqrt{\frac{p_0 q_0}{n}} = \sqrt{\frac{(.5)(.5)}{576}} = .021$$

and the 3-standard-deviation interval around p_0 is

$$p_0 \pm 3\sigma_{\hat{p}} \approx .5 \pm 3(.021) = (.437, .563)$$

As long as this interval does not contain 0 or 1 (i.e., is completely contained in the interval 0 to 1), as is the case here, the normal distribution will provide a reasonable approximation for the sampling distribution of $\hat{p}$.

Returning to the hypothesis test at hand, the proportion of the sampled transactions that resulted in a stock increase is

$$\hat{p} = \frac{327}{576} = .568$$

Finally, we calculate the number of standard deviations (the z value) between the sampled and hypothesized value of the binomial proportion:

$$z = \frac{\hat{p} - p_0}{\sigma_{\hat{p}}} = \frac{\hat{p} - p_0}{\sqrt{p_0 q_0/n}} = \frac{.568 - .5}{.021} = \frac{.068}{.021} = 3.24$$

The implication is that the observed sample proportion is (approximately) 3.24 standard deviations above the null hypothesized proportion .5 (Figure 6.15). Therefore, we reject the null hypothesis, concluding at the .05 level of significance that the true probability of an increase or decrease in a stock's price differs from .5 the day following insider purchase of the stock. It appears that an insider purchase significantly increases the probability that the stock price will increase the following day. (To estimate the magnitude of the probability of an increase, a confidence interval can be constructed.)

The test of hypothesis about a population proportion p is summarized in the next box. Note that the procedure is entirely analogous to that used for conducting large-sample tests about a population mean.

Large-Sample Test of Hypothesis About p

One-Tailed Test	**Two-Tailed Test**
H_0: $p = p_0$ (p_0 = hypothesized value of p)	H_0: $p = p_0$
H_a: $p < p_0$ (or H_a: $p > p_0$)	H_a: $p \neq p_0$
Test statistic: $z = \frac{\hat{p} - p_0}{\sigma_{\hat{p}}}$	*Test statistic:* $z = \frac{\hat{p} - p_0}{\sigma_{\hat{p}}}$

where, according to H_0, $\sigma_{\hat{p}} = \sqrt{p_0 q_0/n}$ and $q_0 = 1 - p_0$

Rejection region: $z < -z_\alpha$ (or $z > z_\alpha$ when H_a: $p > p_0$)	*Rejection region:* $\lvert z \rvert > z_{\alpha/2}$

Assumption:
The experiment is binomial, and the sample size is large enough that the interval $p_0 \pm 3\sigma_{\hat{p}}$ does not include 0 or 1.

EXAMPLE 6.7 The reputations (and hence sales) of many businesses can be severely damaged by shipments of manufactured items that contain a large percentage of defectives. For example, a manufacturer of alkaline batteries may want to be reasonably certain that fewer than 5% of its batteries are defective. Suppose 300 batteries are randomly selected from a very large shipment; each is tested and 10 defective batteries are found. Does this provide sufficient evidence for the manufacturer to conclude that the fraction defective in the entire shipment is less than .05? Use $\alpha = .01$.

Solution Before conducting the test of hypothesis, we check to determine whether the sample size is large enough to use the normal approximation for the sampling distribution of $\hat{p}$. The criterion is tested by the interval

$$p_0 \pm 3\sigma_{\hat{p}} = p_0 \pm 3\sqrt{\frac{p_0q_0}{n}} = .05 \pm 3\sqrt{\frac{(.05)(.95)}{300}}$$

$$= .05 \pm .04 \quad \text{or} \quad (.01, .09)$$

Since the interval lies within the interval (0, 1), the normal approximation will be adequate.

The objective of the sampling is to determine whether there is sufficient evidence to indicate that the fraction defective, p, is less than .05. Consequently, we will test the null hypothesis that $p = .05$ against the alternative hypothesis that $p < .05$. The elements of the test are

H_0: $p = .05$

H_a: $p < .05$

Test statistic: $z = \dfrac{\hat{p} - p_0}{\sigma_{\hat{p}}}$

Rejection region: $z < -z_{.01} = -2.33$ (see Figure 6.16)

We now calculate the test statistic:

$$z = \frac{\hat{p} - .05}{\sigma_{\hat{p}}} = \frac{(10/300) - .05}{\sqrt{p_0q_0/n}} = \frac{.033 - .05}{\sqrt{p_0q_0/300}}$$

Notice that we use p_0 to calculate $\sigma_{\hat{p}}$ because, in contrast to calculating $\sigma_{\hat{p}}$ for a confidence interval, the test statistic is computed on the assumption that the null hypothesis is true—that is, $p = p_0$. Therefore, substituting the values for $\hat{p}$ and p_0 into the z statistic, we obtain

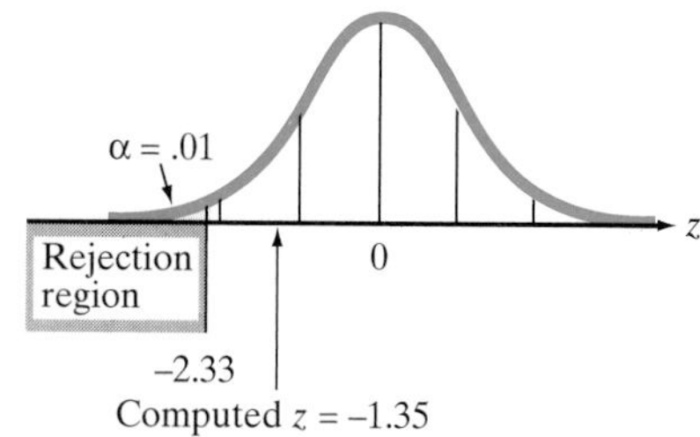

FIGURE 6.16
Rejection region for Example 6.7

$$z \approx \frac{-.017}{\sqrt{(.05)(.95)/300}} = \frac{-.017}{.0126} = -1.35$$

As shown in Figure 6.16, the calculated z value does not fall in the rejection region. Therefore, there is insufficient evidence at the .01 level of significance to indicate that the shipment contains fewer than 5% defective batteries.

EXAMPLE 6.8

In Example 6.7 we found that we did not have sufficient evidence, at the $\alpha = .01$ level of significance, to indicate that the fraction defective p of alkaline batteries was less than $p = .05$. How strong was the weight of evidence favoring the alternative hypothesis (H_a: $p < .05$)? Find the observed significance level for the test.

Solution The computed value of the test statistic z was $z = -1.35$. Therefore, for this lower-tailed test, the observed significance level is

$$\text{Observed significance level} = P(z \leq -1.35)$$

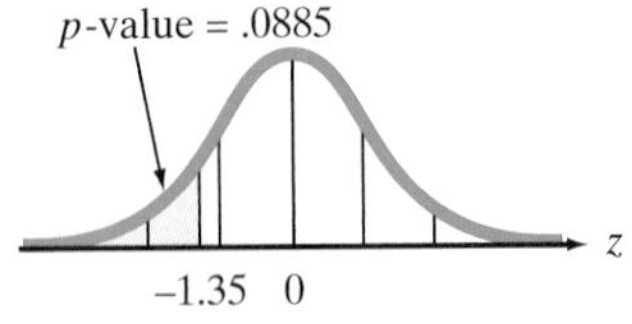

FIGURE 6.17 The observed significance level for Example 6.8

This lower-tail area is shown in Figure 6.17. The area between $z = 0$ and $z = 1.35$ is given in Table IV in Appendix B as .4115. Therefore, the observed significance level is $.5 - .4115 = .0885$. Note that this probability is quite small. Although we did not reject H_0: $p = .05$ at $\alpha = .01$, the probability of observing a z value as small as or smaller than -1.35 is only .0885 if in fact H_0 is true. Therefore, we would reject H_0 if we choose $\alpha = .10$ (since the observed significance level is less than .10), and we would not reject H_0 (the conclusion of Example 6.7) if we choose $\alpha = .05$ or $\alpha = .01$.

Small-sample test procedures are also available for p, although most surveys use samples that are large enough to employ the large-sample tests presented in this section. A test of proportions that can be applied to small samples is discussed in Section 8.3.

EXERCISES 6.53–6.63

Learning the Mechanics

6.53 For the binomial sample sizes and null hypothesized values of p in each part, determine whether the sample size is large enough to use the normal approximation methodology presented in this section to conduct a test of the null hypothesis H_0: $p = p_0$.

a. $n = 900$, $p_0 = .975$ b. $n = 125$, $p_0 = .01$

c. $n = 40$, $p_0 = .75$ d. $n = 15$, $p_0 = .75$

e. $n = 12$, $p_0 = .62$

6.54 Suppose a random sample of 100 observations from a binomial population gives a value of $\hat{p} = .63$ and you wish to test the null hypothesis that the population parameter p is equal to .70 against the alternative hypothesis that p is less than .70.

a. Noting that $\hat{p} = .63$, what does your intuition tell you? Does the value of $\hat{p}$ appear to contradict the null hypothesis?

b. Use the large-sample z-test to test H_0: $p = .70$ against the alternative hypothesis, H_a: $p < .70$. Use $\alpha = .05$. How do the test results compare with your intuitive decision from part **a?**

c. Find and interpret the observed significance level of the test you conducted in part **b.**

6.55 Refer to Exercise 5.26 (p. 285), in which 50 consumers taste tested a new snack food. Their responses (where 0 = do not like; 1 = like; 2 = indifferent) are reproduced below.

SNACK.DAT

1	0	0	1	2	0	1	1	0	0	0	1
0	2	0	2	2	0	0	1	1	0	0	0
0	1	0	2	0	0	0	1	0	0	1	0
0	1	0	1	0	2	0	0	1	1	0	0
0	1										

a. Test H_0: $p = .5$ against H_a: $p > .5$, where p is the proportion of customers who do not like the snack food. Use $\alpha = 10$.

b. Find the observed significance level of your test.

SPSS Output for Exercise 6.56

```
- - - - - - Binomial Test

        Cases
                                  Test Prop. =    .5000
          220      = 1            Obs. Prop. =    .4400
          280      = 0
          --                      Z Approximation
          500    Total            2-Tailed P =   0.3300
```

6.56 A statistics student used a computer program to test the null hypothesis H_0: $p = .5$ against the one-tailed alternative, H_a: $p > .5$. A sample of 500 observations are input into SPSS, which returns the output shown above.

a. The student concludes, based on the p-value, that there is a 33% chance that the alternative hypothesis is true. Do you agree? If not, correct the interpretation.

b. How would the p-value change if the alternative hypothesis were two-tailed, H_a: $p \neq .5$? Interpret this p-value.

Applying the Concepts

6.57 Pond's Age-Defying Complex, a cream with alpha-hydroxy acid, advertises that it can reduce wrinkles and improve the skin. In a study published in *Archives of Dermatology* (June 1996), 33 women over age 40 used a cream with alpha-hydroxy acid for twenty-two weeks. At the end of the study period, 23 of the women exhibited skin improvement (as judged by a dermatologist).

a. Is this evidence that the cream will improve the skin of more than 60% of women over age 40? Test using $\alpha = .05$.

b. Find and interpret the p-value of the test.

6.58 Shoplifting in the U. S. costs retailers about $15 billion a year. Those losses translate into higher prices for consumers. Despite the seriousness of the problem, Shoplifters Alternative of Jericho, N. Y., claims that only 50% of all shoplifters are turned over to police (*Athens Daily News,* Dec. 12, 1999). A random sample of 40 U. S. retailers were questioned concerning the disposition of the most recent shoplifter they apprehended. Only 24 were turned over to police. Do these data provide sufficient evidence to contradict Shoplifters Alternative?

a. Is the sample size large enough to use the inferential procedure presented in this section to answer the question? Explain.

b. Conduct a hypothesis test to answer the question of interest. Use $\alpha = .05$.

c. Find the observed significance level of the hypothesis test in part **b.**

d. For what values of α would the observed significance level be sufficient to reject the null hypothesis of the test you conducted in part **b?**

6.59 The *placebo effect* describes the phenomenon of improvement in the condition of a patient taking a placebo—a pill that looks and tastes real but contains no medically active chemicals. Physicians at a clinic in La Jolla, California, gave what they thought were drugs to 7,000 asthma, ulcer, and herpes patients. Although the doctors later learned that the drugs were really placebos, 70% of the patients reported an improved condition (*Forbes,* May 22, 1995). Use this information to test (at $\alpha = .05$) the placebo effect at the clinic. Assume that if the placebo is ineffective, the probability of a patient's condition improving is .5.

6.60 Refer to the *Nature* (Aug. 27, 1998) study of facial characteristics that are deemed attractive, Exercise 6.35 (p. 318). In another experiment, 67 human subjects viewed side-by-side an image of a Caucasian male face and the same image 50% masculinized. Each subject was asked to select the facial image that they deemed more attractive. Fifty-eight of the 67 subjects felt that masculinization of face shape decreased attractiveness of the male face. The researchers used this sample information to test whether the subjects showed preference for either the unaltered or morphed male face.

a. Set up the null and alternative hypotheses for this test.

b. Compute the test statistic.

c. The researchers reported p-value ≈ 0 for the test. Do you agree?

d. Make the appropriate conclusion in the words of the problem. Use $\alpha = .01$.

6.61 Creative Good, a New York consulting firm, claimed that 39% of shoppers fail in their attempts to purchase merchandise on-line because Web sites are too complex. They estimated that this would translate into a loss of more than $6 billion for on-line merchants during the 1999 holiday season (*Forbes,* Dec. 13, 1999). Another consulting firm asked a random sample of 60 on-line shoppers to each test a different randomly selected e-commerce Web site. Only 15 reported sufficient frustration with their sites to deter making a purchase.

a. Do these data provide sufficient evidence to reject the claim made by Creative Good? Test using $\alpha = .01$.

b. Find the observed significance level of the test and interpret it in the context of the problem.

6.62 In 1895, druggist Asa Candler began distributing handwritten tickets to his customers for free glasses of Coca-Cola at his soda fountain. That was the genesis of the discount coupon. In 1975 it was estimated that 69% of U.S. consumers regularly used discount coupons when shopping. In a 1995 consumer survey, 71% said they regularly redeem coupons (*Newark Star-Ledger*, Oct. 9, 1995). Assume the 1995 survey consisted of a random sample of 1,000 shoppers.

a. Does the 1995 survey provide sufficient evidence that the percentage of shoppers using cents-off coupons exceeds 69%? Test using $\alpha = .05$.
b. Is the sample size large enough to use the inferential procedures presented in this section? Explain.
c. Find the observed significance level for the test you conducted in part **a**, and interpret its value.

6.63 *Consumer Reports* (Sept. 1992) evaluated and rated 46 brands of toothpaste. One attribute examined in the study was whether or not a toothpaste brand carries an American Dental Association (ADA) seal verifying effective decay prevention. The data for the 46 brands (coded 1 = ADA seal, 0 = no ADA seal) are listed here.

ADA.DAT

0	0	0	0	0	0	1	1	1	0	0	1
0	1	0	0	0	0	1	1	1	0	1	1
1	1	0	0	0	0	0	1	0	0	1	1
1	0	1	0	1	1	1	0	0	0		

a. Give the null and alternative hypotheses for testing whether the true proportion of toothpaste brands with the ADA seal verifying effective decay prevention is less than .5.
b. The data were analyzed in SPSS; the results of the test are shown in the SPSS printout below. Interpret the results.

SPSS Output for Exercise 6.63

```
- - - - - - Binomial Test

   ADASEAL

    Cases
                                 Test Prop. =    .5000
        20     = 1.00            Obs. Prop. =    .4348
        26     =  .00
        --                       Z Approximation
        46    Total              2-Tailed P =    .4610
```

6.6 A NONPARAMETRIC TEST ABOUT A POPULATION MEDIAN (OPTIONAL)

In Sections 6.2-6.4 we utilized the z and t statistics for testing hypotheses about a population mean. The z statistic is appropriate for large random samples selected from "general" populations—that is, with few limitations on the probability distribution of the underlying population. The t statistic was developed for small-sample tests in which the sample is selected at random from a *normal* distribution. The question is: How can we conduct a test of hypothesis when we have a small sample from a *nonnormal* distribution? The answer is: Use a procedure that requires fewer or less stringent assumptions about the underlying population, called a **nonparametric method.**

The **sign test** is a relatively simple nonparametric procedure for testing hypotheses about the central tendency of a nonnormal probability distribution. Note that we used the phrase *central tendency* rather than *population mean.* This is because the sign test, like many nonparametric procedures, provides inferences about the population *median* rather than the population mean μ. Denoting the population median by the Greek letter, η, we know (Chapter 2) that η is the 50th percentile of the distribution (Figure 6.18) and as such is less affected by the skewness of the distribution and the presence of outliers (extreme observations). Since the nonparametric test must be suitable for all distributions, not just the normal, it is reasonable for nonparametric tests to focus on the more robust (less sensitive to extreme values) measure of central tendency, the median.

FIGURE 6.18
Location of the population median, η

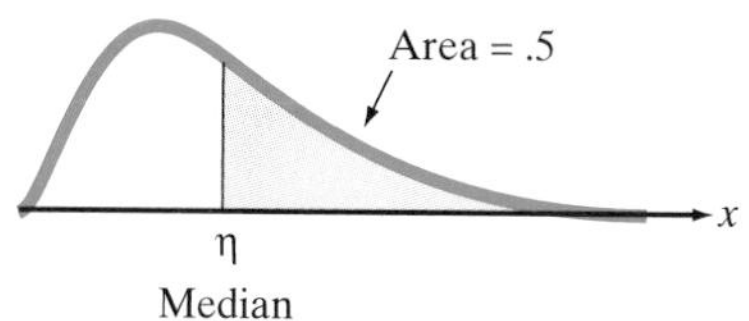

For example, increasing numbers of both private and public agencies are requiring their employees to submit to tests for substance abuse. One laboratory that conducts such testing has developed a system with a normalized measurement scale, in which values less than 1.00 indicate "normal" ranges and values equal to or greater than 1.00 are indicative of potential substance abuse. The lab reports a normal result as long as the median level for an individual is less than 1.00. Eight independent measurements of each individual's sample are made. Suppose, then, that one individual's results were as follows:

.78	.51	3.79	.23	.77	.98	.96	.89

If the objective is to determine whether the *population* median (that is, the true median level if an indefinitely large number of measurements were made on the same individual sample) is less than 1.00, we establish that as our alternative hypothesis and test

$$H_0: \eta = 1.00$$
$$H_a: \eta < 1.00$$

The one-tailed sign test is conducted by counting the number of sample measurements that "favor" the alternative hypothesis—in this case, the number that are less than 1.00. If the null hypothesis is true, we expect approximately half of the measurements to fall on each side of the hypothesized median and if the alternative is true, we expect significantly more than half to favor the alternative—that is, to be less than 1.00. Thus,

Test statistic: S = Number of measurements less than 1.00, the null hypothesized median

If we wish to conduct the test at the $\alpha = .05$ level of significance, the rejection region can be expressed in terms of the observed significance level, or p-value of the test:

Rejection region: p-value $\leq .05$

In this example, $S = 7$ of the 8 measurements are less than 1.00. To determine the observed significance level associated with this outcome, we note that the number of measurements less than 1.00 is a binomial random variable (check the binomial characteristics presented in Section 4.3), and *if H_0 is true,* the binomial probability p that a measurement lies below (or above) the median 1.00 is equal to .5 (Figure 6.18). What is the probability that a result is *as contrary to or more contrary to H_0* than the one observed if H_0 is true? That is, what is the probability that 7 *or more* of 8 binomial measurements will result in Success (be less than 1.00) if the probability of Success is .5? Binomial Table II in Appendix B (using $n = 8$ and $p = .5$) indicates that

$$P(x \geq 7) = 1 - P(x \leq 6) = 1 - .965 = .035$$

Thus, the probability that at least 7 of 8 measurements would be less than 1.00 *if the true median were 1.00* is only .035. The p-value of the test is therefore .035.

FIGURE 6.19
MINITAB printout of sign test

```
SIGN TEST OF MEDIAN = 1.000 VERSUS  L.T.   1.000

                N   BELOW  EQUAL  ABOVE   P-VALUE    MEDIAN
READING         8       7      0      1    0.0352    0.8350
```

This p-value can also be obtained using a statistical software package. The MINITAB printout of the analysis is shown in Figure 6.19, with the p-value highlighted on the printout. Since $p = .035$ is less than $\alpha = .05$, we conclude that this sample provides sufficient evidence to reject the null hypothesis. The implication of this rejection is that the laboratory can conclude at the $\alpha = .05$ level of significance that the true median level for the tested individual is less than 1.00. However, we note that one of the measurements greatly exceeds the others, with a value of 3.79, and deserves special attention. Note that this large measurement is an outlier that would make the use of a t-test and its concomitant assumption of normality dubious. The only assumption necessary to ensure the validity of the sign test is that the probability distribution of measurements is continuous.

The use of the sign test for testing hypotheses about population medians is summarized in the box.

Sign Test for a Population Median η

One-Tailed Test	**Two-Tailed Test**
$H_0: \eta = \eta_0$	$H_0: \eta = \eta_0$
$H_a: \eta > \eta_0$ [or $H_a: \eta < \eta_0$]	$H_a: \eta \neq \eta_0$
Test statistic: S = Number of sample measurements greater than η_0 [or S = number of measurements less then η_0]	S = Larger of S_1 and S_2, where S_1 is the number of measurements less than η_0 and S_2 is the number of measurements greater than η_0
Observed significance level: p-value $= P(x \geq S)$	p-value $= 2P(x \geq S)$

where x has a binomial distribution with parameters n and $p = .5$. (Use Table II, Appendix B.)

Rejection region: Reject H_0 if p-value $\leq .05$.

Assumption: The sample is selected randomly from a continuous probability distribution. [*Note:* No assumptions need to be made about the shape of the probability distribution.]

Recall that the normal probability distribution provides a good approximation for the binomial distribution when the sample size is large. For tests about the median of a distribution, the null hypothesis implies that $p = .5$, and the normal distribution provides a good approximation if $n \geq 10$. (Samples with $n \geq 10$ satisfy the condition that $np \pm 3\sqrt{npq}$ is contained in the interval 0 to n.) Thus, we can use the standard normal z-distribution to conduct the sign test for large samples. The large-sample sign test is summarized in the next box.

Large-Sample Sign Test for a Population Median η

One-Tailed Test	Two-Tailed Test
$H_0: \eta = \eta_0$	$H_0: \eta = \eta_0$
$H_a: \eta > \eta_0$	$H_a: \eta \neq \eta_0$
[or $H_a: \eta < \eta_0$]	

$$\textit{Test statistic: } z = \frac{(S - .5) - .5n}{.5\sqrt{n}}$$

[*Note:* S is calculated as shown in the previous box. We subtract .5 from S as the "correction for continuity." The null hypothesized mean value is $np = .5n$, and the standard deviation is

$$\sqrt{npq} = \sqrt{n(.5)(.5)} = .5\sqrt{n}$$

See Chapter 5 for details on the normal approximation to the binomial distribution.]

Rejection region: $z > z_\alpha$	Rejection region: $z > z_{\alpha/2}$

where tabulated z values can be found in Table IV of Appendix B.

EXAMPLE 6.9 A manufacturer of compact disk (CD) players has established that the median time to failure for its players is 5,250 hours of utilization. A sample of 20 CDs from a competitor is obtained, and they are continuously tested until each fails. The 20 failure times range from five hours (a "defective" player) to 6,575 hours, and 14 of the 20 exceed 5,250 hours. Is there evidence that the median failure time of the competitor differs from 5,250 hours? Use $\alpha = .10$.

Solution The null and alternative hypotheses of interest are

$H_0: \eta = 5{,}250$ hours

$H_a: \eta \neq 5{,}250$ hours

Test statistic: Since $n \geq 10$, we use the standard normal z statistic:

$$z = \frac{(S - .5) - .5n}{.5\sqrt{n}}$$

where S is the maximum of S_1, the number of measurements greater than 5,250, and S_2, the number of measurements less than 5,250.

Rejection region: $z > 1.645$ where $z_{\alpha/2} = z_{.05} = 1.645$

Assumptions: The distribution of the failure times is continuous (time is a continuous variable), but nothing is assumed about the shape of its probability distribution.

Since the number of measurements exceeding 5,250 is $S_2 = 14$ and thus the number of measurements less than 5,250 is $S_1 = 6$, then $S = 14$, the greater of S_1 and S_2. The calculated z statistic is therefore

$$z = \frac{(S - .5) - .5n}{.5\sqrt{n}} = \frac{13.5 - 10}{.5\sqrt{20}} = \frac{3.5}{2.236} = 1.565$$

The value of z is not in the rejection region, so we cannot reject the null hypothesis at the $\alpha = .10$ level of significance. Thus, the CD manufacturer should not conclude, on the basis of this sample, that its competitor's CDs have a median failure time that differs from 5,250 hours.

The one-sample nonparametric sign test for a median provides an alternative to the t-test for small samples from nonnormal distributions. However, if the distribution is approximately normal, the t-test provides a more powerful test about the central tendency of the distribution.

EXERCISES 6.64–6.72

Learning the Mechanics

6.64 What is the probability that a randomly selected observation exceeds the

a. Mean of a normal distribution?
b. Median of a normal distribution?
c. Mean of a nonnormal distribution?
d. Median of a nonnormal distribution?

6.65 Use Table II of Appendix B to calculate the following binomial probabilities:

a. $P(x \geq 7)$ when $n = 8$ and $p = .5$
b. $P(x \geq 5)$ when $n = 8$ and $p = .5$
c. $P(x \geq 8)$ when $n = 8$ and $p = .5$
d. $P(x \geq 10)$ when $n = 15$ and $p = .5$. Also use the normal approximation to calculate this probability, then compare the approximation with the exact value.
e. $P(x \geq 15)$ when $n = 25$ and $p = .5$. Also use the normal approximation to calculate this probability, then compare the approximation with the exact value.

6.66 Consider the following sample of 10 measurements:

 **LM6_66.DAT**

8.4	16.9	15.8	12.5	10.3	4.9	12.9	9.8	23.7	7.3

Use these data to conduct each of the following sign tests using the binomial tables (Table II, Appendix B) and $\alpha = .05$:

a. $H_0: \eta = 9$ versus $H_a: \eta > 9$
b. $H_0: \eta = 9$ versus $H_a: \eta \neq 9$
c. $H_0: \eta = 20$ versus $H_a: \eta < 20$
d. $H_0: \eta = 20$ versus $H_a: \eta \neq 20$
e. Repeat each of the preceding tests using the normal approximation to the binomial probabilities. Compare the results.
f. What assumptions are necessary to ensure the validity of each of the preceding tests?

6.67 Suppose you wish to conduct a test of the research hypothesis that the median of a population is greater than 75. You randomly sample 25 measurements from the population and determine that 17 of them exceed 75. Set up and conduct the appropriate test of hypothesis at the .10 level of significance. Be sure to specify all necessary assumptions.

Applying the Concepts

6.68 One way to assess the benefits of an MBA degree is to investigate the salaries received by MBA students several years after graduation. In 1998, the Graduate Management Admission Council estimated that the median earnings for graduates of full-time, highly-ranked MBA programs four years after graduating was \$96,000 (*Selections,* Winter 1999). A random sample of 50 graduates from the class of 1996 of a particular highly ranked MBA program were mailed a questionnaire and asked to report their earnings for 2000. Fifteen useable responses were received; 9 indicated earnings greater than \$96,000 and 6 indicated earnings below \$96,000.

a. Specify the null and alternative hypotheses that should be used in testing whether the median income of graduates of the MBA program was more than \$96,000 in 2000.
b. Conduct the test of part **a** using $\alpha = .05$ and draw your conclusion in the context of the problem.
c. What assumptions must hold to ensure the validity of your hypothesis test?

6.69 The biting rate of a particular species of fly was investigated in a study reported in the *Journal of the American Mosquito Control Association* (Mar. 1995). Biting rate was defined as the number of flies biting a volunteer during 15 minutes of exposure. This species of fly is known to have a median biting rate of 5 bites per 15 minutes on Stanbury Island, Utah. However, it is theorized that the median biting rate is higher in bright, sunny weather. (This information is of interest to marketers of pesticides.) To test this theory, 122 volunteers were exposed to the flies during a sunny day on Stanbury Island. Of these volunteers, 95 experienced biting rates greater than 5.

a. Set up the null and alternative hypotheses for the test.
b. Calculate the approximate p-value of the test. [*Hint:* Use the normal approximation for a binomial probability.]
c. Make the appropriate conclusion at $\alpha = .01$.

6.70 Reducing the size of a company's workforce in order to reduce costs is referred to as *corporate downsizing* or *reductions in force* (RIF) by the business community and media (*Business Week,* Feb. 24, 1997). Following RIFs, companies are often sued by former employees

MINITAB Output for Exercise 6.70

```
SIGN TEST OF MEDIAN = 37.00 VERSUS  G.T.  37.00

                    N  BELOW  EQUAL  ABOVE   P-VALUE    MEDIAN
AGE                15      4      0     11    0.0592     43.00
```

who allege that the RIFs were discriminatory with regard to age. Federal law protects employees over 40 years of age against such discrimination. Suppose one large company's employees have a median age of 37. Its RIF plan is to fire 15 employees with ages listed in the table below.

FIRE15.DAT

43	32	39	28	54	41	50	62
22	45	47	54	43	33	59	

a. Calculate the median age of the employees who are being terminated.

b. What are the appropriate null and alternative hypotheses to test whether the population from which the terminated employees were selected has a median age that exceeds the entire company's median age?

c. The test of part **b** was conducted using MINITAB. Find the significance level of the test on the MINITAB printout shown above and interpret its value.

d. Assuming that courts generally require statistical evidence at the .10 level of significance before ruling that age discrimination laws were violated, what do you advise the company about its planned RIF? Explain.

6.71 The Federal Aviation Administration (FAA) increased the frequency and thoroughness of its review of aircraft maintenance procedures in response to the admission by ValuJet Airlines that it had not met some maintenance requirements. Suppose that the FAA samples the records of six aircraft currently utilized by one airline and determines the number of flights between the last two complete engine maintenances for each, with the results shown in the table. The FAA requires that this maintenance be performed at least every 30 flights. Although it is obvious that not all aircraft are meeting the requirement, the FAA wishes to test whether the airline is meeting this particular maintenance requirement "on average."

FAA6.DAT

24	27	25
94	29	28

a. Would you suggest the t-test or sign test to conduct the test? Why?

b. Set up the null and alternative hypotheses such that the burden of proof is on the airline to show it is meeting the "on-average" requirement.

c. What are the test statistic and rejection region for this test if the level of significance is $\alpha = .01$? Why would the level of significance be set at such a low value?

d. Conduct the test, and state the conclusion in terms of this application.

6.72 In Exercise 5.18 (p. 276), the average 5-year revenue growth for the 500 fastest growing technology companies in 1999 (i.e., *Forbes' Technology Fast 500*) was investigated. The data are reproduced in the table below.

FAST500.DAT

Rank	Company	1994–1999 Revenue Growth Rate (%)
4	Netscape Communication	64,240
22	Primary Network	10,789
89	WebTrends	3,378
160	CTX	1,864
193	ARIS	1,543
268	Iomega	1,098
274	Medarex	1,075
322	World Access	895
359	Force 3	808
396	Theragenics	704
441	Ascent Solutions	630
485	3 Com	555

Source: *Forbes ASAP*, Nov. 29, 1999, pp. 97–111.

a. Recall that in Exercise 5.18a, the t-distribution was employed to make an inference about the true mean 5-year revenue growth rate for the 1999 *Technology Fast 500*. Explain why the resulting inference may be invalid.

b. Give the null and alternative hypotheses for a nonparametric test designed to determine if the "average" 5-year revenue growth rate is less than 5,000 percent.

c. Conduct the test of part **b** using $\alpha = .05$. Interpret your result in the context of the problem.

STATISTICS IN Action

March Madness: Handicapping the NCAA Basketball Tourney

For three weeks each March, the National Collegiate Athletic Association (NCAA) holds its annual men's basketball championship tournament. The 64 best college basketball teams in the nation play a single-elimination tournament—a total of 63 games—to determine the NCAA champion. Due to its extreme popularity (all 63 games are televised by CBS), the media refers to the tournament as "March Madness."

The NCAA groups the 64 teams into four regions (East, South, Midwest, and West) of 16 teams each. The teams in each region are ranked (seeded) from 1 to 16 based on their performance during the regular season. The NCAA considers such factors as overall record, strength of schedule, average margin of victory, wins on the road, and conference affiliation to determine a team's seeding. In the first round, the number one seed plays the number 16 seed, the second seed plays the fifteenth seed, the third seed plays the fourteenth seed, etc. (See Figure 6.20.) Winners continue playing until the champion is determined.

Tournament followers, from hardcore gamblers to the casual fan who enters the office betting pool, have a strong

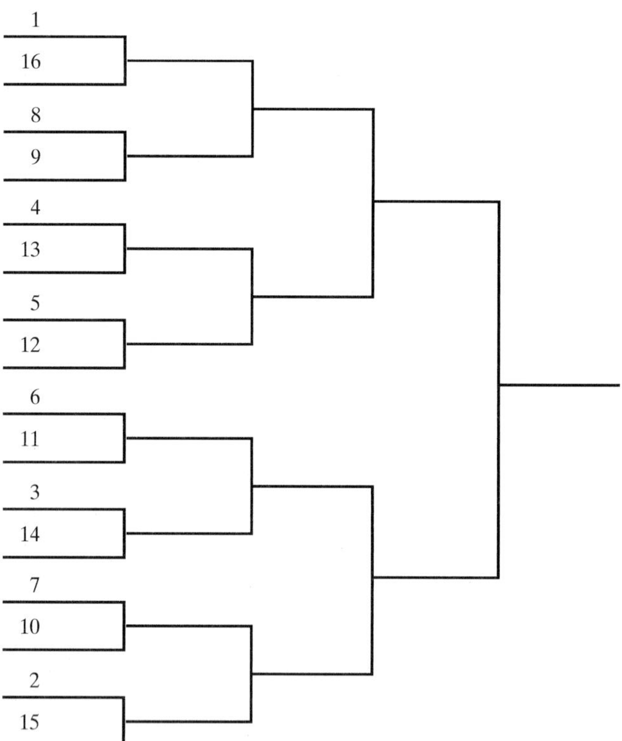

FIGURE 6.20
The design of a 16-team NCAA regional tournament

QUICK REVIEW

Key Terms

Note: Starred (*) items are from the optional section in this chapter.

Alternative (research) hypothesis 300
Conclusion 304
Level of significance 304
Lower-tailed test 307
*Nonparametric Method 332
Null hypothesis 300
Observed significance level (p-value) 313
One-tailed test 306
Rejection region 302
*Sign Test 332
Test statistic 300
Two-tailed test 306
Type I error 301
Type II error 303
Upper-tailed test 307

interest in handicapping the games. Obviously, predicting the eventual champion is a prime interest. However, knowing who will win each game and the margin of victory may be just as important. To provide insight into this phenomenon, statisticians Hal Stern and Barbara Mock analyzed data from the past 13 NCAA tournaments and published their results in *Chance* (Winter 1998). The results of first-round games are summarized in Table 6.4.

Focus

a. A common perception among fans, media, and gamblers is that the higher seeded team has a better than 50-50 chance of winning a first-round game. Is there evidence to support this perception? Conduct the appropriate test for each matchup. What trends do you observe?

b. Is there evidence to support the claim that a 1-, 2-, 3-, or 4-seeded team will win by an average of more than 10 points in first-round games? Conduct the appropriate test for each matchup.

c. Is there evidence to support the claim that a 5-, 6-, 7-, or 8-seeded team will win by an average of less than five points in first-round games? Conduct the appropriate test for each matchup.

d. The researchers also calculated the difference between the game outcome (victory margin, in points) and point spread established by Las Vegas oddsmakers for a sample of 360 recent NCAA tournament games. The mean difference is .7 and the standard deviation of the difference is 11.3. If the true mean difference is 0, then the point spread can be considered a good predictor of the game outcome. Use this sample information to test the hypothesis that the point spread, on average, is a good predictor of the victory margin in NCAA tournament games.

TABLE 6.4 Summary of First-Round NCAA Tournament Games, 1985–1997

Matchup (Seeds)	Number of Games	Number Won by Favorite (Higher Seed)	Margin of Victory (Points)	
			Mean	Standard Deviation
1 vs 16	52	62	22.9	12.4
2 vs 15	52	49	17.2	11.4
3 vs 14	52	41	10.6	12.0
4 vs 13	52	42	10.0	12.5
5 vs 12	52	37	5.3	10.4
6 vs 11	52	36	4.3	10.7
7 vs 10	52	35	3.2	10.5
8 vs 9	52	22	−2.1	11.0

Source: Stern, H. S., and Mock, B. "College basketball upsets: Will a 16-seed ever beat a 1-seed?" *Chance,* Vol. 11, No. 1, Winter 1998, p. 29 (Table 3).

Key Formulas

For testing H_0: $\theta = \theta_0$, the **large-sample test statistic** is $z = \dfrac{\hat{\theta} - \theta_0}{\sigma_{\hat{\theta}}}$ where $\hat{\theta}$, θ_0, and $\sigma_{\hat{\theta}}$ are obtained from the table below:

Parameter,	Hypothesized Parameter Value,	Estimator,	Standard Error of Estimator,	
μ	μ_0	$\bar{x}$	$\dfrac{\sigma}{\sqrt{n}}$	310
p	p_0	$\hat{p}$	$\sqrt{\dfrac{p_0q_0}{n}}$	328

For testing H_0: $\mu = \mu_0$, the **small-sample test statistic** is

$$t = \frac{\bar{x} - \mu_0}{s/\sqrt{n}} \quad 321$$

*For testing H_0: $\eta = \eta_0$, the nonparametric test statistic is:

S = the number of the sample measurements greater than (or less than) η_0 (small samples) 334

$$Z = \frac{(S - .5) - .5n}{.5\sqrt{n}}$$ (large samples) 335

LANGUAGE LAB

Symbol	Pronunciation	Description
H_0	H-oh	Null hypothesis
H_a	H-a	Alternative hypothesis
α	alpha	Probability of Type I error
β	beta	Probability of Type II error
S		Test statistic for sign test
η	eta	Population median

SUPPLEMENTARY EXERCISES 6.73–6.93

Note: Starred (*) exercises refer to the optional section in this chapter.

Learning the Mechanics

6.73 *Complete the following statement:* The smaller the p-value associated with a test of hypothesis, the stronger the support for the ________ hypothesis. Explain your answer.

6.74 Which of the elements of a test of hypothesis can and should be specified *prior* to analyzing the data that are to be utilized to conduct the test?

6.75 A random sample of 20 observations selected from a normal population produced $\bar{x} = 72.6$ and $s^2 = 19.4$

a. Test H_0: $\mu = 80$ against H_a: $\mu < 80$. Use $\alpha = .05$.

b. Test H_0: $\mu = 80$ against H_a: $\mu \neq 80$. Use $\alpha = .01$.

6.76 A random sample of $n = 200$ observations from a binomial population yields $\hat{p} = .29$.

a. Test H_0: $p = .35$ against H_a: $p < .35$. Use $\alpha = .05$.

b. Test H_0: $p = .35$ against H_a: $p \neq .35$. Use $\alpha = .05$.

6.77 A random sample of 175 measurements possessed a mean $\bar{x} = 82$ and a standard deviation $s = .79$.

a. Test H_0: $\mu = 8.3$ against H_a: $\mu \neq 8.3$ Use $\alpha = .05$.

b. Test H_0: $\mu = 8.4$ against H_a: $\mu \neq 8.4$ Use $\alpha = .05$.

6.78 A t-test is conducted for the null hypothesis H_0: $\mu = 10$ versus the alternative H_a: $\mu > 10$ for a random sample of $n = 17$ observations. The data are analyzed using MINITAB, with the results shown below.

a. Interpret the p-value.

b. What assumptions are necessary for the validity of this test?

c. Calculate and interpret the p-value assuming the alternative hypothesis was instead H_a: $\mu \neq 10$.

Applying the Concepts

6.79 "Take the Pepsi Challenge" was a marketing campaign used recently by the Pepsi-Cola Company. Coca-Cola drinkers participated in a blind taste test where they were asked to taste unmarked cups of Pepsi and Coke and were asked to select their favorite. In one Pepsi television commercial, an announcer states that "in recent blind taste tests, more than half the Diet Coke drinkers surveyed said they preferred the taste of Diet Pepsi" (*Consumer's Research,* May 1993). Suppose 100

MINITAB Output for Exercise 6.78

```
TEST OF MU = 10.000 VS MU G.T. 10.000

              N      MEAN     STDEV   SE MEAN       T   P VALUE
X            17     12.50      8.78      2.13   1.174     .1288
```

Diet Coke drinkers took the Pepsi Challenge and 56 preferred the taste of Diet Pepsi. Test the hypothesis that more than half of all Diet Coke drinkers will select Diet Pepsi in the blind taste test. Use $\alpha = .05$. What are the consequences of the test results from Coca-Cola's perspective?

6.80 Medical tests have been developed to detect many serious diseases. A medical test is designed to minimize the probability that it will produce a "false positive" or a "false negative." A false positive refers to a positive test result for an individual who does not have the disease, whereas a false negative is a negative test result for an individual who does have the disease.

a. If we treat a medical test for a disease as a statistical test of hypothesis, what are the null and alternative hypotheses for the medical test?

b. What are the Type I and Type II errors for the test? Relate each to false positives and false negatives.

c. Which of the errors has graver consequences? Considering this error, is it more important to minimize α or β? Explain.

6.81 The trade publication *Potentials in Marketing* (Nov./Dec. 1995) surveyed its readers concerning their opinions of electronic marketing (i.e., marketing via the Internet, e-mail, CD-ROMS, etc.). A questionnaire was faxed to 1,500 randomly selected U.S. readers in August and September 1995. Of the 195 questionnaires that were returned, 37 reported that their company already has a World Wide Web site and 59 indicated that their company had plans to create one.

a. Do these data provide sufficient evidence to reject the claim by a producer of a well-known Web browser that "more than 25% of all U.S. businesses will have Web sites by the middle of 1995"?

b. Discuss potential problems associated with the sampling methodology and the appropriateness of the sample for making generalizations about all U.S. businesses.

6.82 The Lincoln Tunnel (under the Hudson River) connects suburban New Jersey to midtown Manhattan. On Mondays at 8:30 A.M., the mean number of cars waiting in line to pay the Lincoln Tunnel toll is 1,220. Because of the substantial wait during rush hour, the Port Authority of New York and New Jersey is considering raising the amount of the toll between 7:30 and 8:30 A.M. to encourage more drivers to use the tunnel at an earlier or later time (*Newark Star-Ledger,* Aug. 27, 1995). Suppose the Port Authority experiments with peak-hour pricing for six months, increasing the toll from \$4 to \$7 during the rush hour peak. On 10 different workdays at 8:30 A.M. aerial photographs of the tunnel queues are taken and the number of vehicles counted. The results follow:

TUNNEL.DAT

1,260	1,052	1,201	942	1,062	999	931	849	867	735

Analyze the data for the purpose of determining whether peak-hour pricing succeeded in reducing the average number of vehicles attempting to use the Lincoln Tunnel during the peak rush hour. Utilize the information in the accompanying EXCEL printout.

EXCEL Output for Exercise 6.82

Count	
Mean	989.8
Standard Error	50.81006025
Median	970.5
Mode	#N/A
Standard Deviation	160.6755184
Sample Variance	25816.62222
Kurtosis	-0.339458911
Skewness	0.276807237
Range	525
Minimum	735
Maximum	1260
Sum	9898
Count	10
Confidence Level(95.000%)	99.58574067

6.83 In order to be effective, the mean length of life of a certain mechanical component used in a spacecraft must be larger than 1,100 hours. Owing to the prohibitive cost of this component, only three can be tested under simulated space conditions. The lifetimes (hours) of the components were recorded and the following statistics were computed: $\bar{x} = 1{,}173.6$ and $s = 36.3$. These data were analyzed using MINITAB, with the results shown in the printout below.

MINITAB Output for Exercise 6.83

```
TEST OF MU = 1100 VS MU G.T. 1100

           N      MEAN     STDEV   SE MEAN       T   P VALUE
COMP       3   1,173.6      36.3     20.96   3.512     .0362
```

a. Verify that the software has correctly calculated the t statistic and determine whether the p-value is in the appropriate range.
b. Interpret the p-value.
c. Which type of error, I or II, is of greater concern for this test? Explain.
d. Would you recommend that this component be passed as meeting specifications?

6.84 In Exercise 6.25 (p. 312) you tested H_0: $\mu \geq 10$ versus H_a: $\mu < 10$, where μ is the average number of solder joints inspected per second when the joints are spaced .1 inch apart. An SPSS printout of the hypothesis test is shown below.
a. Locate the two-tailed p-value of the test shown on the printout.
b. Adjust the p-value for the one-tailed test (if necessary) and interpret its value.

6.85 Sales promotions that are used by manufacturers to entice retailers to carry, feature, or push the manufacturer's products are called *trade promotions.* A survey of 250 manufacturers conducted by Cannondale Associates, a sales and marketing consulting firm, found that 91% of the manufacturers believe their spending for trade promotions is inefficient (*Potentials in Marketing,* June 1995). Is this sufficient evidence to reject a previous claim by the American Marketing Association that no more than half of all manufacturers are dissatisfied with their trade promotion spending?
a. Conduct the appropriate hypothesis test at $\alpha = .02$. Begin your analysis by determining whether the sample size is large enough to apply the testing methodology presented in this chapter.
b. Report the observed significance level of the test and interpret its meaning in the context of the problem.

6.86 A consumer protection group is concerned that a ketchup manufacturer is filling its 20-ounce family-size containers with less than 20 ounces of ketchup. The group purchases 10 family-size bottles of this ketchup, weighs the contents of each, and finds that the mean weight is equal to 19.86 ounces, and the standard deviation is equal to .22 ounce.
a. Do the data provide sufficient evidence for the consumer group to conclude that the mean fill per family-size bottle is less than 20 ounces? Test using $\alpha = .05$
b. If the test in part **a** were conducted on a periodic basis by the company's quality control department, is the consumer group more concerned about the company's making a Type I error or a Type II error? (The probability of making this type of error is called the *consumer's risk.*)
c. The ketchup company is also interested in the mean amount of ketchup per bottle. It does not wish to overfill them. For the test conducted in part **a,** which type of error is more serious from the company's point of view—a Type I error or a Type II error? (The probability of making this type of error is called the *producer's risk.*)

6.87 The EPA sets an airborne limit of 5 parts per million (ppm) on vinyl chloride, a colorless gas used to make plastics, adhesives, and other chemicals. It is both a carcinogen and a mutagen (New Jersey Department of Health, *Hazardous Substance Fact Sheet,* Dec. 1994). A major plastics manufacturer, attempting to control the amount of vinyl chloride its workers are exposed to, has given instructions to halt production if the mean amount of vinyl chloride in the air exceeds 3.0 ppm. A random sample of 50 air specimens produced the following statistics: $\bar{x} = 3.1$ ppm, $s = .5$ ppm.
a. Do these statistics provide sufficient evidence to halt the production process? Use $\alpha = .01$.
b. If you were the plant manager, would you want to use a large or a small value for α for the test in part **a?** Explain.
c. Find the p-value for the test and interpret its value.

6.88 One way of evaluating a measuring instrument is to repeatedly measure the same item and compare the average of these measurements to the item's known measured value. The difference is used to assess the instrument's accuracy (*Quality Progress,* Jan. 1993). To evaluate a particular Metlar scale, an item whose weight is known to be 16.01 ounces is weighed five times by the same operator. The measurements, in ounces, are as follows:

METLAR.DAT

15.99	16.00	15.97	16.01	15.96

SPSS Output for Exercise 6.84

Variable	Number of Cases	Mean	Standard Deviation	Standard Error
NUMBER	48	9.2917	2.103	.304
MU	48	10.0000	.	.

(Difference) Mean	Standard Deviation	Standard Error	t Value	Degrees of Freedom	2-Tail Prob.
-.7083	2.103	.304	-2.33	47	.024

a. In a statistical sense, does the average measurement differ from 16.01? Conduct the appropriate hypothesis test. What does your analysis suggest about the accuracy of the instrument?
b. List any assumptions you make in conducting the hypothesis test.
*c. Conduct the appropriate nonparametric test of the data. Interpret the results.

6.89 According to the National Restaurant Association, hamburgers are the number one selling fast-food item in the United States (*Newark Star-Ledger,* Mar. 17, 1997). An economist studying the fast-food buying habits of Americans paid graduate students to stand outside two suburban McDonald's restaurants near Boston and ask departing customers whether they spent more or less than \$2.25 on hamburger products for their lunch. Twenty answered "less than"; 50 said "more than"; and 10 refused to answer the question.
a. Is there sufficient evidence to conclude that the median amount spent for hamburgers at lunch at McDonald's is less than \$2.25?
b. Does your conclusion apply to all Americans who eat lunch at McDonald's? Justify your answer.
c. What assumptions must hold to ensure the validity of your test in part **a?**

6.90 One study (*Journal of Political Economy,* Feb. 1988) of gambling newsletters that purport to improve a bettor's odds of winning bets on NFL football games indicates that the newsletters' betting schemes were not profitable. Suppose a random sample of 50 games is selected to test one gambling newsletter. Following the newsletter's recommendations, 30 of the 50 games produced winning wagers.
a. Test whether the newsletter can be said to significantly increase the odds of winning over what one could expect by selecting the winner at random. Use $\alpha = .05$
b. Calculate and interpret the p-value for the test.

6.91 The "beta coefficient" of a stock is a measure of the stock's volatility (or risk) relative to the market as a whole. Stocks with beta coefficients greater than 1 generally bear greater risk (more volatility) than the market, whereas stocks with beta coefficients less than 1 are less risky (less volatile) than the overall market (Alexander, Sharpe, and Bailey, *Fundamentals of Investments,* 1993). A random sample of 15 high-technology stocks was selected at the end of 1996, and the mean and standard deviation of the beta coefficients were calculated: $\bar{x} = 1.23$, $s = .37$
a. Set up the appropriate null and alternative hypotheses to test whether the average high-technology stock is riskier than the market as a whole.
b. Establish the appropriate test statistic and rejection region for the test. Use $\alpha = .10$.
c. What assumptions are necessary to ensure the validity of the test?
d. Calculate the test statistic and state your conclusion.
e. Interpret the p-value on the SAS computer output shown here. (**Prob** > |**T**| on the SAS printout corresponds to a two-tailed test of the null hypothesis $\mu = 1$.)
f. If the alternative hypothesis of interest is $\mu > 1$, what is the appropriate p-value of the test?

SAS Output for Exercise 6.91

```
Analysis Variable : BETA_1

  N Obs              T      Prob>|T|
  ----------------------------------
     15      2.4080000        0.0304
  ----------------------------------
```

6.92 The manufacturer of an over-the-counter analgesic claims that its product brings pain relief to headache sufferers in less than 3.5 minutes, on average. In order to be able to make this claim in its television advertisements, the manufacturer was required by a particular television network to present statistical evidence in support of the claim. The manufacturer reported that for a random sample of 50 headache sufferers, the mean time to relief was 3.3 minutes and the standard deviation was 1.1 minutes.
a. Do these data support the manufacturer's claim? Test using $\alpha = .05$.
b. Report the p-value of the test.
c. In general, do large p-values or small p-values support the manufacturer's claim? Explain.

6.93 According to the U. S. Department of Commerce, the average price for a new home topped \$200,000 for the first time in 1999. In November 1999, the average new-home price was \$209,700 (*Wall Street Journal Interactive Edition,* Jan. 7, 2000). The prices of a random sample of 32 new homes sold in November 2000 yielded $\bar{x} = \$216,981$ and $s = \$19,805$.
a. What are the appropriate null and alternative hypotheses to test whether the mean price of a new home in November 2000 exceeds \$209,700?
b. Compute and interpret the p-value of the test. Do the data provide sufficient evidence to conclude that the mean new-home price in November 2000 exceeded the reported mean price of November 1999?

Chapter 7

COMPARING POPULATION MEANS

CONTENTS

STATISTICS IN ACTION

Where We've Been

We explored two methods for making statistical inferences, confidence intervals and tests of hypotheses, in Chapters 5 and 6. In particular, we studied confidence intervals and tests of hypotheses concerning a single population mean μ and a single population proportion p. We also learned how to select the sample size necessary to obtain a specified amount of information concerning a parameter.

Where We're Going

Now that we've learned to make inferences about a single population, we'll learn how to compare two populations. For example, we may wish to compare the mean gas mileages for two models of automobiles. In this chapter we'll see how to decide whether differences exist and how to estimate the differences between population means. We will learn how to compare population proportions in Chapter 8.

Many experiments involve a comparison of two population means. For instance, a consumer group may want to test whether two major brands of food freezers differ in the mean amount of electricity they use. A golf ball supplier may wish to compare the average distance that two competing brands of golf balls travel when struck with the same club. In this chapter we consider techniques for using two (or more) samples to compare the populations from which they were selected.

7.1 COMPARING TWO POPULATION MEANS: INDEPENDENT SAMPLING

Many of the same procedures that are used to estimate and test hypotheses about a single parameter can be modified to make inferences about two parameters. Both the z and t statistics may be adapted to make inferences about the difference between two population means.

In this section we develop both large-sample and small-sample methodologies for comparing two population means. In the large-sample case we use the z statistic, while in the small-sample case we use the t statistic.

Large Samples

EXAMPLE 7.1

In recent years, the United States and Japan have engaged in intense negotiations regarding restrictions on trade between the two countries. One of the claims made repeatedly by U.S. officials is that many Japanese manufacturers price their goods higher in Japan than in the United States, in effect subsidizing low prices in the United States by extremely high prices in Japan. According to the U.S. argument, Japan accomplishes this by keeping competitive U.S. goods from reaching the Japanese marketplace.

An economist decided to test the hypothesis that higher retail prices are being charged for Japanese automobiles in Japan than in the United States. She obtained random samples of 50 retail sales in the United States and 30 retail sales in Japan over the same time period and for the same model of automobile, converted the Japanese sales prices from yen to dollars using current conversion rates, and obtained the summary information shown in Table 7.1. Form a 95% confidence interval for the difference between the population mean retail prices of this automobile model for the two countries. Interpret the result.

TABLE 7.1 Summary Statistics for Automobile Retail Price Study

	U.S. Sales	Japan Sales
Sample size	50	30
Sample mean	\$16,545	\$17,243
Sample standard deviation	\$ 1,989	\$ 1,843

Solution Recall that the general form of a large-sample confidence interval for a single mean μ is $\bar{x} \pm z_{\alpha/2}\sigma_{\bar{x}}$. That is, we add and subtract $z_{\alpha/2}$ standard deviations of the sample estimate, $\bar{x}$, to the value of the estimate. We employ a similar procedure to form the confidence interval for the difference between two population means.

Let μ_1 represent the mean of the population of retail sales prices for this car model sold in the United States. Let μ_2 be similarly defined for retail sales in Japan. We wish to form a confidence interval for $(\mu_1 - \mu_2)$. An intuitively appealing estimator for $(\mu_1 - \mu_2)$ is the difference between the sample means, $(\bar{x}_1 - \bar{x}_2)$. Thus, we will form the confidence interval of interest by

$$(\bar{x}_1 - \bar{x}_2) \pm z_{\alpha/2}\sigma_{(\bar{x}_1-\bar{x}_2)}$$

Assuming the two samples are independent, the standard deviation of the difference between the sample means is

$$\sigma_{(\bar{x}_1-\bar{x}_2)} = \sqrt{\frac{\sigma_1^2}{n_1} + \frac{\sigma_2^2}{n_2}} \approx \sqrt{\frac{s_1^2}{n_1} + \frac{s_2^2}{n_2}}$$

Using the sample data and noting that $\alpha = .05$ and $z_{.025} = 1.96$, we find that the 95% confidence interval is, approximately,

$$(16{,}545 - 17{,}243) \pm 1.96\sqrt{\frac{(1{,}989)^2}{50} + \frac{(1{,}843)^2}{30}} = -698 \pm (1.96)(438.57)$$

$$= -698 \pm 860$$

or $(-1{,}558, 162)$. Using this estimation procedure over and over again for different samples, we know that approximately 95% of the confidence intervals formed in this manner will enclose the difference in population means $(\mu_1 - \mu_2)$. Therefore, we are highly confident that the difference in mean retail prices in the United States and Japan is between $-\$1{,}558$ and $\$162$. Since 0 falls in this interval, the economist cannot conclude that a significant difference exists between the mean retail prices in the two countries.

The justification for the procedure used in Example 7.1 to estimate $(\mu_1 - \mu_2)$ relies on the properties of the sampling distribution of $(\bar{x}_1 - \bar{x}_2)$. The performance of the estimator in repeated sampling is pictured in Figure 7.1, and its properties are summarized in the box.

Properties of the Sampling Distribution of $(\bar{x}_1 - \bar{x}_2)$

1. The mean of the sampling distribution $(\bar{x}_1 - \bar{x}_2)$ is $(\mu_1 - \mu_2)$.
2. If the two samples are independent, the standard deviation of the sampling distribution is

$$\sigma_{(\bar{x}_1-\bar{x}_2)} = \sqrt{\frac{\sigma_1^2}{n_1} + \frac{\sigma_2^2}{n_2}}$$

   where σ_1^2 and σ_2^2 are the variances of the two populations being sampled and n_1 and n_2 are the respective sample sizes. We also refer to $\sigma_{(\bar{x}_1-\bar{x}_2)}$ as the **standard error** of the statistic $(\bar{x}_1 - \bar{x}_2)$.
3. The sampling distribution of $(\bar{x}_1 - \bar{x}_2)$ is approximately normal for *large samples* by the Central Limit Theorem.

FIGURE 7.1
Sampling distribution of $(\bar{x}_1 - \bar{x}_2)$

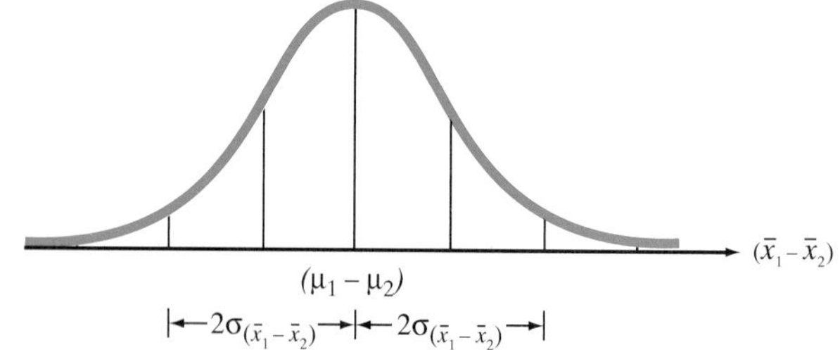

In Example 7.1, we noted the similarity in the procedures for forming a large-sample confidence interval for one population mean and a large-sample confidence interval for the difference between two population means. When we are testing hypotheses, the procedures are again very similar. The general large-sample procedures for forming confidence intervals and testing hypotheses about $(\mu_1 - \mu_2)$ are summarized in the next two boxes.

Large Sample Confidence Interval for $(\mu_1 - \mu_2)$

$$(\bar{x}_1 - \bar{x}_2) \pm z_{\alpha/2}\sigma_{(\bar{x}_1 - \bar{x}_2)} = (\bar{x}_1 - \bar{x}_2) \pm z_{\alpha/2}\sqrt{\frac{\sigma_1^2}{n_1} + \frac{\sigma_2^2}{n_2}}$$

Assumptions: The two samples are randomly selected in an independent manner from the two populations. The sample sizes, n_1 and n_2, are large enough so that $\bar{x}_1$ and $\bar{x}_2$ both have approximately normal sampling distributions and so that s_1^2 and s_2^2 provide good approximations to σ_1^2 and σ_2^2. This will be true if $n_1 \geq 30$ and $n_2 \geq 30$.

Large-Sample Test of Hypothesis for $(\mu_1 - \mu_2)$

One-Tailed Test	**Two-Tailed Test**
H_0: $(\mu_1 - \mu_2) = D_0$	H_0: $(\mu_1 - \mu_2) = D_0$
H_a: $(\mu_1 - \mu_2) < D_0$ [or H_a: $(\mu_1 - \mu_2) > D_0$]	H_a: $(\mu_1 - \mu_2) \neq D_0$

where D_0 = Hypothesized difference between the means (this difference is often hypothesized to be equal to 0)

Test statistic:

$$z = \frac{(\bar{x}_1 - \bar{x}_2) - D_0}{\sigma_{(\bar{x}_1 - \bar{x}_2)}} \quad \text{where} \quad \sigma_{(\bar{x}_1 - \bar{x}_2)} = \sqrt{\frac{\sigma_1^2}{n_1} + \frac{\sigma_2^2}{n_2}}$$

Rejection region: $z < -z_\alpha$ [or $z > z_\alpha$ when H_a: $(\mu_1 - \mu_2) > D_0$]	*Rejection region:* $|z| > z_{\alpha/2}$

Assumptions: Same as for the large-sample confidence interval.

EXAMPLE 7.2 Refer to the study of retail prices of an automobile sold in the United States and Japan, Example 7.1. Another way to compare the mean retail prices for the two countries is to conduct a test of hypothesis. Use the summary data in Table 7.1 to conduct the test. Use $\alpha = .05$.

Solution Again, we let μ_1 and μ_2 represent the population mean retail sales prices in the United States and Japan, respectively. If the claim made by the U.S. government is true, then the mean retail price in Japan will exceed the mean in the U.S., i.e., $\mu_1 < \mu_2$ or $(\mu_1 - \mu_2) < 0$. Thus, the elements of the test are as follows:

H_0: $(\mu_1 - \mu_2) = 0$ (i.e., $\mu_1 = \mu_2$; note that $D_0 = 0$ for this hypothesis test)

H_a: $(\mu_1 - \mu_2) < 0$ (i.e., $\mu_1 < \mu_2$)

Test statistic: $z = \dfrac{(\bar{x}_1 - \bar{x}_2) - D_0}{\sigma_{(\bar{x}_1-\bar{x}_2)}} = \dfrac{\bar{x}_1 - \bar{x}_2 - 0}{\sigma_{(\bar{x}_1-\bar{x}_2)}}$

Rejection region: $z < -z_{.05} = -1.645$ (see Figure 7.2)

Substituting the summary statistics given in Table 7.1 into the test statistic, we obtain

$$z = \frac{(\bar{x}_1 - \bar{x}_2) - 0}{\sigma_{(\bar{x}_1-\bar{x}_2)}} = \frac{(16{,}545 - 17{,}243)}{\sqrt{\dfrac{\sigma_1^2}{n_1} + \dfrac{\sigma_2^2}{n_2}}}$$

$$\approx \frac{-698}{\sqrt{\dfrac{s_1^2}{n_1} + \dfrac{s_2^2}{n_2}}} = \frac{-698}{\sqrt{\dfrac{(1{,}989)^2}{50} + \dfrac{(1{,}843)^2}{30}}} = \frac{-698}{438.57} = -1.59$$

As you can see in Figure 7.2, the calculated z value does not fall in the rejection region. Therefore, the samples do not provide sufficient evidence, at $\alpha = .05$, for the economist to conclude that the mean retail price in Japan exceeds that in the United States.

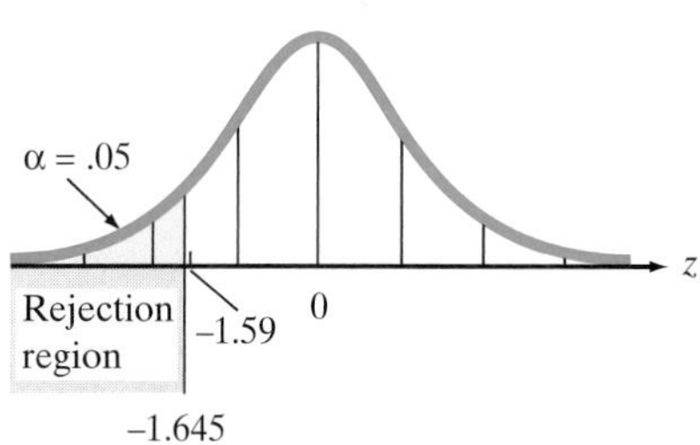

FIGURE 7.2
Rejection region for Example 7.2

Note that this conclusion agrees with the inference drawn from the 95% confidence interval in Example 7.1.

EXAMPLE 7.3 Find the observed significance level for the test in Example 7.2. Interpret the result.

Solution The alternative hypothesis in Example 7.2, H_a: $(\mu_1 - \mu_2) < 0$, required a lower one-tailed test using

$$z = \frac{\bar{x}_1 - \bar{x}_2}{\sigma_{(\bar{x}_1-\bar{x}_2)}}$$

as a test statistic. Since the value z calculated from the sample data was -1.59, the observed significance level (p-value) for the lower-tailed test is the probability of observing a value of z more contradictory to the null hypothesis as $z = -1.59$; that is,

$$p\text{-value} = P(z < -1.59)$$

This probability is computed assuming H_0 is true and is equal to the shaded area shown in Figure 7.3.

FIGURE 7.3
The observed significance level for Example 7.2

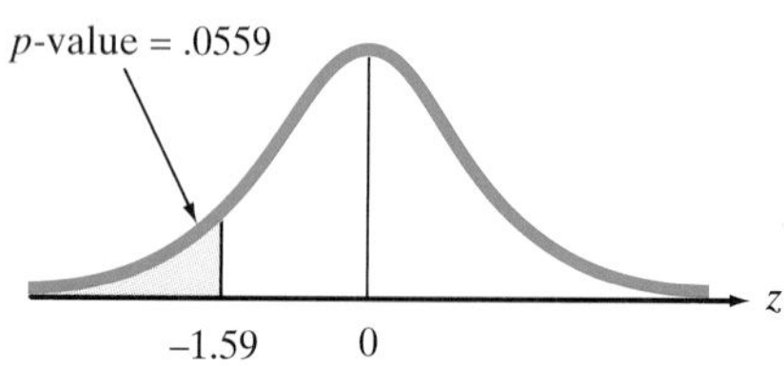

The tabulated area corresponding to $z = 1.59$ in Table IV of Appendix B is .4441. Therefore, the observed significance level of the test is

$$p\text{-value} = .5 - .4441 = .0559$$

Since our selected α value, .05, is less than this p-value, we have insufficient evidence to reject H_0: $(\mu_1 - \mu_2) = 0$ in favor of H_a: $(\mu_1 - \mu_2) < 0$.

The p-value of the test is more easily obtained from a statistical software package. A MINITAB printout for the hypothesis test is displayed in Figure 7.4. The one-tailed p-value, highlighted on the printout, is .056. [Note that MINITAB also gives a 95% confidence interval for $(\mu_1 - \mu_2)$. This interval agrees with the interval calculated in Example 7.1.]

FIGURE 7.4
MINITAB printout for the hypothesis test of Example 7.2

```
Two sample T for US vs JAPAN
          N       Mean       StDev    SE Mean
US       50      16545        1989     281.29
JAPAN    30      17243        1843     336.48

95% CI for mu US - mu JAPAN: (-1558, 162)
T-Test mu US = mu JAPAN (vs <): T= -1.59 P=0.056 DF= 78
```

Note: Like MINITAB, EXCEL and STATISTIX can perform both one-tailed and two-tailed tests. However, SAS and SPSS conduct only two-tailed hypothesis tests. For these packages, obtain the p-value for a one-tailed test as follows:

$p = \dfrac{\text{Reported } p\text{-value}}{2}$ if form of H_a (e.g., $<$) agrees with sign of test statistic (e.g., negative)

$p = 1 - \dfrac{\text{Reported } p\text{-value}}{2}$ if form of H_a (e.g., $<$) disagrees with sign of test statistic (e.g., positive)

Small Samples

When comparing two population means with small samples (say, $n_1 < 30$ and $n_2 < 30$), the methodology of the previous three examples is invalid. The reason? When the sample sizes are small, estimates of σ_1^2 and σ_2^2 are unreliable and the Central Limit Theorem (which guarantees that the z statistic is normal) can no longer be applied. But as in the case of a single mean (Section 6.4), we use the familiar Student's t-distribution described in Chapter 5.

To use the t*-distribution, both sampled populations must be approximately normally distributed with equal population variances, and the random samples must be selected independently of each other.* The normality and equal variances assumptions imply relative frequency distributions for the populations that would appear as shown in Figure 7.5.

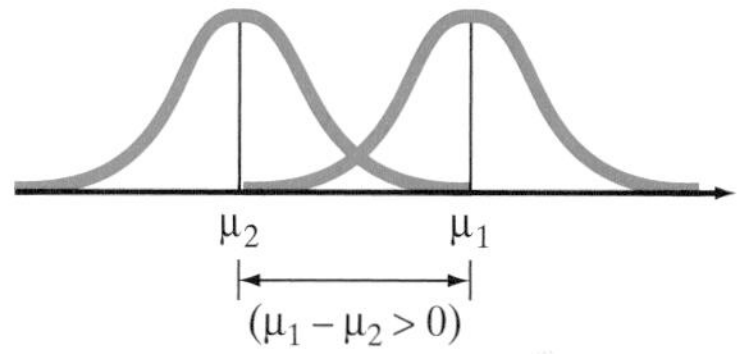

FIGURE 7.5
Assumptions for the two-sample t: (1) normal populations, (2) equal variances

Since we assume the two populations have equal variances ($\sigma_1^2 = \sigma_2^2 = \sigma^2$), it is reasonable to use the information contained in both samples to construct a **pooled sample estimator of σ^2** for use in confidence intervals and test statistics. Thus, if s_1^2 and s_2^2 are the two sample variances (both estimating the variance σ^2 common to both populations), the pooled estimator of σ^2, denoted as s_p^2, is

$$s_p^2 = \frac{(n_1 - 1)s_1^2 + (n_2 - 1)s_2^2}{(n_1 - 1) + (n_2 - 1)} = \frac{(n_1 - 1)s_1^2 + (n_2 - 1)s_2^2}{n_1 + n_2 - 2}$$

or

$$s_p^2 = \frac{\overbrace{\sum (x_1 - \bar{x}_1)^2}^{\textbf{From sample 1}} + \overbrace{\sum (x_2 - \bar{x}_2)^2}^{\textbf{From sample 2}}}{n_1 + n_2 - 2}$$

where x_1 represents a measurement from sample 1 and x_2 represents a measurement from sample 2. Recall that the term *degrees of freedom* was defined in Section 5.2 as 1 less than the sample size. Thus, in this case, we have $(n_1 - 1)$ degrees of freedom for sample 1 and $(n_2 - 1)$ degrees of freedom for sample 2. Since we are pooling the information on σ^2 obtained from both samples, the degrees of freedom associated with the pooled variance s_p^2 is equal to the sum of the degrees of freedom for the two samples, namely, the denominator of s_p^2; that is, $(n_1 - 1) + (n_2 - 1) = n_1 + n_2 - 2$.

Note that the second formula given for s_p^2 shows that the pooled variance is simply a *weighted average* of the two sample variances, s_1^2 and s_2^2. The weight given each variance is proportional to its degrees of freedom. If the two variances have the same number of degrees of freedom (i.e., if the sample sizes are equal), then the pooled variance is a simple average of the two sample variances. The result is an average or "pooled" variance that is a better estimate of σ^2 than either s_1^2 or s_2^2 alone.

Both the confidence interval and the test of hypothesis procedures for comparing two population means with small samples are summarized in the accompanying boxes.

Small-Sample Confidence Interval for $(\mu_1 - \mu_2)$ (Independent Samples)

$$(\bar{x}_1 - \bar{x}_2) \pm t_{\alpha/2}\sqrt{s_p^2\left(\frac{1}{n_1} + \frac{1}{n_2}\right)}$$

where $s_p^2 = \dfrac{(n_1 - 1)s_1^2 + (n_2 - 1)s_2^2}{n_1 + n_2 - 2}$

and $t_{\alpha/2}$ is based on $(n_1 + n_2 - 2)$ degrees of freedom.

Assumptions:
1. Both sampled populations have relative frequency distributions that are approximately normal.
2. The population variances are equal.
3. The samples are randomly and independently selected from the population.

Small-Sample Test of Hypothesis for $(\mu_1 - \mu_2)$ (Independent Samples)

One-Tailed Test	**Two-Tailed Test**
$H_0: (\mu_1 - \mu_2) = D_0$	$H_0: (\mu_1 - \mu_2) = D_0$
$H_a: (\mu_1 - \mu_2) < D_0$ [or $H_a: (\mu_1 - \mu_2) > D_0$]	$H_a: (\mu_1 - \mu_2) \neq D_0$

Test statistic: $t = \dfrac{(\bar{x}_1 - \bar{x}_2) - D_0}{\sqrt{s_p^2\left(\dfrac{1}{n_1} + \dfrac{1}{n_2}\right)}}$

Rejection region: $t < -t_\alpha$ [or $t > t_\alpha$ when $H_a: (\mu_1 - \mu_2) > D_0$]	*Rejection region:* $\lvert t \rvert > t_{\alpha/2}$

where t_α and $t_{\alpha/2}$ are based on $(n_1 + n_2 - 2)$ degrees of freedom.

Assumptions: Same as for the small-sample confidence interval for $(\mu_1 - \mu_2)$ in the previous box.

EXAMPLE 7.4

Behavioral researchers have developed an index designed to measure managerial success. The index (measured on a 100-point scale) is based on the manager's length of time in the organization and his or her level within the firm; the higher the index, the more successful the manager. Suppose a researcher wants to compare the average success index for two groups of managers at a large manufacturing plant. Managers in group 1 engage in a high volume of interactions with people outside the manager's work unit. (Such interactions include phone and face-to-face meetings with customers and suppliers, outside meetings, and public relations work.) Managers in group 2 rarely interact with people outside their work unit. Independent random samples of 12 and 15 managers are selected from groups 1 and 2, respectively, and the success index of each recorded. The results of the study are given in Table 7.2.

TABLE 7.2 Managerial Success Indexes for Two Groups of Managers

Group 1						Group 2					
Interaction with Outsiders						Few Interactions					
65	58	78	60	68	69	62	53	36	34	56	50
66	70	53	71	63	63	42	57	46	68	48	42
						52	53	43			

a. Use the data in the table to estimate the true mean difference between the success indexes of managers in the two groups. Use a 95% confidence interval, and interpret the interval.

b. What assumptions must be made in order that the estimate be valid? Are they reasonably satisfied?

Solution

a. For this experiment, let μ_1 and μ_2 represent the mean success index of group 1 and group 2 managers, respectively. Then, the objective is to obtain a 95% confidence interval for $(\mu_1 - \mu_2)$.

The first step in constructing the confidence interval is to obtain summary statistics (e.g., $\bar{x}$ and s) on the success index for each group of managers. The data of Table 7.2 were entered into a computer, and SAS was used to obtain these descriptive statistics. The SAS printout appears in Figure 7.6. Note that $\bar{x}_1 = 65.33$, $s_1 = 6.61$, $\bar{x}_2 = 49.47$, and $s_2 = 9.33$.

FIGURE 7.6
SAS printout for Example 7.4

```
Analysis Variable : SUCCESS

------------------------- GROUP=1 ---------------------------

N Obs    N      Minimum       Maximum             Mean     Std Dev
-------------------------------------------------------------------
   12   12   53.0000000   78.0000000    65.3333333   6.6103683
-------------------------------------------------------------------

------------------------- GROUP=2 ---------------------------

N Obs    N      Minimum       Maximum             Mean     Std Dev
-------------------------------------------------------------------
   15   15   34.0000000   68.0000000    49.4666667   9.3340136
-------------------------------------------------------------------
```

Next, we calculate the pooled estimate of variance:

$$s_p^2 = \frac{(n_1 - 1)s_1^2 + (n_2 - 1)s_2^2}{n_1 + n_2 - 2}$$

$$= \frac{(12 - 1)(6.61)^2 + (15 - 1)(9.33)^2}{12 + 15 - 2} = 67.97$$

where s_p^2 is based on $(n_1 + n_2 - 2) = (12 + 15 - 2) = 25$ degrees of freedom. Also, we find $t_{\alpha/2} = t_{.025} = 2.06$ (based on 25 degrees of freedom) from Table VI of Appendix B.

Finally, the 95% confidence interval for $(\mu_1 - \mu_2)$, the difference between mean managerial success indexes for the two groups, is

$$(\bar{x}_1 - \bar{x}_2) \pm t_{\alpha/2}\sqrt{s_p^2\left(\frac{1}{n_1} + \frac{1}{n_2}\right)} = 65.33 - 49.47 \pm t_{.025}\sqrt{67.97\left(\frac{1}{12} + \frac{1}{15}\right)}$$

$$= 15.86 \pm (2.06)(3.19)$$

$$= 15.86 \pm 6.58$$

or (9.28, 22.44). Note that the interval includes only positive differences. Consequently, we are 95% confident that $(\mu_1 - \mu_2)$ exceeds 0. In fact, we estimate the mean success index, μ_1, for managers with a high volume of

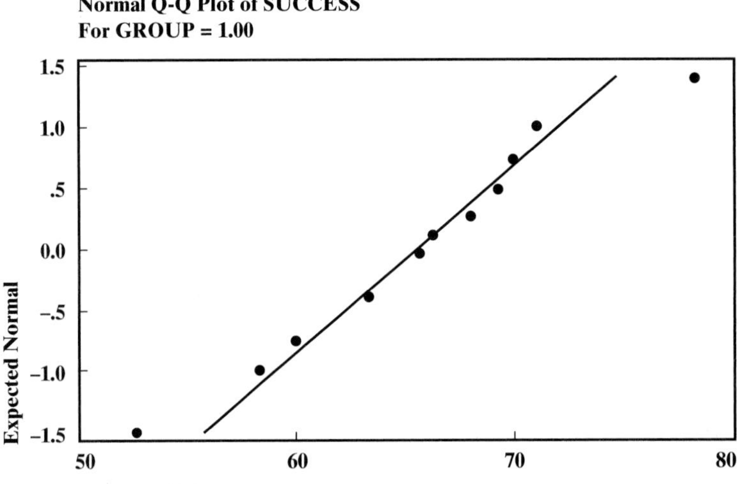

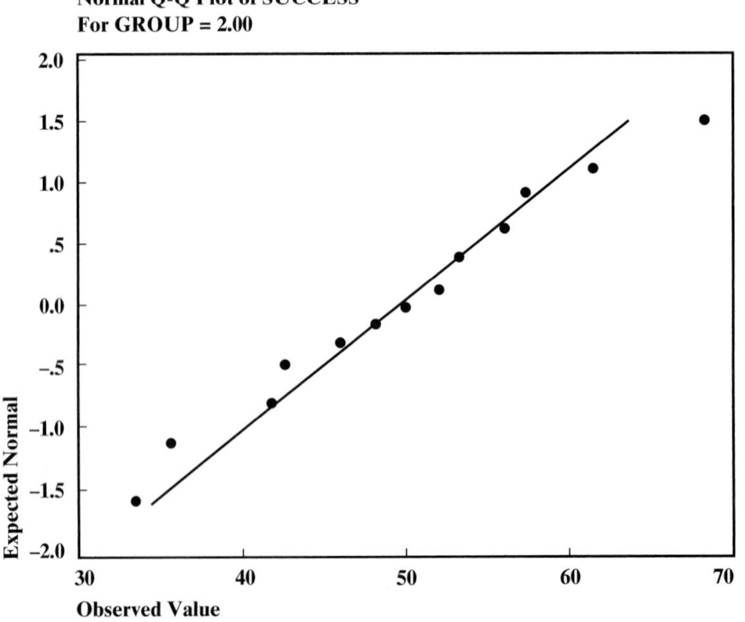

FIGURE 7.7
SPSS normal probability plots for Example 7.4

outsider interaction (group 1) to be anywhere between 9.28 and 22.44 points higher than the mean success index, μ_2, of managers with few interactions (group 2).

b. To properly use the small-sample confidence interval, the following assumptions must be satisfied:

1. The samples of managers are randomly and independently selected from the populations of group 1 and group 2 managers.
2. The success indexes are normally distributed for both groups of managers.
3. The variance of the success indexes are the same for the two populations, i.e., $\sigma_1^2 = \sigma_2^2$.

The first assumption is satisfied, based on the information provided about the sampling procedure in the problem description. To check the plausibility of the remaining two assumptions, we resort to graphical methods. Figure 7.7 is a portion of an SPSS printout that displays normal probability plots (called *Q-Q plots*) for the success indexes of the two samples of managers. The near straight-line trends on both plots indicate that the success index distributions are approximately mound-shaped and symmetric. Consequently, each sample data set appears to come from a population that is approximately normal.

One way to check assumption #3 is to test the null hypothesis H_0: $\sigma_1^2 = \sigma_2^2$. This test is covered in optional Section 7.4. Another approach is to examine box plots for the sample data. Figure 7.8 is an SPSS printout that shows side-by-side vertical box plots for the success indexes in the two samples. Recall, from Section 2.9, that the box plot represents the "spread" of a data set. The two box plots appear to have about the same spread; thus, the samples appear to come from populations with approximately the same variance.

FIGURE 7.8
SPSS box plots for Example 7.4

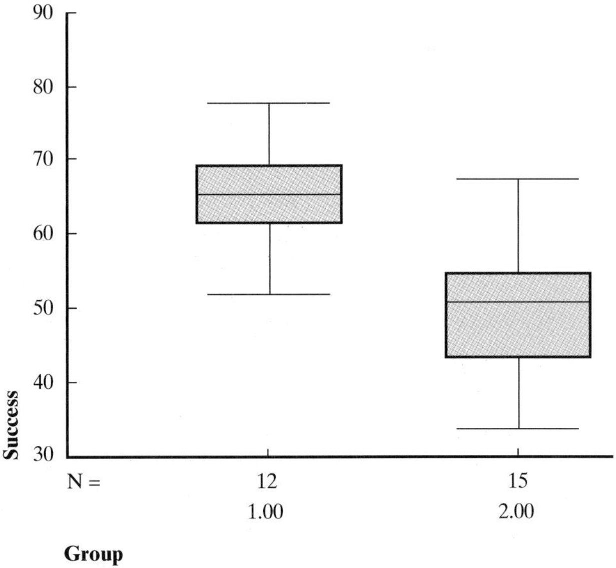

All three assumptions, then, appear to be reasonably satisfied for this application of the small-sample confidence interval.

The two-sample t statistic is a powerful tool for comparing population means when the assumptions are satisfied. It has also been shown to retain its usefulness when the sampled populations are only approximately normally distributed. And when the sample sizes are equal, the assumption of equal population variances can be relaxed. That is, if $n_1 = n_2$, then σ_1^2 and σ_2^2 can be quite different and the test statistic will still possess, approximately, a Student's t-distribution. When the assumptions are not satisfied, you can select larger samples from the populations or you can use other available statistical tests (nonparametric statistical tests). A nonparametric test for independent samples is presented in optional Section 7.5.

EXERCISES 7.1–7.20

Learning the Mechanics

7.1 In order to compare the means of two populations, independent random samples of 400 observations are selected from each population, with the following results:

Sample 1	Sample 2
$\bar{x}_1 = 5{,}275$	$\bar{x}_2 = 5{,}240$
$s_1 = 150$	$s_2 = 200$

a. Use a 95% confidence interval to estimate the difference between the population means $(\mu_1 - \mu_2)$. Interpret the confidence interval.

b. Test the null hypothesis H_0: $(\mu_1 - \mu_2) = 0$ versus the alternative hypothesis H_a: $(\mu_1 - \mu_2) \neq 0$. Give the significance level of the test, and interpret the result.

c. Suppose the test in part **b** was conducted with the alternative hypothesis H_a: $(\mu_1 - \mu_2) > 0$. How would your answer to part **b** change?

d. Test the null hypothesis H_0: $(\mu_1 - \mu_2) = 25$ versus H_a: $(\mu_1 - \mu_2) \neq 25$. Give the significance level, and interpret the result. Compare your answer to the test conducted in part **b.**

e. What assumptions are necessary to ensure the validity of the inferential procedures applied in parts **a–d?**

7.2 To use the t statistic to test for a difference between the means of two populations, what assumptions must be made about the two populations? About the two samples?

7.3 Two populations are described in each of the following cases. In which cases would it be appropriate to apply the small-sample t-test to investigate the difference between the population means?

a. Population 1: Normal distribution with variance σ_1^2. Population 2: Skewed to the right with variance $\sigma_2^2 = \sigma_1^2$.

b. Population 1: Normal distribution with variance σ_1^2. Population 2: Normal distribution with variance $\sigma_2^2 \neq \sigma_1^2$.

c. Population 1: Skewed to the left with variance σ_1^2. Population 2: Skewed to the left with variance $\sigma_2^2 = \sigma_1^2$.

d. Population 1: Normal distribution with variance σ_1^2. Population 2: Normal distribution with variance $\sigma_2^2 = \sigma_1^2$.

e. Population 1: Uniform distribution with variance σ_1^2. Population 2: Uniform distribution with variance $\sigma_2^2 = \sigma_1^2$.

7.4 Assume that $\sigma_1^2 = \sigma_2^2 = \sigma^2$. Calculate the pooled estimator of σ^2 for each of the following cases:

a. $s_1^2 = 120$, $s_2^2 = 100$, $n_1 = n_2 = 25$

b. $s_1^2 = 12$, $s_2^2 = 20$, $n_1 = 20$, $n_2 = 10$

c. $s_1^2 = .15$, $s_2^2 = .20$, $n_1 = 6$, $n_2 = 10$

d. $s_1^2 = 3{,}000$, $s_2^2 = 2{,}500$, $n_1 = 16$, $n_2 = 17$

e. Note that the pooled estimate is a weighted average of the sample variances. To which of the variances does the pooled estimate fall nearer in each of the above cases?

7.5 Independent random samples from normal populations produced the results shown here.

LM7_5.DAT

Sample 1	Sample 2
1.2	4.2
3.1	2.7
1.7	3.6
2.8	3.9
3.0	

a. Calculate the pooled estimate of σ^2.

b. Do the data provide sufficient evidence to indicate that $\mu_2 > \mu_1$? Test using $\alpha = .10$.

c. Find a 90% confidence interval for $(\mu_1 - \mu_2)$.

d. Which of the two inferential procedures, the test of hypothesis in part **b** or the confidence interval in part **c,** provides more information about $(\mu_1 - \mu_2)$?

7.6 Two independent random samples have been selected, 100 observations from population 1 and 100 from population 2. Sample means $\bar{x}_1 = 15.5$ and $\bar{x}_2 = 26.6$ were obtained. From previous experience with these populations, it is known that the variances are $\sigma_1^2 = 9$ and $\sigma_2^2 = 16$.

a. Find $\sigma_{(\bar{x}_1-\bar{x}_2)}$.
b. Sketch the approximate sampling distribution for $(\bar{x}_1 - \bar{x}_2)$ assuming $(\mu_1 - \mu_2) = 10$.
c. Locate the observed value of $(\bar{x}_1 - \bar{x}_2)$ on the graph you drew in part **b.** Does it appear that this value contradicts the null hypothesis H_0: $(\mu_1 - \mu_2) = 10$?
d. Use the z-table on the inside of the front cover to determine the rejection region for the test of H_0: $(\mu_1 - \mu_2) = 10$ against H_0: $(\mu_1 - \mu_2) \neq 10$. Use $\alpha = .05$.
e. Conduct the hypothesis test of part **d** and interpret your result.
f. Construct a 95% confidence interval for $(\mu_1 - \mu_2)$. Interpret the interval.
g. Which inference provides more information about the value of $(\mu_1 - \mu_2)$—the test of hypothesis in part **e** or the confidence interval in part **f?**

7.7 Independent random samples are selected from two populations and used to test the hypothesis H_0: $(\mu_1 - \mu_2) = 0$ against the alternative H_a: $(\mu_1 - \mu_2) \neq 0$. A total of 233 observations from population 1 and 312 from population 2 are analyzed by using MINITAB, with the results shown in the printout.
a. Interpret the results of the computer analysis.
b. If the alternative hypothesis had been H_a: $(\mu_1 - \mu_2) < 0$, how would the p-value change? Interpret the p-value for this one-tailed test.

7.8 Independent random samples from approximately normal populations produced the results shown below:

LM7_8.DAT

Sample 1				Sample 2			
52	33	42	44	52	43	47	56
41	50	44	51	62	53	61	50
45	38	37	40	56	52	53	60
44	50	43		50	48	60	55

a. Do the data provide sufficient evidence to conclude that $(\mu_2 - \mu_1) > 10$? Test using $\alpha = .01$.
b. Construct a 98% confidence interval for $(\mu_2 - \mu_1)$. Interpret your result.

7.9 Independent random samples selected from two normal populations produced the sample means and standard deviations shown below:

Sample 1	Sample 2
$n_1 = 17$	$n_2 = 12$
$\bar{x}_1 = 5.4$	$\bar{x}_2 = 7.9$
$s_1 = 3.4$	$s_2 = 4.8$

a. The test H_0: $(\mu_1 - \mu_2) = 0$ against H_a: $(\mu_1 - \mu_2) \neq 0$ was conducted using SAS, with the results shown in the printout at the bottom of the page. Check and interpret the results.
b. Estimate $(\mu_1 - \mu_2)$ using a 95% confidence interval.

Applying the Concepts

7.10 Many psychologists believe that knowledge of a college student's relationships with his or her parents can be useful in predicting the student's future interpersonal relationships both on the job and in private life. Researchers at the University of South Alabama compared the attitudes of male and female students toward their fathers (*Journal of Genetic Psychology,* Mar. 1998). Using a five-point Likert-type scale, they asked each group to complete the following statement: My relationship with my father can best be described as (1) Awful! (2) Poor, (3) Average, (4) Good, or (5) Great! The data (adapted from the article) are listed in the table on page 358, accompanied by a STATISTIX printout of the analysis.
a. Do male college students tend to have better relationships, on average, with their fathers than female students? Conduct the appropriate hypothesis test using $\alpha = .01$.

MINITAB Output for Exercise 7.7

```
Two sample Z for X1 vs X2
              N         Mean         StDev    SE Mean
X1          233          473            84      15.26
X2          312          485            93      17.66

Z-Test mu X1 = mu X2 (vs n.e.): T= -1.576   P=0.1150
```

SAS Output for Exercise 7.9

```
Variable: X

SAMPLE      N    Mean      Std Dev        Std Error
---------------------------------------------------
  1        17     5.4          3.4            4.123
  2        12     7.9          4.8            3.464

Variances           T         DF      Prob>|T|
---------------------------------------------------
Equal          -1.646         27         .1114
```

STATISTIX Output for Exercise 7.10

```
TWO-SAMPLE T TESTS FOR FATHRATE BY GENDER

                                  SAMPLE
  GENDER         MEAN              SIZE          S.D.          S.E.
----------    ----------        ---------     ---------     ---------
F                 3.6778             90          1.3560        0.1429
M                 3.9091             44          0.9601        0.1447
DIFFERENCE       -0.2313

NULL HYPOTHESIS: DIFFERENCE = 0
ALTERNATIVE HYP: DIFFERENCE <> 0

ASSUMPTION              T          DF          P        95% CI FOR DIFFERENCE
----------------     ------     ------      ------    ---------------------
EQUAL VARIANCES      -1.01      132         0.3128      (-0.6829, 0.2203)
UNEQUAL VARIANCES    -1.14      114.9       0.2568      (-0.6343, 0.1716)

                              F         NUM DF      DEN DF        P
TESTS FOR EQUALITY         -------      ------      ------      ------
      OF VARIANCES           1.99         89          43        0.0068
```

FATHER.DAT

Father Ratings for Females

5	2	5	5	3	3	2	5	2	1	5	4	2	5	3
5	4	2	5	5	2	3	4	3	5	4	4	4	2	1
5	3	5	4	4	5	5	5	3	5	5	4	5	4	5
1	5	4	4	5	4	4	4	2	1	1	4	2	3	4
2	4	2	3	5	2	4	5	5	5	5	5	5	1	2
2	5	4	1	2	5	4	3	5	5	3	5	5	5	2

Father Ratings for Males

4	4	4	3	3	5	4	5	4	5	5	3	4	4	5
2	3	2	5	4	5	3	5	5	4	3	5	4	4	3
5	4	2	4	3	4	4	5	3	4	5	3	2	5	

Data adapted from: Vitulli, William F., and Richardson, Deanna K., "College Student's Attitudes toward Relationships with Parents: A Five-Year Comparative Analysis," *Journal of Genetic Psychology*, Vol. 159, No. 1, Mar. 1998, pp. 45–52.

b. Find the p-value of the test you conducted in part **a.**

c. What assumptions, if any, about the samples did you have to make to ensure the validity of the hypothesis test you conducted?

d. Refer to part **c.** If you made assumptions, check to see if they are reasonably satisfied. If no assumptions were necessary, explain why.

7.11 *Ingratiation* is defined as a class of strategic behaviors designed to make others believe in the attractiveness of one's personal qualities. In organizational settings, individuals use such behaviors to influence superiors in order to attain personal goals. An index that measures ingratiatory behavior, called the Measure of Ingratiatory Behaviors in Organizational Settings (MIBOS) Index, was applied independently to a sample of managers employed by four manufacturing companies in the southeastern United States and to clerical personnel from a large university in the northwestern United States (*Journal of Applied Psychology*, Dec. 1998). Scores are reported on a five-point scale with higher scores indicating more extensive ingratiatory behavior. Summary statistics are show in the table.

Managers	Clerical Personnel
$n_1 = 288$	$n_2 = 110$
$\bar{x}_1 = 2.41$	$\bar{x}_2 = 1.90$
$s_1 = .74$	$s_2 = .59$

Source: Harrison, Allison W., Hochwarter, Wayne A., Perrewe, Pamela L, and Ralston, David A., "The Ingratiation Construct: An Assessment of the Validity of the Measure of Ingratiatory Behaviors in Organization Settings (MIBOS)." *Journal of Applied Psychology*, Vol. 86, No. 6, Dec. 1998, pp. 932–943.

a. Specify the null and alternative hypotheses you would use to test for a difference in ingratiatory behavior between managers and clerical personnel.

b. Conduct the test of part **a** using $\alpha = .05$. Interpret the results of the test in the context of the problem.

c. Construct a 95% confidence interval for $(\mu_1 - \mu_2)$ and interpret the result. Your conclusion should agree with your answer in part **b.**

7.12 Some college professors make bound lecture notes available to their classes in an effort to improve teaching effectiveness. *Marketing Educational Review* (Fall 1994) published a study of business students' opinions of lecture notes. Two groups of students were surveyed—86 students enrolled in a promotional strategy class that required the purchase of lecture notes, and 35 students enrolled in a sales/retailing elective that did not offer lecture notes. At the end of the semester, the students were asked to respond to the statement: "Having a copy of the lecture notes was [would be] helpful in understanding the material." Responses were measured on a nine-point semantic difference scale, where 1 = "strongly disagree" and 9 = "strongly agree." A summary of the results are reported in the table.

Classes Buying Lecture Notes	Classes Not Buying Lecture Notes
$n_1 = 86$	$n_2 = 35$
$\bar{x}_1 = 8.48$	$\bar{x}_2 = 7.80$
$s_1^2 = 0.94$	$s_2^2 = 2.99$

Source: Gray, J. I., and Abernathy, A. M. "Pros and cons of lecture notes and handout packages: Faculty and student opinions," *Marketing Education Review*, Vol. 4, No. 3, Fall 1984, p. 25 (Table 4), American Marketing Association.

a. Describe the two populations involved in the comparison.
b. Do the samples provide sufficient evidence to conclude that there is a difference in the mean responses of the two groups of students? Test using $\alpha = .01$.
c. Construct a 99% confidence interval for $(\mu_1 - \mu_2)$. Interpret the result.
d. Would a 95% confidence interval for $(\mu_1 - \mu_2)$ be narrower or wider than the one you found in part **c?** Why?

7.13 Marketing strategists would like to predict consumer response to new products and their accompanying promotional schemes. Consequently, studies that examine the differences between buyers and nonbuyers of a product are of interest. One classic study conducted by Shuchman and Riesz (*Journal of Marketing Research*, Feb. 1975) was aimed at characterizing the purchasers and nonpurchasers of Crest toothpaste. The researchers demonstrated that both the mean household size (number of persons) and mean household income were significantly larger for purchasers than for nonpurchasers. A similar study utilized independent random samples of size 20 and yielded the data shown in the table on the age of the householder primarily responsible for buying toothpaste. An analysis of the data is provided in the SAS printout at the bottom of the page.

CREST.DAT

Purchasers						Nonpurchasers					
34	35	23	44	52	46	28	22	44	33	55	63
28	48	28	34	33	52	45	31	60	54	53	58
41	32	34	49	50	45	52	52	66	35	25	48
29	59					59	61				

a. Do the data present sufficient evidence to conclude there is a difference in the mean age of purchasers and nonpurchasers? Use $\alpha = .10$.
b. What assumptions are necessary in order to answer part **a?**
c. Find the observed significance level for the test on the printout, and interpret its value.
d. Calculate and interpret a 90% confidence interval for the difference between the mean ages of purchasers and nonpurchasers.

7.14 Valparaiso University professors D. L. Schroeder and K. E. Reichardt conducted a salary survey of members of the Institute of Management Accountants (IMA) and reported the results in *Management Accounting* (June 1995). A salary questionnaire was mailed to a random sample of 4,800 IMA members; 2,287 were returned and form the database for the study. The researchers compared average salaries by management level, education, and gender. Some of the results for entry level managers are shown in the table on p. 360.
a. Suppose you want to make an inference about the difference between salaries of male and female

SAS Output for Exercise 7.13

```
                         TTEST PROCEDURE

Variable: AGE

BUYER           N               Mean            Std Dev         Std Error
---------------------------------------------------------------------------
NONPURCH       20        47.20000000        13.62119092        3.04579088
PURCHASE       20        39.80000000        10.03992032        2.24499443

Variances          T        DF     Prob>|T|
-------------------------------------------
Unequal       1.9557      34.9       0.0585
Equal         1.9557      38.0       0.0579

For HO: Variances are equal, F' = 1.84  DF =  (19,19)  Prob>F' = 0.1927
```

	CPA Degree		Baccalaureate Degree No CPA	
	Men	Women	Men	Women
Mean Salary	$40,084	$35,377	$39,268	$33,159
Number of Respondents	48	39	205	177

Source: Schroeder, D. L., and Reichardt, K. E. "Salaries 1994." *Management Accounting,* Vol. 76, No. 12, June 1995, p. 34 (Table 12).

entry-level managers who earned a CPA degree, at a 95% level of confidence. Why is this impossible to do using the information in the table?

b. Make the inference, part **a,** assuming the salary standard deviation for male and female entry-level managers with CPAs are $4,000 and $3,000, respectively.

c. Repeat part **b,** but assume the male and female salary standard deviations are $16,000 and $12,000, respectively.

d. Compare the two inferences, parts **b** and **c.**

e. Suppose you want to compare the mean salaries of male entry-level managers with a CPA to the mean salary of male entry-level managers without a CPA degree. Give sample standard deviation values that will yield a significant difference between the two means, at $\alpha = .05$.

f. In your opinion, are the sample standard deviations, part **e,** reasonable values for the salary data? Explain.

7.15 As a country's standard of living increases, so does its production of solid waste. The attendant environmental threat makes solid-waste management an important national problem in many countries of the world. The *International Journal of Environmental Health Research* (Vol. 4, 1994) reported on the solid-waste generation rates (in kilograms per capita per day) for samples of cities from industrialized and middle-income countries. The data are provided in the next table.

SOLWASTE.DAT

Industrialized Countries		Middle-Income Countries	
New York (USA)	2.27	Singapore	0.87
Phoenix (USA)	2.31	Hong Kong	0.85
London (UK)	2.24	Medellin (Colombia)	0.54
Hamburg (Germany)	2.18	Kano (Nigeria)	0.46
Rome (Italy)	2.15	Manila (Philippines)	0.50
		Cairo (Egypt)	0.50
		Tunis (Tunisia)	0.56

a. Based on only a visual inspection of the data, does it appear that the mean waste generation rates of cities in industrialized and middle-income countries differ?

b. Conduct a test of hypothesis (at $\alpha = .05$) to support your observation in part **a.** Use the EXCEL printout below to make your conclusion.

7.16 A recent rash of retirements from the U.S. Senate prompted Middlebury College researchers J. E. Trickett and P. M. Sommers to study the ages and lengths of service of members of Congress (*Chance,* Spring 1996). One question of interest to the researchers is: "Did the 13 senators who decided to retire in 1995–1996 begin their careers at a younger average age than did the rest of their colleagues in the Senate?"

a. The average age at which the 13 retiring senators began their service is 45.783 years; the corresponding

EXCEL Output for Exercise 7.15

t-Test: Two-Sample Assuming Equal Variances		
	INDUST	MIDDLE
Mean	2.23	0.611428571
Variance	0.00425	0.029880952
Observations	5	7
Pooled Variance	0.019628571	
Hypothesized Mean Difference	0	
df	10	
t Stat	19.73017433	
P(T<=t) one-tail	1.22537E-09	
t Critical one-tail	1.812461505	
P(T<=t)two-tail	2.45073E-09	
t Critical two-tail	2.228139238	

average for all other senators is 47.201 years. Is this sufficient information to answer the researchers' question? Explain.

b. The researchers conducted a two-sample t-test on the difference between the two means. Specify the null and alternative hypotheses for this test. Clearly define the parameter of interest.

c. The observed significance level for the test, part **b**, was reported as $p = .55$. Interpret this result.

7.17 Many American industries have adopted a participative management style utilizing self-managed work teams (SMWTs). SMWTs require that employees be trained in interpersonal skills such as listening, decision-making, and conflict resolution (*Quality Management Journal*, Summer 1995). Survey data were collected from 114 AT&T employees who work in one of fifteen SMWTs at an AT&T technical division. The workers were divided into two groups: (1) those who reported positive spillover of work skills to family life and (2) those who did not report positive work spillover. The two groups were compared on a variety of job and demographic characteristics, several of which are shown in the table below. (All but the demographic characteristics were measured on a 7-point scale, ranging from 1 = "strongly disagree" to 7 = "strongly agree"; thus, the larger the number, the more of the job characteristic indicated.) Fully interpret the result for each characteristic. Which job-related characteristics are most highly associated with positive work spillover?

7.18 In the United States, high job turnover rates are common in many industries and are associated with high product defect rates. High turnover rates mean more inexperienced workers who are unfamiliar with the company's product lines (Stevenson, *Production/Operations Management*, 1996). In a recent study, five Japanese and five U.S. plants that manufacture air conditioners were randomly sampled; their turnover rates are listed in the accompanying table; a MINITAB descriptive statistics printout is provided at the bottom of the page.

TURNOVER.DAT

U.S. Plants	Japanese Plants
7.11%	3.52%
6.06	2.02
8.00	4.91
6.87	3.22
4.77	1.92

a. Do the data provide sufficient evidence to indicate that the mean annual percentage turnover for U.S. plants exceeds the corresponding mean percentage for Japanese plants? Test using $\alpha = .05$.

b. Report and interpret the observed significance level of the test you conducted in part **a.**

c. List any assumptions you made in conducting the hypothesis test of part **a.** Comment on their validity for this application.

7.19 Helping smokers kick the habit is a big business in today's no-smoking environment. One of the more commonly used treatments according to an article in

Results for Exercise 7.17

	Means		
Characteristic	(1) No Positive Work Spillover ($n = 67$)	(2) Positive Work Spillover ($n = 47$)	$H_0: \mu_1 = \mu_2$ p-Value
Use of creative ideas (7-pt. scale)	4.4	5.3	$p < .001$
Communication (7-pt. scale)	3.6	4.4	$.001 < p < .01$
Utilization of information (7-pt. scale)	4.7	5.2	$p > .05$
Participation in decisions (7-pt. scale)	2.7	3.3	$.01 < p < .05$
Good use of skills (7-pt. scale)	4.8	5.9	$p < .001$
Age (years)	45.0	46.2	$p > .05$
Education (years)	13.1	13.0	$p > .05$

Source: Stanley-Stevens, L., Yeatts, D. E., and Seward, R. R. "Positive effects of work on family-life: A case for self-managed work teams." *Quality Management Journal*, Summer 1995, p. 38 (Table 1).

MINITAB Output for Exercise 7.18

```
TWOSAMPLE T FOR US VS JAPAN
        N      MEAN      STDEV    SE MEAN
US      5      6.56       1.22       0.54
JAPAN   5      3.12       1.23       0.55

95 PCT CI FOR MU US - MU JAPAN:  (1.62, 5.27)

TTEST MU US = MU JAPAN (VS NE): T= 4.46   P=0.0031   DF= 7
```

the *Journal of Imagination, Cognition and Personality* (Vol. 12, 1992/93) is Spiegel's three-point message:

1. For your body, smoking is a poison.
2. You need your body to live.
3. You owe your body this respect and protection.

To determine the effectiveness of this treatment, the authors conducted a study consisting of a sample of 52 smokers placed in two groups, a Spiegel treatment group or a control group (no treatment). Each participant was asked to record the number of cigarettes he or she smoked each week. The results for the study are shown here for the beginning period and four follow-up time periods.

	Number of Cigarettes Smoked In Week		
	n	$\bar{x}$	s
Beginning			
Treatment	35	165.09	71.20
Control	17	159.00	67.45
First follow-up (2 wks)			
Treatment	35	105.00	69.08
Control	17	157.24	66.80
Second follow-up (4 wks)			
Treatment	35	111.11	69.08
Control	17	159.52	65.73
Third follow-up (8 wks)			
Treatment	35	120.20	67.59
Control	17	157.88	64.41
Fourth follow-up (12 wks)			
Treatment	35	123.63	74.09
Control	17	162.17	67.01

a. Create 95% confidence intervals for the difference in the average number of cigarettes smoked per week for the two groups for the beginning and each follow-up period. Interpret the results.

b. What assumptions are necessary for the validity of these confidence intervals?

7.20 Suppose you manage a plant that purifies its liquid waste and discharges the water into a local river. An EPA inspector has collected water specimens of the discharge of your plant and also water specimens in the river upstream from your plant. Each water specimen is divided into five parts, the bacteria count is read on each, and the median count for each specimen is reported. The bacteria counts for each of six specimens are reported in the following table for the two locations.

BACTERIA.DAT

Plant Discharge			Upstream		
30.1	36.2	33.4	29.7	30.3	26.4
28.2	29.8	34.9	27.3	31.7	32.3

a. Why might the bacteria counts shown here tend to be approximately normally distributed?

b. What are the appropriate null and alternative hypotheses to test whether the mean bacteria count for the plant discharge exceeds that for the upstream location? Be sure to define any symbols you use.

c. The data are submitted to SPSS, and part of the output is shown below. Carefully interpret this output.

d. What assumptions are necessary to ensure the validity of this test?

SPSS Output for Exercise 7.20

```
Independent samples of  LOCATION

Group 1:  LOCATION EQ      1.00          Group 2:  LOCATION EQ     2.00
t-test for:  BACOUNT

                  Number                   Standard     Standard
                 of Cases      Mean       Deviation       Error
     Group 1        6        32.1000        3.189         1.302
     Group 2        6        29.6167        2.355          .961

                    | Pooled Variance Estimate | Separate Variance Estimate

  F    2-Tail       |   t   Degrees of 2-Tail  |   t     Degrees of   2-Tail
Value  Prob.        | Value   Freedom   Prob.  | Value    Freedom     Prob.
 1.83   .522        |  1.53     10      .156   |  1.53     9.20       .159
```

7.2 COMPARING TWO POPULATION MEANS: PAIRED DIFFERENCE EXPERIMENTS

Suppose you want to compare the mean daily sales of two restaurants located in the same city. If you were to record the restaurants' total sales for each of 12 randomly selected days during a six-month period, the results might appear as shown in Table 7.3. An SPSS printout of descriptive statistics for the data is displayed in Figure 7.9. Do these data provide evidence of a difference between the mean daily sales of the two restaurants?

TABLE 7.3 Daily Sales for Two Restaurants

Day	Restaurant 1	Restaurant 2
1 (Wednesday)	$1,005	$ 918
2 (Saturday)	2,073	1,971
3 (Tuesday)	873	825
4 (Wednesday)	1,074	999
5 (Friday)	1,932	1,827
6 (Thursday)	1,338	1,281
7 (Thursday)	1,449	1,302
8 (Monday)	759	678
9 (Friday)	1,905	1,782
10 (Monday)	693	639
11 (Saturday)	2,106	2,049
12 (Tuesday)	981	933

FIGURE 7.9
SPSS descriptive statistics for daily restaurant sales

```
Number of Valid Observations (Listwise) =          12.00

Variable      Mean     Std Dev   Minimum    Maximum      N  Label

REST1       1349.00    530.07    693.00    2106.00      12
REST2       1267.00    516.04    639.00    2049.00      12
```

We want to test the null hypothesis that the mean daily sales, μ_1 and μ_2, for the two restaurants are equal against the alternative hypothesis that they differ, i.e.,

$$H_0: (\mu_1 - \mu_2) = 0$$
$$H_a: (\mu_1 - \mu_2) \neq 0$$

If we employ the t statistic for independent samples (Section 7.1) we first calculate s_p^2 using the values of s_1 and s_2 highlighted on the SPSS printout:

$$s_p^2 = \frac{(n_1 - 1)s_1^2 + (n_2 - 1)s_2^2}{n_1 + n_2 - 2}$$
$$= \frac{(12 - 1)(530.07)^2 + (12 - 1)(516.04)^2}{12 + 12 - 2} = 273{,}630.6$$

Then we substitute the values of $\bar{x}_1$ and $\bar{x}_2$, also highlighted on the printout, to form the test statistic:

$$t = \frac{(\bar{x}_1 - \bar{x}_2) - 0}{\sqrt{s_p^2\left(\frac{1}{n_1} + \frac{1}{n_2}\right)}} = \frac{(1{,}349.00 - 1{,}267.00)}{\sqrt{273{,}630.6\left(\frac{1}{12} + \frac{1}{12}\right)}} = \frac{82.0}{213.54} = .38$$

This small t value will not lead to rejection of H_0 when compared to the t-distribution with $n_1 + n_2 - 2 = 22$ df, even if α were chosen as large as .20 ($t_{\alpha/2} = t_{.10} = 1.321$). Thus, from *this* analysis we might conclude that insufficient evidence exists to infer that there is a difference in mean daily sales for the two restaurants.

However, if you examine the data in Table 7.3 more closely, you will find this conclusion difficult to accept. The sales of restaurant 1 exceed those of restaurant 2 *for every one of the randomly selected 12 days.* This, in itself, is strong evidence to indicate that μ_1 differs from μ_2, and we will subsequently confirm this fact. Why, then, was the *t*-test unable to detect this difference? The answer is: *The independent samples t-test is not a valid procedure to use with this set of data.*

The *t*-test is inappropriate because the assumption of independent samples is invalid. We have randomly chosen *days,* and thus, once we have chosen the sample of days for restaurant 1, we have *not* independently chosen the sample of days for restaurant 2. The dependence between observations within days can be seen by examining the pairs of daily sales, which tend to rise and fall together as we go from day to day. This pattern provides strong visual evidence of a violation of the assumption of independence required for the two-sample *t*-test of Section 7.1. In this situation, you will note the *large variation within samples* (reflected by the large value of s_p^2) in comparison to the relatively *small difference between the sample means.* Because s_p^2 is so large, the *t*-test of Section 7.1 is unable to detect a possible difference between μ_1 and μ_2.

We now consider a valid method of analyzing the data of Table 7.3. In Table 7.4 we add the column of differences between the daily sales of the two restaurants. We can regard these daily differences in sales as a random sample of all daily differences, past and present. Then we can use this sample to make inferences about the mean of the population of differences, μ_D, which is equal to the difference $(\mu_1 - \mu_2)$. That is, the mean of the population (and sample) of differences equals the difference between the population (and sample) means. Thus, our test becomes

$$H_0\colon \mu_D = 0 \; [\text{i.e., } (\mu_1 - \mu_2) = 0]$$
$$H_a\colon \mu_D \neq 0 \; [\text{i.e., } (\mu_1 - \mu_2) \neq 0]$$

The test statistic is a one-sample *t* (Section 6.4), since we are now analyzing a single sample of differences for small *n:*

$$\textit{Test statistic: } t = \frac{\bar{x}_D - 0}{s_D/\sqrt{n_D}}$$

where $\bar{x}_D$ = Sample mean difference
s_D = Sample standard deviation of differences
n_D = Number of differences = Number of pairs

Assumptions: The population of differences in daily sales is approximately normally distributed. The sample differences are randomly selected from the

TABLE 7.4 Daily Sales and Differences for Two Restaurants

Day	Restaurant 1	Restaurant 2	Difference (Restaurant 1 − Restaurant 2)
1 (Wednesday)	$1,005	$ 918	$ 87
2 (Saturday)	2,073	1,971	102
3 (Tuesday)	873	825	48
4 (Wednesday)	1,074	999	75
5 (Friday)	1,932	1,827	105
6 (Thursday)	1,338	1,281	57
7 (Thursday)	1,449	1,302	147
8 (Monday)	759	678	81
9 (Friday)	1,905	1,782	123
10 (Monday)	693	639	54
11 (Saturday)	2,106	2,049	57
12 (Tuesday)	981	933	48

population differences. [*Note:* We do not need to make the assumption that $\sigma_1^2 = \sigma_2^2$.]

Rejection region: At significance level $\alpha = .05$, we will reject H_0 if $|t| > t_{.05}$, where $t_{.05}$ is based on $(n_D - 1)$ degrees of freedom.

Referring to Table IV in Appendix B, we find the t value corresponding to $\alpha = .025$ and $n_D - 1 = 12 - 1 = 11$ df to be $t_{.025} = 2.201$. Then we will reject the null hypothesis if $|t| > 2.201$ (see Figure 7.10). Note that the number of degrees of freedom has decreased from $n_1 + n_2 - 2 = 22$ to 11 when we use the paired difference experiment rather than the two independent random samples design.

FIGURE 7.10
Rejection region for restaurant sales example

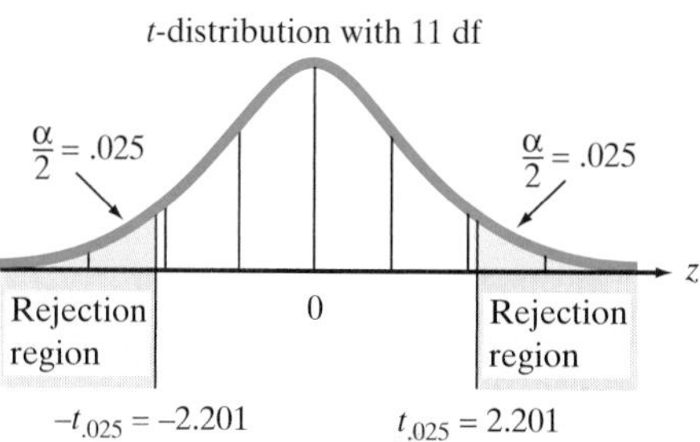

Summary statistics for the $n = 12$ differences are shown on the MINITAB printout, Figure 7.11. Note that $\bar{x}_D = 82.0$ and $s_D = 32.0$ (rounded). Substituting these values into the formula for the test statistic, we have

$$t = \frac{\bar{x}_D - 0}{s_D/\sqrt{n_D}} = \frac{82}{32/\sqrt{12}} = 8.88$$

FIGURE 7.11
MINITAB analysis of differences in Table 7.4

```
TEST OF MU =   0.000 VS MU N.E.   0.000

              N       MEAN      STDEV    SE MEAN          T    P VALUE
DIFF         12     82.000     31.989      9.234       8.88     0.0000
```

Because this value of t falls in the rejection region, we conclude (at $\alpha = .05$) that the difference in population mean daily sales for the two restaurants differs from 0. We can reach the same conclusion by noting that the p-value of the test, highlighted in Figure 7.11, is approximately 0. The fact that $(\bar{x}_1 - \bar{x}_2) = \bar{x}_D = \$82.00$ strongly suggests that the mean daily sales for restaurant 1 exceeds the mean daily sales for restaurant 2.

This kind of experiment, in which observations are paired and the differences are analyzed, is called a **paired difference experiment.** In many cases, a paired difference experiment can provide more information about the difference between population means than an independent samples experiment. The idea is to compare population means by comparing the differences between pairs of experimental units (objects, people, etc.) that were very similar prior to the experiment. The differencing removes sources of variation that tend to inflate σ^2. For instance, in the restaurant example, the day-to-day variability in daily sales is removed by analyzing the differences between the restaurants' daily sales. Making comparisons within groups of similar experimental units is called **blocking,** and the paired difference experiment is an example of a **randomized block experiment.** In our example, the days represent the blocks.

Some other examples for which the paired difference experiment might be appropriate are the following:

1. Suppose you want to estimate the difference $(\mu_1 - \mu_2)$ in mean price per gallon between two major brands of premium gasoline. If you choose two independent random samples of stations for each brand, the variability in price due to geographic location may be large. To eliminate this source of variability you could choose pairs of stations of similar size, one station for each brand, in close geographic proximity and use the sample of differences between the prices of the brands to make an inference about $(\mu_1 - \mu_2)$.
2. A college placement center wants to estimate the difference $(\mu_1 - \mu_2)$ in mean starting salaries for men and women graduates who seek jobs through the center. If it independently samples men and women, the starting salaries may vary because of their different college majors and differences in grade point averages. To eliminate these sources of variability, the placement center could match male and female job seekers according to their majors and grade point averages. Then the differences between the starting salaries of each pair in the sample could be used to make an inference about $(\mu_1 - \mu_2)$.
3. To compare the performance of two automobile salespeople, we might test a hypothesis about the difference $(\mu_1 - \mu_2)$ in their respective mean monthly sales. If we randomly choose n_1 months of salesperson 1's sales and independently choose n_2 months of salesperson 2's sales, the month-to-month variability caused by the seasonal nature of new car sales might inflate s_p^2 and prevent the two-sample t statistic from detecting a difference between μ_1 and μ_2, if such a difference actually exists. However, by taking the difference in monthly sales for the two salespeople for each of n months, we eliminate the month-to-month variability (seasonal variation) in sales, and the probability of detecting a difference between μ_1 and μ_2, if a difference exists, is increased.

The hypothesis-testing procedures and the method of forming confidence intervals for the difference between two means using a paired difference experiment are summarized in the boxes for both large and small n.

Paired Difference Confidence Interval for $\mu_D = (\mu_1 - \mu_2)$

Large Sample

$$\bar{x}_D \pm z_{\alpha/2}\frac{\sigma_D}{\sqrt{n_D}} \approx \bar{x}_D \pm z_{\alpha/2}\frac{s_D}{\sqrt{n_D}}$$

Assumption: The sample differences are randomly selected from the population of differences.

Small Sample

$$\bar{x}_D \pm t_{\alpha/2}\frac{s_D}{\sqrt{n_D}}$$

where $t_{\alpha/2}$ is based on $(n_D - 1)$ degrees of freedom.

Assumptions:

1. The relative frequency distribution of the population of differences is normal.
2. The sample differences are randomly selected from the population of differences.

Paired Difference Test of Hypothesis for $\mu_D = (\mu_1 - \mu_2)$

One-Tailed Test	**Two-Tailed Test**
$H_0: \mu_D = D_0$	$H_0: \mu_D = D_0$
$H_a: \mu_D < D_0$ [or $H_a: \mu_D > D_0$]	$H_a: \mu_D \neq D_0$

Large Sample

Test statistic: $z = \dfrac{\bar{x}_D - D_0}{\sigma_D/\sqrt{n_D}} \approx \dfrac{\bar{x}_D - D_0}{s_D/\sqrt{n_D}}$

Rejection region: $z < -z_\alpha$ [or $z > z_\alpha$ when $H_a: \mu_D > D_0$] *Rejection region:* $|z| > z_{\alpha/2}$

Assumption: The differences are randomly selected from the population of differences.

Small Sample

Test statistic: $t = \dfrac{\bar{x}_D - D_0}{s_D/\sqrt{n_D}}$

Rejection region: $t < -t_\alpha$ [or $t > t_\alpha$ when $H_a: \mu_D > D_0$] *Rejection region:* $|t| > t_{\alpha/2}$

where t_α and $t_{\alpha/2}$ are based on $(n_D - 1)$ degrees of freedom

Assumptions:
1. The relative frequency distribution of the population of differences is normal.
2. The differences are randomly selected from the population of differences.

EXAMPLE 7.5 An experiment is conducted to compare the starting salaries of male and female college graduates who find jobs. Pairs are formed by choosing a male and a female with the same major and similar grade point averages (GPAs). Suppose a random sample of 10 pairs is formed in this manner and the starting annual salary of each person is recorded. The results are shown in Table 7.5. Compare the mean starting salary, μ_1, for males to the mean starting salary, μ_2, for females using a 95% confidence interval. Interpret the results

TABLE 7.5 Data on Annual Salaries for Matched Pairs of College Graduates

Pair	Male	Female	Difference (Male − Female)	Pair	Male	Female	Difference (Male − Female)
1	\$29,300	\$28,800	\$ 500	6	\$27,800	\$28,000	\$−200
2	31,500	31,600	−100	7	29,500	29,200	300
3	30,400	29,800	600	8	31,200	30,100	1,100
4	28,500	28,500	0	9	28,400	28,200	200
5	33,500	32,600	900	10	29,200	28,500	700

Solution Since the data on annual salary are collected in pairs of males and females matched on GPA and major, a paired difference experiment is performed. To conduct the analysis, we first compute the differences between the salaries, as shown in Table 7.5. Summary statistics for these $n = 10$ differences are displayed in the MINITAB printout, Figure 7.12.

FIGURE 7.12
MINITAB analysis of differences in Table 7.5

```
          N      MEAN     STDEV   SE MEAN    95.0 PERCENT C.I.
DIFF     10   400.000   434.613   137.437   (  89.013, 710.987)
```

The 95% confidence interval for $\mu_D = (\mu_1 - \mu_2)$ for this small sample is

$$\bar{x}_D \pm t_{\alpha/2}\frac{s_D}{\sqrt{n_D}}$$

where $t_{\alpha/2} = t_{.025} = 2.262$ (obtained from Table VI, Appendix B) is based on $n - 2 = 8$ degrees of freedom. Substituting the values of $\bar{x}_D$ and s_D shown on the printout, we obtain

$$\bar{x}_D \pm t_{.025}\frac{s_D}{\sqrt{n_D}} = 400 \pm 2.262\left(\frac{434.613}{\sqrt{10}}\right)$$
$$= 400 \pm 310.88 \approx 400 \pm 311 = (\$89, \$711)$$

[*Note:* This interval is also shown on the MINITAB printout, Figure 7.12.] Our interpretation is that the true mean difference between the starting salaries of males and females falls between \$89 and \$711, with 95% confidence. Since the interval falls above 0, we infer that $\mu_1 - \mu_2 > 0$, that is, that the mean salary for males exceeds the mean salary for females.

To measure the amount of information about $(\mu_1 - \mu_2)$ gained by using a paired difference experiment in Example 7.5 rather than an independent samples experiment, we can compare the relative widths of the confidence intervals obtained by the two methods. A 95% confidence interval for $(\mu_1 - \mu_2)$ using the paired difference experiment is, from Example 7.5, (\$89, \$711). If we analyzed the same data as though this were an independent samples experiment,* we would first obtain the descriptive statistics shown in the MINITAB printout, Figure 7.13.

Then we substitute the sample means and standard deviations shown on the printout into the formula for a 95% confidence interval for $(\mu_1 - \mu_2)$ using independent samples:

$$(\bar{x}_1 - \bar{x}_2) \pm t_{.025}\sqrt{s_p^2\left(\frac{1}{n_1} + \frac{1}{n_2}\right)}$$

*This is done only to provide a measure of the increase in the amount of information obtained by a paired design in comparison to an unpaired design. Actually, if an experiment is designed using pairing, an unpaired analysis would be invalid because the assumption of independent samples would not be satisfied.

FIGURE 7.13
MINITAB analysis of data in Table 7.5, assuming independent samples

```
TWOSAMPLE T FOR C1 VS C2
       N         MEAN        STDEV   SE MEAN
C1    10        29930         1735       549
C2    10        29530         1527       483

95 PCT CI FOR MU C1 - MU C2: (-1136, 1936)

TTEST MU C1 = MU C2(VS NE): T= 0.55  P=0.59  DF=  18

POOLED STDEV =          1634
```

where

$$s_p^2 = \frac{(n_1 - 1)s_1^2 + (n_2 - 1)s_2^2}{n_1 + n_2 - 2}$$

MINITAB performed these calculations and obtained the interval (−\$1,136, \$1,936). This interval is highlighted on Figure 7.13.

Notice that the independent samples interval includes 0. Consequently, if we were to use this interval to make an inference about $(\mu_1 - \mu_2)$, we would incorrectly conclude that the mean starting salaries of males and females do not differ! You can see that the confidence interval for the independent sampling experiment is about five times wider than for the corresponding paired difference confidence interval. Blocking out the variability due to differences in majors and grade point averages significantly increases the information about the difference in male and female mean starting salaries by providing a much more accurate (smaller confidence interval for the same confidence coefficient) estimate of $(\mu_1 - \mu_2)$.

You may wonder whether conducting a paired difference experiment is always superior to an independent samples experiment. The answer is: Most of the time, but not always. We sacrifice half the degrees of freedom in the t statistic when a paired difference design is used instead of an independent samples design. This is a loss of information, and unless this loss is more than compensated for by the reduction in variability obtained by blocking (pairing), the paired difference experiment will result in a net loss of information about $(\mu_1 - \mu_2)$. Thus, we should be convinced that the pairing will significantly reduce variability before performing the paired difference experiment. Most of the time this will happen.

One final note: The pairing of the observations is determined before the experiment is performed (that is, by the *design* of the experiment). A paired difference experiment is *never* obtained by pairing the sample observations after the measurements have been acquired.

EXERCISES 7.21–7.33

Learning the Mechanics

7.21 A paired difference experiment yielded n_D pairs of observations. In each case, what is the rejection region for testing H_0: $\mu_D > 2$?
a. $n_D = 12, \alpha = .05$ b. $n_D = 24, \alpha = .10$
c. $n_D = 4, \alpha = .025$ d. $n_D = 8, \alpha = .01$

7.22 The data for a random sample of six paired observations are shown in the table on page 370.
a. Calculate the difference between each pair of observations by subtracting observation 2 from observation 1. Use the differences to calculate $\bar{x}_D$ and s_D^2.

LM7_22.DAT

Pair	Sample from Population 1 (Observation 1)	Sample from Population 2 (Observation 2)
1	7	4
2	3	1
3	9	7
4	6	2
5	4	4
6	8	7

b. If μ_1 and μ_2 are the means of populations 1 and 2, respectively, express μ_D in terms of μ_1 and μ_2.

c. Form a 95% confidence interval for μ_D.

d. Test the null hypothesis H_0: $\mu_D = 0$ against the alternative hypothesis H_a: $\mu_D \neq 0$. Use $\alpha = .05$.

7.23 The data for a random sample of 10 paired observations are shown in the accompanying table.

LM7_23.DAT

Pair	Sample from Population 1	Sample from Population 2
1	19	24
2	25	27
3	31	36
4	52	53
5	49	55
6	34	34
7	59	66
8	47	51
9	17	20
10	51	55

a. If you wish to test whether these data are sufficient to indicate that the mean for population 2 is larger than that for population 1, what are the appropriate null and alternative hypotheses? Define any symbols you use.

b. The data are analyzed using MINITAB, with the results shown below. Interpret these results.

c. The output of MINITAB also included a confidence interval. Interpret this output.

d. What assumptions are necessary to ensure the validity of this analysis?

7.24 A paired difference experiment produced the following data:

$n_D = 18 \quad \bar{x}_1 = 92 \quad \bar{x}_2 = 95.5 \quad \bar{x}_D = -3.5 \quad s_D^2 = 21$

a. Determine the values of t for which the null hypothesis, $\mu_1 - \mu_2 = 0$, would be rejected in favor of the alternative hypothesis, $\mu_1 - \mu_2 < 0$. Use $\alpha = .10$.

b. Conduct the paired difference test described in part **a.** Draw the appropriate conclusions.

c. What assumptions are necessary so that the paired difference test will be valid?

d. Find a 90% confidence interval for the mean difference μ_D.

e. Which of the two inferential procedures, the confidence interval of part **d** or the test of hypothesis of part **b,** provides more information about the differences between the population means?

7.25 A paired difference experiment yielded the data shown in the next table.

LM7_25.DAT

Pair	Obs.1	Obs. 2	Pair	Obs.1	Obs. 2
1	55	44	5	75	62
2	68	55	6	52	38
3	40	25	7	49	31
4	55	56			

a. Test H_0: $\mu_D = 10$ against H_a: $\mu_D \neq 10$, where $\mu_D = (\mu_1 - \mu_2)$. Use $\alpha = .05$.

b. Report the p-value for the test you conducted in part **a.** Interpret the p-value.

Applying the Concepts

7.26 When searching for an item (e.g., a roadside traffic sign, a misplaced file, or a tumor in a mammogram), common sense dictates that you will not re-examine items previously rejected. However, researchers at Harvard Medical School found that a visual search has no memory (*Nature,* Aug. 6, 1998). In their experiment, nine subjects searched for the letter "T" mixed among several letters "L." Each subject conducted the search under two conditions: random and static. In the random condition, the location of the letters were changed every 111 milliseconds; in the static condition, the location of

MINITAB Output for Exercise 7.23

```
TEST OF MU = 0.000 VS MU L.T. 0.000

            N      MEAN    STDEV  SE MEAN        T   P VALUE

DIFF       10    -3.700    2.214    0.700    -5.29    0.0002
----------------------------------------------------------------
            N      MEAN    STDEV  SE MEAN   95.0 PERCENT C.I.
DIFF       10    -3.700    2.214    0.700  (  -5.284,   -2.116)
```

the letters remained unchanged. In each trial, the reaction time (i.e., the amount of time it took the subject to locate the target letter) was recorded in milliseconds.

a. One goal of the research is to compare the mean reaction times of subjects in the two experimental conditions. Explain why the data should be analyzed as a paired-difference experiment.

b. If a visual search had no memory, then the main reaction times in the two conditions will not differ. Specify H_0 and H_a for testing the "no memory" theory.

c. The test statistic was calculated as $t = 1.52$ with p-value $= .15$. Make the appropriate conclusion.

7.27 Lack of sleep costs companies about $18 billion a year in lost productivity, according to the National Sleep Foundation. Companies are waking up to the problem, however. Some even have quiet rooms available for study or sleep. "Power naps" are in vogue (*Athens Daily News,* Jan. 9, 2000). A major airline recently began encouraging reservation agents to nap during their breaks. The table lists the number of complaints received about each of a sample of 10 reservation agents during the six months before naps were encouraged and during the six months after the policy change.

POWERNAP.DAT

Agent	1999 No. of Complaints	2000 No. of Complaints
1	10	5
2	3	0
3	16	7
4	11	4
5	8	6
6	2	4
7	1	2
8	14	3
9	5	5
10	6	1

a. Do the data present sufficient evidence to conclude that the new napping policy reduced the mean number of customer complaints about reservation agents? Test using $\alpha = .05$.

b. What assumptions must hold to ensure the validity of the test?

7.28 Refer to the *Journal of Genetic Psychology* (Mar. 1998) comparison of male and female college students' attitudes toward their fathers, Exercise 7.10 (p. 357). In this exercise, data adapted from the same study are used to compare male students' attitudes toward their fathers with their attitudes toward their mothers. Each of a sample of 13 males from the original sample of 44 males was asked to complete the following statement about each of his parents: My relationship with my father (mother) can best be described as (1) Awful! (2) Poor, (3) Average, (4) Good, or (5) Great! The data obtained are shown in the table:

FATHMOTH.DAT

Student	Attitude toward Father	Attitude toward Mother
1	2	3
2	5	5
3	4	3
4	4	5
5	3	4
6	5	4
7	4	5
8	2	4
9	4	5
10	5	4
11	4	5
12	5	4
13	3	3

Source: Adapted from Vitulli, William F., and Richardson, Deanna K., "College Student's Attitudes toward Relationships with Parents: A Five-Year Comparative Analysis," *Journal of Genetic Psychology,* Vol. 159, No. 1, Mar. 1998, pp. 45–52.

STATISTIX Output for Exercise 7.28

```
PAIRED T TEST FOR FATHERATT - MOTHERATT

NULL HYPOTHESIS: DIFFERENCE =  0
ALTERNATIVE HYP: DIFFERENCE <> 0

MEAN            -0.3077
STD ERROR        0.2861
LO 95% CI       -0.9311
UP 95% CI        0.3157
T                 -1.08
DF                   12
P                0.3033
```

a. Specify the appropriate hypotheses for testing whether male students' attitudes toward their fathers differ from their attitudes toward their mothers, on average.

b. Use the accompanying STATISTIX printout to conduct the test of part **a** (at $\alpha = .05$). Interpret the results in the context of the problem.

c. What assumptions about the sample and its population did you have to make in order to ensure the validity of the hypothesis test?

d. Are you satisfied that your assumption about the population is correct? Justify your answer.

7.29 Twice a year *The Wall Street Journal* asks a panel of economists to forecast interest rates, inflation rates, growth in Gross Domestic Product, and other economic variables. The table (p. 372) reports the inflation forecasts (in percent) made in June 1999 and in January 2000 by nine randomly selected members of the panel.

a. On average, were the economists more optimistic about the prospects for low inflation in late 1999

INFLATE.DAT

	June 1999 Forecast for 11/99	January 2000 Forecast for 5/00
Bruce Steinberg	1.8	2.2
Wayne Angell	2.3	2.3
David Blitzer	2.3	2.3
Michael Cosgrove	2.5	3.0
Gail Fosler	2.3	2.4
John Lonski	2.5	3.0
Donald Ratajczak	2.5	2.5
Thomas Synott	2.3	2.6
Sund Won Sohn	2.5	2.6

Source: Wall Street Journal, January 3, 2000.

than they were for Spring 2000? Specify the hypotheses to be tested.

b. Conduct the hypothesis test using $\alpha = .05$ and answer the question posed in part **a.**

7.30 Facility layout and material flowpath design are major factors in the productivity analysis of automated manufacturing systems. Facility layout is concerned with the location arrangement of machines and buffers for work-in-process. Flowpath design is concerned with the direction of manufacturing material flows (e.g., unidirectional or bidirectional) (Lee, Lei, and Pinedo, *Annals of Operations Research,* 1997). A manufacturer of printed circuit boards (PCBs) is interested in evaluating two alternative existing layout and flowpath designs. The output of each design was monitored for eight consecutive working days.

FLOWPATH.DAT

Working Days	Design 1	Design 2
8/16	1,220 units	1,273 units
8/17	1,092 units	1,363 units
8/18	1,136 units	1,342 units
8/19	1,205 units	1,471 units
8/20	1,086 units	1,299 units
8/23	1,274 units	1,457 units
8/24	1,145 units	1,263 units
8/25	1,281 units	1,368 units

a. Construct a 95% confidence interval for the difference in mean daily output of the two designs.

b. What assumptions must hold to ensure the validity of the confidence interval?

c. Design 2 appears to be superior to Design 1. Is this confirmed by the confidence interval? Explain.

7.31 A *pupillometer* is a device used to observe changes in pupil dilations as the eye is exposed to different visual stimuli. Since there is a direct correlation between the amount an individual's pupil dilates and his or her interest in the stimuli, marketing organizations sometimes use pupillometers to help them evaluate potential consumer interest in new products, alternative package designs, and other factors (*Optical Engineering,* Mar. 1995). The Design and Market Research Laboratories of the Container Corporation of America used a pupillometer to evaluate consumer reaction to different silverware patterns for a client. Suppose 15 consumers were chosen at random, and each was shown two silverware patterns. Their pupillometer readings (in millimeters) are shown in the table on page 373.

a. What are the appropriate null and alternative hypotheses to test whether the mean amount of pupil dilation differs for the two patterns? Define any symbols you use.

b. The data were analyzed using MINITAB, with the results shown in the printout (p. 373). Interpret these results.

c. Is the paired difference design used for this study preferable to an independent samples design? For independent samples we could select 30 consumers, divide them into two groups of 15, and show each group a different pattern. Explain your preference.

7.32 A study reported in the *Journal of Psychology* (Mar. 1991) measures the change in female students' self-concepts as they move from high school to college. A sample of 133 Boston College first-year female students was selected for the study. Each was asked to evaluate several aspects of her life at two points in time: at the end of her senior year of high school, and during her sophomore year of college. Each student was asked to evaluate where she believed she stood on a scale that ranged from top 10% of class (1) to lowest 10% of class (5). The results for three of the traits evaluated are reported in the second table on p. 373.

a. What null and alternative hypotheses would you test to determine whether the mean self-concept of females decreases between the senior year of high school and the sophomore year of college as measured by each of these three traits?

b. Are these traits more appropriately analyzed using an independent samples test or a paired difference test? Explain.

PUPILL.DAT

Consumer	Pattern 1	Pattern 2	Consumer	Pattern 1	Pattern 2
1	1.00	.80	9	.98	.91
2	.97	.66	10	1.46	1.10
3	1.45	1.22	11	1.85	1.60
4	1.21	1.00	12	.33	.21
5	.77	.81	13	1.77	1.50
6	1.32	1.11	14	.85	.65
7	1.81	1.30	15	.15	.05
8	.91	.32			

MINITAB Output for Exercise 7.31

```
TEST OF MU = 0.000 VS MU N.E. 0.000

             N      MEAN     STDEV   SE MEAN        T    P VALUE
DIFF        15      .239      .161     .0415     5.76     0.0000

             N      MEAN     STDEV   SE MEAN     95.0 PERCENT CI
DIFF        15      .239      .161     .0415        (.150, .328)
```

Results for Exercise 7.31

		Senior Year of High School	Sophomore Year of College
Trait	n	$\bar{x}$	$\bar{x}$
Leadership	133	2.09	2.33
Popularity	133	2.48	2.69
Intellectual self-confidence	133	2.29	2.55

c. Noting the size of the sample, what assumptions are necessary to ensure the validity of the tests?

d. The article reports that the leadership test results in a p-value greater than .05, while the tests for popularity and intellectual self-confidence result in p-values less than .05. Interpret these results.

7.33 Merck Research Labs conducted an experiment to evaluate the effect of a new drug using the single-T swim maze. Nineteen impregnated dam rats were allocated a dosage of 12.5 milligrams of the drug. One male and one female rat pup were randomly selected from each resulting litter to perform in the swim maze. Each pup was placed in the water at one end of the maze and allowed to swim until it escaped at the opposite end. If the pup failed to escape after a certain period of time, it was placed at the beginning of the maze and given another chance. The experiment was repeated until each pup accomplished three successful escapes. The next table reports the number of swims required by each pup to perform three successful escapes. Is there sufficient evidence of a difference between the mean number of swims required by male and female pups? Use the MINITAB printout below to conduct the test (at $\alpha = .10$). Comment on the assumptions required for the test to be valid.

RATPUPS.DAT

Litter	Male	Female	Litter	Male	Female
1	8	5	11	6	5
2	8	4	12	6	3
3	6	7	13	12	5
4	6	3	14	3	8
5	6	5	15	3	4
6	6	3	16	8	12
7	3	8	17	3	6
8	5	10	18	6	4
9	4	4	19	9	5
10	4	4			

Source: Thomas E. Bradstreet, Merck Research Labs, BL 3-2, West Point, PA 19486.

MINITAB Output for Exercise 7.33

```
TEST OF MU = 0.000 VS MU N.E. 0.000

               N      MEAN     STDEV   SE MEAN       T   P VALUE
SwimDiff      19     0.368     3.515     0.806    0.46      0.65
```

7.3 DETERMINING THE SAMPLE SIZE

You can find the appropriate sample size to estimate the difference between a pair of population means with a specified degree of reliability by using the method described in Section 5.4. That is, to estimate the difference between a pair of means correct to within B units with probability $(1 - \alpha)$, let $z_{\alpha/2}$ standard deviations of the sampling distribution of the estimator equal B. Then solve for the sample size. To do this, you have to solve the problem for a specific ratio between n_1 and n_2. Most often, you will want to have equal sample sizes, that is, $n_1 = n_2 = n$. We will illustrate the procedure with two examples.

EXAMPLE 7.6 New fertilizer compounds are often advertised with the promise of increased crop yields. Suppose we want to compare the mean yield μ_1 of wheat when a new fertilizer is used to the mean yield μ_2 with a fertilizer in common use. The estimate of the difference in mean yield per acre is to be correct to within .25 bushel with a confidence coefficient of .95. If the sample sizes are to be equal, find $n_1 = n_2 = n$, the number of one-acre plots of wheat assigned to each fertilizer.

Solution To solve the problem, you need to know something about the variation in the bushels of yield per acre. Suppose from past records you know the yields of wheat possess a range of approximately 10 bushels per acre. You could then approximate $\sigma_1 = \sigma_2 = \sigma$ by letting the range equal 4σ. Thus,

$$4\sigma \approx 10 \text{ bushels}$$

$$\sigma \approx 2.5 \text{ bushels}$$

The next step is to solve the equation

$$z_{\alpha/2}\sigma_{(\bar{x}_1 - \bar{x}_2)} = B \qquad \text{or} \qquad z_{\alpha/2}\sqrt{\frac{\sigma_1^2}{n_1} + \frac{\sigma_2^2}{n_2}} = B$$

for n, where $n = n_1 = n_2$. Since we want the estimate to lie within $B = .25$ of $(\mu_1 - \mu_2)$ with confidence coefficient equal to .95, we have $z_{\alpha/2} = z_{.025} = 1.96$. Then, letting $\sigma_1 = \sigma_2 = 2.5$ and solving for n, we have

$$1.96\sqrt{\frac{(2.5)^2}{n} + \frac{(2.5)^2}{n}} = .25$$

$$1.96\sqrt{\frac{2(2.5)^2}{n}} = .25$$

$$n = 768.32 \approx 769 \text{ (rounding up)}$$

Consequently, you will have to sample 769 acres of wheat for each fertilizer to estimate the difference in mean yield per acre to within .25 bushel. Since this would necessitate extensive and costly experimentation, you might decide to allow a larger bound (say, $B = .50$ or $B = 1$) in order to reduce the sample size, or you might decrease the confidence coefficient. The point is that we can obtain an idea of the experimental effort necessary to achieve a specified precision in our final estimate by determining the approximate sample size *before* the experiment is begun.

EXAMPLE 7.7 A laboratory manager wishes to compare the difference in the mean readings of two instruments, A and B, designed to measure the potency (in parts per million) of an antibiotic. To conduct the experiment, the manager plans to select n_D specimens of the antibiotic from a vat and to measure each specimen with both instruments. The difference $(\mu_A - \mu_B)$ will be estimated based on the n_D paired differences $(x_A - x_B)$ obtained in the experiment. If preliminary measurements suggest that the differences will range between plus or minus 10 parts per million, how many differences will be needed to estimate $(\mu_A - \mu_B)$ correct to within 1 part per million with confidence equal to .99?

Solution The estimator for $(\mu_A - \mu_B)$, based on a paired difference experiment, is $\bar{x}_D = (\bar{x}_A - \bar{x}_B)$ and

$$\sigma_{\bar{x}_D} = \frac{\sigma_D}{\sqrt{n_D}}$$

Thus, the number n_D of pairs of measurements needed to estimate $(\mu_A - \mu_B)$ to within 1 part per million can be obtained by solving for n_D in the equation

$$z_{\alpha/2}\frac{\sigma_D}{\sqrt{n_D}} = B$$

where $z_{.005} = 2.58$ and $B = 1$. To solve this equation for n_D, we need to have an approximate value for σ_D.

We are given the information that the differences are expected to range from -10 to 10 parts per million. Letting the range equal $4\sigma_D$, we find

$$\text{Range} = 20 \approx 4\sigma_D$$

$$\sigma_D \approx 5$$

Substituting $\sigma_D = 5$, $B = 1$, and $z_{.005} = 2.58$ into the equation and solving for n_D, we obtain

$$2.58\frac{5}{\sqrt{n_D}} = 1$$

$$n_D = [(2.58)(5)]^2$$

$$= 166.41$$

Therefore, it will require $n_D = 167$ pairs of measurements to estimate $(\mu_A - \mu_B)$ correct to within 1 part per million using the paired difference experiment.

The box summarizes the procedures for determining the sample sizes necessary for estimating $(\mu_1 - \mu_2)$ for the case $n_1 = n_2 = 2$ and for estimating μ_D.

Determination of Samples Sizes for Comparing Two Means

Independent Random Samples

To estimate $(\mu_1 = \mu_2)$ to within a given bound B with probability $(1 - \alpha)$, use the following formula to solve for equal sample sizes that will achieve the desired reliability:

$$n_1 = n_2 = \frac{(z_{\alpha/2})^2(\sigma_1^2 + \sigma_2^2)}{B^2}$$

You will need to substitute estimates for the values of σ_1^2 and σ_2^2 before solving for the sample size. These estimates might be sample variances s_1^2 ands_2^2 from prior sampling (e.g., a pilot sample), or from an educated (and conservatively large) guess based on the range—that is, $s \approx R/4$.

Paired Difference Experiment

To estimate μ_D to within a given bound B with probability $(1 - \alpha)$, use the following formula to solve for n:

$$n = \frac{(z_{\alpha/2})^2\sigma_D^2}{B^2}$$

You will need to substitute an estimate of σ_D^2 before solving for the sample size. This estimate might be the sample variance s_D^2 from prior sampling (e.g., a pilot study), or from an educated (and conservatively large) guess based on the range—that is, $s \approx R/4$.

EXERCISES 7.34–7.41

Learning the Mechanics

7.34 Find the appropriate values of n_1 and n_2 (assume $n_1 = n_2$) needed to estimate $(\mu_1 - \mu_2)$ with:

a. A bound on the error of estimation equal to 3.2 with 95% confidence. From prior experience it is known that $\sigma_1 \approx 15$ and $\sigma_2 \approx 17$.

b. A bound on the error of estimation equal to 8 with 99% confidence. The range of each population is 60.

c. A 90% confidence interval of width 1.0. Assume that $\sigma_1^2 \approx 5.8$ and $\sigma_2^2 \approx 7.5$.

7.35 Suppose you want to use a paired difference experiment to estimate the difference between two population means correct to within 1.8 with a 95% confidence interval. If prior information suggests that the population variances of the differences is approximately equal to $\sigma_D^2 = 28$, how many pairs should be selected?

7.36 Enough money has been budgeted to collect independent random samples of size $n_1 = n_2 = 100$ from populations 1 and 2 in order to estimate $(\mu_1 - \mu_2)$. Prior information indicates that $\sigma_1 = \sigma_2 = 10$. Have sufficient funds been allocated to construct a 90% confidence interval for $(\mu_1 - \mu_2)$ of width 5 or less? Justify your answer.

Applying the Concepts

7.37 Refer to the EPA study of average bacteria counts in water specimens at two river locations, Exercise 7.20 (p. 362). How many water specimens need to be sampled at each location in order for a 95% confidence interval for the true mean difference in bacteria counts to yield an estimate that lies within 1.5 bacteria of the true difference? Assume equal sample sizes will be collected at each location.

7.38 Is housework hazardous to your health? A study in the *Public Health Reports* (July–Aug. 1992) compares the life expectancies of 25-year-old white women in the labor force to those who are housewives. How large a sample would have to be taken from each group in order to be 95% confident that the estimate of difference in average life expectancies for the two groups is within one year of the true difference in average life expectancies?

Assume that equal sample sizes will be selected from the two groups, and that the standard deviation for both groups is approximately 15 years.

7.39 Refer to the Merck Research Labs experiment designed to evaluate the effect of a new drug using rats in a single-T swim maze, Exercise 7.33 (p. 373). How many matched pairs of male and female rat pups need to be included in the experiment in order to estimate the difference between the mean number of swim attempts required to escape to within 1.5 attempts with 95% confidence? Use the value of s_D found in Exercise 7.33 in your calculations.

7.40 *The Professional Geographer* (May 1992) published a study of the proximity of a woman's place of employment in two-income households. One inference involved estimating the difference between the average distances to work for men and women living in suburban residences. Determine the sample sizes required to estimate this difference to within 1 mile with 99% confidence. Assume an equal number of men and women will be sampled and $\sigma_1 = \sigma_2 \approx 6$ miles.

7.41 Even though Japan is an economic superpower, Japanese workers are in many ways worse off than their U.S. and European counterparts. For example, a few years ago the estimated average housing space per person (in square feet) was 665.2 in the United States, and only 269 in Japan (*Minneapolis Star-Tribune,* Jan. 31, 1993). Suppose a team of economists and sociologists from the United Nations plans to reestimate the difference in the mean housing space per person for U.S. and Japanese workers. Assume that equal sample sizes will be used for each country and that the standard deviation is 35 square feet for Japan and 80 for the United States. How many people should be sampled in each country to estimate the difference to within 10 square feet with 95% confidence?

7.4 TESTING THE ASSUMPTION OF EQUAL POPULATION VARIANCES (OPTIONAL)

Consider the problem of comparing two population means with small (independent) samples. Recall, from Section 7.1, that the statistical method employed requires that the variances of the two populations be equal. Before we compare the means we should check to be sure that this assumption is reasonably satisfied. Otherwise, any inferences derived from the t-test for comparing means may be invalid.

To solve problems like these we need to develop a statistical procedure to compare population variances. The common statistical procedure for comparing population variances, σ_1^2 and σ_2^2, makes an inference about the ratio σ_1^2/σ_2^2. In this section, we will show how to test the null hypothesis that the ratio σ_1^2/σ_2^2 equals 1 (the variances are equal) against the alternative hypothesis that the ratio differs from 1 (the variances differ):

$$H_0\colon \frac{\sigma_1^2}{\sigma_2^2} = 1 \qquad (\sigma_1^2 = \sigma_2^2)$$

$$H_a\colon \frac{\sigma_1^2}{\sigma_2^2} \neq 1 \qquad (\sigma_1^2 \neq \sigma_2^2)$$

To make an inference about the ratio σ_1^2/σ_2^2, it seems reasonable to collect sample data and use the ratio of the sample variances, s_1^2/s_2^2. We will use the test statistic

$$F = \frac{s_1^2}{s_2^2}$$

To establish a rejection region for the test statistic, we need to know the sampling distribution of s_1^2/s_2^2. As you will subsequently see, the sampling distribution of s_1^2/s_2^2 is based on two of the assumptions already required for the t-test:

1. The two sampled populations are normally distributed.
2. The samples are randomly and independently selected from their respective populations.

When these assumptions are satisfied and when the null hypothesis is true (that is, $\sigma_1^2 = \sigma_2^2$), the sampling distribution of $F = s_1^2/s_2^2$ is the ***F*-distribution** with $(n_1 - 1)$

numerator degrees of freedom and $(n_2 - 1)$ denominator degrees of freedom, respectively. The shape of the F-distribution depends on the degrees of freedom associated with s_1^2 and s_2^2—that is, on $(n_1 - 1)$ and $(n_2 - 1)$. An F-distribution with 7 and 9 df is shown in Figure 7.14. As you can see, the distribution is skewed to the right, since s_1^2/s_2^2 cannot be less than 0 but can increase without bound.

FIGURE 7.14
An F-distribution with 7 numerator and 9 denominator degrees of freedom

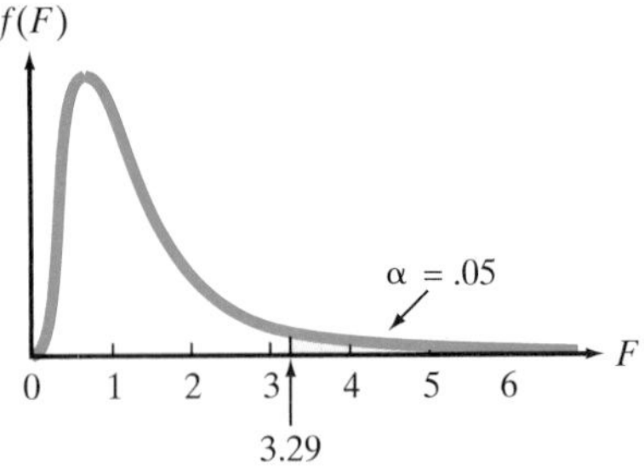

We need to be able to find F values corresponding to the tail areas of this distribution in order to establish the rejection region for our test of hypothesis because we expect the ratio F of the sample variances to be either very large or very small when the population variances are unequal. The upper-tail F values for $\alpha = .10, .05, .025$, and $.01$ can be found in Tables VIII, IX, X, and XI of Appendix B. Table IX is partially reproduced in Table 7.6. It gives F values that correspond to $\alpha = .05$ upper-tail areas for different degrees of freedom ν_1 for the numerator sample variance, s_1^2, whereas the rows correspond to the degrees of freedom ν_2 for

TABLE 7.6 Reproduction of Part of Table IX in Appendix B: Percentage Points of the F-Distribution, $\alpha = .05$

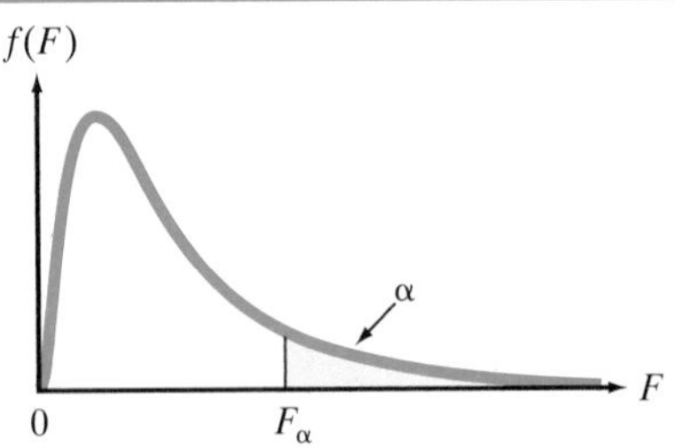

Numerator Degrees of Freedom

Denominator Degrees of Freedom ν_2 \ ν_1	1	2	3	4	5	6	7	8	9
1	161.4	199.5	215.7	224.6	230.2	234.0	236.8	238.9	240.5
2	18.51	19.00	19.16	19.25	19.30	19.33	19.35	19.37	19.38
3	10.13	9.55	9.28	9.12	9.01	8.94	8.89	8.85	8.81
4	7.71	6.94	6.59	6.39	6.26	6.16	6.09	6.04	6.00
5	6.61	5.79	5.41	5.19	5.05	4.95	4.88	4.82	4.77
6	5.99	5.14	4.76	4.53	4.39	4.28	4.21	4.15	4.10
7	5.59	4.74	4.35	4.12	3.97	3.87	3.79	3.73	3.68
8	5.32	4.46	4.07	3.84	3.69	3.58	3.50	3.44	3.39
9	5.12	4.26	3.86	3.63	3.48	3.37	3.29	3.23	3.18
10	4.96	4.10	3.71	3.48	3.33	3.22	3.14	3.07	3.02
11	4.84	3.98	3.59	3.36	3.20	3.09	3.01	2.95	2.90
12	4.75	3.89	3.49	3.25	3.11	3.00	2.91	2.85	2.80
13	4.67	3.81	3.41	3.18	3.03	2.92	2.83	2.77	2.71
14	4.60	3.74	3.34	3.11	2.96	2.85	2.76	2.70	2.65

the denominator sample variance, s_2^2. Thus, if the numerator degrees of freedom is $\nu_1 = 7$ and the denominator degrees of freedom is $\nu_2 = 9$, we look in the seventh column and ninth row to find $F_{.05} = 3.29$. As shown in Figure 7.14, $\alpha = .05$ is the tail area to the right of 3.29 in the F-distribution with 7 and 9 df. That is, if $\sigma_1^2 = \sigma_2^2$, then the probability that the F statistic will exceed 3.29 is $\alpha = .05$.

EXAMPLE 7.8

In Example 7.4 (Section 7.1) we used the two-sample t statistic to compare the success indexes of two groups of managers. The data are repeated in Table 7.7 for convenience followed by a SAS printout of the analysis in Figure 7.15. The use of the t statistic was based on the assumption that the population variances of the managerial success indexes were equal for the two groups. Check this assumption at $\alpha = .10$.

TABLE 7.7 Managerial Success Indexes for Two Groups of Managers

Group 1						Group 2					
Interaction with Outsiders						Few Interactions					
65	58	78	60	68	69	62	53	36	34	56	50
66	70	53	71	63	63	42	57	46	68	48	42
						52	53	43			

```
                              TTEST PROCEDURE

Variable: SUCCESS

GROUP        N          Mean        Std Dev      Std Error       Minimum       Maximum
--------------------------------------------------------------------------------------
    1       12   65.33333333    6.61036835    1.90824897   53.00000000   78.00000000
    2       15   49.46666667    9.33401358    2.41003194   34.00000000   68.00000000

Variances          T        DF      Prob>|T|
--------------------------------------------
Unequal       5.1615      24.7        0.0001
Equal         4.9675      25.0        0.0000

For HO: Variances are equal, F' = 1.99    DF = (14,11)    Prob>F' = 0.2554
```

FIGURE 7.15
SAS F-test for the data in Table 7.7

Solution Let

$$\sigma_1^2 = \text{Population variance of success indexes for Group 1 managers}$$
$$\sigma_2^2 = \text{Population variance of success indexes for Group 2 managers}$$

The hypotheses of interest then are

$$H_0\text{: } \frac{\sigma_1^2}{\sigma_2^2} = 1 \qquad (\sigma_1^2 = \sigma_2^2)$$

$$H_a\text{: } \frac{\sigma_1^2}{\sigma_2^2} \neq 1 \qquad (\sigma_1^2 \neq \sigma_2^2)$$

The nature of the F-tables given in Appendix B affects the form of the test statistic. To form the rejection region for a two-tailed ***F*-test**, we want to make certain that the upper tail is used, because only the upper-tail values of F are shown in Tables VIII, IX, X, and XI. To accomplish this, *we will always place the larger sample variance in the numerator of the* F*-test statistic.* This has the effect of doubling the tabulated value for α, since we double the probability that the F-ratio will fall in the upper tail by always placing the larger sample variance in the numerator. That is, we establish a one-tailed rejection region by putting the larger variance in the numerator rather than establishing rejection regions in both tails.

From the SAS printout in Figure 7.15, we find that $s_1 = 6.610$ and $s_2 = 9.334$. Therefore, the test statistic is:

$$F = \frac{\text{Larger sample variance}}{\text{Smaller sample variance}} = \frac{s_2^2}{s_1^2} = \frac{(9.334)^2}{(6.610)^2} = 1.99$$

For numerator df $\nu_1 = n_2 - 1 = 14$ and denominator df $\nu_2 = n_1 - 1 = 11$, we will reject H_0: $\sigma_1^2 = \sigma_2^2$ at $\alpha = .10$ when the calculated value of F exceeds the tabulated value:

$$F_{\alpha/2} = F_{.05} = 2.74 \quad \text{(see Figure 7.16)}$$

FIGURE 7.16
Rejection region for Example 7.8

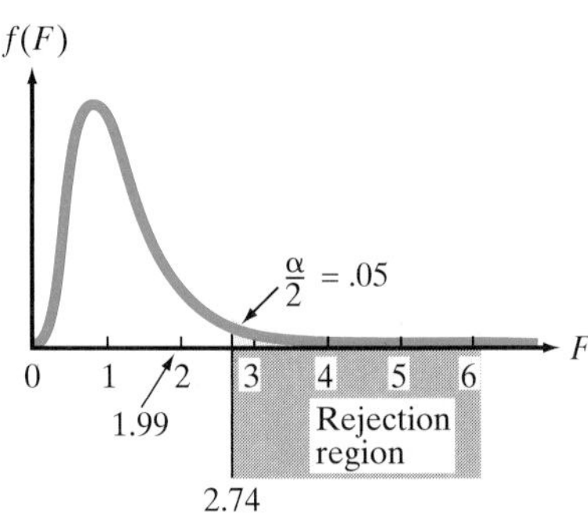

Note that $F = 1.99$ does not fall into the rejection region shown in Figure 7.16. Therefore, the data provide insufficient evidence to reject the null hypothesis of equal population variances.

This F-test is also shown on the SAS printout, Figure 7.15. Both the test statistic, $F = 1.99$, and two-tailed p-value, .2554, are highlighted on the printout. Since $\alpha = .10$ is less than the p-value, our conclusion is confirmed: we do not reject the null hypothesis that the population variances of the success indexes are equal.

Although we must be careful not to accept H_0 (since the probability of a Type II error, β, is unknown), this result leads us to behave as if the assumption of equal population variances is reasonably satisfied. Consequently, the inference drawn from the t-test in Example 7.4 appears to be valid. ✶

We conclude this section with a summary of the F-test for equal population variances.*

*Although a test of a hypothesis of equality of variances is the most common application of the F-test, it can also be used to test a hypothesis that the ratio between the population variances is equal to some specified value, H_0: $\sigma_1^2/\sigma_2^2 = k$. The test is conducted in exactly the same way as specified in the box, except that we use the test statistic

$$F = \frac{s_1^2}{s_2^2}\left(\frac{1}{k}\right)$$

F-Test for Equal Population Variances

One-Tailed Test	Two-Tailed Test
$H_0: \sigma_1^2 = \sigma_2^2$	$H_0: \sigma_1^2 = \sigma_2^2$
$H_a: \sigma_1^2 < \sigma_2^2$ (or $H_a: \sigma_1^2 > \sigma_2^2$)	$H_a: \sigma_1^2 \neq \sigma_2^2$
Test statistic: $F = \frac{s_2^2}{s_1^2}$ $\left(\text{or } F = \frac{s_1^2}{s_2^2} \text{ when } H_a: \sigma_1^2 > \sigma_2^2\right)$	*Test statistic:* $F = \frac{\text{Larger sample variance}}{\text{Smaller sample variance}} = \frac{s_1^2}{s_2^2} \text{ when } s_1^2 > s_2^2$ $\left(\text{or } \frac{s_2^2}{s_1^2} \text{ when } s_2^2 > s_1^2\right)$
Rejection region: $F > F_\alpha$	*Rejection region:* $F > F_{\alpha/2}$

where F_α and $F_{\alpha/2}$ are based on ν_1 = numerator degrees of freedom and ν_2 = denominator degrees of freedom; ν_1 and ν_2 are the degrees of freedom for the numerator and denominator sample variances, respectively.

Assumptions: 1. Both sampled populations are normally distributed.*
2. The samples are random and independent.

Note: Rejecting the null hypothesis $H_0: \sigma_1^2 = \sigma_2^2$ implies that the assumption of equal population variances is violated. Consequently, the small-sample procedure for comparing population means in Section 7.1 may lead to invalid inferences. In this situation, apply the nonparametric procedure for comparing two populations discussed in optional Section 7.5, or consult the chapter references for methods that utilize an adjusted t-statistic.

EXERCISES 7.42–7.52

Learning the Mechanics

7.42 Use Tables VIII, IX, X, and XI of Appendix B to find each of the following F values:

a. $F_{.05}$ where $\nu_1 = 9$ and $\nu_2 = 6$
b. $F_{.01}$ where $\nu_1 = 18$ and $\nu_2 = 14$
c. $F_{.025}$ where $\nu_1 = 11$ and $\nu_2 = 4$
d. $F_{.10}$ where $\nu_1 = 20$ and $\nu_2 = 5$

7.43 For each of the following cases, identify the rejection region that should be used to test $H_0: \sigma_1^2 = \sigma_2^2$ against $H_a: \sigma_1^2 \neq \sigma_2^2$. Assume $\nu_1 = 10$ and $\nu_2 = 12$.

a. $\alpha = .20$ b. $\alpha = .10$ c. $\alpha = .05$ d. $\alpha = .02$

7.44 Specify the appropriate rejection region for testing $H_0: \sigma_1^2 = \sigma_2^2$ in each of the following situations:

a. $H_a: \sigma_1^2 > \sigma_2^2$; $\alpha = .05$, $n_1 = 25$, $n_2 = 20$
b. $H_a: \sigma_1^2 < \sigma_2^2$; $\alpha = .05$, $n_1 = 10$, $n_2 = 15$
c. $H_a: \sigma_1^2 \neq \sigma_2^2$; $\alpha = .10$, $n_1 = 21$, $n_2 = 31$
d. $H_a: \sigma_1^2 < \sigma_2^2$; $\alpha = .01$, $n_1 = 31$, $n_2 = 41$
e. $H_a: \sigma_1^2 \neq \sigma_2^2$; $\alpha = .05$, $n_1 = 7$, $n_2 = 16$

7.45 Independent random samples were selected from each of two normally distributed populations, $n_1 = 12$ from population 1 and $n_2 = 27$ from population 2. The means and variances for the two samples are shown in the table.

Sample 1	Sample 2
$n_1 = 12$	$n_2 = 27$
$\bar{x}_1 = 31.7$	$\bar{x}_2 = 37.4$
$s_1^2 = 3.87$	$s_2^2 = 8.75$

*The F-test is much less robust (i.e., much more sensitive) to departures from normality than the t-test for comparing the population means. If you have doubts about the normality of the population frequency distributions, use a nonparametric method for comparing the two variances. A method can be found in the nonparametric statistics texts listed in the chapter references.

SPSS Output for Exercise 7.46

```
Summaries of    X
By levels of    SAMPLE

Variable          Value  Label                     Mean     Std Dev    Cases

For Entire Population                             3.3000     2.3656       11

SAMPLE             1.00                           2.4167     1.4359        6
SAMPLE             2.00                           4.3600     2.9729        5

  Total Cases =          11
```

a. Test the null hypothesis $H_0: \sigma_1^2 = \sigma_2^2$ against the alternative hypothesis $H_a: \sigma_1^2 \neq \sigma_2^2$. Use $\alpha = .10$.

b. Find the approximate p-value of the test.

7.46 Independent random samples were selected from each of two normally distributed populations, $n_1 = 6$ from population 1 and $n_2 = 5$ from population 2. The data are shown in the table below, and an SPSS descriptive statistics printout is provided above.

a. Test $H_0: \sigma_1^2 = \sigma_2^2$ against $H_a: \sigma_1^2 < \sigma_2^2$. Use $\alpha = .01$.

b. Find the approximate p-value of the test.

LM7_46.DAT

Sample 1	Sample 2
3.1	2.3
4.4	1.4
1.2	3.7
1.7	8.9
.7	5.5
3.4	

Applying the Concepts

7.47 In addition to evaluating the performance of individual companies, securities analysts also evaluate and compare industry sectors. One of the variables used in this analysis is the percentage growth in net incomes for the previous year. The table, extracted from *Forbes* (Jan. 10, 2000), lists the percentage growth in net income for samples of firms from the banking and energy sectors of the U.S. economy.

BANKENER.DAT

Banking		Energy	
Bank of NY	46.5%	Ashland	42.9%
Compass	9.7	Coastal	22.8
First Union	35.1	Duke	3.2
PNC Bank	13.6	Exxon Mobil	−29.7
Regions	30.2	MidAmerican	231.7
State Street	13.2	Nicor	−6.5
Summit	−2.4	OGE	−11.0
Synovus	20.3	Royal Dutch	−56.6
		UGE	38.2

Source: *Forbes*, Jan. 10, 2000, pp. 84–167.

a. Suppose you want to compare the mean growth in net incomes for the banking and energy sectors. What assumption about the variability in growth rates must be true for the inference about the means to be valid?

b. What are the appropriate null and alternative hypotheses to use in comparing the variability of net income growth rates of the banking and energy sectors?

c. Conduct the test of part **b** using $\alpha = .05$. Interpret your results in the context of the problem.

d. What assumptions must hold to ensure the validity of the test?

7.48 A study in the *Journal of Occupational and Organizational Psychology* (Dec. 1992) investigated the relationship of employment status and mental health. A sample of working and unemployed people was selected, and each person was given a mental health examination using the General Health Questionnaire (GHQ), a widely recognized measure of mental health. Although the article focused on comparing the mean GHQ levels, a comparison of the variability of GHQ scores for employed and unemployed men and women is of interest as well.

a. In general terms, what does the amount of variability in GHQ scores tell us about the group?

b. What are the appropriate null and alternative hypotheses to compare the variability of the mental health scores of the employed and unemployed groups? Define any symbols you use.

c. The standard deviation for a sample of 142 employed men was 3.26, while the standard deviation for 49 unemployed men was 5.10. Conduct the test you set up in part **b** using $\alpha = .05$. Interpret the results.

d. What assumptions are necessary to ensure the validity of the test?

7.49 Tests of product quality using human inspectors can lead to serious inspection error problems (*Journal of Quality Technology*, Apr. 1986). To evaluate the performance of inspectors in a new company, a quality manager had a sample of 12 novice inspectors evaluate 200 finished products. The same 200 items were evaluated by 12 experienced inspectors. The quality of each item—whether defective or nondefective—was known to the manager. The table (p. 383) lists the number of inspection errors (classifying a defective item as nondefective or vice versa) made by each inspector. A SAS printout with descriptive statistics for the two types of inspectors is provided on the next page.

SAS Output for Exercise 7.49

```
Analysis Variable : ERRORS

--------------------------INSPECT=EXPER--------------------------

N Obs    N         Minimum         Maximum            Mean         Std Dev
--------------------------------------------------------------------------

   12   12      10.0000000      31.0000000      20.5833333       5.7439032
--------------------------------------------------------------------------

-------------------------INSPECT=NOVICE--------------------------

N Obs    N         Minimum         Maximum            Mean         Std Dev
--------------------------------------------------------------------------

   12   12      20.0000000      48.0000000      32.8333333       8.6427409
--------------------------------------------------------------------------
```

INSPECT.DAT

Novice Inspectors				Experienced Inspectors			
30	35	26	40	31	15	25	19
36	20	45	31	28	17	19	18
33	29	21	48	24	10	20	21

a. Prior to conducting this experiment, the manager believed the variance in inspection errors was lower for experienced inspectors than for novice inspectors. Do the sample data support her belief? Test using $\alpha = .05$.

b. What is the appropriate p-value of the test you conducted in part **a?**

7.50 Refer to the *International Journal of Environmental Health Research* (Vol. 4, 1994) study, Exercise 7.15 (p. 360), in which the mean solid-waste generation rates for middle-income and industrialized countries were compared. The data are reproduced in the table at right.

a. In order to conduct the two-sample t-test in Exercise 7.15, it was necessary to assume that the two population variances were equal. Test this assumption at $\alpha = .05$. Use the SAS printout below to conduct the test.

b. What does your test indicate about the appropriateness of applying a two-sample t-test?

7.51 Following the Persian Gulf War, the Pentagon changed its logistics processes to be more corporate-like. The extravagant "just-in-case" mentality was replaced with "just-in-time" systems. Emulating Federal Express and United Parcel Service, deliveries from factories to foxholes are now expedited using bar codes, laser cards, radio tags, and databases to track supplies. The table on the next page contains order-to-delivery times (in days) for a sample of shipments from the United States to the Persian Gulf in 1991 and a sample of shipments to Bosnia in 1995.

a. Use the SPSS printout on p. 384 to test whether the variances in order-to-delivery times for Persian Gulf and Bosnia shipments are equal. Use $\alpha = .05$.

b. Given your answer to part **a,** is it appropriate to construct a confidence interval for the difference between the mean order-to-delivery times? Explain.

7.52 The *American Educational Research Journal* (Fall, 1998) published a study to compare the mathematics achievement test scores of male and female students.

SOLWASTE.DAT

Industrialized Countries		Middle-Income Countries	
New York (USA)	2.27	Singapore	0.87
Phoenix (USA)	2.31	Hong Kong	0.85
London (UK)	2.24	Medellin (Colombia)	0.54
Hamburg (Germany)	2.18	Kano (Nigeria)	0.46
Rome (Italy)	2.15	Manila (Philippines)	0.50
		Cairo (Egypt)	0.50
		Tunis (Tunisia)	0.56

SAS Output for Exercise 7.50

```
                              TTEST PROCEDURE

Variable: WASTE

COUNTRY        N                Mean                Std Dev            Std Error
---------------------------------------------------------------------------------
INDUS          5          2.23000000             0.06519202           0.02915476
MIDDLE         7          0.61142857             0.17286108           0.06533535

Variances            T      DF      Prob>|T|
---------------------------------------------
Unequal       22.6231     8.1        0.0001
Equal         19.7302    10.0        0.0000

For HO: Variances are equal, F' = 7.03     DF = (6,4)     Prob>F' = 0.0800
```

SPSS Output for Exercise 7.51

```
Independent samples of    LOCATION

Group 1:  LOCATION  EQ      1.00          Group 2:  LOCATION  EQ       2.00

t-test for:  TIME

                    Number                   Standard      Standard
                   of Cases      Mean       Deviation       Error

     Group 1          9        25.2444        10.520        3.507
     Group 2          9         7.3778         3.654        1.218

                 | Pooled Variance Estimate  | Separate Variance Estimate
                 |                           |
  F    2-Tail    |    t   Degrees of 2-Tail  |    t     Degrees of   2-Tail
Value   Prob.    |  Value   Freedom   Prob.  |  Value     Freedom     Prob.
                 |                           |
 8.29    .007    |   4.81     16      .000   |   4.81       9.90      .001
```

ORDTIMES.DAT

Persian Gulf	Bosnia
28.0	15.1
20.0	6.4
26.5	5.0
10.6	11.4
9.1	6.5
35.2	6.5
29.1	3.0
41.2	7.0
27.5	5.5

Source: Adapted from Crock, S. "The Pentagon goes to B-school." *Business Week*, December 11, 1995, p. 98.

a. The researchers hypothesized that the distribution of test scores for males is more variable than the corresponding distribution for females. Use the summary information in the table below to test this claim at $\alpha = .01$.

b. Does the result, part **a,** prevent you from conducting a test to compare the mean scores of males and females? Explain.

	Males	Females
Sample size	1,764	1,739
Mean	48.9	48.4
Standard deviation	12.96	11.85

Source: Bielinski, J., and Davison, M. L. "Gender differences by item difficulty interactions in multiple-choice mathematics items." *American Educational Research Journal*, Vol. 35, No. 3, Fall 1998, p. 464 (Table 1).

7.5 A NONPARAMETRIC TEST FOR COMPARING TWO POPULATIONS: INDEPENDENT SAMPLING (OPTIONAL)

Suppose two independent random samples are to be used to compare the populations and the t-test of Section 7.1 is inappropriate for making the comparison. We may be unwilling to make assumptions about the form of the underlying population probability distributions or we may be unable to obtain exact values of the sample measurements. If the data can be ranked in order of magnitude for either of these situations, the **Wilcoxon rank sum test** (developed by Frank Wilcoxon) can be used to test the hypothesis that the probability distributions associated with the two populations are equivalent.

For example, suppose six economists who work for the federal government and seven university economists are randomly selected, and each is asked to predict next year's percentage change in cost of living as compared with this year's figure. The objective of the study is to compare the government economists' predictions to those of the university economists. The data are shown in Table 7.8.

Experience has shown that the populations of predicted percentage changes often possess probability distributions that are skewed, as shown in Figure 7.17. Consequently, a t-test should not be used to compare the mean predictions of the two groups of economists because the normality assumption that is required for the t-test may not be valid.

TABLE 7.8 Percentage Cost of Living Change, as Predicted by Government and University Economists

Government Economist (1)		University Economist (2)	
Prediction	Rank	Prediction	Rank
3.1	4	4.4	6
4.8	7	5.8	9
2.3	2	3.9	5
5.6	8	8.7	11
0.0	1	6.3	10
2.9	3	10.5	12
		10.8	13

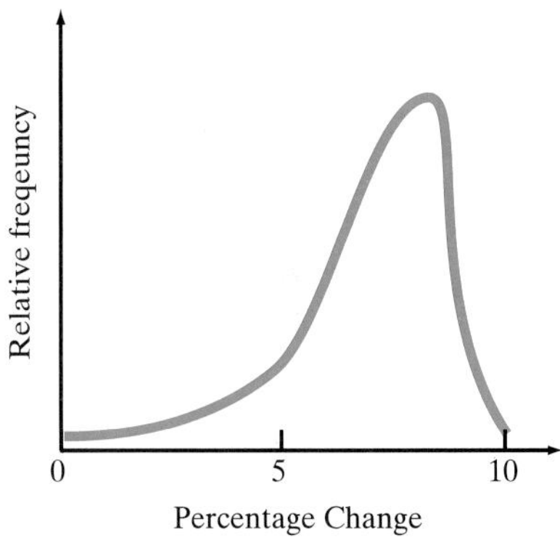

FIGURE 7.17
Typical probability distribution of predicted cost of living changes

The two populations of predictions are those that would be obtained from *all* government and *all* university economists if they could all be questioned. To compare their probability distributions using a nonparametric test, we first *rank the sample observations as though they were all drawn from the same population.* That is, we pool the measurements from both samples and then rank the measurements from the smallest (a rank of 1) to the largest (a rank of 13). The ranks of the 13 economists' predictions are indicated in Table 7.8.

The test statistic for the Wilcoxon test is based on the totals of the ranks for each of the two samples—that is, on the **rank sums.** If the two rank sums are nearly equal, the implication is that there is no evidence that the probability distributions from which the samples were drawn are different. On the other hand, if the two rank sums are very different, the implication is that the two samples may have come from different populations.

For the economists' predictions, we arbitrarily denote the rank sum for government economists by T_1 and that for university economists by T_2. Then

$$T_1 = 4 + 7 + 2 + 8 + 1 + 3 = 25$$

$$T_2 = 6 + 9 + 5 + 11 + 10 + 12 + 13 = 66$$

The sum of T_1 and T_2 will always equal $n(n + 1)/2$, where $n = n_1 + n_2$. So, for this example, $n_1 = 6$, $n_2 = 7$, and

$$T_1 + T_2 = \frac{13(13 + 1)}{2} = 91$$

Since $T_1 + T_2$ is fixed, a small value for T_1 implies a large value for T_2 (and vice versa) and a large difference between T_1 and T_2. Therefore, the smaller the value of one of the rank sums, the greater the evidence to indicate that the samples were selected from different populations.

The test statistic for this test is the rank sum for the smaller sample; or, in the case where $n_1 = n_2$, either rank sum can be used. Values that locate the rejection region for this rank sum are given in Table XII of Appendix B. A partial reproduction of this table is shown in Table 7.9. The columns of the table represent n_1, the first sample size, and the rows represent n_2, the second sample size. *The* T_L *and* T_U *entries in the table are the boundaries of the lower and upper regions, respectively, for the rank sum associated with the sample that has fewer measurements.* If the sample sizes n_1 and n_2 are the same, either rank sum may be used as the test statistic. To illustrate, suppose $n_1 = 8$ and $n_2 = 10$. For a two-tailed test with $\alpha = .05$, we consult part **a** of the table and find that the null hypothesis will be rejected if the rank sum of sample 1 (the sample with fewer measurements), T, is less than or equal to $T_L = 54$ or greater than or equal to $T_U = 98$. (These values are highlighted in Table 7.9.) The Wilcoxon rank sum test is summarized in the box on p. 387.

TABLE 7.9 Reproduction of Part of Table XII in Appendix B: Critical Values for the Wilcoxon Rank Sum Test

$\alpha = .025$ one-tailed; $\alpha = .05$ two-tailed

n_2 \ n_1	3		4		5		6		7		8		9		10	
	T_L	T_U	T_L	T_U	T_L	T_U	T_L	T_U	T_L	T_U	T_L	T_U	T_L	T_U	T_L	T_U
3	5	16	6	18	6	21	7	23	7	26	8	28	8	31	9	33
4	6	18	11	25	12	28	12	32	13	35	14	38	15	41	16	44
5	6	21	12	28	18	37	19	41	20	45	21	49	22	53	24	56
6	7	23	12	32	19	41	26	52	28	56	29	61	31	65	32	70
7	7	26	13	35	20	45	28	56	37	68	39	73	41	78	43	83
8	8	28	14	38	21	49	29	61	39	73	49	87	51	93	54	98
9	8	31	15	41	22	53	31	65	41	78	51	93	63	108	66	114
10	9	33	16	44	24	56	32	70	43	83	54	98	66	114	79	131

Note that the assumptions necessary for the validity of the Wilcoxon rank sum test do not specify the shape or type of probability distribution. However, the distributions are assumed to be continuous so that the probability of tied measurements is 0 (see Chapter 4), and each measurement can be assigned a unique rank. In practice, however, rounding of continuous measurements will sometimes produce ties. As long as the number of ties is small relative to the sample sizes, the Wilcoxon test procedure will still have an approximate significance level of α. The test is not recommended to compare discrete distributions for which many ties are expected.

EXAMPLE 7.9

Test the hypothesis that the government economists' predictions of next year's percentage change in cost of living tend to be lower than the university economists'. That is, test to determine if the probability distribution of government economists' predictions is *shifted to the left* of the probability distribution of university economists' predictions. Conduct the test using the data in Table 7.8 and $\alpha = .05$.

Wilcoxon Rank Sum Test: Independent Samples*

Let D_1 and D_2 represent the probability distributions for populations 1 and 2, respectively.

One-Tailed Test	**Two-Tailed Test**
H_0: D_1 and D_2 are identical	H_0: D_1 and D_2 are identical
H_a: D_1 is shifted to the right of D_2 [or H_a: D_1 is shifted to the left of D_2]	H_a: D_1 is shifted either to the left or to the right of D_2
Test statistic:	*Test statistic:*
T_1, if $n_1 < n_2$; T_2, if $n_2 < n_1$ (Either rank sum can be used if $n_1 = n_2$.)	T_1, if $n_1 < n_2$; T_2, if $n_2 < n_1$ (Either rank sum can be used if $n_1 = n_2$.) We will denote this rank sum as T.
Rejection region:	*Rejection region:*
T_1: $T_1 \geq T_U$ [or $T_1 \leq T_L$] T_2: $T_2 \leq T_L$ [or $T_2 \geq T_U$]	$T \leq T_L$ or $T \geq T_U$

where T_L and T_U are obtained from Table XII of Appendix B.

Assumptions: 1. The two samples are random and independent.
2. The two probability distributions from which the samples are drawn are continuous.

Ties: Assign tied measurements the average of the ranks they would receive if they were unequal but occurred in successive order. For example, if the third-ranked and fourth-ranked measurements are tied, assign each a rank of $(3 + 4)/2 = 3.5$.

Solution

H_0: The probability distributions corresponding to the government and university economists' predictions of inflation rate are identical

H_a: The probability distribution for the government economists' predictions lies below (to the left of) the probability distribution for the university economists' predictions†

Test statistic: Since fewer government economists ($n_1 = 6$) than university economists ($n_2 = 7$) were sampled, the test statistic is T_1, the rank sum of the government economists' predictions.

Rejection region: Since the test is one-sided, we consult part **b** of Table XII for the rejection region corresponding to $\alpha = .05$. We reject H_0 only for $T_1 \leq T_L$, the lower value from Table XII, since we are specifically testing that the distribution of government economists' predictions lies *below* the distribution of university economists' predictions, as shown in Figure 7.18. Thus, we reject H_0 if $T_1 \leq 30$.

*Another statistic used for comparing two populations based on independent random samples is the *Mann-Whitney U statistic.* The U statistic is a simple function of the rank sums. It can be shown that the Wilcoxon rank sum test and the Mann-Whitney U-test are equivalent.

†The alternative hypotheses in this chapter will be stated in terms of a difference in the *location* of the distributions. However, since the shapes of the distributions may also differ under H_a, some of the figures (e.g., Figure 7.18) depicting the alternative hypothesis will show probability distributions with different shapes.

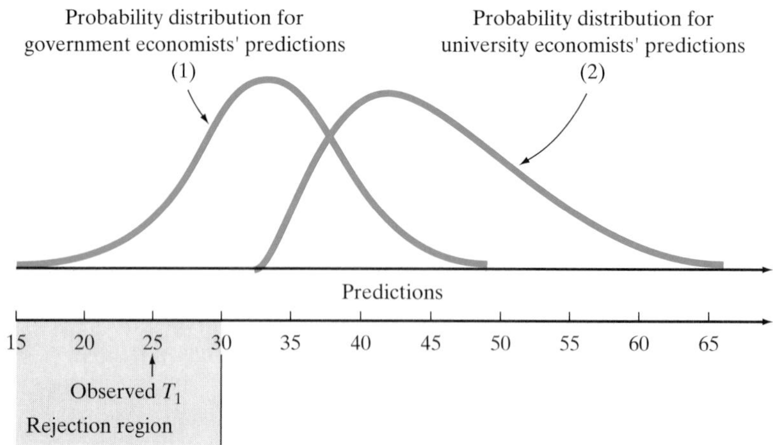

FIGURE 7.18
Alternative hypothesis and rejection region for Example 7.9

Since T_1, the rank sum of the government economists' predictions in Table 7.8, is 25, it is in the rejection region (see Figure 7.18). Therefore, we can conclude that the university economists' predictions tend, in general, to exceed the government economists' predictions. This same conclusion can be reached using a statistical software package. The SAS printout of the analysis is shown in Figure 7.19. Both the test statistic ($T_1 = 25$) and two-tailed p-value ($p = .0184$) are highlighted on the printout. The one-tailed p-value, $p = .0184/2 = .0092$, is less than $\alpha = .05$, leading us to reject H_0.

```
                    N P A R 1 W A Y   P R O C E D U R E

          Wilcoxon Scores (Rank Sums) for Variable PCTCHNG
                   Classified by Variable ECONOMST

                          Sum of      Expected       Std Dev          Mean
ECONOMST        N         Scores      Under H0       Under H0         Score

GOVERN          6           25.0          42.0            7.0    4.16666667
UNIV            7           66.0          49.0            7.0    9.42857143

        Wilcoxon 2-Sample Test (Normal Approximation)
        (with Continuity Correction of .5)

        S=  25.0000      Z= -2.35714      Prob > |Z|  = 0.0184

        T-Test approx. Significance =      0.0362

        Kruskal-Wallis Test (Chi-Square Approximation)
        CHISQ=  5.8980      DF=  1      Prob > CHISQ=     0.0152
```

FIGURE 7.19
SAS printout for Example 7.9

Table XII in Appendix B gives values of T_L and T_U for values of n_1 and n_2 less than or equal to 10. When both sample sizes n_1 and n_2 are 10 or larger, the sampling distribution of T_1 can be approximated by a normal distribution with mean and variance

$$E(T_1) = \frac{n_1(n_1 + n_2 + 1)}{2} \quad \text{and} \quad \sigma^2_{T_1} = \frac{n_1 n_2(n_1 + n_2 + 1)}{12}$$

Therefore, for $n_1 \geq 10$ and $n_2 \geq 10$ we can conduct the Wilcoxon rank sum test using the familiar z-test of Section 7.1. The test is summarized in the next box.

The Wilcoxon Rank Sum Test for Large Samples ($n_1 \geq 10$ and $n_2 \geq 10$)

Let D_1 and D_2 represent the probability distributions for populations 1 and 2, respectively.

One-Tailed Test	Two-Tailed Test
H_0: D_1 and D_2 are identical	H_0: D_1 and D_2 are identical
H_a: D_1 is shifted to the right of D_2 (or H_a: D_1 is shifted to the left of D_2)	H_a: D_1 is shifted either to the right or to the left of D_2

$$\text{Test statistic: } z = \frac{T_1 - \dfrac{n_1(n_1 + n_2 + 1)}{2}}{\sqrt{\dfrac{n_1 n_2(n_1 + n_2 + 1)}{12}}}$$

Rejection region:	Rejection region:
$z > z_\alpha$ (or $z < -z_\alpha$)	$\lvert z \rvert > z_{\alpha/2}$

EXERCISES 7.53–7.63

Learning the Mechanics

7.53 Specify the test statistic and the rejection region for the Wilcoxon rank sum test for independent samples in each of the following situations:

a. $n_1 = 10, n_2 = 6, \alpha = .10$
H_0: Two probability distributions, 1 and 2, are identical
H_a: Probability distribution for population 1 is shifted to the right or left of the probability distribution for population 2

b. $n_1 = 5, n_2 = 7, \alpha = .05$
H_0: Two probability distributions, 1 and 2, are identical
H_a: Probability distribution for population 1 is shifted to the right of the probability distribution for population 2

c. $n_1 = 9, n_2 = 8, \alpha = .025$
H_0: Two probability distributions, 1 and 2, are identical
H_a: Probability distribution for population 1 is shifted to the left of the probability distribution for population 2

d. $n_1 = 15, n_2 = 15, \alpha = .05$
H_0: Two probability distributions, 1 and 2, are identical
H_a: Probability distribution for population 1 is shifted to the right or left of the probability distribution for population 2

7.54 Suppose you want to compare two treatments, A and B. In particular, you wish to determine whether the distribution for population B is shifted to the right of the distribution for population A. You plan to use the Wilcoxon rank sum test.

a. Specify the null and alternative hypotheses you would test.

b. Suppose you obtained the following independent random samples of observations on experimental units subjected to the two treatments. Conduct a test of the hypotheses described in part **a.** Test using $\alpha = .05$.

 **LM7_54.DAT**

Sample A: 37, 40, 33, 29, 42, 33, 35, 28, 34
Sample B: 65, 35, 47, 52

7.55 Explain the difference between the one-tailed and two-tailed versions of the Wilcoxon rank sum test for independent random samples.

7.56 Independent random samples are selected from two populations. The data are shown in the table.

 **LM7_56.DAT**

Sample 1		Sample 2		
15	16	5	9	5
10	13	12	8	10
12	8	9	4	

a. Use the Wilcoxon rank sum test to determine whether the data provide sufficient evidence to indicate a shift in the locations of the probability distributions of the sampled populations. Test using $\alpha = .05$.

b. Do the data provide sufficient evidence to indicate that the probability distribution for population 1 is shifted to the right of the probability distribution for population 2? Use the Wilcoxon rank sum test with $\alpha = .05$.

Applying the Concepts

7.57 University of Queensland researchers J. Hann and R. Weber sampled private sector and public sector organizations in Australia to study the planning undertaken by their information systems departments (*Management Science,* July 1996). As part of that process they asked each sample organization how much it had spent on information systems and technology in the previous fiscal year as a percentage of the organization's total revenues. The results are reported in the table.

INFOSYS.DAT

Private Sector	Public Sector
2.58%	5.40%
5.05	2.55
.05	9.00
2.10	10.55
4.30	1.02
2.25	5.11
2.50	12.42
1.94	1.67
2.33	3.33

Source: Adapted from Hann, J., and Weber, R. "Information systems planning: A model and empirical tests." *Management Science,* Vol. 42, No. 2, July, 1996, pp. 1043–1064.

a. Do the two sampled populations have identical probability distributions or is the distribution for public sector organizations in Australia located to the right of Australia's private sector firms? Test using $\alpha = .05$.

b. Is the p-value for the test less than or greater than .05? Justify your answer.

c. What assumptions must be met to ensure the validity of the test you conducted in part **a?**

7.58 In Exercise 7.15 (p. 360), the solid waste generation rates for cities in industrialized countries and cities in middle-income countries were investigated. In this exercise, the focus is on middle-income countries versus low-income countries. The next table, extracted from the *International Journal of Environmental Health Research* (1994), reports waste generation values (kg per capita per day) for two independent samples. Do the rates differ for the two categories of countries?

a. Which nonparametric hypothesis-testing procedures could be used to answer the question?

SOLWAST2.DAT

Cities of Low-Income Countries		Cities of Middle-Income Countries	
Jakarta	.60	Singapore	.87
Surabaya	.52	Hong Kong	.85
Bandung	.55	Medellin	.54
Lahore	.60	Kano	.46
Karachi	.50	Manila	.50
Calcutta	.51	Cairo	.50
Kanpur	.50	Tunis	.56

Source: Al-Momani, A. H. "Solid-waste management: Sampling, analysis and assessment of household waste in the city of Amman." *International Journal of Environmental Health Research,* Vol. 4, 1994, pp. 208–222.

b. Specify the null and alternative hypotheses of the test.

c. Conduct the test using $\alpha = .01$. Interpret the results in the context of the problem.

7.59 Purchasing organizations such as the National Association of Purchasing Management advocate ethical purchasing practices for purchasing managers including the avoidance of situations that might influence or appear to influence purchasing decisions. In Mexico, the U.S.'s third largest trading partner, purchasing has not fully evolved into a profession with its own standards of ethical behavior. Researchers at Xavier University investigated the question: Do American and Mexican purchasing managers perceive ethical situations differently (*Industrial Marketing Management,* July 1999)? As part of their study, 15 Mexican purchasing managers and 15 American purchasing managers were asked to consider different ethical situations and respond on a 100-point scale with end points "strongly disagree" (1) and "strongly agree" (100). For the situation "accepting free trips from salespeople is okay," the responses shown in the table on p. 391 were obtained.

a. Consider a Wilcoxon rank sum test to determine whether American and Mexican purchasing managers perceive the given ethical situation differently. A STATISTIX printout of the analysis is also shown on p. 391. Verify the rank sums shown on the printout are accurate.

b. Conduct the test of $\alpha = .05$. Use the p-value shown on the printout to make your conclusion. (Note: STATISTIX employs the equivalent Mann-Whitney U-test to analyze the data. The p-values of the two tests are identical.)

c. Under what circumstances could the two-sample t-test of Section 7.1 be used to analyze the data? Check to see whether the t-test is appropriate in this situation.

7.60 The data in the second table on p. 391, extracted from *Technometrics* (Feb. 1986), represent daily accumulated stream flow and precipitation (in inches) for two U.S. Geological Survey stations in Colorado. Conduct a test to determine whether the distributions of daily

ETHICS.DAT

American Purchasing Managers			Mexican Purchasing Managers		
50	15	19	10	15	5
10	8	11	90	60	55
35	40	5	65	80	40
30	80	25	50	85	45
20	75	30	20	35	95

Source: Adapted from Tadepalli, R., Moreno, A., and Trevino, S., "Do American and Mexican Purchasing Managers Perceive Ethical Situations Differently? An Empirical Investigation," *Industrial Marketing Management,* Vol. 28, No. 4, July 1999, pp. 369–380.

STATISTIX Output for Exercise 7.59

```
RANK SUM TWO-SAMPLE (MANN-WHITNEY) TEST FOR FREETRIP BY COUNTRY

                               SAMPLE
 COUNTRY        RANK SUM       SIZE        U STAT          MEAN RANK
----------     ---------      ------     ---------         ---------
MEX              279.00         15        159.00              18.6
US               186.00         15        66.000              12.4
TOTAL            465.00         30

NORMAL APPROXIMATION WITH CONTINUITY CORRECTION             1.908
TWO-TAILED P-VALUE FOR NORMAL APPROXIMATION                0.0564

TOTAL NUMBER OF VALUES THAT WERE TIED           18
MAXIMUM DIFFERENCE ALLOWED BETWEEN TIES 0.00001

CASES INCLUDED 30      MISSING CASES 0
```

COLORAIN.DAT

Station 1			Station 2		
127.96	108.91	100.85	114.79	85.54	280.55
210.07	178.21	85.89	109.11	117.64	145.11
203.24	285.37		330.33	302.74	95.36

Source: Gastwirth, J. L., and Mahmoud, H. "An efficient robust nonparametric test for scale change for data from a gamma distribution." *Technometrics,* Vol. 28, No. 1, Feb. 1986, p. 83 (Table 2).

accumulated stream flow and precipitation for the two stations differ in location. Use $\alpha = .10$. Why is a nonparametric test appropriate for this data?

7.61 Recall that the variance of a binomial sample proportion, $\hat{p}$, depends on the value of the population parameter, p. As a consequence, the variance of a sample percentage, $(100\hat{p})\%$, also depends on p. Thus if you conduct an unpaired t-test (Section 7.1) to compare the means of two populations of percentages, you may be violating the assumption that $\sigma_1^2 = \sigma_2^2$, upon which the t-test is based. If the disparity in the variances is large, you will obtain more reliable test results using the Wilcoxon rank sum test for independent samples. In Exercise 7.18 (p. 361), we used a Student's t-test to compare the mean annual percentages of labor turnover between U.S. and Japanese manufacturers of air conditioners. The annual percentage turnover rates for five U.S. and five Japanese plants are shown in the table (p. 392). Do the data provide sufficient evidence to indicate that the mean annual percentage turnover for American plants exceeds the corresponding mean for Japanese plants? Test using the Wilcoxon rank sum test with $\alpha = .05$. Do your test conclusions agree with those of the t-test in Exercise 7.18?

TURNOVER.DAT

U.S. Plants	Japanese Plants
7.11%	3.52%
6.06	2.02
8.00	4.91
6.87	3.22
4.77	1.92

7.62 A major razor blade manufacturer advertises that its twin-blade disposable razor "gets you lots more shaves" than any single-blade disposable razor on the market. A rival company that has been very successful in selling single-blade razors plans to test this claim. Independent random samples of eight single-blade users and eight twin-blade users are taken, and the number of shaves that each gets before indicating a preference to change blades is recorded. The results are shown in the table.

RAZOR.DAT

Twin Blades		Single Blades	
8	15	10	13
17	10	6	14
9	6	3	5
11	12	7	7

a. Do the data support the twin-blade manufacturer's claim? Use $\alpha = .05$.
b. Do you think this experiment was designed in the best possible way? If not, what design might have been better?
c. What assumptions are necessary for the validity of the test you performed in part **a**? Do the assumptions seem reasonable for this application?

7.63 A *management information system* (MIS) is a computer-based information-processing system designed to support the operations, management, and decision functions of an organization. The development of an MIS involves three stages: definition, physical design, and implementation of the system (*Managing Information,* 1993). Thirty firms that recently implemented an MIS were surveyed: 16 were satisfied with the implementation results, 14 were not. Each firm was asked to rate the quality of the planning and negotiation stages of the development process, using a scale of 0 to 100, with higher numbers indicating better quality. (A score of 100 indicates that all the problems that occurred in the planning and negotiation stages were successfully resolved, while 0 indicates that none were resolved.) The results are shown in the table below.

MIS.DAT

Firms with a Good MIS			Firms with a Poor MIS		
52	59	95	60	40	90
70	60	90	50	55	85
40	90	86	55	65	80
80	75	95	70	55	90
82	80	93	41	70	
65					

a. The Wilcoxon rank sum test was used to compare the quality of the development processes of successfully and unsuccessfully implemented MISs. The results are shown in the SAS printout provided. Determine whether the distribution of quality scores for successfully implemented systems lies above the distribution of scores for unsuccessfully implemented systems. Test using $\alpha = .05$.
b. Under what circumstances could you use the two-sample t-test of Section 7.1 to conduct the same test?

SAS Output for Exercise 7.63

```
                    N P A R 1 W A Y   P R O C E D U R E

            Wilcoxon Scores (Rank Sums) for Variable QUALITY
                       Classified by Variable FIRM

                         Sum of       Expected        Std Dev          Mean
FIRM            N        Scores       Under H0       Under H0         Score

GOOD           16    290.500000          248.0     23.9858196    18.1562500
POOR           14    174.500000          217.0     23.9858196    12.4642857
                  Average Scores were used for Ties
          Wilcoxon 2-Sample Test (Normal Approximation)
          (with Continuity Correction of .5)

          S=  174.500      Z= -1.75103      Prob > |Z| = 0.0799

          T-Test approx. Significance =      0.0905

          Kruskal-Wallis Test (Chi-Square Approximation)
          CHISQ=  3.1396      DF=  1      Prob > CHISQ=     0.0764
```

7.6 A NONPARAMETRIC TEST FOR COMPARING TWO POPULATIONS: PAIRED DIFFERENCE EXPERIMENTS (OPTIONAL)

Nonparametric techniques can also be employed to compare two probability distributions when a paired difference design is used. For example, consumer preferences for two competing products are often compared by having each of a sample of consumers rate both products. Thus, the ratings have been paired on each consumer. Here is an example of this type of experiment.

For some paper products, softness is an important consideration in determining consumer acceptance. One method of determining softness is to have judges give a sample of the products a softness rating. Suppose each of 10 judges is given a sample of two products that a company wants to compare. Each judge rates the softness of each product on a scale from 1 to 10, with higher ratings implying a softer product. The results of the experiment are shown in Table 7.10.

TABLE 7.10 Softness Ratings of Paper

	Product		Difference		
Judge	A	B	(A − B)	Absolute Value of Difference	Rank of Absolute Value
1	6	4	2	2	5
2	8	5	3	3	7.5
3	4	5	−1	1	2
4	9	8	1	1	2
5	4	1	3	3	7.5
6	7	9	−2	2	5
7	6	2	4	4	9
8	5	3	2	2	5
9	6	7	−1	1	2
10	8	2	6	6	10

T_+ = Sum of positive ranks = 46
T_- = Sum of negative ranks = 9

Since this is a paired difference experiment, we analyze the differences between the measurements (see Section 7.2). However, the nonparametric approach—called the **Wilcoxon signed rank test**—requires that we calculate the ranks of the absolute values of the differences between the measurements, that is, the ranks of the differences after removing any minus signs. *Note that tied absolute differences are assigned the average of the ranks they would receive if they were unequal but successive measurements.* After the absolute differences are ranked, the sum of the ranks of the positive differences of the original measurements, T_+, and the sum of the ranks of the negative differences of the original measurements, T_-, are computed.

We are now prepared to test the nonparametric hypotheses:

H_0: The probability distributions of the ratings for products A and B are identical

H_a: The probability distributions of the ratings differ (in location) for the two products (Note that this is a two-sided alternative and that it implies a two-tailed test.)

Test statistic: T = Smaller of the positive and negative rank sums T_+ and T_-

The smaller the value of T, the greater the evidence to indicate that the two probability distributions differ in location. The rejection region for T can be determined by consulting Table XIII in Appendix B (part of the table is shown in Table 7.11).

This table gives a value T_0 for both one-tailed and two-tailed tests for each value of n, the number of matched pairs. For a two-tailed test with $\alpha = .05$, we will reject H_0 if $T \leq T_0$. You can see in Table 7.11 that the value of T_0 that locates the boundary of the rejection region for the judges' ratings for $\alpha = .05$ and $n = 10$ pairs of observations is 8. Thus, the rejection region for the test (see Figure 7.20) is

$$\text{Rejection region: } T \leq 8 \text{ for } \alpha = .05$$

TABLE 7.11 Reproduction of Part of Table XIII of Appendix B: Critical Values for the Wilcoxon Paired Difference Signed Rank Test

One-Tailed	Two-Tailed	$n = 5$	$n = 6$	$n = 7$	$n = 8$	$n = 9$	$n = 10$
$\alpha = .05$	$\alpha = .10$	1	2	4	6	8	11
$\alpha = .025$	$\alpha = .05$		1	2	4	6	8
$\alpha = .01$	$\alpha = .02$			0	2	3	5
$\alpha = .005$	$\alpha = .01$				0	2	3
		$n = 11$	$n = 12$	$n = 13$	$n = 14$	$n = 15$	$n = 16$
$\alpha = .05$	$\alpha = .10$	14	17	21	26	30	36
$\alpha = .025$	$\alpha = .05$	11	14	17	21	25	30
$\alpha = .01$	$\alpha = .02$	7	10	13	16	20	24
$\alpha = .005$	$\alpha = .01$	5	7	10	13	16	19
		$n = 17$	$n = 18$	$n = 19$	$n = 20$	$n = 21$	$n = 22$
$\alpha = .05$	$\alpha = .10$	41	47	54	60	68	75
$\alpha = .025$	$\alpha = .05$	35	40	46	52	59	66
$\alpha = .01$	$\alpha = .02$	28	33	38	43	49	56
$\alpha = .005$	$\alpha = .01$	23	28	32	37	43	49
		$n = 23$	$n = 24$	$n = 25$	$n = 26$	$n = 27$	$n = 28$
$\alpha = .05$	$\alpha = .10$	83	92	101	110	120	130
$\alpha = .025$	$\alpha = .05$	73	81	90	98	107	117
$\alpha = .01$	$\alpha = .02$	62	69	77	85	93	102
$\alpha = .005$	$\alpha = .01$	55	61	68	76	84	92

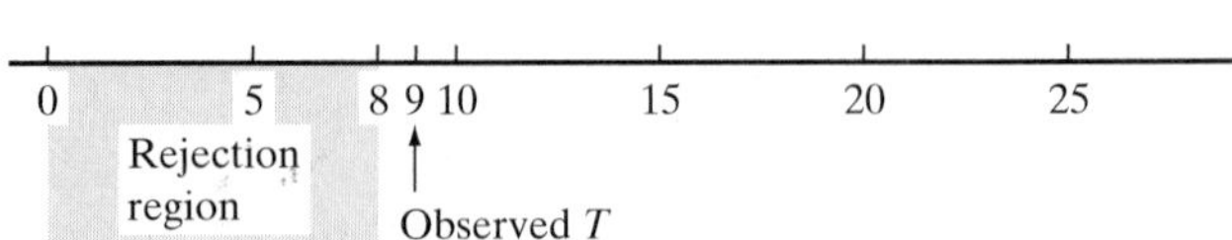

FIGURE 7.20 Rejection region for paired difference experiment

Since the smaller rank sum for the paper data, $T_- = 9$, does not fall within the rejection region, the experiment has not provided sufficient evidence to indicate that the two paper products differ with respect to their softness ratings at the $\alpha = .05$ level.

Note that if a significance level of $\alpha = .10$ had been used, the rejection region would have been $T \leq 11$ and we would have rejected H_0. In other words, the samples do provide evidence that the probability distributions of the softness ratings differ at the $\alpha = .10$ significance level.

The Wilcoxon signed rank test is summarized in the box. Note that the difference measurements are assumed to have a continuous probability distribution so that the absolute differences will have unique ranks. Although tied (absolute) differences can be assigned ranks by averaging, the number of ties should be small relative to the number of observations to ensure the validity of the test.

Wilcoxon Signed Rank Test for a Paired Difference Experiment

Let D_1 and D_2 represent the probability distributions for populations 1 and 2, respectively,

One-Tailed Test	**Two-Tailed Test**
H_0: D_1 and D_2 are identical	H_0: D_1 and D_2 are identical
H_a: D_1 is shifted to the right of D_2 [or H_a: D_1 is shifted to the left of D_2]	H_a: D_1 is shifted either to the left or to the right of D_2

Calculate the difference within each of the n matched pairs of observations. Then rank the absolute value of the n differences from the smallest (rank 1) to the highest (rank n) and calculate the rank sum T_- of the negative differences and the rank sum T_+ of the positive differences. [*Note:* Differences equal to 0 are eliminated, and the number n of differences is reduced accordingly.]

Test statistic:	*Test statistic:*
T_-, the rank sum of the negative differences [or T_+, the rank sum of the positive differences]	T, the smaller of T_+ or T_-
Rejection region:	*Rejection region:*
$T_- \le T_0$ [or $T_+ \le T_0$]	$T \le T_0$

where T_0 is given in Table XIII in Appendix B.

Assumptions:
1. The sample of differences is randomly selected from the population of differences.
2. The probability distribution from which the sample of paired differences is drawn is continuous.

Ties: Assign tied absolute differences the average of the ranks they would receive if they were unequal but occurred in successive order. For example, if the third-ranked and fourth-ranked differences are tied, assign both a rank of $(3 + 4)/2 = 3.5$.

EXAMPLE 7.10

Suppose the U.S. Consumer Product Safety Commission (CPSC) wants to test the hypothesis that New York City electrical contractors are more likely to install unsafe electrical outlets in urban homes than in suburban homes. A pair of homes, one urban and one suburban and both serviced by the same electrical contractor, is chosen for each of ten randomly selected electrical contractors. A CPSC inspector assigns each of the 20 homes a safety rating between 1 and 10, with higher numbers implying safer electrical conditions. The results are shown in Table 7.12. Use the Wilcoxon signed rank test to determine whether the CPSC hypothesis is supported at the $\alpha = .05$ level.

Solution The null and alternative hypotheses are

H_0: The probability distributions of home electrical ratings are identical for urban and suburban homes

TABLE 7.12 Electrical Safety Ratings for 10 Pairs of New York City Homes

Contractor	Location: Urban A	Location: Suburban B	Difference (A − B)	Rank of Absolute Difference
1	7	9	−2	4.5
2	4	5	−1	2
3	8	8	0	(Eliminated)
4	9	8	1	2
5	3	6	−3	6
6	6	10	−4	7.5
7	8	9	−1	2
8	10	8	2	4.5
9	9	4	5	9
10	5	9	−4	7.5
				Positive rank sum = T_+ = 15.5

H_a: The electrical ratings for suburban homes tend to exceed the electrical ratings for urban homes

Since a paired difference design was used (the homes were selected in urban-suburban pairs so that the electrical contractor was the same for both), we first calculate the difference between the ratings for each pair of homes, and then rank the absolute values of the differences (see Table 7.12). Note that one pair of ratings was the same (both 8), and the resulting 0 difference contributes to neither the positive nor the negative rank sum. Thus, we eliminate this pair from the calculation of the test statistic.

Test statistic: T_+, the positive rank sum

In Table 7.12, we compute the urban minus suburban rating differences, and if the alternative hypothesis is true, we would expect most of these differences to be negative. Or, in other words, we would expect the *positive* rank sum T_+ to be small if the alternative hypothesis is true (see Figure 7.21).

Rejection region: For $\alpha = .05$, from Table XIII of Appendix B, we use $n = 9$ (remember, one pair of observations was eliminated) to find the rejection region for this one-tailed test: $T_+ \le 8$

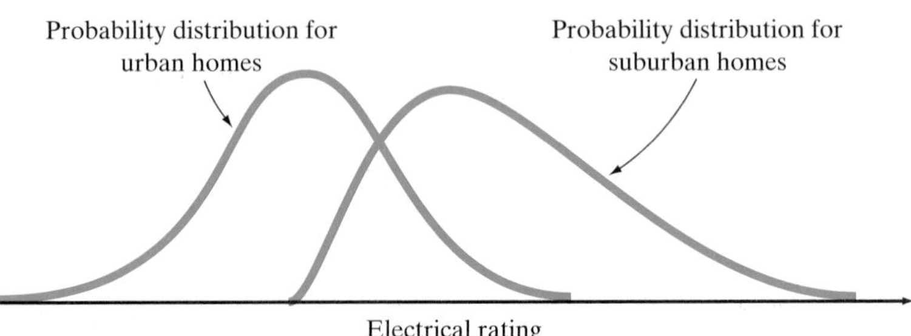

FIGURE 7.21 The alternative hypothesis for Example 7.10: We expect T_+ to be small

Since the computed value $T_+ = 15.5$ exceeds the critical value of 8, we conclude that this sample provides insufficient evidence at $\alpha = .05$ to support the alternative hypothesis. We *cannot* conclude on the basis of this sample information that suburban homes have safer electrical outlets than urban homes. A MINITAB printout of the analysis, shown in Figure 7.22, confirms this conclusion. The p-value of the test (highlighted) is .221, which exceeds $\alpha = .05$.

FIGURE 7.22
MINITAB printout for Example 7.10

```
TEST OF MEDIAN = 0.000000 VERSUS MEDIAN L.T. 0.000000

                   N FOR   WILCOXON            ESTIMATED
            N      TEST    STATISTIC  P-VALUE     MEDIAN
AminusB    10         9         15.5    0.221     -1.000
```

As is the case for the rank sum test for independent samples, the sampling distribution of the signed rank statistic can be approximated by a normal distribution when the number n of paired observations is large (say, $n \geq 25$). The large-sample z-test is summarized in the box below.

Wilcoxon Signed Rank Test for Large Samples ($n \geq 25$)

Let D_1 and D_2 represent the probability distributions for populations 1 and 2, respectively.

One-Tailed Test

H_0: D_1 and D_2 are identical
H_a: D_1 is shifted to the right of D_2
[or H_a: D_1 is shifted to the left of D_2]

Two-Tailed Test

H_0: D_1 and D_2 are identical
H_a: D_1 is shifted either to the left or to the right of D_2

$$\textit{Test statistic: } z = \frac{T_+ - [n(n+1)/4]}{\sqrt{[n(n+1)(2n+1)]/24}}$$

Rejection region (one-tailed): $z > z_\alpha$ [or $z < -z_\alpha$]

Rejection region (two-tailed): $|z| > z_{\alpha/2}$

Assumptions: The sample size n is greater than or equal to 25. Differences equal to 0 are eliminated and the number n of differences is reduced accordingly. Tied absolute differences receive ranks equal to the average of the ranks they would have received had they not been tied.

EXERCISES 7.64–7.75

Learning the Mechanics

7.64 Specify the test statistic and the rejection region for the Wilcoxon signed rank test for the paired difference design in each of the following situations:

a. $n = 30, \alpha = .10$
H_0: Two probability distributions, 1 and 2, are identical
H_a: Probability distribution for population 1 is shifted to the right or left of probability distribution for population 2

b. $n = 20, \alpha = .05$
H_0: Two probability distributions, 1 and 2, are identical
H_a: Probability distribution for population 1 is shifted to the right of the probability distribution for population 2

c. $n = 8, \alpha = .005$
H_0: Two probability distributions, 1 and 2, are identical
H_a: Probability distribution for population 1 is shifted to the left of the probability distribution for population 2

7.65 Suppose you want to test a hypothesis that two treatments, A and B, are equivalent against the alternative hypothesis that the responses for A tend to be larger than those for B. You plan to use a paired difference experiment and to analyze the resulting data (shown below) using the Wilcoxon signed rank test.

LM7_65.DAT

Pair	Treatment A	Treatment B	Pair	Treatment A	Treatment B
1	54	45	6	77	75
2	60	45	7	74	63
3	98	87	8	29	30
4	43	31	9	63	59
5	82	71	10	80	82

a. Specify the null and alternative hypotheses you would test.

b. Suppose the paired difference experiment yielded the data in the table. Conduct the test of part **a.** Test using $\alpha = .025$.

7.66 Explain the difference between the one- and two-tailed versions of the Wilcoxon signed rank test for the paired difference experiment.

7.67 In order to conduct the Wilcoxon signed rank test, why do we need to assume the probability distribution of differences is continuous?

7.68 Suppose you wish to test a hypothesis that two treatments, A and B, are equivalent against the alternative that the responses for A tend to be larger than those for B.

a. If the number of pairs equals 25, give the rejection region for the large-sample Wilcoxon signed rank test for $\alpha = .05$.

b. Suppose that $T_+ = 273$. State your test conclusions.

c. Find the p-value for the test and interpret it.

7.69 A paired difference experiment with $n = 30$ pairs yielded $T_+ = 354$.

a. Specify the null and alternative hypotheses that should be used in conducting a hypothesis test to determine whether the probability distribution for population 1 is located to the right of that for population 2.

b. Conduct the test of part **a** using $\alpha = .05$.

c. What is the approximate p-value of the test of part **b?**

d. What assumptions are necessary to ensure the validity of the test you performed in part **b?**

Applying the Concepts

7.70 An atlas is a compendium of geographic, economic, and social information that describes one or more geographic regions. Atlases are used by the sales and marketing functions of businesses, local chambers of commerce, and educators. One of the most critical aspects of a new atlas design is its thematic content. In a survey of atlas users (*Journal of Geography,* May/June 1995), a large sample of high school teachers in British Columbia ranked 12 thematic atlas topics for usefulness. The consensus rankings of the teachers (based on the percentage of teachers who responded they "would definitely use" the topic) are given in the table above. These teacher rankings were compared to the rankings of a group of university geography alumni made three years earlier. Compare the distributions of theme rankings for the two groups with an appropriate nonparametric test. Use $\alpha = .05$. Interpret the results practically.

ATLAS.DAT

Theme	Rankings: High School Teachers	Rankings: Geography Alumni
Tourism	10	2
Physical	2	1
Transportation	7	3
People	1	6
History	2	5
Climate	6	4
Forestry	5	8
Agriculture	7	10
Fishing	9	7
Energy	2	8
Mining	10	11
Manufacturing	12	12

Source: Keller, C. P., *et al.* "Planning the next generation of regional atlases: Input from educators." *Journal of Geography,* Vol. 94, No. 3, May/June 1995, p. 413 (Table 1).

7.71 According to the National Sleep Foundation, companies are encouraging their workers to take "power naps" (*Athens Daily News,* Jan. 9, 2000). In

POWERNAP.DAT

Agent	1999 Number of Complaints	2000 Number of Complaints
1	10	5
2	3	0
3	16	7
4	11	4
5	8	6
6	2	4
7	1	2
8	14	3
9	5	5
10	6	1

Exercise 7.27 (p. 371), you analyzed data collected by a major airline that recently began encouraging reservation agents to nap during their breaks. The number of complaints received about each of a sample of 10 reservation agents during the six months before naps were encouraged and during the six months after the policy change are reproduced on p. 398. Compare the distributions of number of complaints for the two time periods using the Wilcoxon signed rank test. Use $\alpha = .05$ to make the appropriate inference.

7.72 In Exercise 7.29 (p. 371), the inflation forecasts of nine economists that were made in June 1999 and January 2000 were reported. These forecasts, obtained from the *Wall Street Journal,* are reproduced below. To determine whether the economists were more optimistic about the prospects for low inflation in late 1999 than in mid 2000, apply the Wilcoxon signed rank test.

INFLATE.DAT

	June 1999 Forecast for 11/99	January 2000 Forecast for 5/00
Bruce Steinberg	1.8	2.2
Wayne Angell	2.3	2.3
David Blitzer	2.3	2.3
Michael Cosgrove	2.5	3.0
Gail Fosler	2.3	2.4
John Lonski	2.5	3.0
Donald Ratajczak	2.5	2.5
Thomas Synott	2.3	2.6
Sung Won Sohn	2.5	2.6

Source: Wall Street Journal, January 3, 2000.

a. Specify the null and alternative hypotheses you would employ.
b. Conduct the test using $\alpha = .05$. Interpret your results in the context of the problem.
c. Explain the difference between a Type I and a Type II error in the context of the problem.

7.73 A job-scheduling innovation that has helped managers overcome motivation and absenteeism problems associated with a fixed 8-hour workday is a concept called *flextime.* This flexible working hours program permits employees to design their own 40-hour work week to meet their personal needs (*New York Times,* Mar. 31, 1996). The management of a large manufacturing firm may adopt a flextime program depending on the success or failure of a pilot program. Ten employees were randomly selected and given a questionnaire designed to measure their attitude toward their job. Each was then permitted to design and follow a flextime workday. After six months, attitudes toward their jobs were again measured. The resulting attitude scores are displayed in the table above. The higher the score, the more favorable the employee's attitude toward his or her work. Use a nonparametric test procedure to evaluate the success of the pilot flextime program. Test using $\alpha = .05$.

FLEXTIME.DAT

Employee	Before	After	Employee	Before	After
1	54	68	6	82	88
2	25	42	7	94	90
3	80	80	8	72	81
4	76	91	9	33	39
5	63	70	10	90	93

7.74 The Standard and Poor's 500 Index is a benchmark against which investors compare the performance of individual stocks. A sample of eight of the manufacturing companies included in the index were evaluated for profitability in 1998 and 1999 with the results shown in the table below. The profitability measure used was *net margin*—defined as net income from continuing operations before extraordinary items as a percentage of sales.

NETMARGIN.DAT

Firm	1999 Net Margin (%)	1998 Net Margin (%)
Applied Materials	17.3	2.3
Caterpillar	4.8	7.2
Ingersoll-Rand	7.1	6.2
Johnson Controls	2.6	2.6
3M	11.3	8.1
Black & Decker	6.6	−16.6
Newell Rubbermaid	1.5	7.8
Corning	11.0	9.3

Source: Business Week, March 27, 2000, pp. 182–183.

a. Is there sufficient evidence to conclude that U.S. manufacturing firms were more profitable in 1999 than 1998? Test using $\alpha = .05$.
b. What assumptions must be met to ensure the validity of the test in part **a?**

7.75 It has been known for a number of years that the tailings (waste) of gypsum and phosphate mines in Florida contain radioactive radon 222. The radiation levels in waste gypsum and phosphate mounds in Polk County, Florida, are regularly monitored by the Eastern Environmental Radiation Facility (EERF) and by the Polk County Health Department (PCHD), Winter Haven, Florida. The table (p. 400) shows measurements of the exhalation rate (a measure of radiation) for 15 soil samples obtained from waste mounds in Polk County, Florida. The exhalation rate was

SPSS Output for Exercise 7.75

```
- - - - - Wilcoxon Matched-pairs Signed-ranks Test

     PCHD
with EERF

     Mean Rank      Cases

          8.40        10   - Ranks  (EERF Lt PCHD)
          7.20         5   + Ranks  (EERF Gt PCHD)
                       0     Ties   (EERF Eq PCHD)
                      --
                      15 Total

          Z = -1.3631                2-tailed P = .1728
```

measured for each soil sample by both the PCHD and the EERF. Do the data provide sufficient evidence (at $\alpha = .05$) to indicate that one of the measuring facilities, PCHD or EERF, tends to read higher or lower than the other? Use the SPSS Wilcoxon signed rank printout above to make your conclusions.

EXRATES.DAT

Charcoal Canister No.	PCHD	EERF
71	1,709.79	1,479.0
58	357.17	257.8
84	1,150.94	1,287.0
91	1,572.69	1,395.0
44	558.33	416.5
43	4,132.28	3,993.0
79	1,489.86	1,351.0
61	3,017.48	1,813.0
85	393.55	187.7
46	880.84	630.4
4	2,996.49	3,707.0
20	2,367.40	2,791.0
36	599.84	706.8
42	538.37	618.5
55	2,770.23	2,639.0

Source: Horton, T. R. "Preliminary radiological assessment of radon exhalation from phosphate gypsum piles and inactive uranium mill tailings piles." EPA-520/5-79-004. Washington, D.C.: Environmental Protection Agency, 1979.

7.7 COMPARING THREE OR MORE POPULATION MEANS: ANALYSIS OF VARIANCE (OPTIONAL)

Suppose we are interested in comparing the means of three or more populations. For example, we may want to compare the mean SAT scores of seniors at three different high schools. Or, we could compare the mean income per household of residents in four census districts. Since the methods of Sections 7.1–7.6 apply to two populations only, we require an alternative technique. In this optional section, we discuss a method for comparing two or more populations based on independent random samples, called an **analysis of variance (ANOVA).**

In the Jargon of ANOVA, **treatments** represent the groups or populations of interest. Thus, the primary objective of an analysis of variance is to compare the treatment (or population) means. If we denote the true means of the p treatments as $\mu_1, \mu_2, \ldots, \mu_p$, then we will test the null hypothesis that the treatment means are all equal against the alternative that at least two of the treatment means differ:

$$H_0: \mu_1 = \mu_2 = \cdots = \mu_p$$

H_a: At least two of the p treatment means differ

The μ's might represent the means of *all* female and male high school seniors' SAT scores or the means of *all* households' income in each of four census regions.

To conduct a statistical test of these hypotheses, we will use the means of the independent random samples selected from the treatment populations using the completely randomized design. That is, we compare the p sample means, $\bar{x}_1, \bar{x}_2, \ldots, \bar{x}_p$.

To illustrate the method in a two-sample case, suppose you select independent random samples of five female and five male high school seniors and obtain sample mean SAT scores of 550 and 590, respectively. Can we conclude that males score 40 points higher, on average, than females? To answer this question, we must consider the amount of sampling variability among the experimental units (students). If the scores are as depicted in the dot plot shown in Figure 7.23, then the difference between the means is small relative to the sampling variability of the scores within the treatments, Female and Male. We would be inclined not to reject the null hypothesis of equal population means in this case.

FIGURE 7.23
Dot plot of SAT scores: Difference between means dominated by sampling variability

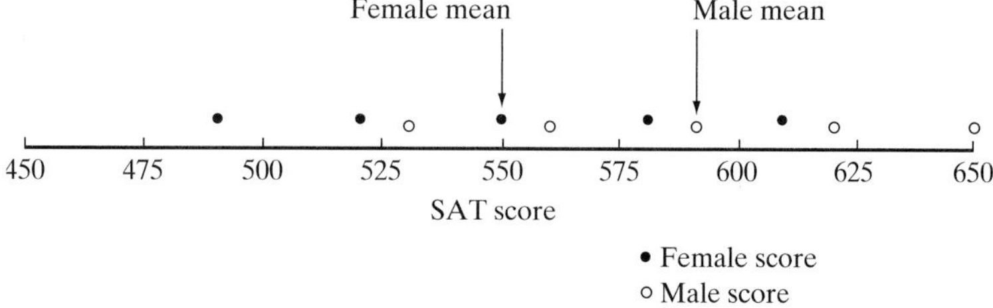

In contrast, if the data are as depicted in the dot plot of Figure 7.24, then the sampling variability is small relative to the difference between the two means. We would be inclined to favor the alternative hypothesis that the population means differ in this case.

FIGURE 7.24
Dot plot of SAT scores: Difference between means large relative to sampling variability

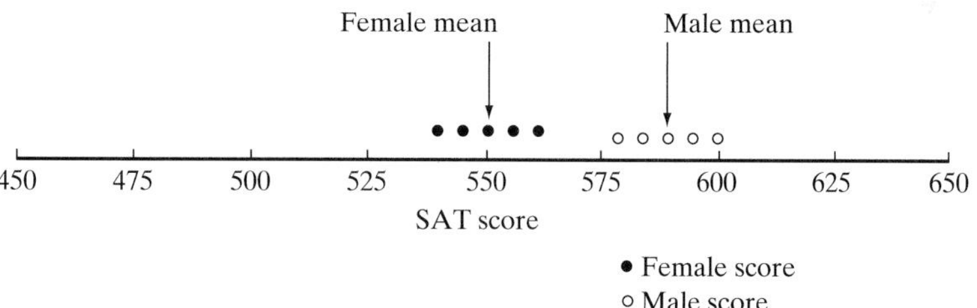

You can see that the key is to compare the difference between the treatment means to the amount of sampling variability. To conduct a formal statistical test of the hypotheses requires numerical measures of the difference between the treatment means and the sampling variability within each treatment. The variation between the treatment means is measured by the **Sum of Squares for Treatments** (SST), which is calculated by squaring the distance between each treatment mean and the overall mean of *all* sample measurements, multiplying each squared distance by the number of sample measurements for the treatment, and adding the results over all treatments:

$$\text{SST} = \sum_{i=1}^{p} n_i(\bar{x}_i - \bar{x})^2 = 5(550 - 570)^2 + 5(590 - 570)^2 = 4{,}000$$

where we use $\bar{x}$ to represent the overall mean response of all sample measurements, that is, the mean of the combined samples. The symbol n_i is used to denote the sample size for the ith treatment. You can see that the value of SST is 4,000 for the two samples of five female and five male SAT scores depicted in Figures 7.23 and 7.24.

Next, we must measure the sampling variability within the treatments. We call this the **Sum of Squares for Error** (SSE) because it measures the variability around the treatment means that is attributed to sampling error. Suppose the 10 measurements in the first dot plot (Figure 7.23) are 490, 520, 550, 580, and 610 for females, and 530, 560, 590, 620, and 650 for males. Then the value of SSE is computed by summing the squared distance between each response measurement and the corresponding treatment mean, and then adding the squared differences over all measurements in the entire sample:

$$\text{SSE} = \sum_{j=1}^{n_1}(x_{1j} - \bar{x}_1)^2 + \sum_{j=1}^{n_2}(x_{2j} - \bar{x}_2)^2 + \cdots + \sum_{j=1}^{n_p}(x_{pj} - \bar{x}_p)^2$$

where the symbol x_{1j} is the jth measurement in sample 1, x_{2j} is the jth measurement in sample 2, and so on. This rather complex-looking formula can be simplified by recalling the formula for the sample variance, s^2, given in Chapter 2:

$$s^2 = \sum_{i=1}^{n}\frac{(x_i - \bar{x})^2}{n - 1}$$

Note that each sum in SSE is simply the numerator of s^2 for that particular treatment. Consequently, we can rewrite SSE as

$$\text{SSE} = (n_1 - 1)s_1^2 + (n_2 - 1)s_2^2 + \cdots + (n_p - 1)s_p^2$$

where $s_1^2, s_2^2, \ldots, s_p^2$ are the sample variances for the p treatments. For our samples of SAT scores, we find $s_1^2 = 2{,}250$ (for females) and $s_2^2 = 2{,}250$ (for males); then we have

$$\text{SSE} = (5 - 1)(2{,}250) + (5 - 1)(2{,}250) = 18{,}000$$

To make the two measurements of variability comparable, we divide each by the degrees of freedom to convert the sums of squares to mean squares. First, the **Mean Square for Treatments** (MST), which measures the variability *among* the treatment means, is equal to

$$\text{MST} = \frac{\text{SST}}{p - 1} = \frac{4{,}000}{2 - 1} = 4{,}000$$

where the number of degrees of freedom for the p treatments is $(p - 1)$. Next, the **Mean Square for Error** (MSE), which measures the sampling variability *within* the treatments, is

$$\text{MSE} = \frac{\text{SSE}}{n - p} = \frac{18{,}000}{10 - 2} = 2{,}250$$

Finally, we calculate the ratio of MST to MSE—an *F statistic:*

$$F = \frac{\text{MST}}{\text{MSE}} = \frac{4{,}000}{2{,}250} = 1.78$$

Values of the F statistic near 1 indicate that the two sources of variation, between treatment means and within treatments, are approximately equal. In this case, the difference between the treatment means may well be attributable to sampling error, which provides little support for the alternative hypothesis that the population treatment means differ. Values of F well in excess of 1 indicate that the variation among treatment means well exceeds that within means and therefore support the alternative hypothesis that the population treatment means differ.

When does F exceed 1 by enough to reject the null hypothesis that the means are equal? This depends on the degrees of freedom for treatments and for error, and on the value of α selected for the test. We compare the calculated F value to a table F value (Tables VIII–XI of Appendix B) with $\nu_1 = (p - 1)$ degrees of freedom in the numerator and $\nu_2 = (n - p)$ degrees of freedom in the denominator and corresponding to a Type I error probability of α. For the SAT score example, the F statistic has $\nu_1 = (2 - 1) = 1$ numerator degree of freedom and $\nu_2 = (10 - 2) = 8$ denominator degrees of freedom. Thus, for $\alpha = .05$ we find (Table IX of Appendix B)

$$F_{.05} = 5.32$$

The implication is that MST would have to be 5.32 times greater than MSE before we could conclude at the .05 level of significance that the two population treatment means differ. Since the data yielded $F = 1.78$, our initial impressions for the dot plot in Figure 7.23 are confirmed—there is insufficient information to conclude that the mean SAT scores differ for the populations of female and male high school seniors. The rejection region and the calculated F value are shown in Figure 7.25.

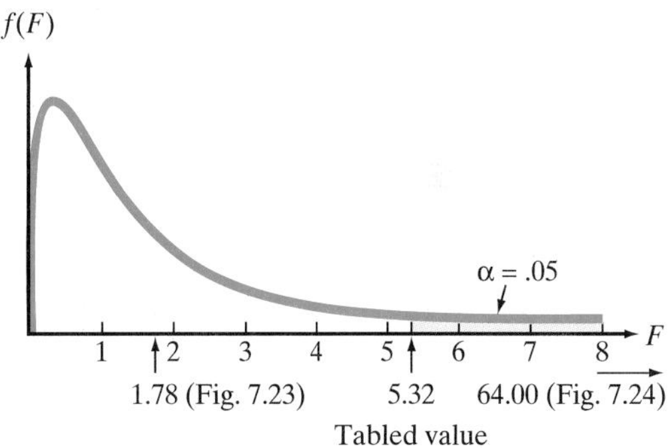

FIGURE 7.25
Rejection region and calculated F values for SAT score samples

In contrast, consider the dot plot in Figure 7.24. Since the means are the same as in the first example, 550 and 590, respectively, the variation between the means is the same, MST = 4,000. But the variation within the two treatments appears to be considerably smaller. The observed SAT scores are 540, 545, 550, 555, and 560 for females, and 580, 585, 590, 595, and 600 for males. These values yield $s_1^2 = 62.5$ and $s_2^2 = 62.5$. Thus, the variation within the treatments is measured by

$$\begin{aligned} \text{SSE} &= (5 - 1)(62.5) + (5 - 1)(62.5) \\ &= 500 \end{aligned}$$

$$\text{MSE} = \frac{\text{SSE}}{n - p} = \frac{500}{8} = 62.5$$

Then the F-ratio is

$$F = \frac{\text{MST}}{\text{MSE}} = \frac{4{,}000}{62.5} = 64.0$$

Again, our visual analysis of the dot plot is confirmed statistically: $F = 64.0$ well exceeds the tabled F value, 5.32, corresponding to the .05 level of significance. We would therefore reject the null hypothesis at that level and conclude that the SAT mean score of males differs from that of females.

Recall that we performed a hypothesis test for the difference between two means in Section 7.1, using a two-sample t statistic for two independent samples. When two independent samples are being compared, the t- and F-tests are equivalent. To see this, recall the formula

$$t = \frac{\bar{x}_1 - \bar{x}_2}{\sqrt{s_p^2\left(\frac{1}{n_1} + \frac{1}{n_2}\right)}} = \frac{590 - 550}{\sqrt{(62.5)\left(\frac{1}{5} + \frac{1}{5}\right)}} = \frac{40}{5} = 8$$

where we used the fact that $s_p^2 = \text{MSE}$, which you can verify by comparing the formulas. Note that the calculated F for these samples ($F = 64$) equals the square of the calculated t for the same samples ($t = 8$). Likewise, the tabled F value (5.32) equals the square of the tabled t value at the two-sided .05 level of significance ($t_{.025} = 2.306$ with 8 df). Since both the rejection region and the calculated values are related in the same way, the tests are equivalent. Moreover, the assumptions that must be met to ensure the validity of the t- and F-tests are the same:

1. The probability distributions of the populations of responses associated with each treatment must all be normal.
2. The probability distributions of the populations of responses associated with each treatment must have equal variances.
3. The samples of experimental units selected for the treatments must be random and independent.

In fact, the only real difference between the tests is that the F-test can be used to compare *more than two* treatment means, whereas the t-test is applicable to two samples only. The F-test is summarized in the accompanying box.

ANOVA Test to Compare p Treatment Means: Independent Sampling

$$H_0\text{: } \mu_1 = \mu_2 = \cdots = \mu_p$$

H_a: At least two treatment means differ

$$\textit{Test statistic: } F = \frac{\text{MST}}{\text{MSE}}$$

Assumptions:
1. Samples are selected randomly and independently from the respective populations.
2. All p population probability distributions are normal.
3. The p population variances are equal.

Rejection region: $F > F_\alpha$, where F_α is based on $(p - 1)$ numerator degrees of freedom (associated with MST) and $(n - p)$ denominator degrees of freedom (associated with MSE).

Computational formulas for MST and MSE are given in Appendix C. We will rely on some of the many statistical software packages available to compute the F statistic, concentrating on the interpretation of the results rather than their calculations.

EXAMPLE 7.11

Suppose the USGA wants to compare the mean distances associated with four different brands of golf balls when struck with a driver. An independent sampling design is employed, with Iron Byron, the USGA's robotic golfer, using a driver to hit a random sample of 10 balls of each brand in a random sequence. The distance is recorded for each hit, and the results are shown in Table 7.13, organized by brand.

TABLE 7.13 Results of Independent Sampling Design: Iron Byron Driver

	Brand A	Brand B	Brand C	Brand D
	251.2	263.2	269.7	251.6
	245.1	262.9	263.2	248.6
	248.0	265.0	277.5	249.4
	251.1	254.5	267.4	242.0
	260.5	264.3	270.5	246.5
	250.0	257.0	265.5	251.3
	253.9	262.8	270.7	261.8
	244.6	264.4	272.9	249.0
	254.6	260.6	275.6	247.1
	248.8	255.9	266.5	245.9
Sample Means	250.8	261.1	270.0	249.3

a. Set up the test to compare the mean distances for the four brands. Use $\alpha = .10$.

b. Use the SAS Analysis of Variance program to obtain the test statistic and p-value. Interpret the results.

Solution

a. To compare the mean distances of the four brands, we first specify the hypotheses to be tested. Denoting the population mean of the ith brand by μ_i, we test

H_0: $\mu_1 = \mu_2 = \mu_3 = \mu_4$

H_a: The mean distances differ for at least two of the brands

The test statistic compares the variation among the four treatment (Brand) means to the sampling variability within each of the treatments.

$$\textit{Test statistic: } F = \frac{\text{MST}}{\text{MSE}}$$

$$\textit{Rejection region: } F > F_{\alpha} = F_{.10}$$

$$\text{with } \nu_1 = (p - 1) = 3 \text{ df and } \nu_2 = (n - p) = 36 \text{ df}$$

From Table VIII of Appendix B, we find $F_{.10} \approx 2.25$ for 3 and 36 df. Thus, we will reject H_0 if $F > 2.25$. (See Figure 7.26.)

The assumptions necessary to ensure the validity of the test are as follows:

1. The samples of 10 golf balls for each brand are selected randomly and independently.

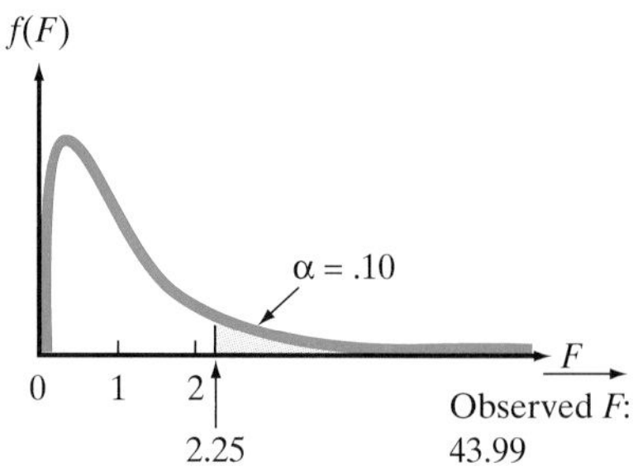

FIGURE 7.26
F-test for golf ball experiment

2. The probability distributions of the distances for each brand are normal.
3. The variances of the distance probability distributions for each brand are equal.

b. The SAS printout for the analysis of the data in Table 7.13 is given in Figure 7.27. The Total Sum of Squares is designated the **Corrected Total,** and it is partitioned into the **Model** (representing treatments) and **Error Sums of Squares.** The bottom part of the printout also gives the treatment (Brand) sum of squares under the column headed **Anova SS.**

```
                 Analysis of Variance Procedure
Dependent Variable: DISTANCE
                                 Sum of          Mean
Source                 DF       Squares        Square   F Value    Pr > F
Model                   3   2794.388750    931.462917     43.99    0.0001
Error                  36    762.301000     21.175028
Corrected Total        39   3556.689750
                 R-Square          C.V.      Root MSE        DISTANCE Mean
                 0.785671      1.785118      4.601633           257.777500
Source                 DF      Anova SS   Mean Square   F Value    Pr > F
BRAND                   3   2794.388750    931.462917     43.99    0.0001
```

FIGURE 7.27
SAS analysis of variance printout for golf ball distance data

The values of the mean squares, MST and MSE (highlighted on the printout), are 931.46 and 21.18, respectively. The *F*-ratio, 43.99, also highlighted on the printout, exceeds the tabled value of 2.25. We therefore reject the null hypothesis at the .10 level of significance, concluding that at least two of the brands differ with respect to mean distance traveled when struck by the driver.

The observed significance level of the *F*-test is also highlighted on the printout: .0001. This is the area to the right of the calculated *F* value and it implies that we would reject the null hypothesis that the means are equal at any α level greater than .0001.

The results of an analysis of variance (ANOVA) can be summarized in a simple tabular format similar to that obtained from the SAS program in Example 7.11. The general form of the table is shown in Table 7.14, where the symbols df, SS, and MS stand for degrees of freedom, Sum of Squares, and Mean Square, respectively. Note that the two sources of variation, Treatments and Error, add to the Total Sum of Squares, SS(Total). The ANOVA summary table for Example 7.11 is given in Table 7.15.

TABLE 7.14 General ANOVA Summary Table for a Completely Randomized Design

Source	df	SS	MS	F
Treatments	$p - 1$	SST	$\text{MST} = \dfrac{\text{SST}}{p-1}$	$\dfrac{\text{MST}}{\text{MSE}}$
Error	$n - p$	SSE	$\text{MSE} = \dfrac{\text{SSE}}{n-p}$	
Total	$n - 1$	SS(Total)		

TABLE 7.15 ANOVA Summary Table for Example 7.11

Source	df	SS	MS	F	p-Value
Brands	3	2,794.39	931.46	43.99	.0001
Error	36	762.30	21.18		
Total	39	3,556.69			

Suppose the F-test results in a rejection of the null hypothesis that the treatment means are equal. Is the analysis complete? Usually, the conclusion that at least two of the treatment means differ leads to other questions. Which of the means differ, and by how much? For example, the F-test in Example 7.11 leads to the conclusion that at least two of the brands of golf balls have different mean distances traveled when struck with a driver. Now the question is, which of the brands differ? How are the brands ranked with respect to mean distance?

One way to obtain this information is to construct a confidence interval for the difference between the means of any pair of treatments using the method of Section 7.1. For example, if a 95% confidence interval for $\mu_A - \mu_C$ in Example 7.11 is found to be $(-24, -13)$, we are confident that the mean distance for Brand C exceeds the mean for Brand A (since all differences in the interval are negative). Constructing these confidence intervals for all possible brand pairs will allow you to rank the brand means. A method for conducting these *multiple comparisons*—one that controls for Type I errors—is beyond the scope of this introductory text. Consult the chapter references to learn more about this methodology.

Using the TI-83 Graphing Calculator

ONE-WAY ANOVA ON THE TI-83

Start from the home screen.

Step 1 Enter each data set into its own list (i.e., sample 1 into List1, sample 2 into List2, sample 3 into List3, etc.).

(continued)

Step 2 Access the Statistical Test Menu.
Press **STAT**
Arrow right to TEST
Arrow up to F: ANOVA(
Press **ENTER**

Step 3 Enter each list, separated by commas, for which you want to perform the analysis (e.g., L1, L2, L3, L4).
Press **ENTER**

Step 4 View Display.
The calculator will display the F-test statistic, as well as the p-value, the Factor degrees of freedom, sum of squares, mean square, and by arrowing down the Error degrees of freedom, sum of squares, mean square, and the pooled standard deviation.

Example Below are four different samples. At the $\alpha = 0.05$ level of significance test whether the four population means are equal. The null hypothesis will be H_0: $\mu_1 = \mu_2 = \mu_3 = \mu_4$. The alternative hypothesis is H_a: At least one mean is different.

SAMPLE 1	SAMPLE 2	SAMPLE 3	SAMPLE 4
60	59	55	58
61	52	55	58
56	51	52	55

Step 1 Enter the data into the lists.

Step 2 Access the Statistical Test Menu.

Step 3 Enter each list for which you wish to perform the analysis (see screen below left).

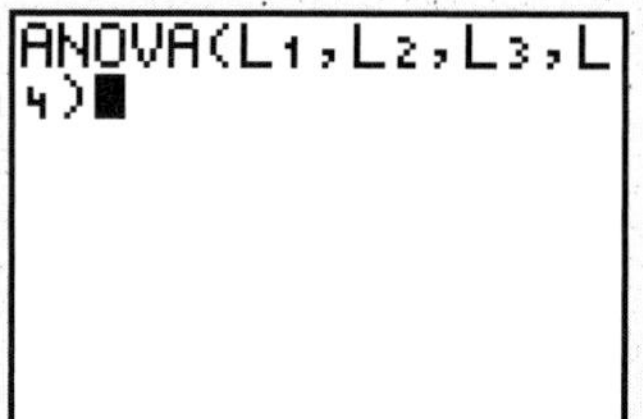

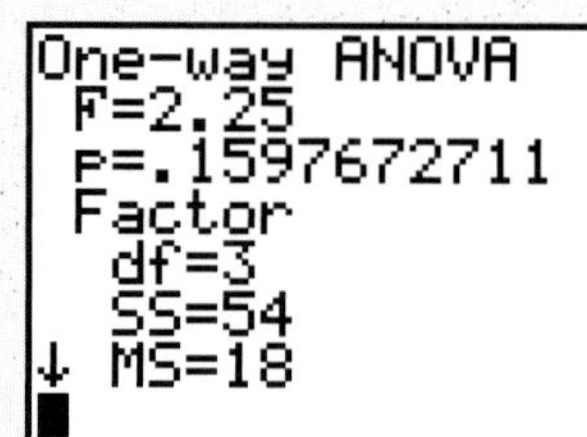

Step 4 Press **ENTER** and view screen (see screen above right.) As you can see from the screen, the p-value is 0.1598 which is **not less than** 0.05 therefore we should **not reject** H_0: $\mu_1 = \mu_2 = \mu_3 = \mu_4$. The differences are not significant.

Step 5 Clear the screen for the next problem. Return to the home screen. Press **CLEAR.**

EXAMPLE 7.12

Refer to the ANOVA conducted in Example 7.11. Are the assumptions required for the test approximately satisfied?

Solution The assumptions for the test are repeated below.

1. The samples of golf balls for each brand are selected randomly and independently.
2. The probability distributions of the distances for each brand are normal.

3. The variances of the distance probability distributions for each brand are equal.

Since the sample consisted of 10 randomly selected balls of each brand and the robotic golfer Iron Byron was used to drive all the balls, the first assumption of independent random samples is satisfied. To check the next two assumptions, we will employ two graphical methods presented in Chapter 2: stem-and-leaf displays and dot plots. A MINITAB stem-and-leaf display for the sample distances of each brand of golf ball is shown in Figure 7.28, followed by a MINITAB dot plot in Figure 7.29.

FIGURE 7.28
MINITAB stem-and-leaf displays for golf ball distance data

```
Stem-and-leaf of BrandA   N = 10
Leaf Unit = 1.0

   2    24 45
   2    24
   4    24 88
  (3)   25 011
   3    25 3
   2    25 4
   1    25
   1    25
   1    26 0

Stem-and-leaf of BrandB   N = 10
Leaf Unit = 1.0

   2    25 45
   3    25 7
   3    25
   4    26 0
  (3)   26 223
   3    26 445

Stem-and-leaf of BrandC   N = 10
Leaf Unit = 1.0

   1    26 3
   2    26 5
   4    26 67
   5    26 9
   5    27 00
   3    27 2
   2    27 5
   1    27 7

Stem-and-leaf of BrandD N = 10
Leaf Unit = 1.0

   1    24 2
   2    24 5
   4    24 67
  (3)   24 899
   3    25 11
   1    25
   1    25
   1    25
   1    25
   1    26 1
```

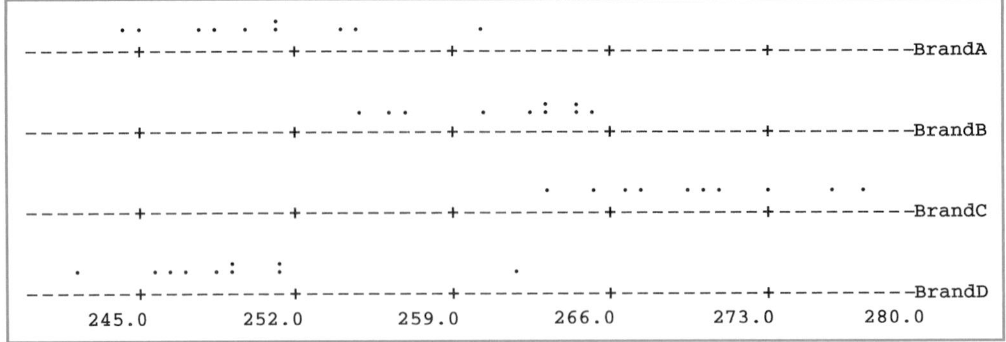

FIGURE 7.29
MINITAB dot plots for golf ball distance data

The normality assumption can be checked by examining the stem-and-leaf displays in Figure 7.28. With only 10 sample measurements for each brand, however, the displays are not very informative. More data would need to be collected for each brand before we could assess whether the distances come from normal distributions. Fortunately, analysis of variance has been shown to be a very **robust method** when the assumption of normality is not satisfied exactly: That is, moderate departures from normality do not have much effect on the significance level of the ANOVA F-test or on confidence coefficients. Rather than spend the time, energy, or money to collect additional data for this experiment in order to verify the normality assumption, we will rely on the robustness of the ANOVA methodology.

Dot plots are a convenient way to obtain a rough check on the assumption of equal variances. With the exception of a possible outlier for Brand D, the dot plots in Figure 7.29 show that the spread of the distance measurements is about the same for each brand. Since the sample variances appear to be the same, the assumption of equal population variances for the brands is probably satisfied. Although robust with respect to the normality assumption, ANOVA is *not robust* with respect to the equal variances assumption. Departures from the assumption of equal population variances can affect the associated measures of reliability (e.g., p-values and confidence levels). Fortunately, the effect is slight when the sample sizes are equal, as in this experiment.

Although graphs can be used to check the ANOVA assumptions, as in Example 7.12, no measures of reliability can be attached to these graphs. When you have a plot that is unclear as to whether or not an assumption is satisfied, you can use formal statistical tests, which are beyond the scope of this text. (Consult the chapter references for information on these tests.) When the validity of the ANOVA assumptions is in doubt, nonparametric statistical methods are useful.

EXERCISES 7.76–7.88

Learning the Mechanics

7.76 A partially completed ANOVA table for an independent sampling design is shown at right.

a. Complete the ANOVA table.
b. How many treatments are involved in the experiment?
c. Do the data provide sufficient evidence to indicate a difference among the population means? Test using $\alpha = .10$.

Source	df	SS	MS	F
Treatments	6	17.5	___	___
Error	___	___	___	
Total	41	46.5		

Dot Plots for Exercise 7.77

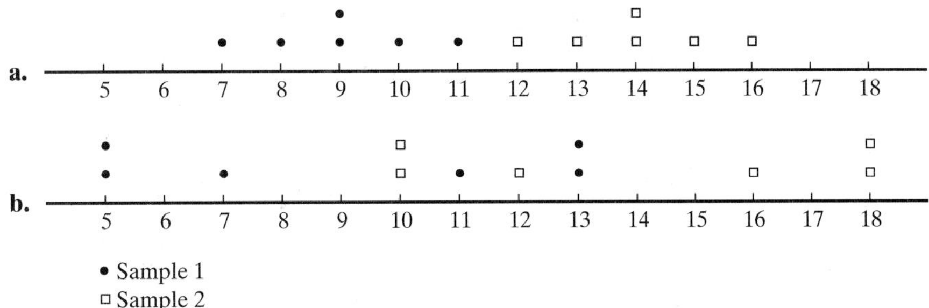

d. Find the approximate observed significance level for the test in part **c**, and interpret it.

e. Suppose that $\bar{x}_1 = 3.7$ and $\bar{x}_2 = 4.1$. Do the data provide sufficient evidence to indicate a difference between μ_1 and μ_2? Assume that there are six observations for each treatment. Test using $\alpha = .10$.

f. Refer to part **e.** Find a 90% confidence interval for $(\mu_1 - \mu_2)$.

g. Refer to part **e.** Find a 90% confidence interval for μ_1.

7.77 Consider dot plots **a** and **b** shown above. In which plot is the difference between the sample means small relative to the variability within the sample observations? Justify your answer.

7.78 Refer to Exercise 7.77. Assume that the two samples represent independent, random samples corresponding to two treatments.

a. Calculate the treatment means, i.e., the means of samples 1 and 2, for both dot plots.

b. Use the means to calculate the Sum of Squares for Treatments (SST) for each dot plot.

c. Calculate the sample variance for each sample and use these values to obtain the Sum of Squares for Error (SSE) for each dot plot.

d. Calculate the Total Sum of Squares [SS(Total)] for the two dot plots by adding the Sums of Squares for Treatments and Error. What percentage of SS(Total) is accounted for by the treatments—that is, what percentage of the Total Sum of Squares is the Sum of Squares for Treatments—in each case?

e. Convert the Sum of Squares for Treatments and Error to mean squares by dividing each by the appropriate number of degrees of freedom. Calculate the F-ratio of the Mean Square for Treatments (MST) to the Mean Square for Error (MSE) for each dot plot.

f. Use the F-ratios to test the null hypothesis that the two samples are drawn from populations with equal means. Use $\alpha = .05$.

g. What assumptions must be made about the probability distributions corresponding to the responses for each treatment in order to ensure the validity of the F-tests conducted in part **f?**

7.79 Refer to Exercises 7.77 and 7.78. Conduct a two-sample t-test (Section 7.1) of the null hypothesis that the two treatment means are equal for each dot plot. Use $\alpha = .05$ and two-tailed tests. In the course of the test, compare each of the following with the F-tests in Exercise 7.78:

a. The pooled variances and the MSEs

b. The t- and F-test statistics

c. The tabled values of t and F that determine the rejection regions

d. The conclusions of the t- and F-tests

e. The assumptions that must be made in order to ensure the validity of the t- and F-tests

7.80 Refer to Exercises 7.77 and 7.78. Complete the following ANOVA table for each of the two dot plots:

Source	df	SS	MS	F
Treatments				
Error				
Total				

7.81 A MINITAB printout for an experiment utilizing independent random samples is shown below.

a. How many treatments are involved in the experiment? What is the total sample size?

MINITAB Output for Exercise 7.81

```
ANALYSIS OF VARIANCE ON Y
SOURCE     DF        SS          MS        F        p
FACTOR      3     57258       19086    14.80    0.002
ERROR      34     43836        1289
TOTAL      37    101094
```

b. Conduct a test of the null hypothesis that the treatment means are equal. Use $\alpha = .10$.

c. What additional information is needed in order to be able to compare specific pairs of treatment means?

Applying the Concepts

7.82 In forming real estate portfolios, investors typically diversify the geographic locations of their holdings. While some choose to own properties in a variety of different metropolitan areas, others diversify across submarkets within the same metropolitan region. J. Rabianski and P. Cheng of Georgia State University investigated the appropriateness of the latter approach as it applies to investing in office properties (*Journal of Real Estate Portfolio Management,* Vol. 3, 1997). Using the office vacancy rate of a submarket as a proxy for total rate of return for the office submarket, the researchers compared submarkets within several U.S. metropolitan areas. The table at left presents the mean vacancy rates of the eight office submarkets of Atlanta, Georgia, for a period of nine years. Quarterly vacancy rates were used in calculating the means.

a. Specify the null and alternative hypotheses to use in comparing the mean vacancy rates of the eight office-property submarkets of Atlanta.

b. The researchers reported an ANOVA F statistic of $F = 17.54$ for the Atlanta data. Conduct the hypothesis test you specified in part **a.** Draw the appropriate conclusions in the context of the problem.

c. Give the approximate p-value for the test you conducted in part **b.**

d. What assumptions must be met to ensure the validity of the inference you made in part **b?** Which of these assumptions do you consider the most questionable in this application? Why?

Submarket	Mean Vacancy Rate (%)
Buckhead	16.85
Downtown	20.73
Midtown	19.75
North Central	16.73
Northeast	16.95
Northwest	16.81
North Lake	20.38
South	28.26

Source: Adapted from: Rabianski, J. S., and Cheng, P., "Intrametropolitan Spatial Diversification," *Journal of Real Estate Portfolio Management,* Vol. 3, No. 2, 1997, pp. 117–128.

7.83 Refer to *Fortune* (Oct. 25, 1999) magazine's study of the 50 most powerful women in America, Exercise 2.36 (p. 59). The data table, reproduced below, gives the age (in years) and title of each of these 50 women. Suppose you want to compare the average ages of powerful women in three groups based on their position (title) within the firm: Group 1 (CEO, CFO, CIO, or COO); Group 2 (Chairman, President, or Director); and Group 3 (Vice President, Vice Chairman, or General Manager). A MINITAB analysis of variance is conducted on the data, with the results shown in the printouts on p. 413–415. Fully interpret the results. Give the null and alternative hypotheses tested. Also, determine whether the ANOVA assumptions are reasonably satisfied.

WOMENPOW.DAT

Rank	Name	Age	Company	Title
1	Carly Fiorina	45	Hewlett-Packard	CEO
2	Heidi Miller	46	Citigroup	CFO
3	Mary Meeker	40	Morgan Stanley	Managing Director
4	Shelly Lazarus	52	Ogilvy & Mather	CEO
5	Meg Whitman	43	eBay	CEO
6	Debby Hopkins	44	Boeing	CFO
7	Marjorie Scardino	52	Pearson	CEO
8	Martha Stewart	58	Martha Stewart Living	CEO
9	Nancy Peretsman	45	Allen & Co.	Ex. V.P.
10	Pat Russo	47	Lucent Technologies	Ex. V.P.
11	Patricia Dunn	46	Barclays Global Investors	Chairman
12	Abby Joseph Cohen	47	Goldman Sachs	Managing Director
13	Ann Livermore	41	Hewlett-Packard	CEO
14	Andrea Jung	41	Avon Products	COO
15	Sherry Lansing	55	Paramount Pictures	Chairman
16	Karen Katen	50	Pfizer	Ex. V.P
17	Marilyn Carlson Nelson	60	Carlson Cos.	CEO
18	Judy McGrath	47	MTV & M2	President
19	Lois Juliber	50	Colgate-Palmolive	COO
20	Gerry Laybourne	52	Oxygen Media	CEO

(continued)

Rank	Name	Age	Company	Title
21	Judith Estrin	44	Cisco Systems	Sr. V.P.
22	Cathleen Black	55	Hearst Magazines	President
23	Linda Sandford	46	IBM	General Manager
24	Ann Moore	49	Time Inc.	President
25	Jill Barad	48	Mattel	CEO
26	Oprah Winfrey	45	Harpo Entertainment	Chairman
27	Judy Lewent	50	Merck	Sr. V.P.
28	Joy Covey	36	Amazon.com	COO
29	Rebecca Mark	45	Azurix	CEO
30	Deborah Willingham	43	Microsoft	V.P.
31	Dina Dubion	46	Chase Manhattan	Ex. V.P.
32	Patricia Woertz	46	Chevron	President
33	Lawton Fitt	46	Goldman Sachs	Man. Dir.
34	Ann Fudge	48	Kraft Foods	Ex. V.P.
35	Carolyn Ticknor	52	Hewlett-Packard	CEO
36	Dawn Lepore	45	Charles Schwab	CIO
37	Jeannine Rivet	51	UnitedHealthcare	CEO
38	Jamie Gorelick	49	Fannie Mae	Vice Chairman
39	Jan Brandt	48	America Online	Mar. President
40	Bridget Macaskill	51	OppenheimerFunds	CEO
41	Jeanne Jackson	48	Banana Republic	CEO
42	Cynthia Trudell	46	General Motors	V.P.
43	Nina DiSesa	53	McCann-Erickson	Chairman
44	Linda Wachner	53	Warnaco	Chairman
45	Darla Moore	45	Rainwater Inc.	President
46	Marion Sandler	68	Golden West	Co-CEO
47	Michelle Anthony	42	Sony Music	Ex. V.P.
48	Orit Gadlesh	48	Bain & Co.	Chairman
49	Charlotte Beers	64	J. Walter Thompson	Chairman
50	Abigail Johnson	37	Fidelity Investments	V.P.

Source: *Fortune,* October 25, 1999.

MINITAB Output for Exercise 7.83

```
Analysis of Variance for Age
Source      DF        SS        MS         F        P
Group        2     114.3      57.1      1.62    0.209
Error       47    1658.5      35.3
Total       49    1772.7
                                     Individual 95% CIs For Mean
                                     Based on Pooled StDev
Level        N      Mean     StDev   ---------+---------+---------+-------
1           21    48.952     7.159                (--------*--------)
2           16    49.188     5.648                (---------*---------)
3           13    45.615     3.595   (----------*----------)
                                     ---------+---------+---------+-------
Pooled StDev     5.940                      45.0      48.0      51.0
```

7.84 Researchers at Pennsylvania State University and Iowa State University jointly studied the attitudes of three groups of professionals that influence U.S. policy governing new technologies: scientists, journalists, and federal government policymakers (*American Journal of Political Science,* Jan. 1998). Random samples of 100 scientists, 100 journalists, and 100 government officials were asked about the safety of nuclear power plants. Responses were made on a seven-point scale, where 1 = very unsafe and 7 = very safe. The mean safety scores for the groups are scientists, 4.1; journalists, 3.7; government officials, 4.2.

a. How many treatments are included in this study? Describe them.

MINITAB Output for Exercise 7.83 (Cont'd.)

```
Stem-and-leaf of Age   Group = 1    N = 21
Leaf Unit = 1.0

    1   3 6
    1   3
    3   4 11
    4   4 3
    8   4 4555
    9   4 6
  (2)   4 88
   10   5 011
    7   5 2222
    3   5
    3   5
    3   5 8
    2   6 0
    1   6
    1   6
    1   6
    1   6 8

Stem-and-leaf of Age   Group = 2  N = 16
Leaf Unit = 1.0
    1   4 0
    1   4
    3   4 55
    8   4 66677
    8   4 899
    5   5
    5   5 33
    3   5 55
    1   5
    1   5
    1   6
    1   6
    1   6 4

Stem-and-leaf of Age   Group = 3  N = 13
Leaf Unit = 1.0

    1   3 7
    1   3
    1   4
    3   4 23
    5   4 45
  (4)   4 6667
    4   4 89
    2   5 00
```

b. Specify the null and alternative hypotheses that should be used to investigate whether there are differences in the attitudes of scientists, journalists, and government officials regarding the safety of nuclear power plants.

c. The MSE for the sample data is 2.355. At least how large must MST be in order to reject the null hypothesis of the test of part **a** using $\alpha = .05$?

d. If the MST = 11.280, what is the approximate p-value of the test of part **a?**

7.85 The Minnesota Multiphasic Personality Inventory (MMPI) is a questionnaire used to gauge personality type. Several scales are built into the MMPI to assess response distortion; these include the Infrequency (I), Obvious (O), Subtle (S), Obvious-subtle (O-S), and Dissimulation (D) scales. *Psychological Assessment* (Mar. 1995) published a study that investigated the effectiveness of these MMPI scales in detecting deliberately distorted responses. An independent sampling design with four treatments was employed. The treatments consisted of independent random samples of females in the following four groups: nonforensic psychiatric patients ($n_1 = 65$), forensic psychiatric patients ($n_2 = 28$), college students who were requested to respond honestly ($n_3 = 140$), and college students who were instructed to provide "fake bad" responses ($n_4 = 45$). All 278 participants were given the MMPI and the I, O, S, O-S, and D scores were recorded for each. Each scale was treated as a response variable and an analysis of variance conducted. The ANOVA F values are reported in the table.

Response Variable	ANOVA F Value
Infrequency (I)	155.8
Obvious (O)	49.7
Subtle (S)	10.3
Obvious-subtle (O-S)	45.4
Dissimulation (D)	39.1

a. For each response variable, determine whether the mean scores of the four groups completing the MMPI differ significantly. Use $\alpha = .05$ for each test.

b. If the MMPI is effective in detecting distorted responses, then the mean score for the "fake bad" treatment group will be largest. Based on the information provided, can the researchers make an inference about the effectiveness of the MMPI? Explain.

7.86 The *Journal of Hazardous Materials* (July 1995) published the results of a study of the chemical properties of three different types of hazardous organic solvents used to clean metal parts: aromatics, chloroalkanes, and esters. One variable studied was sorption rate, measured as mole percentage. Independent samples of solvents from each type were tested and their sorption rates were recorded, as shown in the table on p. 415. An SPSS analysis of variance of the data is shown in the printout above the table.

a. Is there evidence of differences among the mean sorption rates of the three organic solvent types? Test using $\alpha = .10$.

b. List the assumptions required for the analysis, part **a**, to be valid.

MINITAB Output for Exercise 7.83 (Cont'd.)

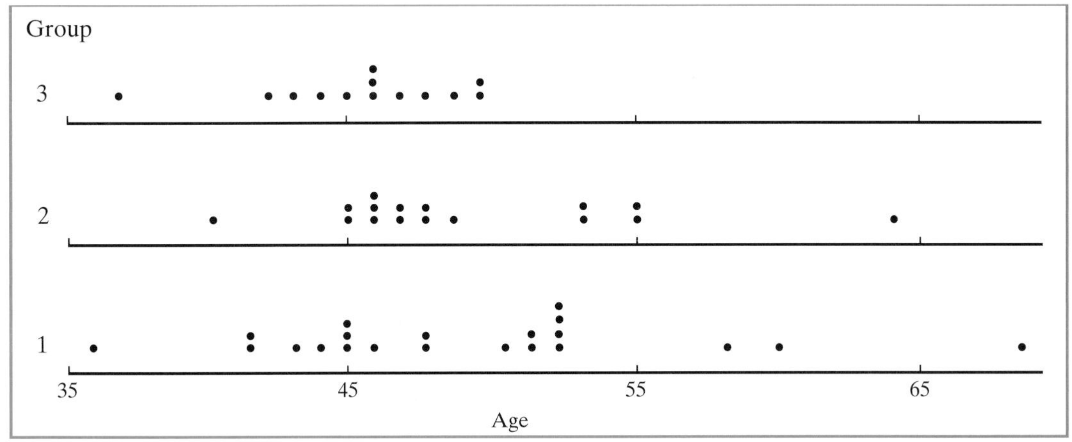

SPSS Output for Exercise 7.86

SORPRATE

	Sum of Squares	df	Mean Square	F	Sig.
Between Groups	3.305	2	1.653	24.512	.000
Within Groups	1.955	29	.067		
Total	5.261	31			

HAZARDS.DAT

Aromatics		Chloroalkanes		Esters		
1.06	.95	1.58	1.12	.29	.43	.06
.79	.65	1.45	.91	.06	.51	.09
.82	1.15	.57	.83	.44	.10	.17
.89	1.12	1.16	.43	.61	.34	.60
1.05				.55	.53	.17

Source: Reprinted from *Journal of Hazardous Materials,* Vol. 42, No. 2, J. D. Ortego *et al.*, "A review of polymeric geosynthetics used in hazardous waste facilities," p. 142 (Table 9), July 1995, Elsevier Science-NL, Sara Burgerhartstraat 25, 1055 KV Amsterdam, The Netherlands.

c. Check the assumptions, part **b.** Do they appear to be reasonably satisfied?

7.87 Industrial sales professionals have long debated the effectiveness of various sales closing techniques. University of Akron researchers S. Hawes, J. Strong, and B. Winick investigated the impact of five different closing techniques and a no-close condition on the level of a sales prospect's trust in the salesperson (*Industrial Marketing Management,* Sept. 1996). Two of the five closing techniques were the *assumed close* and the *impending event technique.* In the former, the salesperson simply writes up the order or behaves as if the sale has been made. In the latter, the salesperson encourages the buyer to buy now before some future event occurs that makes the terms of the sale less favorable for the buyer. Sales scenarios were presented to a sample of 238 purchasing executives. Each subject received one of the five closing techniques or a scenario in which no close was achieved. After reading the sales scenario, each executive was asked to rate their level of trust in the salesperson on a 7-point scale. The table reports the six treatments employed in the study and the number of subjects receiving each treatment.

Treatments: Closing Techniques	Sample Size
1. No close	38
2. Impending event	36
3. Social validation	29
4. If-then	42
5. Assumed close	36
6. Either-or	56

a. The investigator's hypotheses were

H_0: The salesperson's level of prospect trust *is not* influenced by the choice of closing method

H_a: The salesperson's level of prospect trust *is* influenced by the choice of closing method

STATISTICS IN *Action*

On the Trail of the Cockroach

Entomologists have long established that insects such as ants, bees, caterpillars, and termites use chemical or "odor" trails for navigation. These trails are used as highways between sources of food and the insect nest. Until recently, however, "bug" researchers believed that that navigational behavior of cockroaches scavenging for food was random and not linked to a chemical trail.

One of the first researchers to challenge the "random-walk" theory for cockroaches was professor and entomologist Dini Miller of Virginia Tech University. According to Miller, "the idea that roaches forage randomly means that they would have to come out of their hiding places every night and bump into food and water by accident. But roaches never seem to go hungry." Since cockroaches had never before been evaluated for trail-following behavior, Miller designed an experiment to test a cockroach's ability to follow a trail to their fecal material (*Explore,* Research at the University of Florida, Fall 1998).

First, Dr. Miller developed a methanol extract from roach feces—called a pheromone. She theorized that "pheromones are communication devices between cockroaches. If you have an infestation and have a lot of fecal material around, it advertises, 'Hey, this is a good cockroach place.'" Then, she created a chemical trail with the pheromone on a strip of white chromatography paper and placed the paper at the bottom of a plastic, V-shaped container, 122 square centimeters in size. German cockroaches were released into the container at the beginning of the trail, one at a time, and a video surveillance camera was used to monitor the roach's movements.

In addition to the trail containing the fecal extract (the treatment), a trail using methanol only was created. This second trail served as a "control" to compare back against the treated trail. Since Dr. Miller also wanted to determine if trail-following ability differed among cockroaches of different age, sex, and reproductive stage, four roach groups were utilized in the experiment: adult males, adult females, gravid (pregnant) females, and nymphs (immatures). Twenty roaches of each type were randomly assigned to the treatment trail and 10 of each type were randomly assigned to the control trail. Thus, a total of 120 roaches were used in the experiment. A layout of the design is illustrated in Figure 7.30.

The movement pattern of each cockroach tested was translated into *xy* coordinates every one-tenth of a second by the Dynamic Animal Movement Analyzer (DAMA) program. Miller measured the perpendicular distance of each *xy* coordinate from the trail and then averaged these distances, or deviations, for each cockroach. The average trail deviations (measured in pixels*) for 120 cockroaches in the study are listed in Table 7.16 and saved in the file ROACH.DAT.

Focus

Conduct the appropriate analysis of the data. Use the results to answer the following research questions (not necessarily in the order presented):

(1) Is there evidence that cockroaches within a group exhibit the ability to follow fecal extract trails?

(2) Does trail-following ability differ among cockroaches of different age, sex, and reproductive status?

Write up the results of your analysis in a report and present it to your class.

*1 pixel ≈ 2 centimeters

FIGURE 7.30 Layout of Experimental Design for Cockroach Study

		Roach Type			
		Adult Male	Adult Female	Gravid Female	Nymph
Trail	Extract	$n = 20$	$n = 20$	$n = 20$	$n = 20$
	Control	$n = 10$	$n = 10$	$n = 10$	$n = 10$

ROACH.DAT

TABLE 7.16 Average Trail Deviations for 120 Cockroaches

Adult Males		Adult Females		Gravid Females		Nymphs	
Extract	Control	Extract	Control	Extract	Control	Extract	Control
3.1	42.0	7.2	70.2	78.7	54.6	7.7	132.9
6.2	22.7	17.3	49.0	70.3	54.3	27.7	19.7
34.0	93.1	9.1	40.5	79.9	63.5	18.4	32.1
2.1	17.5	13.2	13.3	51.0	52.6	47.6	66.4
2.4	78.1	101.2	31.8	13.6	95.1	22.4	126.0
4.4	74.1	4.6	116.0	20.4	117.9	8.3	131.1
2.4	50.3	18.1	164.0	51.2	53.3	13.5	50.7
7.6	8.9	73.0	30.2	27.5	84.0	45.6	93.8
5.5	11.3	4.8	44.3	63.1	103.5	8.4	59.4
6.9	82.0	20.5	72.6	4.8	53.0	3.3	25.6
25.4		51.6		23.4		51.2	
2.2		5.8		48.2		10.4	
2.5		27.8		13.3		32.0	
4.9		2.8		57.4		6.9	
18.5		4.4		65.4		32.6	
4.6		3.2		10.5		23.8	
7.7		3.6		59.9		5.1	
3.2		1.7		38.4		3.8	
2.4		29.8		27.0		3.1	
1.5		21.7		76.6		2.8	

Source: Dr. Dini Miller, Department of Entomolgy, Virginia Polytechnic Institute and State University.

Rewrite these hypotheses in the form required for an analysis of variance.

b. The researchers reported the ANOVA F statistic as $F = 2.21$. Is there sufficient evidence to reject H_0 at $\alpha = .05$?

c. What assumptions must be met in order for the test of part **a** to be valid?

d. Would you classify this experiment as observational or designed? Explain.

7.88 On average, over a million new businesses are started in the United States every year. An article in the *Journal of Business Venturing* (Vol. 11, 1996) reported on the activities of entrepreneurs during the organization creation process. Among the questions investigated were what activities and how many activities do entrepreneurs initiate in attempting to establish a new business? A total of 71 entrepreneurs were interviewed and divided into three groups: those that were successful in founding a new firm (34), those still actively trying to establish a firm (21), and those who tried to start a new firm, but eventually gave up (16). The total number of activities undertaken (i.e., developed a business plan, sought funding, looked for facilities, etc.) by each group over a specified time period during organization creation was measured and the following incomplete ANOVA table produced:

Source	df	SS	MS	F
Groups	2	128.70	___	___
Error	68	27,124.52	___	

Source: Carter, N., Garner, W., and Reynolds, P. "Exploring start-up event sequences." *Journal of Business Venturing,* Vol. 11, 1996, p. 159.

a. Complete the ANOVA table.

b. Do the data provide sufficient evidence to indicate that the total number of activities undertaken differed among the three groups of entrepreneurs? Test using $\alpha = .05$.

c. What is the p-value of the test you conducted in part **b?**

d. One of the conclusions of the study was that the behaviors of entrepreneurs who have successfully started a new company can be differentiated from the behaviors of entrepreneurs that failed. Do you agree? Justify your answer.

QUICK REVIEW

Key Terms

Note: Starred (*) items are from the optional sections in this chapter.

Analysis of Vairance (ANOVA) 400
Blocking 365
F-distribution* 377
F-test* 381
Mean square for error* 402
Mean square for treatments* 402
Paired difference experiment 365
Pooled sample estimate of variance 351
Randomized block experiment 365
Rank Sum* 385
Robust Method* 410
Sum of squares for error* 402
Standard error 347
Treatments* 400
Wilcoxon rank sum test* 384
Wilcoxon signed rank text* 393

Key Formulas

Note: Starred (*) formulas are from the optional sections in this chapter.

$(1 - \alpha)100\%$ confidence interval forθ: (see table below)

Large samples: $\hat{\theta} \pm z_{\alpha/2}\sigma_{\hat{\theta}}$

Small samples: $\hat{\theta} \pm t_{\alpha/2}\sigma_{\hat{\theta}}$

For testing H_0: $\theta = D_0$: (see table below)

Large samples: $z = \dfrac{\hat{\theta} - D_0}{\sigma_{\hat{\theta}}}$

Small samples: $t = \dfrac{\hat{\theta} - D_0}{\sigma_{\hat{\theta}}}$

Parameter, θ	Estimator, $\hat{\theta}$	Standard Error of Estimator, $\sigma_{\hat{\theta}}$	Estimated Standard Error	
$(\mu_1 - \mu_2)$ (independent samples)	$(\bar{x}_1 - \bar{x}_2)$	$\sqrt{\dfrac{\sigma_1^2}{n_1} + \dfrac{\sigma_2^2}{n_2}}$	Large n: $\sqrt{\dfrac{s_1^2}{n_1} + \dfrac{s_2^2}{n_2}}$	348
			Small n: $\sqrt{s_p^2\left(\dfrac{1}{n_1} + \dfrac{1}{n_2}\right)}$	352
μ_D (paired sample)	$\bar{x}_D$	$\dfrac{\sigma_D}{\sqrt{n_D}}$	$\dfrac{s_D}{\sqrt{n_D}}$	366, 367

$s_p^2 = \dfrac{(n_1 - 1)s_1^2 + (n_2 - 1)s_2^2}{n_1 + n_2 - 2}$	Pooled sample variance	352
$n_1 = n_2 = \dfrac{(z_{\alpha/2})^2(\sigma_1^2 + \sigma_2^2)}{B^2}$	Determining the sample size for estimating $(\mu_1 - \mu_2)$	376
$*F = \begin{cases} \dfrac{\text{larger } s^2}{\text{smaller } s^2} & \text{if } H_a\text{: } \dfrac{\sigma_1^2}{\sigma_2^2} \neq 1 \\ \dfrac{s_1^2}{s_2^2} & \text{if } H_a\text{: } \dfrac{\sigma_1^2}{\sigma_2^2} > 1 \end{cases}$	Test statistic for testing H_0: $\dfrac{\sigma_1^2}{\sigma_2^2}$	381
$*z = \dfrac{T_1 - \dfrac{n_1(n_1 + n_2 + 1)}{2}}{\sqrt{\dfrac{n_1 n_2(n_1 + n_2 + 1)}{12}}}$	Wilcoxon rank sum test (large samples)	389
$*z = \dfrac{T_+ - \dfrac{n(n + 1)}{4}}{\sqrt{\dfrac{n(n + 1)(2n + 1)}{24}}}$	Wilcoxon signed ranks test (large samples)	397
$*F = \dfrac{\text{MST}}{\text{MSE}}$	ANOVA F-test	404

LANGUAGE LAB

Symbol	Pronunciation	Description

Note: Starred (*) symbols are from the optional sections in this chapter.

Symbol	Pronunciation	Description
$(\mu_1 - \mu_2)$	mu-1 minus mu-2	Difference between population means
$(\bar{x}_1 - \bar{x}_2)$	x-bar-1 minus x-bar-2	Difference between sample means
$\sigma_{(\bar{x}_1 - \bar{x}_2)}$	sigma of x-bar-1 minus x-bar-2	Standard deviation of the sampling distribution of $(\bar{x}_1 - \bar{x}_2)$
s_p^2	s-p squared	Pooled sample variance
D_0	D naught	Hypothesized value of difference
μ_D	mu D	Difference between population means, paired data
$\bar{x}_D$	x-bar D	Mean of sample differences
s_D	s-D	Standard deviation of sample differences
n_D	n-D	Number of differences in sample
F_α*	F-alpha	Critical value of F associated with tail area α
ν_1*	nu-1	Numerator degrees of freedom for F statistic
ν_2*	nu-2	Denominator degrees of freedom for F statistic
$\dfrac{\sigma_1^2}{\sigma_2^2}$*	sigma-1 squared over sigma-2 squared	Ratio of two population variances
T_1*		Sum of ranks of observations in sample 1
T_2*		Sum of ranks of observations in sample 2
T_L*		Critical lower Wilcoxon rank sum value
T_U*		Critical upper Wilcoxon rank sum value
T_+*		Sum of ranks of positive differences of paired observations
T_-*		Sum of ranks of negative differences of paired observations
T_0*		Critical value of Wilcoxon signed rank test

ANOVA*	Analysis of Variance
SST*	Sum of Squares for Treatments (i.e., the variation among treatment means)
SSE*	Sum of Squares for Error (i.e., the variability around the treatment means due to sampling error)
MST*	Mean Square for Treatments
MSE*	Mean Square for Error (an estimate of σ^2)

SUPPLEMENTARY EXERCISES 7.89–7.110

Starred (*) exercises refer to the optional sections in this chapter.

Learning the Mechanics

7.89 Independent random samples were selected from two normally distributed populations with means μ_1 and μ_2, respectively. The sample sizes, means, and variances are shown in the following table.

Sample 1	Sample 2
$n_1 = 12$	$n_2 = 14$
$\bar{x}_1 = 17.8$	$\bar{x}_2 = 15.3$
$s_1^2 = 74.2$	$s_2^2 = 60.5$

a. Test H_0: $(\mu_1 - \mu_2) = 0$ against H_a: $(\mu_1 - \mu_2) > 0$. Use $\alpha = .05$.
b. Form a 99% confidence interval for $(\mu_1 - \mu_2)$.
c. How large must n_1 and n_2 be if you wish to estimate $(\mu_1 - \mu_2)$ to within 2 units with 99% confidence? Assume that $n_1 = n_2$.

*7.90 Two independent random samples were selected from normally distributed populations with means and variances (μ_1, σ_1^2) and (μ_2, σ_2^2), respectively. The sample sizes, means, and variances are shown in the table below.

Sample 1	Sample 2
$n_1 = 20$	$n_2 = 15$
$\bar{x}_1 = 123$	$\bar{x}_2 = 116$
$s_1^2 = 31.3$	$s_2^2 = 120.1$

a. Test H_0: $\sigma_1^2 = \sigma_2^2$ against H_a: $\sigma_1^2 \neq \sigma_2^2$. Use $\alpha = .05$.
b. Would you be willing to use a t-test to test the null hypothesis H_0: $(\mu_1 - \mu_2) = 0$ against the alternative hypothesis H_a: $(\mu_1 - \mu_2) \neq 0$? Why?

7.91 Two independent random samples are taken from two populations. The results of these samples are summarized in the next table.
a. Form a 90% confidence interval for $(\mu_1 - \mu_2)$.
b. Test H_0: $(\mu_1 - \mu_2) = 0$ against H_a: $(\mu_1 - \mu_2) \neq 0$. Use $\alpha = .01$.

Sample 1	Sample 2
$n_1 = 135$	$n_2 = 148$
$\bar{x}_1 = 12.2$	$\bar{x}_2 = 8.3$
$s_1^2 = 2.1$	$s_2^2 = 3.0$

c. What sample sizes would be required if you wish to estimate $(\mu_1 - \mu_2)$ to within .2 with 90% confidence? Assume that $n_1 = n_2$.

7.92 List the assumptions necessary for each of the following inferential techniques:
a. Large-sample inferences about the difference $(\mu_1 - \mu_2)$ between population means using a two-sample z statistic
b. Small-sample inferences about $(\mu_1 - \mu_2)$ using an independent samples design and a two-sample t statistic
c. Small-sample inferences about $(\mu_1 - \mu_2)$ using a paired difference design and a single-sample t statistic to analyze the differences
*d. Inferences about the ratio σ_1^2/σ_2^2 of two population variances using an F-test.

7.93 A random sample of five pairs of observations were selected, one of each pair from a population with mean μ_1, the other from a population with mean μ_2. The data are shown in the accompanying table.

LM7_93.DAT

Pair	Value from Population 1	Value from Population 2
1	28	22
2	31	27
3	24	20
4	30	27
5	22	20

a. Test the null hypothesis H_0: $\mu_D = 0$ against H_a: $\mu_D \neq 0$, where $\mu_D = \mu_1 - \mu_2$. Use $\alpha = .05$.
b. Form a 95% confidence interval for μ_D.
c. When are the procedures you used in parts **a** and **b** valid?

*7.94 Two independent random samples produced the measurements listed in the table on page 421. Do the data provide sufficient evidence to conclude that there is a difference between the locations of the probability distributions for the sampled populations? Test using $\alpha = .05$.

LM7_94.DAT

Sample from Population 1		Sample from Population 2	
1.2	1.0	1.5	1.9
1.9	1.8	1.3	2.7
.7	1.1	2.9	3.5
2.5			

*7.95 A random sample of nine pairs of observations are recorded on two variables, x and y. The data are shown in the following table.

LM7_95.DAT

Pair	x	y	Pair	x	y
1	19	12	6	29	10
2	27	19	7	16	16
3	15	7	8	22	10
4	35	25	9	16	18
5	13	11			

Do the data provide sufficient evidence to indicate that the probability distribution for x is shifted to the right of that for y? Test using $\alpha = .05$.

*7.96 Independent random samples are utilized to compare four treatment means. The data are shown in the table below.

LM7_96.DAT

Treatment 1	Treatment 2	Treatment 3	Treatment 4
8	6	9	12
10	9	10	13
9	8	8	10
10	8	11	11
11	7	12	11

a. Given that SST = 36.95 and SS(Total) = 62.55, complete an ANOVA table for this experiment.

b. Is there evidence that the treatment means differ? Use $\alpha = .10$.

c. Place a 90% confidence interval on the mean response for treatment 4.

Applying the Concepts

*7.97 The *Journal of Testing and Evaluation* (July 1992) published an investigation of the mean compression strength of corrugated fiberboard shipping containers. Comparisons were made for boxes of five different sizes: A, B, C, D, and E. Twenty identical boxes of each size were independently selected and tested, and the peak compression strength (pounds) recorded for each box. The figure below shows the sample means for the five box types as well as the variation around each sample mean.

a. Explain why the data is collected as an independent samples design.

b. Refer to box types B and D. Based on the graph, does it appear that the mean compressive strengths of these two box types are significantly different? Explain.

c. Based on the graph, does it appear that the mean compressive strengths of all five box types are significantly different? Explain.

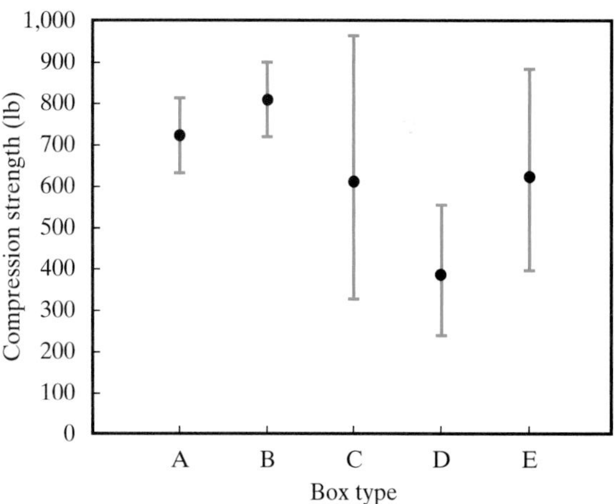

Source: Singh, S. P., et al. "Compression of single-wall corrugated shipping containers using fixed and floating test platens." *Journal of Testing and Evaluation*, Vol. 20, No. 4, July 1992, p. 319 (Figure 3). Copyright American Society for Testing and Materials. Reprinted with permission.

7.98 Refer to the *Marine Technology* (Jan. 1995) study of major oil spills from tankers and carriers, Exercise 2.10 (p. 34). The data for the 50 recent spills are saved in the file OILSPILL.DAT.

a. Construct a 90% confidence interval for the difference between the mean spillage amount of accidents caused by collision and the mean spillage amount of accidents caused by fire/explosion. Interpret the result.

b. Conduct a test of hypothesis to compare the mean spillage amount of accidents caused by grounding to the corresponding mean of accidents caused by hull failure. Use $\alpha = .05$.

c. Refer to parts **a** and **b.** State any assumptions required for the inferences derived from the analyses to be valid. Are these assumptions reasonably satisfied?

*d. Conduct a test of hypothesis to compare the variation in spillage amounts for accidents caused by collision and accidents caused by grounding. Use $\alpha = .02$.

7.99 A manufacturer of automobile shock absorbers was interested in comparing the durability of its shocks with that of the shocks produced by its biggest competitor. To make the comparison, one of the manufacturer's and one of the competitor's shocks were randomly selected and installed on the rear wheels of each of six cars. After the cars had been driven 20,000 miles, the strength of each test shock was measured, coded, and recorded. Results of the examination are shown in the table.

SHOCKABS.DAT

Car Number	Manufacturer's Shock	Competitor's Shock
1	8.8	8.4
2	10.5	10.1
3	12.5	12.0
4	9.7	9.3
5	9.6	9.0
6	13.2	13.0

An EXCEL printout of an analysis of the data is provided below.

a. Do the data present sufficient evidence to conclude that there is a difference in the mean strength of the two types of shocks after 20,000 miles of use? Use $\alpha = .05$.

b. Find the approximate observed significance level for the test, and interpret its value.

c. What assumptions are necessary to apply a paired difference analysis to the data?

d. Construct a 95% confidence interval for $(\mu_1 - \mu_2)$. Interpret the confidence interval.

*e. Analyze the data using a nonparametric test. Interpret the results.

7.100 Suppose the data in Exercise 7.99 are based on independent random samples.

a. Do the data provide sufficient evidence to indicate a difference between the mean strengths for the two types of shocks? Use $\alpha = .05$.

b. Construct a 95% confidence interval for $(\mu_1 - \mu_2)$. Interpret your result.

c. Compare the confidence intervals you obtained in Exercise 7.99 and in part **b** of this exercise. Which is wider? To what do you attribute the difference in width? Assuming in each case that the appropriate assumptions are satisfied, which interval provides you with more information about $(\mu_1 - \mu_2)$? Explain.

d. Are the results of an unpaired analysis valid if the data come from a paired experiment?

7.101 Nontraditional university students, generally defined as those at least 25 years old, comprise an increasingly large proportion of undergraduate student bodies at most universities. A study reported in the *College Student Journal* (Dec. 1992) compared traditional and nontraditional students on a number of factors, including grade point average (GPA). The table below summarizes the information from the sample.

GPA	Traditional Students	Nontraditional Students
n	94	73
$\bar{x}$	2.90	3.50
s	.50	.50

a. What are the appropriate null and alternative hypotheses if we want to test whether the mean GPAs of traditional and nontraditional students differ?

b. Conduct the test using $\alpha = .01$, and interpret the result.

EXCEL Output for Exercise 7.99

t-Test: Paired Two Sample for Means		
	MfgShock	ComShock
Mean	10.71666667	10.3
Variance	3.069666667	3.304
Observations	6	6
Pearson Correlation	0.997902853	
Hypothesized Mean Difference	0	
df	5	
t Stat	7.67868896	
P(T<=t) one-tail	0.000298532	
t Critical one-tail	2.015049176	
P(T<=t)two-tail	0.000597064	
t Critical two-tail	2.570577635	

c. What assumptions are necessary to ensure the validity of the test?

*7.102 An accounting firm that specializes in auditing the financial records of large corporations is interested in evaluating the appropriateness of the fees it charges for its services. As part of its evaluation, it wants to compare the costs it incurs in auditing corporations of different sizes. The accounting firm decided to measure the size of its client corporations in terms of their yearly sales. Accordingly, its population of client corporations was divided into three subpopulations:

A: Those with sales over $250 million

B: Those with sales between $100 million and $250 million

C: Those with sales under $100 million

The firm chose random samples of 10 corporations from each of the subpopulations and determined the costs (in thousands of dollars), given in the accompanying table, from its records.

a. Construct a dot plot for the sample data, using different types of dots for each of the three samples. Indicate the location of each of the sample means. Based on the information reflected in your dot plot, do you believe that a significant difference exists among the subpopulation means? Explain.

b. SAS was used to conduct the analysis of variance calculations, resulting in the printout shown below. Conduct a test to determine whether the three classes of firms have different mean costs incurred in audits. Use $\alpha = .05$.

c. What is the observed significance level for the test in part **b?** Interpret it.

d. What assumptions must be met in order to ensure the validity of the inferences you made in parts **b** and **c?**

ACCOSTS.DAT

A	B	C
250	100	80
150	150	125
275	75	20
100	200	186
475	55	52
600	80	92
150	110	88
800	160	141
325	132	76
230	233	200

7.103 One theory regarding the mobility of college and university faculty members is that those who publish the most scholarly articles are also the most mobile. The logic behind this theory is that good researchers who publish frequently receive more job offers and are therefore more likely to move from one university to another. The *Academy of Management Journal* (Vol. 25, 1982) examined this relationship for persons employed in industry. Using the personnel records of a large national oil company, the researchers obtained the early career performance records for 529 of the company's employees. Of these, 174 were classified as *stayers*, those who stayed with the company; the other 355, who left the company at varying points during a 15-year period, were classified as *leavers*. Summary statistics on three variables—initial performance, rate of career advancement (number of promotions per year), and final performance appraisals—for both stayers and leavers are shown in the table on p. 424. For each variable, compare the means of stayers and leavers using an appropriate statistical method. Interpret the results.

7.104 A study in the *Journal of Psychology and Marketing* (Jan. 1992) investigates the degree to which American

SAS Output for Exercise 7.102

```
                General Linear Models Procedure

Dependent Variable: COST

                               Sum of          Mean
Source                 DF     Squares        Square    F Value    Pr > F

Model                   2  318861.667    159430.833       8.44    0.0014
Error                  27  510163.000     18894.926
Corrected Total        29  829024.667

                 R-Square        C.V.      Root MSE          COST Mean
                 0.384623   72.220043       137.459         190.333333

Source                 DF   Type 1 SS  Mean Square    F Value    Pr > F
TREATMNT                2   318861.67    159430.83       8.44    0.0014
```

Summary Statistics for Exercise 7.103

	Stayers (n_1 = 174)		Leavers (n_2 = 335)	
Variable	$\bar{x}_1$	s_1	$\bar{x}_2$	s_2
Initial performance	3.51	.51	3.24	.52
Rate of career advancement	.43	.20	.31	.31
Final performance appraisal	3.78	.62	3.15	.68

consumers are concerned about product tampering. Large random samples of male and female consumers were asked to rate their concern about product tampering on a scale of 1 (little or no concern) to 9 (very concerned).

a. What are the appropriate null and alternative hypotheses to determine whether a difference exists in the mean level of concern about product tampering between men and women? Define any symbols you use.

b. The statistics reported include those shown in the MINITAB printout below. Interpret these results.

c. What assumptions are necessary to ensure the validity of this test?

7.105 Management training programs are often instituted to teach supervisory skills and thereby increase productivity. Suppose a company psychologist administers a set of examinations to each of 10 supervisors before such a training program begins and then administers similar examinations at the end of the program. The examinations are designed to measure supervisory skills, with higher scores indicating increased skill. The results of the tests are shown in the table at left.

a. Do the data provide evidence that the training program is effective in increasing supervisory skills, as measured by the examination scores? Use α = .10.

b. Find and interpret the approximate p-value for the test on the MINITAB printout below.

7.106 Some power plants are located near rivers or oceans so that the available water can be used for cooling the condensers. Suppose that, as part of an environmental impact study, a power company wants to estimate the difference in mean water temperature between the discharge of its plant and the offshore waters. How many sample measurements must be taken at each site in order to estimate the true difference between means to within .2°C with 95% confidence? Assume that the range in readings will be about 4°C at each site and the same number of readings will be taken at each site.

*7.107 A hotel had a problem with people reserving rooms for a weekend and then not honoring their reservations (no-shows). As a result, the hotel developed a new reservation and deposit plan that it hoped would reduce the number of no-shows. One year after the policy was initiated, management evaluated its effect in comparison with the old policy. Use a nonparametric test to compare the records given in the table (p. 425) on the number of no-shows for the

SUPEXAM.DAT

Supervisor	Pre-Test	Post-Test
1	63	78
2	93	92
3	84	91
4	72	80
5	65	69
6	72	85
7	91	99
8	84	82
9	71	81
10	80	87

MINITAB Output for Exercise 7.104

```
TWOSAMPLE T FOR MSCORE VS FSCORE
            N     MEAN      STDEV    SE MEAN
MSCORE    200    3.209       2.33      0.165
FSCORE    200    3.923       2.94      0.208

TTEST MU MSCORE = MU FSCORE (VS NE): T= -2.69 P=0.0072 DF=398
```

MINITAB Output for Exercise 7.105

```
TEST OF MU = 0.000 VS MU N.E. 0.000

             N        MEAN      STDEV    SE MEAN          T    P VALUE
PRE-POST    10      -6.900      5.425      1.716      -4.02     0.0030
```

10 nonholiday weekends preceding the institution of the new policy and the 10 nonholiday weekends preceding the evaluation time. Has the situation improved under the new policy? Test at $\alpha = .05$.

NOSHOWS.DAT

Before		After	
10	11	4	4
5	8	3	2
3	9	8	5
6	6	5	7
7	5	6	1

7.108 Does the time of day during which one works affect job satisfaction? A study in the *Journal of Occupational Psychology* (Sept. 1991) examined differences in job satisfaction between day-shift and night-shift nurses. Nurses' satisfaction with their hours of work, free time away from work, and breaks during work were measured. The following table shows the mean scores for each measure of job satisfaction (higher scores indicate greater satisfaction), along with the observed significance level comparing the means for the day-shift and night-shift samples:

	Mean Satisfaction		
	Day Shift	Night Shift	*p*-Value
Satisfaction with:			
Hours of work	3.91	3.56	.813
Free time	2.55	1.72	.047
Breaks	2.53	3.75	.0073

a. Specify the null and alternative hypotheses if we wish to test whether a difference in job satisfaction exists between day-shift and night-shift nurses on each of the three measures. Define any symbols you use.
b. Interpret the p-value for each of the tests. (Each of the p-values in the table is two-tailed.)
c. Assume that each of the tests is based on small samples of nurses from each group. What assumptions are necessary for the tests to be valid?

7.109 How does gender affect the type of advertising that proves to be most effective? An article in the *Journal of Advertising Research* (May/June 1990) makes reference to numerous studies that conclude males tend to be more competitive with others than with themselves. To apply this conclusion to advertising, the author creates two ads promoting a new brand of soft drink:

Ad 1: Four men are shown competing in racquetball

Ad 2: One man is shown competing against himself in racquetball

The author hypothesized that the first ad will be more effective when shown to males. To test this hypothesis, 43 males were shown both ads and asked to measure their attitude toward the advertisement (Aad), their attitude toward the brand of soft drink (Ab), and their intention to purchase the soft drink (Intention). Each variable was measured using a seven-point scale, with higher scores indicating a more favorable attitude. The results are shown in the table below.

	Sample Means		
	Aad	Ab	Intention
Ad 1	4.465	3.311	4.366
Ad 2	4.150	2.902	3.813
Level of significance	$p = .091$	$p = .032$	$p = .050$

a. What are the appropriate null and alternative hypotheses to test the author's research hypothesis? Define any symbols you use.
b. Based on the information provided about this experiment, do you think this is an independent samples experiment or a paired difference experiment? Explain.
c. Interpret the p-value for each test.
d. What assumptions are necessary for the validity of the tests?

*7.110 A state highway patrol was interested in knowing whether frequent patrolling of highways substantially reduces the number of speeders. Two similar interstate highways were selected for the study—one heavily patrolled and the other only occasionally patrolled. After 1 month, random samples of 100 cars were chosen on each highway, and the number of cars exceeding the speed limit was recorded. This process was repeated on five randomly selected days. The data are shown in the following table.

HWPATROL.DAT

Day	Highway 1 (heavily patrolled)	Highway 2 (occasionally patrolled)
1	35	60
2	40	36
3	25	48
4	38	54
5	47	63

Use a nonparametric procedure to determine whether the heavily patrolled highway tends to have fewer speeders per 100 cars than the occasionally patrolled highway. Test using $\alpha = .05$.

Real-World Case The Kentucky Milk Case–Part II
(A Case Covering Chapters 5–7)

In The Kentucky Milk Case—Part I, you used graphical and numerical descriptive statistics to investigate bid collusion in the Kentucky school milk market. This case expands your previous analyses, incorporating inferential statistical methodology. The three areas of your focus are described below. (See page 114 for the file layout of MILK.DAT data.) Again, you should prepare a professional document which presents the results of the analyses and any implications regarding collusionary practices in the tri-county Kentucky milk market.

1. *Incumbency rates.* Recall from Part I that market allocation (where the same dairy controls the same school districts year after year) is a common form of collusive behavior in bidrigging conspiracies. Market allocation is typically gauged by the incumbency rate for a market in a given school year—defined as the percentage of school districts that are won by the same milk vendor who won the previous year. Past experience with milk bids in a competitive market reveals that a "normal" incumbency rate is about .7. That is, 70% of the school districts are expected to purchase their milk from the same vendor who supplied the milk the previous year. In the 13-district tri-county Kentucky market, 13 vendor transitions potentially exist each year. Over the 1985–1988 period (when bid collusion was alleged to have occurred), there are 52 potential vendor transitions. Based on the actual number of vendor transitions that occurred each year and over the 1985–1988 period, make an inference regarding bid collusion.
2. *Bid price dispersion.* Recall that in competitive sealed-bid markets, more dispersion or variability among the bids is observed than in collusive markets. (This is due to conspiring vendors sharing information about their bids.) Consequently, if collusion exists, the variation in bid prices in the tri-county market should be significantly smaller than the corresponding variation in the surrounding market. For each milk product, conduct an analysis to compare the bid price variances of the two markets each year. Make the appropriate inferences.
3. *Average winning bid price.* According to collusion theorists, the mean winning bid price in the "rigged" market will exceed the mean winning bid price in the competitive market for each year in which collusion occurs. In addition, the difference between the competitive average and the "rigged" average tends to grow over time when collusionary tactics are employed over several consecutive years. For each milk product, conduct an analysis to compare the winning bid price means of the tri-county and surrounding markets each year. Make the appropriate inferences.

Chapter 8

COMPARING POPULATION PROPORTIONS

CONTENTS

STATISTICS IN ACTION

Where We've Been

Chapter 7 presented both parametric and nonparametric methods for comparing two or more population means.

Where We're Going

In this chapter, we will consider a problem of comparable importance—comparing two or more population proportions. The need to compare population proportions arises because many business and social experiments involve questioning people and classifying their responses. We will learn how to determine whether the proportion of consumers favoring product A differs from the proportion of consumers favoring product B, and we will learn how to estimate the difference with a confidence interval.

Many experiments are conducted in business and the social sciences to compare two or more proportions. (Those conducted to sample the opinions of people are called *sample surveys.*) For example, a state government might wish to estimate the difference between the proportions of people in two regions of the state who would qualify for a new welfare program. Or, after an innovative process change, an engineer might wish to determine whether the proportion of defective items produced by a manufacturing process was less than the proportion of defectives produced before the change. In Section 8.1 we show you how to test hypotheses about the difference between two population proportions based on independent random sampling. We will also show how to find a confidence interval for the difference. Then, in Sections 8.3 and 8.4 we will compare more than two population proportions.

8.1 COMPARING TWO POPULATION PROPORTIONS: INDEPENDENT SAMPLING

Suppose a manufacturer of camper vans wants to compare the potential market for its products in the northeastern United States to the market in the southeastern United States. Such a comparison would help the manufacturer decide where to concentrate sales efforts. Using telephone directories, the company randomly chooses 1,000 households in the northeast (NE) and 1,000 households in the southeast (SE) and determines whether each household plans to buy a camper within the next five years. The objective is to use this sample information to make an inference about the difference $(p_1 - p_2)$ between the proportion p_1 of *all* households in the NE and the proportion p_2 of *all* households in the SE that plan to purchase a camper within five years.

The two samples represent independent binomial experiments. (See Section 4.3 for the characteristics of binomial experiments.) The binomial random variables are the numbers x_1 and x_2 of the 1,000 sampled households in each area that indicate they will purchase a camper within five years. The results are summarized below.

NE	SE
$n_1 = 1{,}000$	$n_2 = 1{,}000$
$x_1 = 42$	$x_2 = 24$

We can now calculate the sample proportions $\hat{p}_1$ and $\hat{p}_2$ of the households in the NE and SE, respectively, that are prospective buyers:

$$\hat{p}_1 = \frac{x_1}{n_1} = \frac{42}{1{,}000} = .042$$

$$\hat{p}_2 = \frac{x_2}{n_2} = \frac{24}{1{,}000} = .024$$

The difference between the sample proportions $(\hat{p}_1 - \hat{p}_2)$ makes an intuitively appealing point estimator of the difference between the population parameters $(p_1 - p_2)$. For our example, the estimate is

$$(\hat{p}_1 - \hat{p}_2) = .042 - .024 = .018$$

To judge the reliability of the estimator $(\hat{p}_1 - \hat{p}_2)$, we must observe its performance in repeated sampling from the two populations. That is, we need to know the **sampling distribution of $(\hat{p}_1 - \hat{p}_2)$.** The properties of the sampling distribution are given in the next box. Remember that $\hat{p}_1$ and $\hat{p}_2$ can be viewed as means of the number of successes per trial in the respective samples, so the Central Limit Theorem applies when the sample sizes are large.

Since the distribution of $(\hat{p}_1 - \hat{p}_2)$ in repeated sampling is approximately normal, we can use the z statistic to derive confidence intervals for $(p_1 - p_2)$ or to test a hypothesis about $(p_1 - p_2)$.

For the camper example, a 95% confidence interval for the difference $(p_1 - p_2)$ is

$$(\hat{p}_1 - \hat{p}_2) \pm 1.96\sigma_{(\hat{p}_1 - \hat{p}_2)} \qquad \text{or} \qquad (\hat{p}_1 - \hat{p}_2) \pm 1.96\sqrt{\frac{p_1q_1}{n_1} + \frac{p_2q_2}{n_2}}$$

Properties of the Sampling Distribution of $(\hat{p}_1 - \hat{p}_2)$

1. The mean of the sampling distribution of $(\hat{p}_1 - \hat{p}_2)$ is $(p_1 - p_2)$; that is,

$$E(\hat{p}_1 - \hat{p}_2) = p_1 - p_2$$

Thus, $(\hat{p}_1 - \hat{p}_2)$ is an unbiased estimator of $(p_1 - p_2)$.

2. The standard deviation of the sampling distribution of $(\hat{p}_1 - \hat{p}_2)$ is

$$\sigma_{(\hat{p}_1 - \hat{p}_2)} = \sqrt{\frac{p_1q_1}{n_1} + \frac{p_2q_2}{n_2}}$$

3. If the sample sizes n_1 and n_2 are large (see Section 5.3 for a guideline), the sampling distribution of $(\hat{p}_1 - \hat{p}_2)$ is approximately normal.

The quantities p_1q_1 and p_2q_2 must be estimated in order to complete the calculation of the standard deviation $\sigma_{(\hat{p}_1 - \hat{p}_2)}$ and hence the calculation of the confidence interval. In Section 5.3 we showed that the value of pq is relatively insensitive to the value chosen to approximate p. Therefore, $\hat{p}_1\hat{q}_1$ and $\hat{p}_2\hat{q}_2$ will provide satisfactory estimates to approximate p_1q_1 and p_2q_2, respectively. Then

$$\sqrt{\frac{p_1q_1}{n_1} + \frac{p_2q_2}{n_2}} \approx \sqrt{\frac{\hat{p}_1\hat{q}_1}{n_1} + \frac{\hat{p}_2\hat{q}_2}{n_2}}$$

and we will approximate the 95% confidence interval by

$$(\hat{p}_1 - \hat{p}_2) \pm 1.96\sqrt{\frac{\hat{p}_1\hat{q}_1}{n_1} + \frac{\hat{p}_2\hat{q}_2}{n_2}}$$

Substituting the sample quantities yields

$$(.042 - .024) \pm 1.96\sqrt{\frac{(.042)(.958)}{1{,}000} + \frac{(.024)(.976)}{1{,}000}}$$

or $.018 \pm .016$. Thus, we are 95% confident that the interval from .002 to .034 contains $(p_1 - p_2)$.

We infer that there are between .2% and 3.4% more households in the northeast than in the southeast that plan to purchase campers in the next five years.

The general form of a confidence interval for the difference $(p_1 - p_2)$ between population proportions is given in the following box.

Large-Sample 100(1 − α)% Confidence Interval for $(p_1 - p_2)$

$$(\hat{p}_1 - \hat{p}_2) \pm z_{\alpha/2}\sigma_{(\hat{p}_1-\hat{p}_2)} = (\hat{p}_1 - \hat{p}_2) \pm z_{\alpha/2}\sqrt{\frac{p_1q_1}{n_1} + \frac{p_2q_2}{n_2}}$$

$$\approx (\hat{p}_1 - \hat{p}_2) \pm z_{\alpha/2}\sqrt{\frac{\hat{p}_1\hat{q}_1}{n_1} + \frac{\hat{p}_2\hat{q}_2}{n_2}}$$

Assumptions: The two samples are independent random samples. Both samples should be large enough that the normal distribution provides an adequate approximation to the sampling distribution of $\hat{p}_1$ and $\hat{p}_2$ (see Section 6.5).

The z statistic,

$$z = \frac{(\hat{p}_1 - \hat{p}_2) - (p_1 - p_2)}{\sigma_{(\hat{p}_1-\hat{p}_2)}}$$

is used to test the null hypothesis that $(p_1 - p_2)$ equals some specified difference, say D_0. For the special case where $D_0 = 0$, that is, where we want to test the null hypothesis H_0: $(p_1 - p_2) = 0$ (or, equivalently, H_0: $p_1 = p_2$), the best estimate of $p_1 = p_2 = p$ is obtained by dividing the total number of successes $(x_1 + x_2)$ for the two samples by the total number of observations $(n_1 + n_2)$; that is

$$\hat{p} = \frac{x_1 + x_2}{n_1 + n_2} \quad \text{or} \quad \hat{p} = \frac{n_1\hat{p}_1 + n_2\hat{p}_2}{n_1 + n_2}$$

The second equation shows that $\hat{p}$ is a weighted average of $\hat{p}_1$ and $\hat{p}_2$, with the larger sample receiving more weight. If the sample sizes are equal, then $\hat{p}$ is a simple average of the two sample proportions of successes.

We now substitute the weighted average $\hat{p}$ for both p_1 and p_2 in the formula for the standard deviation of $(\hat{p}_1 - \hat{p}_2)$:

$$\sigma_{(\hat{p}_1-\hat{p}_2)} = \sqrt{\frac{p_1q_1}{n_1} + \frac{p_2q_2}{n_2}} \approx \sqrt{\frac{\hat{p}\hat{q}}{n_1} + \frac{\hat{p}\hat{q}}{n_2}} = \sqrt{\hat{p}\hat{q}\left(\frac{1}{n_1} + \frac{1}{n_2}\right)}$$

The test is summarized in the next box.

EXAMPLE 8.1

A consumer advocacy group wants to determine whether there is a difference between the proportions of the two leading automobile models that need major repairs (more than \$500) within two years of their purchase. A sample of 400 two-year owners of model 1 is contacted, and a sample of 500 two-year owners of model 2 is contacted. The numbers x_1 and x_2 of owners who report that their cars needed major repairs within the first two years are 53 and 78, respectively. Test the null hypothesis that no difference exists between the proportions in populations 1 and 2 needing major repairs against the alternative that a difference does exist. Use $\alpha = .10$.

Solution

If we define p_1 and p_2 as the true proportions of model 1 and model 2 owners, respectively, whose cars need major repairs within two years, the elements of the test are

Large-Sample Test of Hypothesis About $(p_1 - p_2)$

One-Tailed Test	**Two-Tailed Test**
$H_0: (p_1 - p_2) = 0$*	$H_0: (p_1 - p_2) = 0$
$H_a: (p_1 - p_2) < 0$ [or $H_a: (p_1 - p_2) > 0$]	$H_a: (p_1 - p_2) \neq 0$

$$\textit{Test statistic: } z = \frac{(\hat{p}_1 - \hat{p}_2) - 0}{\sigma_{(\hat{p}_1 - \hat{p}_2)}}$$

Rejection region: $z < -z_\alpha$ [or $z > z_\alpha$ when $H_a: (p_1 - p_2) > 0$]	*Rejection region:* $\lvert z \rvert > z_{\alpha/2}$

Note: $\sigma_{(\hat{p}_1 - \hat{p}_2)} = \sqrt{\dfrac{p_1 q_1}{n_1} + \dfrac{p_2 q_2}{n_2}} \approx \sqrt{\hat{p}\hat{q}\left(\dfrac{1}{n_1} + \dfrac{1}{n_2}\right)}$ where $\hat{p} = \dfrac{x_1 + x_2}{n_1 + n_2}$

Assumption: Same as for large-sample confidence interval for $(p_1 - p_2)$.

$H_0: (p_1 - p_2) = 0$

$H_a: (p_1 - p_2) \neq 0$

$$\textit{Test statistic: } z = \frac{(\hat{p}_1 - \hat{p}_2) - 0}{\sigma_{(\hat{p}_1 - \hat{p}_2)}}$$

Rejection region ($\alpha = .10$): $\lvert z \rvert > z_{\alpha/2} = z_{.05} = 1.645$ (see Figure 8.1)

FIGURE 8.1
Rejection region for Example 8.1

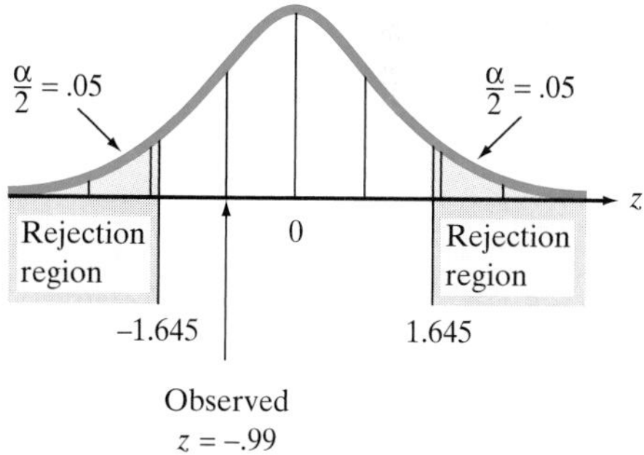

We now calculate the sample proportions of owners who need major car repairs,

$$\hat{p}_1 = \frac{x_1}{n_1} = \frac{53}{400} = .1325$$

$$\hat{p}_2 = \frac{x_2}{n_2} = \frac{78}{500} = .1560$$

*The test can be adapted to test for a difference $D_0 \neq 0$. Because most applications call for a comparison of p_1 and p_2, implying $D_0 = 0$, we will confine our attention to this case.

Then

$$z = \frac{(\hat{p}_1 - \hat{p}_2) - 0}{\sigma_{(\hat{p}_1 - \hat{p}_2)}} \approx \frac{(\hat{p}_1 - \hat{p}_2)}{\sqrt{\hat{p}\hat{q}\left(\frac{1}{n_1} + \frac{1}{n_2}\right)}}$$

where

$$\hat{p} = \frac{x_1 + x_2}{n_1 + n_2} = \frac{53 + 78}{400 + 500} = .1456$$

Note that $\hat{p}$ is a weighted average of $\hat{p}_1$ and $\hat{p}_2$, with more weight given to the larger sample of model 2 owners.

Thus, the computed value of the test statistic is

$$z = \frac{.1325 - .1560}{\sqrt{(.1456)(.8544)\left(\frac{1}{400} + \frac{1}{500}\right)}} = \frac{-.0235}{.0237} = -.99$$

The samples provide insufficient evidence at $\alpha = .10$ to detect a difference between the proportions of the two models that need repairs within two years. Even though 2.35% more sampled owners of model 2 found they needed major repairs, this difference is less than 1 standard deviation ($z = -.99$) from the hypothesized zero difference between the true proportions.

EXAMPLE 8.2 Find the observed significance level for the test in Example 8.1.

Solution The observed value of z for this two-tailed test was $z = -.99$. Therefore, the observed significance level is

$$p\text{-value} = P(|z| > .99) = P(z < -.99 \text{ or } z > .99)$$

This probability is equal to the shaded area shown in Figure 8.2. The area corresponding to $z = .99$ is given in Table IV of Appendix B as .3389. Therefore, the observed significance level for the test, the sum of the two shaded tail areas under the standard normal curve, is

$$p\text{-value} = 2(.5 - .3389) = 2(.1611) = .3222$$

FIGURE 8.2 The observed significance level for the test of Example 8.1

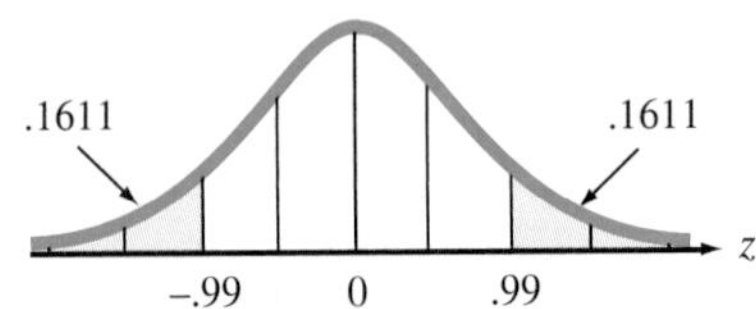

The probability of observing a z as large as .99 or less than $-.99$ if in fact $p_1 = p_2$ is .3222. This large p-value indicates that there is little or no evidence of a difference between p_1 and p_2.

EXERCISES 8.1–8.16

Learning the Mechanics

8.1 Explain why the Central Limit Theorem is important in finding an approximate distribution for $(\hat{p}_1 - \hat{p}_2)$.

8.2 In each case, determine whether the sample sizes are large enough to conclude that the sampling distribution of $(\hat{p}_1 - \hat{p}_2)$ is approximately normal.
a. $n_1 = 12, n_2 = 14, \hat{p}_1 = .42, \hat{p}_2 = .57$
b. $n_1 = 12, n_2 = 14, \hat{p}_1 = .92, \hat{p}_2 = .86$
c. $n_1 = n_2 = 30, \hat{p}_1 = .70, \hat{p}_2 = .73$
d. $n_1 = 100, n_2 = 250, \hat{p}_1 = .93, \hat{p}_2 = .97$
e. $n_1 = 125, n_2 = 200, \hat{p}_1 = .08, \hat{p}_2 = .12$

8.3 For each of the following values of α, find the values of z for which H_0: $(p_1 - p_2) = 0$ would be rejected in favor of H_a: $(p_1 - p_2) < 0$.
a. $\alpha = .01$ b. $\alpha = .025$
c. $\alpha = .05$ d. $\alpha = .10$

8.4 Independent random samples, each containing 800 observations, were selected from two binomial populations. The samples from populations 1 and 2 produced 320 and 400 successes, respectively.
a. Test H_0: $(p_1 - p_2) = 0$ against H_a: $(p_1 - p_2) \neq 0$. Use $\alpha = .05$.
b. Test H_0: $(p_1 - p_2) = 0$ against H_a: $(p_1 - p_2) \neq 0$. Use $\alpha = .01$.
c. Test H_0: $(p_1 - p_2) = 0$ against H_a: $(p_1 - p_2) < 0$. Use $\alpha = .01$.
d. Form a 90% confidence interval for $(p_1 - p_2)$.

8.5 Construct a 95% confidence interval for $(p_1 - p_2)$ in each of the following situations:
a. $n_1 = 400, \hat{p}_1 = .65; n_2 = 400, \hat{p}_2 = .58$
b. $n_1 = 180, \hat{p}_1 = .31; n_2 = 250, \hat{p}_2 = .25$
c. $n_1 = 100, \hat{p}_1 = .46; n_2 = 120, \hat{p}_2 = .61$

8.6 Sketch the sampling distribution of $(\hat{p}_1 - \hat{p}_2)$ based on independent random samples of $n_1 = 100$ and $n_2 = 200$ observations from two binomial populations with success probabilities $\hat{p}_1 = .1$ and $\hat{p}_2 = .5$, respectively.

8.7 Random samples of size $n_1 = 55$ and $n_2 = 65$ were drawn from populations 1 and 2, respectively. The samples yielded $\hat{p}_1 = .7$ and $\hat{p}_2 = .6$. Test H_0: $(p_1 - p_2) = 0$ against H_a: $(p_1 - p_2) > 0$ using $\alpha = .05$.

Applying the Concepts

8.8 In evaluating the usefulness and validity of a questionnaire, researchers often pretest the questionnaire on different independently selected samples of respondents. Knowledge of the differences and similarities of the samples and their respective populations is important for interpreting the questionnaire's validity. *Educational and Psychological Measurement* (Feb. 1998) reported on a newly developed questionnaire for measuring the career success expectations of employees. The instrument was tested on the two independent samples described in the table.

	Managers and Professionals	Part-Time MBA Students
Sample size	162	109
Gender (% males)	95.0	68.9
Marital status (% married)	91.2	53.4

Source: Stephens, Gregory K., Szajna, Bernadette, and Broome, Kirk M., "The Career Success Expectation Scale: An exploratory and Confirmatory Factor Analysis," *Educational and Psychological Measurement*, Vol. 58, No. 1, Feb. 1998, pp. 129–141.

a. Does the population of managers and professionals from which the sample was drawn consist of more males than the part-time MBA population does? Conduct the appropriate test using $\alpha = .05$.
b. Describe any assumptions you made in conducting the test of part **a** and why you made them.
c. Does the population of managers and professionals consist of more married individuals than the part-time MBA population does? Conduct the appropriate hypothesis test using $\alpha = .01$.
d. What assumptions must hold for the test of part **c** to be valid?

8.9 Operation Crossroads was a 1946 military exercise in which atomic bombs were detonated over empty target ships in the Pacific Ocean. The Navy assigned sailors to wash down the test ships immediately after the atomic blasts. The National Academy of Science reported "that the overall death rate among Operation Crossroads sailors was 4.6% higher than among a comparable group of sailors. . . . However, this increase was not statistically significant." (*Tampa Tribune*, Oct. 30, 1996.)
a. Describe the parameter of interest in the National Academy of Science study.
b. Interpret the statement: "This increase was not statistically significant."

8.10 A University of South Florida biologist conducted an experiment to determine whether increased levels of carbon dioxide kill leaf-eating moths (*USF Magazine*, Winter 1999). Moth larvae were placed in open containers filled with oak leaves. Half the containers had normal carbon dioxide levels while the other half had double the normal level of carbon dioxide. Ten percent of the larvae in the containers with high carbon dioxide levels died, compared to five percent in the containers with normal levels. Assume that 80 moth larvae were placed, at random, in each of the two types of containers. Do the experimental results demonstrate that an increased level of carbon dioxide is effective in killing a higher percentage of leaf-eating moth larvae? Test using $\alpha = .01$.

8.11 *Working Women* (June 1999) published the results of a 1999 Gallup poll that found that 92% of adult Americans would vote for a woman president. In 1975, a similar poll found that only 73% would vote for a woman.

a. Let p_{1999} and p_{1975} represent the population parameters of interest for this study. In the words of the problem, define these parameters.

b. Assume the sample sizes were 2,000 in 1999 and 1,500 in 1975. Are these sample sizes large enough ton conclude that the sampling distribution of $(p_{1999} - p_{1975})$ is approximately normally distributed? Justify your answer.

c. Construct a 90% confidence interval for $(p_{1999} - p_{1975})$. Interpret your confidence interval in the context of the problem.

d. Rework part **b** under the assumption that the sample sizes for 1999 and 1975 are 20 and 50, respectively.

8.12 Should marketers use ads that appeal to children to sell adult products? One controversial advertisement campaign was Camel cigarettes' use of the cartoon character "Joe Camel" as its brand symbol. (The Federal Trade Commission eventually banned ads featuring Joe Camel because they supposedly encouraged young people to smoke.) Lucy L. Henke, a marketing professor at the University of New Hampshire, assessed young children's abilities to recognize cigarette brand advertising symbols. She found that 15 out of 28 children under the age of 6, and 46 out of 55 children age 6 and over recognized Joe Camel, the brand symbol of Camel cigarettes (*Journal of Advertising,* Winter 1995).

a. Use a 95% confidence interval to estimate the proportion of all children that recognize Joe Camel. Interpret the interval.

b. Do the data indicate that recognition of Joe Camel increases with age? Test using $\alpha = .05$.

8.13 Price scanners are widely used in U.S. supermarkets. While they are fast and easy to use, they also make mistakes. Over the years, various consumer advocacy groups have complained that scanners routinely gouge the customer by overcharging. A recent Federal Trade Commission study found that supermarket scanners erred 3.47% of the time and department store scanners erred 9.15% of the time ("Scan Errors Help Public," *Newark Star-Ledger,* Oct. 23, 1996).

a. Assume the above error rates were determined from merchandise samples of size 800 and 900, respectively. Are these sample sizes large enough to apply the methods of this section to estimate the difference in the error rates? Justify your answer.

b. Use a 98% confidence interval to estimate the difference in the error rates. Interpret your result.

c. What assumptions must hold to ensure the validity of the confidence interval of part **b?**

8.14 Do you have an insatiable craving for chocolate or some other food? Since many North Americans apparently do, psychologists are designing scientific studies to examine the phenomenon. According to the *New York Times* (Feb. 22, 1995), one of the largest studies of food cravings involved a survey of 1,000 McMaster University (Canada) students. The survey revealed that 97% of the women in the study acknowledged specific food cravings while only 67% of the men did. Assume that 600 of the respondents were women and 400 were men.

a. Is there sufficient evidence to claim that the true proportion of women who acknowledge having food cravings exceeds the corresponding proportion of men? Test using $\alpha = .01$.

b. Why is it dangerous to conclude from the study that women have a higher incidence of food cravings than men?

8.15 *Industrial Marketing Management* (Vol. 25, 1996) published a study that examined the demographics, decision-making roles, and time demands of product managers. Independent samples of $n_1 = 93$ consumer/commercial product managers and $n_2 = 212$ industrial product managers took part in the study. In the consumer/commercial group, 40% of the product managers are 40 years of age or older; in the industrial group, 54% are 40 or more years old. Make an inference about the difference between the true proportions of consumer/commercial and industrial product managers who are at least 40 years old. Justify your choice of method (confidence interval or hypothesis test) and α level. Do industrial product managers tend to be older than consumer/commercial product managers?

8.16 Many female undergraduates at four-year colleges and universities switch from science, mathematics, and engineering (SME) majors into disciplines that are not science based, such as journalism, marketing, and sociology. When female undergraduates switch majors, are their reasons different from those of their male counterparts? This question was investigated in *Science Education* (July 1995). A sample of 335 junior/senior undergraduates—172 females and 163 males—at two large research universities were identified as "switchers," that is, they left a declared SME major for a non-SME major. Each student listed one or more factors that contributed to their switching decision.

a. Of the 172 females in the sample, 74 listed lack or loss of interest in SME (i.e., "turned off" by science) as a major factor, compared to 72 of the 163 males. Conduct a test (at $\alpha = .10$) to determine whether the proportion of female switchers who give "lack of interest in SME" as a major reason for switching differs from the corresponding proportion of males.

b. Thirty-three of the 172 females in the sample admitted they were discouraged or lost confidence due to low grades in SME during their early years, compared to 44 of 163 males. Construct a 90% confidence interval for the difference between the proportions of female and male switchers who lost confidence due to low grades in SME. Interpret the result.

8.2 DETERMINING THE SAMPLE SIZE

The sample sizes n_1 and n_2 required to compare two population proportions can be found in a manner similar to the method described in Section 7.3 for comparing two population means. We will assume equal sized samples, i.e., $n_1 = n_2 = n$, and then choose n so that $(\hat{p}_1 - \hat{p}_2)$ will differ from $(p_1 - p_2)$ by no more than a bound B with a specified probability. We will illustrate the procedure with an example.

EXAMPLE 8.3

A production supervisor suspects that a difference exists between the proportions p_1 and p_2 of defective items produced by two different machines. Experience has shown that the proportion defective for each of the two machines is in the neighborhood of .03. If the supervisor wants to estimate the difference in the proportions to within .005 using a 95% confidence interval, how many items must be randomly sampled from the production of each machine? (Assume that the supervisor wants $n_1 = n_2 = n$)

Solution In this sampling problem, $B = .005$, and for the specified level of reliability, $z_{\alpha/2} = z_{.025} = 1.96$. Then, letting $p_1 = p_2 = .03$ and $n_1 = n_2 = n$, we find the required sample size per machine by solving the following equation for n:

$$z_{\alpha/2}\sigma_{(\hat{p}_1 - \hat{p}_2)} = B$$

or

$$z_{\alpha/2}\sqrt{\frac{p_1 q_1}{n_1} + \frac{p_2 q_2}{n_2}} = B$$

$$1.96\sqrt{\frac{(.03)(.97)}{n} + \frac{(.03)(.97)}{n}} = .005$$

$$1.96\sqrt{\frac{2(.03)(.97)}{n}} = .005$$

$$n = 8{,}943.2$$

You can see that this may be a tedious sampling procedure. If the supervisor insists on estimating $(p_1 - p_2)$ correct to within .005 with 95% confidence, approximately 9,000 items will have to be inspected for each machine.

From the calculations in Example 8.3, note that $\sigma_{(\hat{p}_1 - \hat{p}_2)}$ (and hence the solution, $n_1 = n_2 = n$) depends on the actual (but unknown) values of p_1 and p_2. In fact, the required sample size $n_1 = n_2 = n$ is largest when $p_1 = p_2 = .5$. Therefore, if you have no prior information on the approximate values of p_1 and p_2, use $p_1 = p_2 = .5$ in the formula for $\sigma_{(\hat{p}_1 - \hat{p}_2)}$. If p_1 and p_2 are in fact close to .5, then the values of n_1 and n_2 that you have calculated will be correct. If p_1 and p_2 differ substantially from .5, then your solutions for n_1 and n_2 will be larger than needed. Consequently, using $p_1 = p_2 = .5$ when solving for n_1 and n_2 is a conservative procedure because the sample sizes n_1 and n_2 will be at least as large as (and probably larger than) needed.

The procedure for determining sample sizes necessary for estimating $(p_1 - p_2)$ for the case $n_1 = n_2$ is given in the following box.

Determination of Sample Size for Estimating $p_1 - p_2$

To estimate $(p_1 - p_2)$ to within a given bound B with probability $(1 - \alpha)$, use the following formula to solve for equal sample sizes that will achieve the desired reliability:

$$n_1 = n_2 = \frac{(z_{\alpha/2})^2(p_1q_1 + p_2q_2)}{B^2}$$

You will need to substitute estimates for the values of p_1 and p_2 before solving for the sample size. These estimates might be based on prior samples, obtained from educated guesses or, most conservatively, specified as $p_1 = p_2 = .5$.

EXERCISES 8.17–8.22

Learning the Mechanics

8.17 Assuming that $n_1 = n_2$, find the sample sizes needed to estimate $(p_1 - p_2)$ for each of the following situations:

a. Bound = .01 with 99% confidence. Assume that $p_1 \approx .4$ and $p_2 \approx .7$.

b. A 90% confidence interval of width .05. Assume there is no prior information available to obtain approximate values of p_1 and p_2.

c. Bound = .03 with 90% confidence. Assume that $p_1 \approx .2$ and $p_2 \approx .3$.

Applying the Concepts

8.18 A pollster wants to estimate the difference between the proportions of men and women who favor a particular national candidate using a 90% confidence interval of width .04. Suppose the pollster has no prior information about the proportions. If equal numbers of men and women are to be polled, how large should the sample size be?

8.19 Today, nearly all cable companies carry at least one home shopping channel. Who uses these home shopping services? Are the shoppers primarily men or women? Suppose you want to estimate the difference in the proportions of men and women who say they have used or expect to use televised home shopping using an 80% confidence interval of width .06 or less.

a. Approximately how many people should be included in your samples?

b. Suppose you want to obtain individual estimates for the two proportions of interest. Will the sample size found in part **a** be large enough to provide estimates of each proportion correct to within .02 with probability equal to .90? Justify your response.

8.20 Rat damage creates a large financial loss in the production of sugarcane. One aspect of the problem that has been investigated by the U.S. Department of Agriculture concerns the optimal place to locate rat poison. To be most effective in reducing rat damage, should the poison be located in the middle of the field or on the outer perimeter? One way to answer this question is to determine where the greater amount of damage occurs. If damage is measured by the proportion of cane stalks that have been damaged by rats, how many stalks from each section of the field should be sampled in order to estimate the true difference between proportions of stalks damaged in the two sections to within .02 with probability .95?

8.21 A manufacturer of large-screen televisions wants to compare with a competitor the proportions of its best sets that need repair within 1 year. If it is desired to estimate the difference between proportions to within .05 with 90% confidence, and if the manufacturer plans to sample twice as many buyers (n_1) of its sets as buyers (n_2) of the competitor's sets, how many buyers of each brand must be sampled? Assume that the proportion of sets that need repair will be about .2 for both brands.

8.22 Refer to the *Working Women* (June 1999) comparison of the percentages of adult Americans in 1975 and 1999 who would vote for a woman president, Exercise 8.11 (p. 434). Suppose you want to make a similar comparison for the years 2000 and 2001. How many adults should be sampled each year to estimate the difference in percentages to within 3% with 90% confidence? Assume equal sample sizes will be collected.

8.3 COMPARING POPULATION PROPORTIONS: MULTINOMIAL EXPERIMENT

TABLE 8.1 Consumer Preference Survey

A	B	Store Brand
61	53	36

In this section, we consider a statistical method to compare two or more, say k, population proportions. For example, suppose a large supermarket chain conducts a consumer preference survey by recording the *brand of bread* purchased by customers in its stores. Assume the chain carries three brands of bread—two major brands (A and B) and its own store brand. The brand preferences of a random sample of 150 consumers are observed, and the resulting **count data** (i.e., number of consumers in each brand category) appear in Table 8.1 Do you think these data indicate that a preference exists for any of the brands?

To answer this question with a valid statistical analysis, we need to know the underlying probability distribution of these count data. This distribution, called the **multinomial probability distribution,** is an extension of the binomial distribution (Section 4.3). The properties of a multinomial experiment are given in the following box.

Properties of the Multinomial Experiment

1. The experiment consists of n identical trials.
2. There are k possible outcomes to each trial.
3. The probabilities of the k outcomes, denoted by $p_1, p_2, \ldots, p_k$, remain the same from trial to trial, where $p_1 + p_2 + \cdots, p_k = 1$.
4. The trials are independent.
5. The random variables of interest are the counts $n_1, n_2, \ldots, n_k$ in each of the k cells.

Note that our consumer-preference survey satisfies the properties of a **multinomial experiment.** The experiment consists of randomly sampling $n = 150$ buyers from a large population of consumers containing an unknown proportion p_1 who prefer brand A, a proportion p_2 who prefer brand B, and a proportion p_3 who prefer the store brand. Each buyer represents a single trial that can result in one of three outcomes: The consumer prefers brand A, B, or the store brand with probabilities p_1, p_2, and p_3, respectively. (Assume that all consumers will have a preference.) The buyer preference of any single consumer in the sample does not affect the preference of another; consequently, the trials are independent. And, finally, you can see that the recorded data are the number of buyers in each of three consumer-preference categories. Thus, the consumer-preference survey satisfies the five properties of a multinomial experiment. You can see that the properties of a multinomial experiment closely resemble those of the binomial experiment and that, in fact, a binomial experiment is a multinomial experiment for the special case where $k = 2$.

In the consumer-preference survey, and in most practical applications of the multinomial experiment, the k outcome probabilities $p_1, p_2, \ldots, p_k$ are unknown and we typically want to use the survey data to make inferences about their values. The unknown probabilities in the consumer-preference survey are

p_1 = Proportion of all buyers who prefer brand A

p_2 = Proportion of all buyers who prefer brand B

p_3 = Proportion of all buyers who prefer the store brand

To decide whether the consumers have a preference for any of the brands, we will want to test the null hypothesis that the brands of bread are equally preferred (that is, $p_1 = p_2 = p_3 = \frac{1}{3}$) against the alternative hypothesis that one brand is preferred (that is, at least one of the probabilities p_1, p_2, and p_3 exceeds $\frac{1}{3}$). Thus, we want to test

H_0: $p_1 = p_2 = p_3 = \frac{1}{3}$ (no preference)

H_a: At least one of the proportions exceeds $\frac{1}{3}$ (a preference exists)

If the null hypothesis is true and $p_1 = p_2 = p_3 = \frac{1}{3}$, the expected value (mean value) of the number of customers who prefer brand A is given by

$$E(n_1) = np_1 = (n)\tfrac{1}{3} = (150)\tfrac{1}{3} = 50$$

Similarly, $E(n_2) = E(n_3) = 50$ if the null hypothesis is true and no preference exists.

The following test statistic—the **chi-square test**—measures the degree of disagreement between the data and the null hypothesis:

$$\chi^2 = \frac{[n_1 - E(n_1)]^2}{E(n_1)} + \frac{[n_2 - E(n_2)]^2}{E(n_2)} + \frac{[n_3 - E(n_3)]^2}{E(n_3)}$$

$$= \frac{(n_1 - 50)^2}{50} + \frac{(n_2 - 50)^2}{50} + \frac{(n_3 - 50)^2}{50}$$

Note that the farther the observed numbers n_1, n_2, and n_3, are from their expected value (50), the larger χ^2 will become. That is, large values of χ^2 imply that the null hypothesis is false.

We have to know the distribution of χ^2 in repeated sampling before we can decide whether the data indicate that a preference exists. When H_0 is true, χ^2 can be shown to have (approximately) a **chi-square (χ^2) distribution.** The shape of the chi-square distribution depends on the degrees of freedom (df) associated with the data analyzed. For this application, the χ^2 distribution has $(k - 1)$ degrees of freedom.*

TABLE 8.2 Reproduction of Part of Table VII in Appendix B

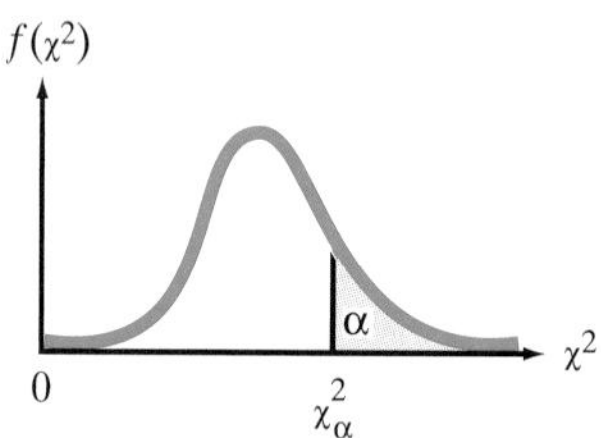

Degrees of Freedom	$\chi^2_{.100}$	$\chi^2_{.050}$	$\chi^2_{.025}$	$\chi^2_{.010}$	$\chi^2_{.005}$
1	2.70554	3.84146	5.02389	6.63490	7.87944
2	4.60517	5.99147	7.37776	9.21034	10.5966
3	6.25139	7.81473	9.34840	11.3449	12.8381
4	7.77944	9.48773	11.1433	13.2767	14.8602
5	9.23635	11.0705	12.8325	15.0863	16.7496
6	10.6446	12.5916	14.4494	16.8119	18.5476
7	12.0170	14.0671	16.0128	18.4753	20.2777

*The derivation of the degrees of freedom for χ^2 involves the number of linear restrictions imposed on the count data. In the present case, the only constraint is that $\sum n_i = n$, where n (the sample size) is fixed in advance. Therefore, df $= k - 1$. For other cases, we will give the degrees of freedom for each usage of χ^2 and refer the interested reader to the references for more detail.

Critical values of χ^2 are provided in Table VII of Appendix B, a portion of which is shown in Table 8.2. To illustrate, the rejection region for the consumer preference survey for $\alpha = .05$ and $k - 1 = 3 - 1 = 2$ df is

$$\textit{Rejection region: } \chi^2 > \chi^2_{.05}$$

The value of $\chi^2_{.05}$ (found in Table VII of Appendix B) is 5.99147. (See Figure 8.3.) The computed value of the test statistic is

$$\chi^2 = \frac{(n_1 - 50)^2}{50} + \frac{(n_2 - 50)^2}{50} + \frac{(n_3 - 50)^2}{50}$$

$$= \frac{(61 - 50)^2}{50} + \frac{(53 - 50)^2}{50} + \frac{(36 - 50)^2}{50} = 6.52$$

Since the computed $\chi^2 = 6.52$ exceeds the critical value of 5.99147, we conclude at the $\alpha = .05$ level of significance that there does exist a consumer preference for one or more of the brands of bread.

FIGURE 8.3
Rejection region for consumer-preference survey

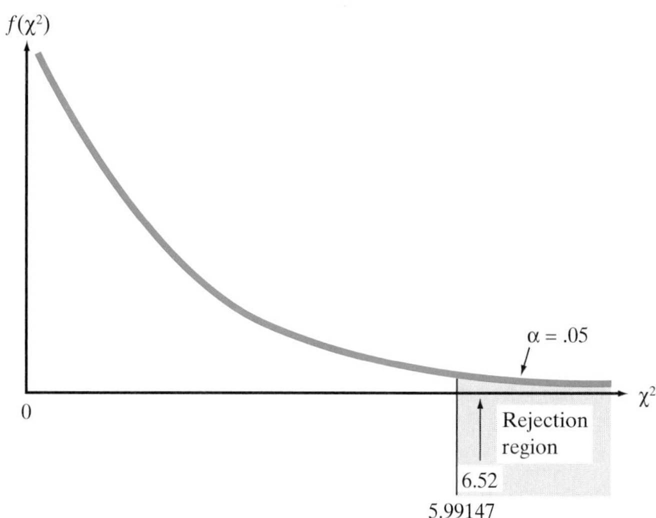

Now that we have evidence to indicate that the proportions p_1, p_2, and p_3 are unequal, we can make inferences concerning their individual values using the methods of Section 6.5. [*Note:* We cannot use the methods of Section 8.1 to compare two proportions because the cell counts are dependent random variables.] The general form for a test of multinomial probabilities is shown in the next box.

EXAMPLE 8.4

A large firm has established what it hopes is an objective system of deciding on annual pay increases for its employees. The system is based on a series of evaluation scores determined by the supervisors of each employee. Employees with scores above 80 receive a merit pay increase, those with scores between 50 and 80 receive the standard increase, and those below 50 receive no increase. The firm designed the plan with the objective that, on the average, 25% of its employees would receive merit increases, 65% would receive standard increases, and 10% would receive no increase. After one year of operation using the new plan, the distribution of pay increases for the 600 company employees was as shown in Table 8.3. Test at $\alpha = .01$ to determine whether the distribution of pay increases differs significantly from the firm's proportions.

TABLE 8.3 Distribution of Pay Increases

None	Standard	Merit
42	365	193

A Test of a Hypothesis About Multinomial Probabilities: One-Way Table

H_0: $p_1 = p_{1,0}, p_2 = p_{2,0}, \ldots, p_k = p_{k,0}$

where $p_{1,0}, p_{2,0}, \ldots, p_{k,0}$ represent the hypothesized values of the multinomial probabilities

H_a: At least one of the multinomial probabilities does not equal its hypothesized value

Test statistic: $\chi^2 = \sum \dfrac{[n_i - E(n_i)]^2}{E(n_i)}$

where $E(n_i) = np_{i,0}$ is the **expected cell count,** that is, the expected number of outcomes of type i assuming that H_0 is true. The total sample size is n.

Rejection region: $\chi^2 > \chi^2_\alpha$,

where χ^2_α has $(k - 1)$ df.

Assumptions:
1. A multinomial experiment has been conducted. This is generally satisfied by taking a random sample from the population of interest.
2. The sample size n will be large enough so that for every cell, the expected cell count $E(n_i)$ will be equal to 5 or more.*

Solution Define the population proportions for the three pay increase categories to be:

p_1 = Proportion of employees who receive no pay increase

p_2 = Proportion of employees who receive a standard increase

p_3 = Proportion of employees who receive a merit increase

Then the null hypothesis representing the distribution of percentages in the firm's proposed plan is:

$$H_0\text{: } p_1 = .10,\ p_2 = .65,\ p_3 = .25$$

and the alternative is

H_a: At least two of the proportions differ from the firm's proposed plan

$$\textit{Test statistic: } \chi^2 = \sum \frac{[n_i - E(n_i)]^2}{E(n_i)}$$

where

*The assumption that all expected cell counts are at least 5 is necessary in order to ensure that the χ^2 approximation is appropriate. Exact methods for conducting the test of a hypothesis exist and may be used for small expected cell counts, but these methods are beyond the scope of this text.

$$E(n_1) = np_{1,0} = 600(.10) = 60$$
$$E(n_2) = np_{2,0} = 600(.65) = 390$$
$$E(n_3) = np_{3,0} = 600(.25) = 150$$

Since all these values are larger than 5, the χ^2 approximation is appropriate.

Rejection region: For $\alpha = .01$ and df $= k - 1 = 2$, reject H_0 if $\chi^2 > \chi^2_{.01}$, where (from Table VII of Appendix B) $\chi^2_{.01} = 9.21034$.

We now calculate the test statistic:

$$\chi^2 = \frac{(42 - 60)^2}{60} + \frac{(365 - 390)^2}{390} + \frac{(193 - 150)^2}{150} = 19.33$$

CHI-SQUARE	P-VALUE
19.33	6.34664E-05

FIGURE 8.4
EXCEL analysis of data in Table 8.3

This value exceeds the table value of χ^2 (9.21034); therefore, the data provide strong evidence $(\alpha = .01)$ that the company's actual pay plan distribution differs from its proposed plan.

The χ^2 test can also be conducted using an available statistical software package. Figure 8.4 is a portion of an EXCEL printout of the analysis of the data in Table 8.3; note that the p-value of the test is .0000634664. Since $\alpha = .01$ exceeds this p-value, there is sufficient evidence to reject H_0.

If we focus on one particular outcome of a multinomial experiment, we can use the methods developed in Section 5.3 for a binomial proportion to establish a confidence interval for any one of the multinomial probabilities.* For example, if we want a 95% confidence interval for the proportion of the company's employees who will receive merit increases under the new system, we calculate

$$\hat{p}_3 \pm 1.96\sigma_{\hat{p}_3} \approx \hat{p}_3 \pm 1.96\sqrt{\frac{\hat{p}_3(1 - \hat{p}_3)}{n}} \quad \text{where } \hat{p}_3 = \frac{n_3}{n} = \frac{193}{600} = .32$$

$$= .32 \pm 1.96\sqrt{\frac{(.32)(1 - .32)}{600}} = .32 \pm .04$$

Thus, we estimate that between 28% and 36% of the firm's employees will qualify for merit increases under the new plan. It appears that the firm will have to raise the requirements for merit increases in order to achieve the stated goal of a 25% employee qualification rate.

EXERCISES 8.23–8.37

Learning the Mechanics

8.23 Use Table VII of Appendix B to find each of the following χ^2 values:
a. $\chi^2_{.05}$ for df = 10
b. $\chi^2_{.990}$ for df = 50
c. $\chi^2_{.10}$ for df = 16
d. $\chi^2_{.005}$ for df = 50

8.24 Find the rejection region for a one-dimensional χ^2 test of a null hypothesis concerning $p_1, p_2, \ldots, p_k$ if

*Note that focusing on one outcome has the effect of lumping the other $(k - 1)$ outcomes into a single group. Thus, we obtain, in effect, two outcomes—or a binomial experiment.

a. $k = 3$; $\alpha = .05$
b. $k = 5$; $\alpha = .10$
c. $k = 4$; $\alpha = .01$

8.25 a. What are the characteristics of a multinomial experiment? Compare the characteristics to those of a binomial experiment.
b. What conditions must n satisfy to make the χ^2 test valid?

8.26 A multinomial experiment with $k = 3$ cells and $n = 320$ produced the data shown in the following one-way table. Do these data provide sufficient evidence to contradict the null hypothesis that $p_1 = .25$, $p_2 = .25$, and $p_3 = .50$? Test using $\alpha = .05$.

	Cell		
	1	2	3
n_i	78	60	182

8.27 A multinomial experiment with $k = 4$ cells and $n = 205$ produced the data shown in the one-way table below.
a. Do these data provide sufficient evidence to conclude that the multinomial probabilities differ? Test using $\alpha = .05$.
b. What are the Type I and Type II errors associated with the test of part **a**?

	Cell			
	1	2	3	4
n_i	43	56	59	47

8.28 Refer to Exercise 8.27. Construct a 95% confidence interval for the multinomial probability associated with cell 3.

Applying the Concepts

8.29 M&M's plain chocolate candies come in six different colors: dark brown, yellow, red, orange, green, and blue. According to the manufacturer (Mars, Inc.), the color ratio in each large production batch is 30% brown, 20% yellow, 20% red, 10% orange, 10% green, and 10% blue. To test this claim, a professor at Carleton College (Minnesota) had students count the colors of M&M's found in "fun size" bags of the candy (*Teaching Statistics*, Spring 1993). The results for 370 M&M's are displayed in the table below.

M&M.DAT

Brown	Yellow	Red	Orange	Green	Blue	Total
84	79	75	49	36	47	370

Source: Johnson, R.W. "Testing colour proportions of M&M's." *Teaching Statistics*, Vol. 15, No. 1, Spring 1993, p. 2 (Table 1).

a. Assuming the manufacturer's stated percentages are accurate, calculate the expected numbers falling into the six categories.
b. Calculate the value of χ^2 for testing the manufacturer's claim.
c. Conduct a test to determine whether the true percentages of the colors produced differ from the manufacturer's stated percentages. Use $\alpha = .05$.

8.30 *Bon Appetit* magazine polled 200 of its readers concerning which of the four vegetables—brussel sprouts, okra, lima beans, and cauliflower—is their least favorite. The results (adapted from *Adweek*, Feb. 21, 2000) are presented in the table. Let p_1, p_2, p_3, and p_4 represent the proportions of all *Bon Appetit* readers who indicate brussel sprouts, okra, lima beans, and cauliflower, respectively, as their least favorite vegetable.

BONAPP.DAT

Brussel Sprouts	Okra	Lima Beans	Cauliflower
46	76	44	34

a. If, in general, *Bon Appetit* readers do not have a preference for their least favorite vegetable, what are the values of p_1, p_2, p_3, and p_4?
b. Specify the null and alternative hypotheses that should be used to determine whether *Bon Appetit* readers have a preference for one of the vegetables as "least favorite."
c. Conduct the test you described in part **b** using $\alpha = .05$. Report your conclusion in the context of the problem.
d. What assumptions must hold to ensure the validity of the test you conducted in part **c**? Which, if any, of these assumptions may be a concern in this application?

8.31 In order to study consumer preferences for health care reform in the U.S., researchers from the University of Michigan surveyed 500 U.S. households (*Journal of Consumer Affairs,* Winter 1999). Heads of household were asked whether they are in favor of, neutral about, or opposed to a national health insurance program in which all Americans are covered and costs are paid by tax dollars. The 434 useable responses are summarized in the table below. A STATISTIX printout of the analysis of the data is shown on p. 443.

 **HEALTH.DAT**

Favor	Neutral	Oppose
234	119	81

Source: Hong, G., and White-Means, S. "Consumer Preferences for Health Care Reform," *Journal of Consumer Affairs,* Vol 33, No. 2, Winter 1999, pp. 237–253.

STATISTIX Output for Exercise 8.31

```
MULTINOMIAL TEST

HYPOTHESIZED PROPORTIONS VARIABLE: HYPPROP
OBSERVED FREQUENCIES VARIABLE:     NUMBER

           HYPOTHESIZED  OBSERVED    EXPECTED    CHI-SQUARE
CATEGORY    PROPORTION   FREQUENCY   FREQUENCY   CONTRIBUTION
   1          0.33333       234       144.67        55.16
   2          0.33333       119       144.67         4.55
   3          0.33333        81       144.67        28.02

OVERALL CHI-SQUARE      87.74
P-VALUE                0.0000
DEGREES OF FREEDOM          2
```

a. Is there sufficient evidence to conclude that opinions are not evenly divided on the issue of national health insurance? Conduct the appropriate test using $\alpha = .01$.
b. Construct a 95% confidence interval for the proportion of heads of household in the U.S. population who favor national health insurance.

8.32 Interferons are proteins produced naturally by the human body that help fight infections and regulate the immune system. A drug developed from interferons, called Avonex, is now available for treating patients with multiple sclerosis (MS). In a clinical study, 85 MS patients received weekly injections of Avonex over a two-year period. The number of exacerbations (i.e., flare-ups of symptoms) was recorded for each patient and is summarized in the accompanying table. For MS patients who take a placebo (no drug) over a similar two-week period, it is known from previous studies that 26% will experience no exacerbations, 30% one exacerbation, 11% two exacerbations, 14% three exacerbations, and 19% four or more exacerbations.

AVONEX.DAT

Number of Exacerbations	Number of Patients
0	32
1	26
2	15
3	6
4 or more	6

Source: Biogen, Inc., 1997.

a. Conduct a test to determine whether the exacerbation distribution of MS patients who take Avonex differs from the percentages reported for placebo patients. Test using $\alpha = .05$
b. Find a 95% confidence interval for the true percentage of Avonex MS patients who are exacerbation–free during a two-year period.
c. Refer to part **b.** Is there evidence that Avonex patients are more likely to have no exacerbations than placebo patients? Explain.

8.33 *Inc. Technology* (Mar. 18, 1997) reported the results of the 1996 Equifax/Harris Consumer Privacy Survey in which 328 Internet users indicated their level of agreement with the following statement: "The government needs to be able to scan Internet messages and user communications to prevent fraud and other crimes." The number of users in each response category is summarized below.

GOVWEB.DAT

Agree Strongly	Agree Somewhat	Disagree Somewhat	Disagree Strongly
59	108	82	79

a. Specify the null and alternative hypotheses you would use to determine if the opinions of Internet users are evenly divided among the four categories.
b. Conduct the test of part **a** using $\alpha = .05$.
c. In the context of this exercise, what is a Type I error? A Type II error?
d. What assumptions must hold in order to ensure the validity of the test you conducted in part **b**?

8.34 Data from supermarket scanners are used by researchers to understand the purchasing patterns and preferences of consumers. Researchers frequently study the purchases of a sample of households, called a *scanner panel.* When shopping, these households present a magnetic identification card that permits their purchase data to be identified and aggregated. Marketing researchers recently studied the extent to which panel households' purchase behavior is representative of the population of households shopping at the same stores (*Marketing Research,* Nov. 1996). The table below reports the peanut butter purchase data collected by A. C. Nielsen Company for a panel of 2,500 households in Sioux Falls, SD, over a 102-week period. The market share percentages in the right column are derived from all peanut butter purchases at the same 15 stores at which the panel shopped during the same 102-week period.

a. Do the data provide sufficient evidence to conclude that the purchases of the household panel are representative of the population of households? Test using $\alpha = .05$.

SCANNER.DAT

Brand	Size	Number of Purchases by Household Panel	Market Shares
Jif	18 oz.	3,165	20.10%
Jif	28	1,892	10.10
Jif	40	726	5.42
Peter Pan	10	4,079	16.01
Skippy	18	6,206	28.65
Skippy	28	1,627	12.38
Skippy	40	1,420	7.32
Total		19,115	

Source: Gupta, S., *et. al.* "Do household scanner data provide representative inferences from brand choices? A comparison with store data." *Journal of Marketing Research,* Vol. 33, Nov. 1996, p. 393 (Table 6).

b. What assumptions must hold to ensure the validity of the testing procedure you used in part **a**?

c. Find the approximate p-value for the test of part **a** and interpret it in the context of the problem.

8.35 Each year, approximately 1.3 million Americans suffer adverse drug effects (ADEs), that is, unintended injuries caused by prescribed medication. A study in the *Journal of the American Medical Association* (July 5, 1995) identified the cause of 247 ADEs that occurred at two Boston hospitals. The researchers found that dosing errors (that is, wrong dosage prescribed and/or dispensed) were the most common.

ADE.DAT

Wrong Dosage Cause	Number of ADEs
(1) Lack of knowledge of drug	29
(2) Rule violation	17
(3) Faulty dose checking	13
(4) Slips	9
(5) Other	27

The previous table summarizes the proximate cause of 95 ADEs that resulted from a dosing error. Conduct a test (at $\alpha = .10$) to determine whether the true percentages of ADEs in the five "cause" categories are different. Use the accompanying EXCEL printout to arrive at your decision.

EXCEL Output for Exercise 8.35

CAUSE	ADEs
NO KNOWLEDGE	29
RULE VIOLATE	17
FAULTY DOSE	13
SLIPS	9
OTHER	27
CHI-SQUARE	16
P-VALUE	0.003019

8.36 In education, the term *instructional technology* refers to products such as computers, spreadsheets, CD-ROMs, videos, and presentation software. How frequently do professors use instructional technology in the classroom? To answer this question, researchers at Western Michigan University surveyed 306 of their fellow faculty (*Educational Technology,* Mar.–Apr. 1995). Responses to the frequency-of-technology use in teaching were recorded as "weekly to every class," "once a semester to monthly," or "never." The faculty responses (number in each response category) for the three technologies are summarized in the next table.

TECHUSE.DAT

Technology	Weekly	Once a Semester/ Monthly	Never
Computer spreadsheets	58	67	181
Word processing	168	61	77
Statistical software	37	82	187

a. Determine whether the percentages in the three frequency-of-use response categories differ for computer spreadsheets. Use $\alpha = .01$.

b. Repeat part **a** for word processing.

c. Repeat part **a** for statistical software.

d. Construct a 99% confidence interval for the true percentage of faculty who never use computer spreadsheets in the classroom. Interpret the interval.

8.37 Although illegal, overloading is common in the trucking industry. A state highway planning agency (Minnesota Department of Transportation) monitored the movements of overweight trucks on an interstate highway using an unmanned, computerized scale that is built into the highway. Unknown to the truckers, the scale weighed their vehicles as they passed over it. Each day's proportion of one week's total truck traffic (five-axle tractor truck semitrailers) is shown in the first table below. During the same week, the number of overweight trucks per day is given in the second table.

a. The planning agency would like to know whether the number of overweight trucks per week is distributed over the seven days of the week in direct proportion to the volume of truck traffic. Test using $\alpha = .05$.

b. Find the approximate p-value for the test of part **a**.

OVERLOAD.DAT

Monday	Tuesday	Wednesday	Thursday	Friday	Saturday	Sunday
.191	.198	.187	.180	.155	.043	.046

Monday	Tuesday	Wednesday	Thursday	Friday	Saturday	Sunday
90	82	72	70	51	18	31

8.4 CONTINGENCY TABLE ANALYSIS

In Section 8.3, we introduced the multinomial probability distribution and considered data classified according to a single qualitative criterion. We now consider multinomial experiments in which the data are classified according to two qualitative criteria, that is, *classification with respect to two factors.*

For example, high gasoline prices have made many consumers more aware of the size of the automobiles they purchase. Suppose an automobile manufacturer is interested in determining the relationship between the size and manufacturer of newly purchased automobiles. One thousand recent buyers of cars made in the United States are randomly sampled, and each purchase is classified with respect to the size and manufacturer of the automobile. The data are summarized in the **two-way table** shown in Table 8.4. This table is called a **contingency table;** it presents multinomial count data classified on two scales, or **dimensions, of classification**—namely, automobile size and manufacturer.

TABLE 8.4 Contingency Table for Automobile Size Example

		Manufacturer				
		A	B	C	D	Totals
Auto Size	Small	157	65	181	10	413
	Intermediate	126	82	142	46	396
	Large	58	45	60	28	191
	Totals	341	192	383	84	1,000

The symbols representing the cell counts for the multinomial experiment in Table 8.4 are shown in Table 8.5a; and the corresponding cell, row, and column probabilities are shown in Table 8.5b. Thus, n_{11} represents the number of buyers who purchase a small car of manufacturer A and p_{11} represents the corresponding cell probability. Note the symbols for the row and column totals and also the symbols for the probability totals. The latter are called **marginal probabilities** for

TABLE 8.5a Observed Counts for Contingency Table 8.4

		Manufacturer				
		A	B	C	D	Totals
Auto Size	Small	n_{11}	n_{12}	n_{13}	n_{14}	r_1
	Intermediate	n_{21}	n_{22}	n_{23}	n_{24}	r_2
	Large	n_{31}	n_{32}	n_{33}	n_{34}	r_3
	Totals	c_1	c_2	c_3	c_4	n

TABLE 8.5b Probabilities for Contingency Table 8.4

		Manufacturer				
		A	B	C	D	Totals
Auto Size	Small	p_{11}	p_{12}	p_{13}	p_{14}	p_{r1}
	Intermediate	p_{21}	p_{22}	p_{23}	p_{24}	p_{r2}
	Large	p_{31}	p_{32}	p_{33}	p_{34}	p_{r3}
	Totals	p_{c1}	p_{c2}	p_{c3}	p_{c4}	1

each row and column. The marginal probability p_{r1} is the probability that a small car is purchased; the marginal probability p_{c1} is the probability that a car by manufacturer A is purchased. Thus,

$$p_{r1} = p_{11} + p_{12} + p_{13} + p_{14} \quad \text{and} \quad p_{c1} = p_{11} + p_{21} + p_{31}$$

Thus, we can see that this really is a multinomial experiment with a total of 1,000 trials, (3)(4) = 12 cells or possible outcomes, and probabilities for each cell as shown in Table 8.5b. If the 1,000 recent buyers are randomly chosen, the trials are considered independent and the probabilities are viewed as remaining constant from trial to trial.

Suppose we want to know whether the two classifications, manufacturer and size, are dependent. That is, if we know which size car a buyer will choose, does that information give us a clue about the manufacturer of the car the buyer will choose? In a probabilistic sense we know (Chapter 3) that independence of events A and B implies $P(\text{AB}) = P(\text{A})P(\text{B})$. Similarly, in the contingency table analysis, if the **two classifications are independent,** the probability that an item is classified in any particular cell of the table is the product of the corresponding marginal probabilities. Thus, under the hypothesis of independence, in Table 8.5b, we must have

$$p_{11} = p_{r1}p_{c1}$$
$$p_{12} = p_{r1}p_{c2}$$

and so forth.

To test the hypothesis of independence, we use the same reasoning employed in the one-dimensional tests of Section 8.3. First, we calculate the *expected,* or *mean, count in each cell* assuming that the null hypothesis of independence is true. We do this by noting that the expected count in a cell of the table is just the total number of multinomial trials, n, times the cell probability. Recall that n_{ij} represents the **observed count** in the cell located in the ith row and jth column. Then the expected cell count for the upper lefthand cell (first row, first column) is

$$E(n_{11}) = np_{11}$$

or, when the null hypothesis (the classifications are independent) is true,

$$E(n_{11}) = np_{r1}p_{c1}$$

Since these true probabilities are not known, we estimate p_{r1} and p_{c1} by the same proportions $\hat{p}_{r1} = r_1/n$ and $\hat{p}_{c1} = c_1/n$. Thus, the estimate of the expected value $E(n_{11})$ is

$$\hat{E}(n_{11}) = n\left(\frac{r_1}{n}\right)\left(\frac{c_1}{n}\right) = \frac{r_1c_1}{n}$$

Similarly, for each i, j,

$$\hat{E}(n_{ij}) = \frac{\text{(Row total)(Column total)}}{\text{Total sample size}}$$

Thus,

$$\hat{E}(n_{12}) = \frac{r_1c_2}{n}$$

$$\vdots \qquad \vdots$$

$$\hat{E}(n_{34}) = \frac{r_3c_4}{n}$$

Using the data in Table 8.4, we find

$$\hat{E}(n_{11}) = \frac{r_1c_1}{n} = \frac{(413)(341)}{1{,}000} = 140.833$$

$$\hat{E}(n_{12}) = \frac{r_1c_2}{n} = \frac{(413)(192)}{1{,}000} = 79.296$$

$$\vdots \qquad \vdots \qquad \vdots \qquad \vdots$$

$$\hat{E}(n_{34}) = \frac{r_3c_4}{n} = \frac{(191)(84)}{1{,}000} = 16.044$$

The observed data and the estimated expected values (in parentheses) are shown in Table 8.6.

TABLE 8.6 Observed and Estimated Expected (in Parentheses) Counts

		Manufacturer				
		A	B	C	D	Totals
Auto Size	Small	157 (140.833)	65 (79.296)	181 (158.179)	10 (34.692)	413
	Intermediate	126 (135.036)	82 (76.032)	142 (151.668)	46 (33.264)	396
	Large	58 (65.131)	45 (36.672)	60 (73.153)	28 (16.044)	191
	Totals	341	192	383	84	1,000

We now use the χ^2 statistic to compare the observed and expected (estimated) counts in each cell of the contingency table:

$$\chi^2 = \frac{[n_{11} - \hat{E}(n_{11})]^2}{\hat{E}(n_{11})} + \frac{[n_{12} - \hat{E}(n_{12})]^2}{\hat{E}(n_{12})} + \cdots + \frac{[n_{34} - \hat{E}(n_{34})]^2}{\hat{E}(n_{34})}$$

$$= \sum \frac{[n_{ij} - \hat{E}(n_{ij})]^2}{\hat{E}(n_{ij})}$$

Note: The use of $\sum$ in the context of a contingency table analysis refers to a sum over all cells in the table.

Substituting the data of Table 8.6 into this expression, we get

$$\chi^2 = \frac{(157 - 140.833)^2}{140.833} + \frac{(65 - 79.296)^2}{79.296} + \cdots + \frac{(28 - 16.044)^2}{16.044} = 45.81$$

Large values of χ^2 imply that the observed counts do not closely agree and hence that the hypothesis of independence is false. To determine how large χ^2 must be before it is too large to be attributed to chance, we make use of the fact that the sampling distribution of χ^2 is approximately a χ^2 probability distribution when the classifications are independent.

When testing the null hypothesis of independence in a two-way contingency table, the appropriate degrees of freedom will be $(r - 1)(c - 1)$, where r is the number of rows and c is the number of columns in the table.

For the size and make of automobiles example, the degrees of freedom for χ^2 is $(r - 1)(c - 1) = (3 - 1)(4 - 1) = 6$. Then, for $\alpha = .05$, we reject the hypothesis of independence when

$$\chi^2 > \chi^2_{.05} = 12.5916$$

Since the computed $\chi^2 = 45.81$ exceeds the value 12.5916, we conclude that the size and manufacturer of a car selected by a purchaser are dependent events.

The pattern of dependence can be seen more clearly by expressing the data as percentages. We first select one of the two classifications to be used as the base variable. In the automobile size preference example, suppose we select manufacturer as the classificatory variable to be the base. Next, we represent the responses for each level of the second categorical variable (size of automobile in our example) as a percentage of the subtotal for the base variable. For example, from Table 8.6 we convert the response for small car sales for manufacturer A (157) to a percentage of the total sales for manufacturer A (341). That is,

$$\left(\frac{157}{341}\right)100\% = 46\%$$

The conversions of all Table 8.6 entries are similarly computed, and the values are shown in Table 8.7. The value shown at the right of each row is the row's total expressed as a percentage of the total number of responses in the entire table. Thus, the small car percentage is $(413/1{,}000)(100\%) = 41\%$ (rounded to the nearest percent).

TABLE 8.7 Percentage of Car Sizes by Manufacturer

		Manufacturer				
		A	B	C	D	All
Auto Size	Small	46	34	47	12	41
	Intermediate	37	43	37	55	40
	Large	17	23	16	33	19
	Totals	100	100	100	100	100

If the size and manufacturer variables are independent, then the percentages in the cells of the table are expected to be approximately equal to the corresponding row percentages. Thus, we would expect the small car percentages for each of the four manufacturers to be approximately 41% if size and manufacturer are independent. The extent to which each manufacturer's percentage departs from this value determines the dependence of the two classifications, with greater variability of the row percentages meaning a greater degree of dependence. A plot of the percentages helps summarize the observed pattern. In Figure 8.5 we show the manufacturer (the base variable) on the horizontal axis, and the size percentages on the vertical axis. The "expected" percentages under the assumption of independence are shown as horizontal lines, and each observed value is represented by a symbol indicating the size category.

Figure 8.5 clearly indicates the reason that the test resulted in the conclusion that the two classifications in the contingency table are dependent. Note that the sales of manufacturers A, B, and C fall relatively close to the expected percentages under the assumption of independence. However, the sales of manufacturer D deviate significantly from the expected values, with much higher percentages for large and intermediate cars and a much smaller percentage for small cars than expected under independence. Also, manufacturer B deviates slightly from the expected pattern, with a greater percentage of intermediate than small car sales. Statistical measures of the degree of dependence and procedures for making comparisons of pairs of levels for classifications are available. They are beyond the scope of this text, but can be found in the references. We will, however, utilize descriptive summaries such as Figure 8.5 to examine the degree of dependence exhibited by the sample data.

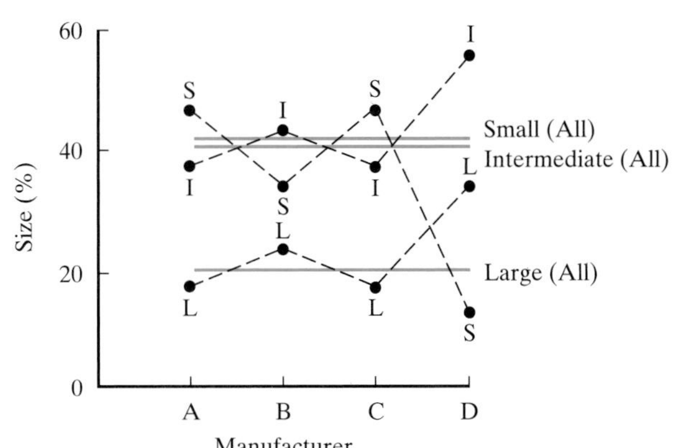

FIGURE 8.5

Size as a percentage of manufacturer subtotals

The general form of a two-way contingency table containing r rows and c columns (called an $r \times c$ contingency table) is shown in Table 8.8. Note that the observed count in the (ij) cell is denoted by n_{ij}, the ith row total is r_i, the jth column total is c_j, and the total sample size is n. Using this notation, we give the general form of the contingency table test for independent classifications in the next box.

TABLE 8.8 General $r \times c$ Contingency Table

		Column				
		1	2	...	c	Row Totals
Row	1	n_{11}	n_{12}	...	n_{1c}	r_1
	2	n_{21}	n_{22}	...	n_{2c}	r_2
	⋮	⋮	⋮		⋮	⋮
	r	n_{r1}	n_{r2}	...	n_{rc}	r_r
Column Totals		c_1	c_2	...	c_c	n

General Form of a Contingency Table Analysis: A Test for Independence

H_0: The two classifications are independent

H_a: The two classifications are dependent

Test statistic: $\chi^2 = \sum \frac{[n_{ij} - \hat{E}(n_{ij})]^2}{\hat{E}(n_{ij})}$

where $\hat{E}(n_{ij}) = \frac{r_i c_j}{n}$.

Rejection region: $\chi^2 > \chi^2_\alpha$, where χ^2_α has $(r-1)(c-1)$ df.

Assumptions:
1. The n observed counts are a random sample from the population of interest. We may then consider this to be a multinomial experiment with $r \times c$ possible outcomes.
2. The sample size, n, will be large enough so that, for every cell, the expected count, $E(n_{ij})$, will be equal to 5 or more.

EXAMPLE 8.5

A large brokerage firm wants to determine whether the service it provides to affluent clients differs from the service it provides to lower-income clients. A sample of 500 clients are selected, and each client is asked to rate his or her broker. The results are shown in Table 8.9.

a. Test to determine whether there is evidence that broker rating and customer income are independent. Use $\alpha = .10$.

TABLE 8.9 Survey Results (Observed Clients), Example 8.5

		Client's Income			
		Under $30,000	$30,000–$60,000	Over $60,000	Totals
Broker Rating	Outstanding	48	64	41	153
	Average	98	120	50	268
	Poor	30	33	16	79
	Totals	176	217	107	500

b. Plot the data and describe the patterns revealed. Is the result of the test supported by the plot?

Solution

a. The first step is to calculate estimated expected cell frequencies under the assumption that the classifications are independent. Rather than compute these values by hand, we resort to a computer. The SAS printout of the analysis of Table 8.9 is displayed in Figure 8.6. Each cell in Figure 8.6 contains the observed (top) and expected (bottom) frequency in that cell. Note that $\hat{E}(n_{11})$, the estimated expected count for the Outstanding, Under $30,000 cell is 53.856. Similarly, the estimated expected count for the Outstanding, $30,000–$60,000 cell is $\hat{E}(n_{12}) = 66.402$. Since all the estimated expected cell frequencies are greater than 5, the χ^2 approximation for the test statistic is appropriate. Assuming the clients chosen were randomly selected from all clients of the brokerage firm, the characteristics of the

FIGURE 8.6
SAS contingency table printout

```
                 TABLE OF RATING BY INCOME

RATING        INCOME

Frequency|          |          |          |
Expected |UNDER30K  |30K-60K   |OVER60K   |   Total
---------+----------+----------+----------+
OUTSTAND |      48  |      64  |      41  |    153
         |  53.856  |  66.402  |  32.742  |
---------+----------+----------+----------+
AVERAGE  |      98  |     120  |      50  |    268
         |  94.336  |  116.31  |  57.352  |
---------+----------+----------+----------+
POOR     |      30  |      33  |      16  |     79
         |  27.808  |  34.286  |  16.906  |
---------+----------+----------+----------+
Total          176        217        107        500

        STATISTICS FOR TABLE OF RATING BY INCOME

Statistic                          DF      Value     Prob
---------------------------------------------------------
Chi-Square                          4      4.278    0.370
Likelihood Ratio Chi-Square         4      4.184    0.382
Mantel-Haenszel Chi-Square          1      2.445    0.118
Phi Coefficient                            0.092
Contingency Coefficient                    0.092
Cramer's V                                 0.065

Sample Size = 500
```

TABLE 8.10 Broker Ratings as Percentage of Income Class

		Client's Income			
		Under $30,000	$30,000–$60,000	Over $60,000	Totals
Broker Rating	Outstanding	27	29	38	31
	Average	56	55	47	54
	Poor	17	15	15	16
	Totals	100	99*	100	101*

*Percentages do not add up to 100 because of rounding.

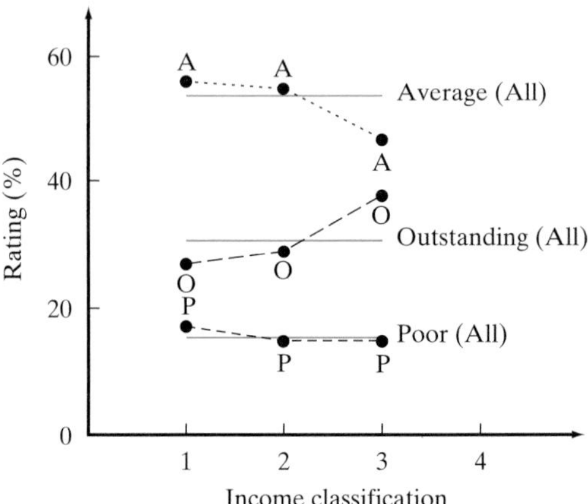

FIGURE 8.7
Plot of broker rating–customer income contingency table

multinomial probability distribution are satisfied. The null and alternative hypotheses we want to test are:

H_0: The rating a client gives his or her broker is independent of client's income

H_a: Broker rating and client income are dependent

The test statistic, $\chi^2 = 4.278$, is highlighted at the bottom of the printout as is the observed significance level (p-value) of the test. Since $\alpha = .10$ is less than $p = .370$, we fail to reject H_0. This survey does not support the firm's alternative hypothesis that affluent clients receive different broker service than lower-income clients.

b. The broker rating frequencies are expressed as percentages of income category frequencies in Table 8.10. The expected percentages under the assumption of independence are shown at the right of each row. The plot of the percentage data is shown in Figure 8.7, where the horizontal lines represent the expected percentages assuming independence. Note that the response percentages deviate only slightly from those expected under the assumption of independence, supporting the result of the test in part **a.** That is, neither the descriptive plot nor the statistical test provides evidence that the rating given the broker services depends on (varies with) the customer's income.

Using the TI-83 Graphing Calculator

Finding *p*-values for Contingency Tables on the TI-83

Start from the home screen.

Step 1 Access the Matrix Menu and enter your observed values as Matrix [A], and your expected values as Matrix [B].

Press **MATRIX**
Arrow right to **EDIT**
Press **ENTER**
Enter the dimensions of your observed Matrix
Enter all values
Press **MATRIX**
Arrow right to **EDIT**
Arrow down to **2:[B]**
Press **ENTER**
Enter the dimensions of the expected values Matrix
(It will be the same as step 1 above)
Enter all values

Step 2 Access the Statistical Tests Menu and perform the χ^2 Test.
Press **STAT**
Arrow right to **TESTS**
Arrow up to **C: χ^2 – Test...**
Press **ENTER**
Enter the names for the Observed and Expected Matrices
(Press Matrix arrow to desired Matrix, Press ENTER)
Arrow down to **Calculate**
Press **ENTER**
View Display

Step 3. Reject H_0 if the p-value $> \alpha$.

Example

Our Observed Matrix will be $[A] = \begin{bmatrix} 39 & 19 & 12 & 28 & 18 \\ 172 & 61 & 44 & 70 & 37 \end{bmatrix}$

Our Expected Matrix will be

$$[B] = \begin{bmatrix} 48.952 & 18.56 & 12.992 & 22.736 & 12.76 \\ 162.05 & 61.44 & 43.008 & 75.264 & 42.24 \end{bmatrix}$$

The hypotheses for this problem are as follows:

H_0: The Matrix entries represent Independent events.

H_a: The Matrix entries represent events that **are not** independent.

Step 1. Access Matrix Menu and enter all values
Press **MATRIX**
Arrow right to **EDIT**

(continued)

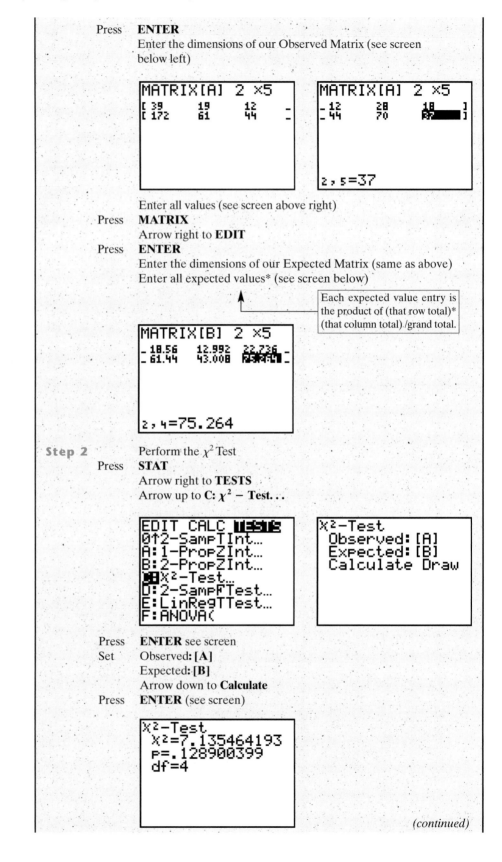

Press **ENTER**
Enter the dimensions of our Observed Matrix (see screen below left)

```
MATRIX[A] 2 ×5
[ 39    19    12   ]
[ 172   61    44   ]
```

```
MATRIX[A] 2 ×5
  12    28    18  ]
  44    70    37  ]

2,5=37
```

Enter all values (see screen above right)
Press **MATRIX**
Arrow right to **EDIT**
Press **ENTER**
Enter the dimensions of our Expected Matrix (same as above)
Enter all expected values* (see screen below)

Each expected value entry is the product of (that row total)* (that column total)/grand total.

```
MATRIX[B] 2 ×5
  18.56   12.992  22.736
  61.44   43.008  75.264

2,4=75.264
```

Step 2 Perform the χ^2 Test
Press **STAT**
Arrow right to **TESTS**
Arrow up to **C: χ^2 − Test. . .**

```
EDIT CALC TESTS
0↑2-SampTInt…
A:1-PropZInt…
B:2-PropZInt…
C:χ²-Test…
D:2-SampFTest…
E:LinRegTTest…
F:ANOVA(
```

```
χ²-Test
 Observed:[A]
 Expected:[B]
 Calculate Draw
```

Press **ENTER** see screen
Set Observed**: [A]**
Expected**: [B]**
Arrow down to **Calculate**
Press **ENTER** (see screen)

```
χ²-Test
 χ²=7.135464193
 p=.128900399
 df=4
```

(continued)

Step 3 **View Screen**

As you can see from the screen the p-value is 0.129. Since the p-value is **not less** than α we **do not** reject H_0.

Step 4 Clear screen for the next problem. Return to the home screen.
Press **CLEAR**

EXERCISES 8.38–8.49

Learning the Mechanics

8.38 Find the rejection region for a test of independence of two classifications where the contingency table contains r rows and c columns.

a. $r = 5, c = 5, \alpha = .05$
b. $r = 3, c = 6, \alpha = .10$
c. $r = 2, c = 3, \alpha = .01$

8.39 Consider the accompanying 2×3 (i.e., $r = 2$ and $c = 3$) contingency table.

LM8_39.DAT

		Column		
		1	2	3
Row	1	9	34	53
	2	16	30	25

a. Specify the null and alternative hypotheses that should be used in testing the independence of the row and column classifications.
b. Specify the test statistic and the rejection region that should be used in conducting the hypothesis test of part **a**. Use $\alpha = .01$.
c. Assuming the row classification and the column classification are independent, find estimates for the expected cell counts.
d. Conduct the hypothesis test of part **a**. Interpret your result.
e. Convert the frequency responses to percentages by calculating the percentage of each column total falling in each row. Also convert the row totals to percentages of the total number of responses. Display the percentages in a table.
f. Create a graph with percentage on the vertical axis and column number on the horizontal axis. Showing the row total percentages as horizontal lines on the graph, plot the cell percentages from part **a** using the row number as a plotting symbol.
g. What pattern do you expect to see if the rows and columns are independent? Does the plot support the result of the test of independence in part **d**?

8.40 Test the null hypothesis of independence of the two classifications, A and B, of the 3×3 contingency table shown here. Test using $\alpha = .05$.

LM8_40.DAT

		B		
		B_1	B_2	B_3
A	A_1	40	72	42
	A_2	63	53	70
	A_3	31	38	30

Applying the Concepts

8.41 In order to create a behavioral profile of pleasure travelers, M. Bonn (Florida State University), L. Forr (Georgia Southern University), and A. Susskind (Cornell University) interviewed 5,026 pleasure travelers in the Tampa Bay region (*Journal of Travel Research,* May 1999). Two of the characteristics they investigated were the travelers' education level and their use of the Internet

NETRAVEL.DAT

	USE INTERNET	
EDUCATION	Yes	No
College Degree or More	1,072	1,287
Less than a College Degree	640	2,027

Source: Bonn, M., Furr, L., and Susskind, A., "Predicting a Behavioral Profile for Pleasure Travelers on the Basis of Internet Use Segmentation," *Journal of Travel Research,* Vol. 37, May 1999, pp. 333–340.

to seek travel information. The table below summarizes the results of the interviews. The researchers concluded that travelers who use the Internet to search for travel information are likely to be people who are college educated. Do you agree? Test using $\alpha = .05$. What assumptions must hold to ensure the validity of your test?

8.42 During the 2000 U.S. presidential campaign, Senator John McCain and Governor George W. Bush competed for the Republican nomination. Immediately prior to the South Carolina primary election, *Newsweek* commissioned a telephone survey of 507 South Carolina voters who intended to vote in the Republican primary. The purpose was to determine where they stood on some of the important campaign issues. Of those surveyed, 218 were Bush supporters, 203 were McCain supporters, and the remainder favored neither. One question asked was: "Should most of the budget surplus be used to pay for a tax cut?" Of the Bush supporters, 61% said yes, 30% said no, and 9% were undecided. Of the McCain supporters, 42% said yes, 50% said no, and 8% were undecided (*Newsweek*, Feb. 21, 2000). Do the data provide sufficient evidence to conclude that a voter's position on the tax cut issue is related to his or her preferred presidential candidate? Test using $\alpha = .05$.

8.43 The *American Journal of Public Health* (July 1995) reported on a population-based study of trauma in Hispanic children. One of the objectives of the study was to compare the use of protective devices in motor vehicles used to transport Hispanic and non-Hispanic white children. On the basis of data collected from the San Diego County Regionalized Trauma System, 792 children treated for injuries sustained in vehicular accidents were classified according to ethnic status (Hispanic or non-Hispanic white) and seatbelt usage (worn or not worn) during the accident. The data are summarized in the table below.

TRAUMA.DAT

	Hispanic	Non-Hispanic White	Totals
Seatbelts worn	31	148	179
Seatbelts not worn	283	330	613
Totals	314	478	792

Source: Matteneci, R. M. *et al.* "Trauma among Hispanic children: A population-based study in a regionalized system of trauma care." *American Journal of Public Health,* Vol. 85, No. 7, July 1995, p. 1007 (Table 2).

a. Calculate the sample proportion of injured Hispanic children who were not wearing seatbelts during the accident.

b. Calculate the sample proportion of injured non-Hispanic white children who were not wearing seatbelts during the accident.

c. Compare the two sample proportions, parts **a** and **b**. Do you think the true population proportions differ?

d. Conduct a test to determine whether seatbelt usage in motor vehicle accidents depends on ethnic status in the San Diego County Regionalized Trauma System. Use $\alpha = .01$.

e. Construct a 99% confidence interval for the difference between the proportions, parts **a** and **b**. Interpret the interval.

8.44 To better understand whether and how Total Quality Management (TQM) is practiced in U.S. companies, University of Scranton researchers N. Tamimi and R. Sebastianelli interviewed one manager in each of a sample of 86 companies in Pennsylvania, New York, and New Jersey (*Production and Inventory Management Journal,* 1996). Concerning whether or not the firms were involved with TQM, the following data were obtained:

 **TQM.DAT**

	Service Firms	Manufacturing Firms
Number practicing TQM	34	23
Number not practicing TQM	18	11
Total	52	34

Source: Adapted from Tamimi, N., and Sebastianelli, R. "How firms define and measure quality." *Production and Inventory Management Journal,* Third Quarter, 1996, p. 35.

a. The researchers concluded that "manufacturing firms were not significantly more likely to be involved with TQM than service firms." Do you agree? Test using $\alpha = .05$.

b. Find and interpret the approximate p-value for the test you conducted in part **a**.

c. What assumptions must hold in order for your test of part **a** and your p-value of part **b** to be valid?

8.45 For over 20 years, movie critics Gene Siskel (formerly of the *Chicago Tribune,* now deceased) and Roger Ebert (*Chicago Sun-Times*) rated the latest film releases on national television, first on PBS with *Sneak Previews,* then in syndication with *At the Movies.* University of Florida statisticians examined data on 160 movie reviews by Siskel and Ebert during the period 1995–1996 (*Chance*, Spring 1997). Each critic's review was categorized as pro ("thumbs up"), con ("thumbs down"), or mixed. Consequently, each movie has a Siskel rating (pro, con, or mixed) and an Ebert rating (pro, con, or mixed). A summary of the data is provided in the SPSS printout on page 457.

a. Verify that the expected cell counts in the table are accurate.

b. Conduct a test of hypothesis to determine whether the movie reviews of the two critics are independent. Use $\alpha = .01$.

SPSS Output for Exercise 8.45

SISKEL * EBERT Crosstabulation

			EBERT			
			Con	Mix	Pro	Total
SISKEL	Con	Count	24	8	13	45
		Expected Count	11.8	8.4	24.8	45.0
	Mix	Count	8	13	11	32
		Expected Count	8.4	6.0	17.6	32.0
	Pro	Count	10	9	64	83
		Expected Count	21.8	15.6	45.7	83.0
Total		Count	42	30	88	160
		Expected Count	42.0	30.0	88.0	160.0

Chi-Square Tests

	Value	df	Asymp. Sig. (2-sided)
Pearson Chi-square	45.357[a]	4	.000
Likelihood Ratio	43.233	4	.000
N of Valid Cases	160		

a. 0 cells (.0%) have expected count less than 5. The minimum expected count is 6.00.

8.46 University of Louisville professor Julia Karcher conducted an experiment to investigate the ethical behavior of accountants (*Journal of Business Ethics*, Vol. 15, 1996). She focused on auditor abilities to detect ethical problems that may not be obvious. Seventy auditors from Big-Six accounting firms were given a detailed case study that contained several problems including tax evasion by the client. In 35 of the cases the tax evasion issue was severe; in the other 35 cases it was moderate. The auditors were asked to identify any problems they detected in the case. The following table summarizes the results for the ethical issue.

ACCETHIC.DAT

	Severity of Ethical Issue	
	Moderate	Severe
Ethical Issue Identified	27	26
Ethical Issue Not Identified	8	9

Source: Karcher, J. "Auditors' ability to discern the presence of ethical problems." *Journal of Business Ethics*, Vol. 15, 1996, p. 1041 (Table V).

a. Did the severity of the ethical issue influence whether the issue was identified or not by the auditors? Test using $\alpha = .05$.

b. Suppose the lefthand column of the table contained the counts 35 and 0 instead of 27 and 8. Should the test of part **a** still be conducted? Explain.

c. Keeping the sample size the same, change the numbers in the contingency table so that the answer you would get for the question posed in part **a** changes.

8.47 Many companies use well-known celebrities in their ads, while other companies create their own spokespersons (such as the Maytag repairman). A study in the *Journal of Marketing* (Fall 1992) investigated the relationship between the gender of the spokesperson and the gender of the viewer in order to see how this relationship affected brand awareness. Three hundred television viewers were asked to identify the products advertised by celebrity spokespersons. The results are presented in two tables on page 460.

a. For the products advertised by male spokespersons, conduct a test to determine whether audience gender and product identification are dependent factors. Test using $\alpha = .05$.

STATISTICS IN Action

Ethics in Computer Technology and Use

Ethics refers to a set of rules or principles used for moral decision-making. Employees in the computer industry face ethical problems every day in the workplace. Illegal and improper actions are practiced knowingly and unknowingly by computer technology users. Some recent examples of unethical practices include Robert Morris's introduction of a "worm" into the Internet and software copyright infringements by several reputable colleges and universities.

Professors Margaret A. Pierce and John W. Henry of Georgia Southern University explored the ethical decision-making behavior of users of computers and computer technology and published their results in the *Journal of Business Ethics* (Vol. 15, 1996). Three primary influencing factors were considered by Pierce and Henry: (1) the individual's own personal code of ethics; (2) any informal code of ethical behavior that is operative in the workplace; and (3) the company's formal code of computer ethics (i.e., policies regarding computer technology).

The researchers mailed a computer ethics questionnaire to a random sample of 2,551 information systems (IS) professionals selected from members of the Data Processing Management Association (DPMA). The issues and questions addressed are given in Figure 8.8. Approximately 14% of the questionnaires were returned, yielding a total of 356 usable responses. Table 8.11 gives a breakdown of the respondents by industry type. Tables 8.12 (What Type of Code Is Important in Making Ethical Decisions?) and 8.13 (Which Code Do You Use?) summarize the responses to two questions and their relationship to the three influencing factors identified by the researchers. (The tables show the number of responses in each category. Due to nonresponse for some questions, the sample size is less than 356.)

Focus

a. Does the existence of a company code of ethics influence computer users' perceptions of the importance of formal, informal, and personal ethics codes? If so, investigate the pattern of dependence by plotting the appropriate percentages on a graph.

b. Does the position of the computer user (professional or employee) influence the use of formal, informal, and personal ethics codes? If so, investigate the pattern of dependence by plotting the appropriate percentages on a graph.

c. With respect to industry type, is the sample of returned questionnaires representative of the 2,551 IS professionals who were mailed the survey? Explain.

Part I. Please answer the following statements/questions regarding ethics. In all parts of this survey "ethics" is defined as ethics related to computer technology/computer use. "Your company" refers to the organization or educational institution where you work.

1. Gender: Female ________ male ________
2. Your age on your last birthday. ________
3. Education (Please circle the highest level attained.) (1) high school (2) 2-yr college (3) 4-yr college (4) master's (5) doctorate
4. Circle the category which best describes your position. (1) CS/MIS educator (2) other educator (3) programmer (4) DP manager (5) system supervisor (6) other ______
5. Do you hold any professional certification or license? (1) no (2) yes, please specify ________
6. Number of years: (1) in profession ________ (2) with present employer ________
7. Type of company you work for: (Please circle one or specify.) (1) Manufacture (2) Government (3) Education (4) Finance (5) Utilities (6) Service (7) Consulting (8) Wholesale/retail (9) Other (specify) ________
8. Size of company (Number of employees) ________
9. Do you think of yourself as (Please circle one.) (1) DP/computer professional (2) an employee of the company
10. Circle the professional organizations listed to which you belong. (1) DPMA (2) ACM (3) IEEE-CS
11. (a) Are you familiar with any of the codes of ethics of the above professional organizations? (1) yes (2) no
    (b) If yes which one(s)? (1) DPMA (2) ACM (3) IEEE-CS
    (c) If yes do you use the code(s) to guide your own behavior? (1) yes (2) no
12. Have you had any formal study concerning theories of ethics or ethical behavior? (1) yes (2) no

FIGURE 8.8 Computer ethics questionnaire, Part I

Part II. Please respond to the following statements/questions about a formal company code of ethics (stated in writing or orally, representing the official position of the company), an informal code of ethics (ethical behavior actually practiced in the workplace), and a personal code of ethics (your own principles) related to computer use/computer technology.

1. Does your company have a formal company code of ethics? (1) yes (2) no
   (If there is a written code, please include a copy of the code.)
2. Which code of ethics is most important in guiding the behavior of employees where you work? (1) formal code (if there is one) (2) informal code (3) personal code
3. Which code of ethics do *you* use most frequently to guide ethical decisions? (1) formal code (if there is one) (2) informal code (3) personal code
4. These codes of ethics are deterrents to unethical behavior.
   a. formal company code of ethics — strongly agree 1 2 3 4 5 strongly disagree
   b. informal code of ethics — strongly agree 1 2 3 4 5 strongly disagree
   c. personal code of ethics — strongly agree 1 2 3 4 5 strongly disagree
5. There are opportunities in my company to engage in unethical behavior. — strongly agree 1 2 3 4 5 strongly disagree
6. Many people in my company engage in what I consider unethical behavior. — strongly agree 1 2 3 4 5 strongly disagree
7. I am aware of the specifics of the informal company code of ethics. — strongly agree 1 2 3 4 5 strongly disagree
8. I have a well-formulated personal code of ethics related to computer use/computer technology — strongly agree 1 2 3 4 5 strongly disagree

FIGURE 8.8 Computer ethics questionnaire, Part II

Source: Margaret A. Pierce and John W. Henry, "Conputer ethics: The role of personal, informal, and formal codes," *Journal of Business Ethics,* Vol. 15/4, 1996, pp. 425–437. Reprinted with kind permission of Kluwer Academic Publishers, Margaret Pierce, and John W. Henry.

TABLE 8.11 TAB8_11.DAT

Industry Type	Number Returned	Percent in Original Sample of 2,551
Manufacturing	67	19
DP Service/Consult	57	16
Utilities	20	5.5
Wholesale/Retail	18	5
Financial/Real Estate	42	12
Education/Medical/Legal	80	22
Government	21	6
Other	51	14.5
Total	356	100.0

Source: Pierce, M. A., and Henry, J. W. "Computer ethics: The role of personal, informal, and formal codes." *Journal of Business Ethics,* Vol. 15, 1996, p. 429 (Table I).

TABLE 8.12 TAB8_12.DAT

	Company Code	
Code	Yes	No
Formal	51	6
Informal	47	69
Personal	70	100

Source: Pierce, M. A., and Henry, J. W. "Computer ethics: The role of personal, informal, and formal codes." *Journal of Business Ethics,* Vol. 15, 1996, p. 431 (Table II).

TABLE 8.13 TAB8_13.DAT

	Position	
Ethics Code	IS Professional	Employee
Formal	27	2
Informal	34	5
Personal	208	63

Source: Pierce, M. A., and Henry, J. W. "Computer ethics: The role of personal, informal, and formal codes." *Journal of Business Ethics,* Vol. 15, 1996, p. 432 (Table IV).

b. Repeat part **a** for the products advertised by female spokespersons.
c. How would you interpret these results?

MALEAD.DAT

Male Spokesperson

	Audience Gender		
	Male	Female	Total
Identified Product	95	41	136
Could Not Identify Product	55	109	164
Total	150	150	300

 **FEMALEAD.DAT**

Female Spokesperson

	Audience Gender		
	Male	Female	Total
Identified Product	47	61	108
Could Not Identify Product	103	89	192
Total	150	150	300

8.48 To study the extent and nature of strategic planning being undertaken by boards of directors, A. Tashakori and W. Boulton questioned a sample of 119 chief executive officers of major U.S. corporations (*Journal of Business Strategy*, Winter 1983). One objective was to determine if a relationship exists between the composition of a board—i.e., a majority of outside directors versus a majority of in-house directors—and its level of participation in the strategic planning process. The questionnaire data were used to classify the responding corporations according to the level of their board's participation in the strategic planning process as follows:

Level 1: Board participates in formulation or implementation or evaluation of strategy

Level 2: Board participates in formulation and implementation, formulation and evaluation, or implementation and evaluation of strategy

Level 3: Board participates in formulation, implementation, and evaluation of strategy

The 119 boards were also classified according to whether a majority of their directors were from inside the firm or outside the firm. The data are summarized in the SAS printout below.

a. The researchers concluded that a relationship exists between a board's level of participation in the strategic planning process and the composition of the

SAS Output for Exercise 8.48

```
                    TABLE OF LEVEL BY COMPOSIT

          LEVEL      COMPOSIT

          Frequency|         |         |
          Expected |INSIDE   |OUTSIDE  |  Total
          ---------+---------+---------+
                 1 |       2 |      20 |     22
                   |  3.5126 |  18.487 |
          ---------+---------+---------+
                 2 |      10 |      27 |     37
                   |  5.9076 |  31.092 |
          ---------+---------+---------+
                 3 |       7 |      53 |     60
                   |  9.5798 |   50.42 |
          ---------+---------+---------+
          Total          19       100      119

       STATISTICS FOR TABLE OF LEVEL BY COMPOSIT

Statistic                        DF      Value      Prob
--------------------------------------------------------
Chi-Square                        2      4.976     0.083
Likelihood Ratio Chi-Square       2      4.696     0.096
Mantel-Haenszel Chi-Square        1      0.120     0.729
Phi Coefficient                          0.204
Contingency Coefficient                  0.200
Cramer's V                               0.204

Sample Size = 119
```

board. Do you agree? Construct the appropriate contingency table, and test using $\alpha = .10$.

b. In the context of this problem, specify the Type I and Type II errors associated with the test of part **a**.

c. Construct a graph that helps to interpret the result of the test in part **a**.

8.49 Research has indicated that the stress produced by today's lifestyles results in health problems for a large proportion of society. An article in the *International Journal of Sports Psychology* (July–Sept. 1990) evaluated the relationship between physical fitness and stress. Five hundred forty-nine employees of companies that participate in the Health Examination Program offered by Health Advancement Services (HAS) were classified into three groups of fitness levels: good, average, and poor. Each person was tested for signs of stress. The table reports the results for the three groups. [*Note:* The proportions given are the proportions of the entire group that show signs of stress and fall into each particular fitness level.] Do the data provide evidence to indicate that the likelihood for stress is dependent on an employee's fitness level?

Fitness Level	Sample Size	Proportions with Signs of Stress
Poor	242	.155
Average	212	.133
Good	95	.108

QUICK REVIEW

Key Terms

Chi-square distribution 438
Chi-square test 438
Contingency table 445
Count data 437
Dimensions of classification 445
Expected cell count 440
Independence of two classifications 446
Marginal probabilities 445
Multinomial experiment 437
Multinomial probability distribution 437
Observed cell count 447
One-way table 440
Sampling distribution of $\hat{p}_1 - \hat{p}_2$ 429
Two-way table 445

Key Formulas

$$(\hat{p}_1 - \hat{p}_2) \pm z_{\alpha/2}\sqrt{\frac{\hat{p}_1\hat{q}_1}{n_1} + \frac{\hat{p}_2\hat{q}_2}{n_2}}$$

Confidence interval for $p_1 - p_2$ 430

$$z = \frac{(\hat{p}_1 - \hat{p}_2) - 0}{\sqrt{\hat{p}\hat{q}\left(\frac{1}{n_1} + \frac{1}{n_2}\right)}}$$

where $\hat{p} = \frac{x_1 + x_2}{n_1 + n_2}$

$\hat{q} = 1 - \hat{p}$

Test statistic for H_0: $(p_1 - p_2) = 0$ 431

$$n_1 = n_2 = \frac{(z_{\alpha/2})^2(p_1q_1 + p_2q_2)}{B^2}$$

Sample size for estimating $p_1 - p_2$ 436

$$\chi^2 = \sum \frac{[n_i - E(n_i)]^2}{E(n_i)}$$

where n_i = count for cell i

$E(n_i) = np_{i,0}$

$p_{i,0}$ = hypothesized value of p_i in H_0

χ^2 test for one-way table 440

$$\chi^2 = \sum \frac{[n_{ij} - \hat{E}(n_{ij})]^2}{\hat{E}(n_{ij})}$$

where n_{ij} = count for cell in row i, column j

$\hat{E}(n_{ij}) = r_ic_j/n$

r_i = total for row i

c_j = total for column j

n = total sample size

χ^2 test for two-way table 450

LANGUAGE LAB

Symbol	Pronunciation	Description
$p_1 - p_2$	*p*-1 minus *p*-2	Difference between population proportions
$\hat{p}_1 - \hat{p}_2$	*p*-1 hat minus *p*-2 hat	Difference between sample proportions
$\sigma_{(\hat{p}_1 - \hat{p}_2)}$	sigma of *p*-1 hat minus *p*-2 hat	Standard deviation of the sampling distribution of $(\hat{p}_1 - \hat{p}_2)$
D_0	*D* naught	Hypothesized value of $p_1 - p_2$
$p_{i,0}$	*p*-*i*-zero	Value of multinomial probability p_i hypothesized in H_0
χ^2	Chi-square	Test statistic used in analysis of count data
n_i	*n*-*i*	Number of observed outcomes in cell *i* of one-way table
$E(n_i)$	Expected value of n_i	Expected number of outcomes in cell *i* of one-way table when H_0 is true
p_{ij}	*p*-*i*-*j*	Probability of an outcome in row *i* and column *j* of a two-way contingency table
n_{ij}	*n*-*i*-*j*	Number of observed outcomes in row *i* and column *j* of a two-way contingency table
$\hat{E}(n_{ij})$	Estimated expected value of n_{ij}	Estimated expected number of outcomes in row *i* and column *j* of a two-way contingency table
r_i	*r*-*i*	Total number of outcomes in row *i* of a contingency table
c_j	*c*-*j*	Total number of outcomes in column *j* of a contingency table

SUPPLEMENTARY EXERCISES 8.50–8.64

Learning the Mechanics

8.50 Independent random samples were selected from two binomial populations. The sizes and number of observed successes for each sample are shown in the table below.

Sample 1	Sample 2
$n_1 = 200$	$n_2 = 200$
$x_1 = 110$	$x_2 = 130$

a. Test H_0: $(p_1 - p_2) = 0$ against H_a: $(p_1 - p_2) < 0$. Use $\alpha = .10$.

b. Form a 95% confidence interval for $(p_1 - p_2)$.

c. What sample sizes would be required if we wish to use a 95% confidence interval of width .01 to estimate $(p_1 - p_2)$?

8.51 A random sample of 150 observations was classified into the categories shown in the table below.

LM8_51.DAT

	Category				
	1	2	3	4	5
n_i	28	35	33	25	29

a. Do the data provide sufficient evidence that the categories are not equally likely? Use $\alpha = .10$.

b. Form a 90% confidence interval for p_2, the probability that an observation will fall in category 2.

8.52 A random sample of 250 observations was classified according to the row and column categories shown in the table.

 **LM8_52.DAT**

		Column		
		1	2	3
Row	1	20	20	10
	2	10	20	70
	3	20	50	30

a. Do the data provide sufficient evidence to conclude that the rows and columns are dependent? Test using $\alpha = .05$.

b. Would the analysis change if the row totals were fixed before the data were collected?

c. Do the assumptions required for the analysis to be valid differ according to whether the row (or column) totals are fixed? Explain.

d. Convert the table entries to percentages by using each column total as a base and calculating each row response as a percentage of the corresponding column total. In addition, calculate the row totals and convert them to percentages of all 250 observations.

e. Plot the row percentages on the vertical axis against the column number on the horizontal axis. Draw horizontal lines corresponding to the row total percentages. Does the deviation (or lack thereof) of the individual row percentages from the row total percentages support the result of the test conducted in part **a?**

Applying the Concepts

8.53 According to a national survey of 1,441 firms by the American Management Association, downsizing is no longer the dominant theme in the workplace (*Newark Star-Ledger*, Oct. 22, 1996). But are there regional differences in this phenomenon? Is there more growth in jobs in the Sunbelt than the Rustbelt? Assuming equal sample sizes for the two regions, how large would the samples need to be to estimate the difference in the proportion of firms that plan to add new jobs in the next year in the two regions? A 90% confidence interval of width no more than .10 is desired.

8.54 The threat of earthquakes is a part of life in California, where scientists have warned about "the big one" for decades. An article in the *Annals of the Association of American Geographers* (June 1992) investigated what influences homeowners in purchasing earthquake insurance. One factor investigated was the proximity to a major fault. The researchers hypothesized that the nearer a county is to a major fault, the more likely residents are to own earthquake insurance. Suppose that a random sample of 700 earthquake-insured residents from four California counties is selected, and the number in each county is counted and recorded in the table:

EARTHQK.DAT

	Contra Costa	Santa Clara	Los Angeles	San Bernardino
Number Insured	103	213	241	143

a. What are the appropriate null and alternative hypotheses to test whether the proportions of all earthquake-insured residents in the four counties differ?

b. Do the data provide sufficient evidence that the proportions of all earthquake-insured residents differ among the four counties? Test using $\alpha = .05$.

c. Los Angeles County is closest to a major earthquake fault. Construct a 95% confidence interval for the proportion of all earthquake-insured residents in the four counties that reside in Los Angeles County.

d. Does the confidence interval you formed in part **c** support the conclusion of the test conducted in part **b**? Explain.

8.55 Research indicates that the highest priority of retirees is travel. A study in the *Annals of Tourism Research* (Vol. 19, 1992) investigates the relationship of retirement status (pre- and postretirement) to various items related to the travel industry. One part of the study investigated the differences in the length of stay of a trip for pre- and postretirees. A sample of 703 travelers were asked how long they stayed on a typical trip. The results are shown in the next table. Use the information in the table to determine whether the retirement status of a traveler and the duration of a typical trip are dependent. Test using $\alpha = .05$.

TRAVTRIP.DAT

Number of Nights	Preretirement	Postretirement
4–7	247	172
8–13	82	67
14–21	35	52
22 or more	16	32
Total	380	323

8.56 Because shareholders control the firm, they can transfer wealth from the firm's bondholders to themselves through several different dividend strategies. This potential conflict of interest between shareholders and bondholders can be reduced through the use of debt covenants. Accountants E. Griner and H. Huss of Georgia State University investigated the effects of insider ownership and the size of the firm on the types of debt covenants required by a firm's bondholders (*Journal of Applied Business Research*, Vol. 11, 1995). As part of the study, they examined a sample of 31 companies whose bondholders required covenants based on tangible assets rather than on liquidity or net assets or retained earnings. Characteristics of those 31 firms are summarized below. The objective of the study is to determine if there is a relationship between the extent of insider ownership and the size of the firm for firms with tangible asset covenants.

INSIDOWN.DAT

		Size	
		Small	**Large**
Inside Ownership	**Low**	3	17
	High	8	3

Source: Griner, E., and Huss, H. "Firm size, insider ownership, and accounting-based debt covenants." *Journal of Applied Business Research*, Vol. 11, No. 4, 1995, p. 7 (Table 4).

a. Assuming the null hypothesis of independence is true, how many firms are expected to fall in each cell of the table above?

b. The researchers were unable to use the chi-square test to analyze the data. Show why.

c. A test of the null hypothesis can be conducted using a small-sample method known as *Fisher's exact test*. This method calculates the exact probability (*p*-value) of observing sample results at least as contradictory to the null hypothesis as those observed for the researchers' data. The researchers reported the *p*-value for this test as .0043. Interpret this result.

d. Investigate the nature of the dependence exhibited by the contingency table by plotting the appropriate contingency table percentages. Describe what you find.

8.57 Over the years, pollsters have found that the public's confidence in big business is closely tied to the economic climate. Harvey Kahalas hypothesized that there is a relationship between the level of confidence in business and job satisfaction, and that this is true for both union and nonunion workers (*Baylor Business Studies*, Feb.–Apr. 1981). He analyzed sample data collected by the National Opinion Research Center (shown in the two tables at the bottom of the page) and concluded that his hypothesis was not supported. Do you agree? Use the accompanying SPSS printouts on page 465 to conduct the appropriate tests using $\alpha = .05$. Be sure to specify your null and alternative hypotheses.

8.58 If a company can identify times of day when accidents are most likely to occur, extra precautions can be instituted during those times. A random sampling of the accident reports over the last year at a plant gives the frequency of occurrence of accidents during the different hours of the workday. Can it be concluded from the data in the table that the proportions of accidents are different for at least two of the four time periods?

JOBACC.DAT

Hours	1–2	3–4	5–6	7–8
Number of Accidents	31	28	45	47

8.59 Many investors believe that the stock market's directional change in January signals the market's direction for the remainder of the year. But is this "January" indicator valid? The table at right summarizes the relevant changes in the Dow Jones Industrial Average for the period December 31, 1927, through January 31, 1981. J. Martinich applied the chi-square test of independence to these data to investigate the January indicator (*Mid-South Business Journal*, Vol. 4, 1984).

JANINDIC.DAT

		Next 11-Month Change	
		Up	Down
January Change	Up	25	10
	Down	9	9

a. Examine the contingency table. Based solely on your visual inspection, do the data appear to confirm the validity of the January indicator? Explain.

b. Construct a plot of the percentage of years for which the 11-month movement is up based on the January change. Compare these two percentages to the percentage of times the market moved up during the last 11 months over all years in the sample. What do you think of the January indicator now?

c. If a chi-square test of independence is to be used to investigate the January indicator, what are the appropriate null and alternative hypotheses?

d. Conduct the test of part **c.** Use $\alpha = .05$. Interpret your results in the context of the problem.

e. Would you get the same result in part **d** if $\alpha = .10$ were used? Explain.

8.60 An economist was interested in knowing whether sons have a tendency to choose the same occupation as their fathers. To investigate this question, 500 males were polled and each questioned concerning his occupation and the occupation of his father. A summary of the numbers of father-son pairs falling in each occupational category is shown in the table on p. 466. Do the data provide sufficient evidence at $\alpha = .05$ to indicate a dependence between a son's choice of occupation and

UNION.DAT

		Job Satisfaction			
		Very Satisfied	Moderately Satisfied	A Little Dissatisfied	Very Dissatisfied
Union Member	A Great Deal	26	15	2	1
Confidence in	Only Some	95	73	16	5
Major Corporations	Hardly Any	34	28	10	9

NONUNION.DAT

		Job Satisfaction			
		Very Satisfied	Moderately Satisfied	A Little Dissatisfied	Very Dissatisfied
Nonunion Confidence	A Great Deal	111	52	12	4
in Major Corporations	Only Some	246	142	37	18
	Hardly Any	73	51	19	9

SPSS Output for Exercise 8.57

```
UNIONCON  by  JOBSAT

                   JOBSAT
         Count   |
         Exp Val |
                 |                                        Row
                 | Little | Moderate|None     | Very    | Total
UNIONCON         +--------+---------+---------+---------+
      GreatDeal  |     2  |    15   |      1  |    26   |   44
                 |   3.9  |  16.3   |    2.1  |  21.7   | 14.0%
                 +--------+---------+---------+---------+
      HardlyAny  |    10  |    28   |      9  |    34   |   81
                 |   7.2  |  29.9   |    3.9  |  40.0   | 25.8%
                 +--------+---------+---------+---------+
      OnlySome   |    16  |    73   |      5  |    95   |  189
                 |  16.9  |  69.8   |    9.0  |  93.3   | 60.2%
                 +--------+---------+---------+---------+
         Column       28       116        15       155      314
          Total     8.9%     36.9%      4.8%     49.4%   100.0%

      Chi-Square                 Value          DF                  Significance
--------------------          ----------       ----                 ------------
Pearson                        13.36744          6                      .03756
Likelihood Ratio               12.08304          6                      .06014

Minimum Expected Frequency -    2.102
Cells with Expected Frequency < 5 -     3 OF     12 (25.0%)
--------------------------------------------------------------------------------
NOUNCON  by  JOBSAT

                   JOBSAT
         Count   |
         Exp Val |
                 |                                        Row
                 | Little | Moderate|None     | Very    | Total
NOUNCON          +--------+---------+---------+---------+
      GreatDeal  |    12  |    52   |      4  |   111   |  179
                 |  15.7  |  56.7   |    7.2  |  99.4   | 23.1%
                 +--------+---------+---------+---------+
      HardlyAny  |    19  |    51   |      9  |    73   |  152
                 |  13.4  |  48.1   |    6.1  |  84.4   | 19.6%
                 +--------+---------+---------+---------+
      OnlySome   |    37  |   142   |     18  |   246   |  443
                 |  38.9  | 140.2   |   17.7  | 246.1   | 57.2%
                 +--------+---------+---------+---------+
         Column       68       245        31       430      774
          Total     8.8%     31.7%      4.0%     55.6%   100.0%

      Chi-Square                 Value          DF                  Significance
--------------------          ----------       ----                 ------------
Pearson                         9.63514          6                      .14088
Likelihood Ratio                9.55907          6                      .14449

Minimum Expected Frequency -    6.088
```

SAS Output for Exercise 8.60

```
                    TABLE OF FATHER BY SON

FATHER        SON

Frequency |        |        |        |        |
Expected  |Farmer  |Prof/Bus|Skill   |Unskill |  Total
----------+--------+--------+--------+--------+
Farmer    |     32 |     15 |     23 |     10 |     80
          |   6.72 |  27.36 |  33.12 |   12.8 |
----------+--------+--------+--------+--------+
Prof/Bus  |      0 |     55 |     38 |      7 |    100
          |    8.4 |   34.2 |   41.4 |     16 |
----------+--------+--------+--------+--------+
Skill     |      0 |     79 |     71 |     25 |    175
          |   14.7 |  59.85 |  72.45 |     28 |
----------+--------+--------+--------+--------+
Unskill   |     10 |     22 |     75 |     38 |    145
          |  12.18 |  49.59 |  60.03 |   23.2 |
----------+--------+--------+--------+--------+
Total           42      171      207       80      500

          STATISTICS FOR TABLE OF FATHER BY SON

Statistic                        DF     Value       Prob
---------------------------------------------------------
Chi-Square                        9   180.874      0.000
Likelihood Ratio Chi-Square       9   160.832      0.000
Mantel-Haenszel Chi-Square        1    52.040      0.000
Phi Coefficient                         0.601
Contingency Coefficient                 0.515
Cramer's V                              0.347

Sample Size = 500
```

FATHSON.DAT

		Son			
		Professional or Business	Skilled	Unskilled	Farmer
Father	Professional or Business	55	38	7	0
	Skilled	79	71	25	0
	Unskilled	22	75	38	10
	Farmer	15	23	10	32

his father's occupation? Use the SAS printout at the top of the page to conduct the analysis.

8.61 Westinghouse Electric Company has experimented with different means of evaluating the performance of solder joint inspectors. One approach involves comparing an individual inspector's classifications with those of the group of experts that comprise Westinghouse's Work Standards Committee. In one experiment conducted by Westinghouse, 153 solder connections were evaluated by the committee and 111 were classified as acceptable. An inspector evaluated the same 153 connections and classified 124 as acceptable. Of the items rejected by the inspector, the committee agreed with 19.

a. Construct a contingency table that summarizes the classifications of the committee and the inspector.

b. Based on a visual examination of the table you constructed in part **a**, does it appear that there is a relationship between the inspector's classifications and the committee's? Explain. (A plot of the percentage rejected by committee and inspector will aid your examination.)

c. Conduct a chi-square test of independence for these data. Use $\alpha = .05$. Carefully interpret the results of your test in the context of the problem.

8.62 Despite company policies allowing unpaid family leave for new fathers, many men fear that exercising this option would be held against them by their superiors (*Minneapolis Star-Tribune*, Feb. 14, 1993). In a random sample of 100 male workers planning to become fathers, 35 agreed with the statement "If I knew there would be no repercussions, I would choose to participate in the family leave program after the birth of a son or daughter." However, of 96 men who became fathers in the previous 16 months, only nine participated in the program.

a. Specify the appropriate null and alternative hypotheses to test whether the sample data provide sufficient evidence to reject the hypothesis that the proportion of new fathers participating in the program is the same as the proportion that would like to participate. Define any symbols you use.
b. Are the sample sizes large enough to conclude that the sampling distribution of $(\hat{p}_1 - \hat{p}_2)$ is approximately normal?
c. Conduct the hypothesis test using $\alpha = .05$. Report the observed significance level of the test.
d. What assumptions must be satisfied for the test to be valid?

8.63 Product or service quality is often defined as *fitness for use*. This means the product or service meets the customer's needs. Generally speaking, fitness for use is based on five quality characteristics: technological (e.g., strength, hardness), psychological (taste, beauty), time-oriented (reliability), contractual (guarantee provisions), and ethical (courtesy, honesty). The quality of a service may involve all these characteristics, while the quality of a manufactured product generally depends on technological and time-oriented characteristics (Schroeder, *Operations Management*, 1993). After a barrage of customer complaints about poor quality, a manufacturer of gasoline filters for cars had its quality inspectors sample 600 filters—200 per work shift—and check for defects. The data in the table resulted.

a. Do the data indicate that the quality of the filters being produced may be related to the shift producing the filter? Test using $\alpha = .05$.
b. Estimate the proportion of defective filters produced by the first shift. Use a 95% confidence interval.

FILTER.DAT

Shift	Defectives Produced
First	25
Second	35
Third	80

8.64 What makes entrepreneurs different from chief executive officers (CEOs) of *Fortune* 500 companies? The *Wall Street Journal* hired the Gallup organization to investigate this question. For the study, entrepreneurs were defined as chief executive officers of companies listed by *Inc.* magazine as among the 500 fastest-growing smaller companies in the United States. The Gallup organization sampled 207 CEOs of *Fortune* 500 companies and 153 entrepreneurs. They obtained the results shown in the table below.

a. In each of the three areas—age, education, and employment record—are the sample sizes large enough to use the inferential methods of this chapter to investigate the differences between *Fortune* 500 CEOs and entrepreneurs? Justify your answer.
b. Test to determine whether the data indicate that the fractions of CEOs and entrepreneurs who have been fired or dismissed from a job differ at the $\alpha = .01$ level of significance.
c. Construct a 99% confidence interval for the difference between the fractions of CEOs and entrepreneurs who have been fired or dismissed from a job.
d. Which inferential procedure provides more information about the difference between employment records, the test of part **b** or the interval of part **c**? Explain.

Variable	*Fortune* 500 CEOs	Entrepreneurs
Age Under 45 years old	19	96
Education Completed 4 years of college	195	116
Employment record Have been fired or dismissed from a job	19	47

Source: Graham, E. "The entrepreneurial mystique." *Wall Street Journal*, May 20, 1985.

Real-World Case: Discrimination in the Workplace

(A Case Covering Chapter 8)

Title VII of the Civil Rights Act of 1964 prohibits discrimination in the workplace on the basis of race, color, religion, gender, or national origin. The Age Discrimination in Employment Act of 1967 (ADEA) protects workers age 40 to 70 against discrimination based on age. The potential for discrimination exists in such processes as hiring, promotion, compensation, and termination.

In 1971 the U.S. Supreme Court established that employment discrimination cases fall into two categories: **disparate treatment** and **disparate impact**. In the former, the issue is whether the employer intentionally discriminated against a worker. For example, if the employer considered an individual's race in deciding whether to terminate him, the case is one of disparate treatment. In a disparate impact case, the issue is whether employment practices have an adverse impact on a protected group or class of people, even when the employer does not intend to discriminate.

PART I: DOWNSIZING AT A COMPUTER FIRM

Disparate impact cases almost always involve the use of statistical evidence and expert testimony by professional statisticians. Attorneys for the plaintiffs frequently use hypothesis test results in the form of p-values in arguing the case for their clients.

Table C4.1 was recently introduced as evidence in a race case that resulted from a round of layoffs during the downsizing of a division of a computer manufacturer. The company had selected 51 of the division's 1,215 employees to lay off. The plaintiffs—in this case 15 of the 20 African Americans who were laid off—were suing the company for $20 million in damages.

The company's lawyers argued that the selections followed from a performance-based ranking of all employees. The plaintiffs legal team and their expert witnesses, citing the results of a statistical test of hypothesis, argued that layoffs were a function of race.

The validity of the plaintiffs interpretation of the data is dependent on whether the assumptions of the test are met in this situation. In particular, like all hypothesis tests presented in this text, the assumption of random sampling must hold. If it does not, the results of the test may be due to the violation of this assumption rather than to discrimination. In general, the appropriateness of the testing procedure is dependent on the test's ability to capture the relevant aspects of the employment process in question (DeGroot, Fienberg, and Kadane, *Statistics and the Law,* 1986).

Prepare a document to be submitted as evidence in the case (i.e., an exhibit), in which you evaluate the validity of the plaintiffs' interpretation of the data. Your evaluation should be based in part on your knowledge of the processes companies use to lay off employees and how well those processes are reflected in the hypothesis-testing procedure employed by the plaintiffs.

PART II: AGE DISCRIMINATION—YOU BE THE JUDGE

In 1996, as part of a significant restructuring of product lines, AJAX Pharmaceuticals (a fictitious name for a real company) laid off 24 of 55 assembly-line workers in its Pittsburgh manufacturing plant. Citing the ADEA, 11 of the laid-off workers claimed they were discriminated against on the basis of age and sued AJAX for $5,000,000. Management disputed the claim, saying that since the workers were essentially interchangeable, they had used random sampling to choose the 24 workers to be terminated.

Table C4.2 lists the 55 assembly-line workers and identifies which were terminated and which remained active. Plaintiffs are denoted by an asterisk. These data were used by both the plaintiffs and the defendants to determine whether the layoffs had an adverse impact on workers age 40 and over and to establish the credibility of management's random sampling claim.

TABC4_1.DAT

TABLE C4.1 Summary of Downsizing Data for Race Case

		Decision	
		Retained	Laid off
RACE	White	1,051	31
	Black	113	20

Source: Confidential personal communication with P. George Benson, 1997.

TABLE C4.2 Data for Age Discrimination Case

Employee	Yearly Wages	Age	Employment Status	Employee	Yearly Wages	Age	Employment Status
*Adler, C.J.	$41,200	45	Terminated	*Huang, T.J.	42,995	48	Terminated
Alario, B.N.	39,565	43	Active	Jatho, J.A.	31,755	40	Active
Anders, J.M.	30,980	41	Active	Johnson, C.H.	29,540	32	Active
Bajwa, K.K.	23,225	27	Active	Jurasik, T.B.	34,300	41	Active
Barny, M.L.	21,250	26	Active	Klein, K.L.	43,700	51	Terminated
*Berger, R.W.	41,875	45	Terminated	Lang, T.F.	19,435	22	Active
Brenn, L.O.	31,225	41	Active	Liao, P.C.	28,750	32	Active
Cain, E.J.	30,135	36	Terminated	*Lostan, W.J.	44,675	52	Terminated
Carle, W.J.	29,850	32	Active	Mak, G.L.	35,505	38	Terminated
Castle, A.L.	21,850	22	Active	Maloff, V.R.	33,425	38	Terminated
Chan, S.D.	43,005	48	Terminated	McCall, R.M.	31,300	36	Terminated
Cho, J.Y.	34,785	41	Active	*Nadeau, S.R.	42,300	46	Terminated
Cohen, S.D.	25,350	27	Active	*Nguyen, O.L.	43,625	50	Terminated
Darel, F.E.	36,300	42	Active	Oas, R.C.	37,650	42	Active
*Davis, D.E.	40,425	46	Terminated	*Patel, M.J.	38,400	43	Terminated
*Dawson, P.K.	39,150	42	Terminated	Porter, K.D.	32,195	35	Terminated
Denker, U.H.	19,435	19	Active	Rosa, L.M.	19,435	21	Active
Dorando, T.R.	24,125	28	Active	Roth, J.H.	32,785	39	Terminated
Dubois, A.G.	30,450	40	Active	Savino, G.L.	37,900	42	Active
England, N.	24,750	25	Active	Scott, I.W.	29,150	30	Terminated
Estis, K.B.	22,755	23	Active	Smith, E.E.	35,125	41	Active
Fenton, C.K.	23,000	24	Active	Teel, Q.V.	27,655	33	Active
Finer, H.R.	42,000	46	Terminated	*Walker, F.O.	42,545	47	Terminated
*Frees, O.C.	44,100	52	Terminated	Wang, T.G.	22,200	32	Active
Gary, J.G.	44,975	55	Terminated	Yen, D.O.	40,350	44	Terminated
Gillen, D.J.	25,900	27	Active	Young, N.L.	28,305	34	Active
Harvey, D.A.	40,875	46	Terminated	Zeitels, P.W.	36,500	42	Active
Higgins, N.M.	38,595	41	Active				

*Denotes plaintiffs

Using whatever statistical methods you think are appropriate, build a case that supports the plaintiffs' position. (Call documents related to this issue Exhibit A.) Similarly, build a case that supports the defendants' position. (Call these documents Exhibit B.) Then discuss which of the two cases is more convincing and why. [*Note:* The data for this case are available in the file DISCRIM.DAT, described in the table.]

DISCRIM.DAT (Number of observations: 55)

Variable	Column(s)	Type
LASTNAME	1–10	QL
WAGES	15–19	QN
AGE	35–36	QN
STATUS	47	QL (A = active, T = terminated)

Chapter 9

SIMPLE LINEAR REGRESSION

CONTENTS

STATISTICS IN ACTION

Where We've Been

We've learned how to estimate and test hypotheses about population parameters based on a random sample of observations from the population. We've also seen how to extend these methods to allow for a comparison of parameters from two populations.

Where We're Going

Suppose we want to predict the assessed value of a house in a particular community. We could select a single random sample of n houses from the community, use the methods of Chapter 5 to estimate the mean assessed value μ, and then use this quantity to predict the house's assessed value. A better method uses information that is available to any property appraiser, e.g., square feet of floor space and age of the house. If we measure square footage and age at the same time as assessed value, we can establish the relationship between these variables—one that lets us use these variables for prediction. This chapter covers the simplest situation—relating two variables. The more complex problem of relating more than two variables is the topic of Chapter 10.

In Chapters 5–7 we described methods for making inferences about population means. The mean of a population was treated as a *constant,* and we showed how to use sample data to estimate or to test hypotheses about this constant mean. In many applications, the mean of a population is not viewed as a constant, but rather as a variable. For example, the mean sale price of residences sold this year in a large city can be treated as a constant and might be equal to \$150,000. But we might also treat the mean sale price as a variable that depends on the square feet of living space in the residence. For example, the relationship might be

$$\text{Mean sale price} = \$30{,}000 + \$60(\text{Square feet})$$

This formula implies that the mean sale price of 1,000-square-foot homes is \$90,000, the mean sale price of 2,000-square-foot homes is \$150,000, and the mean sale price of 3,000-square-foot homes is \$210,000.

What do we gain by treating the mean as a variable rather than a constant? In many practical applications we will be dealing with highly variable data, data for which the standard deviation is so large that a constant mean is almost "lost" in a sea of variability. For example, if the mean residential sale price is \$150,000 but the standard deviation is \$75,000, then the actual sale prices will vary considerably, and the mean price is not a very meaningful or useful characterization of the price distribution. On the other hand, if the mean sale price is treated as a variable that depends on the square feet of living space, the standard deviation of sale prices for any given size of home might be only \$10,000. In this case, the mean price will provide a much better characterization of sale prices when it is treated as a variable rather than a constant.

In this chapter we discuss situations in which the mean of the population is treated as a variable, dependent on the value of another variable. The dependence of residential sale price on the square feet of living space is one illustration. Other examples include the dependence of mean sales revenue of a firm on advertising expenditure, the dependence of mean starting salary of a college graduate on the student's GPA, and the dependence of mean monthly production of automobiles on the total number of sales in the previous month.

In this chapter we discuss the simplest of all models relating a population mean to another variable, *the straight-line model.* We show how to use the sample data to estimate the straight-line relationship between the mean value of one variable, y, as it relates to a second variable, x. The methodology of estimating and using a straight-line relationship is referred to as *simple linear regression analysis.*

9.1 PROBABILISTIC MODELS

An important consideration in merchandising a product is the amount of money spent on advertising. Suppose you want to model the monthly sales revenue of an appliance store as a function of the monthly advertising expenditure. The first question to be answered is this: "Do you think an exact relationship exists between these two variables?" That is, do you think it is possible to state the exact monthly sales revenue if the amount spent on advertising is known? We think you will agree with us that this is *not* possible for several reasons. Sales depend on many variables other than advertising expenditure—for example, time of year, the state of the general economy, inventory, and price structure. Even if many variables are included in a model (the topic of Chapter 10), it is still unlikely that we would be able to predict the monthly sales *exactly*. There will almost certainly be some variation in monthly sales due strictly to *random phenomena* that cannot be modeled or explained.

If we were to construct a model that hypothesized an exact relationship between variables, it would be called a **deterministic model.** For example, if we believe that y, the monthly sales revenue, will be exactly fifteen times x, the monthly advertising expenditure, we write

$$y = 15x$$

This represents a *deterministic relationship* between the variables y and x. It implies that y can always be determined exactly when the value of x is known. *There is no allowance for error in this prediction.*

If, on the other hand, we believe there will be unexplained variation in monthly sales—perhaps caused by important but unincluded variables or by random phenomena—we discard the deterministic model and use a model that accounts for this **random error.** This **probabilistic model** includes both a deterministic component and a random error component. For example, if we hypothesize that the sales y is related to advertising expenditure x by

$$y = 15x + \text{Random error}$$

we are hypothesizing a *probabilistic relationship* between y and x. Note that the deterministic component of this probabilistic model is $15x$.

Figure 9.1a shows the possible values of y and x for five different months, when the model is deterministic. All the pairs of (x, y) data points must fall exactly on the line because a deterministic model leaves no room for error.

FIGURE 9.1
Possible sales revenues, y, for five different months, x

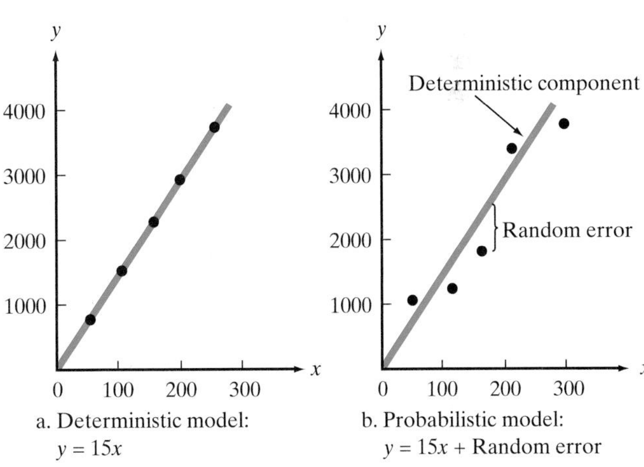

a. Deterministic model: $y = 15x$

b. Probabilistic model: $y = 15x + \text{Random error}$

Figure 9.1b shows a possible set of points for the same values of x when we are using a probabilistic model. Note that the deterministic part of the model (the straight line itself) is the same. Now, however, the inclusion of a random error component allows the monthly sales to vary from this line. Since we know that the sales revenue does vary randomly for a given value of x, the probabilistic model provides a more realistic model for y than does the deterministic model.

General Form of Probabilistic Models

$$y = \text{Deterministic component} + \text{Random error}$$

where y is the variable of interest. We always assume that the mean value of the random error equals 0. This is equivalent to assuming that the mean value of y, $E(y)$, equals the deterministic component of the model; that is

$$E(y) = \text{Deterministic component}$$

In this chapter we present the simplest of probabilistic models—the **straight-line model**—which derives its name from the fact that the deterministic portion of the model graphs as a straight line. Fitting this model to a set of data is an example of **regression analysis,** or **regression modeling.** The elements of the straight-line model are summarized in the next box.

A First-Order (Straight-Line) Probabilistic Model

$$y = \beta_0 + \beta_1 x + \varepsilon$$

where

y = **Dependent** *or* **response variable** (variable to be modeled)
x = **Independent** *or* **predictor variable** (variable used as a predictor of y)*
$E(y) = \beta_0 + \beta_1 x$ = Deterministic component
ε (epsilon) = Random error component
β_0 (beta zero) = **y-intercept of the line**, that is, the point at which the line intercepts or cuts through the y-axis (see Figure 9.2)
β_1 (beta one) = **Slope of the line**, that is, the amount of increase (or decrease) in the deterministic component of y for every 1-unit increase in x. [As you can see in Figure 9.2, $E(y)$ increases by the amount β_1 as x increases from 2 to 3.]

In the probabilistic model, the deterministic component is referred to as the **line of means,** because the mean of y, $E(y)$, is equal to the straight-line component of the model. That is,

$$E(y) = \beta_0 + \beta_1 x$$

Note that the Greek symbols β_0 and β_1, respectively, represent the y-intercept and slope of the model. They are population parameters that will be known only if we have access to the entire population of (x, y) measurements. Together with a specific value of the independent variable x, they determine the mean value of y, which is just a specific point on the line of means (Figure 9.2).

*The word *independent* should not be interpreted in a probabilistic sense, as defined in Chapter 3. The phrase *independent variable* is used in regression analysis to refer to a predictor variable for the response y.

FIGURE 9.2
The straight-line model

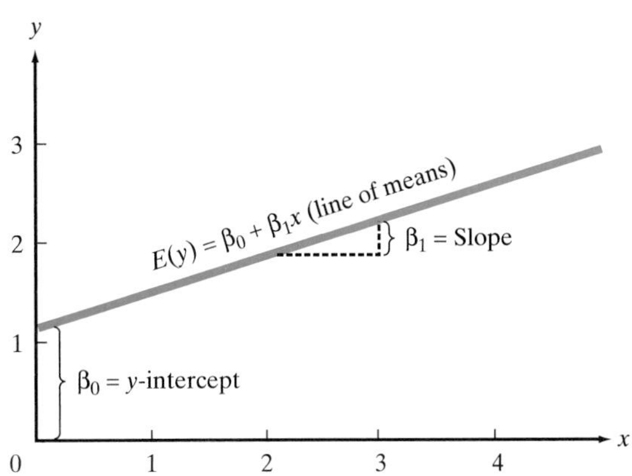

The values of β_0 and β_1 will be unknown in almost all practical applications of regression analysis. The process of developing a model, estimating the unknown parameters, and using the model can be viewed as the five-step procedure shown in the next box.

Step 1 Hypothesize the deterministic component of the model that relates the mean, $E(y)$, to the independent variable x (Section 9.1).

Step 2 Use the sample data to estimate unknown parameters in the model (Section 9.2).

Step 3 Specify the probability distribution of the random error term and estimate the standard deviation of this distribution (Sections 9.3 and 9.4).

Step 4 Statistically evaluate the usefulness of the model (Sections 9.5, 9.6, and 9.7).

Step 5 When satisfied that the model is useful, use it for prediction, estimation, and other purposes (Section 9.8).

EXERCISES 9.1–9.9

Learning the Mechanics

9.1 In each case, graph the line that passes through the given points.
a. (1, 1) and (5, 5) b. (0, 3) and (3, 0)
c. (−1, 1) and (4, 2) d. (−6, −3) and (2, 6)

9.2 Give the slope and y-intercept for each of the lines graphed in Exercise 9.1.

9.3 The equation for a straight line (deterministic model) is

$$y = \beta_0 + \beta_1 x$$

If the line passes through the point (−2, 4), then $x = -2$, $y = 4$ must satisfy the equation; that is,

$$4 = \beta_0 + \beta_1(-2)$$

Similarly, if the line passes through the point (4, 6), then $x = 4$, $y = 6$ must satisfy the equation; that is,

$$6 = \beta_0 + \beta_1(4)$$

Use these two equations to solve for β_0 and β_1; then find the equation of the line that passes through the points (−2, 4) and (4, 6).

9.4 Refer to Exercise 9.3. Find the equations of the lines that pass through the points listed in Exercise 9.1.

9.5 Plot the following lines:
a. $y = 4 + x$ b. $y = 5 - 2x$ c. $y = -4 + 3x$
d. $y = -2x$ e. $y = x$ f. $y = .50 + 1.5x$

9.6 Give the slope and y-intercept for each of the lines defined in Exercise 9.5.

9.7 Why do we generally prefer a probabilistic model to a deterministic model? Give examples for which the two types of models might be appropriate.

9.8 What is the line of means?

9.9 If a straight-line probabilistic relationship relates the mean $E(y)$ to an independent variable x, does it imply that every value of the variable y will always fall exactly on the line of means? Why or why not?

9.2 FITTING THE MODEL: THE LEAST SQUARES APPROACH

After the straight-line model has been hypothesized to relate the mean $E(y)$ to the independent variable x, the next step is to collect data and to estimate the (unknown) population parameters, the y-intercept β_0 and the slope β_1.

To begin with a simple example, suppose an appliance store conducts a five-month experiment to determine the effect of advertising on sales revenue. The results are shown in Table 9.1. (The number of measurements and the measurements themselves are unrealistically simple in order to avoid arithmetic confusion in this introductory example.) This set of data will be used to demonstrate the five-step procedure of regression modeling given in Section 9.1. In this section we hypothesize the deterministic component of the model and estimate its unknown parameters (steps 1 and 2). The model assumptions and the random error component (step 3) are the subjects of Sections 9.3 and 9.4, whereas Sections 9.5–9.7 assess the utility of the model (step 4). Finally, we use the model for prediction and estimation (step 5) in Section 9.8.

TABLE 9.1 Advertising–Sales Data

Month	Advertising Expenditure, x (\$100s)	Sales Revenue, y (\$1,000s)
1	1	1
2	2	1
3	3	2
4	4	2
5	5	4

Step 1 *Hypothesize the deterministic component of the probabilistic model.* As stated before, we will consider only straight-line models in this chapter. Thus, the complete model to relate mean sales revenue $E(y)$ to advertising expenditure x is given by

$$E(y) = \beta_0 + \beta_1 x$$

Step 2 *Use sample data to estimate unknown parameters in the model.* This step is the subject of this section—namely, how can we best use the information in the sample of five observations in Table 9.1 to estimate the unknown y-intercept β_0 and slope β_1?

To determine whether a linear relationship between y and x is plausible, it is helpful to plot the sample data in a **scattergram.** Recall (Section 2.10) that a scattergram locates each of the five data points on a graph, as shown in Figure 9.3.

FIGURE 9.3
Scattergram for data in Table 9.1

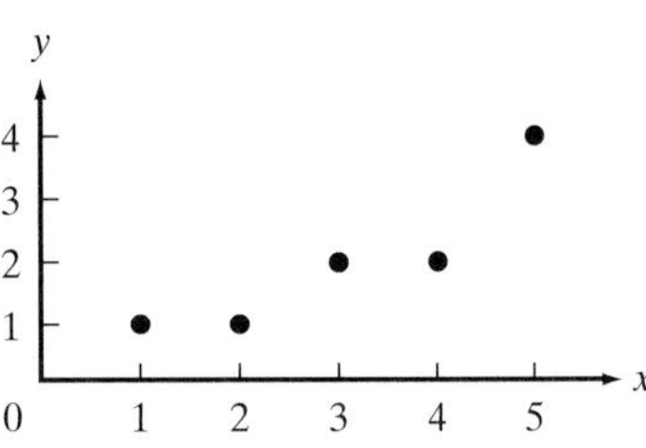

Note that the scattergram suggests a general tendency for y to increase as x increases. If you place a ruler on the scattergram, you will see that a line may be drawn through three of the five points, as shown in Figure 9.4. To obtain the equation of this visually fitted line, note that the line intersects the y-axis at $y = -1$, so the y-intercept is -1. Also, y increases exactly 1 unit for every 1-unit increase in x, indicating that the slope is $+1$. Therefore, the equation is

$$\tilde{y} = -1 + 1(x) = -1 + x$$

where $\tilde{y}$ is used to denote the predicted y from the visual model.

FIGURE 9.4
Visual straight line fitted to the data in Figure 9.3

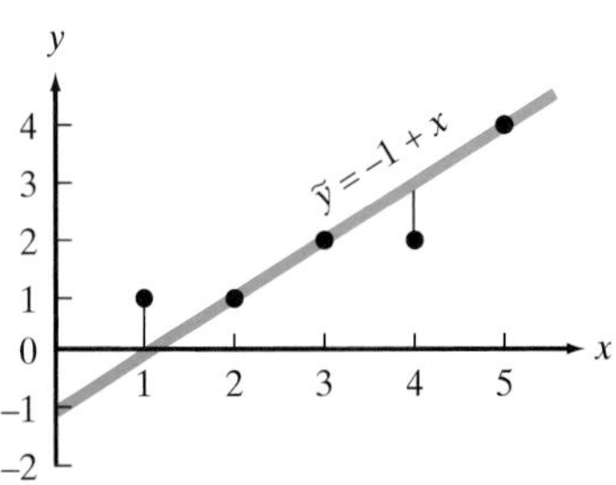

One way to decide quantitatively how well a straight line fits a set of data is to note the extent to which the data points deviate from the line. For example, to evaluate the model in Figure 9.4, we calculate the magnitude of the *deviations,* i.e., the differences between the observed and the predicted values of y. These deviations, or **errors of prediction,** are the vertical distances between observed and predicted values (see Figure 9.4). The observed and predicted values of y, their differences, and their squared differences are shown in Table 9.2. Note that the *sum of errors* equals 0 and the **sum of squares of the errors (SSE),** which gives greater emphasis to large deviations of the points from the line, is equal to 2.

TABLE 9.2 Comparing Observed and Predicted Values for the Visual Model

x	y	$\tilde{y} = -1 + x$	$(y - \tilde{y})$	$(y - \tilde{y})^2$
1	1	0	$(1 - 0) = 1$	1
2	1	1	$(1 - 1) = 0$	0
3	2	2	$(2 - 2) = 0$	0
4	2	3	$(2 - 3) = -1$	1
5	4	4	$(4 - 4) = 0$	0
			Sum of errors = 0	Sum of squared errors (SSE) = 2

You can see by shifting the ruler around the graph that it is possible to find many lines for which the sum of errors is equal to 0, but it can be shown that there is one (and only one) line for which the SSE is a *minimum.* This line is called the **least squares line,** the **regression line,** or the **least squares prediction equation.** The methodology used to obtain this line is called the **method of least squares.**

To find the least squares prediction equation for a set of data, assume that we have a sample of n data points consisting of pairs of values of x and y, say (x_1, y_1), $(x_2, y_2), \ldots, (x_n, y_n)$. For example, the $n = 5$ data points shown in Table 9.2 are

(1, 1), (2, 1), (3, 2), (4, 2), and (5, 4). The fitted line, which we will calculate based on the five data points, is written as

$$\widehat{y} = \widehat{\beta}_0 + \widehat{\beta}_1 x$$

The "hats" indicate that the symbols below them are estimates: $\widehat{y}$ (y-hat) is an estimator of the mean value of y, $E(y)$, and a predictor of some future value of y; and $\widehat{\beta}_0$ and $\widehat{\beta}_1$ are estimators of β_0 and β_1, respectively.

For a given data point, say the point (x_i, y_i), the observed value of y is y_i and the predicted value of y would be obtained by substituting x_i into the prediction equation:

$$\widehat{y}_i = \widehat{\beta}_0 + \widehat{\beta}_1 x_i$$

And the deviation of the ith value of y from its predicted value is

$$(y_i - \widehat{y}_i) = [y_i - (\widehat{\beta}_0 + \widehat{\beta}_1 x_i)]$$

Then the sum of squares of the deviations of the y-values about their predicted values for all the n points is

$$\text{SSE} = \sum [y_i - (\widehat{\beta}_0 + \widehat{\beta}_1 x_i)]^2$$

The quantities $\widehat{\beta}_0$ and $\widehat{\beta}_1$ that make the SSE a minimum are called the **least squares estimates** of the population parameters β_0 and β_1, and the prediction equation $\widehat{y} = \widehat{\beta}_0 + \widehat{\beta}_1 x$ is called the *least squares line.*

DEFINITION 9.1

The **least squares line** $\boldsymbol{\widehat{y} = \widehat{\beta}_0 + \widehat{\beta}_1 x}$ is one that has the following two properties:

1. the sum of the errors (SE) equals 0
2. the sum of squared errors (SSE) is smaller than for any other straight-line model

The values of $\widehat{\beta}_0$ and $\widehat{\beta}_1$ that minimize the SSE are (proof omitted) given by the formulas in the box.*

Preliminary computations for finding the least squares line for the advertising–sales example are presented in Table 9.3. We can now calculate

$$\text{SS}_{xy} = \sum x_i y_i - \frac{(\sum x_i)(\sum y_i)}{5} = 37 - \frac{(15)(10)}{5} = 37 - 30 = 7$$

*Students who are familiar with calculus should note that the values of β_0 and β_1 that minimize SSE $= \Sigma(y_i - \widehat{y}_i)^2$ are obtained by setting the two partial derivatives $\partial\text{SSE}/\partial\beta_0$ and $\partial\text{SSE}/\partial\beta_1$ equal to 0. The solutions to these two equations yield the formulas shown in the box. Furthermore, we denote the *sample* solutions to the equations by $\widehat{\beta}_0$ and $\widehat{\beta}_1$, where the "hat" denotes that these are sample estimates of the true population intercept β_0 and true population slope β_1.

$$SS_{xx} = \sum x_i^2 - \frac{(\sum x_i)^2}{5} = 55 - \frac{(15)^2}{5} = 55 - 45 = 10$$

Formulas for the Least Squares Estimates

Slope: $\hat{\beta}_1 = \frac{SS_{xy}}{SS_{xx}}$

y-intercept: $\hat{\beta}_0 = \bar{y} - \hat{\beta}_1\bar{x}$

where $SS_{xy} = \sum (x_i - \bar{x})(y_i - \bar{y}) = \sum x_i y_i - \frac{(\sum x_i)(\sum y_i)}{n}$

$SS_{xx} = \sum (x_i - \bar{x})^2 = \sum x_i^2 - \frac{(\sum x_i)^2}{n}$

n = Sample size

TABLE 9.3 Preliminary Computations for Advertising–Sales Example

	x_i	y_i	x_i^2	$x_i y_i$
	1	1	1	1
	2	1	4	2
	3	2	9	6
	4	2	16	8
	5	4	25	20
Totals	$\sum x_i = 15$	$\sum y_i = 10$	$\sum x_i^2 = 55$	$\sum x_i y_i = 37$

Then the slope of the least squares line is

$$\hat{\beta}_1 = \frac{SS_{xy}}{SS_{xx}} = \frac{7}{10} = .7$$

and the y-intercept is

$$\hat{\beta}_0 = \bar{y} - \hat{\beta}_1\bar{x} = \frac{\sum y_i}{5} - \hat{\beta}_1\frac{\sum x_i}{5}$$

$$= \frac{10}{5} - (.7)\left(\frac{15}{5}\right) = 2 - (.7)(3) = 2 - 2.1 = -.1$$

The least squares line is thus

$$\hat{y} = \hat{\beta}_0 + \hat{\beta}_1 x = -.1 + .7x$$

The graph of this line is shown in Figure 9.5.

The predicted value of y for a given value of x can be obtained by substituting into the formula for the least squares line. Thus, when $x = 2$ we predict y to be

$$\hat{y} = -.1 + .7x = -.1 + .7(2) = 1.3$$

FIGURE 9.5
The line $\hat{y} = -.1 + .7x$ fitted to the data

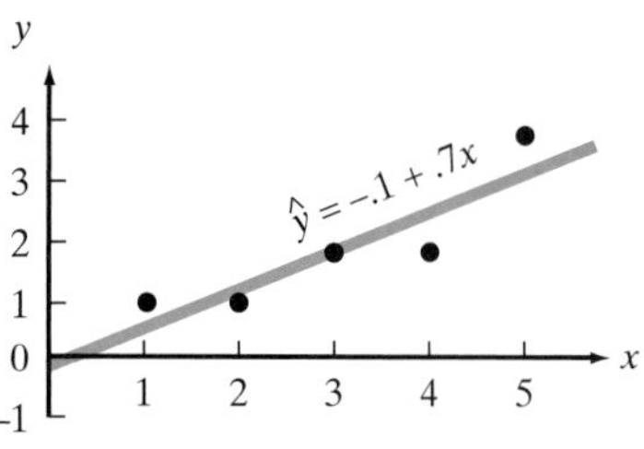

We show how to find a prediction interval for y in Section 9.8.

The observed and predicted values of y, the deviations of the y values about their predicted values, and the squares of these deviations are shown in Table 9.4. Note that the sum of squares of the deviations, SSE, is 1.10, and (as we would expect) this is less than the SSE = 2.0 obtained in Table 9.2 for the visually fitted line.

TABLE 9.4 Comparing Observed and Predicted Values for the Least Squares Prediction Equation

x	y	$\hat{y} = -.1 + .7x$	$(y - \hat{y})$	$(y - \hat{y})^2$
1	1	.6	$(1 - .6) = .4$	.16
2	1	1.3	$(1 - 1.3) = -.3$	.09
3	2	2.0	$(2 - 2.0) = 0$	.00
4	2	2.7	$(2 - 2.7) = -.7$	.49
5	4	3.4	$(4 - 3.4) = .6$	.36
			Sum of errors = 0	SSE = 1.10

The calculations required to obtain $\hat{\beta}_0$, $\hat{\beta}_1$, and SSE in simple linear regression, although straightforward, can become rather tedious. Even with the use of a pocket calculator, the process is laborious and susceptible to error, especially when the sample size is large. Fortunately, the use of a statistical software package can significantly reduce the labor involved in regression calculations. The SAS output for the simple linear regression of the data in Table 9.1 is displayed in Figure 9.6. The values of $\hat{\beta}_0$ and $\hat{\beta}_1$ are highlighted on the SAS printout under the **Parameter Estimate** column in the rows labeled **INTERCEP** and **X,** respectively. These values, $\hat{\beta}_0 = -.1$ and $\hat{\beta}_1 = .7$, agree exactly with our hand-calculated values. The value of SSE = 1.10 is also highlighted in Figure 9.6, under the **Sum of Squares** column in the row labeled **Error.**

Whether you use a hand calculator or a computer, it is important that you be able to interpret the intercept and slope in terms of the data being utilized to fit the model. In the advertising–sales example, the estimated y-intercept, $\hat{\beta}_0 = -.1$, appears to imply that the estimated mean sales revenue is equal to −.1, or −\$100, when the advertising expenditure, x, is equal to \$0. Since negative sales revenues are not possible, this seems to make the model nonsensical. However, *the model parameters should be interpreted only within the sampled range of the independent variable*—in this case, for advertising expenditures between \$100 and \$500. Thus, the y-intercept—which is, by definition, at $x = 0$ (\$0 advertising expenditure)—is not within the range of the sampled values of x and is not subject to meaningful interpretation.

```
Dependent Variable: Y
                        Analysis of Variance

                              Sum of          Mean
        Source        DF     Squares        Square      F Value     Prob>F

        Model          1     4.90000       4.90000       13.364     0.0354
        Error          3     1.10000       0.36667
        C Total        4     6.00000

            Root MSE         0.60553      R-square      0.8167
            Dep Mean         2.00000      Adj R-sq      0.7556
            C.V.            30.27650

                          Parameter Estimates

                        Parameter        Standard      T for HO:
      Variable   DF      Estimate           Error    Parameter=0     Prob>|T|

      INTERCEP    1     -0.100000      0.63508530         -0.157       0.8849
      X           1      0.700000      0.19148542          3.656       0.0354
```

FIGURE 9.6
SAS printout for advertising–sales regression

The slope of the least squares line, $\hat{\beta}_1 = .7$, implies that for every unit increase of x, the mean value of y is estimated to increase by .7 unit. In terms of this example, for every \$100 increase in advertising, the mean sales revenue is estimated to increase by \$700 *over the sampled range of advertising expenditures from \$100 to \$500.* Thus, the model does not imply that increasing the advertising expenditures from \$500 to \$1,000 will result in an increase in mean sales of \$3,500, because the range of x in the sample does not extend to \$1,000 ($x = 10$). Be careful to interpret the estimated parameters only within the sampled range of x.

Using the TI-83 Graphing Calculator

Straight-Line (Linear) Regression on the TI-83

A. Finding the least squares regression equation

Step 1 *Enter the data*
Press **STAT 1** for **STAT Edit**
Enter your x-data in **L1** and your y-data in **L2.**

Step 2 *Find the equation*
Press **STAT** and highlight **CALC**
Press **4** for **LinReg(ax + b)**
Press **ENTER**

The screen will show the values for a and b in the equation $y = ax + b$.

Example: The figures below show a table of data entered on the TI-83 and the regression equation obtained using the steps given above.

(continued)

```
L1      L2      L3      2
2       67      ------
1.9     68
2.3     70
3.9     74
6.4     78
7.4     81
6.8     82
L2(7) =82
```

```
LinReg
 y=ax+b
 a=2.495967742
 b=63.3391129
```

B. Finding r and r^2

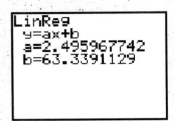

(Note: We discuss these statistics in Sections 9.6 and 9.7.)

If r and r^2 do not already appear on the LinReg screen from part A,

Step 1 *Turn the diagnostics feature on*

Press **2nd 0** for **CATALOG**

Press the x^{-1} key for **D**

Press down the arrow key until **DiagnosticsOn** is highlighted

Press **ENTER** twice

Step 2 *Find the regression equation as shown in part A above*

The values for r and r^2 will appear on the screen as well.

Example: The figures below show a table of data entered on the TI-83 and the regression equation, r, and r^2 obtained using the steps given above.

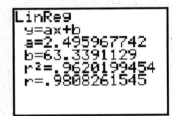

```
L1      L2      L3      2
2       67      ------
1.9     68
2.3     70
3.9     74
6.4     78
7.4     81
6.8     82
L2(7) =82
```

```
LinReg
 y=ax+b
 a=2.495967742
 b=63.3391129
 r²=.9620199454
 r=.9808261545
```

C. Graphing the least squares line with the scatterplot

Step 1 *Enter the data as shown in part A above*

Step 2 *Set up the data plot*

Press **2nd Y=** for **STATPLOT**

Press **1** for **PLOT1**

Use the arrow and **ENTER** keys to set up the screen as shown below.

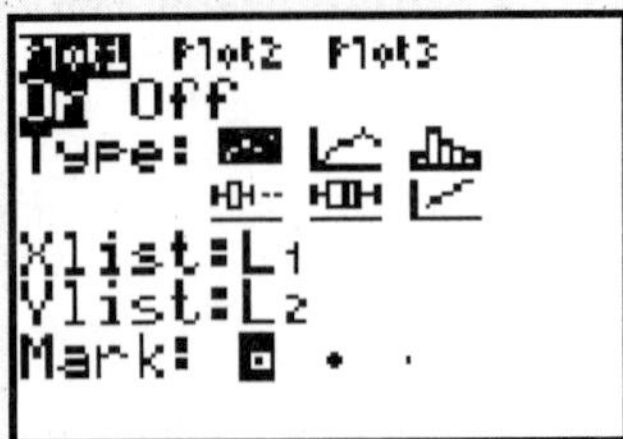

Step 3 *Find the regression equation as shown in part A above*

Step 4 *Enter the regression equation*

Press **Y=**

Press **VARS 5** for **Statistics . . .**

Highlight **EQ** and press **ENTER**

You should see the regression equation in the **Y=** window.

(continued)

Step 5 *View the scatterplot and regression line*
Press ZOOM 9 for ZoomStat

You should see the data graphed along with the regression line.

Example: The figures below show a table of data entered on the TI-83, and the graph of the scatterplot and least squares line obtained using the steps given above.

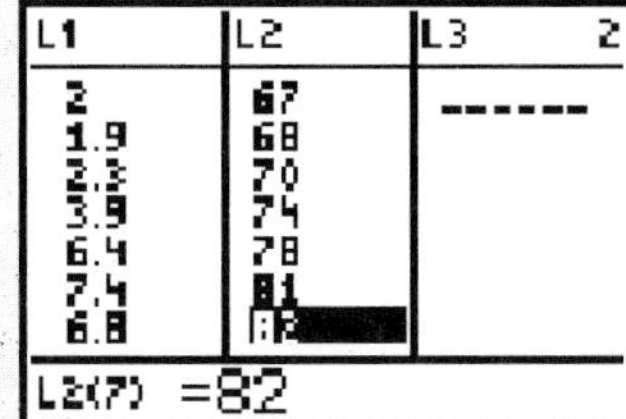

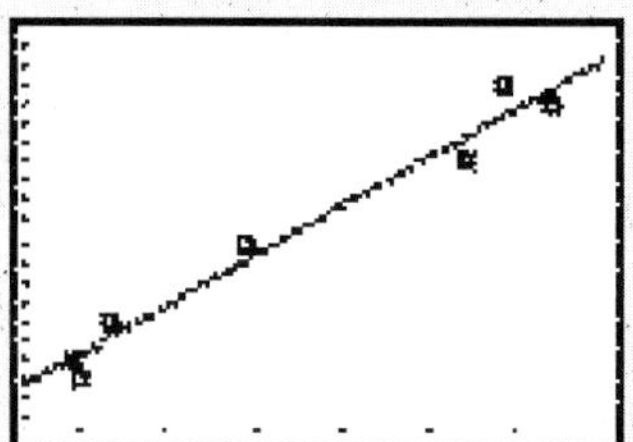

Even when the interpretations of the estimated parameters are meaningful, we need to remember that they are only estimates based on the sample. As such, their values will typically change in repeated sampling. How much confidence do we have that the estimated slope, $\hat{\beta}_1$, accurately approximates the true slope, β_1? This requires statistical inference, in the form of confidence intervals and tests of hypotheses, which we address in Section 9.5.

To summarize, we defined the best-fitting straight line to be the one that minimizes the sum of squared errors around the line, and we called it the least squares line. We should interpret the least squares line only within the sampled range of the independent variable. In subsequent sections we show how to make statistical inferences about the model.

EXERCISES 9.10–9.21

Learning the Mechanics

9.10 The following table is similar to Table 9.3. It is used for making the preliminary computations for finding the least squares line for the given pairs of x and y values.

	x_i	y_i	x_i^2	$x_i y_i$
	7	2		
	4	4		
	6	2		
	2	5		
	1	7		
	1	6		
	3	5		
Totals	$\sum x_i =$	$\sum y_i =$	$\sum x_i^2 =$	$\sum x_i y_i =$

a. Complete the table. b. Find SS_{xy}.
c. Find SS_{xx}. d. Find $\hat{\beta}_1$.
e. Find $\bar{x}$ and $\bar{y}$. f. Find $\hat{\beta}_0$.
g. Find the least squares line.

9.11 Refer to Exercise 9.10. After the least squares line has been obtained, the table below (which is similar to Table 9.4) can be used for (1) comparing the observed and the predicted values of y, and (2) computing SSE.

x	y	$\hat{y}$	$(y - \hat{y})$	$(y - \hat{y})^2$
7	2			
4	4			
6	2			
2	5			
1	7			
1	6			
3	5			
			$\sum(y - \hat{y}) =$	$\text{SSE} = \sum(y - \hat{y})^2 =$

a. Complete the table.
b. Plot the least squares line on a scattergram of the data. Plot the following line on the same graph: $\hat{y} = 14 - 2.5x$
c. Show that SSE is larger for the line in part **b** than it is for the least squares line.

9.12 Construct a scattergram for the data in the following table.

x	.5	1	1.5
y	2	1	3

a. Plot the following two lines on your scattergram:

$$y = 3 - x \quad \text{and} \quad y = 1 + x$$

b. Which of these lines would you choose to characterize the relationship between x and y? Explain.
c. Show that the sum of errors for both of these lines equals 0.
d. Which of these lines has the smaller SSE?
e. Find the least squares line for the data and compare it to the two lines described in part **a.**

9.13 Consider the following pairs of measurements:

LM9_13.DAT

x	8	5	4	6	2	5	3
y	1	3	6	3	7	2	5

a. Construct a scattergram for these data.
b. What does the scattergram suggest about the relationship between x and y?
c. Find the least squares estimates of β_0 and β_1 on the MINITAB printout below.
d. Plot the least squares line on your scattergram. Does the line appear to fit the data well? Explain.
e. Interpret the y-intercept and slope of the least squares line. Over what range of x are these interpretations meaningful?

Applying the Concepts

9.14 The quality of the orange juice produced by a manufacturer (e.g., Minute Maid, Tropicana) is constantly monitored. There are numerous sensory and chemical components that combine to make the best tasting orange juice. For example, one manufacturer has developed a quantitative index of the "sweetness" of orange juice. (The higher the index, the sweeter the juice.) Is there a relationship between the sweetness index and a chemical measure such as the amount of water soluble pectin (parts per million) in the orange juice? Data collected on these two variables for 24 production runs at a juice manufacturing plant are shown in the table. Suppose a manufacturer wants to use simple linear regression to predict the sweetness (y) from the amount of pectin (x).

OJUICE.DAT

Run	Sweetness Index	Pectin (ppm)
1	5.2	220
2	5.5	227
3	6.0	259
4	5.9	210
5	5.8	224
6	6.0	215
7	5.8	231
8	5.6	268
9	5.6	239
10	5.9	212
11	5.4	410
12	5.6	256
13	5.8	306
14	5.5	259
15	5.3	284
16	5.3	383
17	5.7	271
18	5.5	264
19	5.7	227
20	5.3	263
21	5.9	232
22	5.8	220
23	5.8	246
24	5.9	241

Note: The data in the table are authentic. For confidentiality reasons, the manufacturer cannot be disclosed.

MINITAB Output for Exercise 9.13

```
The regression equation is
Y = 8.54 - 0.994 X

Predictor        Coef       Stdev     t-ratio        p
Constant        8.543       1.117        7.65    0.001
X             -0.9939      0.2208       -4.50    0.006

s = 1.069        R-sq = 80.2%      R-sq(adj) = 76.2%

Analysis of Variance

SOURCE       DF          SS          MS          F        p
Regression    1      23.144      23.144      20.25    0.006
Error         5       5.713       1.143
Total         6      28.857
```

a. Find the least squares line for the data.
b. Interpret $\hat{\beta}_0$ and $\hat{\beta}_1$ in the words of the problem.
c. Predict the sweetness index if amount of pectin in the orange juice is 300 ppm. [*Note:* A measure of reliability of such a prediction is discussed in Section 9.8]

9.15 Is the number of games won by a major league baseball team in a season related to the team's batting average? The information in the table, extracted from *Sports Illustrated* and *Sporting News,* shows the number of games won and the batting average for the 14 teams in the American League for the 1998 season.

ALWINS.DAT

Team	Games Won	Batting Ave.
New York	114	.288
Toronto	88	.266
Baltimore	79	.273
Boston	92	.280
Tampa Bay	63	.261
Cleveland	89	.272
Detroit	65	.264
Chicago	80	.271
Kansas City	72	.263
Minnesota	70	.266
Anaheim	85	.272
Texas	88	.289
Seattle	76	.276
Oakland	74	.257

Sources: Sports Illustrated and *Sporting News,* March 29, 1999.

a. If you were to model the relationship between the mean (or expected) number of games won by a major league team and the team's batting average, x, using a straight line, would you expect the slope of the line to be positive or negative? Explain.
b. Construct a scattergram of the data. Does the pattern revealed by the scattergram agree with your answer in part **a?**
c. An SPSS printout of the simple linear regression is provided below. Find the estimates of the β's on the printout and write the equation of the least squares line.
d. Graph the least squares line on the scattergram. Does the least squares line seem to fit the points on the scattergram?
e. Does the mean (or expected) number of games won appear to be strongly related to a team's batting average? Explain.
f. Interpret the values of $\hat{\beta}_0$ and $\hat{\beta}_1$ in the words of the problem.

9.16 Refer to the *Forbes* magazine (Jan. 11, 1999) report on the financial standings of each team in the National Football League (NFL), Exercise 2.113 (p. 113). The table listing the current value (without deduction for debt, except stadium debt) and operating income for each team is reproduced on page 486.
a. Propose a straight-line model relating an NFL team's current value (y) to its operating income (x).
b. Fit the model to the data using the method of least squares.
c. Interpret the least squares estimates of the slope and y-intercept in the words of the problem.

9.17 In recent years U.S. banks have been merging to form mega banks that span many states. The table on page 486, extracted from the *Journal of Banking and Finance* (Feb. 1999) lists the number of U.S. bank mergers each year from 1980 (year 1) to 1993 (year 14) for which $50 million or more changed hands in the transaction.

SPSS Output for Exercise 9.15

```
Equation Number 1    Dependent Variable..    WINS

Block Number 1.   Method:  Enter        BATAVE

Variable(s) Entered on Step Number
    1..    BATAVE

Multiple R              .76684
R Square                .58804
Adjusted R Square       .55371
Standard Error         8.78666

Analysis of Variance
                       DF       Sum of Squares        Mean Square
Regression              1           1322.46420         1322.46420
Residual               12            926.46437           77.20536

F =        17.12918           Signif F =  .0014

------------------Variables in the Equation-------------------

Variable              B           SE B        Beta          T    Sig T

BATAVE       1057.367150    255.480401    .766839     4.139    .0014
(Constant)   -205.777174     69.347955               -2.967    .0118
```

NFLVALUE.DAT

Team	Current Value ($ millions)	Operating Income ($ millions)
Dallas Cowboys	663	56.7
Washington Redskins	607	48.8
Tampa Bay Buccaneers	502	41.2
Carolina Panthers	488	18.8
New England Patriots	460	13.5
Miami Dolphins	446	32.9
Denver Broncos	427	5.0
Jacksonville Jaguars	419	29.3
Baltimore Ravens	408	33.2
Seattle Seahawks	399	6.4
Pittsburgh Steelers	397	15.5
Cincinnati Bengals	394	3.4
St. Louis Rams	390	33.2
New York Giants	376	25.2
San Francisco 49ers	371	12.7
Tennessee Titans	369	4.1
New York Jets	363	12.1
Kansas City Chiefs	353	31.0
Buffalo Bills	326	10.7
San Diego Chargers	323	8.2
Green Bay Packers	320	16.4
Philadelphia Eagles	318	19.1
New Orleans Saints	315	11.3
Chicago Bears	313	19.7
Minnesota Vikings	309	5.1
Atlanta Falcons	306	16.8
Indianapolis Colts	305	15.8
Arizona Cardinals	301	10.6
Oakland Raiders	299	17.3
Detroit Lions	293	16.4

Source: *Forbes*, Jan. 11, 1999.

MERGERS.DAT

Year	Number of Bank Mergers
1	4
2	17
3	19
4	45
5	25
6	37
7	44
8	35
9	27
10	31
11	21
12	38
13	45
14	49

Source: Esty, B., Narasimhan, B., and Tufano P., "Interest-Rate Exposure and Bank Mergers," *Journal of Banking and Finance*, Vol. 23, No. 2-4, Feb. 1999, p. 264.

a. Construct a scattergram for the data, where y = number of mergers and x = year. Is there visual evidence of a linear relationship between x and y? Explain.
b. Use the method of least squares to fit a straight line to the data.
c. Graph the least squares line on your scattergram.
d. According to the least squares line, how many mergers will occur in 1994 (year 15)?
Compare your answer to the actual number of 1994 mergers: 42.

9.18 Due primarily to the price controls of the Organization of Petroleum Exporting Countries (OPEC), a cartel of crude-oil suppliers, the price of crude oil rose

STATISTIX Output for Exercise 9.18

```
UNWEIGHTED LEAST SQUARES LINEAR REGRESSION OF GASOLINE

PREDICTOR
VARIABLES     COEFFICIENT     STD ERROR     STUDENT'S T      P
---------     -----------     ---------     -----------    ------
CONSTANT        30.1348        5.45403          5.53       0.0000
CRUDEOIL        3.01815        0.26542         11.37       0.0000

R-SQUARED               0.8660      RESID. MEAN SQUARE (MSE)   80.2262
ADJUSTED R-SQUARED      0.8593      STANDARD DEVIATION         8.95691

SOURCE         DF        SS          MS          F         P
----------     ---    ---------   ----------   -----    ------
REGRESSION      1      10373.3     10373.3    129.30    0.0000
RESIDUAL       20      1604.52     80.2262
TOTAL          21      11977.9

CASES INCLUDED 22    MISSING CASES 0
```

dramatically from the mid-1970s to the mid-1980s. As a result, motorists saw an upward spiral in gasoline prices. The data in the table below are typical prices for a gallon of regular leaded gasoline and a barrel of crude oil (refiner acquisition cost) for the years 1975–1996.

GASOIL.DAT

Year	Gasoline, y (cents/gal.)	Crude Oil, x (\$/bbl.)
1975	57	10.38
1976	59	10.89
1977	62	11.96
1978	63	12.46
1979	86	17.72
1980	119	28.07
1981	131	35.24
1982	122	31.87
1983	116	28.99
1984	113	28.63
1985	112	26.75
1986	86	14.55
1987	90	17.90
1988	90	14.67
1989	100	17.97
1990	115	22.23
1991	72	16.54
1992	71	15.99
1993	75	14.24
1994	67	13.21
1995	63	14.63
1996	72	18.56

Source: U.S. Bureau of the Census, *Statistical Abstract of the United States: 1982–1998.*

a. Use the STATISTIX printout on p. 486 to find the least squares line that describes the relationship between the price of a gallon of gasoline and the price of a barrel of crude oil over the 22-year period.
b. Construct a scattergram of all the data.
c. Plot your least squares line on the scattergram. Does your least squares line appear to be an appropriate characterization of the relationship between y and x over the 22-year period?
d. According to your model, if the price of crude oil fell to \$15 per barrel, to what level (approximately) would the price of regular leaded gasoline fall? Justify your answer.

9.19 Individuals who report perceived wrongdoing of a corporation or public agency are known as *whistle blowers.* Two researchers developed an index to measure the extent of retaliation against a whistle blower (*Journal of Applied Psychology,* 1986). The index was based on the number of forms of reprisal actually experienced, the number of forms of reprisal threatened, and the number of people within the organization (e.g., coworkers or immediate supervisor) who retaliated against them. The next table lists the retaliation index

RETAL.DAT

Retaliation Index	Salary	Retaliation Index	Salary
301	\$62,000	535	\$19,800
550	36,500	455	44,000
755	21,600	615	46,600
327	24,000	700	15,100
500	30,100	650	70,000
377	35,000	630	21,000
290	47,500	360	16,900
452	54,000		

Source: Data adapted from Near, J. P., and Miceli, M. P. "Retaliation against whistle blowers: Predictors and effects." *Journal of Applied Psychology*, Vol. 71, No. 1, 1986, pp. 137–145.

(higher numbers indicate more extensive retaliation) and salary for a sample of 15 whistle blowers from federal agencies.

a. Construct a scattergram for the data. Does it appear that the extent of retaliation increases, decreases, or stays the same with an increase in salary? Explain.
b. Use the method of least squares to fit a straight line to the data.
c. Graph the least squares line on your scattergram. Does the least squares line support your answer to the question in part **a?** Explain.
d. Interpret the y-intercept, $\hat{\beta}_0$, of the least squares line in terms of this application. Is the interpretation meaningful?
e. Interpret the slope, $\hat{\beta}_1$, of the least squares line in terms of this application. Over what range of x is this interpretation meaningful?

9.20 *Sales and Marketing Management* determined the "effective buying income" (EBI) of the average household in a state. Can the EBI be used to predict retail sales per household in the store-group category "eating and drinking places"?

a. Use the data for 13 states given in the table on page 488 to find the least squares line relating retail sales per household (y) to average household EBI (x).
b. Plot the least squares line, as well as the actual data points, on a scattergram.
c. Based on the graph, part **b,** give your opinion regarding the predictive ability of the least squares line.

9.21 The downsizing and restructuring that took place in corporate America during the 1990s encouraged both laid off middle managers and recent graduates of business schools to become entrepreneurs and start their own businesses. Assuming a business start-up does well, how fast will it grow? Can it expect to need 10 employees in three years or 50 or 100? To answer these questions, a random sample of 12 firms were drawn from the *Inc. Magazine's* "1996 Ranking of the Fastest-Growing Private Companies in America." The age (in years since 1995), x, and number of employees (in 1995), y, of each firm are

EBI.DAT

State	Average Household Buying Income ($)	Retail Sales: Eating and Drinking Places ($ per household)
Connecticut	60,998	2,553.8
New Jersey	63,853	2,154.8
Michigan	46,915	2,523.3
Minnesota	44,717	2,278.6
Florida	42,442	2,475.8
South Carolina	37,848	2,358.4
Mississippi	34,490	1,538.4
Oklahoma	34,830	2,063.1
Texas	44,729	2,363.5
Colorado	44,571	3,214.9
Utah	43,421	2,653.8
California	50,713	2,215.0
Oregon	40,597	2,144.0

Source: Sales and Marketing Management, 1995.

INC12.DAT

Firm	Age, x (years)	Number of Employees, y
General Shelters of Texas	5	43
Productivity Point International	5	52
K.C. Oswald	4	9
Multimax	7	40
Pay + Benefits	5	6
Radio Spirits	6	12
KRA	14	200
Consulting Partners	5	76
Apex Instruments	7	15
Portable Products	6	40
Progressive System Technology	5	65
Viking Components	7	175

Source: Inc. 500, October 22, 1996, pp. 103–132.

recorded in the table at left. SAS was used to conduct a simple linear regression analysis for the model, $E(y) = \beta_0 + \beta_1 x$. The printout is shown below.

a. Plot the data in a scattergram. Does the number of employees at a fast-growing firm appear to increase linearly as the firm's age increases?

b. Find the estimates of β_0 and β_1 in the SAS printout. Interpret their values.

SAS Output for Exercise 9.21

```
Dependent Variable: NUMBER

                          Analysis of Variance

                            Sum of         Mean
       Source       DF     Squares       Square         F Value        Prob>F

       Model         1  23536.50149  23536.50149         11.451        0.0070
       Error        10  20554.41518   2055.44152
       C Total      11  44090.91667

           Root MSE      45.33698      R-square          0.5338
           Dep Mean      61.08333      Adj R-sq          0.4872
           C.V.          74.22152

                          Parameter Estimates

                     Parameter       Standard     T for HO:
     Variable  DF     Estimate          Error   Parameter=0      Prob > |T|

     INTERCEP   1   -51.361607    35.71379104        -1.438          0.1809
     AGE        1    17.754464     5.24673562         3.384          0.0070
```

9.3 MODEL ASSUMPTIONS

In Section 9.2 we assumed that the probabilistic model relating the firm's sales revenue y to the advertising dollars is

$$y = \beta_0 + \beta_1 x + \varepsilon$$

We also recall that the least squares estimate of the deterministic component of the model, $\beta_0 + \beta_1 x$, is

$$\hat{y} = \hat{\beta}_0 + \hat{\beta}_1 x = -.1 + .7x$$

Now we turn our attention to the random component ε of the probabilistic model and its relation to the errors in estimating β_0 and β_1. We will use a probability distribution to characterize the behavior of ε. We will see how the probability distribution of ε determines how well the model describes the relationship between the dependent variable y and the independent variable x.

Step 3 in a regression analysis requires us to specify the probability distribution of the random error ε. We will make four basic assumptions about the general form of this probability distribution:

Assumption 1: The mean of the probability distribution of ε is 0. That is, the average of the values of ε over an infinitely long series of experiments is 0 for each setting of the independent variable x. This assumption implies that the mean value of y, $E(y)$, for a given value of x is $E(y) = \beta_0 + \beta_1 x$.

Assumption 2: The variance of the probability distribution of ε is constant for all settings of the independent variable x. For our straight-line model, this assumption means that the variance of ε is equal to a constant, say σ^2, for all values of x.

Assumption 3: The probability distribution of ε is normal.

Assumption 4: The values of ε associated with any two observed values of y are independent. That is, the value of ε associated with one value of y has no effect on the values of ε associated with other y values.

The implications of the first three assumptions can be seen in Figure 9.7, which shows distributions of errors for three values of x, namely, x_1, x_2, and x_3. Note that the relative frequency distributions of the errors are normal with a

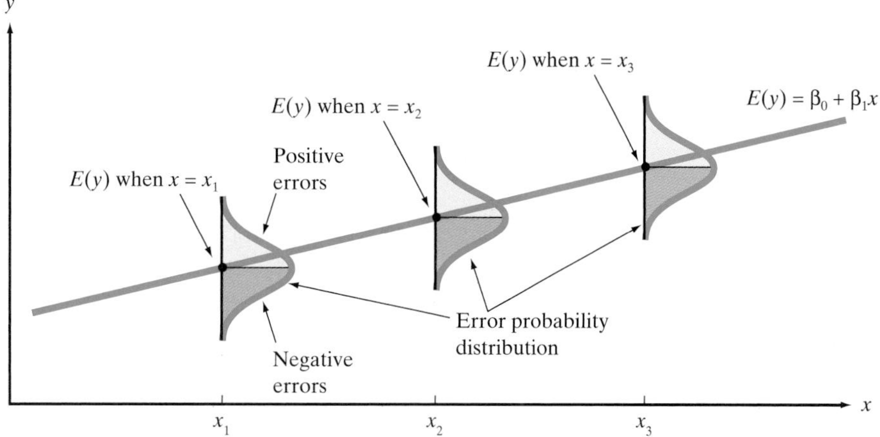

FIGURE 9.7
The probability distribution of ε

mean of 0 and a constant variance σ^2. (All the distributions shown have the same amount of spread or variability.) The straight line shown in Figure 9.7 is the line of means. It indicates the mean value of y for a given value of x. We denote this mean value as $E(y)$. Then, the line of means is given by the equation

$$E(y) = \beta_0 + \beta_1 x$$

These assumptions make it possible for us to develop measures of reliability for the least squares estimators and to develop hypothesis tests for examining the usefulness of the least squares line. We have various techniques for checking the validity of these assumptions, and we have remedies to apply when they appear to be invalid. Several of these remedies are discussed in Chapter 10. Fortunately, the assumptions need not hold exactly in order for least squares estimators to be useful. The assumptions will be satisfied adequately for many applications encountered in practice.

9.4 AN ESTIMATOR OF σ^2

It seems reasonable to assume that the greater the variability of the random error ε (which is measured by its variance σ^2), the greater will be the errors in the estimation of the model parameters β_0 and β_1 and in the error of prediction when $\hat{y}$ is used to predict y for some value of x. Consequently, you should not be surprised, as we proceed through this chapter, to find that σ^2 appears in the formulas for all confidence intervals and test statistics that we will be using.

Estimation of σ^2 for a (First-Order) Straight-Line Model

$$s^2 = \frac{\text{SSE}}{\text{Degrees of freedom for error}} = \frac{\text{SSE}}{n-2}$$

$$\text{where SSE} = \sum (y_i - \hat{y}_i)^2 = \text{SS}_{yy} - \hat{\beta}_1 \text{SS}_{xy}$$

$$\text{SS}_{yy} = \sum (y_i - \bar{y})^2 = \sum y_i^2 - \frac{\left(\sum y_i\right)^2}{n}$$

To estimate the standard deviation σ of ε, we calculate

$$s = \sqrt{s^2} = \sqrt{\frac{\text{SSE}}{n-2}}$$

We will refer to s as the **estimated standard error of the regression model.**

Warning: When performing these calculations, you may be tempted to round the calculated values of SS_{yy}, $\hat{\beta}_1$, and SS_{xy}. Be certain to carry at least six significant figures for each of these quantities to avoid substantial errors in calculation of the SSE.

In most practical situations, σ^2 is unknown and we must use our data to estimate its value. The best estimate of σ^2, denoted by s^2, is obtained by dividing the sum of squares of the deviations of the y values from the prediction line,

$$\text{SSE} = \sum (y_i - \hat{y}_i)^2$$

by the number of degrees of freedom associated with this quantity. We use 2 df to estimate the two parameters β_0 and β_1 in the straight-line model, leaving $(n - 2)$ df for the error variance estimation.

In the advertising–sales example, we previously calculated SSE = 1.10 for the least squares line $\hat{y} = -.1 + .7x$. Recalling that there were $n = 5$ data points, we have $n - 2 = 5 - 2 = 3$ df for estimating σ^2. Thus,

$$s^2 = \frac{\text{SSE}}{n-2} = \frac{1.10}{3} = .367$$

is the estimated variance, and

$$s = \sqrt{.367} = .61$$

is the standard error of the regression model.

The values of s^2 and s can also be obtained from a simple linear regression printout. The SAS printout for the advertising–sales example is reproduced in Figure 9.8. The value of s^2 is highlighted on the printout in the **Mean Square** column in the row labeled **Error.** (In regression, the estimate of σ^2 is called Mean Square for Error, or MSE.) The value, $s^2 = .36667$, rounded to three decimal places agrees with the one calculated by hand. The value of s is highlighted in Figure 9.8 next to the heading **Root MSE.** This value, $s = .60553$, agrees (except for rounding) with our hand-calculated value.

```
Dependent Variable: Y

                          Analysis of Variance

                              Sum of          Mean
Source            DF         Squares        Square      F Value     Prob>F

Model              1         4.90000       4.90000       13.364     0.0354
Error              3         1.10000       0.36667
C Total            4         6.00000

      Root MSE         0.60553       R-square        0.8167
      Dep Mean         2.00000       Adj R-sq        0.7556
      C.V.            30.27650

                          Parameter Estimates

                     Parameter        Standard      T for HO:
Variable    DF        Estimate           Error    Parameter=0    Prob > |T|

INTERCEP     1       -0.100000      0.63508530         -0.157        0.8849
X            1        0.700000      0.19148542          3.656        0.0354
```

FIGURE 9.8
SAS printout for advertising expenditure–sales revenue example

You may be able to grasp s intuitively by recalling the interpretation of a standard deviation given in Chapter 2 and remembering that the least squares line estimates the mean value of y for a given value of x. Since s measures the spread of the distribution of y values about the least squares line, we should not be surprised to find that most of the observations lie within $2s$, or $2(.61) = 1.22$, of the least squares line. For this simple example (only five data points), all five sales revenue values fall within $2s$ (or $1,220) of the least squares line. In Section 9.8, we use s to evaluate the error of prediction when the least squares line is used to predict a value of y to be observed for a given value of x.

Interpretation of s, the Estimated Standard Deviation of ε

We expect most ($\approx$ 95%) of the observed y values to lie within $2s$ of their respective least squares predicted values, $\hat{y}$.

EXERCISES 9.22–9.30

Learning the Mechanics

9.22 Calculate SSE and s^2 for each of the following cases:

a. $n = 20$, $SS_{yy} = 95$, $SS_{xy} = 50$, $\hat{\beta}_1 = .75$

b. $n = 40$, $\sum y^2 = 860$, $\sum y = 50$, $SS_{xy} = 2{,}700$, $\hat{\beta}_1 = .2$

c. $n = 10$, $\sum(y_i - \bar{y})^2 = 58$, $SS_{xy} = 91$, $SS_{xx} = 170$

9.23 Suppose you fit a least squares line to 26 data points and the calculated value of SSE is 8.34.

a. Find s^2, the estimator of σ^2 (the variance of the random error term ε).

b. What is the largest deviation that you might expect between any one of the 26 points and the least squares line?

9.24 Visually compare the scattergrams shown below. If a least squares line were determined for each data set, which do you think would have the smallest variance, s^2? Explain.

9.25 Refer to Exercises 9.10 and 9.13. Calculate SSE, s^2, and s for the least squares lines obtained in these exercises. Interpret the standard error of the regression model, s, for each.

Applying the Concepts

9.26 *Statistical Bulletin* (Oct.–Dec. 1999) reported the average hospital charge and the average length of hospital stay for patients undergoing radical prostatectomies in a sample of 12 states. The data are listed in the accompanying table.

a. Plot the data on a scattergram.

b. Use the method of least squares to model the relationship between average hospital charge (y) and length of hospital stay (x).

c. Find the estimated standard error of the regression model and interpret its value in the context of the problem.

d. For a hospital stay of length $x = 4$ days, find $\hat{y} \pm 2s$.

e. What fraction of the states in the sample have average hospital charges within $\pm 2s$ of the least squares line?

HOSPITAL.DAT

State	Average Hospital Charge ($)	Average Length of Stay (days)
Massachusetts	11,680	3.64
New Jersey	11,630	4.20
Pennsylvania	9,850	3.84
Minnesota	9,950	3.11
Indiana	8,490	3.86
Michigan	9,020	3.54
Florida	13,820	4.08
Georgia	8,440	3.57
Tennessee	8,790	3.80
Texas	10,400	3.52
Arizona	12,860	3.77
California	16,740	3.78

Source: *Statistical Bulletin*, Vol. 80, No. 4, Oct.–Dec. 1999, p. 13.

Scattergrams for Exercise 9.24

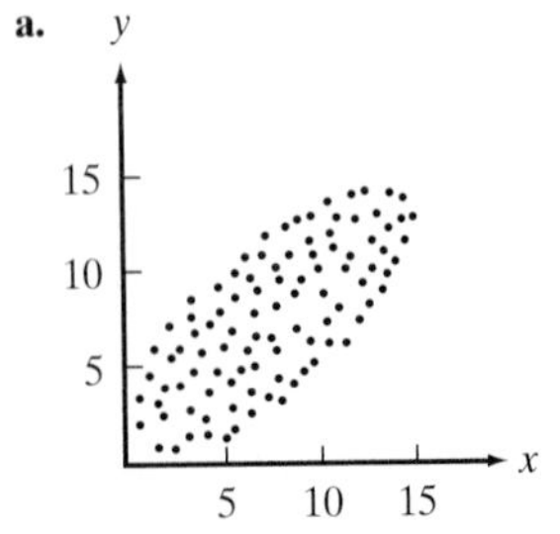

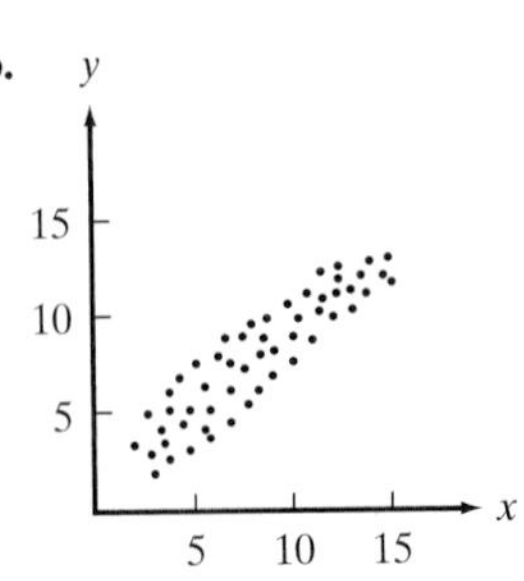

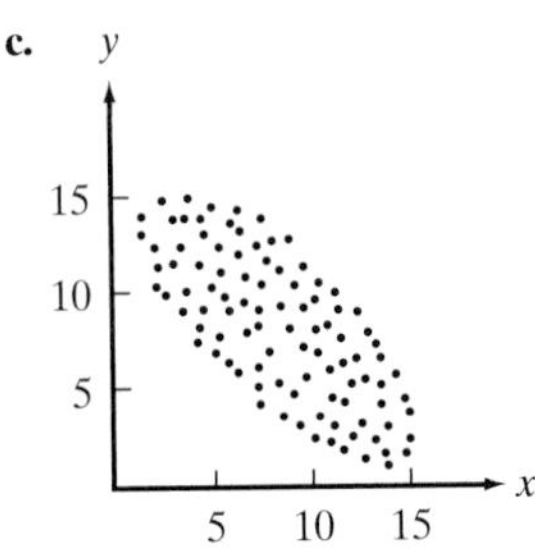

IMPORTS.DAT

	1950	1960	1970	1980	1990
Industrial Countries' Imports, x	39.8	85.4	226.9	1,370.2	2,237.9
Developing Countries' Imports, y	21.1	40.1	75.6	556.4	819.4

9.27 Prior to the 1970s the developing countries played a small role in world trade because their own economic policies hindered integration with the world economy. However, many of these countries have since changed their policies and vastly improved their importance to the global economy (*World Economy,* July 1992). Data (given in billions of U.S. dollars) for investigating the relationship between developing countries' and industrial countries' annual import levels are shown in the table above.

a. Fit a least squares line to the data. Plot the data points and graph the least squares line as a check on your calculations.

b. According to your least squares line, approximately what would you expect annual imports for developing countries to be if annual imports for industrial countries were $1,600 billion?

c. Calculate SSE and s^2.

d. Interpret the standard deviation s in the context of this problem.

9.28 Refer to the simple linear regression relating games won by a major league baseball team y to team batting average x, Exercise 9.15 (p. 485). The SPSS printout is reproduced below.

a. Find SSE, s^2, and s on the printout.

b. Interpret the value of s.

9.29 Refer to the simple linear regression relating number of employees y to age x of a fast-growing firm, Exercise 9.21 (p. 487). The SAS printout is reproduced on the next page.

a. Find SSE, s^2, and s on the printout.

b. Interpret the value of s.

9.30 To improve the quality of the output of any production process, it is necessary first to understand the capabilities of the process (Gitlow, *et al., Quality Management: Tools and Methods for Improvement,* 1995). In a particular manufacturing process, the useful life of a cutting tool is related to the speed at which the tool is operated. The data in the table on page 494 were derived from life tests for the two different

SPSS Output for Exercise 9.28

```
Equation Number 1      Dependent Variable..      WINS

Block Number  1.   Method:  Enter        BATAVE

Variable(s) Entered on Step Number
   1..      BATAVE

Multiple R               .76684
R Square                 .58804
Adjusted R Square        .55371
Standard Error          8.78666

Analysis of Variance
                     DF      Sum of Squares        Mean Square
Regression            1          1322.46420         1322.46420
Residual             12           926.46437           77.20536

F =        17.12918          Signif F =  .0014

------------------ Variables in the Equation --------------------

Variable                 B         SE B         Beta           T   Sig T

BATAVE        1057.367150   255.480401      .766839       4.139   .0014
(Constant)    -205.777174    69.347955                   -2.967   .0118
```

SAS Output for Exercise 9.29

```
Dependent Variable:   NUMBER
                              Analysis of Variance

                                 Sum of          Mean
        Source           DF     Squares         Square         F Value        Prob>F

        Model             1  23536.50149    23536.50149         11.451        0.0070
        Error            10  20554.41518     2055.44152
        C Total          11  44090.91667

            Root MSE        45.33698      R-square           0.5338
            Dep Mean        61.08333      Adj R-sq           0.4872
            C.V.            74.22152

                             Parameter Estimates

                      Parameter        Standard       T for HO:
       Variable  DF    Estimate           Error     Parameter=0     Prob > |T|

       INTERCEP   1  -51.361607     35.71379104          -1.438         0.1809
       AGE        1   17.754464      5.24673562           3.384         0.0070
```

CUTTOOLS.DAT

Cutting Speed (meters per minute)	Useful Life (Hours)	
	Brand A	Brand B
30	4.5	6.0
30	3.5	6.5
30	5.2	5.0
40	5.2	6.0
40	4.0	4.5
40	2.5	5.0
50	4.4	4.5
50	2.8	4.0
50	1.0	3.7
60	4.0	3.8
60	2.0	3.0
60	1.1	2.4
70	1.1	1.5
70	.5	2.0
70	3.0	1.0

brands of cutting tools currently used in the production process.

a. Construct a scattergram for each brand of cutting tool.

b. For each brand, the method of least squares was used to model the relationship between useful life and cutting speed. Find the least squares line for each brand on the EXCEL printouts shown on p. 495.

c. Locate SSE, s^2, and s for each least squares line on the printouts.

d. For a cutting speed of 70 meters per minute, find $\hat{y} \pm 2s$ for each least squares line.

e. For which brand would you feel more confident in using the least squares line to predict useful life for a given cutting speed? Explain.

9.5 ASSESSING THE UTILITY OF THE MODEL: MAKING INFERENCES ABOUT THE SLOPE β_1

Now that we have specified the probability distribution of ε and found an estimate of the variance σ^2, we are ready to make statistical inferences about the model's usefulness for predicting the response y. This is step 4 in our regression modeling procedure.

Refer again to the data of Table 9.1 and suppose the appliance store's sales revenue is *completely unrelated* to the advertising expenditure. What could be said about the values of β_0 and β_1 in the hypothesized probabilistic model

$$y = \beta_0 + \beta_1 x + \varepsilon$$

EXCEL Output for Exercise 9.30: Brand A

SUMMARY OUTPUT						
Regression Statistics						
Multiple R	0.6737515					
R Square	0.453941084					
Adjusted R Square	0.411936552					
Standard Error	1.210721336					
Observations	15					
ANOVA						
	df	SS	MS	F	Significance F	
Regression	1	15.84133333	15.84133333	10.80695494	0.00588884	
Residual	13	19.056	1.465846154			
Total	14	34.89733333				
	Coefficients	Standard Error	t Stat	P-value	Lower 95%	Upper 95%
Intercept	6.62	1.14859111	5.763582829	6.55988E-05	4.138620245	9.101379755
Speed(x)	-0.072666667	0.022104646	-3.287393335	0.00588884	-0.120420842	-0.024912491

EXCEL Output for Exercise 9.30: Brand B

SUMMARY OUTPUT						
Regression Statistics						
Multiple R	0.937007633					
R Square	0.877983304					
Adjusted R Square	0.868597404					
Standard Error	0.609728817					
Observations	15					
ANOVA						
	df	SS	MS	F	Significance F	
Regression	1	34.77633333	34.77633333	93.5427961	2.64643E-07	
Residual	13	4.833	0.371769231			
Total	14	39.60933333				
	Coefficients	Standard Error	t Stat	P-value	Lower 95%	Upper 95%
Intercept	9.31	0.578439545	16.09502683	5.7707E-10	8.060357577	10.55964242
Speed(x)	-0.10766667	0.011132074	-9.67175248	2.6464E-07	-0.13171605	-0.08361729

if x contributes no information for the prediction of y? The implication is that the mean of y—that is, the deterministic part of the model $E(y) = \beta_0 + \beta_1 x$—does not change as x changes. In the straight-line model, this means that the true slope, β_1, is equal to 0 (see Figure 9.9). Therefore, to test the null hypothesis that the linear model contributes no information for the prediction of y against the alternative hypothesis that the linear model is useful for predicting y, we test

$$H_0: \beta_1 = 0$$
$$H_a: \beta_1 \neq 0$$

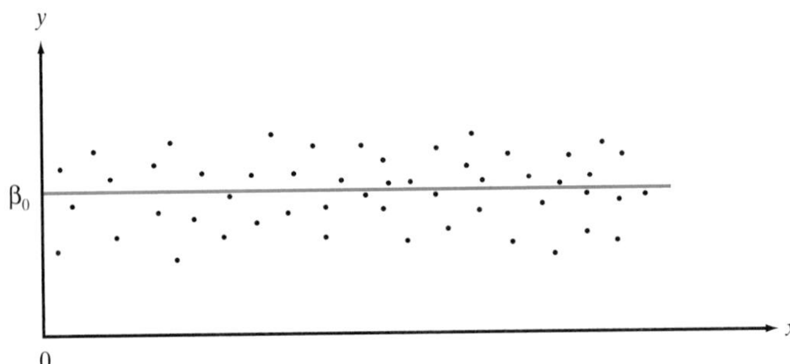

FIGURE 9.9
Graphing the $\beta_1 = 0$ model $y = \beta_0 + \varepsilon$

If the data support the alternative hypothesis, we will conclude that x does contribute information for the prediction of y using the straight-line model (although the true relationship between $E(y)$ and x could be more complex than a straight line). Thus, in effect, this is a test of the usefulness of the hypothesized model.

The appropriate test statistic is found by considering the sampling distribution of $\hat{\beta}_1$, the least squares estimator of the slope β_1, as shown in the following box.

Sampling Distribution of $\hat{\beta}_1$

If we make the four assumptions about ε (see Section 9.3), the sampling distribution of the least squares estimator $\hat{\beta}_1$ of the slope will be normal with mean β_1 (the true slope) and standard deviation

$$\sigma_{\hat{\beta}_1} = \frac{\sigma}{\sqrt{SS_{xx}}} \quad \text{(see Figure 9.10)}$$

We estimate $\sigma_{\hat{\beta}_1}$ by $s_{\hat{\beta}_1} = \frac{s}{\sqrt{SS_{xx}}}$ and refer to this quantity as the estimated standard error of the least squares slope $\hat{\beta}_1$.

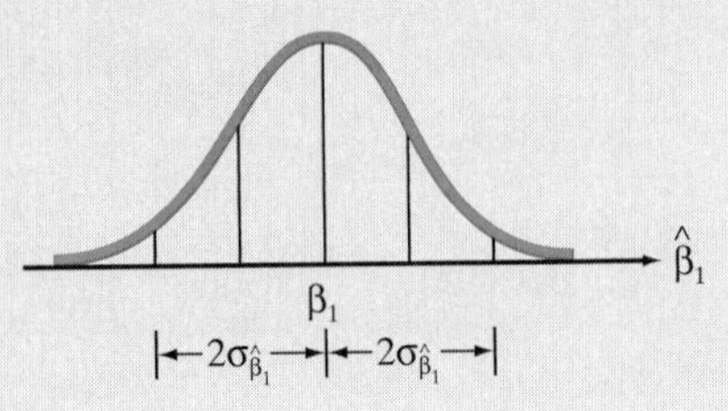

FIGURE 9.10
Sampling distribution of $\hat{\beta}_1$

Since σ is usually unknown, the appropriate test statistic is a t statistic, formed as follows:

$$t = \frac{\hat{\beta}_1 - \text{Hypothesized value of } \beta_1}{s_{\hat{\beta}_1}} \qquad \text{where } s_{\hat{\beta}_1} = \frac{s}{\sqrt{\text{SS}_{xx}}}$$

Thus,

$$t = \frac{\hat{\beta}_1 - 0}{s/\sqrt{\text{SS}_{xx}}}$$

Note that we have substituted the estimator s for σ and then formed the estimated standard error $s_{\hat{\beta}_1}$ by dividing s by $\sqrt{\text{SS}_{xx}}$. The number of degrees of freedom associated with this t statistic is the same as the number of degrees of freedom associated with s. Recall that this number is $(n - 2)$ df when the hypothesized model is a straight line (see Section 9.4). The setup of our test of the usefulness of the straight-line model is summarized in the next box.

A Test of Model Utility: Simple Linear Regression

One-Tailed Test	**Two-Tailed Test**
H_0: $\beta_1 = 0$	H_0: $\beta_1 = 0$
H_a: $\beta_1 < 0$ (or H_a: $\beta_1 > 0$)	H_a: $\beta_1 \neq 0$

Test statistic: $t = \dfrac{\hat{\beta}_1}{s_{\hat{\beta}_1}} = \dfrac{\hat{\beta}_1}{s/\sqrt{\text{SS}_{xx}}}$

Rejection region: $t < -t_\alpha$ (or $t > t_\alpha$ when H_a: $\beta_1 > 0$)	*Rejection region*: $\lvert t\rvert > t_{\alpha/2}$

where t_α and $t_{\alpha/2}$ are based on $(n - 2)$ degrees of freedom

Assumptions: The four assumptions about ε listed in Section 9.3.

For the advertising–sales example, we will choose $\alpha = .05$ and, since $n = 5$, t will be based on $n - 2 = 3$ df and the rejection region will be

$$|t| > t_{.025} = 3.182$$

We previously calculated $\hat{\beta}_1 = .7$, $s = .61$, and $\text{SS}_{xx} = 10$. Thus,

$$t = \frac{\hat{\beta}_1}{s/\sqrt{\text{SS}_{xx}}} = \frac{.7}{.61\sqrt{10}} = \frac{.7}{.19} = 3.7$$

Since this calculated t value falls in the upper-tail rejection region (see Figure 9.11), we reject the null hypothesis and conclude that the slope β_1 is not 0. The sample evidence indicates that advertising expenditure x contributes information for the prediction of sales revenue y when a linear model is used.

We can reach the same conclusion by using the observed significance level (p-value) of the test from a computer printout. The SAS printout for the advertising–sales example is reproduced in Figure 9.12. The test statistic is highlighted on the printout under the **T for HO: Parameter=0** column in the row corresponding to **X,** while the *two-tailed* p-value is highlighted under the column labeled **Prob >|T|.** Since the p-value $= .0354$ is smaller than $\alpha = .05$, we will reject H_0.

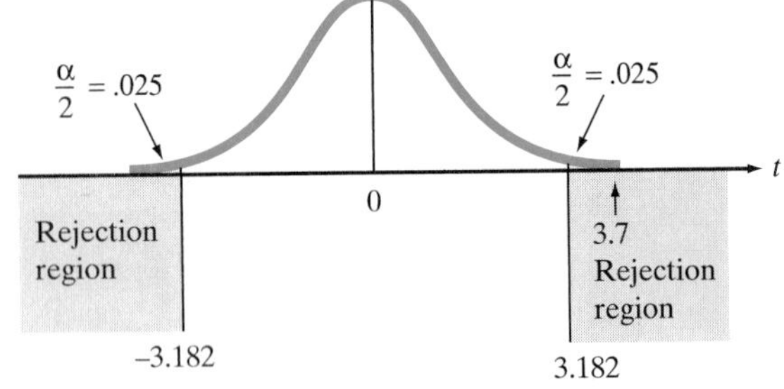

FIGURE 9.11
Rejection region and calculated t value for testing H_0: $\beta_1 = 0$ versus H_a: $\beta_1 \neq 0$

```
Dependent Variable: Y

                    Analysis of Variance

                          Sum of          Mean
     Source       DF     Squares        Square      F Value     Prob>F

     Model         1     4.90000       4.90000       13.364     0.0354
     Error         3     1.10000       0.36667
     C Total       4     6.00000

        Root MSE        0.60553      R-square      0.8167
        Dep Mean        2.00000      Adj R-sq      0.7556
        C.V.           30.27650

                     Parameter Estimates

                    Parameter       Standard     T for HO:
   Variable  DF      Estimate          Error   Parameter=0    Prob > |T|

   INTERCEP   1     -0.100000     0.63508530        -0.157        0.8849
   X          1      0.700000     0.19148542         3.656        0.0354
```

FIGURE 9.12
SAS printout for advertising–sales example

What conclusion can be drawn if the calculated t value does not fall in the rejection region or if the observed significance level of the test exceeds α? We know from previous discussions of the philosophy of hypothesis testing that such a t value does *not* lead us to accept the null hypothesis. That is, we do not conclude that $\beta_1 = 0$. Additional data might indicate that β_1 differs from 0, or a more complex relationship may exist between x and y, requiring the fitting of a model other than the straight-line model.

Interpreting p-Values for β Coefficients in Regression

Almost all statistical computer software packages report a *two-tailed* p-value for each of the β parameters in the regression model. For example, in simple linear regression, the p-value for the two-tailed test H_0: $\beta_1 = 0$ versus H_a: $\beta_1 \neq 0$ is given on the printout. If you want to conduct a *one-tailed* test of hypothesis, you will need to adjust the p-value reported on the printout as follows:

$$\textit{Upper-tailed test } (H_a\!: \beta_1 > 0)\!: \quad p\text{-value} = \begin{cases} p/2 & \text{if } t > 0 \\ 1 - p/2 & \text{if } t < 0 \end{cases}$$

(continued)

Lower-tailed test (H_a: $\beta_1 < 0$): p-value $= \begin{cases} p/2 & \text{if } t < 0 \\ 1 - p/2 & \text{if } t > 0 \end{cases}$

where p is the p-value reported on the printout and t is the value of the test statistic.

Another way to make inferences about the slope β_1 is to estimate it using a confidence interval. This interval is formed as shown in the next box.

A 100(1 − α)% Confidence Interval for the Simple Linear Regression Slope β_1

$$\hat{\beta}_1 \pm t_{\alpha/2} s_{\hat{\beta}_1}$$

where the estimated standard error $\hat{\beta}_1$ is calculated by

$$s_{\hat{\beta}_1} = \frac{s}{\sqrt{\text{SS}_{xx}}}$$

and $t_{\alpha/2}$ is based on $(n - 2)$ degrees of freedom.

Assumptions: The four assumptions about ε listed in Section 9.3.

For the advertising–sales example, $t_{\alpha/2}$ is based on $(n - 2) = 3$ degrees of freedom. Therefore, a 95% confidence interval for the slope β_1, the expected change in sales revenue for a \$100 increase in advertising expenditure, is

$$\hat{\beta}_1 \pm t_{.025} s_{\hat{\beta}_1} = .7 \pm 3.182\left(\frac{s}{\sqrt{\text{SS}_{xx}}}\right) = .7 \pm 3.182\left(\frac{.61}{\sqrt{10}}\right) = .7 \pm .61$$

Thus, the interval estimate of the slope parameter β_1 is .09 to 1.31. In terms of this example, the implication is that we can be 95% confident that the *true* mean increase in monthly sales revenue per additional \$100 of advertising expenditure is between \$90 and \$1,310. This inference is meaningful only over the sampled range of x—that is, from \$100 to \$500 of advertising expenditures.

Since all the values in this interval are positive, it appears that β_1 is positive and that the mean of y, $E(y)$, increases as x increases. However, the rather large width of the confidence interval reflects the small number of data points (and, consequently, a lack of information) in the experiment. Particularly bothersome is the fact that the lower end of the confidence interval implies that we are not even recovering our additional expenditure, since a \$100 increase in advertising may produce as little as a \$90 increase in mean sales. If we wish to tighten this interval, we need to increase the sample size.

EXERCISES 9.31–9.43

Learning the Mechanics

9.31 Construct both a 95% and a 90% confidence interval for β_1 for each of the following cases:

a. $\hat{\beta}_1 = 31$, $s = 3$, $\text{SS}_{xx} = 35$, $n = 10$
b. $\hat{\beta}_1 = 64$, SSE $= 1{,}960$, $\text{SS}_{xx} = 30$, $n = 14$
c. $\hat{\beta}_1 = -8.4$, SSE $= 146$, $\text{SS}_{xx} = 64$, $n = 20$

9.32 Consider the following pairs of observations:

x	1	4	3	2	5	6	0
y	1	3	3	1	4	7	2

a. Construct a scattergram for the data.
b. Use the method of least squares to fit a straight line to the seven data points in the table.
c. Plot the least squares line on your scattergram of part **a.**
d. Specify the null and alternative hypotheses you would use to test whether the data provide sufficient evidence to indicate that x contributes information for the (linear) prediction of y.
e. What is the test statistic that should be used in conducting the hypothesis test of part **d?** Specify the degrees of freedom associated with the test statistic.
f. Conduct the hypothesis test of part **d** using $\alpha = .05$.

9.33 Refer to Exercise 9.32. Construct an 80% and a 98% confidence interval for β_1.

9.34 Do the accompanying data provide sufficient evidence to conclude that a straight line is useful for characterizing the relationship between x and y?

x	4	2	4	3	2	4
y	1	6	5	3	2	4

Applying the Concepts

9.35 Some critics of big business argue that CEOs are overpaid and that their compensation is not related to the performance of their companies. To test this theory, *Chief Executive* (Sept. 1999) collected data on executive's total pay and company's performance for each in a sample of 17 CEOs selected from a variety of industries. The data are listed in the table below. (*Note:* Company performance is the three-year annualized total return to shareholders for the years 1996 to 1998, assuming dividends are reinvested.)

a. Construct a scattergram for these data. Does it appear that CEO pay is related to company performance? Explain.
b. Use the method of least squares to model the relationship between CEO pay (y) and company performance (x).
c. Is CEO compensation related to company performance? Conduct the appropriate hypothesis test using $\alpha = .05$.
d. Interpret the estimate of β_1 in the context of the problem.
e. Construct a 90% confidence interval for β_1 and interpret your result in the context of the problem.
f. How might the results of part **e** change if a sample of CEOs from the *same* industry were used?

9.36 Financial institutions have a legal and social responsibility to serve all communities. Do banks adequately serve both inner city and suburban neighborhoods, both poor and wealthy communities? In New Jersey, banks have been charged with withdrawing from urban areas with a high percentage of minorities. To examine this charge, a regional New Jersey newspaper, the *Asbury Park Press*, compiled county by county data on the number (y) of people in each county per branch bank in the county and the percentage (x) of the popu-

CEO17.DAT

Company	CEO	Total Pay ($ thousands)	Performance (percent)
Cummins Engine	James A. Henderson	4,338	.8
Bank Of New York	Thomas A. Renyi	7,121	52.5
SunTrust Banks	L. Phillip Humann	3,882	33.0
Bear Stearns	James E. Cayne	25,002	46.1
Charles Schwab	Charles R. Schwab	16,506	85.5
Coca-Cola	M. Douglas Ivester	12,712	22.9
Time Warner	Gerald M. Levin	25,136	49.6
Humana	Gregory H. Wolf	4,516	−13.3
Engelhard	Orin R. Smith	6,189	−1.8
Chubb	Dean R. O'Hare	4,052	12.3
American Home Products	John R. Stafford	8,046	35.5
Merck	Raymond V. Gilmartin	7,178	33.4
Schering-Plough	Richard J. Kogan	6,818	61.8
Home Depot	Arthur M. Blank	2,900	58.6
Dell Computer	Michael S. Dell	115,797	222.4
BellSouth	F. Duane Ackerman	18,134	35.8
Delta Air Lines	Leo F. Mullin	17,085	20.8

Source: *Chief Executive*, Sept. 1999, pp. 45–59.

NJBANKS.DAT

County	Number of People per Bank Branch	Percentage of Minority Population
Atlantic	3,073	23.3
Bergen	2,095	13.0
Burlington	2,905	17.8
Camden	3,330	23.4
Cape May	1,321	7.3
Cumberland	2,557	26.5
Essex	3,474	48.8
Gloucester	3,068	10.7
Hudson	3,683	33.2
Hunterdon	1,998	3.7
Mercer	2,607	24.9
Middlesex	3,154	18.1
Monmouth	2,609	12.6
Morris	2,253	8.2
Ocean	2,317	4.7
Passaic	3,307	28.1
Salem	2,511	16.7
Somerset	2,333	12.0
Sussex	2,568	2.4
Union	3,048	25.6
Warren	2,349	2.8

Source: D'Ambrosio, P., and Chambers, S. "No checks and balances." *Asbury Park Press,* September 10, 1995.

lation in each county that is minority. These data for each of New Jersey's 21 counties are provided in the table above.

a. Plot the data in a scattergram. What pattern, if any, does the plot reveal?

b. Consider the linear model $E(y) = \beta_0 + \beta_1 x$. If, in fact, the charge against the New Jersey banks is true, then an increase in the percentage of minorities (x) will lead to a decrease in the number of bank branches in a county and therefore will result in an increase in the number of people (y) per branch. Will the value of β_1 be positive or negative in this situation?

c. Do these data support or refute the charge made against the New Jersey banking community? Test using $\alpha = .01$.

9.37 *Tennis* magazine (Feb. 2000) claims that "tennis players who tie the knot often see their games unravel." The next table lists a sample of players and their rankings on their wedding days and on their first anniversaries.

a. Construct a scattergram for these data. Does it tend to support or refute the magazine's claim? Justify your answer.

b. Use the method of least squares to construct a model of the relationship between wedding day ranking (x) and first anniversary ranking (y).

c. Does the linear model you developed in part **b** contribute information for predicting players' rankings on their first anniversaries? Test at $\alpha = .05$.

TENLOVE.DAT

Player	Ranking on Wedding Day	Ranking on First Anniversary
Arthur Ashe	12	130
Jonathan Stark	67	165
Richey Reneberg	28	97
Paul Haarhuis	28	73
Richard Fromberg	40	79
Byron Black	44	77
Sabine Appelmans	16	49
Petr Korda	7	11
Dominique Van Roost	43	46
Ivan Lendl	1	3
John McEnroe	7	9
Stefan Edberg	2	3
Chris Evert	4	4
Mats Wilander	3	3
Sandrine Testud	14	12
Zina Garrison	6	4
Yevgeny Kafelnikov	8	4
Boris Becker	11	3
Michael Stich	15	6
Julie Halard-Decugis	32	15
Todd Woodbridge	71	27
Jason Stoltenberg	82	31

Source: *Tennis,* Feb. 2000, p. 14.

d. If there were no changes whatsoever in the rankings of the sample of players after getting married, what would the true values of β_0 and β_1 be?

9.38 The U.S. Department of Agriculture has developed and adopted the Universal Soil Loss Equation (USLE) for predicting water erosion of soils. In geographical areas where runoff from melting snow is common, the USLE requires an accurate estimate of snowmelt runoff erosion. An article in the *Journal of Soil and Water Conservation* (Mar.–Apr. 1995) used simple linear regression to develop a snowmelt erosion index. Data for 54 climatological stations in Canada were used to model the McCool winter-adjusted rainfall erosivity index, y, as a straight-line function of the once-in-five-year snowmelt runoff amount, x (measured in millimeters).

a. The data points are plotted in the scattergram shown below. Is there visual evidence of a linear trend?

b. The data for seven stations were removed from the analysis due to lack of snowfall during the study period. Why is this strategy advisable?

c. The simple linear regression on the remaining $n = 47$ data points yielded the following results:

$$\hat{y} = -6.72 + 1.39x; \qquad s_{\hat{\beta}_1} = .06$$

Use this information to construct a 90% confidence interval for β_1.

d. Interpret the interval, part **c.**

9.39 One of the most common types of "information retrieval" processes is document-database searching. An experiment was conducted to investigate the variables that influence search performance in the Medline database and retrieval system (*Journal of Information Science,* Vol. 21, 1995). Simple linear regression was used to model the fraction y of the set of potentially informative documents that are retrieved using Medline as a function of the number x of terms in the search query, based on a sample of $n = 124$ queries. The results are summarized below:

$$\hat{y} = .202 + .135x$$

$$t \text{ (for testing } H_0\text{: } \beta_1 = 0) = 4.98$$

$$\text{Two-tailed } p\text{-value} = .001$$

a. Is there sufficient evidence to indicate that x and y are linearly related? Test using $\alpha = .01$.

b. If appropriate, use the model to predict the fraction of documents retrieved for a search query with $x = 3$ terms.

9.40 One of the most difficult tasks of developing and managing a global portfolio is assessing the risks of potential foreign investments. Duke University researcher C. R. Henry collaborated with two First Chicago Investment Management Company directors to examine the use of country credit ratings as a means of evaluating foreign investments (*Journal of Portfolio Management,* Winter 1995). To be effective, such a measure should help explain and predict the volatility of the foreign market in question. The researchers analyzed data on annualized risk (y) and average credit rating (x) for the 40 countries shown in the table on p. 504. An SPSS printout for a simple linear regression analysis conducted on the data is also provided on p. 503.

a. Locate the least squares estimates of β_0 and β_1 on the printout.

b. Plot the data in a scattergram, then sketch the least squares line on the graph.

c. Do the data provide sufficient evidence to conclude that country credit risk (x) contributes information for the prediction of market volatility (y)?

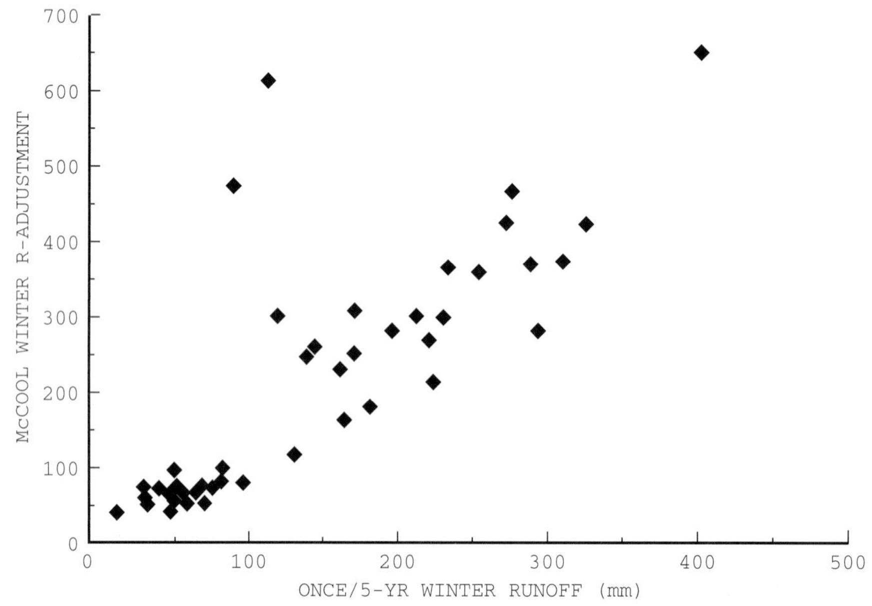

SPSS Output for Exercise 9.40

```
Equation Number 1     Dependent Variable..    RISK

Variable(s) Entered on Step Number
   1..      RATING

Multiple R               .57802
R Square                 .33411
Adjusted R Square        .31658
Standard Error         12.67770

Analysis of Variance
                        DF        Sum of Squares          Mean Square
Regression               1            3064.40538           3064.40538
Residual                38            6107.51862            160.72417

F =        19.06624          Signif F =   .0001

------------------- Variables in the Equation ---------------------

Variable                  B            SE B         Beta           T     Sig T

RATING              -.399606        .091516     -.578020      -4.366     .0001
(Constant)         57.755060       6.127836                    9.425     .0000
```

SAS Output for Exercise 9.41

```
Dependent Variable:   NUMBER

                           Analysis of Variance

                                   Sum of           Mean
          Source          DF      Squares         Square        F Value       Prob>F

          Model            1  23536.50149    23536.50149         11.451       0.0070
          Error           10  20554.41518     2055.44152
          C Total         11  44090.91667

              Root MSE        45.33698     R-square         0.5338
              Dep Mean        61.08333     Adj R-sq         0.4872
              C.V.            74.22152

                           Parameter Estimates

                          Parameter         Standard     T for HO:
        Variable   DF      Estimate            Error   Parameter=0     Prob > |T|

        INTERCEP    1    -51.361607      35.71379104        -1.438         0.1809
        AGE         1     17.754464       5.24673562         3.384         0.0070
```

d. Use the plot, part **b,** to visually locate any unusual data points (outliers).

e. Eliminate the outlier(s), part **d,** from the data set and rerun the simple linear regression analysis. Note any dramatic changes in the results.

9.41 Refer to Exercises 9.21 and 9.29 (p. 487, 493). The SAS simple linear regression printout relating number of employees y to age of a fast-growing firm x is reproduced above.

a. Test to determine whether y is positively linearly related to x. Use $\alpha = .01$.

b. Construct a 99% confidence interval for β_1. Practically interpret the result.

9.42 H. Mintzberg's classic book, *The Nature of Managerial Work* (1973), identified the roles found in all managerial jobs. An observational study of 19 managers from a medium-sized manufacturing plant extended Mintzberg's work by investigating which activities *successful* managers actually perform (*Journal of Applied Behavioral Science,* Aug. 1985). To measure success, the researchers devised an index based on the manager's length of time in the organization and his or her level within the firm; the higher the index, the more successful the manager. The table on p. 505 presents data (which are representative of the data collected by the researchers) that can be used to determine whether managerial success is related to the extensiveness of a manager's network-building interactions with people outside the manager's work unit. Such interactions include phone and face-to-face meetings with customers and suppliers, attending outside meetings, and doing public relations work. A MINITAB printout of the simple linear regression is also provided on page 505.

a. Construct a scattergram for the data.
b. Find the prediction equation for managerial success.
c. Find s for your prediction equation. Interpret the standard deviation s in the context of this problem.
d. Plot the least squares line on your scattergram of part **a.** Does it appear that the number of interactions with outsiders contributes information for the prediction of managerial success? Explain.
e. Conduct a formal statistical hypothesis test to answer the question posed in part **d.** Use $\alpha = .05$.
f. Construct a 95% confidence interval for β_1. Interpret the interval in the context of the problem.

GLOBRISK.DAT (Data for Exercise 9.40)

Country	Annualized Risk (%)	Average Credit Rating
Argentina	87.0	31.8
Australia	26.9	78.2
Austria	26.3	83.8
Belgium	22.0	78.4
Brazil	64.8	36.2
Canada	19.2	87.1
Chile	31.6	38.6
Colombia	31.5	44.4
Denmark	20.6	72.6
Finland	26.1	76.0
France	23.8	85.3
Germany	23.0	93.4
Greece	39.6	51.9
Hong Kong	34.3	69.6
India	30.0	46.6
Ireland	23.4	66.4
Italy	28.0	75.5
Japan	25.7	94.5
Jordan	17.6	33.6
Korea	30.7	62.2
Malaysia	26.7	64.4
Mexico	46.3	43.3
Netherlands	18.5	87.6
New Zealand	26.3	68.9
Nigeria	41.4	30.6
Norway	28.3	83.0
Pakistan	24.4	26.4
Philippines	38.4	29.6
Portugal	47.5	56.7
Singapore	26.4	77.6
Spain	24.8	70.8
Sweden	24.5	79.5
Switzerland	19.6	94.7
Taiwan	53.7	72.9
Thailand	27.0	55.8
Turkey	74.1	32.6
United Kingdom	21.8	87.6
United States	15.4	93.4
Venezuela	46.0	45.0
Zimbabwe	35.6	24.5

Source: Adapted from Erb, C. B., Harvey, C. R., and Viskanta, T. E. "Country risk and global equity selection." *Journal of Portfolio Management,* Vol. 21, No. 2, Winter 1995, p. 76. Published by Institutional Investor, Inc., 488 Madison Ave., New York, NY 10022.

MANAGERS.DAT

Manager	Manager Success Index, y	Number of Interactions with Outsiders, x
1	40	12
2	73	71
3	95	70
4	60	81
5	81	43
6	27	50
7	53	42
8	66	18
9	25	35
10	63	82
11	70	20
12	47	81
13	80	40
14	51	33
15	32	45
16	50	10
17	52	65
18	30	20
19	42	21

MINITAB Output for Exercise 9.42

```
The regression equation is
SUCCESS = 44.1 + 0.237 INTERACT

Predictor        Coef       Stdev      t-ratio        p
Constant       44.130       9.362         4.71    0.000
INTERACT       0.2366      0.1865         1.27    0.222

s = 19.40       R-sq = 8.6%        R-sq(adj) = 3.3%

Analysis of Variance

SOURCE        DF          SS          MS        F        p
Regression     1       606.0       606.0     1.61    0.222
Error         17      6400.6       376.5
Total         18      7006.6
```

9.43 Refer to Exercise 9.19 (p. 487), in which the extent of retaliation against whistle blowers was investigated. Since salary is a reasonably good indicator of a person's power within an organization, the data of Exercise 9.19 can be used to investigate whether the extent of retaliation is related to the power of the whistle blower in the organization. The researchers were unable to reject the hypothesis that the extent of retaliation is unrelated to power. Do you agree? Test using $\alpha = .05$.

9.6 THE COEFFICIENT OF CORRELATION

Recall (from optional Section 2.10) that a **bivariate relationship** describes a relationship between two variables, x and y. Scattergrams are used to graphically describe a bivariate relationship. In this section we will discuss the concept of **correlation** and show how it can be used to measure the linear relationship between two variables x and y. A numerical descriptive measure of correlation is provided by the *Pearson product moment coefficient of correlation, r.*

DEFINITION 9.2

The **Pearson product moment coefficient of correlation,** *r*, is a measure of the strength of the *linear* relationship between two variables *x* and *y*. It is computed (for a sample of *n* measurements on *x* and *y*) as follows:

$$r = \frac{SS_{xy}}{\sqrt{SS_{xx}SS_{yy}}}$$

Note that the computational formula for the correlation coefficient r given in Definition 9.2 involves the same quantities that were used in computing the least squares prediction equation. In fact, since the numerators of the expressions for $\hat{\beta}_1$ and r are identical, you can see that $r = 0$ when $\hat{\beta}_1 = 0$ (the case where x contributes no information for the prediction of y) and that r is positive when the slope is positive and negative when the slope is negative. Unlike $\hat{\beta}_1$, the correlation coefficient r is *scaleless* and assumes a value between -1 and $+1$, regardless of the units of x and y.

A value of r near or equal to 0 implies little or no linear relationship between y and x. In contrast, the closer r comes to 1 or -1, the stronger the linear relationship between y and x. And if $r = 1$ or $r = -1$, all the sample points fall exactly on the least squares line. Positive values of r imply a positive linear relationship between y and x; that is, y increases as x increases. Negative values of r imply a negative linear relationship between y and x; that is, y decreases as x increases. Each of these situations is portrayed in Figure 9.13.

FIGURE 9.13
Values of r and their implications

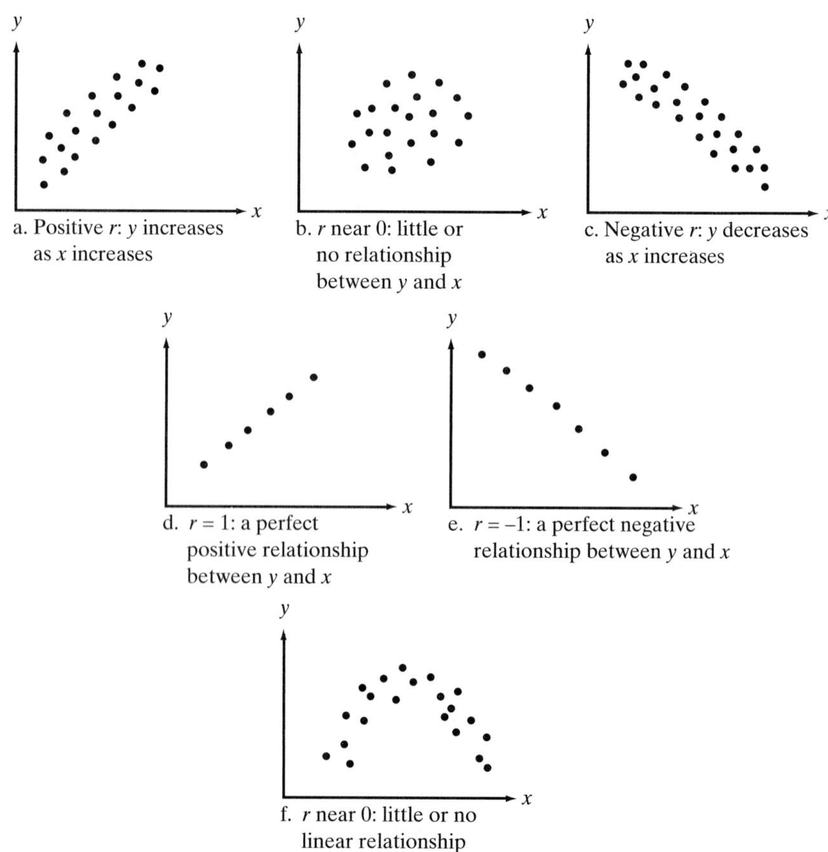

y
x
a. Positive r: y increases as x increases
b. r near 0: little or no relationship between y and x
c. Negative r: y decreases as x increases
d. r = 1: a perfect positive relationship between y and x
e. r = −1: a perfect negative relationship between y and x
f. r near 0: little or no linear relationship between y and x

We demonstrate how to calculate the coefficient of correlation r using the data in Table 9.1 for the advertising–sales example. The quantities needed to calculate r are SS_{xy}, SS_{xx}, and SS_{yy}. The first two quantities have been calculated previously and are repeated here for convenience:

$$SS_{xy} = 7 \qquad SS_{xx} = 10 \qquad SS_{yy} = \sum y^2 - \frac{(\sum y)^2}{n}$$

$$= 26 - \frac{(10)^2}{5} = 26 - 20 = 6$$

We now find the coefficient of correlation:

$$r = \frac{SS_{xy}}{\sqrt{SS_{xx}SS_{yy}}} = \frac{7}{\sqrt{(10)(6)}} = \frac{7}{\sqrt{60}} = .904$$

The fact that r is positive and near 1 in value indicates that the sales revenue y tends to increase as advertising expenditure x increases—*for this sample of five months*. This is the same conclusion we reached when we found the calculated value of the least squares slope to be positive.

EXAMPLE 9.1

Legalized gambling is available on several riverboat casinos operated by a city in Mississippi. The mayor of the city wants to know the correlation between the number of casino employees and the yearly crime rate. The records for the past 10 years are examined, and the results listed in Table 9.5 are obtained. Calculate the coefficient of correlation r for the data.

TABLE 9.5 Data on Casino Employees and Crime Rate, Example 9.1

Year	Number of Casino Employees, x (thousands)	Crime Rate, y (number of crimes per 1,000 population)
1991	15	1.35
1992	18	1.63
1993	24	2.33
1994	22	2.41
1995	25	2.63
1996	29	2.93
1997	30	3.41
1998	32	3.26
1999	35	3.63
2000	38	4.15

Solution Rather than use the computing formula given in Definition 9.2, we resort to a statistical software package. The data of Table 9.5 were entered into a computer and MINITAB was used to compute r. The MINITAB printout is shown in Figure 9.14.

FIGURE 9.14 MINITAB printout for Example 9.1

```
Correlation of NOEMPLOY and CRIMERAT = 0.987
```

The coefficient of correlation, highlighted on the printout, is $r = .987$. Thus, the size of the casino workforce and crime rate in this city are very highly correlated— at least over the past 10 years. The implication is that a strong positive linear relationship exists between these variables (see Figure 9.15). We must be careful, however, not to jump to any unwarranted conclusions. For instance, the mayor may be tempted to conclude that hiring more casino workers next year will increase the crime rate—that is, that there is a *causal relationship* between the two variables. However, high correlation does not imply causality. The fact is, many things have probably contributed both to the increase in the casino workforce and to the increase in crime rate. The city's tourist trade has undoubtedly grown since legalizing riverboat casinos and it is likely that the casinos have expanded both in services offered and in number. *We cannot infer a causal relationship on the basis of high sample correlation. When a high correlation is observed in the sample data, the only safe conclusion is that a linear trend may exist between* x *and* y. Another variable, such as the increase in tourism, may be the underlying cause of the high correlation between x and y.

FIGURE 9.15
Scattergram for Example 9.1

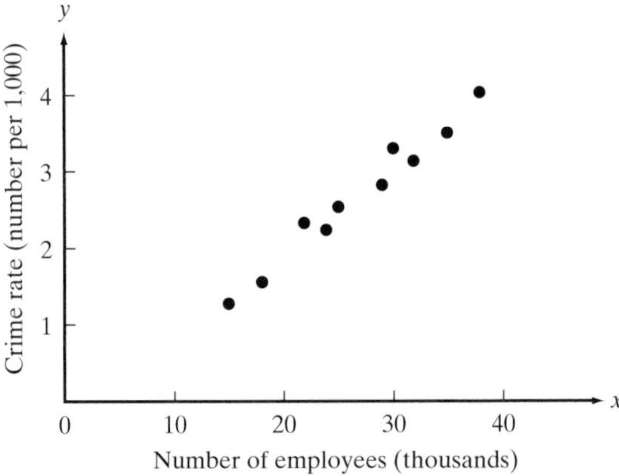

Keep in mind that the correlation coefficient r measures the linear correlation between x values and y values in the sample, and a similar linear coefficient of correlation exists for the population from which the data points were selected. The **population correlation coefficient** is denoted by the symbol ρ (rho). As you might expect, ρ is estimated by the corresponding sample statistic, r. Or, instead of estimating ρ, we might want to test the null hypothesis H_0: $\rho = 0$ against H_a: $\rho \neq 0$—that is, we can test the hypothesis that x contributes no information for the prediction of y by using the straight-line model against the alternative that the two variables are at least linearly related.

However, we already performed this *identical* test in Section 9.5 when we tested H_0: $\beta_1 = 0$ against H_a: $\beta_1 \neq 0$. That is, the null hypothesis H_0: $\rho = 0$ is equivalent to the hypothesis H_0: $\beta_1 = 0$.* When we tested the null hypothesis H_0: $\beta_1 = 0$ in connection with the advertising–sales example, the data led to a rejection of the null hypothesis at the $\alpha = .05$ level. This rejection implies that the null hypothesis of a 0 linear correlation between the two variables (sales revenue and advertising expenditure) can also be rejected at the $\alpha = .05$ level. The only real difference between the least squares slope $\hat{\beta}_1$ and the coefficient of correlation r is the measurement scale. Therefore, the information they provide about the usefulness of the least squares model is to some extent redundant. For this reason,

*The correlation test statistic that is equivalent to $t = \hat{\beta}_1/s_{\hat{\beta}_1}$ is $t = \dfrac{r}{\sqrt{(1 - r^2)/(n - 2)}}$.

we will use the slope to make inferences about the existence of a positive or negative linear relationship between two variables.

9.7 THE COEFFICIENT OF DETERMINATION

Another way to measure the usefulness of the model is to measure the contribution of x in predicting y. To accomplish this, we calculate how much the errors of prediction of y were reduced by using the information provided by x. To illustrate, consider the sample shown in the scattergram of Figure 9.16a. If we assume that x contributes no information for the prediction of y, the best prediction for a value of y is the sample mean $\bar{y}$, which is shown as the horizontal line in Figure 9.16b. The vertical line segments in Figure 9.16b are the deviations of the points about the mean $\bar{y}$. Note that the sum of squares of deviations for the prediction equation $\hat{y} = \bar{y}$ is

$$SS_{yy} = \sum (y_i - \bar{y})^2$$

FIGURE 9.16
A comparison of the sum of squares of deviations for two models

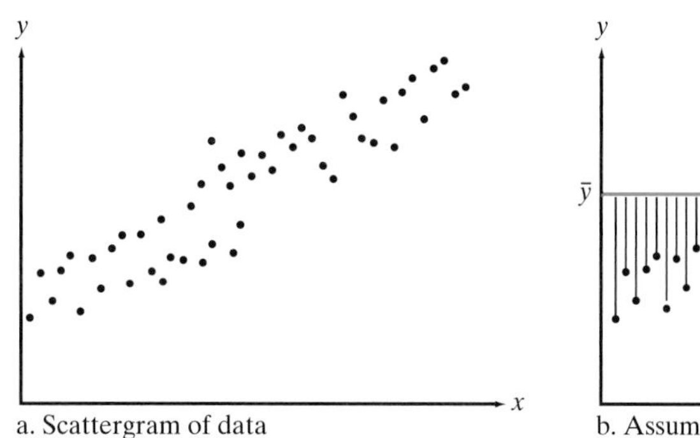

a. Scattergram of data

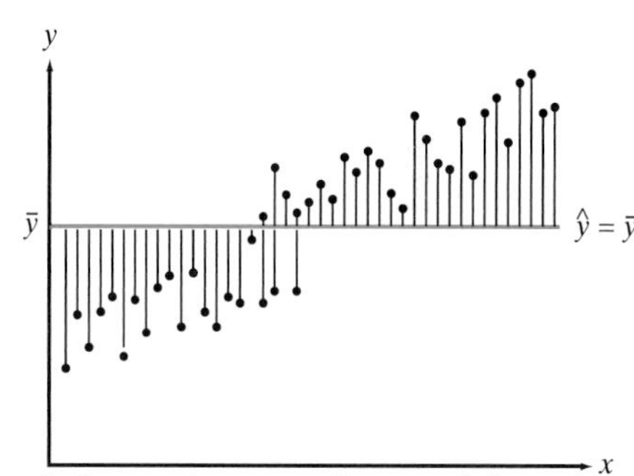

b. Assumption: x contributes no information for predicting y, $\hat{y} = \bar{y}$

y

$\hat{y} = \hat{\beta}_0 + \hat{\beta}_1 x$

x

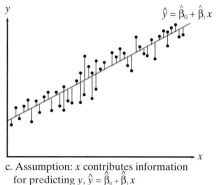

c. Assumption: x contributes information for predicting y, $\hat{y} = \hat{\beta}_0 + \hat{\beta}_1 x$

Now suppose you fit a least squares line to the same set of data and locate the deviations of the points about the line as shown in Figure 9.16c. Compare the deviations about the prediction lines in Figures 9.16b and 9.16c. You can see that

1. If x contributes little or no information for the prediction of y, the sums of squares of deviations for the two lines,

$$SS_{yy} = \sum (y_i - \bar{y})^2 \quad \text{and} \quad SSE = \sum (y_i - \hat{y}_i)^2$$

will be nearly equal.

2. If x does contribute information for the prediction of y, the SSE will be smaller than SS_{yy}. In fact, if all the points fall on the least squares line, then SSE $= 0$.

Then the reduction in the sum of squares of deviations that can be attributed to x, expressed as a proportion of SS_{yy}, is

$$\frac{SS_{yy} - SSE}{SS_{yy}}$$

Note that SS_{yy} is the "total sample variation" of the observations around the mean $\bar{y}$ and that SSE is the remaining "unexplained sample variability" after fitting the line $\hat{y}$. Thus, the difference (SS_{yy} − SSE) is the "explained sample variability" attributable to the linear relationship with x. Then a verbal description of the proportion is

$$\frac{SS_{yy} - SSE}{SS_{yy}} = \frac{\text{Explained sample variability}}{\text{Total sample variability}}$$

$$= \text{Proportion of total sample variability explained by the linear relationship}$$

In simple linear regression, it can be shown that this proportion—called the *coefficient of determination*—is equal to the square of the simple linear coefficient of correlation r (the Pearson product moment coefficient of correlation).

DEFINITION 9.3

The **coefficient of determination** is

$$r^2 = \frac{SS_{yy} - SSE}{SS_{yy}} = 1 - \frac{SSE}{SS_{yy}}$$

It represents the proportion of the total sample variability around $\bar{y}$ that is explained by the linear relationship between y and x. (In simple linear regression, it may also be computed as the square of the coefficient of correlation r.)

Note that r^2 is always between 0 and 1, because r is between −1 and +1. Thus, an r^2 of .60 means that the sum of squares of deviations of the y values about their predicted values has been reduced 60% by the use of the least squares equation $\hat{y}$, instead of $\bar{y}$, to predict y.

EXAMPLE 9.2

Calculate the coefficient of determination for the advertising–sales example. The data are repeated in Table 9.6 for convenience. Interpret the result.

TABLE 9.6 Advertising Expenditure–Sales Revenue Data

Advertising Expenditure, x ($100s)	Sales Revenue, y ($1,000s)
1	1
2	1
3	2
4	2
5	4

Solution From previous calculations,

$$SS_{yy} = 6 \quad \text{and} \quad SSE = \sum (y - \hat{y})^2 = 1.10$$

Then, from Definition 9.3, the coefficient of determination is given by

$$r^2 = \frac{SS_{yy} - SSE}{SS_{yy}} = \frac{6.0 - 1.1}{6.0} = \frac{4.9}{6.0} = .82$$

Another way to compute r^2 is to recall (Section 9.6) that $r = .904$. Then we have $r^2 = (.904)^2 = .82$. A third way to obtain r^2 is from a computer printout. This value is highlighted on the SAS printout reproduced in Figure 9.17, next to the heading **R-square.** Our interpretation is as follows: We know that using advertising expenditure, x, to predict y with the least squares line

$$\hat{y} = -.1 + .7x$$

accounts for 82% of the total sum of squares of deviations of the five sample y values about their mean. Or, stated another way, 82% of the sample variation in sales revenue (y) can be "explained" by using advertising expenditure (x) in a straight-line model.

```
Dependent Variable: Y

                           Analysis of Variance

                                  Sum of             Mean
        Source          DF       Squares           Square     F Value      Prob>F

        Model            1       4.90000          4.90000      13.364      0.0354
        Error            3       1.10000          0.36667
        C Total          4       6.00000

            Root MSE           0.60553      R-square     0.8167
            Dep Mean           2.00000      Adj R-sq     0.7556
            C.V.              30.27650

                           Parameter Estimates

                          Parameter        Standard     T for HO:
      Variable   DF        Estimate           Error   Parameter=0    Prob > |T|

      INTERCEP    1       -0.100000      0.63508530        -0.157        0.8849
      X           1        0.700000      0.19148542         3.656        0.0354
```

FIGURE 9.17
SAS printout for advertising-sales example

Practical Interpretation of the Coefficient of Determination, r^2

About $100(r^2)$% of the sample variation in y (measured by the total sum of squares of deviations of the sample y values about their mean $\bar{y}$) can be explained by (or attributed to) using x to predict y in the straight-line model.

EXERCISES 9.44–9.56

Learning the Mechanics

9.44 Explain what each of the following sample correlation coefficients tells you about the relationship between the x and y values in the sample:

a. $r = 1$ b. $r = -1$ c. $r = 0$
d. $r = .90$ e. $r = .10$ f. $r = -.88$

9.45 Describe the slope of the least squares line if

a. $r = .7$ b. $r = -.7$ c. $r = 0$ d. $r^2 = .64$

9.46 Construct a scattergram for each data set. Then calculate r and r^2 for each data set. Interpret their values.

a.

x	−2	−1	0	1	2
y	−2	1	2	5	6

b.

x	−2	−1	0	1	2
y	6	5	3	2	0

c.

x	1	2	2	3	3	3	4
y	2	1	3	1	2	3	2

d.

x	0	1	3	5	6
y	0	1	2	1	0

9.47 Calculate r^2 for the least squares line in each of the following exercises. Interpret their values.

a. Exercise 9.10 b. Exercise 9.13

Applying the Concepts

9.48 If the economies of the world were tightly interconnected, the stock markets of different countries would move together. If they did, there would be no reason for investors to diversify their stock portfolios with stocks from a variety of countries (Sharpe, Alexander, and Bailey, *Investments,* 1999). The table below lists the correlations of returns on stocks in each of six countries with the returns of U.S. stocks.

Country	Correlation between Foreign and U.S. Stocks
Australia	.48
Canada	.74
France	.50
Germany	.43
Japan	.41
U.K.	.58

Source: Sharpe, W. F., Alexander, G.J., and Bailey, Jeffery V., *Investments*. Upper Saddle River, N.J.: Prentice Hall, 1999, p. 887.

a. Interpret the Australia/U.S. correlation. What does it suggest about the linear relationship between the stocks of the two countries?

b. Sketch a scattergram that is roughly consistent with the magnitude of the France/U.S. correlation.

c. Why must we be careful not to conclude from the information in the table that the country which is most tightly integrated with the U.S. is Canada?

9.49 Many high school students experience "math anxiety," which has been shown to have a negative effect on their learning achievement. Does such an attitude carry over to learning computer skills? A math and computer science researcher at Duquesne University investigated this question and published her results in *Educational Technology* (May–June 1995). A sample of 1,730 high school students—902 boys and 828 girls—from public schools in Pittsburgh, Pennsylvania, participated in the study. Using five-point Likert scales, where 1 = "strongly disagree" and 5 = "strongly agree," the researcher measured the students' interest and confidence in both mathematics and computers.

a. For boys, math confidence and computer interest were correlated at $r = .14$. Fully interpret this result.

b. For girls, math confidence and computer interest were correlated at $r = .33$. Fully interpret this result.

9.50 Studies of Asian (particularly Japanese) and U.S. managers in the 1970s and 1980s found sharp differences of opinion and attitude toward quality management. Do these differences continue to exist? To find out, two California State University researchers (B. F. Yavas and T. M. Burrows) surveyed 100 U.S. and 96 Asian

 **QLAGREE.DAT**

Statement	Percentage of Managers Who Agree: United States	Asian
1	36	38
2	31	42
3	28	43
4	27	48
5	78	58
6	74	49
7	43	46
8	50	56
9	31	65
10	66	58
11	18	21
12	61	69
13	53	45

Source: Yavas, B. F., and Burrows, T. M. "A comparative study of attitudes of U.S. and Asian managers toward product quality." *Quality Management Journal,* Fall 1994, p. 49 (Table 5).

managers in the electronics manufacturing industry (*Quality Management Journal*, Fall 1994). The accompanying table gives the percentages of U.S. and Asian managers who agree with each of 13 randomly selected statements regarding quality. (For example, one statement is "Quality is a problem in my company." Another is "Improving quality is expensive.")

a. Find the coefficient of correlation r for these data on the MINITAB printout below.

```
Correlation of USA and ASIAN = 0.570
```

b. Interpret r in the context of the problem.

c. Refer to part **b.** Using the coefficient of correlation r to make inferences about the difference in attitudes between U.S. and Asian managers regarding quality can be misleading. The value of r measures the strength of the linear relationship between two variables; it does not account for a difference between the means of the variables. To illustrate this, examine the hypothetical data in the table below. Show that $r \approx 1$, but the Asian percentage is approximately 30 points higher for each quality statement. Would you conclude that the attitudes of U.S. and Asian managers are similar?

QLAGREE2.DAT

	Hypothetical Percentage of Managers Who Agree	
Quality Statement	U.S.	Asian
1	20	50
2	30	65
3	40	70
4	50	80
5	55	90

9.51 The booming economy of the 1990s created many new billionaires. The 1999 *Forbes 400* ranks the 400 wealthiest people in the U.S. The top 15 billionaires on this list are described in the table above right.

a. Construct a scattergram for these data. What does the plot suggest about the relationship between age and net worth of billionaires?

b. Find the coefficient of correlation and explain what it tells you about the relationship between age and net worth.

c. If the correlation coefficient of part **b** had the opposite sign, how would that change your interpretation of the relationship between age and net worth?

FORBES400.DAT

Name	Age	Net Worth ($ millions)
Gates, William H. III	43	85,000
Allen, Paul Gardner	40	40,000
Buffett, Warren Edward	69	31,000
Ballmer, Steven Anthony	43	23,000
Dell, Michael	34	20,000
Walton, Jim C.	51	17,300
Walton, Helen R.	80	17,000
Walton, Alice L.	50	16,900
Walton, John T.	53	16,800
Walton, S. Robson	55	16,600
Moore, Gordon Earl	70	15,000
Ellison, Lawrence Joseph	55	13,000
Anschutz, Philip F.	59	11,000
Kluge, John Werner	85	11,000
Anthony, Barbara Cox	76	9,700

Source: Forbes, Oct. 11, 1999, p. 414

d. Find the coefficient of determination for a straight-line model relating net worth (y) to age (x). Interpret the result in the words of the problem.

9.52 The fertility rate of a country is defined as the number of children a woman citizen bears, on average, in her lifetime. *Scientific American* (Dec. 1993) reported on the declining fertility rate in developing countries. The researchers found that family planning can have a great effect on fertility rate. The table on page 514 gives the fertility rate, y, and contraceptive prevalence, x (measured as the percentage of married women who use contraception), for each of 27 developing countries. A SAS printout of the simple linear regression analysis is also provided on p. 504.

a. According to the researchers, "the data reveal that differences in contraceptive prevalence explain about 90% of the variation in fertility rates." Do you concur?

b. The researchers also concluded that "if contraceptive use increases by 15 percent, women bear, on average, one fewer child." Is this statement supported by the data? Explain.

9.53 A negotiable certificate of deposit is a marketable receipt for funds deposited in a bank for a specified period of time at a specified rate of interest (Lee, Finnerty, and Norton, 1997). The table on page 515 lists the end-of-quarter interest rate for three-month certificates of deposit from January 1982 through June 1999 with the concurrent end-of-quarter values of Standard & Poor's 500 Stock Composite Average (an indicator of stock market activity). Find the coefficient of determination and the correlation coefficient for the data

FERTRATE.DAT

Country	Contraceptive Prevalence, x	Fertility Rate, y	Country	Contraceptive Prevalence, x	Fertility Rate, y
Mauritius	76	2.2	Egypt	40	4.5
Thailand	69	2.3	Bangladesh	40	5.5
Colombia	66	2.9	Botswana	35	4.8
Costa Rica	71	3.5	Jordan	35	5.5
Sri Lanka	63	2.7	Kenya	28	6.5
Turkey	62	3.4	Guatemala	24	5.5
Peru	60	3.5	Cameroon	16	5.8
Mexico	55	4.0	Ghana	14	6.0
Jamaica	55	2.9	Pakistan	13	5.0
Indonesia	50	3.1	Senegal	13	6.5
Tunisia	51	4.3	Sudan	10	4.8
El Salvador	48	4.5	Yemen	9	7.0
Morocco	42	4.0	Nigeria	7	5.7
Zimbabwe	46	5.4			

Source: Robey, B., *et al.* "The fertility decline in developing countries." *Scientific American,* December 1993, p. 62. [*Note:* The data values are estimated from a scatterplot.]

SAS Output for Exercise 9.52

```
Dependent Variable: FERTRATE

                         Analysis of Variance

                               Sum of          Mean
        Source          DF    Squares        Square    F Value     Prob>F

        Model            1   35.96633      35.96633     74.309     0.0001
        Error           25   12.10033       0.48401
        C Total         26   48.06667

            Root MSE       0.69571      R-square    0.7483
            Dep Mean       4.51111      Adj R-sq    0.7382
            C.V.          15.42216

                         Parameter Estimates

                      Parameter      Standard    T for HO:
      Variable  DF     Estimate         Error  Parameter=0    Prob > |T|

      INTERCEP   1     6.731929    0.29034252       23.186        0.0001
      CONTPREV   1    -0.054610    0.00633512       -8.620        0.0001
```

and interpret those results. Use the STATISTIX printout on p. 516 to arrive at your answer.

9.54 Refer to the *Journal of Information Science* study of the relationship between the fraction y of documents retrieved using Medline and the number x of terms in the search query, Exercise 9.39. (p. 502)

a. The value of r was reported in the article as $r = .679$. Interpret this result.

b. Calculate the coefficient of determination, r^2, and interpret the result.

9.55 Are college football rankings correlated with the size of athletic department budgets? The table on page 516 lists a sample of athletic department budgets and Associated Press (AP) Top 25 rankings (as of Nov. 21, 1999) for a sample of universities.

a. Construct a scattergram for these data. Does it appear that football ranking and athletic department budget are linearly related? Describe the strength of the relationship in words.

b. Answer the question posed at the beginning of the exercise by finding and interpreting the coefficient of correlation for these data.

9.56 Researchers at the University of Toronto conducted a series of experiments to investigate whether a commercially sold pet food could serve as a substitute diet for baby snow geese (*Journal of Applied Ecology*, Vol. 32,

SP500.DAT (Data for Exercise 9.53)

Year	Quarter	Interest Rate, x	S&P 500, y	Year	Quarter	Interest Rate, x	S&P 500, y
1982	I	14.21	111.96	1991	I	6.71	375.22
	II	14.46	109.61		II	6.01	371.16
	III	10.66	120.42		III	5.70	387.86
	IV	8.66	135.28		IV	4.91	417.09
1983	I	8.69	152.96	1992	I	4.25	403.69
	II	9.20	168.11		II	3.86	408.14
	III	9.39	166.07		III	3.13	417.80
	IV	9.69	164.93		IV	3.48	435.71
1984	I	10.08	159.18	1993	I	3.11	451.67
	II	11.34	153.18		II	3.21	450.53
	III	11.29	166.10		III	3.12	458.93
	IV	8.60	167.24		IV	3.17	466.45
1985	I	9.02	180.66	1994	I	3.77	445.77
	II	7.44	191.85		II	4.52	444.27
	III	7.93	182.08		III	5.03	462.69
	IV	7.80	211.28		IV	6.29	459.27
1986	I	7.24	238.90	1995	I	6.15	500.71
	II	6.73	250.84		II	5.90	544.75
	III	5.71	231.32		III	5.73	584.41
	IV	6.04	242.17		IV	5.62	615.93
1987	I	6.17	291.70	1996	I	5.29	645.50
	II	6.94	304.00		II	5.46	670.63
	III	7.37	321.83		III	5.51	687.31
	IV	7.66	247.08		IV	5.44	740.74
1988	I	6.63	258.89	1997	I	5.53	757.12
	II	7.51	273.50		II	5.66	885.14
	III	8.23	271.91		III	5.60	947.28
	IV	9.25	277.72		IV	5.80	970.43
1989	I	10.09	294.87	1998	I	5.58	1101.75
	II	9.20	317.98		II	5.60	1133.84
	III	8.78	349.15		III	5.41	1017.01
	IV	8.32	353.40		IV	5.14	1229.23
1990	I	8.27	339.94	1999	I	4.91	1286.37
	II	8.33	358.02		II	5.13	1372.71
	III	8.08	306.05				
	IV	7.96	330.22				

Source: Standard & Poor's Statistical Service, Current Statistics. Standard & Poor's Corporation, 1992, 1996, 1999.

1995). Goslings were deprived of food until their guts were empty, then were allowed to feed for 6 hours on a diet of plants or Purina Duck Chow. For each feeding trial, the change in the weight of the gosling after 2.5 hours was recorded as a percentage of initial weight. Two other variables recorded were digestion efficiency (measured as a percentage) and amount of acid-detergent fiber in the digestive tract (also measured as a percentage). The data for 42 feeding trials are listed in the table on page 517.

a. The researchers were interested in the correlation between weight change (y) and digestion efficiency (x). Plot the data for these two variables in a scattergram. Do you observe a trend?

b. On the SPSS printout on page 516, locate the coefficient of correlation relating weight change y to digestion efficiency x. Interpret this value.

c. Conduct a test (at $\alpha = .01$) to determine whether weight change y is correlated with digestion efficiency x. (*Note:* The SPSS printout reports p-values for a test of the null hypothesis of zero correlation.)

d. Repeat parts **b** and **c**, but exclude the data for trials that used duck chow from the analysis. What do you conclude?

e. The researchers were also interested in the correlation between digestion efficiency (y) and acid-detergent fiber (x). Repeat parts **a**–**d** for these two variables.

STATISTIX Output for Exercise 9.53

```
CORRELATIONS (PEARSON)

             SP500
INTRATE    -0.5418

UNWEIGHTED LEAST SQUARES LINEAR REGRESSION OF SP500

PREDICTOR
VARIABLES     COEFFICIENT    STD ERROR      STUDENT'S T        P
---------     -----------    ---------      -----------      ------
CONSTANT         909.430      93.1408           9.76         0.0000
INTRATE         -67.7700      12.7498          -5.32         0.0000

R-SQUARED               0.2935      RESID. MEAN SQUARE (MSE)     66183.7
ADJUSTED R-SQUARED      0.2831      STANDARD DEVIATION           257.262

SOURCE         DF       SS              MS          F        P
----------    ---   ----------      ----------    -----   ------
REGRESSION      1     1869911         1869911     28.25   0.0000
RESIDUAL       68     4500489         66183.7
TOTAL          69     6370401

CASES INCLUDED 70   MISSING CASES 0
```

ADBUDGET.DAT

University	Athletic Dept. Budget (in millions)	AP Ranking
Michigan	$47.6	10
Virginia Tech	20.1	2
Arkansas	24.2	17
Georgia	26.5	16
Texas A&M	27.6	24
Florida State	31.0	1
Alabama	33.4	8
Florida	39.4	5
Tennessee	45.0	6
Wisconsin	41.4	4
Texas	41.2	7
Georgia Tech	21.6	20
Nebraska	36.0	3

Source: *Fortune*, Dec. 20, 1999, p. 172.

SPSS Output for Exercise 9.56

Correlations

		WTCHNG	DIGESTEF	ACIDFIB
WTCHNG	Pearson Correlation	1.000	.612**	-.725**
	Sig. (2-tailed)	.	.000	.000
	N	42	42	42
DIGESTEF	Pearson Correlation	.612**	1.000	-.880**
	Sig. (2-tailed)	.000	.	.000
	N	42	42	42
ACIDFIB	Pearson Correlation	-.725**	-.880**	1.000
	Sig. (2-tailed)	.000	.000	.
	N	42	42	42

**. Correlation is significant at the 0.01 level (2-tailed).

9.8 USING THE MODEL FOR ESTIMATION AND PREDICTION

If we are satisfied that a useful model has been found to describe the relationship between x and y, we are ready for step 5 in our regression modeling procedure: using the model for estimation and prediction.

The most common uses of a probabilistic model for making inferences can be divided into two categories. The first is the use of the model for estimating the mean value of y, E(y), *for a specific value of* x.

SNOWGEES.DAT (Data for Exercise 9.56)

Feeding Trial	Diet	Weight Change (%)	Digestion Efficiency (%)	Acid-Detergent Fiber (%)
1	Plants	−6	0	28.5
2	Plants	−5	2.5	27.5
3	Plants	−4.5	5	27.5
4	Plants	0	0	32.5
5	Plants	2	0	32
6	Plants	3.5	1	30
7	Plants	−2	2.5	34
8	Plants	−2.5	10	36.5
9	Plants	−3.5	20	28.5
10	Plants	−2.5	12.5	29
11	Plants	−3	28	28
12	Plants	−8.5	30	28
13	Plants	−3.5	18	30
14	Plants	−3	15	31
15	Plants	−2.5	17.5	30
16	Plants	−.5	18	22
17	Plants	0	23	22.5
18	Plants	1	20	24
19	Plants	2	15	23
20	Plants	6	31	21
21	Plants	2	15	24
22	Plants	2	21	23
23	Plants	2.5	30	22.5
24	Plants	2.5	33	23
25	Plants	0	27.5	30.5
26	Plants	.5	29	31
27	Plants	−1	32.5	30
28	Plants	−3	42	24
29	Plants	−2.5	39	25
30	Plants	−2	35.5	25
31	Plants	.5	39	20
32	Plants	5.5	39	18.5
33	Plants	7.5	50	15
34	Duck Chow	0	62.5	8
35	Duck Chow	0	63	8
36	Duck Chow	2	69	7
37	Duck Chow	8	42.5	7.5
38	Duck Chow	9	59	8.5
39	Duck Chow	12	52.5	8
40	Duck Chow	8.5	75	6
41	Duck Chow	10.5	72.5	6.5
42	Duck Chow	14	69	7

Source: Gadallah, F.L., and Jefferies, R.L. "Forage quality in brood rearing areas of the lesser snow goose and the growth of captive goslins." *Journal of Applied Biology*, Vol. 32, No. 2, 1995, pp. 281–282 (adapted from Figures 2 and 3).

For our advertising–sales example, we may want to estimate the mean sales revenue for *all* months during which \$400 ($x = 4$) is expended on advertising.

The second use of the model entails predicting a new individual y *value for a given* x.

That is, if we decide to expend \$400 in advertising next month, we may want to predict the firm's sales revenue for that month.

In the first case, we are attempting to estimate the mean value of y for a very large number of experiments at the given x value. In the second case, we are trying to predict the outcome of a single experiment at the given x value. Which of these model uses—estimating the mean value of y or predicting an individual new value of y (for the same value of x)—can be accomplished with the greater accuracy?

Before answering this question, we first consider the problem of choosing an estimator (or predictor) of the mean (or a new individual) y value. We will use the least squares prediction equation

$$\hat{y} = \hat{\beta}_0 + \hat{\beta}_1 x$$

both to estimate the mean value of y and to predict a specific new value of y for a given value of x. For our example, we found

$$\hat{y} = -.1 + .7x$$

so that the estimated mean sales revenue for all months when $x = 4$ (advertising is \$400) is

$$\hat{y} = -.1 + .7(4) = 2.7$$

or \$2,700. (Recall that the units of y are thousands of dollars.) The same value is used to predict a new y value when $x = 4$. That is, both the estimated mean and the predicted value of y are $\hat{y} = 2.7$ when $x = 4$, as shown in Figure 9.18.

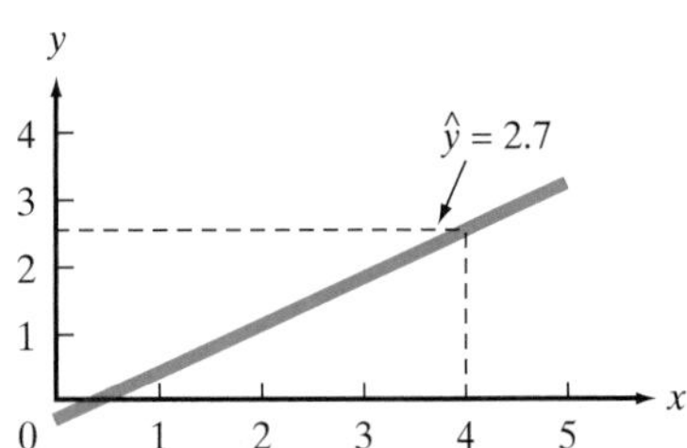

FIGURE 9.18
Estimated mean value and predicted individual value of sales revenue y for $x = 4$

The difference between these two model uses lies in the relative accuracy of the estimate and the prediction. These accuracies are best measured by using the sampling errors of the least squares line when it is used as an estimator and as a predictor, respectively. These errors are reflected in the standard deviations given in the next box.

Sampling Errors for the Estimator of the Mean of *y* and the Predictor of an Individual New Value of *y*

1. The standard deviation of the sampling distribution of the estimator $\hat{y}$ of the mean value of y at a specific value of x, say x_p, is

$$\sigma_{\hat{y}} = \sigma\sqrt{\frac{1}{n} + \frac{(x_p - \bar{x})^2}{SS_{xx}}}$$

where σ is the standard deviation of the random error ε. We refer to $\sigma_{\hat{y}}$ as the standard error of $\hat{y}$.

2. The standard deviation of the prediction error for the predictor $\hat{y}$ of an individual new y value at a specific value of x is

(continued)

$$\sigma_{(y-\hat{y})} = \sigma\sqrt{1 + \frac{1}{n} + \frac{(x_p - \bar{x})^2}{SS_{xx}}}$$

where σ is the standard deviation of the random error ε. We refer to $\sigma_{(y-\hat{y})}$ as the standard error of the prediction.

The true value of σ is rarely known, so we estimate σ by s and calculate the estimation and prediction intervals as shown in the next two boxes.

A 100(1 − α)% Confidence Interval for the Mean Value of y at $x = x_p$

$$\hat{y} \pm t_{\alpha/2}(\text{Estimated standard error of } \hat{y})$$

or

$$\hat{y} \pm t_{\alpha/2}s\sqrt{\frac{1}{n} + \frac{(x_p - \bar{x})^2}{SS_{xx}}}$$

where $t_{\alpha/2}$ is based on $(n - 2)$ degrees of freedom.

A 100(1 − α)% Prediction Interval* for an Individual New Value of y at $x = x_p$

$$\hat{y} \pm t_{\alpha/2}(\text{Estimated standard error of prediction})$$

or

$$\hat{y} \pm t_{\alpha/2}s\sqrt{1 + \frac{1}{n} + \frac{(x_p - \bar{x})^2}{SS_{xx}}}$$

where $t_{\alpha/2}$ is based on $(n - 2)$ degrees of freedom.

EXAMPLE 9.3

Find a 95% confidence interval for the mean monthly sales when the appliance store spends \$400 on advertising.

Solution

For a \$400 advertising expenditure, $x = 4$ and the confidence interval for the mean value of y is

$$\hat{y} \pm t_{\alpha/2}s\sqrt{\frac{1}{n} + \frac{(x_p - \bar{x})^2}{SS_{xx}}} = \hat{y} \pm t_{.025}s\sqrt{\frac{1}{5} + \frac{(4 - \bar{x})^2}{SS_{xx}}}$$

where $t_{.025}$ is based on $n - 2 = 5 - 2 = 3$ degrees of freedom. Recall that $\hat{y} = 2.7$, $s = .61$, $\bar{x} = 3$, and $SS_{xx} = 10$. From Table VI in Appendix B, $t_{.025} = 3.182$. Thus, we have

*The term *prediction interval* is used when the interval formed is intended to enclose the value of a random variable. The term *confidence interval* is reserved for estimation of population parameters (such as mean).

$$2.7 \pm (3.182)(.61)\sqrt{\frac{1}{5} + \frac{(4-3)^2}{10}} = 2.7 \pm (3.182)(.61)(.55)$$
$$= 2.7 \pm (3.182)(.34)$$
$$= 2.7 \pm 1.1 = (1.6, 3.8)$$

Therefore, when the store spends \$400 a month on advertising, we are 95% confident that the mean sales revenue is between \$1,600 and \$3,800. Note that we used a small amount of data (small in size) for purposes of illustration in fitting the least squares line. The interval would probably be narrower if more information had been obtained from a larger sample.

EXAMPLE 9.4 Predict the monthly sales for next month, if \$400 is spent on advertising. Use a 95% prediction interval.

Solution To predict the sales for a particular month for which $x_p = 4$, we calculate the 95% prediction interval as

$$\hat{y} \pm t_{\alpha/2} s\sqrt{1 + \frac{1}{n} + \frac{(x_p - \bar{x})^2}{SS_{xx}}} = 2.7 \pm (3.182)(.61)\sqrt{1 + \frac{1}{5} + \frac{(4-3)^2}{10}}$$
$$= 2.7 \pm (3.182)(.61)(1.14)$$
$$= 2.7 \pm (3.182)(.70)$$
$$= 2.7 \pm 2.2 = (.5, 4.9)$$

Therefore, we predict with 95% confidence that the sales revenue next month (a month in which we spend \$400 in advertising) will fall in the interval from \$500 to \$4,900. Like the confidence interval for the mean value of y, the prediction interval for y is quite large. This is because we have chosen a simple example (only five data points) to fit the least squares line. The width of the prediction interval could be reduced by using a larger number of data points.

Both the confidence interval for $E(y)$ and prediction interval for y can be obtained using a statistical software package. Figures 9.19 and 9.20 are SAS printouts showing confidence intervals and prediction intervals, respectively, for the data in the advertising–sales example.

Obs	X	Dep Var Y	Predict Value	Std Err Predict	Lower95% Mean	Upper95% Mean	Residual
1	1	1.0000	0.6000	0.469	-0.8927	2.0927	0.4000
2	2	1.0000	1.3000	0.332	0.2445	2.3555	-0.3000
3	3	2.0000	2.0000	0.271	1.1382	2.8618	0
4	4	2.0000	2.7000	0.332	1.6445	3.7555	-0.7000
5	5	4.0000	3.4000	0.469	1.9073	4.8927	0.6000

FIGURE 9.19
SAS printout giving 95% confidence intervals for $E(y)$

Obs	X	Dep Var Y	Predict Value	Std Err Predict	Lower95% Predict	Upper95% Predict	Residual
1	1	1.0000	0.6000	0.469	-1.8376	3.0376	0.4000
2	2	1.0000	1.3000	0.332	-0.8972	3.4972	-0.3000
3	3	2.0000	2.0000	0.271	-0.1110	4.1110	0
4	4	2.0000	2.7000	0.332	0.5028	4.8972	-0.7000
5	5	4.0000	3.4000	0.469	0.9624	5.8376	0.6000

FIGURE 9.20
SAS printout giving 95% prediction intervals for y

The 95% confidence interval for $E(y)$ when $x = 4$ is highlighted in Figure 9.19 in the row corresponding to **4** under the columns labeled **Lower95% Mean** and **Upper95% Mean.** The interval shown on the printout, (1.6445, 3.7555), agrees (except for rounding) with the interval calculated in Example 9.3. The 95% prediction interval for y when $x = 4$ is highlighted in Figure 9.20 under the columns **Lower95% Predict** and **Upper95% Predict.** Again, except for rounding, the SAS interval (.5028, 4.8972) agrees with the one computed in Example 9.4.

A comparison of the confidence interval for the mean value of y and the prediction interval for a new value of y when $x = 4$ is illustrated in Figure 9.21. Note that the prediction interval for an individual new value of y is always wider than the corresponding confidence interval for the mean value of y. You can see this by examining the formulas for the two intervals and by studying Figure 9.21.

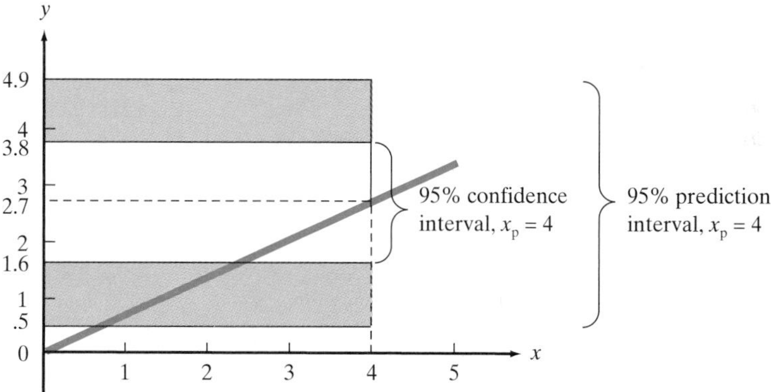

FIGURE 9.21
A 95% confidence interval for mean sales and a prediction interval for sales when $x = 4$

The error in estimating the mean value of y, $E(y)$, for a given value of x, say x_p, is the distance between the least squares line and the true line of means, $E(y) = \beta_0 + \beta_1 x$. This error, $[\hat{y} - E(y)]$, is shown in Figure 9.22. In contrast, *the error* $(y_p - \hat{y})$ *in predicting some future value of* y *is the sum of two errors*—the error of estimating the mean of y, $E(y)$, shown in Figure 9.22, plus the random error that is a component of the value of y to be predicted (see Figure 9.23). Consequently, the error of predicting a particular value of y will be larger than the error of estimating the mean value of y for a particular value of x. Note from their formulas that both the error of estimation and the error of prediction take their

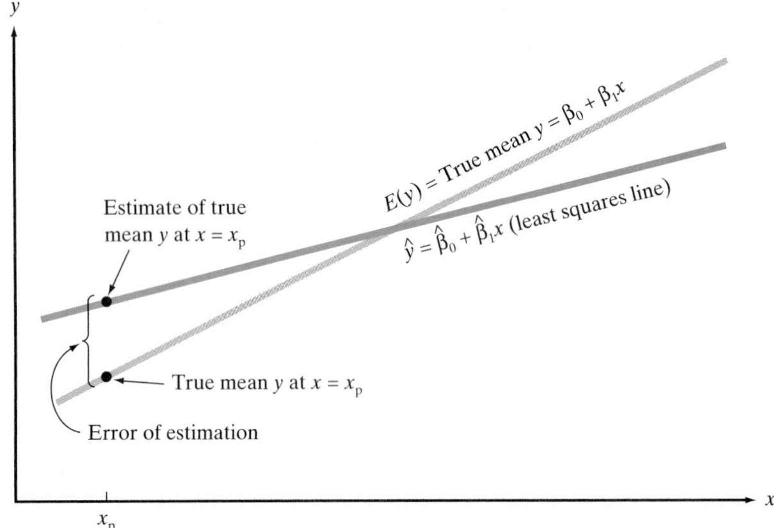

FIGURE 9.22
Error of estimating the mean value of y for a given value of x

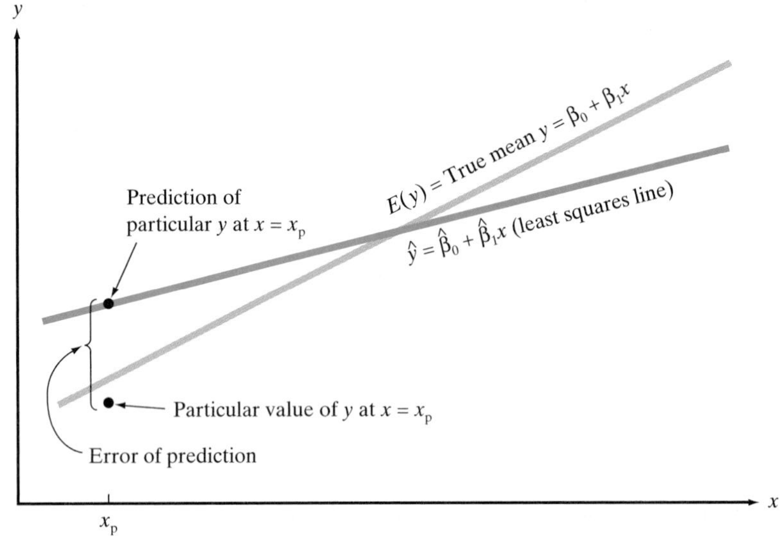

FIGURE 9.23
Error of predicting a future value of y for a given value of x

smallest values when $x_p = \overline{x}$. The farther x_p lies from $\overline{x}$, the larger will be the errors of estimation and prediction. You can see why this is true by noting the deviations for different values of x_p between the line of means $E(y) = \beta_0 + \beta_1 x$ and the predicted line of means $\hat{y} = \hat{\beta}_0 + \hat{\beta}_1 x$ shown in Figure 9.23. The deviation is larger at the extremes of the interval where the largest and smallest values of x in the data set occur.

Both the confidence intervals for mean values and the prediction intervals for new values are depicted over the entire range of the regression line in Figure 9.24. You can see that the confidence interval is always narrower than the prediction interval, and that they are both narrowest at the mean $\overline{x}$, increasing steadily as the distance $|x - \overline{x}|$ increases. In fact, when x is selected far enough away from $\overline{x}$ so that it falls outside the range of the sample data, it is dangerous to make any inferences about $E(y)$, or y.

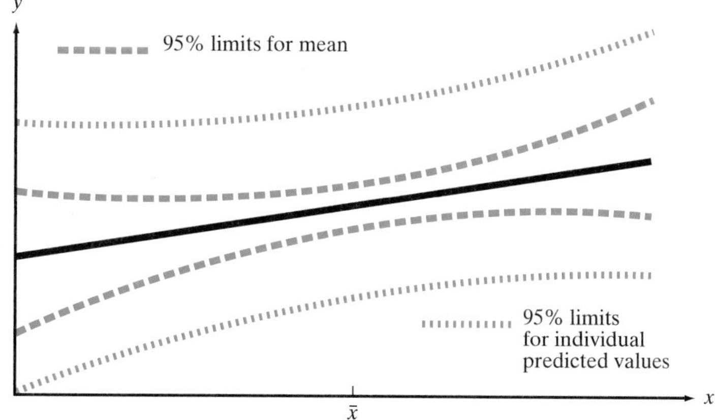

FIGURE 9.24
Confidence intervals for mean values and prediction intervals for new values

> **Caution**
>
> Using the least squares prediction equation to estimate the mean value of y or to predict a particular value of y for values of x that fall *outside the range* of the values of x contained in your sample data may lead to errors of estimation or prediction that are much larger than expected. Although the least squares model may provide a very good fit to the data over the range of x values contained in the sample, it could give a poor representation of the true model for values of x outside this region.

The confidence interval width grows smaller as n is increased; thus, in theory, you can obtain as precise an estimate of the mean value of y as desired (at any given x) by selecting a large enough sample. The prediction interval for a new value of y also grows smaller as n increases, but there is a lower limit on its width. If you examine the formula for the prediction interval, you will see that the interval can get no smaller than $\hat{y} \pm z_{\alpha/2}\sigma$.* Thus, the only way to obtain more accurate predictions for new values of y is to reduce the standard deviation of the regression model, σ. This can be accomplished only by improving the model, either by using a curvilinear (rather than linear) relationship with x or by adding new independent variables to the model, or both. Methods of improving the model are discussed in Chapter 10.

EXERCISES 9.57–9.66

Learning the Mechanics

9.57 Consider the following pairs of measurements:

LM9_57.DAT

x	−2	0	2	4	6	8	10
y	0	3	2	3	8	10	11

a. Construct a scattergram for these data.
b. Find the least squares line, and plot it on your scattergram.
c. Find s^2.
d. Find a 90% confidence interval for the mean value of y when $x = 3$. Plot the upper and lower bounds of the confidence interval on your scattergram.

*The result follows from the facts that, for large n, $t_{\alpha/2} \approx z_{\alpha/2}$, $s \approx \sigma$, and the last two terms under the radical in the standard error of the predictor are approximately 0.

e. Find a 90% prediction interval for a new value of y when $x = 3$. Plot the upper and lower bounds of the prediction interval on your scattergram.
f. Compare the widths of the intervals you constructed in parts **d** and **e**. Which is wider and why?

9.58 Consider the pairs of measurements shown in the next table.

LM9_58.DAT

x	4	6	0	5	2	3	2	6	2	1
y	3	5	−1	4	3	2	0	4	1	1

For these data, $SS_{xx} = 38.9000$, $SS_{yy} = 33.600$, $SS_{xy} = 32.8$, and $\hat{y} = -.414 + .843x$.
a. Construct a scattergram for these data.
b. Plot the least squares line on your scattergram.
c. Use a 95% confidence interval to estimate the mean value of y when $x_p = 6$. Plot the upper and lower bounds of the interval on your scattergram.
d. Repeat part **c** for $x_p = 3.2$ and $x_p = 0$.
e. Compare the widths of the three confidence intervals you constructed in parts **c** and **d** and explain why they differ.

9.59 Refer to Exercise 9.58.
a. Using no information about x, estimate and calculate a 95% confidence interval for the mean value of y. [*Hint:* Use the one-sample t methodology of Section 5.3.]
b. Plot the estimated mean value and the confidence interval as horizontal lines on your scattergram.
c. Compare the confidence intervals you calculated in parts **c** and **d** of Exercise 9.58 with the one you calculated in part **a** of this exercise. Does x appear to contribute information about the mean value of y?
d. Check the answer you gave in part **c** with a statistical test of the null hypothesis $H_0: \beta_1 = 0$ against $H_a: \beta_1 \neq 0$. Use $\alpha = .05$.

9.60 In fitting a least squares line to $n = 10$ data points, the following quantities were computed:

$$SS_{xx} = 32$$
$$\bar{x} = 3$$
$$SS_{yy} = 26$$
$$\bar{y} = 4$$
$$SS_{xy} = 28$$

a. Find the least squares line.
b. Graph the least squares line.
c. Calculate SSE. d. Calculate s^2.
e. Find a 95% confidence interval for the mean value of y when $x_p = 2.5$.
f. Find a 95% prediction interval for y when $x_p = 4$.

Applying the Concepts

9.61 Many variables influence the sales of existing single-family homes. One of these is the interest rate charged for mortgage loans. The table below gives the total number of existing single-family homes sold annually, y, and the average annual conventional mortgage interest rate, x, for 1982–1997. A STATISTIX printout of the simple linear regression is provided on page 525.
a. Plot the data points on graph paper.
b. Find the least squares line relating y to x on the printout. Plot the line on your graph from part **a** to see if the line appears to model the relationship between y and x.
c. Do the data provide sufficient evidence to indicate that mortgage interest rates contribute information for the prediction of annual sales of existing single-family homes? Use $\alpha = .05$.
d. Locate r^2 and interpret its value.

MORTRATE.DAT

Year	Homes Sold, y (1,000s)	Interest Rate, x(%)	Year	Homes Sold, y (1,000s)	Interest Rate, x(%)
1982	1,990	15.82	1991	3,220	9.20
1983	2,719	13.44	1992	3,520	8.43
1984	2,868	13.81	1993	3,802	7.36
1985	3,214	12.29	1994	3,946	8.59
1986	3,565	10.09	1995	3,812	8.05
1987	3,526	10.17	1996	4,087	8.03
1988	3,594	10.31	1997	4,215	7.76
1989	3,346	10.22			
1990	3,211	10.08			

Source: U.S. Bureau of the Census, *Statistical Abstract of the United States: 1998*, pp. 526, 720.

STATISTIX Output for Exercise 9.61

```
UNWEIGHTED LEAST SQUARES LINEAR REGRESSION OF HOMES

PREDICTOR
VARIABLES     COEFFICIENT    STD ERROR      STUDENT'S T      P
---------     -----------    ---------      -----------    ------
CONSTANT         5566.13      253.996          21.95       0.0000
INTRATE         -210.346      24.1940          -8.69       0.0000

R-SQUARED              0.8437     RESID. MEAN SQUARE (MSE)    52438.8
ADJUSTED R-SQUARED     0.8326     STANDARD DEVIATION          228.995

SOURCE        DF       SS            MS           F        P
----------    ---   ----------   ----------     -----   ------
REGRESSION     1     3963719       3963719      75.59   0.0000
RESIDUAL      14      734143       52438.8
TOTAL         15     4697861

PREDICTED/FITTED VALUES OF HOMES

LOWER PREDICTED BOUND      3364.1      LOWER FITTED BOUND     3714.7
PREDICTED VALUE            3883.4            FITTED VALUE     3883.4
UPPER PREDICTED BOUND      4402.7      UPPER FITTED BOUND     4052.0
SE (PREDICTED VALUE)       242.12       SE (FITTED VALUE)     78.635

UNUSUALNESS (LEVERAGE)     0.1179
PERCENT COVERAGE             95.0
CORRESPONDING T              2.14

PREDICTOR VALUES: INTRATE = 8.0000
```

e. A 95% confidence interval for the mean annual number of existing single-family homes sold when the average annual mortgage interest rate is 8.0% is shown next to "Lower/Upper Fitted Bound" on the printout. Interpret this interval.

f. A 95% prediction interval for the annual number of existing single-family homes sold when the average annual mortgage interest rate is 8.0% is shown next to "Lower/Upper Predicted Bound" on the printout. Interpret this interval.

g. Explain why the widths of the intervals found in parts **e** and **f** differ.

9.62 Refer to the simple linear regression of sweetness index y and amount of pectin x for $n = 24$ orange juice samples, Exercise 9.14 (p. 484). A 90% confidence interval for the mean sweetness index, $E(y)$, for each value of x is shown on the SPSS spreadsheet on page 526. Select an observation and interpret this interval.

9.63 Refer to the simple linear regression of number of employees y and age x for fast-growing firms, Exercises 9.21, 9.29, and 9.41. The SAS printout of the analysis is reproduced on page 526.

a. A 95% prediction interval for y when $x = 10$ is shown at the bottom of the printout. Interpret this interval.

b. How would the width of a 95% confidence interval for $E(y)$ when $x = 10$ compare to the interval, part **a**?

c. Would you recommend using the model to predict the number of employees at a firm that has been in business two years? Explain.

9.64 Managers are an important part of any organization's resource base. Accordingly, the organization should be just as concerned about forecasting its future managerial needs as it is with forecasting its needs for, say, the natural resources used in its production process (Northcraft and Neale, *Organizational Behavior: A Management Challenge,* 1994). A common forecasting procedure is to model the relationship between sales and the number of managers needed, since the demand for managers is the result of the increases and decreases

SPSS Spreadsheet for Exercise 9.62

	run	sweet	pectin	lower90m	upper90m
1	1.00	5.20	220.00	5.64898	5.83848
2	2.00	5.50	227.00	5.63898	5.81613
3	3.00	6.00	259.00	5.57819	5.72904
4	4.00	5.90	210.00	5.66194	5.87173
5	5.00	5.80	224.00	5.64337	5.82560
6	6.00	6.00	215.00	5.65564	5.85493
7	7.00	5.80	231.00	5.63284	5.80379
8	8.00	5.60	268.00	5.55553	5.71011
9	9.00	5.60	239.00	5.61947	5.78019
10	10.00	5.90	212.00	5.65946	5.86497
11	11.00	5.40	410.00	5.05526	5.55416
12	12.00	5.60	256.00	5.58517	5.73592
13	13.00	5.80	306.00	5.43785	5.65219
14	14.00	5.50	259.00	5.57819	5.72904
15	15.00	5.30	284.00	5.50957	5.68213
16	16.00	5.30	383.00	5.15725	5.57694
17	17.00	5.70	271.00	5.54743	5.70434
18	18.00	5.50	264.00	5.65691	5.71821
19	19.00	5.70	227.00	5.63898	5.81613
20	20.00	5.30	263.00	5.56843	5.72031
21	21.00	5.90	232.00	5.63125	5.80075
22	22.00	5.80	220.00	5.64898	5.83848
23	23.00	5.80	246.00	5.60640	5.76091
24	24.00	5.90	241.00	5.61587	5.77454

SAS Output for Exercise 9.63

Dependent Variable: NUMBER

Analysis of Variance

Source	DF	Sum of Squares	Mean Square	F Value	Prob>F
Model	1	23536.50149	23536.50149	11.451	0.0070
Error	10	20554.41518	2055.44152		
C Total	11	44090.91667			

Root MSE	45.33698	R-square	0.5338
Dep Mean	61.08333	Adj R-sq	0.4872
C.V.	74.22152		

Parameter Estimates

Variable	DF	Parameter Estimate	Standard Error	T for HO: Parameter=0	Prob > |T|
INTERCEP	1	-51.361607	35.71379104	-1.438	0.1809
AGE	1	17.754464	5.24673562	3.384	0.0070

Obs	AGE	Dep Var NUMBER	Predict Value	Std Err Predict	Lower95% Predict	Upper95% Predict	Residual
1	5	43.0000	37.4107	14.840	-68.8810	143.7	5.5893
2	5	52.0000	37.4107	14.840	-68.8810	143.7	14.5893
3	4	9.0000	19.6563	17.921	-88.9672	128.3	-10.6562
4	7	40.0000	72.9196	13.547	-32.5114	178.4	-32.9196
5	5	6.0000	37.4107	14.840	-68.8810	143.7	-31.4107
6	6	12.0000	55.1652	13.204	-50.0496	160.4	-43.1652
7	14	200.0	197.2	42.301	59.0415	335.4	2.7991
8	5	76.0000	37.4107	14.840	-68.8810	143.7	38.5893
9	7	15.0000	72.9196	13.547	-32.5114	178.4	-57.9196
10	6	40.0000	55.1652	13.204	-50.0496	160.4	-15.1652
11	5	65.0000	37.4107	14.840	-68.8810	143.7	27.5893
12	7	175.0	72.9196	13.547	-32.5114	178.4	102.1
13	10	.	126.2	23.268	12.6384	239.7	.

SPSS Output for Exercise 9.64

```
Equation Number 1    Dependent Variable..      MANAGERS

Variable(s) Entered on Step Number
   1..     UNITS

Multiple R              .96386
R Square                .92903
Adjusted R Square       .92509
Standard Error         2.56642

Analysis of Variance
                       DF        Sum of Squares        Mean Square
Regression              1            1551.99292         1551.99292
Residual               18             118.55708            6.58650

F =      235.63225        Signif F =  .0000

----------------- Variables in the Equation ------------------

Variable                 B          SE B         Beta           T   Sig T

UNITS              .586100       .038182      .963863      15.350   .0000
(Constant)        5.325299      1.179868                    4.513   .0003
```

MANAGERS2.DAT (Data for Exercise 9.64)

Months	Units Sold, x	Managers, y	Month	Units Sold, x	Managers, y
3/95	5	10	9/97	30	22
6/95	4	11	12/97	31	25
9/95	8	10	3/98	36	30
12/95	7	10	6/98	38	30
3/96	9	9	9/98	40	31
6/96	15	10	12/98	41	31
9/96	20	11	3/99	51	32
12/96	21	17	6/99	40	30
3/97	25	19	9/99	48	32
6/97	24	21	12/99	47	32

in the demand for products and services that a firm offers its customers. To develop this relationship, the data shown in the table above are collected from a firm's records. An SPSS printout of the simple linear regression is provided above also.

a. Test the usefulness of the model. Use $\alpha = .05$. State your conclusion in the context of the problem.

b. The company projects that it will sell 39 units in May of 2000. Use the least squares model to construct a 90% prediction interval for the number of managers needed in May 2000.

c. Interpret the interval in part **b**. Use the interval to determine the reliability of the firm's projection.

9.65 The reasons given by workers for quitting their jobs generally fall into one of two categories: (1) worker quits to seek or take a different job, or (2) worker quits to withdraw from the labor force. Economic theory suggests that wages and quit rates are related. The table on page 528 lists quit rates (quits per 100 employees) and the average hourly wage in a sample of 15 manufacturing industries. A MINITAB printout of the simple linear regression of quit rate y on average wage x is shown on p. 528.

a. Do the data present sufficient evidence to conclude that average hourly wage rate contributes useful information for the prediction of quit rates? What does your model suggest about the relationship between quit rates and wages?

b. A 95% prediction interval for the quit rate in an industry with an average hourly wage of \$9.00 is given at the bottom of the MINITAB printout. Interpret the result.

c. A 95% confidence interval for the mean quit rate for industries with an average hourly wage of \$9.00 is also shown on the printout. Interpret this result.

9.66 The data for Exercise 9.30 are reproduced on page 528.

a. Use a 90% confidence interval to estimate the mean useful life of a brand A cutting tool when the cutting speed is 45 meters per minute. Repeat for brand B.

QUITTERS.DAT (Data for Excercise 9.65)

Industry	Quit Rate, y	Average Wage, x
1	1.4	$ 8.20
2	.7	10.35
3	2.6	6.18
4	3.4	5.37
5	1.7	9.94
6	1.7	9.11
7	1.0	10.59
8	.5	13.29
9	2.0	7.99
10	3.8	5.54
11	2.3	7.50
12	1.9	6.43
13	1.4	8.83
14	1.8	10.93
15	2.0	8.80

CUTTOOLS.DAT (Data for Excercise 9.66)

	USEFULE LIFE (HOURS)	
Cutting Speed (meters per minute)	Brand A	Brand B
30	4.5	6.0
30	3.5	6.5
30	5.2	5.0
40	5.2	6.0
40	4.0	4.5
40	2.5	5.0
50	4.4	4.5
50	2.8	4.0
50	1.0	3.7
60	4.0	3.8
60	2.0	3.0
60	1.1	2.4
70	1.1	1.5
70	.5	2.0
70	3.0	1.0

Compare the widths of the two intervals and comment on the reasons for any difference.

b. Use a 90% prediction interval to predict the useful life of a brand A cutting tool when the cutting speed is 45 meters per minute. Repeat for brand B. Compare the widths of the two intervals to each other, and to the two intervals you calculated in part **a**. Comment on the reasons for any differences.

c. Note that the estimation and prediction you performed in parts **a** and **b** were for a value of x that was not included in the original sample. That is, the value $x = 45$ was not part of the sample. However, the value is within the range of x values in the sample, so that the regression model spans the x value for which the estimation and prediction were made. In such situations, estimation and prediction represent *interpolations.* Suppose you were asked to predict the useful life of a brand A cutting tool for a cutting speed of $x = 100$ meters per minute. Since the given value of x is outside the range of the sample x values, the prediction is an example of *extrapolation.* Predict the useful life of a brand A cutting tool that is operated at 100 meters per minute, and construct a 95% confidence interval for the actual useful life of the tool. What additional assumption do you have to make in order to ensure the validity of an extrapolation?

MINITAB Output for Exercise 9.65

```
The regression equation is
QuitRate = 4.86 - 0.347 AveWage

Predictor        Coef       Stdev    t-ratio        p
Constant       4.8615      0.5201       9.35    0.000
AveWage      -0.34655     0.05866      -5.91    0.000

s = 0.4862     R-sq = 72.9%      R-sq(adj) = 70.8%

Analysis of Variance

SOURCE        DF         SS           MS         F        p
Regression     1     8.2507       8.2507     34.90    0.000
Error         13     3.0733       0.2364
Total         14    11.3240

     Fit  Stdev.Fit         95% C.I.            95% P.I.
   1.743      0.128    ( 1.467, 2.018)    ( 0.656, 2.829)
```

9.9 SIMPLE LINEAR REGRESSION: A COMPLETE EXAMPLE

In the preceding sections we have presented the basic elements necessary to fit and use a straight-line regression model. In this section we will assemble these elements by applying them in an example with the aid of a computer.

Suppose a fire insurance company wants to relate the amount of fire damage in major residential fires to the distance between the burning house and the nearest fire station. The study is to be conducted in a large suburb of a major city; a sample of 15 recent fires in this suburb is selected. The amount of damage, y, and the distance between the fire and the nearest fire station, x, are recorded for each fire. The results are given in Table 9.7.

TABLE 9.7 Fire Damage Data

Distance From Fire Station, x (miles)	Fire Damage, y (thousands of dollars)
3.4	26.2
1.8	17.8
4.6	31.3
2.3	23.1
3.1	27.5
5.5	36.0
.7	14.1
3.0	22.3
2.6	19.6
4.3	31.3
2.1	24.0
1.1	17.3
6.1	43.2
4.8	36.4
3.8	26.1

Step 1 First, we hypothesize a model to relate fire damage, y, to the distance from the nearest fire station, x. We hypothesize a straight-line probabilistic model:

$$y = \beta_0 + \beta_1 x + \varepsilon$$

Step 2 Next, we enter the data of Table 9.7 into a computer and use a statistical software package to estimate the unknown parameters in the deterministic component of the hypothesized model. The SAS printout for the simple linear regression analysis is shown in Figure 9.25. The least squares estimate of the slope β_1 and intercept β_0, highlighted on the printout, are

$$\hat{\beta}_1 = 4.919331$$

$$\hat{\beta}_0 = 10.277929$$

and the least squares equation is (rounded)

$$\hat{y} = 10.278 + 4.919x$$

```
Dep Variable: Y
                         Analysis of Variance

                           Sum of          Mean
     Source       DF      Squares        Square      F Value       Prob>F

     Model         1    841.76636     841.76636      156.886       0.0001
     Error        13     69.75098       5.36546
     C Total      14    911.51733

           Root MSE      2.31635        R-Square         0.9235
           Dep Mean     26.41333        Adj R-Sq         0.9176
           C.V.          8.76961

                          Parameter Estimates

                        Parameter      Standard        T for HO:
Variable      DF         Estimate         Error      Parameter=0   Prob > |T|

INTERCEP      1         10.277929    1.42027781            7.237       0.0001
X             1          4.919331    0.39274775           12.525       0.0001

                                      Predict                  Lower95%  Upper95%
     Obs  X                  Y          Value     Residual     Predict   Predict

       1     3.4       26.2000        27.0037      -0.8037     21.8344   32.1729
       2     1.8       17.8000        19.1327      -1.3327     13.8141   24.4514
       3     4.6       31.3000        32.9068      -1.6068     27.6186   38.1951
       4     2.3       23.1000        21.5924       1.5076     16.3577   26.8271
       5     3.1       27.5000        25.5279       1.9721     20.3573   30.6984
       6     5.5       36.0000        37.3342      -1.3342     31.8334   42.8351
       7     0.7       14.1000        13.7215       0.3785      8.1087   19.3342
       8     3.0       22.3000        25.0359      -2.7359     19.8622   30.2097
       9     2.6       19.6000        23.0682      -3.4682     17.8678   28.2686
      10     4.3       31.3000        31.4311      -0.1311     26.1908   36.6713
      11     2.1       24.0000        20.6085       3.3915     15.3442   25.8729
      12     1.1       17.3000        15.6892       1.6108     10.1999   21.1785
      13     6.1       43.2000        40.2858       2.9142     34.5906   45.9811
      14     4.8       36.4000        33.8907       2.5093     28.5640   39.2175
      15     3.8       26.1000        28.9714      -2.8714     23.7843   34.1585
      16     3.5                      27.4956                   22.3239   32.6672

Sum of Residuals                 -3.73035E-14
Sum of Squared Residuals              69.7510
Predicted Resid SS (Press)            93.2117
```

FIGURE 9.25
SAS printout for fire damage regression analysis

This prediction equation is graphed in Figure 9.26 along with a plot of the data points.

The least squares estimate of the slope, $\widehat{\beta}_1 = 4.919$, implies that the estimated mean damage increases by \$4,919 for each additional mile from the fire station. This interpretation is valid over the range of x, or from .7 to 6.1 miles from the station. The estimated y-intercept, $\widehat{\beta}_0 = 10.278$, has the interpretation that a fire 0 miles from the fire station has an estimated mean damage of \$10,278. Although this would seem to apply to the fire station itself, remember that the y-intercept is meaningfully interpretable only if $x = 0$ is within the sampled range of

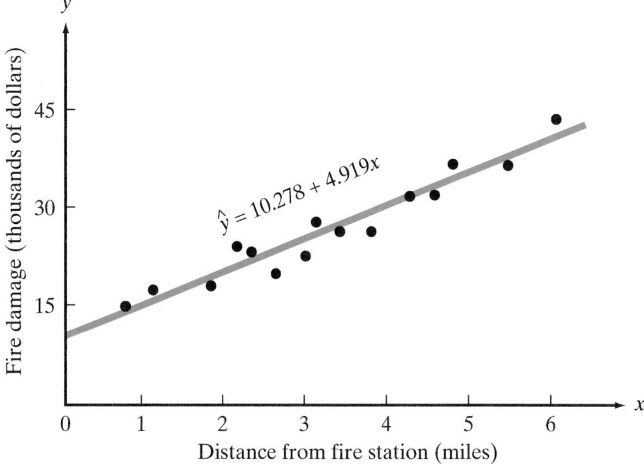

FIGURE 9.26 Least squares model for the fire damage data

the independent variable. Since $x = 0$ is outside the range in this case, $\hat{\beta}_0$ has no practical interpretation.

Step 3 Now we specify the probability distribution of the random error component ε. The assumptions about the distribution are identical to those listed in Section 9.3. Although we know that these assumptions are not completely satisfied (they rarely are for practical problems), we are willing to assume they are approximately satisfied for this example. The estimate of the standard deviation σ of ε, highlighted on the printout, is:

$$s = 2.31635$$

This implies that most of the observed fire damage (y) values will fall within approximately $2s = 4.64$ thousand dollars of their respective predicted values when using the least squares line.

Step 4 We can now check the usefulness of the hypothesized model—that is, whether x really contributes information for the prediction of y using the straight-line model. First, test the null hypothesis that the slope β_1 is 0, that is, that there is no linear relationship between fire damage and the distance from the nearest fire station, against the alternative hypothesis that fire damage increases as the distance increases. We test

$$H_0\colon \beta_1 = 0$$

$$H_a\colon \beta_1 > 0$$

The observed significance level for testing $H_a\colon \beta_1 \neq 0$, highlighted on the printout, is .0001. Thus, the p-value for our one-tailed test is $p = .0001/2 = .00005$. This small p-value leaves little doubt that mean fire damage and distance between the fire and station are at least linearly related, with mean fire damage increasing as the distance increases.

We gain additional information about the relationship by forming a confidence interval for the slope β_1. A 95% confidence interval is

$$\hat{\beta}_1 \pm t_{.025} s_{\hat{\beta}_1}$$

where $\hat{\beta}_1 = 4.919$ and its standard error, $s_{\hat{\beta}_1} = .393$, are both obtained from the printout. The value $t_{.025}$, based on $n - 2 = 13$ df, is 2.160. Therefore, the 95% confidence interval is

$$\hat{\beta}_1 \pm t_{.025}s_{\hat{\beta}_1} = 4.919 \pm (2.160)(.393) = 4.919 \pm .849 = (4.070, 5.768)$$

We estimate that the interval from \$4,070 to \$5,768 encloses the mean increase (β_1) in fire damage per additional mile distance from the fire station.

Another measure of the utility of the model is the coefficient of determination, r^2. The value (highlighted on the printout) is $r^2 = .9235$, which implies that about 92% of the sample variation in fire damage (y) is explained by the distance (x) between the fire and the fire station.

The coefficient of correlation, r, that measures the strength of the linear relationship between y and x is not shown on the SAS printout and must be calculated. Using the facts that $r = \sqrt{r^2}$ in simple linear regression and that r and $\hat{\beta}_1$ have the same sign, we find

$$r = +\sqrt{r^2} = \sqrt{.9235} = .96$$

The high correlation confirms our conclusion that β_1 is greater than 0; it appears that fire damage and distance from the fire station are positively correlated. All signs point to a strong linear relationship between y and x.

Step 5 We are now prepared to use the least squares model. Suppose the insurance company wants to predict the fire damage if a major residential fire were to occur 3.5 miles from the nearest fire station. The predicted value (highlighted at the bottom of the printout) is $\hat{y} = 27.4956$, while the 95% prediction interval (also highlighted) is (22.3239, 32.6672). Therefore, with 95% confidence we predict fire damage in a major residential fire 3.5 miles from the nearest station to be between \$22,324 and \$32,667.

One caution before closing: We would not use this prediction model to make predictions for homes less than .7 mile or more than 6.1 miles from the nearest fire station. A look at the data in Table 9.7 reveals that all the x values fall between .7 and 6.1. It is dangerous to use the model to make predictions outside the region in which the sample data fall. A straight line might not provide a good model for the relationship between the mean value of y and the value of x when stretched over a wider range of x values.

9.10 A NONPARAMETRIC TEST FOR CORRELATION (OPTIONAL)

When the simple linear regression assumptions (Section 9.3) are violated, e.g. the random error ϵ has a highly skewed distribution, an alternative method of analysis is prefered. One technique is to apply a nonparametric test for correlation based on ranks. To illustrate, suppose 10 new car models are evaluated by two consumer magazines and each magazine ranks the braking systems of the cars from 1 (best) to 10 (worst). We want to determine whether the magazines' ranks are related. Does a correspondence exist between their ratings? If a car is ranked high by magazine 1, is it likely to be ranked high by magazine 2? Or do high rankings by one magazine correspond to low rankings by the other? That is, are the rankings of the magazines *correlated?*

If the rankings are as shown in the "Perfect Agreement" columns of Table 9.8, we immediately notice that the magazines agree on the rank of every car. High ranks correspond to high ranks and low ranks to low ranks. This is an example of *perfect positive correlation* between the ranks. In contrast, if the rankings appear as shown in the "Perfect Disagreement" columns of Table 9.8, high ranks for one magazine correspond to low ranks for the other. This is an example of *perfect negative correlation.*

TABLE 9.8 Brake Rankings of 10 New Car Models by Two Consumer Magazines

	Perfect Agreement		Perfect Disagreement	
Car Model	Magazine 1	Magazine 2	Magazine 1	Magazine 2
1	4	4	9	2
2	1	1	3	8
3	7	7	5	6
4	5	5	1	10
5	2	2	2	9
6	6	6	10	1
7	8	8	6	5
8	3	3	4	7
9	10	10	8	3
10	9	9	7	4

In practice, you will rarely see perfect positive or negative correlation between the ranks. In fact, it is quite possible for the magazines' ranks to appear as shown in Table 9.9. You will note that these rankings indicate some agreement between the consumer magazines, but not perfect agreement, thus indicating a need for a measure of **rank correlation.**

TABLE 9.9 Brake Rankings of New Car Models: Less Than Perfect Agreement

	Magazine		Difference Between Rank 1 And Rank 2	
Car Model	1	2	d	d^2
1	4	5	-1	1
2	1	2	-1	1
3	9	10	-1	1
4	5	6	-1	1
5	2	1	1	1
6	10	9	1	1
7	7	7	0	0
8	3	3	0	0
9	6	4	2	4
10	8	8	0	0
				$\Sigma d^2 = 10$

Spearman's rank correlation coefficient, r_s, provides a measure of correlation between ranks. The formula for this measure of correlation is given in the next box. We also give a formula that is identical to r_s when there are no ties in rankings; this provides a good approximation to r_s when the number of ties is small relative to the number of pairs.

Note that if the ranks for the two magazines are identical, as in the second and third columns of Table 9.8, the differences between the ranks, d, will all be 0. Thus,

$$r_s = 1 - \frac{6\sum d^2}{n(n^2-1)} = 1 - \frac{6(0)}{10(99)} = 1$$

That is, *perfect positive correlation* between the pairs of ranks is characterized by a Spearman correlation coefficient of $r_s = 1$. When the ranks indicate perfect disagreement, as in the fourth and fifth columns of Table 9.8, $\Sigma d_i^2 = 330$ and

$$r_s = 1 - \frac{6(330)}{10(99)} = -1$$

Thus, *perfect negative correlation* is indicated by $r_s = -1$.

Spearman's Rank Correlation Coefficient

$$r_s = \frac{SS_{uv}}{\sqrt{SS_{uu}SS_{vv}}}$$

where

$$SS_{uv} = \sum(u_i - \bar{u})(v_i - \bar{v}) = \sum u_i v_i - \frac{(\sum u_i)(\sum v_i)}{n}$$

$$SS_{uu} = \sum(u_i - \bar{u})^2 = \sum u_i^2 - \frac{(\sum u_i)^2}{n}$$

$$SS_{vv} = \sum(v_i - \bar{v})^2 = \sum v_i^2 - \frac{(\sum v_i)^2}{n}$$

u_i = Rank of the ith observation in sample 1

v_i = Rank of the ith observation in sample 2

n = Number of pairs of observations (number of observations in each sample)

Shortcut Formula for r_s*

$$r_s = 1 - \frac{6\sum d_i^2}{n(n^2-1)}$$

where

$d_i = u_i - v_i$ (difference in the ranks of the ith observations for samples 1 and 2)

*The shortcut formula is not exact when there are tied measurements, but it is a good approximation when the total number of ties is not large relative to n.

For the data of Table 9.9,

$$r_s = 1 - \frac{6\sum d^2}{n(n^2 - 1)} = 1 - \frac{6(10)}{10(99)} = 1 - \frac{6}{99} = .94$$

The fact that r_s is close to 1 indicates that the magazines tend to agree, but the agreement is not perfect.

The value of r_s *always falls between* -1 *and* $+1$*, with* $+1$ *indicating perfect positive correlation and* -1 *indicating perfect negative correlation.* The closer r_s falls to $+1$ or -1, the greater the correlation between the ranks. Conversely, the nearer r_s is to 0, the less the correlation.

Note that the concept of correlation implies that two responses are obtained for each experimental unit. In the consumer magazine example, each new car model received two ranks (one for each magazine) and the objective of the study was to determine the degree of positive correlation between the two rankings. Rank correlation methods can be used to measure the correlation between any pair of variables. If two variables are measured on each of n experimental units, we rank the measurements associated with each variable separately. Ties receive the average of the ranks of the tied observations. Then we calculate the value of r_s for the two rankings. This value measures the rank correlation between the two variables. We illustrate the procedure in Example 9.5.

EXAMPLE 9.5

Manufacturers of perishable foods often use preservatives to retard spoilage. One concern is that too much preservative will change the flavor of the food. Suppose an experiment is conducted using samples of a food product with varying amounts of preservative added. Both length of time until the food shows signs of spoiling and a taste rating are recorded for each sample. The taste rating is the average rating for three tasters, each of whom rates each sample on a scale from 1 (good) to 5 (bad). Twelve sample measurements are shown in Table 9.10.

a. Calculate Spearman's rank correlation coefficient between spoiling time and taste rating.

TABLE 9.10 Data and Correlations for Example 9.5

Sample	Days Until Spoilage	Rank	Taste Rating	Rank	d	d^2
1	30	2	4.3	11	−9	81
2	47	5	3.6	7.5	−2.5	6.25
3	26	1	4.5	12	−11	121
4	94	11	2.8	3	8	64
5	67	7	3.3	6	1	1
6	83	10	2.7	2	8	64
7	36	3	4.2	10	−7	49
8	77	9	3.9	9	0	0
9	43	4	3.6	7.5	−3.5	12.25
10	109	12	2.2	1	11	121
11	56	6	3.1	5	1	1
12	70	8	2.9	4	4	16
						Total = 536.5

Note: Tied measurements are assigned the average of the ranks they would be given if they were different but consecutive.

b. Use a nonparametric test to find out whether the spoilage times and taste ratings are negatively correlated. Use $\alpha = .05$.

Solution

a. We first rank the days until spoilage, assigning a 1 to the smallest number (26) and a 12 to the largest (109). Similarly, we assign ranks to the 12 taste ratings. [*Note:* The tied taste ratings receive the average of their respective ranks.] Since the number of ties is relatively small, we will use the shortcut formula to calculate r_s. The differences d between the ranks of days until spoilage and the ranks of taste rating are shown in Table 9.10. The squares of the differences, d^2, are also given. Thus,

$$r_s = 1 - \frac{6\sum d_i^2}{n(n^2-1)} = 1 - \frac{6(536.5)}{12(12^2-1)} = 1 - 1.876 = -.876$$

The value of r_s can also be obtained using a computer. An EXCEL printout of the analysis is shown in Figure 9.27. The value of r_s, highlighted on the printout, is $-.879$ and agrees (except for rounding) with our hand-calculated value. This negative correlation coefficient indicates that in this sample an increase in the number of days until spoilage is *associated with* (but is not necessarily the *cause of*) a decrease in the taste rating.

FIGURE 9.27
EXCEL printout for Example 9.5

Sample	Days	Taste
1	30	4.3
2	47	3.6
3	26	4.5
4	94	2.8
5	67	3.3
6	83	2.7
7	36	4.2
8	77	3.9
9	43	3.6
10	109	2.2
11	56	3.1
12	70	2.9
Spearman r(s)	-0.879160718	0.000165104

b. If we define ρ as the **population rank correlation coefficient** [i.e., the rank correlation coefficient that could be calculated from all (x, y) values in the population], this question can be answered by conducting the test

H_0: $\rho = 0$ (no population correlation between ranks)

H_a: $\rho < 0$ (negative population correlation between ranks)

Test statistic: r_s (the *sample* Spearman rank correlation coefficient)

To determine a rejection region, we consult Table XIV in Appendix B, which is partially reproduced in Table 9.11. Note that the left-hand column gives values of n, the number of pairs of observations. The entries in the table are values for

TABLE 9.11 Reproduction of Part of Table XIV in Appendix B: Critical Values of Spearman's Rank Correlation Coefficient

n	$\alpha = .05$	$\alpha = .025$	$\alpha = .01$	$\alpha = .005$
5	.900	—	—	—
6	.829	.886	.943	—
7	.714	.786	.893	—
8	.643	.738	.833	.881
9	.600	.683	.783	.833
10	.564	.648	.745	.794
11	.523	.623	.736	.818
12	.497	.591	.703	.780
13	.475	.566	.673	.745
14	.457	.545	.646	.716
15	.441	.525	.623	.689
16	.425	.507	.601	.666
17	.412	.490	.582	.645
18	.399	.476	.564	.625
19	.388	.462	.549	.608
20	.377	.450	.534	.591

an upper-tail rejection region, since only positive values are given. Thus, for $n = 12$ and $\alpha = .05$, the value .497 is the boundary of the upper-tailed rejection region, so that $P(r_s > .497) = .05$ if H_0: $\rho = 0$ is true. Similarly, for negative values of r_s, we have $P(r_s < -.497) = .05$ if $\rho = 0$. That is, we expect to see $r_s < -.497$ only 5% of the time if there is really no relationship between the ranks of the variables. The lower-tailed rejection region is therefore

$$\textit{Rejection region } (\alpha = .05)\text{: } r_s < -.497$$

Since the calculated $r_s = -.876$ is less than $-.497$, we reject H_0 at the $\alpha = .05$ level of significance. That is, this sample provides sufficient evidence to conclude that a negative correlation exists between number of days until spoilage and taste rating of the food product. It appears that the preservative does affect the taste of this food adversely. [*Note:* The two-tailed p-value of the test is highlighted on the EXCEL printout next to the value of r_s in Figure 9.27. Since the lower-tailed p-value, $p = .00016/2 = .00008$, is less than $\alpha = .05$, our conclusion is the same: reject H_0.]

A summary of Spearman's nonparametric test for correlation is given in the box on the next page.

EXERCISES 9.67–9.76

Learning the Mechanics

9.67 Use Table XIV of Appendix B to find each of the following probabilities:

a. $P(r_s > .508)$ when $n = 22$
b. $P(r_s > .448)$ when $n = 28$
c. $P(r_s \leq .648)$ when $n = 10$
d. $P(r_s < -.738 \text{ or } r_s > .738)$ when $n = 8$

9.68 Specify the rejection region for Spearman's nonparametric test for rank correlation in each of the following situations:

a. H_0: $\rho = 0$; H_a: $\rho \neq 0$, $n = 10$, $\alpha = .05$
b. H_0: $\rho = 0$; H_a: $\rho > 0$, $n = 20$, $\alpha = .025$

Spearman's Nonparametric Test for Rank Correlation

One-Tailed Test	**Two-Tailed Test**
$H_0: \rho = 0$	$H_0: \rho = 0$
$H_a: \rho > 0$ (or $H_a: \rho < 0$)	$H_a: \rho \neq 0$

Test statistic: r_s, the sample rank correlation (see the formulas for calculating r_s)

Rejection region: $r_s > r_{s,\alpha}$ (or $r_s < -r_{s,\alpha}$ when $H_a: \rho_s < 0$)	*Rejection region:* $\lvert r_s \rvert > r_{s,\alpha/2}$
where $r_{s,\alpha}$ is the value from Table XIV corresponding to the upper-tail area α and n pairs of observations	where $r_{s,\alpha/2}$ is the value from Table XIV corresponding to the upper-tail area $\alpha/2$ and n pairs of observations

Assumptions: 1. The sample of experimental units on which the two variables are measured is randomly selected.
2. The probability distributions of the two variables are continuous.

Ties: Assign tied measurements the average of the ranks they would receive if they were unequal but occurred in successive order. For example, if the third-ranked and fourth-ranked measurements are tied, assign each a rank of $(3 + 4)/2 = 3.5$. The number of ties should be small relative to the total number of observations.

c. $H_0: \rho = 0$; $H_a: \rho < 0$, $n = 30$, $\alpha = .01$

9.69 Compute Spearman's rank correlation coefficient for each of the following pairs of sample observations:

a.

x	33	61	20	19	40
y	26	36	65	25	35

b.

x	89	102	120	137	41
y	81	94	75	52	136

c.

x	2	15	4	10
y	11	2	15	21

d.

x	5	20	15	10	3
y	80	83	91	82	87

9.70 The following sample data were collected on variables x and y:

x	0	3	0	−4	3	0	4
y	0	2	2	0	3	1	2

a. Specify the null and alternative hypotheses that should be used in conducting a hypothesis test to determine whether the variables x and y are correlated.
b. Conduct the test of part **a** using $\alpha = .05$.
c. What is the approximate p-value of the test of part **b?**
d. What assumptions are necessary to ensure the validity of the test of part **b?**

Applying the Concepts

9.71 Refer to the orange juice quality study, Exercise 9.14 (p. 484). Recall that a manufacturer that has developed a quantitative index of the "sweetness" of orange juice is investigating the relationship between the sweetness index and the amount of water soluble pectin in the orange juice it produces. The data for 24 production runs at a juice manufacturing plant are reproduced in the table on page 539.
a. Calculate Spearman's rank correlation coefficient between the sweetness index and the amount of pectin. Interpret the result.
b. Conduct a nonparametric test to determine whether there is a negative association between the sweetness index and the amount of pectin. Use $\alpha = .01$.

9.72 Metropolitan areas with many corporate headquarters are finding it easier to transition from a manufacturing economy to a service economy through job growth in small companies and subsidiaries that service the corporate parent. James O. Wheeler of the University of Georgia studied the relationship between the number of corporate headquarters in eleven metropolitan areas and the number of subsidiaries located there (*Growth and Change*, Spring 1988). He hypothesized that there would be a positive relationship between the variables.

OJUICE.DAT

Run	Sweetness Index	Pectin (ppm)	Run	Sweetness Index	Pectin (ppm)
1	5.2	220	13	5.8	306
2	5.5	227	14	5.5	259
3	6.0	259	15	5.3	284
4	5.9	210	16	5.3	383
5	5.8	224	17	5.7	271
6	6.0	215	18	5.5	264
7	5.8	231	19	5.7	227
8	5.6	268	20	5.3	263
9	5.6	239	21	5.9	232
10	5.9	212	22	5.8	220
11	5.4	410	23	5.8	246
12	5.6	256	24	5.9	241

Note: The data in the table are authentic. For confidentiality reasons, the manufacturer cannot be disclosed.

METRO.DAT

Metropolitan Area	No. of Parent Companies	No. of Subsidiaries
New York	643	2,617
Chicago	381	1,724
Los Angeles	342	1,867
Dallas–Ft. Worth	251	1,238
Detroit	216	890
Boston	208	681
Houston	192	1,534
San Francisco	141	899
Minneapolis	131	492
Cleveland	128	579
Denver	124	672

Source: Wheeler, J. O. "The corporate role of large metropolitan areas in the United States." *Growth and Change,* Spring 1988, pp. 75–88.

a. Calculate Spearman's rank correlation coefficient for the data in the table above. What does it indicate about Wheeler's hypothesis?

b. To conduct a formal test of Wheeler's hypothesis using Spearman's rank correlation coefficient, certain assumptions must hold. What are they? Do they appear to hold? Explain.

9.73 Is there an association between federal government spending for engineering research and the level of employment of scientists in the aircraft and missile industry? The data in the next table lists, for selected years, the amount (in millions of dollars) the federal government allocated to research in engineering and the number (in thousands) of scientists and engineers employed in the aircraft and missile industry. Conduct a nonparametric test to investigate the strength of the relationship between the two variables. Test using $\alpha = .10$.

MISSILE.DAT

Year	Federal Spending for Engineering Research ($ millions)	Number of Scientists and Engineers Employed in Aircraft and Missile Industry (thousands)
1980	2,830	90.6
1985	3,618	130.2
1990	4,227	115.3
1994	5,509	85.4
1995	5,740	68.2
1996	5,680	79.5
1997	5,690	95.1

Source: U.S. Census Bureau, *Statistical Abstract of the United States,* 1999.

9.74 Two expert wine tasters were asked to rank six brands of wine. Their rankings are shown in the table. Do the data present sufficient evidence to indicate a positive correlation in the rankings of the two experts?

WINETAST.DAT

Brand	Expert 1	Expert 2
A	6	5
B	5	6
C	1	2
D	3	1
E	2	4
F	4	3

9.75 An *employee suggestion system* is a formal process for capturing, analyzing, implementing, and recognizing employee-proposed organizational improvements. (The first known system was implemented by the Yale and

STATISTICS IN *Action*

Can "Dowsers" Really Detect Water?

The act of searching for and finding underground supplies of water using nothing more than a divining rod is commonly known as "dowsing." Although widely regarded among scientists as no more than a superstitious relic from medieval times, dowsing remains popular in folklore and, to this day, there are individuals who claim to have this mysterious skill and actually market their "services."

Many dowsers in Germany claim that they respond to "earthrays" that emanate from the water source. These earthrays, say the dowsers, are a subtle form of radiation potentially hazardous to human health. As a result of these claims, the German government in the mid-1980s conducted a 2-year experiment to investigate the possibility that dowsing is a genuine skill. If such a skill could be demonstrated, reasoned government officials, then dangerous levels of radiation in Germany could be detected, avoided, and disposed of.

A group of university physicists in Munich, Germany, were provided a grant of 400,000 marks ($\approx$ \$250,000) to conduct the study. Approximately 500 candidate dowsers were recruited to participate in preliminary tests of their skill. To avoid fraudulent claims, the 43 individuals who seemed to be the most successful in the preliminary tests were selected for the final, carefully controlled, experiment.

The researchers set up a 10-meter-long line on the ground floor of a vacant barn, along which a small wagon could be moved. Attached to the wagon was a short length of pipe, perpendicular to the test line, that was connected by hoses to a pump with running water. The location of the pipe along the line for each trial of the experiment was assigned using a computer-generated random number. On the upper floor of the barn, directly above the experimental line, a 10-meter test line was painted. In each trial, a dowser was admitted to this upper level and required, with his or her rod, stick, or other tool of choice, to ascertain where the pipe with running water on the ground floor was located.

Each dowser participated in at least one test series, that is, a sequence of from 5 to 15 trials (typically 10), with the pipe randomly repositioned after each trial. (Some dowsers undertook only one test series, selected others underwent more than 10 test series.) Over the 2-year experimental period, the 43 dowsers participated in a total of 843 tests. The experiment was "double-blind" in that neither the observer (researcher) on the top floor nor the dowser knew the pipe's location, even after a guess was made. [*Note:* Before the experiment began, a professional magician inspected the entire arrangement for potential deception or cheating by the dowsers.]

For each trial, two variables were recorded: the actual pipe location (in decimeters from the beginning of the line) and the dowser's guess (also measured in decimeters). Based on an examination of these data, the German physicists concluded in their final report that although most dowsers did not do particularly well in the experiments, "Some few dowsers, in particular tests, showed an extraordinarily high rate of success, which can scarcely if at all be explained as due to chance ... a real core of dowser-phenomena can be regarded as empirically proven ... " (Wagner, Betz, and König, 1990).

This conclusion was critically assessed by J.T. Enright, a professor of behavioral physiology at the University of California—San Diego (*Skeptical Inquirer,* Jan./Feb. 1999). Using scatterplots and the notion of correlation, Enright concluded exactly the opposite of the German physicists. According to Enright, "the Munich experiments constitute as decisive and complete a failure as can be imagined of dowsers to do what they claim they can."

Focus

a. Using scatterplots, Enright provided several hypothetical examples of outcomes that might be expected from the dowsing experiments, assuming various arbitrary categories of dowser skill. Let x = dowser's guess and y = pipe location. Construct a scatterplot of hypothetical data that would reflect perfect prediction by the dowsers.

b. Repeat part **a** for dowsers that have good (but not perfect) skill.

c. Repeat part **a** for dowsers that have no skill (i.e., that are making random guesses).

d. Enright presented a scatterplot of the data for all 843 tests performed in the Munich barn. A reproduction of this plot is displayed in Figure 9.28. Based on this graph, what inference would you make about the overall ability of the dowsers? Explain. [*Note:* In this plot, dowser's guess is shown on the vertical axis to make the graph comparable to the scatterplots you drew in parts **a–c.**]

e. Recall that the German physicists found that a "few dowsers ... showed an extraordinarily high rate of success." Consequently, they might argue that the scatterplot in Figure 9.28 on page 542 obscures these outstanding performances since it lumps all 43 dowsers (the majority of which are unskilled) together. In the researchers' final report, they identified three dowsers (those numbered 99, 18, and 108) as having particularly impressive results. All three of these "best" dowsers performed the experiment multiple times. The best test series (sequence of trials) for each of these three dowsers was identified; these data are listed in Table 9.12 and stored in the file DOWSING.DAT. Conduct a complete simple linear regression analysis of the data in order to make an inference about the overall performance of each of the three best dowsers.

f. The data in Table 9.12 represent the outcome of the dowsing experiment in its most favorable light. Can these results be reproduced by the best dowsers in comparable tests? Remember, each of these three dowsers did participate in other test series. Enright plotted the data for these other series in which the three best dowsers performed; this scatterplot is reproduced in Figure 9.29. Comment on the performance of the three best dowsers during these "rest of the best" trials.

g. According to Enright, "there is another way of evaluating the results from those dowsers who produced the best test series ... Suppose that they had always left their dowsing equipment at home in the closet, and had simply, in each and every test, just guessed that the pipe was located exactly at the middle of the test line." Replace the dowsers' guesses in Table 9.12 with the midpoint of the test line, 50 decimeters, and repeat the analysis of part **e.** What do you conclude from the analysis?

h. Give a critical assessment of the Munich dowsing experiments. With whom do you tend to agree, the German physicists or J.T. Enright?

DOWSING.DAT

TABLE 9.12 Dowsing Trial Results: Best Series for the Three Best Dowsers

Trial	Dowser Number	Pipe Location	Dowser's Guess
1	99	4	4
2	99	5	87
3	99	30	95
4	99	35	74
5	99	36	78
6	99	58	65
7	99	40	39
8	99	70	75
9	99	74	32
10	99	98	100
11	18	7	10
12	18	38	40
13	18	40	30
14	18	49	47
15	18	75	9
16	18	82	95
17	108	5	52
18	108	18	16
19	108	33	37
20	108	45	40
21	108	38	66
22	108	50	58
23	108	52	74
24	108	63	65
25	108	72	60
26	108	95	49

Source: Enright, J.T. "Testing dowsing: The failure of the Munich experiments" *Skeptical Inquirer,* Jan./Feb. 1999, p. 45 (Figure 6a).

STATISTICS IN Action

(continued)

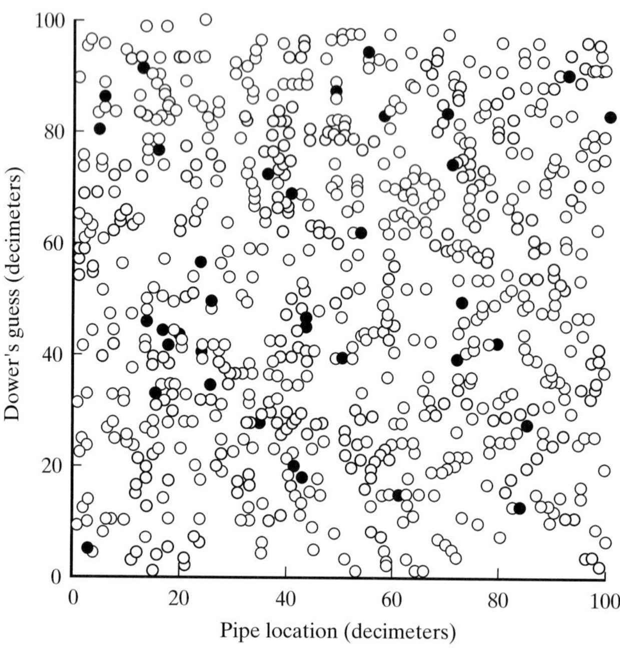

FIGURE 9.28
Results from All 843 Dowsing Trials

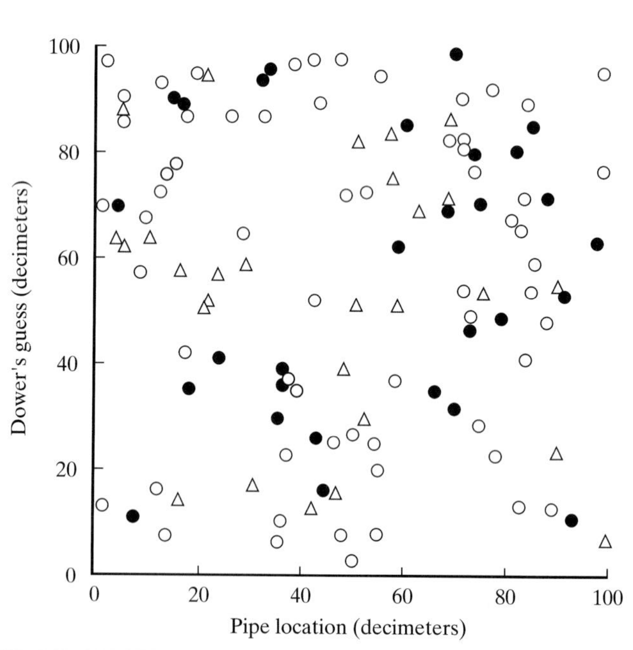

FIGURE 9.29
Results for Other Test Series that Three Best Dowsers Participated In

Towne Manufacturing Company of Stamford, Connecticut, in 1880.) Using data from the National Association of Suggestion Systems, D. Carnevale and B. Sharp examined the strengths of the relationships between the extent of employee participation in suggestion plans and cost savings realized by employers (*Review of Public Personnel Administration*, Spring 1993). The data in the table at right are representative of the data they analyzed for a sample of federal, state, and local government agencies. Savings are calculated from the first year measurable benefits were observed.

a. Explain why the savings data used in this study may understate the total benefits derived from the implemented suggestions.

b. Carnevale and Sharp concluded that a significant moderate positive relationship exists between participation rates and cost savings rates in public sector suggestion systems. Do you agree? Test using $\alpha = .01$.

c. Justify the statistical methodology you used in part **b.**

 **SUGGEST.DAT**

Employee Involvement (% of all employees submitting suggestions)	Savings Rate (% of total budget)
10.1%	8.5%
6.2	6.0
16.3	9.0
1.2	0.0
4.8	5.1
11.5	6.1
.6	1.2
2.8	4.5
8.9	5.4
20.2	15.3
2.7	3.8

Source: Data adapted from Carnevale, D. G., and Sharp, B. S. "The old employee suggestion box." *Review of Public Personnel Administration,* Spring 1993, pp. 82–92.

9.76 A *negotiable certificate of deposit* is a marketable receipt for funds deposited in a bank for a specified period of time at a specified rate of interest (Lee, Finnerty, and Norton, 1997). The table below lists the end-of-quarter

CD3MONTH.DAT

Year	Quarter	Interest Rate, x	S&P 500, y	Year	Quarter	Interest Rate, x	S&P 500, y
1986	I	7.24	232.3	1993	I	3.11	450.2
	II	6.73	245.3		II	3.21	448.1
	III	5.71	238.3		III	3.12	459.2
	IV	6.04	248.6		IV	3.17	466.0
1987	I	6.17	292.5	1994	I	3.77	463.8
	II	6.94	301.4		II	4.52	454.8
	III	7.37	318.7		III	5.03	467.0
	IV	7.66	241.0		IV	6.29	455.2
1988	I	6.63	265.7	1995	I	6.15	493.2
	II	7.51	270.7		II	5.90	539.4
	III	8.23	268.0		III	5.73	578.8
	IV	9.25	276.5		IV	5.62	614.6
1989	I	10.09	292.7	1996	I	5.29	645.5
	II	9.20	323.7		II	5.46	670.6
	III	8.78	347.3		III	5.51	687.3
	IV	8.32	348.6		IV	5.44	740.7
1990	I	8.27	338.5	1997	I	5.53	757.1
	II	8.33	360.4		II	5.66	885.1
	III	8.08	315.4		III	5.60	947.3
	IV	7.96	328.8		IV	5.80	970.4
1991	I	6.71	372.3	1998	I	5.58	1,101.8
	II	6.01	378.3		II	5.60	1,133.8
	III	5.70	387.2		III	5.41	1,017.0
	IV	4.91	388.5		IV	5.14	1,229.2
1992	I	4.25	407.3	1999	I	4.91	1,286.4
	II	3.86	408.27		II	5.13	1,372.7
	III	3.13	418.48		III	5.50	1,282.7
	IV	3.48	435.64		IV	6.05	1,269.3

Source: Standard & Poor's *Current Statistics,* 1992, 1996; Yahoo Finance *Current Statistics,* February 2000; Board of Governors, Federal Reserve Board, *Historical Statistics,* March 2000.

STATISTIX Output for Exercise 9.76

```
SPEARMAN RANK CORRELATIONS, CORRECTED FOR TIES

              INTRATE
SP500   -0.5778

MAXIMUM DIFFERENCE ALLOWED BETWEEN TIES    0.00001

CASES INCLUDED 56     MISSING CASES 0
```

interest rate for three-month certificates of deposit from January 1986 through December 1999 with the concurrent end-of-quarter values of Standard & Poor's 500 Stock Composite Average (an indicator of stock market activity).

a. Locate Spearman's rank correlation coefficient on the STATISTIX printout above. Interpret the result.
b. Test the null hypothesis that the interest rate on certificates of deposit and the S&P 500 are not correlated against the alternative hypothesis that these variables are correlated. Use $\alpha = .10$.
c. Repeat parts **a** and **b** using data from 1996 through the present, which can be obtained at your library in Standard & Poor's *Current Statistics.* Compare your results for the newer data with your results for the earlier period.

QUICK REVIEW

Key Terms

Starred (*) terms refer to the optional section in this chapter.

Bivariate relationship 505
Coefficient of correlation 506
Coefficient of determination 510
Confidence interval for mean of y 519
Dependent variable 474
Deterministic model 473
Errors of prediction 477
Independent variable 474
Least squares line 477
Least squares estimates 478
Line of means 474
Method of least squares 477
Pearson product moment coefficient of correlation 506
Population correlation coefficient 508
Population rank correlation coefficient 536
Prediction interval for y 519
Predictor variable 474
Probabilistic model 473
Random error 473
*Rank correlation 533
Regression analysis 474
Response variable 474
Scattergram 476
Slope 474
*Spearman's rank correlation coeffecient 533
Standard error of regression model 490
Straight-line (first-order) model 474
Sum of squared errors 477
y-intercept 474

Key Formulas

$\hat{y} = \hat{\beta}_0 + \hat{\beta}_1 x$ — Least squares line 478

$\hat{\beta}_1 = \dfrac{SS_{xy}}{SS_{xx}}, \ \hat{\beta}_0 = \bar{y} - \hat{\beta}_1 \bar{x}$ — Least squares estimates of β's 479

$$\text{where } SS_{xy} = \sum xy - \frac{(\sum x)(\sum y)}{n}$$

$$SS_{xx} = \sum x^2 - \frac{(\sum x)^2}{n}$$

$s^2 = \dfrac{SSE}{n-2}$ — Estimated variance of σ^2 of ε 490

$SSE = \sum (y_i - \hat{y}_i)^2 = SS_{yy} - \hat{\beta}_1 SS_{xy}$ — Sum of squared errors 490

$$\text{where } SS_{yy} = \sum y^2 - \frac{(\sum y)^2}{n}$$

$s_{\widehat{\beta}_1} = \dfrac{s}{\sqrt{SS_{xx}}}$	Estimated standard error of $\widehat{\beta}_1$ 496
$t = \dfrac{\widehat{\beta}_1}{s_{\widehat{\beta}_1}}$	Test statistic for H_0: $\beta_1 = 0$ 497
$\widehat{\beta}_1 \pm (t_{\alpha/2})s_{\widehat{\beta}_1}$	$(1 - \alpha)100\%$ confidence interval for β_1 499
$r = \dfrac{SS_{xy}}{\sqrt{SS_{xx}SS_{yy}}} = \pm\sqrt{r^2}$ (same sign as $\widehat{\beta}_1$)	Coefficient of correlation 506
$r^2 = \dfrac{SS_{yy} - SSE}{SS_{yy}}$	Coefficient of determination 510
$\hat{y} \pm (t_{\alpha/2})s\sqrt{\dfrac{1}{n} + \dfrac{(x_p - \bar{x})^2}{SS_{xx}}}$	$(1 - \alpha)100\%$ confidence interval for E(y) when $x = x_p$ 519
$\hat{y} \pm (t_{\alpha/2})s\sqrt{1 + \dfrac{1}{n} + \dfrac{(x_p - \bar{x})^2}{SS_{xx}}}$	$(1 - \alpha)100\%$ prediction interval for y when $x = x_p$ 519
$r_s = 1 - \dfrac{6\sum d_i^2}{n(n^2 - 1)}$	*Spearman's rank correlation coefficient 534

LANGUAGE LAB

Symbol	Pronunciation	Description
y		Dependent variable (variable to be predicted or modeled)
x		Independent (predictor) variable
$E(y)$		Expected (mean) value of y
β_0	beta-zero	y-intercept of true line
β_1	beta-one	Slope of true line
$\widehat{\beta}_0$	beta-zero hat	Least squares estimate of y-intercept
$\widehat{\beta}_1$	beta-one hat	Least squares estimate of slope
ε	epsilon	Random error
$\hat{y}$	y-hat	Predicted value of y
$(y - \hat{y})$		Error of prediction
SE		Sum of errors (will equal zero with least squares line)
SSE		Sum of squared errors (will be smallest for least squares line)
SS_{xx}		Sum of squares of x-values
SS_{yy}		Sum of squares of y-values
SS_{xy}		Sum of squares of cross-products, $x \cdot y$
r		Coefficient of correlation
r^2	R-squared	Coefficient of determination
x_p		Value of x used to predict y
r_s	r-sub-s	*Spearman's rank correlation coefficient
ρ	rho	Population correlation coefficient

SUPPLEMENTARY EXERCISES 9.77–9.91

[Note: Starred (*) exercises are from the optional section in this chapter.]

Learning the Mechanics

9.77 In fitting a least squares line to $n = 15$ data points, the following quantities were computed: $SS_{xx} = 55$, $SS_{yy} = 198$, $SS_{xy} = -88$, $\bar{x} = 1.3$, and $\bar{y} = 35$.

a. Find the least squares line.
b. Graph the least squares line.
c. Calculate SSE.
d. Calculate s^2.
e. Find a 90% confidence interval for β_1. Interpret this estimate.
f. Find a 90% confidence interval for the mean value of y when $x = 15$.
g. Find a 90% prediction interval for y when $x = 15$.

9.78 Consider the following sample data:

y	5	1	3
x	5	1	3

a. Construct a scattergram for the data.
b. It is possible to find many lines for which $\Sigma(y - \hat{y}) = 0$. For this reason, the criterion $\Sigma(y - \hat{y}) = 0$ is not used for identifying the "best-fitting" straight line. Find two lines that have $\Sigma(y - \hat{y}) = 0$.
c. Find the least squares line.
d. Compare the value of SSE for the least squares line to that of the two lines you found in part **b**. What principle of least squares is demonstrated by this comparison?

9.79 Consider the 10 data points at the top of the next column.

a. Plot the data on a scattergram.
b. Calculate the values of r and r^2.

LM9_79.DAT

x	3	5	6	4	3	7	6	5	4	7
y	4	3	2	1	2	3	3	5	4	2

c. Is there sufficient evidence to indicate that x and y are linearly correlated? Test at the $\alpha = .10$ level of significance.
*d. Calculate Spearman's rank correlation r_s.

Applying the Concepts

9.80 Emotional exhaustion, or *burnout*, is a significant problem for people with careers in the field of human services. Regression analysis was used to investigate the relationship between burnout and aspects of the human services professional's job and job-related behavior (*Journal of Applied Behavioral Science*, Vol. 22, 1986). Emotional exhaustion was measured with the Maslach Burnout Inventory, a questionnaire. One of the independent variables considered, called *concentration*, was the proportion of social contacts with individuals who belong to a person's work group. The table below lists the values of the emotional exhaustion index (higher values indicate greater exhaustion) and concentration for a sample of 25 human services professionals who work in a large public hospital. An SPSS printout of the simple linear regression is also provided on page 547.

a. Construct a scattergram for the data. Do the variables x and y appear to be related?
b. Find the correlation coefficient for the data and interpret its value. Does your conclusion mean that concentration causes emotional exhaustion? Explain.

BURNOUT.DAT

Exhaustion Index, y	Concentration, x	Exhaustion Index, y	Concentration, x
100	20%	493	86%
525	60	892	83
300	38	527	79
980	88	600	75
310	79	855	81
900	87	709	75
410	68	791	77
296	12	718	77
120	35	684	77
501	70	141	17
920	80	400	85
810	92	970	96
506	77		

SPSS Output for Exercise 9.80

```
Correlations:   CONCEN

  EXHAUST       .7825**

N of cases:     25          1-tailed Signif:   * - .01    ** - .001
---------------------------------------------------------------------------

        * * * *   M U L T I P L E   R E G R E S S I O N   * * * *

Equation Number 1    Dependent Variable..   EXHAUST

Variable(s) Entered on Step Number
   1..     CONCEN

Multiple R              .78250
R Square                .61231
Adjusted R Square       .59545
Standard Error       174.20742

Analysis of Variance
                      DF        Sum of Squares      Mean Square
Regression             1        1102408.24475    1102408.24475
Residual              23         698009.19525      30348.22588

F =        36.32529         Signif F =   .0000

---------------------- Variables in the Equation ------------------------

Variable               B         SE B      95% Confdnce Intrvl B         T    Sig T

CONCEN          8.865471     1.470948     5.822584    11.908359     6.027   .0000
(Constant)    -29.496718   106.697163  -250.216617   191.223182     -.276   .7847
```

c. Test the usefulness of the straight-line relationship with concentration for predicting burnout. Use $\alpha = .05$.

d. Find the coefficient of determination for the model and interpret it.

e. Find a 95% confidence interval for the slope β_1. Interpret the result.

f. Use a 95% confidence interval to estimate the mean exhaustion level for all professionals who have 80% of their social contacts within their work groups. Interpret the interval.

9.81 *Work standards* specify time, cost, and efficiency norms for the performance of work tasks. They are typically used to monitor job performance. In the distribution center of McCormick and Co., Inc., data were collected to develop work standards for the time to assemble or fill customer orders (*Production and Inventory Management Journal,* 1991). The table to the right contains data for a random sample of 9 orders.

a. Construct a scattergram for these data and interpret it.

b. Fit a least squares line to these data using time as the dependent variable.

c. In general, we would expect the mean time to fill an order to increase with the size of the order. Do the data support this theory? Test using $\alpha = .05$.

d. Find a 95% confidence interval for the mean time to fill an order consisting of 150 cases.

WORKSTD.DAT

Time (mins.)	Order Size (cases)
27	36
15	34
71	255
35	103
8	4
60	555
3	6
10	60
10	96

Source: Boyle, D., Ray, B.A., and Kahan, G. "Work standards—the quality way." *Production and Inventory Management Journal,* Second Quarter, 1991, p. 67.

9.82 Common maize rust is a serious disease of sweet corn. Researchers in New York state have developed an action threshold for initiation of fungicide applications based on a regression equation relating maize rust incidence to severity of the disease (*Phytopathology,* Vol. 80, 1990). In one particular field, data were collected on more than 100 plants of the sweet corn hybrid Jubilee. For each plant, incidence was measured as the percentage of leaves infected (x) and severity was calculated as the log (base 10) of the average number of infections per leaf (y). A simple linear regression analysis of the data produced the following results:

$$\hat{y} = -.939 + .020x$$
$$r^2 = .816$$
$$s = .288$$

a. Interpret the value of $\hat{\beta}_1$.
b. Interpret the value of r^2.
c. Interpret the value of s.
d. Calculate the value of r and interpret it.
e. Use the result, part **d**, to test the utility of the model. Use $\alpha = .05$. (Assume $n = 100$.)
f. Predict the severity of the disease when the incidence of maize rust for a plant is 80%. [*Note:* Take the antilog (base 10) of $\hat{y}$ to obtain the predicted average number of infections per leaf.]

9.83 Refer to Exercise 2.97 (p. 106). The data in the value of 50 Beanie Babies collector's items, published in *Beanie World Magazine*, are reproduced on the next page. Can age (in months as of Sept. 1998) of a Beanie Baby be used to accurately predict its market value? Answer this question by conducting a complete simple linear regression anlysis on the data. Use the SAS printout on page 550.

*9.84 Universities receive gifts and donations from corporations, foundations, friends, and alumni. It has long been argued that universities rise or fall depending on the level of support of their alumni. The table below reports the total dollars raised during a recent academic year by a sample of major U.S. universities. In addition, it reports the percentage of that total donated by alumni.

HIGHERED.DAT

University	Total Funds Raised	Alumni Contribution
Harvard	$323,406,242	47.5%
Yale	199,646,606	54.6
Cornell	198,736,229	56.2
Wisconsin	164,349,458	17.4
Michigan	145,757,642	45.4
Pennsylvania	135,324,761	34.3
Illinois	116,578,975	36.6
Princeton	103,826,392	53.2
Brown	102,513,437	34.7
Northwestern	101,041,213	27.3

Source: The Chronicle of Higher Education, Sept. 2, 1996, p. 27.

a. Do these data indicate that total fundraising and alumni contributions are correlated? Test using $\alpha = .05$.
b. What assumptions must hold to ensure the validity of your test?

9.85 A large proportion of U.S. teenagers work while attending high school. These heavy workloads often result in underachievement in the classroom and lower grades. A study of high school students in California and Wisconsin showed that those who worked only a few hours per week had the highest grade point averages (*Newsweek*, Nov. 16, 1992). The following table shows grade point averages (GPAs) and number of hours worked per week for a sample of five students. Consider a simple linear regression relating GPA (y) to hours worked (x).

TEENWORK.DAT

Grade Point Average, y	2.93	3.00	2.86	3.04	2.66
Hours Worked per Week, x	12	0	17	5	21

a. Find the equation of the least squares line.
b. Plot the data and graph the least squares line.
c. Test whether the model is useful for predicting grade point average. Use $\alpha = .10$.
d. Predict the grade point average of a high school student who works 10 hours per week using a 90% prediction interval. Intrepret the result.

9.86 The Minnesota Department of Transportation installed a state-of-the-art weigh-in-motion scale in the concrete surface of the eastbound lanes of Interstate 494 in Bloomington, Minnesota. After installation, a study was undertaken to determine whether the scale's readings correspond with the static weights of the vehicles being monitored. (Studies of this type are known as *calibration studies.*) After some preliminary comparisons using a two-axle, six-tire truck carrying different loads (see the table on p. 551), calibration adjustments were made in the software of the weigh-in-motion system and the scales were reevaluated.

a. Construct two scattergrams, one of y_1 versus x and the other of y_2 versus x.
b. Use the scattergrams of part **a** to evaluate the performance of the weigh-in-motion scale both before and after the calibration adjustment.
c. Calculate the correlation coefficient for both sets of data and interpret their values. Explain how these correlation coefficients can be used to evaluate the weigh-in-motion scale.
d. Suppose the sample correlation coefficient for y_2 and x was 1. Could this happen if the static weights and the weigh-in-motion readings disagreed? Explain.

9.87 Refer to Exercise 9.42 (p. 503), in which managerial success, y, was modeled as a function of the number of contacts a manager makes with people outside his or her work unit, x, during a specific period of time. The data are repeated in the table on page 551. The MINITAB simple linear regression printout is also provided there.

a. A particular manager was observed for two weeks, as in the *Journal of Applied Behavioral Science*

BEANIE.DAT (Data for Exercise 9.83)

Name	Age (months) as of Sept. 1998	Retired (R)/ Current (C)	Value ($)
1. Ally the Alligator	52	R	55.00
2. Batty the Bat	12	C	12.00
3. Bongo the Brown Monkey	28	R	40.00
4. Blackie the Bear	52	C	10.00
5. Bucky the Beaver	40	R	45.00
6. Bumble the Bee	28	R	600.00
7. Crunch the Shark	21	C	10.00
8. Congo the Gorilla	28	C	10.00
9. Derby the Coarse Mained Horse	28	R	30.00
10. Digger the Red Crab	40	R	150.00
11. Echo the Dolphin	17	R	20.00
12. Fetch the Golden Retriever	5	C	15.00
13. Early the Robin	5	C	20.00
14. Flip the White Cat	28	R	40.00
15. Garcia the Teddy	28	R	200.00
16. Happy the Hippo	52	R	20.00
17. Grunt the Razorback	28	R	175.00
18. Gigi the Poodle	5	C	15.00
19. Goldie the Goldfish	52	R	45.00
20. Iggy the Iguana	10	C	10.00
21. Inch the Inchworm	28	R	20.00
22. Jake the Mallard Duck	5	C	20.00
23. Kiwi the Toucan	40	R	165.00
24. Kuku to Cockatoo	5	C	20.00
25. Mistic the Unicorn	11	R	45.00
26. Mel the Koala Bear	21	C	10.00
27. Nanook the Husky	17	C	15.00
28. Nuts the Squirrel	21	C	10.00
29. Peace the Tie Died Teddy	17	C	25.00
30. Patty the Platypus	64	R	800.00
31. Quacker the Duck	40	R	15.00
32. Puffer the Penguin	10	C	15.00
33. Princess the Bear	12	C	65.00
34. Scottie the Scottie	28	R	28.00
35. Rover the Dog	28	R	15.00
36. Rex the Tyrannosaurus	40	R	825.00
37. Sly the Fox	28	C	10.00
38. Slither the Snake	52	R	1,900.00
39. Skip the Siamese Cat	21	C	10.00
40. Splash the Orca Whale	52	R	150.00
41. Spooky the Ghost	28	R	40.00
42. Snowball the Snowman	12	R	40.00
43. Stinger the Scorpion	5	C	15.00
44. Spot the Dog	52	R	65.00
45. Tank the Armadillo	28	R	85.00
46. Stripes the Tiger (Gold/Black)	40	R	400.00
47. Teddy the 1997 Holiday Bear	12	R	50.00
48. Tuffy the Terrier	17	C	10.00
49. Tracker the Basset Hound	5	C	15.00
50. Zip the Black Cat	28	R	40.00

Source: Beanie World Magazine, Sept. 1998.

study. She made 55 contacts with people outside her work unit. Predict the value of the manager's success index. Use a 90% prediction interval.

b. A second manager was observed for two weeks. This manager made 110 contacts with people outside his work unit. Give two reasons why caution should be

SAS Output for Exercise 9.83

Dependent Variable: VALUE

Analysis of Variance

Source	DF	Sum of Squares	Mean Square	F Value	Probe>F
Model	1	865745.59381	865745.59381	10.548	0.0021
Error	48	3939796.9062	82079.10221		
C Total	49	4805542.5000			

Root MSE	286.49451	R-square	0.1802
Dep Mean	128.90000	Adj R-sq	0.1631
C.V.	222.26106		

Parameter Estimates

Variable	DF	Parameter Estimate	Standard Error	T for H0: Parameter=0	Prob > |T|
INTERCEP	1	-92.457684	79.29105784	-1.166	0.2494
AGE	1	8.346821	2.57005393	3.248	0.0021

Obs	AGE	Dep Var VALUE	Predict Value	Std Err Predict	Lower95% Predict	Upper95% Predict	Residual
1	52	55.0000	341.6	77.006	-254.9	938.1	-286.6
2	12	12.0000	7.7042	55.083	-578.9	594.3	4.2958
3	28	40.0000	141.3	40.695	-440.6	723.1	-101.3
4	52	10.0000	341.6	77.006	-254.9	938.1	-331.6
5	40	45.0000	241.4	53.309	-344.5	827.3	-196.4
6	28	600.0	141.3	40.695	-440.6	723.1	458.7
7	21	10.0000	82.8255	42.928	-499.6	665.3	-72.8255
8	28	10.0000	141.3	40.695	-440.6	723.1	-131.3
9	28	30.0000	141.3	40.695	-440.6	723.1	-111.3
10	40	150.0	241.4	53.309	-344.5	827.3	-91.4151
11	17	20.0000	49.4383	47.331	-534.4	633.3	-29.4383
12	5	15.0000	-50.7236	68.560	-643.0	541.6	65.7236
13	5	20.0000	-50.7236	68.560	-643.0	541.6	70.7236
14	28	40.0000	141.3	40.695	-440.6	723.1	-101.3
15	28	200.0	141.3	40.695	-440.6	723.1	58.7467
16	52	20.0000	341.6	77.006	-254.9	938.1	-321.6
17	28	175.0	141.3	40.695	-440.6	723.1	33.7467
18	5	15.0000	-50.7236	68.560	-643.0	541.6	65.7236
19	52	45.0000	341.6	77.006	-254.6	938.1	-296.6
20	10	10.0000	-8.9895	58.687	-597.0	579.0	18.9895
21	28	20.0000	141.3	40.695	-440.6	723.1	-121.3
22	5	20.0000	-50.7236	68.560	-643.0	541.6	70.7236
23	40	165.0	241.4	53.309	-344.5	827.3	-76.4151
24	5	20.0000	-50.7236	68.560	-643.0	541.6	70.7236
25	11	45.0000	-0.6427	56.856	-587.9	586.6	45.6427
26	21	10.0000	82.8255	42.928	-499.6	665.3	-72.8255
27	17	15.0000	49.4383	47.331	-534.4	633.3	-34.4383
28	21	10.0000	82.8255	42.928	499.6	665.3	-72.8255
29	17	25.0000	49.4383	47.331	-534.4	633.3	-24.4383
30	64	800.0	441.7	104.500	-171.4	1054.9	358.3
31	40	15.0000	241.4	53.309	-344.5	827.3	-226.4
32	10	15.0000	-8.9895	58.687	-597.0	579.0	23.9895
33	12	65.0000	7.7042	55.083	-578.9	594.3	57.2958
34	28	28.0000	141.3	40.695	-440.6	723.1	-113.3
35	28	15.0000	141.3	40.695	-440.6	723.1	-126.3
36	40	825.0	241.4	53.309	-344.5	827.3	583.6
37	28	10.0000	141.3	40.695	-440.6	723.1	-131.3
38	52	1900.0	341.6	77.006	-254.9	938.1	1558.4
39	21	10.0000	82.8255	42.928	-499.6	665.3	-72.8255
40	52	150.0	341.6	77.006	-254.9	938.1	-191.6
41	28	40.0000	141.3	40.695	-440.6	723.1	-101.3
42	12	40.0000	7.7042	55.083	-578.9	594.3	32.2958
43	5	15.0000	-50.7236	68.560	-643.0	541.6	65.7236
44	52	65.0000	341.6	77.006	-254.9	938.1	-276.6
45	28	85.0000	141.3	40.695	-440.6	723.1	-56.2533
46	40	400.0	241.4	53.309	-344.5	827.3	158.6
47	12	50.0000	7.7042	55.083	-578.9	594.3	42.2958
48	17	10.0000	49.4383	47.331	-534.4	633.3	-39.4383
49	5	15.0000	-50.7236	68.560	-643.0	541.6	65.7236
50	28	40.0000	141.3	40.695	-440.6	723.1	-101.3

TRUCKWTS.DAT (Data for Exercise 9.86)

Trial Number	Static Weight of Truck, x (thousand pounds)	Weigh-in-Motion Reading Prior to Calibration Adjustment, y_1 (thousand pounds)	Weigh-in-Motion Reading After Calibration Adjustment, y_2 (thousand pounds)
1	27.9	26.0	27.8
2	29.1	29.9	29.1
3	38.0	39.5	37.8
4	27.0	25.1	27.1
5	30.3	31.6	30.6
6	34.5	36.2	34.3
7	27.8	25.1	26.9
8	29.6	31.0	29.6
9	33.1	35.6	33.0
10	35.5	40.2	35.0

Source: Adapted from data in Wright J. L., Owen, F., and Pena, D. "Status of MN/DOT's weigh-in-motion program." St. Paul: Minnesota Department of Transportation, January 1983.

MINITAB Output for Exercise 9.87

```
The regression equation is
SUCCESS = 44.1 + 0.237 INTERACT

Predictor        Coef        Stdev      t-ratio       p
Constant       44.130        9.362         4.71   0.000
INTERACT       0.2366       0.1865         1.27   0.222

s = 19.40       R-sq = 8.6%       R-sq(adj) = 3.3%

Analysis of Variance

SOURCE        DF          SS            MS         F        p
Regression     1       606.0         606.0      1.61    0.222
Error         17      6400.6         376.5
Total         18      7006.6
```

MANAGERS.DAT (Data for Exercise 9.87)

Manager	Manager Success Index, *y*	Number of Interactions with Outsiders, *x*
1	40	12
2	73	71
3	95	70
4	60	81
5	81	43
6	27	50
7	53	42
8	66	18
9	25	35
10	63	82
11	70	20
12	47	81
13	80	40
14	51	33
15	32	45
16	50	10
17	52	65
18	30	20
19	42	21

exercised in using the least squares model developed from the given data set to construct a prediction interval for this manager's success index.

c. In the context of this problem, determine the value of x for which the associated prediction interval for y is the narrowest.

9.88 Firms planning to build new plants or make additions to existing facilities have become very conscious of the energy efficiency of proposed new structures and are interested in the relation between yearly energy consumption and the number of square feet of building shell. The table on p. 552 lists the energy consumption in British thermal units (a BTU is the amount of heat required to raise 1 pound of water 1°F) for 22 buildings that were all subjected to the same climatic conditions. The SAS printout that fits the straight-line model relating BTU consumption, y, to building shell area, x, is shown on p. 553.

a. Find the least squares estimates of the intercept β_0 and the slope β_1.

b. Investigate the usefulness of the model you developed in part **a.** Is yearly energy consumption

BTU.DAT

BTU/Year (thousands)	Shell Area (square feet)
3,870,000	30,001
1,371,000	13,530
2,422,000	26,060
672,200	6,355
233,100	4,576
218,900	24,680
354,000	2,621
3,135,000	23,350
1,470,000	18,770
1,408,000	12,220
2,201,000	25,490
2,680,000	23,680
337,500	5,650
567,500	8,001
555,300	6,147
239,400	2,660
2,629,000	19,240
1,102,000	10,700
423,500	9,125
423,500	6,510
1,691,000	13,530
1,870,000	18,860

positively linearly related to the shell area of the building? Test using $\alpha = .10$.

c. Calculate the observed significance level of the test of part **b** using the printout. Interpret its value.

d. Find the coefficient of determination r^2 and interpret its value.

e. A company wishes to build a new warehouse that will contain 8,000 square feet of shell area. Find the predicted value of energy consumption and a 95% prediction interval on the printout. Comment on the usefulness of this interval.

f. The application of the model you developed in part **a** to the warehouse problem of part **e** is appropriate only if certain assumptions can be made about the new warehouse. What are these assumptions?

*9.89 The perceptions of accounting professors with respect to the present and desired importance of various factors considered in promotion and tenure decisions at major universities was investigated in the *Journal of Accounting Education* (Spring 1983). One hundred fifteen professors at universities with accredited doctoral programs responded to a mailed questionnaire. The questionnaire asked the professors to rate (1) the actual importance placed on 20 factors in the promotion and tenure decisions at their universities and (2) how they believe the factors *should* be weighted. Responses were obtained on a five-point scale ranging from "no importance" to "extreme importance." The resulting ratings were averaged and converted to the rankings shown in the next table. Calculate Spearman's rank correlation coefficient for the data and carefully interpret its value in the context of the problem.

TENURE.DAT

Factor	Actual	Ideal
I. Teaching (and related items):		
Teaching performance	6	1
Advising and counseling students	19	15
Students' complaints/praise	14	17
II. Research:		
Number of journal articles	1	6.5
Quality of journal articles	4	2
Refereed publications:		
a. Applied studies	5	4
b. Theoretical empirical studies	2	3
c. Educationally oriented	11	8
Papers at professional meetings	10	12
Journal editor or reviewer	9	10
Other (textbooks, etc.)	7.5	11
III. Service and professional interaction:		
Service to profession	15	9
Professional/academic awards	7.5	6.5
Community service	18	19
University service	16	16
Collegiality/cooperativeness	12	13
IV. Other:		
Academic degrees attained	3	5
Professional certification	17	14
Consulting activities	20	20
Grantsmanship	13	18

Source: Campbell, D. K., Gaertner, J., and Vecchio, R. P. "Perceptions of promotion and tenure criteria: A survey of accounting educators." *Journal of Accounting Education,* Vol. 1, Spring 1983, pp. 83–92.

9.90 To develop a compensation plan designed to eliminate pay inequities, a sample of benchmark jobs are evaluated and assigned points, x, based on factors such as responsibility, skill, effort, and working conditions. One market survey was conducted to determine the market rates (or salaries), y, of the benchmark jobs (*Public Personnel Management,* Vol. 20, 1991). The table on page 555 gives the job evaluation points and salaries for a set of 21 benchmark jobs.

a. Construct a scattergram for these data. What does it suggest about the relationship between salary and job evaluation points?

b. The SAS printout on p. 554 shows the results of a straight-line model fit to these data. Identify and interpret the least squares equation.

c. Interpret the value of r^2 for this least squares equation.

d. Is there sufficient evidence to conclude that a straight-line model provides useful information about the relationship in question? Interpret the p-value for this test.

e. A job outside the set of benchmark jobs is evaluated and receives a score of 800 points. Under the compa-

SAS Output for Exercise 9.88

```
Dep Variable: BTU

                          Analysis of Variance

                        Sum of              Mean
    Source     DF      Squares            Square      F Value       Prob>F

    Model       1  1.658498E+13  1.658498E+13       42.028       0.0001
    Error      20   7.89232E+12  394616010047
    C Total    21   2.44773E+13

        Root MSE   628184.69422       R-Square       0.6776
        Dep Mean 1357904.54545        Adj R-Sq       0.6614
        C.V.           46.26133

                          Parameter Estimates

                       Parameter          Standard     T for HO:
Variable    DF          Estimate             Error   Parameter=0   Prob > |T|

INTERCEP     1            -99045      261617.65980        -0.379       0.7090
AREA         1        102.814048       15.85924082         6.483       0.0001

                                          Predict                Lower95%  Upper95%
   Obs   AREA               BTU          Value     Residual     Predict   Predict

     1    30001         3870000        2985479       884521     1546958   4424000
     2    13530         1371000        1292029      78971.2    -47949.3   2632007
     3    26060         2422000        2580289      -158289     1183940   3976637
     4     6355          672200         554338       117862     -810192   1918868
     5     4576          233100         371432      -138332    -1005463   1748327
     6    24680          218900        2438405     -2219505     1054223   3822588
     7     2621          354000         170430       183570    -1222796   1563657
     8    23350         3135000        2301663       833337      927871   3675455
     9    18770         1470000        1830774      -360774      482352   3179196
    10    12220         1408000        1157342       250658     -184021   2498706
    11    25490         2201000        2521685      -320685     1130530   3912840
    12    23680         2680000        2335591       344409      959345   3711838
    13     5650          337500         481854      -144354     -887287   1850995
    14     8001          567500         723570      -156070     -631698   2078838
    15     6147          555300         532953      22347.3     -832898   1898804
    16     2660          239400         174440      64959.9    -1218433   1567313
    17    19240         2629000        1879097       749903      528832   3229362
    18    10700         1102000        1001065       100935     -343656   2345786
    19     9125          423500         839133      -415633     -511035   2189301
    20     6510          423500         570274      -146774     -793294   1933842
    21    13530         1691000        1292029       398971    -47949.3   2632007
    22    18860         1870000        1840028      29972.3      491266   3188789
    23     8000               .         723467            .     -631806   2078740

Sum of Residuals                 1.6298145E-9
Sum of Squared Residuals          7.89232E+12
Predicted Resid SS (Press) 1.012747E+13
```

rable-worth plan, what is a reasonable range within which a fair salary for this job should be found?

9.91 Managers are interested in modeling past cost behavior in order to make more accurete predictions of future costs. Models of past cost behavior are called *cost functions.* Factors that influence costs are called *cost drivers* (Horngren, Foster, and Datar, *Cost Accounting,* 1994). The cost data shown in the second table on page 555 are from a rug manufacturer. Indirect manufacturing labor costs consist of machine maintenance costs and setup labor costs. Machine-hours and direct manufacturing labor-hours are cost drivers.

SAS Output for Exercise 9.90

Dependent Variable: Y

Analysis of Variance

Source	DF	Sum of Squares	Mean Square	F Value	Prob>F
Model	1	66801750.334	66801750.334	74.670	0.0001
Error	19	16997968.904	894629.94232		
C Total	20	83799719.238			

Root MSE	945.84879	R-square	0.7972
Dep Mean	14804.52381	Adj R-sq	0.7865
C.V.	6.38892		

Parameter Estimates

Variable	DF	Parameter Estimate	Standard Error	T for HO: Parameter=0	Prob > |T|
INTERCEP	1	12024	382.31829064	31.449	0.0001
X	1	3.581616	0.41448305	8.641	0.0001

Obs	X	Dep Var Y	Predict Value	Std Err Predict	Lower95% Predict	Upper95% Predict	Residual
1	970	15704.0	15497.8	221.447	13464.6	17531.0	206.2
2	500	13984.0	13814.5	236.070	11774.1	15854.9	169.5
3	370	14196.0	13348.9	266.420	11292.1	15405.6	847.1
4	220	13380.0	12811.6	309.502	10728.6	14894.6	568.4
5	250	13153.0	12919.1	300.351	10842.0	14996.2	233.9
6	1350	18472.0	16858.8	314.833	14772.4	18945.3	1613.2
7	470	14193.0	13707.0	242.349	11663.4	15750.6	486.0
8	2040	20642.0	19330.2	562.933	17026.4	21633.9	1311.8
9	370	13614.0	13348.9	266.420	11292.1	15405.6	265.1
10	1200	16869.0	16321.6	270.968	14262.3	18380.9	547.4
11	820	15184.0	14960.6	207.190	12934.0	16987.2	223.4
12	1865	17341.0	18703.4	496.193	16467.8	20938.9	-1362.4
13	1065	15194.0	15838.1	238.553	13796.4	17879.8	-644.1
14	880	13614.0	15175.5	210.818	13147.2	17203.7	-1561.5
15	340	12594.0	13241.4	274.451	11180.1	15302.7	-647.4
16	540	13126.0	13957.7	228.483	11921.1	15994.4	-831.7
17	490	12958.0	13778.6	238.109	11737.2	15820.1	-820.6
18	940	13894.0	15390.4	217.251	13359.1	17421.6	-1496.4
19	600	13380.0	14172.6	218.972	12140.6	16204.7	-792.6
20	805	15559.0	14906.9	206.741	12880.4	16933.3	652.1
21	220	13844.0	12811.6	309.502	10728.6	14894.6	1032.4
22	800	.	14888.9	206.632	12862.6	16915.3	.

JOBPOINT.DAT

Job Evaluation Points, x	Salary, y	
970	$15,704	Electrician
500	13,984	Semiskilled laborer
370	14,196	Motor equipment operator
220	13,380	Janitor
250	13,153	Laborer
1,350	18,472	Senior engineering technician
470	14,193	Senior janitor
2,040	20,642	Revenue agent
370	13,614	Engineering aide
1,200	16,869	Electrician supervisor
820	15,184	Senior maintenance technician
1,865	17,341	Registered nurse
1,065	15,194	Licensed practical nurse
880	13,614	Principal clerk typist
340	12,594	Clerk typist
540	13,126	Senior clerk stenographer
490	12,958	Senior clerk typist
940	13,894	Principal clerk stenographer
600	13,380	Institutional attendant
805	15,559	Eligibility technician
220	13,844	Cook's helper

Your task is to estimate and compare two alternative cost functions for indirect manufacturing labor costs. In the first, machine-hours is the independent variable; in the second, direct manufacturing labor-hours is the independent variable. Prepare a report that compares the two cost functions and recommends which should be used to explain and predict indirect manufacturing labor costs. Be sure to justify your choice.

RUG.DAT

Week	Indirect Manufacturing Labor Costs	Machine-Hours	Direct Manufacturing Labor-Hours
1	$1,190	68	30
2	1,211	88	35
3	1,004	62	36
4	917	72	20
5	770	60	47
6	1,456	96	45
7	1,180	78	44
8	710	46	38
9	1,316	82	70
10	1,032	94	30
11	752	68	29
12	963	48	38

Source: Data and exercise adapted from Horngren, C. T., Foster, G., and Datar, S. M. *Cost Accounting*, Englewood Cliffs, N.J.: Prentice-Hall, 1994.

Chapter 10

INTRODUCTION TO MULTIPLE REGRESSION

CONTENTS

STATISTICS IN ACTION

Where We've Been

In Chapter 9 we demonstrated how to model the relationship between a dependent variable y and an independent variable x using a straight line. We fit the straight line to the data points, used r and r^2 to measure the strength of the relationship between y and x, and used the resulting prediction equation to estimate the mean value of y or to predict some future value of y for a given value of x.

Where We're Going

This chapter extends the basic concept of Chapter 9, converting it into a powerful estimation and prediction device by modeling the mean value of y as a function of two or more independent variables. The techniques developed will enable you to build a model for a response, y, as a function of two or more variables. As in the case of a simple linear regression, a multiple regression analysis involves fitting the model to a data set, testing the utility of the model, and using it for estimation and prediction.

10.1 MULTIPLE REGRESSION MODELS

Most practical applications of regression analysis utilize models that are more complex than the simple straight-line model. For example, a realistic probabilistic model for reaction time stimulus would include more than just the amount of a particular drug in the bloodstream. Factors such as age, a measure of visual perception, and sex of the subject are a few of the many variables that might be related to reaction time. Thus, we would want to incorporate these and other potentially important independent variables into the model in order to make accurate predictions.

Probabilistic models that include more than one independent variable are called **multiple regression models**. The general form of these models is

$$y = \beta_0 + \beta_1 x_1 + \beta_2 x_2 + \cdots + \beta_k x_k + \varepsilon$$

The dependent variable y is now written as a function of k independent variables, $x_1, x_2, \ldots, x_k$. The random error term is added to make the model probabilistic rather than deterministic. The value of the coefficient β_i determines the contribution of the independent variable x_i, and β_0 is the y-intercept. The coefficients $\beta_0, \beta_1 \ldots, \beta_k$ are usually unknown because they represent population parameters.

At first glance it might appear that the regression model shown above would not allow for anything other than straight-line relationships between y and the independent variables, but this is not true. Actually, $x_1, x_2, \ldots, x_k$ can be functions of variables as long as the functions do not contain unknown parameters. For example, the reaction time, y, of a subject to a visual stimulus could be a function of the independent variables

$$x_1 = \text{Age of the subject}$$

$$x_2 = (\text{Age})^2 = x_1^2$$

$$x_3 = 1 \text{ if male subject, } 0 \text{ if female subject}$$

The x_2 term is called a **higher-order term,** since it is the value of a quantitative variable (x_1) squared (i.e., raised to the second power). The x_3 term is a **dummy (coded) variable** representing a qualitative variable (gender). The multiple regression model is quite versatile and can be made to model many different types of response variables.

The General Multiple Regression Model

$$y = \beta_0 + \beta_1 x_1 + \beta_2 x_2 + \cdots + \beta_k x_k + \varepsilon$$

where

y is the dependent variable
$x_1, x_2, \ldots, x_k$ are the independent variables
$E(y) = \beta_0 + \beta_1 x_1 + \beta_2 x_2 + \cdots + \beta_k x_k$ is the deterministic portion of the model
β_i determines the contribution of the independent variable x_i

Note: The symbols $x_i, x_2, \ldots, x_k$ may represent higher-order terms for quantitative predictors or terms that represent qualitative predictors.

As shown in the box, the steps used to develop the multiple regression model are similar to those used for the simple linear regression model.

Analyzing a Multiple Regression Model

Step 1 Hypothesize the deterministic component of the model. This component relates the mean, $E(y)$, to the independent variables $x_1, x_2, \ldots, x_k$. This involves the choice of the independent variables to be included in the model.

Step 2 Use the sample data to estimate the unknown model parameters $\beta_0, \beta_1, \beta_2, \ldots, \beta_k$ in the model.

Step 3 Specify the probability distribution of the random error term, ϵ, and estimate the standard deviation of this distribution, σ.

Step 4 Check that the assumptions on ϵ are satisfied, and make model modifications if necessary.

Step 5 Statistically evaluate the usefulness of the model.

Step 6 When satisfied that the model is useful, use it for prediction, estimation, and other purposes.

In this introduction to multiple regression, we lay the foundation of **model building** (or useful model construction). We consider the most basic multiple regression model, called the *first-order model.*

10.2 THE FIRST-ORDER MODEL: ESTIMATING AND INTERPRETING THE β PARAMETERS

A model that includes only terms for *quantitative* independent variables, called a **first-order model**, is described in the box. Note that the first-order model does not include any higher-order terms (such as x_1^2).

A First-Order Model in Five Quantitative Independent Variables*

$$E(y) = \beta_0 + \beta_1 x_1 + \beta_2 x_2 + \beta_3 x_3 + \beta_4 x_4 + \beta_5 x_5$$

where $x_1, x_2, \ldots, x_5$ are all quantitative variables that **are not** functions of other independent variables.

Note: β_i represents the slope of the line relating y to x_i when all the other x's are held fixed.

The method of fitting first-order models—and multiple regression models in general—is identical to that of fitting the simple straight-line model: the method of least squares. That is, we choose the estimated model

$$\hat{y} = \hat{\beta}_0 + \hat{\beta}_1 x_1 + \cdots + \hat{\beta}_k x_k$$

*The terminology "first-order" is derived from the fact that each x in the model is raised to the first power.

that minimizes

$$\text{SSE} = \Sigma(y - \hat{y})^2$$

As in the case of the simple linear model, the sample estimates $\hat{\beta}_0, \hat{\beta}_1, \ldots, \hat{\beta}_k$ are obtained as a solution to a set of simultaneous linear equations.*

The primary difference between fitting the simple and multiple regression models is computational difficulty. The $(k + 1)$ simultaneous linear equations that must be solved to find the $(k + 1)$ estimated coefficients $\hat{\beta}_0, \hat{\beta}_1, \ldots, \hat{\beta}_k$ are difficult (sometimes nearly impossible) to solve with a calculator. Consequently, we resort to the use of computers. Instead of presenting the tedious hand calculations required to fit the models, we present output from a variety of statistical software packages.

EXAMPLE 10.1

Suppose a property appraiser wants to model the relationship between the sale price of a residential property in a mid-size city and the following three independent variables: (1) appraised land value of the property, (2) appraised value of improvements (i.e., home value) on the property, and (3) area of living space on the property (i.e., home size). Consider the first-order model

$$y = \beta_0 + \beta_1 x_1 + \beta_2 x_2 + \beta_3 x_3 + \varepsilon$$

where

$$y = \text{Sale price (dollars)}$$
$$x_1 = \text{Appraised land value (dollars)}$$
$$x_2 = \text{Appraised improvements (dollars)}$$
$$x_3 = \text{Area (square feet)}$$

To fit the model, the appraiser selected a random sample of $n = 20$ properties from the thousands of properties that were sold in a particular year. The resulting data are given in Table 10.1.

a. Use scattergrams to plot the sample data. Interpret the plots.

b. Use the method of least squares to estimate the unknown parameters $\beta_0, \beta_1, \beta_2$, and β_3 in the model.

c. Find the value of SSE that is minimized by the least squares method.

Solution

a. SPSS scatterplots for examining the bivariate relationships between y and x_1, y and x_2, and y and x_3 are shown in Figures 10.1a–c. Of the three variables, appraised improvements (x_2) appears to have the strongest linear relationship with sale price (y). (See Figure 10.1b.)

*Students who are familiar with calculus should note that $\hat{\beta}_0, \hat{\beta}_1, \ldots, \hat{\beta}_k$ are the solutions to the set of equations $\partial\text{SSE}/\partial\hat{\beta}_0 = 0, \partial\text{SSE}/\partial\hat{\beta}_1 = 0, \ldots, \partial\text{SSE}/\partial\hat{\beta}_k = 0$. The solution is usually given in matrix form, but we do not present the details here. See the references for details.

TABLE 10.1 Real Estate Appraisal Data for 20 Properties

Property # (Obs.)	Sale Price, y	Land Value, x_1	Improvements Value, x_2	Area, x_3
1	68,900	5,960	44,967	1,873
2	48,500	9,000	27,860	928
3	55,500	9,500	31,439	1,126
4	62,000	10,000	39,592	1,265
5	116,500	18,000	72,827	2,214
6	45,000	8,500	27,317	912
7	38,000	8,000	29,856	899
8	83,000	23,000	47,752	1,803
9	59,000	8,100	39,117	1,204
10	47,500	9,000	29,349	1,725
11	40,500	7,300	40,166	1,080
12	40,000	8,000	31,679	1,529
13	97,000	20,000	58,510	2,455
14	45,500	8,000	23,454	1,151
15	40,900	8,000	20,897	1,173
16	80,000	10,500	56,248	1,960
17	56,000	4,000	20,859	1,344
18	37,000	4,500	22,610	988
19	50,000	3,400	35,948	1,076
20	22,400	1,500	5,779	962

Source: Alachua County (Florida) Property Appraisers Office.

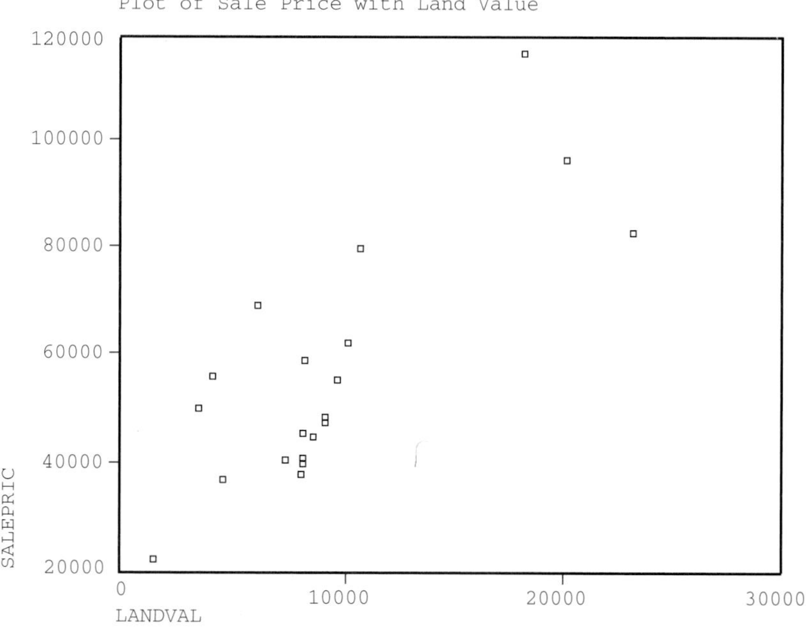

FIGURE 10.1a SPSS scatterplots for the data of Table 10.1

b. The model hypothesized above is fit to the data of Table 10.1 using SAS. A portion of the SAS printout is reproduced in Figure 10.2 (page 563). The least squares estimates of the β parameters appear (highlighted) in the column labeled **Parameter Estimate.** You can see that $\hat{\beta}_0 = 1{,}470.275919$,

FIGURE 10.1b

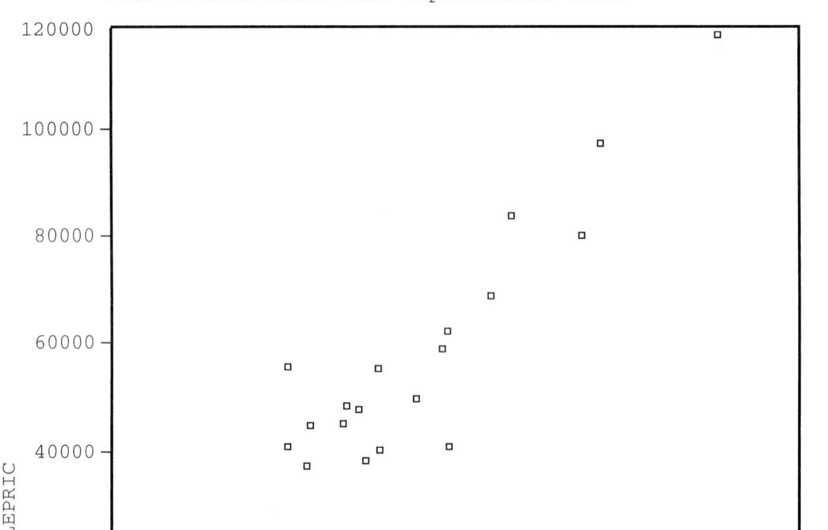

FIGURE 10.1c

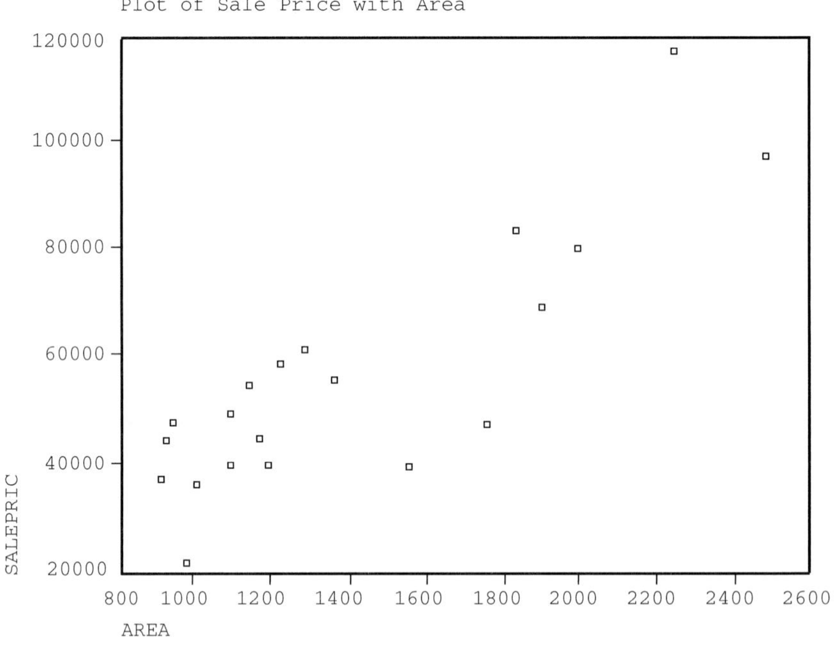

$\hat{\beta}_1 = .814490$, $\hat{\beta}_2 = .820445$, and $\hat{\beta}_3 = 13.528650$. Therefore, the equation that minimizes SSE for this data set (i.e., the **least squares prediction equation**) is

$$\hat{y} = 1{,}470.28 + .8145x_1 + .8204x_2 + 13.53x_3$$

c. The minimum value of the SSE is highlighted in Figure 10.2 in the **Sum of Squares** column and the **Error** row. This value is SSE = 1,003,491,259.4.

Analysis of Variance

Source	DF	Sum of Squares	Mean Square	F Value	Prob>F
Model	3	8779676740.6	2926558913.5	46.662	0.0001
Error	16	1003491259.4	62718203.714		
C Total	19	9783168000.0			

Root MSE	7919.48254	R-Square	0.8974
Dep Mean	56660.00000	Adj R-Sq	0.8782
C.V.	13.97720		

Parameter Estimates

Variable	DF	Parameter Estimate	Standard Error	T for H0: Parameter=0	Prob > |T|
INTERCEP	1	1470.275919	5746.3245832	0.256	0.8013
X1	1	0.814490	0.51221871	1.590	0.1314
X2	1	0.820445	0.21118494	3.885	0.0013
X3	1	13.528650	6.58568006	2.054	0.0567

FIGURE 10.2
SAS output for sale price model, Example 10.1

After obtaining the least squares prediction equation, the analyst will usually want to make meaningful interpretations of the β estimates. Recall that in the straight-line model (Chapter 9)

$$y = \beta_0 + \beta_1 x + \varepsilon$$

β_0 represents the y-intercept of the line and β_1 represents the slope of the line. From our discussion in Chapter 9, β_1 has a practical interpretation—it represents the mean change in y for every 1-unit increase in x. When the independent variables are quantitative, the β parameters in the first-order model specified in Example 10.1 have similar interpretations. The difference is that when we interpret the β that multiplies one of the variables (e.g., x_1), we must be certain to hold the values of the remaining independent variables (e.g., x_2, x_3) fixed.

To see this, suppose that the mean $E(y)$ of a response y is related to two quantitative independent variables, x_1 and x_2, by the first-order model

$$E(y) = 1 + 2x_1 + x_2$$

In other words, $\beta_0 = 1$, $\beta_1 = 2$, and $\beta_2 = 1$.

Now, when $x_2 = 0$, the relationship between $E(y)$ and x_1 is given by

$$E(y) = 1 + 2x_1 + (0) = 1 + 2x_1$$

A graph of this relationship (a straight line) is shown in Figure 10.3. Similar graphs of the relationship between $E(y)$ and x_1 for $x_2 = 1$,

$$E(y) = 1 + 2x_1 + (1) = 2 + 2x_1$$

and for $x_2 = 2$,

$$E(y) = 1 + 2x_1 + (2) = 3 + 2x_1$$

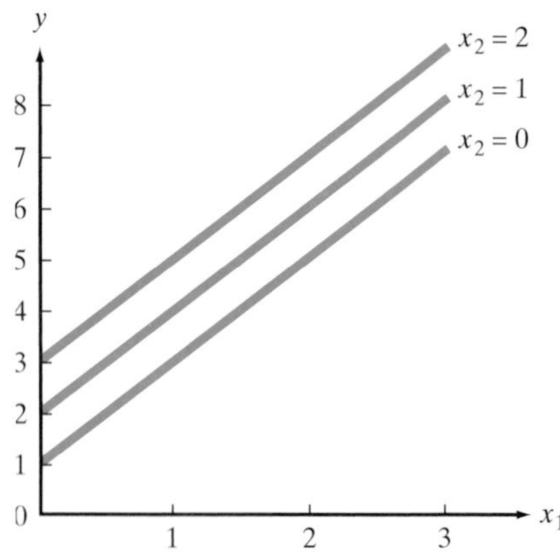

FIGURE 10.3
Graphs of $E(y) = 1 + 2x_1 + x_2$ for $x_2 = 0, 1, 2$

also are shown in Figure 10.3. Note that the slopes of the three lines are all equal to $\beta_1 = 2$, the coefficient that multiplies x_1.

Figure 10.3 exhibits a characteristic of all first-order models: If you graph $E(y)$ versus any one variable—say, x_1—for fixed values of the other variables, the result will always be a *straight line* with slope equal to β_1. If you repeat the process for other values of the fixed independent variables, you will obtain a set of *parallel* straight lines. This indicates that the effect of the independent variable x_i on $E(y)$ is independent of all the other independent variables in the model, and this effect is measured by the slope β_i (see the box on p. 559).

A three-dimensional graph of the model $E(y) = 1 + 2x_1 + x_2$ is shown in Figure 10.4. Note that the model graphs as a plane. If you slice the plane at a particular value of x_2 (say, $x_2 = 0$), you obtain a straight line relating $E(y)$ to x_1 (e.g., $E(y) = 1 + 2x_1$). Similarly, if you slice the plane at a particular value of x_1, you obtain a straight line relating $E(y)$ to x_2. Since it is more difficult to visualize three–dimensional and, in general, k-dimensional surfaces, we will graph all the models presented in this chapter in two dimensions. The key to obtaining these graphs is to hold fixed all but one of the independent variables in the model.

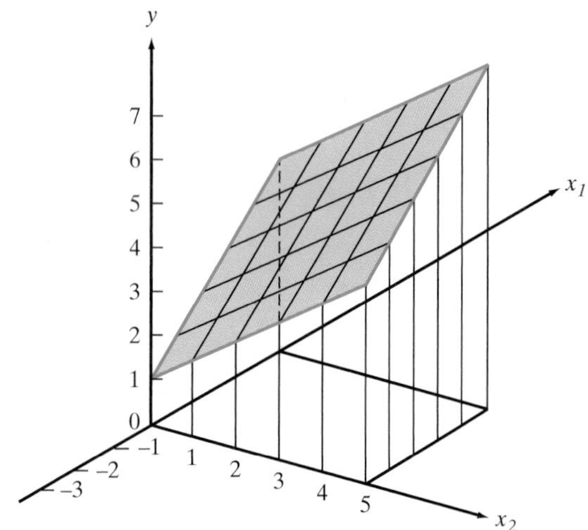

FIGURE 10.4
The plane $E(y) = 1 + 2x_1 + x_2$

EXAMPLE 10.2 Refer to the first-order model for sale price y considered in Example 10.1. Interpret the estimates of the β parameters in the model.

Solution The least squares prediction equation, as given in Example 10.1, is $\hat{y} = 1{,}470.28 + .8145x_1 + .8204x_2 + 13.53x_3$. We know that with first-order models β_1 represents the slope of the y–x_1 line for fixed x_2 and x_3. That is, β_1 measures the change in $E(y)$ for every 1-unit increase in x_1 when all other independent variables in the model are held fixed. Similar statements can be made about β_2 and β_3; e.g., β_2 measures the change in $E(y)$ for every 1-unit increase in x_1 when all other x's in the model are held fixed. Consequently, we obtain the following interpretations:

$\hat{\beta}_1 = .8145$: We estimate the mean sale price of a property, $E(y)$, to increase .8145 dollar for every \$1 increase in appraised land value (x_1) when both appraised improvements (x_2) and area (x_3) are held fixed.

$\hat{\beta}_2 = .8204$: We estimate the mean sale price of a property, $E(y)$, to increase .8204 dollar for every \$1 increase in appraised improvements (x_2) when both appraised land value (x_1) and area (x_3) are held fixed.

$\hat{\beta}_3 = 13.53$: We estimate the mean sale price of a property, $E(y)$, to increase \$13.53 for each additional square foot of living area (x_3) when both appraised land value (x_1) and appraised improvements (x_2) are held fixed.

The value $\hat{\beta}_0 = 1{,}470.28$ does not have a meaningful interpretation in this example. To see this, note that $\hat{y} = \hat{\beta}_0$ when $x_1 = x_2 = x_3 = 0$. Thus, $\hat{\beta}_0 = 1{,}470.28$ represents the estimated mean sale price when the values of all the independent variables are set equal to 0. Since a residential property with these characteristics—appraised land value of \$0, appraised improvements of \$0, and 0 square feet of living area—is not practical, the value of $\hat{\beta}_0$ has no meaningful interpretation. In general, $\hat{\beta}_0$ will not have a practical interpretation unless it makes sense to set the values of the x's simultaneously equal to 0.

Caution

The interpretation of the β parameters in a multiple regression model will depend on the terms specified in the model. The interpretations above are for a first-order linear model only. In practice, you should be sure that a first-order model is the correct model for $E(y)$ before making these β interpretations.

10.3 MODEL ASSUMPTIONS

We noted in Section 10.1 that the general multiple regression model is of the form

$$y = \beta_0 + \beta_1 x_1 + \beta_2 x_2 + \cdots + \beta_k x_k + \varepsilon$$

where y is the response variable that we wish to predict; $\beta_0, \beta_1, \ldots, \beta_k$ are parameters with unknown values; $x_1, x_2, \ldots, x_k$ are information-contributing variables that are measured without error; and ϵ is a random error component. Since $\beta_0, \beta_1, \ldots, \beta_k$ and $x_1, x_2, \ldots, x_k$ are nonrandom, the quantity

$$\beta_0 + \beta_1 x_1 + \beta_2 x_2 + \cdots + \beta_k x_k$$

represents the deterministic portion of the model. Therefore, y is composed of two components—one fixed and one random—and, consequently, y is a random variable.

$$\underbrace{y = \beta_0 + \beta_1 x_1 + \cdots + \beta_k x_k}_{\text{Deterministic portion of model}} + \underbrace{\varepsilon}_{\text{Random error}}$$

We will assume (as in Chapter 9) that the random error can be positive or negative and that for any setting of the x values, $x_1, x_2, \ldots, x_k$, the random error ε has a normal probability distribution with mean equal to 0 and variance equal to σ^2. Further, we assume that the random errors associated with any (and every) pair of y values are probabilistically independent. That is, the error, ε, associated with any one y value is independent of the error associated with any other y value. These assumptions are summarized in the next box.

Assumptions for Random Error ε

1. For any given set of values of $x_1, x_2, \ldots, x_k$, the random error ϵ has a normal probability distribution with mean equal to 0 and variance equal to σ^2.
2. The random errors are independent (in a probabilistic sense).

Note that σ^2 represents the variance of the random error ε. As such, σ^2 is an important measure of the usefulness of the model for the estimation of the mean and the prediction of actual values of y. If $\sigma^2 = 0$, all the random errors will equal 0 and the predicted values, $\hat{y}$, will be identical to $E(y)$; that is $E(y)$ will be estimated without error. In contrast, a large value of σ^2 implies large (absolute) values of ε and larger deviations between the predicted values, $\hat{y}$, and the mean value, $E(y)$. Consequently, the larger the value of σ^2, the greater will be the error in estimating the model parameters $\beta_0, \beta_1, \ldots, \beta_k$ and the error in predicting a value of y for a specific set of values of $x_1, x_2, \ldots, x_k$. Thus, σ^2 plays a major role in making inferences about $\beta_0, \beta_1, \ldots, \beta_k$, in estimating $E(y)$, and in predicting y for specific values of $x_1, x_2, \ldots, x_k$.

Since the variance, σ^2, of the random error, ε, will rarely be known, we must use the results of the regression analysis to estimate its value. Recall that σ^2 is the variance of the probability distribution of the random error, ε, for a given set of values for $x_1, x_2, \ldots, x_k$; hence it is the mean value of the squares of the deviations of the y values (for given values of $x_1, x_2, \ldots, x_k$) about the mean value $E(y)$.* Since the predicted value, $\hat{y}$ estimates $E(y)$ for each of the data points, it seems natural to use

$$\text{SSE} = \sum (y_i - \hat{y}_i)^2$$

to construct an estimator of σ^2.

*Since $y = E(y) + \varepsilon$, ε is equal to the deviation $y - E(y)$. Also, by definition, the variance of a random variable is the expected value of the square of the deviation of the random variable from its mean. According to our model, $E(\varepsilon) = 0$. Therefore, $\sigma^2 = E(\varepsilon^2)$.

For example, in the first-order model of Example 10.2, we found that SSE = 1,003,491,259.4. We now want to use this quantity to estimate the variance of ϵ. Recall that the estimator for the straight-line model is $s^2 = \text{SSE}/(n - 2)$ and note that the denominator is (n − Number of estimated β parameters), which is $(n - 2)$ in the straight-line model. Since we must estimate four parameters, β_0, β_1, β_2, and β_3 for the first-order model, the estimator of σ^2 is

$$s^2 = \frac{\text{SSE}}{n - 4}$$

The numerical estimate for this example is

$$s^2 = \frac{\text{SSE}}{20 - 4} = \frac{1{,}003{,}491{,}259.4}{16} = 62{,}718{,}203.7$$

In many computer printouts and textbooks, s^2 is called the **mean square for error (MSE).** This estimate of σ^2 is shown in the column titled **Mean Square** in the SAS printout in Figure 10.2.

The units of the estimated variance are squared units of the dependent variable y. Since the dependent variable y in this example is sale price in dollars, the units of s^2 are $(\text{dollars})^2$. This makes meaningful interpretation of s^2 difficult, so we use the standard deviation s to provide a more meaningful measure of variability. In this example,

$$s = \sqrt{62{,}718{,}203.7} = 7{,}919.5$$

which is given on the SAS printout in Figure 10.2 next to **Root MSE.** One useful interpretation of the estimated standard deviation s is that the interval $\pm 2s$ will provide a rough approximation to the accuracy with which the model will predict future values of y for given values of x. Thus, in Example 10.2, we expect the model to provide predictions of sale price to within about $\pm 2s = \pm 2(7{,}919.5) = \pm 15{,}839$ dollars.*

For the general multiple regression model

$$y = \beta_0 + \beta_1 x_1 + \beta_2 x_2 + \cdots + \beta_k x_k + \varepsilon$$

we must estimate the $(k + 1)$ parameters $\beta_0, \beta_1, \beta_2, \ldots, \beta_k$. Thus, the estimator of σ^2 is SSE divided by the quantity (n − Number of estimated β parameters).

We will use the estimator of σ^2 both to check the utility of the model (Sections 10.4 and 10.5) and to provide a measure of reliability of predictions and estimates when the model is used for those purposes (Section 10.6). Thus, you can see that the estimation of σ^2 plays an important part in the development of a regression model.

Estimator of σ^2 for a Multiple Regression Model with k Independent Variables

$$s^2 = \frac{\text{SSE}}{n - \text{Number of estimated } \beta \text{ parameters}} = \frac{\text{SSE}}{n - (k + 1)}$$

*The $\pm 2s$ approximation will improve as the sample size is increased. We will provide more precise methodology for the construction of prediction intervals in Section 10.6.

10.4 INFERENCES ABOUT THE β PARAMETERS

Inferences about the individual β parameters in a model are obtained using either a confidence interval or a test of hypothesis, as outlined in the following two boxes.*

Test of an Individual Parameter Coefficient in the Multiple Regression Model

One-Tailed Test	**Two-Tailed Test**
$H_0: \beta_i = 0$	$H_0: \beta_i = 0$
$H_a: \beta_i < 0$ [or $H_a: \beta_i > 0$]	$H_a: \beta_i \neq 0$

$$\textit{Test statistic: } t = \frac{\hat{\beta}_i}{s_{\hat{\beta}_i}}$$

Rejection region: $t < -t_\alpha$ [or $t > t_\alpha$ when $H_a: \beta_i > 0$]	*Rejection region:* $\lvert t\rvert > t_{\alpha/2}$

where t_α and $t_{\alpha/2}$ are based on $n - (k + 1)$ degrees of freedom and

$$n = \text{Number of observations}$$

$$k + 1 = \text{Number of } \beta \text{ parameters in the model}$$

Assumptions: See Section 10.3 for assumptions about the probability distribution for the random error component ε.

A 100(1 − α)% Confidence Interval for a β Parameter

$$\hat{\beta}_i \pm t_{\alpha/2} s_{\hat{\beta}_i}$$

where $t_{\alpha/2}$ is based on $n - (k + 1)$ degrees of freedom and

$$n = \text{Number of observations}$$

$$k + 1 = \text{Number of } \beta \text{ parameters in the model}$$

We illustrate these methods with another example.

EXAMPLE 10.3 A collector of antique grandfather clocks knows that the price received for the clocks increases linearly with the age of the clocks. Moreover, the collector hypothesizes that the auction price of the clocks will increase linearly as the number of bidders increases. Thus, the following first-order model is hypothesized:

$$y = \beta_0 + \beta_1 x_1 + \beta_2 x_2 + \varepsilon$$

*The formulas for computing $\hat{\beta}_i$ and its standard error are so complex, the only reasonable way to present them is by using matrix algebra. We do not assume a prerequisite of matrix algebra for this text and, in any case, we think the formulas can be omitted in an introductory course without serious loss. They are programmed into almost all statistical software packages with multiple regression routines and are presented in some of the texts listed in the references.

TABLE 10.2 Auction Price Data

Age, x_1	Number of Bidders, x_2	Auction Price, y	Age, x_1	Number of Bidders, x_2	Auction Price, y
127	13	$1,235	170	14	$2,131
115	12	1,080	182	8	1,550
127	7	845	162	11	1,884
150	9	1,522	184	10	2,041
156	6	1,047	143	6	845
182	11	1,979	159	9	1,483
156	12	1,822	108	14	1,055
132	10	1,253	175	8	1,545
137	9	1,297	108	6	729
113	9	946	179	9	1,792
137	15	1,713	111	15	1,175
117	11	1,024	187	8	1,593
137	8	1,147	111	7	785
153	6	1,092	115	7	744
117	13	1,152	194	5	1,356
126	10	1,336	168	7	1,262

where

$$y = \text{Auction price}$$
$$x_1 = \text{Age of clock (years)}$$
$$x_2 = \text{Number of bidders}$$

A sample of 32 auction prices of grandfather clocks, along with their age and the number of bidders, is given in Table 10.2. The model $y = \beta_0 + \beta_1 x_1 + \beta_2 x_2 + \varepsilon$ is fit to the data, and a portion of the MINITAB printout is shown in Figure 10.5.

a. Test the hypothesis that the mean auction price of a clock increases as the number of bidders increases when age is held constant, that is, test $\beta_2 > 0$. Use $\alpha = .05$.

b. Form a 90% confidence interval for β_1 and interpret the result.

FIGURE 10.5 MINITAB printout for Example 10.3

```
The regression equation is
Y = -1339 + 12.7 X1 + 86.0 X2

Predictor       Coef        StDev    t-ratio        P
Constant     -1339.0        173.8      -7.70    0.000
X1           12.7406       0.9047      14.08    0.000
X2            85.953        8.729       9.85    0.000

s = 133.5       R-Sq = 89.2%      R-Sq(adj) = 88.5%

Analysis of Variance

SOURCE        DF         SS          MS         F        P
Regression     2    4283063     2141532    120.19    0.000
Error         29     516727       17818
Total         31    4799789
```

Solution

a. The hypotheses of interest concern the parameter β_2. Specifically,

$$H_0: \beta_2 = 0$$
$$H_a: \beta_2 > 0$$

The test statistic is a t statistic formed by dividing the sample estimate $\hat{\beta}_2$ of the parameter β_2 by estimated standard error of $\hat{\beta}_2$ (denoted $s_{\hat{\beta}_2}$). These estimates as well as the calculated t value are shown on the MINITAB printout in the **Coef, Stdev**, and **t-ratio** columns, respectively.

$$\textit{Test statistic: } t = \frac{\hat{\beta}_2}{s_{\hat{\beta}_2}} = \frac{85.953}{8.729} = 9.85$$

The rejection region for the test is found in exactly the same way as the rejection regions for the t-tests in previous chapters. That is, we consult Table VI in Appendix B to obtain an upper-tail value of t. This is a value t_α such that $P(t > t_\alpha) = \alpha$. We can then use this value to construct rejection regions for either one-tailed or two-tailed tests.

For $\alpha = .05$ and $n - (k + 1) = 32 - (2 + 1) = 29$ df, the critical t value obtained from Table VI is $t_{.05} = 1.699$. Therefore,

Rejection region: $t > 1.699$ (see Figure 10.6)

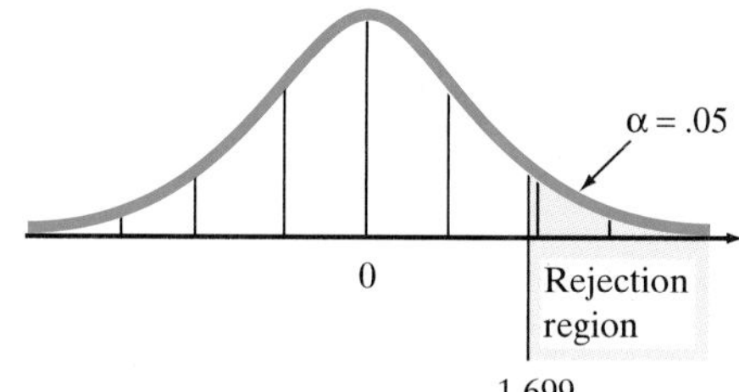

FIGURE 10.6
Rejection region for $H_0: \beta_2 = 0$ vs. $H_a: \beta_2 > 0$

Since the test statistic value, $t = 9.85$, falls in the rejection region, we have sufficient evidence to reject H_0. Thus, the collector can conclude that the mean auction price of a clock increases as the number of bidders increases, when age is held constant. Note that the observed significance level of the test is also given on the printout. Since p-value $= 0$, any nonzero α will lead us to reject H_0.

b. A 90% confidence interval for β_1 is (from the box):

$$\hat{\beta}_1 \pm t_{\alpha/2} s_{\hat{\beta}_1} = \hat{\beta}_1 \pm t_{.05} s_{\hat{\beta}_1}$$

Substituting $\hat{\beta}_1 = 12.74$, $s_{\hat{\beta}_1} = .905$ (both obtained from the MINITAB printout, Figure 10.5) and $t_{.05} = 1.699$ (from part **a**) into the equation, we obtain

$$12.74 \pm 1.699(.905) = 12.74 \pm 1.53$$

or (11.21, 14.27). Thus, we are 90% confident that β_1 falls between 11.21 and 14.27. Since β_1 is the slope of the line relating auction price (y) to age of the clock (x_1), we conclude that price increases between \$11.21 and \$14.27 for every 1-year increase in age, holding number of bidders (x_2) constant.

✶

Caution

It is dangerous to conduct t-tests on the individual β parameters in a *first-order linear model* for the purpose of determining which independent variables are useful for predicting y and which are not. If you fail to reject H_0: $\beta_i = 0$, several conclusions are possible:

1. There is no relationship between y and x_i.
2. A straight-line relationship between y and x exists (holding the other x's in the model fixed), but a Type II error occurred.
3. A relationship between y and x_i (holding the other x's in the model fixed) exists, but is more complex than a straight-line relationship (e.g., a curvilinear relationship may be appropriate). The most you can say about a β parameter test is that there is either sufficient (if you reject H_0: $\beta_i = 0$) or insufficient (if you do not reject H_0: $\beta_i = 0$) evidence of a *linear* (*straight-line*) relationship between y and x_i.

The models presented so far utilized quantitative independent variables (e.g., home size, age of a clock, and number of bidders). Multiple regression models can include qualitative independent variables also. For example, suppose we want to develop a model for the mean operating cost per mile, $E(y)$, of cars as a function of the car manufacturer's country of origin. Further suppose that we are interested only in classifying the manufacturer's origin as "domestic" or "foreign." Then the manufacturer's origin is a single qualitative independent variable with two levels: domestic and foreign. Recall that with a qualitative variable, we cannot attach a meaningful quantitative measure to a given level. Consequently, we utilize a system of coding described below.

To simplify our notation, let μ_D be the mean cost per mile for cars manufactured domestically, and let μ_F be the corresponding mean cost per mile for those foreign-manufactured cars. Our objective is to write a single equation that will give the mean value of y (cost per mile) for both domestic and foreign-made cars. This can be done as follow:

$$E(y) = \beta_0 + \beta_1 x$$

where $x = \begin{cases} 1 & \text{if the car is manufactured domestically} \\ 0 & \text{if the car is not manufactured domestically} \end{cases}$

The variable x is not a meaningful independent variable as in the case of models with quantitative independent variables. Instead, it is a **dummy** (or **indicator**) **variable** that makes the model work. To see how, let $x = 0$. This condition will apply when we are seeking the mean cost of foreign-made cars. (If the car is not domestically produced, it must be foreign-made.) Then the mean cost per mile, $E(y)$, is

$$\mu_F = E(y) = \beta_0 + \beta_1(0) = \beta_0$$

This tells us that the mean cost per mile for foreign cars is β_0. Or, using our notation, it means that $\mu_F = \beta_0$.

Now suppose we want to represent the mean cost per mile, $E(y)$, for cars manufactured domestically. Checking the dummy variable definition, we see that we should let $x = 1$:

$$\mu_D = E(y) = \beta_0 + \beta_1 x = \beta_0 + \beta_1(1) = \beta_0 + \beta_1$$

or, since $\beta_0 = \mu_F$,

$$\mu_D = \mu_F + \beta_1$$

Then it follows that the interpretation of β_1 is

$$\beta_1 = \mu_D - \mu_F$$

which is the difference between the mean costs per mile for domestic and foreign cars. Consequently, a t-test of the null hypothesis H_0: $\beta_1 = 0$ is equivalent to testing H_0: $\mu_D - \mu_F = 0$. Rejecting H_0, then, implies that the mean costs per mile for domestic and foreign cars are different.

It is important to note that β_0 and β_1 in the dummy variable model above *do not* represent the y-intercept and slope, respectively, as in the simple linear regression model of Chapter 9. In general, when using the 1–0 system of coding* for a dummy variable, β_0 will represent the mean value of y for the level of the qualitative variable assigned a value of 0 (called the **base level**) and β_1 will represent a difference between the mean values of y for the two levels (with the mean of the base level always subtracted.)†

EXERCISES 10.1–10.15

Learning the Mechanics

10.1 Write a first-order model relating $E(y)$ to:
- a. two quantitative independent variables
- b. four quantitative independent variables
- c. five quantitative independent variables

10.2 SAS was used to fit the model $E(y) = \beta_0 + \beta_1 x_1 + \beta_2 x_2$ to $n = 20$ data points and the printout shown on page 573 was obtained.
- a. What are the sample estimates of β_0, β_1, and β_2?
- b. What is the least squares prediction equation?
- c. Find SSE, MSE, and s. Interpret the standard deviation in the context of the problem.
- d. Test H_0: $\beta_1 = 0$ against H_a: $\beta_1 \neq 0$. Use $\alpha = .05$.
- e. Use a 95% confidence interval to estimate β_2.

10.3 Suppose you fit the multiple regression model

$$y = \beta_0 + \beta_1 x_1 + \beta_2 x_2 + \beta_3 x_3 + \varepsilon$$

to $n = 30$ data points and obtain the following result:

$$\hat{y} = 3.4 - 4.6x_1 + 2.7x_2 + .93x_3$$

The estimated standard errors of $\hat{\beta}_2$ and $\hat{\beta}_3$ are 1.86 and .29, respectively.
- a. Test the null hypothesis H_0: $\beta_2 = 0$ against the alternative hypothesis H_a: $\beta_2 \neq 0$. Use $\alpha = .05$.
- b. Test the null hypothesis H_0: $\beta_3 = 0$ against the alternative hypothesis H_a: $\beta_3 \neq 0$. Use $\alpha = .05$.
- c. The null hypothesis H_0: $\beta_2 = 0$ is not rejected. In contrast, the null hypothesis H_0: $\beta_3 = 0$ is rejected. Explain how this can happen even though $\hat{\beta}_2 > \hat{\beta}_3$

10.4 Suppose you fit the first-order multiple regression model

$$y = \beta_0 + \beta_1 x_1 + \beta_2 x_2 + \varepsilon$$

to $n = 25$ data points and obtain the prediction equation

$$\hat{y} = 6.4 + 3.1x_1 + .92x_2$$

The estimated standard deviations of the sampling distributions of $\hat{\beta}_1$ and $\hat{\beta}_2$ are 2.3 and .27, respectively.
- a. Test H_0: $\beta_1 = 0$ against H_a: $\beta_1 > 0$. Use $\alpha = .05$.
- b. Test H_0: $\beta_2 = 0$ against H_a: $\beta_2 \neq 0$. Use $\alpha = .05$.
- c. Find a 90% confidence interval for β_1. Interpret the interval.
- d. Find a 99% confidence interval for β_2. Interpret the interval.

10.5 How is the number of degrees of freedom available for estimating σ^2 (the variance of ε) related to the number of independent variables in a regression model?

10.6 Consider the first-order model equation in three quantitative independent variables

$$E(y) = 1 + 2x_1 + x_2 - 3x_3$$

- a. Graph the relationship between y and x_1 for $x_2 = 1$ and $x_3 = 3$.

*You do not have to use a 1–0 system of coding for the dummy variables. Any two-value system will work, but the interpretation given to the model parameters will depend on the code. Using the 1–0 system makes the model parameters easy to interpret.

†The system of coding for a qualitative variable at more than two, say k, levels requires that you create k–1 dummy variables, one for each level except the base level. The interpretation of β_i is $\beta_i = \mu_{\text{level } i} - \mu_{\text{base level}}$.

SAS Output for Excercise 10.2

```
Dep Variable: Y

                         Analysis of Variance

                           Sum of           Mean
     Source      DF       Squares         Square       F Value       Prob>F

     Model        2  128329.27624    64164.63812         7.223       0.0054
     Error       17  151015.72376     8883.27787
     C Total     19  279345.00000

           Root MSE      94.25114       R-Square        0.4594
           Dep Mean     360.50000       Adj R-Sq        0.3958
           C.V.          26.14456

                          Parameter Estimates

                         Parameter        Standard      T for H0:
Variable        DF        Estimate           Error    Parameter=0  Prob > |T|

INTERCEP         1      506.346067     45.16942487         11.210      0.0001
X1               1     -941.900226    275.08555975         -3.424      0.0032
X2               1     -429.060418    379.82566485         -1.130      0.2743
```

b. Repeat part **a** for $x_2 = -1$ and $x_3 = 1$.
c. How do the graphed lines in parts **a** and **b** relate to each other? What is the slope of each line?
d. If a linear model is first-order in three independent variables, what type of geometric relationship will you obtain when $E(y)$ is graphed as a function of one of the independent variables for various combinations of values of the other independent variables?

Applying the Concepts

10.7 Detailed interviews were conducted with over 1,000 street vendors in the city of Puebla, Mexico, in order to study the factors influencing vendors' incomes (*World Development,* Feb. 1998). Vendors were defined as individuals working in the street, and included vendors with carts and stands on wheels and excluded beggars, drug dealers, and prostitutes. The researchers collected data on gender, age, hours worked per day, annual earnings, and education level. A subset of these data appear in the table on page 574.

a. Write a first-order model for mean annual earnings, $E(y)$, as a function of age (x_1) and hours worked (x_2).
b. The model was fit to the data using STATISTIX. Find the least squares prediction equation on the printout shown below.
c. Interpret the estimated β coefficients in your model.
d. Is age x_1 a statistically useful predictor of annual earnings? Test using $\alpha = .01$.

STATISTIX Output for Exercise 10.7

```
UNWEIGHTED LEAST SQUARES LINEAR REGRESSION OF EARNINGS

PREDICTOR
VARIABLES    COEFFICIENT    STD ERROR     STUDENT'S T        P
---------    -----------    ---------     -----------     ------
CONSTANT       -20.3520      652.745         -0.03        0.9756
AGE             13.3504      7.67168          1.74        0.1074
HOURS           243.714      63.5117          3.84        0.0024

R-SQUARED               0.5823     RESID. MEAN SQUARE (MSE)       300016
ADJUSTED R-SQUARED      0.5126     STANDARD DEVIATION            547.737

SOURCE          DF         SS             MS            F        P
----------     ---    ----------     ----------     -----   ------
REGRESSION       2     5018232        2509116        8.36   0.0053
RESIDUAL        12     3600196         300016
TOTAL           14     8618428

CASES INCLUDED 15    MISSING CASES 0
```

e. Construct a 99% confidence interval for β_2. Interpret the interval in the words of the problem.

STREETVN.DAT

Vendor Number	Annual Earnings, y	Age, x_1	Hours Worked per Day, x_2
21	$2841	29	12
53	1876	21	8
60	2934	62	10
184	1552	18	10
263	3065	40	11
281	3670	50	11
354	2005	65	5
401	3215	44	8
515	1930	17	8
633	2010	70	6
677	3111	20	9
710	2882	29	9
800	1683	15	5
914	1817	14	7
997	4066	33	12

Source: Adapted from Smith, Paula A., and Metzger, Michael R., "The Return to Education: Street Vendors in Mexico." *World Development*, Vol. 26, No. 2, Feb. 1998, pp. 289–296.

10.8 Refer to the *Chief Executive* (Sept. 1999) study of chief executive officers (CEOs) from a variety of industries, Exercise 9.35 (p. 500). Recall that a CEO's pay (y) was modeled as a function of company performance (x_1), where performance was measured as a three-year annualized total return to shareholders assuming dividends are reinvested. For this exercise, consider a second independent variable, company sales (x_2). The data for all three variables are listed in the table below.

a. Construct a scattergram of total pay versus company sales. Does your scattergram suggest that company sales will help explain the variation in CEO pay? Explain.

b. The first-order model, $E(y) = \beta_0 + \beta_1 x_1 + \beta_2 x_2$, was fit to the data using EXCEL. Locate the least-squares estimates of the β coefficients on the printout on p. 575 and interpret their values.

c. Test H_0: $\beta_2 = 0$ versus H_a: $\beta_2 < 0$ using $\alpha = .05$. Report your findings in the words of the problem.

d. Locate a 95% confidence interval for β_1 on the printout and interpret it in the words of the problem.

10.9 Many variables influence the price of a company's common stock, including company-specific internal variables such as product quality and financial performance, and external market variables such as interest rates and stock market performance. The table on page 576 contains quarterly data on three such external variables (x_1, x_2, x_3) and the price y of Ford Motor Company's Common stock (adjusted for a stock split). The Japanese Yen Exchange Rate (the value of a U.S. dollar expressed in yen), x_1, measures the strength of the yen versus the U.S. dollar. The higher the rate, the cheaper are Japanese imports—such as the automobiles of Toyota, Nissan, Honda, and Subaru—to U.S. consumers. Similarly, the higher the deutsche mark exchange rate, x_2, the less expensive are BMW's and Mercedes Benz's to U.S. consumers. The S&P 500 Index, x_3, is a general measure of the performance of the market for stocks in U.S. firms.

a. Fit the first-order model $y = \beta_0 + \beta_1 x_1 + \beta_2 x_2 + \beta_3 x_3 + \varepsilon$ to the data. Report the least squares prediction equation.

CEO17.DAT

Company	CEO	Total Pay, y ($ thousands)	Company Performance, x_1	Company Sales, ($ millions), x_2
Cummins Engine	James A. Henderson	4,338	.8	6,266
Bank of New York	Thomas A. Renyi	7,121	52.5	63,579
SunTrust Banks	L. Phillip Humann	3,882	33.0	93,170
Bear Stearns	James E. Cayne	25,002	46.1	7,980
Charles Schwab	Charles R. Schwab	16,506	85.5	3,388
Coca-Cola	M. Douglas Ivester	12,712	22.9	18,813
Time Warner	Gerald M. Levin	25,136	49.6	14,582
Humana	Gregory H. Wolf	4,516	−13.3	9,781
Engelhard	Orin R. Smith	6,189	−1.8	4,172
Chubb	Dean R. O'Hare	4,052	12.3	6,337
American Home Products	John R. Stafford	8,046	35.5	13,463
Merck	Raymond V. Gilmartin	7,178	33.4	26.898
Schering-Plough	Richard J. Kogan	6,818	61.8	8,077
Home Depot	Arthur M. Blank	2,900	58.6	30,219
Dell Computer	Michael S. Dell	115,797	222.4	13,663
BellSouth	F. Duane Ackerman	18,134	35.8	23.123
Delta Air Lines	Leo F. Mullin	17,085	20.8	14,138

Source: *Chief Executive*, Sept. 1999, pp. 45–59.

EXCEL Output for Exercise 10.8

SUMMARY OUTPUT						
Regression Statistics						
Multiple R	0.9037971					
R Square	0.8168492					
Adjusted R Square	0.7906848					
Standard Error	12136.8165					
Observations	17					
ANOVA						
	df	SS	MS	F	Significance F	
Regression	2	9197518606	4598759303	31.21987138	6.91292E-06	
Residual	14	2062232399	147302314.2			
Total	16	11259751005				
	Coefficients	Standard Error	t Stat	P-value	Lower 95%	Upper 95%
Intercept	397.819904	4758.206523	0.083607112	0.934552536	-9807.527182	10603.167
X Variable 1	451.741037	57.9979736	7.788910701	1.86693E-06	327.3476448	576.13443
X Variable 2	-0.17565263	0.129106576	-1.360524294	0.19516709	-0.452558944	0.10125368

FORDSTOCK.DAT (Data for Exercise 10.9)

Date		Ford Motor Co. Common Stock, y	Yen Exchange Rate, x_1	Deutsche Mark Exchange Rate, x_2	S&P 500, x_3
1992	I	38.38	133.2	1.64	407.36
	II	45.88	125.5	1.53	408.21
	III	39.5	119.2	1.41	418.48
	IV	42.88	124.7	1.61	435.64
1993	I	52	121.0	1.61	450.16
	II	52.25	110.1	1.69	447.29
	III	55.25	105.2	1.62	459.24
	IV	64.5	110.9	1.73	465.95
1994	I	58.75	103.2	1.67	463.81
	II	59	99.1	1.60	454.83
	III	27.75	98.5	1.55	466.96
	IV	27.88	99.7	1.55	455.19
1995	I	26.88	89.4	1.38	493.15
	II	29.75	84.6	1.38	539.35
	III	31.12	98.3	1.42	578.77
	IV	28.88	102.8	1.43	614.57
1996	I	34.38	106.3	1.48	647.07
	II	32.38	109.4	1.52	668.50
	III	20.70	111.0	1.53	687.33
	IV	21.28	116.0	1.55	740.74
1997	I	23.02	124.1	1.68	757.12
	II	27.07	114.4	1.74	885.14
	III	28.94	121.0	1.77	947.28
	IV	33.78	130.0	1.79	970.43
1998	I	45.81	132.1	1.85	1101.75
	II	57.00	140.9	1.81	1133.84
	III	54.25	135.3	1.68	1017.01
	IV	61.44	115.6	1.67	1229.23
1999	I	63.94	120.4	0.93	1286.37
	II	48.50	121.1	0.97	1372.71
	III	54.88	106.9	0.94	1282.71

Sources: 1. International Financial Statistics, International Monetary Fund, Washington, D. C., 1998; 2. YahooFinance (*www.yahoo.com*).

b. Find the standard deviation of the regression model and interpret its value in the context of this problem.

c. Do the data provide sufficient evidence to conclude that the price of Ford stock decreases as the yen rate increases? Report the observed significance level and reach a conclusion using $\alpha = .05$.

d. Interpret the value of $\hat{\beta}_2$ in terms of these data. Remember that your interpretation must recognize the presence of the other variables in the model.

10.10 A disabled person's acceptance of a disability is critical to the rehabilitation process. The *Journal of Rehabilitation* (Sept. 1989) published a study that investigated the relationship between assertive behavior level and acceptance of disability in 160 disabled adults. The dependent variable, assertiveness (y), was measured using the Adult Self Expression Scale (ASES). Scores on the ASES range from 0 (no assertiveness) to 192 (extreme assertiveness). The model analyzed was $E(y) = \beta_0 + \beta_1 x_1 + \beta_2 x_2 + \beta_3 x_3$, where

x_1 = Acceptance of disability (AD) score

x_2 = Age (years)

x_3 = Length of disability (years)

The regression results are shown in the table.

Independent Variable	t	Two-Tailed p-Value
AD score (x_1)	5.96	.0001
Age (x_2)	0.01	.9620
Length (x_3)	1.91	.0576

a. Is there sufficient evidence to indicate that AD score is positively linearly related to assertiveness level, once age and length of disability are accounted for? Test using $\alpha = .05$.

b. Test the hypothesis H_0: $\beta_2 = 0$ against H_a: $\beta_2 \neq 0$ Use $\alpha = .05$. Give the conclusion in the words of the problem.

SNOWGEES.DAT

Feeding Trial	Diet	Weight Change (%)	Digestion Efficiency (%)	Acid-Detergent Fiber (%)
1	Plants	−6	0	28.5
2	Plants	−5	2.5	27.5
3	Plants	−4.5	5	27.5
4	Plants	0	0	32.5
5	Plants	2	0	32
6	Plants	3.5	1	30
7	Plants	−2	2.5	34
8	Plants	−2.5	10	36.5
9	Plants	−3.5	20	28.5
10	Plants	−2.5	12.5	29
11	Plants	−3	28	28
12	Plants	−8.5	30	28
13	Plants	−3.5	18	30
14	Plants	−3	15	31
15	Plants	−2.5	17.5	30
16	Plants	−.5	18	22
17	Plants	0	23	22.5
18	Plants	1	20	24
19	Plants	2	15	23
20	Plants	6	31	21
21	Plants	2	15	24
22	Plants	2	21	23
23	Plants	2.5	30	22.5
24	Plants	2.5	33	23
25	Plants	0	27.5	30.5
26	Plants	.5	29	31
27	Plants	−1	32.5	30
28	Plants	−3	42	24
29	Plants	−2.5	39	25
30	Plants	−2	35.5	25
31	Plants	.5	39	20
32	Plants	5.5	39	18.5
33	Plants	7.5	50	15
34	Duck Chow	0	62.5	8
35	Duck Chow	0	63	8
36	Duck Chow	2	69	7
37	Duck Chow	8	42.5	7.5
38	Duck Chow	9	59	8.5
39	Duck Chow	12	52.5	8
40	Duck Chow	8.5	75	6
41	Duck Chow	10.5	72.5	6.5
42	Duck Chow	14	69	7

Source: Gadallah, F. L. and Jefferies, R. L. "Forage quality in brood rearing areas of the lesser snow goose and the growth of captive goslings." *Journal of Applied Biology*, Vol. 32, No. 2, 1995, pp. 281–282 (adapted from Figures 2 and 3).

c. Test the hypothesis H_0: $\beta_3 = 0$ against H_a: $\beta_3 > 0$. Use $\alpha = .05$. Give the conclusion in the words of the problem.

10.11 Refer to the *Journal of Applied Ecology* (Vol. 32, 1995) study of the feeding habits of baby snow geese, Exercise 9.56 (p. 514). The data on gosling weight change, digestion efficiency, acid-detergent fiber (all measured as percentages) and diet (plants or duck chow) for 42 feeding trials are reproduced in the table above. The botanists were interested in predicting weight change (y) as a function of the other variables. The first-order model $E(y) = \beta_0 + \beta_1 x_1 + \beta_2 x_2$, where x_1 is digestion efficiency and x_2 is acid-detergent fiber, was fit to the data. The MINITAB printout is provided on page 578.

a. Find the least squares prediction equation for weight change, y.

b. Interpret the β-estimates in the equation, part **a.**

MINITAB Output for Exercise 10.11

```
The regression equation is
wtchnge = 12.2 - 0.0265 digest - 0.458 acid

Predictor        Coef        StDev          T         P
Constant       12.180        4.402       2.77     0.009
digest       -0.02654      0.05349      -0.50     0.623
acid          -0.4578       0.1283      -3.57     0.001

s = 3.519        R-Sq = 52.9%        R-Sq(adj) = 50.5%

Analysis of Variance

Source        DF          SS          MS          F          P
Regression     2      542.03      271.02      21.88      0.000
Error         39      483.08       12.39
Total         41     1025.12
```

c. Conduct a test to determine if digestion efficiency, x_1, is a useful linear predictor of weight change. Use $\alpha = .01$.
d. Form a 99% confidence interval for β_2. Interpret the result.
e. Explain how to include the qualitative variable diet into the model.

10.12 Empirical research was conducted to investigate the variables that impact the size distribution of manufacturing firms in international markets (*World Development*, Vol. 20, 1992). Data collected on $n = 54$ countries were used to model the country's size distribution y, measured as the share of manufacturing firms in the country with 100 or more workers. The model studied was $E(y) = \beta_0 + \beta_1 x_1 + \beta_2 x_2 + \beta_3 x_3 + \beta_4 x_4 + \beta_5 x_5$, where

x_1 = natural logarithm of Gross National Product (LGNP)

x_2 = geographic area per capita (in thousands of square meters) (AREAC)

x_3 = share of heavy industry in manufacturing value added (SVA)

x_4 = ratio of credit claims on the private sector to Gross Domestic Product (CREDIT)

x_5 = ratio of stock equity shares to Gross Domestic Product (STOCK)

a. The researchers hypothesized that the higher the credit ratio of a country, the smaller the size distribution of manufacturing firms. Explain how to test this hypothesis.
b. The researchers hypothesized that the higher the stock ratio of a country, the larger the size distribution of manufacturing firms. Explain how to test this hypothesis.

10.13 Location is one of the most important decisions for hotel chains and lodging firms. A hotel chain that can select good sites more accurately and quickly than its competition has a distinct competitive advantage. Researchers S. E. Kimes (Cornell University) and J. A. Fitzsimmons (University of Texas) studied the site selection process of La Quinta Motor Inns, a moderately priced hotel chain (*Interfaces*, Mar.–Apr. 1990). Using data collected on 57 mature inns owned by La Quinta, the researchers built a regression model designed to predict the profitability for sites under construction. The least squares model is given below:

$$\hat{y} = 39.05 - 5.41x_1 + 5.86x_2 - 3.09x_3 + 1.75x_4$$

where

$$y = \text{operating margin (measured as a percentage)} = \frac{\text{(profit + interest expenses + depreciation}}{\text{total revenue}}$$

x_1 = state population (in thousands) divided by the total number of inns in the state

x_2 = room rate ($) for the inn

x_3 = square root of the median income of the area (in $ thousands)

x_4 = number of college students within four miles of the inn

All variables were "standardized" to have a mean of 0 and a standard deviation of 1. Interpret the β estimates of the model. Comment on the effect of each independent variable on operating margin, y. [*Note:* A profitable inn is defined as one with an operating margin of over 50%.]

10.14 In the oil industry, water that mixes with crude oil during production and transportation must be

WATEROIL.DAT

Experiment Number	Voltage, y (kw/cm)	Disperse Phase Volume, x_1 (%)	Salinity, x_2 (%)	Temperature, x_3 (°C)	Time Delay, x_4 (hours)	Surfactant Concentration, x_5 (%)	Span: Triton, x_6	Solid Particles, x_7 (%)
1	.64	40	1	4	.25	2	.25	.5
2	.80	80	1	4	.25	4	.25	2
3	3.20	40	4	4	.25	4	.75	.5
4	.48	80	4	4	.25	2	.75	2
5	1.72	40	1	23	.25	4	.75	2
6	.32	80	1	23	.25	2	.75	.5
7	.64	40	4	23	.25	2	.25	2
8	.68	80	4	23	.25	4	.25	.5
9	.12	40	1	4	24	2	.75	2
10	.88	80	1	4	24	4	.75	.5
11	2.32	40	4	4	24	4	.25	2
12	.40	80	4	4	24	2	.25	.5
13	1.04	40	1	23	24	4	.25	.5
14	.12	80	1	23	24	2	.25	2
15	1.28	40	4	23	24	2	.75	.5
16	.72	80	4	23	24	4	.75	2
17	1.08	0	0	0	0	0	0	0
18	1.08	0	0	0	0	0	0	0
19	1.04	0	0	0	0	0	0	0

Source: Førdedal, H., *et al.* "A multivariate analysis of W/O emulsions in high external electric fields as studied by means of dielectric time domain spectroscopy." *Journal of Colloid and Interface Science*, Vol. 173, No. 2, Aug. 1995, p. 398 (Table 2).

removed. Chemists have found that the oil can be extracted from the water/oil mix electrically. Researchers at the University of Bergen (Norway) conducted a series of experiments to study the factors that influence the voltage (y) required to separate the water from the oil (*Journal of Colloid and Interface Science*, Aug. 1995). The seven independent variables investigated in the study are listed in the table above. (Each variable was measured at two levels—a "low" level and a "high" level.) Sixteen water/oil mixtures were prepared using different combinations of the independent variables; then each emulsion was exposed to a high electric field. In addition, three mixtures were tested when all independent variables were set to 0. The data for all 19 experiments are also given in the table.

a. Propose a first-order model for y as a function of all seven independent variables.
b. Use a statistical software package to fit the model to the data in the table.
c. Fully interpret the β estimates.

10.15 The owner of an apartment building in Minneapolis believed that her property tax bill was too high because of an overassessment of the property's value by the city tax assessor. The owner hired an independent real estate appraiser to investigate the appropriateness of the city's assessment. The appraiser used regression analysis to explore the relationship between the sale prices of apartment buildings sold in Minneapolis and various characteristics of the properties. Twenty-five apartment buildings were randomly sampled from all apartment buildings that were sold during a recent year. The table on page 580 lists the data collected by the appraiser. The real estate appraiser hypothesized that the sale price (that is, market value) of an apartment building is related to the other variables in the table according to the model $y = \beta_0 + \beta_1 x_1 + \beta_2 x_2 + \beta_3 x_3 + \beta_4 x_4 + \beta_5 x_5 + \varepsilon$.

a. Fit the real estate appraiser's model to the data in the table. Report the least squares prediction equation.
b. Find the standard deviation of the regression model and interpret its value in the context of this problem.
c. Do the data provide sufficient evidence to conclude that value increases with the number of units in an apartment building? Report the observed significance level and reach a conclusion using $\alpha = .05$.
d. Interpret the value of $\hat{\beta}_1$ in terms of these data. Remember that your interpretation must recognize the presence of the other variables in the model.
e. Construct a scattergram of sale price versus age. What does your scattergram suggest about the relationship between these variables?
f. Test $H_0: \beta_2 = 0$ against $H_a: \beta_2 < 0$ using $\alpha = .01$. Interpret the result in the context of the problem. Does the result agree with your observation in part **e?** Why is it reasonable to conduct a one-tailed rather than a two-tailed test of this null hypothesis?
g. What is the observed significance level of the hypothesis test of part **f?**

MNSALES.DAT (Data for Exercise 10.15)

Code No.	Sale Price, y (\$)	No. of Apartments, x_1	Age of Structure, x_2 (years)	Lot Size, x_3 (sq. ft)	No. of On-Site Parking Spaces, x_4	Gross Building Area, x_5 (sq. ft)
0229	90,300	4	82	4,635	0	4,266
0094	384,000	20	13	17,798	0	14,391
0043	157,500	5	66	5,913	0	6,615
0079	676,200	26	64	7,750	6	34,144
0134	165,000	5	55	5,150	0	6,120
0179	300,000	10	65	12,506	0	14,552
0087	108,750	4	82	7,160	0	3,040
0120	276,538	11	23	5,120	0	7,881
0246	420,000	20	18	11,745	20	12,600
0025	950,000	62	71	21,000	3	39,448
0015	560,000	26	74	11,221	0	30,000
0131	268,000	13	56	7,818	13	8,088
0172	290,000	9	76	4,900	0	11,315
0095	173,200	6	21	5,424	6	4,461
0121	323,650	11	24	11,834	8	9,000
0077	162,500	5	19	5,246	5	3,828
0060	353,500	20	62	11,223	2	13,680
0174	134,400	4	70	5,834	0	4,680
0084	187,000	8	19	9,075	0	7,392
0031	155,700	4	57	5,280	0	6,030
0019	93,600	4	82	6,864	0	3,840
0074	110,000	4	50	4,510	0	3,092
0057	573,200	14	10	11,192	0	23,704
0104	79,300	4	82	7,425	0	3,876
0024	272,000	5	82	7,500	0	9,542

Source: Robinson Appraisal Co., Inc., Mankato, Minnesota

10.5 CHECKING THE OVERALL UTILITY OF A MODEL

Conducting t-tests on each β parameter in a model is *not* the best way to determine whether the overall model is contributing information for the prediction of y. If we were to conduct a series of t-tests to determine whether the independent variables are contributing to the predictive relationship, we would be very likely to make one or more errors in deciding which terms to retain in the model and which to exclude.

For example, suppose you fit a first-order model in 10 quantitative x variables and decide to conduct t-tests on all 10 of the individual β's in the model, each at $\alpha = .05$. Even if all the β parameters (except β_0) are equal to 0, approximately 40% of the time you will incorrectly reject the null hypothesis at least once and conclude that some β parameter differs from 0.* Thus, in multiple regression models for which a large number of independent variables are being considered, conducting a series of t-tests may include a large number of insignificant variables and exclude some useful ones. To test the utility of a multiple regression model, we need a *global test* (one that encompasses all the β parameters). We would also like to find some statistical quantity that measures how well the model fits the data.

*The proof of this result proceeds as follows:

$P(\text{Reject } H_0 \text{ at least once} \mid \beta_1 = \beta_2 = \cdots = \beta_{10} = 0)$

$= 1 - P(\text{Reject } H_0 \text{ no times} \mid \beta_1 = \beta_2 = \cdots = \beta_{10} = 0)$

$\leq 1 - [P(\text{Accept } H_0\text{: } \beta_1 = 0 \mid \beta_1 = 0) \cdot P(\text{Accept } H_0\text{: } \beta_2 = 0 \mid \beta_2 = 0) \cdot \cdots \cdot P(\text{Accept } H_0\text{: } \beta_{10} = 0 \mid \beta_{10} = 0)]$

$= 1 - [(1 - \alpha)^{10}] = 1 - (.05)^{10} = .401$

We commence with the easier problem—finding a measure of how well a linear model fits a set of data. For this we use the multiple regression equivalent of r^2, the coefficient of determination for the straight-line model (Chapter 9), as shown in the box.

DEFINITION 10.1

The **multiple coefficient of determination, R^2,** is defined as

$$R^2 = 1 - \frac{\text{SSE}}{\text{SS}_{yy}} = \frac{\text{SS}_{yy} - \text{SSE}}{\text{SS}_{yy}} = \frac{\text{Explained variability}}{\text{Total variability}}$$

Just as for the simple linear model, R^2 represents the fraction of the sample variation of the y values (measured by SS_{yy}) that is explained by the least squares prediction equation. Thus, $R^2 = 0$ implies a complete lack of fit of the model to the data and $R^2 = 1$ implies a perfect fit with the model passing through every data point. In general, the larger the value of R^2, the better the model fits the data.

To illustrate, the value $R^2 = .8974$ for the sale price model of Example 10.1 is indicated in Figure 10.7. This high value of R^2 implies that using the independent variables land value, appraised improvements, and home size in a first-order model explains 89.7% of the total *sample variation* (measured by SS_{yy}) of sale price y. Thus, R^2 is a sample statistic that tells how well the model fits the data and thereby represents a measure of the usefulness of the entire model.

FIGURE 10.7
SAS printout for sale price model

```
                          Analysis of Variance

                             Sum of          Mean
  Source        DF          Squares        Square       F Value       Prob>F

  Model          3 8779676740.6 2926558913.5           46.662        0.0001
  Error         16 1003491259.4 62718203.714
  C Total       19 9783168000.0

      Root MSE      7919.48254      R-Square            0.8974
      Dep Mean     56660.00000      Adj R-Sq            0.8782
      C.V.            13.97720

                          Parameter Estimates

                    Parameter          Standard       T for H0:
Variable     DF      Estimate             Error     Parameter=0     Prob > |T|

INTERCEP      1   1470.275919      5746.3245832           0.256         0.8013
X1            1      0.814490        0.51221871           1.590         0.1314
X2            1      0.820445        0.21118494           3.885         0.0013
X3            1     13.528650        6.58568006           2.054         0.0567
```

A large value of R^2 computed from the *sample* data does not necessarily mean that the model provides a good fit to all of the data points in the *population*. For example, a first-order linear model that contains three parameters will provide a perfect fit to a sample of three data points and R^2 will equal 1. Likewise, you will always obtain a perfect fit ($R^2 = 1$) to a set of n data points if the model contains exactly n parameters. Consequently, if you want to use the value of R^2 as a measure of how useful the model will be for predicting y, it should be based on a sample that contains substantially more data points than the number of parameters in the model.

Caution

In a multiple regression analysis, use the value of R^2 as a measure of how useful a linear model will be for predicting y only if the sample contains substantially more data points than the number of β parameters in the model.

As an alternative to using R^2 as a measure of model adequacy, the *adjusted multiple coefficient of determination,* denoted R_a^2, is often reported. The formula for R_a^2 is shown in the box.

DEFINITION 10.2

The **adjusted multiple coefficient of determination** is given by

$$R_a^2 = 1 - \left[\frac{(n-1)}{n-(k+1)}\right]\left(\frac{\text{SSE}}{\text{SS}_{yy}}\right)$$

$$= 1 - \left[\frac{(n-1)}{n-(k+1)}\right](1 - R^2)$$

Note: $R_a^2 \leq R^2$

R^2 and R_a^2 have similar interpretations. However, unlike R^2, R_a^2 takes into account ("adjusts" for) both the sample size n and the number of β parameters in the model. R_a^2 will always be smaller than R^2, and more importantly, cannot be "forced" to 1 by simply adding more and more independent variables to the model. Consequently, analysts prefer the more conservative R_a^2 when choosing a measure of model adequacy. In Figure 10.7, R_a^2 is shown directly below the value of R^2. Note that $R_a^2 = .8782$, a value only slightly smaller than R^2.

Despite their utility, R^2 and R_a^2 are only sample statistics. Therefore, it is dangerous to judge the global usefulness of the model based solely on these values. A better method is to conduct a test of hypothesis involving *all* the β parameters (except β_0) in a model. In particular, for the sale price model (Example 10.1), we would test

H_0: $\beta_1 = \beta_2 = \beta_3 = 0$

H_a: At least one of the coefficients is nonzero

The test statistic used to test this hypothesis is an F statistic, and several equivalent versions of the formula can be used (although we will usually rely on the computer to calculate the F statistic):

$$\textit{Test statistic: } F = \frac{(\text{SS}_{yy} - \text{SSE})/k}{\text{SSE}/[n-(k+1)]} = \frac{R^2/k}{(1-R^2)/[n-(k+1)]}$$

Both these formulas indicate that the F statistic is the ratio of the *explained* variability divided by the model degrees of freedom to the *unexplained* variability divided by the error degrees of freedom. Thus, the larger the proportion of the total variability accounted for by the model, the larger the F statistic.

To determine when the ratio becomes large enough that we can confidently reject the null hypothesis and conclude that the model is more useful than no model at all for predicting y, we compare the calculated F statistic to a tabulated F value with k df in the numerator and $[n - (k + 1)]$ df in the denominator. Recall that tabulations of the F-distribution for various values of α are given in Tables VIII, IX, X, and XI of Appendix B.

Rejection region: $F > F_\alpha$, where F is based on k numerator and $n - (k + 1)$ denominator degrees of freedom.

For the sale price example $[n = 20, k = 3, n - (k + 1) = 16$, and $\alpha = .05]$, we will reject H_0: $\beta_1 = \beta_2 = \beta_3 = 0$ if

$$F > F_{.05} = 3.24$$

From the SAS printout (Figure 10.7), we find that the computed F value is 46.66. Since this value greatly exceeds the tabulated value of 3.24, we conclude that at least one of the model coefficients β_1, β_2, and β_3 is nonzero. Therefore, this **global *F*-test** indicates that the first-order model $y = \beta_0 + \beta_1 x_1 + \beta_2 x_2 + \beta_3 x_3 + \varepsilon$ is useful for predicting sale price.

Like SAS, most other regression packages give the F value in a portion of the printout called the "Analysis of Variance." This is an appropriate descriptive term, since the F statistic relates the explained and unexplained portions of the total variance of y. For example, the elements of the SAS printout in Figure 10.7 that lead to the calculation of the F value are:

$$F \text{ Value} = \frac{\text{Sum of Squares (Model)/df (Model)}}{\text{Sum of Squares (Error)/df (Error)}} = \frac{\text{Mean Square (Model)}}{\text{Mean Square (Error)}}$$

$$= \frac{8{,}779{,}676{,}740.6/3}{1{,}003{,}491{,}259.4/16} = \frac{2{,}926{,}558{,}913.5}{62{,}718{,}203.7} = 46.66$$

Note, too, that the observed significance level for the F statistic is given under the heading **Prob > F** as .0001, which means that we would reject the null hypothesis H_0: $\beta_1 = \beta_2 = \beta_3 = 0$ at any α value greater than .0001.

The analysis of variance F-test for testing the usefulness of the model is summarized in the next box.

Testing Global Usefulness of the Model: The Analysis of Variance *F*-Test

H_0: $\beta_1 = \beta_2 = \cdots = \beta_k = 0$ (All model terms are unimportant for predicting y)

H_a: At least one $\beta_i \neq 0$ (At least one model term is useful for predicting y)

Test statistic:
$$F = \frac{(\text{SS}_{yy} - \text{SSE})/k}{\text{SSE}/[n - (k + 1)]} = \frac{R^2/k}{(1 - R^2)/[n - (k + 1)]} = \frac{\text{Mean Square (Model)}}{\text{Mean Square (Error)}}$$

where n is the sample size and k is the number of terms in the model.

(continued)

Rejection region: $F > F_\alpha$, with k numerator degrees of freedom and $[n - (k + 1)]$ denominator degrees of freedom.

Assumptions: The standard regression assumptions about the random error component (Section 10.3).

Caution

A rejection of the null hypothesis H_0: $\beta_1 = \beta_2 = \cdots = \beta_k$ in the global F-test leads to the conclusion [with $100(1 - \alpha)\%$ confidence] that the model is statistically useful. However, statistically "useful" does not necessarily mean "best." Another model may prove even more useful in terms of providing more reliable estimates and predictions. This global F-test is usually regarded as a test that the model *must* pass to merit further consideration.

EXAMPLE 10.4

Refer to Example 10.3, in which an antique collector modeled the auction price y of grandfather clocks as a function of the age of the clock, x_1, and the number of bidders, x_2. The hypothesized first-order model is

$$y = \beta_0 + \beta_1 x_1 + \beta_2 x_2 + \varepsilon$$

A sample of 32 observations is obtained, with the results summarized in the MINITAB printout repeated in Figure 10.8.

FIGURE 10.8 MINITAB printout for Example 10.4

```
The regression equation is
Y = -1339 + 12.7 X1 + 86.0 X2

Predictor      Coef      StDev    t-ratio      P
Constant    -1339.0      173.8      -7.70  0.000
X1          12.7406     0.9047      14.08  0.000
X2           85.953      8.729       9.85  0.000

s = 133.5      R-Sq = 89.2%      R-Sq(adj) = 88.5%

Analysis of Variance

SOURCE       DF        SS         MS        F       P
Regression    2   4283063    2141532   120.19   0.000
Error        29    516727      17818
Total        31   4799789
```

a. Find and interpret the adjusted coefficient of determination R_a^2 for this example.

b. Conduct the global F-test of model usefulness at the $\alpha = .05$ level of significance.

Solution

a. The R_a^2 value (highlighted in Figure 10.8) is .885. This implies that the least squares model has explained about 88.5% of the total sample variation in y values (auction prices), after adjusting for sample size and number of independent variables in the model.

b. The elements of the global test of the model follow:

H_0: $\beta_1 = \beta_2 = 0$ (*Note:* $k = 2$)

H_a: At least one of the two model coefficients is nonzero

Test statistic: $F = 120.19$ (highlighted in Figure 10.8)

p-value: .000

Conclusion: Since $\alpha = .05$ exceeds the observed significance level, $p = .000$, the data provide strong evidence that at least one of the model coefficients is nonzero. The overall model appears to be statistically useful for predicting auction prices.

Can we be sure that the best prediction model has been found if the global F-test indicates that a model is useful? Unfortunately, we cannot. The addition of other independent variables may improve the usefulness of the model. (See the box, p. 583–584.)

To summarize the discussion in this section, both R^2 and R_a^2 are indicators of how well the prediction equation fits the data. Intuitive evaluations of the contribution of the model based on R^2 must be examined with care. Unlike R_a^2, the value of R^2 increases as more and more variables are added to the model. Consequently, you could force R^2 to take a value very close to 1 even though the model contributes no information for the prediction of y. In fact, R^2 equals 1 when the number of terms in the model (including β_0) equals the number of data points. Therefore, you should not rely solely on the value of R^2 (or even R_a^2) to tell you whether the model is useful for predicting y. Use the F-test for testing the global utility of the model.

After we have determined that the overall model is useful for predicting y using the F-test, we may elect to conduct one or more t-tests on the individual β parameters (see Section 10.4). However, the test (or tests) to be conducted should be decided *a priori*, that is, prior to fitting the model. Also, we should limit the number of t-tests conducted to avoid the potential problem of making too many Type I errors. Generally, the regression analyst will conduct t-tests only on the "most important" β's.

Recommendation for Checking the Utility of a Multiple Regression Model

1. First, conduct a test of overall model adequacy using the F-test, that is, test

$$H_0: \beta_1 = \beta_2 = \cdots = \beta_k = 0$$

If the model is deemed adequate (that is, if you reject H_0), then proceed to step 2. Otherwise, you should hypothesize and fit another model. The new model may include more independent variables or higher-order terms.

2. Conduct t-tests on those β parameters in which you are particularly interested (that is, the "most important" β's). These usually involve only the β's associated with higher-order terms (x_2, x_1x_2, etc.). However, it is a safe practice to limit the number of β's that are tested. Conducting a series of t-tests leads to a high overall Type I error rate α.

EXERCISES 10.16–10.30

Learning the Mechanics

10.16 Suppose you fit the first-order model

$$y = \beta_0 + \beta_1 x_1 + \beta_2 x_2 + \beta_3 x_3 + \beta_4 x_4 + \beta_5 x_5 + \varepsilon$$

to $n = 30$ data points and obtain

$$\text{SSE} = .33 \quad R^2 = .92$$

a. Do the values of SSE and R^2 suggest that the model provides a good fit to the data? Explain.
b. Is the model of any use in predicting y? Test the null hypothesis H_0: $\beta_1 = \beta_2 = \beta_3 = \beta_4 = \beta_5 = 0$ against the alternative hypothesis H_a: At least one of the parameters $\beta_1, \beta_2, \ldots, \beta_5$ is nonzero. Use $\alpha = .05$.

10.17 The first-order model $y = \beta_0 + \beta_1 x_1 + \beta_2 x_2 + \varepsilon$ was fit to $n = 19$ data points with the results shown in the SAS printout provided below.
a. Find R^2 and interpret its value.
b. Find R_a^2 and interpret its value.
c. Test the null hypothesis that $\beta_1 = \beta_2 = 0$ against the alternative hypothesis that at least one of β_1 and β_2 is nonzero. Calculate the test statistic using the two formulas given in this section, and compare your results to each other and to that given on the printout. Use $\alpha = .05$ and interpret the result of your test.
d. Find the observed significance level for this test on the printout and interpret it.

10.18 If the analysis of variance F-test leads to the conclusion that at least one of the model parameters is nonzero, can you conclude that the model is the best predictor for the dependent variable y? Can you conclude that all of the terms in the model are important for predicting y? What is the appropriate conclusion?

10.19 Suppose you fit the first-order model

$$y = \beta_0 + \beta_1 x_1 + \beta_2 x_2 + \varepsilon$$

to $n = 20$ data points and obtain

$$\Sigma(y_i - \hat{y}_i)^2 = 12.35 \qquad \Sigma(y_i - \bar{y})^2 = 24.44$$

a. Construct an analysis of variance table for this regression analysis, using the same format as the printout in Exercise 10.17. Be sure to include the sources of variability, the degrees of freedom, the sums of squares, the mean squares, and the F statistic. Calculate R^2 and R_a^2 for the regression analysis.
b. Test the null hypothesis that $\beta_1 = \beta_2 = 0$ against the alternative hypothesis that at least one of the parameters differs from 0. Calculate the test statistic in two different ways and compare the results. Use $\alpha = .05$ to reach a conclusion about whether the model contributes information for the prediction of y.

Applying the Concepts

10.20 Refer to the *World Development* (Feb. 1998) study of street vendors in the city of Puebla, Mexico, Exercise 10.7 (p. 573). Recall that the vendors' mean annual earnings $E(y)$ was modeled as a first-order function of age x_1 and hours worked x_2. Refer to the STATISTIX printout on p. 573 and answer the following:
a. Interpret the value of R^2.
b. Interpret the value of R_a^2. Explain the relationship between R^2 and R_a^2.

SAS Output for Exercise 10.17

```
Dep Variable: Y

                         Analysis of Variance

                          Sum of          Mean
     Source      DF      Squares        Square        F Value       Prob>F

     Model        2     24.22335      12.11167         65.478       0.0001
     Error       16      2.95955       0.18497
     C Total     18     27.18289

         Root MSE        0.43008      R-Square         0.8911
         Dep Mean        3.56053      Adj R-Sq         0.8775
         C.V.           12.07921

                          Parameter Estimates

                        Parameter       Standard      T for H0:
    Variable     DF      Estimate          Error    Parameter=0    Prob > |T|

    INTERCEP      1      0.734606     0.29313351          2.506       0.0234
    X1            1      0.765179     0.08754136          8.741       0.0001
    X2            1     -0.030810     0.00452890         -6.803       0.0001
```

c. Conduct a test of the global utility of the model at $\alpha = .01$. Interpret the result.

10.21 Refer to the *Chief Executive* (Sept. 1999) study of CEOs, Exercise 10.8 (p. 574). Recall that a CEO's pay y was modeled as a function of company performance x_1 and company sales x_2 using a first-order model. Refer to the EXCEL printout on p. 575 and answer the following:

a. Find and interpret the value of the multiple coefficient of determination.

b. Give the null and alternative hypotheses for testing whether the overall model is statistically useful for predicting a CEO's pay.

c. Give the value of the test statistic and corresponding p-value for the test of part **b.**

d. Conduct the test of part **b** using $\alpha = .05$. What is your conclusion?

10.22 The *Journal of Quantitative Criminology* (Vol. 8, 1992) published a paper on the determinants of area property crime levels in the United Kingdom. Several multiple regression models for property crime prevalence, y, measured as the percentage of residents in a geographical area who were victims of at least one property crime, were examined. The results for one of the models, based on a sample of $n = 313$ responses collected for the British Crime Survey, are shown in the table below. [*Note:* All variables except Density are expressed as a percentage of the base area.]

a. Test the hypothesis that the density (x_1) of a region is positively linearly related to crime prevalence (y), holding the other independent variables constant.

b. Do you advise conducting t-tests on each of the 18 independent variables in the model to determine

Results for Exercise 10.22

Variable	$\hat{\beta}$	t	p-value
x_1 = Density (population per hectare)	.331	3.88	$p < .01$
x_2 = Unemployed male population	−.121	−1.17	$p > .10$
x_3 = Professional population	−.187	−1.90	$.01 < p < .10$
x_4 = Population aged less than 5	−.151	−1.51	$p > .10$
x_5 = Population aged between 5 and 15	.353	3.42	$p < .01$
x_6 = Female population	.095	1.31	$p > .10$
x_7 = 10-year change in population	.130	1.40	$p > .10$
x_8 = Minority population	−.122	−1.51	$p > .10$
x_9 = Young adult population	.163	5.62	$p < .01$
x_{10} = 1 if North region, 0 if not	.369	1.72	$.01 < p < .10$
x_{11} = 1 if Yorkshire region, 0 if not	−.210	−1.39	$p > .10$
x_{12} = 1 if East Midlands region, 0 if not	−.192	−0.78	$p > .10$
x_{13} = 1 if East Anglia region, 0 if not	−.548	−2.22	$.01 < p < .10$
x_{14} = 1 if South East region, 0 if not	.152	1.37	$p > .10$
x_{15} = 1 if South West region, 0 if not	−.151	−0.88	$p > .10$
x_{16} = 1 if West Midlands region, 0 if not	−.308	−1.93	$.01 < p < .10$
x_{17} = 1 if North West region, 0 if not	.311	2.13	$.01 < p < .10$
x_{18} = 1 if Wales region, 0 if not	−.019	−0.08	$p > .10$

Source: Osborn, D. R., Tickett, A., and Elder, R. "Area characteristics and regional variates as determinants of area property crime." *Journal of Quantitative Criminology,* Vol. 8, No. 3, 1992, Plenum Publishing Corp.

Results for Exercise 10.23

Independent Variable	Expected Sign of β	β Estimate	t Value	Level of Significance (p-Value)
Constant	−	−4.30	−3.45	.001 (two-tailed)
CHANGE	+	−.002	−0.049	.961 (one-tailed)
SIZE	+	.336	9.94	.000(one-tailed)
COMPLEX	+	.384	7.63	.000(one-tailed)
RISK	+	.067	1.76	.079(one-tailed)
INDUSTRY	−	−.143	−4.05	.000(one-tailed)
BIG8	+	.081	2.18	.030(one-tailed)
NAS	+/−	.134	4.54	.000(two-tailed)
$R^2 = .712$	$F = 111.1$			

Source: Butterworth, S., and Houghton, K. A. "Auditor switching: The pricing of audit services." *Journal of Business Finance and Accounting*, Vol. 22, No. 3, April 1995, p. 334 (Table 4).

which variables are important predictors of crime prevalence? Explain.

c. The model yielded $R^2 = .411$. Use this information to conduct a test of the global utility of the model. Use $\alpha = .05$

10.23 External auditors are hired to review and analyze the financial and other records of an organization and to attest to the integrity of the organization's financial statements. In recent years, the fees charged by auditors have come under increasing scrutiny. S. Butterworth and K. A. Houghton, two University of Melbourne (Australia) researchers, investigated the effects of several variables on the fee charged by auditors. The variables are listed at the bottom of the page.

The multiple regression model $E(y) = \beta_0 + \beta_1 x_1 + \beta_2 x_2 + \beta_3 x_3 + \cdots + \beta_7 x_7$ was fit to data collected for $n = 268$ companies. The results are summarized in the table on page 587.

a. Write the least squares prediction equation.

b. Assess the overall fit of the model.

c. Interpret the estimate of β_3.

d. The researchers hypothesized the direction of the effect of each independent variable on audit fees. These hypotheses are given in the "Expected Sign of β" column in the table on p. 587. (For example, if the expected sign is negative, the alternative hypothesis is H_a: $\beta_i < 0$.) Interpret the results of the hypothesis test for β_4. Use $\alpha = .05$.

e. The main objective of the analysis was to determine whether new auditors charge less than incumbent auditors in a given year. If this hypothesis is true, then the true value of β_1 is negative. Is there evidence to support this hypothesis? Explain.

10.24 An important goal in occupational safety is "active caring." Employees demonstrate active caring (AC) about the safety of their co-workers when they identify environmental hazards and unsafe work practices and then implement appropriate corrective actions for these unsafe conditions or behaviors. Three factors hypothesized to increase the propensity for an employee to actively care for safety are (1) high self-esteem, (2) optimism, and (3) group cohesiveness. *Applied & Preventive Psychology* (Winter 1995) attempted to establish empirical support for the AC hypothesis by fitting the model $E(y) = \beta_0 + \beta_1 x_1 + \beta_2 x_2 + \beta_3 x_3$, where

y = AC score (measuring active caring on a 15-point scale)

x_1 = Self-esteem score

x_2 = Optimism score

x_3 = Group cohesion score

The regression analysis, based on data collected for $n = 31$ hourly workers at a large fiber-manufacturing plant, yielded a multiple coefficient of determination of $R^2 = .362$.

a. Interpret the value of R^2.

b. Use the R^2 value to test the global utility of the model. Use $\alpha = .05$

10.25 Refer to the *Interfaces* (Mar.–Apr. 1990) study of La Quinta Motor Inns, Exercise 10.13 (p. 578). The researchers used state population per inn (x_1), inn room rate (x_2), median income of the area (x_3), and college enrollment (x_4) to build a first-order model for operating margin (y) of a La Quinta Inn. Based on a sample of $n = 57$ inns, the model yielded $R^2 = .51$.

a. Give a descriptive measure of model adequacy.

b. Make an inference about model adequacy by conducting the appropriate test. Use $\alpha = .05$.

10.26 Regression analysis was employed to investigate the determinants of survival size of nonprofit hospitals (*Applied Economics*, Vol. 18, 1986). For a given sample of hospitals, survival size, y, is defined as the largest size hospital (in terms of number of beds) exhibiting growth in market share over a specific time interval. Suppose 10 states are randomly selected and the survival size for all nonprofit hospitals in each state is determined for two time periods five years apart, yielding two observations per state. The 20 survival sizes are listed in the table on page 589, along with the

---

y = Logarithm of audit fee charged to auditee (FEE)

$$x_1 = \begin{cases} 1 \text{ if auditee changed auditors after one year (CHANGE)} \\ 0 \text{ if not} \end{cases}$$

x_2 = Logarithm of auditee's total assets (SIZE)

x_3 = Number of subsidiaries of auditee (COMPLEX)

$$x_4 = \begin{cases} 1 \text{ if auditee receives an audit qualification (RISK)} \\ 0 \text{ if not} \end{cases}$$

$$x_5 = \begin{cases} 1 \text{ if auditee in mining industry (INDUSTRY)} \\ 0 \text{ if not} \end{cases}$$

$$x_6 = \begin{cases} 1 \text{ if auditee is a member of a "Big 8" firm (BIG8)} \\ 0 \text{ if not} \end{cases}$$

x_7 = Logarithm of dollar-value of non-audit services provided by auditor (NAS)

SURVIVAL.DAT

State	Time period	Survival size, y	x_1	x_2	x_3	x_4
1	1	370	.13	.09	5,800	89
1	2	390	.15	.09	5,955	87
2	1	455	.08	.11	17,648	87
2	2	450	.10	.16	17,895	85
3	1	500	.03	.04	7,332	79
3	2	480	.07	.05	7,610	78
4	1	550	.06	.005	11,731	80
4	2	600	.10	.005	11,790	81
5	1	205	.30	.12	2,932	44
5	2	230	.25	.13	3,100	45
6	1	425	.04	.01	4,148	36
6	2	445	.07	.02	4,205	38
7	1	245	.20	.01	1,574	25
7	2	200	.30	.01	1,560	28
8	1	250	.07	.08	2,471	38
8	2	275	.08	.10	2,511	38
9	1	300	.09	.12	4,060	52
9	2	290	.12	.20	4,175	54
10	1	280	.10	.02	2,902	37
10	2	270	.11	.05	2,925	38

Source: Adapted from Bays, C. W. "The determinants of hospital size: A survivor analysis." *Applied Economics*, 1986, Vol. 18, pp. 359-377.

following data for each state, for the second year in each time interval:

x_1 = Percentage of beds that are for-profit hospitals

x_2 = Ratio of the number of persons enrolled in health maintenance organizations (HMOs) to the number of persons covered by hospital insurance

x_3 = State population (in thousands)

x_4 = Percent of state that is urban

The article hypothesized that the following model characterizes the relationship between survival size and the four variables just listed:

$$y = \beta_0 + \beta_1 x_1 + \beta_2 x_2 + \beta_3 x_3 + \beta_4 x_4 + \varepsilon$$

a. The model was fit to the data in the table using SAS, with the results given in the printout below. Report the least squares prediction equation.

b. Find the regression standard deviation s and interpret its value in the context of the problem.

SAS Output for Exercise 10.26

```
Dep Variable: Y

                      Analysis of Variance

                           Sum of            Mean
     Source       DF      Squares          Square      F Value      Prob>F

     Model         4 246537.05939     61634.26485       28.180      0.0001
     Error        15  32807.94061      2187.19604
     C Total      19 279345.00000

          Root MSE     46.76747        R-Square        0.8826
          Dep Mean    360.50000        Adj R-Sq        0.8512
          C.V.         12.97295

                      Parameter Estimates

                        Parameter        Standard      T for H0:
Variable      DF         Estimate           Error    Parameter=0   Prob > |T|

INTERCEP       1       295.327091     40.17888737          7.350       0.0001
X1             1      -480.837576    150.39050364         -3.197       0.0060
X2             1      -829.464955    196.47303539         -4.222       0.0007
X3             1         0.007934      0.00355335          2.233       0.0412
X4             1         2.360769      0.76150774          3.100       0.0073
```

c. Use an F-test to investigate the usefulness of the hypothesized model. Report the observed significance level, and use $\alpha = .025$ to reach your conclusion.

d. Prior to collecting the data it was hypothesized that increases in the number of for-profit hospital beds would decrease the survival size of nonprofit hospitals. Do the data support this hypothesis? Test using $\alpha = .05$.

10.27 Because the coefficient of determination R^2 always increases when a new independent variable is added to the model, it is tempting to include many variables in a model to force R^2 to be near 1. However, doing so reduces the degrees of freedom available for estimating σ^2, which adversely affects our ability to make reliable inferences. Suppose you want to use 18 economic indicators to predict next year's Gross Domestic Product (GDP). You fit the model

$$y = \beta_0 + \beta_1 x_1 + \beta_2 x_2 + \cdots + \beta_{17} x_{17} + \beta_{18} x_{18} + \varepsilon$$

where y = GDP and $x_1, x_2, \ldots, x_{18}$ are the economic indicators. Only 20 years of data ($n = 20$) are used to fit the model, and you obtain $R^2 = .95$. Test to see whether this impressive-looking R^2 is large enough for you to infer that the model is useful, that is, that at least one term in the model is important for predicting GDP. Use $\alpha = .05$.

10.28 Much research—and much litigation—has been conducted on the disparity between the salary levels of men and women. Research reported in *Work and Occupations* (Nov. 1992) analyzes the salaries for a sample of 191 Illinois managers using a regression analysis with the following independent variables:

$$x_1 = \text{Gender of manager} = \begin{cases} 1 & \text{if male} \\ 0 & \text{if not} \end{cases}$$

$$x_2 = \text{Race of manager} = \begin{cases} 1 & \text{if white} \\ 0 & \text{if not} \end{cases}$$

x_3 = Education level (in years)

x_4 = Tenure with firm (in years)

x_5 = Number of hours worked per week

The regression results are shown in the table below as they were reported in the article.

Variable	$\hat{\beta}$	p-Value
x_1	12.774	$< .05$
x_2	.713	$> .10$
x_3	1.519	$< .05$
x_4	.320	$< .05$
x_5	.205	$< .05$
Constant	15.491	—

$R^2 = .240 \qquad n = 191$

a. Write the hypothesized model that was used, and interpret each of the β parameters in the model.

b. Write the least squares equation that estimates the model in part **a,** and interpret each of the β estimates.

c. Interpret the value of R^2. Test to determine whether the model is useful for predicting annual salary. Test using $\alpha = .05$.

d. Test to determine whether the gender variable indicates that male managers are paid more than female managers, even after adjusting for and holding constant the other four factors in the model. Test using $\alpha = .05$. [*Note:* The p-values given in the table are two-tailed.]

e. Why would one want to adjust for these other factors before conducting a test for salary discrimination?

MINITAB Output for Exercise 10.29

```
The regression equation is
wtchnge = 12.2 - 0.0265 digest - 0.458 acid

Predictor        Coef       StDev          T        P
Constant       12.180       4.402       2.77    0.009
digest       -0.02654     0.05349      -0.50    0.623
acid          -0.4578      0.1283      -3.57    0.001

s = 3.519       R-Sq = 52.9%      R-Sq(adj) = 50.5%

Analysis of Variance

Source        DF         SS          MS        F        P
Regression     2     542.03      271.02    21.88    0.000
Error         39     483.08       12.39
Total         41    1025.12
```

10.29 Refer to the *Journal of Applied Ecology* study of the feeding habits of baby snow geese, Exercise 10.11 (p. 577). The MINITAB printout for the model relating weight change (y) to digestion efficiency (x_1) and acid-detergent fiber (x_2) is reproduced on page 590.

a. Locate R^2 and R_a^2 on the MINITAB printout. Interpret these values. Which statistic is the preferred measure of model fit? Explain.

b. Locate the global F value for testing the overall model on the MINITAB printout. Use the statistic to test the null hypothesis H_0: $\beta_1 = \beta_2 = 0$.

10.30 Multiple regression is used by accountants in cost analysis to shed light on the factors that cause costs to be incurred and the magnitudes of their effects. The independent variables of such a regression model are the factors believed to be related to cost, the dependent variable. In some instances, however, it is desirable to use physical units instead of cost as the dependent variable in a cost analysis. This would be the case if most of the cost associated with the activity of interest is a function of some physical unit, such as hours of labor. The advantage of this approach is that the regression model will provide estimates of the number of labor hours required under different circumstances and these hours can then be costed at the current labor rate (Horngren, Foster, and Datar, 1994). The sample data shown in the table below have been collected from a firm's accounting and production records to provide cost information about the firm's shipping department. The EXCEL computer printout for fitting the model $y = \beta_0 + \beta_1 x_1 + \beta_2 x_2 + \beta_3 x_3 + \varepsilon$ is provided on page 592.

a. Find the least squares prediction equation.

b. Use an F-test to investigate the usefulness of the model specified in part **a.** Use $\alpha = .01$, and state your conclusion in the context of the problem.

c. Test H_0: $\beta_2 = 0$ versus H_a: $\beta_2 \neq 0$ using $\alpha = .05$. What do the results of your test suggest about the magnitude of the effects of x_2 on labor costs?

d. Find R^2, and interpret its value in the context of the problem.

e. If shipping department employees are paid \$7.50 per hour, how much less, on average, will it cost the company per week if the average number of pounds per shipment increases from a level of 20 to 21? Assume that x_1 and x_2 remain unchanged. Your answer is an estimate of what is known in economics as the *expected marginal cost* associated with a one-pound increase in x_3.

f. With what approximate precision can this model be used to predict the hours of labor? [*Note:* The precision of multiple regression predictions is discussed in Section 10.6.]

g. Can regression analysis alone indicate what factors *cause* costs to increase? Explain.

SHIPDEPT.DAT

Week	Labor, y (hrs.)	Pounds Shipped, x_1 (1,000s)	Percentage of Units Shipped by Truck, x_2	Average Shipment Weight, x_3 (lbs.)
1	100	5.1	90	20
2	85	3.8	99	22
3	108	5.3	58	19
4	116	7.5	16	15
5	92	4.5	54	20
6	63	3.3	42	26
7	79	5.3	12	25
8	101	5.9	32	21
9	88	4.0	56	24
10	71	4.2	64	29
11	122	6.8	78	10
12	85	3.9	90	30
13	50	3.8	74	28
14	114	7.5	89	14
15	104	4.5	90	21
16	111	6.0	40	20
17	110	8.1	55	16
18	100	2.9	64	19
19	82	4.0	35	23
20	85	4.8	58	25

EXCEL Output for Exercise 10.30

SUMMARY OUTPUT						
Regression Statistics						
Multiple R	0.87755597					
R Square	0.77010448					
Adjusted R Square	0.72699907					
Standard Error	9.810345853					
Observations	20					
ANOVA						
	df	SS	MS	F	Significance F	
Regression	3	5158.313828	1719.437943	17.86561083	2.32332E-05	
Residual	16	1539.886172	96.24288576			
Total	19	6698.2				
	Coefficients	Standard Error	t Stat	P-value	Lower 95%	Upper 95%
Intercept	131.9242521	25.69321439	5.134595076	9.98597E-05	77.45708304	186.3914211
Ship(x1)	2.72608977	2.275004884	1.198278645	0.24825743	-2.096704051	7.548883591
Truck(x2)	0.047218412	0.093348559	0.505829045	0.6198742	-0.150671647	0.245108472
Weight(x3)	-2.587443905	0.642818185	-4.025156669	0.000978875	-3.950157275	-1.224730536

10.6 USING THE MODEL FOR ESTIMATION AND PREDICTION

In Section 9.8 we discussed the use of the least squares line for estimating the mean value of y, $E(y)$, for some particular value of x, say $x = x_p$. We also showed how to use the same fitted model to predict, when $x = x_p$, some new value of y to be observed in the future. Recall that the least squares line yielded the same value for both the estimate of $E(y)$ and the prediction of some future value of y. That is, both are the result of substituting x_p into the prediction equation $\hat{y} = \hat{\beta}_0 + \hat{\beta}_1 x$ and calculating $\hat{y}_p$. There the equivalence ends. The confidence interval for the mean $E(y)$ is narrower than the prediction interval for y because of the additional uncertainty attributable to the random error ϵ when predicting some future value of y.

These same concepts carry over to the multiple regression model. Consider, again, the first-order model relating sale price of a residential property to land value (x_1), improvements (x_2), and home size (x_3). Suppose we want to estimate the mean sale price for a given property with $x_1 = \$15{,}000$, $x_2 = \$50{,}000$, and $x_3 = 1{,}800$ square feet. Assuming that the first-order model represents the true relationship between sale price and the three independent variables, we want to estimate

$$E(y) = \beta_0 + \beta_1 x_1 + \beta_2 x_2 + \beta_3 x_3 = \beta_0 + \beta_1(15{,}000) + \beta_2(50{,}000) + \beta_3(1{,}800)$$

Substituting into the least squares prediction equation, we find the estimate of $E(y)$ to be

$$\begin{aligned}\hat{y} &= \hat{\beta}_0 + \hat{\beta}_1(15{,}000) + \hat{\beta}_2(50{,}000) + \hat{\beta}_3(1{,}800)\\ &= 1{,}470.27 + .814(50{,}000) + .820(50{,}000) + 13.529(1{,}800) = 79{,}061.4\end{aligned}$$

To form a confidence interval for the mean, we need to know the standard deviation of the sampling distribution for the estimator $\hat{y}$. For multiple regression models, the form of this standard deviation is rather complex. However, the regression routines of statistical computer software packages allow us to obtain the confidence intervals for mean values of y for any given combination of values of the independent variables. A portion of the SAS output for the sale price example is shown in Figure 10.9a.

Obs	X1	X2	X3	Y	Predict Value	Residual	Lower95% Mean	Upper95% Mean
21	15000	50000	1800	.	79061.4	.	73380.7	84742.1

FIGURE 10.9a
SAS printout for estimated mean sale price value and corresponding confidence interval

The estimated mean value and corresponding 95% confidence interval for the selected x values are shown in the columns labeled **Predict Value**, **Lower95% Mean**, and **Upper95% Mean,** respectively. We observe that $\hat{y} = 79{,}061.4$, which agrees with our calculation. The corresponding 95% confidence interval for the true mean of y, highlighted on the printout, is (73,380.7, 84,742.1). Thus, with 95% confidence, we conclude that the mean sale price for all properties with $x_1 = \$15{,}000$, $x_2 = \$50{,}000$, and $x_3 = 1{,}800$ square feet will fall between \$73,380.70 and \$84,742.10.

If we were interested in predicting the sale price for a particular (single) property with $x_1 = \$15{,}000$, $x_2 = \$50{,}000$, and $x_3 = 1{,}800$ square feet, we would use $\hat{y} = \$79{,}061.41$ as the predicted value. However, the prediction interval for a new value of y is wider than the confidence interval for the mean value. This is reflected by the SAS printout shown in Figure 10.9b, which gives the predicted value of y and corresponding 95% prediction interval under the columns **Predict Value, Lower95% Predict,** and **Upper95% Predict,** respectively. Note that the prediction interval is (61,337.9, 96,785). Thus, with 95% confidence, we conclude that the sale price for an individual property with the characteristics $x_1 = \$15{,}000$, $x_2 = \$50{,}000$, and $x_3 = 1{,}800$ square feet will fall between \$61,337.90 and \$96,785.

Obs	X1	X2	X3	Y	Predict Value	Residual	Lower95% Predict	Upper95% Predict
21	15000	50000	1800	.	79061.4	.	61337.9	96785

FIGURE 10.9b
SAS printout for predicted sale price value and corresponding prediction interval

EXERCISES 10.31–10.35

Applying the Concepts

10.31 Refer to the *World Development* (Feb. 1998) study of street vendors' earnings, y, Exercises 10.7 and 10.20 (pp. 573, 586). The STATISTIX printout below shows both a 95% prediction interval for y (left side) and a 95% confidence interval for $E(y)$ (right side) for a 45-year-old vendor who works 10 hours a day (i.e., for $x_1 = 45$ and $x_2 = 10$).

a. Interpret the 95% prediction interval for y in the words of the problem.

b. Interpret the 95% confidence interval for $E(y)$ in the words of the problem.

c. Note that the interval of part **a** is wider than the interval of part **b.** Will this always be true? Explain.

10.32 Refer to the *Journal of Applied Ecology* study of the feeding habits of baby snow geese, Exercises 10.11 and 10.29 (pages 577, 591). The MINITAB printout for the first-order model relating gosling weight change y to digestion efficiency x_1 and acid-detergent fiber x_2 is

STATISTIX Output for Exercise 10.31

```
PREDICTED/FITTED VALUES OF EARNINGS

LOWER PREDICTED BOUND      1759.7      LOWER FITTED BOUND     2620.3
PREDICTED VALUE            3017.6      FITTED VALUE           3017.6
UPPER PREDICTED BOUND      4275.4      UPPER FITTED BOUND     3414.9
SE (PREDICTED VALUE)       577.29      SE (FITTED VALUE)      182.35

UNUSUALNESS (LEVERAGE)     0.1108
PERCENT COVERAGE             95.0
CORRESPONDING T              2.18

PREDICTOR VALUES: AGE = 45.000, HOURS = 10.000
```

MINITAB Output for Exercise 10.32

```
The regression equation is
wtchnge = 12.2 - 0.0265 digest - 0.458 acid

Predictor        Coef         StDev          T        P
Constant       12.180         4.402       2.77    0.009
digest       -0.02654       0.05349      -0.50    0.623
acid          -0.4578        0.1283      -3.57    0.001

s = 3.519         R-Sq = 52.9%       R-Sq(adj) = 50.5%

Analysis of Variance

Source          DF          SS          MS          F         P
Regression       2      542.03      271.02      21.88     0.000
Error           39      483.08       12.39
Total           41     1025.12

     Fit   StDev Fit          95.0% CI                  95.0% PI
  -1.687       0.866    (  -3.440,    0.065)   (  -9.020,    5.646)
```

reproduced above. Both a confidence interval for $E(y)$ and a prediction interval for y when $x_1 = 5\%$ and $x_2 = 30\%$ are shown at the bottom of the printout.

a. Interpret the confidence interval for $E(y)$.

b. Interpret the prediction interval for y.

10.33 Refer to Exercise 10.14 (p. 578). The researchers concluded that "in order to break a water-oil mixture with the lowest possible voltage, the volume fraction of the disperse phase x_1 should be high, while the salinity x_2 and the amount of surfactant x_5 should be low." Use this information and the first order model of Exercise 10.14 to find a 95% prediction interval for this "low" voltage y. Interpret the interval.

10.34 An article published in *Geography* (July 1980) used multiple regression to predict annual rainfall levels in California. Data on the average annual precipitation (y), altitude (x_1), latitude (x_2), and distance from the Pacific coast (x_3) for 30 meteorological stations scattered throughout California are listed in the table on page 597. Initially, the first-order model $y = \beta_0 + \beta_1 x_1 + \beta_2 x_2 + \beta_3 x_3 + \varepsilon$ was fit to the data. The SAS printout of the analysis is provided on page 596.

a. Is there evidence that the first-order model is useful for predicting annual precipitation y? Test using $\alpha = .05$.

b. Ninety-five percent prediction intervals for y are shown at the bottom of the printout. Locate and interpret the interval for the Giant Forest meteorological station (station #9).

10.35 In a production facility, an accurate estimate of man-hours needed to complete a task is crucial to management in making such decisions as the proper number of workers to hire, an accurate deadline to quote a client, or cost-analysis decisions regarding budgets. A manufacturer of boiler drums wants to use regression to predict the number of man-hours needed to erect the drums in future projects. To accomplish this, data for 35 boilers were collected. In addition to man-hours (y), the variables measured were boiler capacity (x_1 = lb/hr), boiler design pressure (x_2 = pounds per square inch or psi), boiler type ($x_3 = 1$ if industry field erected, 0 if utility field erected), and drum type ($x_4 = 1$ if steam, 0 if mud). The data are provided in the table on page 598. A MINITAB printout for the model $E(y) = \beta_0 + \beta_1 x_1 + \beta_2 x_2 + \beta_3 x_3 + \beta_4 x_4$ is shown on page 597.

a. Conduct a test for the global utility of the model. Use $\alpha = .01$.

b. Both a 95% confidence interval for $E(y)$ and a 95% prediction interval for y when $x_1 = 150{,}000$, $x_2 = 500$, $x_3 = 1$ and $x_4 = 0$ are shown at the bottom of the MINITAB printout. Interpret both of these intervals.

SAS Output for Exercise 10.34

Model: MODEL1
Dependent Variable: PRECIP

Analysis of Variance

Source	DF	Sum of Squares	Mean Square	F Value	Prob>F
Model	3	4809.35596	1603.11865	13.016	0.0001
Error	26	3202.29762	123.16529		
C Total	29	8011.65359			

Root MSE	11.09799	R-square	0.6003
Dep Mean	19.80733	Adj R-sq	0.5542
C.V.	56.02968		

Parameter Estimates

Variable	DF	Parameter Estimate	Standard Error	T for H0: Parameter=0	Prob > |T|
INTERCEP	1	-102.357429	29.20548173	-3.505	0.0017
ALTITUDE	1	0.004091	0.00121831	3.358	0.0024
LONGTUDE	1	3.451080	0.79486312	4.342	0.0002
COAST	1	-0.142858	0.03634006	-3.931	0.0006

Obs	STATION	Dep Var PRECIP	Predict Value	Std Err Predict	Lower95% Predict	Upper95% Predict	Residual
1	Eureka	39.5700	38.4797	4.568	13.8110	63.1483	1.0903
2	RedBluff	23.2700	23.9136	3.795	-0.1953	48.0226	-0.6436
3	Thermal	18.2000	21.2729	5.132	-3.8600	46.4057	-3.0729
4	FortBrag	37.4800	33.7750	3.815	9.6526	57.8973	3.7050
5	SodaSpri	49.2600	39.4605	5.799	13.7221	65.1990	9.7995
6	SanFranc	21.8200	27.5918	3.144	3.8818	51.3018	-5.7718
7	Sacramen	18.0700	19.1828	2.988	-4.4416	42.8072	-1.1128
8	SanJose	14.1700	23.1015	2.647	-0.3504	46.5535	-8.9315
9	GiantFor	42.6300	29.2534	5.596	3.7056	54.8012	13.3766
10	Salinas	13.8500	22.8856	2.842	-0.6628	46.4340	-9.0356
11	Fresno	9.4400	9.3654	3.029	-14.2809	33.0116	0.0746
12	PtPiedra	19.3300	20.9364	3.147	-2.7752	44.6480	-1.6064
13	PasaRobl	15.6700	19.4445	2.629	-3.9987	42.8877	-3.7745
14	Bakersfi	6.0000	11.0967	2.512	-12.2922	34.4857	-5.0967
15	Bishop	5.7300	14.8859	4.193	-9.5000	39.2717	-9.1559
16	Mineral	47.8200	36.6194	4.392	12.0861	61.1527	11.2006
17	SantaBar	17.9500	16.7077	3.526	-7.2277	40.6432	1.2423
18	Susanvil	18.2000	25.4191	4.571	0.7482	50.0899	-7.2191
19	TuleLake	10.0300	38.7521	4.646	14.0218	63.4823	-28.7221
20	Needles	4.6300	-5.9539	5.224	-31.1665	19.2587	10.5839
21	Burbank	14.7400	11.8145	3.046	-11.8412	35.4701	2.9255
22	LosAngel	15.0200	14.3149	3.416	-9.5536	38.1834	0.7051
23	LongBeac	12.3600	12.7793	3.595	-11.1997	36.7583	-0.4193
24	LosBanos	8.2600	18.0332	2.621	-5.4064	41.4729	-9.7732
25	Blythe	4.0500	-7.4478	4.950	-32.4260	17.5303	11.4978
26	SanDiego	9.9400	9.8563	4.275	-14.5899	34.3025	0.0837
27	Daggett	4.2500	11.7920	3.298	-12.0062	35.5902	-7.5420
28	DeathVal	1.6600	-4.8355	5.843	-30.6159	20.9448	6.4955
29	Crescent	74.8700	41.5529	5.121	16.4295	66.6764	33.3171
30	Colusa	15.9500	20.1703	3.399	-3.6875	44.0280	-4.2203

CALIRAIN.DAT (Data for Exercise 10.34)

Station	Precipitation, y (inches)	Altitude, x_1 (feet)	Latitude, x_2 (degrees)	Distance x_3 (miles)
1. Eureka	39.57	43	40.8	1
2. Red Bluff	23.27	341	40.2	97
3. Thermal	18.20	4152	33.8	70
4. Fort Bragg	37.48	74	39.4	1
5. Soda Springs	49.26	6752	39.3	150
6. San Francisco	21.82	52	37.8	5
7. Sacramento	18.07	25	38.5	80
8. San Jose	14.17	95	37.4	28
9. Giant Forest	42.63	6360	36.6	145
10. Salinas	13.85	74	36.7	12
11. Fresno	9.44	331	36.7	114
12. Pt. Piedras	19.33	57	35.7	1
13. Pasa Robles	15.67	740	35.7	31
14. Bakersfield	6.00	489	35.4	75
15. Bishop	5.73	4108	37.3	198
16. Mineral	47.82	4850	40.4	142
17. Santa Barbara	17.95	120	34.4	1
18. Susanville	18.20	4152	40.3	198
19. Tule Lake	10.03	4036	41.9	140
20. Needles	4.63	913	34.8	192
21. Burbank	14.74	699	34.2	47
22. Los Angeles	15.02	312	34.1	16
23. Long Beach	12.36	50	33.8	12
24. Los Banos	8.26	125	37.8	74
25. Blythe	4.05	268	33.6	155
26. San Diego	9.94	19	32.7	5
27. Daggett	4.25	2105	34.1	85
28. Death Valley	1.66	–178	36.5	194
29. Crescent City	74.87	35	41.7	1
30. Colusa	15.95	60	39.2	91

Source: Taylor, P.J. "A pedagogic application of multiple regression analysis." *Geography*, July 1980, Vol. 65, pp. 203–212.

MINITAB Output for Exercise 10.35

```
The regression equation is
Y = -3783 + 0.00875 X1 + 1.93 X2 + 3444 X3 + 2093 X4

Predictor        Coef        StDev     t-ratio       P
Constant        -3783         1205       -3.14    0.004
X1          0.0087490    0.0009035        9.68    0.000
X2             1.9265       0.6489        2.97    0.006
X3             3444.3        911.7        3.78    0.001
X4             2093.4        305.6        6.85    0.000

s = 894.6       R-Sq = 90.3%     R-Sq(adj) = 89.0%

Analysis of Variance

SOURCE       DF          SS          MS        F        P
Regression    4   230854848    57713712    72.11    0.000
Error        31    24809760      800315
Total        35   255664608

 R denotes an obs. with a large st. resid.

     Fit  StDev.Fit         95% C.I.             95% P.I.
    1936        239   (   1449,    2424)   (     47,    3825)
```

BOILERS.DAT (Data for Exercise 10.35)

Man-Hours, y	Boiler Capacity, x_1	Design Pressure, x_2	Boiler Type, x_3	Drum Type, x_4
3,137	120,000	375	1	1
3,590	65,000	750	1	1
4,526	150,000	500	1	1
10,825	1,073,877	2,170	0	1
4,023	150,000	325	1	1
7,606	610,000	1,500	0	1
3,748	88,200	399	1	1
2,972	88,200	399	1	1
3,163	88,200	399	1	1
4,065	90,000	1,140	1	1
2,048	30,000	325	1	1
6,500	441,000	410	1	1
5,651	441,000	410	1	1
6,565	441,000	410	1	1
6,387	441,000	410	1	1
6,454	627,000	1,525	0	1
6,928	610,000	1,500	0	1
4,268	150,000	500	1	1
14,791	1,089,490	2,170	0	1
2,680	125,000	750	1	1
2,974	120,000	375	1	0
1,965	65,000	750	1	0
2,566	150,000	500	1	0
1,515	150,000	250	1	0
2,000	150,000	500	1	0
2,735	150,000	325	1	0
3,698	610,000	1,500	0	0
2,635	90,000	1,140	1	0
1,206	30,000	325	1	0
3,775	441,000	410	1	0
3,120	441,000	410	1	0
4,206	441,000	410	1	0
4,006	441,000	410	1	0
3,728	627,000	1,525	0	0
3,211	610,000	1,500	0	0
1,200	30,000	325	1	0

Source: Dr. Kelly Uscategui, University of Connecticut

10.7 RESIDUAL ANALYSIS: CHECKING THE REGRESSION ASSUMPTIONS

When we apply regression analysis to a set of data, we never know for certain whether the assumptions of Section 10.3 are satisfied. How far can we deviate from the assumptions and still expect regression analysis to yield results that will have the reliability stated in this chapter? How can we detect departures (if they exist) from the assumptions and what can we do about them? We provide some answers to these questions in this section.

Recall from Section 10.3 that for any given set of values of $x_1, x_2, \ldots, x_k$ we assume that the random error term ε has a normal probability distribution with mean equal to 0 and variance equal to σ^2. Also, we assume that the random errors are probabilistically independent. It is unlikely that these assumptions are ever satisfied exactly in a practical application of regression analysis. Fortunately, experience has shown that least squares regression analysis produces reliable statistical tests, confidence intervals, and prediction intervals as long as the departures from the assumptions are not too great. In this section we present some methods for determining whether the data indicate significant departures from the assumptions.

Because the assumptions all concern the random error component, ε, of the model, the first step is to estimate the random error. Since the actual random error associated with a particular value of y is the difference between the actual y value and its unknown mean, we estimate the error by the difference between the actual y value and the *estimated* mean. This estimated error is called the *regression residual,* or simply the *residual,* and is denoted by $\hat{\varepsilon}$. The actual error ε and residual $\hat{\varepsilon}$ are shown in Figure 10.10.

FIGURE 10.10
Actual random error ε and regression residual $\hat{\varepsilon}$

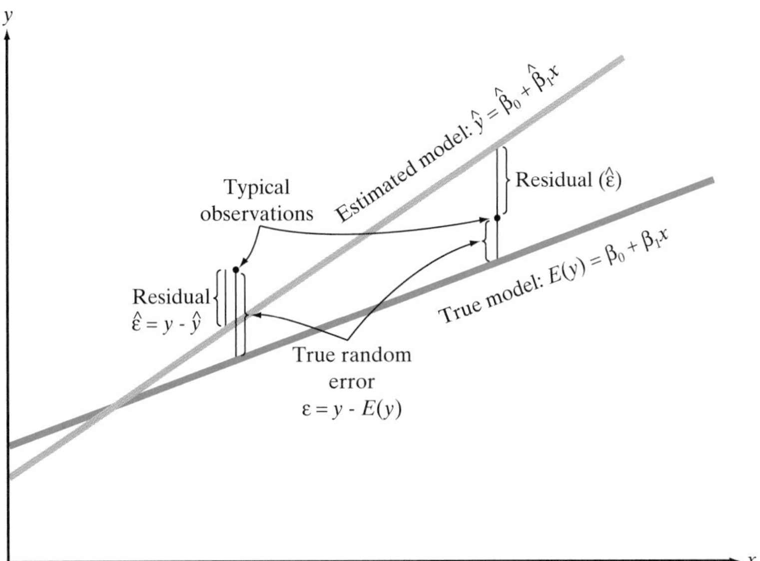

DEFINITION 10.3

A regression **residual,** $\hat{\varepsilon}$, is defined as the difference between an observed y value and its corresponding predicted value:

$$\hat{\varepsilon} = (y - \hat{y}) = y - (\hat{\beta}_0 + \hat{\beta}_1 x_1 + \hat{\beta}_2 x_2 + \cdots + \hat{\beta}_k x_k)$$

Since the true mean of y (that is, the true regression model) is not known, the actual random error cannot be calculated. However, because the residual is based on the estimated mean (the least squares regression model), it can be calculated and used to estimate the random error and to check the regression assumptions. Such checks are generally referred to as **residual analyses**. Two useful properties of residuals are given in the next box.

The following examples show how a graphical analysis of regression residuals can be used to verify the assumptions associated with the model and to support improvements to the model when the assumptions do not appear to be satisfied. Although the residuals can be calculated and plotted by hand, we rely on the statistical software for these tasks in the examples and exercises.

First, we demonstrate how a residual plot can detect a model in which the hypothesized relationship between $E(y)$ and an independent variable x is misspecified. The assumption of mean error of 0 is violated in these types of models.*

Properties of Regression Residuals

1. The mean of the residuals is equal to 0. This property follows from the fact that the sum of the differences between the observed y values and their least squares predicted $\hat{y}$ values is equal to 0.

$$\sum(\text{Residuals}) = \sum(y - \hat{y}) = 0$$

2. The standard deviation of the residuals is equal to the standard deviation of the fitted regression model, s. This property follows from the fact that the sum of the squared residuals is equal to SSE, which when divided by the error degrees of freedom is equal to the variance of the fitted regression model, s^2. The square root of the variance is both the standard deviation of the residuals and the standard deviation of the regression model.

$$\sum(\text{Residuals})^2 = \sum(y - \hat{y})^2 = \text{SSE}$$

$$s = \sqrt{\frac{\Sigma(\text{Residuals})^2}{n - (k + 1)}} = \sqrt{\frac{\text{SSE}}{n - (k + 1)}}$$

EXAMPLE 10.5

In all-electric homes, the amount of electricity expended is of interest to consumers, builders, and energy conservationists. Suppose we wish to investigate the monthly electrical usage, y, in all-electric homes and its relationship to the size, x, of the home. Data were collected for $n = 10$ homes during a particular month and are shown in Table 10.3. A SAS printout for a straight-line model, $E(y) = \beta_0 + \beta_1 x$, fit to the data is shown in Figure 10.11. The residuals from this model is highlighted in the printout. The residuals are then plotted on the vertical axis against the variable x, size of home, on the horizontal axis in Figure 10.12.

TABLE 10.3 Home Size–Electrical Usage Data

Home Size x, (sq. ft.)	Monthly Usage y, (kilowatt-hours)	Home Size x, (sq. ft.)	Monthly Usage y, (kilowatt-hours)
1,290	1,182	1,840	1,711
1,350	1,172	1,980	1,804
1,470	1,264	2,230	1,840
1,600	1,493	2,400	1,956
1,710	1,571	2,930	1,954

a. Verify that each residual is equal to the difference between the observed y value and the estimated mean value, $\hat{y}$.

b. Analyze the residual plot.

*For a misspecified model, the hypothesized mean of y, denoted by $E_h(y)$, will not equal the true mean of y, $E(y)$. Since $y = E_h(y) + \epsilon$, then $\epsilon = y - E_h(y)$ and $E(\epsilon) = E[y - E_h(y)] = E(y) - E_h(y) \neq 0$.

FIGURE 10.11 SAS printout for electrical usage example: Straight-line model

```
Dep Variable: Y

                         Analysis of Variance

                          Sum of            Mean
   Source        DF       Squares          Square       F Value      Prob>F

   Model          1  703957.18342    703957.18342        39.536      0.0002
   Error          8  142444.91658     17805.61457
   C Total        9  846402.10000

        Root MSE     133.43766        R-Square           0.8317
        Dep Mean    1594.70000        Adj R-Sq           0.8107
        C. V.          8.36767

                         Parameter Estimates

                         Parameter        Standard        T for H0:
Variable      DF          Estimate           Error      Parameter=0    Prob > |T|

INTERCEP       1        578.927752    166.96805715            3.467        0.0085
X              1          0.540304      0.08592981            6.288        0.0002

                                             Predict
                     Obs           Y          Value      Residual

                       1      1182.0         1275.9      -93.9204
                       2      1172.0         1308.3        -136.3
                       3      1264.0         1373.2        -109.2
                       4      1493.0         1443.4       49.5852
                       5      1571.0         1502.8       68.1517
                       6      1711.0         1573.1         137.9
                       7      1804.0         1648.7         155.3
                       8      1840.0         1783.8       56.1935
                       9      1956.0         1875.7       80.3417
                      10      1954.0         2162.0        -208.0

Sum of Residuals                        0
Sum of Squared Residuals      142444.9166
```

Solution

a. For the straight-line model the residual is calculated for the first y value as follows:

$$\hat{\varepsilon} = (y - \hat{y}) = 1{,}182 - 1{,}275.9 = -93.9$$

where $\hat{y}$ is the first number in the column labeled **Predict Value** on the SAS printout in Figure 10.11. Similarly, the residual for the second y value is

$$\hat{\varepsilon} = 1{,}172 - 1{,}308.3 = -136.3$$

Both residuals agree (after rounding) with the values given in the column labeled **Residual** in Figure 10.11. Similar calculations produce the remaining residuals.

b. The plot of the residuals for the straight-line model (Figure 10.12) reveals a nonrandom pattern. The residuals exhibit a curved shape, with the residuals for the small values of x below the horizontal 0 (mean of the residuals) line, the residuals corresponding to the middle values of x above the 0 line, and the residual for the largest value of x again below the 0 line. The indication is

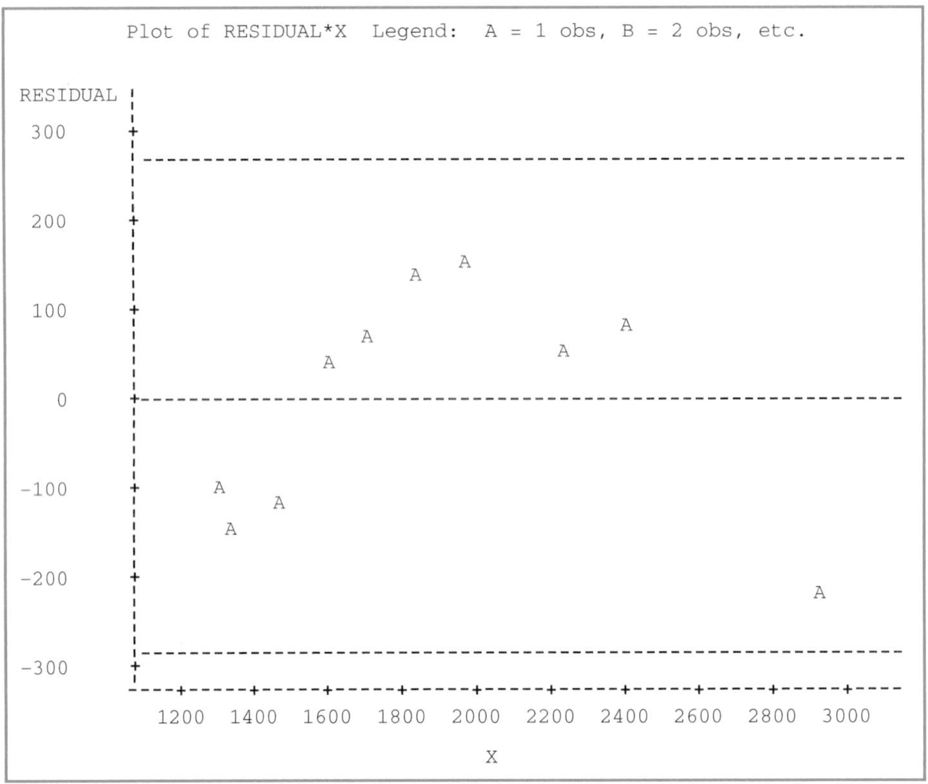

FIGURE 10.12
Residual plot for electrical usage example: Straight-line model

that the mean value of the random error ϵ *within* each of these ranges of x (small, medium, large) may not be equal to 0. Such a pattern usually indicates that **curvature** needs to be added to the model. One way to accomplish this is by adding the term, $\beta_2 x^2$, to the model. This term is called a **second-order** or **quadratic** term.

When the second-order term is added to the model, the nonrandom pattern disappears. Figure 10.13 is a SAS printout for the **quadratic model,** $E(y) = \beta_0 + \beta_1 x + \beta_2 x^2$, with residuals highlighted. These residuals are plotted in Figure 10.14. In Figure 10.14, the residuals appear to be randomly distributed around the 0 line, as expected. Note, too, that the $\pm 2s$ standard deviation lines are at about ± 95 on the quadratic residual plot, compared to (about) ± 275 on the straight-line plot and that the adjusted-R^2 for the quadratic model (.9767) is considerably higher than the adjusted-R^2 for the straight-line model (.8107). The implication is that the quadratic model provides a considerably better model for predicting electrical usage.

Residual analyses are also useful for detecting one or more observations that deviate significantly from the regression model. We expect approximately 95% of the residuals to fall within 2 standard deviations of the 0 line, and all or almost all of them to lie within 3 standard deviations of their mean of 0. Residuals that are extremely far from the 0 line, and disconnected from the bulk of the other residuals, are called *outliers,* and should receive special attention from the regression analyst.

FIGURE 10.13
SAS printout for electrical usage example: Quadratic model

```
Dep Variable: Y

                          Analysis of Variance

                         Sum of              Mean
     Source      DF     Squares            Square         F Value        Prob>F

     Model        2 831069.54637      415534.77319        189.710        0.0001
     Error        7  15332.55363        2190.36480
     C Total      9 846402.10000

          Root MSE      46.80133          R-Square         0.9819
          Dep Mean    1594.70000          Adj R-Sq         0.9767
          C. V.          2.93480

                          Parameter Estimates

                      Parameter          Standard       T for H0:
Variable      DF       Estimate             Error     Parameter=0    Prob > |T|

INTERCEP       1   -1216.143887      242.80636850          -5.009        0.0016
X              1       2.398930        0.24583560           9.758        0.0001
XSQ            1      -0.000450        0.00005908          -7.618        0.0001

                                              Predict
                      Obs           Y           Value       Residual

                        1      1182.0          1129.6        52.4359
                        2      1172.0          1202.2       -30.2136
                        3      1264.0          1337.8       -73.7916
                        4      1493.0          1470.0        22.9586
                        5      1571.0          1570.1         0.9359
                        6      1711.0          1674.2        36.7685
                        7      1804.0          1769.4        34.5998
                        8      1840.0          1895.5       -55.4654
                        9      1956.0          1949.1         6.9431
                       10      1954.0          1949.2         4.8287

Sum of Residuals                  -2.27374E-12
Sum of Squared Residuals            15332.5536
```

DEFINITION 10.4

A residual that is larger than $3s$ (in absolute value) is considered to be an **outlier.**

EXAMPLE 10.6

Refer to Example 10.4 in which we modeled the auction price y of a grandfather clock as a function of age x_1 and number of bidders x_2. The data for this example are repeated in Table 10.4, with one important difference: The auction price of the clock at the top of the second column has been changed from \$2,131 to \$1,131 (highlighted in Table 10.4). The first-order model

$$E(y) = \beta_0 + \beta_1 x_1 + \beta_2 x_2$$

is again fit to these (modified) data, with the MINITAB printout shown in Figure 10.15. The residuals are shown highlighted in the printout and then plotted against the number of bidders, x_2, in Figure 10.16. Analyze the residual plot.

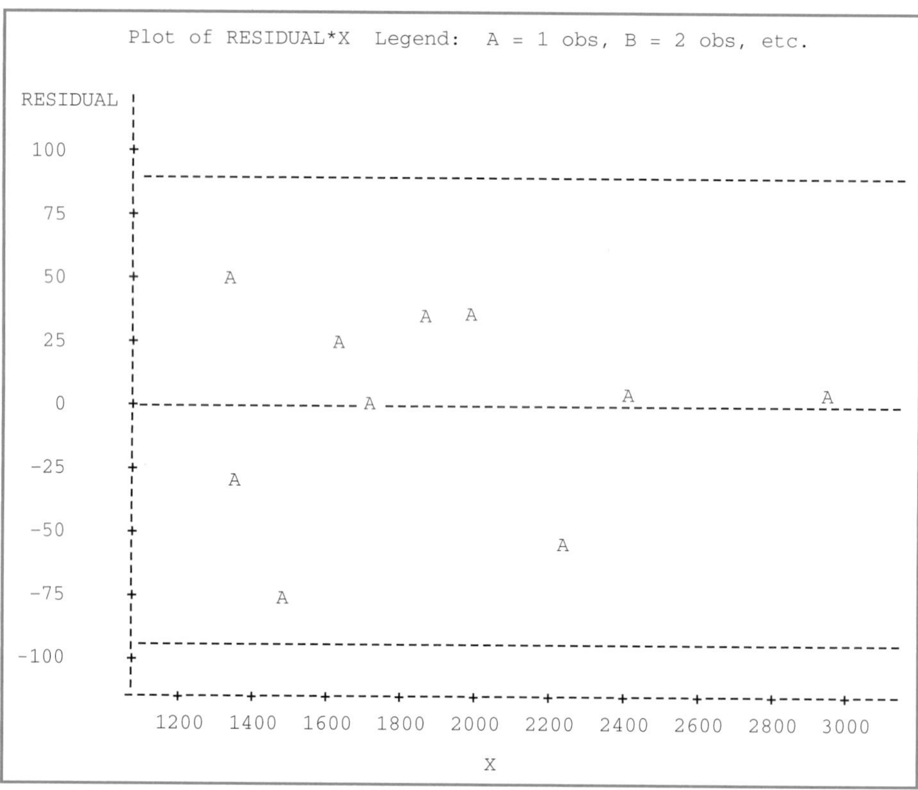

FIGURE 10.14
Residual plot for electrical usage example: Quadratic model

TABLE 10.4 Altered Auction Price Data

Age, x_1	Number of Bidders, x_2	Auction Price, y	Age, x_1	Number of Bidders, x_2	Auction Price, y
127	13	$1,235	170	14	$1,131
115	12	1,080	182	8	1,550
127	7	845	162	11	1,884
150	9	1,522	184	10	2,041
156	6	1,047	143	6	845
182	11	1,979	159	9	1,483
156	12	1,822	108	14	1,055
132	10	1,253	175	8	1,545
137	9	1,297	108	6	729
113	9	946	179	9	1,792
137	15	1,713	111	15	1,175
117	11	1,024	187	8	1,593
137	8	1,147	111	7	785
153	6	1,092	115	7	744
117	13	1,152	194	5	1,356
126	10	1,336	168	7	1,262

Solution The residual plot in Figure 10.16 dramatically reveals the one altered measurement. Note that one of the two residuals at $x_2 = 14$ bidders falls more than 3 standard deviations below 0. Note that no other residual falls more than 2 standard deviations from 0.

What do we do with outliers once we identify them? First, we try to determine the cause. Were the data entered into the computer incorrectly? Was the

FIGURE 10.15
MINITAB printout for grandfather clock example with altered data

```
The regression equation is
Price = - 922 + 11.1 Age + 64.0 Bidders

Predictor      Coef    SE Coef        T        P
Constant     -921.5      258.7    -3.56    0.001
Age          11.087      1.347     8.23    0.000
Bidders       64.03      12.99     4.93    0.000

S = 198.7   R-Sq = 72.5%   R-Sq(adj) = 70.6%

Analysis of Variance

Source          DF        SS        MS        F        P
Regression       2   3015671   1507835    38.20    0.000
Residual Error  29   1144619     39470
Total           31   4160290

Obs        Age   Price      Fit     SE Fit   Residual   St Resid
  1        127  1235.0   1318.9      57.4      -83.9      -0.44
  2        115  1080.0   1121.8      56.8      -41.8      -0.22
  3        127   845.0    934.7      57.5      -89.7      -0.47
  4        150  1522.0   1317.7      36.1      204.3       1.05
  5        156  1047.0   1192.2      56.7     -145.2      -0.76
  6        182  1979.0   1800.6      67.6      178.4       0.96
  7        156  1822.0   1576.3      52.2      245.7       1.28
  8        132  1253.0   1182.2      39.0       70.8       0.36
  9        137  1297.0   1173.6      37.9      123.4       0.63
 10        113   946.0    907.5      57.3       38.5       0.20
 11        137  1713.0   1557.8      77.5      155.2       0.85
 12        117  1024.0   1079.9      51.5      -55.9      -0.29
 13        137  1147.0   1109.6      43.0       37.4       0.19
 14        153  1092.0   1158.9      56.6      -66.9      -0.35
 15        117  1152.0   1208.0      61.8      -56.0      -0.30
 16        126  1336.0   1115.7      42.9      220.3       1.14
 17        170  1131.0   1859.6      82.1     -728.6      -4.03R
 18        182  1550.0   1608.5      60.1      -58.5      -0.31
 19        162  1884.0   1578.8      48.5      305.2       1.58
 20        184  2041.0   1758.7      64.8      282.3       1.50
 21        143   845.0   1048.0      58.4     -203.0      -1.07
 22        159  1483.0   1417.5      39.7       65.5       0.34
 23        108  1055.0   1172.2      74.9     -117.2      -0.64
 24        175  1545.0   1530.9      53.5       14.1       0.07
 25        108   729.0    660.0      83.5       69.0       0.38
 26        179  1792.0   1639.2      56.8      152.8       0.80
 27        111  1175.0   1269.5      82.0      -94.5      -0.52
 28        187  1593.0   1663.9      65.3      -70.9      -0.38
 29        111   785.0    757.3      71.9       27.7       0.15
 30        115   744.0    801.7      67.9      -57.7      -0.31
 31        194  1356.0   1549.4      84.2     -193.4      -1.08
 32        168  1262.0   1389.2      52.5     -127.2      -0.66

R denotes an observation with a large standardized residual
```

FIGURE 10.16
MINITAB residual plot against number of bidders

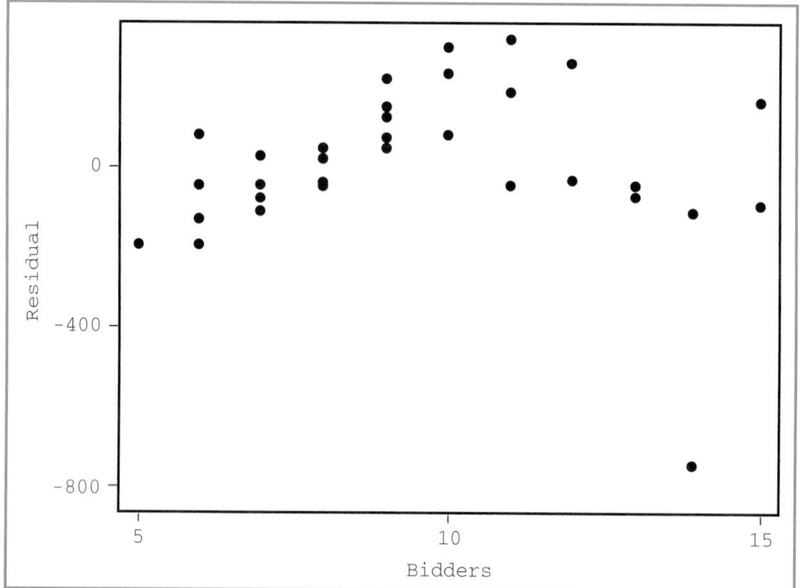

observation recorded incorrectly when the data were collected? If so, we correct the observation and rerun the analysis. Another possibility is that the observation is not representative of the conditions we are trying to model. For example, in this case the low price may be attributable to extreme damage to the clock, or to a clock of inferior quality compared to the others. In these cases we probably would exclude the observation from the analysis. In many cases you may not be able to determine the cause of the outlier. Even so, you may want to rerun the regression analysis excluding the outlier in order to assess the effect of that observation on the results of the analysis.

Figure 10.17 shows the printout when the outlier observation is excluded from the grandfather clock analysis, and Figure 10.18 shows the new plot of the residuals against the number of bidders. Now none of the residuals lies beyond 2 standard deviations from 0. Also, the model statistics indicate a much better model without the outlier. Most notably, the standard deviation (s) has decreased from 198.7 to 134.2, indicating a model that will provide more precise estimates and predictions (narrower confidence and prediction intervals) for clocks that are similar to those in the reduced sample. But remember that if the outlier is removed from the analysis when in fact it belongs to the same population as the rest of the sample, the resulting model may provide misleading estimates and predictions.

Outlier analysis is another example of testing the assumption that the expected (mean) value of the random error ϵ is 0, since this assumption is in doubt for the error terms corresponding to the outliers. The next example in this section checks the assumption of the normality of the random error component.

EXAMPLE 10.7

Refer to Example 10.6. Use a stem-and-leaf display (Section 2.2) to plot the frequency distribution of the residuals in the grandfather clock example, both before and after the outlier residual is removed. Analyze the plots and determine whether the assumption of a normally distributed error term is reasonable.

FIGURE 10.17
MINITAB printout for Example 10.6: Outlier deleted

```
The regression equation is
Price = - 1288 + 12.5 Age + 83.3 Bidders

Predictor      Coef    SE Coef        T        P
Constant    -1288.3      185.3    -6.95    0.000
Age         12.5397     0.9419    13.31    0.000
Bidders      83.290      9.353     8.90    0.000

S = 134.2    R-Sq = 87.8%    R-Sq(adj) = 86.9%

Analysis of Variance

Source           DF        SS        MS        F        P
Regression        2   3627818   1813909   100.67    0.000
Residual Error   28    504496     18018
Total            30   4132314

Souce         DF    Seq SS
Age            1   2199077
Bidders        1   1428741

Obs        Age    Price       Fit    SE Fit    Residual    St Resid
  1        127   1235.0    1387.1      40.4      -152.1       -1.19
  2        115   1080.0    1153.3      38.8       -73.3       -0.57
  3        127    845.0     887.3      39.6       -42.3       -0.33
  4        150   1522.0    1342.3      24.7       179.7        1.36
  5        156   1047.0    1167.7      38.5      -120.7       -0.94
  6        182   1979.0    1910.2      49.2        68.8        0.55
  7        156   1822.0    1667.4      38.4       154.6        1.20
  8        132   1253.0    1199.9      26.5        53.1        0.40
  9        137   1297.0    1179.3      25.6       117.7        0.89
 10        113    946.0     878.3      39.0        67.7        0.53
 11        137   1713.0    1679.0      56.2        34.0        0.28
 12        117   1024.0    1095.1      34.9       -71.1       -0.55
 13        137   1147.0    1096.0      29.2        51.0        0.39
 14        153   1092.0    1130.1      38.5       -38.1       -0.30
 15        117   1152.0    1261.7      42.7      -109.7       -0.86
 16        126   1336.0    1124.7      29.0       211.3        1.61
 17        182   1550.0    1660.3      41.5      -110.3       -0.86
 18        162   1884.0    1659.4      35.4       224.6        1.73
 19        184   2041.0    1852.0      46.5       189.0        1.50
 20        143    845.0    1004.7      40.1      -159.7       -1.25
 21        159   1483.0    1455.2      27.5        27.8        0.21
 22        108   1055.0    1232.1      51.6      -177.1       -1.43
 23        175   1545.0    1572.5      36.8       -27.5       -0.21
 24        108    729.0     565.8      58.6       163.2        1.35
 25        179   1792.0    1706.0      40.0        86.0        0.67
 26        111   1175.0    1353.0      57.1      -178.0       -1.47
 27        187   1593.0    1723.0      45.2      -130.0       -1.03
 28        111    785.0     686.7      50.0        98.3        0.79
 29        115    744.0     736.8      47.2         7.2        0.06
 30        194   1356.0    1560.9      56.9      -204.9       -1.69
 31        168   1262.0    1401.4      35.6      -139.4       -1.08
```

FIGURE 10.18
MINITAB residual plot for Example 10.6: Outlier deleted

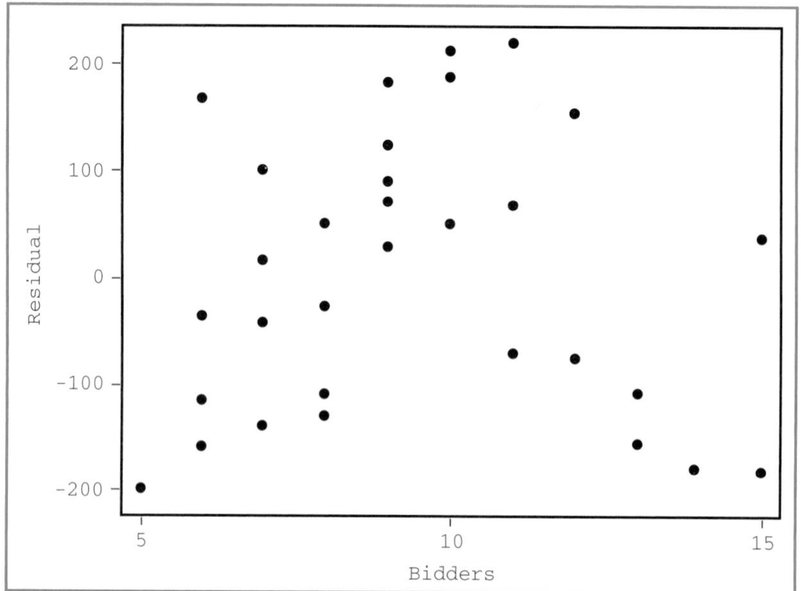

Solution The stem-and-leaf displays for the two sets of residuals are constructed using MINITAB and are shown in Figure 10.19.* Note that the outlier appears to skew the frequency distribution in Figure 10.19a, whereas the stem-and-leaf display in Figure 10.19b appears to be more mound-shaped. Although the displays do not provide formal statistical tests of normality, they do provide a descriptive display. Histograms and normal probability plots can also be used to check the normality assumption. In this example the normality assumption appears to be more plausible after the outlier is removed. Consult the chapter references for methods to conduct statistical tests of normality using the residuals.

FIGURE 10.19a
Stem-and-leaf display for grandfather clock example: Outlier included

```
Stem-and-leaf of Residual   N = 32
Leaf Unit = 10

       1   -7  2
       1   -6
       1   -5
       1   -4
       1   -3
       2   -2  0
       6   -1  9421
      16   -0  9887655554
      16    0  1233667
       9    1  2557
       5    2  0248
       1    3  0
```

*Recall that the left column of the MINITAB printout shows the number of measurements at least as extreme as the stem. In Figure 10.19a, for example, the 6 corresponding to the STEM = −1 means that six measurements are less than or equal to −100. If one of the numbers in the leftmost column is enclosed in parentheses, the number in parentheses is the number of measurements in that row, and the median is contained in that row.

FIGURE 10.19b
Stem-and-leaf display for grandfather clock example: Outlier excluded

```
Stem-and-leaf of Residual    N = 31
Leaf Unit = 10

      1    -2  0
      5    -1  7755
     10    -1  32210
     12    -0  77
     15    -0  432
    (3)     0  023
     13     0  556689
      7     1  1
      6     1  5678
      2     2  12
```

Of all the assumptions in Section 10.3, the assumption that the random error is normally distributed is the least restrictive when we apply regression analysis in practice. That is, moderate departures from a normal distribution have very little effect on the validity of the statistical tests, confidence intervals, and prediction intervals presented in this chapter. In this case, we say that regression analysis is **robust** with respect to nonnormal errors. However, great departures from normality cast doubt on any inferences derived from the regression analysis.

Residual plots can also be used to detect violations of the assumption of constant error variance. For example, a plot of the residuals versus the predicted value $\hat{y}$ may display a pattern as shown in Figure 10.20. In this figure, the range in values of the residuals increases as $\hat{y}$ increases, thus indicating that the variance of the random error, ϵ, becomes larger as the estimate of $E(y)$ increases in value. Since $E(y)$ depends on the x values in the model, this implies that the variance of ϵ is not constant for all settings of the x's.

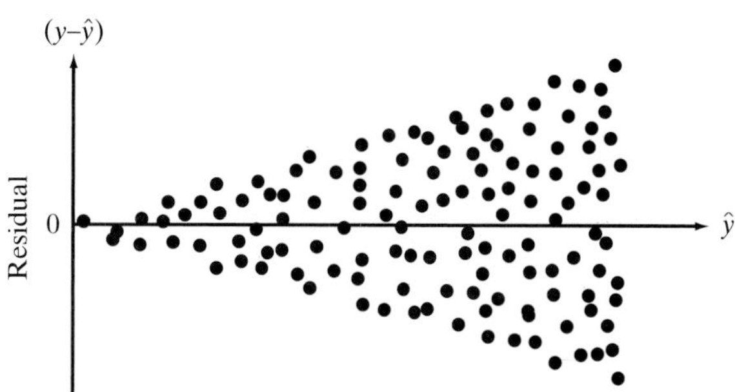

FIGURE 10.20
Residual plot showing changes in the variance of ϵ

In the final example of this section, we demonstrate how to use this plot to detect a nonconstant variance and suggest a useful remedy.

EXAMPLE 10.8

The data in Table 10.5 are the salaries, y, and years of experience, x, for a sample of 50 social workers. The first-order model $E(y) = \beta_0 + \beta_1 x$ was fitted to the data using MINITAB. The MINITAB printout is shown in Figure 10.21, followed by a plot of the residuals versus $\hat{y}$ in Figure 10.22. Interpret the results. Make model modifications, if necessary.

TABLE 10.5 Salary Data for Example 10.8

Years of Experience, x	Salary, y	Years of Experience, x	Salary, y	Years of Experience, x	Salary, y
7	\$26,075	21	\$43,628	28	\$99,139
28	79,370	4	16,105	23	52,624
23	65,726	24	65,644	17	50,594
18	41,983	20	63,022	25	53,272
19	62,308	20	47,780	26	65,343
15	41,154	15	38,853	19	46,216
24	53,610	25	66,537	16	54,288
13	33,697	25	67,447	3	20,844
2	22,444	28	64,785	12	32,586
8	32,562	26	61,581	23	71,235
20	43,076	27	70,678	20	36,530
21	56,000	20	51,301	19	52,745
18	58,667	18	39,346	27	67,282
7	22,210	1	24,833	25	80,931
2	20,521	26	65,929	12	32,303
18	49,727	20	41,721	11	38,371
11	33,233	26	82,641		

```
The regression equation is
Y = 11369 + 2141 X

Predictor        Coef        StDev     t-ratio        P
Constant        11369         3160        3.60    0.001
X              2141.3        160.8       13.31    0.000

s = 8642         R-sq = 78.7%       R-sq(adj) - 78.2%

Analysis of Variance

SOURCE        DF          SS           MS          F          P
Regression     1 13238774784 13238774784     177.25      0.000
Error         48  3585073152    74689024
Total         49 16823847936

Unusual Observations
Obs.          X          Y        Fit  Stdev.Fit   Residual    St.Resid
 31         1.0      24833      13511       3013      11322      1.40 X
 35        28.0      99139      71326       2005      27813      3.31R
 45        20.0      36530      54196       1259     -17666     -2.07R
R denotes an obs. with a large st. resid.
X denotes an obs. whose X value gives it large influence.
```

FIGURE 10.21
MINITAB analysis for first-order model, Example 10.8

Solution The MINITAB printout, Figure 10.21, suggests that the first-order model provides an adequate fit to the data. The R^2 value indicates that the model explains 78.7% of the sample variation in salaries. The t value for testing β_1, 13.31, is highly significant (p-value $\approx$ 0) and indicates that the model contributes information for the prediction of y. However, an examination of the residuals

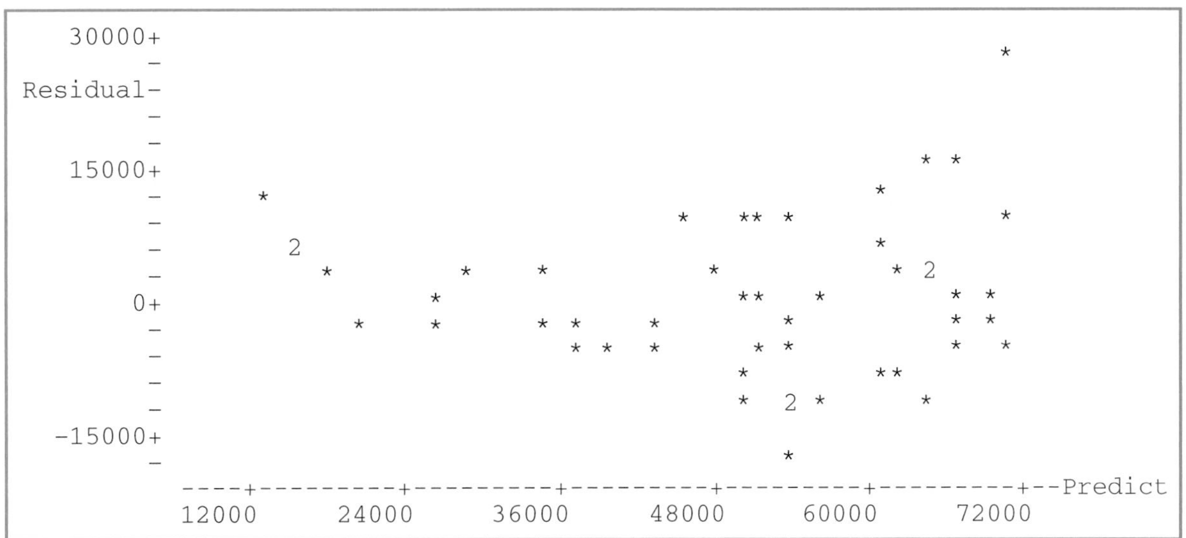

FIGURE 10.22
MINITAB residual plot for first-order model, Example 10.8

plotted against $\hat{y}$ (Figure 10.22) reveals a potential problem. Note the "cone" shape of the residual variability; the size of the residuals increases as the estimated mean salary increases, implying that the constant variance assumption is violated.

One way to stabilize the variance of ϵ is to refit the model using a transformation on the dependent variable y. With economic data (e.g., salaries) a useful **variance-stabilizing transformation** is the natural logarithm of y.* We fit the model

$$\log(y) = \beta_0 + \beta_1 x + \varepsilon$$

to the data of Table 10.5. Figure 10.23 shows the regression analysis printout for the $n = 50$ measurements, while Figure 10.24 shows a plot of the residuals from the log model.

You can see that the logarithmic transformation has stabilized the error variances. Note that the cone shape is gone; there is no apparent tendency of the residual variance to increase as mean salary increases. We therefore are confident that inferences using the logarithmic model are more reliable than those using the untransformed model.

Residual analysis is a useful tool for the regression analyst, not only to check the assumptions, but also to provide information about how the model can be improved. A summary of the residual analyses presented in this section to check the assumption that the random error ε is normally distributed with mean 0 and constant variance is presented in the box on p. 613.

*Other variance-stabilizing transformations that are used successfully in practice are $\sqrt{y}$ and $\sin^{-1}\sqrt{y}$. Consult the chapter references for more details on these transformations.

```
The regression equation is
LOGY = 9.84 + 0.0500 X

Predictor         Coef        StDev     t-ratio        P
Constant       9.84133      0.05636      174.63    0.000
X             0.049978     0.002868       17.43    0.000

s = 1541          R-sq = 86.3%      R-sq(adj) - 86.1%

Analysis of Variance

SOURCE         DF          SS           MS          F          P
Regression      1      7.2118       7.2118     303.65      0.000
Error          48      1.1400       0.0238
Total          49      8.3519

Unusual Observations
Obs.          X        LOGY        Fit  Stdev.Fit   Residual    St.Resid
 19         4.0      9.6869    10.0412     0.0460    -0.3544      _2.41R
 31         1.0     10.1199     9.8913     0.0537     0.2286       1.58 X
 45        20.0     10.5059    10.8409     0.0225    -0.3350      -2.20R
R denotes an obs. with a large st. resid.
X denotes an obs. whose X value gives it large influence.
```

FIGURE 10.23
MINITAB printout for modified model, Example 10.8

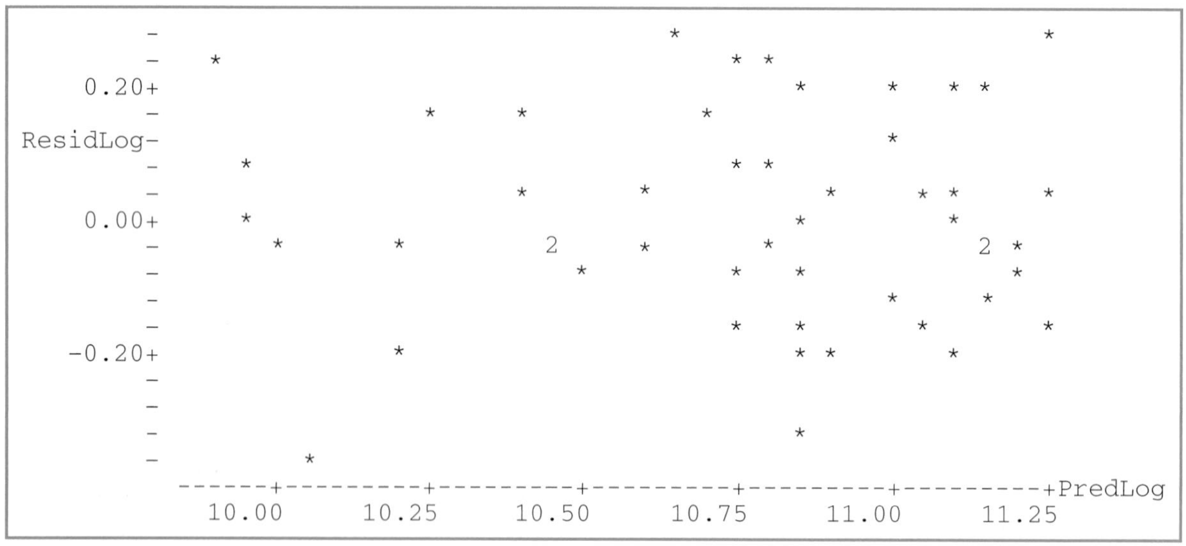

FIGURE 10.24
MINITAB residual plot for modified model, Example 10.8

Using the TI-83 Graphing Calculator

Plotting Residuals on the TI-83

When you compute a regression equation on the TI-83, the residuals are automatically computed and saved to a list called **RESID. RESID** can be found under the **LIST menu (2nd STAT)**.

To make a scatterplot of the residuals,

Step 1 *Enter the data in L1 and L2*

Step 2 *Compute the regression equation* (see Section 9.2)

Step 3 *Set up the data plot*

Press **2nd Y=** for **STATPLOT**
Press **1** for **Plot1**
Use the arrow and **ENTER** keys to set up the screen as shown below.

Note: To enter the **RESID** as your **Ylist:**
1. Use the arrow keys to move the cursor after **Ylist:**
2. Press **2nd STAT** for **LIST**
3. Highlight the listname **RESID** and press **ENTER**

Step 4 *View the scatterplot of the residuals*

Press **ZOOM 9** for **ZoomStat**

Example The figures below show a table of data entered on the TI-83 and the scatterplot of the residuals obtained using the steps given above.

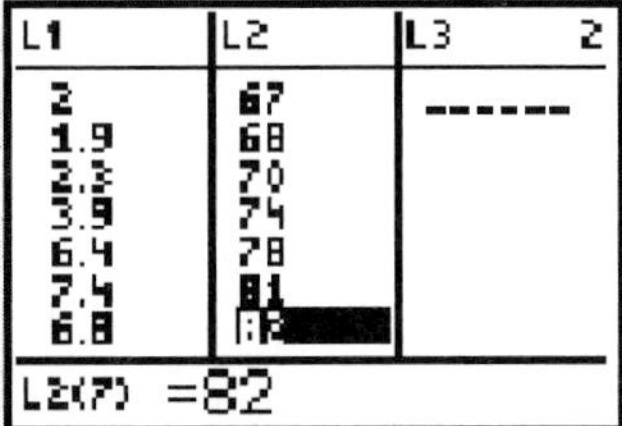

L1	L2	L3 2
2	67	------
1.9	68	
2.3	70	
3.9	74	
6.4	78	
7.4	81	
6.8	82	

L2(7) =82

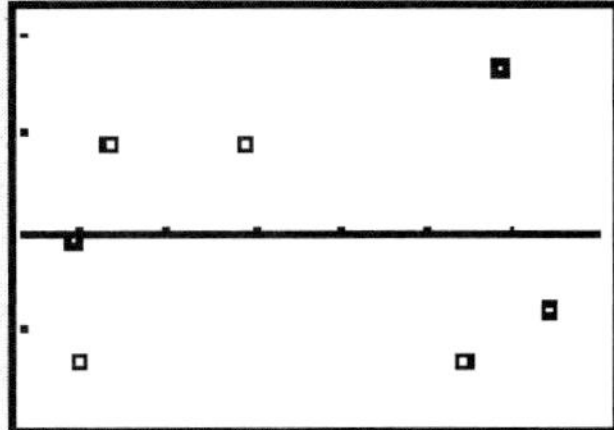

Steps in a Residual Analysis

1. Check for a misspecified model by plotting the residuals against each of the quantitative independent variables. Analyze each plot, looking for a curvilinear trend. This shape signals the need for a quadratic term in the model. Try a second-order term in the variable against which the residuals are plotted.
2. Examine the residual plots for outliers. Draw lines on the residual plots at 2- and 3-standard-deviation distances below and above the 0 line. Examine

(continued)

residuals outside the 3-standard-deviation lines as potential outliers, and check to see that approximately 5% of the residuals exceed the 2-standard-deviation lines. Determine whether each outlier can be explained as an error in data collection or transcription, or corresponds to a member of a population different from that of the remainder of the sample, or simply represents an unusual observation. If the observation is determined to be an error, fix it or remove it. Even if you can't determine the cause; you may want to rerun the regression analysis without the observation to determine its effect on the analysis.

3. Check for nonnormal errors by plotting a frequency distribution of the residuals, using a stem-and-leaf display or a histogram. Check to see if obvious departures from normality exist. Extreme skewness of the frequency distribution may be due to outliers or could indicate the need for a transformation of the dependent variable. (Normalizing transformations are beyond the scope of this book, but you can find information in the references.)
4. Check for unequal error variances by plotting the residuals against the predicted values, $\hat{y}$. If you detect a cone-shaped pattern or some other pattern that indicates that the variance of ϵ is not constant, refit the model using an appropriate variance-stabilizing transformation on y, such as $\log(y)$. (Consult the references for other useful variance-stabilizing transformations.)

10.8 SOME PITFALLS: ESTIMABILITY, MULTICOLLINEARITY, AND EXTRAPOLATION

You should be aware of several potential problems when constructing a prediction model for some response y. A few of the most important are discussed in this final section.

Problem 1 Parameter Estimability

Suppose you want to fit a model relating annual crop yield y to the total expenditure for fertilizer x. We propose the first-order model

$$E(y) = \beta_0 + \beta_1 x$$

Now suppose we have three years of data and \$1,000 is spent on fertilizer each year. The data are shown in Figure 10.25. You can see the problem: The parameters of the model cannot be estimated when all the data are concentrated at a single x value. Recall that it takes two points (x values) to fit a straight line. Thus, the parameters are not estimable when only one x is observed.

FIGURE 10.25
Yield and fertilizer expenditure data: Three years

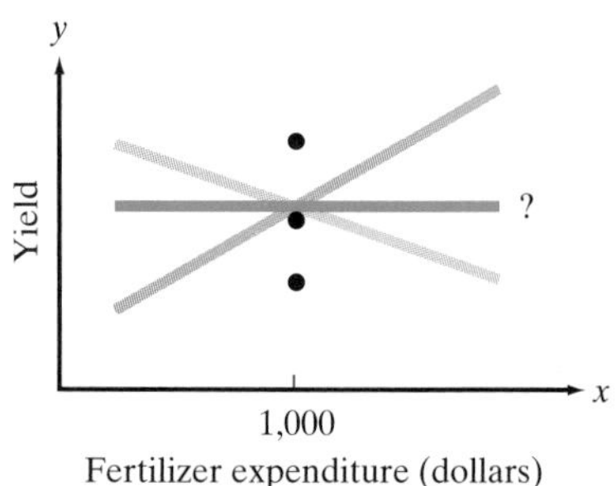

A similar problem would occur if we attempted to fit the quadratic model

$$E(y) = \beta_0 + \beta_1 x + \beta_2 x^2$$

to a set of data for which only one or two different x values were observed (see Figure 10.26). At least three different x values must be observed before a quadratic model can be fit to a set of data (that is, before all three parameters are estimable).

FIGURE 10.26
Only two x values observed: Quadratic model is not estimable

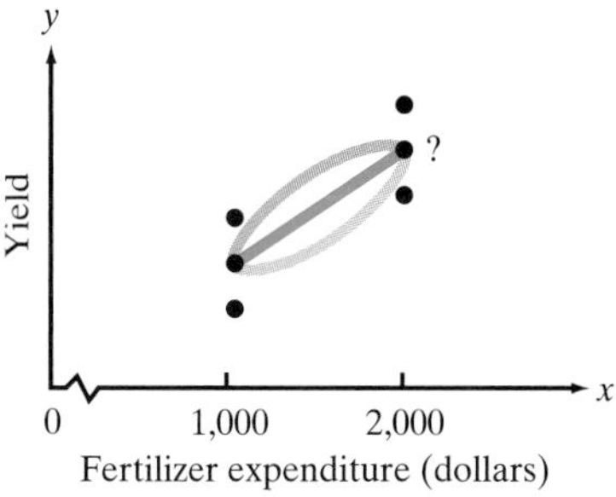

In general, the number of levels of observed x values must be one more than the order of the polynomial in x that you want to fit.

For controlled experiments, the researcher can select experimental designs that will permit estimation of the model parameters. Even when the values of the independent variables cannot be controlled by the researcher, the independent variables are almost always observed at a sufficient number of levels to permit estimation of the model parameters. When the statistical software you use suddenly refuses to fit a model, however, the problem is probably inestimable parameters.

Problem 2 Multicollinearity

Often, two or more of the independent variables used in the model for $E(y)$ contribute redundant information. That is, the independent variables are correlated with each other. Suppose we want to construct a model to predict the gas mileage rating of a truck as a function of its load, x_1, and the horsepower of its engine, x_2. In general, we would expect heavy loads to require greater horsepower and to result in lower mileage ratings. Thus, although both x_1 and x_2 contribute information for the prediction of mileage rating, some of the information is overlapping because x_1 and x_2 are correlated.

If the model

$$E(y) = \beta_0 + \beta_1 x_1 + \beta_2 x_2$$

were fitted to a set of data, we might find that the t values for both $\hat{\beta}_1$ and $\hat{\beta}_2$ (the least squares estimates) are nonsignificant. However, the F-test for H_0: $\beta_1 = \beta_2 = 0$ would probably be highly significant. The tests may seem to produce contradictory conclusions, but really they do not. The t-tests indicate that the contribution of one variable, say x_1 = Load, is not significant after the effect of x_2 = Horsepower has been taken into account (because x_2 is also in the model). The significant F-test, on the other hand, tells us that at least one of the two variables is making a contribution to the prediction of y (that is, either β_1 or β_2, or both, differ from 0). In fact, both are probably contributing, but the contribution of one overlaps with that of the other.

When highly correlated independent variables are present in a regression model, the results are confusing. The researcher may want to include only one of the variables in the final model. One way of deciding which one to include is by using a technique called **stepwise regression.** In stepwise regression, all possible one-variable models of the form $E(y) = \beta_0 + \beta_1 x_i$ are fit and the "best" x_i is selected based on the t-test for β_1. Next, two-variable models of the form $E(y) = \beta_0 + \beta_1 x_1 + \beta_2 x_i$ are fit (where x_1 is the variable selected in the first step); the "second best" x_i is selected based on the test for β_2. The process continues in this fashion until no more "important" x's can be added to the model. Generally, only one of a set of multicollinear independent variables is included in a stepwise regression model, since at each step every variable is tested in the presence of all the variables already in the model. For example, if at one step the variable Load is included as a significant variable in the prediction of the mileage rating, the variable Horsepower will probably never be added in a future step. Thus, if a set of independent variables is thought to be multicollinear, some screening by stepwise regression may be helpful.

Note that it would be fallacious to conclude that an independent variable x_1 is unimportant for predicting y *only* because it is not chosen by a stepwise regression procedure. The independent variable x_1 may be correlated with another one, x_2, that the stepwise procedure did select. The implication is that x_2 contributes *more* for predicting y (in the sample being analyzed), but it may still be true that x_1 alone contributes information for the prediction of y.

Problem 3 Prediction Outside the Experimental Region

By the late 1960s many research economists had developed highly technical models to relate the state of the economy to various economic indices and other independent variables. Many of these models were multiple regression models, where, for example, the dependent variable y might be next year's Gross Domestic Product (GDP) and the independent variables might include this year's rate of inflation, this year's Consumer Price Index (CPI), etc. In other words, the model might be constructed to predict next year's economy using this year's knowledge.

Unfortunately, these models were almost all unsuccessful in predicting the recession in the early 1970s. What went wrong? One of the problems was that many of the regression models were used to **extrapolate,** i.e., predict y values of the independent variables that were outside the region in which the model was developed. For example, the inflation rate in the late 1960s, when the models were developed, ranged from 6% to 8%. When the double-digit inflation of the early 1970s became a reality, some researchers attempted to use the same models to predict future growth in GDP. As you can see in Figure 10.27, the model may be very accurate for predicting y when x is in the range of experimentation, but the use of the model outside that range is a dangerous practice.

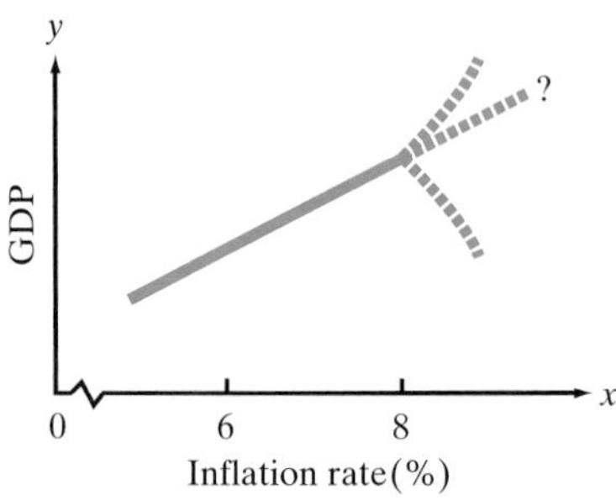

FIGURE 10.27
Using a regression model outside the experimental region

Problem 4 Correlated Errors

Another problem associated with using a regression model to predict a variable y based on independent variables $x_1, x_2, \ldots, x_k$ arises from the fact that the data are frequently *time series.* That is, the values of both the dependent and independent variables are observed sequentially over a period of time. The observations tend to be correlated over time, which in turn often causes the prediction errors of the regression model to be correlated. Thus, the assumption of independent errors is violated, and the model tests and prediction intervals are no longer valid. One solution to this problem is to construct a **time series model;** consult the references for this chapter to learn more about these complex, but powerful, models.

EXERCISES 10.36–10.43

Learning the Mechanics

10.36 Identify the problem(s) in each of the residual plots shown at the bottom of the page.

10.37 Consider fitting the multiple regression model

$$E(y) = \beta_0 + \beta_1 x_1 + \beta_2 x_2 + \beta_3 x_3 + \beta_4 x_4 + \beta_5 x_5$$

A matrix of correlations for all pairs of independent variables is given to the right. Do you detect a multicollinearity problem? Explain.

Correlation Matrix for Exercise 10.37

	x_1	x_2	x_3	x_4	x_5
x_1	—	.17	.02	−.23	.19
x_2		—	.45	.93	.02
x_3			—	.22	−.01
x_4				—	.86
x_5					—

Applying the Concepts

10.38 Chemical engineers at Tokyo Metropolitan University analyzed urban air specimens for the presence of low-molecular-weight dicarboxylic acid (*Environmental Science & Engineering*, Oct. 1993). The dicarboxylic acid (as a percentage of total carbon) and oxidant concentrations for 19 air specimens collected from urban

Residual plots for Exercise 10.36

a.

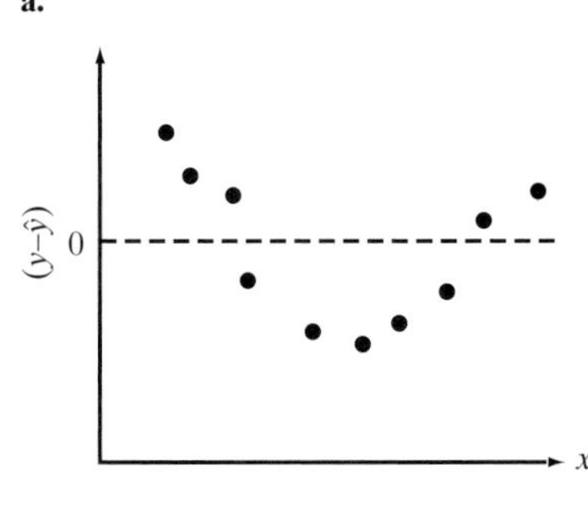

b.

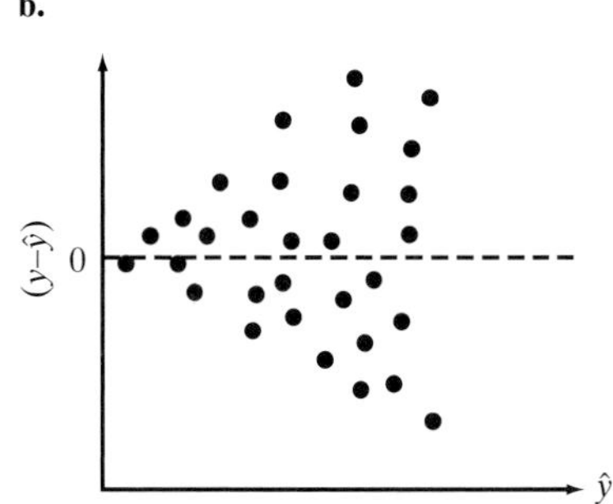

c.

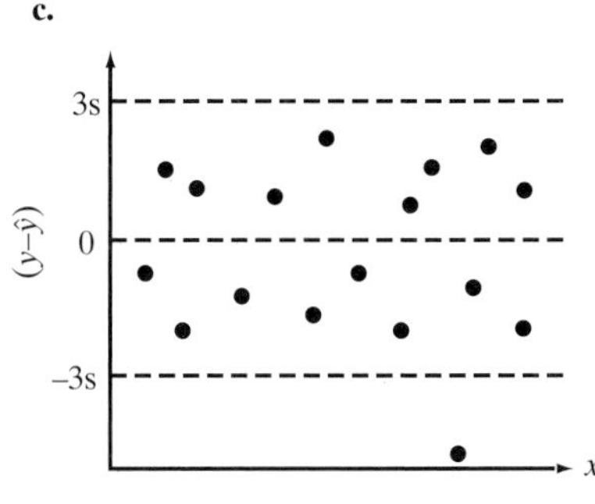

d.

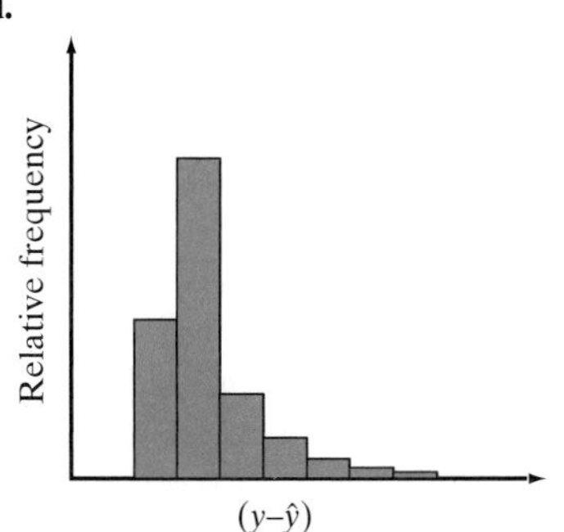

URBANAIR.DAT

Dicarboxylic Acid (%)	Oxidant (ppm)	Dicarboxylic Acid (%)	Oxidant (ppm)
.85	78	.50	32
1.45	80	.38	28
1.80	74	.30	25
1.80	78	.70	45
1.60	60	.80	40
1.20	62	.90	45
1.30	57	1.22	41
.20	49	1.00	34
.22	34	1.00	25
.40	36		

Source: Kawamura, K., and Ikushima, K. "Seasonal changes in the distribution of dicarboxylic acids in the urban atmosphere." *Environmental Science & Technology*, Vol. 27. No. 10, Oct. 1993, p. 2232 (data extracted from Figure 4).

Tokyo are listed in the table above. SAS printouts for the straight-line model relating dicarboxylic acid percentage (y) to oxidant concentration (x) are also provided on pages 619–621. Conduct a complete residual analysis.

10.39 *World Development* (Vol. 20, 1992) published a study of the variables impacting the size distribution of manufacturing firms in international markets. Five independent variables, Gross Domestic Product (GDP), area per capita (AREAC), share of heavy industry in value added (SVA), ratio of credit claims to GDP (CREDIT), and ratio of stock equity of GDP (STOCK), were used to model the share, y, of firms with 100 or more workers. The researchers detected a high correlation between pairs of the following independent variables: GDP and SVA, GDP and STOCK, and CREDIT and STOCK. Describe the problems that may arise if these high correlations are ignored in the multiple regression analysis of the model.

10.40 Passive exposure to environmental tobacco smoke has been associated with growth suppression and an increased frequency of respiratory tract infections in normal children. Is this association more pronounced in children with cystic fibrosis? To answer this question, 43 children (18 girls and 25 boys) attending a 2-week summer camp for cystic fibrosis patients were studied (*The New England Journal of Medicine*, Sept. 20, 1990). Researchers investigated the correlation between a child's weight percentile (y) and the number of cigarettes smoked per day in the child's home (x). The table on page 621 lists the data for the 25 boys. A MINITAB regression printout (with residuals) for the straight-line model relating y to x is also provided on page 622. Examine the residuals. Do you detect any outliers?

10.41 Road construction contracts in the state of Florida are awarded on the basis of competitive, sealed bids; the contractor who submits the lowest bid price wins the contract. During the 1980s, the Office of the Florida Attorney General (FLAG) suspected numerous contractors of practicing bid collusion, i.e., setting the winning bid price above the fair, or competitive, price in order to increase profit margin. FLAG collected data for 279 road construction contracts; the data are available in the file **FLAG.DAT.** For each contract, the following variables were measured:

1. Price of contract ($thousands) bid by lowest bidder
2. Department of Transportaion (DOT) engineer's estimate of fair contract price ($thousands)
3. Ratio of low (winning) bid price to DOT engineer's estimate of fair price.
4. Status (fixed or competitive) of contract
5. District (1, 2, 3, 4, or 5) in which construction project is located
6. Number of bidders on contract
7. Estimated number of days to complete work
8. Length of road project (miles)
9. Percentage of costs allocated to liquid asphalt
10. Percentage of costs allocated to base material
11. Percentage of costs allocated to excavation
12. Percentage of costs allocated to mobilization
13. Percentage of costs allocated to structures
14. Percentage of costs allocated to traffic control
15. Subcontractor utilization (yes or no)

FLAG wants to model the price (y) of the contract bid by lowest bidder in hopes of preventing price-fixing in the future.

a. Do you detect any multicollinearity in these variables? If so, do you recommend that all of these variables be used to predict low bid price y? If not, which variables do you recommend?
b. Using the variables selected in part **a,** fit a first-order model for $E(y)$ to the data stored in the file.
c. Conduct a complete residual analysis on the model fit in part **b.** Do you detect any outliers? Are the standard regression assumptions reasonably satisfied?

SAS Output for Exercise 10.38

```
Dependent Variable: DICARBOX

                         Analysis of Variance

                              Sum of          Mean
          Source       DF    Squares        Square    F Value    Prob>F

          Model         1    2.41362       2.41362     17.080    0.0007
          Error        17    2.40234       0.14131
          C Total      18    4.81597

              Root MSE      0.37592     R-square     0.5012
              Dep Mean      0.92737     Adj R-sq     0.4718
              C.V.         40.53600

                          Parameter Estimates

                         Parameter        Standard     T for H0:
          Variable  DF    Estimate           Error   Parameter=0    Prob > |T|

          INTERCEP   1   -0.023737      0.24576577        -0.097        0.9242
          OXIDANT    1    0.019579      0.00473739         4.133        0.0007

                     Dep Var    Predict    Std Err               Std Err
  Obs   OXIDANT     DICARBOX      Value    Predict   Residual   Residual

    1        78       0.8500     1.5034      0.164    -0.6534      0.338
    2        80       1.4500     1.5425      0.172    -0.0925      0.334
    3        74       1.8000     1.4251      0.148     0.3749      0.346
    4        78       1.8000     1.5034      0.164     0.2966      0.338
    5        60       1.6000     1.1510      0.102     0.4490      0.362
    6        62       1.2000     1.1901      0.107     0.0099      0.360
    7        57       1.3000     1.0922      0.095     0.2078      0.364
    8        49       0.2000     0.9356      0.086    -0.7356      0.366
    9        34       0.2200     0.6419      0.110    -0.4219      0.359
   10        36       0.4000     0.6811      0.105    -0.2811      0.361
   11        32       0.5000     0.6028      0.117    -0.1028      0.357
   12        28       0.3800     0.5245      0.130    -0.1445      0.353
   13        25       0.3000     0.4657      0.141    -0.1657      0.348
   14        45       0.7000     0.8573      0.088    -0.1573      0.365
   15        40       0.8000     0.7594      0.095     0.0406      0.364
   16        45       0.9000     0.8573      0.088     0.0427      0.365
   17        41       1.2200     0.7790      0.093     0.4410      0.364
   18        34       1.0000     0.6419      0.110     0.3581      0.359
   19        25       1.0000     0.4657      0.141     0.5343      0.348
```

(Continued)

10.42 *Teaching Sociology* (July 1995) developed a model for the professional socialization of graduate students working toward their doctorate. One of the dependent variables modeled was professional confidence, y, measured on a 5-point scale. The model included over 20 independent variables and was fitted to data collected for a sample of 309 graduate students. One concern is whether multicollinearity exists in the data. A matrix of Pearson product moment correlations for ten of the independent variables is shown on page 622. [*Note:* Each entry in the table is the correlation coefficient r between the variable in the corresponding row and corresponding column.]

a. Examine the correlation matrix and find the independent variables that are moderately or highly correlated.

b. What modeling problems may occur if the variables, part **a**, are left in the model? Explain.

10.43 The data in the table on p. 624 were collected for a random sample of 26 households in Washington, D.C., during 2000. An economist wants to relate household food consumption, y, to household income, x_1, and household size, x_2, with the first-order model

$$E(y) = \beta_0 + \beta_1 x_1 + \beta_2 x_2$$

SAS Output for Exercise 10.38 (continued)

```
                         UNIVARIATE PROCEDURE
Variable=RESID           Residual

                              Moments

          N                 19     Sum Wgts          19
          Mean               0     Sum                0
          Std Dev     0.365327     Variance    0.133464
          Skewness    -0.41391     Kurtosis    -0.43294
          USS         2.402345     CSS         2.402345
          CV                 .     Std Mean    0.083812
          T:Mean=0           0     Prob> |T|     1.0000
          Sgn Rank           4     Prob> |S|     0.8906
          Num ^=0           19
          W:Normal    0.951334     Prob<W        0.4220

                           Quantiles(Def=5)

          100% Max    0.534273          99%    0.534273
           75% Q3     0.358066          95%    0.534273
           50% Med    0.009867          90%    0.449024
           25% Q1     -0.16573          10%    -0.65339
            0% Min    -0.73561           5%    -0.73561
                                          1%    -0.73561

          Range       1.269885
          Q3-Q1       0.523793
          Mode        -0.73561

                              Extremes

           Lowest        Obs     Highest         Obs
          -0.73561(        8)  0.358066(          18)
          -0.65339(        1)  0.374924(           3)
          -0.42193(        9)  0.441016(          17)
          -0.28109(       10)  0.449024(           5)
          -0.16573(       13)  0.534273(          19)

       Stem Leaf                           #               Boxplot
          4  453                           3                 |
          2  1067                          4              +-----+
          0  144                           3              *--+--*
         -0  76409                         5              +-----+
         -2  8                             1                 |
         -4  2                             1                 |
         -6  45                            2                 |
             ----+----+----+----+
        Multiply Stem.Leaf by 10**-1
```

(*Continued*)

The SPSS printout for the model below is followed by several residual plots on pages 623 and 625.

a. Do you detect any signs of multicollinearity in the data? Explain.
b. Is there visual evidence that a second-order model may be more appropriate for predicting household food consumption? Explain.
c. Comment on the assumption of constant error variance. Does it appear to be satisfied?
d. Are there any outliers in the data? If so, identify them.
e. Does the assumption of normal errors appear to be reasonably satisfied? Explain.

SAS Output for Exercise 10.38 (continued)

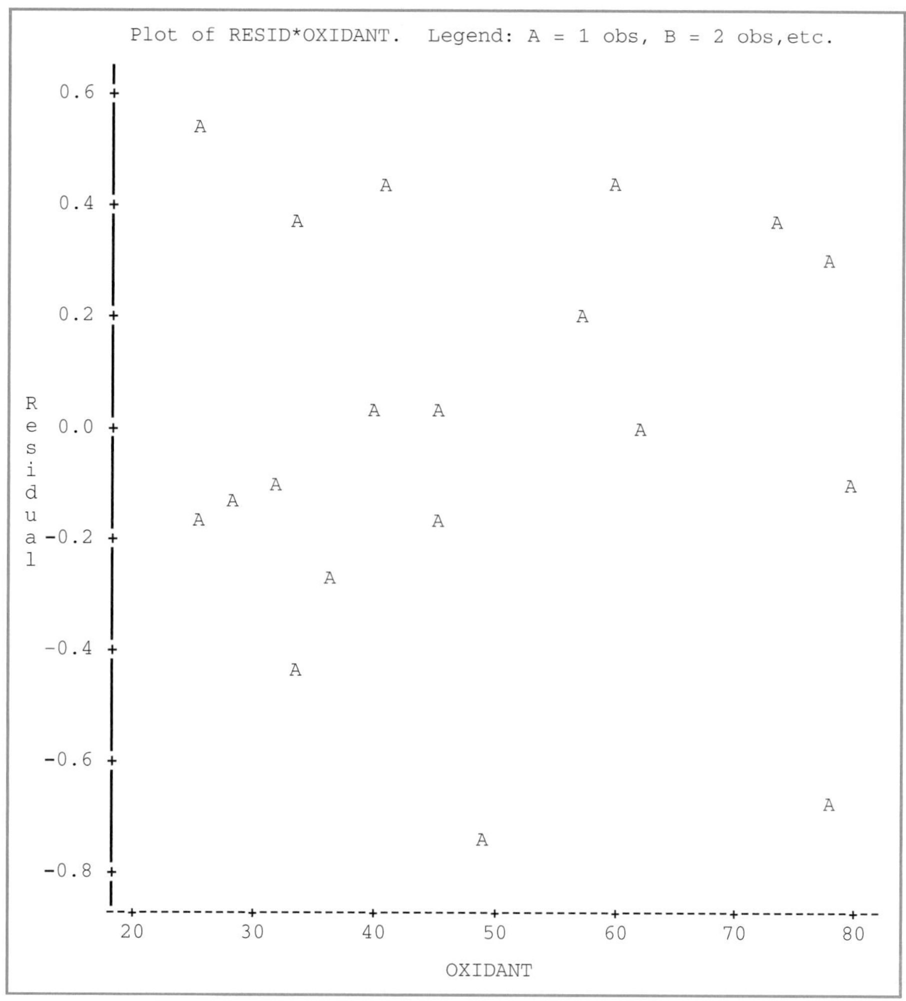

CFSMOKE.DAT (Data for Exercise 10.40)

Weight Percentile, y	No. of Cigarettes Smoked per Day, x	Weight Percentile, y	No. of Cigarettes Smoked per, Day x
6	0	43	0
6	15	49	0
2	40	50	0
8	23	49	22
11	20	46	30
17	7	54	0
24	3	58	0
25	0	62	0
17	25	66	0
25	20	66	23
25	15	83	0
31	23	87	44
35	10		

Source: Rubin, B. K. "Exposure of children with cystic fibrosis to environmental tobacco smoke." *The New England Journal of Medicine,* Sept. 20, 1990. Vol. 323, No. 12, p. 85 (data extracted from Figure 3).

MINITAB Output for Exercise 10.40

```
The regression equation is
WTPCTILE = 41.2 - 0.262 SMOKED

Predictor       Coef       Stdev    t-ratio       p
Constant      41.153       6.843       6.01   0.000
SMOKED       -0.2619      0.3702      -0.71   0.486

s = 24.68       R-sq = 2.1%     R-sq(adj) = 0.0%

Analysis of Variance

SOURCE        DF         SS          MS         F        p
Regression     1      304.9       304.9      0.50    0.486
Error         23    14011.1       609.2
Total         24    14316.0

Obs.   SMOKED   WTPCTILE      Fit  Stdev.Fit  Residual    St.Resid
  1      0.0      6.00      41.15      6.84    -35.15      -1.48
  2     15.0      6.00      37.22      5.00    -31.22      -1.29
  3     40.0      2.00      30.68     11.22    -28.68      -1.30
  4     23.0      8.00      35.13      6.22    -27.13      -1.14
  5     20.0     11.00      35.91      5.61    -24.91      -1.04
  6      7.0     17.00      39.32      5.38    -22.32      -0.93
  7      3.0     24.00      40.37      6.13    -16.37      -0.68
  8      0.0     25.00      41.15      6.84    -16.15      -0.68
  9     25.0     17.00      34.60      6.69    -17.60      -0.74
 10     20.0     25.00      35.91      5.61    -10.91      -0.45
 11     15.0     25.00      37.22      5.00    -12.22      -0.51
 12     23.0     31.00      35.13      6.22     -4.13      -0.17
 13     10.0     35.00      38.53      5.04     -3.53      -0.15
 14      0.0     43.00      41.15      6.84      1.85       0.08
 15      0.0     49.00      41.15      6.84      7.85       0.33
 16      0.0     50.00      41.15      6.84      8.85       0.37
 17     22.0     49.00      35.39      6.00     13.61       0.57
 18     30.0     46.00      33.29      8.06     12.71       0.54
 19      0.0     54.00      41.15      6.84     12.85       0.54
 20      0.0     58.00      41.15      6.84     16.85       0.71
 21      0.0     62.00      41.15      6.84     20.85       0.88
 22      0.0     66.00      41.15      6.84     24.85       1.05
 23     23.0     66.00      35.13      6.22     30.87       1.29
 24      0.0     83.00      41.15      6.84     41.85       1.76
 25     44.0     87.00      29.63     12.56     57.37       2.70
```

Correlation matrix for Exercise 10.42

Independent Variable	(1)	(2)	(3)	(4)	(5)	(6)	(7)	(8)	(9)	(10)
(1) Father's occupation	1.000	.363	.099	−.110	−.047	−.053	−.111	.178	.078	.049
(2) Mother's education	.363	1.000	.228	−.139	−.216	.084	−.118	.192	.125	.068
(3) Race	.099	.228	1.000	.036	−.515	.014	−.120	.112	.117	.337
(4) Sex	−.110	−.139	.036	1.000	.165	−.256	.173	−.106	−.117	.073
(5) Foreign status	−.047	−.216	−.515	.165	1.000	−.041	.159	−.130	−.165	−.171
(6) Undergraduate GPA	−.053	.084	.014	−.256	−.041	1.000	.032	.028	−.034	.092
(7) Year GRE taken	−.111	−.118	−.120	.173	.159	.032	1.000	−.086	−.602	.016
(8) Verbal GRE score	.178	.192	.112	−.106	−.130	.028	−.086	1.000	.132	.087
(9) Years in graduate program	.078	.125	.117	−.117	−.165	−.034	−.602	.132	1.000	−.071
(10) First-year graduate GPA	.049	.068	.337	.073	−.171	.092	.016	.087	−.071	1.000

Source: Keith, B., and Moore, H. A. "Training sociologists: An assessment of professional socializatoin and the emergence of career aspirations." *Teaching Sociology,* Vo. 23, No. 3, July 1995, p. 205 (Table 1).

SPSS Output for Exercise 10.43

```
Equation Number 1.    Dependent Variable..    FOOD

Block Number  1.  Method:  Enter      INCOME   HOMESIZE

Multiple R              .74699         Analysis of Variance
R Square                .55800                             DF      Sum of Squares
Adjusted R Square       .51956         Regression           2            15.00268
Standard Error          .71881         Residual            23            11.88386

                                       F =        14.51808      Signif F =  .0001

----------------- Variables in the Equation -----------------

Variable                  B          SE B        Beta            T   Sig T

INCOME       -1.63937E-04      .006564   -.003495        -.025   .9803
HOMESIZE          .383485      .071887    .746508        5.335   .0000
(Constant)       2.794380      .436335                   6.404   .0000

Residuals Statistics:

               Min         Max        Mean   Std Dev    N

*PRED       3.1664      6.2383      4.1885     .7747   26
*RESID      -.9748      2.7894       .0000     .6895   26
*ZPRED     -1.3194      2.6460       .0000    1.0000   26
*ZRESID    -1.3561      3.8806       .0000     .9592   26

Total Cases =         26
```

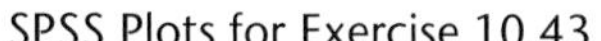
SPSS Plots for Exercise 10.43

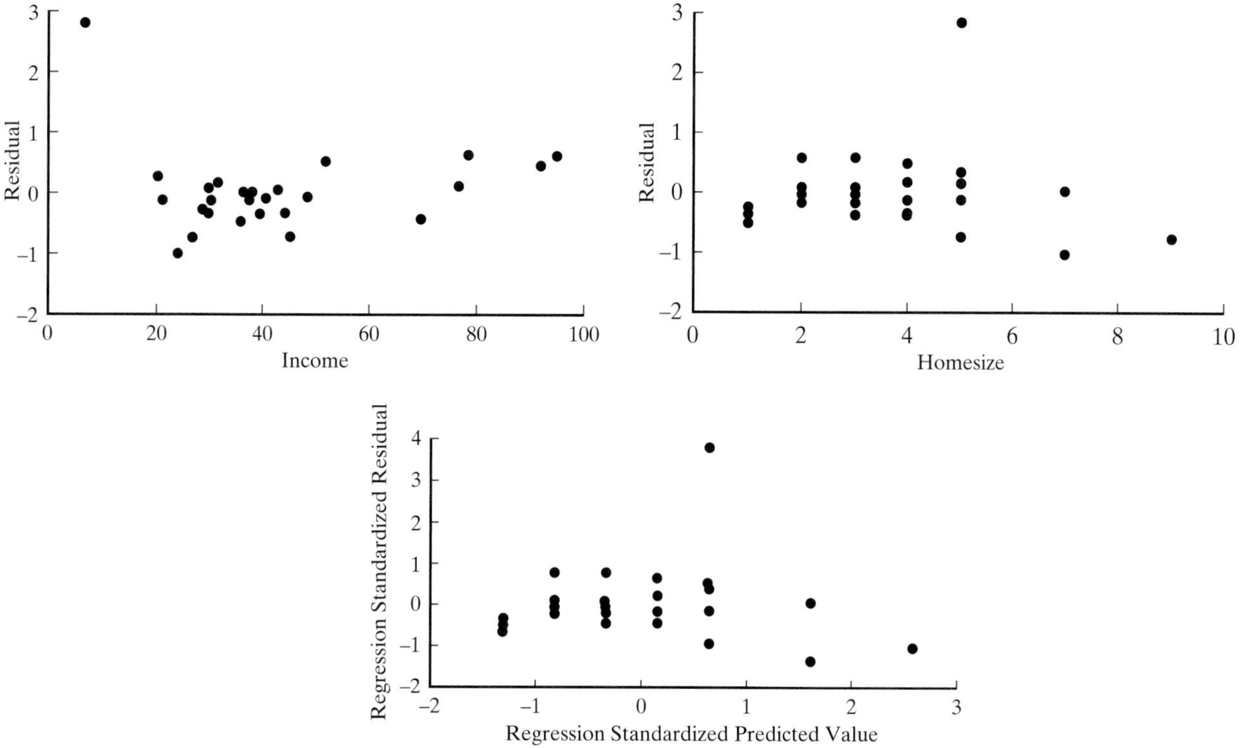

STATISTICS IN 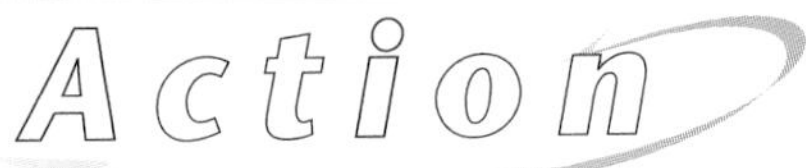

"Wringing" The Bell Curve

In Statistics in Action in Chapter 4, we introduced *The Bell Curve* (Free Press, 1994) by Richard Herrnstein and Charles Murray, a controversial book about race, genes, IQ, and economic mobility. The book heavily employs statistics and statistical methodology in an attempt to support the authors' positions on the relationships among these variables and their social consequences. The main theme of *The Bell Curve* can be summarized as follows:

1. Measured intelligence (IQ) is largely genetically inherited.
2. IQ is correlated positively with a variety of socioeconomic status success measures, such as prestigious job, high annual income, and high educational attainment.
3. From 1 and 2, it follows that socioeconomic successes are largely genetically caused and therefore resistant to educational and environmental interventions (such as affirmative action).

With the help of a major marketing campaign, the book became a best-seller shortly after its publication in October 1994. The underlying theme of the book—that intelligence is hereditary and tied to race and class—apparently appealed to many readers. However, reviews of *The Bell Curve* in popular magazines and newspapers were mostly negative. Social critics have described the authors as "un-American" and "pseudo-scientific racists," and their book as "alien and repellant." (On the other hand, there were defenders who labeled the book as "powerfully written" and "overwhelmingly convincing".) This Statistics in Action is based on two reviews of *The Bell Curve* that critique the statistical methodology employed by the authors and the inferences derived from the statistics. Both reviews, one published in *Chance* (Summer 1995) and the other in *The Journal of the American Statistical Association* (Dec. 1995), were written by Carnegie Mellon University professors Bernie Devlin, Stephen Fienberg, Daniel Resnick, and Kathryn Roeder. (Devlin, Fienberg, and Roeder are all statisticians; Resnick, a historian.)

Here, our focus is on the statistical method used repeatedly by Herrnstein and Murray (H&M) to support their conclusions in *The Bell Curve*: regression analysis. The following are just a few of the problems with H&M's use of regression that are identified by the Carnegie Mellon professors:

Problem 1 H&M consistently use a trio of independent variables—IQ, socioeconomic status, and age—in a series of first-order models designed to predict dependent social outcome variables such as income and unemployment. (Only on a single occasion are interaction terms incorporated.) Consider, for example, the model:

$$E(y) = \beta_0 + \beta_1 x_1 + \beta_2 x_2 + \beta_3 x_3,$$

where y = income, x_1 = IQ,x_2 = socioeconomic status, and x_3 = age. H&M utilize t-tests on the individual β parameters to assess the importance of the independent variables. As with most of the models considered in *The Bell Curve*, the

DCFOOD.DAT

Household	Food Consumption ($1,000s)	Income ($1,000s)	Household Size	Household	Food Consumption ($1,000s)	Income ($1,000s)	Household Size
1	4.2	41.1	4	14	4.1	95.2	2
2	3.4	30.5	2	15	5.5	45.6	9
3	4.8	52.3	4	16	4.5	78.5	3
4	2.9	28.9	1	17	5.0	20.5	5
5	3.5	36.5	2	18	4.5	31.6	4
6	4.0	29.8	4	19	2.8	39.9	1
7	3.6	44.3	3	20	3.9	38.6	3
8	4.2	38.1	4	21	3.6	30.2	2
9	5.1	92.0	5	22	4.6	48.7	5
10	2.7	36.0	1	23	3.8	21.2	3
11	4.0	76.9	3	24	4.5	24.3	7
12	2.7	69.9	1	25	4.0	26.9	5
13	5.5	43.1	7	26	7.5	7.3	5

estimate of β_1 in the income model is positive and statistically significant at $\alpha = .05$, and the associated t value is larger (in absolute value) than the t values associated with the other independent variables. Consequently, *H&M claim that IQ is a better predictor of income than the other two independent variables.* No attempt was made to determine whether the model was properly specified or whether the model provides an adequate fit to the data.

Problem 2 In an appendix, the authors describe multiple regression as a "mathematical procedure that yields coefficients for each of [the independent variables], indicating how much of a change in [the dependent variable] can be anticipated for a given change in any particular [independent] variable, with all the others held constant." Armed with this information and the fact that the estimate of β_1 in the model above is positive, *H&M infer that a high IQ necessarily implies (or causes) a high income, and a low IQ inevitably leads to a low income.* (Cause-and-effect inferences like this are made repeatedly throughout the book.)

Problem 3 The title of the book refers to the normal distribution and its well-known "bell-shaped" curve. There is a misconception among the general public that scores on intelligence tests (IQ) are normally distributed. In fact, most IQ scores have distributions that are decidedly skewed. Traditionally, psychologists and psychometricians have transformed these scores so that the resulting numbers have a precise normal distribution. H&M make a special point to do this. Consequently, *the measure of IQ used in all the regression models is normalized (i.e., transformed so that the resulting distribution is normal), despite the fact that regression methodology does not require predictor (independent) variables to be normally distributed.*

Problem 4 A variable that is not used as a predictor of social outcome in any of the models in *The Bell Curve* is level of education. H&M purposely omit education from the models, arguing that IQ causes education, not the other way around. Other researchers who have examined H&M's data report that *when education is included as an independent variable in the model, the effect of IQ on the dependent variable (say, income) is diminished.*

Focus

a. Comment on each of the problems identified by the Carnegie Mellon University professors in their review of *The Bell Curve*. Why do each of these problems cast a shadow on the inferences made by the authors?

b. Using the variables specified in the model above, describe how you would conduct the multiple regression analysis. (Propose a more complex model and describe the appropriate model tests, including a residual analysis.)

SPSS Histogram for Exercise 10.43

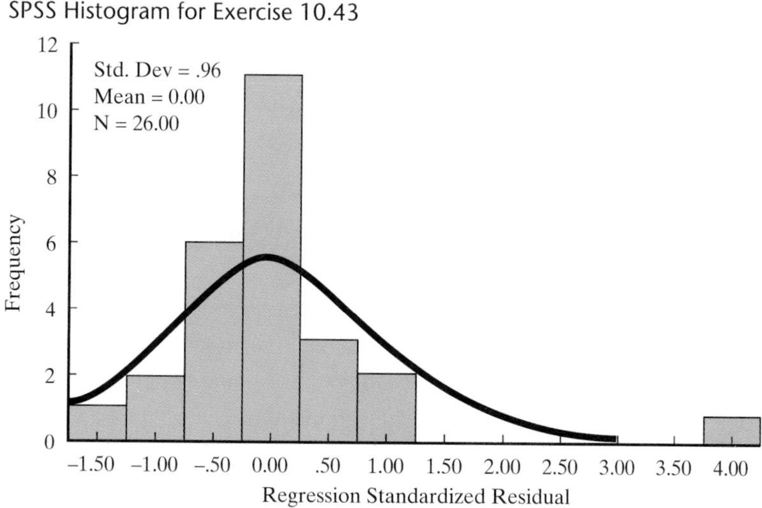

QUICK REVIEW

Key Terms

Key Formulas

$E(y) = \beta_0 + \beta_1 x_1 + \beta_2 x_2$	First-order model with two quantitative independent variables 559
$E(y) = \beta_0 + \beta_1 x + \beta_2 x^2$	Quadratic Model 602
$E(y) = \beta_0 + \beta_1 x$, where $x = \begin{cases} 1 \text{ if level A} \\ 0 \text{ if level B} \end{cases}$	Model with one qualitative variable at 2 levels 571
$s^2 = \text{MSE} = \dfrac{\text{SSE}}{n - (k+1)}$	Estimator of σ^2 for a model with k independent variables 567
$t = \dfrac{\hat{\beta}_i}{s_{\hat{\beta}_i}}$	Test statistic for testing H_0: $\beta_i = 0$ 568
$\hat{\beta}_i \pm (t_{\alpha/2}) s_{\hat{\beta}_i}$, where $t_{\alpha/2}$ depends on $n - (k+1)$ df	$100(1-\alpha)\%$ confidence interval for $\beta_i = 0$ 568
$R^2 = \dfrac{\text{SS}_{yy} - \text{SSE}}{\text{SS}_{yy}}$	Multiple coefficient of determination 581
$R_a^2 = 1 - \left[\dfrac{(n-1)}{n-(k+1)}\right](1 - R^2)$	Adjusted multiple coefficient of determination 582
$F = \dfrac{\text{MS (Model)}}{\text{MSE}} = \dfrac{R^2/k}{(1-R^2)/[n-(k+1)]}$	Test statistic for testing H_0: $\beta_1 = \beta_2 = \cdots = \beta_k = 0$ 583
$y - \hat{y}$	Regression residual 599

LANGUAGE LAB

Symbol	Pronunciation	Description
x^2	x-squared	Quadratic term that allows for curvature in the relationship between y and x
MSE	M-S-E	Mean square for error (estimates σ^2)
β_i	beta-i	Coefficient of x_i in the model
$\hat{\beta}_i$	beta-i-hat	Least squares estimate of β_i
$s_{\hat{\beta}_i}$	s of beta-i-hat	Estimated standard error of $\hat{\beta}_i$

R^2	R-squared	Multiple coefficient of determination
R_a^2	R-squared adjusted	Adjusted multiple coefficient of determination
F		Test statistic for testing global usefulness of model
$\hat{\varepsilon}$	epsilon-hat	Estimated random error, or residual
$\log(y)$	Log of y	Natural logarithm of dependent variable

SUPPLEMENTARY EXERCISES 10.44–10.57

Learning the Mechanics

10.44 Suppose you fit the model

$$y = \beta_0 + \beta_1 x_1 + \beta_2 x_1^2 + \beta_3 x_2 + \beta_4 x_1 x_2 + \varepsilon$$

to $n = 25$ data points with the following results:

$$\hat{\beta}_0 = 1.26 \quad \hat{\beta}_1 = -2.43 \quad \hat{\beta}_2 = .05 \quad \hat{\beta}_3 = .62 \quad \hat{\beta}_4 = 1.81$$

$$s_{\hat{\beta}_1} = 1.21 \quad s_{\hat{\beta}_2} = .16 \quad s_{\hat{\beta}_3} = .26 \quad s_{\hat{\beta}_4} = 1.49$$

$$\text{SSE} = .41 \quad R^2 = .83$$

a. Is there sufficient evidence to conclude that at least one of the parameters β_1, β_2, β_3, or β_4 is nonzero? Test using $\alpha = .05$.
b. Test H_0: $\beta_1 = 0$ against H_a: $\beta_1 < 0$. Use $\alpha = .05$.
c. Test H_0: $\beta_2 = 0$ against H_a: $\beta_2 > 0$. Use $\alpha = .05$.
d. Test H_0: $\beta_3 = 0$ against H_a: $\beta_3 \neq 0$. Use $\alpha = .05$.

10.45 When a multiple regression model is used for estimating the mean of the dependent variable and for predicting a new value of y, which will be narrower—the confidence interval for the mean or the prediction interval for the new y value? Why?

10.46 Suppose you have developed a regression model to explain the relationship between y and x_1, x_2, and x_3. The ranges of the variables you observed were as follows: $10 \le y \le 100$, $5 \le x_1 \le 55$, $.5 \le x_2 \le 1$, and $1{,}000 \le x_3 \le 2{,}000$. Will the error of prediction be smaller when you use the least squares equation to predict y when $x_1 = 30$, $x_2 = .6$, and $x_3 = 1{,}300$, or $x_1 = 60$, $x_2 = .4$, and $x_3 = 900$? Why?

10.47 Suppose you used MINITAB to fit the model

$$y = \beta_0 + \beta_1 x_1 + \beta_2 x_2 + \varepsilon$$

to $n = 15$ data points and you obtained the printout shown below.

a. What is the least squares prediction equation?
b. Find R^2 and interpret its value.
c. Is there sufficient evidence to indicate that the model is useful for predicting y? Conduct an F-test using $\alpha = .05$.
d. Test the null hypothesis H_0: $\beta_1 = 0$ against the alternative hypothesis H_a: $\beta_1 \neq 0$. Test using $\alpha = .05$. Draw the appropriate conclusions.
e. Find the standard deviation of the regression model and interpret it.

10.48 The first-order model $E(y) = \beta_0 + \beta_1 x_1$ was fit to $n = 19$ data points. A residual plot for the model is shown on p. 628. Is the need for a quadratic term in the model evident from the residual plot? Explain.

10.49 To model the relationship between y, a dependent variable, and x, an independent variable, a researcher has taken one measurement on y at each of three different x values. Drawing on his mathematical expertise, the researcher realizes that he can fit the second-order model

MINITAB Output for Exercise 10.47

```
The regression equation is
Y = 90.1 - 1.84 X1 + .285 X2

Predictor        Coef       StDev    t-ratio       P
Constant        90.10       23.10       3.90   0.002
X1             -1.836       0.367      -5.01   0.001
X2              0.285       0.231       1.24   0.465

s = 10.68        R-Sq = 91.6%      R-Sq(adj) = 90.2%

Analysis of Variance

SOURCE        DF        SS        MS        F        P
Regression     2     14801      7400    64.91    0.001
Error         12      1364       114
Total         14     16165
```

Residual Plot for Exercise 10.48

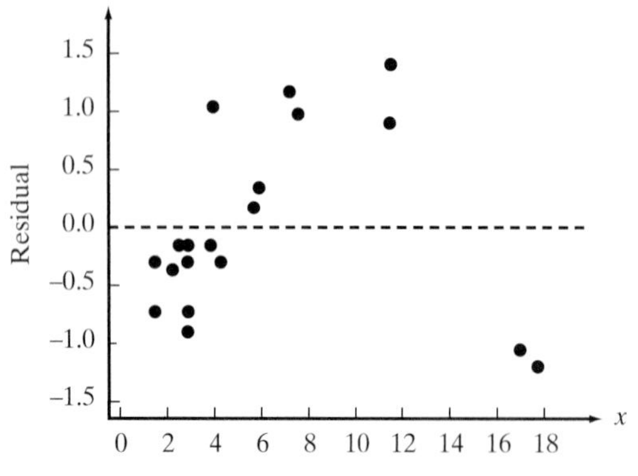

$$E(y) = \beta_0 + \beta_1 x + \beta_2 x^2$$

and it will pass exactly through all three points, yielding SSE = 0. The researcher, delighted with the "excellent" fit of the model, eagerly sets out to use it to make inferences. What problems will he encounter in attempting to make inferences?

Applying the Concepts

10.50 *Best's Review* (June 1999) compared the mortgage loan portfolios for a sample of 25 life/health insurance companies. The information in the table on page 629 is extracted from the article. Suppose you want to model the percentage of problem mortgages (y) of a company as a function of total mortgage loans (x_1), percentage of invested assets (x_2), percentage of commercial mortgages (x_3), and percentage of residential mortgages (x_4).

a. Write a first-order model for $E(y)$.

b. Fit the model of part **a** to the data and evaluate its overall usefulness. Use $\alpha = .05$.

c. Interpret the β estimates in the fitted model.

d. Construct scattergrams of y versus each of the four independent variables in the model. Which variables warrant inclusion in the model as second-order (i.e., squared) terms?

10.51 Emergency services (EMS) personnel are constantly exposed to traumatic situations. However, few researchers have studied the psychological stress that EMS personnel may experience. The *Journal of Consulting and Clinical Psychology* (June 1995) reported on a study of EMS rescue workers who responded to the I-880 freeway collapse during the 1989 San Francisco earthquake. The goal of the study was to identify the predictors of symptomatic distress in the EMS workers. One of the distress variables studied was the Global Symptom Index (GSI). Several models for GSI, y, were considered based on the following independent variables:

x_1 = Critical Incident Exposure scale (CIE)
x_2 = Hogan Personality Inventory-Adjustment scale (HPI-A)
x_3 = Years of experience (EXP)
x_4 = Locus of Control scale (LOC)
x_5 = Social Support scale (SS)
x_6 = Dissociative Experiences scale (DES)
x_7 = Peritraumatic Dissociation Experiences Questionnaire, self-report (PDEQ-SR)

a. Write a first-order model for $E(y)$ as a function of the first five independent variables, x_1–x_5.

b. The model of part **a**, fitted to data collected for $n = 147$ EMS workers, yielded the following results: $R^2 = .469$, $F = 34.47$, p-value $< .001$. Interpret these results.

c. Write a first-order model for $E(y)$ as a function of all seven independent variables, x_1–x_7.

d. The model, part **c**, yielded $R^2 = .603$. Interpret this result.

e. The t-tests for testing the DES and PDEQ-SR variables both yielded a p-value of .001. Interpret these results.

10.52 Since the Great Depression of the 1930s, the link between the suicide rate and the state of the economy has been the subject of much research. Research exploring this link using regression analysis was reported in the *Journal of Socio-Economics* (Spring, 1992). The researchers collected data from a 45-year period on the following variables:

y = Suicide rate
x_1 = Unemployment rate
x_2 = Percentage of females in the labor force
x_3 = Divorce rate
x_4 = Logarithm of Gross National Product (GNP)
x_5 = Annual percent change in GNP

One of the models explored by the researchers was a multiple regression model relating y to linear terms in x_1 through x_5. The least squares model below resulted (the observed significance levels of the β estimates are shown in parentheses beneath the estimates):

$$\hat{y} = .002 + \underset{(.002)}{.0204x_1} - \underset{(.02)}{.0231x_2} + \underset{(>.10)}{.0765x_3} + \underset{(>.10)}{.2760x_4} + \underset{(>.10)}{.0018x_5}$$

$R^2 = .45$

a. Interpret the value of R^2. Is there sufficient evidence to indicate that the model is useful for predicting the suicide rate? Use $\alpha = .05$.

b. Interpret each of the coefficients in the model, and each of the corresponding significance levels.

c. Is there sufficient evidence to indicate that the unemployment rate is a useful predictor of the suicide rate? Use $\alpha = .05$.

10.53 To meet the increasing demand for new software products, many systems development experts have adopted a prototyping methodology. The effects of

BESTINS.DAT

Company	Total Mortgage Loan, x_1	% Invested Assets, x_2	% Commercial Mortgages, x_3	% Residential Mortgages, x_4	% Problem Mortgages, y
TIAA Group	$18,803,163	20.7	100.0	0.0	11.4
Metropolitan Insurance	18,171,162	13.9	77.8	1.6	3.8
Prudential of Am Group	16,213,150	12.9	87.4	2.3	4.1
Principal Mutual IA	11,940,345	30.3	98.8	1.2	32.6
Northwestern Mutual	10,834,616	17.8	99.5	0.0	2.2
Cigna Group	10,181,124	25.1	99.8	0.2	11.1
John Hancock Group	8,229,523	20.4	82.0	0.1	12.2
Aegon USA Inc.	7,695,198	17.7	73.0	24.7	6.4
New York Life	7,088,003	9.4	92.2	7.8	2.4
Nationwide	5,328,142	26.3	100.0	0.0	7.5
Massachusetts Mutual	4,965,287	12.2	78.6	21.4	6.3
Equitable Group	4,905,123	12.7	63.6	0.0	27.0
Aetna US Healthcare Group	3,974,881	10.5	94.1	5.4	8.7
American Express Financial	3,655,292	13.9	100.0	0.0	2.1
ING Group	3,505,206	16.2	99.8	0.2	0.7
American General	3,359,650	6.4	99.8	0.2	2.1
Lincoln National	3,264,860	11.5	99.9	0.1	2.2
SunAmerica Inc.	3,909,177	15.7	100.0	0.0	2.6
Allstate	2,987,144	10.9	100.0	0.0	2.1
Travelers Insurance Group	2,978,628	10.3	74.9	0.1	3.2
GE Capital Corp. Group	2,733,981	7.5	99.7	0.3	0.7
ReliaStar Financial Corp.	2,342,992	16.2	69.9	30.0	6.4
General American Life	2,107,592	15.2	99.8	0.2	1.3
State Farm Group	2,027,648	8.6	97.6	2.4	0.1
Pacific Mutual Life	1,945,392	9.7	96.4	3.6	6.1

Source: *Best's Review*, (Life/Health), June 1999, p. 35.

prototyping on the system development life cycle (SDLC) was investigated in the *Journal of Computer Information Systems* (Spring 1993). A survey of 500 randomly selected corporate level MIS managers was conducted. Three potential independent variables were: (1) *importance* of prototyping to each phase of the SDLC; (2) degree of *support* prototyping provides for the SDLC; and (3) degree to which prototyping *replaces* each phase of the SDLC. The table on the next page gives the pairwise correlations of the three variables in the survey data for one particular phase of the SDLC. Use this information to assess the degree of multicollinearity in the survey data. Would you recommend using all three independent variables in a regression analysis? Explain.

Results for Exercise 10.53

Variable Pairs	Correlation Coefficient, r
Importance–Replace	.2682
Importance–Support	.6991
Replace–Support	−.0531

Source: Hardgrave, B. C., Doke, E. R., and Swanson, N. E. "Prototyping effects of the system development life cycle: An empirical study." *Journal of Computer Information Systems,* Vol. 33, No. 3, Spring 1993, p. 16 (Table 1).

10.54 Traffic forecasters at the Minnesota Department of Transportation (MDOT) use regression analysis to estimate weekday peak-hour traffic volumes on existing and proposed roadways. In particular, they model y, the peak-hour volume (typically, the volume between 7 and 8 A.M.), as a function of x_1, the road's total volume for the day. For one project involving the redesign of a section of Interstate 494, the forecasters collected $n = 72$ observations of peak-hour traffic volume and 24-hour weekday traffic volume using electronic sensors that count vehicles. The data are provided in the table below.

a. Construct a scattergram for the data, plotting peak-hour volume y against 24-hour volume x_1. Note the isolated group of observations at the top of the scattergram. Investigators discovered that all of these data points were collected at the intersection of Interstate 35W and 46th Street. (These are observations 55–72 in the table.) While all other locations in the sample were three-lane highways, this location was unique in that the highway widens to four lanes just north of the electronic sensor. Consequently, the forecasters decided to include a dummy variable to account for a difference between the I-35W location and all other locations.

b. Propose a first-order model for $E(y)$ as a function of 24-hour volume x_1 and the dummy variable for location.

c. Using an available statistical software package, fit the model of part **b** to the data. Interpret the results.

d. Conduct a residual analysis of the model, part **b.** Evaluate the assumptions of normality and constant error variance, and determine whether any outliers exist.

10.55 The audience for a product's advertising can be divided into two segments according to the degree of exposure received as a result of the advertising. These segments are groups of consumers who receive high (H) or low (L) exposure to the advertising. A company is interested in exploring whether its advertising effort affects its product's market share. Accordingly, the company

MINNDOT.DAT

Observation Number	Peak-Hour Volume	24-Hour Volume	I-35	Observation Number	Peak-Hour Volume	24-Hour Volume	I-35	Observation Number	Peak-Hour Volume	24-Hour Volume	I-35
1	1,990.94	20,070	0	25	1,923.87	18,184	0	49	1,978.72	24,249	0
2	1,989.63	21,234	0	26	1,922.79	16,926	0	50	1,975.29	23,321	0
3	1,986.96	20,633	0	27	1,917.64	19,062	0	51	1,973.55	22,842	0
4	1,986.96	20,676	0	28	1,916.17	18,043	0	52	1,973.91	20,626	0
5	1,983.78	19,818	0	29	1,916.17	18,043	0	53	1,972.92	26,166	0
6	1,983.13	19,931	0	30	1,916.13	16,691	0	54	1,966.65	21,755	0
7	1,982.47	19,266	0	31	1,912.49	17,339	0	55	2,120.00	20,250	1
8	1,981.53	19,658	0	32	1,912.49	17,339	0	56	2,140.00	20,251	1
9	1,979.83	19,203	0	33	1,909.98	17,867	0	57	2,160.00	21,852	1
10	1,979.83	19,958	0	34	1,907.04	17,773	0	58	2,186.52	23,511	1
11	1,978.40	19,152	0	35	1,907.46	17,678	0	59	2,180.29	22,431	1
12	1,978.90	21,651	0	36	1,905.14	18,024	0	60	2,174.03	23,734	1
13	1,977.38	20,198	0	37	1,902.37	17,405	0	61	2,174.03	23,734	1
14	1,972.87	20,508	0	38	2,017.76	23,517	0	62	2,167.97	23,387	1
15	1,964.45	19,783	0	39	2,009.38	23,017	0	63	2,160.02	24,885	1
16	1,962.85	20,815	0	40	2,007.10	22,808	0	64	2,160.54	23,332	1
17	1,964.26	20,105	0	41	2,007.28	23,152	0	65	2,159.72	23,838	1
18	1,961.85	20,500	0	42	2,004.17	24,352	0	66	2,155.61	23,662	1
19	1,961.26	19,593	0	43	1,997.58	20,939	0	67	2,147.93	22,948	1
20	1,958.97	20,818	0	44	1,994.53	21,822	0	68	2,147.93	22,948	1
21	1,943.78	17,480	0	45	1,984.70	22,918	0	69	2,147.85	23,551	1
22	1,927.83	17,768	0	46	1,984.01	21,129	0	70	2,144.23	21,637	1
23	1,928.36	17,659	0	47	1,983.17	21,674	0	71	2,142.41	23,543	1
24	1,925.65	18,357	0	48	1,982.02	26,148	0	72	2,137.39	22,594	1

Source: John Sem. Director: Allan E. Pint, State Traffic Forecast Engineer; and James Page Sr., Transportation Planner, Traffic and Commodities Studies Section, Minnesota Department of Transportation, St. Paul, Minnesota.

identifies 24 sample groups of consumers who have been exposed to its advertising, twelve groups at each exposure level. Then, the company determines its product's market share within each group.

a. Write a regression model that expresses the company's market share as a function of advertising exposure level. Define all terms in your model, and list any assumptions you make about them.
b. The data in the table below were obtained by the company. Fit the model you constructed in part **a** to the data.

MKTSHR.DAT

Market Share Within Group	Exposure Level
10.1	L
10.3	L
10.0	L
10.3	L
10.2	L
10.5	L
10.6	L
11.0	L
11.2	L
10.9	L
10.8	L
11.0	L
12.2	H
12.1	H
11.8	H
12.6	H
11.9	H
12.9	H
10.7	H
10.8	H
11.0	H
10.5	H
10.8	H
10.6	H

c. Is there evidence to suggest that the firm's expected market share differs for the two levels of advertising exposure? Test using $\alpha = .05$.

To determine whether extra personnel are needed for the day, the owners of a water adventure park would like to find a model that would allow them to predict the day's attendance each morning before opening based on the day of the week and weather conditions. The model is of the form

$$E(y) = \beta_0 + \beta_1 x_1 + \beta_2 x_2 + \beta_3 x_3$$

where

y = Daily admission

$$x_1 = \begin{cases} 1 & \text{if weekend} \\ 0 & \text{otherwise} \end{cases} \quad \text{(dummy variable)}$$

$$x_2 = \begin{cases} 1 & \text{if sunny} \\ 0 & \text{if overcast} \end{cases} \quad \text{(dummy variable)}$$

x_3 = Predicted daily high temperature (°F)

These data were recorded for a random sample of 30 days, and a regression model was fitted to the data. The least squares analysis produced the following results:

$$\hat{y} = -105 + 25x_1 + 100x_2 + 10x_3$$

with

$$s_{\hat{\beta}_1} = 10 \qquad s_{\hat{\beta}_2} = 30 \qquad s_{\hat{\beta}_3} = 4 \qquad R^2 = .65$$

a. Interpret the estimated model coefficients.
b. Is there sufficient evidence to conclude that this model is useful for the prediction of daily attendance? Use $\alpha = .05$.
c. Is there sufficient evidence to conclude that the mean attendance increases on weekends? Use $\alpha = .10$.
d. Use the model to predict the attendance on a sunny weekday with a predicted high temperature of 95°F.
e. Suppose the 90% prediction interval for part **d** is (645, 1,245). Interpret this interval.

10.57 Many colleges and universities develop regression models for predicting the GPA of incoming freshmen. This predicted GPA can then be used to make admission decisions. Although most models use many independent variables to predict GPA, we will illustrate by choosing two variables:

x_1 = Verbal score on college entrance examination (percentile)
x_2 = Mathematics score on college entrance examination (percentile)

The data in the table on page 632 are obtained for a random sample of 40 freshmen at one college. The SPSS printout corresponding to the model $y = \beta_0 + \beta_1 x_1 + \beta_2 x_2 + \varepsilon$ is shown below the data.

a. Interpret the least squares estimates β_1 and β_2 in the context of this application.
b. Interpret the standard deviation and the adjusted coefficient of determination of the regression model in the context of this application.
c. Is this model useful for predicting GPA? Conduct a statistical test to justify your answer.
d. Sketch the relationship between predicted GPA, $\hat{y}$, and verbal score, x_1, for the following mathematics scores: $x_2 = 60, 75,$ and 90.
e. The residuals from the first-order model are plotted against x_1 and x_2 and shown on p. 633. Analyze the two plots, and determine whether visual evidence exists that curvature (a quadratic term) for either x_1 or x_2 should be added to the model.

COLLGPA.DAT

Verbal, x_1	Mathematics, x_2	GPA, y	Verbal, x_1	Mathematics, x_2	GPA, y	Verbal, x_1	Mathematics, x_2	GPA, y
81	87	3.49	83	76	3.75	97	80	3.27
68	99	2.89	64	66	2.70	77	90	3.47
57	86	2.73	83	72	3.15	49	54	1.30
100	49	1.54	93	54	2.28	39	81	1.22
54	83	2.56	74	59	2.92	87	69	3.23
82	86	3.43	51	75	2.48	70	95	3.82
75	74	3.59	79	75	3.45	57	89	2.93
58	98	2.86	81	62	2.76	74	67	2.83
55	54	1.46	50	69	1.90	87	93	3.84
49	81	2.11	72	70	3.01	90	65	3.01
64	76	2.69	54	52	1.48	81	76	3.33
66	59	2.16	65	79	2.98	84	69	3.06
80	61	2.60	56	78	2.58			
100	85	3.30	98	67	2.73			

SPSS Output for Exercise 10.57

```
Multiple R            .82527
R Square              .68106
Adjusted R Square     .66382
Standard Error        .40228

Analysis of Variance
                    DF      Sum of Squares      Mean Square
Regression           2          12.78595          6.39297
Residual            37           5.98755           .16183

F =        39.50530        Signif F = .0000

------------------Variables in the Equation------------------

Variable                B          SE B          Beta          T  Sig T

X1                 .02573  4.02357E-03       .59719      6.395  .0000
X2                 .03361  4.92751E-03       .63702      6.822  .0000
(Constant)       -1.57054       .49375                  -3.181  .0030
```

SPSS Plots for Exercise 10.57

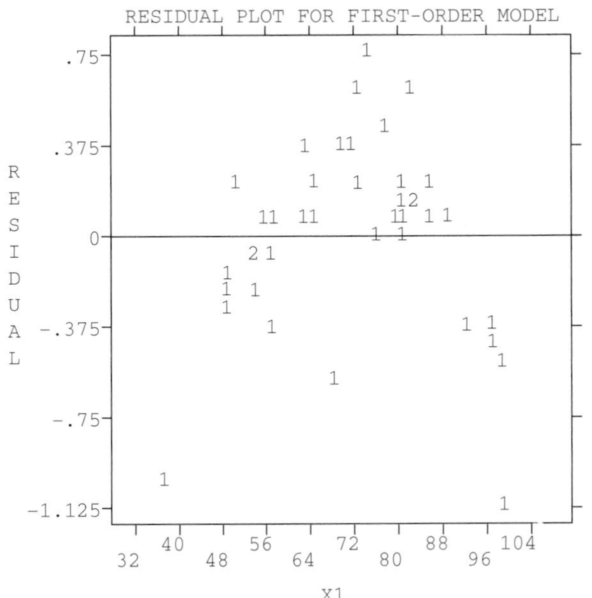

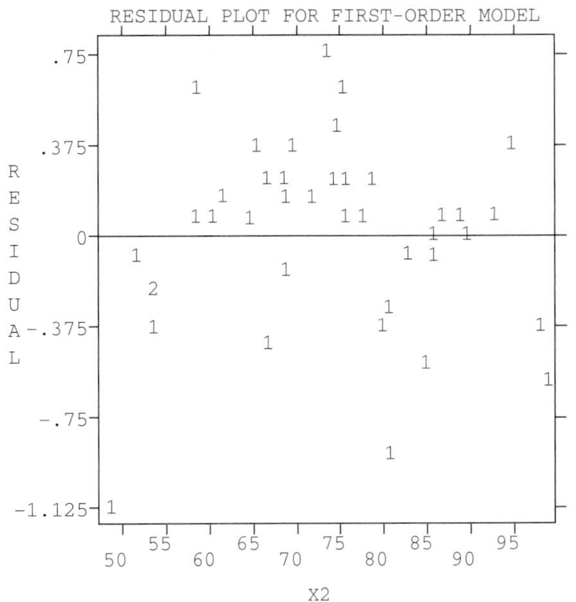

Real-World Case: The Condo Sales Case
(A Case Covering Chapters 9 and 10)

This case involves an investigation of the factors that affect the sale price of oceanside condominium units. It represents an extension of an analysis of the same data by Herman Kelting (1979). Although condo sale prices have increased dramatically over the past 20 years, the relationship between these factors and sale price remain about the same. Consequently, the data provide valuable insight into today's condominium sales market.

The sales data were obtained for a new oceanside condominium complex consisting of two adjacent and connected eight-floor buildings. The complex contains 200 units of equal size (approximately 500 square feet each). The locations of the buildings relative to the ocean, the swimming pool, the parking lot, etc., are shown in the accompanying figure. There are several features of the complex that you should note:

1. The units facing south, called *ocean-view,* face the beach and ocean. In addition, units in building 1 have a good view of the pool. Units to the rear of the building, called *bay-view,* face the parking lot and an area of land that ultimately borders a bay. The view from the upper floors of these units is primarily of wooded, sandy terrain. The bay is very distant and barely visible.
2. The only elevator in the complex is located at the east end of building 1, as are the office and the game room. People moving to or from the higher floor units in

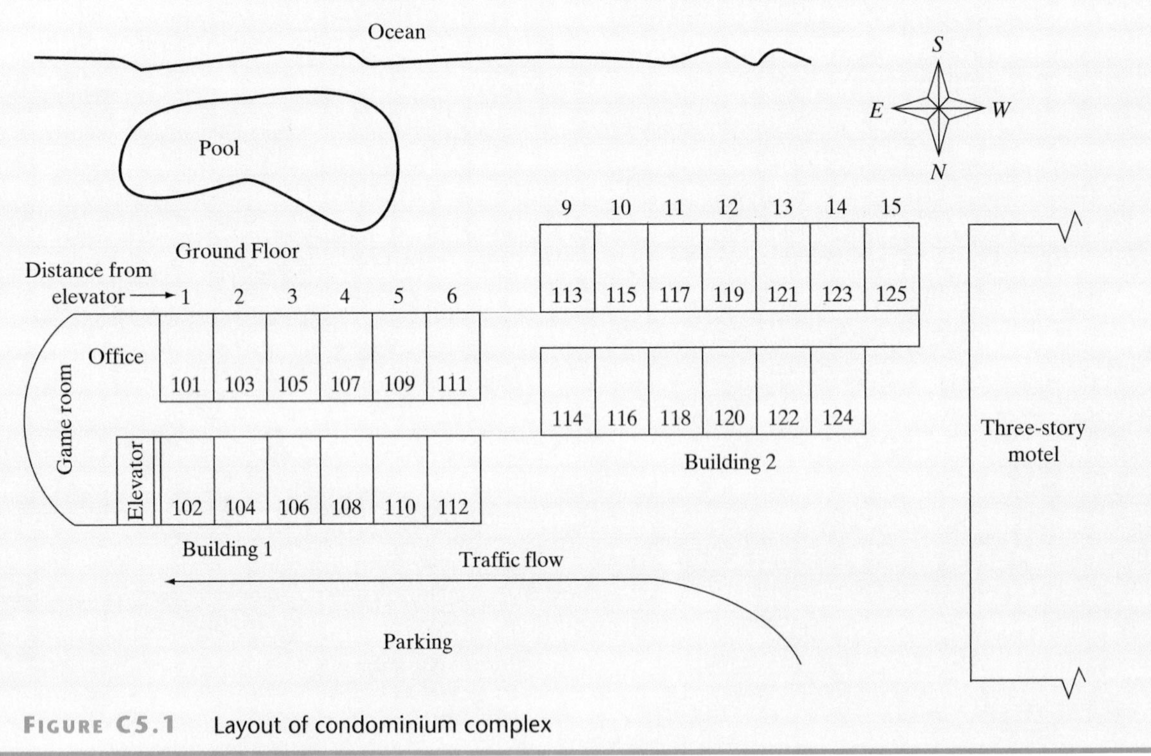

FIGURE C5.1 Layout of condominium complex

building 2 would likely use the elevator and move through the passages to their units. Thus, units on the higher floors and at a greater distance from the elevator would be less convenient; they would require greater effort in moving baggage, groceries, etc., and would be farther away from the game room, the office, and the swimming pool. These units also possess an advantage: there would be the least amount of traffic through the hallways in the area and hence they are the most private.

3. Lower-floor oceanside units are most suited to active people; they open onto the beach, ocean, and pool. They are within easy reach of the game room and they are easily reached from the parking area.
4. Checking the layout of the condominium complex, you discover that some of the units in the center of the complex, units ending in numbers 11 and 14, have part of their view blocked.
5. The condominium complex was completed at the time of the 1975 recession; sales were slow and the developer was forced to sell most of the units at auction approximately 18 months after opening. Consequently, the auction data are completely buyer-specified and hence consumer-oriented in contrast to most other real estate sales data which are, to a high degree, seller and broker specified.
6. Many unsold units in the complex were furnished by the developer and rented prior to the auction. Consequently, some of the units bid on and sold at auction had furniture, others did not.

This condominium complex is obviously unique. For example, the single elevator located at one end of the complex produces a remarkably high level of both inconvenience and privacy for the people occupying units on the top floors in building 2. Consequently, the developer is unsure of how the height of the unit (floor number), distance of the unit from the elevator, presence or absence of an ocean view, etc., affect the prices of the units sold at auction. To investigate these relationships, the following data were recorded for each of the 106 units sold at the auction:

1. *Sale price.* Measured in hundreds of dollars (adjusted for inflation).
2. *Floor height.* The floor location of the unit; the variable levels are 1, 2, . . ., 8.
3. *Distance from elevator.* This distance, measured along the length of the complex, is expressed in number of condominium units. An additional two units of distance was added to the units in building 2 to account for the walking distance in the connecting area between the two buildings. Thus, the distance of unit 105 from the elevator would be 3, and the distance between unit 113 and the elevator would be 9. The variable levels are 1, 2, . . ., 15.
4. *View of ocean.* The presence or absence of an ocean view is recorded for each unit and specified with a dummy variable (1 if the unit possessed an ocean view and 0 if not). Note that units not possessing an ocean view would face the parking lot.
5. *End unit.* We expect the partial reduction of view of end units on the ocean side (numbers ending in 11) to reduce their sale price. The ocean view of these end units is partially blocked by building 2. This qualitative variable is also specified with a dummy variable (1 if the unit has a unit number ending in 11 and 0 if not).
6. *Furniture.* The presence or absence of furniture is recorded for each unit, and represented with a single dummy variable (1 if the unit was furnished and 0 if not).

Your objective for this case is to build a regression model that accurately predicts the sale price of a condominium unit sold at auction. Prepare a professional document that presents the results of your analysis. Include graphs that demonstrate how each of the independent variables in your model affects auction price. A layout of the data file is described below.

CONDO.DAT (Number of Observations: 106)

Variable	Column(s)	Type
PRICE	1—3	QN
FLOOR	5	QN
DISTANCE	7—8	QN
VIEW	10	QL
ENDUNIT	12	QL
FURNISH	14	QL

[*Important Note*: You may want to consider cross-product terms of the form x_1x_2 in your model. These terms, called *interaction* terms, allow the relationship between y and one of the independent variables, say x_1, to change as the value of the other independent variable, x_2, changes.]

Chapter 11

METHODS FOR QUALITY IMPROVEMENT

CONTENTS

STATISTICS IN ACTION

Where We've Been

In Chapters 5–8 we described methods for making inferences about populations based on sample data. In Chapters 9–10 we focused on modeling relationships between variables using regression analysis.

Where We're Going

In this chapter, we turn our attention to processes. Recall from Chapter 1 that a process is a series of actions or operations that transform inputs to outputs. This chapter describes methods for improving processes and the quality of the output they produce.

Over the last two decades U.S. firms have been seriously challenged by products of superior quality from overseas, particularly from Japan. Japan currently produces 25% of the cars sold in the United States. In 1989, for the first time, the top-selling car in the United States was made in Japan: the Honda Accord. Although it's an American invention, virtually all VCRs are produced in Japan. Only one U.S. firm still manufactures televisions; the rest are made in Japan.

To meet this competitive challenge, more and more U.S. firms—both manufacturing and service firms—have begun quality-improvement initiatives of their own. Many of these firms now stress **total quality management** (TQM), i.e., the management of quality in all phases and aspects of their business, from the design of their products to production, distribution, sales, and service.

Broadly speaking, TQM is concerned with (1) finding out what it is that the customer wants, (2) translating those wants into a product or service design, and (3) producing a product or service that meets or exceeds the specifications of the design. In this chapter we focus primarily on the third of these three areas and its major problem—product and service variation.

Variation is inherent in the output of all production and service processes. No two parts produced by a given machine are the same; no two transactions performed by a given bank teller are the same. Why is this a problem? With variation in output comes variation in the quality of the product or service. If this variation is unacceptable to customers, sales are lost, profits suffer, and the firm may not survive.

The existence of this ever-present variation has made statistical methods and statistical training vitally important to industry. In this chapter we present some of the tools and methods currently employed by firms worldwide to monitor and reduce product and service variation.

11.1 QUALITY, PROCESSES, AND SYSTEMS

Quality

Before describing various tools and methods that can be used to monitor and improve the quality of products and services, we need to consider what is meant by the term *quality*. Quality can be defined from several different perspectives. To the engineers and scientists who design products, quality typically refers to the amount of some ingredient or attribute possessed by the product. For example, high-quality ice cream contains a large amount of butterfat. High-quality rugs have a large number of knots per square inch. A high-quality shirt or blouse has 22 to 26 stitches per inch.

To managers, engineers, and workers involved in the production of a product (or the delivery of a service), quality usually means conformance to requirements, or the degree to which the product or service conforms to its design specifications. For example, in order to fit properly, the cap of a particular molded plastic bottle must be between 1.0000 inch and 1.0015 inches in diameter. Caps that do not conform to this requirement are considered to be of inferior quality. For an example in a service operation, consider the service provided to customers in a fast-food restaurant. A particular restaurant has been designed to serve customers within two minutes of the time their order is placed. If it takes more than two minutes, the service does not conform to specifications and is considered to be of inferior quality. Using this production-based interpretation of quality, well-made products are high quality; poorly made products are low quality. Thus, a well-made Rolls Royce and a well-made Chevrolet Nova are both high-quality cars.

Although quality can be defined from either the perspective of the designers or the producers of a product, in the final analysis both definitions should be derived from the needs and preferences of the *user* of the product or service. A firm that produces goods that no one wants to purchase cannot stay in business. We define quality accordingly.

DEFINITION 11.1

The **quality** of a good or service is indicated by the extent to which it satisfies the needs and preferences of its users.

Consumers' needs and wants shape their perceptions of quality. Thus, to produce a high-quality product, it is necessary to study the needs and wants of consumers. This is typically one of the major functions of a firm's marketing department. Once the consumer research has been conducted, it is necessary to translate consumers' desires into a product design. This design must then be translated into a production plan and production specifications that, if properly implemented, will turn out a product with characteristics that will satisfy users' needs and wants. In short, consumer perceptions of quality play a role in all phases and aspects of a firm's operations.

But what product characteristics are consumers looking for? What is it that influences users' perceptions of quality? This is the kind of knowledge that firms need in order to develop and deliver high-quality goods and services. The basic elements of quality are summarized in the eight dimensions shown in the box.

The Eight Dimensions of Quality*

1. **Performance:** The primary operating characteristics of the product. For an automobile, these would include acceleration, handling, smoothness of ride, gas mileage, etc.
2. **Features:** The "bells and whistles" that supplement the product's basic functions. Examples include CD players and digital clocks on cars and the frequent-flyer mileage and free drinks offered by airlines.
3. **Reliability:** Reflects the probability that the product will operate properly within a given period of time.
4. **Conformance:** The extent or degree to which a product meets preestablished standards. This is reflected in, for example, a pharmaceutical manufacturer's concern that the plastic bottles it orders for its drugs have caps that are between 1.0000 and 1.0015 inches in diameter, as specified in the order.
5. **Durability:** The life of the product. If repair is possible, durability relates to the length of time a product can be used before replacement is judged to be preferable to continued repair.
6. **Serviceability:** The ease of repair, speed of repair, and competence and courtesy of the repair staff.
7. **Aesthetics:** How a product looks, feels, sounds, smells, or tastes.
8. **Other perceptions that influence judgments of quality:** Such factors as a firm's reputation and the images of the firm and its products that are created through advertising.

In order to design and produce products of high quality, it is necessary to translate the characteristics described in the box into product attributes that can

*Garvin, D. *Managing Quality.* New York: Free Press/Macmillan, 1988.

be built into the product by the manufacturer. That is, user preferences must be interpreted in terms of product variables over which the manufacturer has control. For example, in considering the performance characteristics of a particular brand of wooden pencil, users may indicate a preference for being able to use the pencil for longer periods between sharpenings. The manufacturer may translate this performance characteristic into one or more measurable physical characteristics such as wood hardness, lead hardness, and lead composition. Besides being used to design high-quality products, such variables are used in the process of monitoring and improving quality during production.

Processes

Much of this textbook focuses on methods for using sample data drawn from a population to learn about that population. In this chapter and the next, however, our attention is not on populations, but on processes—such as manufacturing processes—and the output that they generate. In general, a process is defined as follows:

DEFINITION 11.2

A **process** is a series of actions or operations that transforms inputs to outputs. A process produces output over time.

Processes can be organizational or personal in nature. Organizational processes are those associated with organizations such as businesses and governments. Perhaps the best example is a manufacturing process, which consists of a series of operations, performed by people and machines, whereby inputs such as raw materials and parts are converted into finished products (the outputs). Examples include automobile assembly lines, oil refineries, and steel mills. Personal processes are those associated with your private life. The series of steps you go through each morning to get ready for school or work can be thought of as a process. Through turning off the alarm clock, showering, dressing, eating, and opening the garage door, you transform yourself from a sleeping person to one who is ready to interact with the outside world. Figure 11.1 presents a general description of a process and its inputs.

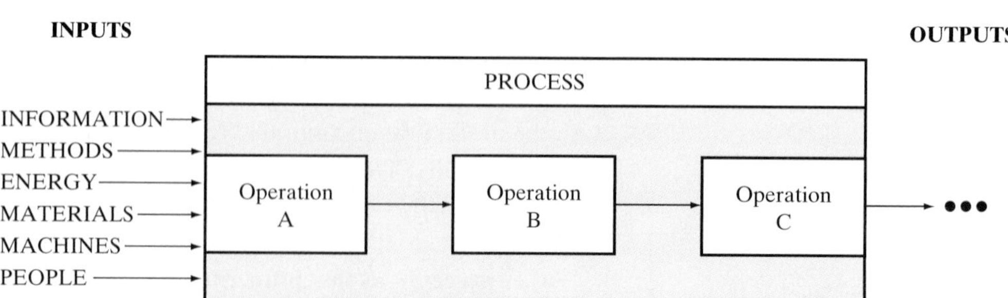

FIGURE 11.1 Graphical depiction of a process and its inputs

It is useful to think of processes as *adding value* to the inputs of the process. Manufacturing processes, for example, are designed so that the value of the outputs to potential customers exceeds the value of the inputs—otherwise the firm would have no demand for its products and would not survive.

Systems

To understand what causes variation in process output and how processes and their output can be improved, we must understand the role that processes play in *systems*.

DEFINITION 11.3

A **system** is a collection or arrangement of interacting processes that has an ongoing purpose or mission. A system receives inputs from its environment, transforms those inputs to outputs, and delivers them to its environment. In order to survive, a system uses feedback (i.e., information) from its environment to understand and adapt to changes in its environment.

Figure 11.2 presents a model of a basic system. As an example of a system, consider a manufacturing company. It has a collection of interacting processes—marketing research, engineering, purchasing, receiving, production, sales, distribution, billing, etc. Its mission is to make money for its owners, to provide high-quality working conditions for its employees, and to stay in business. The firm receives raw materials and parts (inputs) from outside vendors which, through its production processes, it transforms to finished goods (outputs). The finished goods are distributed to its customers. Through its marketing research, the firm "listens" to (receives feedback from) its customers and potential customers in order to change or adapt its processes and products to meet (or exceed) the needs, preferences, and expectations of the marketplace.

FIGURE 11.2 Model of a basic system

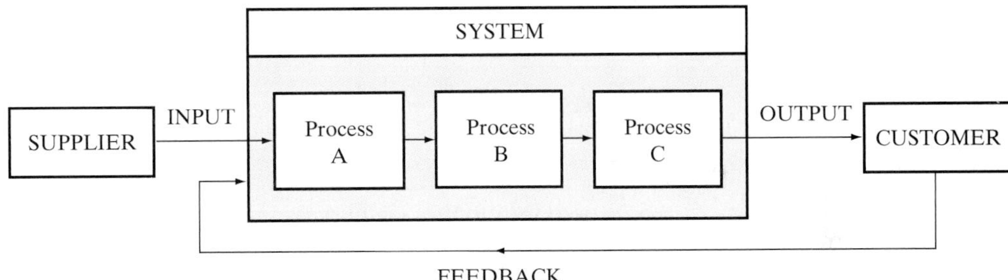

Since systems are collections of processes, the various types of system inputs are the same as those listed in Figure 11.1 for processes. System outputs are products or services. These outputs may be physical objects made, assembled, repaired, or moved by the system; or they may be symbolical, such as information, ideas, or knowledge. For example, a brokerage house supplies customers with information about stocks and bonds and the markets where they are traded.

Two important points about systems and the output of their processes are: (1) No two items produced by a process are the same; (2) Variability is an inherent characteristic of the output of all processes. This is illustrated in Figure 11.3. No two cars produced by the same assembly line are the same: No two windshields are the same; no two wheels are the same; no two tires are the same; no two hubcaps are the same. The same thing can be said for processes that deliver services. Consider the services offered at the teller windows of a bank to two customers waiting in two lines. Will they wait in line the same amount of time? Will they be serviced by tellers with the same degree of expertise and with the same personalities? Assuming the customers' transactions are the same, will they take the same amount of time to execute? The answer to all these questions is no.

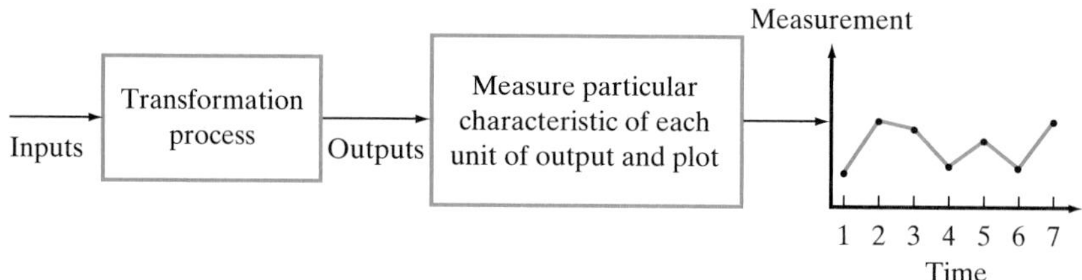

FIGURE 11.3
Output variation

In general, variation in output is caused by the six factors listed in the box.

The Six Major Sources of Process Variation

1. People
2. Machines
3. Materials
4. Methods
5. Measurement
6. Environment

Awareness of this ever-present process variation has made training in statistical thinking and statistical methods highly valued by industry. By **statistical thinking** we mean the knack of recognizing variation, and exploiting it in problem solving and decision-making. The remainder of this chapter is devoted to statistical tools for monitoring process variation.

11.2 STATISTICAL CONTROL

For the rest of this chapter we turn our attention to **control charts**—graphical devices used for monitoring process variation, for identifying when to take action to improve the process, and for assisting in diagnosing the causes of **process variation**. Control charts, developed by Walter Shewhart of Bell Laboratories in the mid 1920s, are the tool of choice for continuously monitoring processes. Before we go into the details of control chart construction and use, however, it is important that you have a fuller understanding of process variation. To this end, we discuss patterns of variation in this section.

As was discussed in Chapter 2, the proper graphical method for describing the variation of process output is a *time series plot*, sometimes called a **run chart.** Recall that in a time series plot the measurements of interest are plotted against time or are plotted in the order in which the measurements were made, as in Figure 11.4. Whenever you face the task of analyzing data that were generated over time, your first reaction should be to plot them. The human eye is one of our most sensitive statistical instruments. Take advantage of that sensitivity by plotting the data and allowing your eyes to seek out patterns in the data.

Let's begin thinking about process variation by examining the plot in Figure 11.4 more closely. The measurements, taken from a paint manufacturing process, are the weights of 50 one-gallon cans of paint that were consecutively filled by the same filling head (nozzle). The weights were plotted in the order of production. Do you detect any systematic, persistent patterns in the sequence of weights? For example, do the weights tend to drift steadily upward or downward over time? Do they oscillate—high, then low, then high, then low, etc.?

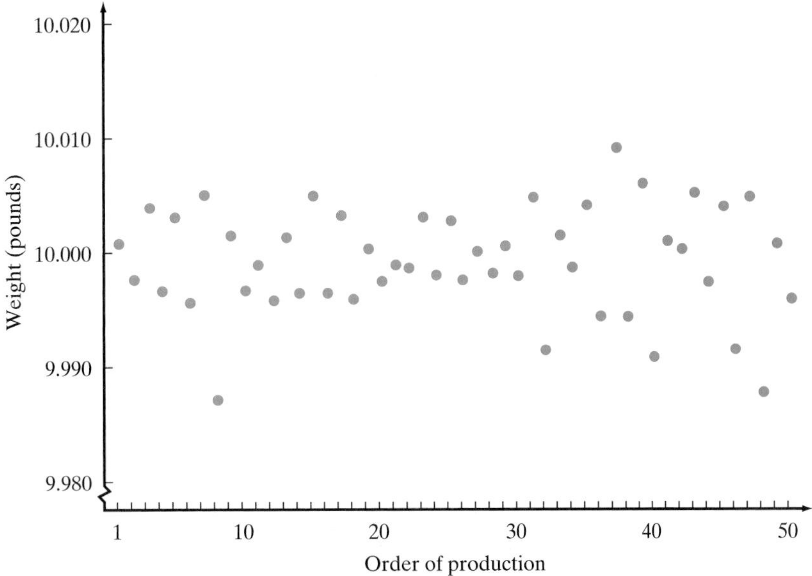

FIGURE 11.4
Time series plot of fill weights for 50 consecutively produced gallon cans of paint

To assist your visual examination of this or any other time series plot, Roberts (1991) recommends enhancing the basic plot in two ways. First, compute (or simply estimate) the mean of the set of 50 weights and draw a horizontal line on the graph at the level of the mean. This **centerline** gives you a point of reference in searching for patterns in the data. Second, using straight lines, connect each of the plotted weights in the order in which they were produced. This helps display the sequence of the measurements. Both enhancements are shown in Figure 11.5.

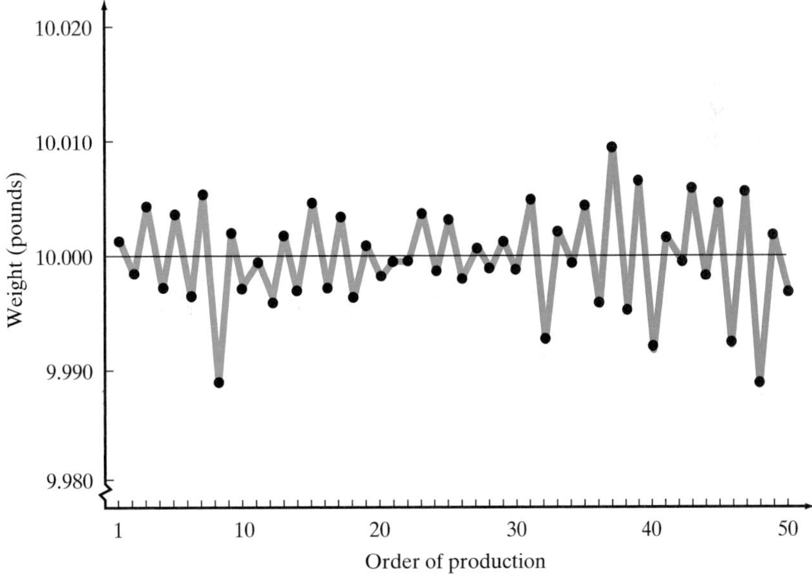

FIGURE 11.5
An enhanced version of the paint fill time series

Now do you see a pattern in the data? Successive points alternate up and down, high then low, in an **oscillating sequence.** In this case, the points alternate above and below the centerline. This pattern was caused by a valve in the paint-filling machine that tended to stick in a partially closed position every other time it operated.

Other patterns of process variation are shown in Figure 11.6. We discuss several of them later.

In trying to describe process variation and diagnose its causes, it helps to think of the sequence of measurements of the output variable (e.g., weight, length, number of defects) as having been generated in the following way:

1. At any point in time, the output variable of interest can be described by a particular probability distribution (or relative frequency distribution). This dis-

FIGURE 11.6
Patterns of process variation: Some examples

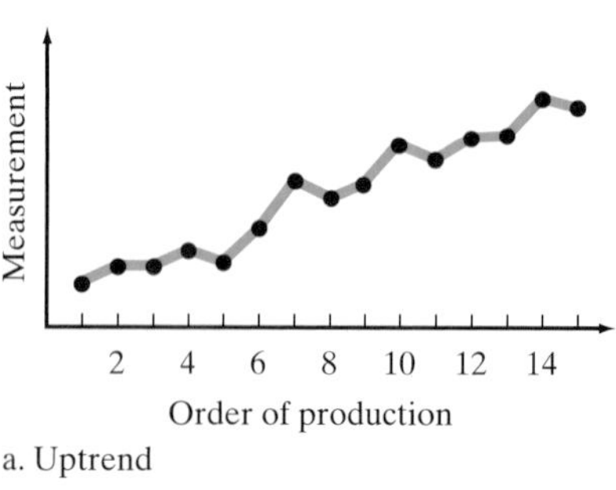

a. Uptrend

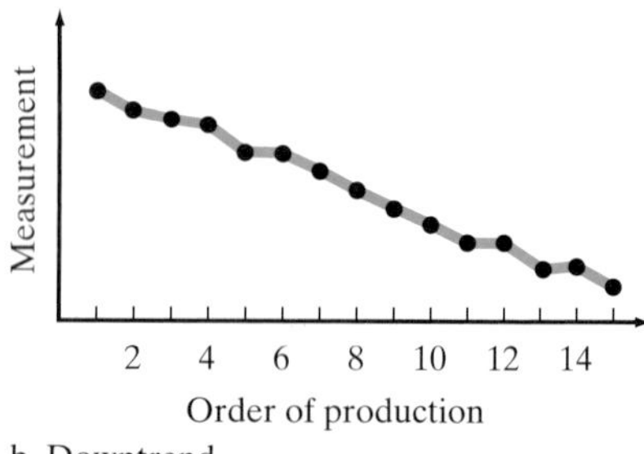
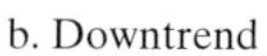

b. Downtrend

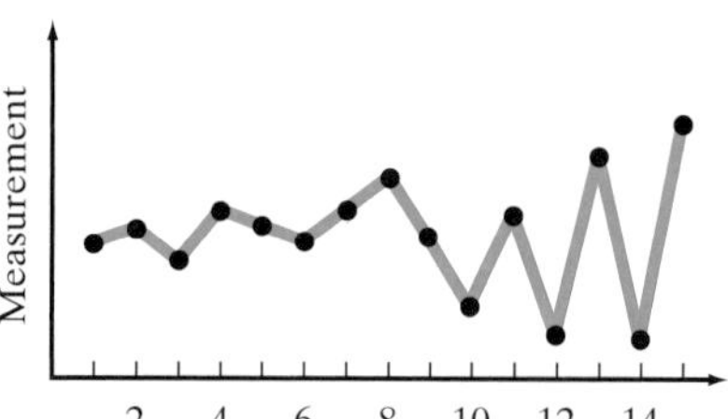
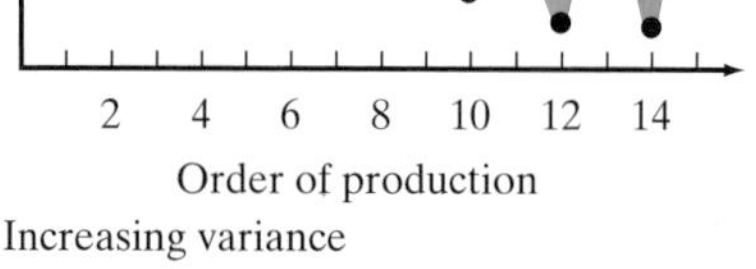

c. Increasing variance

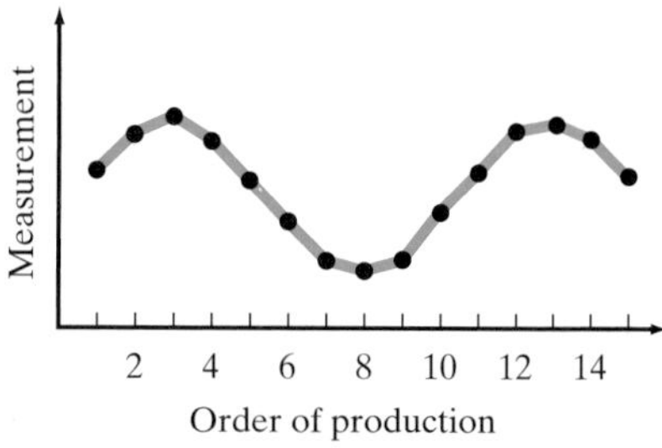

d. Cyclical

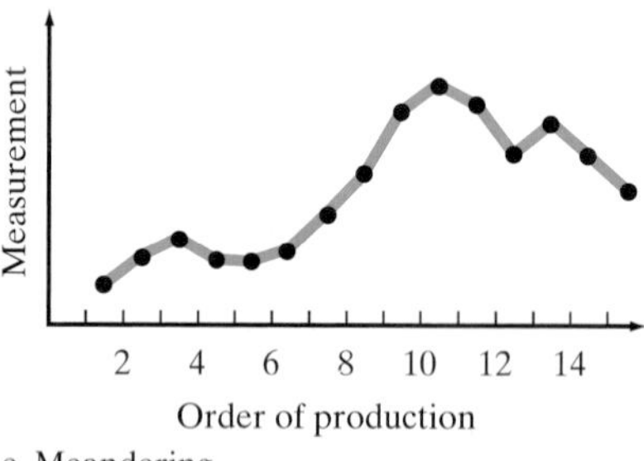

e. Meandering

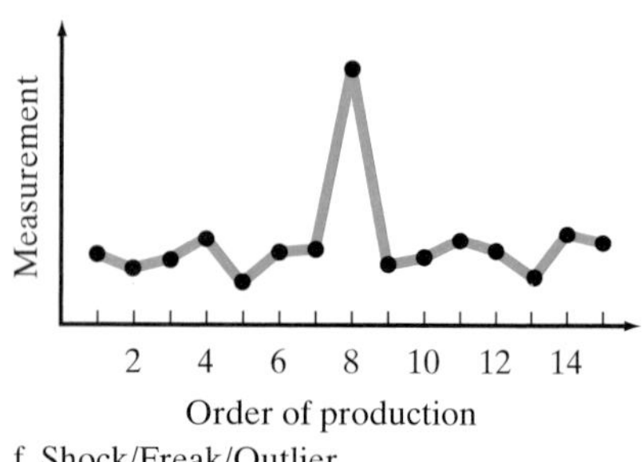

f. Shock/Freak/Outlier

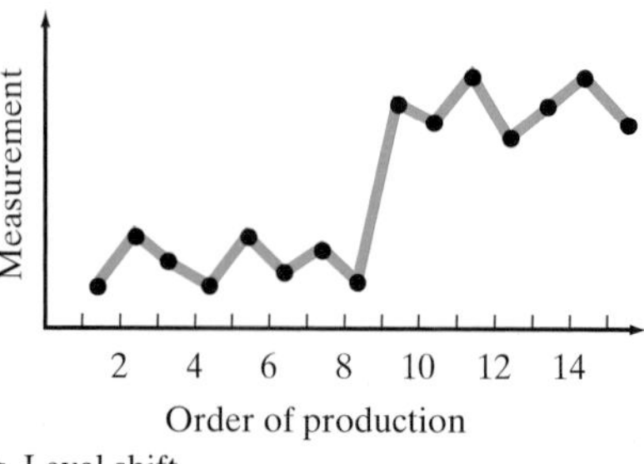

g. Level shift

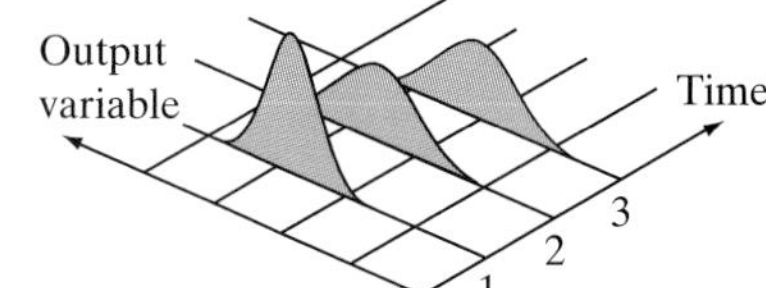

FIGURE 11.7
Distributions describing one output variable at three points in time

tribution describes the possible values that the variable can assume and their likelihood of occurrence. Three such distributions are shown in Figure 11.7.

2. The particular value of the output variable that is realized at a given time can be thought of as being generated or produced according to the distribution described in point 1. (Alternatively, the realized value can be thought of as being generated by a random sample of size $n = 1$ from a population of values whose relative frequency distribution is that of point 1.)
3. The distribution that describes the output variable may change over time. For simplicity, we characterize the changes as being of three types: the mean (i.e., location) of the distribution may change; the variance (i.e., shape) of the distribution may change; or both. This is illustrated in Figure 11.8.

In general, when the output variable's distribution changes over time, we refer to this as a change in the *process.* Thus, if the mean shifts to a higher level, we say that the process mean has shifted. Accordingly, we sometimes refer to the distribution of the output variable as simply the **distribution of the process,** or the **output distribution of the process.**

Let's reconsider the patterns of variation in Figure 11.6 and model them using this conceptualization. This is done in Figure 11.9. The uptrend of Figure 11.6a can be characterized as resulting from a process whose mean is gradually shifting upward over time, as in Figure 11.9a. Gradual shifts like this are a common phenomenon in manufacturing processes. For example, as a machine wears out (e.g., cutting blades dull), certain characteristics of its output gradually change.

The pattern of increasing dispersion in Figure 11.6c can be thought of as resulting from a process whose mean remains constant but whose variance increases over time, as shown in Figure 11.9c. This type of deterioration in a process may be the result of worker fatigue. At the beginning of a shift, workers—whether they be typists, machine operators, waiters, or managers—are fresh and pay close attention to every item that they process. But as the day wears on, concentration may wane and the workers may become more and more careless or more easily distracted. As a result, some items receive more attention than other items, causing the variance of the workers' output to increase.

The sudden shift in the level of the measurements in Figure 11.6g can be thought of as resulting from a process whose mean suddenly increases but whose variance remains constant, as shown in Figure 11.9g. This type of pattern may be caused by such things as a change in the quality of raw materials used in the process or bringing a new machine or new operator into the process.

One thing that all these examples have in common is that the distribution of the output variable *changes over time.* In such cases, we say the process lacks **stability.** We formalize the notion of stability in the following definition.

DEFINITION 11.4

A process whose output distribution does *not* change over time is said to be in a state of **statistical control,** or simply **in control.** If it does change, it is said to be **out of statistical control,** or simply **out of control.**

FIGURE 11.8
Types of changes in output variables

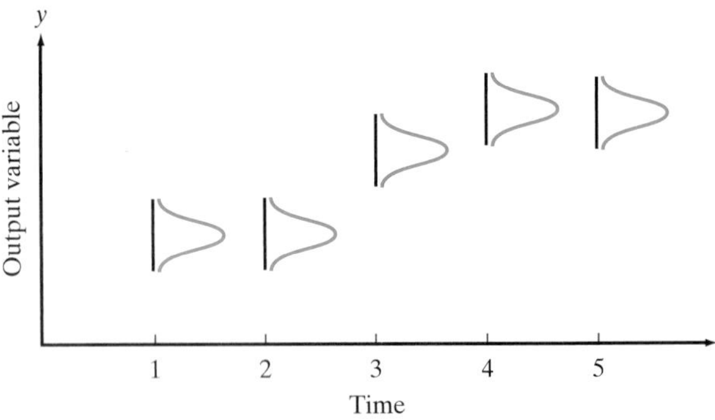

a. Change in mean (i.e., location)

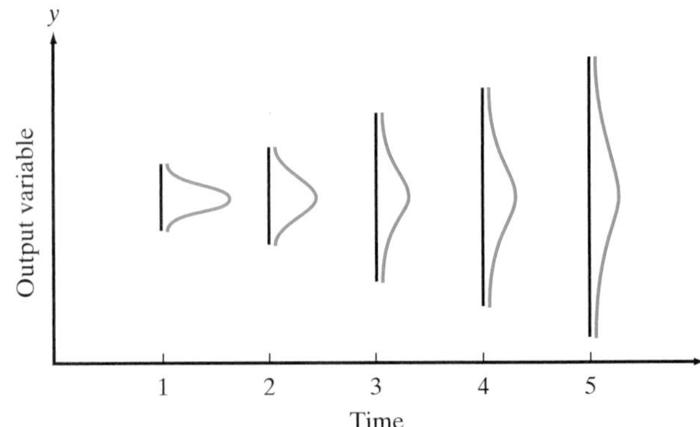

b. Change in variance (i.e., shape)

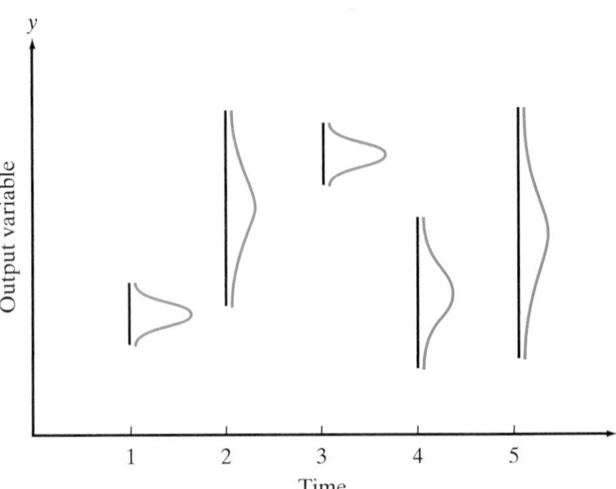

c. Change in mean and variance

Figure 11.10 illustrates a sequence of output distributions for both an in-control and an out-of-control process.

To see what the pattern of measurements looks like on a time series plot for a process that is in statistical control, consider Figure 11.11. These data are from the same paint-filling process we described earlier, but the sequence of measurements was made *after* the faulty valve was replaced. Notice that there are no discernible persistent, systematic patterns in the sequence of measurements such as those in Figures 11.5 and 11.6a–11.6e. Nor are there level shifts

FIGURE 11.9
Patterns of process variation described by changing distributions

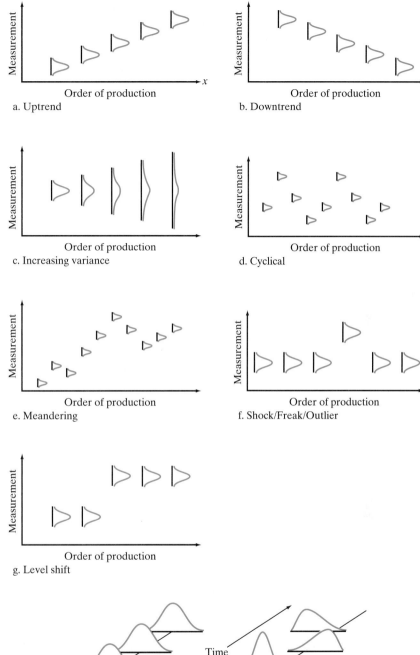

Measurement
Order of production
a. Uptrend

Measurement
Order of production
b. Downtrend

Measurement
Order of production
c. Increasing variance

Measurement
Order of production
d. Cyclical

Measurement
Order of production
e. Meandering

Measurement
Order of production
f. Shock/Freak/Outlier

Measurement
Order of production
g. Level shift

FIGURE 11.10
Comparison of in-control and out-of-control processes

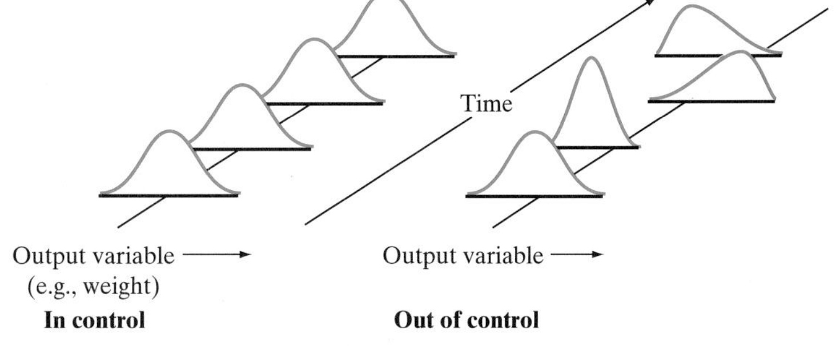

or transitory shocks as in Figures 11.6f–11.6g. This "patternless" behavior is called **random behavior. The output of processes that are in statistical control exhibits random behavior. Thus, even the output of stable processes exhibits variation.**

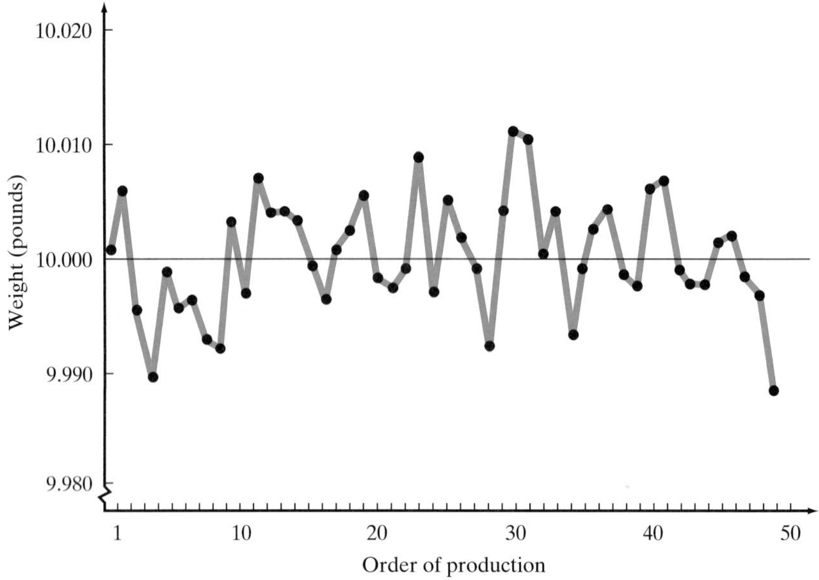

FIGURE 11.11
Time series plot of 50 consecutive paint can fills collected after replacing faulty valve

If a process is in control and remains in control, its future will be like its past. Accordingly, the process is predictable, in the sense that its output will stay within certain limits. This cannot be said about an out-of-control process. As illustrated in Figure 11.12, with most out-of-control processes you have no idea what the future pattern of output from the process may look like.* You simply do not know what to expect from the process. Consequently, a business that operates out-of-control processes runs the risk of (1) providing inferior quality products and services to its internal customers (people within the organization who use the outputs of the processes) and (2) selling inferior products and services to its external customers. In short, it risks losing its customers and threatens its own survival.

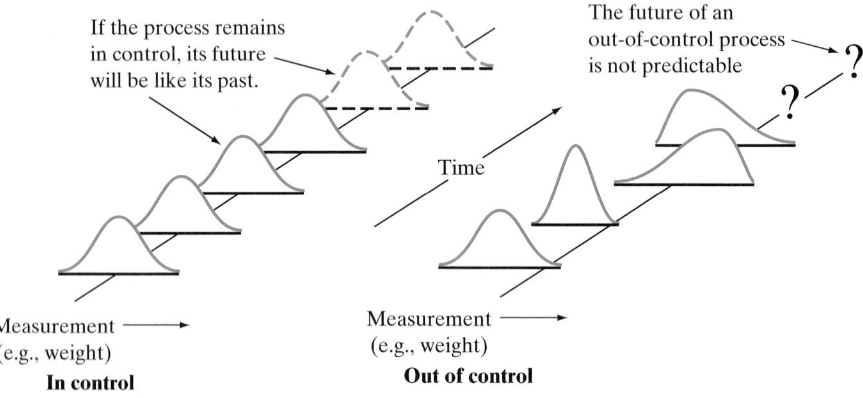

FIGURE 11.12
In-control processes are predictable; out-of-control processes are not

One of the fundamental goals of process management is to identify out-of-control processes, to take actions to bring them into statistical control, and to keep them in a state of statistical control. The series of activities used to attain this goal is referred to as *statistical process control.*

*The output variables of in-control processes may follow approximately normal distributions, as in Figures 11.10 and 11.12, or they may not. But any in-control process will follow the *same* distribution over time. Do not misinterpret the use of normal distributions in many figures in this chapter as indicating that all in-control processes follow normal distributions.

DEFINITION 11.5

The process of monitoring and eliminating variation in order to *keep* a process in a state of statistical control or to *bring* a process into statistical control is called **statistical process control (SPC).**

Everything discussed in this section and the remaining sections of this chapter is concerned with statistical process control. We now continue our discussion of statistical control.

The variation that is exhibited by processes that are in control is said to be due to *common causes of variation.*

DEFINITION 11.6

Common causes of variation are the methods, materials, machines, personnel, and environment that make up a process and the inputs required by the process. Common causes are thus attributable to the design of the process. Common causes affect all output of the process and may affect everyone who participates in the process.

The total variation that is exhibited by an in-control process is due to many different common causes, most of which affect process output in very minor ways. In general, however, each common cause has the potential to affect every unit of output produced by the process. Examples of common causes include the lighting in a factory or office, the grade of raw materials required, and the extent of worker training. Each of these factors can influence the variability of the process output. Poor lighting can cause workers to overlook flaws and defects that they might otherwise catch. Inconsistencies in raw materials can cause inconsistencies in the quality of the finished product. The extent of the training provided to workers can affect their level of expertise and, as a result, the quality of the products and services for which they are responsible.

Since common causes are, in effect, designed into a process, the level of variation that results from common causes is viewed as being representative of the capability of the process. If that level is too great (i.e., if the quality of the output varies too much), the process must be redesigned (or modified) to eliminate one or more common causes of variation. Since process redesign is the responsibility of management, the *elimination of common causes of variation is typically the responsibility of management,* not of the workers.

Processes that are out of control exhibit variation that is the result of both common causes and *special causes of variation.*

DEFINITION 11.7

Special causes of variation (sometimes called **assignable causes**) are events or actions that are not part of the process design. Typically, they are transient, fleeting events that affect only local areas or operations within the process (e.g., a single worker, machine, or batch of materials) for a brief period of time. Occasionally, however, such events may have a persistent or recurrent effect on the process.

Examples of special causes of variation include a worker accidentally setting the controls of a machine improperly, a worker becoming ill on the job and continuing to work, a particular machine slipping out of adjustment, and a negligent supplier shipping a batch of inferior raw materials to the process.

In the latter case, the pattern of output variation may look like Figure 11.6f. If instead of shipping just one bad batch the supplier continued to send inferior materials, the pattern of variation might look like Figure 11.6g. The output of a machine that is gradually slipping out of adjustment might yield a pattern like Figure 11.6a, 11.6b, or 11.6c. All these patterns owe part of their variation to common causes and part to the noted special causes. In general, we treat any pattern of variation other than a random pattern as due to both common and special causes.* Since the effects of special causes are frequently localized within a process, *special causes can often be diagnosed and eliminated by workers or their immediate supervisor.* Occasionally, they must be dealt with by management, as in the case of a negligent or deceitful supplier.

It is important to recognize that **most processes are not naturally in a state of statistical control.** As Deming (1986, p. 322) observed: "*Stability [i.e., statistical control] is seldom a natural state. It is an achievement, the result of eliminating special causes one by one . . . leaving only the random variation of a stable process*" (italics added).

Process improvement first requires the identification, diagnosis, and removal of special causes of variation. Removing all special causes puts the process in a state of statistical control. Further improvement of the process then requires the identification, diagnosis, and removal of common causes of variation. The effects on the process of the removal of special and common causes of variation are illustrated in Figure 11.13.

FIGURE 11.13
The effects of eliminating causes of variation

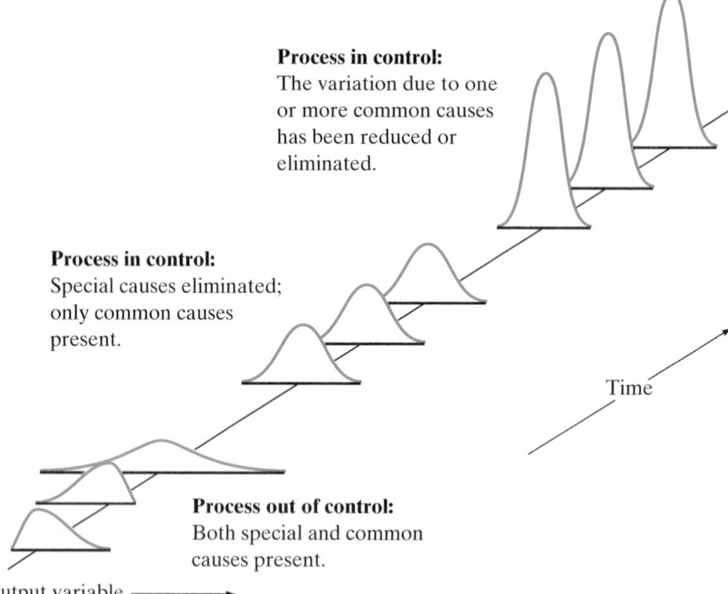
Process in control:
The variation due to one or more common causes has been reduced or eliminated.
Process in control:
Special causes eliminated; only common causes present.
Time
Process out of control:
Both special and common causes present.
Output variable

In the remainder of this chapter, we introduce you to some of the methods of statistical process control. In particular, we address how control charts help us determine whether a given process is in control.

*For certain processes (e.g., those affected by seasonal factors), a persistent systematic pattern—such as the cyclical pattern of Figure 11.6d—is an inherent characteristic. In these special cases, some analysts treat the cause of the systematic variation as a common cause. This type of analysis is beyond the scope of this text. We refer the interested reader to Alwan and Roberts (1988).

11.3 THE LOGIC OF CONTROL CHARTS

We use control charts to help us differentiate between process variation due to common causes and special causes. That is, we use them to determine whether a process is under statistical control (only common causes present) or not (both common and special causes present). Being able to differentiate means knowing when to take action to find and remove special causes and when to leave the process alone. If you take actions to remove special causes that do not exist—that is called tampering with the process—you may actually end up increasing the variation of the process and, thereby, hurting the quality of the output.

In general, control charts are useful for evaluating the past performance of a process and for monitoring its current performance. We can use them to determine whether a process was in control during, say, the past two weeks or to determine whether the process is remaining under control from hour to hour or minute to minute. In the latter case, our goal is the swiftest detection and removal of any special causes of variation that might arise. Keep in mind that **the primary goal of quality-improvement activities is variance reduction.**

In this chapter we show you how to construct and use control charts for both quantitative and qualitative quality variables. Important quantitative variables include such things as weight, width, and time. An important qualitative variable is product status: defective or nondefective.

An example of a control chart is shown in Figure 11.14. A control chart is simply a time series plot of the individual measurements of a quality variable (i.e., an output variable), to which a centerline and two other horizontal lines called **control limits** have been added. The centerline represents the mean of the process (i.e., the mean of the quality variable) *when the process is in a state of statistical control.* The **upper control limit** and the **lower control limit** are positioned so that *when the process is in control* the probability of an individual value of the output variable falling outside the control limits is very small. Most practitioners position the control limits a distance of 3 standard deviations from the centerline (i.e., from the process mean) and refer to them as **3-sigma limits.** If the process is in control and following a normal distribution, the probability of an individual measurement falling outside the control limits is .0027 (less than 3 chances in 1,000). This is shown in Figure 11.15.

FIGURE 11.14
A control chart

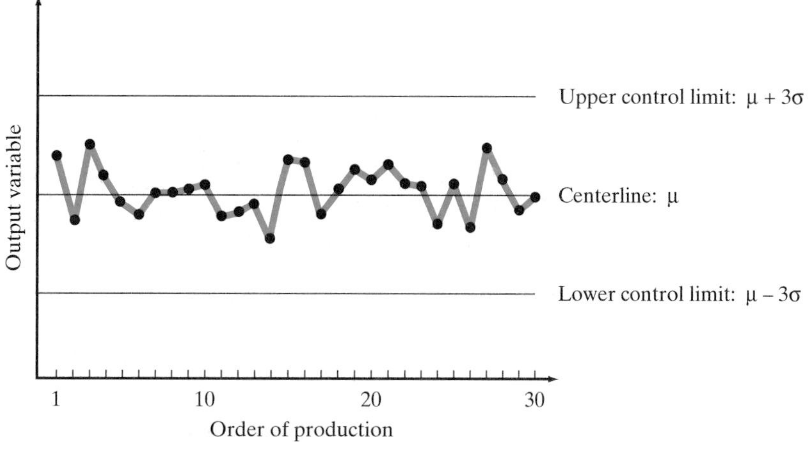

As long as the individual values stay between the control limits, the process is considered to be under control, meaning that no special causes of variation are influencing the output of the process. If one or more values fall outside the control

FIGURE 11.15
The probability of observing a measurement beyond the control limits when the process is in control

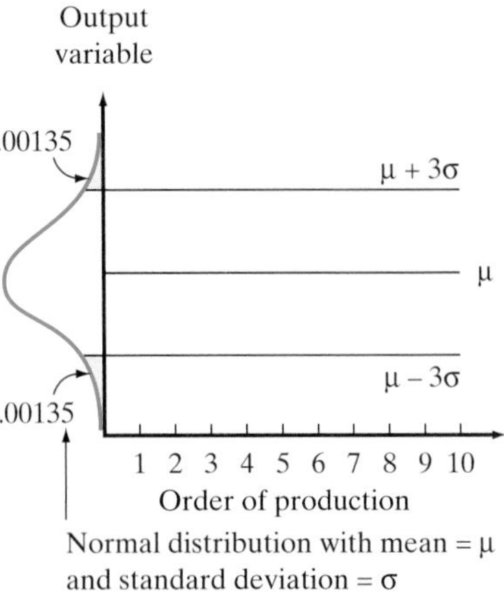

limits, either a **rare event** has occurred or the process is out of control. Following the rare-event approach to inference described earlier in the text, such a result is interpreted as evidence that the process is out of control and that actions should be taken to eliminate the special causes of variation that exist.

Other evidence to indicate that the process is out of control may be present on the control chart. For example, if we observe any of the patterns of variation shown in Figure 11.6, we can conclude the process is out of control *even if all the points fall between the control limits.* In general, any persistent, systematic variation pattern (i.e., any nonrandom pattern) is interpreted as evidence that the process is out of control. We discuss this in detail in the next section.

In Chapter 6 we described how to make inferences about populations using hypothesis-testing techniques. What we do in this section should seem quite similar. Although our focus now is on making inferences about a *process* rather than a *population,* we are again testing hypotheses. In this case, we test

$$H_0\text{: Process is under control}$$
$$H_a\text{: Process is out of control}$$

Each time we plot a new point and see whether it falls inside or outside of the control limits, we are running a two-sided hypothesis test. The control limits function as the critical values for the test.

What we learned in Chapter 6 about the types of errors that we might make in running a hypothesis test holds true in using control charts as well. Any time we reject the hypothesis that the process is under control and conclude that the process is out of control, we run the risk of making a Type I error (rejecting the null hypothesis when the null is true). Anytime we conclude (or behave as if we conclude) that the process is in control, we run the risk of a Type II error (accepting the null hypothesis when the alternative is true). There is nothing magical or mystical about control charts. Just as in any hypothesis test, the conclusion suggested by a control chart may be wrong.

One of the main reasons that 3-sigma control limits are used (rather than 2-sigma or 1-sigma limits, for example) is the small Type I error probability associated with their use. The probability we noted previously of an individual measurement falling outside the control limits—.0027—is a Type I error probability. Since we interpret a sample point that falls beyond the limits as a signal that the process is out of control, the use of 3-sigma limits yields very few signals that are "false alarms."

To make these ideas more concrete, we will construct and interpret a control chart for the paint-filling process discussed in Section 11.2. Our intention is simply to help you better understand the logic of control charts. Structured, step-by-step descriptions of how to construct control charts will be given in later sections.

The sample measurements from the paint-filling process, presented in Table 11.1, were previously plotted in Figure 11.11. We use the mean and standard deviation of the sample, $\bar{x} = 9.9997$ and $s = .0053$, to estimate the mean and the standard deviation of the process. Although these are estimates, in using and interpreting control charts we treat them *as if* they were the actual mean μ and standard deviation σ of the process. This is standard practice in control charting.

TABLE 11.1 Fill Weights of 50 Consecutively Produced Cans of Paint

1. 10.0008	11. 9.9957	21. 9.9977	31. 10.0107	41. 10.0054
2. 10.0062	12. 10.0076	22. 9.9968	32. 10.0102	42. 10.0061
3. 9.9948	13. 10.0036	23. 9.9982	33. 9.9995	43. 9.9978
4. 9.9893	14. 10.0037	24. 10.0092	34. 10.0038	44. 9.9969
5. 9.9994	15. 10.0029	25. 9.9964	35. 9.9925	45. 9.9969
6. 9.9953	16. 9.9995	26. 10.0053	36. 9.9983	46. 10.0006
7. 9.9963	17. 9.9956	27. 10.0012	37. 10.0018	47. 10.0011
8. 9.9925	18. 10.0005	28. 9.9988	38. 10.0038	48. 9.9973
9. 9.9914	19. 10.0020	29. 9.9914	39. 9.9974	49. 9.9958
10. 10.0035	20. 10.0053	30. 10.0036	40. 9.9966	50. 9.9873

The centerline of the control chart, representing the process mean, is drawn so that it intersects the vertical axis at 9.9997, as shown in Figure 11.16. The upper control limit is drawn at a distance of $3s = 3(.0053) = .0159$ above the centerline, and the lower control limit is $3s = .0159$ below the centerline. Then the 50 sample weights are plotted on the chart in the order that they were generated by the paint-filling process.

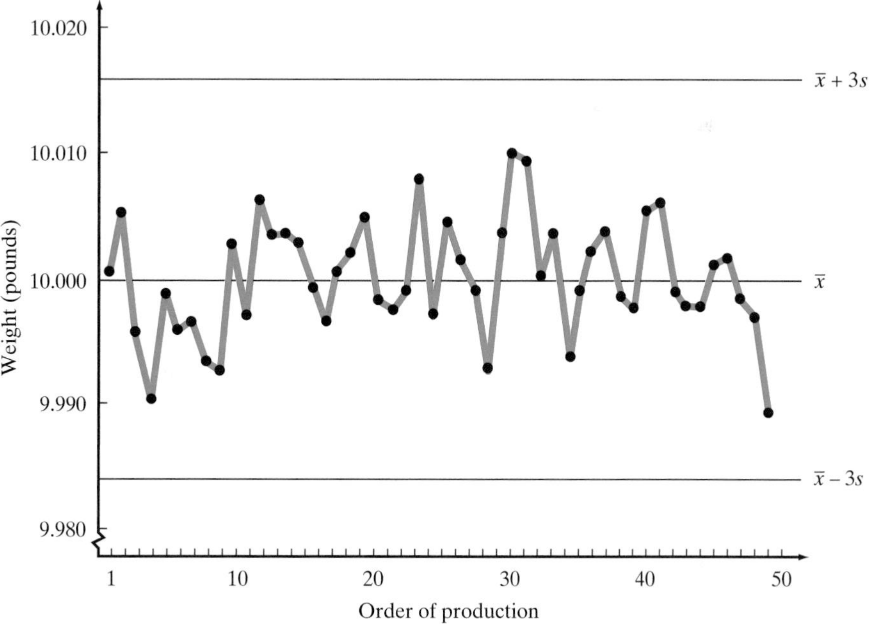

FIGURE 11.16
Control chart of fill weights for 50 consecutive paint can fills

As can be seen in Figure 11.16, all the weight measurements fall within the control limits. Further, there do not appear to be any systematic nonrandom patterns in the data such as displayed in Figures 11.5 and 11.6. Accordingly, we are unable to conclude that the process is out of control. That is, we are unable to reject the null hypothesis that the process is in control. However, instead of using this formal hypothesis-testing language in interpreting control chart results, we prefer simply to say that the data suggest or indicate that the process is in control. We do this, however, with the full understanding that the probability of a Type II error is generally unknown in control chart applications and that we might be wrong in our conclusion. What we are really saying when we conclude that the process is in control is that *the data indicate that it is better to behave as if the process were under control than to tamper with the process.*

We have portrayed the control chart hypothesis test as testing "in control" versus "out of control." Another way to look at it is this: When we compare the weight of an *individual* can of paint to the control limits, we are conducting the following two-tailed hypothesis test:

$$H_0: \mu = 9.9997$$
$$H_0: \mu \neq 9.9997$$

where 9.9997 is the centerline of the control chart. The control limits delineate the two rejection regions for this test. Accordingly, with each weight measurement that we plot and compare to the control limits, we are testing whether the process mean (the mean fill weight) has changed. Thus, what the control chart is monitoring is the mean of the process. **The control chart leads us to accept or reject statistical control on the basis of whether the mean of the process has changed or not.** This type of process instability is illustrated in the top graph of Figure 11.8. In the paint-filling process example, the process mean apparently has remained constant over the period in which the sample weights were collected.

Other types of control charts—one of which we will describe in Section 11.5—help us determine whether the *variance* of the process has changed, as in the middle and bottom graphs of Figure 11.8.

The control chart we have just described is called an **individuals chart,** or an **x-chart.** The term *individuals* refers to the fact that the chart uses individual measurements to monitor the process—that is, measurements taken from individual units of process output. This is in contrast to plotting sample means on the control chart, for example, as we do in the next section.

Students sometimes confuse control limits with product *specification limits.* We have already explained control limits, which are a function of the natural variability of the process. Assuming we always use 3-sigma limits, the position of the control limits is a function of the size of σ, the process standard deviation.

DEFINITION 11.8

Specification limits are boundary points that define the acceptable values for an output variable (i.e., for a quality characteristic) of a particular product or service. They are determined by customers, management, and product designers. Specification limits may be two-sided, with upper and lower limits, or one-sided, with either an upper or a lower limit.

Process output that falls inside the specification limits is said to **conform to specifications.** Otherwise it is said to be **nonconforming.**

Unlike control limits, specification limits are not dependent on the process in any way. A customer of the paint-filling process may specify that all cans contain no more than 10.005 pounds of paint and no less than 9.995 pounds. These are specification limits. The customer has reasons for these specifications but may have no idea whether the supplier's process can meet them. Both the customer's specification limits and the control limits of the supplier's paint-filling process are shown in Figure 11.17. Do you think the customer will be satisfied with the quality of the product received? We don't. Although some cans are within the specification limits, most are not, as indicated by the shaded region on the figure.

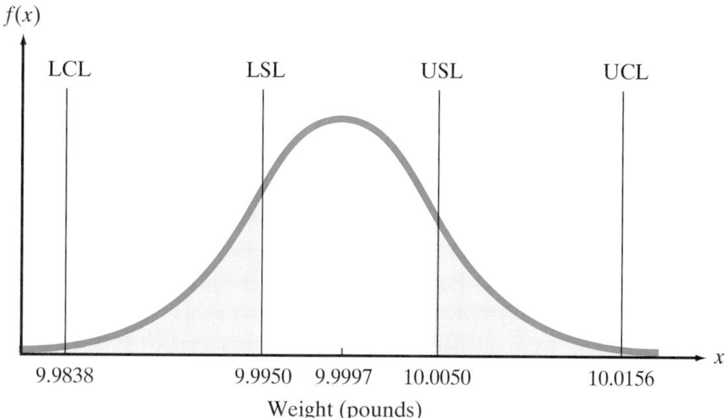

LCL = Lower control limit
UCL = Upper control limit
LSL = Lower specification limit
USL = Upper specification limit

FIGURE 11.17 Comparison of control limits and specification limits

11.4 A CONTROL CHART FOR MONITORING THE MEAN OF A PROCESS: THE $\bar{x}$-CHART

In the last section we introduced you to the logic of control charts by focusing on a chart that reflected the variation in individual measurements of process output. We used the chart to determine whether the process mean had shifted. The control chart we present in this section—the **$\bar{x}$-chart**—is also used to detect changes in the process mean, but it does so by monitoring the variation in the mean of samples that have been drawn from the process. That is, instead of plotting individual measurements on the control chart, in this case we plot sample means. Because of the additional information reflected in sample means (because each sample mean is calculated from n individual measurements), the $\bar{x}$-chart is more sensitive than the individuals chart for detecting changes in the process mean.

In practice, the $\bar{x}$-chart is rarely used alone. It is typically used in conjunction with a chart that monitors the variation of the process, usually a chart called an R-chart. The $\bar{x}$- and R-charts are the most widely used control charts in industry. Used in concert, these charts make it possible to determine whether a process has gone out of control because the variation has changed or because the mean has changed. We present the R-chart in the next section, at the end of which we discuss their simultaneous use. For now, we focus only on the $\bar{x}$-chart. **Consequently, we assume throughout this section that the process variation is stable.***

**To the instructor:* Technically, the R-chart should be constructed and interpreted before the $\bar{x}$-chart. However, in our experience, students more quickly grasp control chart concepts if they are familiar with the underlying theory. We begin with $\bar{x}$-charts because their underlying theory was presented in Chapters 4–6.

Figure 11.18 provides an example of an $\bar{x}$-chart. As with the individuals chart, the centerline represents the mean of the process and the upper and lower control limits are positioned a distance of 3 standard deviations from the mean. However, since the chart is tracking sample means rather than individual measurements, the relevant standard deviation is the standard deviation of $\bar{x}$ not σ, the standard deviation of the output variable.

FIGURE 11.18
$\bar{x}$-Chart

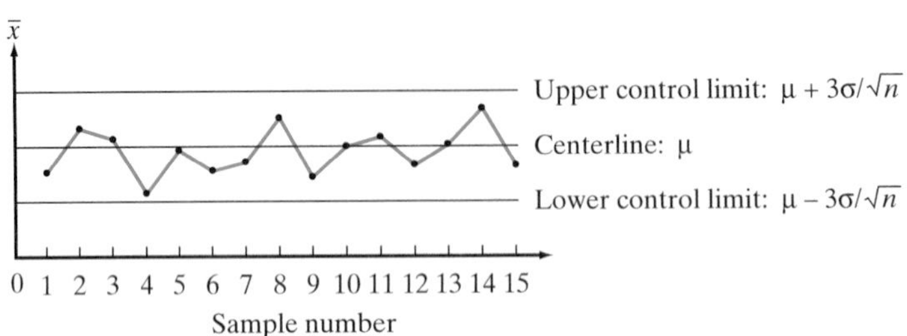

If the process were in statistical control, the sequence of $\bar{x}$'s plotted on the chart would exhibit random behavior between the control limits. Only if a rare event occurred or if the process went out of control would a sample mean fall beyond the control limits.

To better understand the justification for having control limits that involve $\sigma_{\bar{x}}$, consider the following. The $\bar{x}$-chart is concerned with the variation in $\bar{x}$ which, as we saw in Chapter 4, is described by $\bar{x}$'s sampling distribution. But what is the sampling distribution of $\bar{x}$? If the process is in control and its output variable x is characterized at each point in time by a normal distribution with mean μ and standard deviation σ, the distribution of $\bar{x}$ (i.e., $\bar{x}$'s sampling distribution) also follows a normal distribution with mean μ at each point in time. But, as we saw in Chapter 4, its standard deviation is $\sigma_{\bar{x}} = \sigma/\sqrt{n}$. The control limits of the $\bar{x}$-chart are determined from and interpreted with respect to the sampling distribution of $\bar{x}$, not the distribution of x. These points are illustrated in Figure 11.19.*

In order to construct an $\bar{x}$-chart, you should have at least 20 samples of n items each, where $n \geq 2$. This will provide sufficient data to obtain reasonably good estimates of the mean and variance of the process. The centerline, which represents the mean of the process, is determined as follows:

$$\text{Centerline: } \bar{\bar{x}} = \frac{\bar{x}_1 + \bar{x}_2 + \cdots + \bar{x}_k}{k}$$

where k is the number of samples of size n from which the chart is to be constructed and $\bar{x}_i$ is the sample mean of the ith sample. Thus $\bar{\bar{x}}$ is an estimator of μ.

The control limits are positioned as follows:

$$\text{Upper control limit: } \bar{\bar{x}} + \frac{3\sigma}{\sqrt{n}}$$

$$\text{Lower control limit: } \bar{\bar{x}} - \frac{3\sigma}{\sqrt{n}}$$

*The sampling distribution of $\bar{x}$ can also be approximated using the Central Limit Theorem (Chapter 4). That is, when the process is under control and $\bar{x}$ is to be computed from a large sample from the process ($n \geq 30$), the sampling distribution will be approximately normally distributed with the mean μ and standard deviation $\sigma/\sqrt{n}$. Even for samples as small as 4 or 5, the sampling distribution of $\bar{x}$ will be approximately normal as long as the distribution of x is reasonably symmetric and roughly bell-shaped.

FIGURE 11.19
The sampling distribution of $\bar{x}$

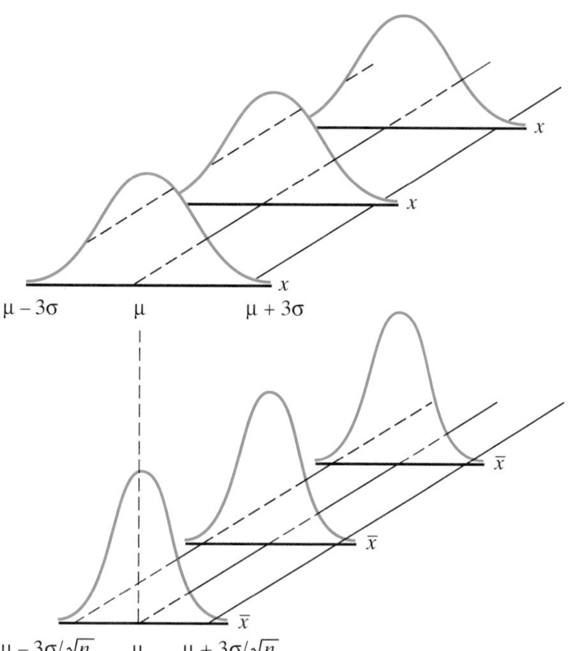
If the process is under control and follows a normal distribution with mean μ and standard deviation σ...
x
x
x
μ − 3σ
μ
μ + 3σ
x̄ also follows a normal distribution with mean μ but has standard deviation σ/√n.
x̄
x̄
x̄
μ − 3σ/√n
μ
μ + 3σ/√n

Since σ, the process standard deviation, is virtually always unknown, it must be estimated. This can be done in several ways. One approach involves calculating the standard deviations for each of the k samples and averaging them. Another involves using the sample standard deviation s from a large sample that was generated while the process was believed to be in control. We employ a third approach, however—the one favored by industry. It has been shown to be as effective as the other approaches for sample sizes of $n = 10$ or less, the sizes most often used in industry.

This approach utilizes the ranges of the k samples to estimate the process standard deviation, σ. Recall from Chapter 2 that the range, R, of a sample is the difference between the maximum and minimum measurements in the sample. It can be shown that dividing the mean of the k ranges, $\bar{R}$, by the constant d_2, obtains an unbiased estimator for σ. [For details, see Ryan (1989).] The estimator, denoted by $\hat{\sigma}$, is calculated as follows:

$$\hat{\sigma} = \frac{\bar{R}}{d_2} = \frac{R_1 + R_2 + \cdots + R_k}{k}\left(\frac{1}{d_2}\right)$$

where R_i is the range of the ith sample and d_2 is a constant that depends on the sample size. Values of d_2 for samples of size $n = 2$ to $n = 25$ can be found in Appendix B, Table XV.

Substituting $\hat{\sigma}$ for σ in the formulas for the upper control limit (UCL) and the lower control limit (LCL), we get

$$\text{UCL: } \bar{\bar{x}} + \frac{3\left(\frac{\bar{R}}{d_2}\right)}{\sqrt{n}} \qquad \text{LCL: } \bar{\bar{x}} - \frac{3\left(\frac{\bar{R}}{d_2}\right)}{\sqrt{n}}$$

Notice that $(\bar{R}/d_2)/\sqrt{n}$ is an estimator of $\sigma_{\bar{x}}$. The calculation of these limits can be simplified by creating the constant

$$A_2 = \frac{3}{d_2\sqrt{n}}$$

Then the control limits can be expressed as

$$\text{UCL: } \bar{\bar{x}} + A_2\bar{R}$$
$$\text{LCL: } \bar{\bar{x}} - A_2\bar{R}$$

where the values for A_2 for samples of size $n = 2$ to $n = 25$ can be found in Appendix B, Table XV.

The degree of sensitivity of the $\bar{x}$-chart to changes in the process mean depends on two decisions that must be made in constructing the chart.

The Two Most Important Decisions in Constructing an $\bar{x}$-Chart

1. The sample size, n, must be determined.
2. The frequency with which samples are to be drawn from the process must be determined (e.g., once an hour, once each shift, or once a day).

In order to quickly detect process change, we try to choose samples in such a way that the change in the process mean occurs *between* samples, not *within* samples (i.e., not during the period when a sample is being drawn). In this way, every measurement in the sample before the change will be unaffected by the change and every measurement in the sample following the change will be affected. The result is that the $\bar{x}$ computed from the latter sample should be substantially different from that of the former sample—a signal that something has happened to the process mean.

DEFINITION 11.9

Samples whose size and frequency have been designed to make it likely that process changes will occur between, rather than within, the samples are referred to as **rational subgroups.**

Rational Subgrouping Strategy

The samples (rational subgroups) should be chosen in a manner that:

1. Gives the maximum chance for the *measurements* in each sample to be similar (i.e., to be affected by the same sources of variation).
2. Gives the maximum chance for the *samples* to differ (i.e., be affected by at least one different source of variation).

The following example illustrates the concept of *rational subgrouping.* An operations manager suspects that the quality of the output in a manufacturing process may differ from shift to shift because of the preponderance of newly hired workers on the night shift. The manager wants to be able to detect such differences quickly, using an $\bar{x}$-chart. Following the rational subgrouping strategy, the control chart should be constructed with samples that are drawn *within* each shift.

None of the samples should span shifts. That is, no sample should contain, say, the last three items produced by shift 1 and the first two items produced by shift 2. In this way, the measurements in each sample would be similar, but the $\bar{x}$'s would reflect differences between shifts.

The secret to designing an effective $\bar{x}$-chart is to anticipate the *types of special causes of variation* that might affect the process mean. Then purposeful rational subgrouping can be employed to construct a chart that is sensitive to the anticipated cause or causes of variation.

The preceding discussion and example focused primarily on the timing or frequency of samples. Concerning the size of the samples, practitioners typically work with samples of size $n = 4$ to $n = 10$ consecutively produced items. Using small samples of consecutively produced items helps to ensure that the measurements in each sample will be similar (i.e., affected by the same causes of variation).

Constructing an $\bar{x}$-Chart: A Summary

1. Using a rational subgrouping strategy, collect at least 20 samples (subgroups), each of size $n \geq 2$.

2. Calculate the mean and range for each sample.

3. Calculate the mean of the sample means, $\bar{\bar{x}}$, and the mean of the sample ranges, $\bar{R}$:

$$\bar{\bar{x}} = \frac{\bar{x}_1 + \bar{x}_2 + \cdots + \bar{x}_k}{k} \qquad \bar{R} = \frac{R_1 + R_2 + \cdots + R_k}{k}$$

where

k = number of samples (i.e., subgroups)

$\bar{x}_i$ = sample mean for the ith sample

R_i = range of the ith sample

4. Plot the centerline and control limits:

Centerline: $\bar{\bar{x}}$

Upper control limit: $\bar{\bar{x}} + A_2\bar{R}$

Lower control limit: $\bar{\bar{x}} - A_2\bar{R}$

where A_2 is a constant that depends on n. Its values are given in Appendix B, Table XV, for samples of size $n = 2$ to $n = 25$.

5. Plot the k sample means on the control chart in the order that the samples were produced by the process.

When interpreting a control chart, it is convenient to think of the chart as consisting of six zones, as shown in Figure 11.20. Each zone is 1 standard deviation wide. The two zones within 1 standard deviation of the centerline are called **C zones;** the regions between 1 and 2 standard deviations from the centerline are called **B zones;** and the regions between 2 and 3 standard deviations from the centerline are called **A zones.** The box describes how to construct the *zone boundaries* for an $\bar{x}$-chart.

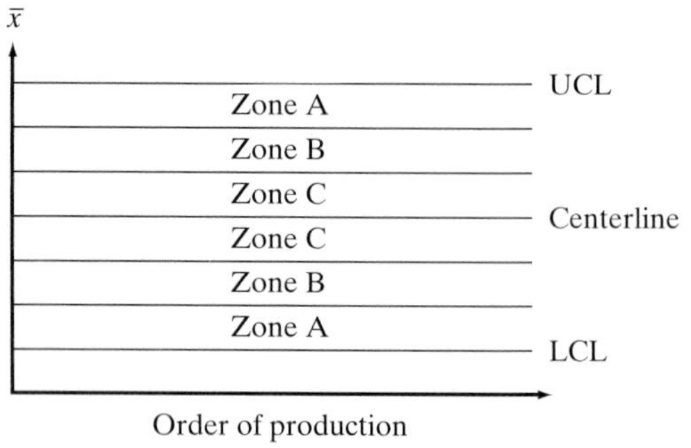

FIGURE 11.20
The zones of a control chart

Constructing Zone Boundaries for an $\bar{x}$-Chart

The zone boundaries can be constructed in either of the following ways:

1. Using the 3-sigma control limits:

$$\textit{Upper A–B boundary: } \bar{\bar{x}} + \frac{2}{3}(A_2\bar{R})$$

$$\textit{Lower A–B boundary: } \bar{\bar{x}} - \frac{2}{3}(A_2\bar{R})$$

$$\textit{Upper B–C boundary: } \bar{\bar{x}} + \frac{1}{3}(A_2\bar{R})$$

$$\textit{Lower B–C boundary: } \bar{\bar{x}} - \frac{1}{3}(A_2\bar{R})$$

2. Using the estimated standard deviation of $\bar{x}$, $(\bar{R}/d_2)/\sqrt{n}$:

$$\textit{Upper A–B boundary: } \bar{\bar{x}} + 2\left[\frac{\left(\frac{\bar{R}}{d_2}\right)}{\sqrt{n}}\right]$$

$$\textit{Lower A–B boundary: } \bar{\bar{x}} - 2\left[\frac{\left(\frac{\bar{R}}{d_2}\right)}{\sqrt{n}}\right]$$

$$\textit{Upper B–C boundary: } \bar{\bar{x}} + \left[\frac{\left(\frac{\bar{R}}{d_2}\right)}{\sqrt{n}}\right]$$

$$\textit{Lower B–C boundary: } \bar{\bar{x}} - \left[\frac{\left(\frac{\bar{R}}{d_2}\right)}{\sqrt{n}}\right]$$

Practitioners use six simple rules that are based on these zones to help determine when a process is out of control. The six rules are summarized in Figure 11.21. They are referred to as **pattern-analysis rules.**

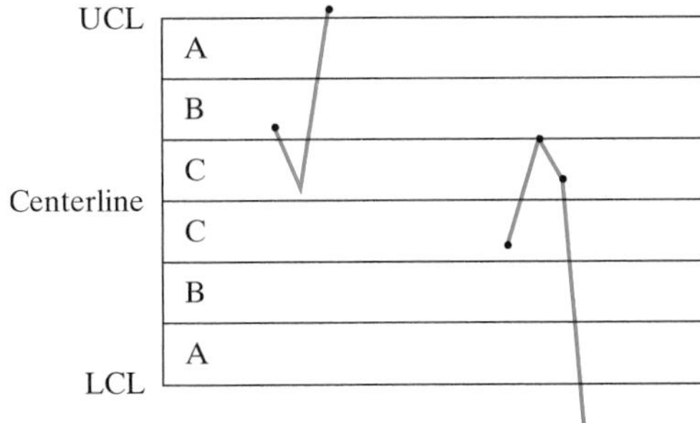

Rule 1: One point beyond Zone A

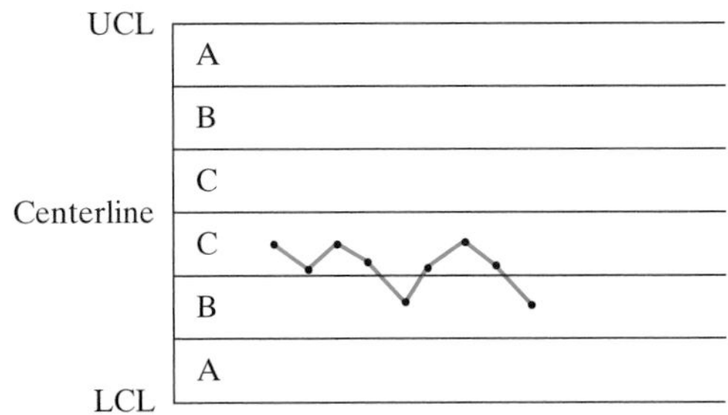

Rule 2: Nine points in a row in Zone C or beyond

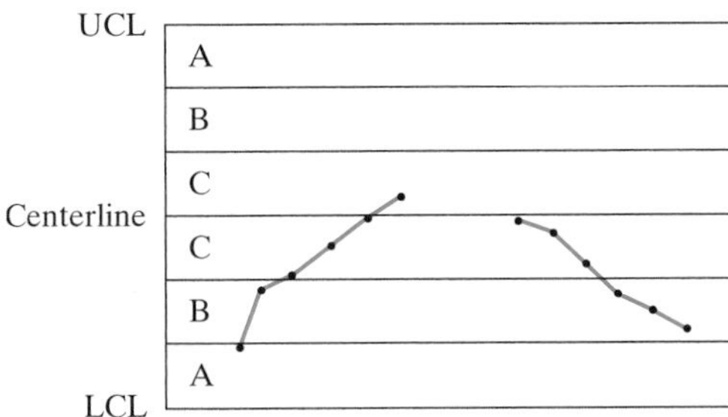

Rule 3: Six points in a row steadily increasing or decreasing

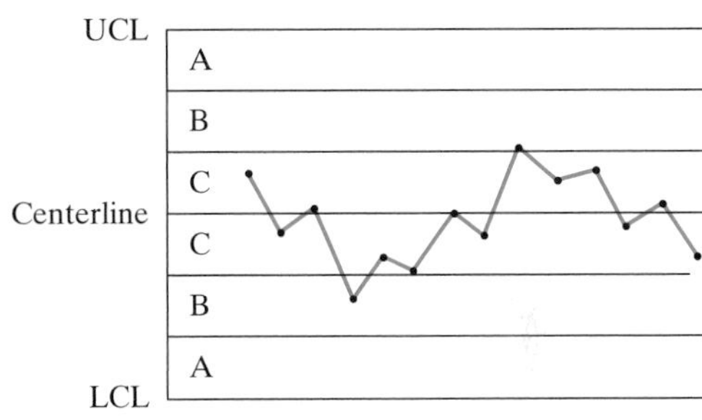

Rule 4: Fourteen points in a row alternating up and down

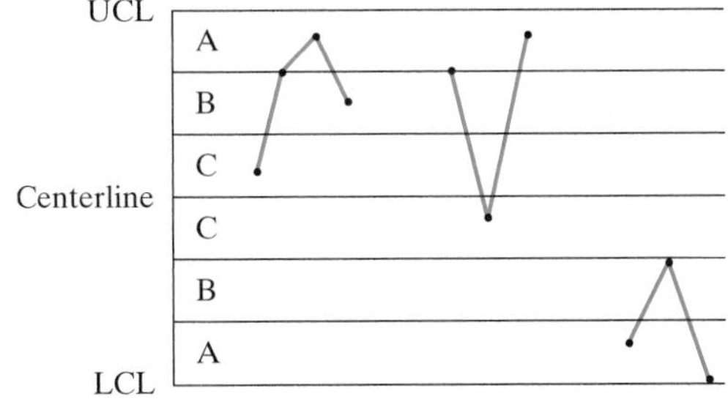

Rule 5: Two out of three points in a row in Zone A or beyond

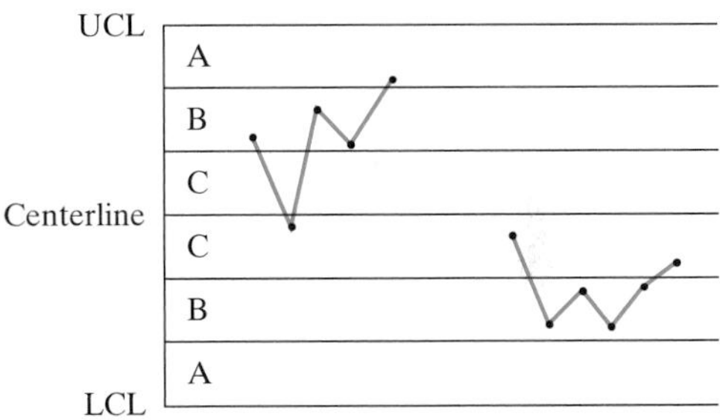

Rule 6: Four out of five points in a row in Zone B or beyond

Rules 1, 2, 5, and 6 should be applied separately to the upper and lower halves of the control chart. Rules 3 and 4 should be applied to the whole chart.

FIGURE 11.21
Pattern-analysis rules for detecting the presence of special causes of variation

Rule 1 is the familiar point-beyond-the-control-limit rule that we have mentioned several times. The other rules all help to determine when the process is out of control *even though all the plotted points fall within the control limits.* That is, the other rules help to identify nonrandom patterns of variation that have not yet broken through the control limits (or may never break through).

All the patterns shown in Figure 11.21 are *rare events* under the assumption that the process is under control. To see this, let's assume that the process is under control and follows a normal distribution. We can then easily work out the probability that an individual point will fall in any given zone. (We dealt with this type of problem in Chapter 4.) Just focusing on one side of the centerline, you can show that the probability of a point falling beyond Zone A is .00135, in Zone A is .02135, in Zone B is .1360, and in Zone C is .3413. Of course, the same probabilities apply to both sides of the centerline.

From these probabilities we can determine the likelihood of various patterns of points. For example, let's evaluate Rule 1. The probability of observing a point outside the control limits (i.e., above the upper control limit or below the lower control limit) is $.00135 + .00135 = .0027$. This is clearly a rare event.

As another example, Rule 5 indicates that the observation of two out of three points in a row in Zone A or beyond is a rare event. Is it? The probability of being in Zone A or beyond is $.00135 + .02135 = .0227$. We can use the binomial distribution (Chapter 4) to find the probability of observing 2 out of 3 points in or beyond Zone A. The binomial probability $P(x = 2)$ when $n = 3$ and $p = .0227$ is .0015. Again, this is clearly a rare event.

In general, when the process is in control and normally distributed, the probability of any one of these rules *incorrectly* signaling the presence of special causes of variation is less than .005, or 5 chances in 1,000. If all of the first four rules are applied, the overall probability of a false signal is about .01. If all six of the rules are applied, the overall probability of a false signal rises to .02, or 2 chances in 100. These three probabilities can be thought of as Type I error probabilities. Each indicates the probability of incorrectly rejecting the null hypothesis that the process is in a state of statistical control.

Explanation of the possible causes of these nonrandom patterns is beyond the scope of this text. We refer the interested reader to AT&T's *Statistical Quality Control Handbook* (1956).

We use these rules again in the next section when we interpret the *R*-chart.

Interpreting an $\bar{x}$-Chart

1. The **process is out of control** if one or more sample means fall beyond the control limits or if any of the other five patterns of variation of Figure 11.21 are observed. Such signals are an indication that one or more special causes of variation are affecting the process mean. We must identify and eliminate them to bring the process into control.
2. The **process is treated as being in control** if none of the previously noted out-of-control signals are observed. Processes that are in control should not be tampered with. However, if the level of variation is unacceptably high, common causes of variation should be identified and eliminated.

Assumption: The variation of the process is stable. (If it were not, the control limits of the $\bar{x}$-chart would be meaningless, since they are a function of the process variation. The *R*-chart, presented in the next section, is used to investigate this assumption.)

In theory, the centerline and control limits should be developed using samples that were collected during a period in which the process was in control. Otherwise, they will not be representative of the variation of the process (or, in the present case, the variation of $\bar{x}$) when the process is in control. However, we will not know whether the process is in control until after we have constructed a control chart. Consequently, when a control chart is first constructed, the centerline and control limits are treated as **trial values.** If the chart indicates that the process was in control during the period when the sample data were collected, then the centerline and control limits become "official" (i.e., no longer treated as trial values). It is then appropriate to extend the control limits and the centerline to the right and to use the chart to monitor future process output.

However, if in applying the pattern-analysis rules of Figure 11.21 it is determined that the process was out of control while the sample data were being collected, the trial values (i.e., the trial chart) should, in general, not be used to monitor the process. The points on the control chart that indicate that the process is out of control should be investigated to see if any special causes of variation can be identified. If special causes of variation are found, (1) they should be eliminated, (2) any points on the chart determined to have been influenced by the special causes—whether inside or outside the control limits—should be discarded, and (3) *new* trial centerline and control limits should be calculated from the remaining data. However, the new trial limits may still indicate that the process is out of control. If so, repeat these three steps until all points fall within the control limits.

If special causes cannot be found and eliminated, the severity of the out-of-control indications should be evaluated and a judgment made as to whether (1) the out-of-control points should be discarded anyway and new trial limits constructed, (2) the original trial limits are good enough to be made official, or (3) new sample data should be collected to construct new trial limits.

EXAMPLE 11.1

Let's return to the paint-filling process described in Sections 11.2 and 11.3. Suppose instead of sampling 50 consecutive gallons of paint from the filling process to develop a control chart, it was decided to sample five consecutive cans once each hour for the next 25 hours. The sample data are presented in Table 11.2. This sampling strategy (rational subgrouping) was selected because several times a month the filling head in question becomes clogged. When that happens, the head dispenses less and less paint over the course of the day. However, the pattern of decrease is so irregular that minute-to-minute or even half-hour-to-half-hour changes are difficult to detect.

a. Explain the logic behind the rational subgrouping strategy that was used.

b. Construct an $\bar{x}$-chart for the process using the data in Table 11.2.

c. What does the chart suggest about the stability of the filling process (whether the process is in or out of statistical control)?

d. Should the control limits be used to monitor future process output?

Solution

a. The samples are far enough apart in time to detect hour-to-hour shifts or changes in the mean amount of paint dispensed, but the individual measurements that make up each sample are close enough together in time to ensure that the process has changed little, if at all, during the time the individual measurements were made. Overall, the rational subgrouping employed affords the opportunity for process changes to occur between samples and therefore show up on the control chart as differences between the sample means.

TABLE 11.2 Twenty-Five Samples of Size 5 from the Paint-Filling Process

Sample	Measurements					Mean	Range
1	10.0042	9.9981	10.0010	9.9964	10.0001	9.99995	.0078
2	9.9950	9.9986	9.9948	10.0030	9.9938	9.99704	.0092
3	10.0028	9.9998	10.0086	9.9949	9.9980	10.00082	.0137
4	9.9952	9.9923	10.0034	9.9965	10.0026	9.99800	.0111
5	9.9997	9.9983	9.9975	10.0078	9.9891	9.99649	.0195
6	9.9987	10.0027	10.0001	10.0027	10.0029	10.00141	.0042
7	10.0004	10.0023	10.0024	9.9992	10.0135	10.00358	.0143
8	10.0013	9.9938	10.0017	10.0089	10.0001	10.00116	.0151
9	10.0103	10.0009	9.9969	10.0103	9.9986	10.00339	.0134
10	9.9980	9.9954	9.9941	9.9958	9.9963	9.99594	.0039
11	10.0013	10.0033	9.9943	9.9949	9.9999	9.99874	.0090
12	9.9986	9.9990	10.0009	9.9947	10.0008	9.99882	.0062
13	10.0089	10.0056	9.9976	9.9997	9.9922	10.00080	.0167
14	9.9971	10.0015	9.9962	10.0038	10.0022	10.00016	.0076
15	9.9949	10.0011	10.0043	9.9988	9.9919	9.99822	.0124
16	9.9951	9.9957	10.0094	10.0040	9.9974	10.00033	.0137
17	10.0015	10.0026	10.0032	9.9971	10.0019	10.00127	.0061
18	9.9983	10.0019	9.9978	9.9997	10.0029	10.00130	.0051
19	9.9977	9.9963	9.9981	9.9968	10.0009	9.99798	.0127
20	10.0078	10.0004	9.9966	10.0051	10.0007	10.00212	.0112
21	9.9963	9.9990	10.0037	9.9936	9.9962	9.99764	.0101
22	9.9999	10.0022	10.0057	10.0026	10.0032	10.00272	.0058
23	9.9998	10.0002	9.9978	9.9966	10.0060	10.00009	.0094
24	10.0031	10.0078	9.9988	10.0032	9.9944	10.00146	.0134
25	9.9993	9.9978	9.9964	10.0032	10.0041	10.00015	.0077

b. Twenty-five samples ($k = 25$ subgroups), each containing $n = 5$ cans of paint, were collected from the process. The first step after collecting the data is to calculate the 25 sample means and sample ranges needed to construct the $\bar{x}$-chart. The mean and range of the first sample are

$$\bar{x} = \frac{10.0042 + 9.9981 + 10.0010 + 9.9964 + 10.0001}{5} = 9.99995$$

$$R = 10.0042 - 9.9964 = .0078$$

All 25 means and ranges are displayed in Table 11.2.

Next, we calculate the mean of the sample means and the mean of the sample ranges:

$$\bar{\bar{x}} = \frac{9.99995 + 9.99704 + \cdots + 10.00015}{25} = 9.9999$$

$$\bar{R} = \frac{.0078 + .0092 + \cdots + .0077}{25} = .01028$$

The centerline of the chart is positioned at $\bar{\bar{x}} = 9.9999$. To determine the control limits, we need the constant A_2, which can be found in Table XV of Appendix B. For $n = 5$, $A_2 = .577$. Then,

$$\text{UCL: } \bar{\bar{x}} + A_2\bar{R} = 9.9999 + .577(.01028) = 10.0058$$

$$\text{LCL: } \bar{\bar{x}} - A_2\bar{R} = 9.9999 - .577(.01028) = 9.9940$$

After positioning the control limits on the chart, we plot the 25 sample means in the order of sampling and connect the points with straight lines. The resulting trial $\bar{x}$-chart is shown in Figure 11.22.

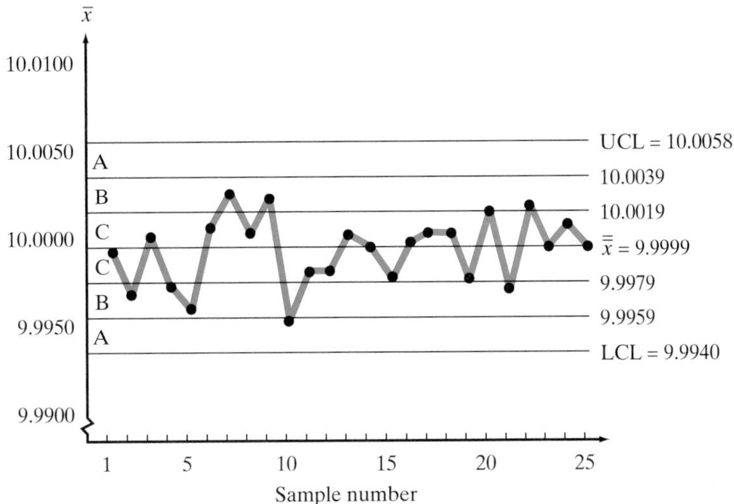

FIGURE 11.22
$\bar{x}$-Chart for the paint-filling process

c. To check the stability of the process, we use the six pattern-analysis rules for detecting special causes of variation, which were presented in Figure 11.21. To apply most of these rules requires identifying the A, B, and C zones of the control chart. These are indicated in Figure 11.22. We describe how they were constructed below.

The boundary between the A and B zones is 2 standard deviations from the centerline, and the boundary between the B and C zones is 1 standard deviation from the centerline. Thus, using $A_2\bar{R}$ and the 3-sigma limits previously calculated, we locate the A, B, and C zones above the centerline:

$$\text{A–B boundary} = \bar{\bar{x}} + \tfrac{2}{3}(A_2\bar{R}) = 9.9999 + \tfrac{2}{3}(.577)(.01028) = 10.0039$$

$$\text{B–C boundary} = \bar{\bar{x}} + \tfrac{1}{3}(A_2\bar{R}) = 9.9999 + \tfrac{1}{3}(.577)(.01028) = 10.0019$$

Similarly, the zones below the centerline are located:

$$\text{A–B boundary} = \bar{\bar{x}} - \tfrac{2}{3}(A_2\bar{R}) = 9.9959$$

$$\text{B–C boundary} = \bar{\bar{x}} - \tfrac{1}{3}(A_2\bar{R}) = 9.9979$$

A careful comparison of the six pattern-analysis rules with the sequence of sample means yields no out-of-control signals. All points are inside the control limits and there appear to be no nonrandom patterns within the control limits. That is, we can find no evidence of a shift in the process mean. Accordingly, we conclude that the process is in control.

d. Since the process was found to be in control during the period in which the samples were drawn, the trial control limits constructed in part **b** can be considered official. They should be extended to the right and used to monitor future process output.

EXAMPLE 11.2 Ten new samples of size $n = 5$ were drawn from the paint-filling process of the previous example. The sample data, including sample means and ranges, are shown in Table 11.3. Investigate whether the process remained in control during the period in which the new sample data were collected.

TABLE 11.3 Ten Additional Samples of Size 5 from the Paint-Filling Process

Sample	Measurements					Mean	Range
26	10.0019	9.9981	9.9952	9.9976	9.9999	9.99841	.0067
27	10.0041	9.9982	10.0028	10.0040	9.9971	10.00125	.0070
28	9.9999	9.9974	10.0078	9.9971	9.9923	9.99890	.0155
29	9.9982	10.0002	9.9916	10.0040	9.9916	9.99713	.0124
30	9.9933	9.9963	9.9955	9.9993	9.9905	9.99498	.0088
31	9.9915	9.9984	10.0053	9.9888	9.9876	9.99433	.0177
32	9.9912	9.9970	9.9961	9.9879	9.9970	9.99382	.0091
33	9.9942	9.9960	9.9975	10.0019	9.9912	9.99614	.0107
34	9.9949	9.9967	9.9936	9.9941	10.0071	9.99726	.0135
35	9.9943	9.9969	9.9937	9.9912	10.0053	9.99626	.0141

Solution We begin by simply extending the control limits, centerline, and zone boundaries of the control chart in Figure 11.22 to the right. Next, beginning with sample number 26, we plot the 10 new sample means on the control chart and connect them with straight lines. This extended version of the control chart is shown in Figure 11.23.

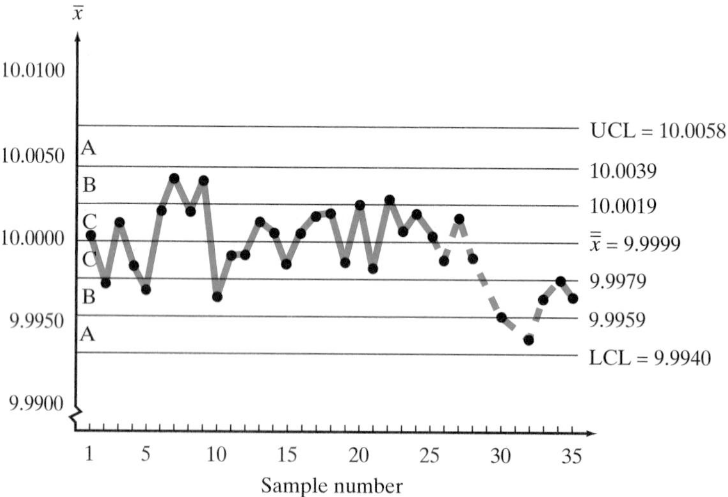

FIGURE 11.23 Extended $\bar{x}$-chart for paint-filling process

Now that the control chart has been prepared, we apply the six pattern-analysis rules for detecting special causes of variation (Figure 11.21) to the new sequence of sample means. No points fall outside the control limits, but we notice six points in a row that steadily decrease (samples 27–32). Rule 3 says that if we observe six points in a row steadily increasing or decreasing, that is an indication of the presence of special causes of variation.

Notice that if you apply the rules from left to right along the sequence of sample means, the decreasing pattern also triggers signals from Rules 5 (samples 29–31) and 6 (samples 28–32).

These signals lead us to conclude that the process has gone out of control. Apparently, the filling head began to clog about the time that either sample 26 or 27 was drawn from the process. As a result, the mean of the process (the mean fill weight dispensed by the process) began to decline.

EXERCISES 11.1–11.17

Learning the Mechanics

11.1 What is a control chart? Describe its use.

11.2 Explain why rational subgrouping should be used in constructing control charts.

11.3 When a control chart is first constructed, why are the centerline and control limits treated as trial values?

11.4 Which process parameter is an $\bar{x}$-chart used to monitor?

11.5 Even if all the points on an $\bar{x}$-chart fall between the control limits, the process may be out of control. Explain.

11.6 What must be true about the variation of a process before an $\bar{x}$-chart is used to monitor the mean of the process? Why?

11.7 Use the six pattern-analysis rules described in Figure 11.21 to determine whether the process being monitored with the accompanying $\bar{x}$-chart is out of statistical control.

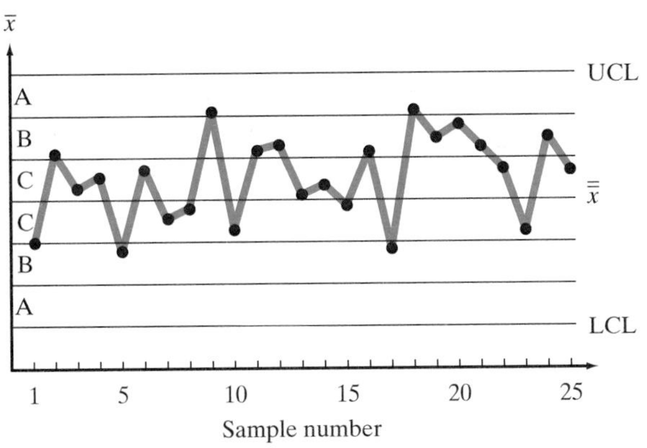

11.8 Is the process for which the $\bar{x}$-chart at right was constructed affected by only special causes of variation, only common causes of variation, or both? Explain.

11.9 Use Table XV in Appendix B to find the value of A_2 for each of the following sample sizes.

a. $n = 3$ b. $n = 10$ c. $n = 22$

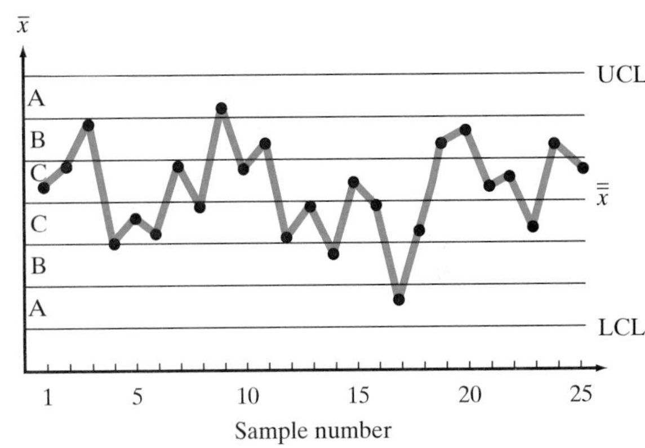

11.10 Twenty-five samples of size $n = 5$ were collected to construct an $\bar{x}$-chart. The accompanying sample means and ranges were calculated for these data.

LM11_10.DAT

Sample	$\bar{x}$	R	Sample	$\bar{x}$	R
1	80.2	7.2	14	83.1	10.2
2	79.1	9.0	15	79.6	7.8
3	83.2	4.7	16	80.0	6.1
4	81.0	5.6	17	83.2	8.4
5	77.6	10.1	18	75.9	9.9
6	81.7	8.6	19	78.1	6.0
7	80.4	4.4	20	81.4	7.4
8	77.5	6.2	21	81.7	10.4
9	79.8	7.9	22	80.9	9.1
10	85.3	7.1	23	78.4	7.3
11	77.7	9.8	24	79.6	8.0
12	82.3	10.7	25	81.6	7.6
13	79.5	9.2			

a. Calculate the mean of the sample means, $\bar{\bar{x}}$, and the mean of the sample ranges, $\bar{R}$.

b. Calculate and plot the centerline and the upper and lower control limits for the $\bar{x}$-chart.

c. Calculate and plot the A, B, and C zone boundaries of the $\bar{x}$-chart.

d. Plot the 25 sample means on the $\bar{x}$-chart and use the six pattern-analysis rules to determine whether the process is under statistical control.

11.11 The data in the next table were collected for the purpose of constructing an $\bar{x}$-chart.

LM11_11.DAT

Sample	Measurements			
1	19.4	19.7	20.6	21.2
2	18.7	18.4	21.2	20.7
3	20.2	18.8	22.6	20.1
4	19.6	21.2	18.7	19.4
5	20.4	20.9	22.3	18.6
6	17.3	22.3	20.3	19.7
7	21.8	17.6	22.8	23.1
8	20.9	17.4	19.5	20.7
9	18.1	18.3	20.6	20.4
10	22.6	21.4	18.5	19.7
11	22.7	21.2	21.5	19.5
12	20.1	20.6	21.0	20.2
13	19.7	18.6	21.2	19.1
14	18.6	21.7	17.7	18.3
15	18.2	20.4	19.8	19.2
16	18.9	20.7	23.2	20.0
17	20.5	19.7	21.4	17.8
18	21.0	18.7	19.9	21.2
19	20.5	19.6	19.8	21.8
20	20.6	16.9	22.4	19.7

a. Calculate $\bar{x}$ and R for each sample.
b. Calculate $\bar{\bar{x}}$ and $\bar{R}$.
c. Calculate and plot the centerline and the upper and lower control limits for the $\bar{x}$-chart.
d. Calculate and plot the A, B, and C zone boundaries of the $\bar{x}$-chart.
e. Plot the 20 sample means on the $\bar{x}$-chart. Is the process in control? Justify your answer.

Applying the Concepts

11.12 The central processing unit (CPU) of a microcomputer is a computer chip containing millions of transistors. Connecting the transistors are slender circuit paths only .5 to .85 micron wide. To understand how narrow these paths are, consider that a micron is a millionth of a meter, and a human hair is 70 microns wide (*Compute,* 1992). A manufacturer of CPU chips knows that if the circuit paths are not .5–.85 micron wide, a variety of problems will arise in the chips' performance. The manufacturer sampled four CPU chips six times a day (every 90 minutes from 8:00 A.M. until 4:30 P.M.) for five consecutive days and measured the circuit path widths. These data and MINITAB were used to construct the $\bar{x}$-chart shown below.

a. Assuming that $\bar{R} = .3162$, calculate the chart's upper and lower control limits, the upper and lower A–B boundaries, and the upper and lower B–C boundaries.
b. What does the chart suggest about the stability of the process used to put circuit paths on the CPU chip? Justify your answer.
c. Should the control limits be used to monitor future process output? Explain.

11.13 A machine at K-Company fills boxes with bran flakes cereal. The target weight for the filled boxes is 24 ounces. The company would like to use an $\bar{x}$-chart to monitor the performance of the machine. To develop the control

MINITAB Output for Exercise 11.12

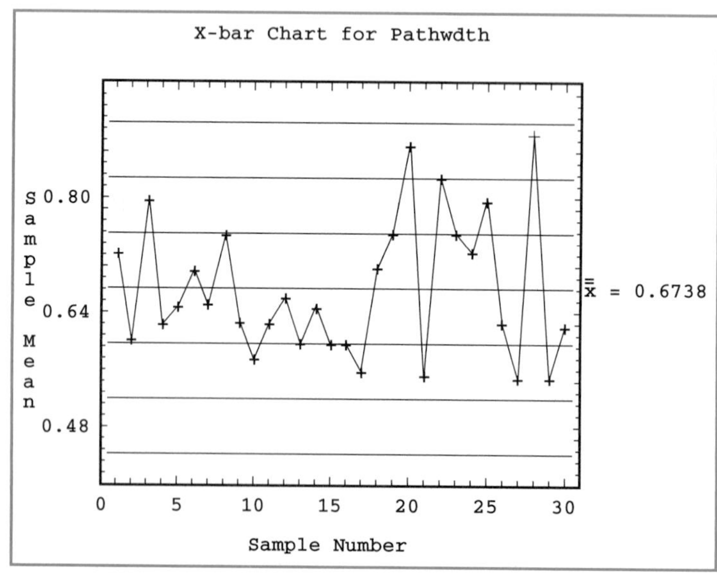

chart, the company decides to sample and weigh five consecutive boxes of cereal five times each day (at 8:00 and 11:00 A.M. and 2:00, 5:00, and 8:00 P.M.) for twenty consecutive days. The data are presented in the table, along with a SAS printout with summary statistics.

a. Construct an $\bar{x}$-chart from the given data.

CEREAL.DAT

Day	Weight of Cereal Boxes (ounces)				
1	24.02	23.91	24.12	24.06	24.13
2	23.89	23.98	24.01	24.00	23.91
3	24.11	24.02	23.99	23.79	24.04
4	24.06	23.98	23.95	24.01	24.11
5	23.81	23.90	23.99	24.07	23.96
6	23.87	24.12	24.07	24.01	23.99
7	23.88	24.00	24.05	23.97	23.97
8	24.01	24.03	23.99	23.91	23.98
9	24.06	24.02	23.80	23.79	24.07
10	23.96	23.99	24.03	23.99	24.01
11	24.10	23.90	24.11	23.98	23.95
12	24.01	24.07	23.93	24.09	23.98
13	24.14	24.07	24.08	23.98	24.02
14	23.91	24.04	23.89	24.01	23.95
15	24.03	24.04	24.01	23.98	24.10
16	23.94	24.07	24.12	24.00	24.02
17	23.88	23.94	23.91	24.06	24.07
18	24.11	23.99	23.90	24.01	23.98
19	24.05	24.04	23.97	24.08	23.95
20	24.02	23.96	23.95	23.89	24.04

SAS Output for Exercise 11.13

	WEIGHT	
	MEAN	RANGE
DAY		
1	24.05	0.22
2	23.96	0.12
3	23.99	0.32
4	24.02	0.16
5	23.95	0.26
6	24.01	0.25
7	23.97	0.17
8	23.98	0.12
9	23.95	0.28
10	24.00	0.07
11	24.01	0.21
12	24.02	0.16
13	24.06	0.16
14	23.96	0.15
15	24.03	0.12
16	24.03	0.18
17	23.97	0.19
18	24.00	0.21
19	24.02	0.13
20	23.97	0.15

b. What does the chart suggest about the stability of the filling process (whether the process is in or out of statistical control)? Justify your answer.

c. Should the control limits be used to monitor future process output? Explain.

d. Two shifts of workers run the filling operation. Each day the second shift takes over at 3:00 P.M. Will the rational subgrouping strategy used by K-Company facilitate or hinder the identification of process variation caused by differences in the two shifts? Explain.

11.14 A precision parts manufacturer produces bolts for use in military aircraft. Ideally, the bolts should be 37 centimeters in length. The company sampled four consecutively produced bolts each hour on the hour for 25 consecutive hours and measured them using a computerized precision instrument. The data are presented below. A MINITAB printout with descriptive statistics for each hour is also shown on page 670.

BOLTS.DAT

Hour	Bolt Lengths (centimeters)			
1	37.03	37.08	36.90	36.88
2	36.96	37.04	36.85	36.98
3	37.16	37.11	36.99	37.01
4	37.20	37.06	37.02	36.98
5	36.81	36.97	36.91	37.10
6	37.13	36.96	37.01	36.89
7	37.07	36.94	36.99	37.00
8	37.01	36.91	36.98	37.12
9	37.17	37.03	36.90	37.01
10	36.91	36.99	36.87	37.11
11	36.88	37.10	37.07	37.03
12	37.06	36.98	36.90	36.99
13	36.91	37.22	37.12	37.03
14	37.08	37.07	37.10	37.04
15	37.03	37.04	36.89	37.01
16	36.95	36.98	36.90	36.99
17	36.97	36.94	37.14	37.10
18	37.11	37.04	36.98	36.91
19	36.88	36.99	37.01	36.94
20	36.90	37.15	37.09	37.00
21	37.01	36.96	37.05	36.96
22	37.09	36.95	36.93	37.12
23	37.00	37.02	36.95	37.04
24	36.99	37.07	36.90	37.02
25	37.10	37.03	37.01	36.90

a. What process is the manufacturer interested in monitoring?

b. Construct an $\bar{x}$-chart from the data.

c. Does the chart suggest that special causes of variation are present? Justify your answer.

d. Provide an example of a special cause of variation that could potentially affect this process. Do the same for a common cause of variation.

MINITAB Output for Exercise 11.14

Descriptive Statistics

Variable	HOUR	N	MEAN	MEDIAN	TR MEAN	STDEV	SE MEAN
LENGTH	1	4	36.973	36.965	36.973	0.098	0.049
	2	4	36.957	36.970	36.957	0.079	0.040
	3	4	37.067	37.060	37.067	0.081	0.040
	4	4	37.065	37.040	37.065	0.096	0.048
	5	4	36.947	36.940	36.947	0.121	0.061
	6	4	36.998	36.985	36.998	0.101	0.051
	7	4	37.000	36.995	37.000	0.054	0.027
	8	4	37.005	36.995	37.005	0.087	0.044
	9	4	37.028	37.020	37.028	0.111	0.055
	10	4	36.970	36.950	36.970	0.106	0.053
	11	4	37.020	37.050	37.020	0.098	0.049
	12	4	36.982	36.985	36.982	0.066	0.033
	13	4	37.070	37.075	37.070	0.132	0.066
	14	4	37.072	37.075	37.072	0.025	0.013
	15	4	36.993	37.020	36.993	0.069	0.035
	16	4	36.955	36.965	36.955	0.040	0.020
	17	4	37.038	37.035	37.038	0.097	0.049
	18	4	37.010	37.010	37.010	0.085	0.043
	19	4	36.955	36.965	36.955	0.058	0.029
	20	4	37.035	37.045	37.035	0.109	0.055
	21	4	36.995	36.985	36.995	0.044	0.022
	22	4	37.023	37.020	37.023	0.096	0.048
	23	4	37.003	37.010	37.003	0.039	0.019
	24	4	36.995	37.005	36.995	0.071	0.036
	25	4	37.010	37.020	37.010	0.083	0.041

Variable	HOUR	MIN	MAX	Q1	Q3
LENGTH	1	36.880	37.080	36.885	37.067
	2	36.850	37.040	36.878	37.025
	3	36.990	37.160	36.995	37.147
	4	36.980	37.200	36.990	37.165
	5	36.810	37.100	36.835	37.068
	6	36.890	37.130	36.907	37.100
	7	36.940	37.070	36.953	37.053
	8	36.910	37.120	36.927	37.092
	9	36.900	37.170	36.927	37.135
	10	36.870	37.110	36.880	37.080
	11	36.880	37.100	36.918	37.092
	12	36.900	37.060	36.920	37.043
	13	36.910	37.220	36.940	37.195
	14	37.040	37.100	37.047	37.095
	15	36.890	37.040	36.920	37.038
	16	36.900	36.990	36.913	36.987
	17	36.940	37.140	36.947	37.130
	18	36.910	37.110	36.927	37.092
	19	36.880	37.010	36.895	37.005
	20	36.900	37.150	36.925	37.135
	21	36.960	37.050	36.960	37.040
	22	36.930	37.120	36.935	37.113
	23	36.950	37.040	36.962	37.035
	24	36.900	37.070	36.922	37.058
	25	36.900	37.100	36.927	37.083

e. Should the control limits be used to monitor future process output? Explain.

11.15 In their text, *Quantitative Analysis of Management* (1997), B. Render (Rollins College) and R. M. Stair (Florida State University), present the case of the Bayfield Mud Company. Bayfield supplies boxcars of 50-pound bags of mud treating agents to the Wet-Land Drilling Company. Mud treating agents are used to control the pH and other chemical properties of the cone during oil drilling operations. Wet-Land has complained to Bayfield that its most recent shipment of bags were underweight by about 5%. (The use of underweight bags may result in poor chemical control during drilling, which may hurt drilling efficiency resulting in serious economic consequences.) Afraid of losing a long-time customer, Bayfield immediately began investigating their production process. Management suspected that the causes of the problem were the recently added third shift and the fact that all three shifts were under pressure to increase output to meet increasing demand for the product. Their quality control staff began randomly sampling and weighing six bags of output each hour. The average weight of each sample over the last three days is recorded in the table along with the weight of the heaviest and lightest bag in each sample.

a. Construct an $\bar{x}$-chart for these data.

b. Is the process under statistical control?

c. Does it appear that management's suspicion about the third shift is correct? Explain?

MUDBAGS.DAT

Time	Average Weight (pounds)	Lightest	Heaviest	Time	Average Weight (pounds)	Lightest	Heaviest
6:00 A.M.	49.6	48.7	50.7	6:00 P.M	46.8	41.0	51.2
7:00	50.2	49.1	51.2	7:00	50.0	46.2	51.7
8:00	50.6	49.6	51.4	8:00	47.4	44.0	48.7
9:00	50.8	50.2	51.8	9:00	47.0	44.2	48.9
10:00	49.9	49.2	52.3	10:00	47.2	46.6	50.2
11:00	50.3	48.6	51.7	11:00	48.6	47.0	50.0
12 noon	48.6	46.2	50.4	12 midnight	49.8	48.2	50.4
1:00 P.M	49.0	46.4	50.0	1:00 A.M.	49.6	48.4	51.7
2:00	49.0	46.0	50.6	2:00	50.0	49.0	52.2
3:00	49.8	48.2	50.8	3:00	50.0	49.2	50.0
4:00	50.3	49.2	52.7	4:00	47.2	46.3	50.5
5:00	51.4	50.0	55.3	5:00	47.0	44.1	49.7
6:00	51.6	49.2	54.7	6:00	48.4	45.0	49.0
7:00	51.8	50.0	55.6	7:00	48.8	44.8	49.7
8:00	51.0	48.6	53.2	8:00	49.6	48.0	51.8
9:00	50.5	49.4	52.4	9:00	50.0	48.1	52.7
10:00	49.2	46.1	50.7	10:00	51.0	48.1	55.2
11:00	49.0	46.3	50.8	11:00	50.4	49.5	54.1
12 midnight	48.4	45.4	50.2	12 noon	50.0	48.7	50.9
1:00 A.M.	47.6	44.3	49.7	1:00 P.M.	48.9	47.6	51.2
2:00	47.4	44.1	49.6	2:00	49.8	48.4	51.0
3:00	48.2	45.2	49.0	3:00	49.8	48.8	50.8
4:00	48.0	45.5	49.1	4:00	50.0	49.1	50.6
5:00	48.4	47.1	49.6	5:00	47.8	45.2	51.2
6:00	48.6	47.4	52.0	6:00	46.4	44.0	49.7
7:00	50.0	49.2	52.2	7:00	46.4	44.4	50.0
8:00	49.8	49.0	52.4	8:00	47.2	46.6	48.9
9:00	50.3	49.4	51.7	9:00	48.4	47.2	49.5
10:00	50.2	49.6	51.8	10:00	49.2	48.1	50.7
11:00	50.0	49.0	52.3	11:00	48.4	47.0	50.8
12 noon	50.0	48.8	52.4	12 midnight	47.2	46.4	49.2
1:00 P.M	50.1	49.4	53.6	1:00 A.M.	47.4	46.8	49.0
2:00	49.7	48.6	51.0	2:00	48.8	47.2	51.4
3:00	48.4	47.2	51.7	3:00	49.6	49.0	50.6
4:00	47.2	45.3	50.9	4:00	51.0	50.5	51.5
5:00	46.8	44.1	49.0	5:00	50.5	50.0	51.9

Source: Kinard, J., Western Carolina University, as reported in Render, B., and Stair, Jr., R., *Quantitative Analysis for Management,* 6th ed. Upper Saddle River, N.J.: Prentice-Hall, 1997.

11.16 University of Waterloo (Canada) statistician S.H. Steiner applied control chart methodology to the manufacturing of a horseshoe-shaped metal fastener called a robotics clamp (*Applied Statistics*, Vol. 47, 1998). Users of the clamp were concerned with the width of the gap between the two ends of the fastener. Their preferred target width is .054 inches. An optical measuring device was used to measure the gap width of the fastener during the manufacturing process. The manufacturer sampled five finished clamps every fifteen minutes throughout its 16-hour daily production schedule and optically measured the gap. Data for four consecutive hours of production are presented in the table below.

CLAMPGAP.DAT

Time	Gap Width (thousandths of an inch)				
00:15	54.2	54.1	53.9	54.0	53.8
00:30	53.9	53.7	54.1	54.4	55.1
00:45	54.0	55.2	53.1	55.9	54.5
01:00	52.1	53.4	52.9	53.0	52.7
01:15	53.0	51.9	52.6	53.4	51.7
01:30	54.2	55.0	54.0	53.8	53.6
01:45	55.2	56.6	53.1	52.9	54.0
02:00	53.3	57.2	54.5	51.6	54.3
02:15	54.9	56.3	55.2	56.1	54.0
02:30	55.7	53.1	52.9	56.3	55.4
02:45	55.2	51.0	56.3	55.6	54.2
03:00	54.2	54.2	55.8	53.8	52.1
03:15	55.7	57.5	55.4	54.0	53.1
03:30	53.7	56.9	54.0	55.1	54.2
03:45	54.1	53.9	54.0	54.6	54.8
04:00	53.5	56.1	55.1	55.0	54.0

Source: Adapted from Steiner, Stefan, H., "Grouped Data Exponentially Weighted Moving Average Control Charts," *Applied Statistics—Journal of the Royal Statistical Society*, Vol. 47, Part 2, 1998, pp. 203–216.

a. Construct an $\bar{x}$-chart from these data.
b. Apply the pattern-analysis rules to the control chart. Does your analysis suggest that special causes of variation are present in the clamp manufacturing process? Which of the six rules led you to your conclusion?
c. Should the control limits be used to monitor future process output? Explain.

11.17 A pharmaceutical company produces vials filled with morphine (*Communications in Statistics*, Vol. 27, 1998). Most of the time the filling process remains stable, but once in a while the mean value shifts off the target of 52.00 grams. To monitor the process, one sample of size 3 is drawn from the process every 27 minutes. Measurements for 20 consecutive samples are shown in the table.

MORPHINE.DAT

Sample	Amount of Morphine in Vials (grams)		
1	51.60	52.35	52.00
2	52.10	53.00	51.90
3	51.75	51.85	52.05
4	52.10	53.50	53.95
5	52.00	52.35	52.40
6	51.70	52.10	51.90
7	52.00	51.50	52.35
8	52.25	52.40	52.05
9	52.00	51.60	51.80
10	52.15	51.65	51.40
11	51.20	52.15	52.35
12	52.00	52.35	51.85
13	51.60	52.15	52.00
14	51.40	52.35	52.10
15	52.90	53.75	54.25
16	54.30	53.90	54.15
17	53.85	53.65	54.90
18	54.25	53.55	54.05
19	54.00	53.60	53.95
20	53.80	54.50	54.20

Source: Adapted from Costa, A.F.B., "VSSI X charts with Sampling at Fixed Times," *Communications in Statistics—Theory and Methods*, Vol. 27, No. 11 (1998), pp. 2853–2869.

a. Construct an $\bar{x}$-chart for these data.
b. What does the $\bar{x}$-chart suggest about the stability of the process?
c. Is the process influenced by both common and special causes of variation? Explain.
d. Should the control limits and centerline of the $\bar{x}$-chart of part **a** be used to monitor future output of the morphine filling process? Explain.

11.5 A CONTROL CHART FOR MONITORING THE VARIATION OF A PROCESS: THE *R*-CHART

Recall from Section 11.2 that a process may be out of statistical control because its mean or variance or both are changing over time (see Figure 11.8). The $\bar{x}$-chart of the previous section is used to detect changes in the process mean. The control chart we present in this section—the ***R*-chart**—is used to detect changes in process variation.

The primary difference between the $\bar{x}$-chart and the R-chart is that instead of plotting *sample means* and monitoring their variation, we plot and monitor the variation of *sample ranges*. Changes in the behavior of the sample range signal changes in the variation of the process.

We could also monitor process variation by plotting *sample standard deviations.* That is, we could calculate s for each sample (i.e., each subgroup) and plot them on a control chart known as an **s-chart**. In this chapter, however, we focus on just the R-chart because (1) when using samples of size 9 or less, the s-chart and the R-chart reflect about the same information, and (2) the R-chart is used much more widely by practitioners than is the s-chart (primarily because the sample range is easier to calculate and interpret than the sample standard deviation). For more information about s-charts, see the references at the end of the book.

The underlying logic and basic form of the R-chart are similar to the $\bar{x}$-chart. In monitoring $\bar{x}$, we use the standard deviation of $\bar{x}$ to develop 3-sigma control limits. Now, since we want to be able to determine when R takes on unusually large or small values, we use the standard deviation of R, or σ_R, to construct 3-sigma control limits. The centerline of the $\bar{x}$-chart represents the process mean μ or, equivalently, the mean of the sampling distribution of $\bar{x}$, $\mu_{\bar{x}}$. Similarly, the centerline of the R-chart represents μ_R, the mean of the sampling distribution of R. These points are illustrated in the R-chart of Figure 11.24.

FIGURE 11.24
R-Chart

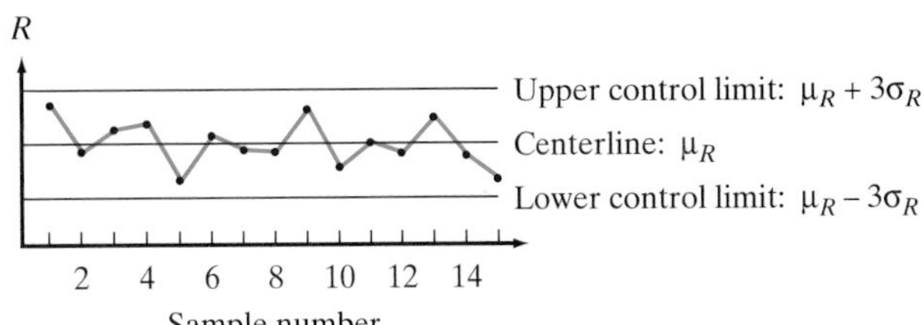

As with the $\bar{x}$-chart, you should have at least 20 samples of n items each ($n \geq 2$) to construct an R-chart. This will provide sufficient data to obtain reasonably good estimates of μ_R and σ_R. Rational subgrouping is again used for determining sample size and frequency of sampling.

The centerline of the R-chart is positioned as follows:

$$\textit{Centerline: } \bar{R} = \frac{R_1 + R_2 + \cdots + R_k}{k}$$

where k is the number of samples of size n and R_i is the range of the ith sample. $\bar{R}$ is an estimate of μ_R.

In order to construct the control limits, we need an estimator of σ_R. The estimator recommended by Montgomery (1991) and Ryan (1989) is

$$\hat{\sigma}_R = d_3\left(\frac{\bar{R}}{d_2}\right)$$

where d_2 and d_3 are constants whose values depend on the sample size, n. Values for d_2 and d_3 for samples of size $n = 2$ to $n = 25$ are given in Table XV of Appendix B.

The control limits are positioned as follows:

$$\textit{Upper control limit: } \bar{R} + 3\hat{\sigma}_R = \bar{R} + 3d_3\left(\frac{\bar{R}}{d_2}\right)$$

$$\textit{Lower control limit: } \bar{R} - 3\hat{\sigma}_R = \bar{R} + 3d_3\left(\frac{\bar{R}}{d_2}\right)$$

Notice that $\overline{R}$ appears twice in each control limit. Accordingly, we can simplify the calculation of these limits by factoring out $\overline{R}$:

$$\text{UCL: } \overline{R}\left(1 + \frac{3d_3}{d_2}\right) = \overline{R}D_4 \qquad \text{LCL: } \overline{R}\left(1 - \frac{3d_3}{d_2}\right) = \overline{R}D_3$$

where

$$D_4 = \left(1 + \frac{3d_3}{d_2}\right) \qquad D_3 = \left(1 - \frac{3d_3}{d_2}\right)$$

The values for D_3 and D_4 have been tabulated for samples of size $n = 2$ to $n = 25$ and can be found in Appendix B, Table XV.

For samples of size $n = 2$ through $n = 6$, D_3 is negative, and the lower control limit falls below zero. Since the sample range cannot take on negative values, such a control limit is meaningless. Thus, when $n \leq 6$ the R-chart contains only one control limit, the upper control limit.

Although D_3 is actually negative for $n \leq 6$, the values reported in Table XV in Appendix B are all zeros. This has been done to discourage the inappropriate construction of negative lower control limits. If the lower control limit is calculated using $D_3 = 0$, you obtain $D_3\overline{R} = 0$. This should be interpreted as indicating that the R-chart has no lower 3-sigma control limit.

Constructing an *R*-Chart: A Summary

1. Using a rational subgrouping strategy, collect at least 20 samples (i.e., subgroups), each of size $n \geq 2$.
2. Calculate the range of each sample.
3. Calculate the mean of the sample ranges, $\overline{R}$:

$$\overline{R} = \frac{R_1 + R_2 + \cdots + R_k}{k}$$

where

$k =$ The number of samples (i.e., subgroups)
$R_i =$ The range of the ith sample

4. Plot the centerline and control limits:

Centerline: $\overline{R}$

Upper control limit: $\overline{R}D_4$

Lower control limit: $\overline{R}D_3$

where D_3 and D_4 are constants that depend on n. Their values can be found in Appendix B, Table XV. When $n \leq 6$, $D_3 = 0$, indicating that the control chart does not have a lower control limit.

5. Plot the k sample ranges on the control chart in the order that the samples were produced by the process.

We interpret the completed R-chart in basically the same way as we did the $\bar{x}$-chart. We look for indications that the process is out of control. Those indications include points that fall outside the control limits as well as any nonrandom patterns of variation that appear between the control limits. To help spot nonrandom behavior, we include the A, B, and C zones (described in the previous section) on the R-chart. The next box describes how to construct the zone boundaries for the R-chart. It requires only Rules 1 through 4 of Figure 11.21, because Rules 5 and 6 are based on the assumption that the statistic plotted on the control chart follows a normal (or nearly normal) distribution, whereas R's distribution is skewed to the right.*

Constructing Zone Boundaries for an R-Chart

The simplest method of construction uses the estimator of the standard deviation of R, which is $\hat{\sigma}_R = d_3(\bar{R}/d_2)$:

$$\textit{Upper A–B boundary: } \bar{R} + 2d_3\left(\frac{\bar{R}}{d_2}\right)$$

$$\textit{Lower A–B boundary: } \bar{R} - 2d_3\left(\frac{\bar{R}}{d_2}\right)$$

$$\textit{Upper B–C boundary: } \bar{R} + d_3\left(\frac{\bar{R}}{d_2}\right)$$

$$\textit{Lower B–C boundary: } \bar{R} - d_3\left(\frac{\bar{R}}{d_2}\right)$$

Note: Whenever $n \leq 6$ the R-chart has no lower 3-sigma control limit. However, the lower A–B, B–C boundaries can still be plotted if they are nonnegative.

Interpreting an R-Chart

1. The **process is out of control** if one or more sample ranges fall beyond the control limits (Rule 1) or if any of the three patterns of variation described by Rules 2, 3, and 4 (Figure 11.21) are observed. Such signals indicate that one or more special causes of variation are influencing the *variation* of the process. These causes should be identified and eliminated to bring the process into control.
2. The **process is treated as being in control** if none of the noted out-of-control signals are observed. Processes that are in control should not be tampered with. However, if the level of variation is unacceptably high, common causes of variation should be identified and eliminated.

As with the $\bar{x}$-chart, the centerline and control limits should be developed using samples that were collected during a period in which the process was in control. Accordingly, when an R-chart is first constructed, the centerline and the control limits are treated as *trial values* (see Section 11.4) and are modified, if necessary, before being extended to the right and used to monitor future process output.

*Some authors (e.g., Kane, 1989) apply all six pattern-analysis rules as long as $n \geq 4$.

EXAMPLE 11.3 Refer to Example 11.1.

a. Construct an R-chart for the paint-filling process.

b. What does the chart indicate about the stability of the filling process during the time when the data were collected?

c. Is it appropriate to use the control limits constructed in part **a** to monitor future process output?

Solution a. The first step after collecting the data is to calculate the range of each sample. For the first sample the range is

$$R_1 = 10.0042 - 9.9964 = .0078$$

All 25 sample ranges appear in Table 11.2.

Next, calculate the mean of the ranges:

$$\overline{R} = \frac{.0078 + .0092 + \cdots + .0077}{25} = .01028$$

The centerline of the chart is positioned at $\overline{R} = .01028$. To determine the control limits, we need the constants D_3 and D_4, which can be found in Table XV of Appendix B. For $n = 5$, $D_3 = 0$ and $D_4 = 2.115$. Since $D_3 = 0$, the lower 3-sigma control limit is negative and is not included on the chart. The upper control limit is calculated as follows:

$$\text{UCL: } \overline{R}D_4 = (.01028)(2.115) = .02174$$

After positioning the upper control limit on the chart, we plot the 25 sample ranges in the order of sampling and connect the points with straight lines. The resulting trial R-chart is shown in Figure 11.25.

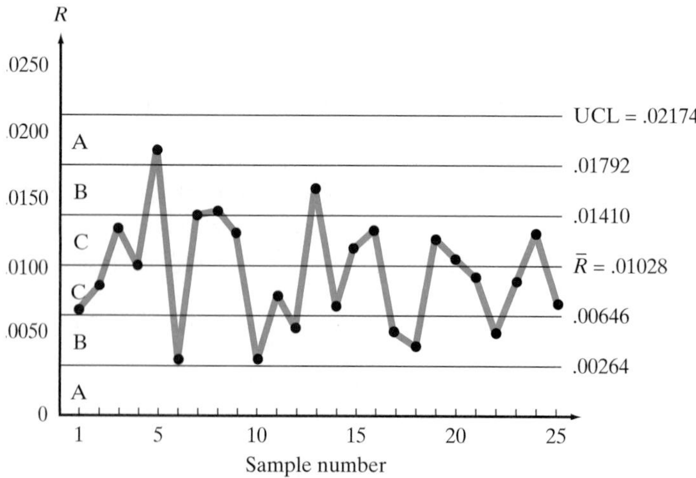

FIGURE 11.25 R-chart for the paint-filling process

b. To facilitate our examination of the R-chart, we plot the four zone boundaries. Recall that in general the A–B boundaries are positioned 2 standard deviations from the centerline and the B–C boundaries are 1 standard deviation from the centerline. In the case of the R-chart, we use the estimated standard deviation of R, $\hat{\sigma}_R = d_3(\overline{R}/d_2)$, and calculate the boundaries:

$$\textit{Upper A–B boundary: } \overline{R} + 2d_3\left(\frac{\overline{R}}{d_2}\right) = .01792$$

$$\textit{Lower A–B boundary: } \overline{R} - 2d_3\left(\frac{\overline{R}}{d_2}\right) = .00264$$

$$\textit{Upper B–C boundary: } \overline{R} + d_3\left(\frac{\overline{R}}{d_2}\right) = .01410$$

$$\textit{Lower B–C boundary: } \overline{R} - d_3\left(\frac{\overline{R}}{d_2}\right) = .00646$$

where (from Table XV of Appendix B) for $n = 5$, $d_2 = 2.326$ and $d_3 = .864$. Notice in Figure 11.25 that the lower A zone is slightly narrower than the upper A zone. This occurs because the lower 3-sigma control limit (the usual lower boundary of the lower A zone) is negative.

All the plotted R values fall below the upper control limit. This is one indication that the process is under control (i.e., is stable). However, we must also look for patterns of points that would be unlikely to occur if the process were in control. To assist us with this process, we use pattern-analysis rules 1–4 (Figure 11.21). None of the rules signal the presence of special causes of variation. Accordingly, we conclude that it is reasonable to treat the process—in particular, the variation of the process—as being under control during the period in question. Apparently, no significant special causes of variation are influencing the variation of the process.

c. Yes. Since the variation of the process appears to be in control during the period when the sample data were collected, the control limits appropriately characterize the variation in R that would be expected when the process is in a state of statistical control. ✶

In practice, the $\bar{x}$-chart and the R-chart are not used in isolation, as our presentation so far might suggest. Rather, they are used together to monitor the mean (i.e., the location) of the process and the variation of the process simultaneously. In fact, many practitioners plot them on the same piece of paper.

One important reason for dealing with them as a unit is that the control limits of the $\bar{x}$-chart are a function of R. That is, the control limits depend on the variation of the process. (Recall that the control limits are $\bar{\bar{x}} \pm A_2\overline{R}$.) Thus, if the process variation is out of control the control limits of the $\bar{x}$-chart have little meaning. This is because when the process variation is changing (as in the bottom two graphs of Figure 11.8), any single estimate of the variation (such as $\overline{R}$ or s) is not representative of the process. Accordingly, **the appropriate procedure is to first construct and then interpret the R-chart. If it indicates that the process variation is in control, then it makes sense to construct and interpret the $\bar{x}$-chart.**

Figure 11.26 is reprinted from Kaoru Ishikawa's classic text on quality-improvement methods, *Guide to Quality Control* (1986). It illustrates how particular changes in a process over time may be reflected in $\bar{x}$- and R-charts. At the top of the figure, running across the page, is a series of probability distributions A, B, and C that describe the process (i.e., the output variable) at different points in time. In practice, we never have this information. For this example, however, Ishikawa

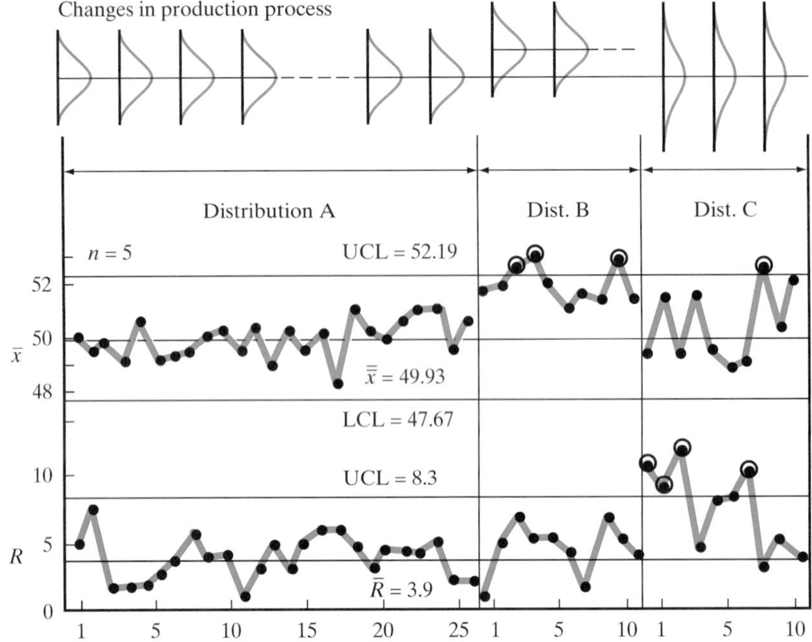

FIGURE 11.26
Combined $\bar{x}$- and R-chart

Source: Reprinted from *Guide to Quality Control,* by Kaoru Ishikawa, © 1986 by Asian Productivity Organization, with permission of the publisher Asian Productivity Organization. Distributed in North America by Quality Resources, New York, NY.

worked with a known process (i.e., with its given probabilistic characterization) to illustrate how sample data from a known process might behave.

The control limits for both charts were constructed from $k = 25$ samples of size $n = 5$. These data were generated by Distribution A. The 25 sample means and ranges were plotted on the $\bar{x}$- and R-charts, respectively. Since the distribution did not change over this period of time, it follows from the definition of statistical control that the process was under control. If you did not know this—as would be the case in practice—what would you conclude from looking at the control charts? (Remember, always interpret the R-chart before the $\bar{x}$-chart.) Both charts indicate that the process is under control. Accordingly, the control limits are made official and can be used to monitor future output, as is done next.

Toward the middle of the figure, the process changes. The mean shifts to a higher level. Now the output variable is described by Distribution B. The process is out of control. Ten new samples of size 5 are sampled from the process. Since the variation of the process has not changed, the R-chart should indicate that the variation remains stable. This is, in fact, the case. All points fall below the upper control limit. As we would hope, it is the $\bar{x}$-chart that reacts to the change in the mean of the process.

Then the process changes again (Distribution C). This time the mean shifts back to its original position, but the variation of the process increases. The process is still out of control but this time for a different reason. Checking the R-chart first, we see that it has reacted as we would hope. It has detected the increase in the variation. Given this R-chart finding, the control limits of the $\bar{x}$-chart become inappropriate (as described before) and we would not use them. Notice, however, how the sample means react to the increased variation in the process. This increased variation in $\bar{x}$ is consistent with what we know about the variance of $\bar{x}$. It is directly proportional to the variance of the process, $\sigma_{\bar{x}}^2 = \sigma^2/n$.

Keep in mind that what Ishikawa did in this example is exactly the opposite of what we do in practice. In practice we use sample data and control charts to make inferences about changes in unknown process distributions. Here, for the purpose of helping you to understand and interpret control charts, known process distributions were changed to see what would happen to the control charts.

EXERCISES 11.18–11.29

Learning the Mechanics

11.18 What characteristic of a process is an R-chart designed to monitor?

11.19 In practice, $\bar{x}$- and R-charts are used together to monitor a process. However, the R-chart should be interpreted before the $\bar{x}$-chart. Why?

11.20 Use Table XV in Appendix B to find the values of D_3 and D_4 for each of the following sample sizes.
a. $n = 4$ b. $n = 12$ c. $n = 24$

11.21 Construct and interpret an R-chart for the data in Exercise 11.10 (p. 667).
a. Calculate and plot the upper control limit and, if appropriate, the lower control limit.
b. Calculate and plot the A, B, and C zone boundaries on the R-chart.
c. Plot the sample ranges on the R-chart and use pattern-analysis rules 1–4 of Figure 11.21 to determine whether the process is under statistical control.

11.22 Construct and interpret an R-chart for the data in Exercise 11.11 (p. 668).
a. Calculate and plot the upper control limit and, if appropriate, the lower control limit.
b. Calculate and plot the A, B, and C zone boundaries on the R-chart.
c. Plot the sample ranges on the R-chart and determine whether the process is in control.

11.23 Construct and interpret an R-chart and an $\bar{x}$-chart from the sample data shown below. Remember to interpret the R-chart *before* the $\bar{x}$-chart.

Applying the Concepts

11.24 Refer to Exercise 11.12 (p. 668), where the desired circuit path widths were .5 to .85 micron. The manufacturer sampled four CPU chips six times a day (every 90 minutes from 8:00 A.M. until 4:30 P.M.) for five consecutive days. The path widths were measured and used to construct the MINITAB R-chart shown on page 680.
a. Calculate the chart's upper and lower control limits.
b. What does the R-chart suggest about the presence of special causes of variation during the time when the data were collected?
c. Should the control limit(s) be used to monitor future process output? Explain.
d. How many different R values are plotted on the control chart? Notice how most of the R values fall along three horizontal lines. What could cause such a pattern?

LM11_23.DAT

Sample	Measurements							$\bar{x}$	R
	1	2	3	4	5	6	7		
1	20.1	19.0	20.9	22.2	18.9	18.1	21.3	20.07	4.1
2	19.0	17.9	21.2	20.4	20.0	22.3	21.5	20.33	4.4
3	22.6	21.4	21.4	22.1	19.2	20.6	18.7	20.86	3.9
4	18.1	20.8	17.8	19.6	19.8	21.7	20.0	19.69	3.9
5	22.6	19.1	21.4	21.8	18.4	18.0	19.5	20.11	4.6
6	19.1	19.0	22.3	21.5	17.8	19.2	19.4	19.76	4.5
7	17.1	19.4	18.6	20.9	21.8	21.0	19.8	19.80	4.7
8	20.2	22.4	22.0	19.6	19.6	20.0	18.5	20.33	3.9
9	21.9	24.1	23.1	22.8	25.6	24.2	25.2	23.84	3.7
10	25.1	24.3	26.0	23.1	25.8	27.0	26.5	25.40	3.9
11	25.8	29.2	28.5	29.1	27.8	29.0	28.0	28.20	3.4
12	28.2	27.5	29.3	30.7	27.6	28.0	27.0	28.33	3.7
13	28.2	28.6	28.1	26.0	30.0	28.5	28.3	28.24	4.0
14	22.1	21.4	23.3	20.5	19.8	20.5	19.0	20.94	4.3
15	18.5	19.2	18.0	20.1	22.0	20.2	19.5	19.64	4.0
16	21.4	20.3	22.0	19.2	18.0	17.9	19.5	19.76	4.1
17	18.4	16.5	18.1	19.2	17.5	20.9	19.6	18.60	4.4
18	20.1	19.8	22.3	22.5	21.8	22.7	23.0	21.74	3.2
19	20.0	17.5	21.0	18.2	19.5	17.2	18.1	18.79	3.8
20	22.3	18.2	21.5	19.0	19.4	20.5	20.0	20.13	4.1

MINITAB Output for Exercise 11.24

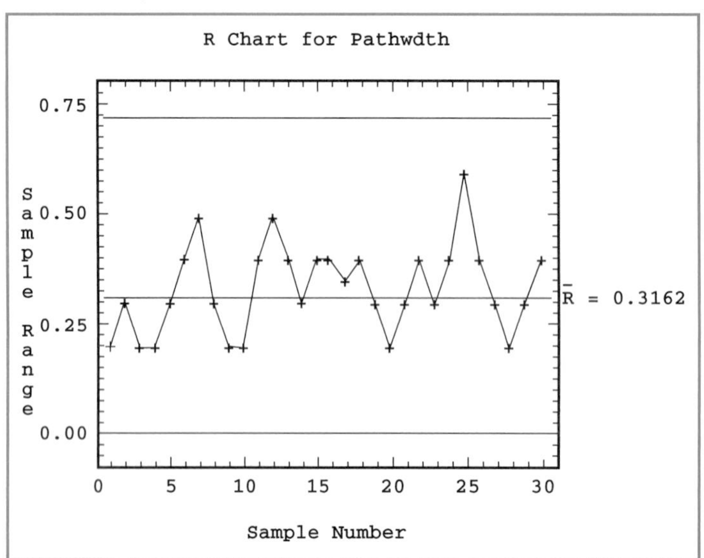

11.25 A soft-drink bottling company is interested in monitoring the amount of cola injected into 16-ounce bottles by a particular filling head. The process is entirely automated and operates 24 hours a day. At 6 A.M. and 6 P.M. each day, a new dispenser of carbon dioxide capable of producing 20,000 gallons of cola is hooked up to the filling machine. In order to monitor the process using control charts, the company decided to sample five consecutive bottles of cola each hour beginning at 6:15 A.M. (i.e., 6:15 A.M., 7:15 A.M., 8:15 A.M., etc.). The data for the first day are given in the table at left. An SPSS descriptive statistics printout is also provided on page 681.

COLAFILL.DAT

Sample	Measurements				
1	16.01	16.03	15.98	16.00	16.01
2	16.03	16.02	15.97	15.99	15.99
3	15.98	16.00	16.03	16.04	15.99
4	16.00	16.03	16.02	15.98	15.98
5	15.97	15.99	16.03	16.01	16.04
6	16.01	16.03	16.04	15.97	15.99
7	16.04	16.05	15.97	15.96	16.00
8	16.02	16.05	16.03	15.97	15.98
9	15.97	15.99	16.02	16.03	15.95
10	16.00	16.01	15.95	16.04	16.06
11	15.95	16.04	16.07	15.93	16.03
12	15.98	16.07	15.94	16.08	16.02
13	15.96	16.00	16.01	16.00	15.98
14	15.98	16.01	16.02	15.99	15.99
15	15.99	16.03	16.00	15.98	16.01
16	16.02	16.02	16.01	15.97	16.00
17	16.01	16.05	15.99	15.99	16.03
18	15.98	16.03	16.04	15.98	16.01
19	15.97	15.96	15.99	15.99	16.01
20	16.03	16.01	16.04	15.96	15.99
21	15.99	16.03	15.97	16.05	16.03
22	15.98	15.95	16.07	16.01	16.04
23	15.99	16.06	15.95	16.03	16.07
24	16.00	16.01	16.08	15.94	15.93

a. Will the rational subgrouping strategy that was used enable the company to detect variation in fill caused by differences in the carbon dioxide dispensers? Explain.

b. Construct an *R*-chart from the data.

c. What does the *R*-chart indicate about the stability of the filling process during the time when the data were collected? Justify your answer.

d. Should the control limit(s) be used to monitor future process output? Explain.

e. Given your answer to part **c,** should an $\bar{x}$-chart be constructed from the given data? Explain.

11.26 In an effort to reduce customer dissatisfaction with delays in replacing lost automated teller machine (ATM) cards, some retail banks monitor the time required to replace a lost ATM card. Called replacement cycle time, it is the elapsed time from when the customer contacts the bank about the loss until the customer receives a new card (*Management Science*, Sept. 1999). A particular retail bank monitors replacement cycle time for the first five requests each week for replacement cards. Variation in cycle times is monitored using an *R*-chart. Data for 20 weeks is presented on page 681.

a. Construct an *R*-chart for these data.

b. What does the *R*-chart suggest about the presence of special causes of variation in the process?

c. Should the control limits of your *R*-chart be used to monitor future replacement cycle times? Explain.

d. Given your conclusion in part **b** and the pattern displayed on the *R*-chart, discuss the possible future impact on the performance of the bank.

SPSS Output for Exercise 11.25

SAMPLE	Variable	Mean	Range	Minimum	Maximum	N
1.00	COLA	16.006	.05	15.98	16.03	5
2.00	COLA	16.000	.06	15.97	16.03	5
3.00	COLA	16.008	.06	15.98	16.04	5
4.00	COLA	16.002	.05	15.98	16.03	5
5.00	COLA	16.008	.07	15.97	16.04	5
6.00	COLA	16.008	.07	15.97	16.04	5
7.00	COLA	16.004	.09	15.96	16.05	5
8.00	COLA	16.010	.08	15.97	16.05	5
9.00	COLA	15.992	.08	15.95	16.03	5
10.00	COLA	16.012	.11	15.95	16.06	5
11.00	COLA	16.004	.14	15.93	16.07	5
12.00	COLA	16.018	.14	15.94	16.08	5
13.00	COLA	15.990	.05	15.96	16.01	5
14.00	COLA	15.998	.04	15.98	16.02	5
15.00	COLA	16.002	.05	15.98	16.03	5
16.00	COLA	16.004	.05	15.97	16.02	5
17.00	COLA	16.014	.06	15.99	16.05	5
18.00	COLA	16.008	.06	15.98	16.04	5
19.00	COLA	15.984	.05	15.96	16.01	5
20.00	COLA	16.006	.08	15.96	16.04	5
21.00	COLA	16.014	.08	15.97	16.05	5
22.00	COLA	16.010	.12	15.95	16.07	5
23.00	COLA	16.020	.12	15.95	16.07	5
24.00	COLA	15.992	.15	15.93	16.08	5

ATM.DAT

Week	Replacement Cycle Time (in days)				
1	7	10	6	6	10
2	7	12	8	8	6
3	7	8	7	11	6
4	8	8	12	11	12
5	3	8	4	7	7
6	6	10	11	5	7
7	5	12	11	8	7
8	7	12	8	7	6
9	8	10	12	10	5
10	12	8	6	6	8
11	10	9	9	5	4
12	3	10	7	6	8
13	9	9	8	7	2
14	7	10	18	20	8
15	8	18	15	18	21
16	10	22	16	8	7
17	3	18	4	8	12
18	11	7	8	17	19
19	10	8	19	20	25
20	6	3	18	18	7

11.27 The *Journal of Quality Technology* (July 1998) published an article examining the effects of the precision of measurement on the R-chart. The authors presented data from a British nutrition company that fills containers labeled "500 grams" with a powdered dietary supplement. Once every 15 minutes, five containers are sampled from the filling process and the fill weight is measured. The table at the top of page 682 lists the measurements for 25 consecutive samples made with a scale that is accurate to .5 gram, followed by a table that gives measurements for the same samples made with a scale that is accurate to only 2.5 grams. Throughout the time period over which the samples were drawn, it is known that the filling process was in statistical control with mean 500 grams and standard deviation 1 gram.

a. Construct an R-chart for the data that is accurate to .5 gram. Is the process under statistical control? Explain.
b. Given your answer to part **a**, is it appropriate to construct an $\bar{x}$-chart for the data? Explain.
c. Construct an R-chart for the data that is accurate to only 2.5 grams. What does it suggest about the stability of the filling process?
d. Based on your answers to parts **a** and **c**, discuss the importance of the accuracy of measurement instruments in evaluating the stability of production processes.

11.28 Refer to Exercise 11.15 (p. 671), in which the Bayfield Mud Company was concerned with discovering why

FILLWT1.DAT

Sample	Fill Weights Accurate to .5 Gram					Range
1	500.5	499.5	502.0	501.0	500.5	2.5
2	500.5	499.5	500.0	499.0	500.0	1.5
3	498.5	499.0	500.0	499.5	500.0	1.5
4	500.5	499.5	499.0	499.0	500.5	1.5
5	500.0	501.0	500.5	500.5	500.0	1.0
6	501.0	498.5	500.0	501.5	500.5	3.0
7	499.5	500.0	499.0	501.0	499.5	2.0
8	498.5	498.0	500.0	500.5	500.5	2.5
9	498.0	499.0	502.0	501.0	501.5	4.0
10	499.0	499.5	499.5	500.0	499.5	1.0
11	502.5	499.5	501.0	501.5	502.0	3.0
12	501.5	501.5	500.0	500.0	501.0	1.5
13	498.5	499.5	501.0	500.5	498.5	2.5
14	499.5	498.0	500.0	499.5	498.5	2.0
15	501.0	500.0	498.0	500.5	500.0	3.0
16	502.5	501.5	502.0	500.5	500.5	2.0
17	499.5	500.5	500.0	499.5	499.5	1.0
18	499.0	498.5	498.0	500.0	498.0	2.0
19	499.0	498.0	500.5	501.0	501.0	3.0
20	501.5	499.5	500.0	500.5	502.0	2.0
21	501.0	500.5	502.0	502.5	502.5	2.0
22	501.5	502.5	502.5	501.5	502.0	1.0
23	499.5	502.0	500.0	500.5	502.0	2.5
24	498.5	499.0	499.0	500.5	500.0	2.0
25	500.0	499.5	498.5	500.0	500.5	2.0

FILLWT2.DAT

Sample	Fill Weights Accurate to 2.5 Grams					Range
1	500.0	500.0	502.5	500.0	500.0	2.5
2	500.0	500.0	500.0	500.0	500.0	0.0
3	500.0	500.0	500.0	500.0	500.0	0.0
4	497.5	500.0	497.5	497.5	500.0	2.5
5	500.0	500.0	500.0	500.0	500.0	0.0
6	502.5	500.0	497.5	500.0	500.0	5.0
7	500.0	500.0	502.5	502.5	500.0	2.5
8	497.5	500.0	500.0	497.5	500.0	2.5
9	500.0	500.0	497.5	500.0	502.5	5.0
10	500.0	500.0	500.0	500.0	500.0	0.0
11	500.0	505.0	502.5	500.0	500.0	5.0
12	500.0	500.0	500.0	500.0	500.0	0.0
13	500.0	500.0	497.5	500.0	500.0	2.5
14	500.0	500.0	500.0	500.0	500.0	0.0
15	502.5	502.5	502.5	500.0	502.5	2.5
16	500.0	500.0	500.0	500.0	500.0	0.0
17	497.5	497.5	497.5	497.5	497.5	0.0
18	500.0	500.0	500.0	500.0	500.0	0.0
19	495.0	497.5	500.0	500.0	500.0	5.0
20	500.0	502.5	500.0	500.0	502.5	2.5
21	500.0	500.0	500.0	500.0	500.0	0.0
22	500.0	500.0	500.0	500.0	500.0	0.0
23	500.0	500.0	500.0	500.0	500.0	0.0
24	497.5	497.5	500.0	497.5	497.5	2.5
25	500.0	500.0	497.5	500.0	500.0	2.5

Source: Adapted from Tricker, A., Coates, E. and Okell, E., "The Effects on the *R*-chart of Precision of Measurement," *Journal of Quality Technology*, Vol. 30, No. 3, July 1998, pp. 232–239.

their filling operation was producing underfilled bags of mud.

a. Construct an R-chart for the filling process.

b. According to the R-chart, is the process under statistical control? Explain.

c. Does the R-chart provide any evidence concerning the cause of Bayfield's underfilling problem? Explain.

12.29 Refer to Exercise 12.16 (p. 712), in which a robotics clamp manufacturer was concerned about gap width.

a. Construct an R-chart for the gap width.

b. Which parameter of the manufacturing process does your R-chart provide information about?

c. What does the R-chart suggest about the presence of special causes of variation during the time when the data were collected?

11.6 A CONTROL CHART FOR MONITORING THE PROPORTION OF DEFECTIVES GENERATED BY A PROCESS: THE p-CHART

Among the dozens of different control charts that have been proposed by researchers and practitioners, the $\bar{x}$- and R-charts are by far the most popular for use in monitoring *quantitative* output variables such as time, length, and weight. Among the charts developed for use with *qualitative* output variables, the chart we introduce in this section is the most popular. Called the ***p*-chart**, it is used when the output variable is categorical (i.e., measured on a nominal scale). With the p-chart, the proportion, p, of units produced by the process that belong to a particular category (e.g., defective or nondefective; successful or unsuccessful; early, on-time, or late) can be monitored.

The p-chart is typically used to monitor the proportion of defective units produced by a process (i.e., the proportion of units that do not conform to specification). This proportion is used to characterize a process in the same sense that the mean and variance are used to characterize a process when the output variable is quantitative. Examples of process proportions that are monitored in industry include the proportion of billing errors made by credit card companies; the proportion of nonfunctional semiconductor chips produced; and the proportion of checks that a bank's magnetic ink character-recognition system is unable to read.

As is the case for the mean and variance, the process proportion can change over time. For example, it can drift upward or downward or jump to a new level. In such cases, the process is out of control. **As long as the process proportion remains constant, the process is in a state of statistical control.**

As with the other control charts presented in this chapter, the p-chart has a centerline and control limits that are determined from sample data. After k samples of size n are drawn from the process, each unit is classified (e.g., defective or nondefective), the proportion of defective units in each sample—$\hat{p}$— is calculated, the centerline and control limits are determined using this information, and the sample proportions are plotted on the p-chart. It is the variation in the $\hat{p}$'s over time that we monitor and interpret. Changes in the behavior of the $\hat{p}$'s signal changes in the process proportion, p.

The p-chart is based on the assumption that the number of defectives observed in each sample is a binomial random variable. What we have called the process proportion is really the binomial probability, p. (We discussed binomial random variables in Chapter 4.) When the process is in a state of statistical control, p remains constant over time. Variation in $\hat{p}$—as displayed on a p-chart—is used to judge whether p is stable.

To determine the centerline and control limits for the p-chart we need to know $\hat{p}$'s sampling distribution. We described the sampling distribution of $\hat{p}$ in Section 5.4. Recall that

$$\hat{p} = \frac{\text{Number of defective items in the sample}}{\text{Number of items in the sample}} = \frac{x}{n}$$

$$\mu_{\hat{p}} = p$$

$$\sigma_{\hat{p}} = \sqrt{\frac{p(1 - p)}{n}}$$

and that for large samples $\hat{p}$ is approximately normally distributed. Thus, if p were known, the centerline would be p and the 3-sigma control limits would be $p \pm 3\sqrt{p(1 - p)/n}$. However, since p is unknown, it must be estimated from the sample data. The appropriate estimator is $\overline{p}$, the overall proportion of defective units in the nk units sampled:

$$\overline{p} = \frac{\text{Total number of defective units in all } k \text{ samples}}{\text{Total number of units sampled}}$$

To calculate the control limits of the p-chart, substitute $\overline{p}$ for p in the preceding expression for the control limits, as illustrated in Figure 11.27.

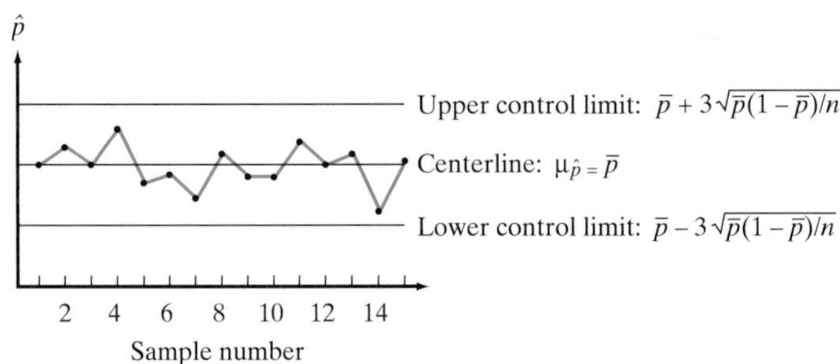

FIGURE 11.27
p-Chart

In constructing a p-chart it is advisable to use a much larger sample size than is typically used for $\overline{x}$- and R-charts. Most processes that are monitored in industry have relatively small process proportions, often less than .05 (i.e., less than 5% of output is nonconforming). In those cases, if a small sample size is used, say $n = 5$, samples drawn from the process would likely not contain any nonconforming output. As a result, most, if not all, $\hat{p}$'s would equal zero.

We present a rule of thumb that can be used to determine a sample size large enough to avoid this problem. This rule will also help protect against ending up with a negative lower control limit, a situation that frequently occurs when both p and n are small. See Montgomery (1991) or Duncan (1986) for further details.

Sample-Size Determination for Monitoring a Process Proportion

Choose n such that $n > \dfrac{9(1 - p_0)}{p_0}$

where

n = Sample size

p_0 = An estimate (perhaps judgmental) of the process proportion p

For example, if p is thought to be about .05, the rule indicates that samples of at least size 171 should be used in constructing the p-chart:

$$n > \frac{9(1 - .05)}{.05} = 171$$

In the next three boxes we summarize how to construct a p-chart and its zone boundaries and how to interpret a p-chart.

Constructing a *p*-Chart: A Summary

1. Using a rational subgrouping strategy, collect at least 20 samples, each of size

$$n > \frac{9(1 - p_0)}{p_0}$$

where p_0 is an estimate of p, the proportion defective (i.e., nonconforming) produced by the process. p_0 can be determined from sample data (i.e., $\hat{p}$) or may be based on expert opinion.

2. For each sample, calculate $\hat{p}$, the proportion of defective units in the sample:

$$\hat{p} = \frac{\text{Number of defective items in the sample}}{\text{Number of items in the sample}}$$

3. Plot the centerline and control limits:

$$\textit{Centerline: } \bar{p} = \frac{\text{Total number of defective units in all } k \text{ samples}}{\text{Total number of units in all } k \text{ samples}}$$

$$\textit{Upper control limit: } \bar{p} + 3\sqrt{\frac{\bar{p}(1 - \bar{p})}{n}}$$

$$\textit{Lower control limit: } \bar{p} - 3\sqrt{\frac{\bar{p}(1 - \bar{p})}{n}}$$

where k is the number of samples of size n and $\bar{p}$ is the overall proportion of defective units in the nk units sampled. $\bar{p}$ is an estimate of the unknown process proportion p.

4. Plot the k sample proportions on the control chart in the order that the samples were produced by the process.

As with the $\bar{x}$- and R-charts, the centerline and control limits should be developed using samples that were collected during a period in which the process was in control. Accordingly, when a p-chart is first constructed, the centerline and the control limits should be treated as *trial values* (see Section 11.4) and, if necessary, modified before being extended to the right on the control chart and used to monitor future process output.

Constructing Zone Boundaries for a *p*-Chart

$$\text{Upper A–B boundary: } \bar{p} + 2\sqrt{\frac{\bar{p}(1-\bar{p})}{n}}$$

$$\text{Lower A–B boundary: } \bar{p} - 2\sqrt{\frac{\bar{p}(1-\bar{p})}{n}}$$

$$\text{Upper B–C boundary: } \bar{p} + \sqrt{\frac{\bar{p}(1-\bar{p})}{n}}$$

$$\text{Lower B–C boundary: } \bar{p} - \sqrt{\frac{\bar{p}(1-\bar{p})}{n}}$$

Note: When the lower control limit is negative, it should not be plotted on the control chart. However, the lower zone boundaries can still be plotted if they are nonnegative.

Interpreting a *p*-Chart

1. The **process is out of control** if one or more sample proportions fall beyond the control limits (Rule 1) or if any of the three patterns of variation described by Rules 2, 3, and 4 (Figure 11.21) are observed. Such signals indicate that one or more special causes of variation are influencing the process proportion, p. These causes should be identified and eliminated in order to bring the process into control.
2. The **process is treated as being in control** if none of the above noted out-of-control signals are observed. Processes that are in control should not be tampered with. However, if the level of variation is unacceptably high, common causes of variation should be identified and eliminated.

EXAMPLE 11.4

A manufacturer of auto parts is interested in implementing statistical process control in several areas within its warehouse operation. The manufacturer wants to begin with the order assembly process. Too frequently orders received by customers contain the wrong items or too few items.

For each order received, parts are picked from storage bins in the warehouse, labeled, and placed on a conveyor belt system. Since the bins are spread over a three-acre area, items that are part of the same order may be placed on different spurs of the conveyor belt system. Near the end of the belt system all spurs converge and a worker sorts the items according to the order they belong to. That information is contained on the labels that were placed on the items by the pickers.

The workers have identified three errors that cause shipments to be improperly assembled: (1) pickers pick from the wrong bin, (2) pickers mislabel items, and (3) the sorter makes an error.

The firm's quality manager has implemented a sampling program in which 90 assembled orders are sampled each day and checked for accuracy. An assembled order is considered nonconforming (defective) if it differs in any way from the order placed by the customer. To date, 25 samples have been evaluated. The resulting data are shown in Table 11.4.

TABLE 11.4 Twenty-Five Samples of Size 90 from the Warehouse Order Assembly Process

Sample	Size	Defective Orders	Sample Proportion
1	90	12	.13333
2	90	6	.06666
3	90	11	.12222
4	90	8	.08888
5	90	13	.14444
6	90	14	.15555
7	90	12	.13333
8	90	6	.06666
9	90	10	.11111
10	90	13	.14444
11	90	12	.13333
12	90	24	.26666
13	90	23	.25555
14	90	22	.24444
15	90	8	.08888
16	90	3	.03333
17	90	11	.12222
18	90	14	.15555
19	90	5	.05555
20	90	12	.13333
21	90	18	.20000
22	90	12	.13333
23	90	13	.14444
24	90	4	.04444
25	90	6	.06666
Totals	2,250	292	

a. Construct a p-chart for the order assembly operation.

b. What does the chart indicate about the stability of the process?

c. Is it appropriate to use the control limits and centerline constructed in part **a** to monitor future process output?

Solution

a. The first step in constructing the p-chart after collecting the sample data is to calculate the sample proportion for each sample. For the first sample,

$$\hat{p} = \frac{\text{Number of defective items in the sample}}{\text{Number of items in the sample}} = \frac{12}{90} = .13333$$

All the sample proportions are displayed in Table 11.4. Next, calculate the proportion of defective items in the total number of items sampled:

$$\overline{p} = \frac{\text{Total number of defective items}}{\text{Total number of items sampled}} = \frac{292}{2{,}250} = .12978$$

The centerline is positioned at $\overline{p}$, and $\overline{p}$ is used to calculate the control limits:

$$\overline{p} \pm 3\sqrt{\frac{\overline{p}(1-\overline{p})}{n}} = .12978 \pm 3\sqrt{\frac{.12978(1-.12978)}{90}}$$

$$= .12978 \pm .10627$$

UCL: .23605

LCL: .02351

After plotting the centerline and the control limits, plot the 25 sample proportions in the order of sampling and connect the points with straight lines. The completed control chart is shown in Figure 11.28.

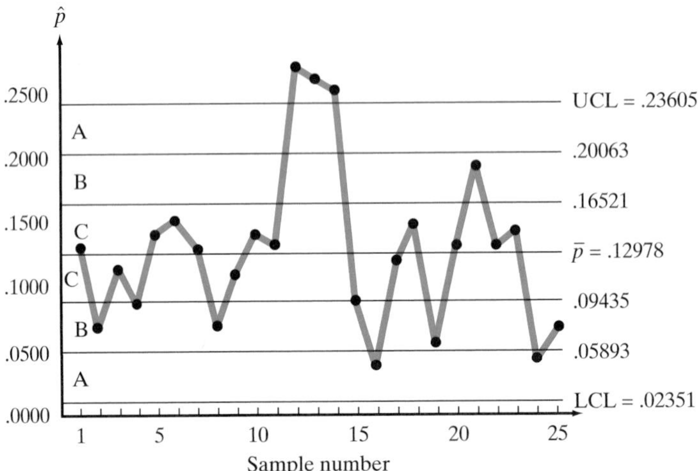

FIGURE 11.28
p-Chart for order assembly process

b. To assist our examination of the control chart, we add the 1- and 2-standard-deviation zone boundaries. The boundaries are located by substituting $\overline{p} = .12978$ into the following formulas:

$$\textit{Upper A–B boundary: } \overline{p} + 2\sqrt{\frac{\overline{p}(1-\overline{p})}{n}} = .20063$$

$$\textit{Lower A–B boundary: } \overline{p} - 2\sqrt{\frac{\overline{p}(1-\overline{p})}{n}} = .05893$$

$$\textit{Upper B–C boundary: } \overline{p} + \sqrt{\frac{\overline{p}(1-\overline{p})}{n}} = .16521$$

$$\textit{Lower B–C boundary: } \overline{p} - \sqrt{\frac{\overline{p}(1-\overline{p})}{n}} = .09435$$

Because three of the sample proportions fall above the upper control limit (Rule 1), there is strong evidence that the process is out of control. None of the nonrandom patterns of Rules 2, 3, and 4 (Figure 11.21) are evident. The process proportion appears to have increased dramatically somewhere around sample 12.

c. Because the process was apparently out of control during the period in which sample data were collected to build the control chart, it is not appropriate to continue using the chart. The control limits and centerline are not representative of the process when it is in control. The chart must be revised before it is used to monitor future output.

In this case, the three out-of-control points were investigated and it was discovered that they occurred on days when a temporary sorter was working in place of the regular sorter. Actions were taken to ensure that in the future better-trained temporary sorters would be available.

Since the special cause of the observed variation was identified and eliminated, all sample data from the three days the temporary sorter was working were dropped from the data set and the centerline and control limits were recalculated:

$$\textit{Centerline: } \overline{p} = \frac{223}{1980} = .11263$$

$$\textit{Control limits: } \overline{p} \pm 3\sqrt{\frac{\overline{p}(1-\overline{p})}{n}} = .11263 \pm 3\sqrt{\frac{.11263(.88737)}{90}}$$

$$= .11263 \pm .09997$$

UCL: .21259 LCL: .01266

The revised zones are calculated by substituting $\overline{p} = .11263$ in the following formulas:

$$\textit{Upper A–B boundary: } \overline{p} + 2\sqrt{\frac{\overline{p}(1-\overline{p})}{n}} = .17927$$

$$\textit{Upper B–C boundary: } \overline{p} + \sqrt{\frac{\overline{p}(1-\overline{p})}{n}} = .14595$$

$$\textit{Lower A–B boundary: } \overline{p} - 2\sqrt{\frac{\overline{p}(1-\overline{p})}{n}} = .04598$$

$$\textit{Lower B–C boundary: } \overline{p} - \sqrt{\frac{\overline{p}(1-\overline{p})}{n}} = .07931$$

The revised control chart appears in Figure 11.29. Notice that now all sample proportions fall within the control limits. These limits can now be treated as official, extended to the right on the chart, and used to monitor future orders.

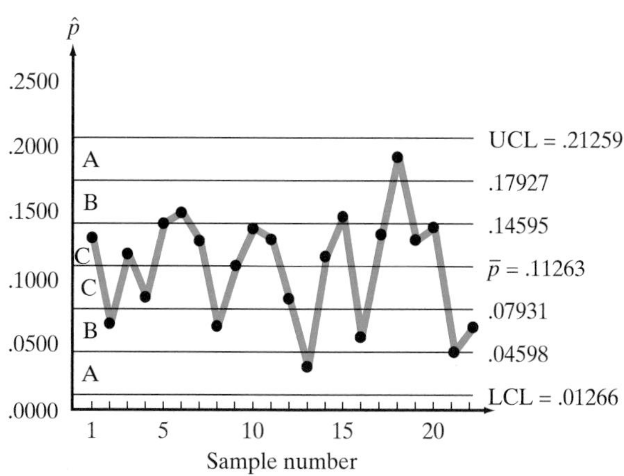

FIGURE 11.29 Revised p-chart for order assembly process

EXERCISES 11.30–11.38

Learning the Mechanics

11.30 What characteristic of a process is a p-chart designed to monitor?

11.31 The proportion of defective items generated by a manufacturing process is believed to be 8%. In constructing a p-chart for the process, determine how large the sample size should be to avoid ending up with a negative lower control limit.

11.32 To construct a p-chart for a manufacturing process, 25 samples of size 200 were drawn from the process. The number of defectives in each sample is listed below.

LM11_32.DAT

Sample	Sample Size	Defectives
1	200	16
2	200	14
3	200	9
4	200	11
5	200	15
6	200	8
7	200	12
8	200	16
9	200	17
10	200	13
11	200	15
12	200	10
13	200	9
14	200	12
15	200	14
16	200	11
17	200	8
18	200	7
19	200	12
20	200	15
21	200	9
22	200	16
23	200	13
24	200	11
25	200	10

a. Calculate the proportion defective in each sample.
b. Calculate and plot $\overline{p}$ and the upper and lower control limits for the p-chart.
c. Calculate and plot the A, B, and C zone boundaries on the p-chart.
d. Plot the sample proportions on the p-chart and connect them with straight lines.
e. Use the pattern-analysis rules 1–4 for detecting the presence of special causes of variation (Figure 11.21) to determine whether the process is out of control.

11.33 To construct a p-chart, 20 samples of size 150 were drawn from a process. The proportion of defective items found in each of the samples is listed in the next table.

LM11_33.DAT

Sample	Proportion Defective	Sample	Proportion Defective
1	.03	11	.07
2	.05	12	.04
3	.10	13	.06
4	.02	14	.05
5	.08	15	.07
6	.09	16	.06
7	.08	17	.07
8	.05	18	.02
9	.07	19	.05
10	.06	20	.03

a. Calculate and plot the centerline and the upper and lower control limits for the p-chart.
b. Calculate and plot the A, B, and C zone boundaries on the p-chart.
c. Plot the sample proportions on the p-chart.
d. Is the process under control? Explain.
e. Should the control limits and centerline of part **a** be used to monitor future process output? Explain.

11.34 In each of the following cases, use the sample size formula to determine a sample size large enough to avoid constructing a p-chart with a negative lower control limit.

a. $p_0 = .01$ b. $p_0 = .05$ c. $p_0 = .10$ d. $p_0 = .20$

Applying the Concepts

11.35 A manufacturer produces micron chips for personal computers. From past experience the production manager believes that 1% of the chips are defective. The company collected a sample of the first 1,000 chips manufactured after 4:00 P.M. every other day for a month. The chips were analyzed for defects, then these data and MINITAB were used to construct the p-chart shown on page 691.

a. From a statistical perspective, is a sample size of 1,000 adequate for constructing the p-chart? Explain.
b. Calculate the chart's upper and lower control limits.
c. What does the p-chart suggest about the presence of special causes during the time when the data were collected?
d. Critique the rational subgrouping strategy used by the disk manufacturer.

11.36 Goodstone Tire & Rubber Company is interested in monitoring the proportion of defective tires generated by the production process at its Akron, Ohio, production plant. The company's chief engineer believes that the proportion is about 7%. Because the tires are destroyed during the testing process, the company would like to keep the number of tires tested to a minimum. However, the engineer would also like to use a

MINITAB Output for Exercise 11.35

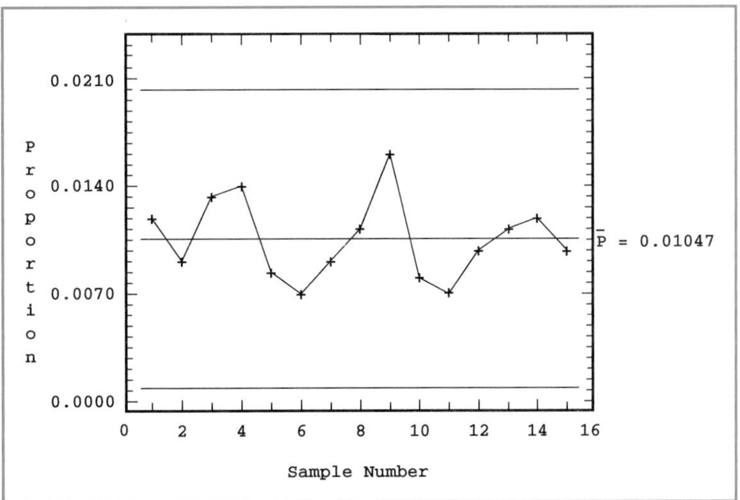

p-chart with a positive lower control limit. A positive lower control limit makes it possible to determine when the process has generated an unusually small proportion of defectives. Such an occurrence is good news and would signal the engineer to look for causes of the superior performance. That information can be used to improve the production process. Using the sample size formula, the chief engineer recommended that the company randomly sample and test 120 tires from each day's production. To date, 20 samples have been taken. The data are presented below.

a. Use the sample size formula to show how the chief engineer arrived at the recommended sample size of 120.

b. Construct a *p*-chart for the tire production process.

c. What does the chart indicate about the stability of the process? Explain.

d. Is it appropriate to use the control limits to monitor future process output? Explain.

e. Is the *p*-chart you constructed in part **b** capable of signaling hour-to-hour changes in *p*? Explain.

11.37 Accurate typesetting is crucial to the production of high-quality newspapers. The editor of the Morristown *Daily Tribune*, a weekly publication with circulation of 27,000, has instituted a process for monitoring the performance of typesetters. Each week 100 paragraphs of the paper are randomly sampled and read for accuracy. The number of paragraphs with errors is recorded in the table below for each of the last 30 weeks.

DEFTIRES.DAT

Sample	Sample Size	Defectives
1	120	11
2	120	5
3	120	4
4	120	8
5	120	10
6	120	13
7	120	9
8	120	8
9	120	10
10	120	11
11	120	10
12	120	12
13	120	8
14	120	6
15	120	10
16	120	5
17	120	10
18	120	10
19	120	3
20	120	8

TYPESET.DAT

Week	Paragraphs with Errors	Week	Paragraphs with Errors
1	2	16	2
2	4	17	3
3	10	18	7
4	4	19	3
5	1	20	2
6	1	21	3
7	13	22	7
8	9	23	4
9	11	24	3
10	0	25	2
11	3	26	2
12	4	27	0
13	2	28	1
14	2	29	3
15	8	30	4

Primary Source: Jerry Kinard, Western Carolina University.

Secondary Source: Render, B., and Stair, Jr., R. *Quantitative Analysis for Management*, 6th ed. Upper Saddle River, N. J.: Prentice-Hall, 1997.

STATISTICS IN Action

Deming's 14 Points

How is it that the Japanese became quality leaders? What inspired their concern for quality? In part, it was the statistical and managerial expertise exported to Japan from the United States following World War II. At the end of the war Japan faced the difficult task of rebuilding its economy. To this end, a group of engineers was assigned by the Allied command to assist the Japanese in improving the quality of their communication systems. These engineers taught the Japanese the statistical quality control methods that had been developed in the United States under the direction of Walter Shewhart of Bell Laboratories in the 1920s and 1930s. Then, in 1950, the Japanese Union of Scientists and Engineers invited W. Edwards Deming, a statistician who had studied with Shewhart, to present a series of lectures on statistical quality-improvement methods to hundreds of Japanese researchers, plant managers, and engineers. During his stay in Japan he also met with many of the top executives of Japan's largest companies. At the time, Japan was notorious for the inferior quality of its products. Deming told the executives that by listening to what consumers wanted and by applying statistical methods in the production of those goods, they could export high-quality products that would find markets all over the world.

In 1951 the Japanese established the *Deming Prize* to be given annually to companies with significant accomplishments in the area of quality. In 1989, for the first time, the Deming Prize was given to a U.S. company—Florida Power and Light Company.

One of Deming's major contributions to the quality movement that is spreading across the major industrialized nations of the world was his recognition that statistical (and other) process improvement methods cannot succeed without the proper organizational climate and culture. Accordingly, he proposed 14 guidelines that, if followed, transform the organizational climate to one in which process-management efforts can flourish. These 14 points are, in essence, Deming's philosophy of management. He argues convincingly that all 14 should be implemented, not just certain subsets. We list all 14 points here, adding clarifying statements where needed. For a fuller discussion of these points, see Deming (1986), Gitlow *et al.* (1995), Walton (1986), and Joiner and Goudard (1990).

1. **Create constancy of purpose toward improvement of product and service, with the aim to become competitive and to stay in business, and to provide jobs.** The organization must have a clear goal or purpose. Everyone in the organization must be encouraged to work toward that goal day in and day out, year after year.
2. **Adopt the new philosophy.** Reject detection-rejection management in favor of a customer-oriented, preventative style of management in which never-ending quality improvement is the driving force.
3. **Cease dependence on inspection to achieve quality.** It is because of poorly designed products and excessive process variation that inspection is needed. If quality is designed into products and process management is used in their production, mass inspection of finished products will not be necessary.
4. **End the practice of awarding business on the basis of price tag.** Do not simply buy from the lowest bidder. Consider the quality of the supplier's products along with the supplier's price. Establish long-term relationships with suppliers based on loyalty and trust. Move toward using a single supplier for each item needed.
5. **Improve constantly and forever the system of production and service, to improve quality and productivity, and thus constantly decrease costs.**

a. Construct a p-chart for the process.
b. Is the process under statistical control? Explain.
c. Should the control limits of part **a** be used to monitor future process output? Explain.
d. Suggest two methods that could be used to facilitate the diagnosis of causes of process variation.

11.38 A Japanese floppy disk manufacturer has a daily production rate of about 20,000 high density 3.5-inch diskettes. Quality is monitored by randomly sampling 200 finished disks every other hour from the production process and testing them for defects. If one or more defects are discovered, the disk is considered defective and is destroyed. The production process operates 20 hours per day, seven days a week. The table on p. 693 reports data for the last three days of production.

a. Construct a p-chart for the diskette production process.
b. What does it indicate about the stability of the process? Explain.
c. What advice can you give the manufacturer to assist them in their search for the special cause(s) of variation that is plaguing the process?

6. **Institute training.** Workers are often trained by other workers who were never properly trained themselves. The result is excessive process variation and inferior products and services. This is not the workers' fault; no one has told them how to do their jobs well.

7. **Institute leadership.** Supervisors should help the workers to do a better job. Their job is to lead, not to order workers around or to punish them.

8. **Drive out fear, so that everyone may work effectively for the company.** Many workers are afraid to ask questions or to bring problems to the attention of management. Such a climate is not conducive to producing high-quality goods and services. People work best when they feel secure.

9. **Break down barriers between departments.** Everyone in the organization must work together as a team. Different areas within the firm should have complementary, not conflicting, goals. People across the organization must realize that they are all part of the same system. Pooling their resources to solve problems is better than competing against each other.

10. **Eliminate slogans, exhortations, and arbitrary numerical goals and targets for the workforce which urge the workers to achieve new levels of productivity and quality.** Simply asking the workers to improve their work is not enough; they must be shown *how* to improve it. Management must realize that significant improvements can be achieved only if management takes responsibility for quality and makes the necessary changes in the design of the system in which the workers operate.

11. **Eliminate numerical quotas.** Quotas are purely quantitative (e.g., number of pieces to produce per day); they do not take quality into consideration. When faced with quotas, people attempt to meet them at any cost, regardless of the damage to the organization.

12. **Remove barriers that rob employees of their pride of workmanship.** People must be treated as human beings, not commodities. Working conditions must be improved, including the elimination of poor supervision, poor product design, defective materials, and defective machines. These things stand in the way of workers' performing up to their capabilities and producing work they are proud of.

13. **Institute a vigorous program of education and self-improvement.** Continuous improvement requires continuous learning. Everyone in the organization must be trained in the modern methods of quality improvement, including statistical concepts and interdepartmental teamwork. Top management should be the first to be trained.

14. **Take action to accomplish the transformation.** Hire people with the knowledge to implement the 14 points. Build a critical mass of people committed to transforming the organization. Put together a top management team to lead the way. Develop a plan and an organizational structure that will facilitate the transformation.

Focus

Contact a company located near your college or university and find out how many (if any) of Deming's 14 points have been implemented at the firm. Pool your results with those of your classmates to obtain a sense of the quality movement in your area. Summarize the results.

DISKS.DAT

Day	Hour	Number of Defectives	Day	Hour	Number of Defectives	Day	Hour	Number of Defectives
1	1	13	2	1	11	3	1	9
	2	5		2	6		2	5
	3	2		3	2		3	2
	4	3		4	3		4	1
	5	2		5	1		5	3
	6	3		6	3		6	2
	7	1		7	1		7	4
	8	2		8	2		8	2
	9	1		9	3		9	1
	10	1		10	1		10	1

QUICK REVIEW

Key Terms

A zone 659
B zone 659
conform to specs 654
centerline 643
common causes of variation 649
control chart 642
control limits 651
C zone 659
in control 645
individuals chart 654
lower control limit 651
nonconforming 654
oscillating sequence 643
out of control 645
output distribution 645
p-chart 683
pattern-analysis rules 660
process 640
process variation 642
quality 639
R-chart 672
random behavior 647
rare event 652
rational subgroups 658
run chart 642
s-chart 673
special (assignable) causes of variation 649
specification limits 654
statistical process control 649
system 641
stability 645
statistical thinking 642
3-sigma limits 651
trial values 663
total quality management 638
upper control limit 651
x-chart 654
$\bar{x}$-chart 655

Key Formulas

Control Chart	Centerline	Control Limits (Lower, Upper)	A–B Boundary (Lower, Upper)	B–C Boundary (Lower, Upper)	
$\bar{x}$-chart	$\bar{\bar{x}} = \dfrac{\sum_{i=1}^{k} \bar{x}_i}{k}$	$\bar{\bar{x}} \pm A_2\bar{R}$	$\bar{\bar{x}} \pm \frac{2}{3}(A_2\bar{R})$ or $\bar{\bar{x}} \pm 2\dfrac{(\bar{R}/d_2)}{\sqrt{n}}$	$\bar{\bar{x}} \pm \frac{1}{3}(A_2\bar{R})$ or $\bar{\bar{x}} \pm \dfrac{(\bar{R}/d_2)}{\sqrt{n}}$	659, 660
R-chart	$\bar{R} = \dfrac{\sum_{i=1}^{k} R_i}{k}$	$(\bar{R}D_3, \bar{R}D_4)$	$\bar{R} \pm 2d_3\left(\dfrac{\bar{R}}{d_2}\right)$	$\bar{R} \pm d_3\left(\dfrac{\bar{R}}{d_2}\right)$	674, 675
p-chart	$\bar{p} = \dfrac{\text{Total number defectives}}{\text{Total number units sampled}}$	$\bar{p} \pm 3\sqrt{\dfrac{\bar{p}(1-\bar{p})}{n}}$	$\bar{p} \pm 2\sqrt{\dfrac{\bar{p}(1-\bar{p})}{n}}$	$\bar{p} \pm \sqrt{\dfrac{\bar{p}(1-\bar{p})}{n}}$	685, 686

$n > \dfrac{9(1-p_0)}{p_0}$ where p_0 estimates the true proportion defective — Sample size for *p*-chart 684

LANGUAGE LAB

Symbol	Pronunciation	Description
LCL	L-C-L	Lower control limit
UCL	U-C-L	Upper control limit
$\bar{\bar{x}}$	*x*-bar-bar	Average of the sample means
$\bar{R}$	*R*-bar	Average of the sample ranges
A_2	*A*-two	Constant obtained from Table XV, Appendix B
D_3	*D*-three	Constant obtained from Table XV, Appendix B
D_4	*D*-four	Constant obtained from Table XV, Appendix B
d_2	*d*-two	Constant obtained from Table XV, Appendix B
d_3	*d*-three	Constant obtained from Table XV, Appendix B

$\hat{p}$	p-hat	Estimated number of defectives in sample
$\overline{p}$	p-bar	Overall proportion of defective units in all nk samples
p_0	p-naught	Estimated overall proportion of defectives for entire process
SPC	S-P-C	Statistical process control

SUPPLEMENTARY EXERCISES 11.39–11.57

Learning the Mechanics

11.39 Define *quality* and list its important dimensions.

11.40 What is a system? Give an example of a system with which you are familiar, and describe its inputs, outputs, and transformation process.

11.41 What is a process? Give an example of an organizational process and a personal process.

11.42 Select a personal process that you would like to better understand or to improve and construct a flowchart for it.

11.43 Describe the six major sources of process variation.

11.44 Suppose all the output of a process over the last year were measured and found to be within the specification limits required by customers of the process. Should you worry about whether the process is in statistical control? Explain.

11.45 Compare and contrast special and common causes of variation.

11.46 Explain the role of the control limits of a control chart.

11.47 Explain the difference between control limits and specification limits.

11.48 A process is under control and follows a normal distribution with mean 100 and standard deviation 10. In constructing a standard $\overline{x}$-chart for this process, the control limits are set 3 standard deviations from the mean—i.e., $100 \pm 3(10/\sqrt{n})$. The probability of observing an $\overline{x}$ outside the control limits is $(.00135 + .00135) = .0027$. Suppose it is desired to construct a control chart that signals the presence of a potential special cause of variation for less extreme values of $\overline{x}$. How many standard deviations from the mean should the control limits be set such that the probability of the chart falsely indicating the presence of a special cause of variation is .10 rather than .0027?

Applying the Concepts

11.49 Consider the following time series data for the weight of a manufactured product.

a. Construct a time series plot. Be sure to connect the points and add a centerline.

b. Which type of variation pattern in Figure 11.6 best describes the pattern revealed by your plot?

TIMEWT.DAT

Order of Production	Weight (grams)	Order of Production	Weight (grams)
1	6.0	9	6.5
2	5.0	10	9.0
3	7.0	11	3.0
4	5.5	12	11.0
5	7.0	13	3.0
6	6.0	14	12.0
7	8.0	15	2.0
8	5.0		

11.50 The accompanying length measurements were made on 20 consecutively produced pencils.

PENCIL.DAT

Order of Production	Length (inches)	Order of Production	Length (inches)
1	7.47	11	7.57
2	7.48	12	7.56
3	7.51	13	7.55
4	7.49	14	7.58
5	7.50	15	7.56
6	7.51	16	7.59
7	7.48	17	7.57
8	7.49	18	7.55
9	7.48	19	7.56
10	7.50	20	7.58

a. Construct a time series plot. Be sure to connect the plotted points and add a centerline.

b. Which type of variation pattern in Figure 11.6 best describes the pattern shown in your plot?

11.51 Use the appropriate pattern-analysis rules to determine whether the process being monitored by the control chart shown on page 696 is under the influence of special causes of variation.

11.52 A company that manufactures plastic molded parts believes it is producing an unusually large number of defects. To investigate this suspicion, each shift drew seven random samples of 200 parts, visually inspected each part to determine whether it was defective, and tallied the primary type of defect

Control Chart for Exercise 11.51

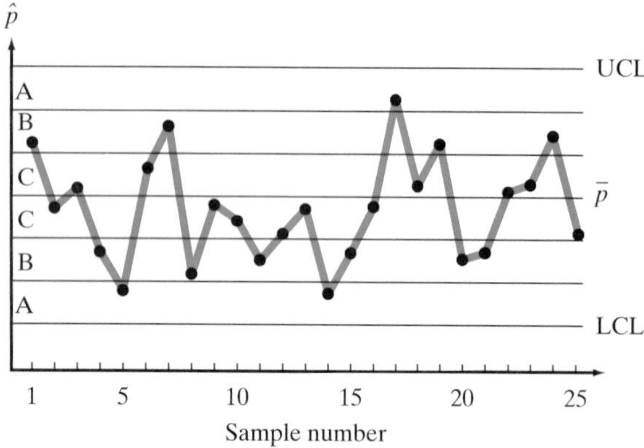

present (Hart, 1992). These data are presented in the table below.

a. From a statistical perspective, are the number of samples and the sample size of 200 adequate for constructing a p-chart for these data? Explain.

b. Construct a p-chart for this manufacturing process.

c. Should the control limits be used to monitor future process output? Explain.

d. Suggest a strategy for identifying the special causes of variation that may be present.

11.53 A hospital has used control charts continuously since 1978 to monitor the quality of its nursing care. A set of 363 scoring criteria, or standards, are applied at critical points in the patients' stay to determine whether the patients are receiving beneficial nursing care. Auditors regularly visit each hospital unit, sample two patients, and evaluate their care. The auditors review patients' records; interview the patients, the nurse, and the head nurse; and observe the nursing care given (*International Journal of Quality and Reliability Management*, Vol. 9, 1992). The data in the table on page 697 were collected over a three-month period for a newly opened unit of the hospital.

a. Construct an R-chart for the nursing care process.

b. Construct an $\bar{x}$-chart for the nursing care process.

c. Should the control charts of parts **a** and **b** be used to monitor future process output? Explain.

d. The hospital would like all quality scores to exceed 335 (their specification limit). Over the three-month periods, what proportion of the sampled patients received care that did not conform to the hospital's requirements?

11.54 AirExpress, an overnight mail service, is concerned about the operating efficiency of the package-sorting departments at its Toledo, Ohio, terminal. The company would like to monitor the time it takes for packages to be put in outgoing delivery bins from the time they are received. The sorting department operates six hours per day, from 6 P.M. to midnight. The company randomly sampled four packages during each hour of operation during four consecutive days. The time for each package to move through the system, in minutes, is given in the second table on the next page.

MOLD.DAT

			Type of Defect				
Sample	Shift	# of Defects	Crack	Burn	Dirt	Blister	Trim
1	1	4	1	1	1	0	1
2	1	6	2	1	0	2	1
3	1	11	1	2	3	3	2
4	1	12	2	2	2	3	3
5	1	5	0	1	0	2	2
6	1	10	1	3	2	2	2
7	1	8	0	3	1	1	3
8	2	16	2	0	8	2	4
9	2	17	3	2	8	2	2
10	2	20	0	3	11	3	3
11	2	28	3	2	17	2	4
12	2	20	0	0	16	4	0
13	2	20	1	1	18	0	0
14	2	17	2	2	13	0	0
15	3	13	3	2	5	1	2
16	3	10	0	3	4	2	1
17	3	11	2	2	3	2	2
18	3	7	0	3	2	2	0
19	3	6	1	2	0	1	2
20	3	8	1	1	2	3	1
21	3	9	1	2	2	2	2

NURSING.DAT

Sample	Scores	Sample	Scores	Sample	Scores
1	345, 341	8	344, 344	15	345, 329
2	331, 328	9	359, 334	16	358, 351
3	343, 355	10	346, 361	17	353, 352
4	351, 352	11	360, 355	18	334, 340
5	360, 348	12	325, 335	19	341, 335
6	342, 336	13	350, 348	20	358, 345
7	328, 331	14	336, 337		

a. Construct an $\bar{x}$-chart from these data. In order for this chart to be meaningful, what assumption must be made about the variation of the process? Why?
b. What does the chart suggest about the stability of the package-sorting process? Explain.
c. Should the control limits be used to monitor future process output? Explain.

TRANSIT.DAT

Sample	Transit Time (mins.)			
1	31.9	33.4	37.8	26.2
2	29.1	24.3	33.2	36.7
3	30.3	31.1	26.3	34.1
4	39.6	29.4	31.4	37.7
5	27.4	29.7	36.5	33.3
6	32.7	32.9	40.1	29.7
7	30.7	36.9	26.8	34.0
8	28.4	24.1	29.6	30.9
9	30.5	35.5	36.1	27.4
10	27.8	29.6	29.0	34.1
11	34.0	30.1	35.9	28.8
12	25.5	26.3	34.8	30.0
13	24.6	29.9	31.8	37.9
14	30.6	36.0	40.2	30.8
15	29.7	33.2	34.9	27.6
16	24.1	26.8	32.7	29.0
17	29.4	31.6	35.2	27.6
18	31.1	33.0	29.6	35.2
19	27.0	29.0	35.1	25.1
20	36.6	32.4	28.7	27.9
21	33.0	27.1	26.2	35.1
22	33.2	41.2	30.7	31.6
23	26.7	35.2	39.7	31.5
24	30.5	36.8	27.9	28.6

11.55 Officials at Mountain Airlines are interested in monitoring the length of time customers must wait in line to check in at their airport counter in Reno, Nevada. In order to develop a control chart, five customers were sampled each day for 20 days. The data, in minutes, are presented next.
a. Construct an R-chart from these data.
b. What does the R-chart suggest about the stability of the process? Explain.

CHECKIN.DAT

Sample	Waiting Time (mins.)				
1	3.2	6.7	1.3	8.4	2.2
2	5.0	4.1	7.9	8.1	.4
3	7.1	3.2	2.1	6.5	3.7
4	4.2	1.6	2.7	7.2	1.4
5	1.7	7.1	1.6	.9	1.8
6	4.7	5.5	1.6	3.9	4.0
7	6.2	2.0	1.2	.9	1.4
8	1.4	2.7	3.8	4.6	3.8
9	1.1	4.3	9.1	3.1	2.7
10	5.3	4.1	9.8	2.9	2.7
11	3.2	2.9	4.1	5.6	.8
12	2.4	4.3	6.7	1.9	4.8
13	8.8	5.3	6.6	1.0	4.5
14	3.7	3.6	2.0	2.7	5.9
15	1.0	1.9	6.5	3.3	4.7
16	7.0	4.0	4.9	4.4	4.7
17	5.5	7.1	2.1	.9	2.8
18	1.8	5.6	2.2	1.7	2.1
19	2.6	3.7	4.8	1.4	5.8
20	3.6	.8	5.1	4.7	6.3

c. Explain why the R-chart should be interpreted prior to the $\bar{x}$-chart.
d. Construct an $\bar{x}$-chart from these data.
e. What does the $\bar{x}$-chart suggest about the stability of the process? Explain.
f. Should the control limits for the R-chart and $\bar{x}$-chart be used to monitor future process output? Explain.

11.56 Over the last year, a company that manufactures golf clubs has received numerous complaints about the performance of its graphite shafts and has lost several market share percentage points. In response, the company decided to monitor its shaft production process to identify new opportunities to improve its product. The process involves pultrusion. A fabric is pulled through a thermosetting polymer bath and then through a long heated steel die. As it moves through the die, the shaft is cured. Finally, it is cut to the desired length. Defects that can occur during the process are internal voids, broken strands, gaps between successive layers, and microcracks caused by improper curing. The company's newly formed quality department sampled 10 consecutive shafts every 30 minutes and nondestructive testing was used to seek out flaws in the shafts. The data from each eight-hour work shift were combined to form a shift sample of 160 shafts. Data on the proportion of defective shafts for 36 shift samples are presented in the table on page 698, followed by data on the types of flaws identified. [*Note:* Each defective shaft may have more than one flaw.]

SHAFT1.DAT

Shift Number	Number of Defective Shafts	Proportion of Defective Shafts
1	9	.05625
2	6	.03750
3	8	.05000
4	14	.08750
5	7	.04375
6	5	.03125
7	7	.04375
8	9	.05625
9	5	.03125
10	9	.05625
11	1	.00625
12	7	.04375
13	9	.05625
14	14	.08750
15	7	.04375
16	8	.05000
17	4	.02500
18	10	.06250
19	6	.03750
20	12	.07500
21	8	.05000
22	5	.03125
23	9	.05625
24	15	.09375
25	6	.03750
26	8	.05000
27	4	.02500
28	7	.04375
29	2	.01250
30	6	.03750
31	9	.05625
32	11	.06875
33	8	.05000
34	9	.05625
35	7	.04375
36	8	.05000

Source: Kolarik, W. *Creating Quality: Concepts, Systems, Strategies, and Tools.* New York: McGraw-Hill, 1995.

SHAFT2.DAT

Type of Defect	Number of Defects
Internal voids	11
Broken strands	96
Gaps between layer	72
Microcracks	150

a. Use the appropriate control chart to determine whether the process proportion remains stable over time.

b. Does your control chart indicate that both common and special causes of variation are present? Explain.

c. To help diagnose the causes of variation in process output, construct a Pareto diagram for the types of shaft defects observed. Which are the "vital few"? The "trivial many"?

11.57 A company called CRW runs credit checks for a large number of banks and insurance companies. Credit history information is typed into computer files by trained administrative assistants. The company is interested in monitoring the proportion of credit histories that contain one or more data entry errors. Based on her experience with the data entry operation, the director of the data processing unit believes that the proportion of histories with data entry errors is about 6%. CRW audited 150 randomly selected credit histories each day for 20 days. The sample data are presented below.

CRW.DAT

Sample	Sample Size	Histories with Errors
1	150	9
2	150	11
3	150	12
4	150	8
5	150	10
6	150	6
7	150	13
8	150	9
9	150	11
10	150	5
11	150	7
12	150	6
13	150	12
14	150	10
15	150	11
16	150	7
17	150	6
18	150	12
19	150	14
20	150	10

a. Use the sample size formula to show that a sample size of 150 is large enough to prevent the lower control limit of the p-chart they plan to construct from being negative.

b. Construct a p-chart for the data entry process.

c. What does the chart indicate about the presence of special causes of variation? Explain.

d. Provide an example of a special cause of variation that could potentially affect this process. Do the same for a common cause of variation.

e. Should the control limits be used to monitor future credit histories produced by the data entry operation? Explain.

Real-World Case The Gasket Manufacturing Case

(A Case Covering Chapter 11)

The Problem A Midwestern manufacturer of gaskets for automotive and off-road vehicle applications was suddenly and unexpectedly notified by a major customer—a U.S. auto manufacturer—that they had significantly tightened the specification limits on the overall thickness of a hard gasket used in their automotive engines. Although the current specification limits were by and large being met by the gasket manufacturer, their product did not come close to meeting the new specification.

The gasket manufacturer's first reaction was to negotiate with the customer to obtain a relaxation of the new specification. When these efforts failed, the customer-supplier relationship became somewhat strained. The gasket manufacturer's next thought was that if they waited long enough, the automotive company would eventually be forced to loosen the requirements and purchase the existing product. However, as time went on it became clear that this was not going to happen and that some positive steps would have to be taken to improve the quality of their gaskets. But what should be done? And by whom?

The Product Figure C6.1 shows the product in question, a hard gasket. A hard gasket is comprised of two outer layers of soft gasket material and an inner layer consisting of a perforated piece of sheet metal. These three pieces are assembled, and some blanking and punching operations follow, after which metal rings are installed around the inside of the cylinder bore clearance holes and the entire outside periphery of the gasket. The quality characteristic of interest in this case is the assembly thickness.

The Process An initial study by the staff engineers revealed that the variation in the thickness of soft gasket material—the two outer layers of the hard gasket—was large and undoubtedly responsible for much of the total variability in the final product. Figure C6.2 shows the roll mill process that fabricates the sheets of soft gasket material from which the two outer layers of the hard gasket are made. To manufacture a sheet of soft gasket material, an operator adds raw material, in a soft pelletlike form, to the gap—called the knip—between the two rolls. The larger roll rotates about its axis with no lateral movement; the smaller roll rotates and moves back and forth laterally to change the size of the knip. As the operator adds more and more material to the knip, the sheet is formed around the larger roll. When the smaller roll reaches a preset destination (i.e., final gap/sheet thickness), a bell rings and a red light goes on telling the operator to stop adding raw material. The operator stops the rolls and cuts the sheet horizontally along the larger roll so that it may be pulled off the roll. The finished sheet, called a pull, is pulled onto a table where the operator checks its thickness with a micrometer. The operator can adjust the final gap if he or she believes that the sheets are coming out too thick or too thin relative to the prescribed nominal value (i.e., the target thickness).

Process Operation Investigation revealed that the operator runs the process in the following way. After each sheet is made, the operator measures the thickness with a micrometer. The thickness values for three consecutive sheets are averaged and the average is plotted on a piece of graph paper that, at the start of the shift, has only a solid horizontal line drawn on it to indicate the target thickness value for the particular soft gasket sheet the operator is making. Periodically, the operator reviews these evolving data and makes a decision as to whether or not the process mean—the sheet thickness—needs to be adjusted. This can be accomplished by stopping the machine, loosening some clamps on the small roll, and jogging the small roll laterally in or out by a few thousandths of an inch—whatever the operator feels is needed. The clamps are tightened, the gap is checked with a taper gage, and if adjusted properly, the operator begins to make sheets again. Typically, this adjustment process takes 10 to 15 minutes. The questions of when to make such adjustments and how much to change the roll gap for each adjustment are completely at the operator's discretion, based on the evolving plot of thickness averages.

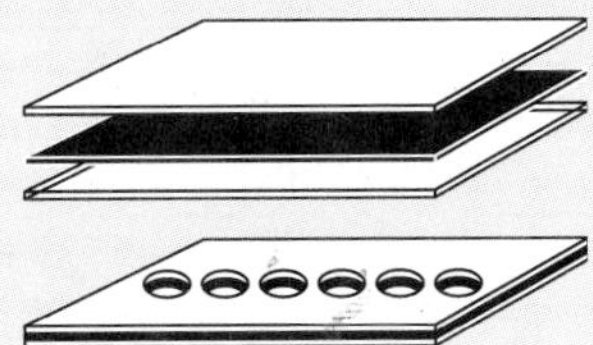

FIGURE C6.1
A hard gasket for automotive applications

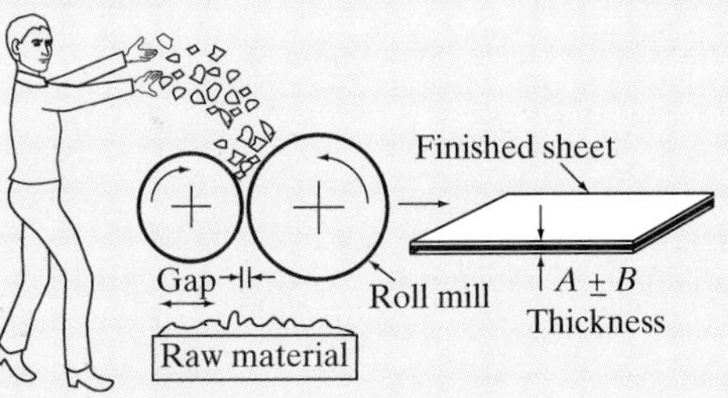

FIGURE C6.2
Roll mill for the manufacture of soft gasket material

Figure C6.3 shows a series of plots that detail the history of one particular work shift over which the operator made several process adjustments. (These data come from the same shift that the staff engineers used to collect data for a process capability study that is described later.) Figure C6.3(a) shows the process data after the first 12 sheets have been made—four averages of three successive sheet thicknesses. At this point the operator judged that the data were telling her that the process was running below the target, so she stopped the process and made an adjustment to slightly increase the final roll gap. She then proceeded to make more sheets. Figure C6.3(b) shows the state of the process somewhat later. Now it appeared to the operator that the sheets were coming out too thick, so she stopped and made another adjustment. As shown in Figure C6.3(c), the process seemed to run well for a while, but then an average somewhat below the target led the operator to believe that another adjustment was necessary. Figures C6.3(d) and C6.3(e) show points in time where other adjustments were made.

Figure C6.3(f) shows the complete history of the shift. A total of 24 × 3, or 72, sheets were made during this shift. When asked, the operator indicated that the history of this shift was quite typical of what happens on a day-to-day basis.

The Company's Stop-Gap Solution While the staff engineers were studying the problem to formulate an appropriate action plan, something had to be done to make it possible to deliver hard gaskets within the new specification limits. Management decided to increase product inspection and, in particular, to grade each piece of material according to thickness so that the wide variation in thickness could be balanced out at the assembly process. Extra inspectors were used to grade each piece of soft gasket material. Sheets of the same thickness were shipped in separate bundles on pallets to a sister plant for assembly. Thick and thin sheets were selected as needed to make a hard gasket that met the specification. The process worked pretty well and there was some discussion about making it permanent. However, some felt it was too costly and did not get at the root cause of the problem.

The Engineering Department's Analysis Meanwhile, the staff engineers in the company were continuing to study the problem and came to the conclusion that the existing roll mill process equipment for making the soft gasket sheets simply was not capable of meeting the new specifications. This conclusion was reached as a result of the examination of production data and scrap logs over the past

FIGURE C6.3
Process adjustment history over one shift

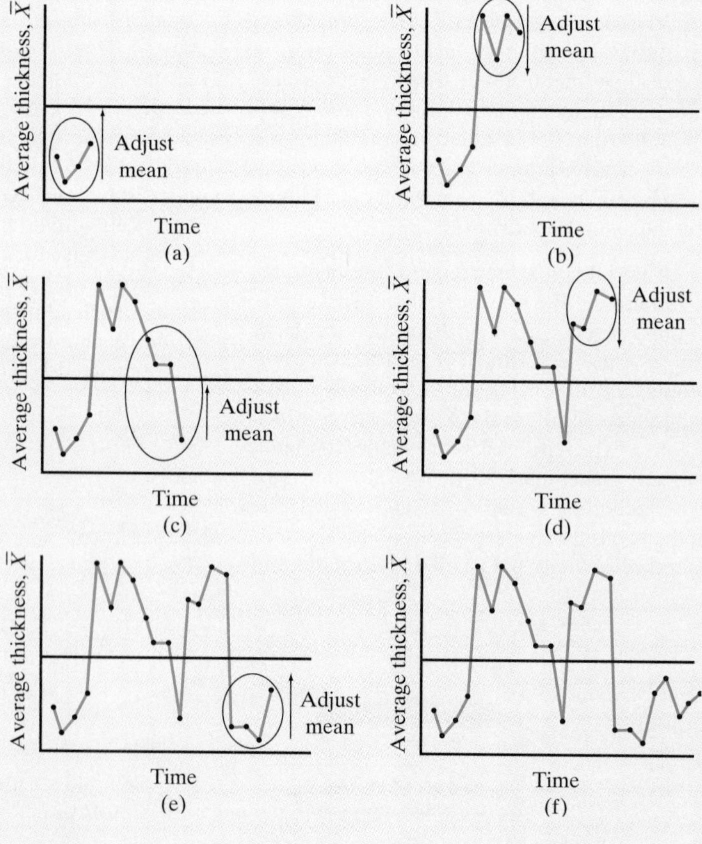

several months. They had researched some new equipment that had a track record for very good sheet-to-sheet consistency and had decided to write a proposal to replace the existing roll mills with this new equipment.

To strengthen the proposal, their boss asked them to include data that demonstrated the poor capability of the existing equipment. The engineers, confident that the equipment was not capable, selected what they thought was the best operator and the best roll mill (the plant has several roll mill lines) and took careful measurements of the thickness of each sheet made on an eight-hour shift. During that shift, a total of 72 sheets/pulls were made. This was considered quite acceptable since the work standard for the process is 70 sheets per shift. The measurements of the sheet thickness (in the order of manufacture) for the 72 sheets are given in Table C6.1. The engineers set out to use these data to conduct a process capability study.

Relying on a statistical methods course that one of the engineers had in college 10 years ago, the group decided to construct a frequency distribution from the data and use it to estimate the percentage of the measurements that fell within the specification limits. Their histogram is shown in Figure C6.4. Also shown in the figure are the upper and lower specification values. The dark shaded part of the histogram represents the amount of the product that lies outside of the specification limits. It is immediately apparent from the histogram that a large proportion of the output does not meet the customer's needs. Eight of the 72 sheets fall outside the specification limits. Therefore, in terms of percent conforming to specifications, the engineers estimated the process capability to be 88.8%. This was clearly unacceptable. This analysis confirmed the engineer's low opinion of the roll mill process equipment. They included it in their proposal and sent their recommendation to replace the equipment to the president's office.

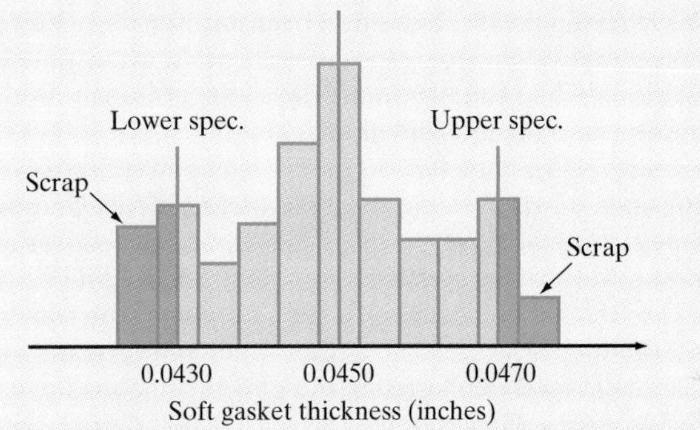

FIGURE C6.4
Histogram of data from process capability study

TABLE C6.1 Measurements of Sheet Thickness

Sheet	Thickness (in.)	Sheet	Thickness (in.)	Sheet	Thickness (in.)
1	0.0440	25	0.0464	49	0.0427
2	0.0446	26	0.0457	50	0.0437
3	0.0437	27	0.0447	51	0.0445
4	0.0438	28	0.0451	52	0.0431
5	0.0425	29	0.0447	53	0.0448
6	0.0443	30	0.0457	54	0.0429
7	0.0453	31	0.0456	55	0.0425
8	0.0428	32	0.0455	56	0.0442
9	0.0433	33	0.0445	57	0.0432
10	0.0451	34	0.0448	58	0.0429
11	0.0441	35	0.0423	59	0.0447
12	0.0434	36	0.0442	60	0.0450
13	0.0459	37	0.0459	61	0.0443
14	0.0466	38	0.0468	62	0.0441
15	0.0476	39	0.0452	63	0.0450
16	0.0449	40	0.0456	64	0.0443
17	0.0471	41	0.0471	65	0.0423
18	0.0451	42	0.0450	66	0.0447
19	0.0472	43	0.0472	67	0.0429
20	0.0477	44	0.0465	68	0.0427
21	0.0452	45	0.0461	69	0.0464
22	0.0457	46	0.0462	70	0.0448
23	0.0459	47	0.0463	71	0.0451
24	0.0472	48	0.0471	72	0.0428

Your Assignment You have been hired as an external consultant by the company's president, Marilyn Carlson. She would like you to critique the engineers' analysis, conclusion, and recommendations.

Suspecting that the engineers' work may be flawed, President Carlson would also like you to conduct your own study and make your own recommendations concerning how to resolve the company's problem. She would like you to use the data reported in Table C6.1 along with the data of Table C6.2, which she ordered be collected for you. These data were collected in the same manner as the data in Table C6.1. However, they were collected during a period of time when the roll mill operator was instructed *not* to adjust the sheet thickness. In your analysis, if you choose to construct control charts, use the same three-measurement subgrouping that the operators use.

Prepare an in-depth, written report for the president that responds to her requests. It should begin with an executive summary and include whatever tables and figures are needed to support your analysis and recommendations. (A layout of the data file available for this case, stored in GASKET.DAT, is described below.)

GASKET.DAT

Variable	Column(s)	Type
SHEET	1–2	QN
THICKNSS	7–11	QN
ADJUST	13	QL (A = operator adjustments, N = no adjustments)

TABLE C6.2 Measurements of Sheet Thickness for a Shift Run with No Operator Adjustment

Sheet	Thickness (in.)	Sheet	Thickness (in.)	Sheet	Thickness (in.)
1	.0445	25	.0443	49	.0445
2	.0455	26	.0450	50	.0471
3	.0457	27	.0441	51	.0465
4	.0435	28	.0449	52	.0438
5	.0453	29	.0448	53	.0445
6	.0450	30	.0467	54	.0472
7	.0438	31	.0465	55	.0453
8	.0459	32	.0449	56	.0444
9	.0428	33	.0448	57	.0451
10	.0449	34	.0461	58	.0455
11	.0449	35	.0439	59	.0435
12	.0467	36	.0452	60	.0443
13	.0433	37	.0443	61	.0440
14	.0461	38	.0434	62	.0438
15	.0451	39	.0454	63	.0444
16	.0455	40	.0456	64	.0444
17	.0454	41	.0459	65	.0450
18	.0461	42	.0452	66	.0467
19	.0455	43	.0447	67	.0445
20	.0458	44	.0442	68	.0447
21	.0445	45	.0457	69	.0461
22	.0445	46	.0454	70	.0450
23	.0451	47	.0445	71	.0463
24	.0436	48	.0451	72	.0456

This case is based on the experiences of an actual company whose identity is disguised for confidentiality reasons. The case was originally written by DeVor, Chang, and Sutherland (*Statistical Quality Design and Control* [New York: Macmillan Publishing Co., 1992] pp. 298–329) and has been adapted to focus on the material presented in Chapter 11.

Appendix A

BASIC COUNTING RULES

Sample points associated with many experiments have identical characteristics. If you can develop a counting rule to count the number of sample points, it can be used to aid in the solution of many probability problems. For example, many experiments involve sampling n elements from a population of N. Then, as explained in Section 3.1, we can use the formula

$$\binom{N}{n} = \frac{N!}{n!(N - n)!}$$

to find the number of different samples of n elements that could be selected from the total of N elements. This gives the number of sample points for the experiment.

Here, we give you a few useful counting rules. You should learn the characteristics of the situation to which each rule applies. Then, when working a probability problem, carefully examine the experiment to see whether you can use one of the rules.

Learning how to decide whether a particular counting rule applies to an experiment takes patience and practice. If you want to develop this skill, try to use the rules to solve some of the exercises in Chapter 3. Proofs of the rules below can be found in the text by W. Feller listed in the references to Chapter 3.

Multiplicative Rule

You have k sets of different elements, n_1 in the first set, n_2 in the second set, ..., and n_k in the kth set. Suppose you want to form a sample of k elements *by taking one element from each of the* k *sets.* The number of different samples that can be formed is the product

$$n_1 \cdot n_2 \cdot n_3 \cdot \cdots \cdot n_k$$

EXAMPLE A.1 A product can be shipped by four airlines and each airline can ship via three different routes. How many distinct ways exist to ship the product?

Solution A method of shipment corresponds to a pairing of one airline and one route. Therefore, $k = 2$, the number of airlines is $n_1 = 4$, the number of routes is $n_2 = 3$, and the number of ways to ship the product is

$$n_1 \cdot n_2 = (4)(3) = 12$$

How the multiplicative rule works can be seen by using a tree diagram, introduced in Section 3.6. The airline choice is shown by three branching lines in Figure A.1.

FIGURE A.1
Tree diagram for airline example

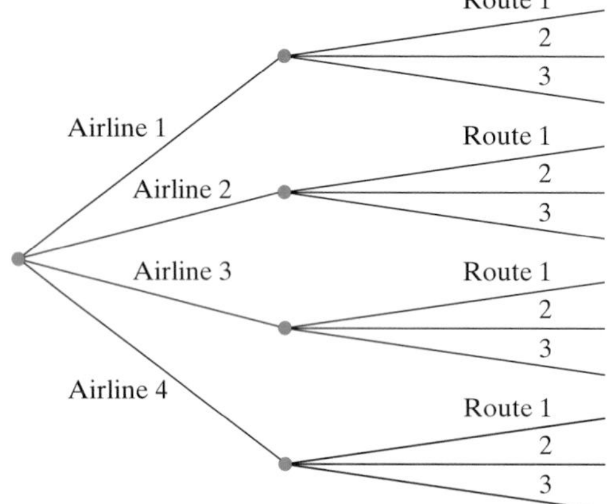

EXAMPLE A.2 You have twenty candidates for three different executive positions, E_1, E_2, and E_3. How many different ways could you fill the positions?

Solution For this example, there are $k = 3$ sets of elements:

Set 1: The candidates available to fill position E_1

Set 2: The candidates remaining (after filling E_1) that are available to fill E_2

Set 3: The candidates remaining (after filling E_1 and E_2) that are available to fill E_3

The numbers of elements in the sets are $n_1 = 20$, $n_2 = 19$, and $n_3 = 18$. Thus, the number of different ways to fill the three positions is

$$n_1 \cdot n_2 \cdot n_3 = (20)(19)(18) = 6{,}480$$

Partitions Rule

You have a *single* set of N distinctly different elements, and you want to partition it into k sets, the first set containing n_1 elements, the second containing n_2 elements, ..., and the kth containing n_k elements. The number of different partitions is

$$\frac{N!}{n_1!n_2! \cdot \cdots \cdot n_k!} \quad \text{where } n_1 + n_2 + n_3 + \cdots + n_k = N$$

EXAMPLE A.3 You have twelve construction workers available for three job sites. Suppose you want to assign three workers to job 1, four to job 2, and five to job 3. How many different ways could you make this assignment?

Solution For this example, $k = 3$ (corresponding to the $k = 3$ job sites), $N = 12$, and $n_1 = 3$, $n_2 = 4$, $n_3 = 5$. Then, the number of different ways to assign the workers to the job sites is

$$\frac{N!}{n_1!n_2!n_3!} = \frac{12!}{3!4!5!} = \frac{12 \cdot 11 \cdot 10 \cdot \cdots \cdot 3 \cdot 2 \cdot 1}{(3 \cdot 2 \cdot 1)(4 \cdot 3 \cdot 2 \cdot 1)(5 \cdot 4 \cdot 3 \cdot 2 \cdot 1)} = 27{,}720$$

Combinations Rule

The combinations rule given in Chapter 3 is a special case ($k = 2$) of the partitions rule. That is, sampling is equivalent to partitioning a set of N elements into $k = 2$ groups: elements that appear in the sample and those that do not. Let $n_1 = n$, the number of elements in the sample, and $n_2 = N - n$, the number of elements remaining. Then the number of different samples of n elements that can be selected from N is

$$\frac{N!}{n_1!n_2!} = \frac{N!}{n!(N-n)!} = \binom{N}{n}$$

This formula was given in Section 3.1.

EXAMPLE A.4 How many samples of four fire fighters can be selected from a group of 10?

Solution We have $N = 10$ and $n = 4$; then,

$$\binom{N}{n} = \binom{10}{4} = \frac{10!}{4!6!} = \frac{10 \cdot 9 \cdot 8 \cdot \cdots \cdot 3 \cdot 2 \cdot 1}{(4 \cdot 3 \cdot 2 \cdot 1)(6 \cdot 5 \cdot \cdots \cdot 2 \cdot 1)} = 210$$

★

Appendix B

TABLES

CONTENTS

TABLE I Random Numbers

Row \ Column	1	2	3	4	5	6	7	8	9	10	11	12	13	14
1	10480	15011	01536	02011	81647	91646	69179	14194	62590	36207	20969	99570	91291	90700
2	22368	46573	25595	85393	30995	89198	27982	53402	93965	34095	52666	19174	39615	99505
3	24130	48360	22527	97265	76393	64809	15179	24830	49340	32081	30680	19655	63348	58629
4	42167	93093	06243	61680	07856	16376	39440	53537	71341	57004	00849	74917	97758	16379
5	37570	39975	81837	16656	06121	91782	60468	81305	49684	60672	14110	06927	01263	54613
6	77921	06907	11008	42751	27756	53498	18602	70659	90655	15053	21916	81825	44394	42880
7	99562	72905	56420	69994	98872	31016	71194	18738	44013	48840	63213	21069	10634	12952
8	96301	91977	05463	07972	18876	20922	94595	56869	69014	60045	18425	84903	42508	32307
9	89579	14342	63661	10281	17453	18103	57740	84378	25331	12566	58678	44947	05585	56941
10	85475	36857	53342	53988	53060	59533	38867	62300	08158	17983	16439	11458	18593	64952
11	28918	69578	88231	33276	70997	79936	56865	05859	90106	31595	01547	85590	91610	78188
12	63553	40961	48235	03427	49626	69445	18663	72695	52180	20847	12234	90511	33703	90322
13	09429	93969	52636	92737	88974	33488	36320	17617	30015	08272	84115	27156	30613	74952
14	10365	61129	87529	85689	48237	52267	67689	93394	01511	26358	85104	20285	29975	89868
15	07119	97336	71048	08178	77233	13916	47564	81056	97735	85977	29372	74461	28551	90707
16	51085	12765	51821	51259	77452	16308	60756	92144	49442	53900	70960	63990	75601	40719
17	02368	21382	52404	60268	89368	19885	55322	44819	01188	65255	64835	44919	05944	55157
18	01011	54092	33362	94904	31273	04146	18594	29852	71585	85030	51132	01915	92747	64951
19	52162	53916	46369	58586	23216	14513	83149	98736	23495	64350	94738	17752	35156	35749
20	07056	97628	33787	09998	42698	06691	76988	13602	51851	46104	88916	19509	25625	58104
21	48663	91245	85828	14346	09172	30168	90229	04734	59193	22178	30421	61666	99904	32812
22	54164	58492	22421	74103	47070	25306	76468	26384	58151	06646	21524	15227	96909	44592
23	32639	32363	05597	24200	13363	38005	94342	28728	35806	06912	17012	64161	18296	22851
24	29334	27001	87637	87308	58731	00256	45834	15398	46557	41135	10367	07684	36188	18510
25	02488	33062	28834	07351	19731	92420	60952	61280	50001	67658	32586	86679	50720	94953
26	81525	72295	04839	96423	24878	82651	66566	14778	76797	14780	13300	87074	79666	95725
27	29676	20591	68086	26432	46901	20849	89768	81536	86645	12659	92259	57102	80428	25280
28	00742	57392	39064	66432	84673	40027	32832	61362	98947	96067	64760	64584	96096	98253
29	05366	04213	25669	26422	44407	44048	37937	63904	45766	66134	75470	66520	34693	90449
30	91921	26418	64117	94305	26766	25940	39972	22209	71500	64568	91402	42416	07844	69618
31	00582	04711	87917	77341	42206	35126	74087	99547	81817	42607	43808	76655	62028	76630
32	00725	69884	62797	56170	86324	88072	76222	36086	84637	93161	76038	65855	77919	88006
33	69011	65795	95876	55293	18988	27354	26575	08625	40801	59920	29841	80150	12777	48501
34	25976	57948	29888	88604	67917	48708	18912	82271	65424	69774	33611	54262	85963	03547
35	09763	83473	73577	12908	30883	18317	28290	35797	05998	41688	34952	37888	38917	88050

(continued)

TABLE I Continued

Row \ Column	1	2	3	4	5	6	7	8	9	10	11	12	13	14
36	91576	42595	27958	30134	04024	86385	29880	99730	55536	84855	29080	09250	79656	73211
37	17955	56349	90999	49127	20044	59931	06115	20542	18059	02008	73708	83517	36103	42791
38	46503	18584	18845	49618	02304	51038	20655	58727	28168	15475	56942	53389	20562	87338
39	92157	89634	94824	78171	84610	82834	09922	25417	44137	48413	25555	21246	35509	20468
40	14577	62765	35605	81263	39667	47358	56873	56307	61607	49518	89656	20103	77490	18062
41	98427	07523	33362	64270	01638	92477	66969	98420	04880	45585	46565	04102	46880	45709
42	34914	63976	88720	82765	34476	17032	87589	40836	32427	70002	70663	88863	77775	69348
43	70060	28277	39475	46473	23219	53416	94970	25832	69975	94884	19661	72828	00102	66794
44	53976	54914	06990	67245	68350	82948	11398	42878	80287	88267	47363	46634	06541	97809
45	76072	29515	40980	07391	58745	25774	22987	80059	39911	96189	41151	14222	60697	59583
46	90725	52210	83974	29992	65831	38857	50490	83765	55657	14361	31720	57375	56228	41546
47	64364	67412	33339	31926	14883	24413	59744	92351	97473	89286	35931	04110	23726	51900
48	08962	00358	31662	25388	61642	34072	81249	35648	56891	69352	48373	45578	78547	81788
49	95012	68379	93526	70765	10592	04542	76463	54328	02349	17247	28865	14777	62730	92277
50	15664	10493	20492	38391	91132	21999	59516	81652	27195	48223	46751	22923	32261	85653
51	16408	81899	04153	53381	79401	21438	83035	92350	36693	31238	59649	91754	72772	02338
52	18629	81953	05520	91962	04739	13092	97662	24822	94730	06496	35090	04822	86774	98289
53	73115	35101	47498	87637	99016	71060	88824	71013	18735	20286	23153	72924	35165	43040
54	57491	16703	23167	49323	45021	33132	12544	41035	80780	45393	44812	12512	98931	91202
55	30405	83946	23792	14422	15059	45799	22716	19792	09983	74353	68668	30429	70735	25499
56	16631	35006	85900	98275	32388	52390	16815	69290	82732	38480	73817	32523	41961	44437
57	96773	20206	42559	78985	05300	22164	24369	54224	35083	19687	11052	91491	60383	19746
58	38935	64202	14349	82674	66523	44133	00697	35552	35970	19124	63318	29686	03387	59846
59	31624	76384	17403	53363	44167	64486	64758	75366	76554	31601	12614	33072	60332	92325
60	78919	19474	23632	27889	47914	02584	37680	20801	72152	39339	34806	08930	85001	87820
61	03931	33309	57047	74211	63445	17361	62825	39908	05607	91284	68833	25570	38818	46920
62	74426	33278	43972	10110	89917	15665	52872	73823	73144	88662	88970	74492	51805	99378
63	09066	00903	20795	95452	92648	45454	09552	88815	16553	51125	79375	97596	16296	66092
64	42238	12426	87025	14267	20979	04508	64535	31355	86064	29472	47689	05974	52468	16834
65	16153	08002	26504	41744	81959	65642	74240	56302	00033	67107	77510	70625	28725	34191
66	21457	40742	29820	96783	29400	21840	15035	34537	33310	06116	95240	15957	16572	06004
67	21581	57802	02050	89728	17937	37621	47075	42080	97403	48626	68995	43805	33386	21597
68	55612	78095	83197	33732	05810	24813	86902	60397	16489	03264	88525	42786	05269	92532
69	44657	66999	99324	51281	84463	60563	79312	93454	68876	25471	93911	25650	12682	73572
70	91340	84979	46949	81973	37949	61023	43997	15263	80644	43942	89203	71795	99533	50501

(continued)

TABLE I Continued

Row \ Column	1	2	3	4	5	6	7	8	9	10	11	12	13	14
71	91227	21199	31935	27022	84067	05462	35216	14486	29891	68607	41867	14951	91696	85065
72	50001	38140	66321	19924	72163	09538	12151	06878	91903	18749	34405	56087	82790	70925
73	65390	05224	72958	28609	81406	39147	25549	48542	42627	45233	57202	94617	23772	07896
74	27504	96131	83944	41575	10573	08619	64482	73923	36152	05184	94142	25299	84387	34925
75	37169	94851	39117	89632	00959	16487	65536	49071	39782	17095	02330	74301	00275	48280
76	11508	70225	51111	38351	19444	66499	71945	05422	13442	78675	84081	66938	93654	59894
77	37449	30362	06694	54690	04052	53115	62757	95348	78662	11163	81651	50245	34971	52924
78	46515	70331	85922	38329	57015	15765	97161	17869	45349	61796	66345	81073	49106	79860
79	30986	81223	42416	58353	21532	30502	32305	86482	05174	07901	54339	58861	74818	46942
80	63798	64995	46583	09785	44160	78128	83991	42865	92520	83531	80377	35909	81250	54238
81	82486	84846	99254	67632	43218	50076	21361	64816	51202	88124	41870	52689	51275	83556
82	21885	32906	92431	09060	64297	51674	64126	62570	26123	05155	59194	52799	28225	85762
83	60336	98782	07408	53458	13564	59089	26445	29789	85205	41001	12535	12133	14645	23541
84	43937	46891	24010	25560	86355	33941	25786	54990	71899	15475	95434	98227	21824	19585
85	97656	63175	89303	16275	07100	92063	21942	18611	47348	20203	18534	03862	78095	50136
86	03299	01221	05418	38982	55758	92237	26759	86367	21216	98442	08303	56613	91511	75928
87	79626	06486	03574	17668	07785	76020	79924	25651	83325	88428	85076	72811	22717	50585
88	85636	68335	47539	03129	65651	11977	02510	26113	99447	68645	34327	15152	55230	93448
89	18039	14367	64337	06177	12143	46609	32989	74014	64708	00533	35398	58408	13261	47908
90	08362	15656	60627	36478	65648	16764	53412	09013	07832	41574	17639	82163	60859	75567
91	79556	29068	04142	16268	15387	12856	66227	38358	22478	73373	88732	09443	82558	05250
92	92608	82674	27072	32534	17075	27698	98204	63863	11951	34648	88022	56148	34925	57031
93	23982	25835	40055	67006	12293	02753	14827	23235	35071	99704	37543	11601	35503	85171
94	09915	96306	05908	97901	28395	14186	00821	80703	70426	75647	76310	88717	37890	40129
95	59037	33300	26695	62247	69927	76123	50842	43834	86654	70959	79725	93872	28117	19233
96	42488	78077	69882	61657	34136	79180	97526	43092	04098	73571	80799	76536	71255	64239
97	46764	86273	63003	93017	31204	36692	40202	35275	57306	55543	53203	18098	47625	88684
98	03237	45430	55417	63282	90816	17349	88298	90183	36600	78406	06216	95787	42579	90730
99	86591	81482	52667	61582	14972	90053	89534	76036	49199	43716	97548	04379	46370	28672
100	38534	01715	94964	87288	65680	43772	39560	12918	86537	62738	19636	51132	25739	56947

Source: Abridged from W. H. Beyer (ed.). *CRC Standard Mathematical Tables,* 24th edition. (Cleveland: The Chemical Rubber Company), 1976. Reproduced by permission of the publisher.

TABLE II Binomial Probabilities

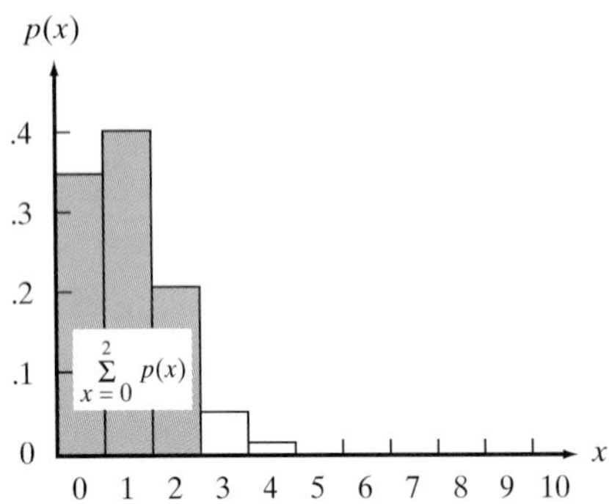

Tabulated values are $\sum_{x=0}^{k} p(x)$. *(Computations are rounded at the third decimal place.)*

a. $n = 5$

k \ p	.01	.05	.10	.20	.30	.40	.50	.60	.70	.80	.90	.95	.99
0	.951	.774	.590	.328	.168	.078	.031	.010	.002	.000	.000	.000	.000
1	.999	.977	.919	.737	.528	.337	.188	.087	.031	.007	.000	.000	.000
2	1.000	.999	.991	.942	.837	.683	.500	.317	.163	.058	.009	.001	.000
3	1.000	1.000	1.000	.993	.969	.913	.812	.663	.472	.263	.081	.023	.001
4	1.000	1.000	1.000	1.000	.998	.990	.969	.922	.832	.672	.410	.226	.049

b. $n = 6$

k \ p	.01	.05	.10	.20	.30	.40	.50	.60	.70	.80	.90	.95	.99
0	.941	.735	.531	.262	.118	.047	.016	.004	.001	.000	.000	.000	.000
1	.999	.967	.886	.655	.420	.233	.109	.041	.011	.002	.000	.000	.000
2	1.000	.998	.984	.901	.744	.544	.344	.179	.070	.017	.001	.000	.000
3	1.000	1.000	.999	.983	.930	.821	.656	.456	.256	.099	.016	.002	.000
4	1.000	1.000	1.000	.998	.989	.959	.891	.767	.580	.345	.114	.033	.001
5	1.000	1.000	1.000	1.000	.999	.996	.984	.953	.882	.738	.469	.265	.059

c. $n = 7$

k \ p	.01	.05	.10	.20	.30	.40	.50	.60	.70	.80	.90	.95	.99
0	.932	.698	.478	.210	.082	.028	.008	.002	.000	.000	.000	.000	.000
1	.998	.956	.850	.577	.329	.159	.063	.019	.004	.000	.000	.000	.000
2	1.000	.996	.974	.852	.647	.420	.227	.096	.029	.005	.000	.000	.000
3	1.000	1.000	.997	.967	.874	.710	.500	.290	.126	.033	.003	.000	.000
4	1.000	1.000	1.000	.995	.971	.904	.773	.580	.353	.148	.026	.004	.000
5	1.000	1.000	1.000	1.000	.996	.981	.937	.841	.671	.423	.150	.044	.002
6	1.000	1.000	1.000	1.000	1.000	.998	.992	.972	.918	.790	.522	.302	.068

(continued)

TABLE II Continued

d. $n = 8$

k \ p	.01	.05	.10	.20	.30	.40	.50	.60	.70	.80	.90	.95	.99
0	.923	.663	.430	.168	.058	.017	.004	.001	.000	.000	.000	.000	.000
1	.997	.943	.813	.503	.255	.106	.035	.009	.001	.000	.000	.000	.000
2	1.000	.994	.962	.797	.552	.315	.145	.050	.011	.001	.000	.000	.000
3	1.000	1.000	.995	.944	.806	.594	.363	.174	.058	.010	.000	.000	.000
4	1.000	1.000	1.000	.990	.942	.826	.637	.406	.194	.056	.005	.000	.000
5	1.000	1.000	1.000	.999	.989	.950	.855	.685	.448	.203	.038	.006	.000
6	1.000	1.000	1.000	1.000	.999	.991	.965	.894	.745	.497	.187	.057	.003
7	1.000	1.000	1.000	1.000	1.000	.999	.996	.983	.942	.832	.570	.337	.077

e. $n = 9$

k \ p	.01	.05	.10	.20	.30	.40	.50	.60	.70	.80	.90	.95	.99
0	.914	.630	.387	.134	.040	.010	.002	.000	.000	.000	.000	.000	.000
1	.997	.929	.775	.436	.196	.071	.020	.004	.000	.000	.000	.000	.000
2	1.000	.992	.947	.738	.463	.232	.090	.025	.004	.000	.000	.000	.000
3	1.000	.999	.992	.914	.730	.483	.254	.099	.025	.003	.000	.000	.000
4	1.000	1.000	.999	.980	.901	.733	.500	.267	.099	.020	.001	.000	.000
5	1.000	1.000	1.000	.997	.975	.901	.746	.517	.270	.086	.008	.001	.000
6	1.000	1.000	1.000	1.000	.996	.975	.910	.768	.537	.262	.053	.008	.000
7	1.000	1.000	1.000	1.000	1.000	.996	.980	.929	.804	.564	.225	.071	.003
8	1.000	1.000	1.000	1.000	1.000	1.000	.998	.990	.960	.866	.613	.370	.086

f. $n = 10$

k \ p	.01	.05	.10	.20	.30	.40	.50	.60	.70	.80	.90	.95	.99
0	.904	.599	.349	.107	.028	.006	.001	.000	.000	.000	.000	.000	.000
1	.996	.914	.736	.376	.149	.046	.011	.002	.000	.000	.000	.000	.000
2	1.000	.988	.930	.678	.383	.167	.055	.012	.002	.000	.000	.000	.000
3	1.000	.999	.987	.879	.650	.382	.172	.055	.011	.001	.000	.000	.000
4	1.000	1.000	.998	.967	.850	.633	.377	.166	.047	.006	.000	.000	.000
5	1.000	1.000	1.000	.999	.953	.834	.623	.367	.150	.033	.002	.000	.000
6	1.000	1.000	1.000	.999	.989	.945	.828	.618	.350	.121	.013	.001	.000
7	1.000	1.000	1.000	1.000	.998	.988	.945	.833	.617	.322	.070	.012	.000
8	1.000	1.000	1.000	1.000	1.000	.998	.989	.954	.851	.624	.264	.086	.004
9	1.000	1.000	1.000	1.000	1.000	1.000	.999	.994	.972	.893	.651	.401	.096

(continued)

TABLE II Continued

g. $n = 15$

k \ p	.01	.05	.10	.20	.30	.40	.50	.60	.70	.80	.90	.95	.99
0	.860	.463	.206	.035	.005	.000	.000	.000	.000	.000	.000	.000	.000
1	.990	.829	.549	.167	.035	.005	.000	.000	.000	.000	.000	.000	.000
2	1.000	.964	.816	.398	.127	.027	.004	.000	.000	.000	.000	.000	.000
3	1.000	.995	.944	.648	.297	.091	.018	.002	.000	.000	.000	.000	.000
4	1.000	.999	.987	.838	.515	.217	.059	.009	.001	.000	.000	.000	.000
5	1.000	1.000	.998	.939	.722	.403	.151	.034	.004	.000	.000	.000	.000
6	1.000	1.000	1.000	.982	.869	.610	.304	.095	.015	.001	.000	.000	.000
7	1.000	1.000	1.000	.996	.950	.787	.500	.213	.050	.004	.000	.000	.000
8	1.000	1.000	1.000	.999	.985	.905	.696	.390	.131	.018	.000	.000	.000
9	1.000	1.000	1.000	1.000	.996	.966	.849	.597	.278	.061	.002	.000	.000
10	1.000	1.000	1.000	1.000	.999	.991	.941	.783	.485	.164	.013	.001	.000
11	1.000	1.000	1.000	1.000	1.000	.998	.982	.909	.703	.352	.056	.005	.000
12	1.000	1.000	1.000	1.000	1.000	1.000	.996	.973	.873	.602	.184	.036	.000
13	1.000	1.000	1.000	1.000	1.000	1.000	1.000	.995	.965	.833	.451	.171	.010
14	1.000	1.000	1.000	1.000	1.000	1.000	1.000	1.000	.995	.965	.794	.537	.140

h. $n = 20$

k \ p	.01	.05	.10	.20	.30	.40	.50	.60	.70	.80	.90	.95	.99
0	.818	.358	.122	.012	.001	.000	.000	.000	.000	.000	.000	.000	.000
1	.983	.736	.392	.069	.008	.001	.000	.000	.000	.000	.000	.000	.000
2	.999	.925	.677	.206	.035	.004	.000	.000	.000	.000	.000	.000	.000
3	1.000	.984	.867	.411	.107	.016	.001	.000	.000	.000	.000	.000	.000
4	1.000	.997	.957	.630	.238	.051	.006	.000	.000	.000	.000	.000	.000
5	1.000	1.000	.989	.804	.416	.126	.021	.002	.000	.000	.000	.000	.000
6	1.000	1.000	.998	.913	.608	.250	.058	.006	.000	.000	.000	.000	.000
7	1.000	1.000	1.000	.968	.772	.416	.132	.021	.001	.000	.000	.000	.000
8	1.000	1.000	1.000	.990	.887	.596	.252	.057	.005	.000	.000	.000	.000
9	1.000	1.000	1.000	.997	.952	.755	.412	.128	.017	.001	.000	.000	.000
10	1.000	1.000	1.000	.999	.983	.872	.588	.245	.048	.003	.000	.000	.000
11	1.000	1.000	1.000	1.000	.995	.943	.748	.404	.113	.010	.000	.000	.000
12	1.000	1.000	1.000	1.000	.999	.979	.868	.584	.228	.032	.000	.000	.000
13	1.000	1.000	1.000	1.000	1.000	.994	.942	.750	.392	.087	.002	.000	.000
14	1.000	1.000	1.000	1.000	1.000	.998	.979	.874	.584	.196	.011	.000	.000
15	1.000	1.000	1.000	1.000	1.000	1.000	.994	.949	.762	.370	.043	.003	.000
16	1.000	1.000	1.000	1.000	1.000	1.000	.999	.984	.893	.589	.133	.016	.000
17	1.000	1.000	1.000	1.000	1.000	1.000	1.000	.996	.965	.794	.323	.075	.001
18	1.000	1.000	1.000	1.000	1.000	1.000	1.000	.999	.992	.931	.608	.264	.017
19	1.000	1.000	1.000	1.000	1.000	1.000	1.000	1.000	.999	.988	.878	.642	.182

(continued)

TABLE II Continued

i. $n = 25$

k \ p	.01	.05	.10	.20	.30	.40	.50	.60	.70	.80	.90	.95	.99
0	.778	.277	.072	.004	.000	.000	.000	.000	.000	.000	.000	.000	.000
1	.974	.642	.271	.027	.002	.000	.000	.000	.000	.000	.000	.000	.000
2	.998	.873	.537	.098	.009	.000	.000	.000	.000	.000	.000	.000	.000
3	1.000	.966	.764	.234	.033	.002	.000	.000	.000	.000	.000	.000	.000
4	1.000	.993	.902	.421	.090	.009	.000	.000	.000	.000	.000	.000	.000
5	1.000	.999	.967	.617	.193	.029	.002	.000	.000	.000	.000	.000	.000
6	1.000	1.000	.991	.780	.341	.074	.007	.000	.000	.000	.000	.000	.000
7	1.000	1.000	.998	.891	.512	.154	.022	.001	.000	.000	.000	.000	.000
8	1.000	1.000	1.000	.953	.677	.274	.054	.004	.000	.000	.000	.000	.000
9	1.000	1.000	1.000	.983	.811	.425	.115	.013	.000	.000	.000	.000	.000
10	1.000	1.000	1.000	.994	.902	.586	.212	.034	.002	.000	.000	.000	.000
11	1.000	1.000	1.000	.998	.956	.732	.345	.078	.006	.000	.000	.000	.000
12	1.000	1.000	1.000	1.000	.983	.846	.500	.154	.017	.000	.000	.000	.000
13	1.000	1.000	1.000	1.000	.994	.922	.655	.268	.044	.002	.000	.000	.000
14	1.000	1.000	1.000	1.000	.998	.966	.788	.414	.098	.006	.000	.000	.000
15	1.000	1.000	1.000	1.000	1.000	.987	.885	.575	.189	.017	.000	.000	.000
16	1.000	1.000	1.000	1.000	1.000	.996	.946	.726	.323	.047	.000	.000	.000
17	1.000	1.000	1.000	1.000	1.000	.999	.978	.846	.488	.109	.002	.000	.000
18	1.000	1.000	1.000	1.000	1.000	1.000	.993	.926	.659	.220	.009	.000	.000
19	1.000	1.000	1.000	1.000	1.000	1.000	.998	.971	.807	.383	.033	.001	.000
20	1.000	1.000	1.000	1.000	1.000	1.000	1.000	.991	.910	.579	.098	.007	.000
21	1.000	1.000	1.000	1.000	1.000	1.000	1.000	.998	.967	.766	.236	.034	.000
22	1.000	1.000	1.000	1.000	1.000	1.000	1.000	1.000	.991	.902	.463	.127	.002
23	1.000	1.000	1.000	1.000	1.000	1.000	1.000	1.000	.998	.973	.729	.358	.026
24	1.000	1.000	1.000	1.000	1.000	1.000	1.000	1.000	1.000	.996	.928	.723	.222

TABLE III Poisson Probabilities

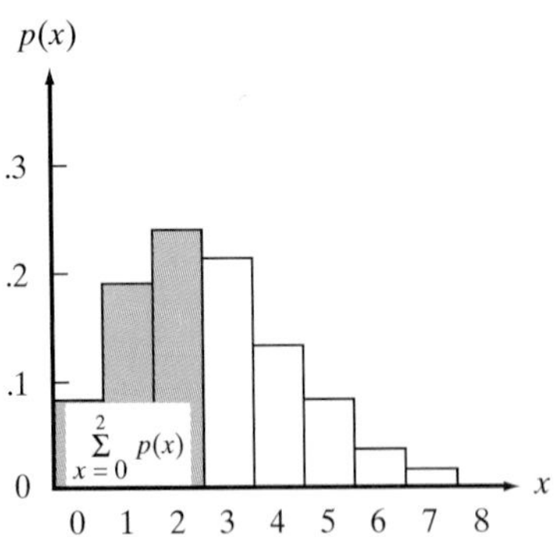

Tabulated values are $\sum_{x=0}^{k} p(x)$. *(Computations are rounded at the third decimal place.)*

λ \ k	0	1	2	3	4	5	6	7	8	9
.02	.980	1.000								
.04	.961	.999	1.000							
.06	.942	.998	1.000							
.08	.923	.997	1.000							
.10	.905	.995	1.000							
.15	.861	.990	.999	1.000						
.20	.819	.982	.999	1.000						
.25	.779	.974	.998	1.000						
.30	.741	.963	.996	1.000						
.35	.705	.951	.994	1.000						
.40	.670	.938	.992	.999	1.000					
.45	.638	.925	.989	.999	1.000					
.50	.607	.910	.986	.998	1.000					
.55	.577	.894	.982	.998	1.000					
.60	.549	.878	.977	.997	1.000					
.65	.522	.861	.972	.996	.999	1.000				
.70	.497	.844	.966	.994	.999	1.000				
.75	.472	.827	.959	.993	.999	1.000				
.80	.449	.809	.953	.991	.999	1.000				
.85	.427	.791	.945	.989	.998	1.000				
.90	.407	.772	.937	.987	.998	1.000				
.95	.387	.754	.929	.981	.997	1.000				
1.00	.368	.736	.920	.981	.996	.999	1.000			
1.1	.333	.699	.900	.974	.995	.999	1.000			
1.2	.301	.663	.879	.966	.992	.998	1.000			
1.3	.273	.627	.857	.957	.989	.998	1.000			
1.4	.247	.592	.833	.946	.986	.997	.999	1.000		
1.5	.223	.558	.809	.934	.981	.996	.999	1.000		

(continued)

TABLE III Continued

λ \ k	0	1	2	3	4	5	6	7	8	9
1.6	.202	.525	.783	.921	.976	.994	.999	1.000		
1.7	.183	.493	.757	.907	.970	.992	.998	1.000		
1.8	.165	.463	.731	.891	.964	.990	.997	.999	1.000	
1.9	.150	.434	.704	.875	.956	.987	.997	.999	1.000	
2.0	.135	.406	.677	.857	.947	.983	.995	.999	1.000	
2.2	.111	.355	.623	.819	.928	.975	.993	.998	1.000	
2.4	.091	.308	.570	.779	.904	.964	.988	.997	.999	1.000
2.6	.074	.267	.518	.736	.877	.951	.983	.995	.999	1.000
2.8	.061	.231	.469	.692	.848	.935	.976	.992	.998	.999
3.0	.050	.199	.423	.647	.815	.916	.966	.988	.996	.999
3.2	.041	.171	.380	.603	.781	.895	.955	.983	.994	.998
3.4	.033	.147	.340	.558	.744	.871	.942	.977	.992	.997
3.6	.027	.126	.303	.515	.706	.844	.927	.969	.988	.996
3.8	.022	.107	.269	.473	.668	.816	.909	.960	.984	.994
4.0	.018	.092	.238	.433	.629	.785	.889	.949	.979	.992
4.2	.015	.078	.210	.395	.590	.753	.867	.936	.972	.989
4.4	.012	.066	.185	.359	.551	.720	.844	.921	.964	.985
4.6	.010	.056	.163	.326	.513	.686	.818	.905	.955	.980
4.8	.008	.048	.143	.294	.476	.651	.791	.887	.944	.975
5.0	.007	.040	.125	.265	.440	.616	.762	.867	.932	.968
5.2	.006	.034	.109	.238	.406	.581	.732	.845	.918	.960
5.4	.005	.029	.095	.213	.373	.546	.702	.822	.903	.951
5.6	.004	.024	.082	.191	.342	.512	.670	.797	.886	.941
5.8	.003	.021	.072	.170	.313	.478	.638	.771	.867	.929
6.0	.002	.017	.062	.151	.285	.446	.606	.744	.847	.916
	10	**11**	**12**	**13**	**14**	**15**	**16**			
2.8	1.000									
3.0	1.000									
3.2	1.000									
3.4	.999	1.000								
3.6	.999	1.000								
3.8	.998	.999	1.000							
4.0	.997	.999	1.000							
4.2	.996	.999	1.000							
4.4	.994	.998	.999	1.000						
4.6	.992	.997	.999	1.000						
4.8	.990	.996	.999	1.000						
5.0	.986	.995	.998	.999	1.000					
5.2	.982	.993	.997	.999	1.000					
5.4	.977	.990	.996	.999	1.000					
5.6	.972	.988	.995	.998	.999	1.000				
5.8	.965	.984	.993	.997	.999	1.000				
6.0	.957	.980	.991	.996	.999	.999	1.000			

(continued)

TABLE III Continued

λ \ k	0	1	2	3	4	5	6	7	8	9
6.2	.002	.015	.054	.134	.259	.414	.574	.716	.826	.902
6.4	.002	.012	.046	.119	.235	.384	.542	.687	.803	.886
6.6	.001	.010	.040	.105	.213	.355	.511	.658	.780	.869
6.8	.001	.009	.034	.093	.192	.327	.480	.628	.755	.850
7.0	.001	.007	.030	.082	.173	.301	.450	.599	.729	.830
7.2	.001	.006	.025	.072	.156	.276	.420	.569	.703	.810
7.4	.001	.005	.022	.063	.140	.253	.392	.539	.676	.788
7.6	.001	.004	.019	.055	.125	.231	.365	.510	.648	.765
7.8	.000	.004	.016	.048	.112	.210	.338	.481	.620	.741
8.0	.000	.003	.014	.042	.100	.191	.313	.453	.593	.717
8.5	.000	.002	.009	.030	.074	.150	.256	.386	.523	.653
9.0	.000	.001	.006	.021	.055	.116	.207	.324	.456	.587
9.5	.000	.001	.004	.015	.040	.089	.165	.269	.392	.522
10.0	.000	.000	.003	.010	.029	.067	.130	.220	.333	.458

λ	10	11	12	13	14	15	16	17	18	19
6.2	.949	.975	.989	.995	.998	.999	1.000			
6.4	.939	.969	.986	.994	.997	.999	1.000			
6.6	.927	.963	.982	.992	.997	.999	.999	1.000		
6.8	.915	.955	.978	.990	.996	.998	.999	1.000		
7.0	.901	.947	.973	.987	.994	.998	.999	1.000		
7.2	.887	.937	.967	.984	.993	.997	.999	.999	1.000	
7.4	.871	.926	.961	.980	.991	.996	.998	.999	1.000	
7.6	.854	.915	.954	.976	.989	.995	.998	.999	1.000	
7.8	.835	.902	.945	.971	.986	.993	.997	.999	1.000	
8.0	.816	.888	.936	.966	.983	.992	.996	.998	.999	1.000
8.5	.763	.849	.909	.949	.973	.986	.993	.997	.999	.999
9.0	.706	.803	.876	.926	.959	.978	.989	.995	.998	.999
9.5	.645	.752	.836	.898	.940	.967	.982	.991	.996	.998
10.0	.583	.697	.792	.864	.917	.951	.973	.986	.993	.997

λ	20	21	22
8.5	1.000		
9.0	1.000		
9.5	.999	1.000	
10.0	.998	.999	1.000

(continued)

TABLE III Continued

λ \ k	0	1	2	3	4	5	6	7	8	9
10.5	.000	.000	.002	.007	.021	.050	.102	.179	.279	.397
11.0	.000	.000	.001	.005	.015	.038	.079	.143	.232	.341
11.5	.000	.000	.001	.003	.011	.028	.060	.114	.191	.289
12.0	.000	.000	.001	.002	.008	.020	.046	.090	.155	.242
12.5	.000	.000	.000	.002	.005	.015	.035	.070	.125	.201
13.0	.000	.000	.000	.001	.004	.011	.026	.054	.100	.166
13.5	.000	.000	.000	.001	.003	.008	.019	.041	.079	.135
14.0	.000	.000	.000	.000	.002	.006	.014	.032	.062	.109
14.5	.000	.000	.000	.000	.001	.004	.010	.024	.048	.088
15.0	.000	.000	.000	.000	.001	.003	.008	.018	.037	.070
	10	**11**	**12**	**13**	**14**	**15**	**16**	**17**	**18**	**19**
10.5	.521	.639	.742	.825	.888	.932	.960	.978	.988	.994
11.0	.460	.579	.689	.781	.854	.907	.944	.968	.982	.991
11.5	.402	.520	.633	.733	.815	.878	.924	.954	.974	.986
12.0	.347	.462	.576	.682	.772	.844	.899	.937	.963	.979
12.5	.297	.406	.519	.628	.725	.806	.869	.916	.948	.969
13.0	.252	.353	.463	.573	.675	.764	.835	.890	.930	.957
13.5	.211	.304	.409	.518	.623	.718	.798	.861	.908	.942
14.0	.176	.260	.358	.464	.570	.669	.756	.827	.883	.923
14.5	.145	.220	.311	.413	.518	.619	.711	.790	.853	.901
15.0	.118	.185	.268	.363	.466	.568	.664	.749	.819	.875
	20	**21**	**22**	**23**	**24**	**25**	**26**	**27**	**28**	**29**
10.5	.997	.999	.999	1.000						
11.0	.995	.998	.999	1.000						
11.5	.992	.996	.998	.999	1.000					
12.0	.988	.994	.987	.999	.999	1.000				
12.5	.983	.991	.995	.998	.999	.999	1.000			
13.0	.975	.986	.992	.996	.998	.999	1.000			
13.5	.965	.980	.989	.994	.997	.998	.999	1.000		
14.0	.952	.971	.983	.991	.995	.997	.999	.999	1.000	
14.5	.936	.960	.976	.986	.992	.996	.998	.999	.999	1.000
15.0	.917	.947	.967	.981	.989	.994	.997	.998	.999	1.000

(continued)

TABLE III Continued

λ \ k	4	5	6	7	8	9	10	11	12	13
16	.000	.001	.004	.010	.022	.043	.077	.127	.193	.275
17	.000	.001	.002	.005	.013	.026	.049	.085	.135	.201
18	.000	.000	.001	.003	.007	.015	.030	.055	.092	.143
19	.000	.000	.001	.002	.004	.009	.018	.035	.061	.098
20	.000	.000	.000	.001	.002	.005	.011	.021	.039	.066
21	.000	.000	.000	.000	.001	.003	.006	.013	.025	.043
22	.000	.000	.000	.000	.001	.002	.004	.008	.015	.028
23	.000	.000	.000	.000	.000	.001	.002	.004	.009	.017
24	.000	.000	.000	.000	.000	.000	.001	.003	.005	.011
25	.000	.000	.000	.000	.000	.000	.001	.001	.003	.006

λ \ k	14	15	16	17	18	19	20	21	22	23
16	.368	.467	.566	.659	.742	.812	.868	.911	.942	.963
17	.281	.371	.468	.564	.655	.736	.805	.861	.905	.937
18	.208	.287	.375	.469	.562	.651	.731	.799	.855	.899
19	.150	.215	.292	.378	.469	.561	.647	.725	.793	.849
20	.105	.157	.221	.297	.381	.470	.559	.644	.721	.787
21	.072	.111	.163	.227	.302	.384	.471	.558	.640	.716
22	.048	.077	.117	.169	.232	.306	.387	.472	.556	.637
23	.031	.052	.082	.123	.175	.238	.310	.389	.472	.555
24	.020	.034	.056	.087	.128	.180	.243	.314	.392	.473
25	.012	.022	.038	.060	.092	.134	.185	.247	.318	.394

λ \ k	24	25	26	27	28	29	30	31	32	33
16	.978	.987	.993	.996	.998	.999	.999	1.000		
17	.959	.975	.985	.991	.995	.997	.999	.999	1.000	
18	.932	.955	.972	.983	.990	.994	.997	.998	.999	1.000
19	.893	.927	.951	.969	.980	.988	.993	.996	.998	.999
20	.843	.888	.922	.948	.966	.978	.987	.992	.995	.997
21	.782	.838	.883	.917	.944	.963	.976	.985	.991	.994
22	.712	.777	.832	.877	.913	.940	.959	.973	.983	.989
23	.635	.708	.772	.827	.873	.908	.936	.956	.971	.981
24	.554	.632	.704	.768	.823	.868	.904	.932	.953	.969
25	.473	.553	.629	.700	.763	.818	.863	.900	.929	.950

λ \ k	34	35	36	37	38	39	40	41	42	43
19	.999	1.000								
20	.999	.999	1.000							
21	.997	.998	.999	.999	1.000					
22	.994	.996	.998	.999	.999	1.000				
23	.988	.993	.996	.997	.999	.999	1.000			
24	.979	.987	.992	.995	.997	.998	.999	.999	1.000	
25	.966	.978	.985	.991	.991	.997	.998	.999	.999	1.000

TABLE IV Normal Curve Areas

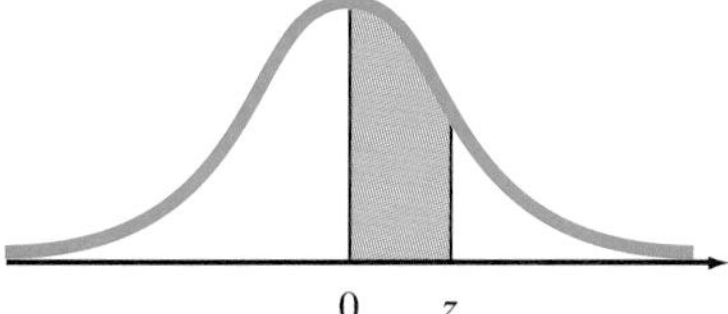

z	.00	.01	.02	.03	.04	.05	.06	.07	.08	.09
.0	.0000	.0040	.0080	.0120	.0160	.0199	.0239	.0279	.0319	.0359
.1	.0398	.0438	.0478	.0517	.0557	.0596	.0636	.0675	.0714	.0753
.2	.0793	.0832	.0871	.0910	.0948	.0987	.1026	.1064	.1103	.1141
.3	.1179	.1217	.1255	.1293	.1331	.1368	.1406	.1443	.1480	.1517
.4	.1554	.1591	.1628	.1664	.1700	.1736	.1772	.1808	.1844	.1879
.5	.1915	.1950	.1985	.2019	.2054	.2088	.2123	.2157	.2190	.2224
.6	.2257	.2291	.2324	.2357	.2389	.2422	.2454	.2486	.2517	.2549
.7	.2580	.2611	.2642	.2673	.2704	.2734	.2764	.2794	.2823	.2852
.8	.2881	.2910	.2939	.2967	.2995	.3023	.3051	.3078	.3106	.3133
.9	.3159	.3186	.3212	.3238	.3264	.3289	.3315	.3340	.3365	.3389
1.0	.3413	.3438	.3461	.3485	.3508	.3531	.3554	.3577	.3599	.3621
1.1	.3643	.3665	.3686	.3708	.3729	.3749	.3770	.3790	.3810	.3830
1.2	.3849	.3869	.3888	.3907	.3925	.3944	.3962	.3980	.3997	.4015
1.3	.4032	.4049	.4066	.4082	.4099	.4115	.4131	.4147	.4162	.4177
1.4	.4192	.4207	.4222	.4236	.4251	.4265	.4279	.4292	.4306	.4319
1.5	.4332	.4345	.4357	.4370	.4382	.4394	.4406	.4418	.4429	.4441
1.6	.4452	.4463	.4474	.4484	.4495	.4505	.4515	.4525	.4535	.4545
1.7	.4554	.4564	.4573	.4582	.4591	.4599	.4608	.4616	.4625	.4633
1.8	.4641	.4649	.4656	.4664	.4671	.4678	.4686	.4693	.4699	.4706
1.9	.4713	.4719	.4726	.4732	.4738	.4744	.4750	.4756	.4761	.4767
2.0	.4772	.4778	.4783	.4788	.4793	.4798	.4803	.4808	.4812	.4817
2.1	.4821	.4826	.4830	.4834	.4838	.4842	.4846	.4850	.4854	.4857
2.2	.4861	.4864	.4868	.4871	.4875	.4878	.4881	.4884	.4887	.4890
2.3	.4893	.4896	.4898	.4901	.4904	.4906	.4909	.4911	.4913	.4916
2.4	.4918	.4920	.4922	.4925	.4927	.4929	.4931	.4932	.4934	.4936
2.5	.4938	.4940	.4941	.4943	.4945	.4946	.4948	.4949	.4951	.4952
2.6	.4953	.4955	.4956	.4957	.4959	.4960	.4961	.4962	.4963	.4964
2.7	.4965	.4966	.4967	.4968	.4969	.4970	.4971	.4972	.4973	.4974
2.8	.4974	.4975	.4976	.4977	.4977	.4978	.4979	.4979	.4980	.4981
2.9	.4981	.4982	.4982	.4983	.4984	.4984	.4985	.4985	.4986	.4986
3.0	.4987	.4987	.4987	.4988	.4988	.4989	.4989	.4989	.4990	.4990

Source: Abridged from Table I of A. Hald, *Statistical Tables and Formulas* (New York: Wiley), 1952. Reproduced by permission of A. Hald.

TABLE V Exponentials

λ	$e^{-\lambda}$	λ	$e^{-\lambda}$	λ	$e^{-\lambda}$	λ	$e^{-\lambda}$	λ	$e^{-\lambda}$
.00	1.000000	**2.05**	.128735	**4.05**	.017422	**6.05**	.002358	**8.05**	.000319
.05	.951229	**2.10**	.122456	**4.10**	.016573	**6.10**	.002243	**8.10**	.000304
.10	.904837	**2.15**	.116484	**4.15**	.015764	**6.15**	.002133	**8.15**	.000289
.15	.860708	**2.20**	.110803	**4.20**	.014996	**6.20**	.002029	**8.20**	.000275
.20	.818731	**2.25**	.105399	**4.25**	.014264	**6.25**	.001930	**8.25**	.000261
.25	.778801	**2.30**	.100259	**4.30**	.013569	**6.30**	.001836	**8.30**	.000249
.30	.740818	**2.35**	.095369	**4.35**	.012907	**6.35**	.001747	**8.35**	.000236
.35	.704688	**2.40**	.090718	**4.40**	.012277	**6.40**	.001661	**8.40**	.000225
.40	.670320	**2.45**	.086294	**4.45**	.011679	**6.45**	.001581	**8.45**	.000214
.45	.637628	**2.50**	.082085	**4.50**	.011109	**6.50**	.001503	**8.50**	.000204
.50	.606531	**2.55**	.078082	**4.55**	.010567	**6.55**	.001430	**8.55**	.000194
.55	.576950	**2.60**	.074274	**4.60**	.010052	**6.60**	.001360	**8.60**	.000184
.60	.548812	**2.65**	.070651	**4.65**	.009562	**6.65**	.001294	**8.65**	.000175
.65	.522046	**2.70**	.067206	**4.70**	.009095	**6.70**	.001231	**8.70**	.000167
.70	.496585	**2.75**	.063928	**4.75**	.008652	**6.75**	.001171	**8.75**	.000158
.75	.472367	**2.80**	.060810	**4.80**	.008230	**6.80**	.001114	**8.80**	.000151
.80	.449329	**2.85**	.057844	**4.85**	.007828	**6.85**	.001059	**8.85**	.000143
.85	.427415	**2.90**	.055023	**4.90**	.007447	**6.90**	.001008	**8.90**	.000136
.90	.406570	**2.95**	.052340	**4.95**	.007083	**6.95**	.000959	**8.95**	.000130
.95	.386741	**3.00**	.049787	**5.00**	.006738	**7.00**	.000912	**9.00**	.000123
1.00	.367879	**3.05**	.047359	**5.05**	.006409	**7.05**	.000867	**9.05**	.000117
1.05	.349938	**3.10**	.045049	**5.10**	.006097	**7.10**	.000825	**9.10**	.000112
1.10	.332871	**3.15**	.042852	**5.15**	.005799	**7.15**	.000785	**9.15**	.000106
1.15	.316637	**3.20**	.040762	**5.20**	.005517	**7.20**	.000747	**9.20**	.000101
1.20	.301194	**3.25**	.038774	**5.25**	.005248	**7.25**	.000710	**9.25**	.000096
1.25	.286505	**3.30**	.036883	**5.30**	.004992	**7.30**	.000676	**9.30**	.000091
1.30	.272532	**3.35**	.035084	**5.35**	.004748	**7.35**	.000643	**9.35**	.000087
1.35	.259240	**3.40**	.033373	**5.40**	.004517	**7.40**	.000611	**9.40**	.000083
1.40	.246597	**3.45**	.031746	**5.45**	.004296	**7.45**	.000581	**9.45**	.000079
1.45	.234570	**3.50**	.030197	**5.50**	.004087	**7.50**	.000553	**9.50**	.000075
1.50	.223130	**3.55**	.028725	**5.55**	.003887	**7.55**	.000526	**9.55**	.000071
1.55	.212248	**3.60**	.027324	**5.60**	.003698	**7.60**	.000501	**9.60**	.000068
1.60	.201897	**3.65**	.025991	**5.65**	.003518	**7.65**	.000476	**9.65**	.000064
1.65	.192050	**3.70**	.024724	**5.70**	.003346	**7.70**	.000453	**9.70**	.000061
1.70	.182684	**3.75**	.023518	**5.75**	.003183	**7.75**	.000431	**9.75**	.000058
1.75	.173774	**3.80**	.022371	**5.80**	.003028	**7.80**	.000410	**9.80**	.000056
1.80	.165299	**3.85**	.021280	**5.85**	.002880	**7.85**	.000390	**9.85**	.000053
1.85	.157237	**3.90**	.020242	**5.90**	.002739	**7.90**	.000371	**9.90**	.000050
1.90	.149569	**3.95**	.019255	**5.95**	.002606	**7.95**	.000353	**9.95**	.000048
1.95	.142274	**4.00**	.018316	**6.00**	.002479	**8.00**	.000336	**10.00**	.000045
2.00	.135335								

TABLE VI Critical Values of t

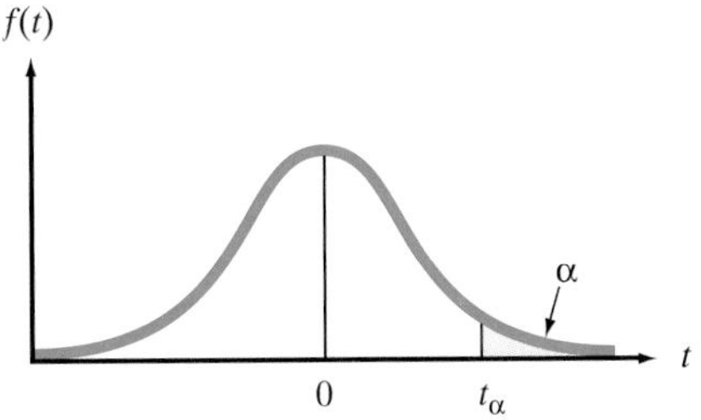

ν	$t_{.100}$	$t_{.050}$	$t_{.025}$	$t_{.010}$	$t_{.005}$	$t_{.001}$	$t_{.0005}$
1	3.078	6.314	12.706	31.821	63.657	318.31	636.62
2	1.886	2.920	4.303	6.965	9.925	22.326	31.598
3	1.638	2.353	3.182	4.541	5.841	10.213	12.924
4	1.533	2.132	2.776	3.747	4.604	7.173	8.610
5	1.476	2.015	2.571	3.365	4.032	5.893	6.869
6	1.440	1.943	2.447	3.143	3.707	5.208	5.959
7	1.415	1.895	2.365	2.998	3.499	4.785	5.408
8	1.397	1.860	2.306	2.896	3.355	4.501	5.041
9	1.383	1.833	2.262	2.821	3.250	4.297	4.781
10	1.372	1.812	2.228	2.764	3.169	4.144	4.587
11	1.363	1.796	2.201	2.718	3.106	4.025	4.437
12	1.356	1.782	2.179	2.681	3.055	3.930	4.318
13	1.350	1.771	2.160	2.650	3.012	3.852	4.221
14	1.345	1.761	2.145	2.624	2.977	3.787	4.140
15	1.341	1.753	2.131	2.602	2.947	3.733	4.073
16	1.337	1.746	2.120	2.583	2.921	3.686	4.015
17	1.333	1.740	2.110	2.567	2.898	3.646	3.965
18	1.330	1.734	2.101	2.552	2.878	3.610	3.922
19	1.328	1.729	2.093	2.539	2.861	3.579	3.883
20	1.325	1.725	2.086	2.528	2.845	3.552	3.850
21	1.323	1.721	2.080	2.518	2.831	3.527	3.819
22	1.321	1.717	2.074	2.508	2.819	3.505	3.792
23	1.319	1.714	2.069	2.500	2.807	3.485	3.767
24	1.318	1.711	2.064	2.492	2.797	3.467	3.745
25	1.316	1.708	2.060	2.485	2.787	3.450	3.725
26	1.315	1.706	2.056	2.479	2.779	3.435	3.707
27	1.314	1.703	2.052	2.473	2.771	3.421	3.690
28	1.313	1.701	2.048	2.467	2.763	3.408	3.674
29	1.311	1.699	2.045	2.462	2.756	3.396	3.659
30	1.310	1.697	2.042	2.457	2.750	3.385	3.646
40	1.303	1.684	2.021	2.423	2.704	3.307	3.551
60	1.296	1.671	2.000	2.390	2.660	3.232	3.460
120	1.289	1.658	1.980	2.358	2.617	3.160	3.373
∞	1.282	1.645	1.960	2.326	2.576	3.090	3.291

Source: This table is reproduced with the kind permission of the Trustees of Biometrika from E. S. Pearson and H. O. Hartley (eds.), *The Biometrika Tables for Statisticians*, Vol. 1, 3d ed., Biometrika, 1966.

TABLE VII Critical Values of χ^2

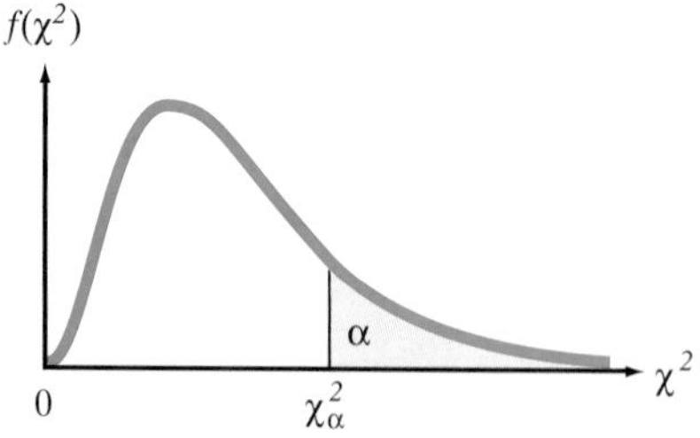

Degrees of Freedom	$\chi^2_{.995}$	$\chi^2_{.990}$	$\chi^2_{.975}$	$\chi^2_{.950}$	$\chi^2_{.900}$
1	.0000393	.0001571	.0009821	.0039321	.0157908
2	.0100251	.0201007	.0506356	.102587	.210720
3	.0717212	.114832	.215795	.351846	.584375
4	.206990	.297110	.484419	.710721	1.063623
5	.411740	.554300	.831211	1.145476	1.61031
6	.675727	.872085	1.237347	1.63539	2.20413
7	.989265	1.239043	1.68987	2.16735	2.83311
8	1.344419	1.646482	2.17973	2.73264	3.48954
9	1.734926	2.087912	2.70039	3.32511	4.16816
10	2.15585	2.55821	3.24697	3.94030	4.86518
11	2.60321	3.05347	3.81575	4.57481	5.57779
12	3.07382	3.57056	4.40379	5.22603	6.30380
13	3.56503	4.10691	5.00874	5.89186	7.04150
14	4.07468	4.66043	5.62872	6.57063	7.78953
15	4.60094	5.22935	6.26214	7.26094	8.54675
16	5.14224	5.81221	6.90766	7.96164	9.31223
17	5.69724	6.40776	7.56418	8.67176	10.0852
18	6.26481	7.01491	8.23075	9.39046	10.8649
19	6.84398	7.63273	8.90655	10.1170	11.6509
20	7.43386	8.26040	9.59083	10.8508	12.4426
21	8.03366	8.89720	10.28293	11.5913	13.2396
22	8.64272	9.54249	10.9823	12.3380	14.0415
23	9.26042	10.19567	11.6885	13.0905	14.8479
24	9.88623	10.8564	12.4011	13.8484	15.6587
25	10.5197	11.5240	13.1197	14.6114	16.4734
26	11.1603	12.1981	13.8439	15.3791	17.2919
27	11.8076	12.8786	14.5733	16.1513	18.1138
28	12.4613	13.5648	15.3079	16.9279	18.9392
29	13.1211	14.2565	16.0471	17.7083	19.7677
30	13.7867	14.9535	16.7908	18.4926	20.5992
40	20.7065	22.1643	24.4331	26.5093	29.0505
50	27.9907	29.7067	32.3574	34.7642	37.6886
60	35.5346	37.4848	40.4817	43.1879	46.4589
70	43.2752	45.4418	48.7576	51.7393	55.3290
80	51.1720	53.5400	57.1532	60.3915	64.2778
90	59.1963	61.7541	65.6466	69.1260	73.2912
100	67.3276	70.0648	74.2219	77.9295	82.3581

Source: From C. M. Thompson, "Tables of the Percentage Points of the χ^2-Distribution," *Biometrika,* 1941, 32, 188–189. Reproduced by permission of the *Biometrika* Trustees.

(continued)

TABLE VII Continued

Degrees of Freedom	$\chi^2_{.100}$	$\chi^2_{.050}$	$\chi^2_{.025}$	$\chi^2_{.010}$	$\chi^2_{.005}$
1	2.70554	3.84146	5.02389	6.63490	7.87944
2	4.60517	5.99147	7.37776	9.21034	10.5966
3	6.25139	7.81473	9.34840	11.3449	12.8381
4	7.77944	9.48773	11.1433	13.2767	14.8602
5	9.23635	11.0705	12.8325	15.0863	16.7496
6	10.6446	12.5916	14.4494	16.8119	18.5476
7	12.0170	14.0671	16.0128	18.4753	20.2777
8	13.3616	15.5073	17.5346	20.0902	21.9550
9	14.6837	16.9190	19.0228	21.6660	23.5893
10	15.9871	18.3070	20.4831	23.2093	25.1882
11	17.2750	19.6751	21.9200	24.7250	26.7569
12	18.5494	21.0261	23.3367	26.2170	28.2995
13	19.8119	22.3621	24.7356	27.6883	29.8194
14	21.0642	23.6848	26.1190	29.1413	31.3193
15	22.3072	24.9958	27.4884	30.5779	32.8013
16	23.5418	26.2962	28.8454	31.9999	34.2672
17	24.7690	27.5871	30.1910	33.4087	35.7185
18	25.9894	28.8693	31.5264	34.8053	37.1564
19	27.2036	30.1435	32.8523	36.1908	38.5822
20	28.4120	31.4104	34.1696	37.5662	39.9968
21	29.6151	32.6705	35.4789	38.9321	41.4010
22	30.8133	33.9244	36.7807	40.2894	42.7956
23	32.0069	35.1725	38.0757	41.6384	44.1813
24	33.1963	36.4151	39.3641	42.9798	45.5585
25	34.3816	37.6525	40.6465	44.3141	46.9278
26	35.5631	38.8852	41.9232	45.6417	48.2899
27	36.7412	40.1133	43.1944	46.9630	49.6449
28	37.9159	41.3372	44.4607	48.2782	50.9933
29	39.0875	42.5569	45.7222	49.5879	52.3356
30	40.2560	43.7729	46.9792	50.8922	53.6720
40	51.8050	55.7585	59.3417	63.6907	66.7659
50	63.1671	67.5048	71.4202	76.1539	79.4900
60	74.3970	79.0819	83.2976	88.3794	91.9517
70	85.5271	90.5312	95.0231	100.425	104.215
80	96.5782	101.879	106.629	112.329	116.321
90	107.565	113.145	118.136	124.116	128.299
100	118.498	124.342	129.561	135.807	140.169

TABLE VIII Percentage Points of the F-distribution, $\alpha = .10$

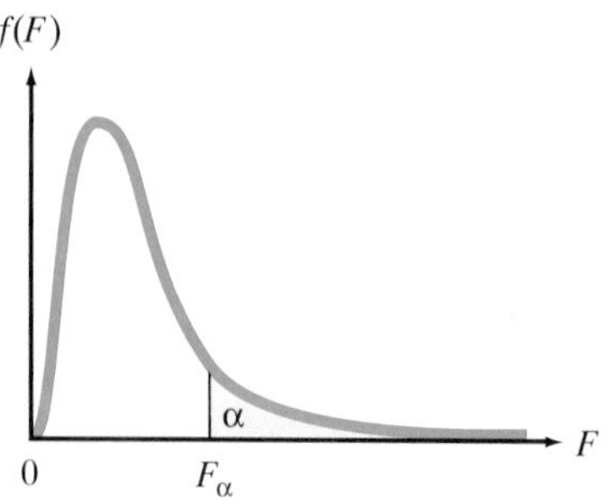

ν_2 \ ν_1 (DENOMINATOR DEGREES OF FREEDOM \ NUMERATOR DEGREES OF FREEDOM)	1	2	3	4	5	6	7	8	9
1	39.86	49.50	53.59	55.83	57.24	58.20	58.91	59.44	59.86
2	8.53	9.00	9.16	9.24	9.29	9.33	9.35	9.37	9.38
3	5.54	5.46	5.39	5.34	5.31	5.28	5.27	5.25	5.24
4	4.54	4.32	4.19	4.11	4.05	4.01	3.98	3.95	3.94
5	4.06	3.78	3.62	3.52	3.45	3.40	3.37	3.34	3.32
6	3.78	3.46	3.29	3.18	3.11	3.05	3.01	2.98	2.96
7	3.59	3.26	3.07	2.96	2.88	2.83	2.78	2.75	2.72
8	3.46	3.11	2.92	2.81	2.73	2.67	2.62	2.59	2.56
9	3.36	3.01	2.81	2.69	2.61	2.55	2.51	2.47	2.44
10	3.29	2.92	2.73	2.61	2.52	2.46	2.41	2.38	2.35
11	3.23	2.86	2.66	2.54	2.45	2.39	2.34	2.30	2.27
12	3.18	2.81	2.61	2.48	2.39	2.33	2.28	2.24	2.21
13	3.14	2.76	2.56	2.43	2.35	2.28	2.23	2.20	2.16
14	3.10	2.73	2.52	2.39	2.31	2.24	2.19	2.15	2.12
15	3.07	2.70	2.49	2.36	2.27	2.21	2.16	2.12	2.09
16	3.05	2.67	2.46	2.33	2.24	2.18	2.13	2.09	2.06
17	3.03	2.64	2.44	2.31	2.22	2.15	2.10	2.06	2.03
18	3.01	2.62	2.42	2.29	2.20	2.13	2.08	2.04	2.00
19	2.99	2.61	2.40	2.27	2.18	2.11	2.06	2.02	1.98
20	2.97	2.59	2.38	2.25	2.16	2.09	2.04	2.00	1.96
21	2.96	2.57	2.36	2.23	2.14	2.08	2.02	1.98	1.95
22	2.95	2.56	2.35	2.22	2.13	2.06	2.01	1.97	1.93
23	2.94	2.55	2.34	2.21	2.11	2.05	1.99	1.95	1.92
24	2.93	2.54	2.33	2.19	2.10	2.04	1.98	1.94	1.91
25	2.92	2.53	2.32	2.18	2.09	2.02	1.97	1.93	1.89
26	2.91	2.52	2.31	2.17	2.08	2.01	1.96	1.92	1.88
27	2.90	2.51	2.30	2.17	2.07	2.00	1.95	1.91	1.87
28	2.89	2.50	2.29	2.16	2.06	2.00	1.94	1.90	1.87
29	2.89	2.50	2.28	2.15	2.06	1.99	1.93	1.89	1.86
30	2.88	2.49	2.28	2.14	2.05	1.98	1.93	1.88	1.85
40	2.84	2.44	2.23	2.09	2.00	1.93	1.87	1.83	1.79
60	2.79	2.39	2.18	2.04	1.95	1.87	1.82	1.77	1.74
120	2.75	2.35	2.13	1.99	1.90	1.82	1.77	1.72	1.68
∞	2.71	2.30	2.08	1.94	1.85	1.77	1.72	1.67	1.63

Source: From M. Merrington and C. M. Thompson, "Tables of Percentage Points of the Inverted Beta (F)-Distribution," *Biometrika*, 1943, 33, 73–88. Reproduced by permission of the *Biometrika* Trustees.

(continued)

TABLE VIII Continued

ν_2 \ ν_1	NUMERATOR DEGREES OF FREEDOM									
DENOMINATOR DEGREES OF FREEDOM	10	12	15	20	24	30	40	60	120	∞
1	60.19	60.71	61.22	61.74	62.00	62.26	62.53	62.79	63.06	63.33
2	9.39	9.41	9.42	9.44	9.45	9.46	9.47	9.47	9.48	9.49
3	5.23	5.22	5.20	5.18	5.18	5.17	5.16	5.15	5.14	5.13
4	3.92	3.90	3.87	3.84	3.83	3.82	3.80	3.79	3.78	3.76
5	3.30	3.27	3.24	3.21	3.19	3.17	3.16	3.14	3.12	3.10
6	2.94	2.90	2.87	2.84	2.82	2.80	2.78	2.76	2.74	2.72
7	2.70	2.67	2.63	2.59	2.58	2.56	2.54	2.51	2.49	2.47
8	2.54	2.50	2.46	2.42	2.40	2.38	2.36	2.34	2.32	2.29
9	2.42	2.38	2.34	2.30	2.28	2.25	2.23	2.21	2.18	2.16
10	2.32	2.28	2.24	2.20	2.18	2.16	2.13	2.11	2.08	2.06
11	2.25	2.21	2.17	2.12	2.10	2.08	2.05	2.03	2.00	1.97
12	2.19	2.15	2.10	2.06	2.04	2.01	1.99	1.96	1.93	1.90
13	2.14	2.10	2.05	2.01	1.98	1.96	1.93	1.90	1.88	1.85
14	2.10	2.05	2.01	1.96	1.94	1.91	1.89	1.86	1.83	1.80
15	2.06	2.02	1.97	1.92	1.90	1.87	1.85	1.82	1.79	1.76
16	2.03	1.99	1.94	1.89	1.87	1.84	1.81	1.78	1.75	1.72
17	2.00	1.96	1.91	1.86	1.84	1.81	1.78	1.75	1.72	1.69
18	1.98	1.93	1.89	1.84	1.81	1.78	1.75	1.72	1.69	1.66
19	1.96	1.91	1.86	1.81	1.79	1.76	1.73	1.70	1.67	1.63
20	1.94	1.89	1.84	1.79	1.77	1.74	1.71	1.68	1.64	1.61
21	1.92	1.87	1.83	1.78	1.75	1.72	1.69	1.66	1.62	1.59
22	1.90	1.86	1.81	1.76	1.73	1.70	1.67	1.64	1.60	1.57
23	1.89	1.84	1.80	1.74	1.72	1.69	1.66	1.62	1.59	1.55
24	1.88	1.83	1.78	1.73	1.70	1.67	1.64	1.61	1.57	1.53
25	1.87	1.82	1.77	1.72	1.69	1.66	1.63	1.59	1.56	1.52
26	1.86	1.81	1.76	1.71	1.68	1.65	1.61	1.58	1.54	1.50
27	1.85	1.80	1.75	1.70	1.67	1.64	1.60	1.57	1.53	1.49
28	1.84	1.79	1.74	1.69	1.66	1.63	1.59	1.56	1.52	1.48
29	1.83	1.78	1.73	1.68	1.65	1.62	1.58	1.55	1.51	1.47
30	1.82	1.77	1.72	1.67	1.64	1.61	1.57	1.54	1.50	1.46
40	1.76	1.71	1.66	1.61	1.57	1.54	1.51	1.47	1.42	1.38
60	1.71	1.66	1.60	1.54	1.51	1.48	1.44	1.40	1.35	1.29
120	1.65	1.60	1.55	1.48	1.45	1.41	1.37	1.32	1.26	1.19
∞	1.60	1.55	1.49	1.42	1.38	1.34	1.30	1.24	1.17	1.00

TABLE IX Percentage Points of the F-distribution, $\alpha = .05$

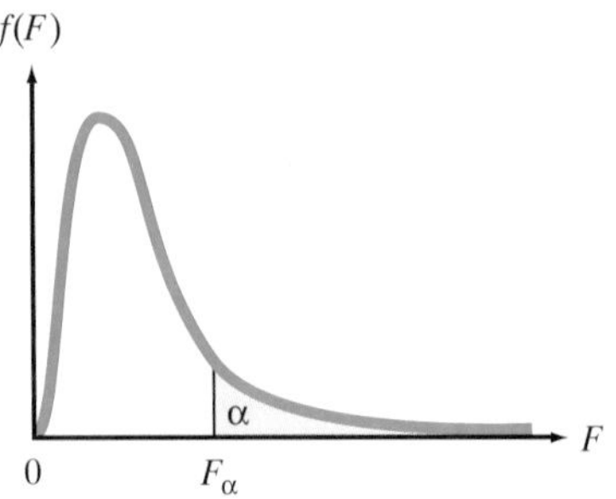

ν_2 \ ν_1 (DENOMINATOR DEGREES OF FREEDOM \ NUMERATOR DEGREES OF FREEDOM)	1	2	3	4	5	6	7	8	9
1	161.4	199.5	215.7	224.6	230.2	234.0	236.8	238.9	240.5
2	18.51	19.00	19.16	19.25	19.30	19.33	19.35	19.37	19.38
3	10.13	9.55	9.28	9.12	9.01	8.94	8.89	8.85	8.81
4	7.71	6.94	6.59	6.39	6.26	6.16	6.09	6.04	6.00
5	6.61	5.79	5.41	5.19	5.05	4.95	4.88	4.82	4.77
6	5.99	5.14	4.76	4.53	4.39	4.28	4.21	4.15	4.10
7	5.59	4.74	4.35	4.12	3.97	3.87	3.79	3.73	3.68
8	5.32	4.46	4.07	3.84	3.69	3.58	3.50	3.44	3.39
9	5.12	4.26	3.86	3.63	3.48	3.37	3.29	3.23	3.18
10	4.96	4.10	3.71	3.48	3.33	3.22	3.14	3.07	3.02
11	4.84	3.98	3.59	3.36	3.20	3.09	3.01	2.95	2.90
12	4.75	3.89	3.49	3.26	3.11	3.00	2.91	2.85	2.80
13	4.67	3.81	3.41	3.18	3.03	2.92	2.83	2.77	2.71
14	4.60	3.74	3.34	3.11	2.96	2.85	2.76	2.70	2.65
15	4.54	3.68	3.29	3.06	2.90	2.79	2.71	2.64	2.59
16	4.49	3.63	3.24	3.01	2.85	2.74	2.66	2.59	2.54
17	4.45	3.59	3.20	2.96	2.81	2.70	2.61	2.55	2.49
18	4.41	3.55	3.16	2.93	2.77	2.66	2.58	2.51	2.46
19	4.38	3.52	3.13	2.90	2.74	2.63	2.54	2.48	2.42
20	4.35	3.49	3.10	2.87	2.71	2.60	2.51	2.45	2.39
21	4.32	3.47	3.07	2.84	2.68	2.57	2.49	2.42	2.37
22	4.30	3.44	3.05	2.82	2.66	2.55	2.46	2.40	2.34
23	4.28	3.42	3.03	2.80	2.64	2.53	2.44	2.37	2.32
24	4.26	3.40	3.01	2.78	2.62	2.51	2.42	2.36	2.30
25	4.24	3.39	2.99	2.76	2.60	2.49	2.40	2.34	2.28
26	4.23	3.37	2.98	2.74	2.59	2.47	2.39	2.32	2.77
27	4.21	3.35	2.96	2.73	2.57	2.46	2.37	2.31	2.25
28	4.20	3.34	2.95	2.71	2.56	2.45	2.36	2.29	2.24
29	4.18	3.33	2.93	2.70	2.55	2.43	2.35	2.28	2.22
30	4.17	3.32	2.92	2.69	2.53	2.42	2.33	2.27	2.21
40	4.08	3.23	2.84	2.61	2.45	2.34	2.25	2.18	2.12
60	4.00	3.15	2.76	2.53	2.37	2.25	2.17	2.10	2.04
120	3.92	3.07	2.68	2.45	2.29	2.17	2.09	2.02	1.96
∞	3.84	3.00	2.60	2.37	2.21	2.10	2.01	1.94	1.88

Source: From M. Merrington and C. M. Thompson, "Tables of Percentage Points of the Inverted Beta (F)-Distribution," *Biometrika,* 1943, 33, 73–88. Reproduced by permission of the *Biometrika* Trustees.

(continued)

TABLE IX Continued

ν_2 \ ν_1	**NUMERATOR DEGREES OF FREEDOM**									
	10	**12**	**15**	**20**	**24**	**30**	**40**	**60**	**120**	∞
DENOMINATOR DEGREES OF FREEDOM										
1	241.9	243.9	245.9	248.0	249.1	250.1	251.1	252.2	253.3	254.3
2	19.40	19.41	19.43	19.45	19.45	19.46	19.47	19.48	19.49	19.50
3	8.79	8.74	8.70	8.66	8.64	8.62	8.59	8.57	8.55	8.53
4	5.96	5.91	5.86	5.80	5.77	5.75	5.72	5.69	5.66	5.63
5	4.74	4.68	4.62	4.56	4.53	4.50	4.46	4.43	4.40	4.36
6	4.06	4.00	3.94	3.87	3.84	3.81	3.77	3.74	3.70	3.67
7	3.64	3.57	3.51	3.44	3.41	3.38	3.34	3.30	3.27	3.23
8	3.35	3.28	3.22	3.15	3.12	3.08	3.04	3.01	2.97	2.93
9	3.14	3.07	3.01	2.94	2.90	2.86	2.83	2.79	2.75	2.71
10	2.98	2.91	2.85	2.77	2.74	2.70	2.66	2.62	2.58	2.54
11	2.85	2.79	2.72	2.65	2.61	2.57	2.53	2.49	2.45	2.40
12	2.75	2.69	2.62	2.54	2.51	2.47	2.43	2.38	2.34	2.30
13	2.67	2.60	2.53	2.46	2.42	2.38	2.34	2.30	2.25	2.21
14	2.60	2.53	2.46	2.39	2.35	2.31	2.27	2.22	2.18	2.13
15	2.54	2.48	2.40	2.33	2.29	2.25	2.20	2.16	2.11	2.07
16	2.49	2.42	2.35	2.28	2.24	2.19	2.15	2.11	2.06	2.01
17	2.45	2.38	2.31	2.23	2.19	2.15	2.10	2.06	2.01	1.96
18	2.41	2.34	2.27	2.19	2.15	2.11	2.06	2.02	1.97	1.92
19	2.38	2.31	2.23	2.16	2.11	2.07	2.03	1.98	1.93	1.88
20	2.35	2.28	2.20	2.12	2.08	2.04	1.99	1.95	1.90	1.84
21	2.32	2.25	2.18	2.10	2.05	2.01	1.96	1.92	1.87	1.81
22	2.30	2.23	2.15	2.07	2.03	1.98	1.94	1.89	1.84	1.78
23	2.27	2.20	2.13	2.05	2.01	1.96	1.91	1.86	1.81	1.76
24	2.25	2.18	2.11	2.03	1.98	1.94	1.89	1.84	1.79	1.73
25	2.24	2.16	2.09	2.01	1.96	1.92	1.87	1.82	1.77	1.71
26	2.22	2.15	2.07	1.99	1.95	1.90	1.85	1.80	1.75	1.69
27	2.20	2.13	2.06	1.97	1.93	1.88	1.84	1.79	1.73	1.67
28	2.19	2.12	2.04	1.96	1.91	1.87	1.82	1.77	1.71	1.65
29	2.18	2.10	2.03	1.94	1.90	1.85	1.81	1.75	1.70	1.64
30	2.16	2.09	2.01	1.93	1.89	1.84	1.79	1.74	1.68	1.62
40	2.08	2.00	1.92	1.84	1.79	1.74	1.69	1.64	1.58	1.51
60	1.99	1.92	1.84	1.75	1.70	1.65	1.59	1.53	1.47	1.39
120	1.91	1.83	1.75	1.66	1.61	1.55	1.50	1.43	1.35	1.25
∞	1.83	1.75	1.67	1.57	1.52	1.46	1.39	1.32	1.22	1.00

TABLE X Percentage Points of the F-distribution, $\alpha = .025$

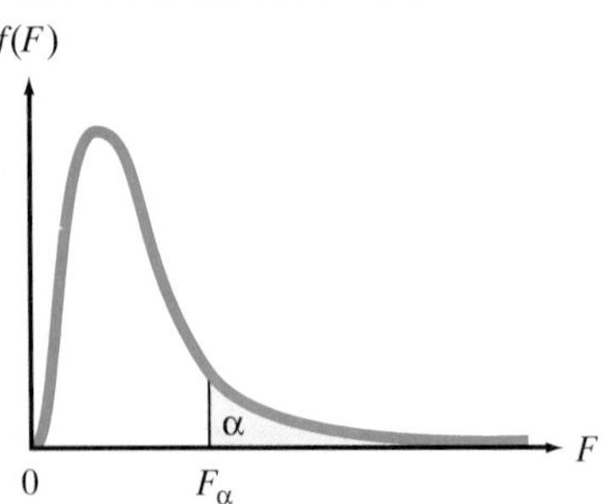

ν_2 \ ν_1	NUMERATOR DEGREES OF FREEDOM								
	1	2	3	4	5	6	7	8	9
1	647.8	799.5	864.2	899.6	921.8	937.1	948.2	956.7	963.3
2	38.51	39.00	39.17	39.25	39.30	39.33	39.36	39.37	39.39
3	17.44	16.04	15.44	15.10	14.88	14.73	14.62	14.54	14.47
4	12.22	10.65	9.98	9.60	9.36	9.20	9.07	8.98	8.90
5	10.01	8.43	7.76	7.39	7.15	6.98	6.85	6.76	6.68
6	8.81	7.26	6.60	6.23	5.99	5.82	5.70	5.60	5.52
7	8.07	6.54	5.89	5.52	5.29	5.12	4.99	4.90	4.82
8	7.57	6.06	5.42	5.05	4.82	4.65	4.53	4.43	4.36
9	7.21	5.71	5.08	4.72	4.48	4.32	4.20	4.10	4.03
10	6.94	5.46	4.83	4.47	4.24	4.07	3.95	3.85	3.78
11	6.72	5.26	4.63	4.28	4.04	3.88	3.76	3.66	3.59
12	6.55	5.10	4.47	4.12	3.89	3.73	3.61	3.51	3.44
13	6.41	4.97	4.35	4.00	3.77	3.60	3.48	3.39	3.31
14	6.30	4.86	4.24	3.89	3.66	3.50	3.38	3.29	3.21
15	6.20	4.77	4.15	3.80	3.58	3.41	3.29	3.20	3.12
16	6.12	4.69	4.08	3.73	3.50	3.34	3.22	3.12	3.05
17	6.04	4.62	4.01	3.66	3.44	3.28	3.16	3.06	2.98
18	5.98	4.56	3.95	3.61	3.38	3.22	3.10	3.01	2.93
19	5.92	4.51	3.90	3.56	3.33	3.17	3.05	2.96	2.88
20	5.87	4.46	3.86	3.51	3.29	3.13	3.01	2.91	2.84
21	5.83	4.42	3.82	3.48	3.25	3.09	2.97	2.87	2.80
22	5.79	4.38	3.78	3.44	3.22	3.05	2.93	2.84	2.76
23	5.75	4.35	3.75	3.41	3.18	3.02	2.90	2.81	2.73
24	5.72	4.32	3.72	3.38	3.15	2.99	2.87	2.78	2.70
25	5.69	4.29	3.69	3.35	3.13	2.97	2.85	2.75	2.68
26	5.66	4.27	3.67	3.33	3.10	2.94	2.82	2.73	2.65
27	5.63	4.24	3.65	3.31	3.08	2.92	2.80	2.71	2.63
28	5.61	4.22	3.63	3.29	3.06	2.90	2.78	2.69	2.61
29	5.59	4.20	3.61	3.27	3.04	2.88	2.76	2.67	2.59
30	5.57	4.18	3.59	3.25	3.03	2.87	2.75	2.65	2.57
40	5.42	4.05	3.46	3.13	2.90	2.74	2.62	2.53	2.45
60	5.29	3.93	3.34	3.01	2.79	2.63	2.51	2.41	2.33
120	5.15	3.80	3.23	2.89	2.67	2.52	2.39	2.30	2.22
∞	5.02	3.69	3.12	2.79	2.57	2.41	2.29	2.19	2.11

(Row label: DENOMINATOR DEGREES OF FREEDOM)

Source: From M. Merrington and C. M. Thompson, "Tables of Percentage Points of the Inverted Beta (F)-Distribution," *Biometrika,* 1943, 33, 73–88. Reproduced by permission of the *Biometrika* Trustees.

(continued)

TABLE X Continued

ν_1 / ν_2	NUMERATOR DEGREES OF FREEDOM									
	10	12	15	20	24	30	40	60	120	∞
1	968.6	976.7	984.9	993.1	997.2	1,001	1,006	1,010	1,014	1,018
2	39.40	39.41	39.43	39.45	39.46	39.46	39.47	39.48	39.49	39.50
3	14.42	14.34	14.25	14.17	14.12	14.08	14.04	13.99	13.95	13.90
4	8.84	8.75	8.66	8.56	8.51	8.46	8.41	8.36	8.31	8.26
5	6.62	6.52	6.43	6.33	6.28	6.23	6.18	6.12	6.07	6.02
6	5.46	5.37	5.27	5.17	5.12	5.07	5.01	4.96	4.90	4.85
7	4.76	4.67	4.57	4.47	4.42	4.36	4.31	4.25	4.20	4.14
8	4.30	4.20	4.10	4.00	3.95	3.89	3.84	3.78	3.73	3.67
9	3.96	3.87	3.77	3.67	3.61	3.56	3.51	3.45	3.39	3.33
10	3.72	3.62	3.52	3.42	3.37	3.31	3.26	3.20	3.14	3.08
11	3.53	3.43	3.33	3.23	3.17	3.12	3.06	3.00	2.94	2.88
12	3.37	3.28	3.18	3.07	3.02	2.96	2.91	2.85	2.79	2.72
13	3.25	3.15	3.05	2.95	2.89	2.84	2.78	2.72	2.66	2.60
14	3.15	3.05	2.95	2.84	2.79	2.73	2.67	2.61	2.55	2.49
15	3.06	2.96	2.86	2.76	2.70	2.64	2.59	2.52	2.46	2.40
16	2.99	2.89	2.79	2.68	2.63	2.57	2.51	2.45	2.38	2.32
17	2.92	2.82	2.72	2.62	2.56	2.50	2.44	2.38	2.32	2.25
18	2.87	2.77	2.67	2.56	2.50	2.44	2.38	2.32	2.26	2.19
19	2.82	2.72	2.62	2.51	2.45	2.39	2.33	2.27	2.20	2.13
20	2.77	2.68	2.57	2.46	2.41	2.35	2.29	2.22	2.16	2.09
21	2.73	2.64	2.53	2.42	2.37	2.31	2.25	2.18	2.11	2.04
22	2.70	2.60	2.50	2.39	2.33	2.27	2.21	2.14	2.08	2.00
23	2.67	2.57	2.47	2.36	2.30	2.24	2.18	2.11	2.04	1.97
24	2.64	2.54	2.44	2.33	2.27	2.21	2.15	2.08	2.01	1.94
25	2.61	2.51	2.41	2.30	2.24	2.18	2.12	2.05	1.98	1.91
26	2.59	2.49	2.39	2.28	2.22	2.16	2.09	2.03	1.95	1.88
27	2.57	2.47	2.36	2.25	2.19	2.13	2.07	2.00	1.93	1.85
28	2.55	2.45	2.34	2.23	2.17	2.11	2.05	1.98	1.91	1.83
29	2.53	2.43	2.32	2.21	2.15	2.09	2.03	1.96	1.89	1.81
30	2.51	2.41	2.31	2.20	2.14	2.07	2.01	1.94	1.87	1.79
40	2.39	2.29	2.18	2.07	2.01	1.94	1.88	1.80	1.72	1.64
60	2.27	2.17	2.06	1.94	1.88	1.82	1.74	1.67	1.58	1.48
120	2.16	2.05	1.94	1.82	1.76	1.69	1.61	1.53	1.43	1.31
∞	2.05	1.94	1.83	1.71	1.64	1.57	1.48	1.39	1.27	1.00

DENOMINATOR DEGREES OF FREEDOM

TABLE XI Percentage Points of the F-distribution, $\alpha = .01$

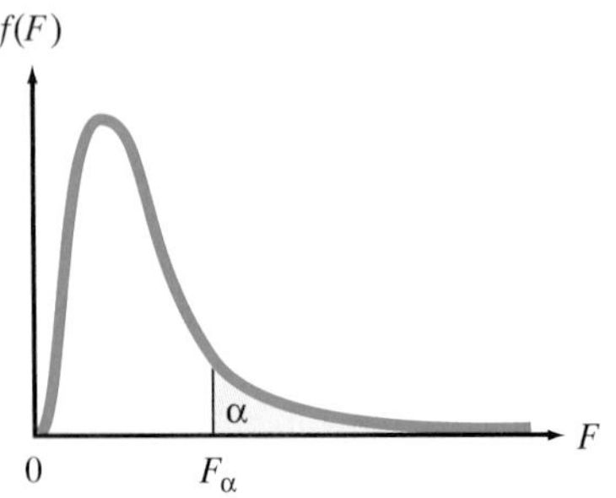

ν_2 \ ν_1	NUMERATOR DEGREES OF FREEDOM								
	1	2	3	4	5	6	7	8	9
DENOMINATOR DEGREES OF FREEDOM									
1	4,052	4,999.5	5,403	5,625	5,764	5,859	5,928	5,982	6,022
2	98.50	99.00	99.17	99.25	99.30	99.33	99.36	99.37	99.39
3	34.12	30.82	29.46	28.71	28.24	27.91	27.67	27.49	27.35
4	21.20	18.00	16.69	15.98	15.52	15.21	14.98	14.80	14.66
5	16.26	13.27	12.06	11.39	10.97	10.67	10.46	10.29	10.16
6	13.75	10.92	9.78	9.15	8.75	8.47	8.26	8.10	7.98
7	12.25	9.55	8.45	7.85	7.46	7.19	6.99	6.84	6.72
8	11.26	8.65	7.59	7.01	6.63	6.37	6.18	6.03	5.91
9	10.56	8.02	6.99	6.42	6.06	5.80	5.61	5.47	5.35
10	10.04	7.56	6.55	5.99	5.64	5.39	5.20	5.06	4.94
11	9.65	7.21	6.22	5.67	5.32	5.07	4.89	4.74	4.63
12	9.33	6.93	5.95	5.41	5.06	4.82	4.64	4.50	4.39
13	9.07	6.70	5.74	5.21	4.86	4.62	4.44	4.30	4.19
14	8.86	6.51	5.56	5.04	4.69	4.46	4.28	4.14	4.03
15	8.68	6.36	5.42	4.89	4.56	4.32	4.14	4.00	3.89
16	8.53	6.23	5.29	4.77	4.44	4.20	4.03	3.89	3.78
17	8.40	6.11	5.18	4.67	4.34	4.10	3.93	3.79	3.68
18	8.29	6.01	5.09	4.58	4.25	4.01	3.84	3.71	3.60
19	8.18	5.93	5.01	4.50	4.17	3.94	3.77	3.63	3.52
20	8.10	5.85	4.94	4.43	4.10	3.87	3.70	3.56	3.46
21	8.02	5.78	4.87	4.37	4.04	3.81	3.64	3.51	3.40
22	7.95	5.72	4.82	4.31	3.99	3.76	3.59	3.45	3.35
23	7.88	5.66	4.76	4.26	3.94	3.71	3.54	3.41	3.30
24	7.82	5.61	4.72	4.22	3.90	3.67	3.50	3.36	3.26
25	7.77	5.57	4.68	4.18	3.85	3.63	3.46	3.32	3.22
26	7.72	5.53	4.64	4.14	3.82	3.59	3.42	3.29	3.18
27	7.68	5.49	4.60	4.11	3.78	3.56	3.39	3.26	3.15
28	7.64	5.45	4.57	4.07	3.75	3.53	3.36	3.23	3.12
29	7.60	5.42	4.54	4.04	3.73	3.50	3.33	3.20	3.09
30	7.56	5.39	4.51	4.02	3.70	3.47	3.30	3.17	3.07
40	7.31	5.18	4.31	3.83	3.51	3.29	3.12	2.99	2.89
60	7.08	4.98	4.13	3.65	3.34	3.12	2.95	2.82	2.72
120	6.85	4.79	3.95	3.48	3.17	2.96	2.79	2.66	2.56
∞	6.63	4.61	3.78	3.32	3.02	2.80	2.64	2.51	2.41

Source: From M. Merrington and C. M. Thompson, "Tables of Percentage Points of the Inverted Beta (F)-Distribution," *Biometrika*, 1943, 33, 73–88. Reproduced by permission of the *Biometrika* Trustees.

(continued)

TABLE XI Continued

ν_2 \ ν_1 (DENOMINATOR DEGREES OF FREEDOM)	NUMERATOR DEGREES OF FREEDOM									
	10	12	15	20	24	30	40	60	120	∞
1	6,056	6,106	6,157	6,209	6,235	6,261	6,287	6,313	6,339	6,366
2	99.40	99.42	99.43	99.45	99.46	99.47	99.47	99.48	99.49	99.50
3	27.23	27.05	26.87	26.69	26.60	26.50	26.41	26.32	26.22	26.13
4	14.55	14.37	14.20	14.02	13.93	13.84	13.75	13.65	13.56	13.46
5	10.05	9.89	9.72	9.55	9.47	9.38	9.29	9.20	9.11	9.02
6	7.87	7.72	7.56	7.40	7.31	7.23	7.14	7.06	6.97	6.88
7	6.62	6.47	6.31	6.16	6.07	5.99	5.91	5.82	5.74	5.65
8	5.81	5.67	5.52	5.36	5.28	5.20	5.12	5.03	4.95	4.86
9	5.26	5.11	4.96	4.81	4.73	4.65	4.57	4.48	4.40	4.31
10	4.85	4.71	4.56	4.41	4.33	4.25	4.17	4.08	4.00	3.91
11	4.54	4.40	4.25	4.10	4.02	3.94	3.86	3.78	3.69	3.60
12	4.30	4.16	4.01	3.86	3.78	3.70	3.62	3.54	3.45	3.36
13	4.10	3.96	3.82	3.66	3.59	3.51	3.43	3.34	3.25	3.17
14	3.94	3.80	3.66	3.51	3.43	3.35	3.27	3.18	3.09	3.00
15	3.80	3.67	3.52	3.37	3.29	3.21	3.13	3.05	2.96	2.87
16	3.69	3.55	3.41	3.26	3.18	3.10	3.02	2.93	2.84	2.75
17	3.59	3.46	3.31	3.16	3.08	3.00	2.92	2.83	2.75	2.65
18	3.51	3.37	3.23	3.08	3.00	2.92	2.84	2.75	2.66	2.57
19	3.43	3.30	3.15	3.00	2.92	2.84	2.76	2.67	2.58	2.49
20	3.37	3.23	3.09	2.94	2.86	2.78	2.69	2.61	2.52	2.42
21	3.31	3.17	3.03	2.88	2.80	2.72	2.64	2.55	2.46	2.36
22	3.26	3.12	2.98	2.83	2.75	2.67	2.58	2.50	2.40	2.31
23	3.21	3.07	2.93	2.78	2.70	2.62	2.54	2.45	2.35	2.26
24	3.17	3.03	2.89	2.74	2.66	2.58	2.49	2.40	2.31	2.21
25	3.13	2.99	2.85	2.70	2.62	2.54	2.45	2.36	2.27	2.17
26	3.09	2.96	2.81	2.66	2.58	2.50	2.42	2.33	2.23	2.13
27	3.06	2.93	2.78	2.63	2.55	2.47	2.38	2.29	2.20	2.10
28	3.03	2.90	2.75	2.60	2.52	2.44	2.35	2.26	2.17	2.06
29	3.00	2.87	2.73	2.57	2.49	2.41	2.33	2.23	2.14	2.03
30	2.98	2.84	2.70	2.55	2.47	2.39	2.30	2.21	2.11	2.01
40	2.80	2.66	2.52	2.37	2.29	2.20	2.11	2.02	1.92	1.80
60	2.63	2.50	2.35	2.20	2.12	2.03	1.94	1.84	1.73	1.60
120	2.47	2.34	2.19	2.03	1.95	1.86	1.76	1.66	1.53	1.38
∞	2.32	2.18	2.04	1.88	1.79	1.70	1.59	1.47	1.32	1.00

TABLE XII Critical Values of T_L and T_U for the Wilcoxon Rank Sum Test: Independent Samples

Test statistic is the rank sum associated with the smaller sample (if equal sample sizes, either rank sum can be used).

a. $\alpha = .025$ one-tailed; $\alpha = .05$ two-tailed

n_2 \ n_1	3		4		5		6		7		8		9		10	
	T_L	T_U	T_L	T_U	T_L	T_U	T_L	T_U	T_L	T_U	T_L	T_U	T_L	T_U	T_L	T_U
3	5	16	6	18	6	21	7	23	7	26	8	28	8	31	9	33
4	6	18	11	25	12	28	12	32	13	35	14	38	15	41	16	44
5	6	21	12	28	18	37	19	41	20	45	21	49	22	53	24	56
6	7	23	12	32	19	41	26	52	28	56	29	61	31	65	32	70
7	7	26	13	35	20	45	28	56	37	68	39	73	41	78	43	83
8	8	28	14	38	21	49	29	61	39	73	49	87	51	93	54	98
9	8	31	15	41	22	53	31	65	41	78	51	93	63	108	66	114
10	9	33	16	44	24	56	32	70	43	83	54	98	66	114	79	131

b. $\alpha = .05$ one-tailed; $\alpha = .10$ two-tailed

n_2 \ n_1	3		4		5		6		7		8		9		10	
	T_L	T_U	T_L	T_U	T_L	T_U	T_L	T_U	T_L	T_U	T_L	T_U	T_L	T_U	T_L	T_U
3	6	15	7	17	7	20	8	22	9	24	9	27	10	29	11	31
4	7	17	12	24	13	27	14	30	15	33	16	36	17	39	18	42
5	7	20	13	27	19	36	20	40	22	43	24	46	25	50	26	54
6	8	22	14	30	20	40	28	50	30	54	32	58	33	63	35	67
7	9	24	15	33	22	43	30	54	39	66	41	71	43	76	46	80
8	9	27	16	36	24	46	32	58	41	71	52	84	54	90	57	95
9	10	29	17	39	25	50	33	63	43	76	54	90	66	105	69	111
10	11	31	18	42	26	54	35	67	46	80	57	95	69	111	83	127

Source: From F. Wilcoxon and R. A. Wilcox, "Some Rapid Approximate Statistical Procedures," 1964, 20–23. Courtesy of Lederle Laboratories Division of American Cyanamid Company, Madison, NJ.

TABLE XIII Critical Values of T_0 in the Wilcoxon Paired Difference Signed Rank Test

One-Tailed	Two-Tailed	$n = 5$	$n = 6$	$n = 7$	$n = 8$	$n = 9$	$n = 10$
$\alpha = .05$	$\alpha = .10$	1	2	4	6	8	11
$\alpha = .025$	$\alpha = .05$		1	2	4	6	8
$\alpha = .01$	$\alpha = .02$			0	2	3	5
$\alpha = .005$	$\alpha = .01$				0	2	3
		$n = 11$	$n = 12$	$n = 13$	$n = 14$	$n = 15$	$n = 16$
$\alpha = .05$	$\alpha = .10$	14	17	21	26	30	36
$\alpha = .025$	$\alpha = .05$	11	14	17	21	25	30
$\alpha = .01$	$\alpha = .02$	7	10	13	16	20	24
$\alpha = .005$	$\alpha = .01$	5	7	10	13	16	19
		$n = 17$	$n = 18$	$n = 19$	$n = 20$	$n = 21$	$n = 22$
$\alpha = .05$	$\alpha = .10$	41	47	54	60	68	75
$\alpha = .025$	$\alpha = .05$	35	40	46	52	59	66
$\alpha = .01$	$\alpha = .02$	28	33	38	43	49	56
$\alpha = .005$	$\alpha = .01$	23	28	32	37	43	49
		$n = 23$	$n = 24$	$n = 25$	$n = 26$	$n = 27$	$n = 28$
$\alpha = .05$	$\alpha = .10$	83	92	101	110	120	130
$\alpha = .025$	$\alpha = .05$	73	81	90	98	107	117
$\alpha = .01$	$\alpha = .02$	62	69	77	85	93	102
$\alpha = .005$	$\alpha = .01$	55	61	68	76	84	92
		$n = 29$	$n = 30$	$n = 31$	$n = 32$	$n = 33$	$n = 34$
$\alpha = .05$	$\alpha = .10$	141	152	163	175	188	201
$\alpha = .025$	$\alpha = .05$	127	137	148	159	171	183
$\alpha = .01$	$\alpha = .02$	111	120	130	141	151	162
$\alpha = .005$	$\alpha = .01$	100	109	118	128	138	149
		$n = 35$	$n = 36$	$n = 37$	$n = 38$	$n = 39$	
$\alpha = .05$	$\alpha = .10$	214	228	242	256	271	
$\alpha = .025$	$\alpha = .05$	195	208	222	235	250	
$\alpha = .01$	$\alpha = .02$	174	186	198	211	224	
$\alpha = .005$	$\alpha = .01$	160	171	183	195	208	
		$n = 40$	$n = 41$	$n = 42$	$n = 43$	$n = 44$	$n = 45$
$\alpha = .05$	$\alpha = .10$	287	303	319	336	353	371
$\alpha = .025$	$\alpha = .05$	264	279	295	311	327	344
$\alpha = .01$	$\alpha = .02$	238	252	267	281	297	313
$\alpha = .005$	$\alpha = .01$	221	234	248	262	277	292
		$n = 46$	$n = 47$	$n = 48$	$n = 49$	$n = 50$	
$\alpha = .05$	$\alpha = .10$	389	408	427	446	466	
$\alpha = .025$	$\alpha = .05$	361	379	397	415	434	
$\alpha = .01$	$\alpha = .02$	329	345	362	380	398	
$\alpha = .005$	$\alpha = .01$	307	323	339	356	373	

Source: From F. Wilcoxon and R. A. Wilcox, "Some Rapid Approximate Statistical Procedures," 1964, p. 28. Courtesy of Lederle Laboratories Division of American Cyanamid Company, Madison, NJ.

TABLE XIV Critical Values of Spearman's Rank Correlation Coefficient

The α values correspond to a one-tailed test of H_0: $\rho = 0$. The value should be doubled for two-tailed tests.

n	$\alpha = .05$	$\alpha = .025$	$\alpha = .01$	$\alpha = .005$	n	$\alpha = .05$	$\alpha = .025$	$\alpha = .01$	$\alpha = .005$
5	.900	—	—	—	**18**	.399	.476	.564	.625
6	.829	.886	.943	—	**19**	.388	.462	.549	.608
7	.714	.786	.893	—	**20**	.377	.450	.534	.591
8	.643	.738	.833	.881	**21**	.368	.438	.521	.576
9	.600	.683	.783	.833	**22**	.359	.428	.508	.562
10	.564	.648	.745	.794	**23**	.351	.418	.496	.549
11	.523	.623	.736	.818	**24**	.343	.409	.485	.537
12	.497	.591	.703	.780	**25**	.336	.400	.475	.526
13	.475	.566	.673	.745	**26**	.329	.392	.465	.515
14	.457	.545	.646	.716	**27**	.323	.385	.456	.505
15	.441	.525	.623	.689	**28**	.317	.377	.448	.496
16	.425	.507	.601	.666	**29**	.311	.370	.440	.487
17	.412	.490	.582	.645	**30**	.305	.364	.432	.478

Source: From E. G. Olds, "Distribution of Sums of Squares of Rank Differences for Small Samples," *Annals of Mathematical Statistics,* 1938, 9. Reproduced with the permission of the Editor, *Annals of Mathematical Statistics*.

TABLE XV Control Chart Constants

Number of Observations in Subgroup, n	A_2	d_2	d_3	D_3	D_4
2	1.880	1.128	.853	.000	3.267
3	1.023	1.693	.888	.000	2.574
4	.729	2.059	.880	.000	2.282
5	.577	2.326	.864	.000	2.114
6	.483	2.534	.848	.000	2.004
7	.419	2.704	.833	.076	1.924
8	.373	2.847	.820	.136	1.864
9	.337	2.970	.808	.184	1.816
10	.308	3.078	.797	.223	1.777
11	.285	3.173	.787	.256	1.744
12	.266	3.258	.778	.283	1.717
13	.249	3.336	.770	.307	1.693
14	.235	3.407	.762	.328	1.672
15	.223	3.472	.755	.347	1.653
16	.212	3.532	.749	.363	1.637
17	.203	3.588	.743	.378	1.622
18	.194	3.640	.738	.391	1.608
19	.187	3.689	.733	.403	1.597
20	.180	3.735	.729	.415	1.585
21	.173	3.778	.724	.425	1.575
22	.167	3.819	.720	.434	1.566
23	.162	3.858	.716	.443	1.557
24	.157	3.895	.712	.451	1.548
25	.153	3.931	.709	.459	1.541
More than 25	$3/\sqrt{n}$				

Source: ASTM Manual on the Presentation of Data and Control Chart Analysis, Philadelphia, PA: American Society for Testing Materials, pp. 134–136, 1976.

CALCULATION FORMULAS FOR ANALYSIS OF VARIANCE: INDEPENDENT SAMPLING

$$\text{CM} = \text{Correction for mean}$$

$$= \frac{(\text{Total of all observations})^2}{\text{Total number of observations}} = \frac{\left(\sum_{i=1}^{n} y_i\right)^2}{n}$$

$$\text{SS(Total)} = \text{Total sum of squares}$$

$$= (\text{Sum of squares of all observations}) - \text{CM} = \sum_{i=1}^{n} y_i^2 - \text{CM}$$

$$\text{SST} = \text{Sum of squares for treatments}$$

$$= \begin{pmatrix} \text{Sum of squares of treatment totals with} \\ \text{each square divided by the number of} \\ \text{observations for that treatment} \end{pmatrix} - \text{CM}$$

$$= \frac{T_1^2}{n_1} + \frac{T_2^2}{n_2} + \cdots + \frac{T_p^2}{n_p} - \text{CM}$$

$$\text{SSE} = \text{Sum of squares for error} = \text{SS(Total)} - \text{SST}$$

$$\text{MST} = \text{Mean square for treatments} = \frac{\text{SST}}{p - 1}$$

$$\text{MSE} = \text{Mean square for error} = \frac{\text{SSE}}{n - p}$$

$$F = \text{Test statistic} = \frac{\text{MST}}{\text{MSE}}$$

where

n = Total number of observations

p = Number of treatments

T_i = Total for treatment i $(i = 1, 2, \ldots, p)$

Answers to Selected Exercises

Chapter 1

1.3 population; variables; summary tools; conclusions **1.5** published source; designed experiment; survey; observationally **1.13** qualitative; qualitative **1.15 a.** all U.S. citizens **b.** president's job performance; qualitative **c.** 2,000 polled individuals **d.** Estimate the proportion of all citizens who believe the president is doing a good job. **e.** survey **f.** not very likely **1.17 a.** all U.S. employees **b.** employee's job status **c.** qualitative **d.** 1,000 employees surveyed **e.** majority of all workers would remain in their jobs **1.19 a.** quantitative **b.** quantitative **c.** qualitative **d.** quantitative **e.** qualitative **f.** quantitative **g.** qualitative **1.21 a.** all department store executives **b.** job satisfaction; Machiavellian rating **c.** 218 department store executives **d.** survey **e.** Executives with higher job-satisfaction scores are likely to have a lower 'mach' rating. **1.25 a.** all major U.S. firms **b.** whether the job offers job-sharing **c.** 1,035 firms **d.** Estimate the proportion of all firms that offer job-sharing to their employees. **1.27** I. qualitative II. quantitative III. quantitative IV. qualitative V. qualitative VI. quantitative **1.29 b.** speed of the deliveries; accuracy of the invoices; quality of the packaging **c.** total numbers of questionnaires received

Chapter 2

2.1 16;.18; .45;.15;.14 **2.3 b.** yes **c.** banks: yes; department stores: no **2.5 a.** .642,.204,.083,.071 **2.7 a.** response time **c.** 3,570 **2.9 a.** length of time small businesses used the Internet per week **c.** .08 **2.13** 50, 75, 125, 100, 25, 50, 50, 25 **2.15 a.** frequency histogram **b.** 14 **c.** 49 **2.17 c.** 28.6% **2.19 b.** 22;.733 **2.25 a.** 44.75% **b.** .325 **2.27 a.** 33 **b.** 175 **c.** 20 **d.** 71 **e.** 1,089 **2.29 a.** 6 **b.** 50 **c.** 42.8 **2.31 a.** $\bar{x} = 2.717, m = 2.65$ **2.33 a.** 2.5; 3; 3 **b.** 3.08; 3; 3 **c.** 49.6; 49; 50 **2.35** $m = 129{,}200.5; \bar{x} = 197{,}632.25$ **2.37 a.** $\bar{x} = 5.24, m = 3$, mode $= 2$ **b.** 48 **c.** $\bar{x} = 4.66$, m $= 3$, mode $= 2$ **2.39 a.** median **b.** mean **2.41 a.** joint: $\bar{x} = 2.6545, m = 1.5$; no prefiling: $\bar{x} = 4.2364, m = 3.2$; prepack: $\bar{x} = 1.8185, m = 1.4$ **b.** three centers **2.43 c.** no; yes (if the data are between 0 and 1) **2.45 a.** $R = 4, s^2 = 2.3, s = 1.52$ **b.** $R = 6, s^2 = 3.619, s = 1.90$ **c.** $R = 10, s^2 = 7.111, s = 2.67$ **d.** $R = 5, s^2 = 1.624, s = 1.274$ **2.47 a.** $\bar{x} = 5.6, s^2 = 17.3, s = 4.1593$ **b.** $\bar{x} = 13.75$ feet, $s^2 = 152.25$ square feet, $s = 12.339$ feet **c.** $\bar{x} = -2.5, s^2 = 4.3, s = 2.0736$ **b.** $\bar{x} = .33$ ounce, $s^2 = .0587$ square ounce, $s = .2422$ ounce **2.49 a.** \$17,360; \$13,700 **b.** \$36,202 **c.** no **2.51 a.** 150.30; 150.95 **b.** 7.5; 7.8 **c.** 2.41; 2.66 **d.** Chicago **2.53 a.** $R = 455.2, s^2 = 25{,}367.88, s = 159.27$ **b.** R and s: million dollars; s^2: million dollars squared **c.** increase; increase **2.55 a.** 68% **b.** 95% **c.** almost all **2.57 a.** $\bar{x} = 8.24, s^2 = 3.357, s = 1.83$ **b.** 18/25 = .72, 24/25 = .96, 25/25 = 1 **d.** $R = 7, s = 1.75$ **2.59 b.** $R = 48, s \approx$ between 8 and 12 **c.** at most 25%, at least 50% **2.61 b.** $(-100.27, 219.91)$ **2.63 a.** no **b.** $(-1.107, 6.205)$ **c.** 47/49 = .959 **d.** no more than 6.2 months **2.65** do not buy **2.67** 11:30 and 4:00 **2.69 a.** 75% **b.** 50% **c.** 20% **d.** 84% **2.71 a.** $z = 2$ **b.** $z = -3$ **c.** $z = -2$ **d.** $z = 1.67$ **2.73** no **2.75 b.** $\bar{x} = -13{,}117.06, s = 21{,}889.6$; Japan: $z = -1.96$; Egypt: $z = .74$ **2.77 a.** 0 **b.** 21 **c.** 5.90 **d.** yes **2.79 a.** $z = .727$, no **b.** $z = -3.273$, yes **c.** $z = 1.364$, no **d.** $z = 3.727$, yes **2.85 c.** no **d.** yes **2.87 b.** customers 268, 269, and 264 **2.91 a.** $-1, 1, 2$ **b.** $-2, 2, 4$ **c.** 1, 3, 4 **d.** .1, .3, .4 **2.93 a.** 6, 27, 5.20 **b.** 6.25, 28.25, 5.32 **c.** 7, 37.67, 6.14 **d.** 3, 0, 0 **2.99 b.** marketing; 6.5 days, engineering: 7.0 days; accounting: 8.5 days **2.103 a.** skewed right **c.** ≈ 38 **d.** no, $z = 3.333$ **2.105 b.** yes, skewed to the right **c.** 370 **d.** 0.46, -1.10 **f.** Carolina, New England, Denver, Seattle, Pittsburgh, Cincinnati **g.** Dallas **h.** operating income increases as current value increases

Chapter 3

3.1 a. .5 **b.** .3 **c.** .6 **3.3** $P(A) = .55, P(B) = .50, P(C) = .70$ **3.5** $P(A) = 1/10, P(B) = 3/5, P(C) = 3/10$ **3.7 b.** .189, .403, .258, .113, .038 **c.** .592 **d.** .812 **3.9** 1/20 **3.11 a.** .990, .010 **b.** .195, .203, .576 **3.13 a.** 1 to 2 **b.** ½ **c.** 2/5 **3.15 b.** 1/16 **c.** 5/16 **3.19 a.** 3/4 **b.** 13/20 **c.** 1 **d.** 2/5 **e.** 1/4 **f.** 7/20 **g.** 1 **h.** 1/4 **3.21 a.** .65 **b.** .72 **c.** .25 **d.** .08 **e.** .35 **f.** .72 **g.** 0 **h.** A and C, B and C, C and D **3.23 a.** $B \cap C$ **b.** A^c **c.** $C \cup B$ **d.** $A \cap C^c$ **3.25 a.** $P(A) = .281, P(B) = .276, P(C) = .044, P(D) = .079, P(E) = .044$ **b.** 0 **c.** .557 **d.** 0 **e.** .325 **f.** A and B, A and C, A and D, A and E **3.27 a.** (1, R), (1, S), (1, E), (2, R), (2, S), (2, E), (3, R), (3, S), (3, E) **b.** sample space **c.** .24 **d.** .10 **e.** .47 **f.** .62 **g.** .28 **3.29 a.** $(D, C), (D, T), (F, C), (F, T), (G, C), (G, T)$ **b.** .450, .550, .338 **c.** .578, 0 **d.** .236, .186 **3.31 a.** yes **b.** $P(A) = .26, P(B) = .35, P(C) = .72, P(D) = .28, P(E) = .05$ **c.** .56, .05, .77 **d.** .74 **e.** C and D, D and E **3.33 a.** .8, .7, .6 **b.** .25, .375, .375 **d.** no **3.35 a.** .37 **b.** .68 **c.** .15 **d.** .2206 **e.** 0 **f.** 0 **g.** no **3.37 a.** A and C, B and C **b.** none **c.** .65, .90 **3.39 a.** .08, .4, .52 **b.** .12, .30 **3.41 a.** .833 **b.** .5 **c.** .333 **3.43 a.** .9224 **b.** .0776 **3.45 a.** .543 **b.** .221 **c.** .052 **d.** .914 **3.47 a.** .02 **b.** .08 **3.49 a.** .116 **b.** .728 **3.51 a.** .3, .6 **b.** dependent **c.** independent **3.53 a.** 35,820,200 **b.** 1/35,820,200 **3.55 a.** .000186 **c.** no **3.61** .5 **3.63 a.** 0, .2, .9, 1, .7, .3, .4, 0

3.65 a. 720 **b.** 10 **c.** 10 **d.** 20 **e.** 1 **3.67 a.** .25 **b.** .13 **c.** .75 **d.** .0325 **3.69 a.** .75 **b.** .2875 **c.** .6 **d.** .06 **e.** no **f.** employee does not plan to retire at age 68 or the employee is not on the technical staff **g.** yes **3.71 a.** 1/10, 1/10 **b.** .641, .359 **c.** upper bounds **3.73 a.** .00000625 **b.** .0135 **c.** doubt validity of the manufacturer's claim **d.** no **3.75** .801 **3.77 b.** .95 **c.** .25 **d.** .5 **3.79 a.** .24 **b.** .1 **c.** .14 **3.81** .79 **3.83 a.** .7127 **b.** .2873 **3.85 b.** 1/10 **c.** 1/10, 3/10 **3.87 a.** .550 **b.** .450 **c.** .272 **d.** .040 **e.** .182 **f.** .857 **g.** .182

Chapter 4

4.3 a. discrete **b.** discrete **c.** discrete **d.** continuous **e.** discrete **f.** continuous **4.11 a.** .25 **b.** .40 **c.** .75 **4.13 a.** .3 **b.** .1 **c.** .2 **d.** .7 **e.** .9 **f.** .9 **4.15 a.** 34.5, 174.75, 13.219 **c.** 1.00 **4.17 a.** .2592 **b.** .0870 **c.** .6826 **4.19 b.** .011, .052, .948, .219 **d.** .138, .196 **4.21** $a_1 = 2.4$; $a_2 = 1.5$; $a_3 = .90$; $a_4 = .90$; $a_5 = .90$; $a_6 = 1.65$ **4.23 b.** 6.5 **c.** 1.9975 **d.** at least 0%, at least 75% **e.** 70%; 95% **4.25 a.** 15 **b.** 10 **c.** 1 **d.** 1 **e.** 4 **4.27 a.** .4096 **b.** .3456 **c.** .027 **d.** .0081 **e.** .3456 **f.** .027 **4.29 a.** 12.5, 6.25, 2.5 **b.** 16, 12.8, 3.578 **c.** 60, 24, 4.899 **d.** 63, 6.3, 2.510 **e.** 48, 9.6, 3.098 **f.** 40, 38.4, 6.197 **4.31 a.** .015, .030 **b.** .0706, .0022 **c.** .1328, .0085 **d.** .9129 **4.33 b.** .60 **c.** .346 **d.** .317 **4.35 a.** ≈ 0 **b.** .4845 **c.** independence of flights **d.** Air Force's **e.** .0803 **4.37 a.** 520, 13.491 **b.** no, $z = -8.895$ **4.39 a.** discrete **b.** Poisson **d.** $\mu = 3, \sigma = 1.7321$ **e.** $\mu = 3, \sigma = 1.7321$ **4.41 a.** .934 **b.** .191 **c.** .125 **d.** .223 **e.** .777 **f.** .001 **4.43 a.** 4, 2 **b.** −1.5 **c.** .889 **4.45 a.** 2 **b.** no, $P(x > 10) = .003$ **4.47 a.** .03 **c.** .0291, .9704 **4.49 a.** .6083 **c.** no, $P(x > 2) = .0064$; yes, $P(x < 1) = .6907$ **4.51 a.** $f(x) = 1/4\,(3 \le x \le 7)$, 0 otherwise **b.** 5, 1.155 **4.53 a.** 0 **b.** 1 **c.** 1 **4.55 a.** $\mu = .03, \sigma = .00013$ **b.** $\mu = .75, \sigma = .0208$ **c.** 1, .375 **d.** .5, .20, 0 **4.57** yes **4.59 a.** continuous **c.** 7, .2887, (6.422, 7.577) **d.** .5 **e.** 0 **f.** .75 **g.** .0002 **4.61 a.** .4772 **b.** .4987 **c.** .4332 **d.** .2881 **4.63 a.** −.81 **b.** .55 **c.** 1.43 **d.** .21 **e.** −2.05 **f.** .50 **4.65 a.** .3830 **b.** .3023 **c.** .1525 **d.** .7333 **e.** .1314 **f.** .9545 **4.67 a.** .6554 **b.** .4295 **c.** .9544 **4.69 a.** .1020 **b.** .6879, .8925 **c.** .0032 **4.71 a.** .5124 **b.** yes **c.** no **4.73 a.** .68% **b.** $P(x < 6) = .0068$ **4.75** 5.068 **4.77 a.** 123 **b.** 1.295 **c.** yes **4.79 b.** 2.765 **c.** $\text{IQR}/s = 1.70$ **4.81** data are not normal **4.85 a.** .345, .3446 **b.** .115, .1151 **c.** .924, .9224 **4.87 a.** 1 **b.** $\mu \pm 3\sigma = (-2.058, 8.658)$ **4.89 a.** 5,000; 25,000 **b.** .5438 **c.** no **4.91 a.** no **b.** .6026, .5155 **c.** no, yes, yes **d.** .7190 **4.93 a.** 300 **b.** 800 **c.** 1.0 **4.95 a.** .367879 **b.** .082085 **c.** .000553 **d.** .223130 **4.97 a.** .999447 **b.** .999955 **c.** .981684 **d.** .632121 **4.99 a.** .0949 **b.** 10.54; 10.54 **d.** .1729 **4.101 a.** $e^{-.5x}$ **b.** .135335 **c.** .367879 **d.** no **e.** 820.85; 3,934.69 **f.** 37 days **4.103 a.** .550671 **b.** .263597 **4.105 c.** 1/16 **4.107 c.** .05 **d.** no **4.109 a.** 5 **b.** $E(\bar{x}) = 5$ **c.** $E(m) = 4.778$ **4.111 a.** 100, 5 **b.** 100, 2 **c.** 100, 1 **d.** 100, 1.414 **e.** 100, .447 **f.** 100, .316 **4.113 a.** 2.9, 3.29, 1.814 **4.115 a.** .0228 **b.** .0668 **c.** .0062 **d.** .8185 **e.** .0013 **4.117 a.** approximately normal **b.** .0322 **c.** .8925 **d.** 19.1 **e.** less than 19.1 **4.119 a.** $\mu_{\bar{x}} = 406$, $\sigma_{\bar{x}} = 1.6833$, approximately normal **b.** .0010 **c.** the first **4.121 a.** ≈ 0 **b.** yes, $\bar{x} = 5.55$ **4.123 a.** discrete **b.** continuous **c.** continuous **d.** continuous **4.125 a.** .2734 **b.** .4096 **c.** .3432 **4.127 a.** .192 **b.** .228 **c.** .772 **d.** .987, .960 **f.** 14, 4.2, 2.049 **g.** .975 **4.129 a.** $f(x) = 1/80, 10 \le x \le 90$, 0 otherwise **b.** 50, 23.09 **d.** .625 **e.** 0 **f.** .875 **g.** .577 **h.** .1875 **4.131 a.** .3821 **b.** .5398 **c.** 0 **d.** .1395 **e.** .0045 **f.** .4602 **4.133 a.** .9975 **b.** .00012 **c.** 0 **d.** 1 **e.** .000006 **4.137 b.** 20, 4.4721 **c.** no, $z = -3.55$ **d.** 0 **4.139** \$9.6582 **4.141 a.** .0918 **b.** 0 **c.** 4.87 decibels **4.143 a.** .221199 **b.** .002394 **c.** .082085 **4.145** No **4.147 a.** nothing about shape **b.** approximately normal **c.** .2843 **d.** .1292

4.105 d.

$\bar{x}$	$p(\bar{x})$
0	1/16
1	2/16
2	3/16
3	4/16
4	3/16
5	2/16
6	1/16

4.107 a.

$\bar{x}$	$p(\bar{x})$
1	.04
1.5	.12
2	.17
2.5	.20
3	.20
3.5	.14
4	.08
4.5	.04
5	.01

4.109 b.

$\bar{x}$	$p(\bar{x})$
2	1/27
8/3	3/27
10/3	3/27
4	1/27
13/3	3/27
5	6/27
17/3	3/27
20/3	3/27
22/3	3/27
9	1/27
	27/27

4.109 c.

m	$p(m)$
2	7/27
4	13/27
9	7/27
	27/27

4.113 b.

$\bar{x}$	$p(\bar{x})$
1	.01
1.5	.08
2	.24
2.5	.32
3	.16
4.5	.02
5	.08
5.5	.08
8	.01
	1.00

Chapter 5

5.1 a. 1.645 **b.** 2.58 **c.** 1.96 **d.** 1.28 **5.3 a.** 28 ± .784 **b.** 102 ± .65 **c.** 15 ± .0588 **d.** 4.05 ± .163 **e.** no **5.5 a.** 33.9 ± .65 **b.** 33.9 ± .32 **c.** width is halved **5.7 d.** claim probably not true **5.9** (.3526, .4921) **5.11 a.** 66.83 ± 4.69 **c.** (41.009, 49.602) **5.13 a.** 2.228 **b.** 2.228 **c.** −1.812 **d.** 1.725 **e.** 4.032 **5.15 a.** 97.94 ± 4.24 **b.** 97.94 ± 6.74 **5.17 a.** 2.886 ± 4.034 **b.** .408 ± .256 **5.19 a.** 49.3 ± 8.6 **b.** 99% confident that the mean amount removed from all soil specimens using the poison is between 40.70% and 57.90%. **5.21** 184.99 ± 133.93 **5.23 a.** 22.46 ± 11.18 **d.** validity is suspect **5.25 a.** yes **b.** no **c.** yes **d.** no **5.27 a.** yes **b.** .46 ± .065 **5.29 b.** .29 ± .028 **5.31 a.** .24 **b.** .24 ± .181 **5.33** .85 ± .002 **5.35** 308 **5.37 a.** 68 **b.** 31 **5.39** 34 **5.41 a.** .226 ± .007 **b.** .014 **c.** 1,680 **5.43** 1,692 **5.45** 43; 171; 385 **5.47** no **5.49 a.** −1.725 **b.** 3.250 **c.** 1.860 **d.** 2.898 **5.51 a.** 32.5 ± 5.16 **b.** 23,964 **5.53 a.** (298.6, 582.3) **5.55 a.** .876 ± .003 **5.57 a.** men: 7.4 ± .979; women: 4.5 ± .755 **b.** men: 9.3 ± 1.185; women: 6.6 ± 1.138 **5.59 a.** 12.2 ± 1.645 **b.** 167 **5.61 a.** 191 **5.63 b.** 3.256 ± .348 **5.65** 154

Chapter 6

6.1 null; alternative **6.3** α **6.7** no **6.9** H_0: $p = .10$, H_a: $p < .10$ **6.11 c.** α **e.** decrease **f.** increase **6.13 a.** unsafe; safe **c.** α **6.15 g.** .025, .05, .005, .10, .10, .01 **6.17 a.** $z = 1.67$, reject H_0 **b.** $z = 1.67$, do not reject H_0 **6.19** $z = -1.86$, do not reject H_0 **6.21 a.** H_0: $\mu = 16$, H_a: $\mu < 16$ **b.** $z = -4.31$, reject H_0 **6.23 a.** yes, $z = 7.02$ **6.25 a.** H_0: $\mu = 10$, H_a: $\mu < 10$ **c.** $z = -2.34$, reject H_0 **6.27 a.** skewed to the right **b.** yes, $z = 1.75$ **c.** yes, no **6.29 a.** do not reject H_0 **b.** reject H_0 **c.** reject H_0 **d.** do not reject H_0 **e.** do not reject H_0 **6.31** .0150 **6.33 a.** do not reject H_0 **b.** reject H_0 **c.** reject H_0 **d.** do not reject H_0 **6.35 b.** reject H_0 **c.** reject H_0 **6.37 a.** H_0: $\mu = 2.5$, H_a: $\mu > 2.5$ **b.** 0 **c.** reject H_0 **6.39 a.** H_0: $\mu = 16.5$, H_a: $\mu > 16.5$ **b.** .0681 **6.43 a.** $|t| > 2.160$ **b.** $t > 2.500$ **c.** $t > 1.397$ **d.** $t < -2.718$ **e.** $|t| > 1.729$ **f.** $t < -2.353$ **6.45 b.** p-value = .0382, reject H_0 **c.** .0764, reject H_0 **6.47 a.** $t = -1.79$, reject H_0 **b.** population of percent repellencies is normally distributed **6.49** yes, $t = 8.75$ **6.51 a.** H_0: $\mu = .004$, H_a: $\mu > .004$ **c.** plant 1: do not reject H_0; plant 2: do not reject H_0 **6.53 a.** yes **b.** no **c.** yes **d.** no **e.** no **6.55 a.** $z = 1.13$, do not reject H_0 **b.** .1292 **6.57 a.** no, $z = 1.14$ **b.** .1271 **6.59** $z = 33.47$, reject H_0 **6.61 a.** $z = -2.22$, do not reject H_0 **b.** .0132 **6.63 a.** H_0: $p = .5$, H_a: $p < .5$ **b.** do not reject H_0 **6.65 a.** .035 **b.** .363 **c.** .004 **d.** .151 **e.** .2119 **6.67** p-value = .054; reject H_0 **6.69 a.** H_0: $\eta = 5$, H_a: $\eta > 5$ **b.** 0 **c.** reject H_0 **6.71 a.** sign test **b.** H_0: $\eta = 30$, H_a: $\eta < 30$ **c.** $S = .5$, p-value < .01 **d.** p-value = .109, do not reject H_0 **6.73** alternative **6.75 a.** $t = -7.51$, reject H_0 **b.** $t = -7.51$, reject H_0 **6.77 a.** $z = -1.67$, do not reject H_0 **b.** $z = -3.35$, reject H_0 **6.79** $z = 1.20$, do not reject H_0 **6.81 a.** yes, $z = -1.93$ **6.83 b.** reject H_0 at $\alpha = .05$ **c.** Type I error **6.85 a.** $z = 12.97$, reject H_0: $p = .5$ **b.** 0 **c.** .6844 **6.87 a.** no, $z = 1.41$ **b.** small **c.** .0793 **6.89 a.** No, $z = -3.47$ **6.91 a.** H_0: $\mu = 1$, H_a: $\mu > 1$ **b.** $t > 1.345$ **d.** $t = 2.408$, reject H_0 **6.93 a.** H_0: $\mu = 209{,}700$, H_a: $\mu > 209{,}700$ **b.** p-value = .0188, reject H_0

Chapter 7

7.1 a. 35 ± 24.5 **b.** $z = 2.8$, p-value = .0052, reject H_0 **c.** p-value = .0026 **d.** $z = .8$, p-value = .4238, do not reject H_0 **e.** independent random samples **7.3 a.** no **b.** no **c.** no **d.** yes **e.** no **7.5 a.** .5989 **b.** yes, $t = -2.39$ **c.** −1.24 ± .98 **d.** confidence interval **7.7 a.** p-value = .1150, do not reject H_0 **b.** .0575 **7.9 a.** p-value = .1114, do not reject H_0 **b.** −2.50 ± 3.12 **7.11 a.** H_0: $\mu_1 = \mu_2$, H_a: $\mu_1 \neq \mu_2$ **b.** $z = 7.71$, reject H_0 **c.** .51 ± .14 **7.13 a.** yes, $t = 1.9557$ **c.** .0579 **d.** −7.4 ± 6.38 **7.15 a.** yes **b.** $t = 19.73$, reject H_0 **7.17** No significant difference for utilization of information, age, and education **7.19 a.** beginning: 6.09 ± 41.84; first: −52.24 ± 40.84; second: −48.41 ± 40.64; third: −37.68 ± 39.78; fourth: −38.54 ± 42.96 **7.21 a.** $t > 1.796$ **b.** $t > 1.319$ **c.** $t > 3.182$ **d.** $t > 2.998$ **7.23 a.** H_0: $\mu_D = 0$, H_a: $\mu_D < 0$ **b.** $t = -5.29$, p-value = .0002, reject H_0 **c.** (−5.284, −2.116) **d.** population of differences is normal **7.25 a.** $t = .81$, do not reject H_0 **b.** p-value ≥ .20 **7.27 a.** yes, $t = 2.864$ **7.29 a.** H_0: $\mu_D = 0$, H_a: $\mu_D < 0$ **b.** $t = -2.948$, reject H_0 **7.31 a.** H_0: $\mu_D = 0$, H_a: $\mu_D \neq 0$ **b.** $t = 5.76$, reject H_0 **c.** yes **7.33** p-value = 0.65, do not reject H_0 **7.35** 34 **7.37** 27 **7.39** $n \approx 21$ **7.41** 293 **7.43 a.** $F > 2.19$ **b.** $F > 2.75$ **c.** $F > 3.37$ **d.** $F > 4.30$ **7.45 a.** $F = 2.26$, do not reject H_0 **b.** .10 < p-value < .20 **7.47 a.** equal variances **b.** H_0: $\sigma_1^2 = \sigma_2^2$, H_a: $\sigma_1^2 \neq \sigma_2^2$ **c.** $F = 28.22$, reject H_0 **7.49 a.** $F = 2.26$, do not reject H_0 **7.51 a.** $F = 8.29$, reject H_0 **b.** no **7.53 a.** T_2; $T_2 \leq 35$ or $T_2 \geq 67$ **b.** T_1; $T_1 \geq 43$ **c.** T_2; $T_2 \geq 93$ **d.** z; $|z| > 1.96$ **7.57 a.** No, $T_2 = 105$ **b.** less than .05 **7.59 b.** p-value = .0564, do not reject H_0 **c.** populations are normal with equal variances; assumption of normality may be violated **7.61** yes, $T_1 = 39$; yes **7.63 a.** $z = -1.75$, reject H_0 **7.65 a.** H_0: Two sampled populations have identical probability distributions **b.** $T_- = 3.5$, reject H_0 **7.69 a.** H_0: Two sampled populations have identical probability distributions **b.** $z = 2.499$, reject H_0 **c.** .0062 **7.71** $T_- = 3.5$, reject H_0 **7.73** $T_+ = 2$, reject H_0 **7.75** No, p-value = .1728 **7.77** dot plot b **7.79 a.** $MSE_a = 2$, $MSE_b = 14.4$ **b.** $t_a = -6.12$, $F_a = 37.5$; $t_b = -2.28$, $F_b = 5.21$ **c.** $|t| > 2.228$, $F > 4.96$ **d.** reject H_0; reject H_0 **7.81 a.** 4; 38 **b.** $F = 14.80$, reject H_0 **c.** sample means **7.83** Do not reject H_0: $\mu_1 = \mu_2 = \mu_3$, $F = 1.62$, p-value = .209; assumption of equal variances may be violated **7.85 a.** Infrequency: reject H_0; obvious: reject H_0; subtle: reject H_0; obvious-subtle: reject H_0; dissimulation: reject H_0 **b.** no **7.87 a.** H_0: $\mu_1 = \mu_2 = \mu_3 = \mu_4 = \mu_5 = \mu_6$ **b.** no **d.** designed **7.89 a.** $t = .78$, do not reject H_0 **b.** 2.50 ± 8.99 **c.** 225 **7.91 a.** 3.90 ± .31 **b.** $z = 20.60$, reject H_0 **c.** 346 **7.93 a.** $t = 5.73$, reject H_0 **b.** 3.8 ± 1.84 **7.95** No, $T = 1.5$ **7.97 b.** yes **c.** no **7.99 a.** yes, = 7.679 **b.** .000597 **d.** .4167 ± .1395 **e.** $T = 0$, reject H_0 **7.101 a.** H_0: $\mu_1 - \mu_2 = 0$, H_a: $\mu_1 - \mu_2 \neq 0$ **b.** $z = -7.69$, reject H_0 **7.103** initial performance: $z = 5.68$, reject H_0; rate of career advancement: $z = 5.36$, reject H_0; final performance appraisal: $z = 10.63$, reject H_0 **7.105 a.** yes, $t = -4.02$ **b.** .0030 **7.107** yes, $T_{before} = 132.5$

7.109 a. H_0: $\mu_D = 0$, H_a: $\mu_D > 0$ **b.** paired difference **c.** Aad: do not reject H_0 for $\alpha = .05$; Ab: reject H_0 for $\alpha = .05$; Intention: do not reject H_0 for $\alpha = .05$

Chapter 8

8.3 a. $z < -2.33$ **b.** $z < -1.96$ **c.** $z < -1.645$ **d.** $z < -1.28$ **8.5 a.** $.07 \pm .067$ **b.** $.06 \pm .086$ **c.** $-.15 \pm .131$ **8.7** $z - 1.14$, do not reject H_0 **8.9 a.** $p_1 - p_2$ **8.11 b.** yes **c.** $.19 \pm .02$ **d.** normal approximation not adequate **8.13 a.** yes **b.** $-.0568 \pm .0270$ **8.15** yes, $z = -2.25$ **8.17 a.** $n_1 = n_2 = 29{,}954$ **b.** $n_1 = n_2 = 2{,}165$ **c.** $n_1 = n_2 = 1{,}113$ **8.19 a.** $n_1 = n_2 = 911$ **b.** no **8.21** $n_1 = 520, n_2 = 260$ **8.23 a.** 18.3070 **b.** 29.7067 **c.** 23.5418 **d.** 79.4900 **8.25 b.** $E(n_i) \geq 5$ **8.27 a.** $\chi^2 = 3.293$ **8.29 a.** 111, 74, 74, 37, 37, 37 **b.** 13.541 **c.** reject H_0 **8.31 a.** yes, $\chi^2 = 87.74$, p-value $= 0$ **b.** $.539 \pm .047$ **8.33 a.** H_0: $p_1 = p_2 = p_3 = p_4 = .25$ **b.** $\chi^2 = 14.805$, reject H_0 **c.** Type I error: conclude opinions of Internet users are not evenly divided among four categories when they are; Type II error: conclude opinions of Internet users are evenly divided among four categories when they are not; **8.35** $\chi^2 = 16$, p-value $= .003$, reject H_0 **8.37 a.** $\chi^2 = 12.734$, do not reject H_0 **b.** $.05 < p$-value $< .10$ **8.39 a.** H_0: row and column classifications are independent **b.** $\chi^2 > 9.21034$ **c.** 14.37, 36.79, 44.84, 10.63, 26.21, 33.16 **d.** $\chi^2 = 8.71$, do not reject H_0 **8.41** yes, $\chi^2 = 256.336$ **8.43 a.** .901 **b.** .690 **d.** $\chi^2 = 48.191$, reject H_0 **e.** $.211 \pm .070$ **8.45 b.** $\chi^2 = 45.357$, p-value $= 0$, reject H_0 **8.47 a.** $\chi^2 = 39.22$, reject H_0 **b.** $\chi^2 = 2.84$, do not reject H_0 **8.49** yes, $\chi^2 = 24.524$ **8.51 a.** no, $\chi^2 = 2.133$ **b.** $.233 \pm .057$ **8.53** 542 **8.55** $\chi^2 = 19.10$, reject H_0 **8.57** union: $\chi^2 = 13.37$, p-value $= .038$, reject H_0; nonunion: $\chi^2 = 9.64$, p-value $= .141$, do not reject H_0 **8.59 a.** no **c.** H_0: Jan. change and next 11-month change are independent **d.** $\chi^2 = 2.373$, do not reject H_0 **e.** yes

8.61 a.

	Committee Accept	Committee Reject	Totals
Inspector Accept	101	23	124
Inspector Reject	10	19	29
Totals	111	42	153

b. yes **c.** $\chi^2 = 26.034$, reject H_0 **8.63 a.** yes, $\chi^2 = 47.98$ **b.** $.125 \pm .046$

Chapter 9

9.3 $\beta_1 = 1/3, \beta_0 = 14/3, y = 14/3 + 1/3x$ **9.9** no **9.11 a.** $\sum(y - \hat{y}) = 0.02$, SSE $= 1.2204$ **c.** SSE $= 108.00$ **9.13 b.** negative linear relationship **c.** $-.9939, 8.543$ **e.** range of x: 2 to 8 **9.15 a.** positive **c.** $-205.777, 1057.367$ **9.17 b.** $\hat{y} = 16.593 + 1.949x$ **d.** 45.828 **9.19 b.** $\hat{y} = 569.5801 - .00192x$ **e.** range of x: \$16,900 to \$70,000 **9.21 b.** $-51.362, 17.754$ **9.23 a.** .3475 **b.** 1.179 **9.25** 10.10: SSE $= 1.22$, $s^2 = .2441$, $s = .4960$; 10.13: SSE $= 5.713$, $s^2 = 1.143$, $s = 1.069$ **9.27 a.** $\hat{y} = 7.381 + .373x$ **b.** \$604.181 billion **c.** SSE $= 2{,}225.63$, $s^2 = 27.24$ **9.29 a.** SSE $= 20{,}554.415$, $s^2 = 2{,}055.442$, $s = 45.337$ **9.31 a.** 95% CI: 31 ± 1.13; 90% CI: $31 \pm .92$ **b.** 95% CI: 64 ± 4.28; 90% CI: 64 ± 3.53 **c.** 95% CI: $-8.4 \pm .67$; 90% CI: $-8.4 \pm .55$ **9.33** $.82 \pm .76$ **9.35 a.** yes **b.** $\hat{y} = -3{,}284.5 + 451.4x$ **c.** yes, $t = 7.57$ **e.** 451.4 ± 104.5 **9.37 a.** support **b.** $\hat{y} = 15.878 + .927x$ **c.** yes, $t = 2.45$ **d.** 0 and 1 **9.39 a.** yes, $t = 4.98$, p-value $= .001$ **b.** .607 **9.41 a.** $t = 3.384$, p-value $= .0035$, reject H_0 **b.** 17.75 ± 16.63 **9.43** yes, $t = -.96$ **9.45 a.** positive **b.** negative **c.** 0 slope **d.** positive or negative **9.47 a.** .9438 **b.** .8020 **9.49 a.** very weak positive linear relationship **b.** weak positive linear relationship **9.51 b.** $-.420$ **d.** .1764 **9.53** $r^2 = 0.2935$, $r = -.5418$ **9.55 a.** yes **b.** $-.423$ **9.57 b.** $\hat{y} = 1.5 + .946x$ **c.** 2.221 **d.** 4.338 ± 1.170 **e.** 4.338 ± 3.223 **f.** prediction interval for y **9.59 a.** 2.2 ± 1.382 **d.** $t = 6.10$, reject H_0 **9.61 b.** $\hat{y} = 5{,}566.13 - 210.346x$ **c.** $t = -8.69$, $p = 0$, reject H_0 **d.** .8437 **e.** (3,714.7, 4,052.0) **f.** (3,364.1, 4,402.7) **9.63 a.** (12.6384, 239.7) **b.** narrower **c.** no **9.65 a.** yes, $t = -5.91$; negative **b.** (.656, 2.829) **c.** (1.467, 2.018) **9.67 a.** .01 **b.** .01 **c.** .975 **d.** .05 **9.69 a.** .4 **b.** $-.9$ **c.** $-.2$ **d.** .2 **9.71 a.** $-.485$ **b.** reject H_0 **9.73** $r_s = -.607$, do not reject H_0 **9.75 b.** $r_s = .972$, reject H_0 **9.77 a.** $\hat{y} = 37.08 - 1.6x$ **c.** 57.2 **d.** 4.4 **e.** $-1.6 \pm .5$ **f.** 13.08 ± 6.93 **g.** 13.08 ± 7.86 **9.79 b.** $r = -.1245$, $r^2 = .0155$ **c.** no, $t = -.35$ **d.** $-.091$ **9.81 b.** $\hat{y} = 12.594 + .10936x$ **c.** yes, $t = 3.50$ **d.** 28.99 ± 12.50 **9.83** $\hat{y} = -92.46 + 8.35x$, reject H_0, p-value $= .0021$ **9.85 a.** $\hat{y} = 3.068 - .015x$ **c.** $t = -3.32$, reject H_0 **d.** $2.913 \pm .207$ **9.87 a.** 57.14 ± 34.82 **b.** 110 is outside range of x **c.** $\bar{x} = 44$ **9.89** .8574 **9.91** machine hours: $t = 3.30$, $p = .008$, reject H_0, $r^2 = .521$; labor hours: $t = 1.43$, $p = .183$, do not reject H_0, $r^2 = .170$

Chapter 10

10.1 a. $E(y) = \beta_0 + \beta_1x_1 + \beta_2x_2$ **b.** $E(y) = \beta_0 + \beta_1x_1 + \beta_2x_2 + \beta_3x_3 + \beta_4x_4$ **c.** $E(y) = \beta_0 + \beta_1x_1 + \beta_2x_2 + \beta_3x_3 + \beta_4x_4 + \beta_5x_5$ **10.3 a.** $t = 1.45$, do not reject H_0 **b.** $t = 3.21$, reject H_0 **10.5** $n - (k + 1)$ **10.7 a.** $E(y) = \beta_0 + \beta_1x_1 + \beta_2x_2$ **b.** $\hat{y} = -20.352 + 13.3504x_1 + 243.714x_2$ **d.** no, $t = 1.74$ **e.** (49.69, 437.74) **10.9 a.** $\hat{y} = 20.9 + 0.261x_1 - 7.8x_2 + .0042x_3$ **b.** 14.01 **c.** no, $t = 1.09$ **10.11 a.** $\hat{y} = 12.2 - .0265x_1 - .458x_2$ **c.** $t = -.50$, $p = .623$, do not reject H_0 **d.** $-.458 \pm .347$ **e.** $x_3 = 1$ if plants, 0 if not **10.15 a.** $\hat{y} = 93{,}074 + 4{,}152x_1 - 855x_2 + .924x_3 + 2{,}692x_4 + 15.5x_5$ **b.** 33,225.9 **c.** yes, $t = 2.78$, p-value $= .0059$ **f.** $t = -2.86$, reject H_0 **g.** .00495 **10.17 a.** .8911 **b.** .8775 **c.** $F = 65.462$, reject H_0 **d.** .0001

10.19 a.

Source	df	SS	MS	F
Model	2	12.09	6.045	8.321
Error	17	12.35	.72647	
Total	19	24.44		

; $R^2 = .4947$; $R_a^2 = .4352$

10.19 b. $F = 8.321$, reject H_0 **10.21 a.** .8168 **b.** H_0: $\beta_1 = \beta_2 = 0$ **c.** $F = 31.22$, $p = .0000069$ **d.** reject H_0 **10.23 a.** $\hat{y} = -4.30 - .002x_1 + .336x_2 + .384x_3 + .067x_4 - .143x_5 + .081x_6 + .134x_7$ **b.** $F = 111.1$, reject H_0 **d.** $t = 1.76$, p-value $= .079$, do not reject H_0 **e.** no, $t = -.049$, p-value $= .961$ **10.25 a.** 51% of the variability in operating margins can be explained by the model **b.** $F = 13.53$, reject H_0 **10.27** $F = 1.06$, do not reject H_0 **10.29 a.** $R^2 = .529$; $R_a^2 = .505$; R_a^2 **b.** $F = 21.88$, p-value $= 0$, reject H_0 **10.31 a.** (1,759.7, 4,275.4) **b.** (2,620.3, 3,414.9) **c.** yes **10.33** (−1.233, 1.038) **10.35 a.** $F = 72.11$, reject H_0 **10.37** yes **10.41 a.** yes **10.43 a.** no **b.** yes **c.** no **d.** yes; 26th household **e.** no **10.45** confidence interval **10.47 a.** $\hat{y} = 90.1 - 1.836x_1 + .285x_2$ **b.** .916 **c.** yes, $F = 64.91$ **d.** $t = -5.01$, reject H_0 **e.** 10.677 **10.49** no degrees of freedom for error **10.51 a.** $E(y) = \beta_0 + \beta_1x_1 + \beta_2x_2 + \beta_3x_3 + \beta_4x_4 + \beta_5x_5$ **b.** reject H_0: $\beta_1 = \beta_2 = \beta_3 = \beta_4 = \beta_5 = 0$ **c.** $E(y) = \beta_0 + \beta_1x_1 + \beta_2x_2 + \beta_3x_3 + \beta_4x_4 + \beta_5x_5 + \beta_6x_6 + \beta_7x_7$ **d.** 60.3% of the variability in GSI scores is explained by the model **e.** both variables contribute to the prediction of GSI **10.53** Importance and Support are correlated at .6991; no **10.55 a.** $E(y) = \beta_0 + \beta_1x$, where $x = \{1 \text{ if H}, 0 \text{ if L}\}$ **b.** $\hat{y} = 10.575 + .917x$ **c.** yes, $t = 3.38$ **10.57 c.** yes, $F = 39.505$, p-value $= .000$ **d.** $x_2 = 60$: $\hat{y} = .47 + .026x_1$; $x_2 = 75$: $\hat{y} = .98 + .026x_1$; $x_2 = 90$: $\hat{y} = 1.49 + .026x_1$ **e.** add x_1^2

Chapter 11

11.7 out of control **11.9 a.** 1.023 **b.** 0.308 **c.** 0.167 **11.11 b.** $\bar{\bar{x}} = 20.11625$, $\bar{R} = 3.31$ **c.** UCL = 22.529, LCL = 17.703 **d.** Upper A-B: 21.725, Lower A-B: 18.507, Upper B-C: 20.920, Lower B-C: 19.312 **e.** yes **11.13 a.** $\bar{\bar{x}} = 23.9971$, $\bar{R} = .1815$, UCL = 24.102, LCL = 23.892, Upper A-B: 24.067, Lower A-B: 23.927, Upper B-C: 24.032, Lower B-C: 23.962 **b.** in control **c.** yes **11.15 a.** $\bar{\bar{x}} = 49.129$, $\bar{R} = 3.733$, UCL = 50.932, LCL = 47.326, Upper A-B: 50.331, Lower A-B: 47.927, Upper B-C: 49.730, Lower B-C: 48.528 **b.** no **c.** no **11.17 a.** $\bar{\bar{x}} = 52.6467$, $\bar{R} = .755$, UCL = 53.419, LCL = 51.874, Upper A-B: 53.162, Lower A-B: 52.132, Upper B-C: 52.904, Lower B-C: 52.389 **b.** out of control **d.** no **11.21 a.** UCL = 16.802 **b.** Upper A-B: 13.853, Lower A-B: 2.043, Upper B-C: 10.900, Lower B-C: 4.996 **c.** in control **11.23** R-chart: $\bar{R} = 4.03$, UCL = 7.754, LCL = 0.306, Upper A-B: 6.513, Lower A-B: 1.547, Upper B-C: 5.271, Lower B-C: 2.789, in control; $\bar{x}$-chart: $\bar{\bar{x}} = 21.728$, UCL = 23.417, LCL = 20.039, Upper A-B: 22.854, Lower A-B: 20.602, Upper B-C: 22.291, Lower B-C: 21.165, out of control **11.25 a.** yes **b.** $\bar{R} = .0796$, UCL = .168, Upper A-B: .139, Lower A-B: .020, Upper B-C: .109, Lower B-C: .050 **c.** in control **d.** yes **e.** yes **11.27 a.** $\bar{R} = 2.08$, UCL = 4.397, Upper A-B: 3.625, Lower A-B: .535, Upper B-C: 2.853, Lower B-C: 1.307; in control **b.** yes **c.** $\bar{R} = 1.7$, UCL = 3.594, Upper A-B: 2.963, Lower A-B: .437, Upper B-C: 2.331, Lower B-C: 1.069; out of control **11.29 a.** $\bar{R} = 2.756$, UCL = 5.826, Upper A-B: 4.803, Lower A-B: .709, Upper B-C: 3.780, Lower B-C: 1.732 **b.** variation **c.** in control **11.31** 104 **11.33 a.** $\bar{p} = .0575$, UCL = .1145, LCL = .0005, Upper A-B: .0955, Lower A-B: .0195, Upper B-C: .0765, Lower B-C: .0385 **d.** no **e.** no **11.35 a.** yes **b.** UCL = .02013, LCL = .00081 **c.** Upper A-B: .01691, Lower A-B: .00403, Upper B-C: .01369, Lower B-C: .00725; in control **11.37 a.** $\bar{p} = .04$, UCL = .099, LCL = −.019, Upper A-B: .079, Lower A-B: .001, Upper B-C: .060, Lower B-C: .020 **b.** no **c.** no **11.49 a.** $\bar{x} = 6.4$ **b.** increasing variance **11.51** out of control **11.53 a.** $\bar{R} = 7.4$, UCL = 24.1758, Upper A-B: 18.5918, Lower A-B: −3.7918, Upper B-C: 12.9959, Lower B-C: 1.8041; out of control **b.** $\bar{\bar{x}} = 344.15$, UCL = 358.062, LCL = 330.238, Upper A-B: 353.425, Lower A-B: 334.875, Upper B-C: 348.787, Lower B-C: 339.513; out of control **c.** no **d.** .25 **11.55 a.** $\bar{R} = 5.455$, UCL = 11.532, Upper A-B: 9.508, Lower A-B: 1.402, Upper B-C: 7.481, Lower B-C: 3.429 **b.** in control **d.** $\bar{\bar{x}} = 3.867$, UCL = 7.015, LCL = .719, Upper A-B: 5.965, Lower A-B: 1.769, Upper B-C: 4.916, Lower B-C: 2.818 **e.** in control **f.** yes **11.57 a.** $n > 141$ **b.** $\bar{p} = .063$, UCL = .123, LCL = .003, Upper A-B: .103, Lower A-B: .023, Upper B-C: .083, Lower B-C: .043 **c.** out of control **e.** no

References

Chapter 1

Careers in Statistics. American Statistical Association, Biometric Society, Institute of Mathematical Statistics and Statistical Society of Canada, 1995.

Chervany, N.L., Benson, P.G., and Iyer, R.K. "The planning stage in statistical reasoning." *The American Statistician,* Nov. 1980, pp. 222–239.

Ethical Guidelines for Statistical Practice. American Statistical Association, 1995.

Tanur, J.M., Mosteller, F., Kruskal, W.H., Link, R.F., Pieters, R.S., and Rising, G.R. *Statistics: A Guide to the Unknown.* (E.L. Lehmann, special editor.) San Francisco: Holden-Day, 1989.

U.S. Bureau of the Census. *Statistical Abstract of the United States: 1998.* Washington, D.C.: U.S. Government Printing Office, 1998.

What is a Survey? Section on Survey Research Methods, American Statistical Association, 1995.

Chapter 2

Adler, P. S., and Clark, K. B. "Behind the learning curve: A sketch of the learning process." *Management Science,* March 1991, p. 267.

Alexander, G. J., Sharpe, W. F., and Bailey, J. V. *Fundamentals of Investments,* 2nd ed. Englewood Cliffs, N.J.: Prentice-Hall, 1993.

Deming, W. E. *Out of the Crisis.* Cambridge, Mass: M.I.T. Center for Advanced Engineering Study, 1986.

Fogarty, D. W., Blackstone, J. H., Jr., and Hoffman, T. R. *Production and Inventory Management.* Cincinnati, Ohio: South-Western, 1991.

Gaither, N. *Production and Operations Management,* 7th ed. Belmont, Calif: Duxbury Press, 1996.

Gitlow, H., Oppenheim, A., and Oppenheim, R. *Quality Management: Methods for Improvement,* 2nd ed., Burr Ridge, Ill.: Irwin 1995.

Huff, D. *How to Lie with Statistics.* New York: Norton, 1954.

Ishikawa, K. Guide to Quality Control, 2nd ed. White Plains, N.Y.: Kraus International Publications, 1982.

Juran, J. M. *Juran on Planning for Quality.* New York: The Free Press, 1988.

Mendenhall, W. *Introduction to Probability and Statistics,* 9th ed. North Scituate, Mass.: Duxbury, 1994.

Schroeder, R. G. *Operations Management,* 4th ed. New York: McGraw-Hill, 1993.

Tufte, E. R. *Visual Explanations.* Cheshire, Conn.: Graphics Press, 1997.

Wasserman, P., and Bernero, J. *Statistics Sources,* 5th ed. Detroit: Gale Research Company, 1978.

Zabel, S. L. "Statistical proof of employment discrimination." *Statistics: A Guide to the Unknown,* 3rd ed. Pacific Grove, Calif.: Wadsworth, 1989

Chapter 3

Benson, G. "Process thinking: The quality catalyst." *Minnesota Management Review,* University of Minnesota, Minneapolis, Fall 1992.

Feller, W. *An Introduction to Probability Theory and Its Applications,* 3d ed., Vol. 1. New York: Wiley, 1968.

Kotler, Philip. *Marketing Management,* 8th ed. Englewood Cliffs, N.J.: Prentice Hall, 1994.

Kuehn, A. A. "An analysis of the dynamics of consumer behavior and its implications for marketing management." Unpublished doctoral dissertation, Graduate School of Industrial Administration, Carnegie Institute of Technology, 1958.

Lindley, D.V. *Making Decisions,* 2d ed. London: Wiley, 1985.

Parzen, E. Modern Probability Theory and Its Applications. New York: Wiley, 1960.

Scheaffer, R. L., and Mendenhall, W. *Introduction to Probability: Theory and Applications.* North Scituate, Mass.: Duxbury, 1975.

Stickney, Clyde P., and Weil, Roman L. *Financial Accounting: An Introduction to Concepts, Methods, and Uses,* 7th ed. Fort Worth: The Dryden Press, 1994.

Williams, B. *A Sampler on Sampling.* New York: Wiley, 1978.

Winkler, R.L. *An Introduction to Bayesian Inference and Decision.* New York: Holt, Rinehart and Winston, 1972.

Chapter 4

Alexander, G. J., and Francis, J. C. *Portfolio Analysis.* Englewood Cliffs, N.J.: Prentice Hall, 1996.

Alexander, G. J., Sharpe, W. F., and Bailey, J. V. *Fundamentals of Investments,* 2nd edition, Englewood Cliffs, N.J.: Prentice Hall, 1993.

Blume, M. "On the assessment of risk." *Journal of Finance,* Mar. 1971, 26, pp. 1–10.

Camm, J. D., and Evans, J. R. *Management Science: Modeling, Analysis, and Interpretation.* Cincinnati: South-Western, 1996.

Clauss, Francis, J. *Applied Management Science and Spreadsheet Modeling.* Belmont, Calif.: Duxbury Press, 1996.

Cowling, A., and James, P. The Essence of Personnel Management and Industrial Relations. New York: Prentice Hall, 1994.

Edwards, Jr., J. P., ed. *Transportation Planning Handbook.* Englewood Cliffs, N.J.: Prentice Hall, 1992.

Elton, E. J., and Gruber, M. J. *Modern Portfolio Theory and Investment Analysis.* New York: Wiley, 1981.

Herrnstein, R. J., and Murray, C. *The Bell Curve.* New York: The Free Press, 1994.

Hogg, R. V., and Craig, A. T. *Introduction to Mathematical Statistics,* 4th ed. New York: Macmillan, 1978.

Lindgren, B. W. Statistical Theory, 3d ed. New York: Macmillan, 1976.

Mendenhall, W. *Introduction to Mathematical Statistics,* 8th ed. Boston: Duxbury, 1991.

Mendenhall, W., Wackerly, D., and Scheaffer, R. L. *Mathematical Statistics with Applications,* 4th ed. Boston: PWS-Kent, 1990.

Mood, A. M., Graybill, F. A., and Boes, D. C. *Introduction to the Theory of Statistics,* 3d ed. New York: McGraw-Hill, 1974.

Moss, M. A. *Applying TQM to Product Design and Development.* New York: Marcel Dekker, 1996.

Neter, J., Wasserman, W., and Whitmore, G. A. *Applied Statistics,* 4th ed. Boston: Allyn & Bacon, 1993.

Parzen, E. *Modern Probability Theory and Its Applications.* New York: Wiley, 1960.

Radcliffe, Robert C. *Investments: Concepts, Analysis, and Strategy,* 4th ed. New York: HarperCollins, 1994.

Ramsey, P. P., and Ramsey, P. H. "Simple tests of normality in small samples." *Journal of Quality Technology,* Vol. 22, 1990, pp. 299–309.

Render, B., and Heizer, J. *Principles of Operations Management.* Englewood Cliffs, N. J.: Prentice Hall, 1995.

Ross, S. M. *Stochastic Processes,* 2d ed. New York: Wiley, 1996.

Willis, R. E., and Chervany, N.L. *Statistical Analysis and Modeling for Management Decision-Making.* Belmont, Calif.: Wadsworth, 1974.

Winkler, R. L., and Hays, W. *Statistics: Probability, Inference, and Decision,* 2d ed. New York: Holt, Rinehart and Winston, 1975.

Chapter 5

Agresti, A., and Coull, B. A. "Approximate is better than 'exact' for interval estimation of binomial proportions." *The American Statistician,* Vol. 52, No. 2, May 1998, pp. 119–126.

Cochran, W. G. *Sampling Techniques,* 3d ed. New York: Wiley, 1997.

Deming, W. E. *Out of the Crisis.* Cambridge, Mass.: MIT Center for Advanced Study of Engineering, 1986.

Freedman, D., Pisani, R., and Purves, R. *Statistics.* New York: Norton, 1978.

Kish, L. *Survey Sampling.* New York: Wiley, 1965.

Mendenhall, W., and Beaver, B. *Introduction to Probability and Statistics,* 8th ed. Boston: PWS-Kent, 1991.

Wilson, E. G. "Probable inference, the law of succession, and statistical inference." *Journal of the American Statistical Association,* Vol. 22, 1927, pp. 209–212.

Chapter 6

Alexander, Gordon J., Sharpe, William F., and Bailey, Jeffery. *Fundamentals of Investments,* 2nd ed. Englewood Cliffs, N.J.: Prentice Hall, 1993

Conover, W. J. *Practical Nonparametric Statistics,* 3rd ed. New York: Wiley, 1999.

Daniel, W. W. *Applied Nonparametric Statistics,* 2nd ed. Boston: PWS-Kent, 1990.

Mendenhall, W., Wackerly, D., and Scheaffer, R. *Mathematical Statistics with Applications,* 4th ed. Boston: PWS-Kent, 1990.

Snedecor, G. W., and Cochran, W. G. *Statistical Methods,* 7th ed. Ames: Iowa State University Press, 1980.

Chapter 7

Conover, W. J. *Practical Nonparametric Statistics,* 2nd ed. New York: Wiley, 1980.

Freedman, D., Pisani, R., and Purves, R. *Statistics.* New York: W. W. Norton and Co., 1978.

Gibbons, J. D. *Nonparametric Statistical Inference,* 2nd ed. New York: McGraw-Hill, 1985.

Hollander, M., and Wolfe, D. A. *Nonparametric Statistical Methods.* New York: Wiley, 1973.

Mendenhall, W. *Introduction to Linear Models and the Design and Analysis of Experiments.* Belmont, Calif.: Wadsworth, 1968.

Mendenhall, W. *Introduction to Probability and Statistics,* 8th ed. Boston: PWS-Kent, 1991.

Miller, R. G., Jr. *Simultaneous Statistical Inference.* New York: Springer-Verlag, 1981.

Neter, J., Kutner, M., Nachtsheim, C., and Wasserman, W. *Applied Linear Statistical Models,* 4th ed. Homewood, Ill.: Richard D. Irwin, 1996.

Satterthwaite, F. W. "An approximate distribution of estimates of variance components." *Biometrics Bulletin,* Vol. 2, 1946, pp. 110–114.

Scheffé, H. "A method for judging all contrasts in the analysis of variance," *Biometrica,* Vol. 40. 1953, pp. 87–104.

Snedecor, G. W., and Cochran, W. *Statistical Methods,* 7th ed. Ames: Iowa State University Press, 1980.

Steel, R. G. D., and Torrie, J. H. *Principles and Procedures of Statistics,* 2nd ed. New York: McGraw-Hill, 1980.

Stevenson, William J. *Production/Operations Management,* 5th ed. Chicago: Irwin, 1996.

Tukey, J. "Comparing individual means in the analysis of variance," *Biometrics,* Vol. 5, 1949. pp. 99–114.

Winer, B. J. *Statistical Principles in Experimental Design,* 2d ed. New York: McGraw–Hill, 1971.

Chapter 8

Agresti, A., *Categorical Data Analysis.* New York: Wiley, 1990.

Cochran, W.G. "The test of goodness of fit." *Annals of Mathematical Statistics,* 1952, 23.

Conover, W.J. *Practical Nonparametric Statistics,* 2nd ed. New York: Wiley, 1980.

Hollander, M., and Wolfe, D. A. *Nonparametric Statistical Methods.* New York: Wiley, 1973.

Savage, I.R. "Bibliography of nonparametric statistics and related topics." *Journal of the American Statistical Association,* 1953, 48.

Schroeder, R. G. *Operations Management,* 4th ed. New York: McGraw-Hill, 1993.

Siegel, S. *Nonparametric Statistics for the Behavioral Sciences.* New York: McGraw-Hill, 1956.

Chapter 9

Chatterjee, S., and Price, B. *Regression Analysis by Example,* 2nd ed. New York: Wiley, 1991.

Draper, N., and Smith, H. *Applied Regression Analysis,* 2nd ed. New York: Wiley, 1981.

Gitlow, H., Oppenheim, A., and Oppenheim, R. *Quality Management: Tools and Methods for Improvement,* 2nd ed. Burr Ridge, Ill.: Irwin, 1995.

Graybill, F. *Theory and Application of the Linear Model.* North Scituate, Mass.: Duxbury, 1976.

Horngren, C.T., Foster, G., and Datar, S.M. *Cost Accounting,* 8th ed. Englewood Cliffs, N.J.: Prentice Hall, 1994.

Kleinbaum, D., and Kupper, L. *Applied Regression Analysis and Other Mutivariable Methods,* 2nd ed. North Scituate, Mass.: Duxbury, 1997.

Lee, C., Finnerty, J. and Norton, E. *Foundations of Financial Management.* Minneapolis, Minn.: West Publishing Co., 1997.

Mendenhall, W. *Introduction to Linear Models and the Design and Analysis of Experiments.* Belmont, Ca.: Wadsworth, 1968.

Mendenhall, W. and Sincich, T. A *Second Course in Statistics: Regression Analysis,* 5th ed. Upper Saddle River, N.J.: Prentice Hall, 1996.

Mintzberg, H. *The Nature of Managerial Work.* New York: Harper and Row, 1973.

Neter, J., Wasserman, W., and Kutner, M. *Applied Linear Statistical Models,* 3rd ed. Homewood, Ill.: Richard Irwin, 1992.

Weisburg, S. *Applied Linear Regression,* 2nd ed. New York: Wiley, 1985.

Chapter 10

Barnett, V., and Lewis, T. *Outliers in Statistical Data.* New York: Wiley, 1978.

Belsley, D. A., Kuh, E., and Welsch, R. E. *Regression Diagnostics: Identifying Influential Data and Sources of Collinearity.* New York: Wiley, 1980.

Chase, R. B., and Aquilano, N. J. *Production and Operations Management,* 6th ed. Homewood, Ill.: Richard D. Irwin, 1992.

Chatterjee, S., and Price, B. *Regression Analysis by Example,* 2d ed. New York: Wiley, 1991.

Draper, N., and Smith, H. *Applied Regression Analysis,* 2nd ed. New York: Wiley, 1981.

Graybill, F. *Theory and Application of the Linear Model. North Scituate,* Mass.: Duxbury, 1976.

Horngren, C. T., Foster, G., and Datar, S. M. *Cost Accounting,* 8th ed. Englewood Cliffs, N. J.: Prentice Hall, 1994.

Lee, C., Finnerty, J., and Norton, E. *Foundations of Financial Management. Minneapolis,* Minn.: West Publishing Co., 1997.

Mendenhall, W. *Introduction to Linear Models and the Design and Analysis of Experiments.* Belmont, Calif.: Wadsworth, 1968.

Mendenhall, W., and Sincich, T. A *Second Course in Statistics: Regression Analysis,* 5th ed. Upper Saddle River, N.J.: Prentice-Hall, 1996.

Neter, J., Kutner, M., Nachtsheim, C., and Wasserman, W. *Applied Linear Statistical Models,* 4th ed. Homewood, Ill.: Richard D. Irwin, 1996.

Rousseeuw, P. J., and Leroy, A. M. *Robust Regression and Outlier Detection.* New York: Wiley, 1987.

Weisberg, S. *Applied Linear Regression,* 2nd ed. New York: Wiley, 1985.

Wonnacott, R. J., and Wonnacott, T. H. *Econometrics,* 2nd ed. New York: Wiley, 1979.

Chapter 11

Alwan, L.C., and Roberts H.V. "Time-series modeling for statistical process control." *Journal of Business and Economic Statistics,* 1988, Vol. 6, pp. 87–95.

Banks, J. *Principles of Quality Control.* New York:Wiley, 1989.

Checkland, P. *Systems Thinking, Systems Practice.* New York: Wiley, 1981.

Deming, W.E. *Out of the Crisis.* Cambridge, Mass.: MIT Center for Advanced Engineering Study, 1986.

DeVor, R.E., Chang, T., and Southerland, J.W. *Statistical Quality Design and Control.* New York: Macmillan, 1992.

Duncan, A.J. Quality *Control and Industrial Statistics.* Homewood, Ill.: Irwin, 1986.

The Ernst and Young Quality Improvement Consulting Group. *Total Quality: An Executive's Guide for the 1990s.* Homewood, Ill.: Dow-Jones Irwin, 1990.

Feigenbaum, A.B. *Total Quality Control,* 3rd ed. New York: McGraw-Hill, 1983.

Garvin, D.A. *Managing Quality.* New York: Free Press/ Macmillan, 1988.

Gitlow, H., Gitlow, S., Oppenheim, A., and Oppenheim, R. *Tools and Methods for the Improvement of Quality.* Homewood, Ill.: Irwin, 1995.

Grant, E.L., and Leavenworth, R.S. *Statistical Quality Control,* 6th ed. New York: McGraw-Hill, 1988.

Hart, Marilyn K. "Quality tools for improvement." *Production and Inventory Management Journal,* First Quarter 1992, Vol. 33, No. 1, p. 59.

Ishikawa, K. *Guide to Quality Control,* 2nd ed. White Plains, N.Y.: Kraus International Publications, 1986.

Joiner, B.L., and Goudard, M.A. "Variation, management, and W. Edwards Deming." *Quality Process,* Dec. 1990, pp. 29–37.

Juran, J. M. *Juran on Planning for Quality.* New York: Free Press/Macmillan, 1988.

Juran, J. M., and Gryna, F. M., Jr. *Quality Planning Analysis,* 2nd ed. New York: McGraw-Hill, 1980.

Kane, V. E. *Defect Prevention.* New York: Marcel Dekker, 1989.

Latzko, W. J. *Quality and Productivity for Bankers and Financial Managers.* New York: Marcel Dekker, 1986.

Moen, R.D., Nolan, T. W., and Provost, L. P. *Improving Quality Through Planned Experimentation.* New York: McGraw-Hill, 1991.

Montgomery, D. C. *Introduction to Statistical Quality Control,* 2nd ed. New York: Wiley, 1991.

Nelson, L. L. "The Shewhart control chart —Tests for special causes." *Journal of Quality Technology,* Oct. 1984, Vol. 16, No. 4, pp. 237–239.

Roberts, H. V. *Data Analysis for Managers,* 2nd ed. Redwood City, Calif.: Scientific Press, 1991.

Rosander, A. C. *Applications of Quality Control in the Service Industries.* New York: Marcel Dekker, 1985.

Rummler, G. A., and Brache, A. P. *Improving Performance: How to Manage the White Space on the Organization Chart.* San Francisco: Jossey-Bass, 1991.

Ryan, T.P. *Statistical Methods for Quality Improvement,* New York: Wiley, 1989.

Statistical Quality Control Handbook. Indianapolis, Ind.: AT&T Technologies, Select Code 700-444 (inquiries: 800-432-6600); originally published by Western Electric Company, 1956.

Wadsworth, H.M., Stephens, K. S., and Godfrey, A. B. *Modern Methods for Quality Control and Improvement.* New York: Wiley, 1986.

Walton, M. *The Deming Management Method.* New York: Dodd, Mead, & Company, 1986.

Wheeler, D. J., and Chambers, D. S. *Understanding Statistical Process Control.* Knoxville, Tenn.: Statistical Process Controls, Inc., 1986.

Index